THE PRENTICE HALL
ANTHOLOGY OF AFRICAN AMERICAN LITERATURE

ROCHELLE SMITH

The University of Mississippi
Oxford, Mississippi

SHARON L. JONES

Earlham College
Richmond, Indiana

Prentice Hall
Upper Saddle River, NJ 07458

Library of Congress Cataloging-in-Publication Data
The Prentice Hall anthology of African American literature /
[edited by] Rochelle Smith, Sharon L. Jones.
     p.   cm.
   Includes bibliographical references (p.   ) and index.
   ISBN 0-13-081367-2
     1. American literature—Afro-American authors. 2. Afro-Americans
Literary collections. I. Smith, Rochelle, 1955– II. Jones, Sharon L.
(Sharon Lynette) III. Title: Anthology of African American literature
PS508.N3 P74   1999
810.8´0896073—dc21

                                        99-32517
                                        CIP

Editorial Director: *Charlyce Jones Owen*
Editor in Chief: *Leah Jewell*
Acquisition Editor: *Carrie Brandon*
Marketing Manager: *Brandy Dawson*
Editorial Assistant: *Gianna Caradonna*
AVP, Director of Manufacturing and
     Production: *Barbara Kittle*
Senior Managing Editor: *Bonnie Biller*
Senior Project Manager: *Shelly Kupperman*
Manufacturing Manager: *Nick Sklitsis*

Prepress and Manufacturing Buyer:
     Mary Ann Gloriande
Creative Design Director: *Leslie Osher*
Interior Designer: *Ximena Tamvakopoulos*
Cover Designer: *Ximena Tamvakopoulos*
Director, Image Resource Center:
     Melinda Reo
Photo Research Supervisor: *Beth Boyd*
Image Permission Supervisor: *Kay Dellosa*
Photo Researcher: *Teri Stratford*

For permission to use copyrighted material, grateful acknowledgment is made to the copyright holders on page xx, which constitute an extension of this copyright page.

Cover Art: Harriet Powers, "Pictorial Quilt" 1895–98. U.S., 1837–1911. Pieced and appliqued cotton embroidered with plain and metallic yarns. L: 69 in. (175 cm.); W: 105 in. (267 cm.). Bequest of Maxim Karolik. Courtesy of Museum of Fine Arts, Boston.

This book was set in 10/12 New Baskerville by Lithokraft II and was printed and bound by Courier-Westford, Inc. The cover was printed by Phoenix Color Corp.

Printed in the United States of America
10 9 8 7 6 5 4 3 2

ISBN 0-13-081367-2

Prentice-Hall International (UK) Limited, *London*
Prentice-Hall of Australia Pty. Limited, *Sydney*
Prentice-Hall Canada Inc., *Toronto*
Prentice-Hall Hispanoamericana, S.A., *Mexico*
Prentice-Hall of India Private Limited, *New Delhi*
Prentice-Hall of Japan, Inc., *Tokyo*
Pearson Asia Pte. Ltd., *Singapore*
Editora Prentice-Hall do Brasil, Ltda., *Rio de Janeiro*

BRIEF CONTENTS

CONTENTS

THE RECONSTRUCTION PERIOD 1865-1900   114

THE HARLEM RENAISSANCE 1900-1940   163

BLACK AESTHETICS MOVEMENT 1960-1969   658

Introduction   658

NEOREALISM MOVEMENT 1970–PRESENT   742

AFRICAN AMERICAN LITERARY CRITICISM   951

FOREWORD

The March has been a long and dangerous one: traps and snares, wide rivers, wicked dogs, scarce food, bitter weather, villains to the left and to the right. But the journey has not been all bad: friendships, unexpected kindness from strangers, reversals of fortune, and, perhaps most precious, the discovery of inner strength and love—the only true definition of courage and of victory.

This volume contains many accounts from various points of view of the rough road, the collective long walk home black folk have made over the last 250 years in North America. These voices do not always agree, and well they should not, for what good would be a chorus of voices sounding constantly the same note throughout the ages? Rather, we have a rich testament—in every form and manner of artistry—bearing witness to the multiple experiences that being of African descent in America has engendered.

Central to the ongoing March toward self-definition for African Americans has been their continual assertion of their humanity. Some might balk at what seems so undeniably obvious, yet again and again what is readily apparent to any thinking person has in fact been denied, revoked, "discredited," disregarded, argued, laughed at, sneered at, misconstrued, misshapen, and misunderstood. Therefore, none should take for granted that every American—even to this day and age—sees African Americans as full human beings, and it behooves us all to say it again and again. This reality makes this volume all the more important.

For those of us, like the authors represented here, for whom the knowledge of the humanity of black folk is a foregone, unshatterable conclusion, there nevertheless remains much to be learned and absorbed, a vast body of works that reveal feelings and facts—the bone of history itself and the sinew of centuries of thought and connective perception. Moreover, herein you will find the artistry spun and respun through the generations, riffs and retakes on the great themes: love, death, and the loneliness of life. These words and images are like vitamins for us all. If you read carefully you can see latter-day Octavia Butler talking to Harlem Renaissance Nella Larsen, and Nella Larsen speaking with antebellum Harriet Jacobs; if you read deeply you can understand how colonial Olaudah Equiano speaks directly to Black Power activist and poet Haki Madhubuti, and how Haki Madhubuti's words reach back and chime with those of Frederick Douglass. Despite the effects of history and time, there are common elements, large and small, that resonate throughout this volume, from slave to freedom fighter, from jazz poet to Reconstruction novelist. The methodology, the specifics of the politics and its circumstances—and even to some extent the language—may have altered, but the core tenets are amazingly similar.

And therein, in that odd contradiction of time and space, in that paradox of art, where so much has changed and yet so much remains constant, we beneficiaries of these gems can tease out the multivarious commonalities that link these extraordinary voices with our own.

Lastly, in the grand enterprise of listening to, reading, and studying these lasting voices, we, as Americans, can begin to see how these linkages are also true for the Irish and for the Chippewa, for the Jew and for the Chinese—for, if we are attentive enough and open our eyes wide enough, we will see that these folk speak not just for African Americans but for all Americans.

Randall Kenan

PREFACE

TO THE STUDENT

This text presents a wide range of African American literature, from colonial times to the present, in a multitude of genres: poetry, drama, fiction, autobiography, nonfiction, music, and art. We, the coeditors, employ an approach that places African American aesthetic contributions within historical context. The anthology is divided according to historical period, moving you through the African American literary tradition in a chronological manner. We believe that you need to understand how African American literature is connected to American society, to see the experiences of African American people within the changing political, social, economic climate of our country. You will learn as much about history as literature: As the book illustrates, one defines the other. We learn about history through literature, and we learn about literature through history.

Placing the literature in historical context is a way to learn about various aspects of history and how African American literature provides a response to historical movements, tensions, and controversies. For example, during the black aesthetics movement, from 1960 to 1969, African American writers produced literary works filled with protest and pride. The voices of writers that had been silenced by racism were being heard because of the changing state of race relations. As this anthology illustrates, freedom of expression for African American writers has increased as limitations based on race have gradually become less stringent. To highlight this move toward freedom, we have chosen "slavery versus freedom" as the book's primary theme—a theme that runs consistently throughout, helping you make connections between authors, genres, and historical events.

Historical overviews introduce each part or section of the text, providing important background information—starting points for the study of African American literature and history during particular time spans. Of course, since one of our goals is to show the breadth of this material, we could only include a limited view of the historical context of which African American literature is a part. In the same way, the readings in the text are a limited representation of this literature. Since we have only skimmed the surface, part of your responsibility as a student using this book is to supplement the text material through both primary and secondary research. Always think of yourself as a source of information; your opinions are valid if you can support them. Use the literature as a point of departure, a way to examine important issues, such as race, in your own lives. Race is not, however, the only issue that students using this text can discuss in spoken and written form.

African American aesthetic contributions to society address not only racial issues but also universal ideas and themes. You do not have to be African American to be able to relate to the anthologized material—the only requirement is that you be human.

An appreciation for differences is just as important as an appreciation for commonalities. The aspects of identity that make us unique individuals, such as language, culture, and experience, should be valued. Problems surface when difference or diversity is used to place limitations on people, to discriminate against persons or groups, or to set people apart because of perceived notions of inferiority. We should strive to know more about those who are different from us, and we should strive to learn more about ourselves. This anthology provides an opportunity to learn about life through African American literature.

Other text components emphasize the importance of reading, writing, and critical thinking skills. In addition to the section overviews, other features of the text include research topics, a Writing About Literature section, a compact disc, art, a timeline, biographical sketches, oral tradition material, and an index. The possibilities for writing are numerous. We encourage you to make connections. For example, you can examine a piece of writing within other contexts, those presented by other races, genders, ethnicities, and viewpoints. In your study of African American literature, focus on topics that you feel strongly about, that you are most interested in, that you can relate to, or that stir emotions within you. Be able to put yourself into your writing; don't view the material as existing outside of your reality. After all, the human element is always a common denominator.

You will gain the most benefit from the works and supplementary material collected in this anthology if you agree to read, write, and discuss the work with an open mind. Narrow points of view will limit your ability to appreciate the African American literature included. A willingness to consider other points of view and appreciate diverse responses to literature is the key to an environment conducive to learning about both literature and writing.

TO THE INSTRUCTOR

This anthology offers a chronological survey of African American literature from the 1700s to the present, with a wide range of selections, including poetry, prose, and drama. In addition, biographical sketches, historical overviews of the literary periods, artwork, topics for research, a timeline, and an oral literature component (including a CD) enhance the distinct qualities of this text. Also, we have provided instructors with a manual to assist in developing strategies for teaching African American literature. The anthology focuses on a unified theme—slavery versus freedom—and traces that theme through several literary periods and movements in the African American literary tradition. The impetus for the text grew out of the coeditors' desire for a comprehensive anthology of African American literature that would be both teacher- and student-friendly in its depth, breadth, and scope.

In pursuit of this goal, the coeditors have chosen the structure very carefully. The text begins with the Introduction, which offers an overview of the key social, historical, and political contexts in which the selections featured in this anthology of African American literature were produced.

The central structure of the anthology is divided into parts that focus on each literary period: The Colonial Period, 1746–1800; The Antebellum Period, 1800–1865; The Reconstruction Period, 1865–1900; The Harlem Renaissance, 1900–1940; The Protest Movement, 1940–1959; Black Aesthetics Movement, 1960–1969; and Neorealism Movement, 1970–Present. Each part has an introduction. This overview frames the social, historical, and political context for the period, emphasizing both literal and figurative examples of the theme, slavery versus freedom. Within each part are selections of works of African American literature from a variety of genres; and at the end of each part is a Topics for Research section, which challenges students to find new directions for examining African American literature.

The coeditors are particularly proud of the oral literature component of this anthology: Oral Traditions sections within each part feature examples of the rich oral tradition in African American literature, including spirituals, folktales, and speeches; and the companion CD adds music and spoken word to the oral tradition and should enhance the breadth and the accessibility of the anthology, particularly for students who are auditory learners. In addition, the anthology contains artwork by African American visual artists. These works reflect the social, political, historical, and economic issues embedded in the oral, written, and musical works we have selected. This distinctive feature further broadens the anthology and will specifically assist visual learners in comprehending the thematic concerns of the African American literary tradition. The oral and visual components reflect our belief in a holistic approach to the teaching of African American literature and cultural traditions.

A section on Writing About African American Literature provides students with the strategies needed for literary analysis. It provides tools students will employ, including discussions of literary terms and strategies for organizing and evaluating literary texts from a variety of genres. Professors may use this section as a means of facilitating writing about African American literature for their students. Next, a timeline marked by important social, historical, and political events from the colonial period to the present will allow students to place the selections they read in a broad framework of both national and international events and will further facilitate their understanding of the contexts for African American literature. The timeline also reinforces the underlying theme of the text—slavery versus freedom.

The anthology ends with a list of sources and an index. The coeditors hope that this bibliography will be valuable for instructors in directing students to the sources of or about the selections in the anthology, particularly since some are published in full while others are excerpts. The index will enable professors to more easily identify page numbers for specific works and names in the anthology. This will make the text more useful as both a research and a teaching tool for professors who teach African American literature.

We view this anthology as a contribution to the study, analysis, and discussion of African American literature in the classroom. This anthology allows the instructor flexibility in terms of the type of course the text can be used in, from surveys in

African American literature to composition and rhetoric courses, and from courses in ethnic American literature to history and interdisciplinary courses as well. The teaching possibilities remain limitless as the desire to explore the African American literary tradition continues to increase and expand due, quite directly we feel, to the universality and relevance of the oral, written, and visual representations of human experience these selections reveal.

ACKNOWLEDGMENTS

The authors wish to thank the following people: Joe, Emily, and Keith Jones, Jay and Evelean Smith, Jay Jr., and Sonya Smith, Mamie L. Smith, Darryl Thurman, Frank Day, Ben W. McClelland, Michael G. Moran, the English Department at Earlham College, the English Department at the University of Mississippi, Donna White, Cheryl Collier, Rose Phillips, Ethel Young-Minor, Yvonne Robinson-Jones, Carrie Brandon, Gianna Caradonna, Shelly Kupperman, and Betty Morgan.

We wish to thank the reviewers for their helpful comments: Dr. Ngwarsungu Chiwengo, Creighton University; Dr. Joanne Gabbin, James Madison University; Professor Joyce Lausch, Department of English, Arizona State University; Professor Mark Mills; Dr. Jewell Parker-Rhodes; Dr. Lisa Pertillar-Brevard, University of Wisconsin, Oshkosh; Professor Kevin Quashie, Department of English, Arizona State University; Dr. Velma Smith, North Harris College; and Dr. John Edgar Tidwell, Miami University. We have benefited greatly from their advice and support.

Rochelle Smith
Sharon L. Jones

LIVING WORDS

AN AUDIO CD OF AFRICAN AMERICAN ORAL TRADITIONS

Oral traditions are a vital component of studying African American life. It is most readily in such traditions—represented by speeches, songs, storytelling, poetry—that the connections to African (and for that matter, Caribbean) cultures are evident; and that the particular rhythms and urgency of texts come alive. On this audio CD, we aim to capture a general sense of the richness oral legacy of African Americans. The selections included here nicely compliment the readings in the anthology.

The CD opens with a piece of Ghanian drum music. Ghana is one of the African countries which serves as a metaphorical and genealogical home to African Americans. The drum rhythms on this track closely parallel similar rhythms in music in the Caribbean, and the United States, which is evidenced here in the Negro spiritual "I Just Came from the Fountain" which follows. It is relevant that the CD open with two musical pieces, because, in the early years of enslavement, it was in music that African traditions were sustained, as many Africans spoke different languages, and were given little (if any) access to education, including reading and writing. The influence of music is not overstated, for music is a central base for the literary and cultural production, and life experiences, of African Americans.

Other musical selections on the CD represent a variety of traditions, and reflect historical moments in African American life. The most common music genre in this collection is the spiritual, one of the earliest African American oral traditions which informs many of the other music genres that develop. The selections here include famous songs performed by equally famous singers: "Go Down Moses" (perhaps the most famous spiritual) by Bill McAdoo; "Come By Hyar" by Bernice Reagon; "Swing Low Sweet Chariot" by Paul Robeson; "I Couldn't Hear Nobody Pray" by the Fisk Jubilee Singers; and "I Sing Because I'm Happy" by Mahalia Jackson. Many spirituals were re-recorded by each generation of African Americans often to give voice to the political and social context of their time. It was in this vein that Marian Anderson's stirring version of "He's Got the Whole World in His Hands" was included in the historic March on Washington in 1963, and "Wade in the Water" became a Civil Rights Movement standard.

The blues and work song traditions learn from and contribute to the spirituals. In Pete Seeger's version of the African American work song classic "Pick a Bale of Cotton," the use of repetition provides an inspiring work rhythm, and resonates with similar uses of repetition in spirituals. Lead Belly performs "Backwater Blues," capturing the blues tradition, and revealing the intimate relationship between blues and spirituals, especially the way both traditions describe everyday and common events as sacred.

The last track, "Zum Zum" is a recording by Six Boys in Trouble in New York. This piece represents an interesting early version of dub poetry and beats which later influences rap and hip hop music. Also, its rhythms and use of drums mirror the opening piece of Ghanian drum music, reflecting the strong overlap between contemporary African American music traditions, and those of the past.

The presence and development of African American music influences other expressions of orality. Many of the aesthetic innovations in poetry echo the repetitions evident in various African American music forms. Furthermore, just as music was intimately connected with reflecting and commenting on social and political condition, so to is the poetry interested in all aspects of life in African America. Harlem Renaissance writer Arna Bontemps reads Lucy Terry's "Bars Fight," the first published poem by an African American. Phillis Wheatley's elegant mediation, "On Being Brought from Africa to America," is read here by Jean Brannon. These two poets establish a foundation for all African American writers who proceed them. The CD also includes a reading of Paul Laurence Dunbar's "Dawn" and James Weldon Johnson's epic piece "The Creation," both read by Bontemps. Claude McKay is heard reading his own poem, "If We Must Die," and Langston Hughes delivers his own "I've Known Rivers" and "I Too." Both of these writers became widely famous during the Harlem Renaissance era, and are best known for the poems they are reading here. Pulitzer Prize winner Gwendolyn Brooks reads her wonderful piece "Song of the Front Yard." Of more contemporary poets, there is Sonia Sanchez reading "liberation/poem," and Nikki Giovanni delivering "Woman."

Finally, there are a variety of prose pieces gathered on this companion, capturing many key moments in African American history. The first are two pieces by former slaves, chronicling their experience. Spoken narratives as these were often the first step toward the production of written autobiographies (for example slave narratives.) In many cases, there are no written accounts by prominent African American figures, but there are stories of their lives and texts of their speeches. Jean Brannon takes a piece of Sojourner Truth's life story, and turns it into a stirring reading about her name and identity. Brannon also offers a glimpse at Harriet Tubman's life, similarly drawing from documents on the great freedom fighter. Maria W. Stewart's speech "What If I Am a Woman," is given a new life here in Ruby Dee's reading; similarly, Frederick Douglass's "If There is No Struggle, There is No Freedom" is vitalized in Ossie Davis's voice.

We hear Booker T. Washington's voice delivering an excerpt from his famous "Address at the Atlanta Exposition," and a contemporary of his, W.E.B. DuBois, in an interview talking about the creation of the N.A.A.C.P. There is Martin Luther King, Jr., delivering a speech at a mass meeting, at the height of the Civil Rights Movement. It is inspiring to hear King at a smaller gathering, and to get a sense of the widespread commitment to political action that existed in the Sixties, manifesting on both national and local fronts. Then, there is Angela Davis's voice of protest, in an interview she gave while still in prison in the early 1970s, a snapshot view of the woman who would become the impressive figure we know today.

The movement of the CD is organized to reflect the diversity of African American oral presentations that exist in our history; and still, it is clear, upon listening to the selections, that there are incredible overlaps, and that many of the pieces are speaking with and in contradistinction with each other and U.S. history. The rhythms, the words, the urgency . . . they are all there in these living words of African American life.

Kevin Everod Quashie
Stuart L. Twite

INTRODUCTION

AFRICAN AMERICAN LITERATURE FROM THE COLONIAL PERIOD to the present represents a journey from slavery to freedom, both literally and figuratively, for African American writers. Social, political, historical, and cultural events shape African American literature as poets, playwrights, novelists, short-story writers, and orators seek to express themselves through the oral and written traditions. An understanding of these movements and the conditions that precipitated these periods in African American literature will enhance the appreciation and evaluation of these rich traditions. The theme of slavery versus freedom unites the authors featured in this anthology, illustrating a common link among the chorus of voices comprising the African American literary tradition.

The history of African Americans dates back to the "divided" selves of blacks transplanted from Africa to the New World via the Middle Passage, the route slave ships followed from Africa to the American colonies. Many African American writers of the colonial period (1746–1800) were slaves who managed to acquire literacy in the English language, such as Phillis Wheatley, Jupiter Hammon, and George Moses Horton. Their literary output and their emphasis on the theme of slavery versus freedom testify to the paradox of slavery in colonial America, particularly in the context of the American Revolutionary War (1775–1781), when the issues of individual and collective liberty gained precedence.

By the antebellum period (1800–1865), resistance to slavery had grown as more blacks achieved literacy and penned tales about the inhumanity of slavery in hopes of achieving freedom for themselves and other African Americans. Blacks and whites cooperated through the establishment of the Underground Railroad, and abolitionist periodicals such as *The Liberator* proliferated as the wave of anti-slavery sentiment swept across the land. Ex-slaves like Frederick Douglass, author of *The Narrative of the Life of Frederick Douglass, an American Slave, Written by Himself*, and Harriet Jacobs, author of *Incidents in the Life of a Slave Girl, Written by Herself*, testified to the injustice of slavery and the need to abolish it. Black literature, like the spirituals, focused on the abolition of slavery, the pressing issue of the day.

Despite the abolition of slavery in 1865 at the end of the Civil War, African Americans found themselves facing rampant discrimination in terms of jobs, housing, and education during the Reconstruction period (1865–1900). The *Plessy v. Ferguson* decision handed down by the U.S. Supreme Court in 1896 sanctioned "separate but equal" policies as the law of the land, upholding legalized segregation of blacks and whites. Still, African Americans fought on for social justice, as revealed in the fiction of Charles Chesnutt; in novels such as *Iola Leroy, or Shadows Uplifted* by Frances E. W. Harper; and in Anna Julia Cooper's *A Voice from the South: By a Black Woman of the South*, a series of essays and speeches. These authors focused on education and moral and spiritual uplift, and they analyzed race, class, and gender prejudice as they sought true emancipation for blacks.

During the Harlem Renaissance (1900–1940), the quest for freedom continued. This interdisciplinary movement in art, literature, politics, and music sought to define the New Negro, a concept that presented blacks as strong, articulate, educated, empowered, and possessing an appreciation of African and African American history and heritage. Harlem Renaissance writers produced many works of lasting value. Activist and writer W. E. B. Du Bois penned *The Souls of Black Folk;* Alain Locke edited *The New Negro: An Interpretation*, which served as a manifesto of the Harlem Renaissance; Zora Neale Hurston critiqued race, class, and gender to provide a female perspective in *Their Eyes Were Watching God;* Langston Hughes illustrated the beauty of African American musical forms through his poetry, which articulated the rhythm of jazz and blues. With their attention to African American aesthetics and their desire to combat racial oppression through organizations such as the NAACP (publisher of *The Crisis*) and the Urban League (publisher of *Opportunity*), artists of the Harlem Renaissance took an important step on the journey from slavery to freedom—a struggle that would be continued by writers of the protest era, the black aesthetics movement, and the neorealism movement.

With their novels, short stories, poetry, drama, and nonfiction, African American writers during the protest movement (1940–1959) helped to advance the journey toward freedom. Although the institution of slavery had been eliminated, African Americans still lived with overt racism. Limited resources and few opportunities for advancement kept blacks in an inferior position, unable to totally break the shackles. The African American male's plight is illustrated in the works of writers such as Richard Wright, Ralph Ellison, James Baldwin, and Robert Hayden. Female perspectives came from Margaret Walker Alexander, Ann Petry, Gwendolyn Brooks, Lorraine Hansberry, and others. These writers presented stories that gave readers insight into what it was like to be an African American facing insurmountable race barriers. For example, in *Native Son* and *Black Boy*, Wright shows the implications of fearing white society, feeling restrained, dehumanized. Fear, as Wright demonstrates, can lead to death, both spiritually and physically. Ellison's protagonist in *Invisible Man* is treated not as an individual but only as a low-class "element" who must endure persecution because of his race. Baldwin explores religious issues, and Hayden deals with political issues. Brooks often writes about African American women in the roles of mother and mate. African

American male and female writers during the 1940s and 1950s clearly painted portraits of blacks enslaved by the dominant societal sector. African Americans protested covertly through their written and oral texts, helping to bridge distance and fill gaps for the audience. Protests outside the literary realm also brought African Americans closer to freedom. Some indicators of the increased freedom were the 1948 ban on segregation in the military, the Supreme Court's 1954 ruling against racial segregation in public schools, and the Alabama bus boycotts brought on when Rosa Parks refused to give up her seat to a white man, which led to the ruling that segregated seating on public transportation was unconstitutional.

Overt protests in literature as well as in society characterized the black aesthetics movement (1960–1969). Some hallmark historical events occurred during this time: the Vietnam War, the March on Washington (for which Martin Luther King, Jr., delivered his famous "I Have a Dream" speech), and the assassinations of King and Malcolm X. The voices, written and oral, of African Americans during the black arts movement carried politically charged messages. In fact, the primary purpose of black art was to promote racial equality. Hence, speeches such as those written and delivered by King and Malcolm X were considered art forms within the black literary arena. Rhetorical analysis of these texts reveals a mastery of the stylistic devices used for persuasion. Amiri Baraka (formerly LeRoi Jones) wrote poetry and essays that exposed the bare truth about living in the grip of racism. His writing has been controversial because he does not "hold his tongue"; he "lets it rip," using a forceful, often angry tone. Haki R. Madhubuti also wrote about controversial topics such as the role of African American race leaders like Malcolm X. Sonia Sanchez and Nikki Giovanni provided strong female voices that dealt with political and social concerns in their poetry. Speaking loudly through their art, African American writers and singers distinguished black aesthetics from white aesthetics. The African American oral and written traditions merged to create a revolutionary period like the Harlem Renaissance, in which the role of the black artist was to move African Americans farther from slavery and closer to freedom.

In some ways, the African American literature that followed the overt protest of black aesthetics is not easy to define. During the neorealism movement (1970–present), African American writers moved even closer to freedom—enjoying wide appreciation from their audience for their work. Also during this time, Jesse Jackson ran for president of the United States, gathering some enthusiastic support, and Martin Luther King Day became a national holiday. Black women writers such as Maya Angelou, Alice Walker, and Toni Morrison have become primary writers with classic works. To a large degree, African American literature has been incorporated into the canon of American literature. Along with this integration comes a separation: specialists in African American literature and Afro-American studies programs became increasingly prominent from the 1970s through the 1990s. English departments have filled academic and cultural gaps by hiring scholars of black literature and multicultural literature. Diversity has become a priority in terms of teachers, students, and course material—across the curriculum. The dominant characteristic of neorealist African American literature is variety, a sense of freedom in artistic presentation. While the common theme of black experience prevails, the neorealism movement represents a culmination of the African American literary tradition from colonial times to the present. Ernest Gaines in *The Autobiography of Miss Jane Pittman* and Charles Johnson in *Middle Passage* provide historical perspectives; Audre Lorde and June Jordan present political perspectives, Octavia Butler writes science fiction; Walter Mosley succeeds at mystery writing; and Randall Kenan explores magic realism. African American literary critics research the important issues of each historical period; as the Los Angeles riots of 1992 emphasized, race is still a major issue in America. Scholars continue to critically examine the vast body of black literature—its authors, rhetorical style, and political leanings.

We have come a long way, but we still have a long way to go. African American literature has a rich and varied history, as this anthology illustrates. During a time when they were not allowed to read and write, blacks used a strong sense of determination and hope to learn in spite of the restrictions. Amazingly, during those early years, they used their voices in speech, writing, and song to argue for equality, and those voices have gotten stronger and more abundant. The use of language for a multitude of purposes—professional and personal—when put in context becomes more meaningful as it is connected to history. Hence, this text puts African American literature within historical context, showing its connections to other aspects of American society. African American writers, singers, and speakers reveal the complexity of the African American experience using a theme that embodies the struggle, the theme of this text: slavery versus freedom.

PART 1

THE COLONIAL PERIOD
1746–1800

INTRODUCTION

MOST SLAVES TRAVELED TO COLONIAL AMERICA THROUGH the Middle Passage (the route from Africa to the New World across the Atlantic Ocean). Cramped inside slave ships with tight, unsanitary quarters, the Africans who were seized, captured, and transported to the New World faced a perilous journey. The Middle Passage, one of the central factors in the history of the African presence in America, is an important theme in African American literature, reflecting the experience of transition between Africa and the New World, the past and the present, freedom and bondage, and oral and written traditions.

In *The Interesting Narrative of the Life of Olaudah Equiano, or Gustavus Vassa, the African, Written by Himself* (pp. 9–19), Olaudah Equiano captures the tumultuous and frightening nature of his transport from Africa to the New World: "In this situation I expected every hour to share the fate of my companions, some of whom were almost daily brought upon deck at the point of death, and I began to hope that death would soon put an end to my miseries. Often did I think many of the inhabitants of the deep much more happy than myself; I envied them the freedom they enjoyed, and as often wished I could change my condition for theirs" (p. 17). His narrative illustrates the emotional aspects of the perilous passage and the tension between the desire for freedom and the reality of entrapment on slave ships.

Not surprisingly, African American literature of the colonial period directly bears upon the "doubleness," the "divided" selves of Africans who were transplanted, against their will, to colonial America. The experience serves as a context for the poetry, letters, songs, and pamphlets produced by early African American writers. Like Equiano, Phillis Wheatley traveled to America on the perilous Middle Passage and documented her experience in her art. Equiano and Wheatley represent those who survived the Middle Passage; many others died because of sickness, suicide, and mutinies on the slave ships. As a child, Wheatley was captured as a slave, transported to colonial America, and later purchased by a wealthy Boston family. Her poetry and letters reveal a divided self, with ambivalent feelings about Africa, the land of her birth and heritage, and New England, the land in which the Wheatleys "Christianized" her as a means of assimilating the young girl to a different land, language, and culture. In her poem "On Being Brought from Africa to America" (p. 19), she meditates on life in "Pagan" Africa in contrast to her experience in the Judeo-Christian world of colonial America; divided between her native and adopted lands, she seeks to negotiate her past and present lives. Tutored in English and Latin, Phillis rose to prominence for her religious poems and elegies, written in a neoclassical style modeled after British writers such as John Milton and Alexander Pope.

Because racist ideology of the period justified the enslavement of blacks by denying the intellectual capabilities of individuals of African descent, Wheatley's authorship of her early poems was called into question. Prominent male citizens therefore verified the authenticity of her work. Wheatley's struggle for authorship anticipates the plight of other black writers, such as Frederick Douglass and Harriet Jacobs, whose writing also had to be validated in prefaces written by prominent whites as a means of authenticating African Americans' experiences and voices in their narratives.

African Americans employed the written word as a means of conveying a desire to break the bonds of slavery and emancipate themselves. African American literature of the colonial period, in the form of poetry, sermons, letters, and the slave narrative, argued for the humanity of blacks and against the evils of slavery, which dehumanized all Americans, black and white. The slave narrative, in fact, set the foundation for African American autobiography and fiction as a prose form that sought to articulate the African American experience in the New World. These early forms of African American literature were a powerful weapon against slavery and served as a source of inspiration and endurance for its victims.

Religion played an important role in early African American literature. Colonists in early America, like the family who owned Phillis Wheatley, often instructed their slaves and indentured servants in the tenets of the Christian faith. Enslaved blacks often looked toward the promise of an afterlife in which they would be free from enforced servitude. Also, a faith in a supreme being often provided them with the sustenance to survive the hardships of slavery. While the newly transplanted Africans often adopted the religious teachings of their masters and owners, they sought to integrate the teachings of Christianity with their African religions, customs, traditions, and beliefs. Poets such as Phillis Wheatley and Jupiter Hammon, steeped in a Protestant tradition, used religion as a source for inspiration and meditation on the plight of African Americans facing oppression in colonial America. Wheatley calls attention to the importance of religion for residents of colonial America in "On the Death of the Rev. Mr. George Whitefield," as a moving elegy for a popular Methodist minister who gained fame during the Great Awakening of religious fervor in the colonies during the eighteenth century. Similarly, Jupiter Hammon reminds his readers that "Salvation comes by Christ alone" in "An Evening Thought: Salvation by Christ with Penentential Cries" (pp. 27–29). The religious concerns of early African American writers reflect life in Puritan America, which dictated that literature be used to serve as a means of moral, spiritual, and religious instruction.

African Americans in colonial America often related biblical stories of captivity and bondage to their own experiences as slaves. They often paralleled their plight with that of the enslaved Israelites of the Old Testament, and in their spirituals they compared the "free" North to the promised land of the King James Bible. Frequently, spirituals contain hidden messages signaling plans to flee the bondage of slavery in the South and escape to the "free" North. The spirituals represent an important aspect of the enduring oral tradition of African American literature and culture. In many contemporary religious services, choirs still perform spirituals such as "Motherless Child" (p. 30).

Like the spirituals, oral storytelling played an important role in the lives of African Americans during the colonial period. In tales such as "All God's Chillen Had Wings" (pp. 24–26), the theme of slavery versus freedom predominates, transmitting the hopes of the storyteller and the audience. Written works such as poems, letters, and slave narratives often conformed to the literary conventions and language of eighteenth-century British and European literature, but the oral tradition often incorporated the language and dialect of early black Americans recently transplanted to the New World. Because many African American slaves could not read or write, and over time laws were enacted to prohibit teaching those skills to slaves, they used their creative and artistic abilities to create work songs, spirituals, and folktales that have survived to this day.

The American Revolutionary War (1775–1781) highlighted the tensions between slavery and freedom for all Americans as the colonists fought the British in a quest for self-rule and self-determination. Literature of the colonial period reflects the irony of an America heralded as a bastion of freedom from British tyranny despite its reliance on slavery and indentured servitude to support the social, political, and economic structure. Forged upon the idea of justice, equality, and freedom from British domination, colonial America exhibited a paradox in its continued tolerance of slavery. The colonists fought for democracy, for freedom from what they perceived as tyrannical rule; the reality of enslavement and bondage became heightened and dramatized in the participation of black soldiers, for both the British and the Americans, in the Revolution. African American writers of the colonial period explore this paradox, which intensified amid tensions breaking out between colonists advocating self-government and those who favored monarchical control. As the issue of freedom from oppression attracted public debate, few could ignore the prevalence of slavery and indentured servitude in the colonies. Early African American writers, such as Phillis Wheatley in "To His Excellency General Washington" (pp. 22–23), identified the tensions between the American colonists desiring freedom from British rule. In her poem, praising George Washington as a moral exemplar and protector of freedom and independence, she articulated the sentiment of many Americans, white and black, in favor of colonial self-rule.

For African American writers of the period, the war often served as a context for their work. Writers like Olaudah Equiano, Phillis Wheatley, Lucy Terry Prince, Jupiter Hammon, George Moses Horton, and Benjamin Banneker all responded to issues of freedom and democracy while overtly or covertly critiquing the status of African Americans in colonial society. In works such as "On Being

Brought from Africa to America," "To S. M., a Young African Painter, on Seeing His Works," "To His Excellency General Washington," and "Letter to Samson Occom" (pp. 19–23), Wheatley comments on slavery in the United States, the artistic capabilities of African Americans, the spiritual equality of all under the eyes of God, and the importance of freedom from tyranny and injustice. Although some critics have asserted that Wheatley fails to address issues of race in her poetry, her work reveals a writer meditating on her African heritage and her assimilation into early American colonial society. As the author of *Poems on Various Subjects, Religious and Moral* (1773), Wheatley stands as significant in ushering in the African American literary tradition.

Like Wheatley, Lucy Terry Prince was African by birth. Brought to America and sold as a slave, she eventually learned to read and write, becoming a trailblazer in the African American literary tradition. Her poem "Bars Fight, August 28, 1746" (pp. 26–27) chronicles an Indian attack against white colonists. The poem reveals the tensions between whites and Indians in colonial America and indicates the poet's sensitivity to the social and political climate of the period. Similarly, George Moses Horton and Jupiter Hammon responded to prevailing issues of the colonial period, including the enslavement of blacks and the importance of religion in early American culture. Like Wheatley and Prince, Horton and Hammon were slaves who acquired literacy and used it to assert their voices and humanity. Horton's "On Liberty and Slavery" (pp. 31–32) signals a heartfelt plea for the abolition of slavery. Hammon's "An Evening Thought: Salvation by Christ with Penetential Cries" (pp. 27–29) chronicles the poet's acceptance of Christianity as the means for ultimate freedom and salvation in heaven.

Although much of early African American literature consists of poetry and slave narratives, Benjamin Banneker is represented through his almanacs and letters. In his "Letter to Thomas Jefferson" (pp. 33–35), arguing for racial equality, he articulates the ideas of freedom and equality for all Americans.

The reality of slavery, the Revolutionary War, and relations between the colonists and Native Americans contributed to the development of African American writing that responded to pressing issues of the colonial period that still find relevancy and resonance in readers today. Colonial African Americans incorporated the style and rhythm of British and European writers, adapted elements of African oral traditions, and transformed their writing into a distinct body of literature. Their poems, letters, and narratives call attention to the plight of early black Americans, divided between the land of their ancestors and the reality of life in colonial America. Their work stands as testimony to their active resistance against slavery while reinforcing the image of African Americans as creative, articulate individuals desirous of freedom.

✠ OLAUDAH EQUIANO (1745–1797)

Equiano's account of his bondage and subsequent freedom, coupled with a vivid account of the effects of slavery upon the enslaved, helped set the stage for the genre of the slave narrative, an important feature of the African American prose tradition. His narrative anticipates works such as Harriet Jacobs's Incidents in the Life of a Slave Girl *and Frederick Douglass's autobiography. By chronicling the harsh realities of slavery and his quest for freedom, Equiano powerfully articulates the experience of blacks in colonial America.*

As the author of one of the earliest slave narratives, Equiano stands as a trailblazer in the African American literary tradition. Born in Africa and sold into slavery, he was transported to Virginia and bought by a British naval officer (while in Virginia), who renamed him Gustavus Vassa. As part of his servitude, Equiano became a sailor. Sympathetic whites taught him how to read and write in the English language. Later, he was bought by a trader from the West Indies, who eventually sold him in Montserrat to a Philadelphia businessman. Purchasing his own freedom in 1766, he relocated to England and married Susanna Cullen, an Englishwoman, in 1792. Equiano's autobiography recounts the Middle Passage and his various travels as a sailor in the 1700s.

From The Interesting Narrative of the Life of Olaudah Equiano, or Gustavus Vassa, the African, Written by Himself (1789)

Chapter 2

The author's birth and parentage—His being kidnapped with his sister—Their separation—Surprise at meeting again—Are finally separated—Account of the different places and incidents the author met with till his arrival *on* the coast—The effect the sight of a slave ship had on him—He sails for the West Indies—Horrors of a slave ship—Arrives at Barbadoes, where the cargo is sold and dispersed.

I. I hope the reader will not think I have trespassed on his patience, in introducing myself to him with some account of the manners and customs of my country. They had been implanted in me with great care, and made an impression on my mind, which time could not erase, and which all the adversity and variety of fortune I have since experienced, served only to rivet and record; for, whether the love of one's country be real or imaginary, a lesson of reason or an instinct of nature, I still look back with pleasure on the first scenes of my life, though that pleasure has been for the most part mingled with sorrow.

I have already acquainted the reader with the time and place of my birth. My father, besides many slaves, had a numerous family, of which seven lived to grow up, including myself and a sister, who was the only daughter. As I was the youngest of the sons, I became, of course, the greatest favourite with my mother, and was always with her, and she used to take particular pains to form my mind.

I was trained up from my earliest years in the art of war: my daily exercise was shooting and throwing javelins; and my mother adorned me with emblems, after the manner of our greatest warriors. In this way I grew up till I was turned the age of eleven, when an end was put to my happiness in the following manner:—When the grown people in the neighbourhood were gone far in the fields to labour, the children generally assembled together in some of the neighbours' premises to play; and some of us often used to get up into a tree to look out for any assailant, or kidnapper, that might come upon us. For they sometimes took those opportunities of our parents' absence, to attack and carry off as many as they could seize. One day, as I was watching at the top of a tree in our yard, I saw one of those people come into the yard of our next neighbour but one, to kidnap, there being many stout young people in it. Immediately on this I gave the alarm of the rogue, and he was surrounded by the stoutest of them, who entangled him with cords, so that he could not escape till some of the grown people came and secured him.

II. But alas! ere long it was my fate to be thus attacked, and to be carried off, when none of the grown people were nigh. One day, when all our people were gone out to their work as usual, and only I and my sister were left to mind the house, two men and a woman got over our walls, and in a moment seized us both; and without giving us time to cry out, or to make any resistance, they stopped our mouths and ran off with us into the nearest wood. Here they tied our hands, and continued to carry us as far as they could, till night came on, when we reached a small house, where the robbers halted for refreshment and spent the night. We were then unbound, but were unable to take any food; and being quite overpowered by fatigue and grief, our only relief was some sleep, which allayed our misfortune for a short time. The next morning we left the house, and continued travelling all the day. For a long time we had kept the woods, but at last we came into a road which I believed I knew. I had now some hopes of being delivered; for we had advanced but a little way before I discovered some people at a distance, on which I began to cry out for their assistance; but my cries had no other effect than to make them tie me faster and stop my mouth; they then put me into a large sack. They also stopped my sister's mouth, and tied her hands; and in this manner we proceeded till we were out of sight of these people.

When we went to rest the following night, they offered us some victuals; but we refused it; and the only comfort we had was in being in one another's arms all that night, and bathing each other with tears. But alas! we were soon deprived of even the small comfort of weeping together. The next day proved one of greater sorrow than I had yet experienced; for my sister and I were then separated, while we lay clasped in each other's arms. It was in vain that we besought them not to part us; she was torn from me, and immediately carried away, while I was left in a state of distraction not to be described. I cried and grieved continually; and for several days did not eat any thing but what they forced into my mouth. At length, after many days' travelling, during which I had often changed masters, I got into the hands of a chieftain, in a pleasant country. This man had two wives and some children, and they all used me extremely well, and did all they could to comfort me; particularly the first wife, who was something like my mother. Although I was a great many days' journey from my father's house, yet these people spoke exactly the same language with us. This first master of mine, as I may call him, was a smith, and my principal employment was working his bellows, which were the same kind as I had seen in my vicinity. They were in some respects not unlike the stoves here in gentlemen's kitchens; and were covered over with leather, and in the middle of that leather a stick was fixed, and a person stood up and worked it, in the same manner as is done to pump water out of a cask with a hand pump. I believe it was gold he worked, for it was of a lovely bright yellow colour, and was worn by the women on their wrists and ankles.

I was there, I suppose, about a month, and they at length used to trust me some little distance from the house. I employed this liberty in embracing every opportunity to inquire the way to my own home: and I also sometimes, for the same purpose, went with the maidens, in the cool of the evenings, to bring pitchers of water from the springs for the use of the house. I had also remarked where the sun rose in the morning, and set in the evening, as I had travelled along: and had observed that my father's house was towards the rising of the sun. I therefore determined to seize the first opportunity of making my escape, and to shape my course for that quarter; for I was quite oppressed and weighed down by grief after my mother and friends; and my love of liberty, ever great, was strengthened by the mortifying circumstance of not daring to eat with the free-born children, although I was mostly their companion.

III. While I was projecting my escape, one day an unlucky event happened, which quite disconcerted my plan, and put an end to my hopes. I used to be sometimes employed in assisting an elderly woman slave to cook and take care of the poultry: and one morning, while I was feeding some chickens, I happened to toss a small pebble at one of them, which hit in on the middle, and directly killed it. The old slave having soon after missed the chicken, inquired after it; and on my relating the accident (for I told her the truth, because my mother would never suffer me to tell a lie) she flew into a violent passion, threatened that I should suffer for it; and, my master being out, she immediately went and told her mistress what I had done. This alarmed me very much, and I expected an instant flogging, which to me was uncommonly dreadful; for I had seldom been beaten at home. I therefore resolved to fly; and accordingly I ran into a thicket that was hard by, and hid myself in the bushes. Soon afterwards my mistress and the slave returned, and, not seeing me, they searched all the house, but not finding me, and I not making answer when they called me, they thought I had run away, and the whole neighbourhood was raised in the pursuit of me.

In that part of the country, as well as in ours, the houses and villages were skirted with woods, or shrubberies, and the bushes were so thick that a man could readily conceal himself in them, so as to elude the strictest search. The neighbours continued the whole day looking for me, and several times many of them came within a few yards of the place where I lay hid. I expected every moment, when I heard a rustling among the trees, to be found out, and punished by my master. But they never discovered me, though they often were so near that I even heard their conjectures, as they were looking about for me; and I now learned from them, that any attempt to return home would be hopeless. Most of them supposed I had fled towards home; but the distance was so great, and the way so intricate, that they thought I could never reach it, and that I should be lost in the woods. When I heard this I was seized with a violent panic, and abandoned myself to despair. Night too began to approach, and aggravated all my fears. I had before entertained hopes of getting home and had determined when it should be dark to make the attempt; but I was now convinced it was fruitless, and began to consider that, if possibly I could escape all other animals, I could not those of the human kind; and that, not knowing the way, I must perish in the woods. Thus was I like the hunted deer:

Ev'ry leaf, and ev'ry whisp'ring breath
Convey'd a foe, and ev'ry foe a death.

I heard frequent rustlings among the leaves, and being pretty sure they were snakes, I expected every instant to be stung by them. This increased my anguish, and the horror of my situation became now quite insupportable. I at length quitted the thicket, very faint and hungry, for I had not eaten nor drunk any thing all the day. I crept to my master's kitchen, from whence I set out at first, which was an open shed, and laid myself down in the ashes with an anxious wish for death to relieve me from all my pains. I was scarcely awake in the morning, when the old woman slave, who was the first up, came to light the fire, and saw me in the fire place. She was very much surprised to see me, and could scarcely believe her own eyes. She now promised to intercede for me, and went for her master, who soon after came, and, having slightly reprimanded me, ordered me to be taken care of, and not ill treated.

IV. Soon after this my master's only daughter and child by his first wife, sickened and died, which affected him so much that for some time he was almost frantic, and really would have killed himself, had he not been watched and prevented. However, in a small time afterwards he recovered, and I was again sold. I was now carried to the left of the sun's rising, through many dreary wastes and dismal woods, amidst the hideous roaring of wild beasts. The people I was sold to used to carry me very often, when I was tired, either on their shoulders or on their backs. I saw many convenient well-built sheds along the road, at proper distances, to accommodate the merchants and travellers. They lie in those buildings along with their wives, who often accompany them: and they always go well armed.

From the time I left my own nation I always found somebody that understood me till I came to the sea coast. The languages of different nations did not totally differ, nor were they so copious as those of the Europeans, particularly the English. They were therefore easily learned; and, while I was journeying thus through Africa, I acquired two or three different tongues. In this manner I had been travelling for a considerable time, when one evening, to my great surprise, whom should I see brought to the house where I was, but my dear sister? As soon as she saw me she gave a loud shriek, and ran into my arms. I was quite overpowered: neither of us could speak; but for a considerable time, clung to each other in mutual embraces, unable to do any thing but weep. Our meeting affected all who saw us; and indeed I must acknowledge, in honour of those sable destroyers of human rights, that I never met with any ill treatment, or saw any offered to their slaves, except tying them, when necessary, to keep them running away.

When these people knew we were brother and sister, they indulged us to be together; and the man, to whom I supposed we belonged, lay with us, he in the middle, while she and I held one another by the hands across his breast all night; and thus for a while we forgot our misfortunes in the joy of being together. But even this small comfort was soon to have an end, for scarcely had the fatal morning appeared, when she was again torn from me for ever! I was now more miserable, if possible, than before. The small relief which her presence gave me from pain was gone, and the wretchedness of my situation was redoubled by my anxiety after her fate, and my apprehensions lest her sufferings should be greater than mine, when I could not be with her to alleviate them.

Yes, dear partner of all my childish sports! Sharer of my joys and sorrows; happy should I have ever esteemed myself to encounter every misery for you, and to procure your freedom by the sacrifice of my own! Though you were early forced from my arms, your image has been always rivetted in my heart, from which neither time nor fortune has been able to remove it: so that, while the thoughts of your sufferings have damped my prosperity, they have mingled with adversity and increased its bitterness. To that Heaven, which protects the weak from the strong, I commit the care of your innocence and virtues, if they have not already received their full reward, and if your youth and delicacy have not long since fallen victims to the violence of the African trader, the pestilential stench of a Guinea ship, the seasoning in the European colonies, or the lash and lust of a brutal and unrelenting overseer.

I did not long remain after my sister. I was again sold, and carried through a number of places, till, after travelling a considerable time, I came to a town called Tinmah, in the most beautiful country I had yet seen in Africa. It was extremely rich, and there were many rivulets which flowed through it, and supplied a large pond in the centre of the town, where the people washed. Here I first saw and tasted cocoa nuts, which I thought superior to any nuts I had ever tasted before; and the trees which were loaded, were also interspersed among the houses, which had commodious shades adjoining, and were in the same manner as ours, the insides being neatly plastered and whitewashed. Here I also saw and tasted, for the first time, sugar-cane. Their money consisted of little white shells, the size of the fingernail. I was sold for one hundred and seventy-two of these, by a merchant who lived at this place. I had been about two or three days at his house, when a wealthy widow, a neighbour of his, came there one evening, and brought with her an only son, a young gentleman about my own age and size. Here they saw me; and, having taken a fancy to me, I was bought of the merchant, and went home with them. Her house and premises were situated close to one of those rivulets I have mentioned, and were the finest I ever saw in Africa: they were very exten-sive, and she had a number of slaves to attend her. The next day I was washed and perfumed, and when meal-time came, I was led into the presence of my mistress, and ate and drank before her with her son. This filled me with astonishment; and I could scarcely avoid expressing my surprise that the young gentleman should suffer me, who was bound, to eat with him who was free; and not only so, but that he would not at any time either eat or drink till I had taken first, because I was the eldest, which was agreeable to our custom. Indeed every thing here, and their treatment of me, made me forget that I was a slave. The language of these people resembled ours so nearly, that we understood each other perfectly. They had also the very same customs as we. There were likewise slaves daily to attend us, while my young master and I, with other boys, sported with our darts, and bows and arrows, as I had been used to do at home. In this resemblance to my former happy state, I passed about two months; and now I began to think I was to be adopted into the family, and was beginning to be reconciled to my situation, and to forget by degrees my misfortunes, when all at once the delusion vanished; for, without the least previous knowledge, one morning, early, while my dear master and companion was still asleep, I was awakened out of my reverie to fresh sorrow, and hurried away even amongst the uncircumcised.

Thus, at the very moment I dreamed of the greatest happiness, I found myself most miserable; and it seemed as if fortune wished to give me this taste of joy, only to render the reverse more poignant. The change I now experienced was as painful as it was sudden and unexpected. It was a change indeed from a state of bliss to a scene which is inexpressible by me, as it discovered to me an element I had never before beheld, and of which till then had no idea; and wherein such instances of hardship and cruelty continually occurred, as I can never reflect on but with horror.

V. All the nations and people I had hitherto passed through resembled our own in their manners, customs, and language: but I came at length to a country, the inhabitants of which differed from us in all these particulars. I was very much struck with this difference, especially when I came among a people who did not circumcise, and who ate without washing their hands. They cooked their provisions also in iron pots, and had European cutlasses and cross bows, which were unknown to us; and fought with their fists among themselves. Their women were not so modest as ours, for they ate, drank, and slept with their men. But, above all, I was amazed to see no sacrifices or offering among them. In some of those places the people ornamented themselves with scars, and likewise filed their teeth very sharp. They sometimes wanted to ornament me in the same manner, but I would not suffer them; hoping that I might sometime be among a people who did not thus disfigure themselves, as I thought they did. At last I came to the banks of a large river, covered with canoes, in which the people appeared to live, with their household utensils, and provisions of all kinds. I was beyond measure astonished at this, as I had never before seen any water larger than a pond or a rivulet: and my surprise was mingled with no small fear when I was put into one of these canoes, and we began to paddle and move along the river. We continued going on thus till night; and when we came to land, and made fires on the banks, each family by themselves, some dragged their canoes on shore, others cooked in theirs, and laid in them all night. Those on the land had mats, of which they made tents, some in the shape of little houses: in these we slept: and after the morning meal, we embarked again, and proceeded as before. I was often very much astonished to see some of the women as well as the men, jump into the water, dive to the bottom, come up again, and swim about. Thus I continued to travel, both by land and by water, through different countries and various nations, till at the end of six or seven months after I had been kidnapped, I arrived at the sea coast.

It would be tedious and uninteresting to relate all the incidents which befell me during this journey, and which I have not yet forgotten, or to mention the various lands I passed through, and the manners and customs of the different people among whom I lived: I shall therefore only observe, that in all the places where I was, the soil was exceedingly rich; the pomkins, aedas, plantains, yams, &c. &c. were in great abundance, and of incredible size. There were also large quantities of different gums, though not used for any purpose; and every where a great deal of tobacco. The cotton even grew quite wild; and there was plenty of red wood. I saw no mechanics whatever in all the way, except such as I have mentioned. The chief employment in all these countries was agriculture, and both the males and females, as with us, were brought up to it, and trained in the arts of war.

The first object that saluted my eyes when I arrived on the coast was the sea, and a slave ship, which was then riding at anchor, and waiting for its cargo. These filled me with astonishment, that was soon converted into terror, which I am yet at a loss to describe, and much more the then feelings of my mind when I was carried on board. I was immediately handled and tossed up to see if I was sound, by some of the crew; and I was now persuaded that I had got into a world of bad spirits, and that they were going to kill me. Their complexions too, differing so much from ours, their long hair, and the language they spoke, which was very different from any I had ever heard, united to confirm me in this belief. Indeed such were the horrors of my views and fears at the moment, that if ten thousand worlds had been my own, I would have freely parted with them all to have exchanged my condition with the meanest slave in my own country. When I looked round the ship too, and saw a large furnace or copper boiling and a multitude of black people, of every description, chained together, every one of their countenances expressing dejection and sorrow, I no longer doubted of my fate; and, quite overpowered with horror and anguish, I fell motionless on the deck, and fainted. When I recovered a little, I found some black people about me, who I believed were some of those who brought me on board, and had been receiving their pay: they talked to me in order to cheer me, but all in vain. I asked them if we were not to be eaten by those white men with horrible looks, red faces, and long hair. They told me I was not: and one of the crew brought me a small portion of spirituous liquor in a wine glass; but, being afraid of him, I would not take it out of his hand. One of the blacks therefore took it from him and gave it to me, and I took a little down my palate, which, instead of reviving me, as they thought it would, threw me into the greatest consternation at the strange feeling it produced, having never tasted any such liquor before.

Soon after this the blacks who brought me on board went off, and left me abandoned to despair. I now saw myself deprived of all chance of returning to my native country, or even the least glimpse of gaining the shore, which I now considered as friendly; and I even wished for my former slavery, in preference to my present situation, which was filled with horrors of every kind, still heightened by my ignorance of what I was to undergo. I was not long suffered to indulge my grief. I was soon put down under the decks, and there I received such a salutation in my nostrils as I had never experienced in my life: so that, with the loathsomeness of the stench, and with my crying together, I became so sick and low that I was not able to eat, nor had I the least desire to taste any thing. I now wished for the last friend, death, to relieve me; but soon, to my grief, two of the white men offered me eatables; and, on my refusing to eat, one of them held me fast by the hands, and laid me across, I think, the windlass, and tied my feet, while the other flogged me severely. I had never experienced any thing of this kind before, and although, not being used to the water, I naturally feared that element the first time I saw it, yet nevertheless, could I have got over the nettings, I would have jumped over the side, but I could not; and besides the crew used to watch us very closely, who were not chained down to the decks, lest we should leap into the water. I have seen some of these poor African prisoners most severely cut for attempting to do so, and hourly whipped for not eating. This indeed was often the case with myself. In a little time after, amongst the poor chained men, I found some of my own nation, which in a small degree gave ease to my mind. I inquired of these what was to be done with us. They gave me to understand we were to be carried to these white people's country to work for them. I was then a little revived, and thought if it were no worse than working, my situation was not so desperate. But still I feared I should be put to death, the white people looked and acted, as I thought, in so savage a manner; for I had never seen among any people such instances of brutal cruelty: and this is not only shewn towards us blacks, but also to some of the whites themselves. One white man in particular I saw, when we were permitted to be on deck, flogged so unmercifully with a large rope near the foremast, that he died in consequence of it; and they tossed him over the side as they would have done a brute. This made me fear these people the more; and I expected nothing less than to be treated in the same manner. I could not help expressing my fearful apprehensions to some of my countrymen. I asked them if these people had no country, but lived in this hollow place, the ship. They told me they did not, but came from a distant one. 'Then,' said I, 'how comes it, that in all our country we never heard of them?' They told me, because they lived so very far off. I then asked, where their women were: had they any like themselves. I was told they had. 'And why,' said I, 'do we not see them?' They answered, because they were left behind. I asked how the vessel could go. They told me they could not tell; but that there was cloth put upon the masts by the help of the ropes I saw, and then the vessel went on; and the white men had some spell or magic they put in the water, when they liked, in order to stop the vessel. I was exceedingly amazed at this account, and really thought they were spirits. I therefore wished much to be from amongst them, for I expected they would sacrifice me; but my wishes were in vain, for we were so quartered that it was impossible for any of us to make our escape.

VI. While we stayed on the coast I was mostly on deck; and one day, to my great astonishment, I saw one of these vessels coming in with the sails up. As soon as the whites saw it, they gave a great shout, at which we were amazed; and the more so as the vessel appeared larger by approaching nearer. At last she came to an anchor in my sight, and when the anchor was let go, I and my countrymen who saw it, were lost in astonishment to observe the vessel stop, and were now convinced it was done by magic. Soon after this the other ship got her boats out, and they came on board of us, and the people of both ships seemed very glad to see each other. Several of the strangers also shook hands with us black people, and made motions with their hands, signifying, I suppose, we were to go to their country; but we did not understand them. At last, when the ship, in which we were, had got in all her cargo, they made ready with many fearful noises, and we were all put under deck, so that we could not see how they managed the vessel.

But this disappointment was the least of my grief. The stench of the hold, while we were an the coast, was so intolerably loathsome, that it was dangerous to remain there for any time, and some of us had been permitted to stay on the deck for the fresh air; but now that the whole ship's cargo were confined together, it became absolutely pestilential. The closeness of the place, and the heat of the climate, added to the number in the ship, being so crowded that each had scarcely room to turn himself, almost suffocated us. This produced copious perspirations, so that the air soon became unfit for respiration, from a variety of loathsome smells, and brought on a sickness among the slaves, of which many died, thus falling victims to the improvident avarice, as I may call it, of their purchasers. This deplorable situation was again aggravated by the galling of the chains, now become insupportable; and the filth of necessary tubs, into which the children often fell, and were almost suffocated. The shrieks of the women, and the groans of the dying, rendered it a scene of horror almost inconceivable. Happily, perhaps, for myself, I was soon reduced so low here that it was thought necessary to keep me almost continually on deck; and from my extreme youth, I was not put in fetters. In this situation I expected every hour to share the fate of my companions, some of whom were almost daily brought upon deck at the point of death, and I began to hope that death would soon put an end to my miseries. Often did I think many of the inhabitants of the deep much more happy than myself; I envied them the freedom they enjoyed, and as often wished I could change my condition for theirs. Every circumstance I met with served only to render my state more painful, and heighten my apprehensions and my opinion of the cruelty of the whites. One day they had taken a number of fishes; and when they had killed and satisfied themselves with as many as they thought fit, to our astonishment who were on the deck, rather than give any of them to us to eat, as we expected, they tossed the remaining fish into the sea again, although we begged and prayed for some as well as we could, but in vain; and some of my countrymen, being pressed by hunger, took an opportunity, when they thought no one saw them, of trying to get a little privately; but were discovered, and the attempt procured for them some very severe floggings.

One day, when we had a smooth sea and a moderate wind, two of my wearied countrymen, who were chained together, (I was near them at the time) preferring death to such a life of misery, somehow made through the nettings and jumped into the sea: immediately another quite dejected fellow, who on account of his illness was suffered to be out of irons also followed their example; and I believe many more would very soon have done the same, if they had not been prevented by the ship's crew, who were instantly alarmed. Those of us who were the most active were in a moment put down under the deck; and there was such a noise and confusion amongst the people of the ship as I never heard before, to stop her and get the boat out to go after the slaves. However, two of the wretches were drowned; but they got the other, and afterward flogged him unmercifully, for thus attempting to prefer death to slavery. In this manner we continued to undergo more hardships than I can now relate, hardships which are inseparable from this accursed trade. Many a time we were near suffocation from the want of fresh air, being deprived thereof for days together. This, and the stench of the necessary tubs, carried off many.

VII. During our passage I first saw flying fishes, which surprised me very much: they used frequently to fly across the ship, and many of them fell on the deck. I also now first saw the use of the quadrant. I had often with astonishment seen the mariners make observations with it, and I could not think what it meant. They at last took notice of my surprise: and one of them, willing to increase it, as well as to gratify my curiosity, made me one day look through it. The clouds appeared to me to be land, which disappeared as they passed along. This heightened my wonder; and I was now more persuaded than ever that I was in another world, and that every thing about me was magic. At last we came in sight of the island of Barbadoes, at which the whites on board gave a great shout, and made many signs of joy to us. We did not know what to think of this, but as the vessel drew nearer we plainly saw the harbour, and other ships of different kinds and sizes; and we soon anchored amongst them off Bridge Town. Many merchants and planters now came on board, though it was in the evening. They put us in separate parcels, and examined us attentively. They also made us jump, and pointed to the land, signifying we were to go there. We thought by this we should be beaten by these ugly men, as they appeared to us; and, when soon after we were all put down under the deck again, there was much dread and trembling among us, and nothing but bitter cries to be heard all the night from these apprehensions, insomuch that at last the white people got some old slaves from the land to pacify us. They told us we were not to be eaten, but to work, and were soon to go on land, where we should see many of our country people. This report eased us much; and, sure enough, soon after we landed, there came to us Africans of all languages.

We were conducted immediately to the merchant's yard, where we were all pent up together like so many sheep in a fold, without regard to sex or age. As every object was new to me, every thing I saw filled me with surprise. What struck me first was that the houses were built with bricks in stories, and were in every other respect different from those I had seen in Africa; but I was still more astonished at seeing people on horseback. I did not know what this could mean; and indeed I thought these people full of nothing but magical arts. While I was in this astonishment one of my fellow prisoners spoke to a countryman of his about the horses, who said they were the same kind they had in their country. I understood them, though they were from a distant part of Africa, and I thought it odd I had not seen any horses there; but afterwards, when I came to converse with different Africans, I found they had many horses amongst them, and much larger than those I then saw.

We were not many days in the merchants' custody before we were sold after the usual manner, which is this:—On a signal given, such as the beat of a drum, the buyers rush at once into the yard where the slaves are confined, and make choice of that parcel they like best. The noise and clamour with which this is attended, and the eagerness visible in the countenances of the buyers, serve not a little to increase the apprehensions of the terrified Africans, who may well be supposed to consider them the ministers of that destruction to which they think themselves devoted. In this manner, without scruple, are relations and friends separated, most of them never to see each other again. I remember in the vessel in which I was brought over in, in the man's apartment, there were several brothers, who, in the sale, were sold in different lots; and it was very moving on this occasion to see their distress and hear their cries at parting. O, ye nominal Christians! might not an African ask you, "learned you this from your God, who says unto you, Do unto all men as you would men should do unto you? Is it not enough that we are torn from our country and friends, to toil for your luxury and lust of gain? Must every tender feeling be likewise sacrificed to your avarice? Are the dearest friends and relations now rendered more dear by their separation from the rest of their kindred, still to be parted from each other, and thus prevented from cheering the gloom of slavery, with the small comfort of being together, and mingling their sufferings and sorrows? Why are parents to lose their children, brothers their sisters, or husbands their wives? Surely this is a new refinement in cruelty, which, while it has no advantage to atone for it, thus aggravates distress, and adds fresh horrors even to the wretchedness of slavery."

PHILLIS WHEATLEY (1753?–1784)

Captured as a slave and transported to the American colonies on the perilous Middle Passage as a child, Phillis Wheatley was purchased in 1761 by John and Susanna Wheatley of Boston. She was placed in the household to perform domestic chores. A precocious child, Phillis learned to read and write with the assistance of Mary Wheatley, the daughter of John and Susanna. A gifted student, Phillis studied Latin, astronomy, history, geography, and the Bible. Strongly influenced by the writing of British poets such as Alexander Pope and John Milton, she mastered the heroic couplet. Many of her early poems consisted of religious meditations and elegies for the dead; at that time it was a widely held belief that literature should have moral and didactic purposes.

In her writing, she focuses on the contrast between slavery and freedom as a black woman in colonial America. In poems such as "On Being Brought from Africa to America," she muses on the meaning of Africa to the African American and considers the importance of religion. Her first collection, Poems on Various Subjects, Religious and Moral *(1773), printed in England, introduced her work to an even wider international audience. Freed around 1778 after John Wheatley's death, Phillis became the wife of John Peters, a freeman. She and John Peters had three children, but none of them lived to adulthood. She died in 1784 while working in a Boston boarding house.*

On Being Brought from Africa to America (1773)

'Twas mercy brought me from my Pagan land,
Taught my benighted soul to understand
That there's a God, that there's a Saviour too:
Once I redemption neither sought nor knew.
Some view our sable race with scornful eye,   5
"Their colour is a diabolic die."
Remember, Christians, Negros, black as Cain,
May be refin'd, and join th' angelic train.

On Imagination (1773)

Thy various works, imperial queen, we see,
How bright their forms! how deck'd with pomp by thee!
Thy wond'rous acts in beauteous order stand,
And all attest how potent is thine hand.

From Helicon's refulgent heights attend,   5
Ye sacred choir, and my attempts befriend:
To tell her glories with a faithful tongue,
Ye blooming graces, triumph in my song.

Now here, now there, the roving Fancy flies,
Till some lov'd object strikes her wand'ring eyes,   10
Whose silken fetters all the senses bind,
And soft captivity involves the mind.

Imagination! who can sing thy force?
Or who describe the swiftness of thy course?
Soaring through air to find the bright abode,   15
Th' empyreal palace of the thund'ring God,
We on thy pinions can surpass the wind,
And leave the rolling universe behind:
From star to star the mental optics rove,
Measure the skies, and range the realms above.   20
There in one view we grasp the mighty whole,
Or with new worlds amaze th' unbounded soul.

Though Winter frowns to Fancy's raptur'd eyes
The fields may flourish, and gay scenes arise;
The frozen deeps may break their iron bands,   25
And bid their waters murmur o'er the sands.
Fair Flora may resume her fragrant reign,
And with her flow'ry riches deck the plain;
Sylvanus may diffuse his honours round,
And all the forest may with leaves be crown'd: 30
Show'rs may descend, and dews their gems disclose,
And nectar sparkle on the blooming rose.

Such is thy pow'r, nor are thine orders vain,
O thou the leader of the mental train:
In full perfection all thy works are wrought,   35
And thine the sceptre o'er the realms of thought.
Before thy throne the subject-passions bow,

Of subject-passions sov'reign ruler Thou;
At thy command joy rushes on the heart,
And through the glowing veins the spirits dart.   40

   Fancy might now her silken pinions try
To rise from earth, and sweep th' expanse on high;
From Tithon's bed now might Aurora rise,
Her cheeks all glowing with celestial dies,
While a pure stream of light o'erflows the skies.   45
The monarch of the day I might behold,
And all the mountains tipt with radiant gold,
But I reluctant leave the pleasing views,
Which Fancy dresses to delight the Muse;
Winter austere forbids me to aspire,   50
And northern tempests damp the rising fire;
They chill the tides of Fancy's flowing sea,
Cease then, my song, cease the unequal lay.

To S. M., a Young African Painter, on Seeing His Works (1773)

To show the lab'ring bosom's deep intent,
And thought in living characters to paint,
When first thy pencil did those beauties give,
And breathing figures learnt from thee to live,
How did those prospects give my soul delight,   5
A new creation rushing on my sight?
Still, wond'rous youth! each noble path pursue,
On deathless glories fix thine ardent view:
Still may the painter's and the poet's fire
To aid thy pencil, and thy verse conspire!   10
And may the charms of each seraphic theme
Conduct thy footsteps to immortal fame!
High to the blissful wonders of the skies
Elate thy soul, and raise thy wishful eyes.
Thrice happy, when exalted to survey   15
That splendid city, crown'd with endless day,
Whose twice six gates on radiant hinges ring:
Celestial Salem blooms in endless spring.

   Calm and serene thy moments glide along,
And may the muse inspire each future song!   20

Still, with the sweets of contemplation bless'd,
May peace with balmy wings your soul invest!
But when these shades of time are chas'd away,
And darkness ends in everlasting day,
On what seraphic pinions shall we move,   25
And view the landscapes in the realms above?
There shall thy tongue in heav'nly murmurs flow,
And there my muse with heav'nly transport glow:
No more to tell of Damon's tender sighs,
Or rising radiance of Aurora's eyes,   30
For nobler themes demand a nobler strain,
And purer language on th' ethereal plain.
Cease, gentle muse! the solemn gloom of night
Now seals the fair creation from my sight.

To His Excellency General Washington (1775)

Celestial choir! enthron'd in realms of light,
   Columbia's scenes of glorious toils I write.
While freedom's cause her anxious breast alarms,
She flashes dreadful in refulgent arms.
See mother earth her offspring's fate bemoan,   5
And nations gaze at scenes before unknown!
See the bright beams of heaven's revolving light
Involved in sorrows and veil of night!

   The goddess comes, she moves divinely fair,
Olive and laurel bind her golden hair: 10
Wherever shines this native of the skies,
Unnumber'd charms and recent graces rise.

   Muse! bow propitious while my pen relates
How pour her armies through a thousand gates,
As when Eolus heaven's fair face deforms,   15
Enwrapp'd in tempest and a night of storms;
Astonish'd ocean feels the wild uproar,
The refluent surges beat the sounding shore;
Or thick as leaves in Autumn's golden reign,
Such, and so many, moves the warrior's train.   20
In bright array they seek the work of war,
Where high unfurl'd the ensign waves in air.
Shall I to Washington their praise recite?

Enough thou know'st them in the fields of fight.
Thee, first in peace and honours,—we demand   25
The grace and glory of thy martial band.
Fam'd for thy valour, for thy virtues more,
Hear every tongue thy guardian aid implore!

   One century scarce perform'd its destined round,
When Gallic powers Columbia's fury found;   30
And so may you, whoever dares disgrace
The land of freedom's heaven-defended race!
Fix'd are the eyes of nations on the scales,
For in their hopes Columbia's arm prevails.
Anon Britannia droops the pensive head,   35
While round increase the rising hills of dead.
Ah! cruel blindness to Columbia's state!
Lament thy thirst of boundless power too late.

   Proceed, great chief, with virtue on thy side,
Thy ev'ry action let the goddess guide.   40
A crown, a mansion, and a throne that shine,
With gold unfading, WASHINGTON! be thine.

Letter to Samson Occom (1774)

Reverend and Honoured Sir,

   I have this Day received your obliging kind Epistle, and am greatly satisfied with your Reasons respecting the Negroes, and think highly reasonable what you offer in Vindication of their natural Rights: Those that invade them cannot be insensible that the divine Light is chasing away the thick Darkness which broods over the Land of Africa; and the Chaos which has reigned so long, is converting into beautiful Order, and reveals more and more clearly, the glorious Dispensation of civil and religious Liberty, which are so inseparably united, that there is little or no Enjoyment of one without the other: Otherwise, perhaps, the Israelites had been less solicitous for their Freedom from Egyptian Slavery; I do not say they would have been contented without it, by no Means, for in every human Breast, God has implanted a Principle, which we call Love of Freedom; it is impatient of Oppression, and pants for Deliverance; and by the Leave of our Modern Egyptians I will assert, that the same Principle lives in us. God grant Deliverance in his own way and Time, and get him honor upon all those whose Avarice impels them to countenance and help forward the Calamities of their Fellow Creatures. This I desire not for their Hurt, but to convince them of the strange Absurdity of their Conduct whose Words and Actions are so diametrically opposite. How well the Cry for Liberty, and the reverse Disposition for the Exercise of oppressive Power over others agree,—I humbly think it does not require the Penetration of a Philosopher to determine.

All God's Chillen Had Wings

As told by Caesar Grant, of John's Island, carter and laborer.

This story exemplifies the oral storytelling tradition in African American liter-
ature. The tale focuses on the injustice of slavery and the desire for freedom
among African slaves who "fly" away to freedom.

Once all Africans could fly like birds; but owing to their many transgres-
sions, their wings were taken away. There remained, here and there, in
the sea islands and out-of-the-way places in the low country, some who
had been overlooked, and had retained the power of flight, though they looked
like other men.

There was a cruel master on one of the sea islands who worked his people till
they died. When they died he bought others to take their places. These also he
killed with overwork in the burning summer sun, through the middle hours of the
day, although this was against the law.

One day, when all the worn-out Negroes were dead of overwork, he bought,
of a broker in the town, a company of native Africans just brought into the country, and put them at once to work in the cottonfield.

He drove them hard. They went to work at sunrise and did not stop until
dark. They were driven with unsparing harshness all day long, men, women and
children. There was no pause for rest during the unendurable heat of the mid-
summer noon, though trees were plenty and near. But through the hardest
hours, when fair plantations gave their Negroes rest, this man's driver pushed the
work along without a moment's stop for breath, until all grew weak with heat
and thirst.

There was among them one young woman who had lately borne a child. It was
her first; she had not fully recovered from bearing, and should not have been sent
to the field until her strength had come back. She had her child with her, as the
other women had, astraddle on her hip, or piggyback.

The baby cried. She spoke to quiet it. The driver could not understand her
words. She took her breast with her hand and threw it over her shoulder that
the child might suck and be content. Then she went back to chopping knot-
grass; but being very weak, and sick with the great heat, she stumbled, slipped
and fell.

The driver struck her with his lash until she rose and staggered on.

She spoke to an old man near her, the oldest man of them all, tall and strong,
with a forked beard. He replied; but the driver could not understand what they
said; their talk was strange to him.

She returned to work; but in a little while she fell again. Again the driver lashed her until she got to her feet. Again she spoke to the old man. But he said: "Not yet, daughter; not yet." So she went on working, though she was very ill.

Soon she stumbled and fell again. But when the driver came running with his lash to drive her on with her work, she turned to the old man and asked: "Is it time yet, daddy?" He answered: "Yes, daughter; the time has come. Go; and peace be with you!" . . . and stretched out his arms toward her . . . so.

With that she leaped straight up into the air and was gone like a bird, flying over field and wood.

The driver and overseer ran after her as far as the edge of the field; but she was gone, high over their heads, over the fence, and over the top of the woods, gone, with her baby astraddle of her hip, sucking at her breast.

Then the driver hurried the rest to make up for her loss; and the sun was very hot indeed. So hot that soon a man fell down. The overseer himself lashed him to his feet. As he got up from where he had fallen the old man called to him in an unknown tongue. My grandfather told me the words that he said; but it was a long time ago, and I have forgotten them. But when he had spoken, the man turned and laughed at the overseer, and leaped up into the air, and was gone, like a gull, flying over field and wood.

Soon another man fell. The driver lashed him. He turned to the old man. The old man cried out to him, and stretched out his arms as he had done for the other two; and he, like them, leaped up, and was gone through the air, flying like a bird over field and wood.

Then the overseer cried to the driver, and the master cried to them both: "Beat the old devil! He is the doer!"

The overseer and the driver ran at the old man with lashes ready; and the master ran too, with a picket pulled from the fence, to beat the life out of the old man who had made those Negroes fly.

But the old man laughed in their faces, and said something loudly to all the Negroes in the field, the new Negroes and the old Negroes.

And as he spoke to them they all remembered what they had forgotten, and recalled the power which once had been theirs. Then all the Negroes, old and new, stood up together; the old man raised his hands; and they all leaped up into the air with a great shout; and in a moment were gone, flying, like a flock of crows, over the field, over the fence, and over the top of the wood; and behind them flew the old man.

The men went clapping their hands; and the women went singing; and those who had children gave them their breasts; and the children laughed and sucked as their mothers flew, and were not afraid.

The master, the overseer, and the driver looked after them as they flew, beyond the wood, beyond the river, miles on miles, until they passed beyond the last rim of the world and disappeared in the sky like a handful of leaves. They were never seen again.

Where they went I do not know; I never was told. Nor what it was that the old man said . . . that I have forgotten. But as he went over the last fence he made a sign in the master's face, and cried "Kuli-ba! Kuli-ba!" I don't know what that means.

But if I could only find the old wood sawyer, he could tell you more; for he was there at the time, and saw the Africans fly away with their women and children. He is an old, old man, over ninety years of age, and remembers a great many strange things.

🔖 LUCY TERRY PRINCE (1730–1821)

Like Phillis Wheatley, Lucy Terry Prince was originally from Africa. After arriving in the colonies, she was purchased by Ebenezer Wells, a resident of Deerfield, Massachusetts. The Wells family had her baptized in 1735 in the midst of the Great Awakening, a period of religious fervor in New England which sought to recapture the early zeal of the Puritans who settled in the area in the 1600s. "Bars Fight, August 28, 1746," Terry's only extant poem, recounts a violent encounter between whites and Native Americans in Massachusetts in 1746.

Terry wed Abijah Prince around 1756. An ex-slave, he purchased his wife from her owners, and the two set up a household in Deerfield. Around 1760, the couple relocated to Guilford, Vermont. While in Vermont, Lucy illustrated her willingness to fight for equal rights by demanding that local authorities protect her household against hostile town residents angry about a black family's presence. Furthermore, she attempted to get one of her six children accepted to Williams College. Although she was not successful, she openly voiced disapproval of racial discrimination, paving the way for other African American women activists such as Sojourner Truth and Ida B. Wells-Barnett in the nineteenth century. Through her activism, Terry highlighted the struggle for freedom and racial equality.

Bars Fight, August 28, 1746 (1746)

August 'twas, the twenty-fifth,
Seventeen hundred forty-six,
The Indians did in ambush lay,
Some very valient men to slay,
The names of whom I'll not leave out: 5
Samuel Allen like a hero fout,
And though he was so brave and bold,

His face no more shall we behold;
Eleazer Hawks was killed outright,
Before he had time to fight,   10
Before he did the Indians see,
Was shot and killed immediately;
Oliver Amsden, he was slain,
Which caused his friends much grief and pain;
Simeon Amsden they found dead,   15
Not many rods off from his head;
Adonijah Gillet, we do hear,
Did lose his life, which was so dear;
John Saddler fled across the water,
And so escaped the dreadful slaughter;   20
Eunice Allen see the Indians comeing,
And hoped to save herself by running,
And had not her petticoats stopt her,
The awful creatures had not cotched her,
And tommyhawked her on the head,   25
And left her on the ground for dead;
Young Samuel Allen, oh! lack-a-day,
Was taken and carried to Canada.

JUPITER HAMMON (1711–1806)

Unlike Phillis Wheatley, Lucy Terry Prince, and Olaudah Equiano, Jupiter Hammon was born in the American colonies. A slave at birth, Terry lived on Long Island, New York. Jupiter Hammon used his abilities in reading and writing as a clerk in a store owned by the Lloyd family (his owners) as well as after he started preaching. He moved to Connecticut with his owners at the time of the American Revolution; later, he and the Lloyds settled again on Long Island. His poems, such as "An Evening Thought: Salvation by Christ with Penetential Cries," and his religious essays bear testimony to the importance of religion in his life; in addition, there is an undertone criticizing the institution of slavery and celebrating the desire for freedom.

An Evening Thought: Salvation by Christ with Penetential Cries (1760)

Salvation comes by Christ alone,
    The only Son of God;
Redemption now to every one,
    That loves his holy Word.
        · · · · · ·

Dear Jesus, give thy Spirit now,   5
   Thy grace to every Nation,
That han't the Lord to whom we bow,
   The Author of Salvation.

Dear Jesus, unto Thee we cry,
   Give us the Preparation;   10
Turn not away thy tender Eye;
   We seek thy true Salvation.

     · · · · · ·

Lord, hear our penetential Cry:
   Salvation from above;
It is the Lord that doth supply,   15
   With his Redeeming Love.

Dear Jesus, by thy precious Blood,
   The World Redemption have:
Salvation now comes from the Lord,
   He being thy captive slave.   20

Dear Jesus, let the Nations cry,
   And all the People say,
Salvation comes from Christ on high,
   Haste on Tribunal Day.

We cry as Sinners to the Lord,   25
   Salvation to obtain;
It is firmly fixed, his holy Word,
   Ye shall not cry in vain.

     · · · · · ·

Lord, turn our dark benighted Souls;
   Give us a true Motion,   30
And let the Hearts of all the World,
   Make Christ their Salvation.

     · · · · · ·

Lord, unto whom now shall we go,
   Or seek a safe abode?
Thou hast the Word, Salvation Too: 35
   The only Son of God.

"Ho! every one that hunger hath,
   Or pineth after me,
Salvation be thy leading Staff,
   To set the Sinner free."   40

Dear Jesus, unto Thee we fly;
   Depart, depart from Sin,
Salvation doth at length supply,
   The glory of our King.

Come, ye Blessed of the Lord,   45
   Salvation greatly given;
O, turn your hearts, accept the Word,
   Your Souls are fit for Heaven.

Dear Jesus, we now turn to Thee,
   Salvation to obtain;   50
Our Hearts and Souls do meet again,
   To magnify thy Name.

Come, holy Spirit, Heavenly Dove,
   The Object of our Care;
Salvation doth increase our Love;   55
   Our Hearts hath felt thy fear.

Now Glory be to God on High,
   Salvation high and low;
And thus the Soul on Christ rely,
   To Heaven surely go.   60

Come, Blessed Jesus, Heavenly Dove,
   Accept Repentance here;
Salvation give, with tender Love;
   Let us with Angels share.

Motherless Child

This African American spiritual testifies to the importance of music among blacks in colonial America as a way of expressing thoughts and emotions.

Sometimes I feel like a motherless child,
Sometimes I feel like a motherless child,
Sometimes I feel like a motherless child,
A long ways from home,
A long ways from home.   5

Sometimes I feel like I'm almost gone,
Sometimes I feel like I'm almost gone,
Sometimes I feel like I'm almost gone,
A long ways from home,
A long ways from home.   10

Sometimes I feel like a feather in the air,
Sometimes I feel like a feather in the air,
Sometimes I feel like a feather in the air,
And I spread my wings and I fly,

I spread my wings and I fly.   15

GEORGE MOSES HORTON (1797–1883)

As an early African American writer, George Moses Horton called attention to the plight of enslaved blacks. His poems focus on the injustice of slavery and the right of all individuals to have freedom. A native of Northampton, North Carolina, he first gained notice for his poetic compositions with love poems he recited to students at the University of North Carolina, Chapel Hill, in the 1800s. Students there helped him in his quest to become skilled in reading and writing. Impressed by his poetic skills and intelligence, writer Caroline Lee Hentz assisted him in having his first volume of poems published. His poem "On Liberty and Slavery" appeared in a newspaper she owned, and The Liberator, *an important abolitionist newspaper in the North, republished it. When Union forces controlled North Carolina during the Civil War, Horton was freed. Later he traveled north, eventually settling in Philadelphia. Horton continued to write until his death.*

The Lover's Farewell (1829)

And wilt thou, love, my soul display,
And all my secret thoughts betray?
I strove, but could not hold thee fast,
My heart flies off with thee at last.

The favorite daughter of the dawn,   5
On love's mild breeze will soon be gone;
I strove, but could not cease to love,
Nor from my heart the weight remove.

And wilt thou, love, my soul beguile,
And gull thy fav'rite with a smile?   10
Nay, soft affection answers, nay,
And beauty wings my heart away.

I steal on tiptoe from these bowers,
All spangled with a thousand flowers;
I sigh, yet leave them all behind,   15
To gain the object of my mind.

And wilt thou, love, command my soul,
And waft me with a light control?
Adieu to all the blooms of May,
Farewell—I fly with love away!   20

I leave my parents here behind,
And all my friends—to love resigned—
'Tis grief to go, but death to stay:
Farewell—I'm gone with love away!

On Liberty and Slavery (1829)

Alas! and am I born for this,
    To wear this slavish chain?
Deprived of all created bliss,
    Through hardship, toil and pain!

How long have I in bondage lain,   5
    And languished to be free!
Alas! and must I still complain—
    Deprived of liberty.

Oh, Heaven! and is there no relief
    This side the silent grave—   10
To soothe the pain—to quell the grief
    And anguish of a slave?

Come Liberty, thou cheerful sound,
   Roll through my ravished ears!
Come, let my grief in joys be drowned,   15
   And drive away my fears.

Say unto foul oppression, Cease:
   Ye tyrants rage no more,
And let the joyful trump of peace,
   Now bid the vassal soar.   20

Soar on the pinions of that dove
   Which long has cooed for thee,
And breathed her notes from Afric's grove,
   The sound of Liberty.

Oh, Liberty! thou golden prize,   25
   So often sought by blood—
We crave thy sacred sun to rise,
   The gift of nature's God!

Bid Slavery hide her haggard face,
   And barbarism fly: 30
I scorn to see the sad disgrace
   In which enslaved I lie.

Dear Liberty! upon thy breast,
   I languish to respire;
And like the Swan unto her nest,   35
   I'd to thy smiles retire.

Oh, blest asylum—heavenly balm!
   Unto thy boughs I flee—
And in thy shades the storm shall calm,
   With songs of Liberty!   40

BENJAMIN BANNEKER (1731–1806)

Literature by African Americans during the colonial period reflects a diversity in forms used to articulate the ideas of freedom and democracy. Benjamin Banneker's almanacs and letters illustrate the use of nonfiction by African Americans during the colonial period in the quest to eradicate slavery and racial discrimination. Banneker was a native of Baltimore County, Maryland. He attended grammar school only briefly, but Banneker's keen innate intelligence enabled him to teach himself astronomy and mathematics. He became so accomplished in math and science that by 1791, he traveled with his neighbor Major Andrew Ellicott to Washington, D.C., on a surveying expedition of the area where the U.S. capital would be established. In addition, Banneker compiled data on astronomical matters. Later, he composed and had printed Benjamin Banneker's Pennsylvania, Delaware, Maryland and Virginia Almanac and Ephemeris, for the Year of Our Lord, 1792. *He mailed the publication to Thomas Jefferson and included his famous antislavery "Letter to Thomas Jefferson." Jefferson replied in writing, and his response and Banneker's letter were printed in pamphlet form. Banneker's letter illustrates the epistolary tradition in African American literature and is an excellent example of early prose work in the vein of abolitionist literature. Banneker died in 1806 in Baltimore, Maryland, known as an abolitionist, astronomer, and successful almanac writer.*

Letter to Thomas Jefferson (1791)

Maryland, Baltimore County
Near Ellicotts' Lower Mills, August 19th, 1791

Thomas Jefferson, Secretary of State.

Sir:—I am fully sensible of the greatness of that freedom, which I take with you on the present occasion, a liberty which seemed to me scarcely allowable, when I reflected on that distinguished and dignified station in which you stand, and the almost general prejudice and prepossession which is so prevalent in the world against those of my complexion.

I suppose it is a truth too well attested to you, to need a proof here, that we are a race of beings who have long laboured under the abuse and censure of the world, that we have long been considered rather as brutish than human, and scarcely capable of mental endowments.

Sir, I hope I may safely admit, in consequence of that report which hath reached me, that you are a man far less inflexible in sentiments of this nature than many others, that you are measurably friendly and well disposed towards us, and that you are willing and ready to lend your aid and assistance to our relief, from those many distresses and numerous calamities, to which we are reduced.

Now, sir, if this is founded in truth, I apprehend you will readily embrace every opportunity to eradicate that train of absurd and false ideas and opinions, which so generally prevails with respect to us, and that your sentiments are concurrent with mine, which are that one universal Father hath given Being to us all, and that he hath not only made us all of one flesh, but that he hath also without partiality afforded us all the same sensations, and endued us all with the same faculties, and that however variable we may be in society or religion, however diversified in situation or colour, we are all of the same family, and stand in the same relation to him.

Sir, if these are sentiments of which you are fully persuaded, I hope you cannot but acknowledge, that it is the indispensable duty of those who maintain for themselves the rights of human nature, and who profess the obligations of christianity, to extend their power and influence to the relief of every part of the human race, from whatever burden or oppression they may unjustly labour under, and this I apprehend a full conviction of the truth and obligation of these principles should lead all to.

Sir, I have long been convinced that if your love for yourselves and for those inesteemable laws, which preserve to you the rights of human nature, was found on sincerity, you could not but be solicitous that every individual of whatever rank or distinction, might with you equally enjoy the blessings thereof, neither could you rest satisfied, short of the most active diffusion of your exertions in order to their promotions from any state of degradation to which the unjustifiable cruelty and barbarism of men have reduced them.

Sir, I freely and cheerfully acknowledge that I am of the African race, and in that colour which is natural to them of the deepest dye, and it is under a sense of the most profound gratitude to the Supreme Being of the universe that I now confess to you that I am not under that state of tyrannical thraldom and inhuman captivity to which too many of my brethren are doomed; but that I have abundantly tasted of the fruition of those blessings which proceed from that free and unequalled liberty with which you are favoured and which, I hope you will willingly allow you have received from the immediate hand of that Being, from whom proceedeth every good and perfect gift.

Sir, suffer me to recall to your mind that time in which the arms and tyranny of the British Crown were exerted with every powerful effort in order to reduce you to a State of Servitude, look back I entreat you on the variety of dangers to which you were exposed; reflect on that time in which every human aid appeared unavailable, and in which even hope and fortitude wore the aspect of inability to the conflict and you cannot but be led to a serious and grateful sense of your miraculous and providential preservation; you cannot but acknowledge that the present freedom and tranquility which you enjoy you have mercifully received and that it is the peculiar blessing of Heaven.

This sir, was a time in which you clearly saw into the injustice of a state of slavery and in which you had just apprehensions of the horrors of its condition, it was now, sir that your abhorence thereof was so excited, that you publickly held forth this true and valuable doctrine, which is worthy to be recorded and remembered in all succeeding ages. "We hold these truths to be self-evident, that all men are created equal, and that they are endowed by their creator with certain unalienable rights, that among these are life, liberty and the pursuit of happiness."

Here, sir, was a time in which your tender feelings for yourselves had engaged you thus to declare, you were then impressed with proper ideas of the great valuation of liberty and the free possession of those blessings to which you were entitled by nature; but, sir, how pitiable is it to reflect that although you were so fully convinced of the benevolence of the Father of mankind and of his equal and impartial distribution of those rights and privileges which he had conferred upon them, that you should at the same time counteract his mercies in detaining by fraud and violence so numerous a part of my brethren under groaning captivity and cruel oppression, that you should at the same time be found guilty of that most criminal act which you professedly detested in others with respect to yourselves.

Sir, I suppose that your knowledge of the situation of my brethren is too extensive to need a recital here; neither shall I presume to prescribe methods by which they may have been relieved, otherwise than by recommending to you and all others to wean yourselves from those narrow prejudices which you have imbibed with respect to them and as Job proposed to his friends, "put your souls in their souls stead," thus shall your hearts be enlarged with kindness and benevolence toward them, and thus shall you need neither the direction of myself or others, in what manner to proceed herein.

And now, sir, although my sympathy and affection for my brethren hath caused my enlargement thus far, I ardently hope that your candour and generosity will plead with you in my behalf when I make known to you that it was not originally my design; but that having taken up my pen in order to direct to you as a present, a copy of an almanac, which I have calculated for the succeeding year, I was unexpectedly and unavoidably led thereto.

This calculation, sir, is the production of my arduous study in this my advanced stage of life; for having long had unbounded desires to become acquainted with the secrets of nature, I have had to gratify my curiosity herein through my own assidous application to astronomical study, in which I need not to recount to you the many difficulties and disadvantages which I have had to encounter.

And although I had almost declined to make my calculation for the ensuing year, in consequence of that time which I had allotted therefor being taken up at the Federal Territory by the request of Mr. Andrew Ellicott, yet finding myself under several engagements to printers of this state, to whom I had communicated my design, on my return to my place of residence I industriously applied myself thereto which I hope I have accomplished with correctness and accuracy, a copy of which I have taken the liberty to direct to you and which I humbly request you will favorably receive. Although you may have the opportunity of perusing it after its publication yet I chose to send it to you in manuscript previous thereto that you might not only have an earlier inspection but that you might also view it in my own handwriting.

And now, sir, I shall conclude and subscribe myself, with the most profound respect, your most obedient humble servant,

B. Banneker

THE COLONIAL PERIOD 1746–1800

Topics for Research

1. The Middle Passage is often a point of entry between the African and the American experience for African American writers. How do they respond to this event? How does the Middle Passage function as a metaphor for the divided self? Is this division resolved? Why? Why not?

2. The colonial period signifies the age of revolution in American history. Analyze the "revolutionary" aspects of writing produced by African Americans and the strategies these writers employed to challenge prevailing notions regarding race, class, and gender.

3. Slavery versus freedom functions as a prevailing theme in African American literature. Compare and contrast responses to the condition of slavery by

African American writers of the colonial period. How are the responses different? similar?

4. Religion plays a central role in colonial literature because the Puritan tradition in early American literature contended that writing should have a moral and didactic purpose. Examine this treatment of religion in African American literature.

5. African American literature begins with the oral tradition. Examine how African American literature of the oral tradition is similar to or different from written texts. Are the narrative forms, themes, and symbols similar or different? Why? Why not?

PART 2

THE ANTEBELLUM PERIOD
1800–1865

INTRODUCTION

THE UNDERGROUND RAILROAD PLAYED AN IMPORTANT ROLE IN antebellum America as a route to freedom. Its existence was vital to the abolitionist movement. Individuals sympathetic to the antislavery cause, black and white, provided safe haven for thousands of black slaves escaping to the North. If it had not been for the Underground Railroad, people such as Frederick Douglass, Harriet Jacobs, and William Wells Brown might not have evaded capture, and we would not have their stories and narratives as records of their bondage, flight, and freedom. The successes of these individuals demonstrated the strength, ingenuity, and resistance of black and white Americans in the nineteenth century.

The quest for freedom and the fight to abolish slavery define literature of the antebellum period. For African American writers of the time, literacy equaled freedom, and they used writing as an instrument to aid the growing sentiment against slavery in the North and the South. Many creative works of the period consist of abolitionist poems and slave narratives testifying to the brutality, evil, and injustice of slavery. The literature reflects the pressing social, political, and economic ramifications of slavery for Americans of all races. Frederick Douglass, William Wells Brown, Harriet Jacobs, Frances E. W. Harper, David Walker, and Sojourner Truth examined the issue of slavery in slave narratives, poems, short stories, speeches, and novels.

Abolitionist newspapers such as *The Liberator* flourished during the period, often serving as forums for escaped slaves to tell their stories or featuring the work of those involved in the antislavery movement. Prominent white antislavery activists and writers authenticated the narratives of fugitive slaves by verifying their accuracy for an audience often unable or unwilling to believe the horrors of slavery or to credit the ability of African Americans to pen their stories. William Lloyd Garrison, editor of *The Liberator*, wrote a preface to *The Narrative of the Life of Frederick Douglass* (1845), and Lydia Maria Child, a short-story writer and novelist, edited Harriet Jacobs's *Incidents in the Life of a Slave Girl* (1861). These rich, vital narratives inspired the people involved in the Underground Railroad and the abolitionist movement.

Antebellum African American literature calls attention to acts of resistance by black Americans to slavery. During the nineteenth century, a number of African Americans organized and led slave revolts, including Gabriel Prosser and Nat Turner in Virginia and Denmark Vesey in South Carolina. Although all the revolts were unsuccessful and eventually led to the execution of the leaders, these men became legends and folk heroes. In *Incidents in the Life of a Slave Girl* (pp. 45– 48), Harriet Jacobs writes of the fear among plantation owners after Turner's revolt, and she tells how the homes of slaves in her native North Carolina were searched for weapons and for documents that might hint at insurrection. She notes the terror and horror of the times:

> Those who never witnessed such scenes can hardly believe what I know was inflicted at this time on innocent men, women, and children, against whom there was not the slightest ground for suspicion. Colored people and slaves who lived in remote parts of the town suffered in an especial manner. In some cases the searchers scattered powder and shot among their clothes, and then sent other parties to find them, and bring them forward as proof that they were plotting insurrection. Every where men, women, and children were whipped till the blood stood in puddles at their feet. (p. 45)

Jacobs's words powerfully convey the graphic and violent nature of slavery in the United States. Because of the violence and mass destruction in its wake, Turner's revolt called attention to the issue of slavery and created bitter debate about the institution.

Until the mid-nineteenth century, African American writers fought against the institution of slavery through their speeches, narratives, poetry, and novels. In 1861, the Civil War broke out between the North and South over the issue of slavery. For Americans of all races, the Civil War was a turning point. For four bloody years, war raged across the land, a chapter in history that still lives in the hearts and minds of many today. Many Americans, black and white, served in the Civil War. The sons of Frederick Douglass enlisted in the 54th Massachusetts Regiment, a black regiment highlighted in the Hollywood film *Glory*.

The antebellum period also showcased a number of African American women writers, whose emphasis on race, class, and gender in relation to slavery anticipates feminist writing of the twentieth century. In *Incidents in the Life of a Slave Girl, Written by Herself*, Harriet Jacobs uses the pseudonym Linda Brent to pen a story about her struggle for freedom. A mother of two, Jacobs hid for seven years in a garret and eluded capture by her owners before eventually fleeing to New York for freedom. Jacobs called attention to the plight of African American women by documenting physical, emotional, and sexual abuse. Similarly, in *Our Nig; or, Sketches from the Life of a Free Black, in a Two-Story White House, North: Showing That Slavery's Shadows Fall Even There* (pp. 85–88), Harriet Wilson critiques the triple jeopardy of race, class, and gender. Her novel focuses on the life of an indentured servant of mixed racial background. By setting the novel in the North, Wilson called attention to the fact that discrimination in America did not occur exclusively in the South.

Writer and orator Frances E. W. Harper focuses on the role of black women in antebellum society in her 1892 novel *Iola Leroy, or Shadows Uplifted* (pp. 88–94). Her short stories and poems also meditate on the injustices of slavery and its impact on black women. *Iola Leroy*, an important work, features a strong, independent young black woman working for the emotional, spiritual, and educational uplift of African Americans in the South. Although Sojourner Truth was illiterate and born a slave (unlike Harper), she too articulated the need for social reform and women's rights in the antebellum period. In her "Address to the Ohio Women's Rights Convention" (p. 112), Truth addresses her right as an African American woman to speak for social, political, and moral equality. Through their commitment to civil rights, individuals like Charlotte Forten Grimke also promoted ideas of uplift for African Americans. Grimke critiqued discrimination in her thought-provoking journals.

During the antebellum period, both the written and oral traditions in African American literature continued to make an impact. Many key figures of the period, such as Frederick Douglass, Frances E. W. Harper, David Walker, and Sojourner Truth, combined the oral and written through the publication of their autobiographies, speeches, novels, poems, and short stories. Douglass, Harper, and Walker relied heavily on more traditional narrative and rhetorical forms for their literary works and speeches. Truth, unable to read and write, relied on the oral tradition as a means of conveying her ideas on justice and equality.

The spirituals and slave work songs still held importance during the antebellum period. Spirituals such as "Follow the Drinkin' Gourd" (p. 84) and "Swing Low, Sweet Chariot" (p. 111) represent the slaves' desire for freedom. Frederick Douglass comments on the power of spirituals and work songs in *The Narrative of the Life of Frederick Douglass*: "They told a tale of woe which was then altogether beyond my feeble comprehension; they were tones loud, long, and deep; they breathed the prayer and complaint of souls boiling over with the bitterest anguish. Every tone was a testimony against slavery, and a prayer to God for deliverance from chains" (p. 110). Through the written word, Douglass conveys the importance of the oral tradition in African American culture, detailing the strategies blacks adopted as a means of coping with their enslavement and their desire for freedom.

Douglass was a noted orator, and his connection with the abolitionist press made him a household name in the nineteenth century. A native of Maryland, he was born a slave but escaped to freedom. His *Narrative of the Life of Frederick Douglass, an American Slave, Written by Himself* (pp. 107–110) chronicles his life and his escape to freedom, serving as a ringing criticism of slavery and hypocrisy. His life and literary legacy illustrate the connection between the abolitionist movement and literature during the nineteenth century.

For African American writers, literature and activism went hand in hand. William Wells Brown, author of *Clotel; or, The President's Daughter: A Narrative of Slave Life in the United States* (1853) and an 1858 play, *The Escape; or, A Leap for Freedom* (pp. 48–83), was a fugitive slave who acquired literacy. *Clotel*, the first novel written by an African American, employs strategies of propagandistic literature of the period, critiquing the injustice of slavery in the United States. In his 1829

Appeal, in Four Articles, Together with a Preamble, to the Coloured Citizens of the World (pp. 41– 44), David Walker examines racial prejudice in America. His powerful critique of race relations in the United States, coupled with his stress on the importance of African American heritage, illustrates the links between political concerns and literature.

The diverse African American literature of the antebellum period features speeches, slave narratives, plays, novels, short stories, and poems that focus on the theme of slavery versus freedom. The works connect to pressing issues of the day—slavery, the changing roles of women, an emerging African American consciousness, and the Civil War. Walker, Jacobs, Brown, Wilson, Harper, Douglass, Truth, and others wove a rich tapestry articulating the African American experience from a variety of perspectives in the quest for freedom, justice, and equality. Their desire for emancipation would be answered with the end of the Civil War and the abolition of slavery.

❧ DAVID WALKER (1785–1830)

The prose of David Walker reflects the growing movement in the nineteenth century to abolish slavery in the United States. Walker was born free in Wilmington, North Carolina; he moved to Boston, where he owned a clothing store, around 1828. Walker's Appeal, in Four Articles, Together with a Preamble, to the Coloured Citizens of the World *(1829) suggests that slaves organize revolts in order to end slavery. The pamphlet immediately created a controversy because of its powerful rhetoric. The urgency and protest strain in Walker's pamphlet anticipate the activists and orators of the 1960s, such as Malcolm X, in the quest for freedom and equality.*

From Appeal, in Four Articles, Together with a Preamble, to the Coloured Citizens of the World (1829)

Preamble

My dearly beloved Brethren and Fellow Citizens:

Having travelled over a considerable portion of these United States, and having, in the course of my travels taken the most accurate observations of things as they exist—the result of my observations has warranted the full and unshakened conviction, that we, (coloured people of these United States) are the most degraded, wretched, and abject set of beings that ever lived since the world began, and I pray God, that none like us ever may live again until time shall be no more. They tell us of the Israelites in Egypt, the Helots in Sparta, and of the Roman Slaves, which last, were made up from almost every nation under heaven, whose sufferings under those ancient and heathen nations were, in comparison with ours, under this enlightened and christian nation, no more than a cypher—or in other words, those heathen nations of antiquity, had but little more among them than the name and form of slavery, while wretchedness and endless miseries were reserved, apparently in a phial, to be poured out upon our fathers, ourselves and our children by *christian* Americans!

These positions, I shall endeavour, by the help of the Lord, to demonstrate in the course of this *appeal*, to the satisfaction of the most incredulous mind—and may God Almighty who is the father of our Lord Jesus Christ, open your hearts to understand and believe the truth.

The *causes*, my brethren, which produce our wretchedness and miseries, are so very numerous and aggravating, that I believe the pen only of a Josephus or a Plutarch, can well enumerate and explain them. Upon subjects, then, of such incomprehensible magnitude, so impenetrable, and so notorious, I shall be obliged to omit a large class of, and content myself with giving you an exposition of a few of those, which do indeed rage to such an alarming pitch, that they cannot but be a perpetual source of terror and dismay to every reflecting mind.

I am fully aware, in making this appeal to my much afflicted and suffering brethren, that I shall not only be assailed by those whose greatest earthly desires are, to keep us in abject ignorance and wretchedness, and who are of the firm conviction that heaven has designed us and our children to be slaves and *beasts of burden* to them and their children.—I say, I do not only expect to be held up to the public as an ignorant, impudent and restless disturber of the public peace, by such avaricious creatures, as well as a mover of insubordination—and perhaps put in prison or to death, for giving a superficial exposition of our miseries, and exposing tyrants. But I am persuaded, that many of my brethren, particularly those who are ignorantly in league with slave-holders or tyrants, who acquire their daily bread by the blood and sweat of their more ignorant brethren—and not a few of those too, who are too ignorant to see an inch beyond their noses, will rise up and call me cursed—Yea, the jealous ones among us will perhaps use more abject subtlety by affirming that this work is not worth perusing; that we are well situated and there is no use in trying to better our condition, for we cannot. I will ask one question here.—Can our condition be any worse?—Can it be more mean and abject? If there are any changes, will they not be for the better, though they may appear for the worse at first? Can they get us any lower? Where can they get us? They are afraid to treat us worse, for they know well, the day they do it they are gone. But against all accusations which may or can be preferred against me, I appeal to heaven for my motive in writing— who knows that my object is, if possible, to awaken in the breasts of my afflicted, degraded and slumbering brethren, a spirit of enquiry and investigation respecting our miseries and wretchedness in this *Republican Land of Liberty!!!!!*

The sources from which our miseries are derived and on which I shall comment, I shall not combine in one, but shall put them under distinct heads and expose them in their turn; in doing which, keeping truth on my side, and not departing from the strictest rules of morality, I shall endeavor to penetrate, search out, and lay them open for your inspection. If you cannot or will not profit by them, I shall have done *my* duty to you, my country and my God.

And as the inhuman system of *slavery*, is the *source* from which most of our miseries proceed, I shall begin with that *curse to nations;* which has spread terror and devastation through so many nations of antiquity, and which is raging to such a pitch at the present day in Spain and in Portugal. It had one tug in England, in France, and in the United States of America; yet the inhabitants thereof, do not learn wisdom, and erase it entirely from their dwellings and from all with whom they have to do. The fact is, the labor of slaves comes so cheap to the avaricious usurpers, and is (as they think) of such great utility to the country where it exists, that those who are actuated by sordid avarice only, overlook the evils, which will as sure as the Lord lives, follow after the good. In fact, they are so happy to keep in ignorance and degradation, and to receive the homage and the labor of the slaves, they forget that God rules in the armies of heaven and among the inhabitants of the earth, having his ears continually open to the cries, tears and groans of his oppressed people; and being a just and holy Being will at one day appear fully in behalf of the oppressed, and arrest the progress of the avaricious oppressors; for although the destruction of the oppressors God may not effect by the oppressed, yet the Lord our God will bring other destructions upon them—for not unfrequently will he cause them to rise up one against another, to be split and divided, and to oppress each other, and sometimes to open hostilities with sword in hand. Some may ask, what is the matter with this enlightened and happy people?—Some say it is the cause of political usurpers, tyrants, oppressors, etc. But has not the Lord an oppressed and suffering people among them? Does the Lord condescend to hear their cries and see their tears in consequence of oppression? Will he let the oppressors rest comfortably and happy always? Will he not cause the very children of the oppressors to rise up against them, and oftimes put them to death? "God works in many ways his wonders to perform."

I will not here speak of the destructions which the Lord brought upon Egypt, in consequence of the oppression and consequent groans of the oppressed—of the hundreds and thousands of Egyptians whom God hurled into the Red Sea for afflicting his people in their land—of the Lord's suffering people in Sparta or Lacedemon, the land of the truly famous Lycurgus—nor have I time to comment upon the cause which produced the fierceness with which Sylla usurped the title, and absolutely acted as dictator of the Roman people—the conspiracy of Cataline—the conspiracy against, and murder of Cæsar in the Senate house— the spirit with which Marc Antony made himself master of the commonwealth— his associating Octavius and Lipidus with himself in power,—their dividing the provinces of Rome among themselves—their attack and defeat on the plains of Phillipi the last defenders of their liberty, (Brutus and Cassius)—the tyranny of Tiberius, and from him to the final overthrow of Constantinople by the Turkish Sultan, Mahomed II, A.D. 1453. 1 say, I shall not take up time to speak of the *causes* which produced so much wretchedness and massacre among those heathen nations, for I am aware that you know too well, that God is just, as well as merciful!—I shall call your attention a few moments to that *christian* nation, the Spaniards, while I shall leave almost unnoticed that avaricious and cruel people, the Portuguese, among whom all true hearted christians and lovers of Jesus Christ, must evidently see the judgments of God displayed. To show the judgments of God upon the Spaniards I shall occupy but little time, leaving a plenty of room for the candid and unprejudiced to reflect.

All persons who are acquainted with history, and particularly the Bible, who are not blinded by the God of this world, and are not actuated solely by avarice— who are able to lay aside prejudice long enough to view candidly and impartially, things as they were, are, and probably will be, who are willing to admit that God made man to serve him *alone*, and that man should have no other Lord or Lords but himself—that God Almighty is the *sole proprietor* or *master* of the WHOLE human family, and will not on any consideration admit of a colleague, being unwilling to divide his glory with another.—And who can dispense with prejudice long enough to admit that we are men, notwithstanding our *improminent noses* and *woolly heads*, and believe that we feel for our fathers, mothers, wives and children as well as they do for theirs.—I say, all who are permitted to see and believe these things, can easily recognize the judgments of God among the Spaniards. Though others may lay the cause of the fierceness with which they cut each other's throats, to some other circumstances, yet they who believe that God is a God of justice, will believe that SLAVERY *is the principal cause.*

While the Spaniards are running about upon the field of battle cutting each other's throats, has not the Lord an afflicted and suffering people in the midst of them, whose cries and groans in consequence of oppression are continually pouring into the ears of the God of justice? Would they not cease to cut each other's throats if they could? But how can they? The very support which they draw from government to aid them in perpetrating such enormities, does it not arise in a great degree from the wretched victims of oppression among them? And yet they are calling for *Peace!—Peace!!* Will any peace be given unto them? Their destruction may indeed be procrastinated awhile, but can it continue long while they are oppressing the Lord's people? Has He not the hearts of all men in His hand? Will he suffer one part of his creatures to go on oppressing another like brutes always, with impunity? And yet those avaricious wretches are calling for *Peace!!!!* I declare it does appear to me, as though some nations think God is asleep, or that he made the Africans for nothing else but to dig their mines and work their farms, or they cannot believe history, sacred or profane. I ask every man who has a heart and is blessed with the privilege of believing—Is not God a God of justice to all his creatures? Do you say he is? Then if he gives peace and tranquility to tyrants, and permits them to keep our fathers, our mothers, ourselves and our children in eternal ignorance and wretchedness to support them and their families, would he be to us a God of *justice*? I ask O ye *christians!!!* who hold us and our children, in the most abject ignorance and degradation, that ever a people were afflicted with since the world began—I say, if God gives you peace and tranquility, and suffers you thus to go on afflicting us and our children, who have never given you the least provocation,—Would he be to us *a God of justice? If* you will allow that we are MEN, who feel for each other, does not the blood of our fathers and of us their children, cry aloud to the Lord of Sabaoth against you, for the cruelties and murders with which you have, and do continue to afflict us. But it is time for me to close my remarks on the suburbs, just to enter more fully into the interior of this system of cruelty and oppression.

HARRIET JACOBS (1813–1897)

A native of Edenton, North Carolina, Harriet Jacobs was born a slave. Tutored by her mistress, she learned to read and write, and found these skills useful years later when penning her slave narrative as a means of providing financial support for herself and her two children, both fathered by a white Southern congressman. According to her narrative, she hid in the garret of a house owned by her grandmother while awaiting an opportunity to escape to the North. After successfully fleeing to New York, she found employment as a domestic in the home of Nathaniel P. and Cornelia Willis. Ironically, Cornelia eventually purchased Jacobs from her owner in the free state of New York, enabling Jacobs to finally have ownership of herself. Writing her narrative to earn money and to call attention to the injustice of slavery, particularly in terms of the racial, class, and sexual oppression that black female slaves faced, Jacobs was championed by white abolitionists, among them Lydia Maria Child, who edited Incidents in the Life of a Slave Girl, Written by Herself *(1861). During the Civil War, Jacobs traveled to Washington, D.C., and gained employment as a nurse. Dying in Washington in 1897, she left a legacy in the tradition of African American women's narratives in her provocative assessment of the effects of slavery on black women.*

From Incidents in the Life of a Slave Girl, Written by Herself (1861)

Chapter 12: Fear of Insurrection

Not far from this time Nat Turner's insurrection broke out; and the news threw our town into great commotion. Strange that they should be alarmed, when their slaves were so "contented and happy"! But so it was.

It was always the custom to have a muster every year. On that occasion every white man shouldered his musket. The citizens and the so-called country gentlemen wore military uniforms. The poor whites took their places in the ranks in every-day dress, some without shoes, some without hats. This grand occasion had already passed; and when the slaves were told there was to be another muster, they were surprised and rejoiced. Poor creatures! They thought it was going to be a holiday. I was informed of the true state of affairs, and imparted it to the few I could trust. Most gladly would I have proclaimed it to every slave; but I dared not. All could not be relied on. Mighty is the power of the torturing lash.

By sunrise, people were pouring in from every quarter within twenty miles of the town. I knew the houses were to be searched; and I expected it would be done by country bullies and the poor whites. I knew nothing annoyed them so much as to see colored people living in comfort and respectability; so I made arrangements for them with especial care. I arranged every thing in my grandmother's house as neatly as possible. I put white quilts on the beds, and decorated some of the rooms with flowers. When all was arranged, I sat down at the window to watch. Far as my eye could reach, it rested on a motley crowd of soldiers. Drums and fifes were discoursing martial music. The men were divided into companies of sixteen, each headed by a captain. Orders were given, and the wild scouts rushed in every direction, wherever a colored face was to be found.

It was a grand opportunity for the low whites, who had no negroes of their own to scourge. They exulted in such a chance to exercise a little brief authority, and show their subserviency to the slaveholders; not reflecting that the power which trampled on the colored people also kept themselves in poverty, ignorance, and moral degradation. Those who never witnessed such scenes can hardly believe what I know was inflicted at this time on innocent men, women, and children, against whom there was not the slightest ground for suspicion. Colored people and slaves who lived in remote parts of the town suffered in an especial manner. In some cases the searchers scattered powder and shot among their clothes, and then sent other parties to find them, and bring them forward as proof that they were plotting insurrection. Every where men, women, and children were whipped till the blood stood in puddles at their feet. Some received five hundred lashes; others were tied hands and feet, and tortured with a bucking paddle, which blisters the skin terribly. The dwellings of the colored people, unless they happened to be protected by some influential white person, who was nigh at hand, were robbed of clothing and every thing else the marauders thought worth carrying away. All day long these unfeeling wretches went round. like a troop of demons, terrifying and tormenting the helpless. At night, they formed themselves into patrol bands, and went wherever they chose among the colored people, acting out their brutal will. Many women hid themselves in woods and swamps, to keep out of their way. If any of the husbands or fathers told of these outrages, they were tied up to the public whipping post, and cruelly scourged for telling lies about white men. The consternation was universal. No two people that had the slightest tinge of color in their faces dared to be seen talking together.

I entertained no positive fears about our household, because we were in the midst of white families who would protect us. We were ready to receive the soldiers whenever they came. It was not long before we heard the tramp of feet and the sound of voices. The door was rudely pushed open; and in they tumbled, like a pack of hungry wolves. They snatched at every thing within their reach. Every box, trunk, closet, and corner underwent a thorough examination. A box in one of the drawers containing some silver change was eagerly pounced upon. When I stepped forward to take it from them, one of the soldiers turned and said angrily, "What d'ye foller us fur? D'ye s'pose white folks is come to steal?"

I replied, "You have come to search; but you have searched that box, and I will take it, if you please."

At that moment I saw a white gentleman who was friendly to us; and I called to him, and asked him to have the goodness to come in and stay till the search was over. He readily complied. His entrance into the house brought in the captain of the company, whose business it was to guard the outside of the house, and see that none of the inmates left it. This officer was Mr. Litch, the wealthy slaveholder whom I mentioned, in the account of neighboring planters, as being notorious for his cruelty. He felt above soiling his hands with the search. He merely gave orders; and, if a bit of writing was discovered, it was carried to him by his ignorant followers, who were unable to read.

My grandmother had a large trunk of bedding and table cloths. When that was opened, there was a great shout of surprise; and one exclaimed, "Where'd the damned niggers git all dis sheet an' table clarf?"

My grandmother, emboldened by the presence of our white protector, said, "You may be sure we didn't pilfer 'em from *your* houses."

"Look here, mammy," said a grim-looking fellow without any coat, "you seem to feel mighty gran' 'cause you got all them 'ere fixens. White folks oughter have 'em all."

His remarks were interrupted by a chorus of voices shouting, "We's got 'em! We's got 'em! Dis 'ere yaller gal's got letters!"

There was a general rush for the supposed letter, which, upon examination, proved to be some verses written to me by a friend. In packing away my things, I had overlooked them. When their captain informed them of their contents, they seemed much disappointed. He inquired of me who wrote them. I told him it was one of my friends. "Can you read them?" he asked. When I told him I could, he swore, and raved, and tore the paper into bits. "Bring me all your letters!" said he, in a commanding tone. I told him I had none. "Don't be afraid," he continued, in an insinuating way. "Bring them all to me. Nobody shall do you any harm." Seeing I did not move to obey him, his pleasant tone changed to oaths and threats. "Who writes to you? half free niggers?" inquired he. I replied, "O, no; most of my letters are from white people. Some request me to burn them after they are read, and some I destroy without reading."

An exclamation of surprise from some of the company put a stop to our conversation. Some silver spoons which ornamented an old-fashioned buffet had just been discovered. My grandmother was in the habit of preserving fruit for many ladies in the town, and of preparing suppers for parties; consequently she had many jars of preserves. The closet that contained these was next invaded, and the contents tasted. One of them, who was helping himself freely, tapped his neighbor on the shoulder, and said, "Wal done! Don't wonder de niggers want to kill all de white folks, when dey live on 'sarves" [meaning preserves]. I stretched out my hand to take the jar, saying, "You were not sent here to watch for sweetmeats."

"And what *were* we sent for?" said the captain, bristling up to me. I evaded the question.

The search of the house was completed, and nothing found to condemn us. They next proceeded to the garden, and knocked about every bush and vine, with no better success. The captain called his men together, and, after a short consultation, the order to march was given. As they passed out of the gate, the captain turned back, and pronounced a malediction on the house. He said it ought to be burned to the ground, and each of its inmates receive thirty-nine lashes. We came out of this affair very fortunately; not losing any thing except some wearing apparel.

Towards evening the turbulence increased. The soldiers, stimulated by drink, committed still greater cruelties. Shrieks and shouts continually rent the air. Not daring to go to the door, I peeped under the window curtain. I saw a mob dragging along a number of colored people, each white man, with his musket upraised, threatening instant death if they did not stop their shrieks. Among the prisoners was a respectable old colored minister. They had found a few parcels of shot in his house, which his wife had for years used to balance her scales. For this they were going to shoot him on Court House Green. What a spectacle was that for a civilized country! A rabble, staggering under intoxication, assuming to be the administrators of justice!

The better class of the community exerted their influence to save the innocent, persecuted people; and in several instances they succeeded, by keeping them shut up in jail till the excitement abated. At last the white citizens found that their own property was not safe from the lawless rabble they had summoned to protect them. They rallied the drunken swarm, drove them back into the country, and set a guard over the town.

The next day, the town patrols were commissioned to search colored people that lived out of the city; and the most shocking outrages were committed with perfect impunity. Every day for a fortnight, if I looked out, I saw horsemen with some poor panting negro tied to their saddles, and compelled by the lash to keep up with their speed, till they arrived at the jail yard. Those who had been whipped too unmercifully to walk were washed with brine, tossed into a cart, and carried to jail. One black man, who had not fortitude to endure scourging, promised to give information about the conspiracy. But it turned out that he knew nothing at all. He had not even heard the name of Nat Turner. The poor fellow had, however, made up a story, which augmented his own sufferings and those of the colored people.

The day patrol continued for some weeks, and at sundown a night guard was substituted. Nothing at all was proved against the colored people, bond or free. The wrath of the slaveholders was somewhat appeased by the capture of Nat Turner. The imprisoned were released. The slaves were sent to their masters, and the free were permitted to return to their ravaged homes. Visiting was strictly forbidden on the plantations. The slaves begged the privilege of again meeting at their little church in the woods, with their burying ground around it. It was built by the colored people, and they had no higher happiness than to meet there and sing hymns together, and pour out their hearts in spontaneous prayer. Their request was denied, and the church was demolished. They were permitted to attend the white churches, a certain portion of the galleries being appropriated to their use. There, when every body else had partaken of the communion, and the benediction had been pronounced, the minister said, "Come down, now, my colored friends." They obeyed the summons, and partook of the bread and wine, in commemoration of the meek and lowly Jesus, who said, "God is your Father, and all ye are brethren."

WILLIAM WELLS BROWN (1814–1884)

A noted playwright and novelist, William Wells Brown was born a slave in 1815. Successfully fleeing his native Kentucky for Ohio, Brown adopted the name Wells Brown to honor the Quaker who had helped him flee his bondage. Later, he penned Narrative of William W. Brown, a Fugitive Slave, Written by Himself *(1847). He traveled abroad to Europe two years later and stayed for a number of years. His novel* Clotel; or, The President's Daughter: A Narrative of Slave Life in the United States, *(1853) was the first published by a black American. His play* The Escape; or, A Leap for Freedom *(1858) heralded the early stages of African American drama. His works focused on the injustice of slavery in America and the irony of its existence in a democratic society. Through his activism and writing, he sounded a powerful voice against slavery and injustice.*

The Escape; or, A Leap for Freedom (1858)

Playwright's Preface

This play was written for my own amusement, and not with the remotest thought that it would ever be seen by the public eye. I read it privately, however, to a circle of my friends, and through them was invited to read it to a Literary Society.

Since then, the drama has been given in various parts of the country. By the earnest solicitation of some in whose judgment I have the greatest confidence, I now present it in a printed form to the public. As I never aspired to be a dramatist, I ask no favor for it, and have little or no solicitude for its fate. If it is not readable, no word of mine can make it so; if it is, to ask favor for it would be needless.

The main features in the drama are true. Glen and Melinda are actual characters, and still reside in Canada. Many of the incidents are drawn from my own experience of eighteen years at the South. The marriage ceremony, as performed in the second act, is still adhered to in many of the southern states, especially in the farming districts.

The ignorance of the slave, as seen in the case of Big Sally, is common wherever chattel slavery exists. The difficulties created in the domestic circle by the presence of beautiful slave women, as found in Dr. Gaines's family is well understood by all who have ever visited the valley of the Mississippi.

The play, no doubt, abounds in defects, but as I was born in slavery, and never had a day's schooling in my life, I owe the public no apology for errors.

—W. W. B.

Characters Represented

DR. GAINES, *propietor of the farm at Muddy Creek*

MR. CAMPBELL, *a neighboring slave owner*

REV. JOHN PINCHEN, *a clergyman*

DICK WALKER, *a slave speculator*

MR. WILDMARSH, *neighbor to Dr. Gaines*

MAJOR MOORE, *a friend of Dr. Gaines*

MR. WHITE, *a citizen of Massachusetts*

BILL JENNINGS, *a slave speculator*

JACOB SCRAGG, *overseer to Dr. Gaines*

MRS. GAINES, *wife of Dr. Gaines*

MR. AND MRS. NEAL, AND DAUGHTER, *Quakers, in Ohio*

THOMAS, *Mr. Neal's hired man*

GLEN, *slave of Mr. Hamilton, brother-in-law of Dr. Gaines*

CATO, SAM, SAMPEY (BOB), MELINDA, DOLLY, SUSAN, AND BIG SALLY, *slaves of Dr. Gaines*

PETE, NED, BILL, AND TAPIOCA, *slaves*

OFFICERS, LOUNGERS, BARKEEPER, *etc.*

ACT 1

SCENE 1

(*A Sitting-Room.* MRS. GAINES, *looking at some drawings*—SAMPEY, *a white slave, stands behind the lady's chair. Enter* DR. GAINES, *right*)

DR. GAINES. Well, my dear, my practice is steadily increasing. I forgot to tell you that neighbor Wyman engaged me yesterday as his family physician; and I hope that the fever and ague, which is now taking hold of the people, will give me more patients. I see by the New Orleans papers that the yellow fever is raging there to a fearful extent. Men of my profession are reaping a harvest in that section this year. I would that we could have a touch of the yellow fever here, for I think I could invent a medicine that would cure it. But the yellow fever is a luxury that we medical men in this climate can't expect to enjoy; yet we may hope for the cholera.

MRS. GAINES. Yes, I would be glad to see it more sickly here, so that your business might prosper. But we are always unfortunate. Everybody here seems to be in good health, and I am afraid that they'll keep so. However, we must hope for the best. We must trust in the Lord. Providence may possibly send some disease among us for our benefit.

(Enter CATO, *right)*

CATO. Mr. Campbell is at de door, massa.

DR. GAINES. Ask him in, Cato.

(Enter MR. CAMPBELL, *right)*

DR. GAINES. Good morning, Mr. Campbell. Be seated.

MR. CAMPBELL. Good morning, doctor. The same to you, Mrs. Gaines. Fine morning, this.

MRS. GAINES. Yes, sir; beautiful day.

MR. CAMPBELL. Well, doctor, I've come to engage you for my family physician. I am tired of Dr. Jones. I've lost another very valuable nigger under his treatment; and, as my old mother used to say, "change of pastures makes fat calves."

DR. GAINES. I shall be most happy to become your doctor. Of course, you want me to attend to your niggers, as well as to your family?

MR. CAMPBELL. Certainly, sir. I have twenty-three servants. What will you charge me by the year?

DR. GAINES. Of course, you'll do as my other patients do, send your servants to me when they are sick, if able to walk?

MR. CAMPBELL. Oh, yes; I always do that.

DR. GAINES. Then I suppose I'll have to lump it, and say $500 per annum.

MR. CAMPBELL. Well, then, we'll consider that matter settled; and as two of the boys are sick, I'll send them over. So I'll bid you good day, doctor. I would be glad if you would come over some time, and bring Mrs. Gaines with you.

DR. GAINES. Yes, I will; and shall be glad if you will pay us a visit, and bring with you Mrs. Campbell. Come over and spend the day.

MR. CAMPBELL. I will. Good morning, doctor. *(exit* MR. CAMPBELL, *right)*

DR. GAINES. There, my dear, what do you think of that? Five hundred dollars more added to our income. That's patronage worth having! And I am glad to get all the negroes I can to doctor, for Cato is becoming very useful to me in the shop. He can bleed, pull teeth, and do almost anything that the blacks require. He can put up medicine as well as any one. A valuable boy, Cato!

MRS. GAINES. But why did you ask Mr. Campbell to visit you, and to bring his wife? I am sure I could never consent to associate with her, for I understand that she was the daughter of a tanner. You must remember, my dear, that I was born with a silver spoon in my mouth. The blood of the Wyleys runs in my veins. I am surprised that you should ask him to visit you at all; you should have known better.

DR. GAINES. Oh, I did not mean for him to visit me. I only invited him for the sake of compliments, and I think he so understood it, for I should be far from wishing you to associate with Mrs. Campbell. I don't forget, my dear, the family you were raised in, nor do I overlook my own family. My father, you know, fought by the side of Washington, and I hope some day to have a handle to my own name. I am certain Providence intended me for something higher than a medical man. Ah! by-the-by, I had forgotten that I have a couple of patients to visit this morning. I must go at once. *(exit* DR. GAINES, *right)*

(Enter HANNAH, *left)*

MRS. GAINES. Go, Hannah, and tell Dolly to kill a couple of fat pullets, and to put the biscuit to rise. I expect brother Pinchen here this afternoon, and I want everything in order. Hannah, Hannah, tell Melinda to come here. *(exit* HANNAH, *left)* We mistresses do have a hard time in this world; I don't see why the Lord should have imposed such heavy duties on us poor mortals. Well, it can't last always. I long to leave this wicked world, and go home to glory. *(enter* MELINDA*)* I am to have company this afternoon, Melinda. I expect brother Pinchen here, and I want everything in order. Go and get one of my new caps, with the lace border, and get out my scolloped-bottomed dimity petticoat, and when you go out, tell Hannah to clean the white-handled knives, and see that not a speck is on them; for I want everything as it should be while brother Pinchen is here. *(exit* MRS. GAINES, *left,* MELINDA, *right)*

SCENE 2

*(Doctor's shop—*CATO *making pills. Enter* DR. GAINES, *left)*

DR. GAINES. Well, Cato, have you made the batch of ointment that I ordered?

CATO. Yes, massa; I dun made de intment, an' now I is making the bread pills. De tater pills is up on the top shelf.

DR. GAINES. I am going out to see some patients. If any gentlemen call, tell them I shall be in this afternoon. If any servants come, you attend to them. I expect two of Mr. Campbell's boys over. You see to them. Feel their pulse, look at their tongues, bleed them, and give them each a dose of calomel. Tell them to drink no cold water, and to take nothing but water gruel.

CATO. Yes, massa; I'll tend to 'em. *(exit* DR. GAINES, *left)* I allers knowed I was a doctor, an' now de ole boss has put me at it, I muss change my coat. Ef any niggers comes in, I want to look suspectable. Dis jacket don't suit a doctor; I'll change it. *(exit* CATO—*immediately returning in a long coat)* Ah! now I looks like a doctor. Now I can bleed, pull teef, or cut off a leg. Oh! well, well, ef I aint put de pill stuff an' de intment stuff togedder. By golly, dat ole cuss will be mad when he finds it out, won't he? Nebber mind, I'll make it up in pills, and when de flour is on dem, he won't know what's in 'em; an' I'll make some new intment. Ah! yonder comes Mr. Campbell's Pete an' Ned; dems de ones massa sed was comin'. I'll see ef I looks right. *(goes to the looking-glass and views himself)* I em some punkins, ain't I? *(knock at the door)* Come in.

(Enter PETE *and* NED, *right)*

PETE. Whar is de doctor?

CATO. Here I is; don't you see me?

PETE. But whar is de ole boss?

CATO. Dat's none you business. I dun tole you dat I is de doctor, an dat's enuff.

NED. Oh! do tell us whar de doctor is. I is almos dead. Oh me! O dear me! I is so sick. *(horrible faces)*

PETE. Yes, do tell us; we don't want to stan' here foolin'.

CATO. I tells you again dat I is de doctor. I larn de trade under massa.

NED. Oh! well, den, give me somethin' to stop dis pain. Oh dear me! I shall die. *(he tries to vomit, but can't—ugly faces)*

CATO. Let me feel your pulse. Now put out your tongue. You is berry sick. Ef you don't mine, you'll die. Come out in de shed, an' I'll bleed you. *(exit all— re-enter)* Dar, now take dese pills, two in de mornin' and two at night, and ef you don't feel better, double de dose. Now, Mr. Pete, what's de matter wid you?

PETE. I got de cole chills, an' has a fever in de night.

CATO. Come out, an' I'll bleed you. *(exit all—re-enter)* Now take dese pills, two in de mornin' and two at night, an' ef dey don't help you, double de dose. Ah! I like to forget to feel your pulse and look at your tongue. Put out your tongue. *(feels his pulse)* Yes, I tells by de feel ob your pulse dat I is gib you de right pills. *(enter Mr. Parker's* BILL, *left)* What you come in dat door widout knockin' for?

BILL. My toof ache so, I didn't tink to knock. Oh, my toof! my toof! Whar is de doctor?

CATO. Here I is; don't you see me?

BILL. What! you de doctor, you brack cuss! You looks like a doctor! Oh, my toof! my toof! Whar is de doctor?

CATO. I tells you I is de doctor. Ef you don't believe me, ax dese men. I can pull your toof in a minnit.

BILL. Well, den, pull it out. Oh, my toof! how it aches! Oh, my toof! *(CATO gets the rusty turnkeys)*

CATO. Now lay down on your back.

BILL. What for?

CATO. Dat's de way massa does.

BILL. Oh, my toof! Well, den, come on. *(lies down,* CATO *gets astraddle of* BILL's *breast, puts the turnkeys on the wrong tooth, and pulls—*BILL *kicks, and cries out)—* Oh, do stop! Oh! oh! oh! *(CATO pulls the wrong tooth—*BILL *jumps up)*

CATO. Dar, now, I tole you I could pull your toof for you.

BILL. Oh, dear me! Oh, it aches yet! Oh me! Oh, Lor-e-massy! You dun pull de wrong toof. Drat your skin! ef I don't pay you for this, you brack cuss! *(they fight, and turn over table, chairs and bench—*PETE *and* NED *look on. Enter* DR. GAINES, *right)*

DR. GAINES. Why, dear me, what's the matter? What's all this about? I'll teach you a lesson, that I will. *(the* DOCTOR *goes at them with his cane)*

CATO. Oh, massa! he's to blame, sir. He's to blame. He struck me fuss.

BILL. No, sir; he's to blame; he pull de wrong toof. Oh, my toof! oh, my toof!

DR. GAINES. Let me see your tooth. Open your mouth. As I live, you've taken out the wrong tooth. I am amazed. I'll whip you for this; I'll whip you well. You're a pretty doctor. Now lie down, Bill, and let him take out the right tooth; and if he makes a mistake this time, I'll cowhide him well. Lie down, Bill. (BILL *lies down, and* CATO *pulls the tooth*) There now, why didn't you do that in the first place?

CATO. He wouldn't hole still, sir.

BILL. He lies, sir. I did hole still.

DR. GAINES. Now go home, boys; go home. (*exit* PETE, NED *and* BILL, *left*)

DR. GAINES. You've made a pretty muss of it, in my absence. Look at the table! Never mind, Cato; I'll whip you well for this conduct of yours today. Go to work now, and clear up the office. (*exit* DR. GAINES, *right*)

CATO. Confound dat nigger! I wish he was in Ginny. He bite my finger and scratch my face. But didn't I give it to him? Well, den, I reckon I did. (*he goes to the mirror, and discovers that his coat is torn—weeps*) Oh, dear me! Oh, my coat—my coat is tore! Dat nigger has tore my coat. (*he gets angry, and rushes about the room frantic*) Cuss dat nigger! Ef I could lay my hands on him, I'd tare him all to pieces,—dat I would. An' de ole boss hit me wid his cane after dat nigger tore my coat. By golly, I wants to fight somebody. Ef ole massa should come in now, I'd fight him. (*rolls up his sleeves*) Let 'em come now, ef dey dare— ole massa, or any body else; I'm ready for 'em.

(*Enter* DR. GAINES, *right*)

DR. GAINES. What's all this noise here?

CATO. Nuffin', sir; only jess I is puttin' things to rights, as you tole me. I didn't hear any noise except de rats.

DR. GAINES. Make haste, and come in; I want you to go to town. (*exit* DR. GAINES, *right*)

CATO. By golly, de ole boss like to cotch me dat time, didn't he? But wasn't I mad! When I is mad, nobody can do nuffin' wid me. But here's my coat, tore to pieces. Cuss dat nigger! (*weeps*) Oh, my coat! oh, my coat! I rudder he had broke my head den to tore my coat. Drat dat nigger! Ef he ever comes here agin, I'll pull out every toof he's got in his head—dat I will. (*exit, right*)

SCENE 3

(*A room in the quarters. Enter* GLEN, *left*)

GLEN. How slowly the time passes away. I've been waiting here two hours, and Melinda has not yet come. What keeps her, I cannot tell. I waited long and late for her last night, and when she approached, I sprang to my feet, caught her in my arms, pressed her to my heart, and kissed away the tears from her moistened cheeks. She placed her trembling hand in mine, and said, "Glen, I am yours; I will never be the wife of another." I clasped her to my bosom, and called God to witness that I would ever regard her as my wife. Old Uncle Joseph joined us in holy wedlock by moonlight; that was the only marriage ceremony. I look upon the vow as ever binding on me, for I am sure that a just God will sanction our union in heaven. Still, this man, who claims Melinda as his property, is unwilling for me to marry the woman of my choice, because he wants her himself. But he shall not have her. What he will say when he finds that we are married, I cannot tell; but I am determined to protect my wife or die. Ah! here comes Melinda. *(enter* MELINDA, *right)* I am glad to see you, Melinda. I've been waiting long, and feared you would not come. Ah! in tears again?

MELINDA. Glen, you are always thinking I am in tears. But what did master say today?

GLEN. He again forbade our union.

MELINDA. Indeed! Can he be so cruel?

GLEN. Yes, he can be just so cruel.

MELINDA. Alas! alas! how unfeeling and heartless! But did you appeal to his generosity?

GLEN. Yes, I did; I used all the persuasive powers that I was master of, but to no purpose; he was inflexible. He even offered me a new suit of clothes, if I would give you up; and when I told him that I could not, he said he would flog me to death if I ever spoke to you again.

MELINDA. And what did you say to him?

GLEN. I answered, that, while I loved life better than death, even life itself could not tempt me to consent to a separation that would make life an unchanging curse. Oh, I would kill myself, Melinda, if I thought that, for the sake of life, I could consent to your degradation. No, Melinda, I can die, but shall never live to see you the mistress of another man. But, my dear girl, I have a secret to tell you, and no one must know it but you. I will go out and see that no person is within hearing. I will be back soon. *(exit* GLEN, *left)*

MELINDA. It is often said that the darkest hour of the night precedes the dawn. It is ever thus with the vicissitudes of human suffering. After the soul has reached the lowest depths of despair, and can no deeper plunge amid its rolling, fetid shades, then the reactionary forces of man's nature begin to operate, resolution takes the place of despondency, energy succeeds instead of apathy, and an upward tendency is felt and exhibited. Men then hope against power, and smile in defiance of despair. I shall never forget when first I saw Glen. It is now more than a year since he came here with his master, Mr. Hamilton. It was a glorious moonlight night in autumn. The wide and fruitful face of nature was silent and buried in repose. The tall trees on the borders of Muddy Creek waved their leafy branches in the breeze, which was wafted from afar, refreshing over hill and vale, over the rippling water, and the waving corn and wheat fields. The starry sky was studded over with a few light, flitting clouds, while the moon, as if rejoicing to witness the meeting of two hearts that should be cemented by the purest love, sailed triumphantly along among the shifting vapors.

Oh, how happy I have been in my acquaintance with Glen! That he loves me, I do well believe it; that I love him, it is most true. Oh, how I would that those who think the slave incapable of the finer feelings, could only see our hearts, and learn our thoughts,—thoughts that we dare not utter in the presence of our masters! But I fear that Glen will be separated from me, for there is nothing too base and mean for master to do, for the purpose of getting me entirely in his power. But, thanks to Heaven, he does not own Glen, and therefore cannot sell him. Yet he might purchase him from his brother-in-law, so as to send him out of the way. But here comes my husband.

(Enter GLEN, *left)*

GLEN. I've been as far as the overseer's house, and all is quiet. Now, Melinda, as you are my wife, I will confide to you a secret. I've long been thinking of making my escape to Canada, and taking you with me. It is true that I don't belong to your master, but he might buy me from Hamilton, and then sell me out of the neighborhood.

MELINDA. But we could never succeed in the attempt to escape.

GLEN. We will make the trial, and show that we at least deserve success. There is a slave trader expected here next week, and Dr. Gaines would sell you at once if he knew that we were married. We must get ready and start, and if we can pass the Ohio river, we'll be safe on the road to Canada. *(exit, right)*

SCENE **4**

(Dining-room. REV. MR. PINCHEN *giving* MRS. GAINES *an account of his experience as a minister—*HANNAH *clearing away the breakfast table—*SAMPEY *standing behind* MRS. GAINES' *chair)*

MRS. GAINES. Now, do give me more of your experience, brother Pinchen. It always does my soul good to hear religious experience. It draws me nearer and nearer to the Lord's side. I do love to hear good news from God's people.

MR. PINCHEN. Well, sister Gaines, I've had great opportunities in my time to study the heart of man. I've attended a great many camp-meetings, revival meetings, protracted meetings, and death-bed scenes, and I am satisfied, sister Gaines, that the heart of man is full of sin, and desperately wicked. This is a wicked world, sister Gaines, a wicked world.

MRS. GAINES. Were you ever in Arkansas, brother Pinchen? I've been told that the people out there are very ungodly.

MR. PINCHEN. Oh, yes, sister Gaines. I once spent a year at Little Rock, and preached in all the towns round about there; and I found some hard cases out there, I can tell you. I was once spending a week in a district where there were a great many horse thieves, and one night, somebody stole my pony. Well, I knowed it was no use to make a fuss, so I told brother Tarbox to say nothing about it, and I'd get my horse by preaching God's everlasting gospel; for I had faith in the truth, and knowed that my Savior would not let me lose my pony. So the next Sunday I preached on horse-stealing, and told the brethren to come up in the evenin' with their hearts filled with the grace of God. So that night the house was crammed brim full with anxious souls, panting for the bread of life. Brother Bingham opened with prayer, and brother Tarbox followed, and I saw right off that we were gwine to have a blessed time. After I got 'em pretty well warmed up, I jumped on to one of the seats, stretched out my hands, and said, "I know who stole my pony; I've found out; and you are in here tryin' to make people believe that you've got religion; but you ain't got it. And if you don't take my horse back to brother Tarbox's pasture this very night,

I'll tell your name right out in meetin' tomorrow night. Take my pony back, you vile and wretched sinner, and come up here and give your heart to God." So the next mornin', I went out to brother Tarbox's pasture, and sure enough, there was my bob-tail pony. Yes, sister Gaines, there he was, safe and sound. Ha, ha, ha.

MRS. GAINES. Oh, how interesting, and how fortunate for you to get your pony! And what power there is in the gospel! God's children are very lucky. Oh, it is so sweet to sit here and listen to such good news from God's people! You Hannah, what are you standing there listening for, and neglecting your work? Never mind, my lady, I'll whip you well when I am done here. Go at your work this moment you lazy huzzy! Never mind, I'll whip you well. *(aside)* Come, do go on, brother Pinchen, with your godly conversation. It is so sweet! It draws me nearer and nearer to the Lord's side.

MR. PINCHEN. Well, sister Gaines, I've had some mighty queer dreams in my time, that I have. You see, one night I dreamed that I was dead and in heaven, and such a place I never saw before. As soon as I entered the gates of the celestial empire, I saw many old and familiar faces that I had seen before. The first person that I saw was good old Elder Pike, the preacher that first called my attention to religion. The next person I saw was Deacon Billings, my first wife's father, and then I saw a host of godly faces. Why, sister Gaines, you knowed Elder Goosbee, didn't you?

MRS. GAINES. Why, yes; did you see him there? He married me to my first husband.

MR. PINCHEN. Oh, yes, sister Gaines, I saw the old Elder, and he looked for all the world as if he had just come out of a revival meetin'.

MRS. GAINES. Did you see my first husband there, brother Pinchen?

MR. PINCHEN. No, sister Gaines, I didn't see brother Pepper there; but I've no doubt but that brother Pepper was there.

MRS. GAINES. Well, I don't know; I have my doubts. He was not the happiest man in the world. He was always borrowing trouble about something or another. Still, I saw some happy moments with Mr. Pepper. I was happy when I made his acquaintance, happy during our courtship, happy a while after our marriage, and happy when he died. *(weeps)*

HANNAH. Massa Pinchen, did you see my ole man Ben up dar in hebben?

MR. PINCHEN. No, Hannah; I didn't go amongst the niggers.

MRS. GAINES. No, of course brother Pinchen didn't go among the blacks. What are you asking questions for? Never mind, my lady, I'll whip you well when I'm done here. I'll skin you from head to foot. *(aside)* Do go on with your heavenly conversation, brother Pinchen; it does my very soul good. This is indeed a precious moment for me. I do love to hear of Christ and Him crucified.

MR. PINCHEN. Well, sister Gaines, I promised sister Daniels that I'd come over and see her this morning, and have a little season of prayer with her, and I suppose I must go. I'll tell you more of my religious experience when I return.

MRS. GAINES. If you must go, then I'll have to let you; but before you do, I wish to get your advice upon a little matter that concerns Hannah. Last week, Hannah stole a goose, killed it, cooked it, and she and her man Sam had a fine time eating the goose; and her master and I would never have known a word about it, if it had not been for Cato, a faithful servant, who told his master. And then, you see, Hannah had to be severely whipped before she'd confess that she stole the goose. Next Sabbath is sacrament day, and I want to know if you think that Hannah is fit to go to the Lord's supper after stealing the goose.

MR. PINCHEN. Well, sister Gaines, that depends on circumstances. If Hannah has confessed that she stole the goose, and has been sufficiently whipped, and has begged her master's pardon, and begged your pardon, and thinks she'll never do the like again, why then I suppose she can go to the Lord's supper; for

While the lamp holds out to burn,
The vilest sinner may return.

But she must be sure that she has repented, and won't steal any more.

MRS. GAINES. Now, Hannah, do you hear that? For my own part, I don't think she's fit to go to the Lord's supper, for she had no occasion to steal the goose. We give our niggers plenty of good wholesome food. They have a full run to the meal tub, meat once a fortnight, and all the sour milk about the place, and I'm sure that's enough for anyone. I do think that our niggers are the most ungrateful creatures in the world, that I do. They aggravate my life out of me.

HANNAH. I know, missis, dat I steal de goose, and massa whip me for it, and I confess it, and I is sorry for it. But, missis, I is gwine to de Lord's supper, next Sunday, kase I ain't agwine to turn my back on my bressed Lord an' Massa for no old tough goose, dat I ain't. *(weeps)*

MR. PINCHEN. Well, sister Gaines, I suppose I must go over and see sister Daniels; she'll be waiting for me. *(exit* MR. PINCHEN, *center)*

MRS. GAINES. Now, Hannah, brother Pinchen is gone, do you get the cowhide and follow me to the cellar, and I'll whip you well for aggravating me as you have today. It seems as if I can never sit down to take a little comfort with the Lord, without you crossing me. The devil always puts it into your head to disturb me, just when I am trying to serve the Lord. I've no doubt but that I'll miss going to heaven on your account. But I'll whip you well before I leave this world, that I will. Get the cowhide and follow me to the cellar. *(exit* MRS. GAINES and HANNAH, *right)*

ACT 2

SCENE 1

(Parlor. DR. GAINES *at a table, letters and papers before him. Enter* SAMPEY, *left)*

SAMPEY. Dar's a gemman at de doe, massa, dat wants to see you, seer.

DR. GAINES. Ask him to walk in, Sampey. *(exit* SAMPEY, *left)*

(Enter WALKER*)*

WALKER. Why, how do you do, Dr. Gaines? I em glad to see you, I'll swear.

DR. GAINES. How do you do, Mr. Walker? I did not expect to see you up here so soon. What has hurried you?

WALKER. Well, you see, doctor, I comes when I em not expected. The price of niggers is up, and I em gwine to take advantage of the times. Now, doctor, ef you've got any niggers that you wants to sell, I em your man. I am paying the highest price of anybody in the market. I pay cash down, and no grumblin'.

DR. GAINES. I don't know that I want to sell any of my people now. Still, I've got to make up a little money next month, to pay in bank; and another thing, the doctors say that we are likely to have a touch of the cholera this summer, and if that's the case, I suppose I had better turn as many of my slaves into cash as I can.

WALKER. Yes, doctor, that is very true. The cholera is death on slaves, and a thousand dollars in your pocket is a great deal better than a nigger in the field, with cholera at his heels. Why, who is that coming up the lane? It's Mr. Wildmarsh as I live! Jest the very man I wants to see. *(enter* MR. WILDMARSH*)* Why, how do you do, Squire? I was jest a thinkin' about you.

WILDMARSH. How are you, Mr. Walker? and how are you, doctor? I am glad to see you both looking so well. You seem in remarkably good health, doctor?

DR. GAINES. Yes, Squire, I was never in the enjoyment of better health. I hope you left all well at Licking?

WILDMARSH. Yes, I thank you. And now, Mr. Walker, how goes times with you?

WALKER. Well, you see, Squire, I em in good spirits. The price of niggers is up in the market, and I am lookin' out for bargains; and I was jest intendin' to come over to Lickin' to see you, to see if you had any niggers to sell. But it seems as ef the Lord knowed that I wanted to see you, and directed your steps over here. Now, Squire, ef you've got any niggers you wants to sell, I em your man. I am payin' the highest cash price of anybody in the market. Now's your time, Squire.

WILDMARSH. No, I don't think I want to sell any of my slaves now. I sold a very valuable gal to Mr. Haskins last week. I tell you, she was a smart one. I got eighteen hundred dollars for her.

WALKER. Why, Squire, how you do talk! Eighteen hundred dollars for one gal? She must have been a screamer to bring that price. What sort of a lookin' critter was she? I should like to have bought her.

WILDMARSH. She was a little of the smartest gal I've ever raised; that she was.

WALKER. Then she was your own raising, was she?

WILDMARSH. Oh, yes; she was raised on my place, and if I could have kept her three or four years longer, and taken her to the market myself, I am sure I could have sold her for three thousand dollars. But you see, Mr. Walker, my wife got a little jealous, and you know jealousy sets women's heads a teetering, and so I had to sell the gal. She's got straight hair, blue eyes, prominent features, and is almost white. Haskins will make a spec, and no mistake.

WALKER. Why, Squire, was she that pretty little gal that I saw on your knee the day that your wife was gone, when I was at your place three years ago?

WILDMARSH. Yes, the same.

WALKER. Well, now, Squire, I thought that was your daughter; she looked mightily like you. She was your daughter, wasn't she? You need not be ashamed to own it to me, for I am mum upon such matters.

WILDMARSH. You know, Mr. Walker, that people will talk, and when they talk, they say a great deal; and people did talk, and many said the gal was my daughter;

and you know we can't help people's talking. But here comes the Rev. Mr. Pinchen; I didn't know that he was in the neighborhood.

WALKER. It is Mr. Pinchen, as I live; jest the very man I wants to see. *(enter* MR. PINCHEN, *right)* Why, how do you do, Mr. Pinchen? What in the name of Jehu brings you down here to Muddy Creek? Any camp-meetins, revival meetins, death-bed scenes, or anything else in your line going on down here? How is religion prosperin' now, Mr. Pinchen? I always like to hear about religion.

MR. PINCHEN. Well, Mr. Walker, the Lord's work is in good condition everywhere now. I tell you, Mr. Walker, I've been in the gospel ministry these thirteen years, and I am satisfied that the heart of man is full of sin and desperately wicked. This is a wicked world, Mr. Walker, a wicked world, and we ought all of us to have religion. Religion is a good thing to live by, and we all want it when we die. Yes, sir, when the great trumpet blows, we ought to be ready. And a man in your business of buying and selling slaves needs religion more than anybody else, for it makes you treat your people as you should. Now, there is Mr. Haskins,—he is a slave-trader, like yourself. Well, I converted him. Before he got religion, he was one of the worst men to his niggers I ever saw; his heart was as hard as stone. But religion has made his heart as soft as a piece of cotton. Before I converted him, he would sell husbands from their wives, and seem to take delight in it; but now he won't sell a man from his wife, if he can get any one to buy both of them together. I tell you, sir, religion has done a wonderful work for him.

WALKER. I know, Mr. Pinchen, that I ought to have religion, and I feel that I am a great sinner; and whenever I get with good pious people like you and the doctor, and Mr. Wildmarsh, it always makes me feel that I am a desperate sinner. I feel it the more, because I've got a religious turn of mind. I know that I would be happier with religion, and the first spare time I get, I am going to try to get it. I'll go to a protracted meeting, and I won't stop till I get religion. Yes, I'll scuffle with the Lord till I gets forgiven. But it always makes me feel bad to talk about religion, so I'll change the subject. Now, doctor, what about them thar niggers you thought you could sell me?

DR. GAINES. I'll see my wife, Mr. Walker, and if she is willing to part with Hannah, I'll sell you Sam and his wife, Hannah. Ah! here comes my wife; I'll mention it. *(enter* MRS. GAINES, *left)* Ah! my dear, I am glad you've come. I was just telling Mr. Walker, that if you were willing to part with Hannah, I'd sell him Sam and Hannah.

MRS. GAINES. Now, Dr. Gaines, I am astonished and surprised that you should think of such a thing. You know what trouble I've had in training up Hannah for a house servant, and now that I've got her so that she knows my ways, you want to sell her. Haven't you niggers enough on the plantation to sell, without selling the servants from under my very nose?

DR. GAINES. Oh, yes, my dear; but I can spare Sam, and I don't like to separate him from his wife; and I thought if you could let Hannah go, I'd sell them both. I don't like to separate husbands from their wives.

MRS. GAINES. Now, gentlemen, that's just the way with my husband. He thinks more about the welfare and comfort of his slaves, than he does of himself or his family. I am sure you need not feel so bad at the thought of separating Sam from Hannah. They've only been married eight months, and their attachment can't be very strong in that short time. Indeed, I shall be glad if you do sell Sam, for then I'll make Hannah *jump the broomstick* with Cato, and I'll have them both here under my eye. I never will again let one of my house servants marry a field hand—never! For when night comes on, the servants are off to the quarters, and I have to holler and holler enough to split my throat before I can make them hear. And another thing: I want you to sell Melinda. I don't intend to keep that mulatto wench about the house any longer.

DR. GAINES. My dear, I'll sell any servant from the place to suit you, except Melinda. I can't think of selling her—I can't think of it.

MRS. GAINES. I tell you that Melinda shall leave this house, or I'll go. There, now you have it. I've had my life tormented out of me by the presence of that yellow wench, and I'll stand it no longer. I know you love her more than you do me, and I'll—I'll—I'll write—write to my father. *(weeps)*. *(Exit* MRS. GAINES, *left)*

WALKER. Why, doctor, your wife's a screamer, ain't she? Ha, ha, ha. Why, doctor, she's got a tongue of her own, ain't she? Why, doctor, it was only last week that I thought of getting a wife myself; but your wife has skeered the idea out of my head. Now, doctor, if you wants to sell the gal, I'll buy her. Husband and wife ought to be on good terms, and your wife won't feel well till the gal is gone. Now, I'll pay you all she's worth, if you wants to sell.

DR. GAINES. No, Mr. Walker; the girl my wife spoke of is not for sale. My wife does not mean what she says; she's only a little jealous. I'll get brother Pinchen to talk to her, and get her mind turned upon religious matters, and then she'll forget it. She's only a little jealous.

WALKER. I tell you what, doctor, ef you call that a little jealous, I'd like to know what's a heap. I tell you, it will take something more than religion to set your wife right. You had better sell me the gal; I'll pay you cash down, and no grumblin'.

DR. GAINES. The girl is not for sale, Mr. Walker; but if you want two good, able-bodied servants, I'll sell you Sam and Big Sally. Sam is trustworthy, and Sally is worth her weight in gold for rough usage.

WALKER. Well, doctor, I'll go out and take a look at 'em, for I never buys slaves without examining them well, because they are sometimes injured by over-work or underfeedin'. I don't say that is the case with yours, for I don't believe it is; but as I sell on honor, I must buy on honor.

DR. GAINES. Walk out, sir, and you can examine them to your heart's content. Walk right out, sir.

SCENE 2

(View in front of the Great House. Examination of SAM *and* BIG SALLY—DR. GAINES, WILDMARSH, MR. PINCHEN *and* WALKER *present)*

WALKER. Well, my boy, what's your name?

SAM. Sam, sir, is my name.

WALKER. How old are you, Sam?

SAM. Ef I live to see next corn plantin' time, I'll be 27, or 30, or 35, or 40—I don't know which, sir.

WALKER. Ha, ha, ha. Well, doctor, this is rather a green boy. Well, mer feller, are you sound?

SAM. Yes, sir, I spec I is.

WALKER. Open your mouth and let me see your teeth. I allers judge a nigger's age by his teeth, same as I dose a hoss. Ah! pretty good set of grinders. Have you got a good appetite?

SAM. Yes, sir.

WALKER. Can you eat your allowance?

SAM. Yes, sir, when I can get it.

WALKER. Get out on the floor and dance; I want to see if you are supple.

SAM. I don't like to dance; I is got religion.

WALKER. Oh, ho! you've got religion, have you? That's so much the better. I likes to deal in the gospel. I think he'll suit me. Now, mer gal, what's your name?

SALLY. I is Big Sally, sir.

WALKER. How old are you, Sally?

SALLY. I don't know, sir; but I heard once dat I was born at sweet pertater diggin' time.

WALKER. Ha, ha, ha. Don't know how old you are! Do you know who made you?

SALLY. I hev heard who it was in de Bible dat made me, but I dun forget de gentman's name.

WALKER. Ha, ha, ha. Well, doctor, this is the greenest lot of niggers I've seen for some time. Well, what do you ask for them?

DR. GAINES. You may have Sam for $1000, and Sally for $900. They are worth all I ask for them. You know I never banter, Mr. Walker. There they are; you can take them at that price, or let them alone, just as you please.

WALKER. Well, doctor, I reckon I'll take 'em; but it's all they are worth. I'll put the handcuffs on 'em, and then I'll pay you. I likes to go accordin' to Scripter. Scripter says ef eatin' meat will offend your brother, you must quit it; and I say, ef leavin' your slaves without the handcuffs will make 'em run away, you must put the handcuffs on 'em. Now, Sam, don't you and Sally cry. I am of a tender heart, and it ollers makes me feel bad to see people cryin'. Don't cry, and the first place I get to, I'll buy each of you a great big *ginger cake*,—that I will. Now, Mr. Pinchen, I wish you were going down the river. I'd like to have your company; for I allers likes the company of preachers.

MR. PINCHEN. Well, Mr. Walker, I would be much pleased to go down the river with you, but it's too early for me. I expect to go to Natchez in four or five weeks, to attend a camp-meetin', and if you were going down then, I'd like it. What kind of niggers sells in the Orleans market, Mr. Walker?

WALKER. Why, field hands. Did you think of goin' in the trade?

MR. PINCHEN. Oh, no; only it's a long way down to Natchez, and I thought I'd just buy five or six niggers, and take 'em down and sell 'em to pay my travellin' expenses. I only want to clear my way.

SCENE 3

(Sitting-room—table and rocking-chair. Enter MRS. GAINES, *right, followed by* SAMPEY*)*

MRS. GAINES. I do wish your master would come; I want supper. Run to the gate, Sampey, and see if he is coming. *(exit* SAMPEY, *left)* That man is enough to break my heart. The patience of an angel could not stand it.

(Enter SAMPEY, *left)*

SAMPEY. Yes, missis, master is coming.

(Enter DR. GAINES, *left. The Doctor walks about with his hands under his coat, seeming very much elated)*

MRS. GAINES. Why, doctor, what is the matter?

DR. GAINES. My dear, don't call me *doctor.*

MRS. GAINES. What should I call you?

DR. GAINES. Call me Colonel, my dear—Colonel. I have been elected Colonel of the Militia, and I want you to call me by my right name. I always felt that Providence had designed me for something great, and He has just begun to shower His blessings upon me.

MRS. GAINES. Dear me, I could never get to calling you Colonel; I've called you Doctor for the last twenty years.

DR. GAINES. Now, Sarah, if you will call me Colonel, other people will, and I want you to set the example. Come, my darling, call me Colonel, and I'll give you anything you wish for.

MRS. GAINES. Well, as I want a new gold watch and bracelets, I'll commence now. Come, Colonel, we'll go to supper. *(aside)* Ah, now for my new shawl. Mrs. Lemme was here today, Colonel, and she had on, Colonel, one of the prettiest shawls, Colonel, I think, Colonel, that I ever saw, Colonel, in my life, Colonel. And there is only one, Colonel, in Mr. Watson's store, Colonel; and that, Colonel, will do, Colonel, for a Colonel's wife.

DR. GAINES. Ah! my dear, you never looked so much the lady since I've known you. Go, my darling, get the watch, bracelets and shawl, and tell them to charge them to Colonel Gaines; and when you say "Colonel," always emphasize the word.

MRS. GAINES. Come, Colonel, let's go to supper.

DR. GAINES. My dear, you're a jewel,—you are! *(exit, right)*

(Enter CATO, *left)*

CATO. Why, whar is massa and missis? I tought dey was here. Ah! by golly, yonder comes a mulatter gal. Yes, its Mrs. Jones's Tapioca. I'll set up to dat gal, dat I will. *(enter* TAPIOCA, *right)* Good ebenin', Miss Tappy. How is your folks?

TAPIOCA. Pretty well, I tank you.

CATO. Miss Tappy, dis wanderin' heart of mine is yours. Come, take a seat! Please to squze my manners; love discommodes me. Take a seat. Now, Miss Tappy, I loves you; an ef you will jess marry me, I'll make you a happy husband, dat I will. Come, take me as I is.

TAPIOCA. But what will Big Jim say?

CATO. Big Jim! Why, let dat nigger go to Ginny.[1] I want to know, now, if you is tinkin' about dat common nigger? Why, Miss Tappy, I is surstonished dat you should tink 'bout frowin' yourself away wid a common, ugly lookin' cuss like Big Jim, when you can get a fine lookin', suspectable man like me. Come, Miss Tappy, choose dis day who you have. Afore I go any furder, give me one kiss. Come, give me one kiss. Come, let me kiss you.

TAPIOCA. No you shan't—dare now! You shan't kiss me widout you is stronger den I is; and I know you is dat. *(he kisses her. Enter* DR. GAINES, *right, and hides)*

CATO. Did you know, Miss Tappy, dat I is de head doctor 'bout dis house? I beats de ole boss all to pieces.

TAPIOCA. I hev hearn dat you bleeds and pulls teef.

CATO. Yes, Miss Tappy; massa could not get along widout me, for massa was made a doctor by books; but I is a natral doctor. I was born a doctor, jess as Lorenzo Dow was born a preacher. So you see I can't be nuffin' but a doctor, while massa is a bunglin' ole cuss at de bissness.

DR. GAINES. *(in a low voice)* Never mind; I'll teach you a lesson, that I will.

CATO. You see, Miss Tappy, I was gwine to say—Ah! but afore I forget, jess give me anudder kiss, jess to keep company wid de one dat you give me jess now,— dat's all. *(kisses her)* Now, Miss Tappy, duse you know de fuss time dat I seed you?

TAPIOCA. No, Mr. Cato, I don't.

CATO. Well, it was at de camp-meetin'. Oh, Miss Tappy, dat pretty red calliker dress you had on dat time did de work for me. It made my heart flutter—

DR. GAINES. *(low voice)* Yes, and I'll make your black hide flutter.

CATO. Didn't I hear some noise? By golly, dar is teves in dis house, and I'll drive 'em out. *(takes a chair and runs at the* DOCTOR, *and knocks him down. The* DOCTOR *chases* CATO *round the table)* Oh, massa, I didn't know 'twas you!

DR. GAINES. You scoundrel! I'll whip you well. Stop! I tell you. *(curtain falls)*

ACT 3

SCENE 1

(Sitting-room. MRS. GAINES, *seated in an arm chair, reading a letter. Enter* HANNAH, *left)*

MRS. GAINES. You need not tell me, Hannah, that you don't want another husband, I know better. Your master has sold Sam, and he's gone down the river, and you'll never see him again. So, go and put on your calico dress, and meet me in the kitchen. I intend for you to *jump the broomstick* with Cato. You need not tell me that you don't want another man. I know that there's no woman living that can be happy and satisfied without a husband.

HANNAH. Oh, missis, I don't want to jump de broomstick wid Cato. I don't love Cato; I can't love him.

---

[1]Virginia.

MRS. GAINES. Shut up, this moment! What do you know about love? I didn't love your master when I married him, and people don't marry for love now. So go and put on your calico dress, and meet me in the kitchen. *(exit* HANNAH, *left)* I am glad that the Colonel has sold Sam; now I'll make Hannah marry Cato, and I have them both here under my eye. And I am also glad that the Colonel has parted with Melinda. Still, I'm afraid that he is trying to deceive me. He took the hussy away yesterday, and says he sold her to a trader; but I don't believe it. At any rate, if she's in the neighborhood, I'll find her, that I will. No man ever fools me. *(exit* MRS. GAINES, *left)*

SCENE 2

(The kitchen—slaves at work. Enter HANNAH, *right)*

HANNAH. Oh, Cato, do go and tell missis dat you don't want to jump de broomstick wid me,—dat's a good man! Do, Cato; kase I nebber can love you. It was only las week dat massa sold my Sammy, and I don't want any udder man. Do go tell missis dat you don't want me.

CATO. No, Hannah, I ain't a-gwine to tell missis no such think, kase I dose want you, and I ain't a-gwine to tell a lie for you ner nobody else. Dar, now you's got it! I don't see why you need to make so much fuss. I is better lookin' den Sam; an' I is a house servant, an' Sam was only a fiel hand; so you ought to feel proud of a change. So go and do as missis tells you. *(exit* HANNAH, *left)* Hannah needn't try to get me to tell a lie; I ain't a-gwine to do it, kase I dose want her, an' I is bin wantin' her dis long time, an' soon as massa sold Sam, I knowed I would get her. By golly, I is gwine to be a married man. Won't I be happy! Now, ef I could only jess run away from ole massa, an' get to Canada wid Hannah, den I'd show 'em who I was. Ah! dat reminds me of my song 'bout ole massa and Canada, an' I'll sing it fer yer. Dis is my moriginal hyme. It comed into my head one night when I was fass asleep under an apple tree, looking up at de moon. Now for my song:—

Air—"Dandy Jim"

Come all ye bondmen far and near,
Let's put a song in massa's ear,
It is a song for our poor race,
Who're whipped and trampled with disgrace.

> [CHORUS]
> My old massa tells me, Oh,
> This is a land of freedom, Oh;
> Let's look about and see if it's so,
> Just as massa tells me, Oh.

He tells us of that glorious one,
I think his name was Washington,
How he did fight for liberty,
To save a threepence tax on tea.

(Chorus)

But now we look about and see
That we poor blacks are not so free;
We're whipped and thrashed about like fools,
And have no chance at common schools.

(Chorus)

They take our wives, insult and mock,
And sell our children on the block,
They choke us if we say a word,
And say that "niggers" shan't be heard.

(Chorus)

Our preachers, too, with whip and cord,
Command obedience in the Lord;
They say they learn it from the big book,
But for ourselves, we dare not look.

(Chorus)

There is a country far away,
I think they call it Canada,
And if we reach Victoria's shore,
They say that we are slaves no more.

> Now haste, all bondmen, let us go,
> And leave this *Christian* country, Oh;
> Haste to the land of the British Queen,
> Where whips for negroes are not seen.

Now, if we go, we must take the night,
And never let them come in sight;
The bloodhounds will be on our track,
And wo to us if they fetch us back.

> Now haste all bondmen, let us go,
> And leave this *Christian* country, Oh;
> God help us to Victoria's shore,
> Where we are free and slaves no more!

(Enter MRS. GAINES, *left)*

MRS. GAINES. Ah! Cato, you're ready, are you? Where is Hannah?

CATO. Yes, missis; I is bin waitin' dis long time. Hannah has bin here tryin' to swade me to tell you dat I don't want her; but I told her dat you sed I must jump de broomstick wid her, an' I is gwine to mind you.

MRS. GAINES. That's right, Cato; servants should always mind their masters and mistresses, without asking a question.

CATO. Yes, missis, I allers dose what you and massa tells me, an' axes nobody.

(*Enter* HANNAH, *right*)

MRS. GAINES. Ah! Hannah; come, we are waiting for you. Nothing can be done till you come.

HANNAH. Oh, missis, I don't want to jump de broomstick wid Cato; I can't love him.

MRS. GAINES. Shut up, this moment. Dolly, get the broom. Susan, you take hold of the other end. There, now hold it a little lower—there, a little higher. There, now, that'll do. Now Hannah, take hold of Cato's hand. Let Cato take hold of your hand.

HANNAH. Oh, missis, do spare me. I don't want to jump de broomstick wid Cato.

MRS. GAINES. Get the cowhide, and follow me to the cellar, and I'll whip you well. I'll let you know how to disobey my orders. Get the cowhide, and follow me to the cellar. (*exit* MRS. GAINES *and* HANNAH, *right*)

DOLLY. Oh, Cato, do go an' tell missis dat you don't want Hannah. Don't you hear how she's whippin' her in de cellar? Do go an' tell missis dat you don't want Hannah, and den she'll stop whippin' her.

CATO. No, Dolly, I ain't a-gwine to do no such a thing, kase ef I tell missis dat I don't want Hannah, den missis will whip me; an' I ain't a-gwine to be whipped fer you, ner Hannah, ner nobody else. No, I'll jump de broomstick wid every woman on de place, ef missis wants me to, before I'll be whipped.

DOLLY. Cato, ef I was in Hannah's place, I'd see you in de bottomless pit before I'd live wid you, you great big wall-eyed, empty-headed, knock-kneed fool. You're as mean as your devilish old missis.

CATO. Ef you don't quit dat busin' me, Dolly, I'll tell missis as soon as she comes in, an' she'll whip you, you know she will.

(*Enter* MRS. GAINES *and* HANNAH, *right.* MRS. GAINES *fans herself with her hand-kerchief, and appears fatigued*)

MRS. GAINES. You ought to be ashamed of yourself, Hannah, to make me fatigue myself in this way, to make you do your duty. It's very naughty in you, Hannah. Now, Dolly, you and Susan get the broom, and get out in the middle of the room. There, hold it a little lower—a little higher; there, that'll do. Now, remember that this is a solemn occasion; you are going to jump into matrimony. Now, Cato, take hold of Hannah's hand. There, now, why couldn't you let Cato take your hand before? Now get ready, and when I count three, do you jump. Eyes on the *broomstick!* All ready. One, two, three, and over you go. There, now you're husband and wife, and if you don't live happy together, it's your own fault; for I am sure there's nothing to hinder it. Now, Hannah, come up to the house, and I'll give you some whiskey, and you can make some apple toddy, and you and Cato can have a fine time. (*exit* MRS. GAINES *and* HANNAH, *left*)

DOLLY. I tell you what, Susan, when I get married, I is gwine to have a preacher to marry me. I ain't a-gwine to jump de broomstick. Dat will do for fiel' hands, but house servants ought to be 'bove dat.

SUSAN. Well, chile, you can't speck any ting else from ole missis. She come from down in Carlina, from 'mong de poor white trash. She don't know any better. You can't speck nothin' more dan a jump from a frog. Missis says she is one of de akastocacy; but she ain't no more of an akastocacy dan I is. Missis says she was born wid a silver spoon in her mouf; ef she was, I wish it had a-choked her, dat's what I wish. Missis wanted to make Linda jump de broomstick wid Glen, but massa ain't a-gwine to let Linda jump de broomstick wid anybody. He's gwine to keep Linda fer heself.

DOLLY. You know massa took Linda 'way las' night, an' tell missis dat he has sold her and sent her down de river; but I don't b'lieve he has sold her at all. He went ober towards de poplar farm, an' I tink Linda is ober dar now. Ef she is dar, missis'll find it out, fer she tell'd massa las' night, dat ef Linda was in de neighborhood, she'd find her. *(exit* DOLLY *and* SUSAN*)*

SCENE 3

(Sitting-room—chairs and table. Enter HANNAH, *right)*

HANNAH. I don't keer what missis says; I don't like Cato, an' I won't live wid him. I always love my Sammy, an' I loves him now. *(knock at the door—goes to the door. Enter* MAJ. MOORE, *center)* Walk in, sir; take a seat. I'll call missis, sir; massa is gone away. *(exit* HANNAH, *right)*

MAJ. MOORE. So I am here at last, and the Colonel is not at home. I hope his wife is a good-looking woman. I rather like fine-looking women, especially when their husbands are from home. Well, I've studied human nature to some purpose. If you wish to get the good will of a man, don't praise his wife, and if you wish to gain the favor of a woman, praise her children, and swear that they are the picture of their father, whether they are nor not. Ah! here comes the lady.

(Enter MRS. GAINES, *right)*

MRS. GAINES. Good morning, sir!

MAJ. MOORE. Good morning, madam! I am Maj. Moore, of Jefferson. The Colonel and I had seats near each other in the last Legislature.

MRS. GAINES. Be seated, sir. I think I've heard the Colonel speak of you. He's away, now; but I expect him every moment. You're a stranger here, I presume?

MAJ. MOORE. Yes, madam, I am. I rather like the Colonel's situation here.

MRS. GAINES. It is thought to be a fine location. *(enter* SAMPEY, *right)* Hand me my fan, will you, Sampey?

*(*SAMPEY *gets the fan and passes near the* MAJOR, *who mistakes the boy for the Colonel's son. He reaches out his hand)*

MAJ. MOORE. How do you do, Bob? Madam, I should have known that this was the Colonel's son, if I had met him in California; for he looks so much like his papa.

MRS. GAINES. *(to the boy)* Get out of here this minute. Go to the kitchen. *(exit* SAMPEY, *right)* That is one of the niggers, sir.

MAJ. MOORE. I beg your pardon, madam; I beg your pardon.

MRS. GAINES. No offence, sir; mistakes will be made. Ah! here comes the Colonel.

(Enter DR. GAINES, *center)*

DR. GAINES. Bless my soul, how are you, Major? I'm exceedingly pleased to see you. Be seated, be seated, Major.

MRS. GAINES. Please excuse me, gentlemen; I must go and look after dinner, for I've no doubt that the Major will have an appetite for dinner, by the time it is ready. *(exit* MRS. GAINES, *right)*

MAJ. MOORE. Colonel, I'm afraid I've played the devil here today.

DR. GAINES. Why, what have you done?

MAJ. MOORE. You see, Colonel, I always make it a point, wherever I go, to praise the children, if there are any, and so today, seeing one of your little servants come in, and taking him to be your son, I spoke to your wife of the marked resemblance between you and the boy. I am afraid I've insulted madam.

DR. GAINES. Oh! don't let that trouble you. Ha, ha, ha. If you did call my son, you didn't miss it much. Ha, ha, ha. Come, we'll take a walk, and talk over matters about old times. *(exit, left)*

SCENE 4

(Forest scenery. Enter GLEN, *left)*

GLEN. Oh, how I want to see Melinda! My heart pants and my soul is moved whenever I hear her voice. Human tongue cannot tell how my heart yearns toward her. Oh, God! thou who gavest me life, and implanted in my bosom the love of liberty, and gave me a heart to love, Oh, pity the poor outraged slave! Thou, who canst rend the veil of centuries, speak, Oh, speak, and put a stop to this persecution! What is death, compared to slavery? Oh, heavy curse, to have thoughts, reason, taste, judgment, conscience, and passions like another man, and not have equal liberty to use them! Why was I born with a wish to be free, and still be a slave? Why should I call another man master? And my poor Melinda, she is taken away from me, and I dare not ask the tyrant where she is. It is childish to stand here weeping. Why should my eyes be filled with tears, when my brain is on fire? I will find my wife—I will; and wo to him who shall try to keep me from her!

SCENE 5

(Room in a small cottage on the Poplar Farm, ten miles from Muddy Creek, and owned by DR. GAINES. *Enter* MELINDA, *right)*

MELINDA. Here I am, watched, and kept a prisoner in this place. Oh, I would that I could escape, and once more get with Glen. Poor Glen! He does not know where I am. Master took the opportunity, when Glen was in the city with his master, to bring me here to this lonely place, and fearing that mistress would know where I was, he brought me here at night. Oh, how I wish I could rush into the arms of sleep!—that sweet sleep, which visits all alike, descending, like the dews of heaven, upon the bond as well as the free. It would drive from my troubled brain the agonies of this terrible night.

(Enter DR. GAINES, *left)*

DR. GAINES. Good evening, Melinda! Are you not glad to see me?

MELINDA. Sir, how can I be glad to see one who has made life a burden, and turned my sweetest moments into bitterness?

DR. GAINES. Come, Melinda, no more reproaches! You know that I love you, and I have told you, and I tell you again, that if you will give up all idea of having Glen for a husband, I will set you free, let you live in this cottage, and be your own mistress, and I'll dress you like a lady. Come, now, be reasonable!

MELINDA. Sir, I am your slave; you can do as you please with the avails of my labor, but you shall never tempt me to swerve from the path of virtue.

DR. GAINES. Now, Melinda, that black scoundrel Glen has been putting these notions into your head. I'll let you know that you are my property, and I'll do as I please with you. I'll teach you that there is no limit to my power.

MELINDA. Sir, let me warn you that if you compass my ruin, a woman's bitterest curse will be laid upon your head, with all the crushing, withering weight that my soul can impart to it; a curse that shall cling to you throughout the remainder of your wretched life; a curse that shall haunt you like a spectre in your dreams by night, and attend upon you by day; a curse, too, that shall embody itself in the ghastly form of the woman whose chastity you will have outraged. Command me to bury myself in yonder stream, and I will obey you. Bid me do anything else, but I beseech you not to commit a double crime,—outrage a woman, and make her false to her husband.

DR. GAINES. You got a husband! Who is your husband, and when were you married?

MELINDA. Glen is my husband, and I've been married four weeks. Old Uncle Joseph married us one night by moonlight. I see you are angry; I pray you not to injure my husband.

DR. GAINES. Melinda, you shall never see Glen again. I have bought him from Hamilton, and I will return to Muddy Creek, and roast him at the stake. A black villain, to get into my way in that manner! Here I've come ten miles tonight to see you, and this is the way you receive me!

MELINDA. Oh, master, I beg you not to injure my husband! Kill me, but spare him! Do! do! he is my husband!

DR. GAINES. You shall never see that black imp again, so good night, my lady! When I come again, you'll give me a more cordial reception. Good night! (*exit* DR. GAINES, *left*)

MELINDA. I shall go distracted. I cannot remain here and know that Glen is being tortured on my account. I must escape from this place,—I must,—I must!

(*Enter* CATO, *right*)

CATO. No, you ain't a-gwine to 'scape, nudder. Massa tells me to keep dese eyes on you, an' I is gwine to do it.

MELINDA. Oh, Cato, do let me get away! I beg you, do!

CATO. No; I tells you massa told me to keep you safe; an' ef I let you go, massa will whip me. (*exit* CATO, *left*)

(*Enter* MRS. GAINES, *right*)

MRS. GAINES. Ah, you trollop! here you are! Your master told me that he had sold you and sent you down the river, but I knew better; I knew it was a lie. And when he left home this evening, he said he was going to the city on business, and I knew that was a lie too, and determined to follow him, and see what he was up to. I rode all the way over here tonight. My side-saddle was lent out, and I had to ride ten miles bare-back, and I can scarcely walk; and your master has just left here. Now deny that, if you dare.

MELINDA. Madam, I will deny nothing which is true. Your husband has just gone from here, but God knows that I am innocent of anything wrong with him.

MRS. GAINES. It's a lie! I know better. If you are innocent, what are you doing here, cooped up in this cottage by yourself? Tell me that!

MELINDA. God knows that I was brought here against my will, and I beg that you will take me away.

MRS. GAINES. Yes, Melinda, I will see that you are taken away, but it shall be after a fashion that you won't like. I know that your master loves you, and I intend to put a stop to it. Here, drink the contents of this vial,—drink it!

MELINDA. Oh, you will not take my life,—you will not!

MRS. GAINES. Drink the poison this moment!

MELINDA. I cannot drink it.

MRS. GAINES. I tell you to drink this poison at once. Drink it, or I will thrust this knife to your heart! The poison or the dagger, this instant! (*she draws a dagger;* MELINDA *retreats to the back of the room, and seizes a broom*)

MELINDA. I will not drink the poison! (*they fight;* MELINDA *sweeps off* MRS. GAINES,—*cap, combs and curls. Curtain falls*)

ACT 4

SCENE 1

(*Interior of a dungeon—*GLEN *in chains*)

GLEN. When I think of my unmerited sufferings, it almost drives me mad. I struck the doctor, and for that, I must remain here loaded with chains. But why did he strike me? He takes my wife from me, sends her off, and then comes and beats me over the head with his cane. I did right to strike him back again. I would I had killed him. Oh! there is a volcano pent up in the hearts of the slaves of these Southern States that will burst forth ere long. When that day comes, wo to those whom its unpitying fury may devour! I would be willing to die, if I could smite down with these chains every man who attempts to enslave his fellowman.

(*Enter* SAMPEY, *right*)

SAMPEY. Glen, I jess bin hear massa call de oberseer, and I spec somebody is gwine to be whipped. Anudder ting: I know whar massa took Linda to. He took her to de poplar farm, an' he went away las' night, an' missis she follow after massa, an' she ain't come back yet. I tell you, Glen, de debil will be to pay on dis place, but don't you tell anybody dat I tole you. (*exit* SAMPEY, *right*)

SCENE 2

(*Parlor.* DR. GAINES, *alone*)

DR. GAINES. Yes, I will have the black rascal well whipped, and then I'll send him. It was most fortunate for me that Hamilton was willing to sell him to me. *(enter* MR. SCRAGG, *left)* I have sent for you, Mr. Scragg. I want you to take Glen out of the dungeon, take him into the tobacco house, fasten him down upon the stretcher, and give him five hundred lashes upon his bare back; and when you have whipped him, feel his pulse, and report to me how it stands, and if he can bear more, I'll have you give him an additional hundred or two, as the case may be.

SCRAGG. I tell you, doctor, that suits me to a charm. I've long wanted to whip that nigger. When your brother-in-law came here to board, and brought that boy with him, I felt bad to see a nigger dressed up in such fine clothes, and I wanted to whip him right off. I tell you, doctor, I had rather whip that nigger than go to heaven, any day,—that I had!

DR. GAINES. Go, Mr. Scragg, and do your duty. Don't spare the whip!

SCRAGG. I will, sir; I'll do it in order. *(exit* SCRAGG, *left)*

DR. GAINES. Everything works well now, and when I get Glen out of the way, I'll pay Melinda another visit, and she'll give me a different reception. But I wonder where my wife is? She left word that she was going to see her brother, but I am afraid that she has got on my track. That woman is the pest of my life. If there's any place in heaven for her, I'd be glad if the Lord would take her home, for I've had her too long already. But what noise is that? What can that be? What is the matter?

(Enter SCRAGG, *left, with face bloody)*

SCRAGG. Oh, dear me! oh, my head! That nigger broke away from me, and struck me over the head with a stick. Oh, dear me! Oh!

DR. GAINES. Where is he, Mr. Scragg?

SCRAGG. Oh! sir, he jumped out of the window; he's gone. Oh! my head; he's cracked my skull. Oh, dear me, I'm kilt! Oh! oh! oh!

(Enter SLAVES, *right)*

DR. GAINES. Go, Dolly, and wash Mr. Scragg's head with some whiskey, and bind it up. Go at once. And Bob, you run over to Mr. Hall, and tell him to come with his hounds; we must go after the rascal. *(exit all except the* DOCTOR, *right)* This will never do. When I catch the scoundrel, I'll make an example of him; I'll whip him to death. Ah! here comes my wife. I wonder what she comes now for? I must put on a sober face, for she looks angry. *(enter* MRS. GAINES, *left)* Ah! my dear, I am glad you've come, I've been so lonesome without you. Oh! Sarah, I don't know what I should do if the Lord should take you home to heaven. I don't think that I should be able to live without you.

MRS. GAINES. Dr. Gaines, you ought to be ashamed to sit there and talk in that way. You know very well that if the Lord should call me home to glory tonight, you'd jump for joy. But you need not think that I am going to leave this world before you. No; with the help of the Lord, I'll stay here to foil you in your meanness. I've been on your track, and a dirty track it is, too. You ought to be ashamed of yourself. See what promises you made me before we were married; and this is the way you keep your word. When I married you, everybody said that it was a pity that a woman of my sweet temper should be linked to such a man as you. (*she weeps and wrings her hands*)

DR. GAINES. Come, my dear, don't make a fool of yourself. Come, let's go to supper, and a strong cup of tea will help your head.

MRS. GAINES. Tea help my head! tea won't help my head. You're a brute of a man; I always knew I was a fool for marrying you. There was Mr. Comstock, he wanted me, and he loved me, and he said I was an angel, so he did; and he loved me, and he was rich; and mother always said that he loved me more than you, for when he used to kiss me, he always squeezed my hand. You never did such a thing in your life. (*she weeps and wrings her hands*)

DR. GAINES. Come, my dear, don't act so foolish.

MRS. GAINES. Yes; everything I do is foolish. You're a brute of a man; I won't live with you any longer. I'll leave you—that I will. I'll go and see a lawyer, and get a divorce from you—so I will.

DR. GAINES. Well, Sarah, if you want a divorce, you had better engage Mr. Barker. He's the best lawyer in town; and if you want some money to facilitate the business, I'll draw a check for you.

MRS. GAINES. So you want me to get a divorce, do you? Well, I won't have a divorce; no, I'll never leave you, as long as the Lord spares me. (*exit* MRS. GAINES, *right*)

SCENE 3

(*Forest at night—large tree. Enter* MELINDA, *left*)

MELINDA. This is indeed a dark night to be out and alone on this road. But I must find my husband, I must. Poor Glen! if he only knew that I was here, and could get to me, he would. What a curse slavery is! It separates husbands from their wives, and tears mothers from their helpless offspring, and blights all our hopes for this world. I must try to reach Muddy Creek before daylight, and seek out my husband. What's that I hear?—footsteps? I'll get behind this tree.

(*Enter* GLEN, *right*)

GLEN. It is so dark, I'm afraid I've missed the road. Still, this must be the right way to the poplar farm. And if Bob told me the truth, when he said that Melinda was at the poplar farm, I will soon be with her; and if I once get her in my arms, it will be a strong man that shall take her from me. Aye, a dozen strong men shall not be able to wrest her from my arms. (MELINDA *rushes from behind the tree*)

MELINDA. Oh, Glen! It is my husband,—it is!

GLEN. Melinda! Melinda! it is, it is. Oh God! I thank Thee for this manifestation of Thy kindness. Come, come, Melinda, we must go at once to Canada. I escaped from the overseer, whom Dr. Gaines sent to flog me. Yes, I struck him over the head with his own club, and I made the wine flow freely; yes, I pounded his old skillet well for him, and then jumped out of the window. It was a leap for freedom. Yes, Melinda, it was a leap for freedom. I've said "master" for the last time. I am free; I'm bound for Canada. Come, let's be off, at once, for the negro dogs will be put upon our track. Let us once get beyond the Ohio river, and all will be right. *(exit, right)*

ACT 5

SCENE 1

(Bar-room in the American Hotel—travellers lounging in chairs, and at the bar. Enter BILL JENNINGS, *right)*

BARKEEPER. Why, Jennings, how do you do?

JENNINGS. Say Mr. Jennings, if you please.

BARKEEPER. Well, Mr. Jennings, if that suits you better. How are times? We've been expecting you, for some days.

JENNINGS. Well, before I talk about the times, I want my horses put up, and want you to tell me where my niggers are to stay tonight. Sheds, stables, barns, and everything else here, seems pretty full, if I am a judge.

BARKEEPER. Oh! I'll see to your plunder.

FIRST LOUNGER. I say, Barkeeper, make me a brandy cocktail, strong. Why, how do you do, Mr. Jennings?

JENNINGS. Pretty well, Mr. Peters. Cold evening, this.

FIRST LOUNGER. Yes, this is cold. I heard you speak of your niggers. Have you got a pretty large gang?

JENNINGS. No, only thirty-three. But they are the best that the country can afford. I shall clear a few dimes, this trip. I hear that the price is up.

(Enter MR. WHITE, *right)*

WHITE. Can I be accommodated here tonight, landlord?

BARKEEPER. Yes, sir; we've bed for man and beast. *(to the waiter)* Go, Dick, and take the gentleman's coat and hat. You're a stranger in these parts, I rec'on.

WHITE. Yes, I am a stranger here.

SECOND LOUNGER. Where mout you come from, ef it's a far question?

WHITE. I am from Massachusetts.

THIRD LOUNGER. I say, cuss Massachusetts!

FIRST LOUNGER. I say so too. There is where the fanatics live; cussed traitors. The President ought to hang 'em all.

WHITE. I say, landlord, if this is the language that I am to hear, I would like to go into a private room.

BARKEEPER. We ain't got no private room empty.

FIRST LOUNGER. Maybe you're mad 'bout what I said 'bout your State. Ef you is, I've only to say that this is a free country, and people talks what they please; an' ef you don't like it, you can better yourself.

WHITE. Sir, if this is a free country, why do you have slaves here? I saw a gang at the door, as I came in.

SECOND LOUNGER. He didn't mean that this was a free country for niggers. He meant that it's free for white people. And another thing, ef you get to talkin 'bout freedom for niggers, you'll catch what you won't like, mister. It's right for niggers to be slaves.

WHITE. But I saw some white slaves.

FIRST LOUNGER. Well, they're white niggers.

WHITE. Well, sir, I am from a free State, and I thank God for it; for the worst act that a man can commit upon his fellow-man, is to make him a slave. Conceive of a mind, a living soul, with the germs of faculties which infinity cannot exhaust, as it first beams upon you in its glad morning of existence, quivering with life and joy, exulting in the glorious sense of its developing energies, beautiful, and brave, and generous, and joyous, and free,—the clear pure spirit bathed in the auroral light of its unconscious immortality,—and then follow it in its dark and dreary passage through slavery, until oppression stifles and kills, one by one, every inspiration and aspiration of its being, until it becomes a dead soul entombed in a living frame!

THIRD LOUNGER. Stop that; stop that, I say. That's treason to the country; that's downright rebellion.

BARKEEPER. Yes, it is. And another thing,—this is not a meeting-house.

FIRST LOUNGER. Yes, if you talk such stuff as that, you'll get a chunk of cold lead in you, that you will.

(*Enter* DR. GAINES *and* SCRAGG, *followed by* CATO, *right*)

DR. GAINES. Gentlemen, I am in pursuit of two valuable slaves, and I will pay five hundred dollars for their arrest. (*exit* MR. WHITE, *left*)

FIRST LOUNGER. I'll bet a picayune that your niggers have been stolen by that cussed feller from Massachusetts. Don't you see he's gone?

DR. GAINES. Where is the man? If I can lay my hands on him, he'll never steal another nigger. Where is the scoundrel?

FIRST LOUNGER. Let's go after the feller. I'll go with you. Come, foller me. (*exit all, left, except* CATO *and the* WAITER)

CATO. Why don't you bring in massa's saddle-bags? What de debil you standin' dar for? You common country niggers don't know nuffin', no how. Go an' get massa's saddle-bags and bring 'em in. (*exit* SERVANT, *right*) By golly! ebry body's gone, an' de bar-keeper too. I'll tend de bar myself now; an' de fuss gemman I waits on will be dis gemman of color. (*goes behind the counter, and drinks*) Ah, dis is de stuff fer me; it makes my head swim; it makes me happy right off. I'll take a little more.

(*Enter* BARKEEPER, *left*)

BARKEEPER. What are you doing behind the bar, you black cuss?

CATO. I is lookin' for massa's saddle-bags, sir. Is dey here?

BARKEEPER. But what were you drinking there?

CATO. Me drinkin'! Why, massa, you muss be mistaken. I ain't drink nuffin'.

BARKEEPER. You infernal whelp, to stand there and lie in that way!

CATO. Oh, yes, seer, I did tase dat coffee in dat bottle; dat's all I did.

(*Enter* MR. WHITE, *left, excited*)

MR. WHITE. I say, sir, is there no place of concealment in your house? They are after me, and my life is in danger. Say, sir, can't you hide me away?

BARKEEPER. Well, you ought to hold your tongue when you come into our State.

MR. WHITE. But, sir, the Constitution gives me the right to speak my sentiments, at all times and in all places.

BARKEEPER. We don't care for Constitutions nor nothin' else. We made the Constitution, and we'll break it. But you had better hide away; they are coming, and they'll lynch you, that they will. Come with me; I'll hide you in the cellar. Foller me. (*exit* BARKEEPER *and* WHITE, *left*)

(*Enter the mob, right*)

DR. GAINES. If I can once lay my hands on that scoundrel, I'll blow a hole through his head.

JENNINGS. Yes, I say so too; for no one knows whose niggers are safe, now-a-days. I must look after my niggers. Who is that I see in the distance? I believe it's that cussed Massachusetts feller. Come, let's go after him. (*exit the mob, right*)

SCENE 2

(*Forest at night. Enter* GLEN *and* MELINDA, *right*)

MELINDA. I am so tired and hungry, that I cannot go further. It is so cloudy that we cannot see the North Star, and therefore cannot tell whether we are going to Canada, or further South. Let's sit down here.

GLEN. I know that we cannot see the North Star, Melinda, and I fear we've lost our way. But, see! the clouds are passing away, and it'll soon be clear. See! yonder is a star; yonder is another and another. Ah! yonder is the North Star, and we are safe!

Star of the North! though night winds drift
    The fleecy drapery of the sky
Between thy lamp and me, I lift,
    Yea, lift with hope my sleepless eye,
To the blue heights wherein thou dwellest,
And of a land of freedom tellest.

Star of the North! while blazing day
    Pours round me its full tide of light,
And hides thy pale but faithful ray,
    I, too, lie hid, and long for night:
For night: I dare not walk at noon,
Nor dare I trust the faithless moon—

Nor faithless man, whose burning lust
    For gold hath riveted my chain,—
Nor other leader can I trust
    But thee, of even the starry train;
For all the host around thee burning,
Like faithless man, keep turning, turning.

I may not follow where they go:—
    Star of the North! I look to thee

While on I press; for well I know,
    Thy light and truth shall set me free:—
Thy light, that no poor slave deceiveth;
Thy truth, that all my soul believeth.

Thy beam is on the glassy breast
    Of the still spring, upon whose brink
I lay my weary limbs to rest,
    And bow my parching lips to drink.
Guide of the friendless negro's way,
I bless thee for this quiet ray!

In the dark top of southern pines
    I nestled, when the Driver's horn
Called to the field, in lengthening lines,
    My fellows, at the break of morn.
And there I lay till thy sweet face
Looked in upon "my hiding place."

The tangled cane-brake, where I crept
    For shelter from the heat of noon,
And where, while others toiled, I slept,
    Till wakened by the rising moon,
As its stalks felt the night wind free,
Gave me to catch a glimpse of thee.

Star of the North! in bright array
    The constellations round thee sweep,
Each holding on its nightly way,
    Rising, or sinking in the deep,
And, as it hangs in mid heaven flaming,
The homage of some nation claiming.

This nation to the Eagle cowers;
    Fit ensign! she's a bird of spoil:—
Like worships like! for each devours
    The earnings of another's toil.
I've felt her talons and her beak,
And now the gentler Lion seek.

The Lion, at the Monarch's feet
    Crouches, and lays his mighty paw
Into her lap!—an emblem meet
    Of England's Queen, and English law:
Queen, that hath made her Islands free!
Law, that holds out its shield to me!

Star of the North! upon that shield
    Thou shinest,—Oh, for ever shine!

The negro, from the cotton field
   Shall, then, beneath its orb recline,
And feed the Lion, crouched before it,
Nor heed the Eagle, screaming o'er it!

With the thoughts of servitude behind us, and the North Star before us, we will go forward with cheerful hearts. Come, Melinda, let's go on. *(exit, left)*

SCENE 3

(A street. Enter MR. WHITE, *right)*

MR. WHITE. I am glad to be once more in a free State. If I am caught again south of Mason and Dixon's line, I'll give them leave to lynch me. I came near losing my life. This is the way our constitutional rights are trampled upon. But what care these men about Constitutions, or anything else that does not suit them? But I must hasten on. *(exit, left)*

(Enter CATO, *in disguise, right)*

CATO. I wonder if dis is me? By golly, I is free as a frog. But maybe I is mistaken; maybe dis ain't me. Cato, is dis you? Yes, seer. Well, now it is me, an' I em a free man. But, stop! I muss change my name, kase ole massa might foller me, and somebody might tell him dat dey seed Cato; so I'll change my name, and den he won't know me ef he sees me. Now, what shall I call myself? I'm now in a suspectable part of de country, an' I muss have a suspectable name. Ah! I'll call myself Alexander Washinton Napoleon Pompey Caesar. Dar, now, dat's a good long, suspectable name, and everybody will suspect me. Let me see; I wonder ef I can't make up a song on my escape! I'll try.

Air—"Dearest Mae"

Now, freemen, listen to my song, a story I'll relate,
It happened in de valley of de ole Kentucky State:
Dey marched me out into de fiel', at every break of day,
And work me dar till late sunset, widout a cent of pay.

   Dey work me all de day,
   Widout a bit of pay,
   And thought, because dey fed me well,
   I would not run away.

Massa gave me his ole coat, an' thought I'd happy be,
But I had my eye on de North Star, an' thought of liberty;
Ole massa lock de door, an' den he went to sleep,
I dress myself in his bess clothes, an' jump into de street.

   [CHORUS]
   Dey work me all de day,
   Widouta bit of pay,

So I took my flight, in the middle of de night,
When de sun was gone away.

Sed I, dis chile's a freeman now, he'll be a slave no more;
I travell'd faster all dat night, dan I ever did before.
I came up to a farmer's house, jest at de break of day,
And saw a white man standin' dar, sed he, "You are a runaway."

(Chorus)

I tole him I had left de whip, an' bayin' of de hound,
To find a place where man is man, ef sich dar can be found;
Dat I had heard, in Canada, dat all mankind are free,
An' dat I was going dar in search of liberty.

(Chorus)

I've not committed any crime, why should I run away?
Oh! shame upon your laws, dat drive me off to Canada.
You loudly boast of liberty, an' say your State is free,
But ef I tarry in your midst, will you protect me?

(Chorus)

SCENE 4

(Dining-room—table spread. MRS. NEAL *and* CHARLOTTE*)*

MRS. NEAL. Thee may put the tea to draw, Charlotte. Thy father will be in soon, and we must have breakfast. *(enter* MR. NEAL, *left)* I think, Simeon, it is time those people were called. Thee knows that they may be pursued, and we ought not to detain them long here.

MR. NEAL. Yes, Ruth, thou art right. Go, Charlotte, and knock on their chamber door, and tell them that breakfast is ready. *(exit* CHARLOTTE, *right)*

MRS. NEAL. Poor creatures! I hope they'll reach Canada in safety. They seem to be worthy persons.

(Enter CHARLOTTE, *right)*

CHARLOTTE. I've called them, mother, and they'll soon be down. I'll put the breakfast on the table.

(Enter NEIGHBOR JONES, *left)*

MR. NEAL. Good morning, James. Thee has heard, I presume, that we have two very interesting persons in the house?

JONES. Yes, I heard that you had two fugitives by the Underground road, last night; and I've come over to fight for them, if any persons come to take them back.

(Enter THOMAS, *right)*

MR. NEAL. Go, Thomas, and harness up the horses and put them to the covered wagon, and be ready to take these people on, as soon as they get their breakfast.

Go, Thomas, and hurry thyself. *(exit* THOMAS, *right)* And so thee wants to fight, this morning, James?

JONES. Yes; as you belongs to a society that don't believe in fighting, and I does believe in that sort of thing, I thought I'd come and relieve you of that work, if there is any to be done.

(Enter GLEN *and* MELINDA, *right)*

MR. NEAL. Good morning, friends. I hope thee rested well, last night.

MRS. NEAL. Yes, I hope thee had a good night's rest.

GLEN. I thank you, madam, we did.

MR. NEAL. I'll introduce thee to our neighbor, James Jones. He's a staunch friend of thy people.

JONES. I am glad to see you. I've come over to render assistance, if any is needed.

MRS. NEAL. Come, friends, take seats at the table. *(to* GLEN *and* MELINDA*)* Thee'll take seats there. *(all take seats at the table)* Does thee take sugar and milk in thy tea?

MELINDA. I thank you, we do.

JONES. I'll look at your *Tribune*, Uncle Simeon, while you're eating.

MR. NEAL. Thee'll find it on the table.

MRS. NEAL. I presume thee's anxious to get to thy journey's end?

GLEN. Yes, madam, we are. I am told that we are not safe in any of the free States.

MR. NEAL. I am sorry to tell thee, that that is too true. Thee will not be safe until thee gets on British soil. I wonder what keeps Thomas; he should have been here with the team.

(Enter THOMAS, *left)*

THOMAS. All's ready; and I've written the prettiest song that was ever sung. I call it "The Underground Railroad."

MR. NEAL. Thomas, thee can eat thy breakfast far better than thee can write a song, as thee calls it. Thee must hurry thyself, when I send thee for the horses, Thomas. Here lately, thee takes thy time.

THOMAS. Well, you see I've been writing poetry; that's the reason I've been so long. If you wish it, I'll sing it to you.

JONES. Do let us hear the song.

MRS. NEAL. Yes, if Thomas has written a ditty, do let us hear it.

MR. NEAL. Well, Thomas, if thee has a ditty, thee may recite it to us.

THOMAS. Well, I'll give it to you. Remember that I call it, "The Underground Railroad."

Air—"Wait for the Wagon"

Oh, where is the invention
   Of this growing age,
Claiming the attention
   Of statesman, priest, or sage,

In the many railways

Through the nation found,
Equal to the Yankees'
    Railway under-ground?

[CHORUS]
No one hears the whistle,
    Or rolling of the cars,
While negroes ride to freedom
    Beyond the stripes and stars.

On the Southern borders
    Are the Railway stations,
Negroes get free orders
    While on the plantations;
For all, of ev'ry color,
    First-class cars are found,
While they ride to freedom
    By Railway under-ground.

    (*Chorus*)

Masters in the morning
    Furiously rage,
Cursing the inventions
    Of this knowing age;
Order out the bloodhounds,
    Swear they'll bring them back,
Dogs return exhausted,
    Cannot find the track.

    (*Chorus*)

Travel is increasing,
    Build a double track,
Cars and engines wanted,
    They'll come, we have no lack.
Clear the track of loafers,
    See that crowded car!
Thousands passing yearly,
    Stock is more than par.

    (*Chorus*)

JONES. Well done! That's a good song. I'd like to have a copy of them verses. (*knock at the door.* CHARLOTTE *goes to the door, and returns. Enter* CATO, *left, still in disguise*)

MR. NEAL. Who is this we have? Another of the outcasts, I presume?

CATO. Yes, seer; I is gwine to Canada, an' I met a man, an' he tole me dat you would give me some wittals an' help me on de way. By golly! ef dar ain't Glen an' Melinda. Dey don't know me in dese fine clothes. *(goes up to them)* Ah, chillen! I is one wid you. I golly, I is here too! *(they shake hands)*

GLEN. Why, it is Cato, as I live!

MELINDA. Oh, Cato, I am so glad to see you! But how did you get here?

CATO. Ah, chile, I come wid ole massa to hunt you; an' you see I get tired huntin' you, an' I am now huntin' for Canada. I leff de ole boss in de bed at de hotel; an' you see I thought, afore I left massa, I'd jess change clothes wid him; so, you see, I is fixed up,—ha, ha, ha. Ah, chillen! I is gwine wid you.

MRS. NEAL. Come, sit thee down, and have some breakfast.

CATO. Tank you, madam, I'll do dat. *(sits down and eats)*

MR. NEAL. This is pleasant for thee to meet one of thy friends.

GLEN. Yes, sir, it is; I would be glad if we could meet more of them. I have a mother and sister still in slavery, and I would give worlds, if I possessed them if by so doing I could release them from their bondage.

THOMAS. We are all ready, sir, and the wagon is waiting.

MRS. NEAL. Yes, thee had better start.

CATO. Ef anybody tries to take me back to ole massa, I'll pull ebry toof out of dar heads, dat I will! As soon as I get to Canada, I'll set up a doctor shop, an' won't I be poplar? Den I rec'on I will. I'll pull teef fer all de people in Canada. Oh, how I wish I had Hannah wid me! It makes me feel bad when I tink I ain't a-gwine to see my wife no more. But, come, chillen, let's be makin' tracks. Dey say we is most to de British side.

MR. NEAL. Yes, a few miles further, and you'll be safe beyond the reach of the Fugitive-Slave Law.

CATO. Ah, dat's de talk fer dis chile. *(exit, center)*

SCENE 5

(The Niagara River—a ferry. FERRYMAN, *fastening his small boat)*

FERRYMAN. *(advancing, takes out his watch)* I swan, if it ain't one o'clock. I thought it was dinner time. Now there's no one here, I'll go to dinner, and if anybody comes, they can wait until I return. I'll go at once. *(exit, left)*

(Enter MR. WHITE, *right, with an umbrella)*

MR. WHITE. I wonder where that ferryman is? I want to cross to Canada. It seems a little showery, or else the mist from the Falls is growing thicker. *(takes out his sketch-book and pencils,—sketches)*

(Enter CANE PEDLAR, *right)*

PEDLAR. Want a good cane today, sir? Here's one from Goat Island,—very good, sir, straight and neat,—only one dollar. I've a wife and nine small children,— youngest is nursing, and the oldest only three years old. Here's a cane from Table Rock, sir. Please buy one! I've had no breakfast today. My wife's got the rheumatics, and the children's got the measles. Come, sit, do buy a cane! I've a lame shoulder, and can't work.

MR. WHITE. Will you stop your confounded talk, and let me alone? Don't you see that I am sketching? You've spoiled a beautiful scene for me, with your nonsense.

(Enter SECOND PEDLAR *right)*

SECOND PEDLAR. Want any bead bags, or money purses? These are all real Ingen bags, made by the Black Hawk Ingens. Here's a pretty bag, sir, only 75 cents. Here's a money purse, 50 cents. Please, sir, buy something! My wife's got the fever and ague, and the house is full of children, and they're all sick. Come, sir, do help a worthy man!

MR. WHITE. Will you hold your tongue? You've spoiled some of the finest pictures in the world. Don't you see that I am sketching? *(exit* PEDLARS, *right, grumbling)* I am glad those fellows have gone; now I'll go a little further up the shore, and see if I can find another boat. I want to get over. *(exit, left)*

(Enter DR. GAINES, SCRAGG, *and an* OFFICER*)*

OFFICER. I don't think that your slaves have crossed yet, and my officers will watch the shore below here, while we stroll up the river. If I once get my hands on them all the Abolitionists in the State shall not take them from me.

DR. GAINES. I hope they have not got over, for I would not lose them for two thousand dollars, especially the gal.

(Enter FIRST PEDLAR*)*

PEDLAR. Wish to get a good cane, sir? This stick was cut on the very spot where Sam Patch jumped over the falls. Only 50 cents. I have a sick wife and thirteen children. Please buy a cane; I ain't had no dinner.

OFFICER. Get out of the way! Gentlemen, we'll go up the shore. *(exit, left)*

(Enter CATO, *right)*

CATO. I is loss fum de cumpny, but dis is de ferry, and I spec dey'll soon come. But didn't we have a good time las' night in Buffalo? Dem dar Buffalo gals make my heart flutter, dat dey did. But, tanks be to de Lord, I is got religion. I got it las' night in de meetin'. Before I got religion, I was a great sinner; I got drunk, an' took de name of de Lord in vain. But now I is a conwerted man; I is bound for hebben; I toats de witness in my bosom; I feel dat my name is rote in de book of life. But dem niggers in de Vine Street Church las' night shout an' make sich a fuss, dey give me de headache. But, tank de Lord, I is got religion, an' now I'll be a preacher, and den dey'll call me de Rev. Alexander Washinton Napoleon Pompey Caesar. Now I'll preach and pull teef, bofe at de same time. Oh, how I wish I had Hannah wid me! Cuss ole massa, fer ef it warn't for him, I could have my wife wid me. Ef I hadn't religion, I'd say "Damn ole massa!" but as I is a religious man, an' belongs to de church, I won't say no sich a thing. But who is dat I see comin'? Oh, it's a whole heap of people. Good Lord! what is de matter?

(Enter GLEN *and* MELINDA, *left, followed by* OFFICERS*)*

GLEN. Let them come; I am ready for them. He that lays hands on me or my wife shall feel the weight of this club.

MELINDA. Oh, Glen, let's die here, rather than again go into slavery.

OFFICER. I am the United States Marshal. I have a warrant from the Commissioner to take you, and bring you before him. I command assistance.

(Enter DR. GAINES, SCRAGG, *and* OFFICER, *right)*

DR. GAINES. Here they are. Down with the villain! down with him! but don't hurt the gal!

(Enter MR. WHITE, *right)*

MR. WHITE. Why, bless me! these are the slaveholding fellows. I'll fight for freedom! *(takes hold of his umbrella with both hands.—The fight commences, in which* GLEN, CATO, DR. GAINES, SCRAGG, WHITE, *and the* OFFICERS, *take part.—*FERRYMAN *enters, and runs to his boat.—*DR. GAINES, SCRAGG *and the* OFFICERS *are knocked down,* GLEN, MELINDA *and* CATO *jump into the boat, and as it leaves the shore and floats away,* GLEN *and* CATO *wave their hats, and shout loudly for freedom.—Curtain falls)*

Follow the Drinkin' Gourd

This song from the 1850s typifies the quest for freedom among fugitive slaves, for the "drinkin' gourd" represents the Big Dipper, which signifies the direction of the North Star. The song was popular among those associated with the Underground Railroad.

When the sun comes back and the first quail calls,
Follow the drinkin' gourd.
For the old man is awaiting for to carry you to freedom
If you follow the drinkin' gourd.   4

Chorus:

Follow the drinkin' gourd,
Follow the drinkin' gourd.
For the old man is awaiting for to carry you to freedom
If you follow the drinkin' gourd.   8

The river banks will make a mighty good road,
The dead trees will show you the way.
Left foot, peg foot, travelin' on,
Follow the drinkin' gourd.   12

Chorus

The river ends between two hills.
Follow the drinkin' gourd.
There's another river on the other side
If you follow the drinkin' gourd.   16

Chorus

HARRIET E. WILSON (1828–1863)

Born in Fredericksburg, Virginia, Harriet Wilson wed Thomas Wilson in 1851 in New Hampshire. A year later she had a child, whom she named George Mason. After being abandoned by her husband, she found herself desperate for money. She moved to Boston and wrote Our Nig; or, Sketches from the Life of a Free Black, in a Two-Story White House, North: Showing That Slavery's Shadows Fall Even There *(1859), hoping to achieve fame and fortune. Meanwhile, her child lived in New Hampshire with individuals who agreed to care for him. Unfortunately, fever claimed the life of George shortly after his mother's book was printed.*

Her book, believed to be the first novel by an African American woman published in America, focuses on the life of a woman of mixed racial heritage who works as an indentured servant for a white family in the North. The novel critiques racism in the North, revealing that race, class, and gender oppression in America were not limited to the South and plantation society. Her novel suggests that indentured servitude was a form of slavery. Wilson spent the remainder of her life in Boston; she died not fully realizing the impact her novel would have.

From Our Nig; or, Sketches from the Life of a Free Black, in a Two-Story White House, North: Showing That Slavery's Shadows Fall Even There (1859)

Chapter 1: Mag Smith, My Mother

> Oh, Grief beyond all other griefs, when fate
> First leaves the young heart lone and desolate
> In the wide world, without that only tie
> For which it loved to live or feared to die;
> Lorn as the hung-up lute, that ne'er hath spoken
> Since the sad day its master-cord was broken!
>
> **Moore**

Lonely Mag Smith! See her as she walks with downcast eyes and heavy heart. It was not always thus. She *had* a loving, trusting heart. Early deprived of parental guardianship, far removed from relatives, she was left to guide her tiny boat over life's surges alone and inexperienced. As she merged into womanhood, unprotected, uncherished, uncared for, there fell on her ear the music of love, awakening an intensity of emotion long dormant. It whispered of an elevation before unaspired to; of ease and plenty her simple heart had never dreamed of as hers. She knew the voice of her charmer, so ravishing, sounded far above her. It seemed like an angel's, alluring her upward and onward. She thought she could ascend to him and become an equal. She surrendered to him a priceless gem, which he proudly garnered as a trophy, with those of other victims, and left her to her fate.

The world seemed full of hateful deceivers and crushing arrogance. Conscious that the great bond of union to her former companions was severed, that the disdain of others would be insupportable, she determined to leave the few friends she possessed, and seek an asylum among strangers. Her offspring came unwelcomed, and before its nativity numbered weeks, it passed from earth, ascending to a purer and better life.

"God be thanked," ejaculated Mag, as she saw its breathing cease; "no one can taunt *her* with my ruin."

Blessed release! may we all respond. How many pure, innocent children not only inherit a wicked heart of their own, claiming life-long scrutiny and restraint, but are heirs also of parental disgrace and calumny, from which only long years of patient endurance in paths of rectitude can disencumber them.

Mag's new home was soon contaminated by the publicity of her fall; she had a feeling of degradation oppressing her; but she resolved to be circumspect, and try to regain in a measure what she had lost. Then some foul tongue would jest of her shame, and averted looks and cold greetings disheartened her. She saw she could not bury in forgetfulness her misdeed, so she resolved to leave her home and seek another in the place she at first fled from.

Alas, how fearful are we to be first in extending a helping hand to those who stagger in the mires of infamy; to speak the first words of hope and warning to those emerging into the sunlight of morality! Who can tell what numbers, advancing just far enough to hear a cold welcome and join in the reserved converse of professed reformers, disappointed, disheartened, have chosen to dwell in unclean places, rather than encounter these "holier-than-thou" of the great brotherhood of man!

Such was Mag's experience; and disdaining to ask favor or friendship from a sneering world, she resolved to shut herself up in a hovel she had often passed in better days, and which she knew to be untenanted. She vowed to ask no favors of familiar faces; to die neglected and forgotten before she would be dependent on any. Removed from the village, she was seldom seen except as upon your introduction, gentle reader, with downcast visage, returning her work to her employer, and thus providing herself with the means of subsistence. In two years many hands craved the same avocation; foreigners who cheapened toil and clamored for a livelihood, competed with her, and she could not thus sustain herself. She was now above no drudgery. Occasionally old acquaintances called to be favored with help of some kind, which she was glad to bestow for the sake of the money it would bring her; but the association with them was such a painful reminder of by-gones, she returned to her hut morose and revengeful, refusing all offers of a better home than she possessed. Thus she lived for years, hugging her wrongs, but making no effort to escape. She had never known plenty, scarcely competency; but the present was beyond comparison with those innocent years when the coronet of virtue was hers.

Every year her melancholy increased, her means diminished. At last no one seemed to notice her, save a kind-hearted African, who often called to inquire after her health and to see if she needed any fuel, he having the responsibility of furnishing that article, and she in return mending or making garments.

"How much you earn dis week, Mag?" asked he one Saturday evening.

▲ Henry Ossawa Tanner, "The Banjo Lesson," 1893. Oil on canvas, 49" x 35 1/2".
Hampton University Museum, Hampton, Virginia.

▲ Aaron Douglas, *Harriet Tubman* (1931). © Bennett College, September 7, 1993.

▲ Aaron Douglas, *Into Bondage* (1936). Oil on canvas, 60 3/8" x 60 1/2". In the collection of the Corcoran Gallery of Art, Washington D.C. Museum purchase and partial gift of Thurlow Tibbs Jr., The Evans-Tibbs Collection (1996.9).

▲ *The Slave Market* (circa 1840). A view of slaves seated around a stove awaiting auction. Painting by unidentified artist. Corbis

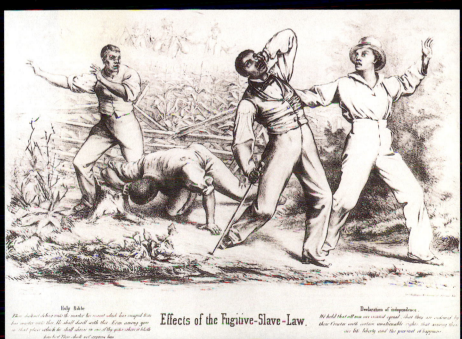

Holy Bible

Effects of the Fugitive-Slave-Law.

Declaration of independence.

▲ *Effects of the Fugitive Slave Law* (1860). Brutally tracking down fugitive slaves on their way to the North. Lithograph by unidentified artist. Corbis

▲ George Smith Cook (American, 1819-1902), *Emancipation Day Celebration,* Richmond, Virginia (1888). Albumen print, 5 1/16" x 7". The Valentine Museum, Richmond, Virginia.

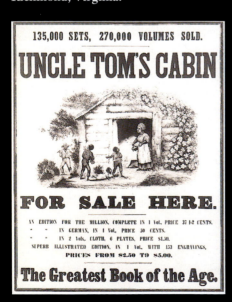

▲ *Advertisement for Uncle Tom's Cabin* (1852). Poster. From the Bella C. Landauer collection of business and advertising art. © Collection of the New-York Historical Society.

▲ Courtesy of the Library of Congress (LC-USZ62-34810).

"Little enough, Jim. Two or three days without any dinner. I washed for the Reeds, and did a small job for Mrs. Bellmont; that's all. I shall starve soon, unless I can get more to do. Folks seem as afraid to come here as if they expected to get some awful disease. I don't believe there is a person in the world but would be glad to have me dead and out of the way."

"No, no, Mag! don't talk so. You shan't starve so long as I have barrels to hoop. Peter Greene boards me cheap. I'll help you, if nobody else will."

A tear stood in Mag's faded eye. "I'm glad," she said, with a softer tone than before, "if there is *one* who isn't glad to see me suffer. I b'lieve all Singleton wants to see me punished, and feel as if they could tell when I've been punished long enough. It's a long day ahead they'll set it, I reckon."

After the usual supply of fuel was prepared, Jim returned home. Full of pity for Mag, he set about devising measures for her relief. "By golly!" said he to himself one day—for he had become so absorbed in Mag's interest that he had fallen into a habit of musing aloud—"By golly! I wish she'd *marry* me."

"Who?" shouted Pete Greene, suddenly starting from an unobserved corner of the rude shop.

"Where you come from, you sly nigger!" exclaimed Jim.

"Come, tell me, who is't?" said Pete; "Mag Smith, you want to marry?"

"Git out, Pete! and when you come in dis shop again, let a nigger know it. Don't steal in like a thief."

Pity and love know little severance. One attends the other. Jim acknowledged the presence of the former, and his efforts in Mag's behalf told also of a finer principle.

This sudden expedient which he had unintentionally disclosed, roused his thinking and inventive powers to study upon the best method of introducing the subject to Mag.

He belted his barrels, with many a scheme revolving in his mind, none of which quite satisfied him, or seemed, on the whole, expedient. He thought of the pleasing contrast between her fair face and his own dark skin; the smooth, straight hair, which he had once, in expression of pity, kindly stroked on her now wrinkled but once fair brow. There was a tempest gathering in his heart, and at last, to ease his pent-up passion, he exclaimed aloud, "By golly!" Recollecting his former exposure, he glanced around to see if Pete was in hearing again. Satisfied on this point, he continued: "She'd be as much of a prize to me as she'd fall short of coming up to the mark with white folks. I don't care for past things. I've done things 'fore now I's 'shamed of. She's good enough for me, any how."

One more glance about the premises to be sure Pete was away.

The next Saturday night brought Jim to the hovel again. The cold was fast coming to tarry its apportioned time. Mag was nearly despairing of meeting its rigor.

"How's the wood, Mag?" asked Jim.

"All gone; and no more to cut, any how," was the reply.

"Too bad!" Jim said. His truthful reply would have been, I'm glad.

"Anything to eat in the house?" continued he.

"No," replied Mag.

"Too bad!" again, orally, with the same *inward* gratulation as before.

"Well, Mag," said Jim, after a short pause, "you's down low enough. I don't see but I've got to take care of ye. 'Sposin' we marry!"

Mag raised her eyes, full of amazement, and uttered a sonorous "What?"

Jim felt abashed for a moment. He knew well what were her objections.

"You's had trial of white folks, any how. They run off and left ye, and now none of 'em come near ye to see if you's dead or alive. I's black outside, I know, but I's got a white heart inside. Which you rather have, a black heart in a white skin, or a white heart in a black one?"

"Oh, dear!" sighed Mag; "Nobody on earth cares for *me*—"

"I do," interrupted Jim.

"I can do but two things," said she, "beg my living, or get it from you."

"Take me, Mag. I can give you a better home than this, and not let you suffer so."

He prevailed; they married. You can philosophize, gentle reader, upon the impropriety of such unions, and preach dozens of sermons on the evils of amalgamation. Want is a more powerful philosopher and preacher. Poor Mag. She has sundered another bond which held her to her fellows. She has descended another step down the ladder of infamy.

✠ FRANCES E. W. HARPER (1825–1911)

African American women writers of the antebellum period combined activism and writing as a tool for advocating equal rights for blacks. Authors such as Frances E. W. Harper stood in the forefront in the quest for civil rights. A native of Baltimore, she relocated to the Midwest to take a position as a teacher in Columbus, Ohio, in 1850. After marrying Fenton Harper, she continued her work with organizations advocating the abolition of slavery and promoting the temperance movement, which preached against the consumption of alcoholic beverages. Her novel Iola Leroy, or Shadows Uplifted *(1892) focuses on a heroine who grows up believing she is white. Learning that she is of black and white parentage only after her father dies, Iola refuses to pass for white and commits herself to the education and uplift of blacks in the South. Iola's commitment to education, religion, and moral uplift mirror the concerns of Harper and other black women involved in the club movement of the late nineteenth century, in which African American females pooled their time, money, and talent to improve the lives of all African Americans. Harper also distinguished herself as a poet with her volume of verse titled* Poems *(1900). When Harper died of a heart condition in Philadelphia, she left a legacy of activism and literature mirroring the concerns of nineteenth-century African Americans but timeless in its stirring appeal to a need for equality and fairness for all.*

From Iola Leroy, or Shadows Uplifted (1892)

Chapter 10: Shadows in the Home

On the next morning after this conversation Leroy left for the North, to attend the commencement and witness the graduation of his ward. Arriving in Ohio, he immediately repaired to the academy and inquired for the principal. He was shown into the reception-room, and in a few moments the principal entered.

"Good morning," said Leroy, rising and advancing towards him; "how is my ward this morning?"

"She is well, and has been expecting you. I am glad you came in time for the commencement. She stands among the foremost in her class."

"I am glad to hear it. Will you send her this?" said Leroy, handing the principal a card. The principal took the card and immediately left the room.

Very soon Leroy heard a light step, and looking up he saw a radiantly beautiful woman approaching him."

"Good morning, Marie," he said, greeting her cordially, and gazing upon her with unfeigned admiration. "You are looking very handsome this morning."

"Do you think so?" she asked, smiling and blushing. "I am glad you are not disappointed; that you do not feel your money has been spent in vain."

"Oh, no, what I have spent on your education has been the best investment I ever made."

"I hope," said Marie, "you may always find it so. But Mas——"

"Hush!" said Leroy, laying his hand playfully on her lips; "you are free. I don't want the dialect of slavery to linger on your lips. You must not call me that name again."

"Why not?"

"Because I have a nearer and dearer one by which I wish to be called."

Leroy drew her nearer, and whispered in her ear a single word. She started, trembled with emotion, grew pale, and blushed painfully. An awkward silence ensued, when Leroy, pressing her hand, exclaimed: "This is the hand that plucked me from the grave, and I am going to retain it as mine; mine to guard with my care until death us do part."

Leroy looked earnestly into her eyes, which fell beneath his ardent gaze. With admirable self-control, while a great joy was thrilling her heart, she bowed her beautiful head and softly repeated, "Until death us do part."

Leroy knew Southern society too well to expect it to condone his offense against its social customs, or give the least recognition to his wife, however cultured, refined, and charming she might be, if it were known that she had the least infusion of negro blood in her veins. But he was brave enough to face the consequences of his alliance, and marry the woman who was the choice of his heart, and on whom his affections were centred.

After Leroy had left the room, Marie sat awhile thinking of the wonderful change that had come over her. Instead of being a lonely slave girl, with the fatal dower of beauty, liable to be bought and sold, exchanged, and bartered, she was to be the wife of a wealthy planter; a man in whose honor she could confide, and on whose love she could lean.

Very interesting and pleasant were the commencement exercises in which Marie bore an important part. To enlist sympathy for her enslaved race, and appear to advantage before Leroy, had aroused all of her energies. The stimulus of hope, the manly love which was environing her life, brightened her eye and lit up the wonderful beauty of her countenance. During her stay in the North she had constantly been brought in contact with anti-slavery people. She was not aware that there was so much kindness among the white people of the country until she had tested it in the North. From the anti-slavery people in private life she had learned some of the noblest lessons of freedom and justice, and had become imbued with their sentiments. Her theme was "American Civilization, its Lights and Shadows."

Graphically she portrayed the lights, faithfully she showed the shadows of our American civilization. Earnestly and feelingly she spoke of the blind Sampson in our land, who might yet shake the pillars of our great Commonwealth. Leroy listened attentively. At times a shadow of annoyance would overspread his face, but it was soon lost in the admiration her earnestness and zeal inspired. Like Esther pleading for the lives of her people in the Oriental courts of a despotic king, she stood before the audience, pleading for those whose lips were sealed, but whose condition appealed to the mercy and justice of the Nation. Strong men wiped the moisture from their eyes, and women's hearts throbbed in unison with the strong, brave words that were uttered in behalf of freedom for all and chains for none. Generous applause was freely bestowed, and beautiful bouquets were showered upon her. When it was known that she was to be the wife of her guardian, warm congratulations were given, and earnest hopes expressed for the welfare of the lonely girl, who, nearly all her life, had been deprived of a parent's love and care. On the eve of starting South Leroy procured a license, and united his destiny with the young lady whose devotion in the darkest hour had won his love and gratitude.

In a few days Marie returned as mistress to the plantation from which she had gone as a slave. But as unholy alliances were common in those days between masters and slaves, no one took especial notice that Marie shared Leroy's life as mistress of his home, and that the family silver and jewelry were in her possession. But Leroy, happy in his choice, attended to the interests of his plantation, and found companionship in his books and in the society of his wife. A few male companions visited him occasionally, admired the magnificent beauty of his wife, shook their heads, and spoke of him as being very eccentric, but thought his marriage the great mistake of his life. But none of his female friends ever entered his doors, when it became known that Marie held the position of mistress of his mansion, and presided at his table. But she, sheltered in the warm clasp of loving arms, found her life like a joyous dream.

Into that quiet and beautiful home three children were born, unconscious of the doom suspended over their heads.

"Oh, how glad I am," Marie would often say, "that these children are free. I could never understand how a cultured white man could have his own children enslaved. I can understand how savages, fighting with each other, could doom their vanquished foes to slavery, but it has always been a puzzle to me how a civilized man could drag his own children, bone of his bone, flesh of his flesh, down to the position of social outcasts, abject slaves, and political pariahs."

"But, Marie," said Eugene, "all men do not treat their illegitimate children in the manner you describe. The last time I was in New Orleans I met Henri Augustine at the depot, with two beautiful young girls. At first I thought that they were his own children, they resembled him so closely. But afterwards I noticed that they addressed him as 'Mister.' Before we parted he told me that his wife had taken such a dislike to their mother that she could not bear to see them on the place. At last, weary of her dissatisfaction, he had promised to bring them to New Orleans and sell them. Instead, he was going to Ohio to give them their freedom, and make provision for their future."

"What a wrong!" said Marie.

"Who was wronged?" said Leroy, in astonishment.

"Every one in the whole transaction," answered Marie. "Your friend wronged himself by sinning against his own soul. He wronged his wife by arousing her hatred and jealousy through his unfaithfulness. He wronged those children by giving them the *status* of slaves and outcasts. He wronged their mother by imposing upon her the burdens and cares of maternity without the rights and privileges of a wife. He made her crown of motherhood a circlet of shame. Under other circumstances she might have been an honored wife and happy mother. And I do think such men wrong their own legitimate children by transmitting to them a weakened moral fibre."

"Oh, Marie, you have such an uncomfortable way of putting things. You make me feel that we have done those things which we ought not to have done, and have left undone those things which we ought to have done."

"If it annoys you," said Marie, "I will stop talking."

"Oh, no, go on," said Leroy, carelessly; and then he continued more thoughtfully, "I know a number of men who have sent such children North, and manumitted, educated, and left them valuable legacies. We are all liable to err, and, having done wrong, all we can do is to make reparation."

"My dear husband, this is a wrong where reparation is impossible. Neither wealth nor education can repair the wrong of a dishonored birth. There are a number of slaves in this section who are servants to their own brothers and sisters; whose fathers have robbed them not simply of liberty but of the right of being well born. Do you think these things will last forever?"

"I suppose not. There are some prophets of evil who tell us that the Union is going to dissolve. But I know it would puzzle their brains to tell where the crack will begin. I reckon we'll continue to jog along as usual. 'Cotton fights, and cotton conquers for American slavery.'"

Even while Leroy dreamed of safety the earthquake was cradling its fire; the ground was growing hollow beneath his tread; but his ear was too dull to catch the sound; his vision too blurred to read the signs of the times.

"Marie," said Leroy, taking up the thread of the discourse, "slavery is a sword that cuts both ways. If it wrongs the negro, it also curses the white man. But we are in it, and what can we do?"

"Get out of it as quickly as possible."

"That is easier said than done. I would willingly free every slave on my plantation if I could do so without expatriating them. Some of them have wives and children on other plantations, and to free them is to separate them from their kith and kin. To let them remain here as a free people is out of the question. My hands are tied by law and custom."

"Who tied them?" asked Marie.

"A public opinion, whose meshes I cannot break. If the negro is the thrall of his master, we are just as much the thralls of public opinion."

"Why do you not battle against public opinion, if you think it is wrong?"

"Because I have neither the courage of a martyr, nor the faith of a saint; and so I drift along, trying to make the condition of our slaves as comfortable as I possibly can. I believe there are slaves on this plantation whom the most flattering offers of freedom would not entice away."

"I do not think," said Marie, "that some of you planters understand your own slaves. Lying is said to be the vice of slaves. The more intelligent of them have so learned to veil their feelings that you do not see the undercurrent of discontent beneath their apparent good humor and jollity. The more discontented they are, the more I respect them. To me a contented slave is an abject creature. I hope that I shall see the day when there will not be a slave in the land. I hate the whole thing from the bottom of my heart."

"Marie, your Northern education has unfitted you for Southern life. You are free, yourself, and so are our children. Why not let well enough alone?"

"Because I love liberty, not only for myself but for every human being. Think how dear these children are to me; and then for the thought to be forever haunting me, that if you were dead they could be turned out of doors and divided among your relatives. I sometimes lie awake at night thinking of how there might be a screw loose somewhere, and, after all, the children and I might be reduced to slavery."

"Marie, what in the world is the matter with you? Have you had a presentiment of my death, or, as Uncle Jack says, 'hab you seed it in a vision?'"

"No, but I have had such sad forebodings that they almost set me wild. One night I dreamt that you were dead; that the lawyers entered the house, seized our property, and remanded us to slavery. I never can be satisfied in the South with such a possibility hanging over my head."

"Marie, dear, you are growing nervous. Your imagination is too active. You are left too much alone on this plantation. I hope that for your own and the children's sake I will be enabled to arrange our affairs so as to find a home for you where you will not be doomed to the social isolation and ostracism that surround you here."

"I don't mind the isolation for myself, but the children. You have enjoined silence on me with respect to their connection with the negro race, but I do not think we can conceal it from them very long. It will not be long before Iola will notice the offishness of girls of her own age, and the scornful glances which, even now, I think, are leveled at her. Yesterday Harry came crying to me, and told me that one of the neighbor's boys had called him 'nigger.'"

A shadow flitted over Leroy's face, as he answered, somewhat soberly, "Oh, Marie, do not meet trouble half way. I have manumitted you, and the children will follow your condition. I have made you all legatees of my will. Except my cousin, Alfred Lorraine, I have only distant relatives, whom I scarcely know and who hardly know me."

"Your cousin Lorraine? Are you sure our interests would be safe in his hands?"

"I think so; I don't think Alfred would do anything dishonorable."

"He might not with his equals. But how many men would be bound by a sense of honor where the rights of a colored woman are in question? Your cousin was bitterly opposed to our marriage, and I would not trust any important interests in his hands. I do hope that in providing for our future you will make assurance doubly sure."

"I certainly will, and all that human foresight can do shall be done for you and our children."

"Oh," said Marie, pressing to her heart a beautiful child of six summers, "I think it would almost make me turn over in my grave to know that every grace and charm which this child possesses would only be so much added to her value as an article of merchandise."

As Marie released the child from her arms she looked wonderingly into her mother's face and clung closely to her, as if to find refuge from some unseen evil. Leroy noticed this, and sighed unconsciously, as an expression of pain flitted over his face.

"Now, Marie," he continued, "stop tormenting yourself with useless fears. Although, with all her faults, I still love the South, I will make arrangements either to live North or go to France. There life will be brighter for us all. Now, Marie, seat yourself at the piano and sing:—

Sing me the songs that to me were so dear,
Long, long ago.
Sing me the songs I delighted to hear,
Long, long ago.

As Marie sang the anxiety faded from her face, a sense of security stole over her, and she sat among her loved ones a happy wife and mother. What if no one recognized her on that lonely plantation! Her world was, nevertheless, there. The love and devotion of her husband brightened every avenue of her life, while her children filled her home with music, mirth, and sunshine.

Marie had undertaken their education, but she could not give them the culture which comes from the attrition of thought, and from contact with the ideas of others. Since her school-days she had read extensively and thought much, and in solitude her thoughts had ripened. But for her children there were no companions except the young slaves of the plantation, and she dreaded the effect of such intercourse upon their lives and characters.

Leroy had always been especially careful to conceal from his children the knowledge of their connection with the negro race. To Marie this silence was oppressive.

One day she said to him, "I see no other way of finishing the education of these children than by sending them to some Northern school."

"I have come," said Leroy, "to the same conclusion. We had better take Iola and Harry North and make arrangements for them to spend several years in being educated. Riches take wings to themselves and fly away, but a good education is an investment on which the law can place no attachment. As there is a possibility of their origin being discovered, I will find a teacher to whom I can confide our story, and upon whom I can enjoin secrecy. I want them well fitted for any emergency in life. When I discover for what they have the most aptitude I will give them especial training in that direction."

A troubled look passed over the face of Marie, as she hesitatingly said: "I am so afraid that you will regret our marriage when you fully realize the complications it brings."

"No, no," said Leroy, tenderly, "it is not that I regret our marriage, or feel the least disdain for our children on account of the blood in their veins; but I do not wish them to grow up under the contracting influence of this race prejudice. I do not wish them to feel that they have been born under a proscription from which no valor can redeem them, nor that any social advancement or individual development can wipe off the ban which clings to them. No, Marie, let them go North, learn all they can, aspire all they may. The painful knowledge will come all too soon. Do not forestall it. I want them simply to grow up as other children; not being patronized by friends nor disdained by foes."

"My dear husband, you may be perfectly right, but are you not preparing our children for a fearful awakening? Are you not acting on the plan, 'After me the deluge?'"

"Not at all, Marie. I want our children to grow up without having their self-respect crushed in the bud. You know that the North is not free from racial prejudice."

"I know it," said Marie, sadly, "and I think one of the great mistakes of our civilization is that which makes color, and not character, a social test."

"I think so, too," said Leroy. "The strongest men and women of a downtrodden race may bare their bosoms to an adverse fate and develop courage in the midst of opposition, but we have no right to subject our children to such crucial tests before their characters are formed. For years, when I lived abroad, I had an opportunity to see and hear of men of African descent who had distinguished themselves and obtained a recognition in European circles, which they never could have gained in this country. I now recall the name of Ira Aldridge, a colored man from New York City, who was covered with princely honors as a successful tragedian. Alexander Dumas was not forced to conceal his origin to succeed as a novelist. When I was in St. Petersburg I was shown the works of Alexander Sergevitch, a Russian poet, who was spoken of as the Byron of Russian literature, and reckoned one of the finest poets that Russia has produced in this century. He was also a prominent figure in fashionable society, and yet he was of African lineage. One of his paternal ancestors was a negro who had been ennobled by Peter the Great. I can't help contrasting the recognition which these men had received with the treatment which has been given to Frederick Douglass and other intelligent colored men in this country. With me the wonder is not that they have achieved so little, but that they have accomplished so much. No, Marie, we will have our children educated without being subjected to the depressing influences of caste feeling. Perhaps by the time their education is finished I will be ready to wind up my affairs and take them abroad, where merit and ability will give them entrance into the best circles of art, literature, and science."

After this conversation Leroy and his wife went North, and succeeded in finding a good school for their children. In a private interview he confided to the principal the story of the cross in their blood, and, finding him apparently free from racial prejudice, he gladly left the children in his care. Gracie, the youngest child, remained at home, and her mother spared no pains to fit her for the seminary against the time her sister should have finished her education.

The Two Offers (1859)

"What is the matter with you, Laura, this morning? I have been watching you this hour, and in that time you have commenced a half dozen letters and torn them all up. What matter of such grave moment is puzzling your dear little head, that you do not know how to decide?"

"Well, it is an important matter: I have two offers for marriage, and I do not know which to choose."

"I should accept neither, or to say the least, not at present."

"Why not?"

"Because I think a woman who is undecided between two offers, has not love enough for either to make a choice; and in that very hesitation, indecision, she has a reason to pause and seriously reflect, lest her marriage, instead of being an affinity of souls or a union of hearts, should only be a mere matter of bargain and sale, or an affair of convenience and selfish interest."

"But I consider them both very good offers, just such as many a girl would gladly receive. But to tell you the truth, I do not think that I regard either as a woman should the man she chooses for her husband. But then if I refuse, there is the risk of being an old maid, and that is not to be thought of."

"Well, suppose there is, is that the most dreadful fate that can befall a woman? Is there not more intense wretchedness in an ill-assorted marriage—more utter loneliness in a loveless home, than in the lot of the old maid who accepts her earthly mission as a gift from God, and strives to walk the path of life with earnest and unfaltering steps?"

"Oh! what a little preacher you are. I really believe that you were cut out for an old maid; that when nature formed you, she put in a double portion of intellect to make up for a deficiency of love; and yet you are kind and affectionate. But I do not think that you know anything of the grand, over-mastering passion, or the deep necessity of woman's heart for loving."

"Do you think so?" resumed the first speaker; and bending over her work she quietly applied herself to the knitting that had lain neglected by her side, during this brief conversation; but as she did so, a shadow flitted over her pale and intellectual brow, a mist gathered in her eyes, and a slight quivering of the lips, revealed a depth of feeling to which her companion was a stranger.

But before I proceed with my story, let me give you a slight history of the speakers. They were cousins, who had met life under different auspices. Laura Lagrange, was the only daughter of rich and indulgent parents, who had spared no pains to make her an accomplished lady. Her cousin, Janette Alston, was the child of parents, rich only in goodness and affection. Her father had been unfortunate in business, and dying before he could retrieve his fortunes, left his business in an embarrassed state. His widow was unacquainted with his business affairs, and when the estate was settled, hungry creditors had brought their claims and the lawyers had received their fees, she found herself homeless and almost penniless, and she who had been sheltered in the warm clasp of loving arms, found them too powerless to shield her from the pitiless pelting storms of adversity. Year after year she struggled with poverty and wrestled with want, till her toil-worn hands became too feeble to hold the shattered chords of existence, and her tear-dimmed eyes grew heavy with the slumber of death. Her daughter had watched over her with untiring devotion, had closed her eyes in death, and gone out into the busy, restless world, missing a precious tone from the voices of earth, a beloved step from the paths of life. Too self reliant to depend on the charity of relations, she endeavored to support herself by her own exertions, and she had succeeded. Her path for a while was marked with struggle and trial, but instead of uselessly repining, she met them bravely, and her life became not a thing of ease and indulgence, but of conquest, victory, and accomplishments. At the time when this conversation took place, the deep trials of her life had passed away. The achievements of her genius had won her a position in the literary world, where she shone as one of its bright particular stars. And with her fame came a competence of worldly means, which gave her leisure for improvement, and the riper development of her rare talents. And she, that pale intellectual woman, whose genius gave life and vivacity to the social circle, and whose presence threw a halo of beauty and grace around the charmed atmosphere in which she moved, had at one period of her life, known the mystic and solemn strength of an all-absorbing love. Years faded into the misty past, had seen the kindling of her eye, the quick flushing of her cheek, and the wild throbbing of her heart, at tones of a voice long since hushed to the stillness of death. Deeply, wildly, passionately, she had loved. Her whole life seemed like the pouring out of rich, warm and gushing affections. This love quickened her talents, inspired her genius, and threw over her life a tender and spiritual earnestness. And then came a fearful shock, a mournful waking from that "dream of beauty and delight." A shadow fell around her path; it came between her and the object of her heart's worship; first a few cold words, estrangement, and then a painful separation; the old story of woman's pride—digging the sepulchre of her happiness, and then a new-made grave, and her path over it to the spirit world; and thus faded out from that young heart her bright, brief and saddened dream of life. Faint and spirit-broken, she turned from the scenes associated with the memory of the loved and lost. She tried to break the chain of sad associations that bound her to the mournful past; and so, pressing back the bitter sobs from her almost breaking heart, like the dying dolphin, whose beauty is born of its death anguish, her genius gathered strength from suffering and wonderous power and brilliancy from the agony she hid within the desolate chambers of her soul. Men hailed her as one of earth's strangely gifted children, and wreathed the garlands of fame for her brow, when it was throbbing with a wild and fearful unrest. They breathed her name with applause, when through the lonely halls of her stricken spirit, was an earnest cry for peace, a deep yearning for sympathy and heart-support.

But life, with its stern realities, met her; its solemn responsibilities confronted her, and turning, with an earnest and shattered spirit, to life's duties and trials, she found a calmness and strength that she had only imagined in her dreams of poetry and song. We will now pass over a period of ten years, and the cousins have met again. In that calm and lovely woman, in whose eyes is a depth of tenderness, tempering the flashes of her genius, whose looks and tones are full of sympathy and love, we recognize the once smitten and stricken Janette Alston. The bloom of her girlhood had given way to a higher type of spiritual beauty, as if some unseen hand had been polishing and refining the temple in which her lovely spirit found its habitation; and this had been the fact. Her inner life had grown beautiful, and it was this that was constantly developing the outer. Never, in the early flush of womanhood, when an absorbing love had lit up her eyes and glowed in her life, had she appeared so interesting as when, with a countenance which seemed overshadowed with a spiritual light, she bent over the death-bed of a young woman, just lingering at the shadowy gates of the unseen land.

"Has he come?" faintly but eagerly exclaimed the dying woman. "Oh! how I have longed for his coming, and even in death he forgets me."

"Oh, do not say so, dear Laura, some accident may have detained him," said Janette to her cousin; for on that bed, from whence she will never rise, lies the once-beautiful and light-hearted Laura Lagrange, the brightness of whose eyes has long since been dimmed with tears, and whose voice had become like a harp whose every chord is tuned to sadness—whose faintest thrill and loudest vibrations are but the variations of agony. A heavy hand was laid upon her once warm and bounding heart, and a voice came whispering through her soul, that she must die. But, to her, the tidings was a message of deliverance—a voice, hushing her wild sorrows to the calmness of resignation and hope. Life had grown so weary upon her head—the future looked so hopeless—she had no wish to tread again the track where thorns had pierced her feet, and clouds overcast her sky; and she hailed the coming of death's angel as the footsteps of a welcome friend. And yet, earth had one object so very dear to her weary heart. It was her absent and recreant husband; for, since that conversation, she had accepted one of her offers, and become a wife. But, before she married, she learned that great lesson of human experience and woman's life, to love the man who bowed at her shrine, a willing worshipper. He had a pleasing address, raven hair, flashing eyes, a voice of thrilling sweetness, and lips of persuasive eloquence; and being well versed in the ways of the world, he won his way to her heart, and she became his bride, and he was proud of his prize. Vain and superficial in his character, he looked upon marriage not as a divine sacrament for the soul's development and human progression, but as the title-deed that gave him possession of the woman he thought he loved. But alas for her, the laxity of his principles had rendered him unworthy of the deep and undying devotion of a pure-hearted woman; but, for awhile, he hid from her his true character, and she blindly loved him, and for a short period was happy in the consciousness of being beloved; though sometimes a vague unrest would fill her soul, when, overflowing with a sense of the good, the beautiful, and the true, she would turn to him, but find no response to the deep yearnings of her soul—no appreciation of life's highest realities—its solemn grandeur and significant importance. Their souls never met, and soon she found a void in her bosom, that his earth-born love could not fill. He did not satisfy the wants of her mental and moral nature—between him and her there was no affinity of minds, no intercommunion of souls.

Talk as you will of woman's deep capacity for loving, of the strength of her affectional nature. I do not deny it; but will the mere possession of any human love, fully satisfy all the demands of her whole being? You may paint her in poetry or fiction, as a frail vine, clinging to her brother man for support, and dying when deprived of it; and all this may sound well enough to please the imaginations of school-girls, or love-lorn maidens. But woman—the true woman—if you would render her happy, it needs more than the mere development of her affectional nature. Her conscience should be enlightened, her faith in the true and right established, and scope given to her Heaven-endowed and God-given faculties. The true aim of female education should be, not a development of one or two, but all the faculties of the human soul, because no perfect womanhood is developed by imperfect culture. Intense love is often akin to intense suffering, and to trust the whole wealth of a woman's nature on the frail bark of human love, may often be like trusting a cargo of gold and precious gems, to a bark that has never battled with the storm, or buffetted the waves. Is it any wonder, then, that so many life-barks go down, paving the ocean of time with precious hearts and wasted hopes? that so many float around us, shattered and dismasted wrecks? that so many are stranded on the shoals of existence, mournful beacons and solemn warnings for the thoughtless, to whom marriage is a careless and hasty rushing together of the affections? Alas that an institution so fraught with good for humanity should be so perverted, and that state of life, which should be filled with happiness, become so replete with misery. And this was the fate of Laura Lagrange. For a brief period after her marriage her life seemed like a bright and beautiful dream, full of hope and radiant with joy. And then there came a change—he found other attractions that lay beyond the pale of home influences. The gambling saloon had power to win him from her side, he had lived in an element of unhealthy and unhallowed excitements, and the society of a loving wife, the pleasures of a well-regulated home, were enjoyments too tame for one who had vitiated his tastes by the pleasures of sin. There were charmed houses of vice, built upon dead men's loves, where, amid a flow of song, laughter, wine, and careless mirth, he would spend hour after hour, forgetting the cheek that was paling through his neglect, heedless of the tear-dimmed eyes, peering anxiously into the darkness, waiting, or watching his return.

The influence of old associations was upon him. In early life, home had been to him a place of ceilings and walls, not a true home, built upon goodness, love and truth. It was a place where velvet carpets hushed his tread, where images of loveliness and beauty invoked into being by painter's art and sculptor's skill, pleased the eye and gratified the taste, where magnificence surrounded his way and costly clothing adorned his person; but it was not the place for the true culture and right development of his soul. His father had been too much engrossed in making money, and his mother in spending it, in striving to maintain a fashionable position in society, and shining in the eyes of the world, to give the proper direction to the character of their wayward and impulsive son. His mother put beautiful robes upon his body, but left ugly scars upon his soul; she pampered his appetite, but starved his spirit. Every mother should be a true artist who knows how to weave into her child's life images of grace and beauty, the true poet capable of writing on the soul of childhood the harmony of love and truth, and teaching it how to produce the grandest of all poems—the poetry of a true and noble life. But in his home, a love for the good, the true and right, had been sacrificed at the shrine of frivolity and fashion. That parental authority which should have been preserved as a string of precious pearls, unbroken and unscattered, was simply the administration of chance. At one time obedience was enforced by authority, at another time by flattery and promises, and just as often it was not enforced at all. His early associations were formed as chance directed, and from his want of home-training, his character received a bias, his life a shade, which ran through every avenue of his existence, and darkened all his future hours. Oh, if we would trace the history of all the crimes that have o'ershadowed this sin-shrouded and sorrow-darkened world of ours, how many might be seen arising from the wrong home influences or the weakening of the home ties. Home should always be the best school for the affections, the birthplace of high resolves, and the altar upon which lofty aspirations are kindled, from whence the soul may go forth strengthened, to act its part aright in the great drama of life, with conscience enlightened, affections cultivated, and reason and judgment dominant. But alas for the young wife. Her husband had not been blessed with such a home. When he entered the arena of life, the voices from home did not linger around his path as angels of guidance about his steps; they were not like so many messages to invite him to deeds of high and holy worth. The memory of no sainted mother arose between him and deeds of darkness; the earnest prayers of no father arrested him in his downward course; and before a year of his married life had waned, his young wife had learned to wait and mourn his frequent and uncalled-for absence. More than once had she seen him come home from his midnight haunts, the bright intelligence of his eye displaced by the drunkard's stare, and his manly gait changed to the inebriate's stagger; and she was beginning to know the bitter agony that is compressed in the mournful words, a drunkard's wife. And then there came a bright but brief episode in her experience; the angel of life gave to her existence a deeper meaning and loftier significance: she sheltered in the warm clasp of her loving arms, a dear babe, a precious child, whose love filled every chamber of her heart, and felt the fount of maternal love gushing so new within her soul. That child was hers. How overshadowing was the love with which she bent over its helplessness, how much it helped to fill the void and chasms in her soul. How many lonely hours were beguiled by its winsome ways, its answering smiles and fond caresses. How exquisite and solemn was the feeling that thrilled her heart when she clasped the tiny hands together and taught her dear child to call God "Our Father."

What a blessing was that child. The father paused in his headlong career, awed by the strange beauty and precocious intellect of his child; and the mother's life had a better expression through her ministrations of love. And then there came hours of bitter anguish, shading the sunlight of her home and hushing the music of her heart. The angel of death bent over the couch of her child and beaconed it away. Closer and closer the mother strained her child to her wildly heaving breast, and struggled with the heavy hand that lay upon its heart. Love and agony contended with death, and the language of the mother's heart was,

> Oh, Death, away! that innocent is mine;
> I cannot spare him from my arms
> To lay him, Death, in thine.
> I am a mother, Death; I gave that darling birth
> I could not bear his lifeless limbs
> Should moulder in the earth.

But death was stronger than love and mightier than agony and won the child for the land of crystal founts and deathless flowers, and the poor, stricken mother sat down beneath the shadow of her mighty grief, feeling as if a great light had gone out from her soul, and that the sunshine had suddenly faded around her path. She turned in her deep anguish to the father of her child, the loved and cherished dead. For awhile his words were kind and tender, his heart seemed subdued, and his tenderness fell upon her worn and weary heart like rain on perishing flowers, or cooling waters to lips all parched with thirst and scorched with fever; but the change was evanescent, the influence of unhallowed associations and evil habits had vitiated and poisoned the springs of his existence. They had bound him in their meshes, and he lacked the moral strength to break his fetters, and stand erect in all the strength and dignity of a true manhood, making life's highest excellence his ideal, and striving to gain it.

And yet moments of deep contrition would sweep over him, when he would resolve to abandon the wine-cup forever, when he was ready to forswear the handling of another card, and he would try to break away from the associations that he felt were working his ruin; but when the hour of temptation came his strength was weakness, his earnest purposes were cobwebs, his well-meant resolutions ropes of sand, and thus passed year after year of the married life of Laura Lagrange. She tried to hide her agony from the public gaze, to smile when her heart was almost breaking. But year after year her voice grew fainter and sadder, her once light and bounding step grew slower and faltering. Year after year she wrestled with agony, and strove with despair, till the quick eyes of her brother read, in the paling of her cheek and the dimming eye, the secret anguish of her worn and weary spirit. On that wan, sad face, he saw the death-tokens, and he knew the dark wing of the mystic angel swept coldly around her path. "Laura," said her brother to her one day, "you are not well, and I think you need our mother's tender care and nursing. You are daily losing strength, and if you will go I will accompany you." At first, she hesitated, she shrank almost instinctively from presenting that pale sad face to the loved ones at home. That face was such a tell-tale; it told of heart-sickness, of hope deferred, and the mournful story of unrequited love. But then a deep yearning for home sympathy woke within her a passionate longing for love's kind words, for tenderness and heart-support, and she resolved to seek the home of her childhood, and lay her weary head upon her mother's bosom, to be folded again in her loving arms, to lay that poor, bruised and aching heart where it might beat and throb closely to the loved ones at home. A kind welcome awaited her. All that love and tenderness could devise was done to bring the bloom to her cheek and the light to her eye; but it was all in vain; hers was a disease that no medicine could cure, no earthly balm would heal. It was a slow wasting of the vital forces, the sickness of the soul. The unkindness and neglect of her husband, lay like a leaden weight upon her heart, and slowly oozed away its life-drops. And where was he that had won her love, and then cast it aside as a useless thing, who rifled her heart of its wealth and spread bitter ashes upon its broken altars? He was lingering away from her when the death-damps were gathering on her brow, when his name was trembling on her lips! lingering away! when she was watching his coming, though the death films were gathering before her eyes, and earthly things were fading from her vision. "I think I hear him now," said the dying woman, "surely that is his step;" but the sound died away in the distance. Again she started from an uneasy slumber, "That is his voice! I am so glad he has come." Tears gathered in the eyes of the sad watchers by that dying bed, for they knew that she was deceived. He had not returned. For her sake they wished his coming. Slowly the hours waned away, and then came the sad, soul-sickening thought that she was forgotten, forgotten in the last hour of human need, forgotten when the spirit, about to be dissolved, paused for the last time on the threshold of existence, a weary watcher at the gates of death. "He has forgotten me," again she faintly murmured, and the last tears she would ever shed on earth sprung to her mournful eyes, and clasping her hands together in silent anguish, a few broken sentences issued from her pale and quivering lips. They were prayers for strength and earnest pleading for him who had desolated her young life, by turning its sunshine to shadows, its smiles to tears. "He has forgotten me," she murmured again, "but I can bear it, the bitterness of death is passed, and soon I hope to exchange the shadows of death for the brightness of eternity, the rugged paths of life for the golden streets of glory, and the care and turmoils of earth for the peace and rest of heaven." Her voice grew fainter and fainter, they saw the shadows that never deceive flit over her pale and faded face, and knew that the death angel waited to soothe their weary one to rest, to calm the throbbing of her bosom and cool the fever of her brain. And amid the silent hush of their grief the freed spirit, refined through suffering, and brought into divine harmony through the spirit of the living Christ, passed over the dark waters of death as on a bridge of light, over whose radiant arches hovering angels bent. They parted the dark locks from her marble brow, closed the waxen lids over the once bright and laughing eye, and left her to the dreamless slumber of the grave. Her cousin turned from that death-bed a sadder and wiser woman. She resolved more earnestly than ever to make the world better by her example, gladder by her presence, and to kindle the fires of her genius on the altars of universal love and truth. She had a higher and better object in all her writings than the mere acquisition of gold, or acquirement of fame. She felt that she had a high and holy mission on the battle-field of existence, that life was not given her to be frittered away in nonsense, or wasted away in trifling pursuits. She would willingly espouse an unpopular cause but not an unrighteous one. In her the down-trodden slave found an earnest advocate; the flying fugitive remembered her kindness as he stepped cautiously through our Republic, to gain his freedom in a monarchial land, having broken the chains on which the rust of centuries had gathered. Little children learned to name her with affection, the poor called her blessed, as she broke her bread to the pale lips of hunger. Her life was like a beautiful story, only it was clothed with the dignity of reality and invested with the sublimity of truth. True, she was an old maid, no husband brightened her life with his love, or shaded it with his neglect. No children nestling lovingly in her arms called her mother. No one appended Mrs. to her name; she was indeed an old maid, not vainly striving to keep up an appearance of girlishness, when departed was written on her youth. Not vainly pining at her loneliness and isolation: the world was full of warm, loving hearts, and her own beat in unison with them. Neither was she always sentimentally sighing for something to love, objects of affection were all around her, and the world was not so wealthy in love that it had no use for hers; in blessing others she made a life and benediction, and as old age descended peacefully and gently upon her, she had learned one of life's most precious lessons, that true happiness consists not so much in the fruition of our wishes as in the regulation of desires and the full development and right culture of our whole natures.

The Slave Mother (1854)

Heard you that shriek? It rose
  So wildly on the air,
It seemed as if a burden'd heart
  Was breaking in despair.

Saw you those hands so sadly clasped—   5
  The bowed and feeble head—
The shuddering of that fragile form—
  That look of grief and dread?

Saw you the sad, imploring eye?
  Its every glance was pain,   10
As if a storm of agony
  Were weeping through the brain.

She is a mother, pale with fear,
  Her boy clings to her side,
And in her kirtle vainly tries   15
  His trembling form to hide.

He is not hers, although she bore
  For him a mother's pains;
He is not hers, although her blood
  Is coursing through his veins!   20

He is not hers, for cruel hands
  May rudely tear apart
The only wreath of household love
  That binds her breaking heart.

His love has been a joyous light   25
  That o'er her pathway smiled,
A fountain gushing ever new,
  Amid life's desert wild.

His lightest word has been a tone
  Of music round her heart,   30

Their lives a streamlet blent in one—
   Oh, Father! must they part?

They tear him from her circling arms,
   Her last and fond embrace.
Oh! never more may her sad eyes   35
   Gaze on his mournful face.

No marvel, then, these bitter shrieks
   Disturb the listening air:
She is a mother, and her heart
   Is breaking in despair.   40

Ethiopia (1853?/1854?)

Yes! Ethiopia yet shall stretch
   Her bleeding hands abroad;
Her cry of agony shall reach
   The burning throne of God.

The tyrant's yoke from off her neck,   5
   His fetters from her soul,
The mighty hand of God shall break,
   And spurn the base control.

Redeemed from dust and freed from chains,
   Her sons shall lift their eyes;   10
From cloud-capt hills and verdant plains
   Shall shouts of triumph rise.

Upon her dark, despairing brow,
   Shall play a smile of peace;
For God shall bend unto her wo,   15
   And bid her sorrows cease.

'Neath sheltering vines and stately palms
   Shall laughing children play,
And aged sires with joyous psalms
   Shall gladden every day.   20

Secure by night, and blest by day,
   Shall pass her happy hours;
Nor human tigers hunt for prey
   Within her peaceful bowers.

Then, Ethiopia! stretch, oh! stretch   25
   Thy bleeding hands abroad;
Thy cry of agony shall reach
   And find redress from God.

✺ CHARLOTTE L. FORTEN GRIMKE (1837–1914)

Charlotte L. Forten Grimke was born in Philadelphia, Pennsylvania. After her mother passed away while Grimke was very young, she grew up in the homes of individuals sympathetic to abolitionist causes. She earned a teaching degree from Salem Normal School in 1856. Although her first teaching assignments were in Massachusetts, where white students were among her pupils, in the 1860s she headed to the South to teach. Her students were ex-slaves who desired to learn how to read and write. Her journals detail her concerns with race, class, and gender in America.

Her journal entries chronicle much of her experience in the South with rituals, customs, and traditions of her students and provide a sense of life for a free black woman amid racial oppression in America. After leaving the South in 1864, she lived in Boston and Washington, D.C., where she was introduced to Francis James Grimke, whom she wed in 1878. She gave birth to a daughter, but the child lived only a few months. Grimke died of a stroke in 1914.

From The Journals of Charlotte Forten Grimke

Journal Three (1860)

Wednesday, October 21. To-day rec'd a note from Mr. McK.[im] asking me if I c'ld possibly be ready to sail for Port Royal perhaps tomorrow. I was astonished, stupefied, and, at first thought it impossible, but on seeing Mr. McK. I found there was an excellent opportunity for me to go. An old Quaker gentleman is going there to keep store, accompanied by his daughter, and he is willing to take charge of me. It will probably be the only opportunity that I shall have of going this winter, so at any cost I *will* go. And so new to work. In greatest haste.

Met John P.[ierce] on the cars. He was very kind.

At Sea. October 27, Monday.—Let me see. Where am I? What do I want to write? I am in a state of utter bewilderment. It was on Wed. I rec'd the note. On Thursday I said "good bye" to the friends that are so dear, and the city that is so hateful, and went to N.Y. Spent the night with Mrs. [Peter] W.[illiams]. The next morn did not hurry myself, having heard that the Steamer "United States" w'ld not sail till twelve. Mrs. W. and I went to "Lovejoy's" to meet the Hunns' and found there a card from Mr. H.[unn] bidding me hasten to the steamer, as it was advertised to sail at nine. It was then between ten and eleven. After hurrying down and wearying ourselves, found when I got on board that it was not to sail till twelve. But I did not go ashore again. It was too bad, for I had not time to get several things that I wanted much, among them "Les Miserables," which my dear brother H.[enry] had kindly given me the money for. He had not had time to get it in Phila.[delphia].

Enjoyed the sail down the harbor perfectly. The shipping is a noble sight. Had no symptoms of sea-sickness until eve. when, being seated at the table an inexpressibly singular sensation caused me to make a hasty retreat to the aft-deck, where by keeping perfectly still sitting on a coil of ropes spent a very comfortable eve. and had a pleasant conversation with one of the passengers. Did not get out of sight of land until after dark. I regretted that.

Went below for the night into the close ladies' cabin with many misgivings which proved not unfounded. Was terribly sea-sick that night and all the next morning. Did not reappear on deck till noon of the next day—Saturday. What an experience. Of all doleful, dismal, desperate experiences sea-sickness is certainly the dolefulest, dismalist, desperate-est!

It was rather a miserable afternoon. Was half sick all the time and scarcely dared to move. There was highly pleasant talk going on around me, to which I could listen in silence—that was all. My companion Lizzie Hunn was sick all the time. Poor girl, she c'ld take no pleasure in anything.

When night came, we both determined that we w'ldn't go below and have a repetition of the agonies of the night before. We heroically resolved to pass the night on deck. A nice little nook was found for us "amidships," and there enveloped in shawls and seated in arm chairs we were made as comfortable as possible, and passed the night without being sick. Two of the passengers—young men from Hilton Head, who were very gentlemanly and attentive, entertained us for some time with some fine singing; then they retired, and we passed the rest of the night in the society of the Ocean alone. How wild and strange it seemed there on deck in the dark night, only the dim outlines of sea and sky to be seen, only the roaring of the waves to be heard. I enjoyed it much. The thought that we were far, far, away from land was a pleasant one to me.

The next day—Sunday—was emphatically a *dismal* day. It rained nearly all the time so that we c'ld not be on deck much of the time. As soon as we established ourselves nicely outside down came the rain and we were driven into the close cabin, which was almost unendurable to me. Tried to read a little in the French Bible which H.[enry Cassey] gave me, but in vain. The day was mostly spent in the interesting occupation of preventing sea-sickness by keeping perfectly quiet and watching the rain drops.

Before night a storm came on. And a terrible storm it was. The steward arranged mattresses and blankets for us in the covered passage way "amidships" and we lay down, but not to rest. It was a veritable grand storm at sea. The vessel rocked and plunged, the planks creaked and groaned; the sea broke upon the boat with thunderous roars, and within one w'ld have thought that all the crockery in the establishment was going to pieces. Such a noise I never heard in my life. Such roaring and plunging, and creaking. Afterward we were told that one of the chains of the vessel broke, and indeed for a time she seemed to be at the mercy of the waves. Some one near us—one of the waiters, I think, was dreadfully frightened, and commenced praying and moaning most piteously, crying "Oh Jesus, dear Jesus," in most lamentable tones, till I began to think we must really be in danger. Then the water came into the ladies' cabin, below. One lady who had a baby with her woke up in the night and c'ld not find the child. It had been rolled away from her by the tossing of the ship, the lamps were out, and after some time, and much terror on the part of the poor woman the baby was found by one of the waiters under the berths. She was very quiet, and did not seem at all alarmed at her involuntary journey. Despite all the alarm and distress and anxiety we c'ld not help being amused at this little episode. During all the storm, however, I felt no fear; and now that the danger has passed, I feel really glad that I have at last experienced a "veritable storm at sea." The most astonishing thing was that I had two or three most refreshing sleeps in the very height of the storm.

This morning the sea was still very rough, but I struggled up, and dressed with great difficulty, and with the aid of one of the waiters made my way on deck. The sky was still very much overcast, the great, white capped waves were rising to a great height and breaking against the sides of the vessel. It was a grand sight, and I enjoyed it greatly. It has quite cleared off now, and the day is most lovely. I am feeling well and *luxuriating* in the glorious beauty of sea and sky. But my poor companion is still quite sick, and while I write, sits before me on a coil of ropes, enveloped in shawls, and looking the picture of dolefulness and despair.

How grand, how glorious the sea is, to-day! It far more than realizes my highest expectations of it. The sky too is beautiful[,] a deep, delicious blue, with soft, white, fleecy clouds floating over it. We have seen several sails today, in the distance, but still no land, whereat I am rejoiced.

There is not much to be said about the passengers on board. There are about a dozen beside ourselves, none of whom seem to me especially interesting, except perhaps our friend from Hilton Head, Mr. B. He is very intelligent, and I sh'ld think even a talented young man. He has read and admires all my favorite authors, and I enjoy talking with him about them. I have rarely found a man with so keen and delicate an appreciation of the beautiful, both in Nature and Art. There are no soldiers on board but one officer who stalks about the boat looking well pleased with himself and evidently trying to look quite grand, but *sans* success, for he was rather insignificant despite his good figure, fierce moustaches, and epaulettes.

Of the three ladies on board two go South to join their husbands, and the third accompanies hers. The first two are quite talkative, the latter very quiet. I believe that is all that can be said of them. There is a sea captain here whom I like very much. He is a Cape Cod man; has been to sea ever since he was nine years old. Has visited many lands, and I enjoy hearing him talk about them. The other gentlemen do not interest me, so I shall let them pass. Have only been able to go to the table twice. Then there was no difficulty—as I feared there might be. People were as kind and polite as possible. Indeed I have had not the least trouble since I have been on board. The waiters are as obliging and attentive as they can be, and bring us our meals out on deck every day.

Afternoon. I have just beheld the most glorious sight I ever saw in my life. With the aid of Mr. B. I staggered to the bow of the ship (which still rolls and pitches terribly) and there saw the sea in all its glory and grandeur. Oh, how beautiful those great waves were as they broke upon the side of the vessel, into foam and spray pure and white as new fallen snow. People talk of the monotony of the sea. I have not found it monotonous for a moment, since I have been well. To me there is "infinite variety," constant enjoyment in it.

I have tried to read, but in vain; there is so much to take off one's attention, besides reading makes my head dizzy. One of the most beautiful sights I have yet seen is the phosphorescence in the water at night—the long line of light in the wake of the steamer, and the stars, and sometimes balls of fire that rise so magically out of the water. It is most strange and beautiful. Had it not been for the storm we should have reached Port Royal to-day. But we shall not get there till to-morrow.

✣ FREDERICK DOUGLASS (1818–1895)

As a writer and activist, Frederick Douglass wrote and spoke eloquently about the injustice of slavery, advocating the emancipation of slaves in the United States. He was born in Tuckahoe, Maryland, on the Lloyd family plantation, the son of a black female slave and an unidentified white male. As a child, Douglass learned to read with instruction from Sophia Auld, the daughter of the manager of the Lloyd estate, after he moved to Baltimore to work in her household. Douglass eventually returned to the Lloyd plantation, but he succeeded in escaping to the North in 1838. After marrying Anna Murray, he became very active in the abolitionist movement in Massachusetts and made speeches that impressed William Lloyd Garrison, editor of The Liberator, *who wrote a preface to* The Narrative of the Life of Frederick Douglass, an American Slave, Written by Himself *(1845). Douglass distinguished himself as an orator and a civil servant, becoming recorder of deeds in the District of Columbia and serving in Haiti as U.S. Minister late in his life. His 1884 marriage to a white woman, Helen Pitts, created controversy in the racial climate of the period. By the time Douglass passed away in 1895, his life and literary legacy had established him as a central figure in the fight against slavery and injustice.*

From The Narrative of the Life of Frederick Douglass, an American Slave, Written by Himself (1845)

Chapter 2

My master's family consisted of two sons, Andrew and Richard, one daughter, Lucretia, and her husband, Captain Thomas Auld. They lived in one house, upon the home plantation of Colonel Edward Lloyd. My master was Colonel Lloyd's clerk and superintendent. He was what might be called the overseer of the overseers. I spent two years of childhood on this plantation in my old master's family. It was here that I witnessed the bloody transaction recorded in the first chapter; and as I received my first impressions of slavery on this plantation, I will give some description of it, and of slavery as it there existed. The plantation is about twelve miles north of Easton, in Talbot county, and is situated on the border of Miles River. The principal products raised upon it were tobacco, corn, and wheat. These were raised in great abundance; so that, with the products of this and the other farms belonging to him, he was able to keep in almost constant employment a large sloop, in carrying them to market at Baltimore. This sloop was named Sally Lloyd, in honor of one of the colonel's daughters. My master's son-in-law, Captain Auld, was master of the vessel; she was otherwise manned by the colonel's own slaves. Their names were Peter, Isaac, Rich, and Jake. These were esteemed very highly by the other slaves, and looked upon as the privileged ones of the plantation; for it was no small affair, in the eyes of the slaves, to be allowed to see Baltimore.

Colonel Lloyd kept from three to four hundred slaves on his home plantation, and owned a large number more on the neighboring farms belonging to him. The names of the farms nearest to the home plantation were Wye Town and New Design. "Wye Town" was under the overseership of a man named Noah Willis. New Design was under the overseership of a Mr. Townsend. The overseers of these, and all the rest of the farms, numbering over twenty, received advice and direction from the managers of the home plantation. This was the great business place. It was the seat of government for the whole twenty farms. All disputes among the overseers were settled here. If a slave was convicted of any high misdemeanor, became unmanageable, or evinced a determination to run away, he was brought immediately here, severely whipped, put on board the sloop, carried to Baltimore, and sold to Austin Woolfolk, or some other slave-trader, as a warning to the slaves remaining.

Here, too, the slaves of all the other farms received their monthly allowance of food, and their yearly clothing. The men and women slaves received, as their monthly allowance of food, eight pounds of pork, or its equivalent in fish, and one bushel of corn meal. Their yearly clothing consisted of two coarse linen shirts, one pair of linen trousers, like the shirts, one jacket, one pair of trousers for winter, made of coarse negro cloth, one pair of stockings, and one pair of shoes; the whole of which could not have cost more than seven dollars. The allowance of the slave children was given to their mothers, or the old women having the care of them. The children unable to work in the field had neither shoes, stockings, jackets, nor trousers, given to them; their clothing consisted of two coarse linen shirts per year. When these failed them, they went naked until the next allowance-day. Children from seven to ten years old, of both sexes, almost naked, might be seen at all seasons of the year.

There were no beds given the slaves, unless one coarse blanket be considered such, and none but the men and women had these. This, however, is not considered a very great privation. They find less difficulty from the want of beds, than from the want of time to sleep; for when their day's work in the field is done, the most of them having their washing, mending, and cooking to do, and having few or none of the ordinary facilities for doing either of these, very many of their sleeping hours are consumed in preparing for the field the coming day; and when this is done, old and young, male and female, married and single, drop down side by side, on one common bed,—the cold, damp floor,—each covering himself or herself with their miserable blankets; and here they sleep till they are summoned to the field by the driver's horn. At the sound of this, all must rise, and be off to the field. There must be no halting; every one must be at his or her post; and woe betides them who hear not this morning summons to the field; for if they are not awakened by the sense of hearing, they are by the sense of feeling: no age nor sex finds any favor. Mr. Severe, the overseer, used to stand by the door of the quarter, armed with a large hickory stick and heavy cowskin, ready to whip any one who was so unfortunate as not to hear, or, from any other cause, was prevented from being ready to start for the field at the sound of the horn.

Mr. Severe was rightly named: he was a cruel man. I have seen him whip a woman, causing the blood to run half an hour at the time; and this, too, in the midst of her crying children, pleading for their mother's release. He seemed to take pleasure in manifesting his fiendish barbarity. Added to his cruelty, he was a profane swearer. It was enough to chill the blood and stiffen the hair of an ordinary man to hear him talk. Scarce a sentence escaped him but that was commenced or concluded by some horrid oath. The field was the place to witness his cruelty and profanity. His presence made it both the field of blood and blasphemy. From the rising till the going down of the sun, he was cursing, raving, cutting, and slashing among the slaves of the field, in the most frightful manner. His career was short. He died very soon after I went to Colonel Lloyd's; and he died as he lived, uttering, with his dying groans, bitter curses and horrid oaths. His death was regarded by the slaves as the result of a merciful providence.

Mr. Severe's place was filled by a Mr. Hopkins. He was a very different man. He was less cruel, less profane, and made less noise, than Mr. Severe. His course was characterized by no extraordinary demonstrations of cruelty. He whipped, but seemed to take no pleasure in it. He was called by the slaves a good overseer.

The home plantation of Colonel Lloyd wore the appearance of a country village. All the mechanical operations for all the farms were performed here. The shoe-making and mending, the blacksmithing, cartwrighting, coopering, weaving, and grain-grinding, were all performed by the slaves on the home plantation. The whole place wore a business-like aspect very unlike the neighboring farms. The number of houses, too, conspired to give it advantage over the neighboring farms. It was called by the slaves the *Great House Farm*. Few privileges were esteemed higher, by the slaves of the out-farms, than that of being selected to do errands at the Great House Farm. It was associated in their minds with greatness. A representative could not be prouder of his election to a seat in the American Congress, than a slave on one of the out-farms would be of his election to do errands at the Great House Farm. They regarded it as evidence of great confidence reposed in them by their overseers; and it was on this account, as well as a constant desire to be out of the field from under the driver's lash, that they esteemed it a high privilege, one worth careful living for. He was called the smartest and most trusty fellow, who had this honor conferred upon him the most frequently. The competitors for this office sought as diligently to please their overseers, as the office-seekers in the political parties seek to please and deceive the people. The same traits of character might be seen in Colonel Lloyd's slaves, as are seen in the slaves of the political parties.

The slaves selected to go to the Great House Farm, for the monthly allowance for themselves and their fellow-slaves, were peculiarly enthusiastic. While on their way, they would make the dense old woods, for miles around, reverberate with their wild songs, revealing at once the highest joy and the deepest sadness. They would compose and sing as they went along, consulting neither time nor tune. The thought that came up, came out—if not in the word, in the sound;— and as frequently in the one as in the other. They would sometimes sing the most pathetic sentiment in the most rapturous tone, and the most rapturous sentiment in the most pathetic tones. Into all of their songs they would manage to weave something of the Great House Farm. Especially would they do this, when leaving home. They would then sing most exultingly the following words:—

I am going away to the Great House Farm!
O, yea! O, yea! O!

This they would sing, as a chorus, to words which to many would seem unmeaning jargon, but which, nevertheless, were full of meaning to themselves. I have sometimes thought that the more hearing of those songs would do more to impress some minds with the horrible character of slavery, than the reading of whole volumes of philosophy on the subject could do.

I did not, when a slave, understand the deep meaning of those rude and apparently incoherent songs. I was myself within the circle; so that I neither saw nor heard as those without might see and hear. They told a tale of woe which was then altogether beyond my feeble comprehension; they were tones loud, long, and deep; they breathed the prayer and complaint of souls boiling over with the bitterest anguish. Every tone was a testimony against slavery, and a prayer to God for deliverance from chains. The hearing of those wild notes always depressed my spirit, and filled me with ineffable sadness. I have frequently found myself in tears while hearing them. The mere recurrence to those songs, even now, afflicts me; and while I am writing these lines, an expression of feeling has already found its way down my cheek. To those songs I trace my first glimmering conception of the dehumanizing character of slavery. I can never get rid of that conception. Those songs still follow me, to deepen my hatred of slavery, and quicken my sympathies for my brethren in bonds. If any one wishes to be impressed with the soul-killing effects of slavery, let him go to Colonel Lloyd's plantation, and, on allowance-day, place himself in the deep pine woods, and there let him, in silence, analyze the sounds that shall pass through the chambers of his soul,—and if he is not thus impressed, it will only be because "there is no flesh in his obdurate heart."

I have often been utterly astonished, since I came to the north, to find persons who could speak of the singing, among slaves, as evidence of their contentment and happiness. It is impossible to conceive of a greater mistake. Slaves sing most when they are most unhappy. The songs of the slave represent the sorrows of his heart; and he is relieved by them, only as an aching heart is relieved by its tears. At least, such is my experience. I have often sung to drown my sorrow, but seldom to express my happiness. Crying for joy, and singing for joy, were alike uncommon to me while in the jaws of slavery. The singing of a man cast away upon a desolate island might be as appropriately considered as evidence of contentment and happiness, as the singing of a slave; the songs of the one and of the other are prompted by the same emotion.

Swing Low, Sweet Chariot

This spiritual, like many during the antebellum period, suggests a double meaning for the singer of the song.

The song conveys a desire to be free from the struggles of daily life as a slave and looks to heaven as a "home" or place of rest; yet it also suggests the desire to escape from slavery in the South by heading North to freedom—to a new "home."

Swing low, sweet chariot,
Coming for to carry me home,
Swing low, sweet chariot,
Coming for to carry me home.   4

I looked over Jordan and what did I see
Coming for to carry me home,
A band of angels, coming after me,
Coming for to carry me home.   8

If you get there before I do,
Coming for to carry me home,
Tell all my friends I'm coming too,
Coming for to carry me home.   12

Swing low, sweet chariot,
Coming for to carry me home,
Swing low, sweet chariot,
Coming for to carry me home.   16

SOJOURNER TRUTH (1797–1883)

A native of Ulster County, New York, Sojourner Truth distinguished herself as an orator fighting for equal rights and the abolition of slavery. Although she was born a slave, she left her owners, the Dumonts, around 1826; she became legally free because of a New York state law prohibiting slavery in 1827. Truth was involved with a number of organizations, including the New York Perfectionists, as well as part of a group of individuals following Robert Matthews, the leader of a religious sect. By 1843, she had renamed herself Sojourner Truth and heeded what she considered to be a call from God to spread the gospel. Her zeal, determination, and sincerity impressed others sympathetic to the call for the abolition of slavery and for women's rights. Olive Gilbert wrote down Truth's life story, Narrative of Sojourner Truth *(1850). Her "Address to the Ohio Women's Rights Convention" (1851) calls attention to the plight of African American women facing race, class, and gender prejudice. Truth's speech was delivered in Akron, Ohio, on May 29, 1851. To the end of her life, she continued to fight for equal rights. At her death in 1883, she had been living in Michigan with Quakers, continuing her struggle for justice.*

Address to the Ohio Women's Rights Convention (1851)

Well, children, where there is so much racket there must be somethin' out o'kilter. I think that 'twixt the Negroes of the North and the South and the women at the North, all talkin' 'bout rights, the white men will be in a fix pretty soon. But what's all this here talkin' 'bout?

That man over there say that women needs to be helped into carriages, and lifted over ditches, and to have the best place everywhere. Nobody ever helps me into carriages, or over mud-puddles, or give me any best place! And ain't I a woman? Look at me? Look at my arm! I have ploughed, and planted, and gathered into barns, and no man could head me! And ain't I a woman? I could work as much and eat as much as a man—when I could get it—and bear the lash as well! And ain't I a woman? I have borne thirteen children, and seen 'em mos' all sold off to slavery, and when I cried out with my mother's grief, none but Jesus heard me! And ain't I a woman?

Then they talk about this thing in the head; what's this they call it? ["Intellect," whispered some one near.] That's it honey. What's that got to do with women's rights or Negro's rights? If my cup won't hold but a pint and yours holds a quart, wouldn't you be mean not to let me have my little half measure full?

Then that little man in black there, he says women can't have as much rights as men, 'cause Christ wasn't a woman! Where did your Christ come from? Where did your Christ come from? From God and a woman! Man had nothin' to do with Him.

If the first woman God ever made was strong enough to turn the world upside down all alone, these women together ought to be able to turn it back, and get it right side up again. And now they is asking to do it, they better let 'em. 'Bliged to you for hearin' me, and now ole Sojourner hasn't got nothin' more to say.

THE ANTEBELLUM PERIOD 1800–1865

Topics for Research

1. Address how writers explore the theme of slavery versus freedom in works written during the antebellum period.

2. African American women writers of the antebellum period genderize African American life in pre–Civil War America. In an essay, compare and contrast how African American women authors write their experience into literature.

3. Discuss the oral tradition in antebellum literature and how it frames a discussion of key social, political, and cultural issues of the period. Does oral literature of the period differ from the written tradition? Why? Why not?

4. Select an author from the antebellum period and one from the colonial period, and analyze the similarities and differences in their writing in terms of narrative technique, theme, symbolism, or character development.

5. Choose a historical incident from the antebellum period, and examine how a literary work or works respond to that incident. Is the literary work a faithful rendering, or does the author employ artistic license in shaping or framing the event?

PART 3

THE RECONSTRUCTION PERIOD 1865–1900

INTRODUCTION

AFRICAN AMERICAN LITERATURE FROM 1865 TO 1900 REFLECTS the fact that despite the abolition of slavery, the United States was far from being a place of freedom, equality, and justice for everyone. Thus, African American writers continued to emphasize the theme of slavery versus freedom in the ever-present struggle for equality. In their writing they represented the hopes, dreams, and aspirations of blacks. The central debate surrounded the question of social, economic, and political enfranchisement. To black poets, orators, playwrights, novelists, and short-story writers of the Reconstruction period, literature was a means of liberating and transforming the lives of African Americans in a society in which "separate but equal" policies held sway. Central concerns included education, literacy, enfranchisement, Pan-Africanism, and spirituality.

In the Reconstruction era, African American writers viewed education and literacy as a means of attaining social, economic, and political freedom. Because many African Americans, particularly in the South, could not read or write (laws had prohibited the education of slaves), the federal government established schools to teach reading and writing to the newly emancipated citizens. The Freedmen's Bureau, created by Congress to provide health care and educational facilities for blacks and poor whites in the South after the Civil War, set up schools ranging from elementary to university-level institutions.

Many nineteenth-century African American writers taught school, and many more heralded education to a populace who had been denied equal access to learning. For educated African American women and men of the period, teaching served as one of the few vocational opportunities. Anna Julia Cooper, in her 1892 text *A Voice from the South: By a Black Woman of the South* (pp. 146–153), extols the virtues of education for African Americans, particularly women, as a means of attaining fulfillment. An educator herself, Cooper taught at the famous Washington Colored High School, or M Street School, in Washington, D.C., which educated many African Americans who later attended prestigious Ivy League institutions. She writes, "Not unfelt, then, if unproclaimed has been the work and influence of the colored women of America. Our list of chieftains in the service, though not long, is not inferior in strength and excellence, I dare believe, to any similar list which this country can produce" (p. 151). In her early feminist text, Cooper valorizes the black woman as an agent of spiritual, educational, and moral uplift for all African Americans. Elizabeth Keckley, best known for her exposé of the Lincoln household, *Behind the Scenes; or, Thirty Years a Slave, and Four Years in the White House* (pp. 118–121), taught domestic science at Wilberforce University after leaving the employment of the Lincolns, illustrating her commitment to education for African Americans.

During the Reconstruction era, African American writers, like their antebellum predecessors, used the pen to wage war for political enfranchisement, ensuring that blacks would have not only physical freedom but political freedom as well. Through periodicals like *The Colored American Magazine* (which writers such as Pauline Hopkins helped to found), African Americans sought a means to voice their concerns in relation to pressing issues of the period, such as equal rights for all Americans under the law, Pan-Africanism, and black art and culture. Pan-Africanism, a movement that sought to connect the concerns of blacks facing social, economic, and political oppression in the United States, the Caribbean, and Africa, proved to be a powerful force in shaping a collective black identity throughout the world. African American writers promoted African heritage as essential to black identity in serialized novels like Hopkins's *Hagar's Daughter: A Story of Southern Caste Prejudice* (pp. 143–145). Anna Julia Cooper supported Pan-Africanism by speaking before an audience at a Pan-African Conference held in London in 1900. The early interest in Pan-Africanism in the Reconstruction period gave African Americans a sense of pride in black history and culture and provided a background to the emphasis on racial identity in literature of the Harlem Renaissance.

The oral tradition in African American literature features sermons, speeches, spirituals, and stories. Victoria Earle Matthews's "The Awakening of the Afro-American Woman" (pp. 122–127) promotes moral and spiritual uplift. Her speech illustrates the role black women played during Reconstruction as agents of change. Reverend Henry McNeal Turner's sermon "How Long? How Long, O Heaven?" (pp. 154–155) responds to racial violence in the South and calls for strategies to combat social injustice. His sermon reveals the influence and power of the black church in nineteenth-century America. Both Matthews and Turner illustrate how the oral tradition in African American literature functioned to promote social, economic, and political equality.

Literature of the Reconstruction period also fostered an appreciation of black "folk" culture as African American writers and educators sought to valorize black artistic expression, both oral and written. In fact, during Reconstruction, many writers sought to integrate the oral and written traditions by incorporating black dialect in their literature. Charles Chesnutt, in tales such as "The Goophered Grapevine" (pp. 127–136) and "Po' Sandy" (pp. 136–143), presents oral storytelling, through the character Uncle Julius, who spins tales about antebellum days and the harsh realities of slavery. Chesnutt successfully intertwines the oral and the written in his works, illustrating the significance of black folk culture and traditions.

African American poets of the Reconstruction period also captured the black vernacular expression in their work and anticipated the emphasis by twentieth-century African American poets on voice and freedom of expression. Paul Laurence Dunbar turned to the plantation past for many of his most famous poems. Often using dialect to capture the voices of his speakers, his poems emphasize the resilience and endurance of African Americans facing discrimination in the nineteenth century. In "When Malindy Sings" (pp. 158–159), Dunbar's speaker uses nonstandard American English as he conveys the power of a woman singing powerful spirituals such as "Swing Low, Sweet Chariot." Dunbar calls attention to the spiritual as the root of African American poetry and highlights the beauty of the language his folk speaker employs. In "Sympathy" (pp. 155–156), Dunbar comments on the plight of nineteenth-century African Americans desirous of equality at a time when they were treated as second-class citizens. He uses the symbol of the caged bird warbling a song:

It is not a carol of joy or glee,
But a prayer that he sends from his heart's deep core,
But a plea, that upward to Heaven he flings—
I know why the caged bird sings! (18–21)

The caged bird represents the African American, and specifically the African American artist attempting to use art as a means of achieving freedom. Although Dunbar wrote poems in standard American English, such as "Sympathy" and "We Wear the Mask" (p. 156), his poem "When Malindy Sings" stands as significant in its articulation of folk expression in the nineteenth century.

The Reconstruction period marks a time in American history when racial, gender, and class roles were reevaluated. The abolition of slavery, the gaining of limited suffrage rights for black men, and the burgeoning feminist movement were factors in social change. African American women demanded equality in their public and private lives. Because of the institution of slavery, which had dictated that women work alongside men, and because of economic necessity after the Civil War, black women were a vital part of the American work force in professions ranging from domestics to teachers. Black female writers such as Anna Julia Cooper, Pauline Hopkins, and noted suffragist and antilynching crusader Ida B. Wells Barnett challenged prevailing notions about the role of women in American society. Their words proved particularly poignant during the late nineteenth century. The *Plessy v. Ferguson* Supreme Court decision in 1896, which favored a "separate but equal" policy of legalized segregation of blacks and whites, led to eradication of the limited rights African Americans had gained at the end of the Civil War in terms of suffrage and access to public facilities and institutions. In spite of setbacks, outspoken activists in the black women's club movement anticipated the feminist consciousness of Harlem Renaissance women writers, such as Zora Neale Hurston in *Their Eyes Were Watching God* (pp. 301–403), and neorealist writers, such as Alice Walker in *The Color Purple* and *In Search of Our Mothers' Gardens* (pp. 1003–1010).

The Reconstruction period represents a crossroads in American cultural history. It ushered in a host of issues for the country to come to terms with, including racial, gender, and social equity. Its literary legacy stems from autobiographies, stories, novels, speeches, and poems that reflect the society of the period, emphasizing the theme of slavery versus freedom. Writers sought to make the personal more public, and the local more universal, in their attempts to voice their concerns. Through the works of Keckley, Chesnutt, Hopkins, Cooper, and Dunbar, the reader sees the struggle ultimately to obtain freedom and equality.

❧ ELIZABETH KECKLEY (1824?–1907)

Born a slave in Virginia, Elizabeth Keckley lived much of her early life in Kentucky and Missouri with friends and relatives of her owners. While in St. Louis, Missouri, Keckley earned money by sewing for wealthy whites. After marrying James Keckley, whom she had known in Virginia, she used the funds she earned to buy herself from her owners. An independent woman, she went to work as a seamstress in Baltimore and Washington, D.C., where she designed clothing for Mrs. Jefferson Davis and later for Mary Todd Lincoln. The income proved necessary for the support of herself and her young son, who was fathered by a friend of her master's son when Keckley was 18 years old and living in North Carolina.

Keckley penned Behind the Scenes; or, Thirty Years a Slave, and Four Years in the White House *(1868) about her experiences and desire for freedom when she was a slave, her life in the Lincoln White House, and her experiences facing racism and sexism in America. Her autobiography functions as both a slave narrative and a chronicle of life in antebellum and Reconstruction-era America, and it provides glimpses into the lives of black female domestics in the nineteenth century. By 1892, Keckley had relocated to Ohio, where she taught domestic arts at Wilberforce University. Later, she worked for the Home for Destitute Women and Children in Washington, D.C. A stroke claimed her life in 1907.*

From Behind the Scenes; or, Thirty Years a Slave, and Four Years in the White House (1868)

Chapter 9: Behind the Scenes

Some of the freedmen and freedwomen had exaggerated ideas of liberty. To them it was a beautiful vision, a land of sunshine, rest, and glorious promise. They flocked to Washington, and since their extravagant hopes were not realized, it was but natural that many of them should bitterly feel their disappointment. The colored people are wedded to associations, and when you destroy these you destroy half of the happiness of their lives. They make a home, and are so fond of it that they prefer it, squalid though it be, to the comparative ease and luxury of a shifting, roaming life. Well, the emancipated slaves, in coming North, left old associations behind them, and the love for the past was so strong that they could not find much beauty in the new life so suddenly opened to them. Thousands of the disappointed, huddled together in camps, fretted and pined like children for the "good old times." In visiting them in the interests of the Relief Society of which I was president, they would crowd around me with pitiful stories of distress. Often I heard them declare that they would rather go back to slavery in the South, and be with their old masters, than to enjoy the freedom of the North. I believe they were sincere in these declarations, because dependence had become a part of their second nature, and independence brought with it the cares and vexations of poverty.

I was very much amused one day at the grave complaints of a good old, simple-minded woman, fresh from a life of servitude. She had never ventured beyond a plantation until coming North. The change was too radical for her, and she could not exactly understand it. She thought, as many others thought, that Mr. and Mrs. Lincoln were the government, and that the President and his wife had nothing to do but to supply the extravagant wants of every one that applied to them. The wants of this old woman, however, were not very extravagant.

"Why, Missus Keckley," said she to me one day, "I is been here eight months, and Missus Lingom an't even give me one shife. Bliss God, childen, if I had ar know dat de Government, and Mister and Missus Government, was going to do dat ar way, I neber would've comed here in God's wurld. My old missus us't gib me two shifes eber year."

I could not restrain a laugh at the grave manner in which this good old woman entered her protest. Her idea of freedom was two or more old shifts every year. Northern readers may not fully recognize the pith of the joke. On the Southern plantation, the mistress, according to established custom, every year made a present of certain under-garments to her slaves, which articles were always anxiously looked forward to, and thankfully received. The old woman had been in the habit of receiving annually two shifts from her mistress, and she thought the wife of the President of the United States very mean for overlooking this established custom of the plantation.

While some of the emancipated blacks pined for the old associations of slavery, and refused to help themselves, others went to work with commendable energy, and planned with remarkable forethought. They built themselves cabins, and each family cultivated for itself a small patch of ground. The colored people are fond of domestic life, and with them domestication means happy children, a fat pig, a dozen or more chickens, and a garden. Whoever visits the Freedmen's Village now in the vicinity of Washington will discover all of these evidences of prosperity and happiness. The schools are objects of much interest. Good teachers, white and colored, are employed, and whole brigades of bright-eyed dusky children are there taught the common branches of education. These children are studious, and the teachers inform me that their advancement is rapid. I number among my personal friends twelve colored girls employed as teachers in the schools at Washington. The Colored Mission Sabbath School, established through the influence of Gen. Brown at the Fifteenth Street Presbyterian Church, is always an object of great interest to the residents of the Capital, as well as to the hundreds of strangers visiting the city.

In 1864 the receptions again commenced at the White House. For the first two years of Mr. Lincoln's administration, the President selected a lady to join in the promenade with him, which left Mrs. Lincoln free to choose an escort from among the distinguished gentlemen that always surrounded her on such occasions. This custom at last was discontinued by Mrs. Lincoln.

"Lizabeth!"—I was sewing in her room, and she was seated in a comfortable arm-chair—"Lizabeth, I have been thinking over a little matter. As you are well aware, the President, at every reception, selects a lady to lead the promenade with him. Now it occurs to me that this custom is an absurd one. On such occasions our guests recognize the position of the President as first of all; consequently, he takes the lead in everything; well, now, if they recognize his position they should also recognize mine. I am his wife, and should lead with him. And yet he offers his arm to any other lady in the room, making her first with him and placing me second. The custom is an absurd one, and I mean to abolish it. The dignity that I owe to my position, as Mrs. President, demands that I should not hesitate any longer to act."

Mrs. Lincoln kept her word. Ever after this, she either led the promenade with the President, or the President walked alone or with a gentleman. The change was much remarked, but the reason why it was made, I believe, was never generally known.

In 1864 much doubt existed in regard to the re-election of Mr. Lincoln, and the White House was besieged by all grades of politicians. Mrs. Lincoln was often blamed for having a certain class of men around her.

"I have an object in view, Lizabeth," she said to me in reference to this matter. "In a political canvass it is policy to cultivate every element of strength. These men have influence, and we require influence to re-elect Mr. Lincoln. I will be clever to them until after the election, and then, if we remain at the White House, I will drop every one of them, and let them know very plainly that I only made tools of them. They are an unprincipled set, and I don't mind a little double-dealing with them."

"Does Mr. Lincoln know what your purpose is?" I asked.

"God! no; he would never sanction such a proceeding, so I keep him in the dark, and will tell him of it when all is over. He is too honest to take the proper care of his own interests, so I feel it to be my duty to electioneer for him."

Mr. Lincoln, as every one knows, was far from handsome. He was not admired for his graceful figure and finely moulded face, but for the nobility of his soul and the greatness of his heart. His wife was different. He was wholly unselfish in every respect, and I believe that he loved the mother of his children very tenderly. He asked nothing but affection from her, but did not always receive it. When in one of her wayward impulsive moods, she was apt to say and do things that wounded him deeply. If he had not loved her, she would have been powerless to cloud his thoughtful face, or gild it with a ray of sunshine as she pleased. We are indifferent to those we do not love, and certainly the President was not indifferent to his wife. She often wounded him in unguarded moments, but calm reflection never failed to bring regret.

Mrs. Lincoln was extremely anxious that her husband should be re-elected President of the United States. In endeavoring to make a display becoming her exalted position, she had to incur many expenses. Mr. Lincoln's salary was inadequate to meet them, and she was forced to run in debt, hoping that good fortune would favor her, and enable her to extricate herself from an embarrassing situation. She bought the most expensive goods on credit, and in the summer of 1864 enormous unpaid bills stared her in the face.

"What do you think about the election, Lizabeth?" she said to me one morning.

"I think that Mr. Lincoln will remain in the White House four years longer," I replied, looking up from my work.

"What makes you think so? Somehow I have learned to fear that he will be defeated."

"Because he has been tried, and has proved faithful to the best interests of the country. The people of the North recognize in him an honest man, and they are willing to confide in him, at least until the war has been brought to a close. The Southern people made his election a pretext for rebellion, and now to replace him by some one else, after years of sanguinary war, would look too much like a surrender of the North. So, Mr. Lincoln is certain to be re-elected. He represents a principle, and to maintain this principle the loyal people of the loyal States will vote for him, even if he had no merits to commend him."

"Your view is a plausible one, Lizabeth, and your confidence gives me new hope. If he should be defeated, I do not know what would become of us all. To me, to him, there is more at stake in this election than he dreams of."

"What can you mean, Mrs. Lincoln? I do not comprehend."

"Simply this. I have contracted large debts, of which he knows nothing, and which he will be unable to pay if he is defeated."

"What are your debts, Mrs. Lincoln?"

"They consist chiefly of store bills. I owe altogether about twenty-seven thousand dollars; the principal portion at Stewart's, in New York. You understand, Lizabeth, that Mr. Lincoln has but little idea of the expense of a woman's wardrobe. He glances at my rich dresses, and is happy in the belief that the few hundred dollars that I obtain from him supply all my wants. I must dress in costly materials. The people scrutinize every article that I wear with critical curiosity. The very fact of having grown up in the West, subjects me to more searching observation. To keep up appearances, I must have money—more than Mr. Lincoln can spare for me. He is too honest to make a penny outside of his salary; consequently I had, and still have, no alternative but to run in debt."

"And Mr. Lincoln does not even suspect how much you owe?"

"God, no!"—this was a favorite expression of hers—"and I would not have him suspect. If he knew that his wife was involved to the extent that she is, the knowledge would drive him mad. He is so sincere and straightforward himself, that he is shocked by the duplicity of others. He does not know a thing about any debts, and I value his happiness, not to speak of my own, too much to allow him to know anything. This is what troubles me so much. If he is re-elected, I can keep him in ignorance of my affairs; but if he is defeated, then the bills will be sent in, and he will know all;" and something like a hysterical sob escaped her.

Mrs. Lincoln sometimes feared that the politicians would get hold of the particulars of her debts, and use them in the Presidential campaign against her husband; and when this thought occurred to her, she was almost crazy with anxiety and fear.

When in one of these excited moods, she would fiercely exclaim—

"The Republican politicians must pay my debts. Hundreds of them are getting immensely rich off the patronage of my husband, and it is but fair that they should help me out of my embarrassment. I will make a demand of them, and when I tell them the facts they cannot refuse to advance whatever money I require."

The Awakening of the Afro-American Woman (1897)

Victoria Earle Matthews

In this speech given in San Francisco in 1897, African American orator and writer Victoria Earle Matthews addresses the Annual Convention of the Society of Christian Endeavor. In this speech, she focuses on the values of Christianity and its importance in teaching individuals the concepts of equality and justice for all.

The awakening to life of any of the forces of nature is the most mysterious as it is the sublimest of spectacles. Through all nature there runs a thread of life. We watch with equal interest and awe the transformation of the rosebud into the flower and the babe into manhood. The philosopher has well said that the element of life runs through all nature and links the destinies of earth with the destinies of the stars. This is a beautiful and ennobling thought; while it binds to earth it yet lifts us to heaven. It gives us strength in adversity, when the storms beat and the thunders peal forth their diapason and confusion reigns supreme everywhere; it tempers our joys with soberness when prosperity hedges us about as the dews of the morning hedge about with gladness the modest violet shyly concealed by the wayside. Life is the most mysterious as it is the most revealed force in nature. Death does not compare with it in these qualities, for there can be no death without life. It is from this point of view that we must regard the tremendous awakening of the Afro-American womanhood, during the past three decades from the double night of ages of slavery in which it was locked in intellectual and moral eclipse. It has been the awakening of a race from the nightmare of 250 years of self-effacement and debasement. It is not within the power of any one who has stood outside of Afro-American life to adequately estimate the extent of the effacement and debasement, and, therefore, of the gracious awakening which has quickened into life the slumbering forces and filled with hope and gladness the souls of millions of the womanhood of our land. To the God of love and tenderness and pity and justice we ascribe the fullness of our thanks and prayers for the transformation from the death of slavery to the life of freedom. All the more are we grateful to the moral and Christian forces of the world, the Christian statesmen and soldiers and scholars who were the divine instruments who made it possible for this womanhood to stand in this august presence to-day, this vast army laboring for the upbuilding of the Master's kingdom among men; for it is true as Longfellow said:

Were half the power that fills the world with terror,
Were half the wealth bestowed on camps and courts,
Given to redeem the human mind from error,
There were no need of arsenals and forts.

The auction block of brutality has been changed into the forum of reason, the slave mart has been replaced by the schoolroom and the church.

As I stand here to-day clothed in the garments of Christian womanhood, the horrible days of slavery, out of which I came, seem as a dream that is told, some horror incredible. Indeed, could they have been, and are not? They were; they are not; this is the sum and substance, the shame and the glory of the tale that I would tell, of the message that I would bring.

In the vast economy of nature, cycles of time are of small moment, years are as hours, and seconds bear but small relation to the problem, yet they are as the drops of rain that fall to earth and lodge in the fastnesses of the mountain from which our rivers are formed that feed the vast expanse of ocean. So in the history of a race lifting itself out of its original condition of helplessness, time is as necessary an element as is opportunity, in the assisting forces of humankind.

When we remember that the God who created all things is no respector [sic] of persons, that the black child is beloved of Him as the white child, we can more easily fix the responsibility that rests upon the Christian womanhood of the country to join with us in elevating the head, the heart and the soul of Afro-American womanhood. As the great Frederick Douglass once said, in order to measure the heights to which we have risen we must first measure the depths to which we were dragged. It is from this point of observation that we must regard the awakening of the Afro-American womanhood of the land. And what is this awakening? What is its distinguishing characteristics? It would seem superfluous to ask or to answer questions so obvious, but the lamentable truth is, that the womanhood of the United States, of the world, knows almost absolutely nothing of the hope and aspirations, of the joys and the sorrows, of the wrongs, and of the needs of the black women of this country, who came up out of the effacement and debasement of American slavery into the dazzling sunlight of freedom. My friends, call to mind the sensations of the prisoner of Chillon, as he walked out of the dungeon where the flower of his life had been spent, into the open air, and you will be able to appreciate in some sense our feelings in 1865,

When the war drums throbbed no longer,
And the battle flags were furled.

What a past was ours! There was no attribute of womanhood which had not been sullied—aye, which had not been despoiled in the crucible of slavery. Virtue, modesty, the joys of maternity, even hope of mortality, all those were the heritage of this womanhood when the voice of Lincoln and the sword of Grant, as the expression of the Christian opinion of the land, bade them stand forth, without let or hindrance, as arbiters of their own persons and wills. They had no past to which they could appeal for anything. It had destroyed, more than in the men, all that a woman holds sacred, all that ennobles womanhood. She had but the future.

From such small beginnings she was compelled to construct a home. She who had been an outcast, the caprice of brutal power and passion, who had been educated to believe that morality was an echo, and womanly modesty a name; she who had seen father and brother and child torn from her and hurried away into everlasting separation—this creature was born to life in an hour and expected to create a home.

Home, sweet home;
Be it ever so humble,
There's no place like home.

My friends, more, home is the noblest, the most sacred spot in a Christian nation. It is the foundation upon which nationality rests, the pride of the citizen and the glory of the Republic. This woman was expected to build a home for 4,500,000 people, of whom she was the decisive unit. No Spartan mother ever had a larger task imposed upon her shoulders; no Spartan mother ever acquitted herself more heroically than this Afro-American woman has done. She has done it almost without any assistance from her white sister; who, in too large a sense, has left her to work out her own destiny in fear and trembling. The color of the skin has been an almost insurmountable barrier between them, despite the beautiful lines of the gentle Cowper, that—

Skin may differ,
But affection
Dwells in black and white the same.

I am not unmindful, however, of the Northern women who went into the South after the war as the missionary goes into the dark places of the world, and helped the Afro-American women to lay the foundation of her home broad and deep in the Christian virtues. For years they did this in the schoolroom and their labors naturally had their reflex in the home life of their pupils.

Broadly speaking, my main statement holds, however, that these women, starting empty handed, were left to make Christian homes where a Christian citizenship should be nurtured. The marvel is not that they have succeeded, not that they are succeeding, but that they did not fail, *utterly fail.* I believe the God who brought them out of the Valley of the Shadow, who snatched them from the hand of the white rapist, the base slave master whose unacknowledged children are to be found in every hamlet of the Republic, guided these women, and guides them in the supreme work of building their Christian homes. The horrors of the past were forgotten in the joyous labor that presented itself. Even the ineffaceable wrongs of the past, while not forgotten, were forgiven in the spirit of the Master, who even forgave those who took His life.

If there had been no other awakening than this, if this woman who had stood upon the auction block possessed of no rights that a white man was bound to respect, and none which he did respect, if there had been no other awakening of the Afro-American woman than this, that she made a home for her race, an abiding place for husband, and son, and daughter, it would be glory enough to embalm her memory in song and story. As it is, it will be her sufficient monument through all time that out of nothing she created something, and that something the dearest, the sweetest, the strongest institution in Christian government.

But she has done more than this. The creation of a home is the central feature of her awakening, but around this are many other features which show her strong title to the countenance and respect of the sisterhood of the world. She has meekly taken her place by her husband, in the humble occupations of life as a bread winner, and by her labors and sacrifices has helped to rear and educate 50,000 young women, who are active instructors in the Christian churches of the land. In the building up of the Master's kingdom she has been and she is an active and a positive influence; indeed, in this field she has proven, as her white sister has proven, the truth of Napoleon Bonaparte's sententious but axiomatic truth, that "The hand that rocks the cradle rules the world." It is not too much to say that the 7,000,000 Afro-American church memberships would fall to pieces as a rope of sand if the active sympathy and support of the Afro-American women were withdrawn. It is demonstrable that these women are the arch of the Afro-American temple. But these women who came out of slavery have done more than this. They have not only made Christian homes for their families, and educated 50,000 Sunday-school workers, but they have given to the State 25,000 educated school teachers, who are to-day the hope and inspiration of the whole race. The black women who came out of slavery in the past thirty years, have accomplished these tremendous results as farm-laborers and house servants, and they deserve the admiration of mankind for the glorious work that they have accomplished. In the past few years the educated daughters of these ex-slave women have aroused themselves to the necessity of systematic organization for their own protection, and for strengthening their race where they find it is weak, and to this end they have in the several States 243 regularly organized and officered clubs in the Afro-American Women's National Association; there are besides hundreds of social clubs and temperance organizations working in their own way for a strong Christian womanhood. Indeed, the impulse of aspiration after the strong and the good in our civilization is manifest on all hands in our womanhood. It is all so grounded in Christian morality that we may safely conclude that it is built upon a rock and cannot be shaken by the fury of the storms.

The awakening of the Afro-American woman is one of the most promising facts in our national life. That she deserves the active sympathy and co-operation of all the female forces of the Republic, I think I have sufficiently shown. We need them. We have always needed them. We need them in the work of religion, of education, of temperance, of morality, of industrialism; and above all we need their assistance in combatting the public opinion and laws that degrade our womanhood because it is black and not white; for of a truth, and as a universal law, an injury to one woman is an injury to all women. As long as the affections are controlled by legislation in defiance of Christian law, making infamous the union of black and white, we shall have unions without the sanction of the law, and children without legal parentage, to the degradation of black womanhood and the disgrace of white manhood. As one woman, as an Afro-American woman, I stand in this great Christian presence to-day and plead that the marriage and divorce laws be made uniform throughout the Republic, and that they shall not control, but legalize, the union of mutual affections. Until this shall have been done, Afro-American womanhood will have known no full and absolute awakening. As the laws now stand, they are the greatest demoralizing forces with which our womanhood has to contend. They serve as the protection of the white man, but they leave us defenceless, indeed. I ask the Christian womanhood of this great organized Army of Christ, to lend us their active co-operation in coercing the law-makers of the land in throwing around our womanhood the equal protection of the State to which it is entitled. A slave regulation should not be allowed to prevail in a free government. A barbarous injustice should not receive the sanction of a Christian nation. The stronger forces of society should scorn to crush to the earth one of the weakest forces.

Next to these degrading marriage and divorce laws which prevail in two [sic] many States of the Republic, the full awakening of the Afro-American woman to her rightful position in society, are the separate car regulations which prevail in most of the States of the South. They were conceived in injustice; they are executed with extraordinary cowardice. Their entire operation tends to degrade Afro-American womanhood. None who are familiar with their operation will dispute this statement of facts. From this exalted forum, and in the name of the large army of Afro-American women, I appeal to the Christian sentiment which dominates this organization, to assist us in righting the wrongs growing out of these regulations, to the end that our womanhood may be sustained in its dignity and protected in its weakness, and the heavenly Father, who hath declared, "righteousness exalteth a nation, but sin is a reproach to any people," will give His benediction to the laws made just.

I am moved here further to invoke your patience and sympathy in the efforts of our awakening womanhood to care for the aged and infirm, for the orphan and outcast; for the reformation of the penal institutions of the Southern States, for the separation of male and female convicts, and above all for the establishment of juvenile reformatories [in] those States for both races, to the end that the shame of it may be removed that children of tender age should be herded with hardened criminals from whose life all of moral sensibility has vanished forever.

I feel moved to speak here in this wise for a whole race of women whose rise or fall, whose happiness or sorrow, whose degradation or exaltation are the concern of Christian men and women everywhere. I feel moved to say in conclusion that in all Christian and temperance work, in all that lifts humanity from its fallen condition to a more perfect resemblance of Him in whose image it was made, in all that goes to make our common humanity stronger and better and more beautiful; the Afro-American women of the Republic will "do their duty as God shall give them light to do it."

CHARLES CHESNUTT (1858–1932)

Many African American writers of the Reconstruction era articulated the folk experience and culture in their works, illustrating the richness of the black experience. A native of Cleveland, Ohio, Charles Chesnutt grew up in Fayetteville, North Carolina, where he was exposed to black Southern folk culture by the town residents who came to his father's store. By 1884, he had returned to Cleveland, where he studied to become a lawyer. In addition, he wrote fiction. The Conjure Woman *(1899) features short stories focusing on folk culture in the rural South.* The Wife of His Youth, and Other Stories of the Color Line *(1899) focuses on race relations in America. He also wrote novels, including* The House Behind the Cedars *(1900) as well as* The Marrow of Tradition *(1901). Many of his early stories focus on the injustice of slavery and the quest for freedom. In "The Goophered Grapevine" and "Po' Sandy," Chesnutt's authentic rendering of customs, traditions, rituals, and Southern black dialect at the turn of the century anticipates the works of later writers such as Zora Neale Hurston and Ernest Gaines. Chesnutt died during the heyday of the Harlem Renaissance in 1932, but prior to his death his achievements were honored with the 1928 Spingarn Medal from the NAACP.*

The Goophered Grapevine (1899)

Some years ago my wife was in poor health, and our family doctor, in whose skill and honesty I had implicit confidence, advised a change of climate. I shared, from an unprofessional standpoint, his opinion that the raw winds, the chill rains, and the violent changes of temperature that characterized the winters in the region of the Great Lakes tended to aggravate my wife's difficulty, and would undoubtedly shorten her life if she remained exposed to them. The doctor's advice was that we seek, not a temporary place of sojourn, but a permanent residence, in a warmer and more equable climate. I was engaged at the time in grape-culture in northern Ohio, and, as I liked the business and had given it much study, I decided to look for some other locality suitable for carrying it on. I thought of sunny France, of sleepy Spain, of Southern California, but there were objections to them all. It occurred to me that I might find what I wanted in some one of our own Southern States. It was a sufficient time after the war for conditions in the South to have become somewhat settled; and I was enough of a pioneer to start a new industry, if I could not find a place where grape-culture had been tried. I wrote to a cousin who had gone into the turpentine business in central North Carolina. He assured me, in response to my inquiries, that no better place could be found in the South than the State and neighborhood where he lived; the climate was perfect for health, and, in conjunction with the soil, ideal for grape-culture; labor was cheap, and land could be bought for a mere song. He gave us a cordial invitation to come and visit him while we looked into the matter. We accepted the invitation, and after several days of leisurely travel, the last hundred miles of which were up a river on a sidewheel steamer, we reached our destination, a quaint old town, which I shall call Patesville, because, for one reason, that is not its name. There was a red brick market-house in the public square, with a tall tower, which held a four-faced clock that struck the hours, and from which there pealed out a curfew at nine o'clock. There were two or three hotels, a court-house, a jail, stores, offices, and all the appurtenances of a county seat and a commercial emporium; for while Patesville numbered only four or five thousand inhabitants, of all shades of complexion, it was one of the principal towns in North Carolina, and had a considerable trade in cotton and naval stores. This business activity was not immediately apparent to my unaccustomed eyes. Indeed, when I first saw the town, there brooded over it a calm that seemed almost sabbatic in its restfulness, though I learned later on that underneath its somnolent exterior the deeper currents of life—love and hatred, joy and despair, ambition and avarice, faith and friendship—flowed not less steadily than in livelier latitudes.

We found the weather delightful at that season, the end of summer, and were hospitably entertained. Our host was a man of means and evidently regarded our visit as a pleasure, and we were therefore correspondingly at our ease, and in a position to act with the coolness of judgment desirable in making so radical a change in our lives. My cousin placed a horse and buggy at our disposal, and himself acted as our guide until I became somewhat familiar with the country.

I found that grape-culture, while it had never been carried on to any great extent, was not entirely unknown in the neighborhood. Several planters thereabouts had attempted it on a commercial scale, in former years, with greater or less success; but like most Southern industries, it had felt the blight of war and had fallen into desuetude.

I went several times to look at a place that I thought might suit me. It was a plantation of considerable extent, that had formerly belonged to a wealthy man by the name of McAdoo. The estate had been for years involved in litigation between disputing heirs, during which period shiftless cultivation had well-nigh exhausted the soil. There had been a vineyard of some extent on the place, but it had not been attended to since the war, and had lapsed into utter neglect. The vines—here partly supported by decayed and broken-down trellises, there twining themselves among the branches of the slender saplings which had sprung up among them—grew in wild and unpruned luxuriance, and the few scattered grapes they bore were the undisputed prey of the first comer. The site was admirably adapted to grape-raising; the soil, with a little attention, could not have been better; and with the native grape, the luscious scuppernong, as my main reliance in the beginning, I felt sure that I could introduce and cultivate successfully a number of other varieties.

One day I went over with my wife to show her the place. We drove out of the town over a long wooden bridge that spanned a spreading mill-pond, passed the long whitewashed fence surrounding the county fair-ground, and struck into a road so sandy that the horse's feet sank to the fetlocks. Our route lay partly up hill and partly down, for we were in the sand-hill county; we drove past cultivated farms, and then by abandoned fields grown up in scrub-oak and short-leaved pine, and once or twice through the solemn aisles of the virgin forest, where the tall pines, well-nigh meeting over the narrow road, shut out the sun, and wrapped us in cloistral solitude. Once, at a cross-roads, I was in doubt as to the turn to take, and we sat there waiting ten minutes—we had already caught some of the native infection of restfulness—for some human being to come along, who could direct us on our way. At length a little negro girl appeared, walking straight as an arrow, with a piggin full of water on her head. After a little patient investigation, necessary to overcome the child's shyness, we learned what we wished to know, and at the end of about five miles from the town reached our destination.

We drove between a pair of decayed gateposts—the gate itself had long since disappeared—and up a straight sandy lane, between two lines of rotting rail fence, partly concealed by jimson-weeds and briers, to the open space where a dwelling-house had once stood, evidently a spacious mansion, if we might judge from the ruined chimneys that were still standing, and the brick pillars on which the sills rested. The house itself, we had been informed, had fallen a victim to the fortunes of war.

We alighted from the buggy, walked about the yard for a while, and then wandered off into the adjoining vineyard. Upon Annie's complaining of weariness I led the way back to the yard, where a pine log, lying under a spreading elm, afforded a shady though somewhat hard seat. One end of the log was already occupied by a venerable-looking colored man. He held on his knees a hat full of grapes, over which he was smacking his lips with great gusto, and a pile of grapeskins near him indicated that the performance was no new thing. We approached him at an angle from the rear, and were close to him before he perceived us. He respectfully rose as we drew near, and was moving away, when I begged him to keep his seat.

"Don't let us disturb you," I said. "There is plenty of room for us all."

He resumed his seat with somewhat of embarrassment. While he had been standing, I had observed that he was a tall man, and, though slightly bowed by the weight of years, apparently quite vigorous. He was not entirely black, and this fact, together with the quality of his hair, which was about six inches long and very bushy, except on the top of his head, where he was quite bald, suggested a slight strain of other than negro blood. There was a shrewdness in his eyes, too, which was not altogether African, and which, as we afterwards learned from experience, was indicative of a corresponding shrewdness in his character. He went on eating the grapes, but did not seem to enjoy himself quite so well as he had apparently done before he became aware of our presence.

"Do you live around here?" I asked, anxious to put him at his ease.

"Yas, suh. I lives des ober yander, behine de nex' san'-hill, on de Lumberton plank-road."

"Do you know anything about the time when this vineyard was cultivated?"

"Lawd bless you, suh, I knows all about it. Dey ain' na'er a man in dis settlement w'at won' tell you ole Julius McAdoo 'uz bawn en raise' on dis yer same plantation. Is you de Norv'n gemman w'at's gwine ter buy de ole vimya'd?"

"I am looking at it," I replied; "but I don't know that I shall care to buy unless I can be reasonably sure of making something out of it."

"Well, suh, you is a stranger ter me, en I is a stranger ter you, en we is bofe strangers ter one anudder, but 'f I 'uz in yo' place, I would n' buy dis vimya'd."

"Why not?" I asked.

"Well, I dunno whe'r you b'lieves in cunj'in' er not,—some er de w'ite folks don't, er says dey don't,—but de truf er de matter is dat dis yer ole vimya'd is goophered."

"Is what?" I asked, not grasping the meaning of this unfamiliar word.

"Is goophered,—cunju'd, bewitch'."

He imparted this information with such solemn earnestness, and with such an air of confidential mystery, that I felt somewhat interested, while Annie was evidently much impressed, and drew closer to me.

"How do you know it is bewitched?" I asked.

"I would n' spec' fer you ter b'lieve me 'less you know all 'bout de fac's. But ef you en young miss dere doan' min' lis'nin' ter a ole nigger run on a minute er two w'ile you er restin', I kin 'splain to you how it all happen'."

We assured him that we would be glad to hear how it all happened, and he began to tell us. At first the current of his memory—or imagination—seemed somewhat sluggish; but as his embarrassment wore off, his language flowed more freely, and the story acquired perspective and coherence. As he became more and more absorbed in the narrative, his eyes assumed a dreamy expression, and he seemed to lose sight of his auditors, and to be living over again in monologue his life on the old plantation.

"Ole Mars Dugal' McAdoo," he began, "bought dis place long many years befo' de wah, en I 'member well w'en he sot out all dis yer part er de plantation in scuppernon's. De vimes growed monst'us fas', en Mars Dugal' made a thousan' gallon er scuppernon' wine eve'y year.

"Now, ef dey's an'thing a nigger lub, nex' ter 'possum, en chick'n, en watermillyums, it's scuppernon's. Dey ain' nuffin dat kin stan' up side'n de scuppernon' fer sweetness; sugar ain't a suckumstance ter scuppernon'. W'en de season is nigh 'bout ober, en de grapes begin ter swivel up des a little wid de wrinkles er ole age,—w'en de skin git sof' en brown,—den de scuppernon' make you smack yo' lip en roll yo' eye en wush fer mo'; so I reckon it ain' very 'stonishin' dat niggers lub scuppernon'.

"Dey wuz a sight er niggers in de naberhood er de vimya'd. Dere wuz ole Mars Henry Brayboy's niggers, en ole Mars Jeems McLean's niggers, en Mars Dugal's own niggers; den dey wuz a settlement er free niggers en po' buckrahs down by de Wim'l'ton Road, en Mars Dugal' had de only vimya'd in de naberhood. I reckon it ain' so much so nowadays, but befo' de wah, in slab'ry times, a nigger did n' mine goin' fi' er ten mile in a night, w'en dey wuz sump'n good ter eat at de yuther een'.

"So atter a w'ile Mars Dugal' begin ter miss his scuppernon's. Co'se he 'cuse' de niggers er it, but dey all 'nied it ter de las'. Mars Dugal' sot spring guns en steel traps, en he en de oberseah sot up nights once't er twice't, tel one night Mars Dugal'—he 'uz a monst'us keerless man—got his leg shot full er cow-peas. But somehow er nudder dey could n' nebber ketch none er de niggers. I dunner how it happen, but it happen des like I tell you, en de grapes kep' on a-goin' des de same.

"But bimeby ole Mars Dugal' fix' up a plan ter stop it. Dey wuz a cunjuh 'oman livin' down 'mongs' de free niggers on de Wim'l'ton Road, en all de darkies fum Rockfish ter Beaver Crick wuz feared er her. She could wuk de mos' powerfulles' kin' er goopher,—could make people hab fits, er rheumatiz, er make 'em des dwinel away en die; en dey say she went out ridin' de niggers at night, fer she wuz a witch 'sides bein' a cunjuh 'oman. Mars Dugal' hearn 'bout Aun' Peggy's doin's, en begun ter 'flect whe'r er no he could n' git her ter he'p him keep de niggers off'n de grapevimes. One day in de spring er de year, ole miss pack' up a basket er chick'n en poun'-cake, en a bottle er scuppernon' wine, en Mars Dugal' tuk it in his buggy en driv ober ter Aun' Peggy's cabin. He tuk de basket in, en had a long talk wid Aun' Peggy.

"De nex' day Aun' Peggy come up ter de vimya'd. De niggers seed her slippin' 'roun', en dey soon foun' out what she 'uz doin' dere. Mars Dugal' had hi'ed her ter goopher de grapevimes. She sa'ntered 'roun' 'mongs' de vimes, en tuk a leaf fum dis one, en a grape-hull fum dat one, en a grape-seed fum anudder one; en den a little twig fum here, en a little pinch er dirt fum dere,—en put it all in a big black bottle, wid a snake's toof en a speckle' hen's gall en some ha'rs fum a black cat's tail, en den fill' de bottle wid scuppernon' wine. Wen she got de goopher all ready en fix', she tuk 'n went out in de woods en buried it under de root uv a red oak tree, en den come back en tole one er de niggers she done goopher de grape-vimes, en a'er a nigger w'at eat dem grapes 'ud be sho ter die inside'n twel' mont's.

"Atter dat de niggers let de scuppernon's 'lone, en Mars Dugal' did n' hab no 'casion ter fine no mo' fault; en de season wuz mos' gone, w'en a strange gemman stop at de plantation one night ter see Mars Dugal' on some business; en his coachman, seein' de scuppernon's growin' so nice en sweet, slip 'roun' behine de smoke-house, en et all de scuppernon's he could hole. Nobody did n' notice it at de time, but dat night, on de way home, de gemman's hoss runned away en kill' de coachman. W'en we hearn de noos, Aun' Lucy, de cook, she up'n say she seed de strange nigger eat'n' er de scuppernon's behine de smoke-house; en den we knowed de goopher had b'en er wukkin'. Den one er de nigger chilluns runned away fum de quarters one day, en got in de scuppernon's, en died de nex' week. W'ite folks say he die' er de fevuh, but de niggers knowed it wuz de goopher. So you k'n be sho de darkies did n' hab much ter do wid dem scuppernon' vimes.

"W'en de scuppernon' season 'uz ober fer dat year, Mars Dugal' foun' he had made fifteen hund'ed gallon er wine; en one er de niggers hearn him laffin' wid de oberseah fit ter kill, en sayin' dem fifteen hund'ed gallon er wine wuz monst'us good intrus' on de ten dollars he laid out on de vimya'd. So I 'low ez he paid Aun' Peggy ten dollars fer to goopher de grapevimes.

"De goopher did n' wuk no mo' tel de nex' summer, w'en 'long to'ds de middle er de season one er de fiel' han's died; en ez dat lef' Mars Dugal' sho't er han's, he went off ter town fer ter buy anudder. He fotch de noo nigger home wid 'im. He wuz er ole nigger, er de color er a gingy-cake, en ball ez a hoss-apple on de top er his head. He wuz a peart ole nigger, do', en could do a big day's wuk.

"Now it happen dat one er de niggers on de nex' plantation, one er ole Mars Henry Brayboy's niggers, had runned away de day befo', en tuk ter de swamp, en ole Mars Dugal' en some er de yuther nabor w'ite folks had gone out wid dere guns en dere dogs fer ter he'p 'em hunt fer de nigger; en de han's on our own plantation wuz all so flusterated dat we fuhgot ter tell de noo han' 'bout de goopher on de scuppernon' vimes. Co'se he smell de grapes en see de vimes, an atter dahk de fus' thing he done wuz ter slip off ter de grapevimes 'dout sayin' nuffin ter nobody. Nex' mawnin' he tole some er de niggers 'bout de fine bait er scuppernon' he et de night befo'.

"W'en dey tole 'im 'bout de goopher on de grapevimes, he 'uz dat tarrified dat he turn pale, en look des like he gwine ter die right in his tracks. De oberseah come up en axed w'at 'uz de matter; en w'en dey tole 'im Henry be'n eatin' er de scuppernon's, en got de goopher on 'im, he gin Henry a big drink er w'iskey, en 'low dat de nex' rainy day he take 'im ober ter Aun' Peggy's, en see ef she would n' take de goopher off'n him, seein' ez he did n' know nuffin erbout it tel he done et de grapes.

"Sho nuff, it rain de nex' day, en de oberseah went ober ter Aun' Peggy's wid Henry. En Aun' Peggy say dat bein' ez Henry did n' know 'bout de goopher, en et de grapes in ign'ance er de conseq'ences, she reckon she mought be able fer ter take de goopher off'n him. So she fotch out er bottle wid some cunjuh medicine in it, en po'd some out in a go'd fer Henry ter drink He manage ter git it down; he say it tas'e like whiskey wid sump'n bitter in it. She 'lowed dat 'ud keep de goopher off'n him tel de spring; but w'en de sap begin ter rise in de grapevimes he ha' ter come en see her ag'in, en she tell him w'at e's ter do.

"Nex' spring, w'en de sap commence' ter rise in de scuppernon' vime, Henry tuk a ham one night. Whar'd he git de ham? *I* doan know; dey wa'n't no hams on de plantation 'cep'n' w'at 'uz in de smoke-house, but *I* never see Henry 'bout de smoke-house. But ez I wuz a-sayin', he tuk de ham ober ter Aun' Peggy's; en Aun' Peggy tole 'im dat w'en Mars Dugal' begin ter prune de grapevimes, he mus' go en take 'n scrape off de sap whar it ooze out'n de cut een's er de vimes, en 'n'int his ball head wid it; en ef he do dat once't a year de goopher would n' wuk agin 'im long ez he done it. En bein' ez he fotch her de ham, she fix' it so he kin eat all de scuppernon' he want.

"So Henry 'n'int his head wid de sap out'n de big grapevime des ha'f way 'twix' de quarters en de big house, en de goopher nebber wuk agin him dat summer. But de beatenes' thing you eber see happen ter Henry. Up ter dat time he wuz ez ball ez a sweeten' 'tater, but des ez soon ez de young leaves begun ter come out on de grapevimes, de ha'r begun ter grow out on Henry's head, en by de middle er de summer he had de bigges' head er ha'r on de plantation. Befo' dat, Henry had tol'able good ha'r 'roun' de aidges, but soon ez de young grapes begun ter come, Henry's ha'r begun to quirl all up in little balls, des like dis yer reg'lar grapy ha'r, en by de time de grapes got ripe his head look des like a bunch er grapes. Combin' it did n' do no good; he wuk at it ha'f de night wid er Jim Crow,[1] en think he git it straighten' out, but in de mawnin' de grapes 'ud be dere des de same. So he gin it up, en tried ter keep de grapes down by havin' his ha'r cut sho't.

"But dat wa'n't de quares' thing 'bout de goopher. When Henry come ter de plantation, he wuz gittin' a little ole an stiff in de j'ints. But dat summer he got des ez spry en libely ez any young nigger on de plantation; fac', he got so biggity dat Mars Jackson, de oberseah, ha' ter th'eaten ter whip 'im, ef he did n' stop cuttin' up his didos en behave hisse'f. But de mos' cur'ouses' thing happen' in de fall, when de sap begin ter go down in de grapevimes. Fus', when de grapes 'uz gethered, de knots begun ter straighten out'n Henry's ha'r; en w'en de leaves begin ter fall, Henry's ha'r 'mence' ter drap out; en when de vimes 'uz bar', Henry's head wuz baller 'n it wuz in de spring, en he begin ter git ole en stiff in de j'ints ag'in, en paid no mo' 'tention ter de gals dyoin' er de whole winter. En nex' spring, w'en he rub de sap on ag'in, he got young ag'in, en so soopl en libely dat none er de young niggers on de plantation could n' jump, ner dance, ner hoe ez much cotton ez Henry. But in de fall er de year his grapes 'mence' ter straighten out, en his j'ints ter git stiff, en his ha'r drap off, en de rheumatiz begin ter wrastle wid 'im.

"Now, ef you'd 'a' knowed ole Mars Dugal' McAdoo, you'd 'a' knowed dat it ha' ter be a mighty rainy day when he could n' fine sump'n fer his niggers ter do, en it ha' ter be a mighty little hole he could n' crawl thoo, en ha' ter be a monst'us cloudy night when a dollar git by him in de dahkness; en w'en he see how Henry git young in de spring en ole in de fall, he 'lowed ter hisse'f ez how he could make mo' money out'n Henry dan by wukkin' him in de cotton-fiel'. 'Long de nex' spring, atter de sap 'mence' ter rise, en Henry 'n'int 'is head en sta'ted fer ter git young en soopl, Mars Dugal' up 'n tuk Henry ter town, en sole 'im fer fifteen hunder' dollars. Co'se de man w'at bought Henry did n' know nuffin 'bout de goopher, en Mars Dugal' did n' see no 'casion fer ter tell 'im. Long to'ds de fall, w'en de sap went down, Henry begin ter git ole ag'in same ez yuzhal, en his noo marster begin ter git skeered les'n he gwine ter lose his fifteen-hunder'-dollar nigger. He sent fer a mighty fine doctor, but de med'cine did n' 'pear ter do no good; de goopher had a good holt. Henry tole de doctor 'bout de goopher, but de doctor des laff at 'im.

"One day in de winter Mars Dugal' went ter town, en wuz santerin' long de Main Street, when who should he meet but Henry's noo marster. Dey said 'Hoddy,' en Mars Dugal' ax 'im ter hab a seegyar; en atter dey run on awhile 'bout de craps en de weather, Mars Dugal' ax 'im, sorter keerless, like ez ef he des thought of it,—

"'How you like de nigger I sole you las' spring?'

"Henry's marster shuck his head en knock de ashes off'n his seegyar.

---

[1] A small card, resembling a currycomb in construction, and used by negroes in the rural districts instead of a comb.

"'Spec' I made a bad bahgin when I bought dat nigger. Henry done good wuk all de summer, but sence de fall set in he 'pears ter be sorter pinin' away. Dey ain' nuffin pertickler de matter wid 'im—leastways de doctor say so—'cep'n' a tech er de rheumatiz; but his ha'r is all fell out, en ef he don't pick up his strenk mighty soon, I spec' I'm gwine ter lose 'im.'

"Dey smoked on awhile, en bimeby ole mars say, 'Well, a bahgin 's a bahgin, but you en me is good fren's, en I doan wan' ter see you lose all de money you paid fer dat nigger; en ef w'at you say is so, en I ain't 'sputin' it, he ain't wuf much now. I 'spec's you wukked him too ha'd dis summer, er e'se de swamps down here don't agree wid de san'-hill nigger. So you des lemme know, en ef he gits any wusser I'll be willin' ter gib yer five hund'ed dollars fer 'im, en take my chances on his livin'.'

"Sho 'nuff, when Henry begun ter draw up wid de rheumatiz en it look like he gwine ter die fer sho, his noo marster sen' fer Mars Dugal', en Mars Dugal' gin him what he promus, en brung Henry home ag'in. He tuk good keer uv 'im dyoin' er de winter,—give 'im w'iskey ter rub his rheumatiz, en terbacker ter smoke, en all he want ter eat,—'caze a nigger w'at he could make a thousan' dollars a year off'n did n' grow on eve'y huckleberry bush.

"Nex' spring, w'en de sap ris en Henry's ha'r commence' ter sprout, Mars Dugal' sole 'im ag'in, down in Robeson County dis time; en he kep' dat sellin' business up fer five year er mo'. Henry nebber say nuffin 'bout de goopher ter his noo marsters, 'caze he know he gwine ter be tuk good keer uv de nex' winter, w'en Mars Dugal' buy him back. En Mars Dugal' made 'nuff money off'n Henry ter buy anudder plantation ober on Beaver Crick.

"But 'long 'bout de een' er dat five year dey come a stranger ter stop at de plantation. De fus' day he 'uz dere he went out wid Mars Dugal' en spent all de mawnin' lookin' ober de vimya'd, en atter dinner dey spent all de evenin' playin' kya'ds. De niggers soon 'skiver' dat he wuz a Yankee, en dat he come down ter Norf C'lina fer ter l'arn de w'ite folks how to raise grapes en make wine. He promus Mars Dugal' he c'd make de grapevimes b'ar twicet ez many grapes, en dat de noo winepress he wuz a-sellin' would make mo' d'n twice't ez many gallons er wine. En ole Mars Dugal' des drunk it all in, des 'peared ter be bewitch' wid dat Yankee. W'en de darkies see dat Yankee runnin' 'roun' de vimya'd en diggin' under de grapevimes, dey shuk dere heads, en 'lowed dat dey feared Mars Dugal' losin' his min'. Mars Dugal' had all de dirt dug away fum under de roots er all de scuppernon' vimes, an' let 'em stan' dat away fer a week er mo'. Den dat Yankee made de niggers fix up a mixtry er lime en ashes en manyo, en po' it 'roun' de roots er de grapevimes. Den he 'vise Mars Dugal' fer ter trim de vimes close't, en Mars Dugal' tuck 'n done eve'ything de Yankee tole him ter do. Dyoin' all er dis time, mind yer, dis yer Yankee wuz libbin' off'n de fat er de lan', at de big house, en playin' kya'ds wid Mars Dugal' eve'y night; en dey say Mars Dugal' los' mo'n a thousan' dollars dyoin' er de week dat Yankee wuz a-ruinin' de grapevimes.

"W'en de sap ris nex' spring, ole Henry 'n'inted his head ez yuzhal, en his ha'r 'mence' ter grow des de same ez it done eve'y year. De scuppernon' vimes growed monst's fas', en de leaves wuz greener en thicker dan dey eber be'n dyoin' my rememb'ance; en Henry's ha'r growed out thicker dan eber, en he 'peared ter git younger 'n younger, en soopler 'n soopler; en seein' ez he wuz sho't er han's dat spring, havin' tuk in consid'able noo groun', Mars Dugal' 'cluded he would n' sell Henry 'tel he git de crap in en de cotton chop'. So he kep' Henry on de plantation.

"But 'long 'bout time fer de grapes ter come on de scuppernon' vimes, dey 'peared ter come a change ober 'em; de leaves withered en swivel' up, en de young grapes turn' yaller, en bimeby eve'ybody on de plantation could see dat de whole vimya'd wuz dyin'. Mars Dugal' tuk 'n water de vimes en done all he could, but 't wa'n' no use: dat Yankee had done bus' de watermillyum. One time de vimes picked up a bit, en Mars Dugal' 'lowed dey wuz gwine ter come out ag'in; but dat Yankee done dug too close under de roots, en prune de branches too close ter de vime, en all dat lime en ashes done burn' de life out'n de vimes, en dey des kep' a-with'in' en a-swivelin'.

"All dis time de goopher wuz a-wukkin'. When de vimes sta'ted ter wither, Henry 'mence' ter complain er his rheumatiz; en when de leaves begin ter dry up, his ha'r 'mence' ter drap out. When de vimes fresh' up a bit, Henry 'd git peart ag'in, en when de vimes wither' ag'in, Henry 'd git ole ag'in, en des kep' gittin' mo' en mo' fitten fer nuffin; he des pined away, en pined away, en fine'ly tuk ter his cabin; en when de big vime whar he got de sap ter 'n'int his head withered en turned yaller en died, Henry died too,—des went out sorter like a cannel. Dey did n't 'pear ter be nuffin de matter wid 'im, 'cep'n' de rheumatiz, but his strenk des dwinel' away 'tel he did n' hab ernuff lef' ter draw his bref. De goopher had got de under holt, en th'owed Henry dat time fer good en all.

"Mars Dugal' tuk on might'ly 'bout losin' his vimes en his nigger in de same year; en he swo' dat ef he could git holt er dat Yankee he'd wear 'im ter a frazzle, en den chaw up de frazzle; en he'd done it, too, for Mars Dugal' 'uz a monst'us brash man w'en he once git started. He sot de vimya'd out ober ag'in, but it wuz th'ee er fo' year befo' de vimes got ter b'arin' any scuppernon's.

"W'en de wah broke out, Mars Dugal' raise' a comp'ny, en went off ter fight de Yankees. He say he wuz mighty glad dat wah come, en he des want ter kill a Yankee fer eve'y dollar he los' 'long er dat grape-raisin' Yankee. En I 'spec' he would 'a' done it, too, ef de Yankees had n' s'picioned sump'n, en killed him fus. Atter de s'render ole miss move' ter town, de niggers all scattered 'way fum de plantation, en de vimya'd ain' be'n cultervated sence."

"Is that story true?" asked Annie doubtfully, but seriously, as the old man concluded his narrative.

"It 's des ez true ez I 'm a-settin' here, miss. Dey's a easy way ter prove it: I kin lead de way right ter Henry's grave ober yander in de plantation buryin'-groun'. En I tell yer w'at, marster, I would n' 'vise you to buy dis yer ole vimya'd, 'caze de goopher's on it yit, en dey ain' no tellin' w'en it's gwine ter crap out."

"But I thought you said all the old vines died."

"Dey did 'pear ter die, but a few un 'em come out ag'in, en is mixed in 'mongs' de yuthers. I ain' skeered ter eat de grapes, 'caze I knows de old vimes fum de noo ones; but wid strangers dey ain' no tellin' w'at mought happen. I would n' 'vise yer ter buy dis vimya'd."

I bought the vineyard, nevertheless, and it has been for a long time in a thriving condition, and is often referred to by the local press as a striking illustration of the opportunities open to Northern capital in the development of Southern industries. The luscious scuppernong holds first rank among our grapes, though we cultivate a great many other varieties, and our income from grapes packed and shipped to the Northern markets is quite considerable. I have not noticed any developments of the goopher in the vineyard, although I have a mild suspicion that our colored assistants do not suffer from want of grapes during the season.

I found, when I bought the vineyard, that Uncle Julius had occupied a cabin on the place for many years, and derived a respectable revenue from the product of the neglected grapevines. This, doubtless, accounted for his advice to me not to buy the vineyard, though whether it inspired the goopher story I am unable to state. I believe, however, that the wages I paid him for his services as coachman, for I gave him employment in that capacity, were more than an equivalent for anything he lost by the sale of the vineyard.

Po' Sandy (1899)

On the northeast corner of my vineyard in central North Carolina, and fronting on the Lumberton plank-road, there stood a small frame house, of the simplest construction. It was built of pine lumber, and contained but one room, to which one window gave light and one door admission. Its weather-beaten sides revealed a virgin innocence of paint. Against one end of the house, and occupying half its width, there stood a huge brick chimney: the crumbling mortar had left large cracks between the bricks; the bricks themselves had begun to scale off in large flakes, leaving the chimney sprinkled with unsightly blotches. These evidences of decay were but partially concealed by a creeping vine, which extended its slender branches hither and thither in an ambitious but futile attempt to cover the whole chimney. The wooden shutter, which had once protected the unglazed window, had fallen from its hinges, and lay rotting in the rank grass and jimson-weeds beneath. This building, I learned when I bought the place, had been used as a schoolhouse for several years prior to the breaking out of the war, since which time it had remained unoccupied, save when some stray cow or vagrant hog had sought shelter within its walls from the chill rains and nipping winds of winter.

One day my wife requested me to build her a new kitchen. The house erected by us, when we first came to live upon the vineyard, contained a very conveniently arranged kitchen; but for some occult reason my wife wanted a kitchen in the back yard, apart from the dwelling-house, after the usual Southern fashion. Of course I had to build it.

To save expense, I decided to tear down the old schoolhouse, and use the lumber, which was in a good state of preservation, in the construction of the new kitchen. Before demolishing the old house, however, I made an estimate of the amount of material contained in it, and found that I would have to buy several hundred feet of lumber additional, in order to build the new kitchen according to my wife's plan.

One morning old Julius McAdoo, our colored coachman, harnessed the gray mare to the rockaway, and drove my wife and me over to the sawmill from which I meant to order the new lumber. We drove down the long lane which led from our house to the plank-road; following the plank-road for about a mile, we turned into a road running through the forest and across the swamp to the sawmill beyond. Our carriage jolted over the half-rotted corduroy road which traversed the swamp, and then climbed the long hill leading to the sawmill. When we reached the mill, the foreman had gone over to a neighboring farmhouse, probably to smoke or gossip, and we were compelled to await his return before we could transact our business. We remained seated in the carriage, a few rods from the mill, and watched the leisurely movements of the mill-hands. We had not waited long before a huge pine log was placed in position, the machinery of the mill was set in motion, and the circular saw began to eat its way through the log, with a loud whir which resounded throughout the vicinity of the mill. The sound rose and fell in a sort of rhythmic cadence, which, heard from where we sat, was not unpleasing, and not loud enough to prevent conversation. When the saw started on its second journey through the log, Julius observed, in a lugubrious tone, and with a perceptible shudder:—

"Ugh! but dat des do cuddle my blood!"

"What's the matter, Uncle Julius?" inquired my wife, who is of a very sympathetic turn of mind. "Does the noise affect your nerves?"

"No, Mis' Annie," replied the old man, with emotion, "I ain' narvous; but dat saw, a-cuttin' en grindin' thoo dat stick er timber, en moanin', en groanin,' en sweekin', kyars my 'memb'ance back ter ole times, en 'min's me er po' Sandy." The pathetic intonation with which he lengthened out the "po' Sandy" touched a responsive chord in our own hearts.

"And who was poor Sandy?" asked my wife, who takes a deep interest in the stories of plantation life which she hears from the lips of the older colored people. Some of these stories are quaintly humorous; others wildly extravagant, revealing the Oriental cast of the negro's imagination; while others, poured freely into the sympathetic ear of a Northern-bred woman, disclose many a tragic incident of the darker side of slavery.

"Sandy," said Julius, in reply to my wife's question, "was a nigger w'at useter b'long ter ole Mars Marrabo McSwayne. Mars Marrabo's place wuz on de yuther side'n de swamp, right nex 'ter yo' place. Sandy wuz a monst'us good nigger, en could do so many things erbout a plantation, en alluz 'ten' ter his wuk so well, dat w'en Mars Marrabo's chilluns growed up en married off, dey all un 'em wanted dey daddy fer ter gin 'em Sandy fer a weddin' present. But Mars Marrabo knowed de res' would n' be satisfied ef he gin Sandy ter a'er one un 'em; so w'en dey wuz all done married, he fix it by 'lowin' one er his chilluns ter take Sandy fer a mont' er so, en den ernudder for a mont' er so, en so on dat erway tel dey had all had 'im de same lenk er time; en den dey would all take him roun' ag'in, 'cep'n' oncet in a w'ile w'en Mars Marrabo would len' 'im ter some er his yuther kinfolks 'roun' de country, w'en dey wuz short er han's; tel bimeby it got so Sandy did n' hardly knowed whar he wuz gwine ter stay fum one week's een' ter de yuther.

"One time w'en Sandy wuz lent out ez yushal, a spekilater come erlong wid a lot er niggers, en Mars Marrabo swap' Sandy's wife off fer a noo 'oman. W'en Sandy come back, Mars Marrabo gin 'im a dollar, en 'lowed he wuz monst'us sorry fer ter break up de fambly, but de spekilater had gin 'im big boot, en times wuz hard en money skase, en so he wuz bleedst ter make de trade. Sandy tuk on some 'bout losin' his wife, but he soon seed dey want no use cryin' ober spilt mer-lasses; en bein' ez he lacked de looks er de noo 'oman, he tuk up wid her atter she'd be'n on de plantation a mont' er so.

"Sandy en his noo wife got on mighty well tergedder, en de niggers all 'mence' ter talk about how lovin' dey wuz. W'en Tenie wuz tuk sick oncet, Sandy useter set up all night wid 'er, en den go ter wuk in de mawnin' des lack he had his reg'lar sleep; en Tenie would 'a' done anythin' in de worl' for her Sandy.

"Sandy en Tenie had n' be'n libbin' tergedder fer mo' d'n two mont's befo' Mars Marrabo's old uncle, w'at libbed down in Robeson County, sent up ter fin' out ef Mars Marrabo could n' len' 'im er hire 'im a good han' fer a mont' er so. Sandy's marster wuz one er dese yer easy-gwine folks w'at wanter please eve'y-body, en he says yas, he could len' 'im Sandy. En Mars Marrabo tol' Sandy fer ter git ready ter go down ter Robeson nex' day, fer ter stay a mont' er so.

"It wuz monst'us hard on Sandy fer ter take 'im 'way fum Tenie. It wuz so fur down ter Robeson dat he did n' hab no chance er comin' back ter see her tel de time wuz up; he would n' 'a' mine comin' ten er fifteen mile at night ter see Tenie, but Mars Marrabo's uncle's plantation wuz mo' d'n forty mile off. Sandy wuz mighty sad en cas' down atter w'at Mars Marrabo tol' 'im, en he says ter Tenie, sezee:—

"'I'm gittin' monst'us ti'ed er dish yer gwine roun' so much. Here I is lent ter Mars Jeems dis mont', en I got ter do so-en-so; en ter Mars Archie de nex' mont', en I got ter do so-en-so; den I got ter go ter Miss Jinnie's: en hit 's Sandy dis en Sandy dat, en Sandy yer en Sandy dere, tel it 'pears ter me I ain' got no home, ner no marster, ner no mistiss, ner no nuffin. I can't eben keep a wife: my yuther ole 'oman wuz sol' away widout my gittin' a chance fer ter tell her good-by; en now I got ter go off en leab you, Tenie, en I dunno whe'r I'm eber gwine ter see you ag'in er no. I wisht I wuz a tree, er a stump, er a rock, er sump'n w'at could stay on de plantation fer a w'ile.'

"Atter Sandy got thoo talkin', Tenie did n' say naer word, but des sot dere by de fier, studyin' en studyin'. Bimeby she up'n' says:—

"'Sandy, is I eber tol' you I wuz a cunjuh 'oman?'

"Co'se Sandy had n' nebber dremp' er nuffin lack dat, en he made a great 'miration w'en he hear w'at Tenie say. Bimeby Tenie went on:—

"'I ain' goophered nobody, ner done no cunjuh wuk, fer fifteen year er mo'; en w'en I got religion I made up my mine I would n' wuk no mo' goopher. But dey is some things I doan b'lieve it 's no sin fer ter do; en ef you doan wanter be sent roun' fum pillar ter pos', en ef you doan wanter go down ter Robeson, I kin fix things so you won't haf ter. Ef you'll des say de word, I kin turn you ter w'ateber you wanter be, en you kin stay right whar you wanter, ez long ez you mineter.'

"Sandy say he doan keer; he's willin' fer ter do anythin' fer ter stay close ter Tenie. Den Tenie ax 'im ef he doan wanter be turnt inter a rabbit.

"Sandy say, 'No, de dogs mought git atter me.'

"'Shill I turn you ter a wolf?' sez Tenie.

"'No, eve'ybody's skeered er a wolf, en I doan want nobody ter be skeered er me.'

"'Shill I turn you ter a mawkin'-bird?'

"'No, a hawk mought ketch me. I wanter be turnt inter sump'n w'at 'll stay in one place.'

"'I kin turn you ter a tree,' sez Tenie. 'You won't hab no mouf ner years, but I kin turn you back oncet in a w'ile, so you kin git sump'n ter eat, en hear w'at's gwine on.'

"Well, Sandy say dat'll do. En so Tenie tuk 'im down by de aidge er de swamp, not fur fum de quarters, en turnt 'im inter a big pine-tree, en sot 'im out 'mongs' some yuther trees. En de nex' mawnin', ez some er de fiel' han's wuz gwine long dere, dey seed a tree w'at dey did n' 'member er habbin' seed befo'; it wuz monst'us quare, en dey wuz bleedst ter 'low dat dey had n' 'membered right, er e'se one er de saplin's had be'n growin' monst'us fas'.

"W'en Mars Marrabo 'skiver' dat Sandy wuz gone, he 'lowed Sandy had runned away. He got de dogs out, but de las' place dey could track Sandy ter wuz de foot er dat pine-tree. En dere de dogs stood en barked, en bayed, en pawed at de tree, en tried ter climb up on it; en w'en dey wuz tuk roun' thoo de swamp ter look fer de scent, dey broke loose en made fer dat tree ag'in. It wuz de beatenis' thing de w'ite folks eber hearn of, en Mars Marrabo 'lowed dat Sandy must 'a' clim' up on de tree en jump' off on a mule er sump'n, en rid fur ernuff fer ter spile de scent. Mars Marrabo wanted ter 'cuse some er de yuther niggers er heppin' Sandy off, but dey all 'nied it ter de las'; en eve'ybody knowed Tenie sot too much sto' by Sandy fer ter he'p 'im run away whar she could n' nebber see 'im no mo'.

"W'en Sandy had be'n gone long ernuff fer folks ter think he done got clean away, Tenie useter go down ter de woods at night en turn 'im back, en den dey'd slip up ter de cabin en set by de fire en talk. But dey ha' ter be monst'us keerful, er e'se somebody would 'a' seed 'em, en dat would 'a' spile' de whole thing; so Tenie alluz turnt Sandy back in de mawnin' early, befo' anybody wuz a-stirrin'.

"But Sandy did n' git erlong widout his trials en tribberlations. One day a woodpecker come erlong en 'mence' ter peck at de tree; en de nex' time Sandy wuz turnt back he had a little roun' hole in his arm, des lack a sharp stick be'n stuck in it. Atter dat Tenie sot a sparrer-hawk fer ter watch de tree; en w'en de woodpecker come erlong nex' mawnin' fer ter finish his nes', he got gobble' up mos' 'fo' he stuck his bill in de bark.

"Nudder time, Mars Marrabo sent a nigger out in de woods fer ter chop tuppentime boxes. De man chop a box in dish yer tree, en hack' de bark up two er th'ee feet, fer ter let de tuppentime run. De nex' time Sandy wuz turnt back he had a big skyar on his lef' leg, des lack it be'n skint; en it tuk Tenie nigh 'bout all night fer ter fix a mixtry ter kyo it up. Atter dat, Tenie sot a hawnet fer ter watch de tree; en w'en de nigger come back ag'in fer ter cut ernudder box on de yuther side'n de tree, de hawnet stung 'im so hard dat de ax slip en cut his foot nigh 'bout off.

"W'en Tenie see so many things happenin' ter de tree, she 'cluded she'd ha' ter turn Sandy ter sump'n e'se; en atter studyin' de matter ober, en talkin' wid Sandy one ebenin', she made up her mine fer ter fix up a goopher mixtry w'at would turn herse'f en Sandy ter foxes, er sump'n, so dey could run away en go some'rs whar dey could be free en lib lack w'ite folks.

"But dey ain' no tellin' w'at 's gwine ter happen in dis worl'. Tenie had got de night sot fer her en Sandy ter run away, w'en dat ve'y day one er Mars Marrabo's sons rid up ter de big house in his buggy, en say his wife wuz monst'us sick, en he want his mammy ter len' 'im a 'oman fer ter nuss his wife. Tenie's mistiss say sen' Tenie; she wuz a good nuss. Young mars wuz in a tarrible hurry fer ter git back home. Tenie wuz washin' at de big house dat day, en her mistiss say she should go right 'long wid her young marster. Tenie tried ter make some 'scuse fer ter git away en hide 'tel night, w'en she would have eve'ything fix' up fer her en Sandy; she say she wanter go ter her cabin fer ter git her bonnet. Her mistiss say it doan matter 'bout de bonnet; her head-hankcher wuz good ernuff. Den Tenie say she wanter git her bes' frock; her mistiss say no, she doan need no mo' frock, en w'en dat one got dirty she could git a clean one whar she wuz gwine. So Tenie had ter git in de buggy en go 'long wid young Mars Dunkin ter his plantation, w'ich wuz mo' d'n twenty mile away; en dey wa'n't no chance er her seein' Sandy no mo' 'tel she come back home. De po' gal felt monst'us bad 'bout de way things wuz gwine on, en she knowed Sandy mus' be a wond'rin' why she did n' come en turn 'im back no mo'.

"W'iles Tenie wuz away nussin' young Mars Dunkin's wife, Mars Marrabo tuk a notion fer ter buil' 'im a noo kitchen; en bein' ez he had lots er timber on his place, he begun ter look 'roun' 'fer a tree ter hab de lumber sawed out'n. En I dunno how it come to be so, but he happen fer ter hit on de ve'y tree w'at Sandy wuz turnt inter. Tenie wuz gone, en dey wa'n't nobody ner nuffin fer ter watch de tree.

"De two men w'at cut de tree down say dey nebber had sech a time wid a tree befo': dey axes would glansh off, en did n' 'pear ter make no progress thoo de wood; en of all de creakin', en shakin', en wobblin' you eber see, dat tree done it w'en it commence' ter fall. It wuz de beatenis' thing!

"W'en dey got de tree all trim' up, dey chain it up ter a timber waggin, en start fer de sawmill. But dey had a hard time gittin' de log dere: fus' dey got stuck in de mud w'en dey wuz gwine crosst de swamp, en it wuz two er th'ee hours befo' dey could git out. W'en dey start' on ag'in, de chain kep' a-comin' loose, en dey had ter keep a-stoppin' en a-stoppin' fer ter hitch de log up ag'in. W'en dey commence' ter climb de hill ter de sawmill, de log broke loose, en roll down de hill en in 'mongs' de trees, en hit tuk nigh 'bout half a day mo' ter git it haul' up ter de sawmill.

"De nex' mawnin' atter de day de tree wuz haul' ter de sawmill, Tenie come home. W'en she got back ter her cabin, de fus' thing she done wuz ter run down ter de woods en see how Sandy wuz gittin' on. W'en she seed de stump standin' dere, wid de sap runnin' out'n it, en de limbs layin' scattered roun', she nigh 'bout went out'n her min'. She run ter her cabin, en got her goopher mixtry, en den follered de track er de timber waggin ter de sawmill. She knowed Sandy could n' lib mo' d'n a minute er so ef she turnt him back, fer he wuz all chop' up so he 'd 'a' be'n bleedst ter die. But she wanted ter turn 'im back long ernuff fer ter 'splain ter 'im dat she had n' went off a-purpose, en lef' 'im ter be chop' down en sawed up. She did n' want Sandy ter die wid no hard feelin's to'ds her.

"De han's at de sawmill had des got de big log on de kerridge, en wuz startin' up de saw, w'en dey seed a 'oman runnin' up de hill, all out er bref, cryin' en gwine on des lack she wuz plumb 'stracted. It wuz Tenie; she come right inter de mill, en th'owed herse'f on de log, right in front er de saw, a-hollerin' en cryin' ter her Sandy ter fergib her, en not ter think hard er her, fer it wa'n't no fault er hern. Den Tenie 'membered de tree did n' hab no years, en she wuz gittin' ready fer ter wuk her goopher mixtry so ez ter turn Sandy back, w'en de mill-hands kotch holt er her en tied her arms wid a rope, en fasten' her to one er de posts in de sawmill; en den dey started de saw up ag'in, en cut de log up inter bo'ds en scantlin's right befo' her eyes. But it wuz mighty hard wuk; fer of all de sweekin, en moanin', en groanin', dat log done it w'iles de saw wuz a-cuttin' thoo it. De saw wuz one er dese yer ole-timey, up-en-down saws, en hit tuk longer dem days ter saw a log 'en it do now. Dey greased de saw, but dat did n' stop de fuss; hit kep' right on, tel fin'ly dey got de log all sawed up.

"W'en de berseah w'at run de sawmill come fum breakfas', de han's up en tell him 'bout de crazy 'oman—ez dey s'posed she wuz—w'at had come runnin' in de sawmill, a-hollerin' en gwine on, en tried ter th'ow herse'f befo' de saw. En de oberseah sent two er th'ee er de han's fer ter take Tenie back ter her marster's plantation.

"Tenie 'peared ter be out'n her min' fer a long time, en her marster ha' ter lock her up in de smoke-'ouse 'tel she got ober her spells. Mars Marrabo wuz monst'us mad, en hit would 'a' made yo' flesh crawl fer ter hear him cuss, 'caze he say de spekilater w'at he got Tenie fum had fooled 'im by wukkin' a crazy 'oman off on him. W'iles Tenie wuz lock up in de smoke-'ouse, Mars Marrabo tuk 'n' haul de lumber fum de sawmill, en put up his noo kitchen.

"W'en Tenie got quiet' down, so she could be 'lowed ter go 'roun' de plantation, she up'n' tole her marster all erbout Sandy en de pine-tree; en w'en Mars Marrabo hearn it, he 'lowed she wuz de wuss 'stracted nigger he eber hearn of. He did n' know w'at ter do wid Tenie: fus' he thought he'd put her in de po 'house; but fin'ly, seein' ez she did n' do no harm ter nobody ner nuffin, but des went 'roun' moanin', en groanin', en shakin' her head, he 'cluded ter let her stay on de plantation en nuss de little nigger chilluns w'en dey mammies wuz ter wuk in de cotton-fiel'.

"De noo kitchen Mars Marrabo buil' wuz n' much use, fer it had n' be'n put up long befo' de niggers 'mence' ter notice quare things erbout it. Dey could hear sump'n moanin' en groanin' 'bout de kitchen in de night-time, en w'en de win' would blow dey could hear sump'n a-hollerin' en sweekin' lack it wuz in great pain en sufferin'. En it got so atter a w'ile dat it wuz all Mars Marrabo's wife could do ter git a 'oman ter stay in de kitchen in de daytime long ernuff ter do de cookin'; en dey wa'n't naer nigger on de plantation w'at would n' rudder take forty dan ter go 'bout dat kitchen atter dark,—dat is, 'cep'n' Tenie; she did n' 'pear ter min' de ha'nts. She useter slip 'roun' at night, en set on de kitchen steps, en lean up agin de do'-jamb, en run on ter herse'f wid some kine er foolishness w'at nobody could n' make out; fer Mars Marrabo had th'eaten' ter sen' her off'n de plantation ef she say anything ter any er de yuther niggers 'bout de pine-tree. But somehow er 'nudder de niggers foun' out all erbout it, en dey all knowed de kitchen wuz ha'nted by Sandy's sperrit. En bimeby hit got so Mars Marrabo's wife herse'f wuz skeered ter go out in de yard atter dark.

"W'en it come ter dat, Mars Marrabo tuk en to' de kitchen down, en use' de lumber fer ter buil' dat ole school'ouse w'at you er talkin' 'bout pullin' down. De school'ouse wuz n' use' 'cep'n' in de daytime, en on dark nights folks gwine 'long de road would hear quare soun's en see quare things. Po' ole Tenie useter go down dere at night, en wander 'roun' de school'ouse; en de niggers all 'lowed she went fer ter talk wid Sandy's sperrit. En one winter mawnin', w'en one er de boys went ter school early fer ter start de fire, w'at should he fin' but po' ole Tenie, layin' on de flo', stiff, en col', en dead. Dere did n' 'pear ter be nuffin pertickler de matter wid her,—she had des grieve' herse'f ter def fer her Sandy. Mars Marrabo did n' shed no tears. He thought Tenie wuz crazy, en dey wa'n't no tellin' w'at she mought do nex'; en dey ain' much room in dis worl' fer crazy w'ite folks, let 'lone a crazy nigger.

"Hit wa'n't long atter dat befo' Mars Marrabo sol' a piece er his track er lan' ter Mars Dugal' McAdoo,—*my* ole marster,—en dat's how de ole school'ouse happen to be on yo' place. W'en de wah broke out, de school stop', en de ole school'ouse be'n stannin' empty ever sence,—dat is, 'cep'n' fer de ha'nts. En folks sez dat de ole school'ouse, er any yuther house w'at got any er dat lumber in it w'at wuz sawed out'n de tree w'at Sandy wuz turnt inter, is gwine ter be ha'nted tel de las' piece er plank is rotted en crumble' inter dus'."

Annie had listened to this gruesome narrative with strained attention.

"What a system it was," she exclaimed, when Julius had finished, under which such things were possible!"

"What things?" I asked, in amazement. "Are you seriously considering the possibility of a man's being turned into a tree?"

"Oh, no," she replied quickly, "not that;" and then she murmured absently, and with a dim look in her fine eyes, "Poor Tenie!"

We ordered the lumber, and returned home. That night, after we had gone to bed, and my wife had to all appearances been sound asleep for half an hour, she startled me out of an incipient doze by exclaiming suddenly,—

"John, I don't believe I want my new kitchen built out of the lumber in that old schoolhouse."

"You would n't for a moment allow yourself," I replied, with some asperity, "to be influenced by that absurdly impossible yarn which Julius was spinning to-day?"

"I know the story is absurd," she replied dreamily, "and I am not so silly as to believe it. But I don't think I should ever be able to take any pleasure in that kitchen if it were built out of that lumber. Besides, I think the kitchen would look better and last longer if the lumber were all new."

Of course she had her way. I bought the new lumber, though not without grumbling. A week or two later I was called away from home on business. On my return, after an absence of several days, my wife remarked to me,—

"John, there has been a split in the Sandy Run Colored Baptist Church, on the temperance question. About half the members have come out from the main body, and set up for themselves. Uncle Julius is one of the seceders, and he came to me yesterday and asked if they might not hold their meetings in the old schoolhouse for the present."

"I hope you did n't let the old rascal have it," I returned, with some warmth. I had just received a bill for the new lumber I had bought.

"Well," she replied, "I could n't refuse him the use of the house for so good a purpose."

"And I'll venture to say," I continued, "that you subscribed something toward the support of the new church?"

She did not attempt to deny it.

"What are they going to do about the ghost?" I asked, somewhat curious to know how Julius would get around this obstacle.

"Oh," replied Annie, "Uncle Julius says that ghosts never disturb religious worship, but that if Sandy's spirit *should* happen to stray into meeting by mistake, no doubt the preaching would do it good."

⚜ PAULINE E. HOPKINS (1859–1930)

An editor, activist, and novelist, Pauline E. Hopkins stands as one of the pioneers in the development of the African American novel. Although Portland, Maine, was her birth-place, Hopkins lived in Boston during her childhood and the majority of her adulthood. In novels such as Hagar's Daughter: A Story of Southern Caste Prejudice, *she focuses on themes such as color prejudice, gender roles for women, education, and uplift for African Americans.*

When she worked as an editor of Colored American Magazine, *she helped to shape a philosophy of self-determination and advocating of equal rights for African Americans. In 1916, Hopkins attempted another foray into publishing as editor of* New Era, *a Boston-based publication. Hopkins died of burns caused by a fire from her stove. Her work with the African American press, her novels, and her activism had helped pave the way for later African American writers in the twentieth century.*

From Hagar's Daughter: A Story of Southern Caste Prejudice (1901–1903)

Chapter 1

In the fall of 1860 a stranger visiting the United States would have thought that nothing short of a miracle could preserve the union of states so proudly proclaimed by the signers of the Declaration of Independence, and so gloriously maintained by the gallant Washington.

The nomination of Abraham Lincoln for the presidency by the Republican party was inevitable. The proslavery Democracy was drunk with rage at the prospect of losing control of the situation, which, up to that time, had needed scarcely an effort to bind in riveted chains impenetrable alike to the power of man or the frowns of the Godhead; they had inaugurated a system of mob-law and terrorism against all sympathizers with the despised party. The columns of partisan newspapers teemed each day in the year with descriptions of disgraceful scenes enacted North and South by proslavery men, due more to the long-accustomed subserviency of Northern people to the slaveholders than to a real, personal hatred of the Negro.

The free negroes North and South, and those slaves with the hearts of freemen who had boldly taken the liberty denied by man, felt the general spirit of unrest and uncertainty which was spreading over the country to such an alarming extent. The subdued tone of the liberal portion of the press, the humiliating offers of compromise from Northern political leaders, and the numerous cases of surrendering fugitive slaves to their former masters, sent a thrill of mortal fear into the very heart of many a household where peace and comfort had reigned for many years. The fugitive slave had perhaps won the heart of some Northern free woman; they had married, prospered, and were happy. Now came the haunting dread of a stealthy tread, an ominous knock, a muffled cry at midnight, and the sunlight of the new day would smile upon a broken-hearted woman with baby hands clinging to her skirts, and children's voices asking in vain for their father lost to them forever. The Negro felt that there was no safety for him beneath the Stars and Stripes, and, so feeling, sacrificed his home and personal effects and fled to Canada.

The Southerners were in earnest, and would listen to no proposals in favor of their continuance in the Union under existing conditions; namely, Lincoln and the Republican party. The vast wealth of the South made them feel that they were independent of the world. Cotton was not merely king; it was God. Moral considerations were nothing. Drunk with power and dazzled with prosperity, monopolizing cotton and raising it to the influence of a veritable fetich, the authors of the Rebellion did not admit a doubt of the success of their attack on the Federal government. They dreamed of perpetuating slavery, though all history shows the decline of the system as industry, commerce, and knowledge advance. The slaveholders proposed nothing less than to reverse the currents of humanity, and to make barbarism flourish in the bosom of civilization.

The South argued that the principle of right would have no influence over starving operatives; and England and France, as well as the Eastern States of the Union, would stand aghast, and yield to the master stroke which should deprive them of the material of their labor. Millions of the laboring class were dependent upon it in all the great centers of civilization; it was only necessary to wave this sceptre over the nations and all of them would acknowledge the power which wielded it. But, alas! the supreme error of this anticipation was in omitting from the calculation the power of principle. Right still had authority in the councils of nations. Factories might be closed, men and women out of employment, but truth and justice still commanded respect among men. The proslavery men in the North encouraged the rebels before the breaking out of the war. They promised the South that civil war should reign in every free state in case of an uprising of the Southern oligarchy, and that men should not be permitted to go South to put down their brothers in rebellion.

Weak as were the Southern people in point of numbers and political power, compared with those of the North, yet they easily persuaded themselves that they could successfully cope in arms with a Northern foe, whom they affected to despise for his cowardly and mercenary disposition. They indulged the belief, in proud confidence, that their great political prestige would continue to serve them among party associates at the North, and that the counsels of the adversary would be distracted and his power weakened by the effects of dissension.

When the Republican banner bearing the names of Abraham Lincoln for President and Hannibal Hamlin for Vice-President flung its folds to the breeze in 1860, there was a panic of apprehension at such bold manœuvering; mob-law reigned in Boston, Utica and New York City, which witnessed the greatest destruction of property in the endeavor to put down the growing public desire to abolish slavery. Elijah Lovejoy's innocent blood spoke in trumpet tones to the reformer from his quiet grave by the rolling river. William Lloyd Garrison's outraged manhood brought the blush of shame to the cheek of the honest American who loved his country's honor better than any individual institution. The memory of Charles Sumner's brutal beating by Preston Brooks stamped the mad passions of the hour indelibly upon history's page. Debate in the Senate became fiery and dangerous as the crisis approached in the absorbing question of the perpetuation of slavery.

At the South laws were enacted abridging the freedom of speech and press; it was difficult for Northerners to travel in slave states. Rev. Charles T. Torrey was sentenced to the Maryland penitentiary for aiding slaves to escape; Jonathan Walker had been branded with a red-hot iron for the same offense. In the midst of the tumult came the "Dred Scott Decision," and the smouldering fire broke forth with renewed vigor. Each side waited impatiently for the result of the balloting.

In November the Rubicon was passed, and Abraham Lincoln was duly elected President contrary to the wishes and in defiance of the will of the haughty South. There was much talk of a conspiracy to prevent by fraud or violence a declaration of the result of the election by the Vice-President before the two Houses, as provided by law. As the eventful day drew near patriotic hearts were sick with fear or filled with forebodings. Would the certificates fail to appear; would they be wrested by violence from the hands ordered to bear them across the rotunda from the Senate Chamber to the hall of the House, or would they be suppressed by the only official who could open them, John C. Breckenridge of Kentucky, himself a candidate and in full sympathy with the rebellion.

A breathless silence, painfully intense, reigned in the crowded chamber as the Vice-President arose to declare the result of the election. Six feet in height, lofty in carriage, youthful, dashing, he stood before them pale and nervous. The galleries were packed with hostile conspirators. It was the supreme moment in the life of the Republic. With unfaltering utterance his voice broke the oppressive stillness:

"I therefore declare Abraham Lincoln duly elected President of the United States for the term of four years from the fourth of March next."

It was the signal for secession, and the South let loose the dogs of war.

ANNA JULIA COOPER (1859–1964)

Born in Raleigh, North Carolina, Anna Julia Cooper was the daughter of a slave. Anna was educated at St. Augustine Normal School and Collegiate Institute, and in 1877 she married one of her teachers, George A. C. Cooper. By 1881, Cooper (a widow since her husband's death in 1879) was attending Oberlin College in Ohio. Earning a degree in 1884, she accepted a position in Ohio at Wilberforce University, but she stayed only a year, leaving to take a position at St. Augustine. After being awarded an M.A. from Oberlin College, she relocated to Washington, D.C., to teach at M Street School, where she served as principal from 1901 to 1906. Her speeches and essays were collected in A Voice from the South: By a Black Woman of the South *(1892)*. *She advocated civil rights, women's rights, suffrage for women, and an American literature that would be more inclusive and would render respectful images of African Americans. Believing in the importance of education for black Americans, she became one of the first African American women to receive a Ph.D. when she earned a doctorate from the Sorbonne at age 65. Cooper gave a voice to the disenfranchised black women of the nineteenth century while anticipating the feminist movement of the twentieth century.*

From A Voice from the South: By a Black Woman of the South (1892)

The Status of Woman in America

Just four hundred years ago an obscure dreamer and castle builder, prosaically poor and ridiculously insistent on the reality of his dreams, was enabled through the devotion of a noble woman to give to civilization a magnificent continent.

What the lofty purpose of Spain's pure-minded queen had brought to the birth, the untiring devotion of pioneer women nourished and developed. The dangers of wild beasts and of wilder men, the mysteries of unknown wastes and unexplored forests, the horrors of pestilence and famine, of exposure and loneliness, during all those years of discovery and settlement, were braved without a murmur by women who had been most delicately constituted and most tenderly nurtured.

And when the times of physical hardship and danger were past, when the work of clearing and opening up was over and the struggle for accumulation began, again woman's inspiration and help were needed and still was she loyally at hand. A Mary Lyon, demanding and making possible equal advantages of education for women as for men, and, in the face of discouragement and incredulity, bequeathing to women the opportunities of Holyoke.[1]

A Dorothea Dix,[2] insisting on the humane and rational treatment of the insane and bringing about a reform in the lunatic asylums of the country, making a great step forward in the tender regard for the weak by the strong throughout the world.

A Helen Hunt Jackson,[3] convicting the nation of a century of dishonor in regard to the Indian.

A Lucretia Mott,[4] gentle Quaker spirit, with sweet insistence, preaching the abolition of slavery and the institution, in its stead, of the brotherhood of man;

---

[1]Holyoke refers to Mount Holyoke College, a women's college in South Hadley, Massachusetts, founded in 1837 by Mary Lyon. Originally, the school was called Mount Holyoke Seminary, and it became a college in 1893.

[2]Dorothea Dix (1804–1887) was an educator, writer, and social reformer. She worked as a tireless advocate for the rights of the mentally ill.

[3]Helen Hunt Jackson (1803–1885) was a novelist, poet, essayist, and champion of equal rights for Native Americans.

[4]Lucretia Mott (1793–1880) was a Quaker minister, an educator, and an abolitionist. She advocated for women's rights.

her life and words breathing out in tender melody the injunction

Have love. Not love alone for one
But man as man thy brother call;
And scatter, like the circling sun,
Thy charities *on all*.

And at the most trying time of what we have called the Accumulative Period, when internecine war, originated through man's love of gain and his determination to subordinate national interests and black men's rights alike to considerations of personal profit and loss, was drenching our country with its own best blood, who shall recount the name and fame of the women on both sides the senseless strife,—those uncomplaining souls with a great heart ache of their own, rigid features and pallid cheek their ever effective flag of truce, on the battle field, in the camp, in the hospital, binding up wounds, recording dying whispers for absent loved ones, with tearful eyes pointing to man's last refuge, giving the last earthly hand clasp and performing the last friendly office for strangers whom a great common sorrow had made kin, while they knew that somewhere—somewhere a husband, a brother, a father, a son, was being tended by stranger hands—or mayhap those familiar eyes were even then being closed forever by just such another ministering angel of mercy and love.

But why mention names? Time would fail to tell of the noble army of women who shine like beacon lights in the otherwise sordid wilderness of this accumulative period—prison reformers and tenement cleansers, quiet unnoted workers in hospitals and homes, among imbeciles, among outcasts—the sweetening, purifying antidotes for the poisons of man's acquisitiveness,—mollifying and soothing with the tenderness of compassion and love the wounds and bruises caused by his overreaching and avarice.

The desire for quick returns and large profits tempts capital ofttimes into unsanitary, well nigh inhuman investments,—tenement tinder boxes, stifling, stunting, sickening alleys and pestiferous slums; regular rents, no waiting, large percentages,—rich coffers coined out of the life-blood of human bodies and souls. Men and women herded together like cattle, breathing in malaria and typhus from an atmosphere seething with moral as well as physical impurity, revelling in vice as their native habitat and then, to drown the whisperings of their higher consciousness and effectually to hush the yearnings and accusations within, flying to narcotics and opiates—rum, tobacco, opium, binding hand and foot, body and soul, till the proper image of God is transformed into a fit associate for demons,—a besotted, enervated, idiotic wreck, or else a monster of wickedness terrible and destructive.

These are some of the legitimate products of the unmitigated tendencies of the wealth-producing period. But, thank Heaven, side by side with the cold, mathematical, selfishly calculating, so-called practical and unsentimental instinct of the business man, there comes the sympathetic warmth and sunshine of good women, like the sweet and sweetening breezes of spring, cleansing, purifying, soothing, inspiring, lifting the drunkard from the gutter, the outcast from the pit. Who can estimate the influence of these "daughters of the king," these lend-a-hand forces, in counteracting the selfishness of an acquisitive age?

To-day America counts her millionaires by the thousand; questions of tariff and questions of currency are the most vital ones agitating the public mind. In this period, when material prosperity and well earned ease and luxury are assured facts from a national standpoint, woman's work and woman's influence are needed as never before; needed to bring a heart power into this money getting, dollar-worshipping civilization; needed to bring a moral force into the utilitarian motives and interests of the time; needed to stand for God and Home and Native Land *versus gain and greed and grasping selfishness.*

There can be no doubt that this fourth centenary of America's discovery which we celebrate at Chicago, strikes the keynote of another important transition in the history of this nation; and the prominence of woman in the management of its celebration is a fitting tribute to the part she is destined to play among the forces of the future. This is the first congressional recognition of woman in this country, and this Board of Lady Managers constitute the first women legally appointed by any government to act in a national capacity. This of itself marks the dawn of a new day.

Now the periods of discovery, of settlement, of developing resources and accumulating wealth have passed in rapid succession. Wealth in the nation as in the individual brings leisure, repose, reflection. The struggle with nature is over, the struggle with ideas begins. We stand then, it seems to me, in this last decade of the nineteenth century, just in the portals of a new and untried movement on a higher plain and in a grander strain than any the past has called forth. It does not require a prophet's eye to divine its trend and image its possibilities from the forces we see already at work around us; nor is it hard to guess what must be the status of woman's work under the new regime.

In the pioneer days her role was that of a camp-follower, an additional something to fight for and be burdened with, only repaying the anxiety and labor she called forth by her own incomparable gifts of sympathy and appreciative love; unable herself ordinarily to contend with the bear and the Indian, or to take active part in clearing the wilderness and constructing the home.

In the second or wealth producing period her work is abreast of man's, complementing and supplementing, counteracting excessive tendencies, and mollifying over rigorous proclivities.

In the era now about to dawn, her sentiments must strike the keynote and give the dominant tone. And this because of the nature of her contribution to the world.

Her kingdom is not over physical forces. Not by might, nor by power can she prevail. Her position must ever be inferior where strength of muscle creates leadership. If she follows the instincts of her nature, however, she must always stand for the conservation of those deeper moral forces which make for the happiness of homes and the righteousness of the country. In a reign of moral ideas she is easily queen.

There is to my mind no grander and surer prophecy of the new era and of woman's place in it, than the work already begun in the waning years of the nineteenth century by the W.C.T.U.[5] in America, an organization which has even now reached not only national but international importance, and seems destined to

---

[5] W.C.T.U. refers to Women's Christian Temperance Union.

permeate and purify the whole civilized world. It is the living embodiment of woman's activities and woman's ideas, and its extent and strength rightly prefigure her increasing power as a moral factor.

The colored woman of to-day occupies, one may say, a unique position in this country. In a period of itself transitional and unsettled, her status seems one of the least ascertainable and definitive of all the forces which make for our civilization. She is confronted by both a woman question and a race problem, and is as yet an unknown or an unacknowledged factor in both. While the women of the white race can with calm assurance enter upon the work they feel by nature appointed to do, while their men give loyal support and appreciative countenance to their efforts, recognizing in most avenues of usefulness the propriety and the need of woman's distinctive co-operation, the colored woman too often finds herself hampered and shamed by a less liberal sentiment and a more conservative attitude on the part of those for whose opinion she cares most. That this is not universally true I am glad to admit. There are to be found both intensely conservative white men and exceedingly liberal colored men. But as far as my experience goes the average man of our race is less frequently ready to admit the actual need among the sturdier forces of the world for woman's help or influence. That great social and economic questions await her interference, that she could throw any light on problems of national import, that her intermeddling could improve the management of school systems, or elevate the tone of public institutions, or humanize and sanctify the far reaching influence of prisons and reformatories and improve the treatment of lunatics and imbeciles,—that she has a word worth hearing on mooted questions in political economy, that she could contribute a suggestion on the relations of labor and capital, or offer a thought on honest money and honorable trade, I fear the majority of "Americans of the colored variety" are not yet prepared to concede. It may be that they do not yet see these questions in their right perspective, being absorbed in the immediate needs of their own political complications. A good deal depends on where we put the emphasis in this world; and our men are not perhaps to blame if they see everything colored by the light of those agitations in the midst of which they live and move and have their being. The part they have had to play in American history during the last twenty-five or thirty years has tended rather to exaggerate the importance of mere political advantage, as well as to set a fictitious valuation on those able to secure such advantage. It is the astute politician, the manager who can gain preferment for himself and his favorites, the demagogue known to stand in with the powers at the White House and consulted on the bestowal of government plums, whom we set in high places and denominate great. It is they who receive the hosannas of the multitude and are regarded as leaders of the people. The thinker and the doer, the man who solves the problem by enriching his country with an invention worth thousands or by a thought inestimable and precious is given neither bread nor a stone. He is too often left to die in obscurity and neglect even if spared in his life the bitterness of fanatical jealousies and detraction.

And yet politics, and surely American politics, is hardly a school for great minds. Sharpening rather than deepening, it develops the faculty of taking advantage of present emergencies rather than the insight to distinguish between the true and the false, the lasting and the ephemeral advantage. Highly cultivated self-ishness rather than consecrated benevolence is its passport to success. Its votaries are never seers. At best they are but manipulators—often only jugglers. It is conducive neither to profound statesmanship nor to the higher type of manhood. Altruism is its *mauvais succes* and naturally enough it is indifferent to any factor which cannot be worked into its own immediate aims and purposes. As woman's influence as a political element is as yet nil in most of the commonwealths of our republic, it is not surprising that with those who place the emphasis on mere political capital she may yet seem almost a nonentity so far as it concerns the solution of great national or even racial perplexities.

There are those, however, who value the calm elevation of the thoughtful spectator who stands aloof from the heated scramble; and, above the turmoil and din of corruption and selfishness, can listen to the teachings of eternal truth and righteousness. There are even those who feel that the black man's unjust and unlawful exclusion temporarily from participation in the elective franchise in certain states is after all but a lesson "in the desert" fitted to develop in him insight and discrimination against the day of his own appointed time. One needs occasionally to stand aside from the hum and rush of human interests and passions to hear the voices of God. And it not unfrequently happens that the All-loving gives a great push to certain souls to thrust them out, as it were, from the distracting current for awhile to promote their discipline and growth, or to enrich them by communion and reflection. And similarly it may be woman's privilege from her peculiar coigne of vantage as a quiet observer, to whisper just the needed suggestion or the almost forgotten truth. The colored woman, then, should not be ignored because her bark is resting in the silent waters of the sheltered cove. She is watching the movements of the contestants none the less and is all the better qualified, perhaps, to weigh and judge and advise because not herself in the excitement of the race. Her voice, too, has always been heard in clear, unfaltering tones, ringing the changes on those deeper interests which make for permanent good. She is always sound and orthodox on questions affecting the well-being of her race. You do not find the colored woman selling her birthright for a mess of pottage. Nay, even after reason has retired from the contest, she has been known to cling blindly with the instinct of a turtle dove to those principles and policies which to her mind promise hope and safety for children yet unborn. It is notorious that ignorant black women in the South have actually left their husbands' homes and repudiated their support for what was understood by the wife to be race disloyalty, or "voting away," as she expresses it, the privileges of herself and little ones.

It is largely our women in the South to-day who keep the black men solid in the Republican party. The latter as they increase in intelligence and power of discrimination would be more apt to divide on local issues at any rate. They begin to see that the Grand Old Party regards the Negro's cause as an outgrown issue, and on Southern soil at least finds a too intimate acquaintanceship with him a somewhat unsavory recommendation. Then, too, their political wits have been sharpened to appreciate the fact that it is good policy to cultivate one's neighbors and not depend too much on a distant friend to fight one's home battles. But the black woman can never forget—however lukewarm the party may to-day appear—that it was a Republican president who struck the manacles from her own wrists and gave the possibilities of manhood to her helpless little ones; and to her mind a Democratic Negro is a traitor and a time-server. Talk as much as you like of venality and manipulation in the South, there are not many men, I can tell you, who would dare face a wife quivering in every fiber with the consciousness that her husband is a coward who could be paid to desert her deepest and dearest interests.

Not unfelt, then, if unproclaimed has been the work and influence of the colored women of America. Our list of chieftains in the service, though not long, is not inferior in strength and excellence, I dare believe, to any similar list which this country can produce.

Among the pioneers, Frances Watkins Harper could sing with prophetic exaltation in the darkest days, when as yet there was not a rift in the clouds overhanging her people:

> Yes, Ethiopia shall stretch
> Her bleeding hands abroad;
> Her cry of agony shall reach the burning throne of God.
> Redeemed from dust and freed from chains
> Her sons shall lift their eyes,
> From cloud-capt hills and verdant plains
> Shall shouts of triumph rise.

Among preachers of righteousness, an unanswerable silencer of cavilers and objectors, was Sojourner Truth, that unique and rugged genius who seemed carved out without hand or chisel from the solid mountain mass; and in pleasing contrast, Amanda Smith, sweetest of natural singers and pleaders in dulcet tones for the things of God and of His Christ.

Sarah Woodson Early[6] and Martha Briggs,[7] planting and watering in the school room, and giving off from their matchless and irresistible personality an impetus and inspiration which can never die so long as there lives and breathes a remote descendant of their disciples and friends.

Charlotte Forten Grimke, the gentle spirit whose verses and life link her so beautifully with America's great Quaker poet and loving reformer.

Hallie Quinn Brown,[8] charming reader, earnest, effective lecturer and devoted worker of unflagging zeal and unquestioned power.

Fannie Jackson Coppin,[9] the teacher and organizer, pre-eminent among women of whatever country or race in constructive and executive force.

---

[6]Sarah Woodson Early (1825–1907) earned the distinction of being the first African American female college professor when she joined the faculty of Wilberforce University in 1859.

[7]Martha Briggs (1838–1889) was an African American educator who served on the faculty at Howard University as principal of the Normal Department from 1883 to 1889. She was responsible for training many young teachers, who went to teach in the South.

[8]Hallie Quinn Brown (1850–1949) was an African American educator and writer who founded the National Association of Colored Women.

[9]Fannie Jackson Coppin (1837–1913) was a missionary, a member of the National Association of Colored Women, and an educator. She promoted the ideas of racial equality.

These women represent all shades of belief and as many departments of activity; but they have one thing in common—their sympathy with the oppressed race in America and the consecration of their several talents in whatever line to the work of its deliverance and development.

Fifty years ago woman's activity according to orthodox definitions was on a pretty clearly cut "sphere," including primarily the kitchen and the nursery, and rescued from the barrenness of prison bars by the womanly mania for adorning every discoverable bit of china or canvass with forlorn looking cranes balanced idiotically on one foot. The woman of to-day finds herself in the presence of responsibilities which ramify through the profoundest and most varied interests of her country and race. Not one of the issues of this plodding, toiling, sinning, repenting, falling, aspiring humanity can afford to shut her out, or can deny the reality of her influence. No plan for renovating society, no scheme for purifying politics, no reform in church or in state, no moral, social, or economic question, no movement upward or downward in the human plane is lost on her. A man once said when told his house was afire: "Go tell my wife; I never meddle with household affairs." But no woman can possibly put herself or her sex outside any of the interests that affect humanity. All departments in the new era are to be hers, in the sense that her interests are in all and through all; and it is incumbent on her to keep intelligently and sympathetically *en rapport* with all the great movements of her time, that she may know on which side to throw the weight of her influence. She stands now at the gateway of this new era of American civilization. In her hands must be moulded the strength, the wit, the statesmanship, the morality, all the psychic force, the social and economic intercourse of that era. To be alive at such an epoch is a privilege, to be a woman then is sublime.

In this last decade of our century, changes of such moment are in progress, such new and alluring vistas are opening out before us, such original and radical suggestions for the adjustment of labor and capital, of government and the governed, of the family, the church and the state, that to be a possible factor though an infinitesimal in such a movement is pregnant with hope and weighty with responsibility. To be a woman in such an age carries with it a privilege and an opportunity never implied before. But to be a woman of the Negro race in America, and to be able to grasp the deep significance of the possibilities of the crisis, is to have a heritage, it seems to me, unique in the ages. In the first place, the race is young and full of the elasticity and hopefulness of youth. All its achievements are before it. It does not look on the masterly triumphs of nineteenth century civilization with that *blasé* world-weary look which characterizes the old washed out and worn out races which have already, so to speak, seen their best days.

Said a European writer recently: "Except the Sclavonic, the Negro is the only original and distinctive genius which has yet to come to growth—and the feeling is to cherish and develop it."

Everything to this race is new and strange and inspiring. There is a quickening of its pulses and a glowing of its self-consciousness. Aha, I can rival that! I can aspire to that! I can honor my name and vindicate my race! Something like this, it strikes me, is the enthusiasm which stirs the genius of young Africa in America; and the memory of past oppression and the fact of present attempted repression only serve to gather momentum for its irrepressible powers. Then again, a race in such a stage of growth is peculiarly sensitive to impressions. Not the photographer's sensitized plate is more delicately impressionable to outer influences than is this high strung people here on the threshold of a career.

What a responsibility then to have the sole management of the primal lights and shadows! Such is the colored woman's office. She must stamp weal or woe on the coming history of this people. May she see her opportunity and vindicate her high prerogative.

How Long? How Long, O Heaven?

Reverend Henry McNeal Turner

This sermon represents an important aspect of the oral tradition in African American literature as ministers combined both secular and religious concerns to address problems of the period. This sermon addresses racial violence in Southern states. Reverend Henry McNeal Turner, who preached the sermon to his congregation at a Philadelphia church on August 5, 1876, criticizes racial violence and injustice while suggesting that African Americans might enlist the aid of European countries in their desire for justice in the United States.

In 1833 the authorities of South Carolina hanged twenty-eight colored men because they were suspicioned of conspiring to assert and take their freedom— six at one time, twenty-two at another—and yet the blood of a mouse was not shed, throughout the whole so-called conspiracy. Nevertheless, upon this trumped-up charge, they hanged several colored men, who, for Christian integrity and loyalty to law and order, were as far ahead of the Calhouns, Rhetts, Brookses, Adamses, et cetera, as Gabriel is ahead of the devil. Yet, when a disloyal white general and his diabolical crew, incarnate fiends, brutally murder and maim for life nearly or quite a dozen of the colored defenders of that state and of the nation, scores of newspapers loom up with wicked apologies, and thousands of pretended church members openly endorse the act. Still we talk about this being a Christian country. Did you ever read the history of the Dark Ages? I have, and I have read of nothing being perpetrated during that long night of dissipation and cruelty, which surpassed the deeds of horror that have been committed in Louisiana, Georgia, Mississippi, South Carolina, and other states, where not only do men pretend to be civilized, but Christianized.

The acts of blood and carnage which have disgraced this nation for the last half-dozen years and are justified by a whole party that even essays to make a President are so revolting to the very instincts of a savage that I should not be surprised to see Hottentots coming as missionaries to this country. The cold-blooded murders that have been perpetrated in this country with impunity and silent approval could not have gone on in any European country without causing a war and arousing the whole continent.

And if we colored people were not so blind and stupid, we would hold a convention somewhere and send a delegation to England, Germany, France, or to all the civilized countries in the Old World, and ask them to interfere in our behalf and save us from mad frenzy of infuriated mobs, before whom the national government, with its immense army and navy, quails and sinks in the dust. I had rather live under a monarch, autocrat, despot, or under any impartial authority than pretend to live under a mobocracy, with no power in the state or nation to quell and bid them stop. How long? How long, O Heaven, before this condition of things will change? When will thy justice, O God, avenge our wrongs?

PAUL LAURENCE DUNBAR (1872–1906)

As an African American writer of the Reconstruction period, Paul Laurence Dunbar used the poetic resonance of folk life and culture in many of his best-known poems. A native of Dayton, Ohio, Dunbar was the son of ex-slaves. His mother's tales of life on the plantation served as the context for the dialect he employed in his verse. His first book of poems, Oak and Ivy *(1893), garnered him attention as a promising poet. American writer William Dean Howells, a proponent of realism, praised Dunbar's second collection,* Majors and Minors *(1895).* Lyrics of Lowly Life *(1896) earned him praise and financial success. His poems, such as "Sympathy" and "The Colored Soldiers," emphasize the African American struggle for dignity and equality. He wed Alice Ruth Moore, an accomplished Harlem Renaissance writer, in 1898. Dunbar's published novels, including* The Uncalled *(1898) and* The Sport of the Gods *(1902), received less critical attention. A bout with tuberculosis, coupled with excessive consumption of alcohol, led to his death.*

Sympathy (1899)

I know what the caged bird feels, alas!
   When the sun is bright on the upland slopes;
When the wind stirs soft through the springing grass,
And the river flows like a stream of glass;
   When the first bird sings and the first bud opes,   5
And the faint perfume from its chalice steals—
I know what the caged bird feels!

I know why the caged bird beats his wing
   Till its blood is red on the cruel bars;
For he must fly back to his perch and cling   10
When he fain would be on the bough a-swing;
   And a pain still throbs in the old, old scars
And they pulse again with a keener sting—
I know why he beats his wing!

I know why the caged bird sings, ah me,   15
   When his wing is bruised and his bosom sore,—
When he beats his bars and he would be free;
It is not a carol of joy or glee,
   But a prayer that he sends from his heart's deep core,
But a plea, that upward to Heaven he flings—   20
I know why the caged bird sings!

We Wear the Mask (1896)

We wear the mask that grins and lies,
   It hides our cheeks and shades our eyes,—
This debt we pay to human guile;
With torn and bleeding hearts we smile,
And mouth with myriad subtleties.   5

Why should the world be over-wise,
In counting all our tears and sighs?
Nay, let them only see us, while
    We wear the mask.

We smile, but, O great Christ, our cries   10
To thee from tortured souls arise.
We sing, but oh the clay is vile
Beneath our feet, and long the mile;
But let the world dream otherwise,
    We wear the mask!   15

Frederick Douglass (1896)

A hush is over all the teeming lists,
   And there is pause, a breath-space in the strife;
A spirit brave has passed beyond the mists
   And vapors that obscure the sun of life.
And Ethiopia, with bosom torn,   5
Laments the passing of her noblest born.

She weeps for him a mother's burning tears—
   She loved him with a mother's deepest love.
He was her champion thro' direful years,
   And held her weal all other ends above.   10
When Bondage held her bleeding in the dust,
He raised her up and whispered, "Hope and Trust."

For her his voice, a fearless clarion, rung
   That broke in warning on the ears of men;
For her the strong bow of his power he strung,   15
   And sent his arrows to the very den
Where grim Oppression held his bloody place
And gloated o'er the mis'ries of a race.

And he was no soft-tongued apologist;
   He spoke straightforward, fearlessly uncowed;   20
The sunlight of his truth dispelled the mist,
   And set in bold relief each dark-hued cloud;
To sin and crime he gave their proper hue,
And hurled at evil what was evil's due.

Through good and ill report he cleaved his way   25
   Right onward, with his face set toward the heights,
Nor feared to face the foeman's dread array,—
   The lash of scorn, the sting of petty spites.
He dared the lightning in the lightning's track,
And answered thunder with his thunder back.   30

When men maligned him, and their torrent wrath
   In furious imprecations o'er him broke,
He kept his counsel as he kept his path;
   'Twas for his race, not for himself, he spoke.
He knew the import of his Master's call,   35
And felt himself too mighty to be small.

No miser in the good he held was he,—
   His kindness followed his horizon's rim.
His heart, his talents, and his hands were free
   To all who truly needed aught of him.   40
Where poverty and ignorance were rife,
He gave his bounty as he gave his life.

The place and cause that first aroused his might
   Still proved its power until his latest day.
In Freedom's lists and for the aid of Right   45
   Still in the foremost rank he waged the fray;
Wrong lived; his occupation was not gone.
He died in action with his armor on!

We weep for him, but we have touched his hand,
   And felt the magic of his presence nigh,   50
The current that he sent throughout the land,
   The kindling spirit of his battle-cry.
O'er all that holds us we shall triumph yet,
And place our banner where his hopes were set!

Oh, Douglass, thou hast passed beyond the shore,   55
   But still thy voice is ringing o'er the gale!
Thou'st taught thy race how high her hopes may soar,
   And bade her seek the heights, nor faint, nor fail.
She will not fail, she heeds thy stirring cry,
She knows thy guardian spirit will be nigh,   60
And, rising from beneath the chast'ning rod,
She stretches out her bleeding hands to God!

When Malindy Sings (1896)

G'way an' quit dat noise, Miss Lucy—
   Put dat music book away;
What 's de use to keep on tryin'?
   Ef you practise twell you 're gray,
You cain't sta't no notes a-flyin'   5
   Lak de ones dat rants and rings
F'om de kitchen to de big woods
   When Malindy sings.

You ain't got de nachel o'gans
   Fu' to make de soun' come right,   10
You ain't got de tu'ns an' twistin's
   Fu' to make it sweet an' light.
Tell you one thing now, Miss Lucy,
   An' I 'm tellin' you fu' true,
When hit comes to raal right singin',   15
   'T ain't no easy thing to do.

Easy 'nough fu' folks to hollah,
   Lookin' at de lines an' dots,
When dey ain't no one kin sence it,
   An' de chune comes in, in spots;   20
But fu' real melojous music,
   Dat jes' strikes yo' hea't and clings,
Jes' you stan' an' listen wif me
   When Malindy sings.

Ain't you nevah hyeahd Malindy?   25
   Blessed soul, tek up de cross!
Look hyeah, ain't you jokin', honey?
   Well, you don't know whut you los'.
Y' ought to hyeah dat gal a-wa'blin',
   Robins, la'ks, an' all dem things,   30

Heish dey moufs an' hides dey faces
　　When Malindy sings.

Fiddlin' man jes' stop his fiddlin',
　　Lay his fiddle on de she'f;
Mockin'-bird quit tryin' to whistle,　　　　　　35
　　'Cause he jes' so shamed hisse'f.
Folks a-playin' on de banjo
　　Draps dey fingahs on de strings—
Bless yo' soul—fu'gits to move 'em,
　　When Malindy sings.　　　　　　　　　　　40

She jes' spreads huh mouf and hollahs,
　　"Come to Jesus," twell you hyeah
Sinnahs' tremblin' steps and voices,
　　Timid-lak a-drawin' neah;
Den she tu'ns to "Rock of Ages,"　　　　　　45
　　Simply to de cross she clings,
An' you fin' yo' teahs a-drappin'
　　When Malindy sings.

Who dat says dat humble praises
　　Wif de Master nevah counts?　　　　　　　50
Heish yo' mouf, I hyeah dat music,
　　Ez hit rises up an' mounts—
Floatin' by de hills an' valleys,
　　Way above dis buryin' sod,
Ez hit makes its way in glory　　　　　　　55
　　To de very gates of God!

Oh, hit 's sweetah dan de music
　　Of an edicated band;
An' hit 's dearah dan de battle's
　　Song o' triumph in de lan'.　　　　　　　60
It seems holier dan evenin'
　　When de solemn chu'ch bell rings,
Ez I sit an' ca'mly listen
　　While Malindy sings.

Towsah, stop dat ba'kin', hyeah me!　　　　　65
　　Mandy, mek dat chile keep still;
Don't you hyeah de echoes callin'
　　F'om de valley to de hill?
Let me listen, I can hyeah it,
　　Th'oo de bresh of angel's wings,　　　　　70
Sof' an' sweet, "Swing Low, Sweet Chariot,"
　　Ez Malindy sings.

The Colored Soldiers (1896)

If the muse were mine to tempt it
  And my feeble voice were strong,
If my tongue were trained to measures,
  I would sing a stirring song.
I would sing a song heroic   5
  Of those noble sons of Ham,
Of the gallant colored soldiers
  Who fought for Uncle Sam!

In the early days you scorned them,
  And with many a flip and flout   10
Said "These battles are the white man's,
  And the whites will fight them out."
Up the hills you fought and faltered,
  In the vales you strove and bled,
While your ears still heard the thunder   15
  Of the foes' advancing tread.

Then distress fell on the nation,
  And the flag was drooping low;
Should the dust pollute your banner?
  No! the nation shouted, No!   20
So when War, in savage triumph,
  Spread abroad his funeral pall—
Then you called the colored soldiers,
  And they answered to your call.

And like hounds unleashed and eager   25
  For the life blood of the prey,
Sprung they forth and bore them bravely
  In the thickest of the fray.
And where'er the fight was hottest,
  Where the bullets fastest fell,   30
There they pressed unblanched and fearless
  At the very mouth of hell.

Ah, they rallied to the standard
  To uphold it by their might;
None were stronger in the labors,   35
  None were braver in the fight.
From the blazing breach of Wagner
  To the plains of Olustee,
They were foremost in the fight
  Of the battles of the free.   40

And at Pillow! God have mercy
  On the deeds committed there,

And the souls of those poor victims
  Sent to Thee without a prayer.
Let the fulness of Thy pity   45
  O'er the hot wrought spirits sway
Of the gallant colored soldiers
  Who fell fighting on that day!

Yes, the Blacks enjoy their freedom,
  And they won it dearly, too;   50
For the life blood of their thousands
  Did the southern fields bedew.
In the darkness of their bondage,
  In the depths of slavery's night,
Their muskets flashed the dawning,   55
  And they fought their way to light.

They were comrades then and brothers,
  Are they more or less to-day?
They were good to stop a bullet
  And to front the fearful fray.   60
They were citizens and soldiers,
  When rebellion raised its head;
And the traits that made them worthy,—
  Ah! those virtues are not dead.

They have shared your nightly vigils,   65
  They have shared your daily toil;
And their blood with yours commingling
  Has enriched the Southern soil.
They have slept and marched and suffered
  'Neath the same dark skies as you,   70
They have met as fierce a foeman,
  And have been as brave and true.

And their deeds shall find a record
  In the registry of Fame;
For their blood has cleansed completely   75
  Every blot of Slavery's shame.
So all honor and all glory
  To those noble sons of Ham—
The gallant colored soldiers
  Who fought for Uncle Sam!   80

THE RECONSTRUCTION PERIOD 1865–1900

Topics for Research

1. African American writers of the Reconstruction period valorize the folk in their literature. In an essay, examine the treatment of the "folk" in literature of this period. What strategies do writers employ to present the folk experience as vital to an understanding of African American life and culture?

2. African American women writers of the Reconstruction period reflect an emerging concern with women's rights in the post-slavery era. In an essay, examine how women writers analyze the tripartite race, class, and gender discrimination that black women often faced.

3. Trace the oral tradition in Reconstruction literature in post–Civil War America. How does the oral tradition differ from or bear resemblance to the written tradition?

4. Examine the theme of slavery versus freedom in literature of the Reconstruction period. How do works that treat this theme differ from works in earlier periods?

5. Select a writer from the Reconstruction period, and compare and contrast that writer's treatment of African American life and experience with that of writers from the colonial and antebellum periods.

PART 4

THE HARLEM RENAISSANCE
1900-1940

INTRODUCTION

ESPITE THE END OF SLAVERY IN THE UNITED STATES, African Americans still faced discrimination in the early part of the twentieth century. Artists associated with the Harlem Renaissance reinforced the theme of slavery versus freedom, highlighting the progress still to be made before blacks would achieve total emancipation in terms of equal rights and privileges. The Harlem Renaissance, a movement in music, art, literature, and politics from the early 1900s to the 1940s, emphasized the importance of freedom—political, economic, social, and artistic—for African Americans. Currently, debates exist in regard to the dates of the movement, with some centering its beginning around the end of World War I and the return to the United States of black troops demanding equal rights, while others see its beginning as 1925 with publication of *The New Negro*, an anthology featuring writings about the creativity and vitality of African American culture. Most critics concur that the Harlem Renaissance ended with the stock market crash of 1929 and the Great Depression of the 1930s. Many writers and artists of the movement had received stipends from wealthy patrons of the arts, and because of their own precarious financial situations, individuals who previously freely gave money to fund artistic projects became reluctant to provide subsidies for writers and artists.

International tensions during the period between 1900 and 1940 heightened concern for human rights. African American soldiers who fought in Western Europe during World War I (1914–1918) experienced the irony of risking their lives for the sake of freedom and democracy in Europe while not receiving equitable treatment in the United States. With the end of the war and the return of black soldiers, many African Americans agitated for civil rights. Literature of the Harlem Renaissance reflects the social and political activism of the early twentieth century, when organizations such as the NAACP and the Urban League fought for civil rights, signaling their desire to make African Americans truly free. The organizations' desire to eradicate Jim Crow ("separate but equal") policies and to halt mob violence against blacks coincided with the creation of journals that promoted civil rights. In fact, *The Crisis* (published by the NAACP) and *Opportunity* (published by the Urban League) promoted the works of African American writers of the period, including Zora Neale Hurston and Langston Hughes. Jessie Redmon Fauset, poet, short-story writer, and novelist, was literary editor of *The Crisis* from 1919 to 1926, publishing her own works and those of her peers, such as Hughes. Both *The Crisis* and *Opportunity* illustrate the marriage of politics and art during the Harlem Renaissance. As racial violence and intolerance spread across the land, the Urban League and the NAACP rose to the vanguard in protecting the rights of African American citizens. Through literature, and through encouragement of literary and visual productions by black artists, these organizations sought to eradicate existing racial stereotypes and misconceptions about African Americans.

Harlem in the 1920s and 1930s nurtured the African American artistic heritage and fostered an appreciation of the contributions blacks had made to American society. The preeminence of this part of the country as a site of black life and culture followed the influx of African Americans into Northern industrial areas in the early part of the twentieth century, seeking social, political, economic, and artistic freedom. As blacks from the South and West migrated to New York City, Philadelphia, and Boston, a sizable black population emerged in areas such as Harlem, where real estate prices were low and opportunities for entrepreneurship presented themselves. Harlem Renaissance–era writers such as Dorothy West chronicled the lives of rural Southern blacks who moved to the North in search of better economic opportunities, often to find that the American Dream remained elusive. Other writers of the era, such as Zora Neale Hurston, exemplified the great black migration through their own lives and travel. Hurston, like many other black authors of the Harlem Renaissance, was not originally from Harlem. She relocated to New York City because it was the scene of artistic and cultural life, as well as the hub of the publishing world, during the 1920s and 1930s.

Writers such as Zora Neale Hurston, Dorothy West, and Claude McKay embraced the idea of the New Negro, a concept that emphasized self-sufficiency, education, black pride, a sense of African American history, and cultural advancement. The concept found shape in an anthology, *The New Negro* (pp. 422–430). Edited by Alain Locke, a professor at Howard University, the text features a number of fiction and nonfiction pieces. Connecting to the tone of the times, Locke writes:

> In Harlem, Negro life is seizing upon its first chances for group expression and self-determination. It is—or promises at least to be—a race capital. That is why our comparison is taken with those nascent centers of folk-expression and self-determination which are playing a creative part in the world to-day. Without pretense to their political significance, Harlem has the same rôle to play for the New Negro as Dublin has had for the New Ireland or Prague for the New Czechoslovakia. (p. 424)

The New Negro highlights concerns of black intellectuals of the period in regard to social and political rights for African Americans. By embracing the ideas of black pride and self-determination, African American writers of the Harlem Renaissance sought to revise what they considered to be stereotypical notions of African American life, art, and culture.

The Harlem Renaissance also reflected the oral tradition in African American literature through its interdisciplinary nature and the valorization of music, particularly jazz and blues. The Harlem Renaissance coincided with the Jazz Age of the 1920s and 1930s, when Harlem nightspots became popular among blacks and whites, showcasing the talents of dancers such as Josephine Baker; blues singers such as Bessie Smith, Florence Mills, and Billie Holiday; and bandleaders such as Duke Ellington and Cab Calloway. Many artists attempted to capture aspects of the oral tradition through narrative form and language. Poet Langston Hughes used the blues and jazz rhythms as the basis for many of his poems, including "Dream Boogie: Variation" (pp. 445–446). By incorporating the rhythms of African American music and black vernacular expression into literature, Hughes sought to connect written and oral traditions of African American artistic expression. Similarly, anthropologist and author Zora Neale Hurston used the black vernacular in her texts, capitalizing on the oral tradition. In *Their Eyes Were Watching God*, Hurston's protagonist Janie tells her life story to her friend Pheoby as a means of empowerment. Hurston's use of dialect and oral storytelling pays tribute to the oral tradition in African American culture. Speeches represent another aspect of the oral tradition. Marcus Garvey, a social and political activist from Jamaica, delivered rousing speeches of black pride amid his "Back to Africa" rhetoric. James Weldon Johnson, in speeches such as "Our Democracy and the Ballot" (p. 203), addressed political concerns such as voting rights for African Americans. As an interdisciplinary movement involving music, literature, art, politics, and dance, the Harlem Renaissance supported experiment with a variety of forms and sources of inspiration.

Visual arts flourished as individuals such as sculptor Augusta Savage, illustrator Laura Wheeler Waring (whose work often appeared in *The Crisis*), and painter Aaron Douglass translated the black experience in their respective media. The end result promoted an awareness and appreciation of black Americans' artistic abilities and skills and of their life and culture as a viable source for art. Still, like their counterparts in music and literature, African American visual artists faced discrimination. Augusta Savage, for example, was denied admission to an art academy because of the color of her skin. Jessie Redmon Fauset examined the plight of the black artist in works such as *Plum Bun: A Novel Without a Moral* (1929), which details the life of Angela Murray, a young black woman who passes for white because she believes knowledge of her true racial heritage will prevent her from receiving critical acclaim as an artist. Nevertheless, the legacy of these forerunners represents the scope of black artistic endeavor during the period.

Literature of the Harlem Renaissance period centers around the debates regarding social, political, and economic advancement for African Americans and the desire for America to uphold its dream of equality for all. W. E. B. Du Bois, one of the leading figures of the Harlem Renaissance as editor of *The Crisis* and a founder of the NAACP, led the vanguard with his 1903 masterpiece *The Souls of Black Folk* (pp. 168–181), which critiques racism in the United States and advocates appreciation of African American culture. Du Bois helped shape the political and artistic aims of the movement by focusing on both the national and international implications of race relations: "The problem of the twentieth century is the problem of the color-line,— the relation of the darker to the lighter races of men in Asia and Africa, in America and the islands of the sea" (p. 168). His provocative account of his own experiences as a black man is a compelling work that emphasizes black consciousness and cultural awareness. Booker T. Washington, founder of Tuskegee Institute and author of the autobiography *Up from Slavery* (1901), championed the notions of hard work, thrift, patience, and industry. He and Du Bois are often viewed as opposites in terms of their ideas on education, suffrage, and the best strategies for obtaining equal rights for African Americans; their difference of opinion illustrates the complexities of political thought during the period.

A number of poets rose to the forefront, thanks to publishing opportunities in *The Crisis* and *Opportunity*. Anne Spencer and Alice Ruth Moore Dunbar-Nelson offered a feminine perspective in their poetry, which often focused on the triple jeopardy of race, class, and gender for African American women in the early 1900s. Countee Cullen, often referred to as the Black Keats because of his admiration of British Romantic poets, articulated the divided nature of African Americans in poems such as "Heritage," dealt with racism in "Incident," and focused on the black artist's struggle in "Yet Do I Marvel" (pp. 447–451). Langston Hughes, like Paul Laurence Dunbar, used black vernacular English in many fine poems, including the dramatic monologue "Mother to Son" (p. 444), which details the hardships of a black mother in a racist society. Arna Bontemps also articulated many of the concerns of African American artists in regard to the racial climate in America in poems such as "A Black Man Talks of Reaping" (p. 466).

Drama also proved an important forum for African American writers of the Harlem Renaissance: Angelina Weld Grimke wrote the 1916 drama *Rachel* (pp. 209–256), and Marita Bonner wrote the 1928 play *The Purple Flower* (pp. 458–465). Both playwrights dealt with issues such as social, political, and economic oppression in other forums as well, including short stories. Grimke was also a poet, and her verse articulates many of the same concerns as her drama. As playwrights, Grimke and Bonner anticipate the concerns of later dramatists, including Lorraine Hansberry in *A Raisin in the Sun* (1959), Ntozake Shange in *For Colored Girls Who Have Considered Suicide/When the Rainbow is Enuf* (1975), and August Wilson in *The Piano Lesson* (1990).

In their exploration of the theme of slavery versus freedom, writers of the Harlem Renaissance analyzed both the progress and the impediments toward racial equality evident in the United States. Black consciousness was heightened by the activities of the NAACP and the Urban League. Publications such as *The Crisis* and *Opportunity*, as well as an interest in African American music, dance, and art, inspired many creative writers to use the issue of color consciousness as a theme in their works. The story or novel of passing, in which a black character "passes" for white in hopes of social, economic, and political advancement, became a popular vehicle for mediating on race, class, and gender in American society. Jessie Redmon Fauset penned several novels and stories dealing with the issue, including "The Sleeper Wakes" (pp. 270–289) and *Comedy: American Style* (pp. 289–294). Nella Larsen, in her novellas *Quicksand* (pp. 416–421) and *Passing* written in the 1920s, examined the impact that socially prescribed racial and gender roles had on black women in America during the first half of the twentieth century. Wallace Thurman, in his 1929 critique of racism *The Blacker the Berry* (pp. 430–443), and James Weldon Johnson, in his 1912 novel *The Autobiography of an Ex-Colored Man* (pp. 193–199), also dealt with interracial and intraracial color consciousness in America and its damaging effects upon society. In her 1937 novel *Their Eyes Were Watching God* (pp. 301–403), Zora Neale Hurston explored how interracial and intraracial color prejudice, sexism, and class discrimination affected the life of Janie Crawford, a black woman living in rural Florida during the early part of the twentieth century. Although Hurston died relatively unknown and in dire economic straits in 1960, her message of black female empowerment has brought her to the forefront as one of the central writers of the Harlem Renaissance.

A number of writers of the Harlem Renaissance period are difficult to classify because of the structure and variety of their work. Some, such as Dorothy West, transcend literary periods because of the chronological scope of their writing. West critiqued economic injustice in stories such as "The Typewriter" (pp. 295–301), in which she profiles a thwarted attempt by an African American man to realize the American Dream. Her novels *The Living Is Easy* (1948) and *The Wedding* (1995) focus on issues such as the great black migration, the legacy of slavery, color, and class prejudice. Like West, Jean Toomer, author of the 1923 collection *Cane* (pp. 407–413), is difficult to classify, mainly because of his experimentation with literary genre. *Cane* consists of a series of stories and poems. The text can be read alternatively as a short-story cycle or as a novella interspersed with poetry. Toomer's work presents African Americans of various social, educational, and economic levels in a society fraught with injustice.

The Harlem Renaissance catapulted a number of writers to the forefront of the civil rights movement as they recognized that despite the end of legalized slavery in America, blacks still faced discrimination and a long road to freedom. These writers responded to the call for literature articulating the concerns of blacks in the early part of the twentieth century. Against the backdrop of the great black migration to the North, the founding of the NAACP and the Urban League, the establishment of publications such as *The Crisis* and *Opportunity*, and the consciousness of the New Negro, the writers of the Harlem Renaissance represented a diversity in genre. Their work has proved long-lasting, as shown by the renewed interest in writers such as Hurston, Hughes, and Du Bois.

The root of this renewed interest in literature of the Harlem Renaissance lies in the black consciousness of the 1960s and the feminist movement of the 1970s, when scholars in African American studies and women's studies found that explorations of race, class, and gender dating back to the Harlem Renaissance of the 1920s and 1930s were relevant to emerging black consciousness and feminism in contemporary society. The Harlem Renaissance is important because of its treatment of the concerns held by writers of the colonial and Reconstruction eras and its anticipation of issues ranging from feminism to black aesthetics articulated in later movements. The Harlem Renaissance signifies a milestone on the road from slavery to freedom for African American artists.

W. E. B. DU BOIS (1868–1963)

As a leading writer, social activist, scholar, professor, and administrator, W. E. B. Du Bois helped shaped the intellectual life of the Harlem Renaissance era. A native of Great Barrington, Massachusetts, Du Bois earned a B.A. from Fisk University in 1888, a B.A. from Harvard University by 1890, and a master of arts degree a year later. By 1896, he had been awarded a Ph.D. by Harvard University. He was employed as a professor and researcher at a number of institutions, including the University of Pennsylvania, where his research led to a book called The Philadelphia Negro *(1899).*

His book The Souls of Black Folk *(1903), which focuses on race relations in the United States, has been heralded as a classic for its insightful view of the African American as a divided self, both black and American, and for its focus on the theme of slavery versus freedom. Six years after the book's publication, Du Bois would help to found the NAACP, and he served for many years as editor of* The Crisis. *He also created* Phylon, *a journal in the field of African American studies. An independent thinker, Du Bois became disenchanted with racism in America; he died in Ghana in 1963.*

From The Souls of Black Folk (1903)

Chapter 2: Of the Dawn of Freedom

> Careless seems the great Avenger;
>   History's lessons but record
> One death-grapple in the darkness
>   'Twixt old systems and the Word;
> Truth forever on the scaffold,
>   Wrong forever on the throne;
> Yet that scaffold sways the future,
>   And behind the dim unknown
> Standeth God within the shadow
>   Keeping watch above His own.

Lowell

The problem of the twentieth century is the problem of the color-line,—the relation of the darker to the lighter races of men in Asia and Africa, in America and the islands of the sea. It was a phase of this problem that caused the Civil War; and however much they who marched South and North in 1861 may have fixed on the technical points of union and local autonomy as a shibboleth, all nevertheless knew, as we know, that the question of Negro slavery was the real cause of the conflict. Curious it was, too, how this deeper question ever forced itself to the surface despite effort and disclaimer. No sooner had Northern armies touched Southern soil than this old question, newly guised, sprang from the earth,—What shall be done with Negroes? Peremptory military commands this way and that, could not answer the query; the Emancipation Proclamation seemed but to broaden and intensify the difficulties; and the War Amendments made the Negro problems of to-day.

It is the aim of this essay to study the period of history from 1861 to 1872 so far as it relates to the American Negro. In effect, this tale of the dawn of Freedom is an account of that government of men called the Freedmen's Bureau,—one of the most singular and interesting of the attempts made by a great nation to grapple with vast problems of race and social condition.

The war has naught to do with slaves, cried Congress, the President, and the Nation; and yet no sooner had the armies, East and West, penetrated Virginia and Tennessee than fugitive slaves appeared within their lines. They came at night, when the flickering camp-fires shone like vast unsteady stars along the black horizon: old men and thin, with gray and tufted hair; women with frightened eyes, dragging whimpering hungry children; men and girls, stalwart and gaunt,—a horde of starving vagabonds, homeless, helpless, and pitiable, in their dark distress. Two methods of treating these newcomers seemed equally logical to opposite sorts of minds. Ben Butler, in Virginia, quickly declared slave property contraband of war, and put the fugitives to work; while Fremont, in Missouri, declared the slaves free under martial law. Butler's action was approved, but Fremont's was hastily countermanded, and his successor, Halleck, saw things differently. "Hereafter," he commanded, "no slaves should be allowed to come into your lines at all; if any come without your knowledge, when owners call for them deliver them." Such a policy was difficult to enforce; some of the black refugees declared themselves freemen, others showed that their masters had deserted them, and still others were captured with forts and plantations. Evidently, too, slaves were a source of strength to the Confederacy, and were being used as laborers and producers. "They constitute a military resource," wrote Secretary Cameron, late in 1861; "and being such, that they should not be turned over to the enemy is too plain to discuss." So gradually the tone of the army chiefs changed; Congress forbade the rendition of fugitives, and Butler's "contrabands" were welcomed as military laborers. This complicated rather than solved the problem, for now the scattering fugitives became a steady stream, which flowed faster as the armies marched.

Then the long-headed man with care-chiselled face who sat in the White House saw the inevitable, and emancipated the slaves of rebels on New Year's, 1863. A month later Congress called earnestly for the Negro soldiers whom the act of July, 1862, had half grudgingly allowed to enlist. Thus the barriers were levelled and the deed was done. The stream of fugitives swelled to a flood, and anxious army officers kept inquiring: "What must be done with slaves, arriving almost daily? Are we to find food and shelter for women and children?"

It was a Pierce of Boston who pointed out the way, and thus became in a sense the founder of the Freedmen's Bureau. He was a firm friend of Secretary Chase; and when, in 1861, the care of slaves and abandoned lands developed upon the Treasury officials, Pierce was specially detailed from the ranks to study the conditions. First, he cared for the refugees at Fortress Monroe; and then, after Sherman had captured Hilton Head, Pierce was sent there to found his Port Royal experiment of making free workingmen out of slaves. Before his experiment was barely started, however, the problem of the fugitives had assumed such proportions that it was taken from the hands of the over-burdened Treasury

Department and given to the army officials. Already centres of massed freedmen were forming at Fortress Monroe, Washington, New Orleans, Vicksburg and Corinth, Columbus, Ky., and Cairo, Ill., as well as at Port Royal. Army chaplains found here new and fruitful fields; "superintendents of contrabands" multiplied, and some attempt at systematic work was made by enlisting the able-bodied men and giving work to the others.

Then came the Freedmen's Aid societies, born of the touching appeals from Pierce and from these other centres of distress. There was the American Missionary Association, sprung from the *Amistad*, and now full-grown for work; the various church organizations, the National Freedmen's Relief Association, the American Freedmen's Union, the Western Freedmen's Aid Commission,—in all fifty or more active organizations, which sent clothes, money, school-books, and teachers southward. All they did was needed, for the destitution of the freedmen was often reported as "too appalling for belief," and the situation was daily growing worse rather than better.

And daily, too, it seemed more plain that this was no ordinary matter of temporary relief, but a national crisis; for here loomed a labor problem of vast dimensions. Masses of Negroes stood idle, or, if they worked spasmodically, were never sure of pay; and if perchance they received pay, squandered the new thing thoughtlessly. In these and other ways were camp-life and the new liberty demoralizing the freedmen. The broader economic organization thus clearly demanded sprang up here and there as accident and local conditions determined. Here it was that Pierce's Port Royal plan of leased plantations and guided workmen pointed out the rough way. In Washington the military governor, at the urgent appeal of the superintendent, opened confiscated estates to the cultivation of the fugitives, and there in the shadow of the dome gathered black farm villages. General Dix gave over estates to the freedmen of Fortress Monroe, and so on, South and West. The government and benevolent societies furnished the means of cultivation, and the Negro turned again slowly to work. The systems of control, thus started, rapidly grew, here and there, into strange little governments, like that of General Banks in Louisiana, with its ninety thousand black subjects, its fifty thousand guided laborers, and its annual budget of one hundred thousand dollars and more. It made out four thousand pay-rolls a year, registered all freedmen, inquired into grievances and redressed them, laid and collected taxes, and established a system of public schools. So, too, Colonel Eaton, the superintendent of Tennessee and Arkansas, ruled over one hundred thousand freedmen, leased and cultivated seven thousand acres of cotton land, and fed ten thousand paupers a year. In South Carolina was General Saxton, with his deep interest in black folk. He succeeded Pierce and the Treasury officials, and sold forfeited estates, leased abandoned plantations, encouraged schools, and received from Sherman, after that terribly picturesque march to the sea, thousands of the wretched camp followers.

Three characteristic things one might have seen in Sherman's raid through Georgia, which threw the new situation in shadowy relief: the Conqueror, the Conquered, and the Negro. Some see all significance in the grim front of the destroyer, and some in the bitter sufferers of the Lost Cause. But to me neither soldier nor fugitive speaks with so deep a meaning as that dark human cloud that clung like remorse on the rear of those swift columns, swelling at times to half their size, almost engulfing and choking them. In vain were they ordered back, in vain were bridges hewn from beneath their feet; on they trudged and writhed and surged, until they rolled into Savannah, a starved and naked horde of tens of thousands. There too came the characteristic military remedy: "The islands from Charleston south, the abandoned rice-fields along the rivers for thirty miles back from the sea, and the country bordering the St. John's River, Florida, are reserved and set apart for the settlement of Negroes now made free by act of war." So read the celebrated "Field-order Number Fifteen."

All these experiments, orders, and systems were bound to attract and perplex the government and the nation. Directly after the Emancipation Proclamation, Representative Eliot had introduced a bill creating a Bureau of Emancipation; but it was never reported. The following June a committee of inquiry, appointed by the Secretary of War, reported in favor of a temporary bureau for the "improvement, protection, and employment of refugee freedmen," on much the same lines as were afterwards followed. Petitions came in to President Lincoln from distinguished citizens and organizations, strongly urging a comprehensive and unified plan of dealing with the freedmen, under a bureau which should be "charged with the study of plans and execution of measures for easily guiding, and in every way judiciously and humanely aiding, the passage of our emancipated and yet to be emancipated blacks from the old condition of forced labor to their new state of voluntary industry."

Some half-hearted steps were taken to accomplish this, in part, by putting the whole matter again in charge of the special Treasury agents. Laws of 1863 and 1864 directed them to take charge of and lease abandoned lands for periods not exceeding twelve months, and to "provide in such leases, or otherwise, for the employment and general welfare" of the freedmen. Most of the army officers greeted this as a welcome relief from perplexing "Negro affairs," and Secretary Fessenden, July 29, 1864, issued an excellent system of regulations, which were afterward closely followed by General Howard. Under Treasury agents, large quantities of land were leased in the Mississippi Valley, and many Negroes were employed; but in August, 1864, the new regulations were suspended for reasons of "public policy," and the army was again in control.

Meanwhile Congress had turned its attention to the subject; and in March the House passed a bill by a majority of two establishing a Bureau for Freedmen in the War Department. Charles Sumner, who had charge of the bill in the Senate, argued that freedmen and abandoned lands ought to be under the same department, and reported a substitute for the House bill attaching the Bureau to the Treasury Department. This bill passed, but too late for action by the House. The debates wandered over the whole policy of the administration and the general question of slavery, without touching very closely the specific merits of the measure in hand. Then the national election took place; and the administration, with a vote of renewed confidence from the country, addressed itself to the matter more seriously. A conference between the two branches of Congress agreed upon a carefully drawn measure which contained the chief provisions of Sumner's bill, but made the proposed organization a department independent of both the

War and the Treasury officials. The bill was conservative, giving the new department "general superintendence of all freedmen." Its purpose was to "establish regulations" for them, protect them, lease them lands, adjust their wages, and appear in civil and military courts as their "next friend." There were many limitations attached to the powers thus granted, and the organization was made permanent. Nevertheless, the Senate defeated the bill, and a new conference committee was appointed. This committee reported a new bill, February 28, which was whirled through just as the session closed, and became the act of 1865 establishing in the War Department a "Bureau of Refugees, Freedmen, and Abandoned Lands."

This last compromise was a hasty bit of legislation, vague and uncertain in outline. A Bureau was created, "to continue during the present War of Rebellion, and for one year thereafter," to which was given "the supervision and management of all abandoned lands and the control of all subjects relating to refugees and freedmen," under "such rules and regulations as may be presented by the head of the Bureau and approved by the President." A Commissioner, appointed by the President and Senate, was to control the Bureau, with an office force not exceeding ten clerks. The President might also appoint assistant commissioners in the seceded States, and to all these offices military officials might be detailed at regular pay. The Secretary of War could issue rations, clothing, and fuel to the destitute, and all abandoned property was placed in the hands of the Bureau for eventual lease and sale to ex-slaves in forty-acre parcels.

Thus did the United States government definitely assume charge of the emancipated Negro as the ward of the nation. It was a tremendous undertaking. Here at a stroke of the pen was erected a government of millions of men,—and not ordinary men either, but black men emasculated by a peculiarly complete system of slavery, centuries old; and now, suddenly, violently, they come into a new birthright, at a time of war and passion, in the midst of the stricken and embittered population of their former masters. Any man might well have hesitated to assume charge of such a work, with vast responsibilities, indefinite powers, and limited resources. Probably no one but a soldier would have answered such a call promptly; and, indeed, no one but a soldier could be called, for Congress had appropriated no money for salaries and expenses.

Less than a month after the weary Emancipator passed to his rest, his successor assigned Major-Gen. Oliver O. Howard to duty as Commissioner of the new Bureau. He was a Maine man, then only thirty-five years of age. He had marched with Sherman to the sea, had fought well at Gettysburg, and but the year before had been assigned to the command of the Department of Tennessee. An honest man, with too much faith in human nature, little aptitude for business and intricate detail, he had had large opportunity of becoming acquainted at first hand with much of the work before him. And of that work it has been truly said that "no approximately correct history of civilization can ever be written which does not throw out in bold relief, as one of the great landmarks of political and social progress, the organization and administration of the Freedmen's Bureau."

On May 12, 1865, Howard was appointed; and he assumed the duties of his office promptly on the 15th, and began examining the field of work. A curious mess he looked upon: little despotisms, communistic experiments, slavery, peonage, business speculations, organized charity, unorganized almsgiving,—all reeling on under the guise of helping the freedmen, and all enshrined in the smoke and blood of the war and the cursing and silence of angry men. On May 19 the new government—for a government it really was—issued its constitution; commissioners were to be appointed in each of the seceded states, who were to take charge of "all subjects relating to refugees and freedmen," and all relief and rations were to be given by their consent alone. The Bureau invited continued cooperation with benevolent societies, and declared: "It will be the object of all commissioners to introduce practicable systems of compensated labor," and to establish schools. Forthwith nine assistant commissioners were appointed. They were to hasten to their fields of work; seek gradually to close relief establishments, and make the destitute self-supporting; act as courts of law where there were no courts, or where Negroes were not recognized in them as free; establish the institution of marriage among ex-slaves, and keep records; see that freedmen were free to choose their employers, and help in making fair contracts for them; and finally, the circular said: "Simple good faith, for which we hope on all hands for those concerned in the passing away of slavery, will especially relieve the assistant commissioners in the discharge of their duties toward the freedmen, as well as promote the general welfare."

No sooner was the work thus started, and the general system and local organization in some measure begun, than two grave difficulties appeared which changed largely the theory and outcome of Bureau work. First, there were the abandoned lands of the South. It had long been the more or less definitely expressed theory of the North that all the chief problems of Emancipation might be settled by establishing the slaves on the forfeited lands of their masters,—a sort of poetic justice, said some. But this poetry done into solemn prose meant either wholesale confiscation of private property in the South, or vast appropriations. Now Congress had not appropriated a cent, and no sooner did the proclamations of general amnesty appear than the eight hundred thousand acres of abandoned lands in the hands of the Freedmen's Bureau melted quickly away. The second difficulty lay in perfecting the local organization of the Bureau throughout the wide field of work. Making a new machine and sending out officials of duly ascertained fitness for a great work of social reform is no child's task; but this task was even harder, for a new central organization had to be fitted on a heterogeneous and confused but already existing system of relief and control of ex-slaves; and the agents available for this work must be sought for in an army still busy with war operations,—men in the very nature of the case ill fitted for delicate social work,—or among the questionable camp followers of an invading host. Thus, after a year's work, vigorously as it was pushed, the problem looked even more difficult to grasp and solve than at the beginning. Nevertheless, three things that year's work did, well worth the doing: it relieved a vast amount of physical suffering; it transported seven thousand fugitives from congested centres back to the farm; and, best of all, it inaugurated the crusade of the New England schoolma'am.

The annals of this Ninth Crusade are yet to be written,—the tale of a mission that seemed to our age far more quixotic than the quest of St. Louis seemed to his.

Behind the mists of ruin and rapine waved the calico dresses of women who dared, and after the hoarse mouthings of the field guns rang the rhythm of the alphabet. Rich and poor they were, serious and curious. Bereaved now of a father, now of a brother, now of more than these, they came seeking a life work in planting New England schoolhouses among the white and black of the South. They did their work well. In that first year they taught one hundred thousand souls, and more.

Evidently, Congress must soon legislate again on the hastily organized Bureau, which had so quickly grown into wide significance and vast possibilities. An institution such as that was well-nigh as difficult to end as to begin. Early in 1866 Congress took up the matter, when Senator Trumbull, of Illinois, introduced a bill to extend the Bureau and enlarge its powers. This measure received, at the hands of Congress, far more thorough discussion and attention than its predecessor. The war cloud had thinned enough to allow a clearer conception of the work of Emancipation. The champions of the bill argued that the strengthening of the Freedmen's Bureau was still a military necessity; that it was needed for the proper carrying out of the Thirteenth Amendment, and was a work of sheer justice to the ex-slave, at a trifling cost to the government. The opponents of the measure declared that the war was over, and the necessity for war measures past; that the Bureau, by reason of its extraordinary powers, was clearly unconstitutional in time of peace, and was destined to irritate the South and pauperize the freedmen, at a final cost of possibly hundreds of millions. These two arguments were unanswered, and indeed unanswerable: the one that the extraordinary powers of the Bureau threatened the civil rights of all citizens; and the other that the government must have power to do what manifestly must be done, and that present abandonment of the freedmen meant their practical re-enslavement. The bill which finally passed enlarged and made permanent the Freedmen's Bureau. It was promptly vetoed by President Johnson as "unconstitutional," "unnecessary," and "extrajudicial," and failed of passage over the veto. Meantime, however, the breach between Congress and the President began to broaden, and a modified form of the lost bill was finally passed over the President's second veto, July 16.

The act of 1866 gave the Freedmen's Bureau its final form,—the form by which it will be known to posterity and judged of men. It extended the existence of the Bureau to July, 1868; it authorized additional assistant commissioners, the retention of army officers mustered out of regular service, the sale of certain forfeited lands to freedmen on nominal terms, the sale of Confederate public property for Negro schools, and a wider field of judicial interpretation and cognizance. The government of the unreconstructed South was thus put very largely in the hands of the Freedmen's Bureau, especially as in many cases the departmental military commander was now made also assistant commissioner. It was thus that the Freedmen's Bureau became a full-fledged government of men. It made laws, executed them and interpreted them; it laid and collected taxes, defined and punished crime, maintained and used military force, and dictated such measures as it thought necessary and proper for the accomplishment of its varied ends. Naturally, all these powers were not exercised continuously nor to their fullest extent; and yet, as General Howard has said, "scarcely any subject that has to be legislated upon in civil society failed, at one time or another, to demand the action of this singular Bureau."

To understand and criticise intelligently so vast a work, one must not forget an instant the drift of things in the later sixties. Lee had surrendered, Lincoln was dead, and Johnson and Congress were at loggerheads; the Thirteenth Amendment was adopted, the Fourteenth pending, and the Fifteenth declared in force in 1870. Guerrilla raiding, the ever-present flickering after-flame of war, was spending its forces against the Negroes, and all the Southern land was awakening as from some wild dream to poverty and social revolution. In a time of perfect calm, amid willing neighbors and streaming wealth, the social uplifting of four million slaves to an assured and self-sustaining place in the body politic and economic would have been a herculean task; but when to the inherent difficulties of so delicate and nice a social operation were added the spite and hate of conflict, the hell of war; when suspicion and cruelty were rife, and gaunt Hunger wept beside Bereavement,—in such a case, the work of any instrument of social regeneration was in large part foredoomed to failure. The very name of the Bureau stood for a thing in the South which for two centuries and better men had refused even to argue,—that life amid free Negroes was simply unthinkable, the maddest of experiments.

The agents that the Bureau could command varied all the way from unselfish philanthropists to narrow-minded busybodies and thieves; and even though it be true that the average was far better than the worst, it was the occasional fly that helped spoil the ointment.

Then amid all crouched the freed slave, bewildered between friend and foe. He had emerged from slavery,—not the worst slavery in the world, not a slavery that made all life unbearable, rather a slavery that had here and there something of kindliness, fidelity, and happiness,—but withal slavery, which, so far as human aspiration and desert were concerned, classed the black man and the ox together. And the Negro knew full well that, whatever their deeper convictions may have been, Southern men had fought with desperate energy to perpetuate this slavery under which the black masses, with half-articulate thought, had writhed and shivered. They welcomed freedom with a cry. They shrank from the master who still strove for their chains; they fled to the friends that had freed them, even though those friends stood ready to use them as a club for driving the recalcitrant South back into loyalty. So the cleft between the white and black South grew. Idle to say it never should have been; it was as inevitable as its results were pitiable. Curiously incongruous elements were left arrayed against each other,—the North, the government, the carpet-bagger, and the slave, here; and there, all the South that was white, whether gentleman or vagabond, honest man or rascal, lawless murderer or martyr to duty.

Thus it is doubly difficult to write of this period calmly, so intense was the feeling, so mighty the human passions that swayed and blinded men. Amid it all, two figures ever stand to typify that day to coming ages,—the one, a gray-haired gentleman, whose fathers had quit themselves like men, whose sons lay in nameless graves; who bowed to the evil of slavery because its abolition threatened untold ill to all; who stood at last, in the evening of life, a blighted, ruined form, with hate in his eyes;—and the other, a form hovering dark and mother-like, her awful face black with the mists of centuries, had aforetime quailed at that white master's command, had bent in love over the cradles of his sons and daughters, and closed in death the sunken eyes of his wife,—aye, too, at his behest had laid herself low to his lust, and borne a tawny man-child to the world, only to see her dark boy's limbs scattered to the winds by midnight marauders riding after "damned Niggers." These were the saddest sights of that woful day; and no man clasped the hands of these two passing figures of the present-past; but, hating, they went to their long home, and, hating, their children's children live to-day.

Here, then, was the field of work for the Freedmen's Bureau; and since, with some hesitation, it was continued by the act of 1868 until 1869, let us look upon four years of its work as a whole. There were, in 1868, nine hundred Bureau officials scattered from Washington to Texas, ruling, directly and indirectly, many millions of men. The deeds of these rulers fall mainly under seven heads: the relief of physical suffering, the overseeing of the beginnings of free labor, the buying and selling of land, the establishment of schools, the paying of bounties, the administration of justice, and the financiering of all these activities.

Up to June, 1869, over half a million patients had been treated by Bureau physicians and surgeons, and sixty hospitals and asylums had been in operation. In fifty months twenty-one million free rations were distributed at a cost of over four million dollars. Next came the difficult question of labor. First, thirty thousand black men were transported from the refuges and relief stations back to the farms, back to the critical trial of a new way of working. Plain instructions went out from Washington: the laborers must be free to choose their employers, no fixed rate of wages was prescribed, and there was to be no peonage or forced labor. So far, so good; but where local agents differed *toto cœlo* in capacity and character, where the *personnel* was continually changing, the outcome was necessarily varied. The largest element of success lay in the fact that the majority of the freedmen were willing, even eager, to work. So labor contracts were written,—fifty thousand in a single State,—laborers advised, wages guaranteed, and employers supplied. In truth, the organization became a vast labor bureau,—not perfect, indeed, notably defective here and there, but on the whole successful beyond the dreams of thoughtful men. The two great obstacles which confronted the officials were the tyrant and the idler,—the slaveholder who was determined to perpetuate slavery under another name; and the freedman who regarded freedom as perpetual rest,—the Devil and the Deep Sea.

In the work of establishing the Negroes as peasant proprietors, the Bureau was from the first handicapped and at last absolutely checked. Something was done, and larger things were planned; abandoned lands were leased so long as they remained in the hands of the Bureau, and a total revenue of nearly half a million dollars derived from black tenants. Some other lands to which the nation had gained title were sold on easy terms, and public lands were opened for settlement to the very few freedmen who had tools and capital. But the vision of "forty acres and a mule"—the righteous and reasonable ambition to become a landholder, which the nation had all but categorically promised the freedmen—was destined in most cases to bitter disappointment. And those men of marvellous hindsight who are today seeking to preach the Negro back to the present peonage of the soil know well, or ought to know, that the opportunity of binding the Negro peasant willingly to the soil was lost on that day when the Commissioner of the Freedmen's Bureau had to go to South Carolina and tell the weeping freedmen, after their years of toil, that their land was not theirs, that there was a mistake—somewhere. If by 1874 the Georgia Negro alone owned three hundred and fifty thousand acres of land, it was by grace of his thrift rather than by bounty of the government.

The greatest success of the Freedmen's Bureau lay in the planting of the free school among Negroes, and the idea of free elementary education among all classes in the South. It not only called the school-mistresses through the benevolent agencies and built them schoolhouses, but it helped discover and support such apostles of human culture as Edmund Ware,[1] Samuel Armstrong,[2] and Erastus Cravath.[3] The opposition to Negro education in the South was at first bitter, and showed itself in ashes, insult, and blood; for the South believed an educated Negro to be a dangerous Negro. And the South was not wholly wrong; for education among all kinds of men always has had, and always will have, an element of danger and revolution, of dissatisfaction and discontent. Nevertheless, men strive to know. Perhaps some inkling of this paradox, even in the unquiet days of the Bureau, helped the bayonets allay an opposition to human training which still to-day lies smouldering in the South, but not flaming. Fisk, Atlanta, Howard, and Hampton were founded in these days, and six million dollars were expended for educational work, seven hundred and fifty thousand dollars of which the freedmen themselves gave of their poverty.

Such contributions, together with the buying of land and various other enterprises, showed that the ex-slave was handling some free capital already. The chief initial source of this was labor in the army, and his pay and bounty as a soldier. Payments to Negro soldiers were at first complicated by the ignorance of the recipients, and the fact that the quotas of colored regiments from Northern States were largely filled by recruits from the South, unknown to their fellow soldiers. Consequently, payments were accompanied by such frauds that Congress, by joint resolution in 1867, put the whole matter in the hands of the Freedmen's Bureau. In two years six million dollars was thus distributed to five thousand claimants, and in the end the sum exceeded eight million dollars. Even in this system fraud was frequent; but still the work put needed capital in the hands of practical paupers, and some, at least, was well spent.

The most perplexing and least successful part of the Bureau's work lay in the exercise of its judicial functions. The regular Bureau court consisted of one representative of the employer, one of the Negro, and one of the Bureau. If the Bureau could have maintained a perfectly judicial attitude, this arrangement would have been ideal, and must in time have gained confidence; but the nature of its other activities and the character of its *personnel* prejudiced the Bureau in favor of the black litigants, and led without doubt to much injustice and annoyance. On the other hand, to leave the Negro in the hands of Southern courts was impossible. In a distracted land where slavery had hardly fallen, to keep the strong

---

[1]Edmund Ware (1837–1885) established Atlanta University.

[2]Samuel Armstrong (1839–1893) founded Hampton Institute.

[3]Erastus Cravath (1833–1900) was the first president at Fisk University.

from wanton abuse of the weak, and the weak from gloating insolently over the half-shorn strength of the strong, was a thankless, hopeless task. The former masters of the land were peremptorily ordered about, seized, and imprisoned, and punished over and again, with scant courtesy from army officers. The former slaves were intimidated, beaten, raped, and butchered by angry and revengeful men. Bureau courts tended to become centres simply for punishing whites, while the regular civil courts tended to become solely institutions for perpetuating the slavery of blacks. Almost every law and method ingenuity could devise was employed by the legislatures to reduce the Negroes to serfdom,—to make them the slaves of the State, if not of individual owners; while the Bureau officials too often were found striving to put the "bottom rail on top," and gave the freedmen a power and independence which they could not yet use. It is all well enough for us of another generation to wax wise with advice to those who bore the burden in the heat of the day. It is full easy now to see that the man who lost home, fortune, and family at a stroke, and saw his land ruled by "mules and niggers," was really benefited by the passing of slavery. It is not difficult now to say to the young freedman, cheated and cuffed about who has seen his father's head beaten to a jelly and his own mother namelessly assaulted, that the meek shall inherit the earth. Above all, nothing is more convenient than to heap on the Freedmen's Bureau all the evils of that evil day, and damn it utterly for every mistake and blunder that was made.

All this is easy, but it is neither sensible nor just. Someone had blundered, but that was long before Oliver Howard[4] was born; there was criminal aggression and heedless neglect, but without some system of control there would have been far more than there was. Had that control been from within, the Negro would have been re-enslaved, to all intents and purposes. Coming as the control did from without, perfect men and methods would have bettered all things; and even with imperfect agents and questionable methods, the work accomplished was not undeserving of commendation.

Such was the dawn of Freedom; such was the work of the Freedmen's Bureau, which, summed up in brief, may be epitomized thus: for some fifteen million dollars, beside the sums spent before 1865, and the dole of benevolent societies, this Bureau set going a system of free labor, established a beginning of peasant proprietorship, secured the recognition of black freedmen before courts of law, and founded the free common school in the South. On the other hand, it failed to begin the establishment of good-will between ex-masters and freedmen, to guard its work wholly from paternalistic methods which discouraged self-reliance, and to carry out to any considerable extent its implied promises to furnish the freedmen with land. Its successes were the result of hard work, supplemented by the aid of philanthropists and the eager striving of black men. Its failures were the result of bad local agents, the inherent difficulties of the work, and national neglect.

Such an institution, from its wide powers, great responsibilities, large control of moneys, and generally conspicuous position, was naturally open to repeated and bitter attack. It sustained a searching Congressional investigation at the

---

[4]Oliver Howard (1830–1909) served as commissioner for the Freedmen's Bureau in 1865.

instance of Fernando Wood in 1870. Its archives and few remaining functions were with blunt discourtesy transferred from Howard's control, in his absence, to the supervision of Secretary of War Belknap in 1872, on the Secretary's recommendation. Finally, in consequence of grave intimations of wrong-doing made by the Secretary and his subordinates, General Howard was court-martialed in 1874. In both of these trials the Commissioner of the Freedmen's Bureau was officially exonerated from any wilful misdoing, and his work commended. Nevertheless, many unpleasant things were brought to light,—the methods of transacting the business of the Bureau were faulty; several cases of defalcation were proved, and other frauds strongly suspected; there were some business transactions which savored of dangerous speculation, if not dishonesty; and around it all lay the smirch of the Freedmen's Bank.

Morally and practically, the Freedmen's Bank was part of the Freedmen's Bureau, although it had no legal connection with it. With the prestige of the government back of it, and a directing board of unusual respectability and national reputation, this banking institution had made a remarkable start in the development of that thrift among black folk which slavery had kept them from knowing. Then in one sad day came the crash,—all the hard-earned dollars of the freedmen disappeared; but that was the least of the loss,—all the faith in saving went too, and much of the faith in men; and that was a loss that a Nation which to-day sneers at Negro shiftlessness has never yet made good. Not even ten additional years of slavery could have done so much to throttle the thrift of the freedmen as the mismanagement and bankruptcy of the series of savings banks chartered by the Nation for their especial aid. Where all the blame should rest, it is hard to say; whether the Bureau and the Bank died chiefly by reason of the blows of its selfish friends or the dark machinations of its foes, perhaps even time will never reveal, for here lies unwritten history.

Of the foes without the Bureau, the bitterest were those who attacked not so much its conduct or policy under the law as the necessity for any such institution at all. Such attacks came primarily from the Border States and the South; and they were summed up by Senator Davis, of Kentucky, when he moved to entitle the act of 1866 a bill "to promote strife and conflict between the white and black races . . . by a grant of unconstitutional power." The argument gathered tremendous strength South and North; but its very strength was its weakness. For, argued the plain common-sense of the nation, if it is unconstitutional, unpractical, and futile for the nation to stand guardian over its helpless wards, then there is left but one alternative,—to make those wards their own guardians by arming them with the ballot. Moreover, the path of the practical politician pointed the same way; for, argued this opportunist, if we cannot peacefully reconstruct the South with white votes, we certainly can with black votes. So justice and force joined hands.

The alternative thus offered the nation was not between full and restricted Negro suffrage; else every sensible man, black and white, would easily have chosen the latter. It was rather a choice between suffrage and slavery, after endless blood and gold had flowed to sweep human bondage away. Not a single Southern legislature stood ready to admit a Negro, under any conditions, to the polls; not a single Southern legislature believed free Negro labor was possible without a system of restrictions that took all its freedom away; there was scarcely a white man in the South who did not honestly regard Emancipation as a crime, and its practical nullification as a duty. In such a situation, the granting of the ballot to the black man was a necessity, the very least a guilty nation could grant a wronged race, and the only method of compelling the South to accept the results of the war. Thus Negro suffrage ended a civil war by beginning a race feud. And some felt gratitude toward the race thus sacrificed in its swaddling clothes on the altar of national integrity; and some felt and feel only indifference and contempt.

Had political exigencies been less pressing, the opposition to government guardianship of Negroes less bitter, and the attachment to the slave system less strong, the social seer can well imagine a far better policy,—a permanent Freedmen's Bureau, with a national system of Negro schools; a carefully supervised employment and labor office; a system of impartial protection before the regular courts; and such institutions for social betterment as savings-banks, land and building associations, and social settlements. All this vast expenditure of money and brains might have formed a great school of prospective citizenship, and solved in a way we have not yet solved the most perplexing and persistent of the Negro problems.

That such an institution was unthinkable in 1870 was due in part to certain acts of the Freedmen's Bureau itself. It came to regard its work as merely temporary, and Negro suffrage as a final answer to all present perplexities. The political ambition of many of its agents and *protégés* led it far afield into questionable activities, until the South, nursing its own deep prejudices, came easily to ignore all the good deeds of the Bureau and hate its very name with perfect hatred. So the Freedmen's Bureau died, and its child was the Fifteenth Amendment.

The passing of a great human institution before its work is done, like the untimely passing of a single soul, but leaves a legacy of striving for other men. The legacy of the Freedmen's Bureau is the heavy heritage of this generation. To-day, when new and vaster problems are destined to strain every fibre of the national mind and soul, would it not be well to count this legacy honestly and carefully? For this much all men know: despite compromise, war, and struggle, the Negro is not free. In the backwoods of the Gulf States, for miles and miles, he may not leave the plantation of his birth; in well-nigh the whole rural South the black farmers are peons, bound by law and custom to an economic slavery, from which the only escape is death or the penitentiary. In the most cultured sections and cities of the South the Negroes are a segregated servile caste, with restricted rights and privileges. Before the courts, both in law and custom, they stand on a different and peculiar basis. Taxation without representation is the rule of their political life. And the result of all this is, and in nature must have been, lawlessness and crime. That is the large legacy of the Freedmen's Bureau, the work it did not do because it could not.

I have seen a land right merry with the sun, where children sing, and rolling hills lie like passioned women wanton with harvest. And there in the King's Highways sat and sits a figure veiled and bowed, by which the traveller's footsteps hasten as they go. On the tainted air broods fear. Three centuries' thought has been the raising and unveiling of that bowed human heart, and now behold a century new for the duty and the deed. The problem of the Twentieth Century is the problem of the color-line.

BOOKER T. WASHINGTON (1856–1915)

Born a slave in Roanoke, Virginia, Booker T. Washington grew up in Malden, West Virginia. By 1872, he began attending Hampton Institute, earning a degree in 1875. After accepting a position as head of Tuskegee Institute in 1881, Washington promoted the idea of industrial education as a means for African American students to achieve prosperity and social equality. He succeeded with his fund-raising techniques, creating a huge endowment for the college. He died from arteriosclerosis in 1915.

Up from Slavery (1901), his autobiography, documents his journey from slavery to freedom and his views on racial integration and suffrage for blacks. Because of his ideology, often seen as accommodationist in his lack of public critique of social segregation of blacks and whites, scholars have viewed Booker T. Washington as politically conservative in comparison to W. E. B. Du Bois, who more openly criticized social segregation.

From Up from Slavery (1901)

Chapter 14: The Atlanta Exposition Address

The Atlanta Exposition, at which I had been asked to make an address as a representative of the Negro race, . . . was opened with a short address from Governor Bullock. After other interesting exercises, including an invocation from Bishop Nelson, of Georgia, a dedicatory ode by Albert Howell, Jr., and addresses by the President of the Exposition and Mrs. Joseph Thompson, the President of the Woman's Board, Governor Bullock introduced me with the words, "We have with us to-day a representative of Negro enterprise and Negro civilization."

When I arose to speak, there was considerable cheering, especially from the coloured people. As I remember it now, the thing that was uppermost in my mind was the desire to say something that would cement the friendship of the races and bring about hearty cooperation between them. So far as my outward surroundings were concerned, the only thing that I recall distinctly now is that when I got up, I saw thousands of eyes looking intently into my face. The following is the address which I delivered:—

Mr. President and Gentlemen of the Board of Directors and Citizens:

One-third of the population of the South is of the Negro race. No enterprise seeking the material, civil, or moral welfare of this section can disregard this element of our population and reach the highest success. I but convey to you, Mr. President and Directors, the sentiment of the masses of my race when I say that in no way have the value and manhood of the American Negro been more fittingly and generously recognized than by the managers of this magnificent Exposition at every stage of its progress. It is a recognition that will do more to cement the friendship of the two races than any occurrence since the dawn of our freedom.

Not only this, but the opportunity here afforded will awaken among us a new era of industrial progress. Ignorant and inexperienced, it is not strange that in the first years of our new life we began at the top instead of at the bottom; that a seat in Congress or the state legislature was more sought than real estate or industrial skill; that the political convention or stump speaking had more attractions than starting a dairy farm or truck garden.

A ship lost at sea for many days suddenly sighted a friendly vessel. From the mast of the unfortunate vessel was seen a signal, 'Water, water; we die of thirst!' The answer from the friendly vessel at once came back, 'Cast down your bucket where you are.' A second time the signal, 'Water, water; send us water!' ran up from the distressed vessel, and was answered, 'Cast down your bucket where you are.' And a third and fourth signal for water was answered, 'Cast down your bucket where you are.' The captain of the distressed vessel, at last heeding the injunction, cast down his bucket, and it came up full of fresh, sparkling water from the mouth of the Amazon River. To those of my race who depend on bettering their condition in a foreign land or who underestimate the importance of cultivating friendly relations with the Southern white man, who is their next-door neighbour, I would say: 'Cast down your bucket where you are'—cast it down in making friends in every manly way of the people of all races by whom we are surrounded.

Cast it down in agriculture, mechanics, in commerce, in domestic service, and in the professions. And in this connection it is well to bear in mind that whatever other sins the South may be called to bear, when it comes to business, pure and simple, it is in the South that the Negro is given a man's chance in the commercial world, and in nothing is this Exposition more eloquent than in emphasizing this chance. Our greatest danger is that in the great leap from slavery to freedom we may overlook the fact that the masses of us are to live by the productions of our hands, and fail to keep in mind that we shall prosper in proportion as we learn to dignify and glorify common labour and put brains and skill into the common occupations of life; shall prosper in proportion as we learn to draw the line between the superficial and the substantial, the ornamental gewgaws of life and the useful. No race can prosper till it learns that there is as much dignity in tilling a field as in writing a poem. It is at the bottom of life we must begin, and not at the top. Nor should we permit our grievances to overshadow our opportunities.

To those of the white race who look to the incoming of those of foreign birth and strange tongue and habits for the prosperity of the South, were I permitted I would repeat what I say to my own race, 'Cast down your bucket where you are.' Cast it down among the eight millions of Negroes whose habits you know, whose fidelity and love you have tested in days when to have proved treacherous meant the ruin of your firesides. Cast down your bucket among these people who have, without strikes and labour wars, tilled your fields, cleared your forests, builded your railroads and cities, and brought forth treasures from the bowels of the earth, and helped make possible this magnificent representation of the progress of the South. Casting down your bucket among my people, helping and encouraging them as you are doing on these grounds, and to education of head, hand, and heart, you will find that they will buy your surplus land, make blossom the waste places in your fields, and run your factories. While doing this, you can be sure in the future, as in the past, that you and your families will be surrounded by the most patient, faithful, law-abiding, and unresentful people that the world has seen. As we have proved our loyalty to you in the past, in nursing your children, watching by the sick-bed of your mothers and fathers, and often following them with tear-dimmed eyes to their graves, so in the future, in our humble way, we shall stand by you with a devotion that no foreigner can approach, ready to lay down our lives, if need be, in defence of yours, interlacing our industrial, commercial, civil, and religious life with yours in a way that shall make the interests of both races one. In all things that are purely social we can be as separate as the fingers, yet one as the hand in all things essential to mutual progress.

There is no defence or security for any of us except in the highest intelligence and development of all. If anywhere there are efforts tending to curtail the fullest growth of the Negro, let these efforts be turned into stimulating, encouraging, and making him the most useful and intelligent citizen. Effort or means so invested will pay a thousand per cent interest. These efforts will be twice blessed—'blessing him that gives and him that takes.'

There is no escape through law of man or God from the inevitable:—

The laws of changeless justice bind
   Oppressor with oppressed;
And close as sin and suffering joined
   We march to fate abreast.

Nearly sixteen millions of hands will aid you in pulling the load upward, or they will pull against you the load downward. We shall constitute one-third and more of the ignorance and crime of the South, or one-third its intelligence and progress; we shall contribute one-third to the business and industrial prosperity of the South, or we shall prove a veritable body of death, stagnating, depressing, retarding every effort to advance the body politic.

Gentlemen of the Exposition, as we present to you our humble effort at an exhibition of our progress, you must not expect overmuch. Starting thirty years ago with ownership here and there in a few quilts and pumpkins and chickens (gathered from miscellaneous sources), remember the path that has led from these to the inventions and production of agricultural implements, buggies, steam-engines, newspapers, books, statuary, carving, paintings, the management of drug-stores and banks, has not been trodden without contact with thorns and thistles. While we take pride in what we exhibit as a result of our independent efforts, we do not for a moment forget that our part in this exhibition would fall far short of your expectations but for the constant help that has come to our educational life, not only from the Southern states, but especially from Northern philanthropists, who have made their gifts a constant stream of blessing and encouragement.

The wisest among my race understand that the agitation of questions of social equality is the extremest folly, and that progress in the enjoyment of all the privileges that will come to us must be the result of severe and constant struggle rather than of artificial forcing. No race that has anything to contribute to the markets of the world is long in any degree ostracized. It is important and right that all privileges of the law be ours, but it is vastly more important that we be prepared for the exercises of these privileges. The opportunity to earn a dollar in a factory just now is worth infinitely more than the opportunity to spend a dollar in an opera-house.

In conclusion, may I repeat that nothing in thirty years has given us more hope and encouragement, and drawn us so near to you of the white race, as this opportunity offered by the Exposition; and here bending, as it were, over the altar that represents the results of the struggles of your race and mine, both starting practically empty-handed three decades ago, I pledge that in your effort to work out the great and intricate problem which God has laid at the doors of the South, you shall have at all times the patient, sympathetic help of my race; only let this be constantly in mind, that, while from representations in these buildings of the product of field, of forest, of mine, of factory, letters, and art, much good will come, yet far above and beyond material benefits will be that higher good, that, let us pray God, will come, in a blotting out of sectional differences and racial animosities and suspicions, in a determination to administer absolute justice, in a willing obedience among all classes to the mandates of law. This, this, coupled with our material prosperity, will bring into our beloved South a new heaven and a new earth.

The first thing that I remember, after I had finished speaking, was that Governor Bullock rushed across the platform and took me by the hand, and that others did the same. I received so many and such hearty congratulations that I found it difficult to get out of the building. I did not appreciate to any degree, however, the impression which my address seemed to have made, until the next morning, when I went into the business part of the city. As soon as I was recognized, I was surprised to find myself pointed out and surrounded by a crowd of men who wished to shake hands with me. This was kept up on every street on to which I went, to an extent which embarrassed me so much that I went back to my boarding-place. The next morning I returned to Tuskegee. At the station in Atlanta, and at almost all of the stations at which the train stopped between that city and Tuskegee, I found a crowd of people anxious to shake hands with me.

The papers in all parts of the United States published the address in full, and for months afterward there were complimentary editorial references to it. Mr. Clark Howell, the editor of the Atlanta *Constitution*, telegraphed to a New York paper, among other words, the following, 'I do not exaggerate when I say that Professor Booker T. Washington's address yesterday was one of the most notable speeches, both as to character and as to the warmth of its reception, ever delivered to a Southern audience. The address was a revelation. The whole speech is a platform upon which blacks and whites can stand with full justice to each other.'

The Boston *Transcript* said editorially: 'The speech of Booker T. Washington at the Atlanta Exposition, this week, seems to have dwarfed all the other proceedings and the Exposition itself. The sensation that it has caused in the press has never been equalled.'

I very soon began receiving all kinds of propositions from lecture bureaus, and editors of magazines and papers, to take the lecture platform, and to write articles. One lecture bureau offered me fifty thousand dollars, or two hundred dollars a night and expenses, if I would place my services at its disposal for a given period. To all these communications I replied that my life-work was at Tuskegee; and that whenever I spoke it must be in the interests of the Tuskegee school and my race, and that I would enter into no arrangements that seemed to place a mere commercial value upon my services.

Some days after its delivery I sent a copy of my address to the President of the United States, the Hon. Grover Cleveland. I received from him the following autograph reply:—

> GRAY GABLES, BUZZARD'S BAY, MASS.,
> October 6, 1895.

BOOKER T. WASHINGTON, ESQ.:

MY DEAR SIR: I thank you for sending me a copy of your address delivered at the Atlanta Exposition.

I thank you with much enthusiasm for making the address. I have read it with intense interest, and I think the Exposition would be fully justified if it did not do more than furnish the opportunity for its delivery. Your words cannot fail to delight and encourage all who wish well for your race; and if our coloured fellow-citizens do not from your utterances gather new hope and form new determinations to gain every valuable advantage offered them by their citizenship, it will be strange indeed.

> Yours very truly,
> GROVER CLEVELAND.

Later I met Mr. Cleveland, for the first time, when, as President, he visited the Atlanta Exposition. At the request of myself and others he consented to spend an hour in the Negro Building, for the purpose of inspecting the Negro exhibit and of giving the coloured people in attendance an opportunity to shake hands with him. As soon as I met Mr. Cleveland I became impressed with his simplicity, greatness, and rugged honesty. I have met him many times since then, both at public functions and at his private residence in Princeton, and the more I see of him the more I admire him. When he visited the Negro Building in Atlanta he seemed to give himself up wholly, for that hour, to the coloured people. He seemed to be as careful to shake hands with some old coloured 'auntie' clad partially in rags, and to take as much pleasure in doing so, as if he were greeting some millionnaire. Many of the coloured people took advantage of the occasion to get him to write his name in a book or on a slip of paper. He was as careful and patient in doing this as if he were putting his signature to some great state document.

Mr. Cleveland has not only shown his friendship for me in many personal ways, but has always consented to do anything I have asked of him for our school. This he has done, whether it was to make a personal donation or to use his influence in securing the donations of others. Judging from my personal acquaintance with Mr. Cleveland, I do not believe that he is conscious of possessing any colour prejudice. He is too great for that. In my contact with people I find that, as a rule, it is only the little, narrow people who live for themselves, who never read good books, who do not travel, who never open up their souls in a way to permit them to come into contact with other souls—with the great outside world. No man whose vision is bounded by colour can come into contact with what is highest and best in the world. In meeting men, in many places, I have found that the happiest people are those who do the most for others; the most miserable are those who do the least. I have also found that few things, if any, are capable of making one so blind and narrow as race prejudice. I often say to our students, in the course of my talks to them on Sunday evenings in the chapel, that the longer I live and the more experience I have of the world, the more I am convinced that, after all, the one thing that is most worth living for—and dying for, if need be—is the opportunity of making some one else more happy and more useful.

The coloured people and the coloured newspapers at first seemed to be greatly pleased with the character of my Atlanta address, as well as with its reception. But after the first burst of enthusiasm began to die away, and the coloured people began reading the speech in cold type, some of them seemed to feel that they had been hypnotized. They seemed to feel that I had been too liberal in my remarks toward the Southern whites, and that I had not spoken out strongly enough for what they termed the 'rights' of the race. For a while there was a reaction, so far as a certain element of my own race was concerned, but later these reactionary ones seemed to have been won over to my way of believing and acting.

While speaking of changes in public sentiment, I recall that about ten years after the school at Tuskegee was established, I had an experience that I shall never forget. Dr. Lyman Abbott, then the pastor of Plymouth Church, and also editor of the *Outlook* (then the *Christian Union*), asked me to write a letter for his paper giving my opinion of the exact condition, mental and moral, of the coloured ministers in the South, as based upon my observations. I wrote the letter, giving the exact facts as I conceived them to be. The picture painted was a rather black one—or, since I am black, shall I say 'white'? It could not be otherwise with a race but a few years out of slavery, a race which had not had time or opportunity to produce a competent ministry.

What I said soon reached every Negro minister in the country, I think, and the letters of condemnation which I received from them were not few. I think that for a year after the publication of this article every association and every conference or religious body of any kind, of my race, that met, did not fail before adjourning to pass a resolution condemning me, or calling upon me to retract or modify what I had said. Many of these organizations went so far in their resolutions as to advise parents to cease sending their children to Tuskegee. One association even appointed a 'missionary' whose duty it was to warn the people against sending their children to Tuskegee. This missionary had a son in the school, and I noticed that, whatever the 'missionary' might have said or done with regard to others, he was careful not to take his son away from the institution. Many of the coloured papers, especially those that were the organs of religious bodies, joined in the general chorus of condemnation or demands for retraction.

During the whole time of the excitement, and through all the criticism, I did not utter a word of explanation or retraction. I knew that I was right, and that time and the sober second thought of the people would vindicate me. It was not long before the bishops and other church leaders began to make a careful investigation of the conditions of the ministry, and they found out that I was right. In fact, the oldest and most influential bishop in one branch of the Methodist Church said that my words were far too mild. Very soon public sentiment began making itself felt, in demanding a purifying of the ministry. While this is not yet complete by any means, I think I may say, without egotism, and I have been told by many of our most influential ministers, that my words had much to do with starting a demand for the placing of a higher type of men in the pulpit. I have had the satisfaction of having many who once condemned me thank me heartily for my frank words.

The change of the attitude of the Negro ministry, so far as regards myself, is so complete that at the present time I have no warmer friends among any class than I have among the clergymen. The improvement in the character and life of the Negro ministers is one of the most gratifying evidences of the progress of the race. My experience with them, as well as other events in my life, convince me that the thing to do, when one feels sure that he has said or done the right thing, and is condemned, is to stand still and keep quiet. If he is right, time will show it.

In the midst of the discussion which was going on concerning my Atlanta speech, I received the letter which I give below, from Dr. Gilman, the President of Johns Hopkins University, who had been made chairman of the judges of award in connection with the Atlanta Exposition:—

> Johns Hopkins University, Baltimore,
> President's Office, September 30, 1895.

> Dear Mr. Washington: Would it be agreeable to you to be one of the Judges of Award in the Department of Education at Atlanta? If so, I shall be glad to place your name upon the list. A line by telegraph will be welcomed.

> Yours very truly,
> D. C. Gilman.

I think I was even more surprised to receive this invitation than I had been to receive the invitation to speak at the opening of the Exposition. It was to be a part of my duty, as one of the jurors, to pass not only upon the exhibits of the coloured schools, but also upon those of the white schools. I accepted the position, and spent a month in Atlanta in performance of the duties which it entailed. The board of jurors was a large one, consisting in all of sixty members. It was about equally divided between Southern white people and Northern white people. Among them were college presidents, leading scientists and men of letters, and specialists in many subjects. When the group of jurors to which I was assigned met for organization, Mr. Thomas Nelson Page, who was one of the number, moved that I be made secretary of that division, and the motion was unanimously adopted. Nearly half of our division were Southern people. In performing my duties in the inspection of the exhibits of white schools I was in every case treated with respect, and at the close of our labours I parted from my associates with regret.

I am often asked to express myself more freely than I do upon the political condition and the political future of my race. These recollections of my experience in Atlanta give me the opportunity to do so briefly. My own belief is, although I have never before said so in so many words, that the time will come when the Negro in the South will be accorded all the political rights which his ability, character, and material possessions entitle him to. I think, though, that the opportunity to freely exercise such political rights will not come in any large degree through outside or artificial forcing, but will be accorded to the Negro by the Southern white people themselves, and that they will protect him in the exercise of those rights. Just as soon as the South gets over the old feeling that it is being forced by 'foreigners,' or 'aliens,' to do something which it does not want to do, I believe that the change in the direction that I have indicated is going to begin. In fact, there are indications that it is already beginning in a slight degree.

Let me illustrate my meaning. Suppose that some months before the opening of the Atlanta Exposition there had been a general demand from the press and public platform outside the South that a Negro be given a place on the opening programme, and that a Negro be placed upon the board of jurors of award. Would any such recognition of the race have taken place? I do not think so. The Atlanta officials went as far as they did because they felt it to be a pleasure, as well as a duty, to reward what they considered merit in the Negro race. Say what we will, there is something in human nature which we cannot blot out, which makes one man, in the end, recognize and reward merit in another, regardless of colour or race.

I believe it is the duty of the Negro—as the greater part of the race is already doing—to deport himself modestly in regard to political claims, depending upon the slow but sure influences that proceed from the possession of property, intelligence, and high character for the full recognition of his political rights. I think that the according of the full exercise of political rights is going to be a matter of natural, slow growth, not an over-night, gourd-vine affair. I do not believe that the Negro should cease voting, for a man cannot learn the exercise of self-government by ceasing to vote, any more than a boy can learn to swim by keeping out of the water, but I do believe that in his voting he should more and more be influenced by those of intelligence and character who are his next-door neighbours.

I know coloured men who, through the encouragement, help, and advice of Southern white people, have accumulated thousands of dollars' worth of property, but who, at the same time, would never think of going to those same persons for advice concerning the casting of their ballots. This, it seems to me, is unwise and unreasonable, and should cease. In saying this I do not mean that the Negro should truckle, or not vote from principle, for the instant he ceases to vote from principle he loses the confidence and respect of the Southern white man even.

I do not believe that any state should make a law that permits an ignorant and poverty-stricken white man to vote, and prevents a black man in the same condition from voting. Such a law is not only unjust, but it will react, as all unjust laws do, in time; for the effect of such a law is to encourage the Negro to secure education and property, and at the same time it encourages the white man to remain in ignorance and poverty. I believe that in time, through the operation of intelligence and friendly race relations, all cheating at the ballot-box in the South will cease. It will become apparent that the white man who begins by cheating a Negro out of his ballot soon learns to cheat a white man out of his, and that the man who does this ends his career of dishonesty by the theft of property or by some equally serious crime. In my opinion, the time will come when the South will encourage all of its citizens to vote. It will see that it pays better, from every standpoint, to have healthy, vigorous life than to have that political stagnation which always results when one-half of the population has no share and no interest in the Government.

As a rule, I believe in universal, free suffrage, but I believe that in the South we are confronted with peculiar conditions that justify the protection of the ballot in many of the states, for a while at least, either by an educational test, a property test, or by both combined; but whatever tests are required, they should be made to apply with equal and exact justice to both races.

JAMES WELDON JOHNSON (1871–1938)

Originally from Jacksonville, Florida, James Weldon Johnson came from a family that valued education. He attended Atlanta University and by 1894 had earned a degree. He engaged in a number of professions, including teaching, editing, and law. Later, he was appointed U.S. consul in Venezuela and Nicaragua. He penned The Autobiography of an Ex-Colored Man *(1912), a novel of passing that chronicles a light-skinned black man's attempt to pretend he is white. The novel suggests that although blacks in twentieth-century America were no longer slaves, they were not truly free but suffered from racial discrimination and injustice. Like Du Bois, Johnson was heavily involved in the NAACP, becoming executive secretary in 1920. He edited* The Book of American Negro Poetry *(1922), an important text in the evolution of African American literature. He followed this collection with* God's Trombones: Seven Negro Sermons in Verse *(1927) and* Black Manhattan *(1930), which documents the presence of African American culture in New York. He died in 1958 in a car accident that occurred in Maine.*

O Black and Unknown Bards (1908)

O black and unknown bards of long ago,
How came your lips to touch the sacred fire?
How, in your darkness, did you come to know
The power and beauty of the minstrel's lyre?
Who first from midst his bonds lifted his eyes?   5

Who first from out the still watch, lone and long,
Feeling the ancient faith of prophets rise
Within his dark-kept soul, burst into song?

Heart of what slave poured out such melody
As "Steal away to Jesus"? On its strains   10
His spirit must have nightly floated free,
Though still about his hands he felt his chains.
Who heard great "Jordan roll"? Whose starward eye
Saw chariot "swing low"? And who was he
That breathed that comforting, melodic sigh,   15
"Nobody knows de trouble I see"?

What merely living clod, what captive thing,
Could up toward God through all its darkness grope,
And find within its deadened heart to sing
These songs of sorrow, love, and faith, and hope?   20
How did it catch that subtle undertone,
That note in music heard not with the ears?
How sound the elusive reed so seldom blown,
Which stirs the soul or melts the heart to tears.

Not that great German master in his dream   25
Of harmonies that thundered amongst the stars
At the creation, ever heard a theme
Nobler than "Go down, Moses." Mark its bars,
How like a mighty trumpet-call they stir
The blood. Such are the notes that men have sung   30
Going to valorous deeds; such tones there were
That helped make history when Time was young.

There is a wide, wide wonder in it all,
That from degraded rest and servile toil
The fiery spirit of the seer should call   35
These simple children of the sun and soil.
O black slave singers, gone, forgot, unfamed,
You—you alone, of all the long, long line
Of those who've sung untaught, unknown, unnamed,
Have stretched out upward, seeking the divine.   40

You sang not deeds of heroes or of kings;
No chant of bloody war, no exulting pean
Of arms-won triumphs; but your humble strings
You touched in chord with music empyrean.
You sang far better than you knew; the songs   45
That for your listeners' hungry hearts sufficed
Still live,—but more than this to you belongs:
You sang a race from wood and stone to Christ.

The Creation (1927)

And God stepped out on space,
And he looked around and said:
I'm lonely—
I'll make me a world.

And far as the eye of God could see   5
Darkness covered everything,
Blacker than a hundred midnights
Down in a cypress swamp.

Then God smiled,
And the light broke,   10
And the darkness rolled up on one side,
And the light stood shining on the other,
And God said: That's good!

Then God reached out and took the light in his hands,
And God rolled the light around in his hands   15
Until he made the sun;
And he set that sun a-blazing in the heavens.
And the light that was left from making the sun
God gathered it up in a shining ball
And flung it against the darkness,   20
Spangling the night with the moon and stars.
Then down between
The darkness and the light
He hurled the world;
And God said: That's good!   25

Then God himself stepped down—
And the sun was on his right hand,
And the moon was on his left;
The stars were clustered about his head,
And the earth was under his feet.   30
And God walked, and where he trod
His footsteps hollowed the valleys out
And bulged the mountains up.

Then he stopped and looked and saw
That the earth was hot and barren.   35
So God stepped over to the edge of the world
And he spat out the seven seas—
He batted his eyes, and the lightnings flashed—
He clapped his hands, and the thunders rolled—
And the waters above the earth came down,   40
The cooling waters came down.

Then the green grass sprouted,
And the little red flowers blossomed,
The pine tree pointed his finger to the sky,
And the oak spread out his arms,   45
The lakes cuddled down in the hollows of the ground,
And the rivers ran down to the sea;
And God smiled again,
And the rainbow appeared,
And curled itself around his shoulder.   50

Then God raised his arm and he waved his hand
Over the sea and over the land,
And he said: Bring forth! Bring forth!
And quicker than God could drop his hand,
Fishes and fowls   55
And beasts and birds
Swam the rivers and the seas,
Roamed the forests and the woods,
And split the air with their wings.
And God said: That's good!   60

Then God walked around,
And God looked around
On all that he had made.
He looked at his sun,
And he looked at his moon,   65
And he looked at his little stars;
He looked on his world
With all its living things,
And God said: I'm lonely still.

Then God sat down—   70
On the side of a hill where he could think;
By a deep, wide river he sat down;
With his head in his hands,
God thought and thought,
Till he thought: I'll make me a man!   75

Up from the bed of the river
God scooped the clay;
And by the bank of the river
He kneeled him down;
And there the great God Almighty   80
Who lit the sun and fixed it in the sky,
Who flung the stars to the most far corner of the night,
Who rounded the earth in the middle of his hand;
This Great God,
Like a mammy bending over her baby,   85

Kneeled down in the dust
Toiling over a lump of clay
Till he shaped it in his own image;

Then into it he blew the breath of life,
And man became a living soul.   90
Amen. Amen.

From The Autobiography of an Ex-Colored Man
(1912)

Chapter 1

I know that in writing the following pages I am divulging the great secret of my life, the secret which for some years I have guarded far more carefully than any of my earthly possessions; and it is a curious study to me to analyse the motives which prompt me to do it. I feel that I am led by the same impulse which forces the un-found-out criminal to take somebody into his confidence, although he knows that the act is likely, even almost certain, to lead to his undoing. I know that I am playing with fire, and I feel the thrill which accompanies that most fascinating pastime; and, back of it all, I think I find a sort of savage and diabolical desire to gather up all the little tragedies of my life, and turn them into a practical joke on society.

And, too, I suffer a vague feeling of unsatisfaction, of regret, of almost remorse, from which I am seeking relief, and of which I shall speak in the last paragraph of this account.

I was born in a little town of Georgia a few years after the close of the Civil War. I shall not mention the name of the town, because there are people still living there who could be connected with this narrative. I have only a faint recollection of the place of my birth. At times I can close my eyes and call up in a dreamlike way things that seem to have happened ages ago in some other world. I can see in this half vision a little house—I am quite sure it was not a large one—I can remember that flowers grew in the front yard, and that around each bed of flowers was a hedge of vari-coloured glass bottles stuck in the ground neck down. I remember that once, while playing round in the sand, I became curious to know whether or not the bottles grew as the flowers did, and I proceeded to dig them up to find out; the investigation brought me a terrific spanking, which indelibly fixed the incident in my mind. I can remember, too, that behind the house was a shed under which stood two or three wooden wash-tubs. These tubs were the earliest aversion of my life, for regularly on certain evenings I was plunged into one of them and scrubbed until my skin ached. I can remember to this day the pain caused by the strong, rank soap's getting into my eyes.

Back from the house a vegetable garden ran, perhaps seventy-five or one hundred feet; but to my childish fancy it was an endless territory. I can still recall the thrill of joy, excitement, and wonder it gave me to go on an exploring expedition through it, to find the blackberries, both ripe and green, that grew along the edge of the fence.

I remember with what pleasure I used to arrive at, and stand before, a little enclosure in which stood a patient cow chewing her cud, how I would occasionally offer her through the bars a piece of my bread and molasses, and how I would jerk back my hand in half fright if she made any motion to accept my offer.

I have a dim recollection of several people who moved in and about this little house, but I have a distinct mental image of only two: one, my mother; and the other, a tall man with a small, dark moustache. I remember that his shoes or boots were always shiny, and that he wore a gold chain and a great gold watch with which he was always willing to let me play. My admiration was almost equally divided between the watch and chain and the shoes. He used to come to the house evenings, perhaps two or three times a week; and it became my appointed duty whenever he came to bring him a pair of slippers and to put the shiny shoes in a particular corner; he often gave me in return for this service a bright coin, which my mother taught me to promptly drop in a little tin bank. I remember distinctly the last time this tall man came to the little house in Georgia; that evening before I went to bed he took me up in his arms and squeezed me very tightly; my mother stood behind his chair wiping tears from her eyes. I remember how I sat upon his knee and watched him laboriously drill a hole through a ten-dollar gold piece, and then tie the coin around my neck with a string. I have worn that gold piece around my neck the greater part of my life, and still possess it, but more than once I have wished that some other way had been found of attaching it to me besides putting a hole through it.

On the day after the coin was put around my neck my mother and I started on what seemed to me an endless journey. I knelt on the seat and watched through the train window the corn- and cotton-fields pass swiftly by until I fell asleep. When I fully awoke, we were being driven through the streets of a large city—Savannah. I sat up and blinked at the bright lights. At Savannah we boarded a steamer which finally landed us in New York. From New York we went to a town in Connecticut, which became the home of my boyhood.

My mother and I lived together in a little cottage which seemed to me to be fitted up almost luxuriously: there were horse-hair covered chairs in the parlour, and a little square piano; there was a stairway with red carpet on it leading to a half second story; there were pictures on the walls, and a few books in a glass-doored case. My mother dressed me very neatly, and I developed that pride which well-dressed boys generally have. She was careful about my associates, and I myself was quite particular. As I look back now I can see that I was a perfect little aristocrat. My mother rarely went to anyone's house, but she did sewing, and there were a great many ladies coming to our cottage. If I was round they would generally call me, and ask me my name and age and tell my mother what a pretty boy I was. Some of them would pat me on the head and kiss me.

My mother was kept very busy with her sewing; sometimes she would have another woman helping her. I think she must have derived a fair income from her work. I know, too, that at least once each month she received a letter; I used to watch for the postman, get the letter, and run to her with it; whether she was busy or not, she would take it and instantly thrust it into her bosom. I never saw her read one of these letters. I knew later that they contained money and what was to her more than money. As busy as she generally was, she found time, however, to teach me my letters and figures and how to spell a number of easy words. Always on Sunday evenings she opened the little square piano and picked out hymns. I can recall now that whenever she played hymns from the book her *tempo* was always decidedly *largo*. Sometimes on other evenings, when she was not sewing, she would play simple accompaniments to some old Southern songs which she sang. In these songs she was freer, because she played them by ear. Those evenings on which she opened the little piano were the happiest hours of my childhood. Whenever she started toward the instrument, I used to follow her with all the interest and irrepressible joy that a pampered pet dog shows when a package is opened in which he knows there is a sweet bit for him. I used to stand by her side and often interrupt and annoy her by chiming in with strange harmonies which I found on either the high keys of the treble or the low keys of the bass. I remember that I had a particular fondness for the black keys. Always on such evenings, when the music was over, my mother would sit with me in her arms, often for a very long time. She would hold me close, softly crooning some old melody without words, all the while gently stroking her face against my head; many and many a night I thus fell asleep. I can see her now, her great dark eyes looking into the fire, to where? No one knew but her. The memory of that picture has more than once kept me from straying too far from the place of purity and safety in which her arms held me.

At a very early age I began to thump on the piano alone, and it was not long before I was able to pick out a few tunes. When I was seven years old, I could play by ear all of the hymns and songs that my mother knew. I had also learned the names of the notes in both clefs, but I preferred not to be hampered by notes. About this time several ladies for whom my mother sewed heard me play and they persuaded her that I should at once be put under a teacher; so arrangements were made for me to study the piano with a lady who was a fairly good musician; at the same time arrangements were made for me to study my books with this lady's daughter. My music teacher had no small difficulty at first in pinning me down to the notes. If she played my lesson over for me, I invariably attempted to reproduce the required sounds without the slightest recourse to the written characters. Her daughter, my other teacher, also had her worries. She found that, in reading, whenever I came to words that were difficult or unfamiliar, I was prone to bring my imagination to the rescue and read from the picture. She has laughingly told me, since then, that I would sometimes substitute whole sentences and even paragraphs from what meaning I thought the illustrations conveyed. She said she not only was sometimes amused at the fresh treatment I would give an author's subject, but, when I gave some new and sudden turn to the plot of the story, often grew interested and even excited in listening to hear what kind of a denouement I would bring about. But I am sure this was not due to dullness, for I made rapid progress in both my music and my books.

And so for a couple of years my life was divided between my music and my school-books. Music took up the greater part of my time. I had no playmates, but amused myself with games—some of them my own invention—which could be played alone. I knew a few boys whom I had met at the church which I attended with my mother, but I had formed no close friendships with any of them. Then, when I was nine years old, my mother decided to enter me in the public school, so all at once I found myself thrown among a crowd of boys of all sizes and kinds; some of them seemed to me like savages. I shall never forget the bewilderment, the pain, the heart-sickness, of that first day at school. I seemed to be the only stranger in the place; every other boy seemed to know every other boy. I was fortunate enough, however, to be assigned to a teacher who knew me; my mother made her dresses. She was one of the ladies who used to pat me on the head and kiss me. She had the tact to address a few words directly to me; this gave me a certain sort of standing in the class and put me somewhat at ease.

Within a few days I had made one staunch friend and was on fairly good terms with most of the boys. I was shy of the girls, and remained so; even now a word or look from a pretty woman sets me all a-tremble. This friend I bound to me with hooks of steel in a very simple way. He was a big awkward boy with a face full of freckles and a head full of very red hair. He was perhaps fourteen years of age; that is, four or five years older than any other boy in the class. This seniority was due to the fact that he had spent twice the required amount of time in several of the preceding classes. I had not been at school many hours before I felt that "Red Head"—as I involuntarily called him—and I were to be friends. I do not doubt that this feeling was strengthened by the fact that I had been quick enough to see that a big, strong boy was a friend to be desired at a public school; and, perhaps, in spite of his dullness, "Red Head" had been able to discern that I could be of service to him. At any rate there was a simultaneous mutual attraction.

The teacher had strung the class promiscuously round the walls of the room for a sort of trial heat for places of rank; when the line was straightened out, I found that by skilful manœuvring I had placed myself third and had piloted "Red Head" to the place next to me. The teacher began by giving us to spell the words corresponding to our order in the line. "Spell *first*." "Spell *second*." "Spell *third*." I rattled off: "T-h-i-r-d, third," in a way which said: "Why don't you give us something hard?" As the words went down the line, I could see how lucky I had been to get a good place together with an easy word. As young as I was, I felt impressed with the unfairness of the whole proceeding when I saw the tailenders going down before *twelfth* and *twentieth*, and I felt sorry for those who had to spell such words in order to hold a low position. "Spell *fourth*." "Red Head," with his hands clutched tightly behind his back, began bravely: "F-o-r-t-h." Like a flash a score of hands went up, and the teacher began saying: "No snapping of fingers, no snapping of fingers." This was the first word missed, and it seemed to me that some of the scholars were about to lose their senses; some were dancing up and down on one foot with a hand above their heads, the fingers working furiously, and joy beaming all over their faces; others stood still, their hands raised not so high, their fingers working less rapidly, and their faces expressing not quite so much happiness; there were still others who did not move or raise their hands, but stood with great wrinkles on their foreheads, looking very thoughtful.

The whole thing was new to me, and I did not raise my hand, but slyly whispered the letter "u" to "Red Head" several times. "Second chance," said the teacher. The hands went down and the class became quiet. "Red Head," his face now red, after looking beseechingly at the ceiling, then pitiably at the floor, began very haltingly: "F-u—" Immediately an impulse to raise hands went through the class, but the teacher checked it, and poor "Red Head," though he knew that each letter he added only took him farther out of the way, went doggedly on and finished: "—r-t-h." The handraising was now repeated with more hubbub and excitement than at first. Those who before had not moved a finger were now waving their hands above their heads. "Red Head" felt that he was lost. He looked very big and foolish, and some of the scholars began to snicker. His helpless condition went straight to my heart, and gripped my sympathies. I felt that if he failed, it would in some way be my failure. I raised my hand, and, under cover of the excitement and the teacher's attempts to regain order, I hurriedly shot up into his ear twice, quite distinctly: "F-o-u-r-t-h, f-o-u-r-t-h." The teacher tapped on her desk and said: "Third and last chance." The hands came down, the silence became oppressive. "Red Head" began: "F—" Since that day I have waited anxiously for many a turn of the wheel of fortune, but never under greater tension than when I watched for the order in which those letters would fall from "Red's" lips—"o-u-r-t-h." A sigh of relief and disappointment went up from the class. Afterwards, through all our school-days, "Red Head" shared my wit and quickness and I benefited by his strength and dogged faithfulness.

There were some black and brown boys and girls in the school, and several of them were in my class. One of the boys strongly attracted my attention from the first day I saw him. His face was as black as night, but shone as though it were polished; he had sparkling eyes, and when he opened his mouth, he displayed glistening white teeth. It struck me at once as appropriate to call him "Shiny Face," or "Shiny Eyes," or "Shiny Teeth," and I spoke of him often by one of these names to the other boys. These terms were finally merged into "Shiny," and to that name he answered goodnaturedly during the balance of his public school days.

"Shiny" was considered without question to be the best speller, the best reader, the best penman—in a word, the best scholar, in the class. He was very quick to catch anything, but, nevertheless, studied hard; thus he possessed two powers very rarely combined in one boy. I saw him year after year, on up into the high school, win the majority of the prizes for punctuality, deportment, essay writing, and declamation. Yet it did not take me long to discover that, in spite of his standing as a scholar, he was in some way looked down upon.

The other black boys and girls were still more looked down upon. Some of the boys often spoke of them as "niggers." Sometimes on the way home from school a crowd would walk behind them repeating:

Nigger, nigger, never die,
Black face and shiny eye.

On one such afternoon one of the black boys turned suddenly on his tormentors and hurled a slate; it struck one of the white boys in the mouth, cutting a slight gash in his lip. At sight of the blood the boy who had thrown the slate ran, and his companions quickly followed. We ran after them pelting them with stones until they separated in several directions. I was very much wrought up over the affair, and went home and told my mother how one of the "niggers" had struck a boy with a slate. I shall never forget how she turned on me. "Don't you ever use that word again," she said, "and don't you ever bother the coloured children at school. You ought to be ashamed of yourself." I did hang my head in shame, not because she had convinced me that I had done wrong, but because I was hurt by the first sharp word she had ever given me.

My school-days ran along very pleasantly. I stood well in my studies, not always so well with regard to my behaviour. I was never guilty of any serious misconduct, but my love of fun sometimes got me into trouble. I remember, however, that my sense of humour was so sly that most of the trouble usually fell on the head of the other fellow. My ability to play on the piano at school exercises was looked upon as little short of marvellous in a boy of my age. I was not chummy with many of my mates, but, on the whole, was about as popular as it is good for a boy to be.

One day near the end of my second term at school the principal came into our room and, after talking to the teacher, for some reason said: "I wish all of the white scholars to stand for a moment." I rose with the others. The teacher looked at me and, calling my name, said: "You sit down for the present, and rise with the others." I did not quite understand her, and questioned: "Ma'm?" She repeated, with a softer tone in her voice: "You sit down now, and rise with the others." I sat down dazed. I saw and heard nothing. When the others were asked to rise, I did not know it. When school was dismissed, I went out in a kind of stupor. A few of the white boys jeered at me, saying: "Oh, you're a nigger too." I heard some black children say: "We knew he was coloured." "Shiny" said to them: "Come along, don't tease him," and thereby won my undying gratitude.

I hurried on as fast as I could, and had gone some distance before I perceived that "Red Head" was walking by my side. After a while he said to me: "Le' me carry your books." I gave him my strap without being able to answer. When we got to my gate, he said as he handed me my books: "Say, you know my big red agate? I can't shoot with it any more. I'm going to bring it to school for you tomorrow." I took my books and ran into the house. As I passed through the hallway, I saw that my mother was busy with one of her customers; I rushed up into my own little room, shut the door, and went quickly to where my looking-glass hung on the wall. For an instant I was afraid to look, but when I did, I looked long and earnestly. I had often heard people say to my mother: "What a pretty boy you have!" I was accustomed to hear remarks about my beauty; but now, for the first time, I became conscious of it and recognized it. I noticed the ivory whiteness of my skin, the beauty of my mouth, the size and liquid darkness of my eyes, and how the long, black lashes that fringed and shaded them produced an effect that was strangely fascinating even to me. I noticed the softness and glossiness of my dark hair that fell in waves over my temples, making my forehead appear whiter than it really was. How long I stood there gazing at my image I do not know. When I came out and reached the head of the stairs, I heard the lady who had been with my mother going out. I ran downstairs and rushed to where my mother was sitting, with a piece of work in her hands. I buried my head in her lap and blurted out: "Mother, mother, tell me, am I a nigger?" I could not see her face, but I knew the piece of work dropped to the floor and I felt her hands on my head. I looked up into her face and repeated: "Tell me, mother, am

I a nigger?" There were tears in her eyes and I could see that she was suffering for me. And then it was that I looked at her critically for the first time. I had thought of her in a childish way only as the most beautiful woman in the world; now I looked at her searching for defects. I could see that her skin was almost brown, that her hair was not so soft as mine, and that she did differ in some way from the other ladies who came to the house; yet, even so, I could see that she was very beautiful, more beautiful than any of them. She must have felt that I was examining her, for she hid her face in my hair and said with difficulty: "No, my darling, you are not a nigger." She went on: "You are as good as anybody; if anyone calls you a nigger, don't notice them." But the more she talked, the less was I reassured, and I stopped her by asking: "Well, mother, am I white? Are you white?" She answered tremblingly: "No, I am not white, but you—your father is one of the greatest men in the country—the best blood of the South is in you—" This suddenly opened up in my heart a fresh chasm of misgiving and fear, and I almost fiercely demanded: "Who is my father? Where is he?" She stroked my hair and said: "I'll tell you about him some day." I sobbed: "I want to know now." She answered: "No, not now."

Perhaps it had to be done, but I have never forgiven the woman who did it so cruelly. It may be that she never knew that she gave me a sword-thrust that day in school which was years in healing.

From Black Manhattan (1930)

Chapter 1

The fact that within New York, the greatest city of the New World, there is found the greatest single community anywhere of people descended from age-old Africa appears at a thoughtless glance to be the climax of the incongruous. Harlem is today the Negro metropolis and as such is everywhere known. In the history of New York the name Harlem has changed from Dutch to Irish to Jewish to Negro; but it is through this last change that it has gained its most widespread fame. Throughout coloured America Harlem is the recognized Negro capital. Indeed, it is Mecca for the sightseer, the pleasure-seeker, the curious, the adventurous, the enterprising, the ambitious, and the talented of the entire Negro world; for the lure of it has reached down to every island of the Carib Sea and penetrated even into Africa. It is almost as well known to the white world, for it has been much talked and written about.

So here we have Harlem—not merely a colony or a community or a settlement—not at all a "quarter" or a slum or a fringe—but a black city, located in the heart of white Manhattan, and containing more Negroes to the square mile than any other spot on earth. It strikes the uninformed observer as a phenomenon, a miracle straight out of the skies.

But the seeming incongruity and wonder of this black metropolis in the heart of the great Western white metropolis grows less and less and disappears as we glance backward from Harlem and become familiar with the story of the Negro in the City and State of New York. The anomaly of the situation starts to fade out the moment we take account of how far back the story begins.

Henry Hudson, under the flag of the Dutch East India Company, sailed up the Hudson River in 1609; the Dutch West India Company was established in 1614; and New Netherland was founded as a Dutch colony in 1623. Governor Peter Minuit bought Manhattan Island from the Indians and established the settlement of New Amsterdam—New York City—in 1626. Within the same year there were eleven Negroes in the colony, constituting a little above five per cent of the total non-Indian population. There is a record of the names of four of these eleven Negroes: Paul d'Angola, Simon Congo, Anthony Portuguese, and John Francisco. These names appear to have some bearing on the origins of the men who bore them, and they also carry a suggestion of romance. What was the history of these first Negroes landed on Manhattan? There is nothing to tell the tale. The eleven were all men, and the probabilities are that they were captured seamen, for the Dutch West India Company was actually a naval power and waged war upon the high seas. These Negroes were landed at New Amsterdam and made bondservants; but there were instances at a later date when Dutch commanders, not knowing what to do with them, let captured blacks go free. Two years later three Negro women were landed at New Amsterdam.

Under a system of patroonship the number of Negroes in the colony increased, but only slowly; and it was not until a definite system of slavery was established that it grew rapidly. Slavery was never quite profitable in New Netherland under the Dutch; so it never actually flourished. But the Dutch surrendered to the English in 1664; and under the English, who had found slave labour profitable in Virginia, slavery became an institution in New York. Thirty years after the English occupation of the colony there were 2,170 Negroes in New York, a little more than thirteen per cent of the whole colonial population. Under English rule the trade in black human beings was extended and became lucrative. The laying out of plantations in Westchester County and on Long Island and Staten Island was an important factor in the development of the trade. The settling of whites and blacks on the land in these three sections began at the same time. In 1709 a slave-market was established at the foot of Wall Street.

Slavery under the Dutch was comparatively mild. The Dutch West India Company in 1644 manumitted eleven Negro slaves who had been long in its service. It is interesting to take their names from the record, if for no other reason than that they shed an additional light on the original eleven. The names of those manumitted because they had "served the Company seventeen or eighteen years" and had been "long since promised their freedom on the same footing as other free peoples here in New Netherland" were: Paul d'Angola, Big Manuel, Little Manuel, Manuel de Gerrit de Rens, Simon Congo, Anthony Portuguese, Gracia, Peter Santome, John Francisco, Little Anthony, John Fort Orange. The manumission of these eleven slaves marked a cardinal epoch in the history of the Negro in New York—the beginning of a colony of black freemen in the midst of slavery. This policy of manumission was followed by numbers of individuals.

Slaves in New Netherland differed but little from indentured servants. They had almost full freedom of motion and assembly; they were allowed to marry; wives and daughters had legal protection against the lechery of masters, and they had the right to acquire and hold property. Slaves in New Netherland never became mere merchandise, nor did the slave system ever reach the dehumanized stage which it reached in the English-speaking colonies and states. Perhaps the system under the Dutch lacked, among other things, sufficient time for development; be that as it may, under the English, slavery in the colony flourished and took on all the harsh and cruel traits of the system farther south. Laws were enacted annulling those few rights which the slaves had possessed, and the most severe restrictions and drastic practices were adopted.

The slaves had been far from content under the soft system of the Dutch. They were continually striving for freedom through manumission. It was upon their own petition that the first group was manumitted. As conditions grew harsher, they tried swifter methods. They escaped to Canada or ran away and took refuge with the Indians. In 1705 the General Assembly found it necessary to pass an act forbidding all Negro slaves from "travelling forty miles above the city of Albany, at or above a place called Sarachtoge [Saratoga], on pain of death," unless accompanied by master or mistress. Later a treaty was made with the Six Nations, in which these Indian tribes agreed to deliver up all Negro slaves that might take refuge among them. Such treaties were never lived up to by the Indians.

The increasing cruelty of slavery was attended by the increasing bitterness and resentment of the slaves, until, driven to the extreme, they struck a blind blow at their oppressors. The blow, of course, was futile; indeed, it was followed by laws and practices still more severe and galling. In striking it, however, the Negro wrote his first full-length page in New York history—and a bloody page it is. The report on the "Negro Insurrection of 1712" made by Governor Robert Hunter to the Lords of Trade may be paraphrased briefly: On April 6, 1712 twenty-three Negro slaves met about midnight in the orchard of one Mr. Cook, in the middle of the town, for the purpose of destroying as many of the inhabitants as they could to revenge themselves for the hard usage they felt they had received from their masters. Some of them were armed with fire-arms, some with swords, and others with knives and hatchets. One of them, Coffee (or Cuffee), slave of one Peter Vantilburg, set fire to an outhouse of his master, whereupon the whole band sallied forth and marched to the fire. News of the fire spread through the town, and a crowd of townspeople flocked to it. The band of insurgents opened fire on the crowd, killing nine citizens and wounding five or six others. Alarm was given. The Governor ordered a detachment from the fort to march against the revolting slaves, but they, under cover of night, made their escape into the woods. The Governor, by placing sentries and having the militia of New York and Westchester counties drive the island, captured all the rebels, except six who preferred suicide to capture. In the "tryal before ye Justices" twenty-seven were condemned. Twenty-one were executed—"some were burnt, others hanged, one broke on the wheele and one hung alive in ye towne." The Governor did not strain his words in saying: "There has been the most exemplary punishment inflicted that could be thought of."

Twenty-nine years later the city was again thrown into a panic by the so-called "conspiracy to burn New York and murder its inhabitants." On March 18, 1741 the fort at what is now the Battery was destroyed by fire. A number of fires followed in quick succession throughout the town. Wild rumours began to fly that the fires were the result of a slave conspiracy to destroy the city and massacre the whites. Negroes were arrested wholesale and put into prison, but no clue to the origin of the fires could be found. The mystery was deepened by the fact that none of the fires was connected with any attempt at violence. A month or so after the burning of the fort, Mary Burton, a white indentured servant to John Hughson, an innkeeper, was called before the grand jury to testify regarding a robbery which, it was alleged, had been planned in her master's place. The jury came to feel that in Mary Burton they had the key to the mystery of the fires. The girl at first refused to give any testimony on that point, but under pressure she told a story that involved three Negroes known as Cæsar, Prince, and Coffee (or Cuffee) not only in the robbery, but also in the conspiracy to burn the town, massacre the whites, and make themselves the rulers. She testified that the three had met often at her master's house to lay these plans. In her story she also implicated John Hughson, her master, Sara Hughson, her master's wife, and another white woman, named Peggy Kerry, known as "the Irish beauty," who lived at Hughson's and was the kept mistress of Cæsar, having had a child by him. It cannot be known how trustworthy Mary Burton's testimony was, but through it scores of persons were eventually involved in the charge. The trial was held in an atmosphere of apprehension and terror. There were, of course, many persons alive who had vivid recollections of the "Insurrection of 1712." In such an atmosphere justice could not have a breathing chance. Many a time has a legal trial served as a sort of substitute for a Roman circus for New Yorkers, but, without doubt, no other legal show has ever approached this 1741 trial in sensationalism and importance. And it is certain that not only New York but every other slave-holding community in the country was deeply interested in the outcome. So important was this case deemed that Chief Justice Horsmanden, in 1744, published a *Journal of the Proceedings against the Conspirators*. This volume was republished in England in 1748, and in 1810 it was republished in New York as a *History of the Negro Plot*, a book of nearly four hundred pages. The chief purpose of the book was to justify the drastic punishments that had been meted out.

As a result of the trial eighteen were hanged, fourteen were executed in the manner of one, Tom, who was condemned to be "burned alive with a slow fire until he is dead and consumed to ashes." In addition, seventy-odd Negroes were transported out of the country. Among those hanged were John Hughson and his wife, the white girl, Peggy, and an Englishman, a priest, named John Ury.

After the "Conspiracy of 1741" the state of the Negro in New York sank to the nadir, but in the last quarter of the century a change in sentiment regarding slavery began to make itself felt. The doctrine of the Declaration of Independence was not without some collateral effect upon the status of the black man. During the Revolutionary War the Legislature of New York passed an act granting freedom to all slaves who served in the Army for three years or until honourably discharged. Later a bill was passed providing for two Negro regiments. Coloured men of New York formed a good proportion of the nearly four thousand Negro soldiers that fought in the colonial armies. At the close of the Revolutionary War—to be more precise, according to the census of 1790—there were 25,978 Negroes in the State of New York—21,324 slaves and 4,654 freemen.

Our Democracy and the Ballot

James Weldon Johnson

In 1923, James Weldon Johnson gave this speech in New York City. His subject matter focuses on voting rights for blacks. African American writers during the Harlem Renaissance used the written and oral word to advocate civil rights.

Ladies and Gentlemen:

For some time since I have had growing apprehensions about any subject—especially the subject of a speech—that contained the word "'democracy." The word "democracy" carries so many awe-inspiring implications. As the key-word of the subject of an address it may be the presage of an outpour of altitudinous and platitudinous expressions regarding "the most free and glorious government of the most free and glorious people that the world has ever seen." On the other hand, it may hold up its sleeve, if you will permit such a figure, a display of abstruse and recondite theorizations or hypotheses of democracy as a system of government. In choosing between either of these evils it is difficult to decide which is the lesser.

Indeed, the wording of my subject gave me somewhat more concern than the speech. I am not sure that it contains the slightest idea of what I shall attempt to say; but if the wording of my subject is loose it only places upon me greater reason for being more specific and definite in what I shall say. This I shall endeavor to do; at the same time, however, without being so confident or so cocksure as an old preacher I used to listen to on sundry Sundays when I taught school one summer down in the backwoods of Georgia, sometimes to my edification and often to my amazement.

On one particular Sunday, after taking a rather cryptic text, he took off his spectacles and laid them on the pulpit, closed the Bible with a bang, and said, "Brothers and sisters, this morning I intend to explain the inexplainable, to find out the indefinable, to ponder over the imponderable, and to unscrew the inscrutable."

Our Democracy and the Ballot

It is one of the commonplaces of American thought that we have a democracy based upon the free will of the governed. The popular idea of the strength of this democracy is that it is founded upon the fact that every American citizen, through the ballot, is a ruler in his own right; that every citizen of age and outside of jail or the insane asylum has the undisputed right to determine through his vote by what laws he shall be governed and by whom these laws shall be enforced.

I could be cynical or flippant and illustrate in how many ways this popular idea is a fiction, but it is not my purpose to deal in *cleverisms*. I wish to bring to your attention seriously a situation, a condition, which not only runs counter to the popular conception of democracy in America but which runs counter to the fundamental law upon which that democracy rests and which, in addition, is a negation of our principles of government and a menace to our institutions.

Without any waste of words, I come directly to a condition which exists in that section of our country which we call "the South," where millions of American citizens are denied both the right to vote and the privilege of qualifying themselves to vote. I refer to the wholesale disfranchisement of Negro citizens. There is no need at this time of going minutely into the methods employed to bring about this condition or into the reasons given as justification for those methods. Neither am I called upon to give proof of my general statement that millions of Negro citizens in the South are disfranchised. It is no secret. There are the published records of state constitutional conventions in which the whole subject is set forth with brutal frankness. The purpose of these state constitutional conventions is stated over and over again, that purpose being to exclude from the right of franchise the Negro, however literate, and to include the white man, however illiterate.

The press of the South, public men in public utterances, and representatives of those states in Congress, have not only admitted these facts but have boasted of them. And so we have it as an admitted and undisputed fact that there are upwards of four million Negroes in the South who are denied the right to vote but who in any of the great northern, mid-western or western states would be allowed to vote or would at least have the privilege of qualifying themselves to vote.

Now, nothing is further from me than the intention to discuss this question either from an anti-South point of view or from a pro-Negro point of view. It is my intention to put it before you purely as an American question, a question in which is involved the political life of the whole country.

Let us first consider this situation as a violation, not merely a violation but a defiance, of the Constitution of the United States. The Fourteenth and Fifteenth Amendments to the Constitution taken together express so plainly that a grammar school boy can understand it that the Negro is created a citizen of the United States and that as such he is entitled to all the rights of every other citizen and that those rights, specifically among them the right to vote, shall not be denied or abridged by the United States or by any state. This is the expressed meaning of these amendments in spite of all the sophistry and fallacious pretense which have been invoked by the courts to overcome it.

There are some, perhaps even here, who feel that it is no more serious a matter to violate or defy one amendment to the constitution than another. Such persons will have in mind the Eighteenth Amendment. This is true in a strictly legal sense, but any sort of analysis will show that violation of the two Civil War Amendments strikes deeper. As important as the Eighteenth Amendment may be, it is not fundamental; it contains no grant of rights to the citizen nor any requirement of service from him. It is rather a sort of welfare regulation for his personal conduct and for his general moral uplift.

But the two Civil War Amendments are grants of citizenship rights and a guarantee of protection in those rights, and therefore their observation is fundamental and vital not only to the citizen but to the integrity of the government.

We may next consider it as a question of political franchise equality between the states. We need not here go into a list of figures. A few examples will strike the difference:

In the elections of 1920 it took 82,492 votes in Mississippi to elect two senators and eight representatives. In Kansas it took 570,220 votes to elect exactly the same representation. Another illustration from the statistics of the same election shows that one vote in Louisiana has fifteen times the political power of one vote in Kansas.

In the Congressional elections of 1918 the total vote for the ten representatives from the State of Alabama was 62,345, while the total vote for ten representatives in Congress from Minnesota was 299,127, and the total vote in Iowa, which has ten representatives, was 316,377.

In the Presidential election of 1916 the states of Alabama, Arkansas, Georgia, Louisiana, Mississippi, North Carolina, South Carolina, Tennessee, Texas and Virginia cast a total vote for the Presidential candidates of 1,870,209. In Congress these states have a total of 104 representatives and 126 votes in the electoral college. The State of New York alone cast a total vote for Presidential candidates of 1,706,354, a vote within 170,000 of all the votes cast by the above states, and yet New York has only 43 representatives and 45 votes in the electoral college.

What becomes of our democracy when such conditions of inequality as these can be brought about through chicanery, the open violation of the law and defiance of the Constitution?

But the question naturally arises, What if there is violation of certain clauses of the Constitution; what if there is an inequality of political power among the states? All this may be justified by necessity.

In fact, the justification is constantly offered. The justification goes back and makes a long story. It is grounded in memories of the Reconstruction period. Although most of those who were actors during that period have long since died, and although there is a new South and a new Negro, the argument is still made that the Negro is ignorant, the Negro is illiterate, the Negro is venal, the Negro is inferior; and, therefore, for the preservation of civilized government in the South, he must be debarred from the polls. This argument does not take into account the fact that the restrictions are not against ignorance, illiteracy and venality, because by the very practices by which intelligent, decent Negroes are debarred, ignorant and illiterate white men are included.

Is this pronounced desire on the part of the South for an enlightened franchise sincere, and what has been the result of these practices during the past forty years?

What has been the effect socially, intellectually and politically, on the South? In all three of these vital phases of life the South is, of all sections of the country, at the bottom. Socially, it is that section of the country where public opinion allows it to remain the only spot in the civilized world—no, more than that, we may count in the blackest spots of Africa and the most unfrequented islands of the sea—it is a section where public opinion allows it to remain the only spot on the earth where a human being may be publicly burned at the stake.

And what about its intellectual and political life? As to intellectual life I can do nothing better than quote from Mr. H. L. Mencken, himself a Southerner. In speaking of the intellectual life of the South, Mr. Mencken says:

> It is, indeed, amazing to contemplate so vast a vacuity. One thinks of the interstellar spaces, of the colossal reaches of the now mythical ether. One could throw into the South France, Germany and Italy, and still have room for the British Isles. And yet, for all its size and all its wealth and all the "progress" it babbles of, it is almost as sterile, artistically, intellectually, culturally, as the Sahara Desert. . . . If the whole of the late Confederacy were to be engulfed by a tidal wave tomorrow, the effect on the civilized minority of men in the world would be but little greater than that of a flood on the Yang-tse-kiang. It would be impossible in all history to match so complete a drying-up of a civilization. In all that section there is not a single poet, not a serious historian, not a creditable composer, not a critic good or bad, not a dramatist dead or alive.

In a word, it may be said that this whole section where, at the cost of the defiance of the Constitution, the perversion of law, the stultification of men's consciousness, injustice and violence upon a weaker group, the "purity" of the ballot has been preserved and the right to vote restricted to only lineal survivors of Lothrop Stoddard's mystical Nordic supermen—that intellectually it is dead and politically it is rotten.

If this experiment in super-democracy had resulted in one one-hundredth of what was promised, there might be justification for it, but the result has been to make the South a section not only in which Negroes are denied the right to vote, but one in which white men dare not express their honest political opinions. Talk about political corruption through the buying of votes, here is political corruption which makes a white man fear to express a divergent political opinion. The actual and total result of this practice has been not only the disfranchisement of the Negro but the disfranchisement of the white man. The figures which I quoted a few moments ago prove that not only Negroes are denied the right to vote but that white men fail to exercise it; and the latter condition is directly dependent upon the former.

The whole condition is intolerable and should be abolished. It has failed to justify itself even upon the grounds which it is claimed made it necessary. Its results and its tendencies make it more dangerous and more damaging than anything which might result from an ignorant and illiterate electorate. How this iniquity might be abolished is, however, another story.

I said that I did not intend to present this subject either as anti-South or pro-Negro, and I repeat that I have not wished to speak with anything that approached bitterness toward the South. Indeed, I consider the condition of the South unfortunate, more than unfortunate. The South is in a state of superstition which makes it see ghosts and bogymen, ghosts which are the creation of its own mental processes.

With a free vote in the South the specter of Negro domination would vanish into thin air. There would naturally follow a breaking up of the South into two parties. There would be political light, political discussion, the right to differences of opinion, and the Negro vote would naturally divide itself. No other procedure would be probable. The idea of a solid party, a minority party at that, is inconceivable.

But perhaps the South will not see the light. Then, I believe, in the interest of the whole country, steps should be taken to compel compliance with the Constitution, and that should be done through the enforcement of the Fourteenth Amendment, which calls for a reduction in representation in proportion to the number of citizens in any state denied the right to vote.

And now I cannot sit down after all without saying one word for the group of which I am a member.

The Negro in the matter of the ballot demands only that he should be given the right as an American citizen to vote under the identical qualifications required of other citizens. He cares not how high those qualifications are made—whether they include the ability to read and write, or the possession of five hundred dollars, or a knowledge of the Einstein Theory—just so long as these qualifications are impartially demanded of white men and black men.

In this controversy over which have been waged battles of words and battles of blood, where does the Negro himself stand?

The Negro in the matter of the ballot demands only that he be given his right as an American citizen. He is justified in making this demand because of his undoubted Americanism, an Americanism which began when he first set foot on the shores of this country more than three hundred years ago, antedating even the Pilgrim Fathers; an Americanism which has woven him into the woof and warp of the country and which has impelled him to play his part in every war in which the country has been engaged, from the Revolution down to the late World War.

Through his whole history in this country he has worked with patience, and in spite of discouragement he has never turned his back on the light. Whatever may be his shortcomings, however slow may have been his progress, however disappointing may have been his achievements, he has never consciously sought the backward path. He has always kept his face to the light and continued to struggle forward and upward in spite of obstacles, making his humble contributions to the common prosperity and glory of our land. And it is his land. With conscious pride the Negro can say:

"This land is ours by right of birth,
　This land is ours by right of toil;
We helped to turn its virgin earth,
　Our sweat is in its fruitful soil.

"Where once the tangled forest stood.—
　Where flourished once rank weed and thorn,—
Behold the path-traced, peaceful wood.
　The cotton white, the yellow corn.

"To gain these fruits that have been earned,
　To hold these fields that have been won.
Our arms have strained, our backs have burned
　Bent bare beneath a ruthless sun.

"That banner which is now the type
　Of victory on field and flood—
Remember, its first crimson stripe
　Was dyed by Attucks' willing blood.

"And never yet has come the cry—
　When that fair flag has been assailed—
For men to do, for men to die,
　That we have faltered or have failed."

　　The Negro stands as the supreme test of the civilization, the Christianity and the common decency of the American people. It is upon the answer demanded of America today by the Negro that there depends the fulfillment or the failure of democracy in America. I believe that that answer will be the right and just answer. I believe that the spirit in which American democracy was founded, though often turned aside and often thwarted, can never be defeated or destroyed but that ultimately it will triumph.

　　If American democracy cannot stand the test of giving to any citizen who measures up to the qualifications required of others the full rights and privileges of American citizenship, then we had just as well abandon that democracy in name as in deed. If the Constitution of the United States cannot extend the arm of protection around the weakest and humblest of American citizens as around the strongest and proudest, then it is not worth the paper it is written on.

ANGELINA WELD GRIMKE (1880–1958)

African American women writers of the Harlem Renaissance era often wrote about the influence of race, class, and gender in their lives. Angelina Weld Grimke illustrates the concerns of many African American women of the early twentieth century. A native of Boston, Massachusetts, Grimke was the daughter of an NAACP vice president. A well-educated woman, she spent six years as a student at Harvard. Later, she relocated to Washington, D.C., where she worked as an English teacher. She wrote poetry, short stories, and plays, critiquing discrimination in America and calling for freedom from racial, sexual, and class prejudice. Her play Rachel *(1916) indicts racism in America. Grimke died in 1958, but her work lives on in its poignant treatment of race, gender, and class issues.*

Rachel (1916)

Cast of Characters

Mrs. Loving, *mother*
Rachel Loving, *her daughter*
Tom Loving, *her son*
John Strong, *Tom's friend*

Jimmy, *the neighbor's small boy*
Mrs. Lane, *a black woman*
Ethel, Louise, Nancy, Mary,
  Martha, Jenny, *children*

ACT 1

(The scene is a room scrupulously neat and clean and plainly furnished. The walls are painted green, the woodwork white. In the rear at the left [left and right are from the spectator's point of view] an open doorway leads into a hall. Its bare green wall and white baseboard are all that can be seen of it. It leads into the other rooms of the flat. In the center of the rear wall of the room is a window. It is shut. The white sash curtains are pushed to right and left as far as they will go. The green shade is rolled up to the top. Through the window can be seen the red bricks of a house wall, and the tops of a couple of trees moving now and then in the wind. Within the window, and just below the sill, is a shelf upon which are a few potted plants. Between the window and the door is a bookcase full of books and above it, hanging on the wall, a simply framed, inexpensive copy of Millet's "The Reapers." There is a run extending from the right center to just below the right upper entrance. It is the vestibule of the flat. Its open doorway faces the left wall. In the right wall near the front is another window. Here the sash curtains are drawn together and the green shade is partly lowered. The window is up from the bottom. Through it street noises can be heard. In front of this window is an open, threaded sewing-machine. Some frail, white fabric is lying upon it. There is a chair in front of the machine and at the machine's left a small table covered with a green cloth. In the rear of the left wall and directly opposite to the entrance to the flat is the doorway leading into the kitchenette, dishes on shelves can be seen behind glass doors.

In the center of the left wall is a fireplace with a grate in it for coals; over this is a wooden mantel painted white. In the center is a small clock. A pair of vases, green and white in coloring, one at each end, complete the ornaments. Over the mantel is a narrow mirror; and over this, hanging on the wall Burne-Jones' "Golden Stairs" simply framed. Against the front end of the left wall is an upright piano with a stool in front of it. On top is music neatly piled. Hanging over the piano is Raphael's "Sistine Madonna." In the center of the floor is a green rug, and in the center of this, a rectangular dining-room table, the long side facing front. It is covered with a green table-cloth. Three dining-room chairs are at the table, one at either end and one at the rear facing front. Above the table is a chandelier with four gas jets enclosed by glass globes. At the right front center is a rather shabby arm-chair upholstered in green.

Before the sewing-machine, MRS. LOVING *is seated. She looks worried. She is sewing swiftly and deftly by hand upon a waist in her lap. It is a white, beautiful thing and she sews upon it delicately. It is about half-past four in the afternoon; and the light is failing.* MRS. LOVING *pauses in her sewing, rises and lets the window-shade near her go up to the top. She pushes the sash-curtains to either side, the corner of a red brick house wall being thus brought into view. She shivers slightly, then pushes the window down at the bottom and lowers it a trifle from the top. The street noises become less distinct. She takes off her thimble, rubs her hands gently, puts the thimble on again, and looks at the clock on the mantel. She then reseats herself, with her chair as close to the window as possible and begins to sew. Presently a key is heard, and the door opens and shuts noisily.* RACHEL *comes in from the vestibule. In her left arm she carries four or five books strapped together; under her right, a roll of music. Her hat is twisted over her left ear and her hair is falling in tendrils about her face. She brings into the room with her the spirit of abounding life, health, joy, youth.* MRS. LOVING *pauses, needle in hand, as soon as she hears the turning key and the banging door. There is a smile at each other. Then* RACHEL *throws her books upon the dining-room table, places the music there also, but with care, and rushing to her mother, gives her a bear hug and a kiss)*

RACHEL. Ma dear! dear, old Ma dear!

MRS. LOVING. Look out for the needle, Rachel! The waist! Oh, Rachel!

RACHEL. *(on her knees and shaking her finger directly under her mother's nose)* You old, old fraud! You know you adore being hugged. I've a good mind . . .

MRS. LOVING. Now, Rachel, please! Besides, I know your tricks. You think you can make me forget you are late. What time is it?

RACHEL. *(looking at the clock and expressing surprise)* Jiminy Christmas! *(whistles)* Why, it's five o'clock!

MRS. LOVING. *(severely)* Well!

RACHEL. *(plaintively)* Now, Ma dear, you're going to be horrid and cross.

MRS. LOVING. *(laughing)* Really, Rachel, that expression is not particularly affecting, when your hat is over your ear, and you look, with your hair over your eyes, exactly like someone's pet poodle. I wonder if you are ever going to grow up and be ladylike.

RACHEL. Oh! Ma dear, I hope not, not for the longest time, two long, long years at least. I just want to be silly and irresponsible, and have you to love and torment, and, of course, Tom, too.

MRS. LOVING. *(smiling down at* RACHEL*)* You'll not make me forget, young lady. Why are you late, Rachel?

RACHEL. Well, Ma dear, I'm your pet poodle, and my hat is over my ear, and I'm late, for the loveliest reason.

MRS. LOVING. Don't be silly, Rachel.

RACHEL. That may sound silly, but it isn't. And please don't "Rachel" me so much. It was honestly one whole hour ago when I opened the front door down stairs. I know it was, because I heard the postman telling some one it was four o'clock. Well, I climbed the first flight, and was just starting up the second when a little shrill voice said, "Lo!" I raised my eyes, and there, half-way up the stairs, sitting in the middle of a step, was just the dearest, cutest, darlingest little brown baby boy you ever saw. "Lo! yourself," I said. "What are you doing, and who are you anyway?" "I'm Jimmy; and I'm widing to New York on the choo-choo tars." As he looked entirely too young to be going such a distance by himself, I asked him if I might go too. For a minute or two he considered the question and me very seriously, and then he said, "Es," and made room for me on the step beside him. We've been everywhere: New York, Chicago, Boston, London, Paris and Oshkosh. I wish you could have heard him say that last place. I suggested going there just to hear him. Now, Ma dear, is it any wonder I am late? See all the places we have been in just one "teeny, weeny" hour? We would have been traveling yet, but his horrid, little mother came out and called him in. They're in the flat below, the new people. But before he went, Ma dear, he said the "cunningest" thing. He said, "Will you turn out an' p'ay wif me aden in two minutes?" I nearly hugged him to death, and it's a wonder my hat is on my head at all. Hats are such unimportant nuisances anyway!

MRS. LOVING. Unimportant nuisances! What ridiculous language you do use, Rachel! Well, I'm no prophet, but I see very distinctly what is going to happen. This little brown baby will be living here night and day. You're not happy unless some child is trailing along in your rear.

RACHEL. (*mischievously*) Now, Ma dear, who's a hypocrite? What? I suppose you don't like children! I can tell you one thing, though, it won't be my fault if he isn't here night and day. Oh, I wish he were all mine, every bit of him! Ma dear, do you suppose that "she woman" he calls mother would let him come up here until it is time for him to go to bed! I'm going down there this minute. (*rises impetuously*)

MRS. LOVING. Rachel, for Heaven's sake! No! I am entirely too busy and tired today without being bothered with a child romping around in here.

RACHEL. (*reluctantly and a trifle petulantly*) Very well, then. (*for several moments she watches her mother, who has begun to sew again. The displeasure vanishes from her face*) Ma dear!

MRS. LOVING. Well.

RACHEL. Is there anything wrong today?

MRS. LOVING. I'm just tired, chickabiddy, that's all.

RACHEL. (*moves over to the table. Mechanically takes off her hat and coat and carries them out into the entryway of the flat. She returns and goes to the looking glass over the fireplace and tucks in the tendrils of her hair in rather a preoccupied manner. The electric doorbell rings. She returns to the speaking tube in the vestibule. Her voice is heard answering*) Yes!—Yes!—No, I'm not Mrs. Loving. She's here, yes!— What? Oh! come right up! (*appearing in the doorway*) Ma dear, it's some man, who is coming for Mrs. Strong's waist.

MRS. LOVING. *(pausing and looking at* RACHEL*)* It is probably her son. She said she would send for it this afternoon. *(*RACHEL *disappears. A door is heard opening and closing. There is the sound of a man's voice.* RACHEL *ushers in* MR. JOHN STRONG*)*

STRONG. *(bowing pleasantly to* MRS. LOVING*)* Mrs. Loving? *(*MRS. LOVING *bows, puts down her sewing, rises and goes toward* STRONG*)* My name is Strong. My mother asked me to come by and get her waist this afternoon. She hoped it would be finished.

MRS. LOVING. Yes, Mr. Strong, it is all ready. If you'll sit down a minute, I'll wrap it up for you. *(she goes into hallway leading to other rooms in flat)*

RACHEL. *(manifestly ill at ease at being left alone with a stranger; attempting, however, to be the polite hostess)* Do sit down, Mr. Strong. *(they both sit)*

RACHEL. *(nervously after a pause)* It's a very pleasant day, isn't it, Mr. Strong?

STRONG. Yes, very. *(he leans back composedly, his hat on his knee, the faintest expression of amusement in his eyes)*

RACHEL. *(after a pause)* It's quite a climb up to our flat, don't you think?

STRONG. Why, no! It didn't strike me so. I'm not old enough yet to mind stairs.

RACHEL. *(nervously)* Oh! I didn't mean that you are old! Anyone can see you are quite young, that is, of course, not too young, but—(STRONG *laughs quietly)* There! I don't blame you for laughing. I'm always clumsy just like that.

MRS. LOVING. *(calling from the other room)* Rachel, bring me a needle and the sixty cotton, please.

RACHEL. All right, Ma dear! *(rummages for the cotton in the machine drawer, and upsets several spools upon the floor. To* STRONG*)* You see! I can't even get a spool of cotton without spilling things all over the floor. *(*STRONG *smiles,* RACHEL *picks up the spools and finally gets the cotton and needle)* Excuse me! *(goes out door leading to other rooms.* STRONG*, left to himself, looks around casually. The "Golden Stairs" interests him and the "Sistine Madonna")*

RACHEL. *(reenters, evidently continuing her function of hostess)* We were talking about the climb to our flat, weren't we? You see, when you're poor, you have to live in a top flat. There is always a compensation, though; we have bully—I mean nice air, better light, a lovely view, and nobody "thud-thudding" up and down over our heads night and day. The people below have our "thud-thudding," and it must be something *awful*, especially when Tom and I play "Ivanhoe" and have a tournament up here. We're entirely too old, but we still play. Ma dear rather dreads the climb up three flights, so Tom and I do all the errands. We don't mind climbing the stairs, particularly when we go up two or three at a time,—that is— Tom still does. I can't, Ma dear stopped me. *(sighs)* I've got to grow up it seems.

STRONG. *(evidently amused)* It is rather hard being a girl, isn't it?

RACHEL. Oh, no! It's not hard at all. That's the trouble, they won't let me be a girl. I'd love to be.

MRS. LOVING. *(reentering with parcel. She smiles)* My chatterbox, I see, is entertaining you, Mr. Strong. I'm sorry to have kept you waiting, but I forgot, I found, to sew the ruching in the neck. I hope everything is satisfactory. If it isn't, I'll be glad to make any changes.

STRONG. *(who has risen upon her entrance)* Thank you, Mrs. Loving, I'm sure everything is all right.

(He takes the package and bows to her and RACHEL. *He moves towards the vestibule,* MRS. LOVING *following him. She passes through the doorway first. Before leaving,* STRONG *turns for a second and looks back quietly at* RACHEL. *He goes out too.* RACHEL *returns to the mirror, looks at her face for a second, and then begins to touch and pat her hair lightly and delicately here and there.* MRS. LOVING *returns)*

RACHEL. *(still at the glass)* He *was* rather nice, wasn't he Ma dear?—for a man? *(laughs)* I guess my reason's a vain one,—he let me do all the talking. *(pauses)* Strong? Strong? Ma dear, is his mother the little woman with the sad, black eyes?

MRS. LOVING. *(resuming her sewing; sitting before the machine)* Yes. I was rather curious, I confess, to see this son of hers. The whole time I'm fitting her she talks of nothing else. She worships him. *(pauses)* It's rather a sad case, I believe. She is a widow. Her husband was a doctor and left her a little money. She came up from the South to educate this boy. Both of them worked hard and the boy got through college. Three months he hunted for work that a college man might expect to get. You see he had the tremendous handicap of being colored. As the two of them had to live, one day, without her knowing it, he hired himself out as a waiter. He has been one now for two years. He is evidently goodness itself to his mother.

RACHEL. *(slowly and thoughtfully)* Just because he is *colored!* *(pauses)* We sing a song at school, I believe, about "the land of the free and the home of the brave." What an amusing nation it is.

MRS. LOVING. *(watching* RACHEL *anxiously)* Come, Rachel, you haven't time for "amusing nations." Remember, you haven't practised any this afternoon. And put your books away; don't leave them on the table. You didn't practice any this morning either, did you?

RACHEL. No, Ma dear,—didn't wake up in time. *(goes to the table and in an abstracted manner puts books on the bookcase; returns to the table; picks up the roll of sheet music she has brought home with her; brightens; impulsively)* Ma dear, just listen to this lullaby. It's the sweetest thing. I was so "daffy" over it, one of the girls at school lent it to me. *(she rushes to the piano with the music and plays the accompaniment through softly and then sings, still softly and with great expression, Jessie Gaynor's "Slumber Boat")*

Baby's boat's the silver moon;
    Sailing in the sky,
Sailing o'er the sea of sleep,
    While the clouds float by.

Sail, baby, sail,
    Out upon that sea,
Only don't forget to sail
    Back again to me.

Baby's fishing for a dream,
    Fishing near and far,

His line a silver moon beam is,
    His bait a silver star.

Sail, baby, sail,
>   Out upon that sea,

Listen, Ma dear, right here. Isn't it lovely? *(plays and sings very softly and slowly)*

Only don't forget to sail
>   Back again to me.

(pauses; in hushed tones) Ma dear, it's so beautiful—it—it hurts.

MRS. LOVING. *(quietly)* Yes, dear, it is pretty.

RACHEL. *(for several minutes watches her mother's profile from the piano stool. Her expression is rather wistful)* Ma dear!

MRS. LOVING. Yes, Rachel.

RACHEL. What's the matter?

MRS. LOVING. *(without turning)* Matter! What do you mean?

RACHEL. I don't know. I just *feel* something is not quite right with you.

MRS. LOVING. I'm only tired—that's all.

RACHEL. Perhaps. But—*(watches her mother a moment or two longer; shakes her head; turns back to the piano. She is thoughtful; looks at her hands in her lap)* Ma dear, wouldn't it be nice if we could keep all the babies in the world—always little babies? Then they'd be always little, and cunning, and lovable; and they could never grow up, then, and—and—be bad. I'm so sorry for mothers whose little babies—grow up—and—and—are bad.

MRS. LOVING. *(startled; controlling herself, looks at* RACHEL *anxiously, perplexedly.* RACHEL's *eyes are still on her hands. Attempting a light tone)* Come, Rachel, what experience have you had with mothers whose babies have grown up to be bad? You—you talk like an old, old woman.

RACHEL. *(without raising her eyes, quietly)* I know I'm not old; but, just the same I know that is true. *(softly)* And I'm so sorry for the mothers.

MRS. LOVING. *(with a forced laugh)* Well, Miss Methuselah, how do you happen to know all this? Mothers whose babies grow up to be bad don't, as a rule, parade their faults before the world.

RACHEL. That's just it—that's *how* you know. They don't talk at all.

MRS. LOVING. *(involuntarily)* Oh! *(ceases to sew; looks at* RACHEL *sharply; she is plainly worried. There is a long silence. Presently* RACHEL *raises her eyes to Raphael's "Madonna" over the piano. Her expression becomes rapt; then, very softly, her eyes still on the picture, she plays and sings Nevin's "Mighty Lak' a Rose")*

Sweetest li'l feller,
>   Ev'rybody knows;
Dunno what to call him,
>   But he mighty lak' a rose!
Lookin' at his Mammy
>   Wid eyes so shiny blue,
Mek' you think that heav'n
>   Is comin' clost ter you!

W'en his dar a sleepin'
> In his li'l place
Think I see de angels
> Lookin' thro' de lace.
W'en de dark is fallin',
> W'en de shadders creep,
Den dey comes on tip-toe,
> Ter kiss him in his sleep.

Sweetest li'l feller, etc.

(with head still raised, after she has finished, she closes her eyes. Half to herself and slowly) I think the loveliest thing of all the lovely things in this world is just *(almost in a whisper)* being a mother!

MRS. LOVING. *(turns and laughs)* Well, of all the startling children, Rachel! I am getting to feel, when you're around, as though I'm shut up with dynamite. What next? (RACHEL *rises, goes slowly to her mother, and kneels down beside her. She does not touch her mother)* Why so serious, chickabiddy?

RACHEL. *(slowly and quietly)* It is not kind to laugh at sacred things. When you laughed, it was as though you laughed—at God!

MRS. LOVING. *(startled)* Rachel!

RACHEL. *(still quietly)* It's true. It was the best in me that said that—it was God! *(pauses)* And, Ma dear, if I believed that I should grow up and not be a mother, I'd pray to die now. I've thought about it a lot, Ma dear, and once I dreamed, and a voice said to me—oh! it was so real—"Rachel, you are to be a mother to little children." Wasn't that beautiful? Ever since I have known how Mary felt at the "Annunciation." *(almost in a whisper) God spoke to me through some one, and I believe.* And it has explained so much to me. I know now why I just can't resist any child. I have to love it—it calls me—it—draws me. I want to take care of it, wash it, dress it, live for it. I want the feel of its little warm body against me, its breath on my neck, its hands against my face. *(pauses thoughtfully for a few moments)* Ma dear, here's something I don't understand: I love the little black and brown babies best of all. There is something about them that—that—clutches at my heart. Why—why—should they be—oh!—pathetic? I don't understand. It's dim. More than the other babies, I feel that I must protect them. They're in danger, but from what? I don't know. I've tried so hard to understand, but I can't. *(her face radiant and beautiful)* Ma dear, I think their white teeth and the clear whites of their big black eyes and their dimples everywhere—are—are—*(breaks off)* and, Ma dear, because I love them best, I pray God every night to give me, when I grow up, little black and brown babies—to protect and guard. *(wistfully)* Now, Ma dear, don't you see why you must never laugh at me again? Dear, dear, Ma dear? *(buries her head in her mother's lap and sobs)*

MRS. LOVING. *(for a few seconds, sits as though dazed, and then instinctively begins to caress the head in her lap. To herself)* And I suppose my experience is every mother's. Sooner or later—of a sudden she finds her own child a stranger to her. *(to RACHEL, very tenderly)* Poor little girl! Poor little chickabiddy!

RACHEL. *(raising her head)* Why do you say, "Poor little girl," like that? I don't understand. Why, Ma dear, I never saw tears in your eyes before. Is it—is it—because you know the things I do not understand? Oh! It *is* that.

MRS. LOVING. *(simply)* Yes, Rachel, and I cannot save you.

RACHEL. Ma dear, you frighten me. Save me from what?

MRS. LOVING. Just life, my little chickabiddy!

RACHEL. Is life so terrible? I had found it mostly beautiful. How can life be terrible, when the world is full of little children?

MRS. LOVING. *(very sadly)* Oh, Rachel! Rachel!

RACHEL. Ma dear, what have I said?

MRS. LOVING. *(forcing a smile)* Why, the truth, of course, Rachel. Life is not terrible when there are little children—and you—and Tom—and a roof over our heads—and work—and food—and clothes—and sleep at night. *(pauses)* Rachel, I am not myself today. I'm tired. Forget what I've said. Come, chickabiddy, wipe your eyes and smile. That's only an imitation smile, but it's better than none. Jump up now, and light the lamp for me, will you? Tom's late, isn't he? I shall want you to go, too, for the rolls and pie for supper.

RACHEL. *(rises rather wearily and goes into the kitchenette. While she is out of the room* MRS. LOVING *does not move. She sits staring in front of her.* MRS. LOVING *can just be seen when* RACHEL *reenters with the lamp. She places it on the small table near her mother, adjusts it, so the light falls on her mother's work, and then lowers the window shades at the windows. She still droops.* MRS. LOVING, *while* RACHEL *is in the room, is industrious.* RACHEL *puts on her hat and coat listlessly. She does not look in the glass)* Where is the money, Ma dear? I'm ready.

MRS. LOVING. Before you go, Rachel, just give a look at the meat and see if it is cooking all right, will you, dearie?

RACHEL. *(goes out into the kitchenette and presently returns)* It's all right, Ma dear.

MRS. LOVING. *(while* RACHEL *is out of the room, she takes her pocket book out of the machine drawer, opens it, takes out money and gives it to* RACHEL *upon her return)* A dozen brown rolls, Rachel. Be sure they're brown! And, I guess,—an apple pie. As you and Tom never seem to get enough apple pie, get the largest she has. And here is a quarter. Get some candy—any kind *you* like, chickabiddy. Let's have a party tonight, I feel extravagant. Why, Rachel! Why are you crying?

RACHEL. Nothing, dear Ma dear. I'll be all right when I get in the air. Goodbye! *(rushes out of the flat.* MRS. LOVING *sits idle. Presently the outer door of the flat opens and shuts with a bang, and* TOM *appears.* MRS. LOVING *begins to work as soon as she hears the banging door)*

TOM. 'Lo, Ma! Where's Sis,—out? The door's off the latch. *(kisses his mother and hangs hat in entryway)*

MRS. LOVING. *(greeting him with the same beautiful smile with which she greeted* RACHEL*)* Rachel just went after the rolls and pie. She'll be back in a few minutes. You're late, Tommy.

TOM. No, Ma—you forget—it's pay day. *(with decided shyness and awkwardness he hands her his wages)* Here, Ma!

MRS. LOVING. *(proudly counting it)* But, Tommy, this is every bit of it. You'll need some.

TOM. Not yet! *(constrainedly)* I only wish—. Say, Ma, I hate to see you work so hard. *(fiercely)* Some day—some day—. *(breaks off)*

MRS. LOVING. Son, I'm as proud as though you have given me a million dollars.

TOM. *(emphatically)* I may some day,—you see. *(abruptly changing the subject)* Gee! Ma, I'm hungry. What's for dinner? Smells good.

MRS. LOVING. Lamb and dumplings and rice.

TOM. Gee! I'm glad I'm living—and a pie too?

MRS. LOVING. Apple pie, Tommy.

TOM. Say, Ma, don't wake me up. And shall "muzzer's" own little boy set the table?

MRS. LOVING. Thank you, Son.

TOM. *(folds the green cloth, hangs it over the back of the arm-chair, gets white table-cloth from kitchenette and sets the table. The whole time he is whistling blithely a popular air. He lights one of the gas jets over the table)* Ma!

MRS. LOVING. Yes, Son.

TOM. I made "squad" today,—I'm quarter-back. Five other fellows tried to make it. We'll all have to buy new hats, now.

MRS. LOVING. *(with surprise)* Buy new hats! Why?

TOM. *(makes a ridiculous gesture to show that his head and hers are both swelling)* Honest, Ma, I had to carry my hat in my hand tonight,—couldn't even get it to perch aloft.

MRS. LOVING. *(smiling)* Well, I for one, Son, am not going to say anything to make you more conceited.

TOM. You don't *have* to say anything. Why, Ma, ever since I told you, you can almost look down your own back your head is so high. What? *(MRS. LOVING laughs. The outer door of the flat opens and shuts. RACHEL's voice is heard)*

RACHEL. *(without)* My! That was a "dreful" climb, wasn't it? Ma, I've got something here for you. *(appears in the doorway carrying packages and leading a little boy by the hand. The little fellow is shy but smiling)* Hello, Tommy! Here, take these things for me. This is Jimmy. Isn't he a dear? Come, Jimmy. *(TOM carries the packages into the kitchenette. RACHEL leads JIMMY to MRS. LOVING)* Ma dear, this is my brown baby. I'm going to take him right down stairs again. His mother is as sweet as can be, and let me bring him up just to see you. Jimmy, this is Ma dear. *(MRS. LOVING turns expectantly to see the child. Standing before her, he raises his face to hers with an engaging smile. Suddenly, without word or warning, her body stiffens; her hands grip her sewing convulsively; her eyes stare. She makes no sound)*

RACHEL. *(frightened)* Ma dear! What is the matter? Tom! Quick! *(TOM reenters and goes to them)*

MRS. LOVING. *(controlling herself with an effort and breathing hard)* Nothing, dears, nothing. I must be—I am—nervous tonight. *(with a forced smile)* How-do-you-do, Jimmy? Now, Rachel—perhaps—don't you think—you had better take him back to his mother? Goodnight, Jimmy! *(eyes the child in a fascinated way the whole time he is in the room. RACHEL, very much perturbed, takes the child out)* Tom, open that window, please! There! That's better! *(still breathing deeply)* What a fool I am!

TOM. *(patting his mother awkwardly on the back)* You're all pegged out, that's the trouble—working entirely too hard. Can't you stop for the night and go to bed right after supper?

MRS. LOVING. I'll see, Tommy dear. Now I must look after the supper.

TOM. Huh! Well, I guess not. How old do you think Rachel and I are anyway? I see; you think we'll break some of this be-au-tiful Hav-i-land china, we bought at the "Five and Ten Cent Store." *(to* RACHEL *who has just reentered wearing a puzzled and worried expression. She is without hat and coat)* Say, Rachel, do you think you're old enough?

RACHEL. Old enough for what, Tommy?

TOM. To dish up the supper for Ma.

RACHEL. *(with attempted sprightliness)* Ma dear thinks nothing can go on in this little flat unless she does it. Let's show her a thing or two. *(they bring in the dinner.* MRS. LOVING *with trembling hands tries to sew.* TOM *and* RACHEL *watch her covertly. Presently she gets up)*

MRS. LOVING. I'll be back in a minute, children. *(goes out the door that leads to the other rooms of the flat.* TOM *and* RACHEL *look at each other)*

RACHEL. *(in a low voice keeping her eyes on the door)* Why do you suppose she acted so strangely about Jimmy?

TOM. Don't know—nervous, I guess,—worn out. I wish—*(breaks off)*

RACHEL. *(slowly)* It may be that; but she hasn't been herself this afternoon. I wonder—Look out! Here she comes!

TOM. *(in a whisper)* Liven her up. *(*RACHEL *nods.* MRS. LOVING *reenters. Both rush to her and lead her to her place at the right end of the table. She smiles and tries to appear cheerful. They sit down,* TOM *opposite* MRS. LOVING *and* RACHEL *at the side facing front.* MRS. LOVING *asks grace. Her voice trembles. She helps the children bountifully, herself sparingly. Every once in a while she stops eating and stares blankly into her plate; then, remembering where she is suddenly, looks around with a start and goes on eating.* TOM *and* RACHEL *appear not to notice her)*

TOM. Ma's "some" cook, isn't she?

RACHEL. Is she! Delmonico's isn't in it.

TOM. *(presently)* Say, Rachel, do you remember that Reynolds boy in the fourth year?

RACHEL. Yes. You mean the one who is flat-nosed, freckled, and who squints and sneers?

TOM. *(looking at* RACHEL *admiringly)* The same.

RACHEL. *(vehemently)* I hate him!

MRS. LOVING. Rachel, you do use such violent language. Why hate him?

RACHEL. I do—that's all.

TOM. Ma, if you saw him just once, you'd understand. No one likes him. But, then, what can you expect? His father's in "quod" doing time for something, I don't know just what. One of the fellows says he has a real decent mother, though. She never mentions him in any way, shape or form, he says. Hard on her, isn't it? Bet I'd keep my head shut too;—you'd never get a yap out of me. *(*RACHEL *looks up quickly at her mother;* MRS. LOVING *stiffens perceptibly, but keeps her eyes on her plate.* RACHEL *catches* TOM'S *eye; silently draws his attention to their mother; and shakes her head warningly at him)*

TOM. *(continuing hastily and clumsily)* Well, anyway, he called me "nigger" today. If his face isn't black, his eye is.

RACHEL. Good! Oh! Why did you let the other one go?

TOM. *(grinning)* I knew he said things behind my back; but today he was hopping mad, because I made quarter-back. He didn't!

RACHEL. Oh, Tommy! How lovely! Ma dear, did you hear that? *(chants)* Our Tommy's on the team! Our Tommy's on the team!

TOM. *(trying not to appear pleased)* Ma dear, what did I say about er—er "capital" enlargements?

MRS. LOVING. *(smiling)* You're right, Son.

TOM. I hope you got that "capital," Rachel. How's that for Latin knowledge? Eh?

RACHEL. I don't think much of your knowledge, Tommy dear; but *(continuing to chant)* Our Tommy's on the team! Our Tommy's on the team! Our—*(breaks off)* I've a good mind to kiss you.

TOM. *(threateningly)* Don't you dare.

RACHEL. *(rising and going toward him)* I will! I will! I will!

TOM. *(rising, too, and dodging her)* No, you don't, young lady. *(a tremendous tussle and scuffle ensues)*

MRS. LOVING. *(laughing)* For Heaven's sake! children, do stop playing and eat your supper. *(they nod brightly at each other behind her back and return smiling to the table)*

RACHEL. *(sticking out her tongue at* TOM*)* I will!

TOM. *(mimicking her)* You won't!

MRS. LOVING. Children! *(they eat for a time in silence)*

RACHEL. Ma dear, have you noticed Mary Shaw doesn't come here much these days?

MRS. LOVING. Why, that's so, she doesn't. Have you two quarreled?

RACHEL. No, Ma dear. *(uncomfortably)* I—think I know the reason—but I don't like to say, unless I'm certain.

TOM. Well, I know. I've seen her lately with those two girls who have just come from the South. Twice she bowed stiffly, and the last time made believe she didn't see me.

RACHEL. Then you think—? Oh! I was afraid it was that.

TOM. *(bitterly)* Yes—we're "niggers"—that's why.

MRS. LOVING. *(slowly and sadly)* Rachel, that's one of the things I can't save you from. I worried considerably about Mary, at first—you do take your friendships so seriously. I knew exactly how it would end. *(pauses)* And then I saw that if Mary Shaw didn't teach you the lesson—some one else would. They don't want you, dearies, when you and they grow up. You may have everything in your favor—but they don't *dare* to like you.

RACHEL. I know all that is generally true—but I had hoped that Mary—*(breaks off)*

TOM. Well, I guess we can still go on living even if people don't speak to us. I'll never bow to *her* again—that's certain.

MRS. LOVING. But, Son, that wouldn't be polite, if she bowed to you first.

TOM. Can't help it. I guess I can be blind, too.

MRS. LOVING. *(wearily)* Well—perhaps you are right—I don't know. It's the way I feel about it too—but—but I wish my son always to be a *gentleman*.

TOM. If being a *gentleman* means not being a *man*—I don't wish to be one.

RACHEL. Oh! well, perhaps we're wrong about Mary—I hope we are. *(sighs)* Anyway, let's forget it. Tommy, guess what I've got. *(rises, goes out into entryway swiftly, and returns holding up a small bag)* Ma dear treated. Guess!

TOM. Ma, you're a thoroughbred. Well, let's see—it's—a dozen dill pickles?

RACHEL. Oh! stop fooling.

TOM. I'm not. Tripe?

RACHEL. Silly!

TOM. Hog's jowl?

RACHEL. Ugh! Give it up—quarter-back.

TOM. Pig's feet?

RACHEL. *(in pretended disgust)* Oh! Ma dear—send him from the table. It's CANDY!

TOM. Candy? Funny, I never thought of that! And I was just about to say some nice, delicious chitlings. Candy! Well! Well! *(RACHEL disdainfully carries the candy to her mother, returns to her own seat with the bag and helps herself. She ignores TOM)*

TOM. *(in an aggrieved voice)* You see, Ma, how she treats me. *(in affected tones)* I have a good mind, young lady, to punish you, er—er, corporeally speaking. Tut! Tut! I have a mind to master thee—I mean—you. Methinks that if I should advance upon you, apply, perchance, two or three digits to your glossy locks and extract—aha!—say, a strand—you would no more defy me. *(he starts to rise)*

MRS. LOVING. *(quickly and sharply)* Rachel! give Tom the candy and stop playing. *(RACHEL obeys. They eat in silence. The old depression returns. When the candy is all gone, RACHEL pushes her chair back, and is just about to rise, when her mother, who very evidently nerving herself for something, stops her)* Just a moment, Rachel. *(pauses, continuing slowly and very seriously)* Tom and Rachel! I have been trying to make up my mind for some time whether a certain thing is my duty or not. Today—I have decided it is. You are old enough, now,—and I see you ought to be told. Do you know what day this is? *(both TOM and RACHEL have been watching their mother intently)* It's the sixteenth of October. Does that mean anything to either of you?

TOM and RACHEL. *(wonderingly)* No.

MRS. LOVING. *(looking at both of them thoughtfully, half to herself)* No—I don't know why it should. *(slowly)* Ten years ago—today—your father and your half-brother died.

TOM. I do remember, now, that you told us it was in October.

RACHEL. *(with a sigh)* That explains—today.

MRS. LOVING. Yes, Rachel. *(pauses)* Do you know—how they—died?

TOM and RACHEL. Why, no.

MRS. LOVING. Did it ever strike you as strange—that they—died—the same day?

TOM. Well, yes.

RACHEL. We often wondered, Tom and I; but—but somehow we never quite dared to ask you. You—you—always refused to talk about them, you know, Ma dear.

MRS. LOVING. Did you think—that—perhaps—the reason—I—I—wouldn't talk about them—was—because, because—I was ashamed—of them? *(TOM and RACHEL look uncomfortable)*

RACHEL. Well, Ma dear—we—we—did—wonder.

MRS. LOVING. *(questioningly)* And you thought?

RACHEL. *(haltingly)* W-e-l-l—

MRS. LOVING. *(sharply)* Yes?

TOM. Oh! come, now, Rachel, you know we haven't bothered about it at all. Why should we? We've been happy.

MRS. LOVING. But when you have thought—you've been ashamed? *(intensely)* Have you?

TOM. Now, Ma, aren't you making a lot out of nothing?

MRS. LOVING. *(slowly)* No. *(half to herself)* You evade—both—of you. You *have* been ashamed. And I never dreamed until today you *could* take it this way. How blind—how almost criminally blind, I have been.

RACHEL. *(tremulously)* Oh! Ma dear, don't! (TOM *and* RACHEL *watch their mother anxiously and uncomfortably.* MRS. LOVING *is very evidently nerving herself for something)*

MRS. LOVING. *(very slowly, with restrained emotion)* Tom—and Rachel!

TOM. Ma!

RACHEL. Ma dear! *(a tense, breathless pause)*

MRS. LOVING. *(bracing herself)* They—they—were lynched!!

TOM and RACHEL. *(in a whisper)* Lynched!

MRS. LOVING. *(slowly, laboring under strong but restrained emotion)* Yes—by Christian people—in a Christian land. We found out afterwards they were all church members in good standing—the best people. *(a silence)* Your father was a man among men. He was a fanatic. He was a Saint!

TOM. *(breathing with difficulty)* Ma—can you—will you—tell us—about it?

MRS. LOVING. I believe it to be my duty. *(a silence)* When I married your father I was a widow. My little George was seven years old. From the very beginning he worshiped your father. He followed him around—just like a little dog. All children were like that with him. I myself have never seen anybody like him. "Big" seems to fit him better than any other word. He was big-bodied— big-souled. His loves were big and his hates. You can imagine, then, how the wrongs of the Negro—ate into his soul. *(pauses)* He was utterly fearless. *(a silence)* He edited and owned, for several years, a small Negro paper. In it he said a great many daring things. I used to plead with him to be more careful. I was always afraid for him. For a long time, nothing happened—he was too important to the community. And then—one night—ten years ago—a mob made up of the respectable people in the town lynched an innocent black man—and what was worse—they knew him to be innocent. A white man was guilty. I never saw your father so wrought up over anything: he couldn't eat; he couldn't sleep; he brooded night and day over it. And then—realizing fully the great risk he was running, although I begged him not to—and all his friends also—he deliberately and calmly went to work and published a most terrific denunciation of that mob. The old prophets in the Bible were not more terrible than he. A day or two later, he received an anonymous letter, very evidently from an educated man, calling upon him to retract his words in the next issue. If he refused his life was threatened. The next week's issue contained an arraignment as frightful, if not more so, than the previous one. Each word was white-hot, searing. That night, some dozen masked men came to our house.

RACHEL. (moaning) Oh, Ma dear! Ma dear!

MRS. LOVING. (too absorbed to hear) We were not asleep—your father and I. They broke down the front door and made their way to our bedroom. Your father kissed me—and took up his revolver. It was always loaded. They broke down the door. (a silence. She continues slowly and quietly) I tried to shut my eyes—I could not. Four masked men fell—they did not move any more—after a little. (pauses) Your father was finally overpowered and dragged out. In the hall—my little seventeen-year-old George tried to rescue him. Your father begged him not to interfere. He paid no attention. It ended in their dragging them both out. (pauses) My little George—was—a man! (controls herself with an effort) He never made an outcry. His last words to me were: "Ma, I am glad to go with Father." I could only nod to him. (pauses) While they were dragging them down the steps, I crept into the room where you were. You were both asleep. Rachel, I remember, was smiling. I knelt down by you—and covered my ears with my hands—and waited. I could not pray—I couldn't for a long time—afterwards. (a silence) It was very still when I finally uncovered my ears. The only sounds were the faint rustle of leaves and the "tap-tapping of the twig of a tree" against the window. I hear it still—sometimes in my dreams. It was the tree—where they were. (a silence) While I had knelt there waiting—I had made up my mind what to do. I dressed myself and then I woke you both up and dressed you. (pauses) We set forth. It was a black, still night. Alternately dragging you along and carrying you—I walked five miles to the house of some friends. They took us in, and we remained there until I had seen my dead laid comfortably at rest. They lent me money to come North—I couldn't bring you up—in the South. (a silence) Always remember this: There never lived anywhere—or at any time—any two whiter or more beautiful souls. God gave me one for a husband and one for a son and I am proud. (brokenly) You—must—be—proud—too. (a long silence. MRS. LOVING bows her head in her hands. TOM controls himself with an effort. RACHEL creeps softly to her mother, kneels beside her and lifts the hem of her dress to her lips. She does not dare touch her. She adores her with her eyes)

MRS. LOVING. (presently raising her head and glancing at the clock) Tom, it's time, now, for you to go to work. Rachel and I will finish up here.

TOM. (still laboring under great emotion goes out into the entryway and comes back and stands in the doorway with his cap. He twirls it around and around nervously) I want you to know, Ma, before I go—how—how proud I am. Why, I didn't believe two people could be like that—and live. And then to find out that one—was your own father—and one—your own brother.—It's wonderful! I'm—not much yet, Ma, but—I've—I've just got to be something now. (breaks off. His face becomes distorted with passion and hatred) When I think—when I think—of those devils with white skins—living somewhere today—living and happy—I—see—red! I—I—goodbye! (rushes out, the door bangs)

MRS. LOVING. (half to herself) I was afraid of just that. I wonder—if I did the wise thing—after all.

RACHEL. (*with a gesture infinitely tender, puts her arm around her mother*) Yes, Ma dear, you did. And, hereafter, Tom and I share and share alike with you. To think, Ma dear, of ten years of this—all alone. It's wicked! (*a short silence*)

MRS. LOVING. And, Rachel, about that dear little boy, Jimmy.

RACHEL. Now, Ma dear, tell me tomorrow. You've stood enough for one day.

MRS. LOVING. No, it's better over and done with—all at once. If I had seen that dear child suddenly any other day than this—I might have borne it better. When he lifted his little face to me—and smiled—for a moment—I thought it was the end—of all things. Rachel, he is the image of my boy—my George!

RACHEL. Ma dear!

MRS. LOVING. And, Rachel—it will hurt—to see him again.

RACHEL. I understand, Ma dear. (*a silence. Suddenly*) Ma dear, I am beginning to see—to understand—so much. (*slowly and thoughtfully*) Ten years ago, all things being equal, Jimmy might have been—George? Isn't that so?

MRS. LOVING. Why—yes, if I understand you.

RACHEL. I guess that doesn't sound very clear. It's only getting clear to me, little by little. Do you mind my thinking out loud to you?

MRS. LOVING. No, chickabiddy.

RACHEL. If Jimmy went South now—and grew up—he might be—a George?

MRS. LOVING. Yes.

RACHEL. Then, the South is full of tens, hundreds, thousands of little boys, who, one day may be—and some of them with certainty—Georges?

MRS. LOVING. Yes, Rachel.

RACHEL. And the little babies, the dear, little, helpless babies, being born today—now—and those who will be, tomorrow, and all the tomorrows to come—have *that* sooner or later to look forward to? They will laugh and play and sing and be happy and grow up, perhaps, and be ambitious—just for *that*?

MRS. LOVING. Yes, Rachel.

RACHEL. Then, everywhere, everywhere, throughout the South, there are hundreds of dark mothers who live in fear, terrible, suffocating fear, whose rest by night is broken, and whose joy by day in their babies on their hearts is three parts—pain. Oh, I know this is true—for this is the way I should feel, if I were little Jimmy's mother. How horrible! Why—it would be more merciful—to strangle the little things at birth. And so this nation—this white Christian nation—has deliberately set its curse upon the most beautiful—the most holy thing in life—motherhood! Why—it—makes—you doubt—God!

MRS. LOVING. Oh, hush! little girl. Hush!

RACHEL. (*suddenly with a great cry*) Why, Ma dear, *you know. You* were a mother, *George's mother.* So, this is what it means. Oh, Ma dear! Ma dear! (*faints in her mother's arms*)

ACT 2

(TIME: *October sixteenth, four years later; seven o'clock in the morning.*

SCENE: *The same room. There have been very evident improvements made. The room is not so bare; it is cosier. On the shelf, before each window, are potted red geraniums.*

At the windows are green denim drapery curtains covering fresh white dotted Swiss inner curtains. At each doorway are green denim portieres. On the wall between the kitchenette and the entrance to the outer rooms of the flat, a new picture is hanging, Millet's "The Man With the Hoe." Hanging against the side of the run that faces front is Watts's "Hope." There is another easy-chair at the left front. The table in the center is covered with a white table-cloth. A small asparagus fern is in the middle of this. When the curtain rises there is the clatter of dishes in the kitchenette. Presently RACHEL *enters with dishes and silver in her hands. She is clad in a bungalow apron. She is noticeably all of four years older. She frowns as she sets the table. There is a set expression about the mouth. A child's voice is heard from the rooms within)*

JIMMY. *(still unseen)* Ma Rachel!

RACHEL. *(pauses and smiles)* What is it, Jimmy boy?

JIMMY. *(appearing in rear doorway, half-dressed, breathless, and tremendously excited over something. Rushes toward* RACHEL*)* Three guesses! Three guesses! Ma Rachel!

RACHEL. *(her whole face softening)* Well, let's see—maybe there is a circus in town.

JIMMY. No sirree! *(in a sing-song)* You're not right! You're not right!

RACHEL. Well, maybe Ma Loving's going to take you somewhere.

JIMMY. No! *(vigorously shaking his head)* It's—

RACHEL. *(interrupting quickly)* You said I could have three guesses, honey. I've only had two.

JIMMY. I thought you had three! How many are three!

RACHEL. *(counting on her fingers)* One! Two! Three! I've only had one! two!—See? Perhaps Uncle Tom is going to give you some candy.

JIMMY. *(dancing up and down)* No! No! No! *(catches his breath)* I leaned over the bath-tub, way over, and got hold of the chain with the button on the end, and dropped it into the little round place in the bottom. And then I runned lots of water in the tub and climbed over and fell in splash! just like a big stone; *(loudly)* and took a bath all by myself alone.

RACHEL. *(laughing and hugging him)* All by yourself, honey? You ran the water, too, boy, not "runned" it. What I want to know is, where was Ma Loving all this time?

JIMMY. I stole in "creepy-creep" and looked at Ma Loving and she was awful fast asleep. *(proudly)* Ma Rachel, I'm a "nawful," big boy now, aren't I? I are almost a man, aren't I?

RACHEL. Oh! Boy, I'm getting tired of correcting you—"I am almost a man, am I not?" Jimmy, boy, what will Ma Rachel do, if you grow up? Why, I won't have a little boy any more! Honey, you mustn't grow up, do you hear? You mustn't.

JIMMY. Oh, yes, I must; and you'll have me just the same, Ma Rachel. I'm going to be a policeman and make lots of money for you and Ma Loving and Uncle Tom, and I'm going to buy you some trains and fire-engines, and little, cunning ponies, and some rabbits, and some great 'normous banks full of money— lots of it. And then, we are going to live in a great, big castle and eat lots of ice cream, all the time, and drink lots and lots of nice pink lemonade.

RACHEL. What a generous Jimmy boy! *(hugs him)* Before I give you "morning kiss," I must see how clean my boy is. *(inspects teeth, ears and neck)* Jimmy, you're sweet and clean enough to eat. *(kisses him; he tries to strangle her with hugs)* Now the hands. Oh! Jimmy, look at those nails! Oh! Jimmy! (JIMMY *wriggles and tries to get his hands away)* Honey, get my file off of my bureau and go to Ma Loving; she must be awake by this time. Why, honey, what's the matter with your feet?

JIMMY. I don't know. I thought they looked kind of queer, myself. What's the matter with them?

RACHEL. *(laughing)* You have your shoes on the wrong feet.

JIMMY. *(bursts out laughing)* Isn't that most 'normously funny? I'm a case, aren't I—*(pauses thoughtfully)* I mean—am I not, Ma Rachel?

RACHEL. Yes, honey, a great big case of molasses. Come, you must hurry now, and get dressed. You don't want to be late for school, you know.

JIMMY. Ma Rachel! *(shyly)* I—I have been making something for you all the morning—ever since I waked up. It's awful nice. It's—stoop down, Ma Rachel, please—a great, big *(puts both arms about her neck and gives her a noisy kiss.* RACHEL *kisses him in return, then pushes his head back. For a long moment they look at each other; and, then, laughing joyously, he makes believe he is a horse, and goes prancing out of the room.* RACHEL, *with a softer, gentler expression, continues setting the table. Presently,* MRS. LOVING, *bent and worn-looking, appears in the doorway in the rear. She limps a trifle)*

MRS. LOVING. Good morning dearie. How's my little girl, this morning? *(looks around the room)* Why, where's Tom? I was certain I heard him running the water in the tub, some time ago. *(limps into the room)*

RACHEL. *(laughing)* Tom isn't up yet. Have you seen Jimmy?

MRS. LOVING. Jimmy? No. I didn't know he was awake, even.

RACHEL. *(going to her mother and kissing her)* Well! What do you think of that! I sent the young gentleman to you, a few minutes ago, for help with his nails. He is very much grown up this morning, so I suppose that explains why he didn't come to you. Yesterday, all day, you know, he was a puppy. No one knows what he will be by tomorrow. All of this, Ma dear, is preliminary to telling you that Jimmy boy has stolen a march on you, this morning.

MRS. LOVING. Stolen a march! How?

RACHEL. It appears that he took his bath all by himself and, as a result, he is so conceited, peacocks aren't in it with him.

MRS. LOVING. I heard the water running and thought, of course, it was Tom. Why, the little rascal! I must go and see how he has left things. I was just about to wake him up.

RACHEL. Rheumatism's not much better this morning, Ma dear. *(confronting her mother)* Tell me the truth now, did you or did you not try that liniment I bought you yesterday?

MRS. LOVING. *(guiltily)* Well, Rachel, you see—it was this way, I was—I was so tired, last night,—I—I really forgot it.

RACHEL. I thought as much. Shame on you!

MRS. LOVING. As soon as I walk around a bit it will be all right. It always is. It's bad, when I first get up—that's all. I'll be spry enough in a few minutes. *(limps to the door; pauses)* Rachel, I don't know why the thought should strike me, but how very strangely things turn out. If any one had told me four years ago that Jimmy would be living with us, I should have laughed at him. Then it hurt to see him; now it would hurt not to. *(softly)* Rachel, sometimes—I wonder—if, perhaps, God—hasn't relented a little—and given me back my boy,—my George.

RACHEL. The whole thing was strange, wasn't it?

MRS. LOVING. Yes, God's ways are strange and often very beautiful; perhaps all would be beautiful—if we only understood.

RACHEL. God's ways are certainly very mysterious. Why, of all the people in this apartment-house, should Jimmy's father and mother be the only two to take the smallpox, and the only two to die. It's queer!

MRS. LOVING. It doesn't seem like two years ago, does it?

RACHEL. Two years, Ma dear! Why it's three the third of January.

MRS. LOVING. Are you sure, Rachel?

RACHEL. *(gently)* I don't believe I could ever forget that, Ma dear.

MRS. LOVING. No, I suppose not. That is one of the differences between youth and old age—youth attaches tremendous importance to dates,—old age does not.

RACHEL. *(quickly)* Ma dear, don't talk like that. You're not old.

MRS. LOVING. Oh! yes, I am, dearie. It's sixty long years since I was born; and I am much older than that, much older.

RACHEL. Please, Ma dear, please!

MRS. LOVING. *(smiling)* Very well, dearie, I won't say it any more. *(a pause)* By the way,—how—does Tom strike you, these days?

RACHEL. *(avoiding her mother's eye)* The same old, bantering, cheerful Tom. Why?

MRS. LOVING. I know he's all that, dearie, but it isn't possible for him to be really cheerful. *(pauses; goes on wistfully)* When you are little, we mothers can kiss away all the trouble, but when you grow up—and go out—into the world—and get hurt—we are helpless. There is nothing we can do.

RACHEL. Don't worry about Tom, Ma dear, he's game. He doesn't show the white feather.

MRS. LOVING. Did you see him, when he came in, last night?

RACHEL. Yes.

MRS. LOVING. Had he had—any luck?

RACHEL. No. *(firmly)* Ma dear, we may as well face it—it's hopeless, I'm afraid.

MRS. LOVING. I'm afraid—you are right. *(shakes her head sadly)* Well, I'll go and see how Jimmy has left things and wake up Tom, if he isn't awake yet. It's the waking up in the mornings that's hard. *(goes limping out rear door.* RACHEL *frowns as she continues going back and forth between the kitchenette and the table. Presently* TOM *appears in the door at the rear. He watches* RACHEL *several moments before he speaks or enters.* RACHEL *looks grim enough)*

TOM. *(entering and smiling)* Good-morning, "Merry Sunshine"! Have you, perhaps, been taking a—er—prolonged draught of that very delightful beverage—vinegar? *(*RACHEL, *with a knife in her hand, looks up unsmiling. In pretended fright)* I take it all back, I'm sure. May I request, humbly, that before I press my chaste, morning salute upon your forbidding lips, that you—that you—that you—er—in some way rid yourself of that—er—knife? *(bows as* RACHEL *puts it down)* I thank you. *(he comes to her and tips her head back; gently)* What's the matter with my little Sis?

RACHEL. *(her face softening)* Tommy dear, don't mind me. I'm getting wicked, I guess. At present I feel just like—like curdled milk. Once upon a time, I used to have quite a nice disposition, didn't I, Tommy?

TOM. *(smiling)* Did you, indeed! I'm not going to flatter you. Well, brace yourself, old lady. Ready, One! Two! Three! Go! *(kisses her, then puts his hands on either side of her face, and raising it looks down into it)* You're a pretty, decent little sister, Sis, that's what T. Loving thinks about it; and he knows a thing or two. *(abruptly looking around)* Has the paper come yet?

RACHEL. I haven't looked, it must have, though, by this time. *(TOM, hands in his pockets, goes into the vestibule. He whistles. The outer door opens and closes, and presently he saunters back, newspaper in hand. He lounges carelessly in the arm-chair and looks at RACHEL)*

TOM. May T. Loving be of any service to you?

RACHEL. Service! How?

TOM. May he run, say, any errands, set the table, cook the breakfast? Anything?

RACHEL. *(watching the lazy figure)* You look like working.

TOM. *(grinning)* It's at least—polite—to offer.

RACHEL. You can't do anything; I don't trust you to do it right. You may just sit there, and read your paper—and try to behave yourself.

TOM. *(in affectedly meek tones)* Thank you, ma'am. *(opens the paper, but does not read. JIMMY presently enters riding around the table on a cane. RACHEL peeps in from the kitchenette and smiles. TOM puts down his paper)* 'Lo! Big Fellow, what's this?

JIMMY. *(disgustedly)* How can I hear? I'm miles and miles away yet. *(prances around and around the room; presently stops near TOM, attempting a gruff voice)* Good-morning!

TOM. *(lowering his paper again)* Bless my stars! Who's this? Well, if it isn't Mr. Mason! How-do-you-do, Mr. Mason! That's a beautiful horse you have there. He limps a trifle in his left, hind, front foot, though.

JIMMY. He doesn't!

TOM. He does!

JIMMY. *(fiercely)* He doesn't!

TOM. *(as fiercely)* I say he does!

MRS. LOVING. *(appearing in the doorway in the rear)* For Heaven's sake! What is this? Good-morning, Tommy.

TOM. *(rising and going toward his mother, JIMMY following astride of the cane in his rear)* Good-morning, Ma. *(kisses her; lays his head on her shoulder and makes believe he is crying; in a high falsetto)* Ma! Jimmy says his horse doesn't limp in his hind, front right leg, and I say he does.

JIMMY. *(throws his cane aside, rolls on the floor and kicks up his heels. He roars with laughter)* I think Uncle Tom is funnier than any clown in the "Kickus."

TOM. *(raising his head and looking down at JIMMY; RACHEL stands in the kitchenette doorway)* In the *what*, Jimmy?

JIMMY. In the "kickus," of course.

TOM. "Kickus"! "Kickus"! Oh, Lordy! *(TOM and RACHEL shriek with laughter; MRS. LOVING looks amused; JIMMY, very much affronted, gets upon his feet again. TOM leans over and swings* JIMMY *high in the air)* Boy, you'll be the death of me yet. Circus, son! Circus!

JIMMY. *(from on high, soberly and with injured dignity)* Well, I thinks "kickus" and circus are very much alike. Please put me down.

RACHEL. *(from the doorway)* We laugh, honey, because we love you so much.

JIMMY. *(somewhat mollified, to* TOM*)* Is that so, Uncle Tom?

TOM. Surest thing in the world! *(severely)* Come, get down, young man. Don't you know you'll wear my arms out? Besides, there is something in my lower vest pocket, that's just dying to come to you. Get down, I say.

JIMMY. *(laughing)* How can I get down? *(wriggles around)*

TOM. How should I know! Just get down, of course. *(very suddenly puts* JIMMY *down on his feet.* JIMMY *tries to climb up over him)*

JIMMY. Please sit down, Uncle Tom?

TOM. *(in feigned surprise)* Sit down! What for?

JIMMY. *(pummeling him with his little fists, loudly)* Why, you said there was something for me in your pocket.

TOM. *(sitting down)* So I did. How forgetful I am!

JIMMY. *(finding a bright, shiny penny, shrieks)* Oh! Oh! Oh! *(climbs up and kisses* TOM *noisily)*

TOM. Why, Jimmy! You embarrass me. My! My!

JIMMY. What is 'barrass?

TOM. You make me blush.

JIMMY. What's that?

MRS. LOVING. Come, come, children! Rachel has the breakfast on the table. *(*TOM *sits in* JIMMY's *place and* JIMMY *tries to drag him out)*

TOM. What's the matter, now?

JIMMY. You're in *my* place.

TOM. Well, can't you sit in mine?

JIMMY. *(wistfully)* I wants to sit by my Ma Rachel.

TOM. Well, so do I.

RACHEL. Tom, stop teasing Jimmy. Honey, don't you let him bother you; ask him please prettily.

JIMMY. Please prettily, Uncle Tom.

TOM. Oh! well then. *(gets up and takes his own place. They sit as they did in Act 1 only* JIMMY *sits between* TOM, *at the end, and* RACHEL*)*

JIMMY. *(loudly)* Oh, goody! goody! goody! We've got sau-sa-ges.

MRS. LOVING. Sh!

JIMMY. *(silenced for a few moments;* RACHEL *ties a big napkin around his neck, and prepares his breakfast. He breaks forth again suddenly and excitedly)* Uncle Tom!

TOM. Sir?

JIMMY. I took a bath this morning, all by myself alone, in the bath-tub, and I ranned, no *(doubtfully)* I runned, I think—the water all in it, and got in it all by myself; and Ma Loving thought it was you; but it was *me*.

TOM. *(in feignedly severe tones)* See here, young man, this won't do. Don't you know I'm the only one who is allowed to do that here? It's a perfect waste of water—that's what it is.

JIMMY. *(undaunted)* Oh! no, you're not the only one, 'cause Ma Loving and Ma Rachel and me—alls takes baths every single morning. So, there!

TOM. You 'barrass me. (JIMMY *opens his mouth to ask a question;* TOM *quickly)* Young gentleman, your mouth is open. Close it, sir; close it.

MRS. LOVING. Tom, you're as big a child exactly as Jimmy.

TOM. *(bowing to right and left)* You compliment me. I thank you, I am sure.

(*They finish in silence)*

JIMMY. *(sighing with contentment)* I'm through, Ma Rachel.

MRS. LOVING. Jimmy, you're a big boy, now, aren't you? (JIMMY *nods his head vigorously and looks proud)* I wonder if you're big enough to wash your own hands, this morning?

JIMMY. *(shrilly)* Yes, ma'am.

MRS. LOVING. Well, if they're beautifully clean, I'll give you another penny.

JIMMY. *(excitedly to* RACHEL*)* Please untie my napkin, Ma Rachel! (RACHEL *does so)* "Excoose" me, please.

MRS. LOVING and RACHEL. Certainly. (JIMMY *climbs down and rushes out of the rear doorway)*

MRS. LOVING. *(solemnly and slowly; breaking the silence)* Rachel, do you know what day this is?

RACHEL. *(looking at her plate; slowly)* Yes, Ma dear.

MRS. LOVING. Tom.

TOM. *(grimly and slowly)* Yes, Ma.

(A silence)

MRS. LOVING. *(impressively)* We must never—as long—as we live—forget this day.

RACHEL. No, Ma dear.

TOM. No, Ma.

(Another silence)

TOM. *(slowly; as though thinking aloud)* I hear people talk about God's justice—and I wonder. There, are you, Ma. There isn't a sacrifice—that you haven't made. You're still working your fingers to the bone—sewing—just so all of us may keep on living. Rachel is a graduate in Domestic Science; she was high in her class; most of the girls below her in rank have positions in the schools. I'm an electrical engineer—and I've tried steadily for several months—to practice my profession. It seems our educations aren't of much use to us: we aren't allowed to make good—because our skins are dark. *(pauses)* And, in the South today, there are white men—*(controls himself)* They have everything; they're well-dressed, well-fed, well-housed; they're prosperous in business; they're important politically; they're pillars in the church. I know all this is true—I've inquired. Their children (our ages, some of them) are growing up around them; and they are having a square deal handed out to them—college, position, wealth, and best of all, freedom, without galling restrictions, to work out their own salvations. With ability, they may become—anything; and all this will be true of their children's children after them. *(a pause)* Look at us—and look at them. We are destined to failure—they, to success. Their children shall grow up in hope; ours, in despair. Our hands are clean;—theirs are red with blood—red with the blood of a noble man—and a boy. They're nothing but low, cowardly, bestial murderers. The scum of the earth shall succeed.—God's justice, I suppose.

Mrs. Loving. (*rising and going to* Tom; *brokenly*) Tom, promise me—one thing.

Tom. (*rises gently*) What is it, Ma?

Mrs. Loving. That—you'll try—not to lose faith—in God. I've been where you are now—and it's black. Tom, we don't understand God's ways. My son, I know, now—He is beautiful. Tom, won't you try to believe, again?

Tom. (*slowly, but not convincingly*) I'll try, Ma.

Mrs. Loving. (*sighs*) Each one, I suppose, has to work out his own salvation. (*after a pause*) Rachel, if you'll get Jimmy ready, I'll take him to school. I've got to go down town shopping for a customer, this morning. (Rachel *rises and goes out the rear doorway;* Mrs. Loving, *limping very slightly now, follows. She turns and looks back yearningly at* Tom, *who has seated himself again and is staring unseeingly at his plate. She goes out.* Tom *sits without moving until he hears* Mrs. Loving's *voice within and* Rachel's *faintly; then he gets the paper, sits in the arm-chair and pretends to read*)

Mrs. Loving. (*from within*) A yard, you say, Rachel? You're sure that will be enough. Oh! you've measured it. Anything else?—What?—Oh, all right. I'll be back by one o'clock, anyway. Good-bye. (*enters with* Jimmy. *Both are dressed for the street.* Tom *looks up brightly at* Jimmy)

Tom. Hello! Big Fellow, where are you taking *my* mother, I'd like to know? This is a pretty kettle of fish.

Jimmy. (*laughing*) Aren't you funny, Uncle Tom! Why, I'm not taking her anywhere. She's taking me. (*importantly*) I'm going to school.

Tom. Big Fellow, come here. (Jimmy *comes with a rush*) Now, where's that penny I gave you? No, I don't want to see it. All right. Did Ma Loving give you another? (*vigorous noddings of the head from* Jimmy) I wish you to promise me solemnly—Now, listen! Here, don't wriggle so! not to buy—Listen! too many pints of ice-cream with my penny. Understand?

Jimmy. (*very seriously*) Yes, Uncle Tom, cross my "tummy"! I promise.

Tom. Well, then, you may go. I guess that will be all for the present. (Jimmy *loiters around looking up wistfully into his face*) Well?

Jimmy. Haven't you—aren't you—isn't you—forgetting something?

Tom. (*grabbing at his pockets*) Bless my stars! what now?

Jimmy. If you could kind of lean over this way. (Tom *leans forward*) No, not that way. (Tom *leans toward the side away from* Jimmy) No, this way! (*laughs and pummels him with his little fists*) This way!

Tom. (*leaning toward* Jimmy) Well, why didn't you say so, at first?

Jimmy. (*puts his arms around* Tom's *neck and kisses him*) Good-bye, dear old Uncle Tom. (Tom *catches him and hugs him hard*) I likes to be hugged like that—I can taste—sau-sa-ges.

Tom. You 'barrass me, son. Here, Ma, take your boy. Now remember all I told you, Jimmy.

Jimmy. I 'members.

MRS. LOVING. God bless you, Tom. Good luck.

JIMMY. *(to* TOM*)* God bless you, Uncle Tom. Good luck!

TOM. *(much affected, but with restraint, rising)* Thank you—Good-bye. (MRS. LOV-ING *and* JIMMY *go out through the vestibule.* TOM *lights a cigarette and tries to read the paper. He soon sinks into a brown study. Presently* RACHEL *enters humming.* TOM *relights his cigarette; and* RACHEL *proceeds to clear the table. In the midst of this, the bell rings three distinct times)*

RACHEL and TOM. John!

TOM. I wonder what's up—It's rather early for him.—I'll go. *(rises leisurely and goes out into the vestibule. The outer door opens and shuts. Men's voices are heard.* TOM *and* JOHN STRONG *enter. During the ensuing conversation* RACHEL *finishes clearing the table, takes the fern off, puts on the green table-cloth, places a doily carefully in the centre, and replaces the fern. She apparently pays no attention to the conversation between her brother and* STRONG. *After she has finished, she goes to the kitchenette. The rattle of dishes can be heard now and then)*

RACHEL. *(brightly)* Well, stranger, how does it happen you're out so early in the morning?

STRONG. I hadn't seen any of you for a week, and I thought I'd come by, on my way to work, and find out how things are going. There is no need of asking how you are, Rachel. And the mother and the boy?

RACHEL. Ma dear's rheumatism still holds on.—Jimmy's fine.

STRONG. I'm sorry to hear that your mother is not well. There isn't a remedy going that my mother doesn't know about. I'll get her advice and let you know. *(turning to* TOM*)* Well, Tom, how goes it? (STRONG *and* TOM *sit)*

TOM. *(smiling grimly)* There's plenty of "go," but no "git there."

(There is a pause)

STRONG. I was hoping for better news.

TOM. If I remember rightly, not so many years ago, you tried—and failed. Then, a colored man had hardly a ghost of a show;—now he hasn't even the ghost of a ghost.

STRONG. That's true enough. *(a pause)* What are you going to do?

TOM. *(slowly)* I'll do this little "going act" of mine the rest of the week; *(pauses)* and then, I'll do anything I can get to do. If necessary, I suppose, I can be "white-wing."

STRONG. Tom, I came—*(breaks off; continuing slowly)* Six years ago, I found I was up against a stone wall—your experience, you see, to the letter. I couldn't let my mother starve, so I became a waiter. *(pauses)* I studied waiting; I made a science of it, an art. In a comparatively short time, I'm a head-waiter and I'm up against another stone wall. I've reached my limit. I'm thirty-two now, and I'll die a head-waiter. *(a pause)* College friends, so-called, and acquaintances used to come into the restaurant. One or two at first—attempted to commiserate with me. They didn't do it again. I waited upon them—I did my best. Many of them tipped me. *(pauses and smiles grimly)* I can remember my first tip, still. They come in yet; many of them are already powers, not only in this city, but in the country. Some of them make a personal request that I wait upon them.

I am an artist, now, in my proper sphere. They tip me well, extremely well—the larger the tip, the more pleased they are with me. Because of me, in their own eyes, they're philanthropists. Amusing, isn't it? I can stand their attitude now. My philosophy—learned hard, is to make the best of everything you can, and go on. At best, life isn't so very long. You're wondering why I'm telling you all this. I wish you to see things exactly as they are. There are many disadvantages and some advantages in being a waiter. My mother can live comfortably; I am able, even, to see that she gets some of the luxuries. Tom, it's this way—I can always get you a job as a waiter; I'll teach you the art. If you care to begin the end of the week—all right. And remember this, as long as I keep my job—this offer holds good.

Tom. I—I—*(breaks off)* Thank you. *(a pause; then smiling wryly)* I guess it's safe enough to say, you'll see me at the end of the week. John you're—*(breaking off again. A silence interrupted presently by the sound of much vigorous rapping on the outer door of the flat.* RACHEL *appears and crosses over toward the vestibule)*

Rachel. Hear the racket! My kiddies gently begging for admittance. It's about twenty minutes of nine, isn't it? *(TOM nods)* I thought so.

(Goes into the entryway; presently reappears with a group of six little girls ranging in age from five to about nine. All are fighting to be close to her; and all are talking at once. There is one exception: the smallest tot is self-possessed and self-sufficient. She carries a red geranium in her hand and gives it her full attention)

Little Mary. It's my turn to get "Morning kiss" first, this morning, Miss Rachel. You kissed Louise first yesterday. You said you'd kiss us "alphabettically." *(ending in a shriek)* You promised! *(RACHEL kisses MARY, who subsides)*

Little Nancy. *(imperiously)* Now, me. *(RACHEL kisses her, and then amid shrieks, recriminations, pulling of hair, jostling, etc., she kisses the rest. The small tot is still oblivious to everything that is going on)*

Rachel. *(laughing)* You children will pull me limb from limb and then I'll be all dead; and you'll be sorry—see, if you aren't. *(they fall back immediately.* TOM *and* JOHN *watch in amused silence.* RACHEL *loses all self-consciousness, and seems to bloom in the children's midst)* Edith! come here this minute, and let me tie your hair-ribbon again. Nancy, I'm ashamed of you, I saw you trying to pull it off. *(NANCY looks abashed but mischievous)* Louise, you look as sweet as sweet, this morning; and Jenny, where did you get the pretty, pretty dress?

Little Jenny. *(snuffling, but proud)* My mother made it. *(pauses with more snuffles)* My mother says I have a very bad cold. *(there is a brief silence interrupted by the small tot with the geranium)*

Little Martha. *(in a sweet, little voice)* I—have—a—pitty—'ittle flower.

Rachel. Honey, it's beautiful. Don't you want "Morning kiss" too?

Little Martha. Yes, I do.

Rachel. Come, honey. *(RACHEL kisses her)* Are you going to give the pretty flower to Jenny's teacher? *(vigorous shakings of the head in denial)* Is it for—mother? *(more shakings of the head)* Is it for—let's see—Daddy? *(more shakings of the head)* I give up. To whom are you going to give the pretty flower, honey?

Little Martha. *(shyly)* "Oo."

RACHEL. You, darling!

LITTLE MARTHA. Muzzer and I picked it—for "oo." Here 't is. *(puts her finger in her mouth, and gives it shyly)*

RACHEL. Well, I'm going to pay you with three big kisses. One! Two! Three!

LITTLE MARTHA. I can count, One! Two! Free! Tan't I? I am going to school soon; and I wants to put the flower in your hair.

RACHEL. *(kneels)* All right, baby. (LITTLE MARTHA *fumbles and* RACHEL *helps her)*

LITTLE MARTHA. *(dreamily)* Miss Rachel, the little flower loves you. It told me so. It said it wanted to lie in your hair. It is going to tell you a pitty 'ittle secret. You listen awful hard—and you'll hear. I wish I were a fairy and had a little wand. I'd turn everything into flowers. Wouldn't that be nice, Miss Rachel?

RACHEL. Lovely, honey!

LITTLE JENNY. *(snuffling loudly)* If I were a fairy and had a wand, I'd turn you, Miss Rachel, into a queen—and then I'd always be near you and see that you were happy.

RACHEL. Honey, how beautiful!

LITTLE LOUISE. I'd make my mother happy—if I were a fairy. She cries all the time. My father can't get anything to do.

LITTLE NANCY. If I were a fairy, I'd turn a boy in my school into a spider. I hate him.

RACHEL. Honey, why?

LITTLE NANCY. I'll tell you sometime—I hate him.

LITTLE EDITH. Where's Jimmy, Miss Rachel?

RACHEL. He went long ago; and chickies, you have to clear out, all of you, now, or you'll be late. Shoo! Shoo! *(she drives them out prettily before her. They laugh merrily. They all go into the vestibule)*

TOM. *(slowly)* Does it ever strike you—how pathetic and tragic a thing—a little colored child is?

STRONG. Yes.

TOM. Today, we colored men and women, everywhere—are up against it. Every year, we are having a harder time of it. In the South, they make it as impossible as they can for us to get an education. We're hemmed in on all sides. Our one safeguard—the ballot—in most states, is taken away already, or is being taken away. Economically, in a few lines, we have a slight show—but at what a cost! In the North, they make a pretense of liberality: they give us the ballot and a good education, and then—snuff us out. Each year, the problem just to live, gets more difficult to solve. How about these children—if we're fools enough to have any? *(RACHEL *reenters. Her face is drawn and pale. She returns to the kitchenette)*

STRONG. *(slowly, with emphasis)* That part—is damnable! *(a silence)*

TOM. *(suddenly looking at the clock)* It's later than I thought. I'll have to be pulling out of here now, if you don't mind. *(raising his voice)* Rachel! (RACHEL *still drawn and pale, appears in the doorway of the kitchenette. She is without her apron)* I've got to go now, Sis. I leave John in your hands.

STRONG. I've got to go, myself, in a few minutes.

TOM. Nonsense, man! Sit still. I'll begin to think, in a minute, you're afraid of the ladies.

STRONG. I am.

TOM. What! And not ashamed to acknowledge it?

STRONG. No.

TOM. You're lots wiser than I dreamed. So long! (*gets hat out in the entry-way and returns; smiles wryly*) "Morituri Salutamus." (*they nod at him—*RACHEL *wistfully. He goes out. There is the sound of an opening and closing door.* RACHEL *sits down. A rather uncomfortable silence, on the part of* RACHEL, *ensues.* STRONG *is imperturbable*)

RACHEL. (*nervously*) John!

STRONG. Well?

RACHEL. I—I listened.

STRONG. Listened! To what?

RACHEL. To you and Tom.

STRONG. Well,—what of it?

RACHEL. I didn't think it was quite fair not to tell you. It—it seemed, well, like eavesdropping.

STRONG. Don't worry about it. Nonsense!

RACHEL. I'm glad—I want to thank you for what you did for Tom. He needs you, and will need you. You'll help him?

STRONG. (*thoughtfully*) Rachel, each one—has his own little battles. I'll do what I can. After all, an outsider doesn't help much.

RACHEL. But friendship—just friendship—helps.

STRONG. Yes. (*a silence*) Rachel, do you hear anything encouraging from the schools? Any hope for you yet?

RACHEL. No, nor ever will be. I know that now. There's no more chance for me than there is for Tom,—or than there was for you—or for any of us with dark skins. It's lucky for me that I love to keep house, and cook, and sew. I'll never get anything else. Ma dear's sewing, the little work Tom has been able to get, and the little sewing I sometimes get to do—keep us from the poorhouse. We live. According to your philosophy, I suppose, make the best of it—it might be worse.

STRONG. (*quietly*) You don't want to get morbid over these things, you know.

RACHEL. (*scornfully*) That's it. If you see things as they are, you're either pessimistic or morbid.

STRONG. In the long run, do you believe, that attitude of mind—will be—beneficial to you? I'm ten years older than you. I tried your way. I know. Mine is the only sane one. (*goes over to her slowly; deliberately puts his hands on her hair, and tips her head back. He looks down into her face quietly without saying anything*)

RACHEL. (*nervous and startled*) Why, John, don't! (*he pays no attention, but continues to look down into her face*)

STRONG. (*half to himself*) Perhaps—if you had—a little more fun in your life, your point of view would be—more normal. I'll arrange it so I can take you to some theatre, one night, this week.

RACHEL. (*irritably*) You talk as though I were a—a jelly-fish. You'll take me, how do you know *I'll* go?

STRONG. You will.

RACHEL. (*sarcastically*) Indeed! (STRONG *makes no reply*) I wonder if you know how—how—maddening you are. Why, you talk as though my will counts for nothing. It's as if you're trying to master me. I think a domineering man is detestable.

STRONG. *(softly)* If he's, perhaps, *the* man?

RACHEL. *(hurriedly, as though she had not heard)* Besides, some of these theatres put you off by yourself as though you had leprosy. I'm not going.

STRONG. *(smiling at her)* You know I wouldn't ask you to go, under those circumstances. *(a silence)* Well, I must be going now *(he takes her hand, and looks at it reverently.* RACHEL, *at first, resists; but he refuses to let go. When she finds it useless, she ceases to resist. He turns his head and smiles down into her face)* Rachel, I am coming back to see you, this evening.

RACHEL. I'm sure *we'll* all be very glad to see you.

STRONG. *(looking at her calmly)* I said—you. *(very deliberately, he turns her hand palm upwards, leans over and kisses it; then he puts it back into her lap. He touches her cheek lightly)* Good-bye—little Rachel. *(turns in the vestibule door and looks back, smiling)* Until tonight. *(He goes out.* RACHEL *sits for some time without moving. She is lost in a beautiful day-dream. Presently she sighs happily, and after looking furtively around the room, lifts the palm* JOHN *has kissed to her lips. She laughs shyly and jumping up, begins to hum. She opens the window at the rear of the room and then commences to thread the sewing-machine. She hums happily the whole time. A light rapping is heard at the outer door.* RACHEL *listens. It stops, and begins again. There is something insistent, and yet hopeless in the sound.* RACHEL *looking puzzled, goes out into the vestibule. . . . The door closes.* RACHEL, *and a black woman, poorly dressed, and a little ugly, black child come in. There is the stoniness of despair in the woman's face. The child is thin, nervous, suspicious, frightened)*

MRS. LANE. *(in a sharp, but toneless voice)* May I sit down? I'm tired.

RACHEL. *(puzzled, but gracious; draws up a chair for her)* Why, certainly.

MRS. LANE. No, you don't know me—never even heard of me—nor I of you. I was looking at the vacant flat on this floor—and saw your name—on your door,— "Loving!" It's a strange name to come across—in this world.—I thought, perhaps, you might give me some information. *(the child hides behind her mother and looks around at* RACHEL *in a frightened way)*

RACHEL. *(smiling at the woman and child in a kindly manner)* I'll be glad to tell you anything, I am able Mrs.—

MRS. LANE. What I want to know is, how do they treat the colored children in the school I noticed around the corner? *(the child clutches at her mother's dress)*

RACHEL. *(perplexed)* Very well—I'm sure.

MRS. LANE. *(bluntly)* What reason have you for being sure?

RACHEL. Why, the little boy I've adopted goes there; and he's very happy. All the children in this apartment-house go there too; and I know they're happy.

MRS. LANE. Do you know how many colored children there are in the school?

RACHEL. Why, I should guess around thirty.

MRS. LANE. I see. *(pauses)* What color is this little adopted boy of yours?

RACHEL. *(gently)* Why—he's brown.

MRS. LANE. Any black children there?

RACHEL. *(nervously)* Why—yes.

Mrs. Lane. Do you mind if I send Ethel over by the piano to sit?

Rachel. N—no, certainly not. *(places a chair by the piano and goes to the little girl holding out her hand. She smiles beautifully. The child gets farther behind her mother)*

Mrs. Lane. She won't go to you—she's afraid of everybody now but her father and me. Come, Ethel. (mrs. lane *takes the little girl by the hand and leads her to the chair. In a gentler voice)* Sit down, Ethel. (ethel *obeys. When her mother starts back again toward* rachel, *she holds out her hands pitifully. She makes no sound)* I'm not going to leave you, Ethel. I'll be right over here. You can see me. *(the look of agony on the child's face, as her mother leaves her, makes* rachel *shudder)* Do you mind if we sit over here by the sewing machine? Thank you. *(they move their chairs)*

Rachel. *(looking at the little, pitiful figure watching its mother almost unblinkingly)* Does Ethel like apples, Mrs. Lane?

Mrs. Lane. Yes.

Rachel. Do you mind if I give her one?

Mrs. Lane. No. Thank you, very much.

Rachel. *(goes into the kitchenette and returns with a fringed napkin, a plate, and a big, red apple cut into quarters, She goes to the little girl, who cowers away from her; very gently)* Here, dear, little girl, is a beautiful apple for you. *(the gentle tones have no appeal for the trembling child before her)*

Mrs. Lane. *(coming forward)* I'm sorry, but I'm afraid she won't take it from you. Ethel, the kind lady has given you an apple. Thank her nicely. Here! I'll spread the napkin for you, and put the plate in your lap. Thank the lady like a good little girl.

Ethel. *(very low)* Thank you. *(They return to their seats.* ethel *with difficulty holds the plate in her lap. During the rest of the interview between* rachel *and her mother, she divides her attention between the apple on the plate and her mother's face. She makes no attempt to eat the apple, but holds the plate in her lap with a care that is painful to watch. Often, too, she looks over her shoulder fearfully. The conversation between* rachel *and her mother is carried on in low tones)*

Mrs. Lane. I've got to move—it's *Ethel.*

Rachel. What is the matter with that child? It's—it's heartbreaking to see her.

Mrs. Lane. I understand how you feel,—I don't feel anything, myself, any more. *(a pause)* My husband and I are poor, and we're ugly and we're Black. Ethel looks like her father more than she does like me. We live in 55th Street—near the railroad. It's a poor neighborhood, but the rent's cheap. My husband is a porter in a store; and, to help out, I'm a caretaker. *(pauses)* I don't know why I'm telling you all this. We had a nice little home—and the three of us were happy. Now we've got to move.

Rachel. Move! Why?

Mrs. Lane. It's Ethel. I put her in school this September. She stayed two weeks. *(pointing to* ethel) That's the result.

Rachel. *(in horror)* You mean—that just two weeks—in school—did that?

Mrs. Lane. Yes. Ethel never had a sick day in her life—before. *(a brief pause)* I took her to the doctor at the end of the two weeks. He says she's a nervous wreck.

Rachel. But what could they have done to her?

Mrs. Lane. *(laughs grimly and mirthlessly)* I'll tell you what they did the first day. Ethel is naturally sensitive and backward. She's not assertive. The teacher saw that, and, after I had left, told her to sit in a seat in the rear of the class. She was alone there—in a corner. The children, immediately feeling there was something wrong with Ethel because of the teacher's attitude, turned and stared at her. When the teacher's back was turned they whispered about her, pointed their fingers at her and tittered. The teacher divided the class into two parts, divisions, I believe, they are called. She forgot all about Ethel, of course, until the last minute, and then, looking back, said sharply: "That little girl there may join this division," meaning the group of pupils standing around her. Ethel naturally moved slowly. The teacher called her sulky and told her to lose a part of her recess. When Ethel came up—the children drew away from her in every direction. She was left standing alone. The teacher then proceeded to give a lesson about kindness to animals. Funny, isn't it, *kindness to animals?* The children forgot Ethel in the excitement of talking about their pets. Presently, the teacher turned to Ethel and said disagreeably: "Have you a pet?" Ethel said, "Yes," very low. "Come, speak up, you sulky child, what is it?" Ethel said: "A blind puppy." They all laughed, the teacher and all. Strange, isn't it, but Ethel loves that puppy. She spoke up: "It's mean to laugh at a little blind puppy. I'm glad he's blind." This remark brought forth more laughter. "Why are you glad?" the teacher asked curiously. Ethel refused to say. *(pauses)* When I asked her why, do you know what she told me? "If he saw me, he might not love me any more." *(a pause)* Did I tell you that Ethel is only seven years old?

Rachel. *(drawing her breath sharply)* Oh! I didn't believe any one could be as cruel as that—to a little child.

Mrs. Lane. It isn't very pleasant, is it? When the teacher found out that Ethel wouldn't answer, she said severely: "Take your seat!" At recess, all the children went out. Ethel could hear them playing and laughing and shrieking. Even the teacher went too. She was made to sit there all alone—in that big room—because God made her ugly—and Black. *(pauses)* When the recess was half over the teacher came back. "You may go now," she said coldly. Ethel didn't stir. "Did you hear me!" "Yes'm." "Why don't you obey!" "I don't want to go out, please." "You don't, don't you, you stubborn child! Go immediately!" Ethel went. She stood by the school steps. No one spoke to her. The children near her moved away in every direction. They stopped playing, many of them, and watched her. They stared as only children can stare. Some began whispering about her. Presently one child came up and ran her hand roughly over Ethel's face. She looked at her hand and Ethel's face and ran screaming back to the others, "It won't come off! See!" Other children followed the first child's example. Then one boy spoke up loudly: "I know what she is, she's a nigger!" Many took up the cry. God or the devil interfered—the bell rang. The children filed in. One boy boldly called her "Nigger!" before the teacher. She said, "That isn't nice,"—but she smiled at the boy. Things went on about the same for the rest of the day. At the end of school, Ethel put on her hat and coat—the teacher made her hang them at a distance from the other pupils' wraps; and started for home. Quite a crowd escorted her. They called her "Nigger!" all the way. I *made* Ethel go the next day. I complained to the authorities. They treated me lightly. I was determined not to let them force my child out of school. At the end of two weeks—I had to take her out.

RACHEL. *(brokenly)* Why,—I never—in all my life—heard anything—so—pitiful.

MRS. LANE. Did you ever go to school here?

RACHEL. Yes. I was made to feel my color—but I never had an experience like that.

MRS. LANE. How many years ago were you in the graded schools?

RACHEL. Oh!—around ten.

MRS. LANE. *(laughs grimly)* Ten years! Every year things are getting worse. Last year wasn't as bad as this. *(pauses)* So they treat the children all right in this school?

RACHEL. Yes! Yes! I know that.

MRS. LANE. I can't afford to take this flat here, but I'll take it. I'm going to have Ethel educated. Although, when you think of it,—it's all rather useless—this education! What are our children going to do with it, when they get it? We strive and save and sacrifice to educate them—and the whole time—down underneath, we know—they'll have no chance.

RACHEL. *(sadly)* Yes, that's true, all right.—God seems to have forgotten us.

MRS. LANE. God! It's all a lie about God. I know.—This fall I sent Ethel to a white Sunday-school near us. She received the same treatment there she did in the day school. Her being there, nearly broke up the school. At the end, the superintendent called her to him and asked her if she didn't know of some nice colored Sunday-school. He told her she must feel out of place, and uncomfortable there. That's your Church of God!

RACHEL. Oh! how unspeakably brutal. *(controls herself with an effort; after a pause)* Have you any other children?

MRS. LANE. *(dryly)* Hardly! If I had another—I'd kill it. It's kinder. *(rising presently)* Well, I must go, now. Thank you, for your information—and for listening. *(suddenly)* You aren't married, are you?

RACHEL. No.

MRS. LANE. Don't marry—that's my advice. Come, Ethel. (ETHEL *gets up and puts down the things in her lap, carefully upon her chair. She goes in a hurried, timid way to her mother and clutches her hand)* Say good-bye to the lady.

ETHEL. *(faintly)* Good-bye.

RACHEL. *(kneeling by the little girl—a beautiful smile on her face)* Dear little girl, won't you let me kiss you good-bye? I love little girls. *(the child hides behind her mother; continuing brokenly)* Oh!—no child ever did—that to me—before!

MRS. LANE. *(in a gentler voice)* Perhaps, when we move in here, the first of the month, things may be better. Thank you, again. Good-morning! You don't belie your name. *(all three go into the vestibule. The outside door opens and closes.* RACHEL *as though dazed and stricken returns. She sits in a chair, leans forward, and clasping her hands loosely between her knees, stares at the chair with the apple on it where* ETHEL LANE *has sat. She does not move for some time. Then she gets up and goes to the window in the rear center and sits there. She breathes in the air deeply and then goes to the sewing-machine and begins to sew on something she is making.*

Presently her feet slow down on the pedals; she stops; and begins brooding again. After a short pause, she gets up and begins to pace up and down slowly, mechanically, her head bent forward. The sharp ringing of the electric bell breaks in upon this. RACHEL *starts and goes slowly into the vestibule. She is heard speaking dully through the tube)*

RACHEL. Yes!—All right! Bring it up! *(presently she returns with a long flower box. She opens it listlessly at the table. Within are six, beautiful crimson rosebuds with long stems.* RACHEL *looks at the name on the card. She sinks down slowly on her knees and leans her head against the table. She sighs wearily)* Oh! John! John!—What are we to do?—I'm—I'm afraid! Everywhere—it is the same thing. My mother! My little brother! Little, Black, crushed Ethel! *(in a whisper)* Oh! God! You who I have been taught to believe are so good, so beautiful how could—You permit—these—things? *(pauses, raises her head and sees the rosebuds. Her face softens and grows beautiful, very sweetly)* Dear little rosebuds—you—make me think—of sleeping, curled up, happy babies. Dear beautiful, little rosebuds! *(pauses; goes on thoughtfully to the rosebuds)* When I look—at you—I believe—God is beautiful. He who can make a little exquisite thing like this, and this can't be cruel. Oh! He can't mean me—to give up—love—and the hope of little children. *(there is the sound of a small hand knocking at the outer door.* RACHEL *smiles)* My Jimmy! It must be twelve o'clock. *(rises)* I didn't dream it was so late. *(starts for the vestibule)* Oh! the world can't be so bad. I don't believe it. I won't. I *must* forget that little girl. My little Jimmy is happy—and today John—sent me beautiful rosebuds. Oh, there are lovely things, yet. *(goes into the vestibule. A child's eager cry is heard; and* RACHEL *carrying* JIMMY *in her arms comes in. He has both arms about her neck and is hugging her. With him in her arms, she sits down in the armchair at the right front)*

RACHEL. Well, honey, how was school today?

JIMMY. *(sobering a trifle)* All right, Ma Rachel. *(suddenly sees the roses)* Oh! look at the pretty flowers. Why, Ma Rachel, you forgot to put them in water. They'll die.

RACHEL. Well, so will. Hop down this minute, and I'll put them in right away. *(gathers up box and flowers and goes into the kitchenette.* JIMMY *climbs back into the chair. He looks thoughtful and serious.* RACHEL *comes back with the buds in a tall, glass vase. She puts the fern on top of the table)* There, honey, that's better, isn't it? Aren't they lovely?

JIMMY. Yes, that's lots better. Now they won't die, will they? Rosebuds are just like little "chilyun," aren't they, Ma Rachel? If you are good to them, they'll grow up into lovely roses, won't they? And if you hurt them, they'll die. Ma Rachel, do you think all people are kind to little rosebuds?

RACHEL. *(watching* JIMMY *shortly)* Why, of course. Who could hurt little children? Who would have the heart to do such a thing?

JIMMY. If you hurt them, it would be lots kinder, wouldn't it, to kill them all at once, and not a little bit and a little bit?

RACHEL. *(sharply)* Why, honey boy, why are you talking like this?

JIMMY. Ma Rachel, what is a "Nigger"?

*(*RACHEL *recoils as though she had been struck)*

RACHEL. Honey boy, why—why do you ask that?

JIMMY. Some big boys called me that when I came out of school just now. They said: "Look at the little nigger!" and they laughed. One of them runned, no ranned, after me and threw stones; and they all kept calling "Nigger! Nigger! Nigger!" One stone struck me hard in the back, and it hurt awful bad; but I didn't cry, Ma Rachel. I wouldn't let them make me cry. The stone hurts me there, Ma Rachel; but what they called me hurts and hurts here. What is a "nigger," Ma Rachel?

RACHEL. *(controlling herself with a tremendous effort. At last she sweeps down upon him and hugs and kisses him)* Why, honey, boy, those boys didn't mean anything. Silly, little, honey boy! They're rough, that's all. How *could* they mean anything?

JIMMY. You're only saying that, Ma Rachel, so I won't be hurt. I know. It wouldn't ache here like it does—if they didn't mean something.

RACHEL. *(abruptly)* Where's Mary, honey?

JIMMY. She's in her flat. She came in just after I did.

RACHEL. Well, honey, I'm going to give you two big cookies and two to take to Mary; and you may stay in there and play with her, till I get your lunch ready. Won't that be jolly?

JIMMY. *(brightening a little)* Why, you never give me but one at a time. You'll give me two?—One? Two?

RACHEL. *(gets the cookies and brings them to him.* JIMMY *climbs down from the chair)* Shoo! now, little honey boy. See how many laughs you can make for me, before I come after you. Hear? Have a good time, now.

*(*JIMMY *starts for the door quickly; but he begins to slow down. His face gets long and serious again.* RACHEL *watches him)*

RACHEL. *(jumping at him)* Shoo! Shoo! Get out of here quickly, little chicken. *(she follows him out. The outer door opens and shuts. Presently she returns. She looks old and worn and grey; calmly. Pauses)* First, it's little, Black Ethel—and then it's Jimmy. Tomorrow, it will be some other little child. The blight—sooner or later— strikes all. My little Jimmy, only seven years old poisoned! *(through the open window comes the laughter of little children at play.* RACHEL, *shuddering, covers her ears)* And once I said, centuries ago, it must have been: "How can life be so terrible, when there are little children in the world?" Terrible! Terrible! *(in a whisper, slowly)* That's the reason it *is* so terrible. *(the laughter reaches her again; this time she listens)* And, suddenly, some day, from out of the black, the blight shall descend, and shall still forever—the laughter on those little lips, and in those little hearts. *(pauses thoughtfully)* And the loveliest thing—almost, that ever happened to me, that beautiful voice, in my dream, those beautiful words: "Rachel, you are to be the mother to little children." *(pauses, then slowly and with dawning surprise)* Why, God, you were making a mock of me; you were laughing at me. I didn't believe God could laugh at our sufferings, but He can. We are accursed, accursed! We have nothing, absolutely nothing. *(*STRONG'S *rosebuds attract her attention. She goes over to them, puts her hand out as if to touch them, and then shakes her head, very sweetly)* No, little rosebuds, I may not touch you. Dear, little, baby rosebuds,—I am accursed. *(gradually her whole form stiffens, she breathes deeply; at last slowly)* You God!—You terrible, laughing God! Listen! I swear—and may my soul be damned to all eternity, if I do break this oath—I swear—that no child of mine shall ever lie upon my breast, for I will not have it rise up, in the terrible days that are to be—and call me cursed. *(a pause, very wistfully; questioningly)* Never to know the loveliest thing in all the world—the feel of a little head, the touch of little hands, the beautiful utter dependence—of a little child? *(with sudden frenzy)* You can laugh, Oh God! Well, so can I. *(bursts into terrible, racking laughter)* But I can be kinder than You. *(fiercely she snatches the rosebuds from the vase, grasps them roughly, tears each head from the stem, and grinds it under her feet. The vase goes over with a crash; the water drips unheeded over the table-cloth and floor)* If I kill, You Mighty God, I kill at once—I do not torture. *(falls face downward on the floor. The laughter of the children shrills loudly through the window)*

ACT 3

*(*TIME: *Seven o'clock in the evening, one week later.*

PLACE: *The same room. There is a cool fire in the grate. The curtains are drawn. A lighted oil lamp with a dark green porcelain shade is in the center of the table.* MRS. LOVING *and* TOM *are sitting by the table,* MRS. LOVING *sewing,* TOM *reading. There is the sound of much laughter and the shrill screaming of a child from the bedrooms. Presently* JIMMY *clad in a flannelet sleeping suit, covering all of him but his head and hands, chases a pillow, which has come flying through the doorway at the rear. He struggles with it, finally gets it in his arms, and rushes as fast as he can through the doorway again.* RACHEL *jumps at him with a cry. He drops the pillow and shrieks. There is a tussle for possession of it, and they disappear. The noise grows louder and merrier.* TOM *puts down his paper and grins. He looks at his mother)*

TOM. Well, who's the giddy one in this family now?

MRS. LOVING. *(shaking her head in troubled manner)* I don't like it. It worries me. Rachel—*(breaks off)*

TOM. Have you found out, yet—

MRS. LOVING. *(turning and looking toward the rear doorway, quickly interrupting him)* Sh! (RACHEL, *laughing, her hair tumbling over her shoulders, comes rushing into the room.* JIMMY *is in close pursuit. He tries to catch her, but she dodges him. They are both breathless)*

MRS. LOVING. *(deprecatingly)* Really, Rachel, Jimmy will be so excited he won't be able to sleep. It's after his bedtime, now. Don't you think you had better stop?

RACHEL. All right, Ma dear. Come on, Jimmy; let's play "Old Folks" and sit by the fire. *(she begins to push the big arm-chair over to the fire.* TOM *jumps up, moves her aside, and pushes it himself.* JIMMY *renders assistance)*

TOM. Thanks, Big Fellow, you are "sure some" strong. I'll remember you when these people around here come for me to move pianos and such things around. Shake! *(they shake hands)*

JIMMY. *(proudly)* I am awful strong, am I not?

TOM. You "sure" are a Hercules. *(hurriedly, as* JIMMY's *mouth and eyes open wide)* And see here! Don't ask me tonight who that was. I'll tell you the first thing tomorrow morning. Hear? *(returns to his chair and paper)*

RACHEL. *(sitting down)* Come on, honey boy, and sit in my lap.

JIMMY. *(doubtfully)* I thought we were going to play "Old Folks."

RACHEL. We are.

JIMMY. Do old folks sit in each other's laps?

RACHEL. Old folks do anything. Come on.

JIMMY. *(hesitatingly climbs into her lap, but presently snuggles down and sighs audibly from sheer content;* RACHEL *starts to bind up her hair)* Ma Rachel, don't please! I like your hair like that. You're—you're pretty. I like to feel of it; and it smells like—like—oh!—like a barn.

RACHEL. My! how complimentary! I like that. Like a barn, indeed!

JIMMY. What's "complimentary"?

RACHEL. Oh! saying nice things about me. *(pinching his cheek and laughing)* That my hair is like a barn, for instance.

JIMMY. *(stoutly)* Well, that is "complimentary." It smells like hay—like the hay in the barn you took me to, one day, last summer. 'Member?

RACHEL. Yes, honey.

JIMMY. *(after a brief pause)* Ma Rachel!

RACHEL. Well?

JIMMY. Tell me a story, please. It's "storytime" now, isn't it?

RACHEL. Well, let's see. *(they both look into the fire for a space; beginning softly)* Once upon a time, there were two, dear, little boys, and they were all alone in the world. They lived with a cruel, old man and woman, who made them work hard, very hard—all day, and beat them when they did not move fast enough, and always, every night, before they went to bed. They slept in an attic on a rickety, narrow bed, that went screech! screech! whenever they moved. And, in summer, they nearly died with the heat up there, and in winter, with the cold. One wintry night, when they were both weeping very bitterly after a particularly hard beating, they suddenly heard a pleasant voice saying: "Why are you crying, little boys?" They looked up, and there, in the moonlight, by their bed, was the dearest, little old lady. She was dressed all in grey, from the peak of her little pointed hat to her little, buckled shoes. She held a black cane much taller than her little self. Her hair fell about her ears in tiny, grey corkscrew curls, and they bobbed about as she moved. Her eyes were black and bright—as bright as—well, as that lovely, white light there. No, there! And her cheeks were as red as the apple I gave you yesterday. Do you remember?

JIMMY. *(dreamily)* Yes.

RACHEL. "Why are you crying, little boys?" she asked again, in a lovely, low, little voice. "Because we are tired and sore and hungry and cold; and we are all alone in the world; and we don't know how to laugh any more. We should so like to laugh again." "Why, that's easy," she said, "it's just like this." And she laughed a little, joyous, musical laugh. "Try!" she commanded. They tried, but their laughing boxes were very rusty, and they made horrid sounds. "Well," she said, "I advise you to pack up, and go away, as soon as you can, to the Land of Laughter. You'll soon learn there, I can tell you." "Is there such a land?" they asked doubtfully. "To be sure there is," she answered the least bit sharply. "We never heard of it," they said. "Well, I'm sure there must be plenty of things you never heard about," she said just the "leastest" bit more sharply. "In a moment you'll be telling me flowers don't talk together, and the birds." "We never heard of such a thing," they said in surprise, their eyes like saucers. "There!" she said, bobbing her little curls. "What did I tell you? You have much to learn." "How do you get to the Land of Laughter?" they asked. "You go out of the eastern gate of the town, just as the sun is rising; and you take the highway there, and follow it; and if you go with it long enough, it will bring you to the very gates of the Land of Laughter. It's a long, long way from here; and it will take you many days." The words had scarcely left her mouth, when, lo! the little lady disappeared, and where she had stood was the white square of moonlight—nothing else. And without more ado these two little boys put their arms around each other and fell fast asleep. And in the grey, just before daybreak, they awoke and dressed; and, putting on their ragged caps and mittens, for it was a wintry day, they stole out of the house and made for the eastern gate. And just as they reached it and passed through, the whole east leapt into fire. All day they walked, and many days thereafter, and kindly people, by the way, took them in and gave them food and drink and sometimes a bed at night. Often they slept by the roadside, but they didn't mind that for the climate was delightful—not too hot, and not too cold. They soon threw away their ragged little mittens. They walked for many days, and there was no Land of Laughter. Once they met an old man, richly dressed, with shining jewels on his fingers, and he stopped them and asked: "Where are you going so fast, little boys?" "We are going to the Land of Laughter," they said together gravely. "That," said the old man, "is a very foolish thing to do. Come with me, and I will take you to the Land of Riches. I will cover you with garments of beauty, and give you jewels and a castle to live in and servants and horses and many things besides." And they said to him: "No, we wish to learn how to laugh again; we have forgotten how, and we are going to the Land of Laughter." "You will regret not going with me. See, if you don't," he said; and he left them in quite a huff. And they walked again, many days, and again they met an old man. He was tall and imposing-looking and very dignified. And he said: "Where are you going so fast, little boys?" "We are going to the Land of Laughter," they said together very seriously. "What!" he said, "that is an extremely foolish thing to do. Come with me, and I will give you power. I will make you great men: generals, kings, emperors. Whatever you desire to accomplish will be permitted you." And they smiled politely: "Thank you very much, but we have forgotten how to laugh, and we are going there to learn how." He looked upon them haughtily, without speaking, and disappeared. And they walked and walked more days; and they met another old man. And he was clad in rags, and his face was thin, and his eyes were unhappy. And he whispered to them: "Where are you going so fast, little boys?" "We are going to the Land of Laughter," they answered, without a smile. "Laughter! Laughter! that is useless. Come with me and I will show you the beauty of life through sacrifice, suffering for others. That is the only life. I come from the Land of Sacrifice." And they thanked him kindly, but said: "We have suffered long enough. We have forgotten how to laugh. We would learn again." And they went on; and he looked after them very wistfully. They walked more days, and at last they came to the Land of Laughter. And how do you suppose they knew this? Because they could hear, over the wall, the sound of joyous laughter,—the laughter of men, women, and children. And one sat guarding the gate, and they went to her. "We have come a long distance; and we would enter the Land of Laughter." "Let me see you smile, first," she said gently. "I sit at the gate; and no one who does not know how to smile may enter the Land of Laughter." And they tried to smile, but could not. "Go away and practice," she said kindly, "and come back tomorrow." And they went away, and practiced all night how to smile; and in the morning they returned, and the gentle lady at the gate said: "Dear little boys, have you learned how to smile?" and they said: "We have tried. How is this?" "Better," she said, "much better. Practice some more, and come back tomorrow." And they went away obediently and practiced. And they came the third day. And she said: "Now try again." And tears of delight came into her lovely eyes. "Those were very beautiful smiles," she said. "Now, you may enter." And she unlocked the gate, and kissed them both, and they entered the Land—the beautiful Land of Laughter. Never had they seen such blue skies, such green trees and grass; never had they heard such birds' songs. And people, men, women and children, laughing softly, came to meet them, and took them in, and made them at home; and soon, very soon, they learned to sleep. And they grew up here, and married, and had laughing, happy children. And sometimes they thought of the Land of Riches, and said: "Ah! well!" and sometimes of the Land of Power, and sighed a little; and sometimes of the Land of Sacrifice—and their eyes were wistful. But they soon forgot, and laughed again. And they grew old, laughing. And then when they died—a laugh was on their lips. Thus are things in the beautiful Land of Laughter. *(there is a long pause)*

JIMMY. I like that story, Ma Rachel. It's nice to laugh, isn't it? Is there such a land?

RACHEL. *(softly)* What do you think, honey?

JIMMY. I thinks it would be awful nice if there was. Don't you?

RACHEL. *(wistfully)* If there only were! If there only were!

JIMMY. Ma Rachel.

RACHEL. Well?

JIMMY. It makes you think—kind of—doesn't it—of sunshine medicine?

RACHEL. Yes, honey,—but it isn't medicine there. It's always there—just like—well—like our air here. It's *always* sunshine there.

JIMMY. Always sunshine? Never any dark?

RACHEL. No, honey.

JIMMY. *(with a big sigh)* Oh!—Oh! I *wisht* it was here—not there. *(puts his hand up to* RACHEL's *face; suddenly sits up and looks at her)* Why, Ma Rachel dear, you're crying. Your face is all wet. Why! Don't cry! Don't cry!

RACHEL. *(gently)* Do you remember that I told you the lady at the gate had tears of joy in her eyes, when the two, dear, little boys smiled that beautiful smile?

JIMMY. Yes.

RACHEL. Well, these are tears of joy, honey, that's all—tears of joy.

JIMMY. It must be awful queer to have tears of joy, 'cause you're happy. I never did. *(with a sigh)* But, if you say they are, dear Ma Rachel, they must be. You knows everything, don't you?

RACHEL. *(sadly)* Some things, honey, some things. *(a silence)*

JIMMY. *(sighing happily)* This is the beautifulest night I ever knew. If you would do just one more thing, it would be lots more beautiful. Will you, Ma Rachel?

RACHEL. Well, what, honey?

JIMMY. Will you sing—at the piano, I mean, it's lots prettier that way—the little song you used to rock me to sleep by? You know, the one about the "Slumber Boat"?

RACHEL. Oh! honey, not tonight. You're too tired. It's bedtime now.

JIMMY. *(patting her face with his little hand; wheedlingly)* Please! Ma Rachel, please! pretty please!

RACHEL. Well, honey boy, this once, then. Tonight, you shall have the little song—I used to sing you to sleep by *(half to herself)* perhaps, for the last time.

JIMMY. Why, Ma Rachel, why the last time?

RACHEL. *(shaking her head sadly, goes to the piano; in a whisper)* The last time. *(she twists up her hair into a knot at the back of her head and looks at the keys for a few moments; then she plays the accompaniment of the "Slumber Boat" through softly, and, after a moment, sings. Her voice is full of pent-up longing, and heartbreak, and hopelessness. She ends in a little sob, but attempts to cover it by singing, lightly and daintily, the chorus of "The Owl and the Moon,"* . . . *Then softly and with infinite tenderness, almost against her will, she plays and sings again the refrain of "Slumber Boat")*

Sail, baby, sail
    Out from the sea,
Only don't forget to sail
    Back again to me.

(Presently she rises and goes to JIMMY, *who is lolling back happily in the big chair. During the singing,* TOM *and* MRS. LOVING *apparently do not listen; when she sobs, however,* TOM's *hand on his paper tightens;* MRS. LOVING's *needle poises for a moment in mid-air. Neither looks at* RACHEL. JIMMY *evidently has not noticed the sob)*

RACHEL. *(kneeling by* JIMMY*)* Well, honey, how did you like it?

JIMMY. *(proceeding to pull down her hair from the twist)* It was lovely, Ma Rachel. *(yawns audibly)* Now, Ma Rachel, I'm just beautifully sleepy. *(dreamily)* I think that p'r'aps I'll go to the Land of Laughter tonight in my dreams. I'll go in the "Slumber Boat" and come back in the morning and tell you all about it. Shall I?

RACHEL. Yes, honey. *(whispers)*

Only don't forget to sail
    Back again to me.

TOM. *(suddenly)* Rachel! *(*RACHEL *starts slightly)* I nearly forgot. John is coming here tonight to see how you are. He told me to tell you so.

RACHEL. *(stiffens perceptibly, then in different tones)* Very well. Thank you. *(suddenly with a little cry she puts her arms around* JIMMY*)* Jimmy! honey! Don't go tonight. Don't go without Ma Rachel. Wait for me, honey. I do so wish to go, too, to the Land of Laughter. Think of it, Jimmy; nothing but birds always singing, and flowers always blooming, and skies always blue—and people, all of them, always laughing, laughing. You'll wait for Ma Rachel, won't you, honey?

JIMMY. Is there really and truly, Ma Rachel, a Land of Laughter?

RACHEL. Oh! Jimmy let's hope so; let's pray so.

JIMMY. *(frowns)* I've been thinking—*(pauses)* You have to smile at the gate, don't you, to get in?

RACHEL. Yes, honey.

JIMMY. Well, I guess I couldn't smile if my Ma Rachel wasn't somewhere close to me. So I couldn't get in after all, could I? Tonight, I'll go somewhere else, and tell you all about it. And then, some day, we'll go together, won't we?

RACHEL. *(sadly)* Yes, honey, some day—some day. *(a short silence)* Well, this isn't going to "sleepy-sleep," is it? Go, now, and say goodnight to Ma Loving and Uncle Tom.

JIMMY. *(gets down obediently, and goes first to* MRS. LOVING. *She leans over, and he puts his little arms around her neck. They kiss, very sweetly)* Sweet dreams! God keep you all the night!

MRS. LOVING. The sweetest of sweet dreams to you, dear little boy! Good-night! *(*RACHEL *watches, unwatched, the scene. Her eyes are full of yearning)*

JIMMY. *(going to* TOM, *who makes believe he does not see him)* Uncle Tom!

TOM. *(jumps as though tremendously startled;* JIMMY *laughs)* My! how you frightened me. You'll put my gizzard out of commission, if you do that often. Well, sir, what can I do for you?

JIMMY. I came to say good-night.

TOM. *(gathering* JIMMY *up in his arms and kissing him; gently and with emotion)* Good-night, dear little Big Fellow! Good-night!

JIMMY. Sweet dreams! God keep you all the night! *(goes sedately to* RACHEL, *and holds out his little hand)* I'm ready, Ma Rachel, *(yawns)* I'm so nice and sleepy.

RACHEL. *(with* JIMMY'S *hand in hers, she hesitates a moment, and then approaches* TOM *slowly. For a short time she stands looking down at him; suddenly leaning over him)* Why, Tom, what a pretty tie! Is it new?

TOM. Well, no, not exactly. I've had it about a month. It is rather a beauty, isn't it?

RACHEL. Why, I never remember seeing it.

TOM. *(laughing)* I guess not. I saw to that.

RACHEL. Stingy!

TOM. Well, I am—where my ties are concerned. I've had experience.

RACHEL. *(tentatively)* Tom!

TOM. Well?

RACHEL. *(nervously and wistfully)* Are you—will you—I mean, won't you be home this evening?

TOM. You've got a long memory, Sis. I've that engagement, you know. Why?

RACHEL. *(slowly)* I forgot; so you have.

TOM. Why?

RACHEL. *(hastily)* Oh! nothing—nothing. Come on, Jimmy boy, you can hardly keep those little peepers open, can you? Come on, honey. *(*RACHEL *and* JIMMY *go out the rear doorway. There is a silence)*

MRS. LOVING. *(slowly, as though thinking aloud)* I try to make out what could have happened; but it's no use—I can't. Those four days, she lay in bed hardly moving, scarcely speaking. Only her eyes seemed alive. I never saw such a wide, tragic look in my life. It was as though her soul had been mortally wounded. But how? how? What could have happened?

TOM. *(quietly)* I don't know. She generally tells me everything; but she avoids me now. If we are alone in a room—she gets out. I don't know what it means.

MRS. LOVING. She will hardly let Jimmy out of her sight. While he's at school, she's nervous and excited. She seems always to be listening, but for what? When he returns, she nearly devours him. And she always asks him in a frightened sort of way, her face as pale and tense as can be: "Well, honey boy, how was school today?" And he always answers, "Fine, Ma Rachel, fine! I learned—"; and then he goes on to tell her everything that has happened. And when he has finished, she says in an uneasy sort of way: "Is—is that all?" And when he says "Yes," she relaxes and becomes limp. After a little while she becomes feverishly happy. She plays with Jimmy and the children more than ever she did—and she played a good deal, as you know. They're here, or she's with them. Yesterday, I said in remonstrance, when she came in, her face pale and haggard and black hollows under her eyes: "Rachel, remember you're just out of a sickbed. You're not well enough to go on like this." "I know," was all she would say, "but I've got to. I can't help myself. This part of their little lives must be happy—it just must be." *(pauses)* The last couple of nights, Jimmy has awakened and cried most pitifully. She wouldn't let me go to him; said I had enough trouble, and she could quiet him. She never will let me know why he cries; but she stays with him, and soothes him until, at last, he falls asleep again. Every time she has come out like a rag; and her face is like a dead woman's. Strange isn't it, this is the first time we have ever been able to talk it over? Tom, what could have happened?

TOM. I don't know, Ma, but I feel, as you do; something terrible and sudden has hurt her soul; and, poor little thing, she's trying bravely to readjust herself to life again. *(pauses, looks at his watch and then rises, and goes to her. He pats her back awkwardly)* Well, Ma, I'm going now. Don't worry too much. Youth, you know, gets over things finally. It takes them hard, that's all—. At least, that's what the older heads tell us. *(gets his hat and stands in the vestibule doorway)* Ma, you know, I begin with John tomorrow. *(with emotion)* I don't believe we'll ever forget John. Good-night! *(exit.* MRS. LOVING *continues to sew.* RACHEL, *her hair arranged, reenters, through the rear doorway. She is humming)*

RACHEL. He's sleeping like a top. Aren't little children, Ma dear, the sweetest things, when they're all helpless and asleep? One little hand is under his cheek; and he's smiling. *(stops suddenly, biting her lips. A pause)* Where's Tom?

MRS. LOVING. He went out a few minutes ago.

RACHEL. *(sitting in* TOM's *chair and picking up his paper. She is exceedingly nervous. She looks the paper over rapidly; presently trying to make her tone casual)* Ma,—you—you—aren't going anywhere tonight, are you?

MRS. LOVING. I've got to go out for a short time about half-past eight. Mrs. Jordan, you know. I'll not be gone very long, though. Why?

RACHEL. Oh! nothing particular. I just thought it would be cosy if we could sit here together the rest of the evening. Can't you—can't you go tomorrow?

MRS. LOVING. Why, I don't see how I can. I've made the engagement. It's about a new reception gown; and she's exceedingly exacting, as you know. I can't afford to lose her.

RACHEL. No, I suppose not. All right, Ma dear. (*presently, paper in hand, she laughs, but not quite naturally*) Look! Ma dear! How is that for fashion, anyway? Isn't it the "limit"? (*rises and shows her mother a picture in the paper. As she is in the act, the bell rings. With a startled cry*) Oh! (*drops the paper, and grips her mother's hand*)

MRS. LOVING. (*anxiously*) Rachel, your nerves are right on edge; and your hand feels like fire. I'll have to see a doctor about you; and that's all there is to it.

RACHEL. (*laughing nervously, and moving toward the vestibule*) Nonsense, Ma dear! Just because I let out a whoop now and then, and have nice warm hands? (*goes out, is heard talking through the tube*) Yes! (*her voice emitting tremendous relief*) Oh! bring it right up! (*appearing in the doorway*) Ma dear, did you buy anything at Goddard's today?

MRS. LOVING. Yes; and I've been wondering why they were so late in delivering it. I bought it early this morning. (RACHEL *goes out again. A door opens and shuts. She reappears with a bundle*)

MRS. LOVING. Put it on my bed, Rachel, please. (*exit* RACHEL *rear doorway; presently returns empty-handed; sits down again at the table with the paper between herself and mother; sinks in a deep revery. Suddenly there is the sound of many loud knocks made by numerous small fists.* RACHEL *drops the paper, and comes to a sitting posture, tense again. Her mother looks at her, but says nothing. Almost immediately* RACHEL *relaxes*)

RACHEL. My kiddies! They're late, this evening. (*goes out into the vestibule. A door opens and shuts. There is the shrill, excited sound of childish voices.* RACHEL *comes in surrounded by the children, all trying to say something to her at once.* RACHEL *puts her finger on her lip and points toward the doorway in the rear. They all quiet down. She sits on the floor in the front of the stage, and the children all cluster around her. Their conversation takes place in a half-whisper. As they enter they nod brightly at* MRS. LOVING, *who smiles in return*) Why so late, kiddies? It's long past "sleepy-time."

LITTLE NANCY. We've been playing "Hide and Seek," and having the mostest fun. We promised, all of us, that if we could play until half-past seven tonight we wouldn't make any fuss about going to bed at seven o'clock the rest of the week. It's awful hard to go. I *hate* to go to bed!

LITTLE MARY, LOUISE and EDITH. So do I! So do I! So do I!

LITTLE MARTHA. I don't. I love bed. My bed, after my muzzer tucks me all in, is like a nice warm bag. I just stick my nose out. When I lifts my head up I can see the light from the dining-room come in the door. I can hear my muzzer and fazzer talking nice and low; and then, before I know it, I'm fast asleep, and I dream pretty things, and in about a minute it's morning again. I love my little bed, and I love to dream.

LITTLE MARY. (*aggressively*) Well, I guess I love to dream too. I wish I could dream, though, without going to bed.

LITTLE NANCY. When I grow up, I'm never going to bed at night! (*darkly*) You see.

LITTLE LOUISE. "Grown-ups" just love to poke their heads out of windows and cry, "Child'run, it's time for bed now; and you'd better hurry, too, I can tell you." They "sure" are queer, for sometimes when I wake up, it must be about twelve o'clock, I can hear my big sister giggling and talking to some silly man. If it's good for me to go to bed early—I should think—

RACHEL. *(interrupting suddenly)* Why, where is my little Jenny? Excuse me, Louise dear.

LITTLE MARTHA. Her cold is awful bad. She coughs like this *(giving a distressing imitation)* and snuffles all the time. She can't talk out loud, and she can't go to sleep. Muzzer says she's fev'rish—I thinks that's what she says. Jenny says she knows she could go to sleep, if you would come and sit with her a little while.

RACHEL. I certainly will. I'll go when you do, honey.

LITTLE MARTHA. *(softly stroking* RACHEL'S *arm)* You're the very nicest "grown-up," *(loyally)* except my muzzer, of course, I ever knew. You knows all about little chil'run, and you can be one, although you're all grown up. I think you would make a lovely muzzer. *(to the rest of the children)* Don't you?

ALL. *(in excited whispers)* Yes, I do.

RACHEL. *(winces, then says gently)* Come, kiddies, you must go now, or your mothers will blame me for keeping you. *(rises, as do the rest.* LITTLE MARTHA *puts her hand into* RACHEL'S*)* Ma dear, I'm going to sit a little while with Jenny. I'll be back before you go, though. Come, kiddies, say good-night to my mother.

ALL. *(gravely)* Good-night! Sweet dreams! God keep you all the night.

MRS. LOVING. Good-night dears! Sweet dreams, all!

(Exeunt RACHEL *and the children.* MRS. LOVING *continues to sew. The bell presently rings three distinct times. In a few moments,* MRS. LOVING *gets up and goes out into the vestibule. A door opens and closes.* MRS. LOVING *and* JOHN STRONG *come in. He is a trifle pale but his imperturbable self.* MRS. LOVING, *somewhat nervous, takes her seat and resumes her sewing. She motions* STRONG *to a chair. He returns to the vestibule, leaves his hat, returns, and sits down)*

STRONG. Well, how is everything?

MRS. LOVING. Oh, about the same, I guess. Tom's out. John, we'll never forget you—and your kindness.

STRONG. That was nothing. And Rachel?

MRS. LOVING. She'll be back presently. She went to sit with a sick child for a little while.

STRONG. And how is she?

MRS. LOVING. She's not herself yet, but I think she is better.

STRONG. *(after a short pause)* Well, what *did* happen—exactly?

MRS. LOVING. That's just what I don't know.

STRONG. When you came home—you couldn't get in—was that it?

MRS. LOVING. Yes. *(pauses)* It was just a week ago today. I was down town all the morning. It was about one o'clock when I got back. I had forgotten my key. I rapped on the door and then called. There was no answer. A window was open, and I could feel the air under the door, and I could hear it as the draught sucked it through. There was no other sound. Presently I made such a noise the people began to come out into the hall. Jimmy was in one of the flats playing with a little girl named Mary. He told me he had left Rachel here a short time before. She had given him four cookies, two for him and two for Mary, and had told him he could play with her until she came to tell him his lunch was ready. I saw he was getting frightened, so I got the little girl and her mother to keep him in their flat. Then, as no man was at home, I sent out for help. Three men broke the door down. *(pauses)* We found Rachel unconscious, lying on her face. For a few minutes I thought she was dead. *(pauses)* A vase had fallen over on the table and the water had dripped through the cloth and onto the floor. There had been flowers in it. When I left, there were no flowers here. What she could have done to them, I can't say. The long stems were lying everywhere, and the flowers had been ground into the floor. I could tell that they must have been roses from the stems. After we had put her to bed and called the doctor, and she had finally regained consciousness, I very naturally asked her what had happened. All she would say was, "Ma dear, I'm too—tired—please." For four days she lay in bed scarcely moving, speaking only when spoken to. That first day, when Jimmy came in to see her, she shrank away from him. We had to take him out, and comfort him as best we could. We kept him away, almost by force, until she got up. And then, she was utterly miserable when he was out of her sight. What happened, I don't know. She avoids Tom, and she won't tell me. *(pauses)* Tom and I both believe her soul has been hurt. The trouble isn't with her body. You'll find her highly nervous. Sometimes she is very much depressed; again she is feverishly gay—almost reckless. What do you think about it, John?

STRONG. *(who has listened quietly)* Had anybody been here, do you know?

MRS. LOVING. No, I don't. I don't like to ask Rachel; and I can't ask the neighbors.

STRONG. And the flowers were ground into the carpet?

MRS. LOVING. Yes.

STRONG. Did you happen to notice the box? They must have come in a box, don't you think?

MRS. LOVING. Yes, there was a box in the kitchenette. It was from "Marcy's." I saw no card.

STRONG. *(slowly)* It is rather strange. *(a long silence during which the outer door opens and shuts.* RACHEL *is heard singing. She stops abruptly. In a second or two she appears in the door. There is an air of suppressed excitement about her)*

RACHEL. Hello! John. (STRONG *rises, nods at her, and brings forward for her the big arm-chair near the fire)* I thought that was your hat in the hall. It's brand new, I know—but it looks—"Johnlike." How are you? Ma! Jenny went to sleep like a little lamb. I don't like her breathing, though. *(looks from one to the other; flippantly)* Who's dead? *(nods her thanks to* STRONG *for the chair and sits down)*

MRS. LOVING. Dead, Rachel?

RACHEL. Yes. The atmosphere here is so funereal,—it's positively "crapey."

STRONG. I don't know why it should be—I was just asking how you are.

RACHEL. Heavens! Does the mere inquiry into my health precipitate such an atmosphere? Your two faces were as long, as long—*(breaks off)* Kind sir, let me assure you, I am in the very best of health. And how are you, John?

STRONG. Oh! I'm always well. *(sits down)*

MRS. LOVING. Rachel, I'll have to get ready to go now. John, don't hurry. I'll be back shortly, probably in three-quarters of an hour—maybe less.

RACHEL. And maybe more, if I remember Mrs. Jordan. However, Ma dear, I'll do the best I can—while you are away. I'll try to be a credit to your training. (MRS. LOV-ING *smiles and goes out the rear doorway*) Now, let's see—in the books of etiquette, I believe, the properly reared young lady, always asks the young gentleman caller—you're young enough, aren't you, to be classed still as a "young gentleman caller"? *(no answer)* Well, anyway, she always asks the young gentleman caller sweetly something about the weather. *(primly)* This has been an exceedingly beautiful day, hasn't it, Mr. Strong? *(No answer from STRONG, who, with his head resting against the back of the chair, and his knees crossed is watching her in an amused, quizzical manner)* Well, really, every properly brought up young gentleman, I'm sure, ought to know, that it's exceedingly rude not to answer a civil question.

STRONG. *(lazily)* Tell me what to answer, Rachel.

RACHEL. Say, "Yes, very"; and look interested and pleased when you say it.

STRONG. *(with a half-smile)* Yes, very.

RACHEL. Well, I certainly wouldn't characterize that as a particularly animated remark. Besides, when you look at me through half-closed lids like that—and kind of smile—what are you thinking? *(no answer)* John Strong, are you deaf or—just plain stupid?

STRONG. Plain stupid, I guess.

RACHEL. *(in wheedling tones)* What were you thinking, John?

STRONG. *(slowly)* I was thinking—*(breaks off)*

RACHEL. *(irritably)* Well?

STRONG. I've changed my mind.

RACHEL. You're not going to tell me?

STRONG. No.

(MRS. LOVING *dressed for the street comes in*)

MRS. LOVING. Good-bye, children. Rachel, don't quarrel so much with John. Let me see—if I have my key. *(feels in her bag)* Yes, I have it. I'll be back shortly. Good-bye. (STRONG *and* RACHEL *rise. He bows*)

RACHEL. Good-bye, Ma dear. Hurry back as soon as you can, won't you? *(exit* MRS. LOVING *through the vestibule.* STRONG *leans back again in his chair, and watches* RACHEL *through half-closed eyes.* RACHEL *sits in her chair nervously)*

STRONG. Do you mind, if I smoke?

RACHEL. You know I don't.

STRONG. I am trying to behave like—Reginald—"the properly reared young gentleman caller." *(lights a cigar; goes over to the fire, and throws his match away.* RACHEL *goes into the kitchenette, and brings him a saucer for his ashes. She places it on the table near him)* Thank you. *(they both sit again,* STRONG *very evidently enjoying his cigar and* RACHEL*)* Now this is what I call cosy.

RACHEL. Cosy! Why?

STRONG. A nice warm room—shut in—curtains drawn—a cheerful fire crackling at my back—a lamp, not an electric or gas one, but one of your plain, old-fashioned kerosene ones—

RACHEL. (*interrupting*) Ma dear would like to catch you, I am sure, talking about *her* lamp like that. "Old-fashioned! plain!"—You have nerve.

STRONG. (*continuing as though he had not been interrupted*) A comfortable chair—a good cigar—and not very far away, a little lady, who is looking charming, so near, that if I reached over, I could touch her. You there—and I here.—It's living.

RACHEL. Well! of all things! A compliment—and from *you!* How did it slip out, pray? (*no answer*) I suppose that you realize that a conversation between two persons is absolutely impossible, if one has to do her share all alone. Soon my ingenuity for introducing interesting subjects will be exhausted; and then will follow what, I believe, the story books call, "an uncomfortable silence."

STRONG. (*slowly*) Silence—between friends—isn't such a bad thing.

RACHEL. Thanks awfully. (*leans back; cups her cheek in her hand, and makes no pretense at further conversation. The old look of introspection returns to her eyes. She does not move*)

STRONG. (*quietly*) Rachel! (RACHEL *starts perceptibly*) You must remember I'm here. I don't like looking into your soul—when you forget you're not alone.

RACHEL. I hadn't forgotten.

STRONG. Wouldn't it be easier for you, little girl, if you could tell—some one?

RACHEL. No. (*a silence*)

STRONG. Rachel,—you're fond of flowers,—aren't you?

RACHEL. Yes.

STRONG. Rosebuds—red rosebuds—particularly?

RACHEL. (*nervously*) Yes.

STRONG. Did you—dislike—the giver?

RACHEL. (*more nervously; bracing herself*) No, of course not.

STRONG. Rachel,—why—why—did you—kill the roses—then?

RACHEL. (*twisting her hands*) Oh, John! I'm so sorry, Ma dear told you that. She didn't know you sent them.

STRONG. So I gathered. (*pauses and then leans foward; quietly*) Rachel, little girl, why—did you kill them?

RACHEL. (*breathing quickly*) Don't you believe—it—a—a—kindness—sometimes—to kill?

STRONG. (*after a pause*) You—considered it—a kindness—to kill them?

RACHEL. Yes. (*another pause*)

STRONG. Do you mean—just—the roses?

RACHEL. (*breathing more quickly*) John!—Oh! must I say?

STRONG. Yes, little Rachel.

RACHEL. (*in a whisper*) No. (*there is a long pause.* RACHEL *leans back limply, and closes her eyes. Presently* STRONG *rises, and moves his chair very close to hers. She does not stir. He puts his cigar on the saucer*)

STRONG. (*leaning forward; very gently*) Little girl, little girl, can you tell me why?

RACHEL. (*wearily*) I can't.—It hurts—too much—to talk about it yet,—please.

STRONG. (*takes her hand; looks at it a few minutes and then at her quietly*) You—don't care, then? (*she winces*) Rachel!—Look at me, little girl! (*as if against her will, she looks at him. Her eyes are fearful, hunted. She tries to look away, to draw away her hand; but he holds her gaze and her hands steadily*) Do you?

RACHEL. *(almost sobbing)* John! John! don't ask me. You are drawing my very soul out of my body with your eyes. You must not talk this way. You mustn't look—John, don't. *(tries to shield her eyes)*

STRONG. *(quietly takes both of her hands, and kisses the backs and the palms slowly. A look of horror creeps into her face. He deliberately raises his eyes and looks at her mouth. She recoils as though she expected him to strike her. He resumes slowly)* If—you—do—care, and I know now—that you do—nothing else, *nothing should count.*

RACHEL. *(wrenching herself from his grasp and rising. She covers her ears; she breathes rapidly)* No! No! No!—You *must* stop. *(laughs nervously; continues feverishly)* I'm not behaving very well as a hostess, am I? Let's see. What shall I do? I'll play you something, John. How will that do? Or I'll sing to you. You used to like to hear me sing; you said my voice, I remember, was sympathetic, didn't you? *(moves quickly to the piano)* I'll sing you a pretty little song. I think it's beautiful. You've never heard it, I know. I've never sung it to you before. It's Nevin's "At Twilight." *(pauses, looks down, before she begins, then turns toward him and says quietly and sweetly)* Sometimes—in the coming years—I want—you to remember—I sang you this little song.—Will you?—I think it will make it easier for me—when I—when I—*(breaks off and begins the first chords.* STRONG *goes slowly to the piano. He leans there watching intently.* RACHEL *sings)*

The roses of yesteryear
    Were all of the white and red;
It fills my heart with silent fear
    To find all their beauty fled.

The roses of white are sere,
    All faded the roses red,
And one who loves me is not here
    And one that I love is dead.

(A long pause. Then STRONG *goes to her and lifts her from the piano-stool. He puts one arm around her very tenderly and pushes her head back so he can look into her eyes. She shuts them, but is passive)*

STRONG. *(gently)* Little girl, little girl, don't you know that suggestions—suggestions—like those you are sending yourself constantly—are wicked things? You, who are so gentle, so loving, so warm—*(breaks off and crushes her to him. He kisses her many times. She does not resist, but in the midst of his caresses she breaks suddenly into convulsive laughter. He tries to hush the terrible sound with his mouth; then brokenly)* Little girl— don't laugh—like that.

RACHEL. *(interrupted throughout by her laughter)* I have to.—God is laughing.—We're his puppets.—He pulls the wires,—and we're so funny to Him.—I'm laughing too—because I can hear—my little children—weeping. They come to me generally while I'm asleep,—but I can hear them now.—They've begged me—do you understand?—begged me—not to bring them here;—and I've promised them—not to—I've promised. I can't stand the sound of their crying.—I have to laugh—Oh! John! laugh!—laugh too!—I can't drown their weeping.

(STRONG picks her up bodily and carries her to the arm-chair)

STRONG. *(harshly)* Now, stop that!

RACHEL. *(in sheer surprise)* W-h-a-t?

STRONG. *(still harshly)* Stop that!—You've lost your self-control.—Find yourself
again!

*(He leaves her and goes over to the fireplace, and stands looking down into it for some
little time. RACHEL, little by little, becomes calmer. STRONG returns and sits beside her
again. She doesn't move. He soothes her hair back gently, and kisses her forehead—and
then, slowly, her mouth. She does not resist; simply sits there, with shut eyes, inert, limp)*

STRONG. Rachel! *(pauses)* There is a little flat on 43rd Street. It faces south and
overlooks a little park. Do you remember it?—it's on the top floor?—Once I
remember your saying—you liked it. That was over a year ago. That same
day—I rented it. I've never lived there. No one knows about it—not even my
mother. It's completely furnished now—and waiting—do you know for whom?
Every single thing in it, I've bought myself—even to the pins on the little bird's
eye maple dresser. It has been the happiest year I have ever known. I furnished
it—one room at a time. It's the prettiest, the most homelike little flat I've ever
seen. *(very low)* Everything there—breathes love. Do you know for whom it is
waiting? On the sitting-room floor is a beautiful, Turkish rug—red, and blue
and gold. It's soft—and rich—and do you know for whose little feet it is waiting? There are delicate curtains at the windows and a bookcase full of friendly, eager, little books.—Do you know for whom they are waiting? There are
comfortable leather chairs, just the right size and a beautiful piano—that I
leave open—sometimes, and lovely pictures of Madonnas. Do you know for
whom they are waiting? There is an open fireplace with logs of wood, all carefully piled on gleaming andirons—and waiting. There is a bellows and a pair
of shining tongs—waiting. And in the kitchenette painted blue and white, and
smelling sweet with paint is everything: bright pots and pans and kettles, and
blue and white enamel-ware, and all kinds of knives and forks and spoons—
and on the door—a roller-towel. Little girl, do you know for whom they
are all waiting? And somewhere—there's a big, strong man—with broad
shoulders. And he's willing and anxious to do anything—everything, and he's
waiting very patiently. Little girl, is it to be—yes or no?

RACHEL. *(during STRONG's speech life has come flooding back to her. Her eyes are shining; her face, eager. For a moment she is beautifully happy)* Oh! You're too good to
me and mine, John. I—didn't dream any one—could be—so good. *(leans forward and puts his big hand against her cheek and kisses it shyly)*

STRONG. *(quietly)* Is it—yes—or no, little girl?

RACHEL. *(feverishly, gripping his hands)* Oh, yes! yes! yes! and take me quickly,
John. Take me before I can think any more. You mustn't let me think, John.
And you'll be good to me, won't you? Every second of every minute, of every
hour, of every day, you'll have me in your thoughts, won't you? And you'll be
with me every minute that you can? And, John, John!—you'll keep away
the weeping of my little children. You won't let me hear it, will you? You'll
make me forget everything everything—won't you?—Life is so short, John.

(shivers and then fearfully and slowly) And eternity so—long. *(feverishly again)* And, John, after I am dead—promise me, promise me you'll love me more. *(shivers again)* I'll need love then. Oh! I'll need it. *(suddenly there comes to their ears the sound of a child's weeping. It is monotonous, hopeless, terribly afraid.* RACHEL *recoils)* Oh! John! Listen! It's my boy, again.—I—John—I'll be back in a little while. *(goes swiftly to the door in the rear, pauses and looks back. The weeping continues. Her eyes are tragic. Slowly she kisses her hand to him and disappears.* JOHN *stands where she has left him looking down. The weeping stops. Presently* RACHEL *appears in the doorway. She is haggard, and grey. She does not enter the room. She speaks as one dead might speak—tonelessly, slowly)*

RACHEL. Do you wish to know why Jimmy is crying?

STRONG. Yes.

RACHEL. I am twenty-two—and I'm old; you're thirty-two—and you're old; Tom's twenty-three—and he is old. Ma dear's sixty—and she said once she is much older than that. She is. We are all blighted; we are all accursed—all of us—, everywhere, we whose skins are dark—our lives blasted by the white man's prejudice. *(pause)* And my little Jimmy—seven years old, that's all—is blighted too. In a year or two, at best, he will be made old by suffering. *(pause)* One week ago, today, some white boys, older and larger than my little Jimmy, as he was leaving the school—called him "Nigger"! They chased him through the streets calling him, "Nigger! Nigger! Nigger!" One boy threw stones at him. There is still a bruise on his little back where one struck him. That will get well; but they bruised his soul—and that—will never—get well. He asked me what "Nigger" meant. I made light of the whole thing, laughed it off. He went to his little playmates, and very naturally asked them. The oldest of them is nine!—and they knew, poor little things—and they told him. *(pauses)* For the last couple of nights he has been dreaming—about these boys. And he always awakes—in the dark—afraid—afraid—of the now—and the future—I have seen that look of deadly fear—in the eyes—of other little children. I know what it is myself.—I was twelve—when some big boys chased me and called me names. I never left the house afterwards—without being afraid. I was afraid, in the streets—in the school—in the church, everywhere, always, afraid of being hurt. And I—was not—afraid in vain. *(the weeping begins again)* He's only a baby—and he's blighted. *(to* JIMMY*)* Honey, I'm right here. I'm coming in just a minute. Don't cry. *(to* STRONG*)* If it nearly kills me to hear my Jimmy's crying, do you think I could stand it, when my own child, flesh of my flesh, blood of my blood—learned the same reason for weeping? Do you? *(pauses)* Ever since I fell here—a week ago—I am afraid—to go—to sleep, for every time I do—my children come—and beg me—weeping—not to—bring them here— to suffer. Tonight, they came—when I was awake. *(pauses)* I have promised them again, now—by Jimmy's bed. *(in a whisper)* I have damned—my soul to all eternity—if I do. *(to* JIMMY*)* Honey, don't! I'm coming. *(to* STRONG*)* And John,—dear John—you see—it can never be—all the beautiful, beautiful things—you have—told me about. *(wistfully)* No—they—can never be—now. *(*STRONG *comes toward her)* No,—John dear,—you—must not—touch me—any more. *(pauses)* Dear, this—is—"Good-bye."

STRONG. *(quietly)* It's not fair—to you, Rachel, to take you—at your word—tonight. You're sick; you've brooded so long, so continuously,—you've lost—your perspective. Don't answer, yet. Think it over for another week and I'll come back.

RACHEL. *(wearily)* No,—I can't think—any more.

STRONG. You realize—fully—you're sending me—for always?

RACHEL. Yes.

STRONG. And you care?

RACHEL. Yes.

STRONG. It's settled, then for all time—"Good-bye!"

RACHEL. *(after a pause)* Yes.

STRONG. *(stands looking at her steadily a long time, and then moves to the door and turns, facing her; with infinite tenderness)* Good-bye, dear, little Rachel—God bless you.

RACHEL. Good-bye, John! (STRONG *goes out. A door opens and shuts. There is finality in the sound. The weeping continues. Suddenly; with a great cry)* John! John! *(runs out into the vestibule. She presently returns. She is calm again. Slowly)* No! No! John. Not for us. *(a pause; with infinite yearning)* Oh! John,—if it only—if it only—(breaks off, controls herself. Slowly again; thoughtfully)* No—no sunshine— no laughter—always—darkness. That is it. Even our little flat—*(in a whisper)* John's and mine—the little flat—that calls, calls us—through darkness. It shall wait—and wait—in vain—in darkness. Oh, John! *(pauses)* And my little children! my little children! *(the weeping ceases; pauses)* I shall never—see—you— now. Your little, brown, beautiful bodies—I shall never see.—Your dimples— everywhere—your laughter—your tears—the beautiful, lovely feel of you here. *(puts her hands against her heart)* Never—never—to be. *(a pause, fiercely)* But you are somewhere—and wherever you are you are mine! You are mine! All of you! Every bit of you! Even God can't take you away. *(a pause; very sweetly; pathetically)* Little children!—My little children!—No more need you come to me— weeping—weeping. You may be happy now—you are safe. Little weeping, voices, hush! hush! *(the weeping begins again. To* JIMMY, *her whole soul in her voice)* Jimmy! My little Jimmy! Honey! I'm coming.—Ma Rachel loves you so. *(sobs and goes blindly, unsteadily to the rear doorway; she leans her head there one second against the door; and then stumbles through and disappears. The light in the lamp flickers and goes out. . . . It is black. The terrible, heart-breaking weeping continues.)*

CURTAIN

🎴 ANNE SPENCER (1882–1975)

Like Angelina Weld Grimke, Anne Spencer sought to express the lives of black women in her verse. Born in Henry County, Virginia, she was educated at Virginia Seminary, where she earned a degree in 1899. Later, she married Edward Alexander Spencer, and the family moved to Lynchburg, Virginia, where she gave birth to three children. She wrote most of her poems in a cottage behind her home. She rose to fame when James

Weldon Johnson published her work in The Book of American Negro Poetry *(1922). Her home served as a literary salon during the Harlem Renaissance, with distinguished visitors such as W. E. B. Du Bois, Claude McKay, and James Weldon Johnson. In her poems, such as "The Wife-Woman," she critiques race, class, and gender issues, anticipating later poets like Gwendolyn Brooks, Nikki Giovanni, and Maya Angelou.*

Dunbar (1920)

Ah, how poets sing and die!
Make one song and Heaven takes it;
Have one heart and Beauty breaks it;
Chatterton, Shelley, Keats and I—
Ah, how poets sing and die!   5

The Wife-Woman (1931)

Maker-of-Sevens in the scheme of things
From earth to star;
Thy cycle holds whatever is fate, and
Over the border the bar.
Though rank and fierce the mariner   5
Sailing the seven seas,
He prays, as he holds his glass to his eyes,
Coaxing the Pleiades.

I cannot love them; and I feel your glad
Chiding from the grave,   10
That my all was only worth at all, what
Joy to you it gave.
These seven links the *Law* compelled
For the human chain—
I cannot love *them;* and *you*, oh,   15
Seven-fold months in Flanders slain!

A jungle there, a cave here, bred six
And a million years,
Sure and strong, mate for mate, such
Love as culture fears;   20
I gave you clear the oil and wine;
You saved me your hob and hearth—
See how *even* life may be ere the
Sickle comes and leaves a swath.

But I can wait the seven of moons,   25
Or years I spare,
Hoarding the heart's plenty, nor spend

A drop, nor share—
So long but outlives a smile and
A silken gown;   30
Then gaily I reach up from my shroud,
And you, glory-clad, reach down.

✿ CLAUDE McKAY (1889-1948)

*Claude McKay was a native of Sunny Ville, Jamaica. His early work was infused with the
sounds and sights of his homeland, and he won recognition with* Songs of Jamaica *and*
Constab Ballads *(both published in 1912). Money he earned from the Jamaican Medal
of the Institute of Arts and Science enabled him to travel to America. He found wealth and
fame hard to achieve in the United States, where he elicited negative reactions from editors because of the strong black consciousness and protest in his poems. The protest element
in his work points out the political context of the Harlem Renaissance. "If We Must Die"
(1919) has a strident quality calling on the oppressed to fight valiantly against their
oppressors. The poem, included in his volume* Harlem Shadows *(1922), is one of McKays's
best known. He lived abroad from 1923 to 1934, writing novels, including* Home to
Harlem *(1928), a best-seller. He later returned to the United States, becoming a Catholic
in 1944, and died of heart failure in Chicago in 1948. His literary legacy shows that
despite the abolition of slavery in the nineteenth century, blacks were not truly free to enjoy
equal treatment in early-twentieth-century America.*

If We Must Die (1919)

If we must die, let it not be like hogs
Hunted and penned in an inglorious spot,
While round us bark the mad and hungry dogs,
Making their mock at our accursed lot.
If we must die, O let us nobly die,   5
So that our precious blood may not be shed
In vain; then even the monsters we defy
Shall be constrained to honor us though dead!
O kinsmen! we must meet the common foe!
Though far outnumbered, let us show us brave,   10
And for their thousand blows deal one deathblow!
What though before us lies the open grave?
Like men we'll face the murderous, cowardly pack,
Pressed to the wall, dying, but fighting back!

The Tropics in New York (1920)

Bananas ripe and green, and ginger-root,
   Cocoa in pods and alligator pears,

And tangerines and mangoes and grape fruit,
   Fit for the highest prize at parish fairs,

Set in the window, bringing memories   5
   Of fruit-trees laden by low-singing rills,
And dewy dawns, and mystical blue skies
   In benediction over nun-like hills.

My eyes grew dim, and I could no more gaze;
   A wave of longing through my body swept,   10
And, hungry for the old, familiar ways,
   I turned aside and bowed my head and wept.

America (1921)

Although she feeds me bread of bitterness,
And sinks into my throat her tiger's tooth,
Stealing my breath of life, I will confess
I love this cultured hell that tests my youth!
Her vigor flows like tides into my blood,   5
Giving me strength erect against her hate.
Her bigness sweeps my being like a flood.
Yet as a rebel fronts a king in state,
I stand within her walls with not a shred
Of terror, malice, not a word of jeer.   10
Darkly I gaze into the days ahead,
And see her might and granite wonders there,
Beneath the touch of Time's unerring hand,
Like priceless treasures sinking in the sand.

Spring in New Hampshire (1920)

(*To J. L. J. F. E.*)

Too green the springing April grass,
   Too blue the silver-speckled sky,
For me to linger here, alas,
   While happy winds go laughing by,
Wasting the golden hours indoors,   5
Washing windows and scrubbing floors.

Too wonderful the April night,
   Too faintly sweet the first May flowers,
The stars too gloriously bright,
   For me to spend the evening hours,   10

When fields are fresh and streams are leaping,
Wearied, exhausted, dully sleeping.

JESSIE REDMON FAUSET (1882–1961)

Born in Camden County, New Jersey, Jessie Redmon Fauset earned a B.A. from Cornell University in 1904 and an M.A. from the University of Pennsylvania in 1919. She attended the Sorbonne in France in 1925. Like many African American writers of the Harlem Renaissance period, she was an educator, teaching at the prestigious M Street High School in Washington, D.C., beginning in 1906. From 1919 to 1926, she served as literary editor of The Crisis, *publishing notable writers such as Langston Hughes. She wrote four novels:* There Is Confusion *(1924),* Plum Bun: A Novel Without a Moral *(1929),* The Chinaberry Tree *(1931), and* Comedy: American Style *(1933). Her novels often focus on protagonists who feel enslaved because of racial, sexual, and class prejudices. Her last novel,* Comedy: American Style, *is a scathing critique of racial self-hatred. Fauset married Herbert Harris in 1929, and the couple lived in Harlem until the 1940s, when they moved to New Jersey. After her husband's death, Fauset moved to Philadelphia, where she spent the rest of her life. As literary editor of* The Crisis, *a short-story writer, and a novelist, Fauset helped shape the tone of the Harlem Renaissance through her own creative writing and her attempts to mentor other writers.*

Double Trouble (1923)

I

Angélique came walking delicately down Cedarwood Street. You could see by the way she advanced, a way which fell just short of dancing that she was feeling to the utmost the pleasant combination of her youth, the weather and the season. Angélique was seventeen, the day was perfect and the year was at the spring.

Just before Cedarwood crosses Tenth, she stopped, her nice face crinkling with amusement and untied and retied the ribbon which fastened her trim oxford. Before she had finished this ritual Malory Fordham turned the corner and asked rather sternly if he might not perform the task. "Allow me to tie it for you," he had said with unrelieved formality.

"Sure I'll allow you." Angélique was never shy with those whom she liked. She replaced the subtler arts of the coquette with a forthrightness which might have proved her undoing with another boy. But not with Malory Fordham. Shy, pensive, and enveloped by the aura of malaise which so mysteriously and perpetually hung over his household he found Angélique's manner a source both of attraction and wonder. To him she was a radiant, generous storehouse of light and warmth which constantly renewed his chilled young soul.

"We're in luck this afternoon," said Angélique resuming her happy gait. "Sometimes I have to tie my shoes a dozen times. Once I took one shoe off and shook it and shook it, trying to get rid of make believe dust. I was glad you didn't turn up just then for I happened to look across the street and there was cousin Laurentine walking, you know that stiff poker-like way she goes—" Angélique bubbling with merriment imitated it—"I know she was disgusted seeing me like 'my son John, one shoe off and one shoe on.'"

"It's a wonder she didn't take you home," said Malory, admiring her.

"Oh, no! Cousin Laurentine wouldn't be seen walking up the street with me! She doesn't like me. Funny isn't it? But you know what's funnier still, Malory, not many folks around here do like me. Strange, don't you think, and living all my life almost in this little place? I never knew what it was to be really liked before you came except for Aunt Sal. I say to myself lots of times: 'Well, anyway, Malory likes me,' and then I'm completely happy."

"I'm glad of that," Malory told her, flushing. He was darker than Angélique for his father and mother had both been brown-skinned mulattoes, with a trace of Indian on his mother's side. Angélique's mother, whom she rarely saw, was a mulatto, too, but a very light one, quite yellow, and though she could not remember her father, she had in her mind's eye a concept of him which made him only the least shade darker than her mother. He had to be darker, for Angélique always associated masculinity with a dark complexion. She did not like to see men fairer than their wives.

Malory dwelt for several moments on Angélique's last remark. You could see him patiently turning the idea over and over. His high, rather narrow, forehead contracted, his almond, liquid eyes narrowed. His was a type which in any country but America would have commanded immediate and admiring attention. As it was even in Edendale he received many a spontaneous, if surreptitious, glance of approval.

He evolved an answer. "I don't know but you're right, Angélique. I think I must have been home six months before I met you, though I knew your name. I seem to have known your name a long time," he said musing slowly over some evasive idea. "But I never saw you, I guess, until that night when Evie Thompson's mother introduced us at Evie's party. I remember old Mrs. Rossiter seemed so queer. She said—"

"Yes, I know," Angélique interrupted, mimicking, "Oh, Miz Thompson, you didn't ever introduce them! That," concluded the girl with her usual forthrightness, "was because she wanted you to meet her Rosie—such a name Rosie Rossiter!—and have you dance attendance on her all evening!"

Fordham blushed again. "I don't know about that. Anyhow, what I was going to say was if I were you I wouldn't bother if the folks around here didn't like me. They don't like me either."

"No, I don't think they do very much. And yet it's different." Angélique explained puzzling out something. "They may not like you probably because you've lived away from home so long but they're willing to go with you. Now I think it's the other way around with me. They sort of like me, lots of the girls at times have liked me a great deal, new girls especially. But they shy away after a time. When Evie Thompson first came to this town she liked me better than she did any one else. I know she did. But after her mother gave that big party she acted different. She has never had me at a real party since and you know she entertains a lot—you're always there. Yet she's forever asking me over to her house when she hasn't company and then she's just as nice and her mother is always too sweet."

They were nearing the corner where they always parted. Cousin Laurentine did not allow Angélique to have beaux. "Perhaps they're jealous," Malory proposed as a last solution.

The girl's nice, round face clouded. She was not pretty but she bore about her an indefinable atmosphere of niceness, of freshness and innocence. "Jealous of the boys, you mean?" She bit her full red lip. "No, it's not that, none of the boys ever treats me very nicely, none of them ever has except you and Asshur Judson."

"Asshur Judson!" Malory echoed in some surprise. "You mean that tall, rough, farmer fellow? I'd have thought he'd be the last fellow in the world to know how to treat a nice girl like you."

"Mmh. He does, he did. You know the boys most of them" for the first time Fordham saw her shy, wistful—"when I say they're not nice I mean they are usually too nice. They try to kiss me, put their arms around me. Sometimes when I used to go skating I'd have horrid things happen. They'd tease the other girls, too, but with me they're different. They act as though it didn't matter how they treated me. Maybe it's because my father's dead."

"Perhaps," Malory acquiesced doubtfully, but he was completely bewildered. "And you say Asshur Judson was polite?"

"I'd forgotten Asshur. You didn't know him well, I think he came while you were in Philadelphia and he went away right after you came back. We'd been skating everyday. I wasn't with anyone, just down there in the crowd, and I struck off all alone. Bye and bye who should come racing after me but Asshur. I looked back and saw him and went on harder than ever. Of course he caught up to me, and when he did he took me right in his arms and held me tight. I struggled and fought so that I knew he understood I didn't like it, so he let me go. And then that hateful Harry Robbins came up and said: 'Don't you mind her, Jud, she's just pretending, she'll come around!'" Her voice shook with the shame of it.

"And then?" Malory prompted her fiercely.

"I heard Judson say just as mad, 'What the deuce you talking about Robbins?'"

Malory failed to see any extraordinary exhibition of politeness in that.

"Oh, but afterwards! You know my Cousin Laurentine doesn't allow me to have company. Of course he didn't know that, and that night he came to the house. Cousin Laurentine let him in and I heard her say: 'Yes, Angélique is in but she doesn't have callers.' And he answered: 'But I must see her, Miss Fletcher, I must explain something.' His voice sounded all funny and different. So I came running down stairs and asked him what he wanted.

"It was all so queer, Malory. He came over to me past Cousin Laurentine standing at the door like a dragon and he took both my hands, sort of frightened me. He said: 'You kid, you decent little kid! Treat 'em all like you treated me this afternoon, and try to forgive me. If you see me a thousand times you'll never have to complain of me again.' And he went."

"Funny," was Malory's comment. "Didn't he say anything more?"

"No, just went and I've got to go. Got to memorize a lot of old Shakespeare for tomorrow. Silly stuff from Macbeth. 'Double, double, toil and trouble.' Bye Malory."

"Good-bye," he echoed, turning in the direction of his home where his mother and his three plain older sisters awaited him. On his way he captured the idea which had earlier eluded him. He remembered speaking once before he had met her, of Angélique Murray to his old subdued household and of receiving a momentary impression of shock, of horror even, passing over his mother's face. He looked at his sisters and received the same impression. He looked at all four women again and saw nothing, just nothing, utter blankness, out of which came the voice of Gracie, his hostile middle sister. "Good heavens, Malory! Don't tell me that you know that Angélique Murray. I won't have you meeting her. She is ordinary, her whole family is the last thing in ordinariness. Now mind if you meet her, you let her alone."

At the time he had acquiesced, deeming this one of the thousand queer phases of his household with which he was striving so hard to become reacquainted. He had been a very little boy when he had been taken so hurriedly to live in Philadelphia, but his memory had painted them all so different.

In spite of his sister's warning Angélique's brightness when he met her, her frankness, her merriment proved too much for him. She was like an unfamiliar but perfectly recognizable part of himself. Pretty soon he was fathoms deep in love. But because he was a boy of practically no ingenuities but mechanical ones he could hit on nothing better than walking home from school with her. She was the one picture in the daily book of his life and having seen her he retired home each day like Browning's lovers to think up a scheme which would enable him sometime to tear it out for himself.

Angélique, hastening on flying feet, hoped that Cousin Laurentine would be out when she reached home. She could manage Laurentine's mother, Aunt Sal, even when she was as late as she was today. But before she entered the house she realized that for tonight at least she would be free from her cousin's hateful and scornful espionage. For peeping through the window which gave from the front room on to the porch she was able to make out against the soft inner gloom the cameo-like features of the Misses Courtney, the two young white women who came so often to see Aunt Sal and Laurentine. They were ladies of indubitable breeding and refinement, but for all their culture and elegance they could not eclipse Laurentine whose eyes shone as serene, whose forehead rose as smooth and classical as did their own. The only difference lay in their coloring. The Misses Courtney's skin shone as white as alabaster, their eyes lay, blue corn-flowers, in that lake of dazzling purity. But Laurentine was crimson and gold like the flesh of the mango, her eyes were dark emeralds. Her proud head glowed like all amber carving rising from the green perfection of her dress. She was a replica of the Courtney sisters startlingly vivified. Angélique, on her way to the kitchen poising on noiseless feet in the outside hall, experienced anew her thrill at the shocking resemblance between the two white women and the colored one; a resemblance which missed completely the contribution of white Mrs. Courtney and black Aunt Sal, and took into account only the remarkable beauty of Ralph Courtney, the father of all three of these women.

Aunt Sal in the background of the picture was studying with her customary unwavering glance the three striking figures. The Misses Courtney had travelled in Europe, they spoke French fluently. But Laurentine had travelled in the West Indies and spoke Spanish. When the time came for the Misses Courtney to go, they would kiss Laurentine lightly on both cheeks, they would murmur: "Good-bye, Sister," and would trail off leaving behind them the unmistakable aura of their loyal, persistent, melancholic determination to atone for their father's ancient wrong. And Laurentine, beautiful, saffron creature, would rise and gaze after them, enveloped in a sombre evanescent triumph.

But afterwards!

Up in her room Angélique envisaged the reaction which inevitably befell her cousin after the departure of these visitors. For the next three weeks Laurentine would be more than ever hateful, proud, jealous, scornful, intractable. The older woman, the young girl shrewdly guessed, was jealous of her; jealous of her unblemished parentage, of her right to race pride, of her very youth, though her own age could not be more than twenty-eight. "Poor Cousin Laurentine," the child thought, "as though she could help her father's being white. Anything was liable to happen in those old slavery times. I must try to be nicer to her."

When later she opened the door to her cousin's tap her determination was put to a severe test, for Laurentine was in one of her nastiest moods. "Here is another one of those letters," she said bitingly, "from that young ruffian who pushed his way past me that night. If I had my way I'd burn up every one of them. I can't think how you manage to attract such associates. It will be the best thing in the world for all of us when your mother sends for you."

Angélique took Asshur's letter somewhat sullenly, though she knew the feeling which her cousin's outburst concealed. In that household of three women this young girl was the only one who could be said to receive mail. Even hers was, until very lately, almost negligible—a note or two from a proudly travelling schoolmate, some directions for making candy from Evie Thompson or from the girl who at that moment was espousing her inexplicable cause, a card or so from a boy and now this constant stream of letters from Asshur Judson. As she opened these last or sat down to answer them in the shaded green glow of the dining-room, she had seen Cousin Laurentine's face pale with envy under the saffron satin of her skin.

Laurentine received letters and cards from the Misses Courtney when they were abroad—a few bills—she made rather a practice of having charge accounts—and an occasional note from the white summer transient expressing the writer's pleasure with "that last dress you made me." Once the young divinity student who, while the pastor was on his vacation, took over the services of the African Methodist Episcopal Church, sent her a post card from Niagara Falls. Laurentine exhibited a strange negligence with regard to this card, it was always to be found in the litter of the sewing table. "Oh," she would say casually to the customer whom she was fitting, "that's a card from Mr. Deaver who substituted here last summer. Yes, he does seem to be a fine young man."

Angélique did not at once open Asshur's letter. She had too many lessons to get. Besides she knew what it would contain, his constant and unvarying injunction "to be good, to be decent" coupled with an account of his latest success in some branch of scientific agriculture; he was an enthusiastic farmer. She liked to hear from him, but she wished his interests were broader. Laying the letter aside unregretfully she fell to memorizing the witches' speech in Macbeth and then in her little English Handbook under the chapter on "The Drama—Greek Tragedy," she made a brief but interested foray among the peculiarities of the ancient stage. Reading of Greek masks, buskins and "unities" she forgot all about Asshur's letter until as usual Aunt Sal put her fine dark head in the door and told her in mild but unanswerable tones that it was "most nigh bedtime."

She jumped up then and began to undress. But first she read the letter. Just as she thought it began like all his former letters and would probably end the same. No, here was something different. Asshur had written:

"My father says I'm making great headway, and so does Mr. Ellis, the man on whose farm I'm experimenting. Next year I'll be twenty-one and father's going to let me work a small farm he owns right up here in northern New Jersey. But first I'm coming for you. Only you must keep good and straight like you were when I first met you. You darn spunky little kid. Mind, you be good, you be decent. I'm sure coming for you."

It was a queer love-letter. "So you'll come for me," said Angélique to her image in the glass. She shook out her short, black, rather wiry hair till it misted like a cloud about her childishly round face. "How do you know I'll go with you? I may find someone I like ten times better." Dimpling and smiling she imitated Malory's formality: "May I tie your shoe for you?"

All night she dreamed she was chasing Malory Fordham. Was it a game? If so why did he so doggedly elude her? Then when, laughing, she had overtaken him, why did he turn on her with round gaping mouth and horrid staring eyes that transformed him into a Greek tragic mask? Through open, livid lips came whistling strange words, terrible phrases whose import at first she could not grasp. When she did she threw her arm across her face with a fearful cry and fell back convulsed and shuddering into the arms of a dark, muffled figure whose features she fought vainly to discover.

II

Edendale, like many another Jersey town, as well as all Gaul, was divided into three parts. In one section, the prettiest from a natural point of view, lived Italians, Polacks and Hungarians who had drifted in as laborers. In another section, elegant and cultivated, dwelt a wealthy and leisure class of white men of affairs, commuters, having big business interests in Philadelphia, Trenton, Newark and even New York. Occupying the traditional middle ground were Jews, small tradesmen, country lawyers and a large group of colored people ranging in profession from Phil Baltimore, successful ash-contractor to the equally successful physician, Dr. Thompson. This last group was rather closely connected with the wealthy white group, having in far preceding generations, dwelt with them as slaves or more recently as house servants. Sometimes as in the case of Aunt Sal Fletcher and the Courtneys, who following the Civil War had drifted into Jersey from Delaware, they had served in both capacities.

Malory and Angélique came to know the foreign quarters well. Here on the old Hopewell Road beginning nowhere and going nowhither they were surest of escaping the eye of a too vigilant colored townsman as well as that of the occasional white customer for whom the girl's cousin sewed. Malory was in no danger from a possibility like this last for the Fordhams on the maternal side had been small but independent householders for nearly a century. Even now Mrs. Fordham lived on a small income which came partly from her father's legacy, partly from the sale of produce from a really good truck-farm. Her husband had showed a tendency to dissipate this income but he had died before he had crippled it too sorely. Malory was determined to have more money when he grew older, money which he would obtain by his own methods. He never meant to ask his family for anything. The thought of a possible controversy with the invincible Gracie turned him sick.

He would be an engineer, how or where he did not know. But there would be plenty of money for him and Angélique. Already all his dreams included Angélique. He had not told her but he loved her fervently with an ardor excelling ordinary passion, for his included gratitude, a rapt consciousness of the miracle which daily she wrought for him in the business of living. She was so vivid, so joyous, so generous, so much what he would wish to be that almost it was as though she were his very self. Every day he warmed his hands at that fire which she alone could create for him.

He it was who fought so keenly against the clandestine nature of their meetings. Not so Angélique. This child so soon, so tragically to be transformed into a woman, was still a romantic dreaming girl. Half the joy of this new experience lay in its secrecy. This was fun, great fun, to run counter to imperious, unhappy Laurentine, to know that while her cousin endured the condescending visit of the son of the ash-contractor in the hope that some day, somehow she might receive the son of the colored physician, she herself was the eagerly and respectfully chosen of the son of the first colored family in the county. This was nectar and ambrosia, their taste enhanced by secrecy.

But Malory hated it. He had not told his family about the girl because clearly for some fool reason they were prejudiced against her, and as for Angélique's family—no males allowed. Hence this impasse. But he wanted like many another fond lover to acquaint others with his treasure, to show off not only this unparalleled gem, but himself too. For in her presence he himself shone, he became witty, his shyness vanished. The Methodist Sunday School picnic was to be held the first week in June. His sisters never went; proud Laurentine would not think of attending. He told Angélique that he would take her.

"Wonderful!" she breathed. She had a white dress with red ribbons.

They met on that memorable day, rather late. Laurentine could not keep Angélique from attending the picnic, but she could make her late; she could make her feel the exquisite torture which envelops a young girl who has to enter alone and unattended the presence of a crowd of watchful acquaintances. Angélique, inwardly unperturbed,—she knew Malory would wait for her forever,—outwardly greatly chafing, enjoyed her cousin's barely concealed satisfaction at her pretended discomfiture. With a blithe indifference she went from task to task, from chore to chore. "Greek tragedy," she whispered gaily into the ear of Marcus, an adored black kitten.

Malory did not mind her lateness. Indeed he was glad of it. So much the more conspicuous their entrance to the grounds. As it chanced, practically the whole party was in or around the large pavilion grouped there to receive instructions from Mrs. Evie Thompson who had charge of the picnic. A great church worker, Mrs. Evie. When the two arrived the place was in an uproar, Mrs. Evie balanced perilously on a stool tried to out talk the noise. Presently she realized that her voice was unnecessarily loud, the sea of black, yellow, and of white faces had ebbed into quiet but not because of her. Malory just outside the wide entrance, in the act of helping Angélique up the rustic steps caught that same fleeting shadow of horror and dismay, that shadow which he had marked on the faces of his household, rippling like a wave over the faces of the crowd, touching for a second Mrs. Thompson's face and vanishing. Appalled, bewildered, he stood still.

Mrs. Thompson rushed to them. "You just happened to meet Angélique, Malory? You—you didn't bring her?" Her voice was low but anxious.

"Of course I brought her," he replied testily. What possessed these staring people? "Why shouldn't I bring her?"

"Why not indeed?" soothed Mrs. Thompson. She herself came from a "best family" in some nearby city. "It's such luck that's all. I was wishing for Angélique. She's such a help at a time like this, so skillful. I want her to help me cut sandwiches."

Malory, rather sulkily accepting this, allowed his guest to be spirited away to exercise this skill. The crowd drawing a vast, multi-throated breath dispersed. Mrs. Thompson was anything but skillful herself. In the course of the afternoon she cut her assistant's hand. "I don't anticipate any infection," she remarked, peering at the small wound with an oddly unrepentant air, but you'd better come home with me and let Doctor dress it. Sorry I can't invite you too, Malory, but there's hardly room in the buggy for four. Evie and I are both fat."

Malory passed a night of angry sleeplessness. "I don't know what to think of these people," he told Angélique when they met the next day. "Do you know what I want you to do? You come home with me now and meet my mother and sisters. When they get to know you, they'll like you too and I know they can make these others step around." It was the first time he had betrayed any consciousness of the Fordham social standing.

Angélique, nothing loth, agreed with him. She too had thought Mrs. Thompson extraordinary the day before, but she had not seen as Malory had the strange shadowy expression of horror. And in any case would have had no former memory to emphasize it.

The two moved joyously up the tree-lined street, Malory experiencing his usual happy reaction to Angélique's buoyancy. Nothing would ever completely destroy her gay equanimity he thought, feeling his troubled young spirit relax. There was no one like her he knew. His people, even Gracie, must love her. He was living at this time in the last years of the nineties and so was given to much reading of Tennyson. Angélique made him think of the Miller's daughter, who had "grown so dear, so dear." What of life and youth and cheerfulness would she not introduce into his drab household, musty with old memories, inexplicably tainted with the dessication of some ancient imperishable grief!

At the corner of the street he took her arm. They would march into the house bravely and he would say, "Mother, this is Angélique whom I love. I want you to love her too; you will when you know her." He perceived as he opened the gate that Angélique was nervous, frightened. Timidity was in her such an unusual thing that he felt a new wave of tenderness rising within him. On the porch just before he touched the knob of the screen door he laid his hand on hers.

"Don't be frightened," he murmured.

"Look," she returned faintly.

He spun about and saw pressed against the window-pane a face, the small, brown face of his sister Gracie. In the background above her shoulder hovered the head of the oldest girl Reba, her body so completely hidden behind Gracie's that for a second, it seemed to him fantastically, her head swung suspended in space. But only for a second did he think this, so immediately was his attention drawn, riveted to the look of horror, of hatred, of pity which was frozen, seared on the faces of his sisters.

"For God's sake, what is it?" he cried.

Gracie's hands made a slight outward movement toward Angélique, a warding off motion of faintness and disgust such as one might make involuntarily towards a snake.

"I'm going in; come Angélique," the boy said in exasperation. "Has the whole world gone crazy?"

Before he could open the door Reba appeared, that expression still on her face, like a fine veil blurring out her features. Would it remain there forever he wondered.

"You can't bring her in Malory, you musn't."

"Why musn't I? What are you talking about?" Strange oaths rose to his lips. "What's the matter with her?" He started to pull the door from his sister's grasp when Gracie came, pushed the door open and stepped out on the porch beside him.

"Oh Malory you must send her away! Come in and I'll tell you." She burst into tears.

Gracie his tyrant, his arch-enemy weeping! That startled him far more than that inexplicable look. The foundations of the world were tottering. He turned to his trembling companion. "Go home, Angel," he bade her tenderly. "Meet me tomorrow and we'll fix all this up." He watched her waver down the porch-steps then turned to his sisters:

"Now girls?"

Together they got him into the house and told him.

III

Angélique said to herself, "I'll ask Aunt Sal,—Cousin Laurentine,—but what could they know about it? No I'll wait for Malory. Can I have the leprosy I wonder?" She went home, stripped and peered a long time in the mirror at her delicate, yellow body.

Next afternoon near the corner of Cedarwood and Tenth she untied and retied her shoes twenty times. Malory did not come. She shook out bushels of imaginary dust. He had not come, was never coming.

At the end of an hour she went to the corner and peered down Tenth Street. Yes—no—yes it was he coming slowly, slowly down the steps of the Boys' High School. Perhaps he was sick; when he saw her, he would be better. . . . He did not look in her direction; without so much as turning his head he came down the steps and started due west. Cedarwood Street lay east.

Without a second's hesitation she followed him. He was turning now out of Tenth north on Wheaton Avenue. After all you could go this way to the old Hopewell Road. Perhaps he had meant for her to meet him there. A block behind him, she saw him turn from Wheaton into the narrow footpath that later broadened into Hopewell Road. Yes, that was what he meant. She began to run then feeling something vaguely familiar about the act. On Hopewell Road she gained on him, called his name, "Malory, oh Malory." He turned around an instant shading his eyes from the golden June sunlight to make sure and spinning back began to run, almost leap away from her.

Bewildered, horrified, she plodded behind, leaving little clouds of white dust spiraling after her footsteps. As she ran she realized that he was fleeing from her in earnest; this was no game, no lover's playfulness.

He tripped over a tree root, fell, reeled to his feet and, breathless, found her upon him. She knew that this was her dream but even so she was unprepared for the face he turned upon her, a face with horrid staring eyes, with awful gaping lips, the face of a Greek tragic mask!

She came close to him. "Malory," she besought pitifully. Her hand moved out to touch his arm.

"Don't come near me!" His breath came whistling from his ghastly lips. "Don't touch me!" He broke into terrible weeping. "You're my sister—my sister!" he raised tragic arms to the careless sky. "Oh God how could you! I loved her, I wanted to marry her, and she's my sister!"

To proud Laurentine sitting in haughty dejection in the littered sewing-room, fingering a dog-eared postcard from Niagara Falls came the not unwelcome vision of her stricken cousin swaying, stumbling toward her.

"Laurentine, tell me! I saw Malory, Malory Fordham, he says, he says I'm his sister. How can that be? Oh Laurentine be kind to me, tell me it isn't true!" She would have thrown herself about the older woman's neck.

Inflexible arms held her off, pushed her down. "So you've found it out have you? You sailing about me with your pitying ways and your highty tighty manner. Sorry for Cousin Laurentine, weren't you? because her father was white and her mother wasn't married to him. But my mother couldn't help it. She had been a slave until she became a woman and she carried a slave's traditions into freedom.

"But her sister, your mother," the low hating voice went on, "whom my mother had shielded and guarded, to whom she held up herself and me—me—" she struck her proud breast—"as horrible examples,—your mother betrayed Mrs. Fordham, a woman of her own race who had been kind to her, and ran away with her husband." She spurned the grovelling girl with a disdainful foot. "Stop snivelling. Did you ever see me cry? No and you never will."

Angélique asked irrelevantly: "Why did you hate me so? I should think you'd pity me."

Her cousin fingered the postcard. "Look at me." She rose in her trailing red dress. "Young, beautiful, educated,—and nobody wants me, nobody who is anybody will have me. The ash-contractor's son offers,—not asks,—to marry me. Mr Deaver," she looked long at the postcard, "liked me, wrote me,—once—"

"Why did he stop?" Angélique asked in all innocence.

Laurentine flushed on her. "Because of you. You little fool, because of you! Must I say it again? Because my mother was the victim of slavery. People looked at me when I was a little girl; they used to say: 'Her mother couldn't help it, and she is beautiful.' They would have forgotten all about it. Oh why did your mother have to bring you home with us! Now they see you and they say: 'What! And her mother too! A colored man this time. Broke up a home. No excuse for that. Bad blood there. Best leave them alone.'"

She looked at Angélique with a furious mounting hatred. "Well you'll know all about it too. Wait a few years longer. You'll never be as beautiful as I, but you'll be pretty. And you'll sit and watch the years go by, and dread to look in your mirror for fear of what you'll find there. And at night you'll curse God,—but pshaw you won't,—" she broke off scornfully, "you'll only cry—"

Angélique crept up to her room to contemplate a future like Laurentine's.

Hours later Aunt Sal came in, her inscrutable dark face showing a blurred patch against the grey of the room. In her hand something gleamed whitely.

"Thought you might want yore letter," she said in her emotionless, husky voice.

Her letter, her letter from Asshur! Her letter that would reiterate: "Be a good kid and I'll come for you. . . ."

She seized it and fell half-fainting in the old woman's arms. "Oh Asshur I'll be good, I'll be good! Oh Aunt Sal, help me, keep me. . . ."

The Sleeper Wakes (1920)

Amy recognized the incident as the beginning of one of her phases. Always from a child she had been able to tell when "something was going to happen." She had been standing in Marshall's store, her young, eager gaze intent on the lovely little sample dress which was not from Paris, but quite as dainty as anything that Paris could produce. It was not the lines or even the texture that fascinated Amy so much, it was the grouping of colors—of shades. She knew the combination was just right for her.

"Let me slip it on, Miss," said the saleswoman suddenly. She had nothing to do just then, and the girl was so evidently charmed and so pretty—it was a pleasure to wait on her.

"Oh, no," Amy had stammered. "I haven't time." She had already wasted two hours at the movies, and she knew at home they were waiting for her.

The saleswoman slipped the dress over the girl's pink blouse, and tucked the linen collar under so as to bring the edge of the dress next to her pretty neck. The dress was apricot-color shading into a shell pink and the shell pink shaded off again into the pearl and pink whiteness of Amy's skin. The saleswoman beamed as Amy, entranced, surveyed herself naively in the tall looking-glass.

Then it was that the incident befell. Two men walking idly through the dress-salon stopped and looked—she made an unbelievably pretty picture. One of them with a short, soft brown beard,—"fuzzy" Amy thought to herself as she caught his glance in the mirror—spoke to his companion.

"Jove, how I'd like to paint her!" But it was the look on the other man's face that caught her and thrilled her. "My God! Can't a girl be beautiful!" he said half to himself. The pair passed on.

Amy stepped out of the dress and thanked the saleswoman half absently. She wanted to get home and think, think to herself about that look. She had seen it before in men's eyes, it had been in the eyes of the men in the moving-picture which she had seen that afternoon. But she had not thought *she* could cause it. Shut up in her little room she pondered over it. Her beauty,—she was really good-looking then—she could stir people—men! A girl of seventeen has no psychology, she does not go beneath the surface, she accepts. But she knew she was entering on one of her phases.

She was always living in some sort of story. She had started it when as a child of five she had driven with the tall, proud, white woman to Mrs. Boldin's home. Mrs. Boldin was a bride of one year's standing then. She was slender and very, very comely, with her rich brown skin and her hair that crinkled thick and soft above a low forehead. The house was still redolent of new furniture; Mr. Boldin was spick and span—he, unlike the furniture, remained so for that matter. The white woman had told Amy that this henceforth was to be her home.

Amy was curious, fond of adventure; she did not cry. She did not, of course, realize that she was to stay here indefinitely, but if she had, even at that age she would hardly have shed tears, she was always too eager, too curious to know, to taste what was going to happen next. Still since she had had almost no dealings with colored people and she knew absolutely none of the class to which Mrs. Boldin belonged, she did venture one question.

"Am I going to be colored now?"

The tall white woman had flushed and paled. "You—" she began, but the words choked her. "Yes, you are going to be colored now," she ended finally. She was a proud woman, in a moment she had recovered her usual poise. Amy carried with her for many years the memory of that proud head. She never saw her again.

When she was sixteen she asked Mrs. Boldin the question which in the light of that memory had puzzled her always. "Mrs. Boldin, tell me—am I white or colored?"

And Mrs. Boldin had told her and told her truly that she did not know.

"A—a—mee!" Mrs. Boldin's voice mounted on the last syllable in a shrill crescendo. Amy rose and went downstairs.

Down the comfortable, but rather shabby dining-room which the Boldin's used after meals to sit in, Mr. Boldin, a tall black man, with aristocratic features, sat practicing on a cornet, and Mrs. Boldin sat rocking. In all of their eyes was the manifestation of the light that Amy loved, but how truly she loved it, she was not to guess till years later.

"Amy," Mrs. Boldin paused in her rocking, "did you get the braid?" Of course she had not, though that was the thing she had gone to Marshall's for. Amy always forgot essentials. If she went on an errand, and she always went willingly, it was for the pure joy of going. Who knew what angels might meet one unawares? Not that Amy thought in biblical or in literary phrases. She was in the High School it is true, but she was simply passing through, "getting by" she would have said carelessly. The only reading that had ever made any impression on her had been fairy tales read to her in those long remote days when she had lived with the tall proud woman; and descriptions in novels or histories of beautiful, stately palaces tenanted by beautiful, stately women. She could pore over such pages for hours, her face flushed, her eyes eager.

At present she cast about for an excuse. She had so meant to get the braid. "There was a dress—" she began lamely, she was never deliberately dishonest.

Mr. Boldin cleared his throat and nervously fingered his paper. Cornelius ceased his awful playing and blinked at her short-sightedly through his thick glasses. Both of these, the man and the little boy, loved the beautiful, inconsequent creature with her airy, irresponsible ways. But Mrs. Boldin loved her too, and because she loved her she could not scold.

"Of course you forgot," she began chidingly. Then she smiled. "There was a dress that you looked at *perhaps*. But confess, didn't you go to the movies first?"

Yes, Amy confessed she had done just that. "And oh, Mrs. Boldin, it was the most wonderful picture—a girl—such a pretty one—and she was poor, awfully. And somehow she met the most wonderful people and they were so kind to her. And she married a man who was just tremendously rich and he gave her everything. I did so want Cornelius to see it."

"Huh!" said Cornelius who had been listening not because he was interested, but because he wanted to call Amy's attention to his playing as soon as possible. "Huh! I don't want to look at no pretty girl. Did they have anybody looping the loop in an airship?"

"You'd better stop seeing pretty girl pictures, Amy," said Mr. Boldin kindly. "They're not always true to life. Besides, I know where you can see all the pretty girls you want without bothering to pay twenty-five cents for it."

Amy smiled at the implied compliment and went on happily studying her lessons. They were all happy in their own way. Amy because she was sure of their love and admiration, Mr. and Mrs. Boldin because of her beauty and innocence and Cornelius because he knew he had in his foster-sister a listener whom his terrible practicing could never bore. He played brokenly a piece he had found in an old music-book. "*There's an aching void in every heart, brother.*"

"Where do you pick up those old things, Neely?" said his mother fretfully. But Amy could not have her favorite's feelings injured.

"I think it's lovely," she announced defensively. "Cornelius, I'll ask Sadie Murray to lend me her brother's book. He's learning the cornet, too, and you can get some new pieces. Oh, isn't it awful to have to go to bed? Good-night, everybody." She smiled her charming, ever ready smile, the mere reflex of youth and beauty and content.

"You do spoil her, Mattie," said Mr. Boldin after she had left the room. "She's only seventeen—here, Cornelius, you go to bed—but it seems to me she ought to be more dependable about errands. Though she is splendid about some things," he defended her. "Look how willingly she goes off to bed. She'll be asleep before she knows it when most girls of her age would want to be up in the street."

But upstairs Amy was far from asleep. She lit one gas-jet and pulled down the shades. Then she stuffed tissue paper in the keyhole and under the doors, and lit the remaining gas-jets. The light thus thrown on the mirror of the ugly oak dresser was perfect. She slipped off the pink blouse and found two scarfs, a soft yellow and a soft pink,—she had had them in a scarf-dance for a school entertainment. She wound them and draped them about her pretty shoulders and loosened her hair. In the mirror she apostrophized the beautiful, glowing vision of herself.

"There," she said, "I'm like the girl in the picture. She had nothing but her beautiful face—and she did so want to be happy." She sat down on the side of the rather lumpy bed and stretched out her arms. "I want to be happy, too." She intoned it earnestly, almost like an incantation. "I want wonderful clothes, and people around me, men adoring me, and the world before me. I want—everything! It will come, it will all come because I want it so." She sat frowning intently as she was apt to do when very much engrossed. "And we'd all be so happy. I'd give Mr. and Mrs. Boldin money! And Cornelius—he'd go to college and learn all about his old airships. Oh, if I only knew how to begin!"

Smiling, she turned off the lights and crept to bed.

II

Quite suddenly she knew she was going to run away. That was in October. By December she had accomplished her purpose. Not that she was the least bit unhappy but because she must get out in the world,—she felt caged, imprisoned. "Trenton is stifling me," she would have told you, in her unconsciously adopted "movie" diction. New York she knew was the place for her. She had her plans all made. She had sewed steadily after school for two months—as she frequently did when she wanted to buy her season's wardrobe, so besides her carfare she had $25. She went immediately to a white Y.W.C.A., stayed there two nights, found and answered an advertisement for clerk and waitress in a small confectionery and bakery-shop, was accepted and there she was launched.

Perhaps it was because of her early experience when as a tiny child she was taken from that so different home and left at Mrs. Boldin's, perhaps it was some fault in her own disposition, concentrated and egotistic as she was, but certainly she felt no pangs of separation, no fear of her future. She was cold too,—unfired though so to speak rather than icy,—and fastidious. This last quality kept her safe where morality or religion, of neither of which had she any conscious endowment, would have availed her nothing. Unbelievably then she lived two years in New York, unspoiled, untouched, going to work on the edge of Greenwich Village early and coming back late, knowing almost no one and yet altogether happy in the expectation of some thing wonderful, which she knew some day must happen.

It was at the end of the second year that she met Zora Harrison. Zora used to come into lunch with a group of habitués of the place—all of them artists and writers Amy gathered. Mrs. Harrison (for she was married as Amy later learned) appealed to the girl because she knew so well how to afford the contrast to her blonde, golden beauty. Purple, dark and regal, enveloped in velvets and heavy silks, and strange marine blues she wore, and thus made Amy absolutely happy. Singularly enough, the girl, intent as she was on her own life and experiences, had felt up to this time no yearning to know these strange, happy beings who surrounded her. She did miss Cornelius, but otherwise she was never lonely, or if she was she hardly knew it, for she had always lived an inner life to herself. But Mrs. Harrison magnetized her—she could not keep her eyes from her face, from her wonderful clothes. She made conjectures about her.

The wonderful lady came in late one afternoon—an unusual thing for her. She smiled at Amy invitingly, asked some banal questions and their first conversation began. The acquaintance once struck up progressed rapidly—after a few weeks Mrs. Harrison invited the girl to come to see her. Amy accepted quietly, unaware that anything extraordinary was happening. Zora noticed this and liked it. She had an apartment in 12th Street in a house inhabited only by artists—she was by no means one herself. Amy was fascinated by the new world into which she found herself ushered; Zora's surroundings were very beautiful and Zora herself was a study. She opened to the girl's amazed vision fields of thought and conjecture, phases of whose existence Amy, who was a builder of phases, had never dreamed. Zora had been a poor girl of good family. She had wanted to study art, she had deliberately married a rich man and as deliberately obtained in the course of four years a divorce, and she was now living in New York studying by means of her alimony and enjoying to its fullest the life she loved. She took Amy on a footing with herself—the girl's refinement, her beauty, her interest in colors (though this in Amy at that time was purely sporadic, never consciously encouraged), all this gave Zora a figure about which to plan and build romance. Amy had told her the truth, but not all about her coming to New York. She had grown tired of Trenton—her people were all dead—the folks with whom she lived were kind and good but not "inspiring" (she had borrowed the term from Zora and it was true, the Boldins, when one came to think of it, were not "inspiring"), so she had run away.

Zora had gone into raptures. "What an adventure! My dear, the world is yours. Why, with your looks and your birth, for I suppose you really belong to the Kildares who used to live in Philadelphia, I think there was a son who ran off and married an actress or someone—they disowned him I remember,—you can reach any height. You must marry a wealthy man—perhaps someone who is interested in art and who will let you pursue your studies." She insisted always that Amy had run away in order to study art. "But luck like that comes to few," she sighed, remembering her own plight, for Mr. Harrison had been decidedly unwilling to let her pursue her studies, at least to the extent she wished. "Anyway you must marry wealth,— one can always get a divorce," she ended sagely.

Amy—she came to Zora's every night now—used to listen dazedly at first. She had accepted willingly enough Zora's conjecture about her birth, came to believe it in fact—but she drew back somewhat at such wholesale exploitation of people to suit one's own convenience, still she did not probe too far into this thought—nor did she grasp at all the infamy of exploitation of self. She ventured one or two objections however, but Zora brushed everything aside.

"Everybody is looking out for himself," she said fairly. "I am interested in you, for instance, not for philanthropy's sake, not because I am lonely, and you are charming and pretty and don't get tired of hearing me talk. You'd better come and live with me awhile, my dear, six months or a year. It doesn't cost any more for two than for one, and you can always leave when we get tired of each other. A girl like you can always get a job. If you are worried about being dependent you can pose for me and design my frocks, and oversee Julienne"—her maid-of-all-work—"I'm sure she's a stupendous robber."

Amy came, not at all overwhelmed by the good luck of it—good luck was around the corner more or less for everyone, she supposed. Moreover, she was beginning to absorb some of Zora's doctrine—she, too, must look out for herself. Zora *was* lonely, she *did* need companionship, Julienne *was* careless about change and old blouses and left-over dainties. Amy had her own sense of honor. She carried out faithfully her share of the bargain, cut down waste, renovated Zora's clothes, posed for her, listened to her endlessly and bore with her fitfulness. Zora was truly grateful for this last. She was temperamental but Amy had good nerves and her strong natural inclination to let people do as they wanted stood her in good stead. She was a little stolid, a little unfeeling under her lovely exterior. Her looks at this time belied her—her perfect ivory-pink face, her deep luminous eyes,—very brown they were with purple depths that made one think of pansies—her charming, rather wide mouth, her whole face set in a frame of very soft, very live, brown hair which grew in wisps and tendrils and curls and waves back from her smooth, young forehead. All this made one look for softness and ingenuousness. The ingenuousness was there, but not the softness—except of her fresh, vibrant loveliness.

On the whole then she progressed famously with Zora. Sometimes the latter's callousness shocked her, as when they would go strolling through the streets south of Washington Square. The children, the people all foreign, all dirty, often very artistic, always immensely human, disgusted Zora except for "local color"—she really could reproduce them wonderfully. But she almost hated them for being what they were.

"Br-r-r, dirty little brats!" she would say to Amy. "Don't let them touch me." She was frequently amazed at her protégée's utter indifference to their appearance, for Amy herself was the pink of daintiness. They were turning from MacDougall into Bleecker Street one day and Amy had patted a child—dirty, but lovely—on the head.

"They are all people just like anybody else, just like you and me, Zora," she said in answer to her friend's protest.

"You *are* the true democrat," Zora returned with a shrug. But Amy did not understand her.

Not the least of Amy's services was to come between Zora and the too pressing attention of the men who thronged about her.

"Oh, go and talk to Amy," Zora would say, standing slim and gorgeous in some wonderful evening gown. She was an extraordinarily attractive creature, very white and pink, with great ropes of dazzling gold hair, and that look of no-age which only American women possess. As a matter of fact she was thirty-nine, immensely sophisticated and selfish, even, Amy thought, a little cruel. Her present mode of living just suited her; she could not stand any condition that bound her, anything at all *exigeant*. It was useless for anyone to try to influence her. If she did not want to talk, she would not.

The men used to obey her orders and seek Amy sulkily at first, but afterwards with considerably more interest. She was so lovely to look at. But they really, as Zora knew, preferred to talk to the older woman, for while with Zora indifference was a role, second nature now but still a role—with Amy it was natural and she was also a trifle shallow. She had the admiration she craved, she was comfortable, she asked no more. Moreover she thought the men, with the exception of Stuart James Wynne, rather uninteresting—they were faddists for the most part, crazy not about art or music, but merely about some phase such as cubism or syncopation.

Wynne, who was much older than the other half-dozen men who weekly paid Zora homage—impressed her by his suggestion of power. He was a retired broker, immensely wealthy (Zora, who had known him since childhood, informed her), very set and purposeful and polished. He was perhaps fifty-five, widely traveled, of medium height, very white skin and clear, frosty blue eyes, with sharp, proud features. He liked Amy from the beginning, her childishness touched him. In particular he admired her pliability—not knowing it was really indifference. He had been married twice; one wife had divorced him, the other had died. Both marriages were unsuccessful owing to his dominant, rather unsympathetic nature. But he had softened considerably with years, though he still had decided views, [and] was glad to see that Amy, in spite of Zora's influence, neither smoked nor drank. He liked her shallowness—she fascinated him.

Zora had told him much—just the kind of romantic story to appeal to the rich, powerful man. Here was beauty forlorn, penniless, of splendid birth,—for Zora once having connected Amy with the Philadelphia Kildares never swerved from that belief. Amy seemed to Wynne everything a girl should be—she was so unspoiled, so untouched. He asked her to marry him. If she had tried she could not have acted more perfectly. She looked at him with her wonderful eyes.

"But I am poor, ignorant—a nobody," she stammered. "I'm afraid I don't love you either," she went on in her pretty troubled voice, "though I do like you very, very much."

He liked her honesty and her self-depreciation, even her coldness. The fact that she was not flattered seemed to him an extra proof of her native superiority. He, himself, was a representative of one of the South's oldest families, though he had lived abroad lately.

"I have money and influence," he told her gravely, "but I count them nothing without you." And as for love—he would teach her that, he ended, his voice shaking a little. Underneath all his chilly, polished exterior he really cared.

"It seems an unworthy thing to say," he told her wistfully, for she seemed very young beside his experienced fifty-five years, "but anything you wanted in this world could be yours. I could give it to you—clothes, houses and jewels."

"Don't be an idiot," Zora had said when Amy told her. "Of course, marry him. He'll give you a beautiful home and position. He's probably no harder to get along with than anybody else, and if he is, there is always the divorce court."

It seemed to Amy somehow that she was driving a bargain—how infamous a one she could not suspect. But Zora's teachings had sunk deep. Wynne loved her, and he could secure for her what she wanted. "And after all," she said to herself once, "it really is my dream coming true."

She resolved to marry him. There were two weeks of delirious, blissful shopping. Zora was very generous. It seemed to Amy that the whole world was contributing largely to her happiness. She was to have just what she wanted and as her taste was perfect she afforded almost as much pleasure to the people from whom she bought as to herself. In particular she brought rapture to an exclusive modiste in Forty-second Street who exclaimed at her "so perfect taste."

"Mademoiselle is of a marvelous, of an absolute correctness," she said.

Everything whirled by. After the shopping there was the small, impressive wedding. Amy stumbled somehow through the service, struck by its awful solemnity. Then later there was the journey and the big house waiting them in the small town, fifty miles south of Richmond. Wynne was originally from Georgia, but business and social interests had made it necessary for him to be nearer Washington and New York.

Amy was absolute mistress of himself and his home, he said, his voice losing its coldness. "Ah, my dear, you'll never realize what you mean to me—I don't envy any other man in this world. You are so beautiful, so sweet, so different!"

III

From the very beginning *he* was different from what she had supposed. To start with he was far, far wealthier, and he had, too, a tradition, a family-pride which to Amy was inexplicable. Still more inexplicably he had a race-pride. To his wife this was not only strange but foolish. She was as Zora had once suggested, the true democrat. Not that she preferred the company of her maids, though the reason for this did not lie *per se* in the fact that they were maids. There was simply no common ground. But she was uniformly kind, a trait which had she been older would have irritated her husband. As it was, he saw in it only an additional indication of her freshness, her lack of worldliness which seemed to him the attributes of an inherent refinement and goodness untouched by experience.

He, himself, was intolerant of all people of inferior birth or standing and looked with contempt on foreigners, except the French and English. All the rest were variously "guineys," "niggers," and "wops," and all of them he genuinely despised and hated, and talked of them with the huge intolerant carelessness characteristic of occidental civilization. Amy was never able to understand it. People were always first and last, just people to her. Growing up as the average colored American girl does grow up, surrounded by types of every hue, color and facial configuration she had

had no absolute ideal. She was not even aware that there was one. Wynne, who in his grim way had a keen sense of humor, used to be vastly amused at the artlessness with which she let him know that she did not consider him to be good-looking. She never wanted him to wear anything but dark blue, or sombre mixtures always.

"They take away from that awful whiteness of your skin," she used to tell him, "and deepen the blue of your eyes."

In the main she made no attempt to understand him, as indeed she made no attempt to understand anything. The result, of course, was that such ideas as seeped into her mind stayed there, took growth and later bore fruit. But just at this period she was like a well-cared for, sleek, house-pet, delicately nurtured, velvety, content to let her days pass by. She thought almost nothing of her art just now except as her sensibilities were jarred by an occasional disharmony. Likewise, even to herself, she never criticized Wynne, except when some act or attitude of his stung. She could never understand why he, so fastidious, so versed in elegance of word and speech, so careful in his surroundings, even down to the last detail of glass and napery, should take such evident pleasure in literature of a certain prurient type. He fairly revelled in the realistic novels which to her depicted sheer badness. He would get her to read to him, partly because he liked to be read to, mostly because he enjoyed the realism and in a slighter degree because he enjoyed seeing her shocked. Her point of view amused him.

"What funny people," she would say naively, "to do such things." She could not understand the liaisons and intrigues of women in the society novels, such infamy was stupid and silly. If one starved, it was conceivable that one might steal; if one were intentionally injured, one might hit back, even murder; but deliberate nastiness she could not envisage. The stories, after she had read them to him, passed out of her mind as completely as though they had never existed.

Picture the two of them spending three years together with practically no friction. To his dominance and intolerance she opposed a soft and unobtrusive indifference. What she wanted she had, ease, wealth, adoration, love, too, passionate and imperious, but she had never known any other kind. She was growing cleverer also, her knowledge of French was increasing, she was acquiring a knowledge of politics, of commerce and of the big social questions, for Wynne's interests were exhaustive and she did most of his reading for him. Another woman might have yearned for a more youthful companion, but her native coldness kept her content. She did not love him, she had never really loved anybody, but little Cornelius Boldin—he had been such an enchanting, such a darling baby, she remembered,—her heart contracted painfully when she thought as she did very often of his warm softness.

"He must be a big boy now," she would think almost maternally, wondering— once she had been so sure!—if she would ever see him again. But she was very fond of Wynne, and he was crazy over her just as Zora had predicted. He loaded her with gifts, dresses, flowers, jewels—she amused him because none but colored stones appealed to her.

"Diamonds are so hard, so cold, and pearls are dead," she told him.

Nothing ever came between them, but his ugliness, his hatefulness to dependents. It hurt her so, for she was naturally kind in her careless, uncomprehending way. True, she had left Mrs. Boldin without a word, but she did not guess how completely Mrs. Boldin loved her. She would have been aghast had she realized how stricken her flight had left them. At twenty-two, Amy was still as good, as unspoiled, as pure as a child. Of course with all this she was too unquestioning, too selfish, too vain, but they were all faults of her lovely, lovely flesh. Wynne's intolerance finally got on her nerves. She used to blush for his unkindness. All the servants were colored, but she had long since ceased to think that perhaps she, too, was colored, except when he, by insult toward an employee, overt, always at least implied, made her realize his contemptuous dislike and disregard for a dark skin or Negro blood.

"Stuart, how can you say such things?" she would expostulate. "You can't expect a man to stand such language as that." And Wynne would sneer, "A man— you don't consider a nigger a man, do you? Oh, Amy, don't be such a fool. You've got to keep them in their places."

Some innate sense of the fitness of things kept her from condoling outspokenly with the servants, but they knew she was ashamed of her husband's ways. Of course, they left—it seemed to Amy that Peter, the butler, was always getting new "help,"—but most of the upper servants stayed, for Wynne paid handsomely and although his orders were meticulous and insistent the retinue of employees was so large that the individual's work was light.

Most of the servants who did stay on in spite of Wynne's occasional insults had a purpose in view. Callie, the cook, Amy found out, had two children at Howard University—of course she never came in contact with Wynne. The chauffeur had a crippled sister. Rose, Amy's maid and purveyor of much outside information, was the chief support of the family. About Peter, Amy knew nothing: he was a striking, taciturn man, very competent, who had left the Wynnes' service years before and had returned in Amy's third year. Wynne treated him with comparative respect. But Stephen, the new valet, met with entirely different treatment. Amy's heart yearned toward him, he was like Cornelius, with short-sighted, patient eyes, always willing, a little over-eager. Amy recognized him for what he was: a boy of respectable, ambitious parentage, striving for the means for an education; naturally far above his present calling, yet willing to pass through all this as a means to an end. She questioned Rosa about him.

"Oh, Stephen," Rosa told her, "yes'm, he's workin' for fair. He's got a brother at the Howard's and a sister at the Smith's. Yes'm, it do seem a little hard on him, but Stephen, he say, they're both goin' to turn roun' and help him when they get through. That blue silk has a rip in it, Miss Amy, if you was thinkin' of wearin' that. Yes'm, somehow I don't think Steve's very strong, kinda worries like. I guess he's sorta nervous."

Amy told Wynne, "He's such a nice boy, Stuart," she pleaded, "it hurts me to have you so cross with him. Anyway don't call him names." She was both surprised and frightened at the feeling in her that prompted her to interfere. She had held so aloof from other people's interests all these years.

"I *am* colored," she told herself that night. "I feel it inside of me. I must be or I couldn't care so about Stephen. Poor boy, I suppose Cornelius is just like him. I wish Stuart would let him alone. I wonder if all white people are like that. Zora was hard, too, on unfortunate people." She pondered over it a bit. "I wonder what Stuart would say if he knew I was colored?" She lay perfectly still, her smooth brow knitted, thinking hard. "But he loves me," she said to herself still silently. "He'll always love my looks," and she fell to thinking that all the wonderful happenings in her sheltered, pampered life had come to her through her beauty. She reached out an exquisite arm, switched on a light, and picking up a hand-mirror from a dressing-table, fell to studying her face. She was right. It was her chiefest asset. She forgot Stephen and fell asleep.

But in the morning her husband's voice, issuing from his dressing-room across the hall, awakened her. She listened drowsily. Stephen, leaving the house the day before, had been met by a boy with a telegram. He had taken it, slipped it into his pocket, (he was just going to the mailbox) and had forgotten to deliver it until now, nearly twenty-four hours later. She could hear Stuart's storm of abuse—it was terrible, made up as it was of oaths and insults to the boy's ancestry. There was a moment's lull. Then she heard him again.

"If your brains are a fair sample of that black wench of a sister of yours—"

She sprang up then thrusting her arms as she ran into her pink dressing-gown. She got there just in time. Stephen, his face quivering, was standing looking straight into Wynne's smoldering eyes. In spite of herself, Amy was glad to see the boy's bearing. But he did not notice her.

"You devil!" he was saying. "You white-faced devil! I'll make you pay for that!" He raised his arm. Wynne did not blench.

With a scream she was between them. "Go, Stephen, go,—get out of the house. Where do you think you are? Don't you know you'll be hanged, lynched, tortured?" Her voice shrilled at him.

Wynne tried to thrust aside her arms that clung and twisted. But she held fast till the door slammed behind the fleeing boy.

"God, let me by, Amy!" As suddenly as she had clasped him she let him go, ran to the door, fastened it and threw the key out the window.

He took her by the arm and shook her. "Are you mad? Didn't you hear him threaten me, me, a nigger threaten me?" His voice broke with nigger, "And you're letting him get away! Why, I'll get him. I'll set bloodhounds on him, I'll have every white man in this town after him! He'll be hanging so high by midnight—" he made for the other door, cursing, half-insane.

How, *how* could she keep him back! She hated her weak arms with their futile beauty! She sprang toward him. "Stuart, wait," she was breathless and sobbing. She said the first thing that came into her head. "Wait, Stuart, you cannot do this thing." She thought of Cornelius—suppose it had been he—"Stephen,—that boy,—he is my brother."

He turned on her. "What!" he said fiercely, then laughed a short laugh of disdain. "You are crazy," he said roughly. "My God, Amy! How can you even in jest associate yourself with these people? Don't you suppose I know a white girl when I see one? There's no use in telling a lie like that."

Well, there was no help for it. There was only one way. He had turned back for a moment, but she must keep him many moments—an hour. Stephen must get out of town.

She caught his arm again. "Yes," she told him, "I did lie. Stephen is not my brother, I never saw him before." The light of relief that crept into his eyes did not escape her, it only nerved her. "But I *am* colored," she ended.

Before he could stop her she had told him all about the tall white woman. "She took me to Mrs. Boldin's and gave me to her to keep. She would never have taken me to her if I had been white. If you lynch this boy, I'll let the world, your world, know that your wife is a colored woman."

He sat down like a man suddenly stricken old, his face ashen. "Tell me about it again," he commanded. And she obeyed, going mercilessly into every damning detail.

IV

Amazingly her beauty availed her nothing. If she had been an older woman, if she had had Zora's age and experience, she would have been able to gauge exactly her influence over Wynne. Though even then in similar circumstances she would have taken the risk and acted in just the same manner. But she was a little bewildered at her utter miscalculation. She had thought he might not want his friends—his world by which he set such store—to know that she was colored, but she had not dreamed it could make any real difference to him. He had chosen her, poor and ignorant, but of a host of women, and had told her countless times of his love. To herself Amy Wynne was in comparison with Zora for instance, stupid and uninteresting. But his constant, unsolicited iterations had made her accept his idea.

She was just the same woman she told herself, she had not changed, she was still beautiful, still charming, still "different." Perhaps, that very difference had its being in the fact of her mixed blood. She had been his wife—there were memories—she could not see how he could give her up. The suddenness of the divorce carried her off her feet. Dazedly she left him—though almost without a pang for she had only liked him. She had been perfectly honest about this, and he, although consumed by the fierceness of his emotion toward her, had gradually forced himself to be content, for at least she had never made him jealous.

She was to live in a small house of his in New York, up town in the 80's. Peter was in charge and there was a new maid and a cook. The servants, of course, knew of the separation, but nobody guessed why. She was living on a much smaller basis than the one to which she had become so accustomed in the last three years. But she was very comfortable. She felt, at any rate she manifested, no qualms at receiving alimony from Wynne. That was the way things happened, she supposed when she thought of it at all. Moreover, it seemed to her perfectly in keeping with Wynne's former attitude toward her; she did not see how he could do less. She expected people to be consistent. That was why she was so amazed that he in spite of his oft iterated love, could let her go. If she had felt half the love for him which he had professed for her, she would not have sent him away if he had been a leper.

"Why I'd stay with him," she told herself, "if he were one, even as I feel now."

She was lonely in New York. Perhaps it was the first time in her life that she had felt so. Zora had gone to Paris the first year of her marriage and had not come back.

The days dragged on emptily. One thing helped her. She had gone one day to the modiste from whom she had bought her trousseau. The woman remembered her perfectly—"The lady with the exquisite taste for colors—ah, madame, but you have the rare gift." Amy was grateful to be taken out of her thoughts. She bought one or two daring but altogether lovely creations and let fall a few suggestions:

"That brown frock, Madame,—you say it has been on your hands a long time? Yes? But no wonder. See, instead of that dead white you should have a shade of ivory, that white cheapens it." Deftly she caught up a bit of ivory satin and worked out her idea. Madame was ravished.

"But yes, Madame Ween is correct,—as always. Oh, what a pity that the Madame is so wealthy. If she were only a poor girl—Mlle. Antoine with the best eye for color in the place has just left, gone back to France to nurse her brother—this World War is of such a horror! If someone like Madame, now, could be found, to take the little Antoine's place!"

Some obscure impulse drove Amy to accept the half proposal: "Oh! I don't know, I have nothing to do just now. My husband is abroad." Wynne had left her with that impression. "I could contribute the money to the Red Cross or to charity."

The work was the best thing in the world for her. It kept her from becoming too introspective, though even then she did more serious, connected thinking than she had done in all the years of her varied life.

She missed Wynne definitely, chiefly as a guiding influence for she had rarely planned even her own amusements. Her dependence on him had been absolute. She used to picture him to herself as he was before the trouble—and his changing expressions as he looked at her, of amusement, interest, pride, a certain little teasing quality that used to come into his eyes, which always made her adopt her "spoiled child air," as he used to call it. It was the way he liked her best. Then last, there was that look he had given her the morning she had told him she was colored—it had depicted so many emotions, various and yet distinct. There were dismay, disbelief, coldness, a final aloofness.

There was another expression, too, that she thought of sometimes—the look on the face of Mr. Packard, Wynne's lawyer. She, herself, had attempted no defense.

"For God's sake why did you tell him, Mrs. Wynne?" Packard asked her. His curiosity got the better of him. "You couldn't have been in love with that yellow rascal," he blurted out. "She's too cold really, to love anybody," he told himself. "If you didn't care about the boy why should you have told?"

She defended herself feebly. "He looked so like little Cornelius Boldin," she replied vaguely, "and he couldn't help being colored." A clerk came in then and Packard said no more. But into his eyes had crept a certain reluctant respect. She remembered the look, but could not define it.

She was so sorry about the trouble now, she wished it had never happened. Still if she had it to repeat she would act in the same way again. "There was nothing else for me to do," she used to tell herself.

But she missed Wynne unbelievably.

If it had not been for Peter, her life would have been almost that of a nun. But Peter, who read the papers and kept abreast of times, constantly called her attention, with all due respect, to the meetings, the plays, the sights which she ought to attend or see. She was truly grateful to him. She was very kind to all three of the servants. They had the easiest "places" in New York, the maids used to tell their friends. As she never entertained, and frequently dined out, they had a great deal of time off.

She had been separated from Wynne for ten months before she began to make any definite plans for her future. Of course, she could not go on like this always. It came to her suddenly that probably she would go to Paris and live there—why or how she did not know. Only Zora was there and lately she had begun to think that her life was to be like Zora's. They had been amazingly parallel up to this time. Of course she would have to wait until after the war.

She sat musing about it one day in the big sitting-room which she had had fitted over into a luxurious studio. There was a sewing-room off to the side from which Peter used to wheel into the room waxen figures of all colorings and contours so that she could drape the various fabrics about them to be sure of the best results. But today she was working out a scheme for one of Madame's customers, who was of her own color and size and she was her own lay-figure. She sat in front of the huge pier glass, a wonderful soft yellow silk draped about her radiant loveliness.

"I could do some serious work in Paris," she said half aloud to herself. "I suppose if I really wanted to, I could be very successful along this line."

Somewhere downstairs an electric bell buzzed, at first softly, then after a slight pause, louder, and more insistently.

"If Madame sends me that lace today," she was thinking, idly, "I could finish this and start on the pink. I wonder why Peter doesn't answer the bell."

She remembered then that Peter had gone to New Rochelle on business and she had sent Ellen to Altman's to find a certain rare velvet and had allowed Mary to go with her. She would dine out, she told them, so they need not hurry. Evidently she was alone in the house.

Well she could answer the bell. She had done it often enough in the old days at Mrs. Boldin's. Of course it was the lace. She smiled a bit as she went downstairs thinking how surprised the delivery-boy would be to see her arrayed thus early in the afternoon. She hoped he wouldn't go. She could see him through the long, thick panels of glass in the vestibule and front door. He was just turning about as she opened the door.

This was no delivery-boy, this man whose gaze fell on her hungry and avid. This was Wynne. She stood for a second leaning against the doorjamb, a strange figure surely in the sharp November weather. Some leaves—brown, skeleton shapes—rose and swirled unnoticed about her head. A passing letter-carrier looked at them curiously.

"What are you doing answering the door?" Wynne asked her roughly. "Where is Peter? Go in, you'll catch cold."

She was glad to see him. She took him into the drawing room—a wonderful study in browns—and looked at him and looked at him.

"Well," he asked her, his voice eager in spite of the commonplace words, "are you glad to see me? Tell me what you do with yourself."

She could not talk fast enough, her eyes clinging to his face. Once it struck her that he had changed in some indefinable way. Was it a slight coarsening of that refined aristocratic aspect? Even in her subconsciousness she denied it.

He had come back to her.

"So I design for Madame when I feel like it, and send the money to the Red Cross and wonder when you are coming back to me." For the first time in their acquaintanceship she was conscious deliberately of trying to attract, to hold him. She put on her spoiled child air which had once been so successful.

"It took you long enough to get here," she pouted. She was certain of him now. His mere presence assured her.

They sat silent a moment, the late November sun bathing her head in an austere glow of chilly gold. As she sat there in the big brown chair she was, in her yellow dress, like some mysterious emanation, some wraith-like aura developed from the tone of her surroundings.

He rose and came toward her, still silent. She grew nervous, and talked incessantly with sudden unusual gestures. "Oh, Stuart, let me give you tea. It's right there in the pantry off the dining-room. I can wheel the table in." She rose, a lovely creature in her yellow robe. He watched her intently.

"Wait," he bade her.

She paused almost on tiptoe, a dainty golden butterfly.

"You are coming back to live with me?" he asked her hoarsely.

For the first time in her life she loved him.

"Of course I am coming back," she told him softly. "Aren't you glad? Haven't you missed me? I didn't see how you *could* stay away. Oh! Stuart, what a wonderful ring!"

For he had slipped on her finger a heavy dull gold band, with an immense sapphire in an oval setting—a beautiful thing of Italian workmanship.

"It is so like you to remember," she told him gratefully. "I love colored stones." She admired it, turning it around and around on her slender finger.

How silent he was, standing there watching her with his sombre yet eager gaze. It made her troubled, uneasy. She cast about for something to say.

"You can't think how I've improved since I saw you, Stuart. I've read all sorts of books—Oh! I'm learned," she smiled at him. "And Stuart," she went a little closer to him, twisting the button on his perfect coat, "I'm so sorry about it all,—about Stephen, that boy, you know. I just couldn't help interfering. But when we're married again, if you'll just remember how it hurts me to have you so cross—"

He interrupted her. "I wasn't aware that I spoke of our marrying again," he told her, his voice steady, his blue eyes cold.

She thought he was teasing. "Why you just asked me to. You said 'aren't you coming back to live with me—'"

Still she didn't comprehend. "But what do you mean?" she asked bewildered.

"What do you suppose a man means," he returned deliberately, "when he asks a woman to live with him but not to marry him?"

She sat down heavily in the brown chair, all glowing ivory and yellow against its sombre depths.

"Like the women in those awful novels?" she whispered. "Not like those women!—Oh Stuart! you don't mean it!" Her very heart was numb.

"But you must care a little—" she was amazed at her own depth of feeling. "Why I care—there are all those memories back of us—you must want me really—"

"I do want you," he told her tensely. "I want you damnably. But—well—I might as well out with it—A white man like me simply doesn't marry a colored woman. After all what difference need it make to you? We'll live abroad—you'll travel, have all the things you love. Many a white woman would envy you." He stretched out an eager hand.

She evaded it, holding herself aloof as though his touch were contaminating. Her movement angered him.

"Oh, hell!" he snarled at her roughly. "Why don't you stop posing? What do you think you are anyway? Do you suppose I'd take you for my wife—what do you think can happen to you? What man of your own race could give you what you want? You don't suppose I am going to support you this way forever, do you? The court imposed no alimony. You've got to come to it sooner or later—you're bound to fall to some white man. What's the matter—I'm not rich enough?"

Her face flamed at that—"As though it were *that* that mattered!"

He gave her a deadly look. "Well, isn't it? Ah, my girl, you forget you told me you didn't love me when you married me. You sold yourself to me then. Haven't I reason to suppose you are waiting for a higher bidder?"

At these words something in her died forever, her youth, her illusions, her happy, happy blindness. She saw life leering mercilessly in her face. It seemed to her that she would give all her future to stamp out, to kill the contempt in his frosty insolent eyes. In a sudden rush of savagery she struck him, struck him across his hateful sneering mouth with the hand which wore his ring.

As *she* fell, reeling under the fearful impact of his brutal but involuntary blow, her mind caught at, registered two things. A little thin stream of blood was trickling across his chin. She had cut him with the ring, she realized with a certain savage satisfaction. And there was something else which she must remember, which she *would* remember if only she could fight her way out of this dreadful clinging blackness, which was bearing down upon her—closing her in.

When she came to she sat up holding her bruised, aching head in her palms, trying to recall what it was that had impressed her so.

Oh yes, her very mind ached with the realization. She lay back again on the floor, prone, anything to relieve that intolerable pain. But her memory, her thoughts went on.

"Nigger," he had called her as she fell, "nigger, nigger," and again, "nigger."

"He despised me absolutely," she said to herself wonderingly, "because I was colored. And yet he wanted me."

V

Somehow she reached her room. Long after the servants had come in, she lay face downward across her bed, thinking. How she hated Wynne, how she hated herself! And for ten months she had been living off his money although in no way had she a claim on him. Her whole body burned with the shame of it.

In the morning she rang for Peter. She faced him, white and haggard, but if the man noticed her condition, he made no sign. He was, if possible, more imperturbable than ever.

"Peter," she told him, her eyes and voice very steady, "I am leaving this house today and shall never come back."

"Yes, Miss."

"And, Peter, I am very poor now and shall have no money besides what I can make for myself."

"Yes, Miss."

Would nothing surprise him, she wondered dully. She went on, "I don't know whether you knew it or not, Peter, but I am colored, and hereafter I mean to live among my own people. Do you think you could find a little house or little cottage not too far from New York?"

He had a little place in New Rochelle, he told her, his manner altering not one whit, or better yet his sister had a four-room house in Orange, with a garden, if he remembered correctly. Yes, he was sure there was a garden. It would be just the thing for Mrs. Wynne.

She had four hundred dollars of her very own which she had earned by designing for Madame. She paid the maids a month in advance—they were to stay as long as Peter needed them. She, herself, went to a small hotel in Twenty-eighth Street, and here Peter came for her at the end of ten days, with the acknowledgement of the keys and receipts from Mr. Packard. Then he accompanied her to Orange and installed her in her new home.

"I wish I could afford to keep you, Peter," she said a little wistfully, "but I am very poor. I am heavily in debt and I must get that off my shoulders at once."

Mrs. Wynne was very kind, he was sure; he could think of no one with whom he would prefer to work. Furthermore, he often ran down from New Rochelle to see his sister; he would come in from time to time, and in the spring would plant the garden if she wished.

She hated to see him go, but she did not dwell long on that. Her only thought was to work and work and work and save until she could pay Wynne back. She had not lived very extravagantly during those ten months and Peter was a perfect manager—in spite of her remonstrances he had given her every month an account of his expenses. She had made arrangements with Madame to be her regular designer. The French woman guessing that more than whim was behind this move drove a very shrewd bargain, but even then the pay was excellent. With care, she told herself, she could be free within two years, three at most.

She lived a dull enough existence now, going to work steadily every morning and getting home late at night. Almost it was like those early days when she had first left Mrs. Boldin, except that now she had no high sense of adventure, no expectation of great things to come, which might buoy her up. She no longer thought of phases and the proper setting for her beauty. Once indeed catching sight of her face late one night in the mirror in her tiny work-room in Orange, she stopped and scanned herself, loathing what she saw there.

"You *thing!*" she said to the image in the glass, "if you hadn't been so vain, so shallow!" And she had struck herself violently again and again across the face until her head ached.

But such fits of passion were rare. She had a curious sense of freedom in these days, a feeling that at last her brain, her senses were liberated from some hateful clinging thralldom. Her thoughts were always busy. She used to go over that last scene with Wynne again and again trying to probe the inscrutable mystery which she felt was at the bottom of the affair. She groped her way toward a solution, but always something stopped her. Her impulse to strike, she realized, and his brutal rejoinder had been actuated by something more than mere sex antagonism, there was *race* antagonism there—two elements clashing. That much she could fathom. But that he despising her, hating her for not being white should yet desire her! It seemed to her that his attitude toward her—hate and yet desire, was the attitude in microcosm of the whole white world toward her own, toward that world to which those few possible strains of black blood so tenuously and yet so tenaciously linked her.

Once she got hold of a big thought. Perhaps there *was* some root, some racial distinction woven in with the stuff of which she was formed which made her persistently kind and unexacting. And perhaps in the same way this difference, helplessly, inevitably operated in making Wynne and his kind, cruel or at best indifferent. Her reading for Wynne reacted to her thought—she remembered the grating insolence of white exploiters in foreign lands, the wrecking of African villages, the destruction of homes in Tasmania. She couldn't imagine where Tasmania was, but wherever it was, it had been the realest thing in the world to its crude inhabitants.

Gradually she reached a decision. There were two divisions of people in the world—on the one hand insatiable desire for power; keenness, mentality; a vast and cruel pride. On the other there was ambition, it is true, but modified, a certain humble sweetness, too much inclination to trust, an unthinking, unswerving loyalty. All the advantages in the world accrued to the first division. But without bitterness she chose the second. She wanted to be colored, she hoped she was colored. She wished even that she did not have to take advantage of her appearance to earn a living. But that was to meet an end. After all she had contracted her debt with a white man, she would pay him with a white man's money.

The years slipped by—four of them. One day a letter came from Mr. Packard. Mrs. Wynne had sent him the last penny of the sum received from Mr. Wynne from February to November, 1914. Mr. Wynne had refused to touch the money, it was and would be indefinitely at Mrs. Wynne's disposal.

She never even answered the letter. Instead she dismissed the whole incident,—Wynne and all,—from her mind and began to plan for her future. She was free, free! She had paid back her sorry debt with labor, money and anguish. From now on she could do as she pleased. Almost she caught herself saying "something is going to happen." But she checked herself, she hated her old attitude.

But something *was* happening. Insensibly from the moment she knew of her deliverance, her thoughts turned back to a stifled hidden longing, which had lain, it seemed to her, an eternity in her heart. Those days with Mrs. Boldin! At night,—on her way to New York,—in the work-rooms,—her mind was busy with little intimate pictures of that happy, wholesome, unpretentious life. She could see Mrs. Boldin, clean and portly, in a lilac chambray dress, upbraiding her for some trifling, yet exasperating fault. And Mr. Boldin, immaculate and slender, with his noticeably polished air—how kind he had always been, she remembered. And lastly, Cornelius: Cornelius in a thousand attitudes and engaged in a thousand occupations, brown and near-sighted and sweet—devoted to his pretty sister, as he used to call her; Cornelius, who used to come to her as a baby as willingly as to his mother; Cornelius spelling out colored letters on his blocks, pointing to them stickily with a brown, perfect finger; Cornelius singing like an angel in his breathy, sexless voice and later murdering everything possible on his terrible cornet. How had she ever been able to leave them all and the dear shabbiness of that home! Nothing, she realized, in all these years had touched her inmost being, had penetrated to the core of her cold heart like the memories of those early, misty scenes.

One day she wrote a letter to Mrs. Boldin. She, the writer, Madame A. Wynne, had come across a young woman, Amy Kildare, who said that as a girl she had run away from home and now she would like to come back. But she was ashamed to write. Madame Wynne had questioned the girl closely and she was quite sure that this Miss Kildare had in no way incurred shame or disgrace. It had been some time since Madame Wynne had seen the girl but if Mrs. Boldin wished, she would try to find her again—perhaps Mrs. Boldin would like to get in touch with her. The letter ended on a tentative note.

The answer came at once.

My dear Madame Wynne:

My mother told me to write you this letter. She says even if Amy Kildare had done something terrible, she would want her to come home again. My father says so too. My mother says, please find her as soon as you can and tell her to come back. She still misses her. We all miss her. I was a little boy when she left, but though I am in the High School now and play in the school orchestra, I would rather see her than do anything I know. If you see her, be sure to tell her to come right away. My mother says thank you.

> Yours respectfully,
> Cornelius Boldin

The letter came to the modiste's establishment in New York. Amy read it and went with it to Madame. "I must go away immediately. I can't come back—you may have these last two weeks for nothing." Madame, who had surmised long since the separation, looked curiously at the girl's flushed cheeks, and decided that "Monsieur Ween" had returned. She gave her fatalistic shrug. All Americans were crazy.

"But, yes, Madame, if you must go, absolument."

When she reached the ferry, Amy looked about her searchingly. "I hope I'm seeing you for the last time. I'm going home, home!" Oh, the unbelievable kindness! She had left them without a word and they still wanted her back!

Eventually she got to Orange and to the little house. She sent a message to Peter's sister and set about her packing. But first she sat down in the little house and looked about her. She would go home, home—how she loved the word, she would stay there a while, but always there was life, still beckoning. It would beckon forever she realized to her adventurousness. Afterwards she would set up an establishment of her own,—she reviewed possibilities—in a rich suburb, where white women would pay for her expertness, caring nothing for realities, only for externals.

"As I myself used to care," she sighed. Her thoughts flashed on. "Then some day I'll work and help with colored people—the only ones who have really cared for and wanted me." Her eyes blurred.

She would never make any attempt to find out who or what she was. If she were white, there would always be people urging her to keep up the silliness of racial prestige. How she hated it all!

"Citizen of the world, that's what I'll be. And now I'll go home."

Peter's sister's little girl came over to be with the pretty lady whom she adored.

"You sit here, Angel, and watch me pack," Amy said, placing her in a little arm-chair. And the baby sat there in silent observation, one tiny leg crossed over the other, surely the quaintest, gravest bit of bronze, Amy thought, that ever lived.

"Miss Amy cried," the child told her mother afterwards.

Perhaps Amy did cry, but if so she was unaware. Certainly she laughed more happily, more spontaneously than she had done for years. Once she got down on her knees in front of the little arm-chair and buried her face in the baby's tiny bosom.

"Oh Angel, Angel," she whispered, "do you suppose Cornelius still plays on that cornet?"

From Comedy: American Style (1933)

Chapter 1

Mrs. Olivia Blanchard Cary glanced out of the window of her pleasant residence in West Philadelphia and saw her daughter Teresa, her books under her arm, strolling down the street, with two other little girls similarly laden. One of her companions, a very fair blonde with dark blue eyes and gay gilt hair, Mrs. Cary identified immediately as Phebe Grant. She was not so sure of the identity of the third youngster. Closer inspection revealed to her however the dark brown skin, the piquant features, the sparkling black eyes and the abundant, silky and intensely curly locks of Marise Davies. Mrs. Cary frowned. "As often as I've told Teresa to keep away from that Davies child!" she murmured angrily to herself.

She met them at the front door. The countenances of the three children were in striking contrast. Teresa's wore a look of apprehension, Phebe's of bland indifference, Marise's of acute expectancy.

"Good-afternoon, Teresa," Olivia said. "Good-afternoon children. I'm afraid it's not best for Teresa to have so much company today. She gets excited and worn out and it's hard afterwards for her to settle down to her lessons. I don't mind if one of you stays. Phebe, suppose you come in and play with her a while, and, Marise, you can come back another time."

"Tomorrow?" asked Marise, whose black eyes had never left Olivia's face.

"Well, hardly tomorrow," the woman replied, flushing a little. She really disliked this child. "Horrid, little pushing thing," she inwardly apostrophized. But aloud she continued. "Hardly tomorrow, but some other day very soon, I am sure. Come on in Phebe."

"No, thank you, Mrs. Cary," the child answered, pushing back the thick gilt hair which framed her face. "I was with Marise first, so I'll go on with her. We were just going to ask you to let Teresa come along with us. My mother expects me to be at Marise's if I'm not home." She spoke simply, no trace of the avenging angel about her.

The two children, hand in hand, backed off the bottom step on which they had been precariously teetering. Marise, ignoring Olivia completely, waved a slender hand toward Teresa. "Come on over whenever you can. My mother doesn't mind."

From the pavement both looked back once more to wave a careless farewell to their school-mate. "G'bye, Treesa!"

"Treesa!" Olivia echoed angrily. "Why can't they pronounce your name right?" She glanced sharply at her daughter's tear-stained face. "What's the matter, Teresa?"

The little girl wiped away a tear with the back of her hand.

"Mamma, why can't I play with Marise? Of course Phebe's all right and I like her very, very much. But I like Marise best. She's such fun."

Her mother sighed. "I have," she thought, "the stupidest children and husband too in the world. Why can't they see this thing the way I want it?" Not unkindly she took out her handkerchief and wiped the child's eyes.

"Now, Teresa, it isn't worth while going all over this matter again. I don't mind your having Phebe here; in fact I rather like Phebe. But I don't like to have colored people in the house if we can possibly avoid it."

"But, Mamma, Phebe is colored too."

"I know she is but nobody would ever guess it."

"They don't have to guess it; she tells it; she stood right up in class and said so."

"What nonsense!" Olivia countered angrily. "What occasion would a girl, looking like her, have to talk about color?"

"She didn't say it of her own accord, Mamma. The teacher was having a review lesson on races one day and she asked Phebe what race she belonged to and Phebe said: 'I belong to the black or Negro race.'"

"What did the teacher say?"

"She just giggled at first and then she said: 'Well, Phebe, we all know that isn't true. Don't try to be funny. Now tell us what race you do belong to, dear!' And Phebe said it all over again. She said: 'I belong to the black or Negro race.'"

Olivia gasped. "Silly little thing! The idea of a girl as white as she saying that! What happened then?"

"The teacher had her stay after school and Phebe showed her the picture of her mother. She wears it in a locket around her throat all the time. And her mother *is* colored. Not black, you know, Mamma, but real, real brown. Almost as brown as Marise, you know. You should have seen how surprised Miss Packer was!"

In spite of herself her mother was interested. "What did she say then?"

"She looked awful queer and asked Phebe if she looked like her father and Phebe said she looked exactly like him . . . and that he didn't live here and that he was married to someone else. . . . And then Miss Packer turned kind of red and never said another word. . . . How can Phebe's father not be married to her mother, Mamma?"

"Oh, I don't know . . . probably they couldn't get along so they separated. Married people often do that. They call it getting a divorce." Hurriedly she changed the subject: "Did the children act any different to Phebe after that?"

Teresa considered this a moment. "Well, you see, Mamma, the children don't act any special kind of way to Phebe anyway, because Phebe don't care anything about them. The only child Phebe likes a whole lot in school is Marise."

"I thought she liked you."

"O she does, but not the same way she likes Marise. Marise is so smart you know. She can think up all the most wonderful things. Why she changed her name herself. It used to be Maria. And she said that was all wrong. She said she didn't look like a Maria person and she didn't feel like a Maria person. . . . Isn't that funny, Mamma? And she can sing and play and dance. You never saw anyone dance like her. And she can think up such smart things to say. I don't see why you don't like her, Mamma."

"I don't dislike her," her mother retorted in exasperation. "You don't understand these things, yet, Teresa. But you will when you're older . . . and you'll be grateful to me. I just don't want you to have Marise and people like that around because I don't want you to grow up among folks who live the life that most colored people have to live . . . narrow and stultified and stupid. Always pushed in the background . . . out of everything. Looked down upon and despised! . . .

"Teresa, how many times must I tell you these things? You and your father and Christopher almost drive me crazy! You're so willfully perverse about it all! Here we could all be as white as the whitest people in Philadelphia. When we moved in this neighborhood not a soul here but thought we were white! And your father is never happy unless he has some typical Negro hanging about. I believe he does it to tease me. And now here you are, all wrapped up in this Davies child!"

"But, Mamma, what difference does it make? And anyway, there's Oliver!"

There indeed was Oliver.

Olivia with very little love for her husband, Dr. Cary, with no enthusiasm, as such, for the institution of matrimony and with absolutely no urge for the maternal life, had none the less gone cheerfully and willingly into both marriage and motherhood because she believed that through her children she might obtain her heart's desire. She could, she was sure, imbue her offspring with precept and example to such an extent that it would never enter their minds to acknowledge the strain of black blood which in considerable dilution would flow through their veins.

She could be certain of their color. Her twin sister and brother, only two years older than her own children, had proven that. It was worth every one, she felt, of her labor pains not to hold in her arms little Teresa, her first-born,—but to gaze on that tiny, unremarkable face and note the white skin, the thick, "good" dark hair which covered the frail skull; to note that the tell-tale half-moons of which she had so often read were conspicuously absent. It seemed to her that the tenuous bonds holding her never so slightly to her group, and its station in America, were perceptibly weakened. Every time she appeared in public with the little girl she was presenting the incontestable proof of her white womanhood. . . .

And when Christopher, the second child was born, she was not the least fraction worried over the closely curling tendency of his slightly reddish hair. She had known Jews with hair much kinkier. Time and care would attend to all that. And meanwhile his skin was actually fairer than that of his little sister, his features finer and better chiselled. He had, she felt, a look of "race," by which she meant of course the only race which God, or Nature, for hidden, inscrutable purposes, meant should rule.

But she had not reckoned with the children's father. Christopher had finally established in his mind the fact of his chaste wife's frigidity. When he fully realized that her much-prized "aloofness," instead of being the *insigne* of a wealth of feeling, was merely the result of an absolute vacuum of passion, young as he was, he resolved not to kick against the pricks.

He had, he told himself, been sold, as many a man before him had; tricked as completely by his deliberate submission to ideals, entirely false to his nature and his desires, as a young girl might be by her first surrender to a passion which her heart tells her is natural, though her mind and breeding might warn her of its inexpediency. The first of that hardening process which was so to change him did have its inception during this period, but as he had some humor and a sense of justice beyond his years he refused to let the iron enter his soul.

Moreover, Olivia, though not a "comfortable" housekeeper, was a clean and a considerate one. She really never interfered with his "papers"; she never, even from the beginning, troubled him with the delinquencies of the help. And in those days, and for some years to come, she never exceeded the budget which he allowed her. Also her obvious willingness, even eagerness, to have children pleased and touched him. In his total ignorance of the plans which nestled eternally in the back of her sleek, dark head, he reasoned that a woman so fond of children must by a very natural extension develop eventually a certain tenderness for their father. So he hoped for many things and forgave her much with a somewhat rueful and yet amused indulgence.

Until he found in her the unalterable determination to carry himself and his children definitely across the narrow border-line of race! This too he at first regarded with some indulgence, but her unimaginative persistence finally irritated him. He was too busy to undertake completely the education of the children—he was responsible for their maintenance. But he could let them see his manifest respect and liking for many men who had been his boyhood friends and who bore the badge of their mixed blood plainly upon them.

He told the children every story he knew about the heroes of the race. Olivia would have preferred them to be ignorant of their own remote connection with slavery. But he did strive to make them realize the contrast between their present status and that of their black forebears. He emphasized the racial progress, stressing the brief span of years in which it had been accomplished.

And the children, straightforward, serious little things without an ounce of perversity in their make-up, were entranced, thrilled. Perhaps because they never met with any open expression of prejudice they seemed to find their greatest interest and amusement among the children of their father's friends who most definitely showed color. For a brief while Christopher's hero was Crispus Attucks; Teresa's brave Sojourner Truth. But later, through lack of nourishment, their interest in this phase of history died.

When the children were four and a half, and six, respectively, Olivia found she was going to have another baby. She was really very happy about it with a naiveté and a frankness which, Dr. Cary, as before, found inexpressibly moving and charming. Within herself she was making plans. This child should be her very own. She would make her husband believe that she needed a change, she would take the child away and live with him apart for two, three, perhaps for five years. In appearance, in rearing, in beliefs he should be completely, unrelievedly a member of the dominant race. She was a much wiser woman than she had been six years ago. The prospect made her gay and charming, almost girlish; far younger too than her twenty-eight years, younger indeed it seemed to her husband than she had ever been in those remote, so precious years of training.

"This one will be a boy," she told big Christopher gaily. "He'll be the handsomest and most attractive of us all. And I'll name him after myself. An Oliver for your Christopher."

Her prophecy was, except in one respect, absolutely true. She had boasted of the ease with which her children had entered the world. But this one she was confident would outstrip them all.

"I'm sure I'll be up very soon, Chris," she told her husband. She adopted one of her rare moods of coquetry. "And when I do get up, you ought to reward a dutiful wife. How would you like to send her and your baby son on a little trip to England?" Her eyes were bright with secrecy. He would, he assured her, do anything, give her anything she wanted within his range.

But the unforeseen happened. The baby arrived in due course. "Hale and hearty," said his beaming father. There never was a baby haler and heartier. But Olivia did not fare so well. She had one sinking spell after another. For the first time she was unable to nurse her child. She was to meet with no excitement or shock and as the baby was doing very well it was best for her not to be concerned with him for a while. She was to concentrate on recovering her strength. So that it was a full month before the baby was set before her, crowing and laughing and persistently and futilely striking his little hands together.

Olivia sat up, arms outstretched to receive him. Her baby! Her eyes stretched wide to behold every fraction of his tiny person. But the expectant smile faded as completely as though an unseen hand had wiped it off. She turned to her husband sharply:

"That's not my baby!"

But it was her baby. It was a boy, handsomer and more attractive than the other children. He was named Oliver. . . . They had been calling him that for a month, her delighted children assured her . . . his hair was black and soft and curly . . . and he had the exact bronze gold complexion of Lee Blanchard!

She had reckoned without her own father!

For the first time since she had known the futile anger of her early childhood she slipped into a black, though silent, rage. Her early anger had been directed against her father. This later ebullition included both her husband and her helpless little boy. She had no special beliefs about prenatal influences but she did observe to herself in the dark and tortuous recesses of her mind that if big Christopher had not been so decidedly a Negrophile, the appearance of their child would have been otherwise.

The little fellow was of a remarkable beauty. Through one pretext and another Olivia contrived not to be seen on the street with him. But the two older children and his father would proudly conduct him anywhere. And wherever he went he attracted attention . . . infinitely more so than his brother and sister had ever earned. Added to this was an undeniable charm of manner and of mind. He possessed not only a winning smile and a genuine sweetness of attitude and conduct but he was unquestionably of remarkable mental endowment. . . . If he had possessed an ounce of self-confidence, or even of the ordinary childish conceit which so often marks the "bright boy," he might easily have become unbearable. But even from babyhood little Oliver sensed in himself one lack which early automatically destroyed any root of undue self-esteem. He knew he did not have his mother's love. . . . Worse than that through some strange childish, unfailing perception he was sure of her active but hidden dislike for him.

When he was home Olivia fed him with the same food, watched over and satisfied his physical welfare as completely and meticulously as she watched over that of the other members of her household. But she never sought his company, she never took him riding or walking as she did the others, never bestowed on him more than the perfunctory kiss of salutation. . . . When people, struck with his appearance and healthy grace, praised him before his face as so often they did, he would turn sometimes toward her thinking dimly that now she must be proud of this fine little boy who was her son. But he never surprised on her countenance a single flash of delight or pride or love.

It saddened his childish days. . . . As soon as he became old enough to be from under her surveillance Olivia saw to it that he spent most of his time with her own mother in Boston or with her husband's mother in South Philadelphia. In both of these homes he met with the intense affection and generous esteem which his finely keyed little nature so craved. Gradually he became able to adjust himself to the inexplicable phenomenon of a mother who not only did not love with especial signal fondness, but who did not love at all, her youngest son. By sheer strength of will he forced himself to steel his brave and loyal heart against this defection and to crush down his pain.

His father had some sense of what was happening and in his heart he bore his wife a deep and unyielding dislike.

◈ DOROTHY WEST (1907–1998)

*Dorothy West's impressive literary output spans several decades in the twentieth cen-
tury. Her novels and short stories illustrate the relevancy that issues which concerned
writers of the Harlem Renaissance have to today's readers. A native of Boston, Dorothy
West was born in a middle-class family. Her father, a successful fruit exporter in
Boston, was an ex-slave. Consequently, slavery versus freedom functions as a primary
theme in many of her works. Well educated, she earned a diploma from Girls Latin
School in 1923, then later attended Columbia University, where she studied philosophy
and journalism. She received an award from* Opportunity *magazine in 1926, which
led to publication of her story "The Typewriter" that year. The story focuses on an
African American man with dreams of economic prosperity. In the 1930s she traveled
to Russia with Langston Hughes and others to make a film called* Black and White,
which was never finished.

She returned to the United States and later started Challenge *magazine and another
version called* New Challenge, *which she hoped would revive the protest spirit of the
Harlem Renaissance of the 1930s. In 1945, she relocated to Martha's Vineyard, where
her family owned a summer home. Her novel* The Living Is Easy *(1948) denounces
intraracial color and class prejudice by showing its negative effects on the Judsons, a black
family.* The Wedding *(1995), made into a television movie produced by Oprah Winfrey,
chronicles the lives of an affluent black family on Martha's Vineyard and the disastrous
emotional and psychic conflicts of race and class prejudice. West stands as an important
bridge between the literature of the Harlem Renaissance and the neo-realism movement
in her critique of race and class prejudice.*

The Typewriter (1926)

It occurred to him, as he eased past the bulging knees of an Irish wash lady and forced
an apologetic passage down the aisle of the crowded car, that more than anything in
all the world he wanted not to go home. He began to wish passionately that he had
never been born, that he had never been married, that he had never been the means
of life's coming into the world. He knew quite suddenly that he hated his flat and his
family and his friends. And most of all the incessant thing that would "clatter clatter"
until every nerve screamed aloud, and the words of the evening paper danced crazily
before him, and the insane desire to crush and kill set his fingers twitching.

He shuffled down the street, an abject little man of fifty-odd years, in an age-
less overcoat that flapped in the wind. He was cold, and he hated the North, and
particularly Boston, and saw suddenly a barefoot pickaninny sitting on a fence in
the hot, Southern sun with a piece of steaming corn bread and a piece of fried salt
pork in either grimy hand.

He was tired, and he wanted his supper, but he didn't want the beans, and
frankfurters, and light bread that Net would undoubtedly have. That Net had had
every Monday night since that regrettable moment fifteen years before when he
had told her—innocently—that such a supper tasted "right nice. Kinda change
from what we always has."

He mounted the four brick steps leading to his door and pulled at the bell; but there was no answering ring. It was broken again, and in a mental flash he saw himself with a multitude of tools and a box of matches shivering in the vestibule after supper. He began to pound lustily on the door and wondered vaguely if his hand would bleed if he smashed the glass. He hated the sight of blood. It sickened him.

Someone was running down the stairs. Daisy probably. Millie would be at that infernal thing, pounding, pounding. . . . He entered. The chill of the house swept him. His child was wrapped in a coat. She whispered solemnly, "Poppa, Miz Hicks an' Miz Berry's orful mad. They gointa move if they can't get more heat. The furnace's bin out all day. Mama couldn't fix it." He said hurriedly, "I'll go right down. I'll go right down." He hoped Mrs. Hicks wouldn't pull open her door and glare at him. She was large and domineering, and her husband was a bully. If her husband ever struck him it would kill him. He hated life, but he didn't want to die. He was afraid of God, and in his wildest flights of fancy couldn't imagine himself an angel. He went softly down the stairs.

He began to shake the furnace fiercely. And he shook into it every wrong, mumbling softly under his breath. He began to think back over his uneventful years, and it came to him as rather a shock that he had never sworn in all his life. He wondered uneasily if he dared say "damn." It was taken for granted that a man swore when he tended a stubborn furnace. And his strongest interjection was "Great balls of fire!"

The cellar began to warm, and he took off his inadequate overcoat that was streaked with dirt. Well, Net would have to clean that. He'd be damned—! It frightened him and thrilled him. He wanted suddenly to rush upstairs and tell Mrs. Hicks if she didn't like the way he was running things, she could get out. But he heaped another shovelful of coal on the fire and sighed. He would never be able to get away from himself and the routine of years.

He thought of that eager Negro lad of seventeen who had come North to seek his fortune. He had walked jauntily down Boylston Street, and even his own kind had laughed at the incongruity of him. But he had thrown up his head and promised himself: "You'll have an office here some day. With plate-glass windows and a real mahogany desk." But, though he didn't know it then, he was not the progressive type. And he became successively, in the years, bell boy, porter, waiter, cook, and finally janitor in a downtown office building.

He had married Net when he was thirty-three and a waiter. He had married her partly because—though he might not have admitted it—there was no one to eat the expensive delicacies the generous cook gave him every night to bring home. And partly because he dared hope there might be a son to fulfill his dreams. But Millie had come, and after her, twin girls who had died within two weeks, then Daisy, and it was tacitly understood that Net was done with childbearing.

Life, though flowing monotonously, had flowed peacefully enough until that sucker of sanity became a sitting room fixture. Intuitively at the very first he had felt its undesirability. He had suggested hesitatingly that they couldn't afford it. Three dollars the eighth of every month. Three dollars: food and fuel. Times were hard, and the twenty dollars apiece the respective husbands of Miz Hicks and Miz Berry irregularly paid was only five dollars more than the thirty-five a month he paid his own Hebraic landlord. And the Lord knew his salary was little enough. At which point Net spoke her piece, her voice rising shrill. "God knows I never complain 'bout nothin'. Ain't no other woman got less than me. I bin wearin' this same dress here five years, an' I'll wear it another five. But I don't want nothin'. I ain't never wanted nothin'. An' when I does as', it's only for my children. You're a poor sort of father if you can't give that child jes' three dollars a month to rent that typewriter. Ain't 'nother girl in school ain't got one. An' mos' of 'ems bought an paid for. You know yourself how Millie is. She wouldn't as' me for it till she had to. An' I ain't going to disappoint her. She's goin' to get that typewriter Saturday, mark my words."

On a Monday then it had been installed. And in the months that followed, night after night he listened to the murderous "tack, tack, tack" that was like a vampire slowly drinking his blood. If only he could escape. Bar a door against the sound of it. But tied hand and foot by the economic fact that "Lord knows we can't afford to have fires burnin' an' lights lit all over the flat. You'all gotta set in one room. An' when y'get tired setting y'c'n go to bed. Gas bill was somep'n scandalous last month."

He heaped a final shovelful of coal on the fire and watched the first blue flames. Then, his overcoat under his arm, he mounted the cellar stairs. Mrs. Hicks was standing in her kitchen door, arms akimbo. "It's warmin'," she volunteered.

"Yeh," he was conscious of his grime-streaked face and hands, "it's warmin'. I'm sorry 'bout all day."

She folded her arms across her ample bosom. "Tending a furnace ain't a woman's work. I don't blame you wife none 'tall."

Unsuspecting, he was grateful. "Yeh, it's pretty hard for a woman. I always look after it 'fore I goes to work, but some days it jes' ac's up."

"Y'oughta have a janitor, that's what y'ought," she flung at him. "The same cullud man that tends them apartments would be willin'. Mr. Taylor has him. It takes a man to run a furnace, and when the man's away all day—"

"I know," he interrupted, embarrassed and hurt. "I know. Tha's right, Miz Hicks, tha's right. But I ain't in a position to make no improvements. Times is hard."

She surveyed him critically. "Your wife called down 'bout three times while you was in the cellar. I reckon she wants you for supper."

"Thanks," he mumbled and escaped up the back stairs.

He hung up his overcoat in the closet, telling himself, a little lamely, that it wouldn't take him more than a minute to clean it up himself after supper. After all, Net was tired and probably worried what with Mrs. Hicks and all. And he hated men who made slaves of their womenfolk. Good old Net.

He tidied up in the bathroom, washing his face and hands carefully and cleanly so as to leave no—or very little—stain on the roller towel. It was hard enough for Net, God knew.

He entered the kitchen. The last spirals of steam were rising from his supper. One thing about Net, she served a full plate. He smiled appreciatively at her unresponsive back, bent over the kitchen sink. There was no one who could bake beans just like Net's. And no one who could find a market with frankfurters quite so fat.

He sat down at his place. "Evenin', hon."

He saw her back stiffen. "If your supper's cold, 'tain't my fault. I called and called."

He said hastily, "It's fine, Net, fine. Piping."

She was the usual tired housewife. "Y'oughta et your supper 'fore you fooled with that furnace. I ain't bothered 'bout them niggers. I got all my dishes washed 'cept yours. An' I hate to mess up my kitchen after I once get it straightened up."

He was humble. "I'll give that old furnace an extra lookin' after in the mornin'. It'll last all day tomorrow, hon."

"An' on top of that," she continued, unheeding him and giving a final wrench to her dish towel, "that confounded bell don't ring. An'—"

"I'll fix it after supper," he interposed quickly.

She hung up her dish towel and came to stand before him looming large and yellow. "An' that old Miz Berry, she claim she was expectin' comp'ny. An' she know they must 'a' come an' gone while she was in her kitchen an' couldn't be at her winder to watch for 'em. Old liar." She brushed back a lock of naturally straight hair. "She wasn't expectin' nobody."

"Well, you know how some folks are—"

"Fools! Half the world," was her vehement answer. "I'm goin' in the front room an' set down a spell. I bin on my feet all day. Leave them dishes on the table. God knows I'm tired, but I'll come back an' wash 'em." But they both knew, of course, that he, very clumsily, would.

At precisely quarter past nine when he, strained at last to the breaking point, uttering an inhuman, strangled cry, flung down his paper, clutched at his throat, and sprang to his feet, Millie's surprised young voice, shocking him to normalcy, heralded the first of that series of great moments that every humble little middle-class man eventually experiences.

"What's the matter, Poppa? You sick? I wanted you to help me."

He drew out his handkerchief and wiped his hot hands. "I declare I must 'a' fallen asleep an' had a nightmare. No, I ain't sick. What you want, hon?"

"Dictate me a letter, Poppa. I c'n do sixty words a minute. You know, like a business letter. You know, like those men in your building dictate to their stenographers. Don't you hear 'em sometimes?"

"Oh sure, I know, hon. Poppa'll help you. Sure. I hear that Mr. Browning. Sure."

Net rose, "Guess I'll put this child to bed. Come on now, Daisy, without no fuss. Then I'll run up to Pa's. He ain't bin well all week."

When the door closed behind them, he crossed to his daughter, conjured the image of Mr. Browning in the process of dictating, so arranged himself, and coughed importantly.

"Well, Millie—"

"Oh, Poppa, is that what you'd call your stenographer?" she teased. "And anyway pretend I'm really one—and you're really my boss, and this letter's real important."

A light crept into his dull eyes. Vigor through his thin blood. In a brief moment the weight of years fell from him like a cloak. Tired, bent, little old man that he was, he smiled, straightened, tapped impressively against his teeth with a toil-stained finger, and became that enviable emblem of American life: a businessman.

"You be Miz Hicks, huh, honey? Course we can't both use the same name. I'll be J. Lucius Jones. J. Lucius. All them real big men use their middle names. Jus' kinda looks big doin', doncha think, hon? Looks like money, huh? J. Lucius." He uttered a sound that was like the proud cluck of a strutting hen. "J. Lucius." It rolled like oil from his tongue.

His daughter twisted impatiently. "Now, Poppa—I mean Mr. Jones, sir—please begin. I am ready for dictation, sir."

He was in that office on Boylston Street, looking with visioning eyes through its plate-glass windows, tapping with impatient fingers on its real mahogany desk. "Ah—Beaker Brothers, Park Square Building, Boston, Mass. Ah—Gentlemen: In reply to yours of the seventh instant would state—"

Every night thereafter in the weeks that followed, with Daisy packed off to bed, and Net "gone up to Pa's" or nodding unobtrusively in her corner, there was the chameleon change of a Court Street janitor to J. Lucius Jones, dealer in stocks and bonds. He would stand, posturing, importantly flicking imaginary dust from his coat lapel, or, his hands locked behind his back, he would stride up and down, earnestly and seriously debating the advisability of buying copper with the market in such a fluctuating state. Once a week, too, he stopped in at Jerry's, and after a preliminary purchase of cheap cigars, bought the latest trade papers, mumbling an embarrassed explanation: "I got a little money. Think I'll invest it in reliable stock."

The letters Millie typed and subsequently discarded, he rummaged for later, and under cover of writing to his brother in the South, laboriously, with a great many fancy flourishes, signed each neatly typed sheet with the exalted J. Lucius Jones.

Later, when he mustered the courage, he suggested tentatively to Millie that it might be fun—just fun, of course—to answer his letters. One night—he laughed a good deal louder and longer than necessary—he'd be J. Lucius Jones, and the next night—here he swallowed hard and looked a little frightened—Rockefeller or Vanderbilt or Morgan—just for fun, y'understand! To which Millie gave consent. It mattered little to her one way or the other. It was practice, and that was what she needed. Very soon now she'd be in the hundred class. Then maybe she could get a job!

He was growing very careful of his English. Occasionally—and it must be admitted, ashamedly—he made surreptitious ventures into the dictionary. He had to, of course. J. Lucius Jones would never say "Y'got to" when he meant "It is expedient." And, old brain though he was, he learned quickly and easily, juggling words with amazing facility.

Eventually, he bought stamps and envelopes—long, important-looking envelopes—and stammered apologetically to Millie, "Honey, Poppa thought it'd help you if you learned to type envelopes, too. Reckon you'll have to do that, too, when y'get a job. Poor old man," he swallowed painfully, "came round selling these envelopes. You know how 'tis. So I had to buy 'em." Which was satisfactory to Millie. If she saw through her father, she gave no sign. After all, it was practice, and Mr. Hennessey had promised the smartest girl in the class a position in the very near future. And she, of course, was smart as a steel trap. Even Mr. Hennessey had said that—though not in just those words.

He had gotten in the habit of carrying those self-addressed envelopes in his inner pocket where they bulged impressively. And occasionally he would take them out—on the car usually—and smile upon them. This one might be from J. P. Morgan. This one from Henry Ford. And a million-dollar deal involved in each. That narrow, little spinster who, upon his sitting down, had drawn herself away from his contact, was shunning J. Lucius Jones!

Once, led by some sudden, strange impulse, as an outgoing car rumbled up out of the subway, he got out a letter, darted a quick shamed glance about him, dropped it in an adjacent box, and swung aboard the car, feeling, dazedly, as if he had committed a crime. And the next night he sat in the sitting room quite on edge until Net said suddenly, "Look here, a real important letter come today for you, Pa. Here 'tis. What you s'pose it says?" And he reached out a hand that trembled. He made brief explanation. "Advertisement, hon. Thassal."

They came quite frequently after that, and despite the fact that he knew them by heart, he read them quite slowly and carefully, rustling the sheet, and making inaudible, intelligent comments. He was, in these moments, pathetically earnest.

Monday, as he went about his janitor's duties, he composed in his mind the final letter from J. P. Morgan that would consummate a big business deal. For days now, letters had passed between them. J. P. had been at first quite frankly uninterested. He had written tersely and briefly. Which was meat to J. Lucius. The compositions of his brain were really the work of an artist. He wrote glowingly of the advantages of a pact between them. Daringly he argued in terms of billions. And at last J. P. had written his next letter would be decisive. Which next letter, this Monday, as he trailed about the office building, was writing itself in his brain.

That night Millie opened the door for him. Her plain face was transformed. "Poppa—Poppa, I got a job! Twelve dollars a week to start with! Isn't that swell!"

He was genuinely pleased. "Honey, I'm glad. Right glad," and went upstairs, unsuspecting.

He ate his supper hastily, went down into the cellar to see about his fire, returned and carefully tidied up, informing his reflection in the bathroom mirror, "Well, J. Lucius, you c'n expect that final letter any day now."

He entered the sitting room. The phonograph was playing. Daisy was singing lustily. Strange. Net was talking animatedly to Millie, busy with needle and thread over a neat, little frock. His wild glance darted to the table. The pretty little centerpiece of the bowl and wax flowers all neatly arranged: the typewriter gone from its accustomed place. It seemed an hour before he could speak. He felt himself trembling. Went hot and cold.

"Millie—your typewriter's—gone!"

She made a deft little in-and-out movement with her needle. "It's the eighth, you know. When the man came today for the money, I sent it back. I won't need it no more—now! The money's on the mantelpiece, Poppa."

"Yeh," he muttered. "All right."

He sank down in his chair, fumbled for the paper, found it.

Net said, "Your poppa wants to read. Stop your noise, Daisy."

She obediently stopped both her noise and the phonograph, took up her book, and became absorbed. Millie went on with her sewing in placid anticipation of the morrow. Net immediately began to nod, gave a curious snort, slept.

Silence. That crowded in on him, engulfed him. That blurred his vision, dulled his brain. Vast, white, impenetrable. . . . His ears strained for the old, familiar sound. And silence beat upon them. . . . The words of the evening paper jumbled together. He read: "J. P. Morgan goes—"

It burst upon him. Blinded him. His hands groped for the bulge beneath his coat. Why this—this was the end! The end of those great moments—the end of everything! Bewildering pain tore through him. He clutched at his heart and felt, almost, the jagged edges drive into his hand. A lethargy swept down upon him. He could not move, nor utter a sound. He could not pray, nor curse.

Against the wall of that silence J. Lucius Jones crashed and died.

ZORA NEALE HURSTON (1891–1960)

*Zora Neale Hurston has been viewed as a literary foremother by many African American women writers, including Alice Walker, who praises Hurston's legacy in the essay "In Search of Our Mothers' Gardens" (pp. 1003–1010). Born in Notasulga, Alabama, Zora Neale Hurston was primarily raised in Eatonville, Florida, which she claimed as her birthplace. She attended Morgan Academy, Barnard College, and Columbia University. She went on expeditions to the South in the late 1920s and 1930s with the aid of grants to collect folklore, which often became the source of her novels. Her four novels—*Jonah's Gourd Vine *(1934),* Their Eyes Were Watching God *(1937),* Moses, Man of the Mountain *(1939), and* Seraph on the Suwanee *(1948)—feature protagonists who feel enslaved by socially prescribed race, class, and gender roles in American society.* Their Eyes Were Watching God, *in its exploration of marriage, sexuality, and female spirituality and community, has been heralded by many critics as a feminist text. Hurston's autobiography,* Dust Tracks on a Road *was published in 1942. She died impoverished in Florida, not living to see her worldwide fame.*

Their Eyes Were Watching God (1937)

Chapter 1

Ships at a distance have every man's wish on board. For some they come in with the tide. For others they sail forever on the horizon, never out of sight, never landing until the Watcher turns his eyes away in resignation, his dreams mocked to death by Time. That is the life of men.

Now, women forget all those things they don't want to remember, and remember everything they don't want to forget. The dream is the truth. Then they act and do things accordingly.

So the beginning of this was a woman and she had come back from burying the dead. Not the dead of sick and ailing with friends at the pillow and the feet. She had come back from the sodden and the bloated; the sudden dead, their eyes flung wide open in judgment.

The people all saw her come because it was sundown. The sun was gone, but he had left his footprints in the sky. It was the time for sitting on porches beside the road. It was the time to hear things and talk. These sitters had been tongue-less, earless, eyeless conveniences all day long. Mules and other brutes had occupied their skins. But now, the sun and the bossman were gone, so the skins felt powerful and human. They became lords of sounds and lesser things. They passed nations through their mouths. They sat in judgment.

Seeing the woman as she was made them remember the envy they had stored up from other times. So they chewed up the back parts of their minds and swallowed with relish. They made burning statements with questions, and killing tools out of laughs. It was mass cruelty. A mood come alive. Words walking without masters; walking altogether like harmony in a song.

"What she doin' coming back here in dem overhalls? Can't she find no dress to put on?—Where's dat blue satin dress she left here in?—Where all dat money her husband took and died and left her?—What dat ole forty year ole 'oman doin' wid her hair swingin' down her back lak some young gal?—Where she left dat young lad of a boy she went off here wid?—Thought she was going to marry?—Where he left *her*?—What he done wid all her money?—Betcha he off wid some gal so young she ain't even got no hairs—why she don't stay in her class?—"

When she got to where they were she turned her face on the bander log and spoke. They scrambled a noisy "good evenin'" and left their mouths setting open and their ears full of hope. Her speech was pleasant enough, but she kept walking straight on to her gate. The porch couldn't talk for looking.

The men noticed her firm buttocks like she had grape fruits in her hip pockets; the great rope of black hair swinging to her waist and unraveling in the wind like a plume; then her pugnacious breasts trying to bore holes in her shirt. They, the men, were saving with the mind what they lost with the eye. The women took the faded shirt and muddy overalls and laid them away for remembrance. It was a weapon against her strength and if it turned out of no significance, still it was a hope that she might fall to their level some day.

But nobody moved, nobody spoke, nobody even thought to swallow spit until after her gate slammed behind her.

Pearl Stone opened her mouth and laughed real hard because she didn't know what else to do. She fell all over Mrs. Sumpkins while she laughed. Mrs. Sumpkins snorted violently and sucked her teeth.

"Humph! Y'all let her worry yuh. You ain't like me. Ah ain't got her to study 'bout. If she ain't got manners enough to stop and let folks know how she been makin' out, let her g'wan!"

"She ain't even worth talkin' after," Lulu Moss drawled through her nose. "She sits high, but she looks low. Dat's what Ah say 'bout dese ole women runnin' after young boys."

Pheoby Watson hitched her rocking chair forward before she spoke. "Well, nobody don't know if it's anything to tell or not. Me, Ah'm her best friend, and *Ah* don't know."

"Maybe us don't know into things lak you do, but we all know how she went 'way from here and us sho seen her come back. 'Tain't no use in your tryin' to cloak no ole woman lak Janie Starks, Pheoby, friend or no friend."

"At dat she ain't so ole as some of y'all dat's talking."

"She's way past forty to my knowledge, Pheoby."

"No more'n forty at de outside."

"She's 'way too old for a boy like Tea Cake."

"Tea Cake ain't been no boy for some time. He's round thirty his ownself."

"Don't keer what it was, she could stop and say a few words with us. She act like we done done something to her," Pearl Stone complained. "She de one been doin' wrong."

"You mean, you mad 'cause she didn't stop and tell us all her business. Anyhow, what you ever know her to do so bad as y'all make out? The worst thing Ah ever knowed her to do was taking a few years offa her age and dat ain't never harmed nobody. Y'all makes me tired. De way you talkin' you'd think de folks in dis town didn't do nothin' in de bed 'cept praise de Lawd. You have to 'scuse me, 'cause Ah'm bound to go take her some supper." Pheoby stood up sharply.

"Don't mind us," Lulu smiled, "just go right ahead, us can mind yo' house for you till you git back. Mah supper is done. You bettah go see how she feel. You kin let de rest of us know."

"Lawd," Pearl agreed, "Ah done scorched-up dat lil meat and bread too long to talk about. Ah kin stay 'way from home long as Ah please. Mah husband ain't fussy."

"Oh, er, Pheoby, if youse ready to go, Ah could walk over dere wid you," Mrs. Sumpkins volunteered. "It's sort of duskin' down dark. De booger man might ketch yuh."

"Naw, Ah thank yuh. Nothin' couldn't ketch me dese few steps Ah'm goin'. Anyhow mah husband tell me say no first class booger would have me. If she got anything to tell yuh, you'll hear it."

Pheoby hurried on off with a covered bowl in her hands. She left the porch pelting her back with unasked questions. They hoped the answers were cruel and strange. When she arrived at the place, Pheoby Watson didn't go in by the front gate and down the palm walk to the front door. She walked around the fence corner and went in the intimate gate with her heaping plate of mulatto rice. Janie must be round that side.

She found her sitting on the steps of the back porch with the lamps all filled and the chimneys cleaned.

"Hello, Janie, how you comin'?"

"Aw, pretty good, Ah'm tryin' to soak some uh de tiredness and de dirt outa mah feet." She laughed a little.

"Ah see you is. Gal, you sho looks *good*. You looks like youse yo' own daughter." They both laughed. "Even wid dem overhalls on, you shows yo' womanhood."

"G'wan! G'wan! You must think Ah brought yuh somethin'. When Ah ain't brought home a thing but mahself."

"Dat's a gracious plenty. Yo' friends wouldn't want nothin' better."

"Ah takes dat flattery offa you, Pheoby, 'cause Ah know it's from de heart." Janie extended her hand. "Good Lawd, Pheoby! ain't you never goin' tuh gimme dat lil rations you brought me? Ah ain't had a thing on mah stomach today exceptin' mah hand." They both laughed easily. "Give it here and have a seat."

"Ah knowed you'd be hongry. No time to be huntin' stove wood after dark. Mah mulatto rice ain't so good dis time. Not enough bacon grease, but Ah reckon it'll kill hongry."

"Ah'll tell you in a minute," Janie said, lifting the cover. "Gal, it's *too* good! you switches a mean fanny round in a kitchen."

"Aw, dat ain't much to eat, Janie. But Ah'm liable to have something sho nuff good tomorrow, 'cause you done come."

Janie ate heartily and said nothing. The varicolored cloud dust that the sun had stirred up in the sky was settling by slow degrees.

"Here, Pheoby, take yo' ole plate. Ah ain't got a bit of use for a empty dish. Dat grub sho come in handy."

Pheoby laughed at her friend's rough joke. "Youse just as crazy as you ever was."

"Hand me dat wash-rag on dat chair by you, honey. Lemme scrub mah feet." She took the cloth and rubbed vigorously. Laughter came to her from the big road.

"Well, Ah see Mouth-Almighty is still sittin' in de same place. And Ah reckon they got *me* up in they mouth now."

"Yes indeed. You know if you pass some people and don't speak tuh suit 'em dey got tuh go way back in yo' life and see whut you ever done. They know mo' 'bout yuh than you do yo' self. An envious heart makes a treacherous ear. They done 'heard' 'bout you just what they hope done happened."

"If God don't think no mo' 'bout 'em then Ah do, they's a lost ball in de high grass."

"Ah hears what they say 'cause they just will collect round mah porch 'cause it's on de big road. Mah husband git so sick of 'em sometime he makes 'em all git for home."

"Sam is right too. They just wearin' out yo' sittin' chairs."

"Yeah, Sam say most of 'em goes to church so they'll be sure to rise in Judgment. Dat's de day dat every secret is s'posed to be made known. They wants to be there and hear it *all*."

"Sam is *too* crazy! You can't stop laughin' when youse round him."

"Uuh hunh. He says he aims to be there hisself so he can find out who stole his corn-cob pipe."

"Phoeby, dat Sam of your'n just won't quit! Crazy thing!"

"Most of dese zigaboos is so het up over yo' business till they liable to hurry theyself to Judgment to find out about you if they don't soon know. You better make haste and tell 'em 'bout you and Tea Cake gittin' married, and if he taken all yo' money and went off wid some young gal, and where at he is now and where at is all yo' clothes dat you got to come back here in overhalls."

"Ah don't mean to bother wid tellin' 'em nothin', Pheoby. 'Tain't worth de trouble. You can tell 'em what Ah say if you wants to. Dat's just de same as me 'cause mah tongue is in mah friend's mouf."

"If you so desire Ah'll tell 'em what you tell me to tell 'em."

"To start off wid, people like dem wastes up too much time puttin' they mouf on things they don't know nothin' about. Now they got to look into me loving Tea Cake and see whether it was done right or not! They don't know if life is a mess of corn-meal dumplings, and if love is a bed-quilt!"

"So long as they get a name to gnaw on they don't care whose it is, and what about, 'specially if they can make it sound like evil."

"If they wants to see and know, why they don't come kiss and be kissed? Ah could then sit down and tell 'em things. Ah been a delegate to de big 'ssociation of life. Yessuh! De Grand Lodge, de big convention of livin' is just where Ah been dis year and a half y'all ain't seen me."

They sat there in the fresh young darkness close together. Pheoby eager to feel and do through Janie, but hating to show her zest for fear it might be thought mere curiosity. Janie full of that oldest human longing—self revelation. Pheoby held her tongue for a long time, but she couldn't help moving her feet. So Janie spoke.

"They don't need to worry about me and my overhalls long as Ah still got nine hundred dollars in de bank. Tea Cake got me into wearing 'em—following behind him. Tea Cake ain't wasted up no money of mine, and he ain't left me for no young gal, neither. He give me every consolation in de world. He'd tell 'em so too, if he was here. If he wasn't gone."

Pheoby dilated all over with eagerness, "Tea Cake gone?"

"Yeah, Pheoby, Tea Cake is gone. And dat's de only reason you see me back here—cause Ah ain't got nothing to make me happy no more where Ah was at. Down in the Everglades there, down on the muck."

"It's hard for me to understand what you mean, de way you tell it. And then again Ah'm hard of understandin' at times."

"Naw, 'tain't nothin' lak you might think. So 'tain't no use in me telling you somethin' unless Ah give you de understandin' to go 'long wid it. Unless you see de fur, a mink skin ain't no different from a coon hide. Looka heah, Pheoby, is Sam waitin' on you for his supper?"

"It's all ready and waitin'. If he ain't got sense enough to eat it, dat's his hard luck."

"Well then, we can set right where we is and talk. Ah got the house all opened up to let dis breeze get a little catchin'."

"Pheoby, we been kissin'-friends for twenty years, so Ah depend on you for a good thought. And Ah'm talking to you from dat standpoint."

Time makes everything old so the kissing, young darkness became a monstropolous old thing while Janie talked.

Chapter 2

Janie saw her life like a great tree in leaf with the things suffered, things enjoyed, things done and undone. Dawn and doom was in the branches.

"Ah know exactly what Ah got to tell yuh, but it's hard to know where to start at.

"Ah ain't never seen mah papa. And Ah didn't know 'im if Ah did. Mah mama neither. She was gone from round dere long before Ah wuz big enough tuh know. Mah grandma raised me. Mah grandma and de white folks she worked wid. She had a house out in de back-yard and dat's where Ah wuz born. They was quality white folks up dere in West Florida. Named Washburn. She had four gran'chillun on de place and all of us played together and dat's how come Ah never called mah

Grandma nothin' but Nanny, 'cause dat's what everybody on de place called her. Nanny used to ketch us in our devilment and lick every youngun on de place and Mis' Washburn did de same. Ah reckon dey never hit us ah lick amiss 'cause dem three boys and us two girls wuz pretty aggravatin', Ah speck.

"Ah was wid dem white chillun so much till Ah didn't know Ah wuzn't white till Ah was round six years old. Wouldn't have found it out then, but a man come long takin' pictures and without askin' anybody, Shelby, dat was de oldest boy, he told him to take us. Round a week later de man brought de picture for Mis' Washburn to see and pay him which she did, then give us all a good lickin'.

"So when we looked at de picture and everybody got pointed out there wasn't nobody left except a real dark little girl with long hair standing by Eleanor. Dat's where Ah was s'posed to be, but Ah couldn't recognize dat dark chile as me. So Ah ast, 'where is me? Ah don't see me.'

"Everybody laughed, even Mr. Washburn. Miss Nellie, de Mama of de chillun who come back home after her husband dead, she pointed to de dark one and said, 'Dat's you, Alphabet, don't you know yo' ownself?'

"Dey all useter call me Alphabet 'cause so many people had done named me different names. Ah looked at de picture a long time and seen it was mah dress and mah hair so Ah said:

"'Aw, aw! Ah'm colored!'

"Den dey all laughed real hard. But before Ah seen de picture Ah thought Ah wuz just like de rest.

"Us lived dere havin' fun till the chillun at school got to teasin' me 'bout livin' in de white folks' back-yard. Dere wuz uh knotty head gal name Mayrella dat useter git mad every time she look at me. Mis' Washburn useter dress me up in all de clothes her gran'chillun didn't need no mo' which still wuz better'n whut de rest uh de colored chillun had. And then she useter put hair ribbon on mah head fuh me tuh wear. Dat useter rile Mayrella uh lot. So she would pick at me all de time and put some others up tuh do de same. They'd push me 'way from de ring plays and make out they couldn't play wid nobody dat lived on premises. Den they'd tell me not to be takin' on over mah looks 'cause they mama told 'em 'bout de hound dawgs huntin' mah papa all night long. 'Bout Mr. Washburn and de sheriff puttin' de bloodhounds on de trail tuh ketch mah papa for whut he done tuh mah mama. Dey didn't tell about how he wuz seen tryin' tuh git in touch wid mah mama later on so he could marry her. Naw, dey didn't talk dat part of it atall. Dey made it sound real bad so as tuh crumple mah feathers. None of 'em didn't even remember whut his name wuz, but dey all knowed de bloodhound part by heart. Nanny didn't love tuh see me wid mah head hung down, so she figgered it would be mo' better fuh me if us had uh house. She got de land and everything and then Mis' Washburn helped out uh whole heap wid things."

Pheoby's hungry listening helped Janie to tell her story. So she went on thinking back to her young years and explaining them to her friend in soft, easy phrases while all around the house, the night time put on flesh and blackness.

She thought awhile and decided that her conscious life had commenced at Nanny's gate. On a late afternoon Nanny had called her to come inside the house because she had spied Janie letting Johnny Taylor kiss her over the gatepost.

It was a spring afternoon in West Florida. Janie had spent most of the day under a blossoming pear tree in the back-yard. She had been spending every minute that she could steal from her chores under that tree for the last three days. That was to say, ever since the first tiny bloom had opened. It had called her to come and gaze on a mystery. From barren brown stems to glistening leaf-buds; from the leaf-buds to snowy virginity of bloom. It stirred her tremendously. How? Why? It was like a flute song forgotten in another existence and remembered again. What? How? Why? This singing she heard that had nothing to do with her ears. The rose of the world was breathing out smell. It followed her through all her waking moments and caressed her in her sleep. It connected itself with other vaguely felt matters that had struck her outside observation and buried themselves in her flesh. Now they emerged and quested about her consciousness.

She was stretched on her back beneath the pear tree soaking in the alto chant of the visiting bees, the gold of the sun and the panting breath of the breeze when the inaudible voice of it all came to her. She saw a dust-bearing bee sink into the sanctum of a bloom; the thousand sister-calyxes arch to meet the love embrace and the ecstatic shiver of the tree from root to tiniest branch creaming in every blossom and frothing with delight. So this was a marriage! She had been summoned to behold a revelation. Then Janie felt a pain remorseless sweet that left her limp and languid.

After a while she got up from where she was and went over the little garden field entire. She was seeking confirmation of the voice and vision, and everywhere she found and acknowledged answers. A personal answer for all other creations except herself. She felt an answer seeking her, but where? When? How? She found herself at the kitchen door and stumbled inside. In the air of the room were flies tumbling and singing, marrying and giving in marriage. When she reached the narrow hallway she was reminded that her grandmother was home with a sick headache. She was lying across the bed asleep so Janie tipped on out of the front door. Oh to be a pear tree—*any* tree in bloom! With kissing bees singing of the beginning of the world! She was sixteen. She had glossy leaves and bursting buds and she wanted to struggle with life but it seemed to elude her. Where were the singing bees for her? Nothing on the place nor in her grandma's house answered her. She searched as much of the world as she could from the top of the front steps and then went on down to the front gate and leaned over to gaze up and down the road. Looking, waiting, breathing short with impatience. Waiting for the world to be made.

Through pollinated air she saw a glorious being coming up the road. In her former blindness she had known him as shiftless Johnny Taylor, tall and lean. That was before the golden dust of pollen had beglamored his rags and her eyes.

In the last stages of Nanny's sleep, she dreamed of voices. Voices far-off but persistent, and gradually coming nearer. Janie's voice. Janie talking in whispery snatches with a male voice she couldn't quite place. That brought her wide awake. She bolted upright and peered out of the window and saw Johnny Taylor lacerating her Janie with a kiss.

"Janie!"

The old woman's voice was so lacking in command and reproof, so full of crumbling dissolution,—that Janie half believed that Nanny had not seen her. So she extended herself outside of her dream and went inside of the house. That was the end of her childhood.

Nanny's head and face looked like the standing roots of some old tree that had been torn away by storm. Foundation of ancient power that no longer mattered. The cooling palma christi leaves that Janie had bound about her grandma's head with a white rag had wilted down and become part and parcel of the woman. Her eyes didn't bore and pierce. They diffused and melted Janie, the room and the world into one comprehension.

"Janie, youse uh 'oman, now, so—"

"Naw, Nanny, naw Ah ain't no real 'oman yet."

The thought was too new and heavy for Janie. She fought it away.

Nanny closed her eyes and nodded a slow, weary affirmation many times before she gave it voice.

"Yeah, Janie, youse got yo' womanhood on yuh. So Ah mout ez well tell yuh whut Ah been savin' up for uh spell. Ah wants to see you married right away."

"Me, married? Naw, Nanny, no ma'am! Whut Ah know 'bout uh husband?"

"Whut Ah seen just now is plenty for me, honey, Ah don't want no trashy nigger, no breath-and-britches, lak Johnny Taylor usin' yo' body to wipe his foots on."

Nanny's words made Janie's kiss across the gatepost seem like a manure pile after a rain.

"Look at me, Janie. Don't set dere wid yo' head hung down. Look at yo' ole grandma!" Her voice began snagging on the prongs of her feelings. "Ah don't want to be talkin' to you lak dis. Fact is Ah done been on mah knees to mah Maker many's de time askin' *please*—for Him not to make de burden too heavy for me to bear."

"Nanny, Ah just—Ah didn't mean nothin' bad."

"Dat's what makes me skeered. You don't mean no harm. You don't even know where harm is at. Ah'm ole now. Ah can't be always guidin' yo' feet from harm and danger. Ah wants to see you married right away."

"Who Ah'm goin' tuh marry off-hand lak dat? Ah don't know nobody."

"De Lawd will provide. He know Ah done bore de burden in de heat uh de day. Somebody done spoke to me 'bout you long time ago. Ah ain't said nothin' 'cause dat wasn't de way Ah placed you. Ah wanted yuh to school out and pick from a higher bush and a sweeter berry. But dat ain't yo' idea, Ah see."

"Nanny, who—who dat been askin' you for me?"

"Brother Logan Killicks. He's a good man, too."

"Naw, Nanny, no ma'am! Is dat whut he been hangin' round here for? He look like some ole skullhead in de grave yard."

The older woman sat bolt upright and put her feet to the floor, and thrust back the leaves from her face.

"So you don't want to marry off decent like, do yuh? You just wants to hug and kiss and feel around with first one man and then another, huh? You wants to make me suck de same sorrow yo' mama did, eh? Mah ole head ain't gray enough. Mah back ain't bowed enough to suit yuh!"

The vision of Logan Killicks was desecrating the pear tree, but Janie didn't know how to tell Nanny that. She merely hunched over and pouted at the floor.

"Janie."

"Yes, ma'am."

"You answer me when Ah speak. Don't you set dere poutin' wid me after all Ah done went through for you!"

She slapped the girl's face violently, and forced her head back so that their eyes met in struggle. With her hand uplifted for the second blow she saw the huge tear that welled up from Janie's heart and stood in each eye. She saw the terrible agony and the lips tightened down to hold back the cry and desisted. Instead she brushed back the heavy hair from Janie's face and stood there suffering and loving and weeping internally for both of them.

"Come to yo' Grandma, honey. Set in her lap lak yo' use tuh. Yo' Nanny wouldn't harm a hair uh yo' head. She don't want nobody else to do it neither if she kin help it. Honey, de white man is de ruler of everything as fur as Ah been able tuh find out. Maybe it's some place way off in de ocean where de black man is in power, but we don't know nothin' but what we see. So de white man throw down de load and tell de nigger man tuh pick it up. He pick it up because he have to, but he don't tote it. He hand it to his womenfolks. De nigger woman is de mule uh de world so fur as Ah can see. Ah been prayin' fuh it tuh be different wid you. Lawd, Lawd, Lawd!"

For a long time she sat rocking with the girl held tightly to her sunken breast. Janie's long legs dangled over one arm of the chair and the long braids of her hair swung low on the other side. Nanny half sung, half sobbed a running chant-prayer over the head of the weeping girl.

"Lawd have mercy! It was a long time on de way but Ah reckon it had to come. Oh Jesus! Do, Jesus! Ah done de best Ah could."

Finally, they both grew calm.

"Janie, how long you been 'lowin' Johnny Taylor to kiss you?"

"Only dis one time, Nanny. Ah don't love him at all. Whut made me do it is— oh, Ah don't know."

"Thank yuh, Massa Jesus."

"Ah ain't gointuh do it no mo', Nanny. Please don't make me marry Mr. Killicks."

"'Tain't Logan Killicks Ah wants you to have, baby, it's protection. Ah ain't git-tin' ole, honey. Ah'm *done* ole. One mornin' soon, now, de angel wid de sword is gointuh stop by here. De day and de hour is hid from me, but it won't be long. Ah ast de Lawd when you was uh infant in mah arms to let me stay here till you got grown. He done spared me to see de day. Mah daily prayer now is tuh let dese golden moments rolls on a few days longer till Ah see you safe in life."

"Lemme wait, Nanny, please, jus' a lil bit mo'."

"Don't think Ah don't feel wid you Janie, 'cause Ah do. Ah couldn't love yuh no more if Ah had uh felt yo' birth pains mahself. Fact uh de matter, Ah loves yuh a whole heap more'n Ah do yo' mama, de one Ah did birth. But you got to take in consideration you ain't no everyday chile like most of 'em. You ain't got no papa, you might jus' as well say no mama, for de good she do yuh. You ain't got nobody but me. And mah head is ole and tilted towards de grave. Neither can you stand alone by yo'self. De thought uh you bein' kicked around from pillar tuh post is uh hurtin' thing. Every tear you drop squeezes a cup uh blood outa mah heart. Ah got tuh try and do for you befo' mah head is cold."

A sobbing sigh burst out of Janie. The old woman answered her with little soothing pats of the hand.

"You know, honey, us colored folks is branches without roots and that makes things come round in queer ways. You in particular. Ah was born back due in slavery so it wasn't for me to fulfill my dreams of whut a woman oughta be and to do. Dat's one of de hold-backs of slavery. But nothing can't stop you from wishin'. You can't beat nobody down so low till you can rob 'em of they will. Ah didn't want to be used for a work-ox and a brood-sow and Ah didn't want mah daughter used dat way neither. It sho wasn't mah will for things to hap-pen lak they did. Ah even hated de way you was born. But, all de same Ah said thank God, Ah got another chance. Ah wanted to preach a great sermon about colored women sittin' on high, but they wasn't no pulpit for me. Freedom found me wid a baby daughter in mah arms, so Ah said Ah'd take a broom and a cook-pot and throw up a highway through de wilderness for her. She would expound what Ah felt. But somehow she got lost offa de highway and next thing Ah knowed here you was in de world. So whilst Ah was tendin' you of nights Ah said Ah'd save de text for you. Ah been waitin' a long time, Janie, but nothin' Ah been through ain't too much if you just take a stand on high ground lak Ah dreamed."

Old Nanny sat there rocking Janie like an infant and thinking back and back. Mind-pictures brought feelings, and feelings dragged out dramas from the hol-lows of her heart.

"Dat mornin' on de big plantation close to Savannah, a rider come in a gallop tellin' 'bout Sherman takin' Atlanta. Marse Robert's son had done been kilt at Chickamauga. So he grabbed his gun and straddled his best horse and went off wid de rest of de gray-headed men and young boys to drive de Yankees back into Tennessee.

"They was all cheerin' and cryin' and shoutin' for de men dat was ridin' off. Ah couldn't see nothin' cause yo' mama wasn't but a week old, and Ah was flat uh mah back. But pretty soon he let on he forgot somethin' and run into mah cabin and made me let down mah hair for de last time. He sorta wropped his hand in it, pulled mah big toe, lak he always done, and was gone after de rest lak lightnin'. Ah heard 'em give one last whoop for him. Then de big house and de quarters got sober and silent.

"It was de cool of de evenin' when Mistis come walkin' in mah door. She throwed de door wide open and stood dere lookin' at me outa her eyes and her face. Look lak she been livin' through uh hundred years in January without one day of spring. She come stood over me in de bed.

"'Nanny, Ah come to see that baby uh yourn.'

"Ah tried not to feel de breeze off her face, but it got so cold in dere dat Ah was freezin' to death under the kivvers. So Ah couldn't move right away lak Ah aimed to. But Ah knowed Ah had to make haste and do it.

" 'You better git dat kivver offa dat youngun and dat quick!' she clashed at me. 'Look lak you don't know who is Mistis on dis plantation, Madam. But Ah aims to show you.'

"By dat time I had done managed tuh unkivver mah baby enough for her to see de head and face.

" 'Nigger, whut's yo' baby doin' wid gray eyes and yaller hair?' She begin tuh slap mah jaws ever which a'way. Ah never felt the fust ones 'cause Ah wuz too busy gittin' de kivver back over mah chile. But dem last lick burnt me lak fire. Ah had too many feelin's tuh tell which one tuh follow so Ah didn't cry and Ah didn't do nothin' else. But then she kept on astin me how come mah baby look white. She asted me dat maybe twenty-five or thirty times, lak she got tuh sayin' dat and couldn't help herself. So Ah told her, 'Ah don't know nothin' but what Ah'm told tuh do, 'cause Ah ain't nothin' but uh nigger and uh slave.'

"Instead of pacifyin' her lak Ah thought, look lak she got madder. But Ah reckon she was tired and wore out 'cause she didn't hit me no more. She went to de foot of de bed and wiped her hands on her handksher. 'Ah wouldn't dirty mah hands on yuh. But first thing in de mornin' de overseer will take you to de whippin' post and tie you down on yo' knees and cut de hide offa yo' yaller back. One hundred lashes wid a raw-hide on yo' bare back. Ah'll have you whipped till de blood run down to yo' heels! Ah mean to count de licks mahself. And if it kills you Ah'll stand de loss. Anyhow, as soon as dat brat is a month old Ah'm going to sell it offa dis place.'

"She flounced on off and left her wintertime wid me. Ah knowed mah body wasn't healed, but Ah couldn't consider dat. In de black dark Ah wrapped mah baby de best Ah knowed how and made it to de swamp by de river. Ah knowed de place was full uh moccasins and other bitin' snakes, but Ah was more skeered uh whut was behind me. Ah hide in dere day and night and suckled de baby every time she start to cry, for fear somebody might hear her and Ah'd git found. Ah ain't sayin' uh friend or two didn't feel mah care. And den de Good Lawd seen to it dat Ah wasn't taken. Ah don't see how come mah milk didn't kill mah chile, wid me so skeered and worried all de time. De noise uh de owls skeered me; de limbs of dem cypress trees took to crawlin' and movin' round after dark, and two three times Ah heered panthers prowlin' round. But nothin' never hurt me 'cause de Lawd knowed how it was.

"Den, one night Ah heard de big guns boomin' lak thunder. It kept up all night long. And de next mornin' Ah could see uh big ship at a distance and a great stirrin' round. So Ah wrapped Leafy up in moss and fixed her good in a tree and picked mah way on down to de landin'. The men was all in blue, and Ah heard people say Sherman was comin' to meet de boats in Savannah, and all of us slaves was free. So Ah run got mah baby and got in quotation wid people and found a place Ah could stay.

"But it was a long time after dat befo' de Big Surrender at Richmond. Den de big bell ring in Atlanta and all de men in gray uniforms had to go to Moultrie, and bury their swords in de ground to show they was never to fight about slavery no mo'. So den we knowed we was free.

"Ah wouldn't marry nobody, though Ah could have uh heap uh times, cause Ah didn't want nobody mistreating mah baby. So Ah got with some good white people and come down here in West Florida to work and make de sun shine on both sides of de street for Leafy.

"Mah Madam help me wid her just lak she been doin' wid you. Ah put her in school when it got so it was a school to put her in. Ah was 'spectin' to make a school teacher outa her.

"But one day she didn't come home at de usual time and Ah waited and waited, but she never come all dat night. Ah took a lantern and went round askin' everybody but nobody ain't seen her. De next mornin' she come crawlin' in on her hands and knees. A sight to see. Dat school teacher had done hid her in de woods all night long, and he had done raped mah baby and run on off just before day.

"She was only seventeen, and somethin' lak dat to happen! Lawd a'mussy! Look lak Ah kin see it all over again. It was a long time before she was well, and by dat time we knowed you was on de way. And after you was born she took to drinkin' likker and stayin' out nights. Couldn't git her to stay here and nowhere else. Lawd knows where she is right now. She ain't dead, 'cause Ah'd know it by mah feelings, but sometimes Ah wish she was at rest.

"And, Janie, maybe it wasn't much, but Ah done de best Ah kin by you. Ah raked and scraped and bought dis lil piece uh land so you wouldn't have to stay in de white folks' yard and tuck yo' head befo' other chillun at school. Dat was all right when you was little. But when you got big enough to understand things, Ah wanted you to look upon yo'self. Ah don't want yo' feathers always crumpled by folks throwin' up things in yo' face. And Ah can't die easy thinkin' maybe de menfolks white or black is makin' a spit cup outa you: Have some sympathy fuh me. Put me down easy, Janie, Ah'm a cracked plate."

Chapter 3

There are years that ask questions and years that answer. Janie had had no chance to know things, so she had to ask. Did marriage end the cosmic loneliness of the unmated? Did marriage compel love like the sun the day?

In the few days to live before she went to Logan Killicks and his often-mentioned sixty acres, Janie asked inside of herself and out. She was back and forth to the pear tree continuously wondering and thinking. Finally out of Nanny's talk and her own conjectures she made a sort of comfort for herself. Yes, she would love Logan after they were married. She could see no way for it to come about, but Nanny and the old folks had said it, so it must be so. Husbands and wives always loved each other, and that was what marriage meant. It was just so. Janie felt glad of the thought, for then it wouldn't seem so destructive and mouldy. She wouldn't be lonely anymore.

Janie and Logan got married in Nanny's parlor of a Saturday evening with three cakes and big platters of fried rabbit and chicken. Everything to eat in abundance. Nanny and Mrs. Washburn had seen to that. But nobody put anything on the seat of Logan's wagon to make it ride glorious on the way to his house. It was a lonesome place like a stump in the middle of the woods where nobody had ever been. The house was absent of flavor, too. But anyhow Janie went on inside to wait for love to begin. The new moon had been up and down three times before she got worried in mind. Then she went to see Nanny in Mrs. Washburn's kitchen on the day for beaten biscuits.

Nanny beamed all out with gladness and made her come up to the bread board so she could kiss her.

"Lawd a'mussy, honey, Ah sho is glad tuh see mah chile! G'wan inside and let Mis' Washburn know youse heah. Umph! Umph! Umph! How is dat husband uh yourn?"

Janie didn't go in where Mrs. Washburn was. She didn't say anything to match up with Nanny's gladness either. She just fell on a chair with her hips and sat there. Between the biscuits and her beaming pride Nanny didn't notice for a minute. But after a while she found the conversation getting lonesome so she looked up at Janie.

"Whut's de matter, sugar? You ain't none too spry dis mornin'."

"Oh, nothin' much, Ah reckon. Ah come to get a lil information from you."

The old woman looked amazed, then gave a big clatter of laughter. "Don't tell me you done got knocked up already, less see—dis Saturday it's two month and two weeks."

"No'm, Ah don't think so anyhow." Janie blushed a little.

"You ain't got nothin' to be shamed of, honey, youse uh married 'oman. You got yo' lawful husband same as Mis' Washburn or anybody else!"

"Ah'm all right dat way. Ah *know* 'tain't nothin' dere."

"You and Logan been fussin'? Lawd, Ah know dat grass-gut, liver-lipted nigger ain't done took and beat mah baby already! Ah'll take a stick and salivate 'im!"

"No'm, he ain't even talked 'bout hittin' me. He says he never mean to lay de weight uh his hand on me in malice. He chops all de wood he think Ah wants and den he totes it inside de kitchen for me. Keeps both water buckets full."

"Humph! don't 'spect all dat tuh keep up. He ain't kissin' yo' mouf when he carry on over yuh lak dat. He's kissin' yo' foot and 'tain't in uh man tuh kiss foot long. Mouf kissin' is on uh equal and dat's natural but when dey got to bow down tuh love, dey soon straightens up."

"Yes'm."

"Well, if he do all dat whut you come in heah wid uh face long as mah arm for?"

"'Cause you told me Ah mus gointer love him, and, and Ah don't. Maybe if somebody was to tell me how, Ah could do it."

"You come heah wid yo' mouf full uh foolishness on uh busy day. Heah you got uh prop tuh lean on all yo' bawn days, and big protection, and everybody got tuh tip dey hat tuh you and call you Mis' Killicks, and you come worryin' me 'bout love."

"But Nanny, Ah wants to want him sometimes. Ah don't want him to do all de wantin'."

"If you don't want him, you sho oughta. Heah you is wid de onliest organ in town, amongst colored folks, in yo' parlor. Got a house bought and paid for and sixty acres uh land right on de big road and . . . Lawd have mussy! Dat's de very prong all us black women gits hung on. Dis love! Dat's just whut's got us uh pullin' and uh haulin' and sweatin' and doin' from can't see in de mornin' till can't see at night. Dat's how come de ole folks say dat bein' uh fool don't kill nobody. It jus' makes you sweat. Ah betcha you wants some dressed up dude dat got to look at de sole of his shoe everytime he cross de street tuh see whether he got enough leather dere tuh make it across. You can buy and sell such as dem wid what you got. In fact you can buy 'em and give 'em away."

"Ah ain't studyin' 'bout none of 'em. At de same time Ah ain't takin' dat ole land tuh heart neither. Ah could throw ten acres of it over de fence every day and never look back to see where it fell. Ah feel de same way 'bout Mr. Killicks too. Some folks never was meant to be loved and he's one of 'em."

"How come?"

"'Cause Ah hates de way his head is so long one way and so flat on de sides and dat pone uh fat back uh his neck."

"He never made his own head. You talk so silly."

"Ah don't keer who made it, Ah don't like de job. His belly is too big too, now, and his toe-nails look lak mule foots. And 'tain't nothin' in de way of him washin' his feet every evenin' before he comes tuh bed. 'Tain't nothin' tuh hinder him 'cause Ah places de water for him. Ah'd ruther be shot wid tacks than tuh turn over in de bed and stir up de air whilst he is in dere. He don't even never mention nothin' pretty."

She began to cry.

"Ah wants things sweet wid mah marriage lak when you sit under a pear tree and think. Ah . . ."

"'Tain't no use in you cryin', Janie. Grandma done been long uh few roads herself. But folks is meant to cry 'bout somethin' or other. Better leave things de way dey is. Youse young yet. No tellin' whut mout happen befo' you die. Wait awhile, baby. Yo' mind will change."

Nanny sent Janie along with a stern mien, but she dwindled all the rest of the day as she worked. And when she gained the privacy of her own little shack she stayed on her knees so long she forgot she was there herself. There is a basin in the mind where words float around on thought and thought on sound and sight. Then there is a depth of thought untouched by words, and deeper still a gulf of formless feelings untouched by thought. Nanny entered this infinity of conscious pain again on her old knees. Towards morning she muttered, "Lawd, you know mah heart. Ah done de best Ah could do. De rest is left to you." She scuffled up from her knees and fell heavily across the bed. A month later she was dead.

So Janie waited a bloom time, and a green time and an orange time. But when the pollen again gilded the sun and sifted down on the world she began to stand around the gate and expect things. What things? She didn't know exactly. Her breath was gusty and short. She knew things that nobody had ever told her. For instance, the words of the trees and the wind. She often spoke to falling seeds and said, "Ah hope you fall on soft ground," because she had heard seeds saying that to each other as they passed. She knew the world was a stallion rolling in the blue pasture of ether. She knew that God tore down the old world every evening and built a new one by sun-up. It was wonderful to see it take form with the sun and emerge from the gray dust of its making. The familiar people and things had failed her so she hung over the gate and looked up the road towards way off. She knew now that marriage did not make love. Janie's first dream was dead, so she became a woman.

Chapter 4

Long before the year was up, Janie noticed that her husband had stopped talking in rhymes to her. He had ceased to wonder at her long black hair and finger it. Six months back he had told her, "If Ah kin haul de wood heah and chop it fuh yuh, look lak you oughta be able tuh tote it inside. Mah fust wife never bothered me 'bout choppin' no wood nohow. She'd grab dat ax and sling chips lak uh man. You done been spoilt rotten."

So Janie had told him, "Ah'm just as stiff as you is stout. If you can stand not to chop and tote wood Ah reckon you can stand not to git no dinner. 'Scuse mah freezolity, Mist' Killicks, but Ah don't mean to chop de first chip."

"Aw you know Ah'm gwine chop de wood fuh yuh. Even if you is stingy as you can be wid me. Yo' Grandma and me myself done spoilt yuh now, and Ah reckon Ah have tuh keep on wid it."

One morning soon he called her out of the kitchen to the barn. He had the mule all saddled at the gate.

"Looka heah, LilBit, help me out some. Cut up dese seed taters fuh me. Ah got tuh go step off a piece."

"Where you goin'?"

"Over tuh Lake City tuh see uh man about uh mule."

"Whut you need two mules fuh? Lessen you aims to swap off dis one."

"Naw, Ah needs two mules dis yeah. Taters is goin' tuh be taters in de fall. Bringin' big prices. Ah aims tuh run two plows, and dis man Ah'm talkin' 'bout is got uh mule all gentled up so even uh woman kin handle 'im."

Logan held his wad of tobacco real still in his jaw like a thermometer of his feelings while he studied Janie's face and waited for her to say something.

"So Ah thought Ah mout as well go see." He tagged on and swallowed to kill time but Janie said nothing except, "Ah'll cut de p'taters fuh yuh. When yuh comin' back?"

"Don't know exactly. Round dust dark Ah reckon. It's uh sorta long trip—specially if Ah hafter lead one on de way back."

When Janie had finished indoors she sat down in the barn with the potatoes. But springtime reached her in there so she moved everything to a place in the yard where she could see the road. The noon sun filtered through the leaves of the fine oak tree where she sat and made lacy patterns on the ground. She had been there a long time when she heard whistling coming down the road.

It was a cityfied, stylish dressed man with his hat set at an angle that didn't belong in these parts. His coat was over his arm, but he didn't need it to represent his clothes. The shirt with the silk sleeveholders was dazzling enough for the world. He whistled, mopped his face and walked like he knew where he was going. He was a seal-brown color but he acted like Mr. Washburn or somebody like that to Janie. Where would such a man be coming from and where was he going? He didn't look her way nor no other way except straight ahead, so Janie ran to the pump and jerked the handle hard while she pumped. It made a loud noise and also made her heavy hair fall down. So he stopped and looked hard, and then he asked her for a cool drink of water.

Janie pumped it off until she got a good look at the man. He talked friendly while he drank.

Joe Starks was the name, yeah Joe Starks from in and through Georgy. Been workin' for white folks all his life. Saved up some money—round three hundred dollars, yes indeed, right here in his pocket. Kept hearin' 'bout them buildin' a new state down heah in Floridy and sort of wanted to come. But he was makin' money where he was. But when he heard all about 'em makin' a town all outa colored folks, he knowed dat was de place he wanted to be. He had always wanted to be a big voice, but de white folks had all de sayso where he come from and everywhere else, exceptin' dis place dat colored folks was buildin' theirselves. Dat was right too. De man dat built things oughta boss it. Let colored folks build things too if dey wants to crow over somethin'. He was glad he had his money all saved up. He meant to git dere whilst de town wuz yet a baby. He meant to buy in big. It had always been his wish and desire to be a big voice and he had to live nearly thirty years to find a chance. Where was Janie's papa and mama?

"Dey dead, Ah reckon. Ah wouldn't know 'bout 'em 'cause mah Grandma raised me. She dead too."

"She dead too! Well, who's lookin' after a lil girl-chile lak you?"

"Ah'm married."

"You married? You ain't hardly old enough to be weaned. Ah betcha you still craves sugar-tits, doncher?"

"Yeah, and Ah makes and sucks 'em when de notion strikes me. Drinks sweeten' water too."

"Ah loves dat mahself. Never specks to get too old to enjoy syrup sweeten' water when it's cools and nice."

"Us got plenty syrup in de barn. Ribbon-cane syrup. If you so desires—"

"Where yo' husband at, Mis' er-er."

"Mah name is Janie Mae Killicks since Ah got married. Useter be name Janie Mae Crawford. Mah husband is gone tuh buy a mule fuh me tuh plow. He left me cuttin' up seed p'taters."

"You behind a plow! You ain't got no mo' business wid uh plow than uh hog is got wid uh holiday! You ain't got no business cuttin' up no seed p'taters neither. A pretty doll-baby lak you is made to sit on de front porch and rock and fan yo'self and eat p'taters dat other folks plant just special for you."

Janie laughed and drew two quarts of syrup from the barrel and Joe Starks pumped the water bucket full of cool water. They sat under the tree and talked. He was going on down to the new part of Florida, but no harm to stop and chat. He later decided he needed a rest anyway. It would do him good to rest a week or two.

Every day after that they managed to meet in the scrub oaks across the road and talk about when he would be a big ruler of things with her reaping the benefits. Janie pulled back a long time because he did not represent sun-up and pollen and blooming trees, but he spoke for far horizon. He spoke for change and chance. Still she hung back. The memory of Nanny was still powerful and strong.

"Janie, if you think Ah aims to tole you off and make a dog outa you, youse wrong. Ah wants to make a wife outa you."

"You mean dat, Joe?"

"De day you puts yo' hand in mine, Ah wouldn't let de sun go down on us single. Ah'm uh man wid principles. You ain't never knowed what it was to be treated lak a lady and Ah wants to be de one tuh show yuh. Call me Jody lak you do sometime."

"Jody," she smiled up at him, "but s'posin'—"

"Leave de s'posin' and everything else to me. Ah'll be down dis road uh little after sunup tomorrow mornin' to wait for you. You come go wid me. Den all de rest of yo' natural life you kin live lak you oughta. Kiss me and shake yo' head. When you do dat, yo' plentiful hair breaks lak day."

Janie debated the matter that night in bed.

"Logan, you 'sleep?"

"If Ah wuz, you'd be done woke me up callin' me."

"Ah wuz thinkin' real hard about us; about you and me."

"It's about time. Youse powerful independent around here sometime considerin'."

"Considerin' whut for instance?"

"Considerin' youse born in a carriage 'thout no top to it, and yo' mama and you bein' born and raised in de white folks back-yard."

"You didn't say all dat when you wuz begging Nanny for me to marry you."

"Ah thought you would 'preciate good treatment. Thought Ah'd take and make somethin' outa yuh. You think youse white folks by de way you act."

"S'posin' Ah wuz to run off and leave yuh sometime."

There! Janie had put words in his held-in fears. She might run off sure enough. The thought put a terrible ache in Logan's body, but he thought it best to put on scorn.

"Ah'm gettin' sleepy, Janie. Let's don't talk no mo'. 'Tain't too many mens would trust yuh, knowin' yo' folks lak dey do."

"Ah might take and find somebody dat did trust me and leave yuh."

"Shucks! 'Tain't no mo' fools lak me. A whole lot of mens will grin in yo' face, but dey ain't gwine tuh work and feed yuh. You won't git far and you won't be long, when dat big gut reach over and grab dat little one, you'll be too glad to come back here."

"You don't take nothin' to count but sow-belly and cornbread."

"Ah'm sleepy. Ah don't aim to worry mah gut into a fiddle-string wid no s'posin'." He flopped over resentful in his agony and pretended sleep. He hoped that he had hurt her as she had hurt him.

Janie got up with him the next morning and had the breakfast halfway done when he bellowed from the barn.

"Janie!" Logan called harshly. "Come help me move dis manure pile befo' de sun gits hot. You don't take a bit of interest in dis place. 'Tain't no use in foolin' round in dat kitchen all day long."

Janie walked to the door with the pan in her hand still stirring the cornmeal dough and looked towards the barn. The sun from ambush was threatening the world with red daggers, but the shadows were gray and solid-looking around the barn. Logan with his shovel looked like a black bear doing some clumsy dance on his hind legs.

"You don't need mah help out dere, Logan. Youse in yo' place and Ah'm in mine."

"You ain't got no particular place. It's wherever Ah need yuh. Git uh move on yuh, and dat quick."

"Mah mamma didn't tell me Ah wuz born in no hurry. So whut business Ah got rushin' now? Anyhow dat ain't whut youse mad about. Youse mad 'cause Ah don't fall down and wash-up dese sixty acres uh ground yuh got. You ain't done me no favor by marryin' me. And if dat's what you call yo'self doin', Ah don't thank yuh for it. Youse mad 'cause Ah'm tellin' yuh whut you already knowed."

Logan dropped his shovel and made two or three clumsy steps towards the house, then stopped abruptly.

"Don't you change too many words wid me dis mawnin', Janie, do Ah'll take and change ends wid yuh! Heah, Ah just as good as take you out de white folks' kitchen and set you down on yo' royal diasticutis[1] and you take and low-rate me! Ah'll take holt uh dat ax and come in dere and kill yuh! You better dry up in dere! Ah'm too honest and hard-workin' for anybody in yo' family, dat's de reason you don't want me!" The last sentence was half a sob and half a cry. "Ah guess some low-lifed nigger is grinnin' in yo' face and lyin' tuh yuh. God damn yo' hide!"

Janie turned from the door without answering, and stood still in the middle of the floor without knowing it. She turned wrongside out just standing there and feeling. When the throbbing calmed a little she gave Logan's speech a hard thought and placed it beside other things she had seen and heard. When she had finished with that she dumped the dough on the skillet and smoothed it over with her hand. She wasn't even angry. Logan was accusing her of her mamma, her grandmama and her feelings, and she couldn't do a thing about any of it. The sow-belly in the pan needed turning. She flipped it over and shoved it back. A little cold water in the coffee pot to settle it. Turned the hoe-cake with a plate and then made a little laugh. What was she losing so much time for? A feeling of sudden newness and change came over her. Janie hurried out of the front gate and turned south. Even if Joe was not there waiting for her, the change was bound to do her good.

The morning road air was like a new dress. That made her feel the apron tied around her waist. She untied it and flung it on a low bush beside the road and walked on, picking flowers and making a bouquet. After that she came to where Joe Starks was waiting for her with a hired rig. He was very solemn and helped her to the seat beside him. With him on it, it sat like some high, ruling chair. From now on until death she was going to have flower dust and springtime sprinkled over everything. A bee for her bloom. Her old thoughts were going to come in handy now, but new words would have to be made and said to fit them.

"Green Cove Springs," he told the driver. So they were married there before sundown, just like Joe had said. With new clothes of silk and wool.

They sat on the boarding house porch and saw the sun plunge into the same crack in the earth from which the night emerged.

---

[1]diasticutis mean "buttocks," according to the Notes section of ed. Cheryl Wall, *Novels and Stories*, Zora Neale Hurston, New York: Library of America, 1995.

Chapter 5

On the train the next day, Joe didn't make many speeches with rhymes to her, but he bought her the best things the butcher had, like apples and a glass lantern full of candies. Mostly he talked about plans for the town when he got there. They were bound to need somebody like him. Janie took a lot of looks at him and she was proud of what she saw. Kind of portly like rich white folks. Strange trains, and people and places didn't scare him neither. Where they got off the train at Maitland he found a buggy to carry them over to the colored town right away.

It was early in the afternoon when they got there, so Joe said they must walk over the place and look around. They locked arms and strolled from end to end of the town. Joe noted the scant dozen of shame-faced houses scattered in the sand and palmetto roots and said, "God, they call this a town? Why, 'tain't nothing but a raw place in de woods."

"It is a whole heap littler than Ah thought." Janie admitted her disappointment.

"Just like Ah thought," Joe said. "A whole heap uh talk and nobody doin' nothin'. I god, where's de Mayor?" he asked somebody. "Ah want tuh speak wid de Mayor."

Two men who were sitting on their shoulderblades under a huge live oak tree almost sat upright at the tone of his voice. They stared at Joe's face, his clothes and his wife.

"Where y'all come from in sich uh big haste?" Lee Coker asked.

"Middle Georgy," Starks answered briskly. "Joe Starks is mah name, from in and through Georgy."

"You and yo' daughter goin' tuh join wid us in fellowship?" the other reclining figure asked. "Mighty glad tuh have yuh. Hicks is the name. Guv'nor Amos Hicks from Buford, South Carolina. Free, single, disengaged."

"I god, Ah ain't nowhere near old enough to have no grown daughter. This here is mah wife."

Hicks sank back and lost interest at once.

"Where is de Mayor?" Starks persisted. "Ah wants tuh talk wid *him*."

"Youse uh mite too previous for dat," Coker told him. "Us ain't got none yit."

"Ain't got no Mayor! Well, who tells y'all what to do?"

"Nobody. Everybody's grown. And then agin, Ah reckon us just ain't thought about it. Ah know Ah ain't."

"Ah did think about it one day," Hicks said dreamily, "but then Ah forgot it and ain't thought about it since then."

"No wonder things ain't no better," Joe commented. "Ah'm buyin' in here, and buyin' in big. Soon's we find some place to sleep tonight us menfolks got to call people together and form a committee. Then we can get things movin' round here."

"Ah kin point yuh where yuh kin sleep," Hicks offered. "Man got his house done built and his wife ain't come yet."

Starks and Janie moved on off in the direction indicated with Hicks and Coker boring into their backs with looks.

"Dat man talks like a section foreman," Coker commented. "He's mighty compellment."

"Shucks!" said Hicks. "Mah britches is just as long as his. But dat wife uh hisn! Ah'm uh son of uh Combunction if Ah don't go tuh Georgy and git me one just like her."

"Whut wid?"

"Wid mah talk, man."

"It takes money tuh feed pretty women. Dey gits uh lavish uh talk."

"Not lak mine. Dey loves to hear me talk because dey can't understand it. Mah co-talkin' is too deep. Too much co to it."

"Umph!"

"You don't believe me, do yuh? You don't know de women Ah kin git to mah command."

"Umph!"

"You ain't never seen me when Ah'm out pleasurin' and givin' pleasure."

"Umph!"

"It's uh good thing he married her befo' she seen me. Ah kin be some trouble when Ah take uh notion."

"Umph!"

"Ah'm uh bitch's baby round lady people."

"Ah's much ruther see all dat than to hear 'bout it. Come on less go see whut he gointuh do 'bout dis town."

They got up and sauntered over to where Starks was living for the present. Already the town had found the strangers. Joe was on the porch talking to a small group of men. Janie could be seen through the bedroom window getting settled. Joe had rented the house for a month. The men were all around him, and he was talking to them by asking questions.

"Whut is de real name of de place?"

"Some say West Maitland and some say Eatonville. Dat's 'cause Cap'n Eaton give us some land along wid Mr. Laurence. But Cap'n Eaton give de first piece."

"How much did they give?"

"Oh 'bout fifty acres."

"How much is y'all got now?"

"Oh 'bout de same."

"Dat ain't near enough. Who owns de land joining on to whut yuh got?"

"Cap'n Eaton."

"Where *is* dis Cap'n Eaton?"

"Over dere in Maitland, 'ceptin' when he go visitin' or somethin'."

"Lemme speak to mah wife a minute and Ah'm goin' see de man. You cannot have no town without some land to build it on. Y'all ain't got enough here to cuss a cat on without gittin' yo' mouf full of hair."

"He ain't got no mo' land tuh give away. Yuh needs plenty money if yuh wants any mo'."

"Ah specks to pay him."

The idea was funny to them and they wanted to laugh. They tried hard to hold it in, but enough incredulous laughter burst out of their eyes and leaked from the corners of their mouths to inform anyone of their thoughts. So Joe walked off abruptly. Most of them went along to show him the way and to be there when his bluff was called.

Hicks didn't go far. He turned back to the house as soon as he felt he wouldn't be missed from the crowd and mounted the porch.

"Evenin', Miz Starks."

"Good evenin'."

"You reckon you gointuh like round here?"

"Ah reckon so."

"Anything *Ah* kin do tuh help out, why you kin call on me."

"Much obliged."

There was a long dead pause. Janie was not jumping at her chance like she ought to. Look like she didn't hardly know he was there. She needed waking up.

"Folks must be mighty close-mouthed where you come from."

"Dat's right. But it must be different at yo' home."

He was a long time thinking but finally he saw and stumbled down the steps with a surly "'Bye."

"Good bye."

That night Coker asked him about it.

"Ah saw yuh when yuh ducked back tuh Starks' house. Well, how didju make out?"

"Who, me? Ah ain't been near de place, man. Ah been down tuh de lake tryin' tuh ketch me uh fish."

"Umph!"

"Dat 'oman ain't so awfully pretty no how when yuh take de second look at her. Ah had to sorta pass by de house on de way back and seen her good. 'Tain't nothin' to her 'ceptin' dat long hair."

"Umph!"

"And anyhow, Ah done took uh likin' tuh de man. Ah wouldn't harm him at all. She ain't half ez pretty ez uh gal Ah run off and left up in South Cal'lina."

"Hicks, Ah'd git mad and say you wuz lyin' if Ah didn't know yuh so good. You just talkin' to consolate yo'self by word of mouth. You got uh willin' mind, but youse too light behind. A whole heap uh men seen de same thing you seen but they got better sense than you. You oughta know you can't take no 'oman lak dat from no man lak him. A man dat ups and buys two hundred acres uh land at one whack and pays cash for it."

"Naw! He didn't buy it sho nuff?"

"He sho did. Come off wid de papers in his pocket. He done called a meetin' on his porch tomorrow. Ain't never seen no sich uh colored man befo' in all mah bawn days. He's gointuh put up uh store and git uh post office from de Goven'ment."

That irritated Hicks and he didn't know why. He was the average mortal. It troubled him to get used to the world one way and then suddenly have it turn different. He wasn't ready to think of colored people in post offices yet. He laughed boisterously.

"Y'all let dat stray darky tell y'all any ole lie! Uh colored man sittin' up in uh post office!" He made an obscene sound.

"He's liable tuh do it too, Hicks. Ah hope so anyhow. Us colored folks is too envious of one 'nother. Dat's how come us don't git no further than us do. Us talks about de white man keepin' us down! Shucks! He don't have tuh. Us keeps our own selves down."

"Now who said Ah didn't want de man tuh git us uh post office? He kin be de king uh Jerusalem fuh all Ah keer. Still and all, 'tain't no use in telling lies just 'cause uh heap uh folks don't know no better. Yo' common sense oughta tell yuh de white folks ain't goin' tuh 'low him tuh run no post office."

"Dat we don't know, Hicks. He say he kin and Ah b'lieve he know whut he's talkin' 'bout. Ah reckon if colored folks got they own town they kin have post offices and whatsoever they please, regardless. And then agin, Ah don't speck de white folks way off yonder give uh damn. Less us wait and see."

"Oh, Ah'm waitin' all right. Specks tuh keep on waitin' till hell freeze over."

"Aw, git reconciled! Dat woman don't want you. You got tuh learn dat all de women in de world ain't been brought up on no teppentine still, and no saw-mill camp. There's some women dat jus' ain't for you tuh broach. You can't git *her* wid no fish sandwich."

They argued a bit more then went on to the house where Joe was and found him in his shirt-sleeves, standing with his legs wide apart, asking questions and smoking a cigar.

"Where's de closest saw-mill?" He was asking Tony Taylor.

"'Bout seben miles goin' t'wards Apopka," Tony told him. "Thinkin' 'bout buildin' right away?"

"I god, yeah. But not de house Ah specks tuh live in. Dat kin wait till Ah make up mah mind where Ah wants it located. Ah figgers we all needs uh store in uh big hurry."

"Uh store?" Tony shouted in surprise.

"Yeah, uh store right heah in town wid everything in it you needs. 'Tain't uh bit uh use in everybody proagin'[2] way over tuh Maitland tuh buy uh little meal and flour when they could git it right heah."

"Dat would be kinda nice, Brother Starks, since you mention it."

"I god, course it would! And then agin uh store is good in other ways. Ah got tuh have a place tuh be at when folks comes tuh buy land. And furthermo' everything is got tuh have uh center and uh heart tuh it, and uh town ain't no different from nowhere else. It would be natural fuh de store tuh be meetin' place fuh de town."

"Dat sho is de truth, now."

"Oh, we'll have dis town all fixed up tereckly. Don't miss bein' at de meetin' tuhmorrow."

Just about time for the committee meeting called to meet on his porch next day, the first wagon load of lumber drove up and Jody went to show them where to put it. Told Janie to hold the committee there until he got back, he didn't want to miss them, but he meant to count every foot of that lumber before it touched

---

[2]proagin' means "to prowl, poke, or search about, to forage, to hunt out, to progress," according to the Notes section of ed. Cheryl Wall, *Novels and Stories*, Zora Neale Hurston, New York: Library of America, 1995.

the ground. He could have saved his breath and Janie could have kept right on with what she was doing. In the first place everybody was late in coming; then the next thing as soon as they heard where Jody was, they kept right on up there where the new lumber was rattling off the wagon and being piled under the big live oak tree. So that's where the meeting was held with Tony Taylor acting as chairman and Jody doing all the talking. A day was named for roads and they all agreed to bring axes and things like that and chop out two roads running each way. That applied to everybody except Tony and Coker. They could carpenter, so Jody hired them to go to work on his store bright and soon the next morning. Jody himself would be busy driving around from town to town telling people about Eatonville and drumming up citizens to move there.

Janie was astonished to see the money Jody had spent for the land come back to him so fast. Ten new families bought lots and moved to town in six weeks. It all looked too big and rushing for her to keep track of. Before the store had a complete roof, Jody had canned goods piled on the floor and was selling so much he didn't have time to go off on his talking tours. She had her first taste of presiding over it the day it was complete and finished. Jody told her to dress up and stand in the store all that evening. Everybody was coming sort of fixed up, and he didn't mean for nobody else's wife to rank with her. She must look on herself as the bell-cow, the other women were the gang. So she put on one of her bought dresses and went up the new-cut road all dressed in wine-colored red. Her silken ruffles rustled and muttered about her. The other women had on percale and calico with here and there a headrag among the older ones.

Nobody was buying anything that night. They didn't come there for that. They had come to make a welcome. So Joe knocked in the head of a barrel of soda crackers and cut some cheese.

"Everybody come right forward and make merry. I god, it's mah treat." Jody gave one of his big heh heh laughs and stood back. Janie dipped up the lemonade like he told her. A big tin cup full for everybody. Tony Taylor felt so good when it was all gone that he felt to make a speech.

"Ladies and gent'men, we'se come tuhgether and gethered heah tuh welcome tuh our midst one who has seen fit tuh cast in his lot amongst us. He didn't just come hisself neither. He have seen fit tuh bring his, er, er, de light uh his home, dat is his wife amongst us also. She couldn't look no mo' better and no nobler if she wuz de queen uh England. It's uh pledger fuh her tuh be heah amongst us. Brother Starks, we welcomes you and all dat you have seen fit tuh bring amongst us—yo' belov-ed wife, yo' store, yo' land—"

A big-mouthed burst of laughter cut him short.

"Dat'll do, Tony," Lige Moss yelled out. "Mist' Starks is uh smart man, we'se all willin' tuh acknowledge tuh dat, but de day he comes waggin' down de road wid two hund'ed acres uf land over his shoulder, Ah wants tuh be dere tuh see it."

Another big blow-out of a laugh. Tony was a little peeved at having the one speech of his lifetime ruined like that.

"All y'all know whut wuz meant. Ah don't see how come—"

"'Cause you jump up tuh make speeches and don't know how," Lige said.

"Ah wuz speakin' jus' all right befo' you stuck yo' bill in."

"Naw, you wuzn't, Tony. Youse way outa jurisdiction. You can't welcome uh man and his wife 'thout you make comparison about Isaac and Rebecca at de well, else it don't show de love between 'em if you don't."

Everybody agreed that that was right. It was sort of pitiful for Tony not to know he couldn't make a speech without saying that. Some tittered at his ignorance. So Tony said testily, "If all them dat's goin-tuh cut de monkey is done cut it and through wid, we'll thank Brother Starks fuh a respond."

So Joe Starks and his cigar took the center of the floor.

"Ah thanks you all for yo' kind welcome and for extendin' tuh me de right hand uh fellowship. Ah kin see dat dis town is full uh union and love. Ah means tuh put mah hands tuh de plow heah, and strain every nerve tuh make dis our town de metropolis uh de state. So maybe Ah better tell yuh in case you don't know dat if we expect tuh move on, us got tuh incorporate lak every other town. Us got tuh incorporate, and us got tuh have uh mayor, if things is tuh be done and done right. Ah welcome you all on behalf uh me and mah wife tuh dis store and tuh de other things tuh come. Amen."

Tony led the loud hand-clapping and was out in the center of the floor when it stopped.

"Brothers and sisters, since us can't never expect tuh better our choice, Ah move dat we make Brother Starks our Mayor until we kin see further."

"Second dat motion!!!" It was everybody talking at once, so it was no need of putting it to a vote.

"And now we'll listen tuh uh few words uh encouragement from Mrs. Mayor Starks."

The burst of applause was cut short by Joe taking the floor himself.

"Thank yuh fuh yo' compliments, but mah wife don't know nothin' 'bout no speech-makin'. Ah never married her for nothin' lak dat. She's uh woman and her place is in de home."

Janie made her face laugh after a short pause, but it wasn't too easy. She had never thought of making a speech, and didn't know if she cared to make one at all. It must have been the way Joe spoke out without giving her a chance to say anything one way or another that took the bloom off of things. But anyway, she went down the road behind him that night feeling cold. He strode along invested with his new dignity, thought and planned out loud, unconscious of her thoughts.

"De mayor of uh town lak dis can't lay round home too much. De place needs buildin' up. Janie, Ah'll git hold uh somebody tuh help out in de store and you kin look after things whilst Ah drum up things otherwise."

"Oh Jody, Ah can't do nothin' wid no store lessen youse there. Ah could maybe come in and help you when things git rushed, but—"

"I god, Ah don't see how come yuh can't. 'Tain't nothin' atall tuh hinder yuh if yuh got uh thimble full uh sense. You got tuh. Ah got too much else on mah hands as Mayor. Dis town needs some light right now."

"Unh hunh, it *is* uh little dark right long heah."

"'Course it is. 'Tain't no use in scufflin' over all dese stumps and roots in de dark. Ah'll call uh meetin' 'bout de dark and de roots right away. Ah'll sit on dis case first thing."

The very next day with money out of his own pocket he sent off to Sears, Roebuck and Company for the street lamp and told the town to meet the following Thursday night to vote on it. Nobody had ever thought of street lamps and some of them said it was a useless notion. They went so far as to vote against it, but the majority ruled.

But the whole town got vain over it after it came. That was because the Mayor didn't just take it out of the crate and stick it up on a post. He unwrapped it and had it wiped off carefully and put it up on a showcase for a week for everybody to see. Then he set a time for the lighting and sent word all around Orange County for one and all to come to the lamplighting. He sent men out to the swamp to cut the finest and the straightest cypress post they could find, and kept on sending them back to hunt another one until they found one that pleased him. He had talked to the people already about the hospitality of the occasion.

"Y'all know we can't invite people to our town just dry long so. I god, naw. We got tuh feed 'em something, and 'tain't nothin' people laks better'n barbecue. Ah'll give one whole hawg mah ownself. Seem lak all de rest uh y'all put tuhgether oughta be able tuh scrape up two mo'. Tell yo' womenfolks tuh do 'round 'bout some pies and cakes and sweet p'tater pone."

That's the way it went, too. The women got together the sweets and the men looked after the meats. The day before the lighting, they dug a big hole in back of the store and filled it full of oak wood and burned it down to a glowing bed of coals. It took them the whole night to barbecue the three hogs. Hambo and Pearson had full charge while the others helped out with turning the meat now and then while Hambo swabbed it all over with the sauce. In between times they told stories, laughed and told more stories and sung songs. They cut all sorts of capers and whiffed the meat as it slowly came to perfection with the seasoning penetrating to the bone. The younger boys had to rig up the saw-horses with boards for the women to use as tables. Then it was after sun-up and everybody not needed went home to rest up for the feast.

By five o'clock the town was full of every kind of a vehicle and swarming with people. They wanted to see that lamp lit at dusk. Near the time, Joe assembled everybody in the street before the store and made a speech.

"Folkses, de sun is goin' down. De Sun-maker brings it up in de mornin', and de Sun-maker sends it tuh bed at night. Us poor weak humans can't do nothin' tuh hurry it up nor to slow it down. All we can do, if we want any light after de settin' or befo' de risin', is tuh make some light ourselves. So dat's how come lamps was made. Dis evenin' we'se all assembled heah tuh light uh lamp. Dis occasion is something for us all tuh remember tuh our dyin' day. De first street lamp in uh colored town. Lift yo' eyes and gaze on it. And when Ah touch de match tuh dat lamp-wick let de light penetrate inside of yuh, and let it shine, let it shine, let it shine. Brother Davis, lead us in a word uh prayer. Ask uh blessin' on dis town in uh most particular manner."

While Davis chanted a traditional prayer-poem with his own variations, Joe mounted the box that had been placed for the purpose and opened the brazen door of the lamp. As the word Amen was said, he touched the lighted match to the wick, and Mrs. Bogle's alto burst out in:

We'll walk in de light, de beautiful light
Come where the dew drops of mercy shine bright
Shine all around us by day and by night
Jesus, the light of the world.

They, all of them, all of the people took it up and sung it over and over until it was wrung dry, and no further innovations of tone and tempo were conceivable. Then they hushed and ate barbecue.

When it was all over that night in bed Jody asked Janie, "Well, honey, how yuh lak bein' Mrs. Mayor?"

"It's all right Ah reckon, but don't yuh think it keeps us in uh kinda strain?"

"Strain? You mean de cookin' and waitin' on folks?"

"Naw, Jody, it jus' looks lak it keeps us in some way we ain't natural wid one 'nother. You'se always off talkin' and fixin' things, and Ah feels lak Ah'm jus' markin' time. Hope it soon gits over."

"Over, Janie? I god, Ah ain't even started good. Ah told you in de very first beginnin' dat Ah aimed tuh be uh big voice. You oughta be glad, 'cause dat makes uh big woman outa you."

A feeling of coldness and fear took hold of her. She felt far away from things and lonely.

Janie soon began to feel the impact of awe and envy against her sensibilities. The wife of the Mayor was not just another woman as she had supposed. She slept with authority and so she was part of it in the town mind. She couldn't get but so close to most of them in spirit. It was especially noticeable after Joe had forced through a town ditch to drain the street in front of the store. They had murmured hotly about slavery being over, but every man filled his assignment.

There was something about Joe Starks that cowed the town. It was not because of physical fear. He was no fist fighter. His bulk was not even imposing as men go. Neither was it because he was more literate than the rest. Something else made men give way before him. He had a bow-down command in his face, and every step he took made the thing more tangible.

Take for instance that new house of his. It had two stories with porches, with bannisters and such things. The rest of the town looked like servants' quarters surrounding the "big house." And different from everybody else in the town he put off moving in until it had been painted, in and out. And look at the way he painted it—a gloaty, sparkly white. The kind of promenading white that the houses of Bishop Whipple, W. B. Jackson and the Vanderpool's wore. It made the village feel funny talking to him—just like he was anybody else. Then there was the matter of the spittoons. No sooner was he all set as the Mayor—post master—landlord—storekeeper, than he bought a desk like Mr. Hill or Mr. Galloway over in Maitland with one of those swing-around chairs to it. What with him biting down on cigars and saving his breath on talk and swinging round in that chair, it weakened people. And then he spit in that gold-looking vase that anybody else would have been glad to put on their front-room table. Said it was a spittoon just like his used-to-be bossman used to have in his bank up there in Atlanta. Didn't have to get up and go to the door every time he had to spit. Didn't spit on his floor neither. Had that golded-up spitting pot right handy. But he went further than that. He bought a little lady-size spitting for Janie to spit in. Had it right in the parlor with little sprigs of flowers painted all around the sides. It took people by surprise because most of the women dipped snuff and of course had a spit-cup in the house. But how could they know up-to-date folks was spitting in flowery little things like that? It sort of made the rest of them feel that they had been taken advantage of. Like things had been kept from them. Maybe more things in the world besides spitting pots had been hid from them, when they wasn't told no better than to spit in tomato cans. It was bad enough for white people, but when one of your own color could be so different it put you on a wonder. It was like seeing your sister turn into a 'gator. A familiar strangeness. You keep seeing your sister in the 'gator and the 'gator in your sister, and you'd rather not. There was no doubt that the town respected him and even admired him in a way. But any man who walks in the way of power and property is bound to meet hate. So when speakers stood up when the occasion demanded and said "Our beloved Mayor," it was one of those statements that everybody says but nobody actually believes like "God is everywhere." It was just a handle to wind up the tongue with. As time went on and the benefits he had conferred upon the town receded in time they sat on his store porch while he was busy inside and discussed him. Like one day after he caught Henry Pitts with a wagon load of his ribbon cane and took the cane away from Pitts and made him leave town. Some of them thought Starks ought not to have done that. He had so much cane and everything else. But they didn't say that while Joe Starks was on the porch. When the mail came from Maitland and he went inside to sort it out everybody had their say.

Sim Jones started off as soon as he was sure that Starks couldn't hear him.

"It's uh sin and uh shame runnin' dat po' man way from here lak dat. Colored folks oughtn't tuh be so hard on one 'nother."

"Ah don't see it dat way atall," Sam Watson said shortly. "Let colored folks learn to work for what dey git lak everybody else. Nobody ain't stopped Pitts from plantin' de cane he wanted tuh. Starks give him uh job, what mo' do he want?"

"Ah know dat too," Jones said, "but, Sam, Joe Starks is too exact wid folks. All he got he done made it offa de rest of us. He didn't have all dat when he come here."

"Yeah, but none uh all dis you see and you'se settin' on wasn't here neither, when he come. Give de devil his due."

"But now, Sam, you know dat all he do is big-belly round and tell other folks what tuh do. He loves obedience out of everybody under de sound of his voice."

"You kin feel a switch in his hand when he's talkin' to yuh," Oscar Scott complained. "Dat chastisin' feelin' he totes sorter gives yuh de protolapsis uh de cutinary linin'."

"He's uh whirlwind among breezes," Jeff Bruce threw in.

"Speakin' of winds, he's de wind and we'se de grass. We bend which ever way he blows," Sam Watson agreed, "but at dat us needs him. De town wouldn't be nothin' if it wasn't for him. He can't help bein' sorta bossy. Some folks needs thrones, and ruling-chairs and crowns tuh make they influence felt. He don't. He's got uh throne in de seat of his pants."

"Whut Ah don't lak 'bout de man is, he talks tuh unlettered folks wid books in his jaws," Hicks complained. "Showin' off his learnin'. To look at me you wouldn't think it, but Ah got uh brother pastorin' up round Ocala dat got good learnin'. If he wuz here, Joe Starks wouldn't make no fool outa him lak he do de rest uh y'all."

"Ah often wonder how dat lil wife uh hisn makes out wid him, 'cause he's uh man dat changes everything, but nothin' don't change him."

"You know many's de time Ah done thought about dat mahself. He gits on her ever now and then when she make little mistakes round de store."

"Whut make her keep her head tied up lak some ole 'oman round de store? Nobody couldn't *git* me tuh tie no rag on mah head if Ah had hair lak dat."

"Maybe he make her do it. Maybe he skeered some de rest of us mens might touch it round dat store. It sho is uh hidden mystery tuh me."

"She sho don't talk much. De way he rears and pitches in de store sometimes when she make uh mistake is sort of ungodly, but she don't seem to mind at all. Reckon dey understand one 'nother."

The town had a basketful of feelings good and bad about Joe's positions and possessions, but none had the temerity to challenge him. They bowed down to him rather, because he was all of these things, and then again he was all of these things because the town bowed down.

Chapter 6

Every morning the world flung itself over and exposed the town to the sun. So Janie had another day. And every day had a store in it, except Sundays. The store itself was a pleasant place if only she didn't have to sell things. When the people sat around on the porch and passed around the pictures of their thoughts for the others to look at and see, it was nice. The fact that the thought pictures were always crayon enlargements of life made it even nicer to listen to.

Take for instance the case of Matt Bonner's yellow mule. They had him up for conversation every day the Lord sent. Most especial if Matt was there himself to listen. Sam and Lige and Walter were the ringleaders of the mule-talkers. The others threw in whatever they could chance upon, but it seemed as if Sam and Lige and Walter could hear and see more about that mule than the whole county put together. All they needed was to see Matt's long spare shape coming down the street and by the time he got to the porch they were ready for him.

"Hello, Matt."

"Evenin', Sam."

"Mighty glad you come 'long right now, Matt. Me and some others wuz jus' about tuh come hunt yuh."

"Whut fuh, Sam?"

"Mighty serious matter, man. Serious!!"

"Yeah man," Lige would cut in, dolefully. "It needs yo' strict attention. You ought not tuh lose no time."

"Whut is it then? You oughta hurry up and tell me."

"Reckon we better not tell yuh heah at de store. It's too fur off tuh do any good. We better all walk on down by Lake Sabelia."

"Whut's wrong, man? Ah ain't after none uh y'alls foolishness now."

"Dat mule uh yourn, Matt. You better go see 'bout him. He's bad off."

"Where 'bouts? Did he wade in de lake and uh alligator ketch him?"

"Worser'n dat. De womenfolks got yo' mule. When Ah come round de lake 'bout noontime mah wife and some others had 'im flat on de ground usin' his sides fuh uh wash board."

The great clap of laughter that they have been holding in, bursts out. Sam never cracks a smile. "Yeah, Matt, dat mule so skinny till de women is usin' his rib bones fuh uh rub-board, and hangin' things out on his hock-bones tuh dry."

Matt realizes that they have tricked him again and the laughter makes him mad and when he gets mad he stammers.

"You'se uh stinkin' lie, Sam, and yo' feet ain't mates. Y-y-y-you!"

"Aw, man, 'tain't no use in you gittin' mad. Yuh know yuh don't feed de mule. How he gointuh git fat?"

"Ah-ah-ah d-d-does feed 'im! Ah g-g-gived 'im uh full cup uh cawn every feedin'."

"Lige knows all about dat cup uh cawn. He hid round yo' barn and watched yuh. 'Tain't no feed cup you measures dat cawn outa. It's uh tea cup."

"Ah does feed 'im. He's jus' too mean tuh git fat. He stay poor and rawbony jus' fuh spite. Skeered he'll hafta work some."

"Yeah, you feeds 'im. Feeds 'im offa 'come up' and seasons it wid raw-hide."

"Does feed de ornery varmint! Don't keer whut Ah do Ah can't git long wid 'im. He fights every inch in front uh de plow, and even lay back his ears tuh kick and bite when Ah go in de stall tuh feed 'im."

"Git reconciled, Matt," Lige soothed. "Us all knows he's mean. Ah seen 'im when he took after one uh dem Roberts chillun in de street and woulda caught 'im and maybe trompled 'im tuh death if de wind hadn't of changed all of a sudden. Yuh see de youngun wuz tryin' tuh make it tuh de fence uh Starks' onion patch and de mule wuz dead in behind 'im and gainin' on 'im every jump, when all of a sudden de wind changed and blowed de mule way off his course, him bein' so poor and everything, and before de ornery varmint could tack, de youngun had done got over de fence." The porch laughed and Matt got mad again.

"Maybe de mule takes out after everybody," Sam said, "'cause he thinks everybody he hear comin' is Matt Bonner comin' tuh work 'im on uh empty stomach."

"Aw, naw, aw, naw. You stop dat right now," Walter objected. "Dat mule don't think Ah look lak no Matt Bonner. He ain't dat dumb. If Ah thought he didn't know no better Ah'd have mah picture took and give it tuh dat mule so's he could learn better. Ah ain't gointuh 'low 'im tuh hold nothin' lak dat against me."

Matt struggled to say something but his tongue failed him so he jumped down off the porch and walked away as mad as he could be. But that never halted the mule talk. There would be more stories about how poor the brute was; his age; his evil disposition and his latest caper. Everybody indulged in mule talk. He was next to the Mayor in prominence, and made better talking.

Janie loved the conversation and sometimes she thought up good stories on the mule, but Joe had forbidden her to indulge. He didn't want her talking after such trashy people. "You'se Mrs. Mayor Starks, Janie. I god, Ah can't see what uh woman uh yo' stability would want tuh be treasurin' all dat gum-grease from folks dat don't even own de house dey sleep in. 'Tain't no earthly use. They's jus' some puny humans playin' round de toes uh Time."

Janie noted that while he didn't talk the mule himself, he sat and laughed at it. Laughed his big heh, heh laugh too. But then when Lige or Sam or Walter or some of the other big picture talkers were using a side of the world for a canvas, Joe would hustle her off inside the store to sell something. Look like he took pleasure in doing it. Why couldn't he go himself sometimes? She had come to hate the inside of that store anyway. That Post Office too. People always coming and asking for mail at the wrong time. Just when she was trying to count up something or write in an account book. Get her so hackled she'd make the wrong change for stamps. Then too, she couldn't read everybody's writing. Some folks wrote so funny and spelt things different from what she knew about. As a rule, Joe put up the mail himself, but sometimes when he was off she had to do it herself and it always ended up in a fuss.

The store itself kept her with a sick headache. The labor of getting things down off of a shelf or out of a barrel was nothing. And so long as people wanted only a can of tomatoes or a pound of rice it was all right. But supposing they went on and said a pound and a half of bacon and a half pound of lard? The whole thing changed from a little walking and stretching to a mathematical dilemma. Or maybe cheese was thirty-seven cents a pound and somebody came and asked for a dime's worth. She went through many silent rebellions over things like that. Such a waste of life and time. But Joe kept saying that she could do it if she wanted to and he wanted her to use her privileges. That was the rock she was battered against.

This business of the head-rag irked her endlessly. But Jody was set on it. Her hair was NOT going to show in the store. It didn't seem sensible at all. That was because Joe never told Janie how jealous he was. He never told her how often he had seen the other men figuratively wallowing in it as she went about things in the store. And one night he had caught Walter standing behind Janie and brushing the back of his hand back and forth across the loose end of her braid ever so lightly so as to enjoy the feel of it without Janie knowing what he was doing. Joe was at the back of the store and Walter didn't see him. He felt like rushing forth with the meat knife and chopping off the offending hand. That night he ordered Janie to tie up her hair around the store. That was all. She was there in the store for *him* to look at, not those others. But he never said things like that. It just wasn't in him. Take the matter of the yellow mule, for instance.

Late one afternoon Matt came from the west with a halter in his hand. "Been huntin' fuh mah mule. Anybody seen 'im?" he asked.

"Seen 'im soon dis mornin' over behind the schoolhouse," Lum said. "'Bout ten o'clock or so. He musta been out all night tuh be way over dere dat early."

"He wuz," Matt answered. "Seen 'im last night but Ah couldn't ketch 'im. Ah'm 'bliged tuh git 'im in tuhnight 'cause Ah got some plowin' fuh tuhmorrow. Done promised tuh plow Thompson's grove."

"Reckon you'll ever git through de job wid dat mule-frame?" Lige asked.

"Aw dat mule is plenty strong. Jus' evil and don't want tuh be led."

"Dat's right. Dey tell me he brought you heah tuh dis town. Say you started tuh Miccanopy but de mule had better sense and brung yuh on heah."

"It's uh l-l-lie! Ah set out fuh dis town when Ah left West Floridy."

"You mean tuh tell me you rode dat mule all de way from West Floridy down heah?"

"Sho he did, Lige. But he didn't mean tuh. He wuz satisfied up dere, but de mule wuzn't. So one mornin' he got straddle uh de mule and he took and brought 'im on off. Mule had sense. Folks up dat way don't eat biscuit bread but once uh week."

There was always a little seriousness behind the teasing of Matt, so when he got huffed and walked on off nobody minded. He was known to buy side-meat by the slice. Carried home little bags of meal and flour in his hand. He didn't seem to mind too much so long as it didn't cost him anything.

About half an hour after he left they heard the braying of the mule at the edge of the woods. He was coming past the store very soon.

"Less ketch Matt's mule fuh 'im and have some fun."

"Now, Lum, you know dat mule ain't aimin' tuh let hisself be caught. Less watch *you* do it."

When the mule was in front of the store, Lum went out and tackled him. The brute jerked up his head, laid back his ears and rushed to the attack. Lum had to run for safety. Five or six more men left the porch and surrounded the fractious beast, goosing him in the sides and making him show his temper. But he had more spirit left than body. He was soon panting and heaving from the effort of spinning his old carcass about. Everybody was having fun at the mule-baiting. All but Janie.

She snatched her head away from the spectacle and began muttering to herself. "They oughta be shamed uh theyselves! Teasin' dat poor brute beast lak they is! Done been worked tuh death; done had his disposition ruint wid mistreatment, and now they got tuh finish devilin' 'im tuh death. Wisht Ah had mah way wid 'em all."

She walked away from the porch and found something to busy herself with in the back of the store so she did not hear Jody when he stopped laughing. She didn't know that he had heard her, but she did hear him yell out, "Lum, I god, dat's enough! Y'all done had yo' fun now. Stop yo' foolishness and go tell Matt Bonner Ah wants tuh have uh talk wid him right away."

Janie came back out front and sat down. She didn't say anything and neither did Joe. But after a while he looked down at his feet and said, "Janie, Ah reckon you better go fetch me dem old black gaiters. Dese tan shoes sets mah feet on fire. Plenty room in 'em, but they hurts regardless."

She got up without a word and went off for the shoes. A little war of defense for helpless things was going on inside her. People ought to have some regard for helpless things. She wanted to fight about it. "But Ah hates disagreement and confusion, so Ah better not talk. It makes it hard tuh git along." She didn't hurry back. She fumbled around long enough to get her face straight. When she got back, Joe was talking with Matt.

"Fifteen dollars? I god you'se as crazy as uh betsy bug! Five dollars."

"L-l-less we strack uh compermise, Brother Mayor. Less m-make it ten."

"Five dollars." Joe rolled his cigar in his mouth and rolled his eyes away indifferently.

"If dat mule is wuth somethin' tuh *you*, Brother Mayor, he's wuth mo' tuh me. More special when Ah got uh job uh work tuhmorrow."

"Five dollars."

"All right, Brother Mayor. If you wants tuh rob uh poor man lak me uh everything he got tuh make uh livin' wid, Ah'll take de five dollars. Dat mule been wid me twenty-three years. It's mighty hard."

Mayor Starks deliberately changed his shoes before he reached into his pocket for the money. By that time Matt was wringing and twisting like a hen on a hot brick. But as soon as his hand closed on the money his face broke into a grin.

"Beatyuh tradin' dat time, Starks! Dat mule is liable tuh be dead befo' de week is out. You won't git no work outa him."

"Didn't buy 'im fuh no work. I god, Ah bought dat varmint tuh let 'im rest. You didn't have gumption enough tuh do it."

A respectful silence fell on the place. Sam looked at Joe and said, "Dat's uh new idea 'bout varmints, Mayor Starks. But Ah laks it mah ownself. It's uh noble thing you done." Everybody agreed with that.

Janie stood still while they all made comments. When it was all done she stood in front of Joe and said, "Jody, dat wuz uh mighty fine thing fuh you tuh do. 'Tain't everybody would have thought of it, 'cause it ain't no everyday thought. Freein' dat mule makes uh mighty big man outa you. Something like George Washington and Lincoln. Abraham Lincoln, he had de whole United States tuh rule so he freed de Negroes. You got uh town so you freed uh mule. You have tuh have power tuh free things and dat makes you lak uh king uh something."

Hambo said, "Yo' wife is uh born orator, Starks. Us never knowed dat befo'. She put jus' de right words tuh our thoughts."

Joe bit down hard on his cigar and beamed all around, but he never said a word. The town talked it for three days and said that's just what they would have done if they had been rich men like Joe Starks. Anyhow a free mule in town was something new to talk about. Starks piled fodder under the big tree near the porch and the mule was usually around the store like the other citizens. Nearly everybody took the habit of fetching along a handful of fodder to throw on the pile. He almost got fat and they took a great pride in him. New lies sprung up about his free-mule doings. How he pushed open Lindsay's kitchen door and slept in the place one night and fought until they made coffee for his breakfast; how he stuck his head in the Pearsons' window while the family was at the table and Mrs. Pearson mistook him for Rev. Pearson and handed him a plate; he ran Mrs. Tully off of the croquet ground for having such an ugly shape; he ran and caught up with Becky Anderson on the way to Maitland so as to keep his head out of the sun under her umbrella; he got tired of listening to Redmond's long-winded prayer, and went inside the Baptist church and broke up the meeting. He did everything but let himself be bridled and visit Matt Bonner.

But way after a while he died. Lum found him under the big tree on his rawbony back with all four feet up in the air. That wasn't natural and it didn't look right, but Sam said it would have been more unnatural for him to have laid down on his side and died like any other beast. He had seen Death coming and had stood his ground and fought it like a natural man. He had fought it to the last breath. Naturally he didn't have time to straighten himself out. Death had to take him like it found him.

When the news got around, it was like the end of a war or something like that. Everybody that could knocked off from work to stand around and talk. But finally there was nothing to do but drag him out like all other dead brutes. Drag him out to the edge of the hammock which was far enough off to satisfy sanitary conditions in the town. The rest was up to the buzzards. Everybody was going to the dragging-out. The news had got Mayor Starks out of bed before time. His pair of gray horses was out under the tree and the men were fooling with the gear when Janie arrived at the store with Joe's breakfast.

"I god, Lum, you fasten up dis store good befo' you leave, you hear me?" He was eating fast and talking with one eye out of the door on the operations.

"Whut you tellin' 'im tuh fasten up for, Jody?" Janie asked, surprised.

"'Cause it won't be nobody heah tuh look after de store. Ah'm goin' tuh de draggin'-out mahself."

"'Tain't nothin' so important Ah got tuh do tuhday, Jody. How come Ah can't go long wid you tuh de draggin'-out?"

Joe was struck speechless for a minute. "Why, Janie! You wouldn't be seen at uh draggin'-out, wouldja? Wid any and everybody in uh passle pushin' and shovin' wid they no-manners selves? Naw, naw!"

"You would be dere wid me, wouldn't yuh?"

"Dat's right, but Ah'm uh man even if Ah is de Mayor. But de mayor's wife is somethin' different again. Anyhow they's liable tuh need me tuh say uh few words over de carcass, dis bein' uh special case. But *you* ain't goin' off in all dat mess uh commonness. Ah'm surprised at yuh fuh askin'."

He wiped his lips of ham gravy and put on his hat. "Shet de door behind yuh, Janie. Lum is too busy wid de hawses."

After more shouting of advice and orders and useless comments, the town escorted the carcass off. No, the carcass moved off with the town, and left Janie standing in the doorway.

Out in the swamp they made great ceremony over the mule. They mocked everything human in death. Starks led off with a great eulogy on our departed citizen, our most distinguished citizen and the grief he left behind him, and the people loved the speech. It made him more solid than building the schoolhouse had done. He stood on the distended belly of the mule for a platform and made gestures. When he stepped down, they hoisted Sam up and he talked about the mule as a school teacher first. Then he set his hat like John Pearson and imitated his preaching. He spoke of the joys of mule-heaven to which the dear brother had departed this valley of sorrow; the mule-angels flying around; the miles of green corn and cool water, a pasture of pure bran with a river of molasses running through it; and most glorious of all, *No* Matt Bonner with plow lines and halters to come in and corrupt. Up there, mule-angels would have people to ride on and from his place beside the glittering throne, the dear departed brother would look down into hell and see the devil plowing Matt Bonner all day long in a hell-hot sun and laying the raw-hide to his back.

With that the sisters got mock-happy and shouted and had to be held up by the menfolks. Everybody enjoyed themselves to the highest and then finally the mule was left to the already impatient buzzards. They were holding a great flying-meet way up over the heads of the mourners and some of the nearby trees were already peopled with the stoop-shouldered forms.

As soon as the crowd was out of sight they closed in circles. The near ones got nearer and the far ones got near. A circle, a swoop and a hop with spread-out wings. Close in, close in till some of the more hungry or daring perched on the carcass. They wanted to begin, but the Parson wasn't there, so a messenger was sent to the ruler in a tree where he sat.

The flock had to wait the white-headed leader, but it was hard. They jostled each other and pecked at heads in hungry irritation. Some walked up and down the beast from head to tail, tail to head. The Parson sat motionless in a dead pine tree about two miles off. He had scented the matter as quickly as any of the rest, but decorum demanded that he sit oblivious until he was notified. Then he took off with ponderous flight and circled and lowered, circled and lowered until the others danced in joy and hunger at his approach.

He finally lit on the ground and walked around the body to see if it were really dead. Peered into its nose and mouth. Examined it well from end to end and leaped upon it and bowed, and the others danced a response. That being over, he balanced and asked:

"What killed this man?"

The chorus answered, "Bare, bare fat."

"What killed this man?"

"Bare, bare fat."

"What killed this man?"

"Bare, bare fat."

"Who'll stand his funeral?"

"We!!!!!"

"Well, all right now."

So he picked out the eyes in the ceremonial way and the feast went on. The yaller mule was gone from the town except for the porch talk, and for the children visiting his bleaching bones now and then in the spirit of adventure.

Joe returned to the store full of pleasure and good humor but he didn't want Janie to notice it because he saw that she was sullen and he resented that. She had no right to be, the way he thought things out. She wasn't even appreciative of his efforts and she had plenty cause to be. Here he was just pouring honor all over her; building a high chair for her to sit in and overlook the world and she here pouting over it! Not that he wanted anybody else, but just too many women would be glad to be in her place. He ought to box her jaws! But he didn't feel like fighting today, so he made an attack upon her position backhand.

"Ah had tuh laugh at de people out dere in de woods dis mornin', Janie. You can't help but laugh at de capers they cuts. But all the same, Ah wish mah people would git mo' business in 'em and not spend so much time on foolishness."

"Everybody can't be lak you, Jody. Somebody is bound tuh want tuh laugh and play."

"Who don't love tuh laugh and play?"

"You make out like you don't, anyhow."

"I god, Ah don't make out no such uh lie! But it's uh time fuh all things. But it's awful tuh see so many people don't want nothin' but uh full belly and uh place tuh lay down and sleep afterwards. It makes me sad sometimes and then agin it makes me mad. They say things sometimes that tickles me nearly tuh death, but Ah won't laugh jus' tuh dis-incourage 'em." Janie took the easy way away from a fuss. She didn't change her mind but she agreed with her mouth. Her heart said, "Even so, but you don't have to cry about it."

But sometimes Sam Watson and Lige Moss forced a belly laugh out of Joe himself with their eternal arguments. It never ended because there was no end to reach. It was a contest in hyperbole and carried on for no other reason.

Maybe Sam would be sitting on the porch when Lige walked up. If nobody was there to speak of, nothing happened. But if the town was there like on Saturday night, Lige would come up with a very grave air. Couldn't even pass the time of day, for being so busy thinking. Then when he was asked what was the matter in order to start him off, he'd say, "Dis question done 'bout drove me crazy. And Sam, he know so much into things, Ah wants some information on de subject."

Walter Thomas was due to speak up and egg the matter on. "Yeah, Sam always got more information than he know what to do wid. He's bound to tell yuh whatever it is you wants tuh know."

Sam begins an elaborate show of avoiding the struggle. That draws everybody on the porch into it.

"How come you want me *tuh* tell yuh? You always claim God done met you round de corner and talked His inside business wid yuh. 'Tain't no use in you askin' *me* nothin'. Ah'm questionizin' *you*."

"How you gointuh do dat, Sam, when Ah arrived dis conversation mahself? Ah'm askin' *you*."

"Askin' me what? You ain't told me de subjick yit."

"Don't aim tuh tell yuh! Ah aims tuh keep yuh in de dark all de time. If you'se smart lak you let on you is, you kin find out."

"Yuh skeered to lemme know whut it is, 'cause yuh know Ah'll tear it tuh pieces. You got to have a subjick tuh talk from, do yuh can't talk. If uh man ain't got no bounds, he ain't got no place tuh stop."

By this time, they are the center of the world.

"Well all right then. Since you own up you ain't smart enough tuh find out whut Ah'm takin' 'bout, Ah'll tell you. Whut is it dat keeps uh man from gettin' burnt on uh red-hot stove—caution or nature?"

"Shucks! Ah thought you had somethin' hard tuh ast me. Walter kin tell yuh dat."

"If de conversation is too deep for yuh, how come yuh don't tell me so, and hush up? Walter can't tell me nothin' uh de kind. Ah'm uh educated man, Ah keeps mah arrangements in mah hands, and if it kept me up all night long studyin' 'bout it, Walter ain't liable tuh be no help to me. Ah needs uh man lak you."

"And then agin, Lige, Ah'm gointuh tell yuh. Ah'm gointuh run dis conversation from uh gnat heel to uh lice. It's nature dat keeps uh man off of uh red-hot stove."

"Uuh huuh! Ah knowed you would going tuh crawl up in dat holler! But Ah aims tuh smoke yuh right out. 'Tain't no nature at all, it's caution, Sam."

"'Tain't no sich uh thing! Nature tells yuh not tuh fool wid no red-hot stove, and you don't do it neither."

"Listen, Sam, if it was nature, nobody wouldn't have tuh look out for babies touchin' stoves, would they? 'Cause dey just naturally wouldn't touch it. But dey sho will. So it's caution."

"Naw it ain't, it's nature, cause nature makes caution. It's de strongest thing dat God ever made, now. Fact is it's de onliest thing God ever made. He made nature and nature made everything else."

"Naw nature didn't neither. A whole heap of things ain't even been made yit."

"Tell me somethin' you know of dat nature ain't made."

"She ain't made it so you kin ride uh butt-headed cow and hold on tuh de horns."

"Yeah, but dat ain't yo' point."

"Yeah it is too."

"Naw it ain't neither."

"Well what *is* mah point?"

"You ain't got none, so far."

"Yeah he is too," Walter cut in. "De red-hot stove is his point."

"He know mighty much, but he ain't proved it yit."

"Sam, Ah say it's caution, not nature dat keeps folks off uh red-hot stove."

"How is de son gointuh be before his paw? Nature is de first of everything. Ever since self was self, nature been keepin' folks off of red-hot stoves. Dat caution you talkin' 'bout ain't nothin' but uh humbug. He's uh inseck dat nothin' he got belongs to him. He got eyes, lak somethin' else; wings lak somethin' else—everything! Even his hum is de sound of somebody else."

"Man, whut you talkin' 'bout? Caution is de greatest thing in de world. If it wasn't for caution—"

"Show me somethin' dat caution ever made! Look whut nature took and done. Nature got so high in uh black hen she got tuh lay uh white egg. Now you tell me, how come, whut got intuh man dat he got tuh have hair round his mouth? Nature!"

"Dat ain't—"

The porch was boiling now. Starks left the store to Hezekiah Potts, the delivery boy, and come took a seat in his high chair.

"Look at dat great big ole scoundrel-beast up dere at Hall's fillin' station—uh great big old scoundrel. He eats up all de folks outa de house and den eat de house."

"Aw 'tain't no sich a varmint nowhere dat kin eat no house! Dat's uh lie. Ah wuz dere yiste'ddy and Ah ain't seen nothin' lak dat. Where is he?"

"Ah didn't see him but Ah reckon he is in de back-yard some place. But dey got his picture out front dere. They was nailin' it up when Ah come pass dere dis evenin'."

"Well all right now, if he eats up houses how come he don't eat up de fillin' station?"

"Dat's 'cause dey got him tied up so he can't. Dey got uh great big picture tellin' how many gallons of dat Sinclair high-compression gas he drink at one time and how he's more'n uh million years old."

"'Tain't *nothin'* no million years old!"

"De picture is right up dere where anybody kin see it. Dey can't make de picture till dey see de thing, kin dey?"

"How dey goin' to tell he's uh million years old? Nobody wasn't born dat fur back."

"By de rings on his tail Ah reckon. Man, dese white folks got ways for tellin' anything dey wants tuh know."

"Well, where he been at all dis time, then?"

"Dey caught him over dere in Egypt. Seem lak he used tuh hang round dere and eat up dem Pharaohs' tombstones. Dey got de picture of him doin' it. Nature is high in uh varmint lak dat. Nature and salt. Dat's whut makes up strong man lak Big John de Conquer. He was uh man wid salt in him. He could give uh flavor to *anything*."

"Yeah, but he was uh man dat wuz more'n man. 'Tain't no mo' lak him. He wouldn't dig potatoes, and he wouldn't rake hay: He wouldn't take a whipping, and he wouldn't run away."

"Oh yeah, somebody else could if dey tried hard enough. Me mahself, Ah got salt in *me*. If Ah like man flesh, Ah could eat some man every day, some of 'em is so trashy they'd let me eat 'em."

"Lawd, Ah loves to talk about Big John. Less we tell lies on Ole John."

But here come Bootsie, and Teadi and Big 'oman down the street making out they are pretty by the way they walk. They have got that fresh, new taste about them like young mustard greens in the spring, and the young men on the porch are just bound to tell them about it and buy them some treats.

"Heah come mah order right now," Charlie Jones announces and scrambles off the porch to meet them. But he has plenty of competition. A pushing, shoving show of gallantry. They all beg the girls to just buy anything they can think of. Please let them pay for it. Joe is begged to wrap up all the candy in the store and order more. All the peanuts and soda water—everything!

"Gal, Ah'm crazy 'bout you," Charlie goes on to the entertainment of everybody. "Ah'll do anything in the world except work for you and give you mah money."

The girls and everybody else help laugh. They know it's not courtship. It's acting-out courtship and everybody is in the play. The three girls hold the center of the stage till Daisy Blunt comes walking down the street in the moonlight.

Daisy is walking a drum tune. You can almost hear it by looking at the way she walks. She is black and she knows that white clothes look good on her, so she wears them for dress up. She's got those big black eyes with plenty shiny white in them that makes them shine like brand new money and she knows what God gave women eyelashes for, too. Her hair is not what you might call straight. It's negro hair, but it's got a kind of white flavor. Like the piece of string out of a ham. It's not ham at all, but it's been around ham and got the flavor. It was spread down thick and heavy over her shoulders and looked just right under a big white hat.

"Lawd, Lawd, Lawd," that same Charlie Jones exclaims rushing over to Daisy. "It must be uh recess in heben if St. Peter is lettin' his angels out lak dis. You got three men already layin' at de point uh death 'bout yuh, and heah's uhnother fool dat's willin' tuh make time on yo' gang."

All the rest of the single men have crowded around Daisy by this time. She is parading and blushing at the same time.

"If you know anybody dat's 'bout tuh die 'bout me, yuh know more'n Ah do," Daisy bridled. "Wisht Ah knowed who it is."

"Now, Daisy, *you* know Jim, and Dave and Lum is 'bout tuh kill one 'nother 'bout you. Don't stand up here and tell dat big ole got-dat-wrong."

"Dey a mighty hush-mouf about it if dey is. Dey ain't never told me nothin'."

"Unhunh, you talked too fast. Heah, Jim and Dave is right upon de porch and Lum is inside de store."

A big burst of laughter at Daisy's discomfiture. The boys had to act out their rivalry too. Only this time, everybody knew they meant some of it. But all the same the porch enjoyed the play and helped out whenever extras were needed.

David said, "Jim don't love Daisy. He don't love yuh lak Ah do."

Jim bellowed indignantly, "Who don't love Daisy? Ah know you ain't talkin' 'bout me."

Dave: "Well all right, less prove dis thing right now. We'll prove right now who love dis gal de best. How much time is you willin' tuh make fuh Daisy?"

Jim: "Twenty yeahs!"

Dave: "See? Ah told yuh dat nigger didn't love yuh. Me, Ah'll beg de Judge tuh hang me, and wouldn't take nothin' less than life."

There was a big long laugh from the porch. Then Jim had to demand a test.

"Dave, how much would you be willin' tuh do for Daisy if she was to turn fool enough tuh marry yuh?"

"Me and Daisy done talked dat over, but if you just got tuh know, Ah'd buy Daisy uh passenger train and give it tuh her."

"Humph! Is dat all? Ah'd buy her uh steamship and then Ah'd hire some mens tuh run it fur her."

"Daisy, don't let Jim fool you wid his talk. He don't aim tuh do nothin' fuh yuh. Uh lil ole steamship! Daisy, Ah'll take uh job cleanin' out de Atlantic Ocean fuh you any time you say you so desire." There was a great laugh and then they hushed to listen.

"Daisy," Jim began, "you know mah heart and all de ranges uh mah mind. And you know if Ah wuz ridin' up in uh earoplane way up in de sky and Ah looked down and seen you walkin' and knowed you'd have tuh walk ten miles tuh git home, Ah'd step backward offa dat earoplane just to walk home wid you."

There was one of those big blow-out laughs and Janie was wallowing in it. Then Jody ruined it all for her.

Mrs. Bogle came walking down the street towards the porch. Mrs. Bogle who was many times a grandmother, but had a blushing air of coquetry about her that cloaked her sunken cheeks. You saw a fluttering fan before her face and magnolia blooms and sleepy lakes under the moonlight when she walked. There was no obvious reason for it, it was just so. Her first husband had been a coachman but "studied jury" to win her. He had finally become a preacher to hold her till his death. Her second husband worked in Fohnes orange grove—but tried to preach when he caught her eye. He never got any further than a class leader, but that was something to offer her. It proved his love and pride. She was a wind on the ocean. She moved men, but the helm determined the port. Now, this night she mounted the steps and the men noticed her until she passed inside the door.

"I god, Janie," Starks said impatiently, "why don't you go on and see whut Mrs. Bogle want? Whut you waitin' on?"

Janie wanted to hear the rest of the play-acting and how it ended, but she got up sullenly and went inside. She came back to the porch with her bristles sticking out all over her and with dissatisfaction written all over her face. Joe saw it and lifted his own hackles a bit.

Jim Weston had secretly borrowed a dime and soon he was loudly beseeching Daisy to have a treat on him. Finally she consented to take a pickled pig foot on him. Janie was getting up a large order when they came in, so Lum waited on them. That is, he went back to the keg but came back without the pig foot.

"Mist' Starks, de pig feets is all gone!" he called out.

"Aw naw dey ain't, Lum. Ah bought uh whole new kag of 'em wid dat last order from Jacksonville. It come in yistiddy."

Joe came and helped Lum look but he couldn't find the new keg either, so he went to the nail over his desk that he used for a file to search for the order.

"Janie, where's dat last bill uh ladin'?"

"It's right dere on de nail, ain't it?"

"Naw it ain't neither. You ain't put it where Ah told yuh tuh. If you'd git yo' mind out de streets and keep it on yo' business maybe you could git somethin' straight sometimes."

"Aw, look around dere, Jody. Dat bill ain't apt tuh be gone off nowheres. If it ain't hangin' on de nail, it's on yo' desk. You bound tuh find it if you look."

"Wid you heah, Ah oughtn't tuh hafta do all dat lookin' and searchin'. Ah done told you time and time agin tuh stick all dem papers on dat nail! All you got tuh do is mind me. How come you can't do lak Ah tell yuh?"

"You sho loves to tell me whut to do, but Ah can't tell you nothin' Ah see!"

"Dat's 'cause you need tellin'," he rejoined hotly. "It would be pitiful if Ah didn't. Somebody got to think for women and chillun and chickens and cows. I god, they sho don't think none theirselves."

"Ah knows uh few things, and womenfolks thinks sometimes too!"

"Aw naw they don't. They just think they's thinkin'. When Ah see one thing Ah understands ten. You see ten things and don't understand one."

Times and scenes like that put Janie to thinking about the inside state of her marriage. Time came when she fought back with her tongue as best she could, but it didn't do her any good. It just made Joe do more. He wanted her submission and he'd keep on fighting until he felt he had it.

So gradually, she pressed her teeth together and learned to hush. The spirit of the marriage left the bedroom and took to living in the parlor. It was there to shake hands whenever company came to visit, but it never went back inside the bedroom again. So she put something in there to represent the spirit like a Virgin Mary image in a church. The bed was no longer a daisy-field for her and Joe to play in. It was a place where she went and laid down when she was sleepy and tired.

She wasn't petal-open anymore with him. She was twenty-four and seven years married when she knew. She found that out one day when he slapped her face in the kitchen. It happened over one of those dinners that chasten all women some-times. They plan and they fix and they do, and then some kitchen-dwelling fiend slips a scorchy, soggy, tasteless mess into their pots and pans. Janie was a good cook, and Joe had looked forward to his dinner as a refuge from other things. So when the bread didn't rise, and the fish wasn't quite done at the bone, and the rice was scorched, he slapped Janie until she had a ringing sound in her ears and told her about her brains before he stalked on back to the store.

Janie stood where he left her for unmeasured time and thought. She stood there until something fell off the shelf inside her. Then she went inside there to see what it was. It was her image of Jody tumbled down and shattered. But look-ing at it she saw that it never was the flesh and blood figure of her dreams. Just something she had grabbed up to drape her dreams over. In a way she turned her back upon the image where it lay and looked further. She had no more blos-somy openings dusting pollen over her man, neither any glistening young fruit where the petals used to be. She found that she had a host of thoughts she had never expressed to him, and numerous emotions she had never let Jody know about. Things packed up and put away in parts of her heart where he could never find them. She was saving up feelings for some man she had never seen. She had an inside and an outside now and suddenly she knew how not to mix them.

She bathed and put on a fresh dress and head kerchief and went on to the store before Jody had time to send for her. That was a bow to the outside of things.

Jody was on the porch and the porch was full of Eatonville as usual at this time of the day. He was baiting Mrs. Tony Robbins as he always did when she came to the store. Janie could see Jody watching her out of the corner of his eye while he joked roughly with Mrs. Robbins. He wanted to be friendly with her again. His big, big laugh was as much for her as for the baiting. He was longing for peace but on his own terms.

"I god, Mrs. Robbins, whut make you come heah and worry me when you see Ah'm readin' mah newspaper?" Mayor Starks lowered the paper in pretended annoyance.

Mrs. Robbins struck her pity-pose and assumed the voice.

"'Cause Ah'm hungry, Mist' Starks. 'Deed Ah is. Me and mah chillun is hon-gry. Tony don't fee-eed me!"

This was what the porch was waiting for. They burst into a laugh.

"Mrs. Robbins, how can you make out you'se hongry when Tony comes in here every Satitday and buys groceries lak a man? Three weeks' shame on yuh!"

"If he buy all dat you talkin' 'bout, Mist' Starks, God knows whut he do wid it. He sho don't bring it home, and me and mah po' chillun is *so* hungry! Mist' Starks, please gimme uh lil piece uh meat fur me and mah chillun."

"Ah know you don't need it, but come on inside. You ain't goin' tuh lemme read till Ah give it to yuh."

Mrs. Tony's ecstasy was divine. "Thank you, Mist' Starks. You'se noble! You'se du most gentlemanfied man Ah ever did see. You'se uh king!"

The salt pork box was in the back of the store and during the walk Mrs. Tony was so eager she sometimes stepped on Joe's heels, sometimes she was a little before him. Something like a hungry cat when somebody approaches her pan with meat. Running a little, caressing a little and all the time making little urging-on cries.

"Yes, indeedy, Mist' Starks, you'se noble. You got sympathy for me and mah po' chillun. Tony don't give us nothin' tuh eat and we'se *so* hongry. Tony don't fee-eed me!"

This brought them to the meat box. Joe took up the big meat knife and selected a piece of side meat to cut. Mrs. Tony was all but dancing around him.

"Dat's right, Mist' Starks! Gimme uh lil piece 'bout dis wide." She indicated as wide as her wrist and hand. "Me and mah chillun is *so* hongry!"

Starks hardly looked at her measurements. He had seen them too often. He marked off a piece much smaller and sunk the blade in. Mrs. Tony all but fell to the floor in her agony.

"Lawd a'mussy! Mist' Starks, you ain't gointuh gimme dat lil tee-ninchy piece fuh me and all mah chillun, is yuh? Lawd, we'se *so* hongry!"

Starks cut right on and reached for a piece of wrapping paper. Mrs. Tony leaped away from the proffered cut of meat as if it were a rattlesnake.

"Ah wouldn't tetch it! Dat lil eyeful uh bacon for me and all mah chillun! Lawd, some folks is got everything and they's so gripin' and so mean!"

Starks made as if to throw the meat back in the box and close it. Mrs. Tony swooped like lightning and seized it, and started towards the door.

"Some folks ain't got no heart in dey bosom. They's willin' tuh see uh po' woman and her helpless chillun starve tuh death. God's gointuh put 'em under arrest, some uh dese days, wid dey stingy gripin' ways."

She stepped from the store porch and marched off in high dudgeon! Some laughed and some got mad.

"If dat wuz *mah* wife," said Walter Thomas, "Ah'd kill her cemetery dead."

"More special after Ah done bought her everything mah wages kin stand, lak Tony do," Coker said. "In de fust place Ah never would spend on *no* woman whut Tony spend on *her*."

Starks came back and took his seat. He had to stop and add the meat to Tony's account.

"Well, Tony tells me tuh humor her along. He moved here from up de State hopin' tuh change her, but it ain't. He say he can't bear tuh leave her and he hate to kill her, so 'tain't nothin' tuh do but put up wid her."

"Dat's 'cause Tony love her too good," said Coker. "Ah could break her if she wuz mine. Ah'd break her or kill her. Makin' uh fool outa me in front of everybody."

"Tony won't never hit her. He says beatin' women is just like steppin' on baby chickens. He claims 'tain't no place on uh woman tuh hit," Joe Lindsay said with scornful disapproval, "but Ah'd kill uh baby just born dis mawnin' fuh uh thing lak dat. 'Tain't nothin' but low-down spitefulness 'ginst her husband make her do it."

"Dat's de God's truth," Jim Stone agreed. "Dat's de very reason."

Janie did what she had never done before, that is, thrust herself into the conversation.

"Sometimes God gits familiar wid us womenfolks too and talks His inside business. He told me how surprised He was 'bout y'all turning out so smart after Him makin' yuh different; and how surprised y'all is goin' tuh be if you ever find out you don't know half as much 'bout us as you think you do. It's so easy to make yo'self out God Almighty when you ain't got nothin' tuh strain against but women and chickens."

"You gettin' too moufy, Janie," Starks told her. "Go fetch me de checker-board *and* de checkers. Sam Watson, you'se mah fish."

Chapter 7

The years took all the fight out of Janie's face. For a while she thought it was gone from her soul. No matter what Jody did, she said nothing. She had learned how to talk some and leave some. She was a rut in the road. Plenty of life beneath the surface but it was kept beaten down by the wheels. Sometimes she stuck out into the future, imagining her life different from what it was. But mostly she lived between her hat and her heels, with her emotional disturbances like shade patterns in the woods—come and gone with the sun. She got nothing from Jody except what money could buy, and she was giving away what she didn't value.

Now and again she thought of a country road at sun-up and considered flight. To where? To what? Then too she considered thirty-five is twice seventeen and nothing was the same at all.

"Maybe he ain't nothin'," she cautioned herself, "but he is something in my mouth. He's got tuh be else Ah ain't got nothin' tuh live for. Ah'll lie and say he is. If Ah don't, life won't be nothin' but uh store and uh house."

She didn't read books so she didn't know that she was the world and the heavens boiled down to a drop. Man attempting to climb to painless heights from his dung hill.

Then one day she sat and watched the shadow of herself going about tending store and prostrating itself before Jody, while all the time she herself sat under a shady tree with the wind blowing through her hair and her clothes. Somebody near about making summertime out of lonesomeness.

This was the first time it happened, but after a while it got so common she ceased to be surprised. It was like a drug. In a way it was good because it reconciled her to things. She got so she received all things with the stolidness of the earth which soaks up urine and perfume with the same indifference.

One day she noticed that Joe didn't sit down. He just stood in front of a chair and fell in it. That made her look at him all over. Joe wasn't so young as he used to be. There was already something dead about him. He didn't rear back in his knees any longer. He squatted over his ankles when he walked. That stillness at the back of his neck. His prosperous-looking belly that used to thrust out so pugnaciously and intimidate folks, sagged like a load suspended from his loins. It didn't seem to be a part of him anymore. Eyes a little absent too.

Jody must have noticed it too. Maybe, he had seen it long before Janie did, and had been fearing for her to see. Because he began to talk about her age all the time, as if he didn't want her to stay young while he grew old. It was always "You oughta throw somethin' over yo' shoulders befo' you go outside. You ain't no young pullet no mo'. You'se uh ole hen now." One day he called her off the cro-quet grounds. "Dat's somethin' for de young folks, Janie, you out dere jumpin' round and won't be able tuh git out de bed tuhmorrer." If he thought to deceive her, he was wrong. For the first time she could see a man's head naked of its skull. Saw the cunning thoughts race in and out through the caves and promontories of his mind long before they darted out of the tunnel of his mouth. She saw he was hurting inside so she let it pass without talking. She just measured out a little time for him and set it aside to wait.

It got to be terrible in the store. The more his back ached and his muscle dis-solved into fat and the fat melted off his bones, the more fractious he became with Janie. Especially in the store. The more people in there the more ridicule he poured over her body to point attention away from his own. So one day Steve Mixon wanted some chewing tobacco and Janie cut it wrong. She hated that tobacco knife anyway. It worked very stiff. She fumbled with the thing and cut way away from the mark. Mixon didn't mind. He held it up for a joke to tease Janie a little.

"Looka heah, Brother Mayor, whut yo' wife done took and done." It was cut comical, so everybody laughed at it. "Uh woman and uh knife—no kind of uh knife, don't b'long tuhgether." There was some more good-natured laughter at the expense of women.

Jody didn't laugh. He hurried across from the post office side and took the plug of tobacco away from Mixon and cut it again. Cut it exactly on the mark and glared at Janie.

"I god amighty! A woman stay round uh store till she get old as Methusalem and still can't cut a little thing like a plug of tobacco! Don't stand dere rollin' yo' pop eyes at me wid yo' rump hangin' nearly to yo' knees!"

A big laugh started off in the store but people got to thinking and stopped. It was funny if you looked at it right quick, but it got pitiful if you thought about it awhile. It was like somebody snatched off part of a woman's clothes while she wasn't looking and the streets were crowded. Then too, Janie took the middle of the floor to talk right into Jody's face, and that was something that hadn't been done before.

"Stop mixin' up mah doings wid mah looks, Jody. When you git through tellin' me how tuh cut uh plug uh tobacco, then you kin tell me whether mah behind is on straight or not."

"Wha—whut's dat you say, Janie? You must be out yo' head."

"Naw, Ah ain't outa mah head neither."

"You must be. Talkin' any such language as dat."

"You de one started talkin' under people's clothes. Not me."

"Whut's de matter wid you, nohow? You ain't no young girl to be gettin' all insulted 'bout yo' looks. You ain't no young courtin' gal. You'se uh ole woman, nearly forty."

"Yeah, Ah'm nearly forty and you'se already fifty. How come you can't talk about dat sometimes instead of always pointin' at me?"

"'Tain't no use in gettin' all mad, Janie, 'cause Ah mention you ain't no young gal no mo'. Nobody in heah ain't lookin' for no wife outa yuh. Old as you is."

"Naw, Ah ain't no young gal no mo' but den Ah ain't no old woman neither. Ah reckon Ah looks mah age too. But Ah'm uh woman every inch of me, and Ah know it. Dat's uh whole lot more'n *you* kin say. You big-bellies round here and put out a lot of brag, but 'tain't nothin' to it but yo' big voice. Humph! Talkin' 'bout *me* lookin' old! When you pull down yo' britches, you look lak de change uh life."

"Great God from Zion!" Sam Watson gasped. "Y'all really playin' de dozens tuhnight."

"Wha—whut's dat you said?" Joe challenged, hoping his ears had fooled him.

"You heard her, you ain't blind," Walter taunted.

"Ah ruther be shot with tacks than tuh hear dat 'bout mahself," Lige Moss commiserated.

Then Joe Starks realized all the meanings and his vanity bled like a flood. Janie had robbed him of his illusion of irresistible maleness that all men cherish, which was terrible. The thing that Saul's daughter had done to David. But Janie had done worse, she had cast down his empty armor before men and they had laughed, would keep on laughing. When he paraded his possessions hereafter, they would not consider the two together. They'd look with envy at the things and pity the man that owned them. When he sat in judgment it would be the same. Good-for-nothing's like Dave and Lum and Jim wouldn't change place with him. For what can excuse a man in the eyes of other men for lack of strength? Raggedy-behind squirts of sixteen and seventeen would be giving him their merciless pity out of their eyes while their mouths said something humble. There was nothing to do in life anymore. Ambition was useless. And the cruel deceit of Janie! Making all that show of humbleness and scorning him all the time! Laughing at him, and now putting the town up to do the same. Joe Starks didn't know the words for all this, but he knew the feeling. So he struck Janie with all his might and drove her from the store.

Chapter 8

After that night Jody moved his things and slept in a room downstairs. He didn't really hate Janie, but he wanted her to think so. He had crawled off to lick his wounds. They didn't talk too much around the store either. Anybody that didn't know would have thought that things had blown over, it looked so quiet and peaceful around. But the stillness was the sleep of swords. So new thoughts had to be thought and new words said. She didn't want to live like that. Why must Joe be so mad with her for making him look small when he did it to her all the time? Had been doing it for years. Well, if she must eat out of a long-handled spoon, she must. Jody might get over his mad spell any time at all and begin to act like somebody towards her.

Then too she noticed how baggy Joe was getting all over. Like bags hanging from an ironing board. A little sack hung from the corners of his eyes and rested on his cheek-bones; a loose-filled bag of feathers hung from his ears and rested on his neck beneath his chin. A sack of flabby something hung from his loins and rested on his thighs when he sat down. But even these things were running down like candle grease as time moved on.

He made new alliances too. People he never bothered with one way or another now seemed to have his ear. He had always been scornful of root-doctors and all their kind, but now she saw a faker from over around Altamonte Springs, hanging around the place almost daily. Always talking in low tones when she came near, or hushed altogether. She didn't know that he was driven by a desperate hope to appear the old-time body in her sight. She was sorry about the root-doctor because she feared that Joe was depending on the scoundrel to make him well when what he needed was a doctor, and a good one. She was worried about his not eating his meals, till she found out he was having old lady Davis to cook for him. She knew that she was a much better cook than the old woman, and cleaner about the kitchen. So she bought a beef-bone and made him some soup.

"Naw, thank you," he told her shortly. "Ah'm havin' uh hard enough time tuh try and git well as it is."

She was stunned at first and hurt afterwards. So she went straight to her bosom friend, Pheoby Watson, and told her about it.

"Ah'd ruther be dead than for Jody tuh think Ah'd hurt him," she sobbed to Pheoby. "It ain't always been too pleasant, 'cause you know how Joe worships de works of his own hands, but God in heben knows Ah wouldn't do one thing tuh hurt nobody. It's too underhand and mean."

"Janie, Ah thought maybe de thing would die down and you never would know nothin' 'bout it, but it's been singin' round here ever since de big fuss in de store dat Joe was 'fixed' and you wuz de one dat did it."

"Pheoby, for de longest time, Ah been feelin' dat somethin' set for still-bait, but dis is—is—oh Pheoby! Whut *kin* I do?"

"You can't do nothin' but make out you don't know it. It's too late fuh y'all tuh be splittin' up and gittin' divorce. Just g'wan back home and set down on yo' royal diasticutis and say nothin'. Nobody don't b'lieve it nohow."

"Tuh think Ah been wid Jody twenty yeahs and Ah just now got tuh bear de name uh poisonin' him! It's 'bout to kill me, Pheoby. Sorrow dogged by sorrow is in mah heart."

"Dat's lie dat trashy nigger dat calls hisself uh two-headed doctor brought tuh 'im in order tuh git in wid Jody. He seen he wuz sick—everybody been knowin' dat for de last longest, and den Ah reckon he heard y'all wuz kind of at variance, so dat wuz his chance. Last summer dat multiplied cockroach wuz round heah tryin' tuh sell gophers!"

"Pheoby, Ah don't even b'lieve Jody b'lieve dat lie. He ain't never took no stock in de mess. He just make out he b'lieve it tuh hurt me. Ah'm stone dead from standin' still and tryin' tuh smile."

She cried often in the weeks that followed. Joe got too weak to look after things and took to his bed. But he relentlessly refused to admit her to his sick room. People came and went in the house. This one and that one came into her house with covered plates of broth and other sick-room dishes without taking the least notice of her as Joe's wife. People who never had known what it was to enter the gate of the Mayor's yard unless it were to do some menial job now paraded in and out as his confidants. They came to the store and ostentatiously looked over whatever she was doing and went back to report to him at the house. Said things like "Mr. Starks need *somebody* tuh sorta look out for 'im till he kin git on his feet again and look for hisself."

But Jody was never to get on his feet again. Janie had Sam Watson to bring her the news from the sick room, and when he told her how things were, she had him bring a doctor from Orlando without giving Joe a chance to refuse, and without saying she sent for him.

"Just a matter of time," the doctor told her. "When a man's kidneys stop working altogether, there is no way for him to live. He needed medical attention two years ago. Too late now."

So Janie began to think of Death. Death, that strange being with the huge square toes who lived way in the West. The great one who lived in the straight house like a platform without sides to it, and without a roof. What need has Death for a cover, and what winds can blow against him? He stands in his high house that overlooks the world. Stands watchful and motionless all day with his sword drawn back, waiting for the messenger to bid him come. Been standing there before there was a where or a when or a then. She was liable to find a feather from his wings lying in her yard any day now. She was sad and afraid too. Poor Jody! He ought not to have to wrassle in there by himself. She sent Sam in to suggest a visit, but Jody said No. These medical doctors wuz all right with the Godly sick, but they didn't know a thing about a case like his. He'd be all right just as soon as the two-headed man found what had been buried against him. He wasn't going to die at all. That was what he thought. But Sam told her different, so she knew. And then if he hadn't, the next morning she was bound to know, for people began to gather in the big yard under the palm and china-berry trees. People who would not have dared to foot the place before crept in and did not come to the house. Just squatted under the trees and waited. Rumor, that wingless bird, had shadowed over the town.

She got up that morning with the firm determination to go on in there and have a good talk with Jody. But she sat a long time with the walls creeping in on her. Four walls squeezing her breath out. Fear lest he depart while she sat trembling upstairs nerved her and she was inside the room before she caught her breath. She didn't make the cheerful, casual start that she had thought out. Something stood like an oxen's foot on her tongue, and then too, Jody, no Joe, gave her a ferocious look. A look with all the unthinkable coldness of outer space. She must talk to a man who was ten immensities away.

He was lying on his side facing the door like he was expecting somebody or something. A sort of changing look on his face. Weak-looking but sharp-pointed about the eyes. Through the thin counterpane she could see what was left of his belly huddled before him on the bed like some helpless thing seeking shelter.

The half-washed bedclothes hurt her pride for Jody. He had always been so clean.

"Whut you doin' in heah, Janie?"

"Come tuh see 'bout you and how you wuz makin' out."

He gave a deep-growling sound like a hog dying down in the swamp and trying to drive off disturbance. "Ah come in heah tuh git shet uh you but look lak 'tain't doin' me no good. G'wan out. Ah needs tuh rest."

"Naw, Jody, Ah come in heah tuh talk widja and Ah'm gointuh do it too. It's for both of our sakes Ah'm talkin'."

He gave another ground grumble and eased over on his back.

"Jody, maybe Ah ain't been sich uh good wife tuh you, but Jody—"

"Dat's 'cause you ain't got de right feelin' for nobody. You oughter have some sympathy 'bout yo'self. You ain't no hog."

"But, Jody, Ah meant tuh be awful nice."

"Much as Ah done fuh yuh. Holdin' me up tuh scorn. No sympathy!"

"Naw, Jody, it wasn't because Ah didn't have no sympathy. Ah had uh lavish uh dat. Ah just didn't never git no chance tuh use none of it. You wouldn't let me."

"Dat's right, blame everything on me. Ah wouldn't let you show no feelin'! When, Janie, dat's all Ah ever wanted or desired. Now you come blamin' me!"

"'Tain't dat, Jody. Ah ain't here tuh blame nobody. Ah'm just tryin' tuh make you know what kinda person Ah is befo' it's too late."

"Too late?" he whispered.

His eyes buckled in a vacant-mouthed terror and she saw the awful surprise in his face and answered it.

"Yeah, Jody, don't keer whut dat multiplied cockroach told yuh tuh git yo' money, you got tuh die, and yuh can't live."

A deep sob came out of Jody's weak frame. It was like beating a bass drum in a hen-house. Then it rose high like pulling in a trombone.

"Janie! Janie! don't tell me Ah got tuh die, and Ah ain't used tuh thinkin' 'bout it."

"'Tain't really no need of you dying, Jody, if you had of—de doctor—but it don't do no good bringin' dat up now. Dat's just whut Ah wants tuh say, Jody. You wouldn't listen. You done lived wid me for twenty years and you don't half know me atall. And you could have but you was so busy worshippin' de works of yo' own hands, and cuffin' folks around in their minds till you didn't see uh whole heap uh things yuh could have."

"Leave heah, Janie. Don't come heah—"

"Ah knowed you wasn't gointuh lissen tuh me. You changes everything but nothin' don't change you—not even death. But Ah ain't goin' outa here and Ah ain't gointuh hush. Naw, you gointuh listen tuh me one time befo' you die. Have yo' way all yo' life, trample and mash down and then die ruther than tuh let yo'self heah 'bout it. Listen, Jody, you ain't de Jody ah run off down de road wid. You'se whut's left after he died. Ah run off tuh keep house wid you in uh wonderful way. But you wasn't satisfied wid me de way Ah was. Naw! Mah own mind had tuh be squeezed and crowded out tuh make room for yours in me."

"Shut up! Ah wish thunder and lightnin' would kill yuh!"

"Ah know it. And now you got tuh die tuh find out dat you got tuh pacify somebody besides yo'self if you wants any love and any sympathy in dis world. You ain't tried tuh pacify *nobody* but yo'self. Too busy listening tuh yo' own big voice."

"All dis tearin' down talk!" Jody whispered with sweat globules forming all over his face and arms. "Git outa heah!"

"All dis bowin' down, all dis obedience under yo' voice—dat ain't whut Ah rushed off down de road tuh find out about you."

A sound of strife in Jody's throat, but his eyes stared unwillingly into a corner of the room so Janie knew the futile fight was not with her. The icy sword of the square-toed one had cut off his breath and left his hands in a pose of agonizing protest. Janie gave them peace on his breast, then she studied his dead face for a long time.

"Dis sittin' in de rulin' chair is been hard on Jody," she muttered out loud. She was full of pity for the first time in years. Jody had been hard on her and others, but life had mishandled him too. Poor Joe! Maybe if she had known some other way to try, she might have made his face different. But what that other way could be, she had no idea. She thought back and forth about what had happened in the making of a voice out of a man. Then thought about herself. Years ago, she had told her girl self to wait for her in the looking glass. It had been a long time since she had remembered. Perhaps she'd better look. She went over to the dresser and looked hard at her skin and features. The young girl was gone, but a handsome woman had taken her place. She tore off the kerchief from her head and let down her plentiful hair. The weight, the length, the glory was there. She took careful stock of herself, then combed her hair and tied it back up again. Then she starched and ironed her face, forming it into just what people wanted to see, and opened up the window and cried, "Come heah people! Jody is dead. Mah husband is gone from me."

Chapter 9

Joe's funeral was the finest thing Orange County had ever seen with Negro eyes. The motor hearse, the Cadillac and Buick carriages; Dr. Henderson there in his Lincoln; the hosts from far and wide. Then again the gold and red and purple, the gloat and glamor of the secret orders, each with its insinuations of power and glory undreamed of by the uninitiated. People on farm houses and mules; babies riding astride of brothers' and sisters' backs. The Elks band ranked at the church door and playing "Safe in the Arms of Jesus" with such a dominant drum rhythm that it could be stepped off smartly by the long line as it filed inside. The Little Emperor of the cross-roads was leaving Orange County as he had come—with the out-stretched hand of power.

Janie starched and ironed her face and came set in the funeral behind her veil. It was like a wall of stone and steel. The funeral was going on outside. All things concerning death and burial were said and done. Finish. End. Nevermore. Darkness. Deep hole. Dissolution. Eternity. Weeping and wailing outside. Inside the expensive black folds were resurrection and life. She did not reach outside for anything, nor did the things of death reach inside to disturb her calm. She sent her face to Joe's funeral, and herself went rollicking with the springtime across the world. After a while the people finished their celebration and Janie went on home.

Before she slept that night she burnt up every one of her head rags and went about the house next morning with her hair in one thick braid swinging well below her waist. That was the only change people saw in her. She kept the store in the same way except of evenings she sat on the porch and listened and sent Hezekiah in to wait on late custom. She saw no reason to rush at changing things around. She would have the rest of her life to do as she pleased.

Most of the day she was at the store, but at night she was there in the big house and sometimes it creaked and cried all night under the weight of lonesomeness. Then she'd lie awake in bed asking lonesomeness some questions. She asked if she wanted to leave and go back where she had come from and try to find her mother. Maybe tend her grandmother's grave. Sort of look over the old stamping ground generally. Digging around inside of herself like that she found that she had no interest in that seldom-seen mother at all. She hated her grandmother and had hidden it from herself all these years under a cloak of pity. She had been getting ready for her great journey to the horizons in search of *people*; it was important to all the world that she should find them and they find her. But she had been whipped like a cur dog, and run off down a back road after *things*. It was all according to the way you see things. Some people could look at a mud-puddle and see an ocean with ships. But Nanny belonged to that other kind that loved to deal in scraps. Here Nanny had taken the biggest thing God ever made, the horizon—for no matter how far a person can go the horizon is still way beyond you—and pinched it in to such a little bit of a thing that she could tie it about her granddaughter's neck tight enough to choke her. She hated the old woman who had twisted her so in the name of love. Most humans didn't love one another nohow, and this mis-love was so strong that even common blood couldn't overcome it all the time. She had found a jewel down inside herself and she had wanted to walk where people could see her and gleam it around. But she had been set in the market-place to sell. Been set for still-bait. When God had made The Man, he made him out of stuff that sung all the time and glittered all over. Then after that some angels got jealous and chopped him into millions of pieces, but still he glittered and hummed. So they beat him down to nothing but sparks but each little spark had a shine and a song. So they covered each one over with mud. And the lonesomeness in the sparks make them hunt for one another, but the mud is deaf and dumb. Like all the other tumbling mud-balls, Janie had tried to show her shine.

Janie found out very soon that her widowhood and property was a great challenge in South Florida. Before Jody had been dead a month, she noticed how often men who had never been intimates of Joe, drove considerable distances to ask after her welfare and offer their services as advisor.

"Uh woman by herself is uh pitiful thing," she was told over and again. "Dey needs aid and assistance. God never meant 'em tuh try tuh stand by theirselves. You ain't been used tuh knockin' round and doin' fuh yo'self, Mis' Starks. You been well taken keer of, you needs uh man."

Janie laughed at all these well-wishers because she knew that they knew plenty of women alone; that she was not the first one they had ever seen. But most of the others were poor. Besides she liked being lonesome for a change. This freedom feeling was fine. These men didn't represent a thing she wanted to know about. She had already experienced them through Logan and Joe. She felt like slapping some of them for sitting around grinning at her like a pack of chessy cats,[3] trying to make out they looked like love.

Ike Green sat on her case seriously one evening on the store porch when he was lucky enough to catch her alone.

"You wants be keerful 'bout who you marry, Mis' Starks. Dese strange men runnin' heah tryin' tuh take advantage of yo' condition."

"Marry!" Janie almost screamed. "Joe ain't had time tuh git cold yet. Ah ain't even give marryin' de first thought."

"But you will. You'se too young uh 'oman tuh stay single, and you'se too pretty for de mens tuh leave yuh alone. You'se bound tuh marry."

"Ah hope not. Ah mean, at dis present time it don't come befo' me. Joe ain't been dead two months. Ain't got settled down in his grave."

"Dat's whut you say now, but two months mo' and you'll sing another tune. Den you want tuh be keerful. Womenfolks is easy taken advantage of. You know what tuh let none uh dese stray niggers dat's settin' round heah git de inside track on yuh. They's jes lak uh pack uh hawgs, when dey see uh full trough. Whut yuh needs is uh man dat yuh done lived uhround and know all about tuh sort of manage yo' things fuh yuh and ginerally do round."

Janie jumped upon her feet. "Lawd, Ike Green, you'se uh case! Dis subjick you bringin' up ain't fit tuh be talked about at all. Lemme go inside and help Hezekiah weigh up dat barrel uh sugar dat just come in." She rushed on inside the store and whispered to Hezekiah, "Ah'm gone tuh de house. Lemme know when dat ole pee-de-bed is gone and Ah'll be right back."

Six months of wearing black passed and not one suitor had ever gained the house porch. Janie talked and laughed in the store at times, but never seemed to want to go further. She was happy except for the store. She knew by her head that she was absolute owner, but it always seemed to her that she was still clerking for Joe and that soon he would come in and find something wrong that she had done. She almost apologized to the tenants the first time she collected the rents. Felt like a usurper. But she hid that feeling by sending Hezekiah who was the best imitation of Joe that his seventeen years could make. He had even taken to smoking, and smoking cigars, since Joe's death and tried to bite 'em tight in one side of his mouth like Joe. Every chance he got he was reared back in Joe's swivel chair trying to thrust out his lean belly into a paunch. She'd laugh quietly at his no-harm posing and pretend she didn't see it. One day as she came in the back door of the store she heard him bawling at Tripp Crawford, "Naw indeed, we can't do nothin' uh de kind! I god, you ain't paid for dem last rations you done et up. I god, you won't git no mo' outa dis store than you got money tuh pay for. I god, dis ain't Gimme, Florida, dis is Eatonville." Another time she overheard him using Joe's favorite expression for pointing out the differences between himself and the careless-living, mouthy town. "Ah'm an educated man, Ah keep mah arrangements in mah hands."

---

[3]Cheshire cats.

She laughed outright at that. His acting didn't hurt nobody and she wouldn't know what to do without him. He sensed that and came to treat her like baby-sister, as if to say "You poor little thing, give it to big brother. He'll fix it for you." His sense of ownership made him honest too, except for an occasional jaw-breaker, or a packet of sen-sen. The sen-sen was to let on to the other boys and the pullet-size girls that he had a liquor breath to cover. This business of managing stores and women store-owners was trying on a man's nerves. He needed a drink of liquor now and then to keep up.

When Janie emerged into her mourning white, she had hosts of admirers in and out of town. Everything open and frank. Men of property too among the crowd, but nobody seemed to get any further than the store. She was always too busy to take them to the house to entertain. They were all so respectful and stiff with her, that she might have been the Empress of Japan. They felt that it was not fitting to mention desire to the widow of Joseph Starks. You spoke of honor and respect. And all that they said and did was refracted by her inattention and shot off towards the rim-bones of nothing. She and Pheoby Watson visited back and forth and once in awhile sat around the lakes and fished. She was just basking in freedom for the most part without the need for thought. A Sanford undertaker was pressing his cause through Pheoby, and Janie was listening pleasantly but undisturbed. It might be nice to marry him, at that. No hurry. Such things take time to think about, or rather she pretended to Pheoby that that was what she was doing.

"'Tain't dat Ah worries over Joe's death, Pheoby. Ah jus' loves dis freedom."

"Sh-sh-sh! Don't let nobody hear you say dat, Janie. Folks will say you ain't sorry he's gone."

"Let 'em say whut dey wants tuh, Pheoby. To my thinkin' mourning oughtn't tuh last no longer'n grief."

Chapter 10

One day Hezekiah asked off from work to go off with the ball team. Janie told him not to hurry back. She could close up the store herself this once. He cautioned her about the catches on the windows and doors and swaggered off to Winter Park.

Business was dull all day, because numbers of people had gone to the game. She decided to close early, because it was hardly worth the trouble of keeping open on an afternoon like this. She had set six o'clock as her limit.

At five-thirty a tall man came into the place. Janie was leaning on the counter making aimless pencil marks on a piece of wrapping paper. She knew she didn't know his name, but he looked familiar.

"Good evenin', Mis' Starks," he said with a sly grin as if they had a good joke together. She was in favor of the story that was making him laugh before she even heard it.

"Good evenin'," she answered pleasantly. "You got all de advantage 'cause Ah don't know yo' name."

"People wouldn't know me lak dey would *you*."

"Ah guess standin' in uh store do make uh person git tuh be known in de vicinity. Look lak Ah seen you somewhere."

"Oh, Ah don't live no further than Orlandah. Ah'm easy tuh see on Church Street most any day or night. You got any smokin' tobacco?"

She opened the glass case. "What kind?"

"Camels."

She handed over the cigarettes and took the money. He broke the pack and thrust one between his full, purple lips.

"You got a lil piece uh fire over dere, lady?"

They both laughed and she handed him two kitchen matches out of a box for that purpose. It was time for him to go but he didn't. He leaned on the counter with one elbow and cold-cocked her a look.

"Why ain't *you* at de ball game, too? Everybody else is dere."

"Well, Ah see somebody else besides me ain't dere. Ah just sold some cigarettes." They laughed again.

"Dat's 'cause Ah'm dumb. Ah got de thing all mixed up. Ah thought de game was gointuh be out at Hungerford. So Ah got uh ride tuh where dis road turns off from de Dixie Highway and walked over here and then Ah find out de game is in Winter Park."

That was funny to both of them too.

"So what you gointuh do now? All de cars in Eatonville is gone."

"How about playin' *you* some checkers? You looks hard tuh beat."

"Ah is, 'cause Ah can't play uh lick."

"You don't cherish de game, then?"

"Yes, Ah do, and then agin Ah don't know whether Ah do or not, 'cause nobody ain't never showed me how."

"Dis is de last day for *dat* excuse. You got uh board round heah?"

"Yes indeed. De men folks treasures de game round heah. Ah just ain't never learnt how."

He set it up and began to show her and she found herself glowing inside. Somebody wanted her to play. Somebody thought it natural for her to play. That was even nice. She looked him over and got little thrills from every one of his good points. Those full, lazy eyes with the lashes curling sharply away like drawn scimitars. The lean, over-padded shoulders and narrow waist. Even nice!

He was jumping her king! She screamed in protest against losing the king she had had such a hard time acquiring. Before she knew it she had grabbed his hand to stop him. He struggled gallantly to free himself. That is he struggled, but not hard enough to wrench a lady's fingers.

"Ah got uh right tuh take it. You left it right in mah way."

"Yeah, but Ah wuz lookin' off when you went and stuck yo' men right up next tuh mine. No fair!"

"You ain't supposed tuh look off, Mis' Starks. It's de biggest part uh de game tuh watch out! Leave go mah hand."

"No suh! Not mah king. You kin take another one, but not dat one."

They scrambled and upset the board and laughed at that.

"Anyhow it's time for uh Coca-Cola," he said. "Ah'll come teach yuh some mo' another time."

"It's all right tuh come teach me, but don't come tuh cheat me."

"Yuh can't beat uh woman. Dey jes won't stand fuh it. But Ah'll come teach yuh agin. You gointuh be uh good player too, after while."

"You reckon so? Jody useter tell me Ah never would learn. It wuz too heavy fuh mah brains."

"Folks is playin' it wid sense and folks is playin' it without. But you got good meat on yo' head. You'll learn. Have uh cool drink on me."

"Oh all right, thank yuh. Got plenty cold ones tuhday. Nobody ain't been heah tuh buy none. All gone off tuh de game."

"You oughta be at de next game. 'Tain't no use in *you* stayin' heah if everybody else is gone. You don't buy from yo'self, do yuh?"

"You crazy thing! 'Course Ah don't. But Ah'm worried 'bout you uh little."

"How come? 'Fraid Ah ain't gointuh pay fuh dese drinks?"

"Aw naw! How you gointuh git back home?"

"Wait round heah fuh a car. If none don't come, Ah got good shoe leather. 'Tain't but seben miles nohow. Ah could walk dat in no time. Easy."

"If it wuz me, Ah'd wait on uh train. Seben miles is uh kinda long walk."

"It would be for you, 'cause you ain't used to it. But Ah'm seen women walk further'n dat. You could too, if yuh had it tuh do."

"Maybe so, but Ah'll ride de train long as Ah got railroad fare."

"Ah don't need no pocket-full uh money to ride de train lak uh woman. When Ah takes uh notion Ah rides anyhow—money or no money."

"Now ain't you somethin'! Mr. er—er—You never did tell me whut yo' name wuz."

"Ah sho didn't. Wuzn't expectin' fuh it to be needed. De name mah mama gimme is Vergible Woods. Dey calls me Tea Cake for short."

"Tea Cake! So you sweet as all dat?" She laughed and he gave her a little cut-eye look to get her meaning.

"Ah may be guilty. You better try me and see."

She did something halfway between a laugh and a frown and he set his hat on straight.

"B'lieve Ah done cut uh hawg, so Ah guess Ah better ketch air." He made an elaborate act of tipping to the door stealthily. Then looked back at her with an irresistible grin on his face. Janie burst out laughing in spite of herself. "You crazy thing!"

He turned and threw his hat at her feet. "If she don't throw it at me, Ah'll take a chance on comin' back," he announced, making gestures to indicate he was hidden behind a post. She picked up the hat and threw it after him with a laugh. "Even if she had uh brick she couldn't hurt yuh wid it," he said to an invisible companion. "De lady can't throw." He gestured to his companion, stepped out from behind the imaginary lamp post, set his coat and hat and strolled back to where Janie was; as if he had just come in the store.

"Evenin', Mis' Starks. Could yuh lemme have uh pound uh knuckle puddin'[4] till Saturday? Ah'm sho tuh pay yuh then."

---

[4] A beating with the fist.

"You needs ten pounds, Mr. Tea Cake. Ah'll let yuh have all Ah got and you needn't bother 'bout payin' it back."

They joked and went on till the people began to come in. Then he took a seat and made talk and laughter with the rest until closing time. When everyone else had left he said, "Ah reckon Ah done over-layed mah leavin' time, but Ah figgured you needed somebody tuh help yuh shut up de place. Since nobody else ain't round heah, maybe Ah kin git de job."

"Thankyuh, Mr. Tea Cake. It is kinda strainin' fuh me."

"Who ever heard of uh teacake bein' called Mister! If you wanta be real high-toned and call me Mr. Woods, dat's de way you feel about it. If yuh wants tuh be uh lil friendly and call me Tea Cake, dat would be real nice." He was closing and bolting windows all the time he talked.

"All right, then. Thank yuh, Tea Cake. How's dat?"

"Jes lak uh lil girl wid her Easter dress on. Even nice!" He locked the door and shook it to be sure and handed her the key. "Come on now, Ah'll see yuh inside yo' door and git on down de Dixie."

Janie was halfway down the palm-lined walk before she had a thought for her safety. Maybe this strange man was up to something! But it was no place to show her fear there in the darkness between the house and the store. He had hold of her arm too. Then in a moment it was gone. Tea Cake wasn't strange. Seemed as if she had known him all her life. Look how she had been able to talk with him right off! He tipped his hat at the door and was off with the briefest good night.

So she sat on the porch and watched the moon rise. Soon its amber fluid was drenching the earth, and quenching the thirst of the day.

Chapter 11

Janie wanted to ask Hezekiah about Tea Cake, but she was afraid he might misunderstand her and think she was interested. In the first place he looked too young for her. Must be around twenty-five and here *she* was around forty. Then again he didn't look like he had too much. Maybe he was hanging around to get in with her and strip her of all that she had. Just as well if she never saw him again. He was probably the kind of man who lived with various women but never married. Fact is, she decided to treat him so cold if he ever did foot the place that he'd be sure not to come hanging around there again.

He waited a week exactly to come back for Janie's snub. It was early in the afternoon and she and Hezekiah were alone. She heard somebody humming like they were feeling for pitch and looked towards the door. Tea Cake stood there mimicking the tuning of a guitar. He frowned and struggled with the pegs of his imaginary instrument watching her out of the corner of his eye with that secret joke playing over his face. Finally she smiled and he sung middle C, put his guitar under his arm and walked on back to where she was.

"Evenin', folks. Thought y'all might lak uh lil music this evenin' so Ah brought long mah box."

"Crazy thing!" Janie commented, beaming out with light.

He acknowledged the compliment with a smile and sat down on a box. "Anybody have uh Coca-Cola wid me?"

"Ah just had one," Janie temporized with her conscience.

"It'll hafter be done all over agin, Mis' Starks."

"How come?"

"'Cause it wasn't done right dat time. 'Kiah bring us two bottles from de bottom uh de box."

"How you been makin' out since Ah seen yuh last, Tea Cake?"

"Can't kick. Could be worse. Made four days dis week and got de pay in mah pocket."

"We got a rich man round here, then. Buyin' passenger trains uh battleships this week?"

"Which one do *you* want? It all depends on you."

"Oh, if you'se treatin' me tuh it, Ah b'lieve Ah'll take de passenger train. If it blow up Ah'll still be on land."

"Choose de battleship if dat's whut you really want. Ah know where one is right now. Seen one round Key West de other day."

"How you gointuh git it?"

"Ah shucks, dem Admirals is always ole folks. Can't no ole man stop me from gittin' no ship for yuh if dat's whut you want. Ah'd git dat ship out from under him so slick till he'd be walkin' de water lak ole Peter befo' he knowed it."

They played away the evening again. Everybody was surprised at Janie playing checkers but they liked it. Three or four stood behind her and coached her moves and generally made merry with her in a restrained way. Finally everybody went home but Tea Cake.

"You kin close up, 'Kiah," Janie said. "Think Ah'll g'wan home."

Tea Cake fell in beside her and mounted the porch this time. So she offered him a seat and they made a lot of laughter out of nothing. Near eleven o'clock she remembered a piece of pound cake she had put away. Tea Cake went out to the lemon tree at the corner of the kitchen and picked some lemons and squeezed them for her. So they had lemonade too.

"Moon's too pretty fuh anybody tuh be sleepin' it away," Tea Cake said after they had washed up the plates and glasses. "Less us go fishin'."

"Fishin'? Dis time uh night?"

"Unhhunh, fishin'. Ah know where de bream is beddin'. Seen 'em when Ah come round de lake dis evenin'. Where's yo' fishin' poles? Less go set on de lake."

It was so crazy digging worms by lamp light and setting out for Lake Sabelia after midnight that she felt like a child breaking rules. That's what made Janie like it. They caught two or three and got home just before day. Then she had to smuggle Tea Cake out by the back gate and that made it seem like some great secret she was keeping from the town.

"Mis' Janie," Hezekiah began sullenly next day, "you oughtn't 'low dat Tea Cake tuh be walkin' tuh de house wid yuh. Ah'll go wid yuh mahself after dis, if you'se skeered."

"What's de matter wid Tea Cake, 'Kiah? Is he uh thief uh somethin'?"

"Ah ain't never heard nobody say he stole nothin'."

"Is he bad 'bout totin' pistols and knives tuh hurt people wid?"

"Dey don't say he ever cut nobody or shot nobody neither."

"Well, is he—he—is he got uh wife or something lak dat? Not dat it's any uh mah business." She held her breath for the answer.

"No'm. And nobody wouldn't marry Tea Cake tuh starve tuh death lessen it's somebody jes lak him—ain't used to nothin'. 'Course he always keep hisself in changin' clothes. Dat long-legged Tea Cake ain't got doodly squat. He ain't got no business makin' hissef familiar wid nobody lak you. Ah said Ah wuz goin' to tell yuh so yuh could know."

"Oh dat's all right, Hezekiah. Thank yuh mighty much."

The next night when she mounted her steps Tea Cake was there before her, sitting on the porch in the dark. He had a string of fresh-caught trout for a present.

"Ah'll clean 'em, you fry 'em and let's eat," he said with the assurance of not being refused. They went out into the kitchen and fixed up the hot fish and corn muffins and ate. Then Tea Cake went to the piano without so much as asking and began playing blues and singing, and throwing grins over his shoulder. The sounds lulled Janie to soft slumber and she woke up with Tea Cake combing her hair and scratching the dandruff from her scalp. It made her more comfortable and drowsy.

"Tea Cake, where you git uh comb from tuh be combin' mah hair wid?"

"Ah brought it wid me. Come prepared tuh lay mah hands on it tuhnight."

"Why, Tea Cake? Whut good do combin' mah hair do *you*? It's *mah* comfortable, not yourn."

"It's mine too. Ah ain't been sleepin' so good for more'n uh week cause Ah been wishin' so bad tuh git mah hands in yo' hair. It's so pretty. It feels jus' lak underneath uh dove's wing next to mah face."

"Umph! You'se mighty easy satisfied. Ah been had dis same hair next tuh mah face ever since Ah cried de fust time, and 'tain't never gimme me no thrill."

"Ah tell you lak you told me—you'se mighty hard tuh satisfy. Ah betcha dem lips don't satisfy yuh neither."

"Dat's right, Tea Cake. They's dere and Ah make use of 'em whenever it's necessary, but nothin' special tuh me."

"Umph! umph! umph! Ah betcha you don't never go tuh de lookin' glass and enjoy yo' eyes yo'self. You lets other folks git all de enjoyment out of 'em 'thout takin' in any of it yo'self."

"Naw, Ah never gazes at 'em in de lookin' glass. If anybody else gits any pleasure out of 'em Ah ain't been told about it."

"See dat? You'se got de world in uh jug and make out you don't know it. But Ah'm glad tuh be de one tuh tell yuh."

"Ah guess you done told plenty women all about it."

"Ah'm de Apostle Paul tuh de Gentiles. Ah tells 'em and then agin Ah shows 'em."

"Ah thought so." She yawned and made to get up from the sofa. "You done got me so sleepy wid yo' head-scratchin' Ah kin hardly make it tuh de bed." She stood up at once, collecting her hair. He sat still.

"Naw, you ain't sleepy, Mis' Janie. You jus' want me tuh go. You figger Ah'm uh rounder and uh pimp and you done wasted too much time talkin' wid me."

"Why, Tea Cake! Whut ever put dat notion in yo' head?"

"De way you looked at me when Ah said whut Ah did. Yo' face skeered me so bad till mah whiskers drawed up."

"Ah ain't got no business bein' mad at nothin' you do and say. You got it all wrong. Ah ain't mad atall."

"Ah know it and dat's what puts de shamery on me. You'se jus' disgusted wid me. Yo' face jus' left here and went off somewhere else. Naw, you ain't mad wid me. Ah be glad if you was, 'cause then Ah might do somethin' tuh please yuh. But lak it is—"

"Mah likes and dislikes ought not tuh make no difference wid you, Tea Cake. Dat's fuh yo' lady friend. Ah'm jus' uh sometime friend uh yourn."

Janie walked towards the stairway slowly, and Tea Cake sat where he was, as if he had frozen to his seat, in fear that once he got up, he'd never get back in it again. He swallowed hard and looked at her walk away.

"Ah didn't aim tuh let on tuh yuh 'bout it, leastways not right away, but Ah ruther be shot wid tacks than fuh you tuh act wid me lak you is right now. You got me in de go-long."

At the newel post Janie whirled around and for the space of a thought she was lit up like a transfiguration. Her next thought brought her crashing down. *He's just saying anything for the time being, feeling he's got me so I'll b'lieve him.* The next thought buried her under tons of cold futility. *He's trading on being younger than me. Getting ready to laugh at me for an old fool. But oh, what wouldn't I give to be twelve years younger so I could b'lieve him!*

"Aw, Tea Cake, you just say dat tuhnight because de fish and corn bread tasted sort of good. Tomorrow yo' mind would change."

"Naw, it wouldn't neither. Ah know better."

"Anyhow from what you told me when we wuz back dere in de kitchen Ah'm nearly twelve years older than you."

"Ah done thought all about dat and tried tuh struggle aginst it, but it don't do me no good. De thought uh mah youngness don't satisfy me lak yo' presence do."

"It makes uh whole heap uh difference wid most folks, Tea Cake."

"Things lak dat got uh whole lot tuh do wid convenience, but it ain't got nothin' tuh do wid love."

"Well, Ah love tuh find out whut you think after sun-up tomorrow. Dis is jus' yo' night thought."

"You got yo' ideas and Ah got mine. Ah got uh dollar dat says you'se wrong. But Ah reckon you don't bet money, neither."

"Ah never have done it so fur. But as de old folks always say, Ah'm born but Ah ain't dead. No tellin' whut Ah'm liable tuh do yet."

He got up suddenly and took his hat. "Good night, Mis' Janie. Look lak we done run our conversation from grass roots tuh pine trees. G'bye." He almost ran out of the door.

Janie hung over the newel post thinking so long that she all but went to sleep there. However, before she went to bed she took a good look at her mouth, eyes and hair.

All next day in the house and store she thought resisting thoughts about Tea Cake. She even ridiculed him in her mind and was a little ashamed of the association. But every hour or two the battle had to be fought all over again. She couldn't make him look just like any other man to her. He looked like the love thoughts of women. He could be a bee to a blossom—a pear tree blossom in the spring. He seemed to be crushing scent out of the world with his footsteps. Crushing aromatic herbs with every step he took. Spices hung about him. He was a glance from God.

So he didn't come that night and she laid in bed and pretended to think scornfully of him. "Bet he's hangin' round some jook or 'nother. Glad Ah treated him cold. Whut do Ah want wid some trashy nigger out de streets? Bet he's livin' wid some woman or 'nother and takin' me for uh fool. Glad Ah caught mahself in time." She tried to console herself that way.

The next morning she awoke hearing a knocking on the front door and found Tea Cake there.

"Hello, Mis' Janie, Ah hope Ah woke you up."

"You sho did, Tea Cake. Come in and rest yo' hat. Whut you doin' out so soon dis mornin'?"

"Thought Ah'd try tuh git heah soon enough tuh tell yuh mah daytime thoughts. Ah see yuh needs tuh know mah daytime feelings. Ah can't sense yuh intuh it at night."

"You crazy thing! Is dat whut you come here for at daybreak?"

"Sho is. You needs tellin' and showin', and dat's whut Ah'm doin'. Ah picked some strawberries too, Ah figgered you might like."

"Tea Cake, Ah 'clare Ah don't know whut tuh make outa you. You'se so crazy. You better lemme fix you some breakfast."

"Ain't got time. Ah got uh job uh work. Gottuh be back in Orlandah at eight o'clock. See yuh later, tell you straighter."

He bolted down the walk and was gone. But that night when she left the store, he was stretched out in the hammock on the porch with his hat over his face pretending to sleep. She called him. He pretended not to hear. He snored louder. She went to the hammock to shake him and he seized and pulled her in with him. After a little, she let him adjust her in his arms and laid there for a while.

"Tea Cake, Ah don't know 'bout you, but Ah'm hongry, come on let's eat some supper."

They went inside and their laughter rang out first from the kitchen and all over the house.

Janie awoke next morning by feeling Tea Cake almost kissing her breath away. Holding her and caressing her as if he feared she might escape his grasp and fly away. Then he must dress hurriedly and get to his job on time. He wouldn't let her get him any breakfast at all. He wanted her to get her rest. He made her stay where she was. In her heart she wanted to get his breakfast for him. But she stayed in bed long after he was gone.

So much had been breathed out by the pores that Tea Cake still was there. She could feel him and almost see him bucking around the room in the upper air. After a long time of passive happiness, she got up and opened the window and let Tea Cake leap forth and mount to the sky on a wind. That was the beginning of things.

In the cool of the afternoon the fiend from hell specially sent to lovers arrived at Janie's ear. Doubt. All the fears that circumstance could provide and the heart feel, attacked her on every side. This was a new sensation for her, but no less excruciating. If only Tea Cake would make her certain! He did not return that night nor the next and so she plunged into the abyss and descended to the ninth darkness where light has never been.

But the fourth day after he came in the afternoon driving a battered car. Jumped out like a deer and made the gesture of tying it to a post on the store porch. Ready with his grin! She adored him and hated him at the same time. How could he make her suffer so and then come grinning like that with that darling way he had? He pinched her arm as he walked inside he door.

"Brought me somethin' tuh haul you off in," he told her with that secret chuckle. "Git yo' hat if you gointuh wear one. We got tuh go buy groceries."

"Ah sells groceries right here in dis store, Tea Cake, if you don't happen tuh know." She tried to look cold but she was smiling in spite of herself.

"Not de kind we want fuh de occasion. You sells groceries for ordinary people. We'se gointuh buy for *you*. De big Sunday School picnic is tomorrow—bet you done forget it—and we got tuh be dere wid uh swell basket and ourselves."

"Ah don't know 'bout dat, Tea Cake. Tell yuh whut you do. G'wan down tuh de house and wait for me. Be dere in uh minute."

As soon as she thought it looked right she slipped out of the back and joined Tea Cake. No need of fooling herself. Maybe he was just being polite.

"Tea Cake, you sure you want me tuh go tuh dis picnic wid yuh?"

"Me scramble 'round tuh git de money tuh take yuh—been workin' lak uh dawg for two whole weeks—and she come astin' me if Ah want her tuh go! Puttin' mahself tuh uh whole heap uh trouble tuh git dis car so you kin go over tuh Winter Park or Orlandah tuh buy de things you might need and dis woman set dere and ast me if Ah want her tuh go!"

"Don't git mad, Tea Cake, Ah just didn't want you doin' nothin' outa politeness. If dere's somebody else you'd ruther take, it's all right wid me."

"Naw, it ain't all right wid you. If it was you wouldn't be sayin' dat. Have de nerve tuh say whut you mean."

"Well, all right, Tea Cake, Ah wants tuh go wid you real bad, but,—oh, Tea Cake, don't make no false pretense wid me!"

"Janie, Ah hope God may kill me, if Ah'm lyin'. Nobody else on earth kin hold uh candle tuh you, baby. You got de keys to de kingdom."

Chapter 12

It was after the picnic that the town began to notice things and got mad. Tea Cake and Mrs. Mayor Starks! All the men that she could get, and fooling with somebody like Tea Cake! Another thing, Joe Starks hadn't been dead but nine months and here she goes sashaying off to a picnic in pink linen. Done quit attending church, like she used to. Gone off to Sanford in a car with Tea Cake and her all dressed in blue! It was a shame. Done took to high heel slippers and a ten dollar hat! Looking like some young girl, always in blue because Tea Cake told her to wear it. Poor Joe Starks. Bet he turns over in his grave every day. Tea Cake and Janie gone hunting. Tea Cake and Janie gone fishing. Tea Cake and

Janie gone to Orlando to the movies. Tea Cake and Janie gone to a dance. Tea Cake making flower beds in Janie's yard and seeding the garden for her. Chopping down that tree she never did like by the dining room window. All those signs of possession. Tea Cake in a borrowed car teaching Janie to drive. Tea Cake and Janie playing checkers; playing coon-can; playing Florida flip[5] on the store porch all afternoon as if nobody else was there. Day after day and week after week.

"Pheoby," Sam Watson said one night as he got in the bed, "Ah b'lieve yo' buddy is all tied up with dat Tea Cake shonough. Didn't b'lieve it at first."

"Aw she don't mean nothin' by it. Ah think she's sort of stuck on dat undertaker up at Sanford."

"It's somebody 'cause she looks might good dese days. New dresses and her hair combed a different way nearly every day. You got to have something to comb hair over. When you see uh woman doin' so much rakin' in her head, she's combin' at some man or 'nother."

"'Course she kin do as she please, but dat's uh good chance she got up at Sanford. De man's wife died and he got uh lovely place tuh take her to—already furnished. Better'n her house Joe left her."

"You better sense her intuh things then 'cause Tea Cake can't do nothin' but help her spend whut she got. Ah reckon dat's whut he's after. Throwin' away whut Joe Starks worked hard tuh git tuhgether."

"Dat's de way it looks. Still and all, she's her own woman. She oughta know by now whut she wants tuh do."

"De men wuz talkin' 'bout it in de grove tuhday and givin' her and Tea Cake both de devil. Dey figger he's spendin' on her now in order tuh make her spend on him later."

"Umph! Umph! Umph!"

"Oh dey got it all figgered out. Maybe it ain't as bad as they say, but they talk it and make it sound real bad on her part."

"Dat's jealousy and malice. Some uh dem very mens wants tuh do whut dey claim deys skeered Tea Cake is doin'."

"De Pastor claim Tea Cake don't 'low her tuh come tuh church only once in awhile 'cause he want dat change tuh buy gas wid. Just draggin' de woman away from church. But anyhow, she's yo' bosom friend, so you better go see 'bout her. Drop uh lil hint here and dere and if Tea Cake is tryin' tuh rob her she kin see and know. Ah laks de woman and Ah sho would hate tuh see her come up lak Mis' Tyler."

"Aw mah God, naw! Reckon Ah better step over dere tomorrow and have some chat wid Janie. She jus' ain't thinkin' whut she doin', dat's all."

The next morning Pheoby picked her way over to Janie's house like a hen to a neighbor's garden. Stopped and talked a little with everyone she met, turned aside momentarily to pause at a porch or two—going straight by walking crooked. So her firm intention looked like an accident and she didn't have to give her opinion to folks along the way.

---

[5]Coon-can and Florida flip are card games.

Janie acted glad to see her and after a while Pheoby broached her with, "Janie, everybody's talkin' 'bout how dat Tea Cake is draggin' you round tuh places you ain't used tuh. Baseball games and huntin' and fishin'. He don't know you'se useter uh more high time crowd than dat. You always did class off."

"Jody classed me off. Ah didn't. Naw, Pheoby, Tea Cake ain't draggin' me off nowhere Ah don't want tuh go. Ah always did want tuh git round uh whole heap, but Jody wouldn't 'low me tuh. When Ah wasn't in de store he wanted me tuh jes sit wid folded hands and sit dere. And Ah'd sit dere wid de walls creepin' up on me and squeezin' all de life outa me. Pheoby, dese educated women got uh heap of things to sit down and consider. Somebody done tole 'em what to set down for. Nobody ain't told poor me, so sittin' still worries me. Ah wants tuh utilize mah-self all over."

"But, Janie, Tea Cake, whilst he ain't no jail-bird, he ain't got uh dime tuh cry. Ain't you skeered he's jes after yo' money—him bein' younger than you?"

"He ain't never ast de first penny from me yet, and if he love property he ain't no different from all de rest of us. All dese ole men dat's settin' round me is after de same thing. They's three mo' widder women in town, how come dey don't break dey neck after dem? 'Cause dey ain't got nothin', dat's why."

"Folks seen you out in colors and dey thinks you ain't payin' de right amount uh respect tuh yo dead husband."

"Ah ain't grievin' so why do Ah hafta mourn? Tea Cake love me in blue, so Ah wears it. Jody ain't never in his life picked out no color for me. De world picked out black and white for mournin', Joe didn't. So Ah wasn't wearin' it for him. Ah was wearin' it for de rest of y'all."

"But anyhow, watch yo'self, Janie, and don't be took advantage of. You know how dese young men is wid older women. Most of de time dey's after whut dey kin git, then dey's gone lak uh turkey through de corn."

"Tea Cake don't talk dat way. He's aimin' tuh make hisself permanent wid me. We done made up our mind tuh marry."

"Janie, you'se yo' own woman, and Ah hope you know whut you doin'. Ah sho hope you ain't lak uh possum—de older you gits, de less sense yuh got. Ah'd feel uh whole heap better 'bout yuh if you wuz marryin' dat man up dere in Sanford. He got somethin' tuh put long side uh whut you got and dat make it more better. He's endurable."

"Still and all Ah'd ruther be wid Tea Cake."

"Well, if yo' mind is already made up, 'tain't nothin' nobody kin do. But you'se takin' uh awful chance."

"No mo' than Ah took befo' and no mo' than anybody else takes when dey gits married. It always changes folks, and sometimes it brings out dirt and meanness dat even de person didn't know they had in 'em theyselves. You know dat. Maybe Tea Cake might turn out lak dat. Maybe not. Anyhow Ah'm ready and willin' tuh try 'im."

"Well, when you aim tuh step off?"

"Dat we don't know. De store is got tuh be sold and then we'se goin' off somewhere tuh git married."

"How come you sellin' out de store?"

"'Cause Tea Cake ain't no Jody Starks, and if he tried tuh be, it would be uh complete flommuck. But de minute Ah marries 'im everybody is gointuh be makin' comparisons. So us is goin' off somewhere and start all over in Tea Cake's way. Dis ain't no business proposition, and no race after property and titles. Dis is uh love game. Ah done lived Grandma's way, now Ah means tuh live mine."

"What you mean by dat, Janie?"

"She was borned in slavery time when folks, dat is black folks, didn't sit down anytime dey felt lak it. So sittin' on porches lak de white madam looked lak uh mighty fine thing tuh her. Dat's whut she wanted for me—don't keer whut it cost. Git up on uh high chair and sit dere. She didn't have time tuh think whut tuh do after you got up on de stool uh do nothin'. De object wuz tuh git dere. So Ah got up on de high stool lak she told me, but Pheoby, Ah done nearly languished tuh death up dere. Ah felt like de world wuz cryin' extry and Ah ain't read de common news yet."

"Maybe so, Janie. Still and all Ah'd love tuh experience it for just one year. It look lak heben tuh me from where Ah'm at."

"Ah reckon so."

"But anyhow, Janie, you be keerful 'bout dis sellin' out and goin' off wid strange men. Look whut happened tuh Annie Tyler. Took whut little she had and went off tuh Tampa wid dat boy dey call Who Flung. It's somethin' tuh think about."

"It sho is. Still Ah ain't Mis' Tyler and Tea Cake ain't no Who Flung, and he ain't no stranger tuh me. We'se just as good as married already. But Ah ain't puttin' it in de street. Ah'm tellin *you*."

"Ah jus lak uh chicken. Chicken drink water, but he don't pee-pee."

"Oh, Ah know you don't talk. We ain't shame faced. We just ain't ready tuh make no big kerflommuck as yet."

"You doin' right not tuh talk it, but Janie, you'se takin' uh mighty big chance."

"'Tain't so big uh chance as it seem lak, Pheoby. Ah'm older than Tea Cake, yes. But he done showed me where it's de thought dat makes de difference in ages. If people thinks de same they can make it all right. So in the beginnin' new thoughts had tuh be thought and new words said. After Ah got used tuh dat, we gits 'long jus' fine. He done taught me de maiden language all over. Wait till you see de new blue satin Tea Cake done picked out for me tuh stand up wid him in. High heel slippers, necklace, earrings, *everything* he wants tuh see me in. Some of dese mornin's and it won't be long, you gointuh wake up callin' me and Ah'll be gone."

Chapter 13

Jacksonville. Tea Cake's letter had said Jacksonville. He had worked in the railroad shops up there before and his old boss had promised him a job come next pay day. No need for Janie to wait any longer. Wear the new blue dress because he meant to marry her right from the train. Hurry up and come because he was about to turn into pure sugar thinking about her. Come on, baby, papa Tea Cake never could be mad with you!

Janie's train left too early in the day for the town to witness much, but the few who saw her leave bore plenty witness. They had to give it to her, she sho looked good, but she had no business to do it. It was hard to love a woman that always made you feel so wishful.

The train beat on itself and danced on the shiny steel rails mile after mile. Every now and then the engineer would play on his whistle for the people in the towns he passed by. And the train shuffled on to Jacksonville, and to a whole lot of things she wanted to see and to know.

And there was Tea Cake in the big old station in a new blue suit and straw hat, hauling her off to a preacher's house first thing. Then right on to the room he had been sleeping in for two weeks all by himself waiting for her to come. And such another hugging and kissing and carrying on you never saw. It made her so glad she was scared of herself. They stayed at home and rested that night, but the next night they went to a show and after that they rode around on the trolley cars and sort of looked things over for themselves. Tea Cake was spending and doing out of his own pocket, so Janie never told him about the two hundred dollars she had pinned inside her shirt next to her skin. Pheoby had insisted that she bring it along and keep it secret just to be on the safe side. She had ten dollars over her fare in her pocket book. Let Tea Cake think that was all she had. Things might not turn out like she thought. Every minute since she had stepped off the train she had been laughing at Pheoby's advice. She meant to tell Tea Cake the joke some time when she was sure she wouldn't hurt his feelings. So it came around that she had been married a week and sent Pheoby a card with a picture on it.

That morning Tea Cake got up earlier than Janie did. She felt sleepy and told him to go get some fish to fry for breakfast. By the time he had gone and come back she would have finished her nap out. He told her he would and she turned over and went back to sleep. She woke up and Tea Cake still wasn't there and the clock said it was getting late, so she got up and washed her face and hands. Perhaps he was down in the kitchen fixing around to let her sleep. Janie went down and the landlady made her drink some coffee with her because she said her husband was dead and it was bad to be having your morning coffee by yourself.

"Yo' husband gone tuh work dis mornin', Mis' Woods? Ah seen him go out uh good while uh go. Me and you kin be comp'ny for one 'nother, can't us?"

"Oh yes, indeed, Mis' Samuels. You puts me in de mind uh mah friend back in Eatonville. Yeah, you'se nice and friendly jus' lak her."

Therefore Janie drank her coffee and sankled on back to her room without asking her landlady anything. Tea Cake must be hunting all over the city for that fish. She kept that thought in front of her in order not to think too much. When she heard the twelve o'clock whistle she decided to get up and dress. That was when she found out her two hundred dollars was gone. There was the little cloth purse with the safety pin on the chair beneath her clothes and the money just wasn't nowhere in the room. She knew from the beginning that the money wasn't any place she knew of if it wasn't in that little pocket book pinned to her pink silk vest. But the exercise of searching the room kept her busy and that was good for her to keep moving, even though she wasn't doing anything but turning around in her tracks.

But, don't care how firm your determination is, you can't keep turning round in one place like a horse grinding sugar cane. So Janie took to sitting over the room. Sit and look. The room inside looked like the mouth of an alligator—gaped wide open to swallow something down. Outside the window Jacksonville looked like it needed a fence around it to keep it from running out on ether's bosom. It was too big to be warm, let alone to need somebody like her. All day and night she worried time like a bone.

Way late in the morning the thought of Annie Tyler and Who Flung came to pay her a visit. Annie Tyler who at fifty-two had been left a widow with a good home and insurance money.

Mrs. Tyler with her dyed hair, newly straightened and her uncomfortable new false teeth, her leathery skin, blotchy with powder and her giggle. Her love affairs, affairs with boys in their late teens or early twenties for all of whom she spent her money on suits of clothes, shoes, watches and things like that and how they all left her as soon as their wants were satisfied. Then when her ready cash was gone, had come Who Flung to denounce his predecessor as a scoundrel and took up around the house himself. It was he who persuaded her to sell her house and come to Tampa with him. The town had seen her limp off. The undersized high-heel slippers were punishing her tired feet that looked like bunions all over. Her body squeezed and crowded into a tight corset that shoved her middle up under her chin. But she had gone off laughing and sure. As sure as Janie had been.

Then two weeks later the porter and conductor of the north bound local had helped her off the train at Maitland. Hair all gray and black and bluish and red-dish in streaks. All the capers that cheap dye could cut was showing in her hair. Those slippers bent and griped just like her work-worn feet. The corset gone and the shaking old woman hanging all over herself. Everything that you could see was hanging. Her chin hung from her ears and rippled down her neck like drapes. Her hanging bosom and stomach and buttocks and legs that draped down over her ankles. She groaned but never giggled.

She was broken and her pride was gone, so she told those who asked what had happened. Who Flung had taken her to a shabby room in a shabby house in a shabby street and promised to marry her next day. They stayed in the room two whole days then she woke up to find Who Flung and her money gone. She got up to stir around and see if she could find him, and found herself too worn out to do much. All she found out was that she was too old a vessel for new wine. The next day hunger had driven her out to shift. She had stood on the streets and smiled and smiled, and then smiled and begged and then just begged. After a week of world-bruising a young man from home had come along and seen her. She couldn't tell him how it was. She just told him she got off the train and somebody had stolen her purse. Naturally, he had believed her and taken her home with him to give her time to rest up a day or two, then he had bought her a ticket for home.

They put her to bed and sent for her married daughter from up around Ocala to come see about her. The daughter came as soon as she could and took Annie Tyler away to die in peace. She had waited all her life for something, and it had killed her when it found her.

The thing made itself into pictures and hung around Janie's bedside all night long. Anyhow, she wasn't going back to Eatonville to be laughed at and pitied. She had ten dollars in her pocket and twelve hundred in the bank. But oh God, don't let Tea Cake be off somewhere hurt and Ah not know nothing about it. And God, please suh, don't let him love nobody else but me. Maybe Ah'm is uh fool, Lawd, lak dey say, but Lawd, Ah been so lonesome, and Ah been waitin', Jesus. Ah done waited uh long time.

Janie dozed off to sleep but she woke up in time to see the sun sending up spies ahead of him to mark out the road through the dark. He peeped up over the door sill of the world and made a little foolishness with red. But pretty soon, he laid all that aside and went about his business dressed all in white. But it was always going to be dark to Janie if Tea Cake didn't soon come back. She got out of the bed but a chair couldn't hold her. She dwindled down on the floor with her head in a rocking chair.

After a while there was somebody playing a guitar outside her door. Played right smart while. It sounded lovely too. But it was sad to hear it feeling blue like Janie was. Then whoever it was started to singing "Ring de bells of mercy. Call de sinner man home." Her heart all but smothered her.

"Tea Cake, is dat you?"

"You know so well it's me, Janie. How come you don't open de door?"

But he never waited. He walked on in with a guitar and a grin. Guitar hanging round his neck with a red silk cord and a grin hanging from his ears.

"Don't need tuh ast me where Ah been all dis time, 'cause it's mah all day job tuh tell yuh."

"Tea Cake, Ah—"

"Good Lawd, Janie, whut you doin' settin' on de floor?"

He took her head in his hands and eased himself into the chair. She still didn't say anything. He sat stroking her head and looking down into her face.

"Ah see whut it is. You doubted me 'bout de money. Thought Ah had done took it and gone. Ah don't blame yuh but it wasn't lak you think. De girl baby ain't born and her mama is dead, dat can git me tuh spend our money on her. Ah told yo' before dat you got de keys tuh de kingdom. You can depend on dat."

"Still and all you went off and left me all day and all night."

"'Twasn't 'cause Ah wanted tuh stay off lak dat, and it sho Lawd, wuzn't no woman. If you didn't have de power tuh hold me and hold me tight, Ah wouldn't be callin' yuh Mis' Woods. Ah met plenty women before Ah knowed you tuh talk tuh. You'se de onliest woman in de world Ah ever even mentioned gitting married tuh. You bein' older don't make no difference. Don't never consider dat no mo'. If Ah ever gits tuh messin' round another woman it won't be on account of her age. It'll be because she got me in de same way you got me—so Ah can't help mahself."

He sat down on the floor beside her and kissed and playfully turned up the corner of her mouth until she smiled.

"Looka here, folks," he announced to an imaginary audience, "Sister Woods is 'bout tuh quit her husband!"

Janie laughed at that and let herself lean on him. Then she announced to the same audience, "Mis' Woods got herself uh new lil boy rooster, but he been off somewhere and won't tell her."

"First thing, though, us got tuh eat together, Janie. Then we can talk."

"One thing, Ah won't send you out after no fish."

He pinched her in the side and ignored what she said.

"'Tain't no need of neither one of us workin' dis mornin'. Call Mis' Samuels and let her fix whatever you want."

"Tea Cake, if you don't hurry up and tell me, Ah'll take and beat yo' head flat as uh dime."

Tea Cake stuck out till he had some breakfast, then he talked and acted out the story.

He spied the money while he was tying his tie. He took it up and looked at it out of curiosity and put it in his pocket to count it while he was out to find some fish to fry. When he found out how much it was, he was excited and felt like letting folks know who he was. Before he found the fish market he met a fellow he used to work with at the round house. One word brought on another one and pretty soon he made up his mind to spend some of it. He never had had his hand on so much money before in his life, so he made up his mind to see how it felt to be a millionaire. They went on out to Callahan round the railroad shops and he decided to give a big chicken and macaroni supper that night, free to all.

He bought up the stuff and they found somebody to pick the guitar so they could all dance some. So they sent the message all around for people to come. And come they did. A big table loaded down with fried chicken and biscuits and a wash-tub full of macaroni with plenty cheese in it. When the fellow began to pick the box the people begin to come from east, west, north and Australia. And he stood in the door and paid all the ugly women two dollars *not* to come in. One big meriny colored woman was so ugly till it was worth five dollars for her not to come in, so he gave it to her.

They had a big time till one man come in who thought he was bad. He tried to pull and haul over all the chickens and pick out the livers and gizzards to eat. Nobody else couldn't pacify him so they called Tea Cake to come see if he could stop him. So Tea Cake walked up and asked him, "Say, whut's de matter wid you, nohow?"

"Ah don't want nobody handin' me nothin'. Specially don't issue me out no rations. Ah always chooses mah rations." He kept right on plowing through the pile uh chicken. So Tea Cake got mad.

"You got mo' nerve than uh brass monkey. Tell me, what post office did *you* ever pee in? Ah craves tuh know."

"Whut you mean by dat now?" the fellow asked.

"Ah means dis—it takes jus' as much nerve tuh cut caper lak dat in uh United States Government Post Office as it do tuh comes pullin' and haulin' over any chicken Ah pay for. Hit de ground. Damned if Ah ain't gointuh try you dis night."

So they all went outside to see if Tea Cake could handle the boogerboo. Tea Cake knocked out two of his teeth, so that man went on off from there. Then two men tried to pick a fight with one another, so Tea Cake said they had to kiss and make up. They didn't want to do it. They'd rather go to jail, but everybody else liked the idea, so they made 'em do it. Afterwards, both of them spit and gagged and wiped their mouths with the back of their hands. One went outside and chewed a little grass like a sick dog, he said to keep it from killing him.

Then everybody began to holler at the music because the man couldn't play but three pieces. So Tea Cake took the guitar and played himself. He was glad of the chance because he hadn't had his hand on a box since he put his in the pawn shop to get some money to hire a car for Janie soon after he met her. He missed his music. So that put him in the notion he ought to have one. He bought the guitar on the spot and paid fifteen dollars cash. It was really worth sixty-five any day.

Just before day the party wore out. So Tea Cake hurried on back to his new wife. He had done found out how rich people feel and he had a fine guitar and twelve dollars left in his pocket and all he needed now was a great big old hug and kiss from Janie.

"You musta thought yo' wife was powerful ugly. Dem ugly women dat you paid two dollars not to come in, could git tuh de door. You never even 'lowed me tuh git dat close." She pouted.

"Janie, Ah would have give Jacksonville wid Tampa for a jump-back for you to be dere wid me. Ah started to come git yuh two three times."

"Well, how come yuh didn't come git me?"

"Janie, would you have come if Ah did?"

"Sho Ah would. Ah laks fun just as good as you do."

"Janie, Ah wanted tuh, mighty much, but Ah was skeered. Too skeered Ah might lose yuh."

"Why?"

"Dem wuzn't no high muckty mucks. Dem wuz railroad hands and dey womenfolks. You ain't usetuh folks lak dat and Ah wuz skeered you might git all mad and quit me for takin' you 'mongst 'em. But Ah wanted yuh wid me jus' de same. Befo' us got married Ah made up mah mind not tuh let you see no commonness in me. When Ah git mad habits on, Ah'd go off and keep it out yo' sight. 'Tain't mah notion tuh drag *you* down wid me."

"Looka heah, Tea Cake, if you ever go off from me and have a good time lak dat and then come back heah tellin' me how nice Ah is, Ah specks tuh kill yuh dead. You heah me?"

"So you aims tuh partake wid everything, hunh?"

"Yeah, Tea Cake, don't keer what it is."

"Dat's all Ah wants tuh know. From now on you'se mah wife and mah woman and everything else in de world Ah needs."

"Ah hope so."

"And honey, don't you worry 'bout yo' lil ole two hundred dollars. It's big pay day dis comin' Saturday at de railroad yards. Ah'm gointuh take dis twelve dollars in mah pocket and win it all back and mo'."

"How?"

"Honey, since you loose me and gimme privilege tuh tell yuh all about mahself, Ah'll tell yuh. You done married one uh de best gamblers God ever made. Cards or dice either one. Ah can take uh shoe string and win uh tan-yard. Wish yuh could see me rollin'. But dis time it's gointuh be nothin' but tough men's talkin' all kinds uh talk so it ain't no place for you tuh be, but 'twon't be long befo' you see me."

All the rest of the week Tea Cake was busy practising up on his dice. He would flip them on the bare floor, on the rug and on the bed. He'd squat and throw, sit in a chair and throw and stand and throw. It was very exciting to Janie who had never touched dice in her life. Then he'd take his deck of cards and shuffle and cut, shuffle and cut and deal out then examine each hand carefully, and do it again. So Saturday came. He went out and bought a new switch-blade knife and two decks of star-back playing cards that morning and left Janie around noon.

"They'll start to paying off, pretty soon now. Ah wants tuh git in de game whilst de big money is in it. Ah ain't fuh no spuddin' tuhday. Ah'll come home wid de money or Ah'll come back on uh stretcher." He cut nine hairs out of the mole of her head for luck and went off happy.

Janie waited till midnight without worrying, but after that she began to be afraid. So she got up and sat around scared and miserable. Thinking and fearing all sorts of dangers. Wondering at herself as she had many times this week that she was not shocked at Tea Cake's gambling. It was part of him, so it was all right. She rather found herself angry at imaginary people who might try to criticize. Let the old hypocrites learn to mind their own business, and leave other folks alone. Tea Cake wasn't doing a bit more harm trying to win hisself a little money than they was always doing with their lying tongues. Tea Cake had more good nature under his toe-nails than they had in their so-called Christian hearts. She better not hear none of them old backbiters talking about *her* husband! Please, Jesus, don't let them nasty niggers hurt her boy. If they do, Master Jesus, grant her a good gun and a chance to shoot 'em. Tea Cake had a knife it was true, but that was only to protect hisself. God knows, Tea Cake wouldn't harm a fly.

Daylight was creeping around the cracks of the world when Janie heard a feeble rap on the door. She sprung to the door and flung it wide. Tea Cake was out there looking like he was asleep standing up. In some strange way it was frightening. Janie caught his arm to arouse him and he stumbled into the room and fell.

"Tea Cake! You chile! What's de matter, honey?"

"Dey cut me, dat's all. Don't cry. Git me out dis coat quick as yuh can."

He told her he wasn't cut but twice but she had to have him naked so she could look him all over and fix him up to a certain extent. He told her not to call a doctor unless he got much worse. It was mostly loss of blood anyhow.

"Ah won the money jus' lak ah told yuh. Round midnight Ah had yo' two hundred dollars and wuz ready tuh quit even though it wuz uh heap mo' money in de game. But dey wanted uh chance tuh win it back so Ah set back down tuh play some mo'. Ah knowed ole Double-Ugly wuz 'bout broke and wanted tuh fight 'bout it, so Ah set down tuh give 'im his chance tuh git back his money and then to give 'im uh quick trip tuh hell if he tried tuh pull dat razor Ah glimpsed in his pocket. Honey, no up-to-date man don't fool wid no razor. De man wid his switch-blade will be done cut yuh tuh death while you foolin' wid uh razor. But Double-Ugly brags he's too fast wid it tuh git hurt, but Ah knowed better.

"So round four o'clock Ah had done cleaned 'em out complete—all except two men dat got up and left while dey had money for groceries, and one man dat wuz lucky. Then Ah rose tuh bid 'em good bye agin. None of 'em didn't lak it, but dey all realized it wuz fair. Ah had done give 'em a fair chance. All but Double-Ugly. He claimed Ah switched de dice. Ah shoved de money down deep in mah pocket and picked up mah hat and coat wid mah left hand and kept mah right hand on mah knife. Ah didn't keer what he *said* long as he didn't try tuh *do* nothin'. Ah got mah hat on and one arm in mah coat as Ah got to de door. Right dere he jumped at me as Ah turned to see de doorstep outside and cut me twice in de back.

"Baby, Ah run mah other arm in mah coat-sleeve and grabbed dat nigger by his necktie befo' he could bat his eye and then Ah wuz all over 'im jus' lak gravy over rice. He lost his razor tryin' tuh git loose from me. He wuz hollerin' for me tuh turn him loose, but baby, Ah turnt him every way *but* loose. Ah left him on the doorstep and got here to yuh de quickest way Ah could. Ah know Ah ain't cut too deep 'cause he was too skeered tuh run up on me close enough. Sorta pull de flesh together with stickin' plaster. Ah'll be all right in uh day or so."

Janie was painting on iodine and crying.

"You ain't de one to be cryin', Janie. It's his ole lady oughta do dat. You done gimme luck. Look in mah left hand pants pocket and see whut yo' daddy brought yuh. When Ah tell yuh Ah'm gointuh bring it, Ah don't lie."

They counted it together—three hundred and twenty-two dollars. It was almost like Tea Cake had held up the Paymaster. He made her take the two hundred and put it back in the secret place. Then Janie told him about the other money she had in the bank.

"Put dat two hundred back wid de rest, Janie. Mah dice. Ah no need no assistance tuh help me feed mah woman. From now on, you gointuh eat whutever mah money can buy yuh and wear de same. When Ah ain't got nothin' you don't git nothin'."

"Dat's all right wid me."

He was getting drowsy, but he pinched her leg playfully because he was glad she took things the way he wanted her to. "Listen, mama, soon as Ah git over dis lil cuttin' scrape, we gointuh do somethin' crazy."

"Whut's dat?"

"We goin' on de muck."

"Whut's de muck, and where is it at?"

"Oh down in de Everglades round Clewiston and Belle Glade where dey raise all dat cane and string-beans and tomatuhs. Folks don't do nothin' down dere but make money and fun and foolishness. We must go dere."

He drifted off into sleep and Janie looked down on him and felt a self-crushing love. So her soul crawled out from its hiding place.

Chapter 14

To Janie's strange eyes, everything in the Everglades was big and new. Big Lake Okechobee, big beans, big cane, big weeds, big everything. Weeds that did well to grow waist high up the state were eight and often ten feet tall down there. Ground so rich that everything went wild. Volunteer cane just taking the place. Dirt roads so rich and black that a half mile of it would have fertilized a Kansas wheat field. Wild cane on either side of the road hiding the rest of the world. People wild too.

"Season don't open up till last of September, but we had tuh git heah ahead uh time tuh git us uh room," Tea Cake explained. "Two weeks from now, it'll be so

many folks heah dey won't be lookin' fuh rooms, dey'll be jus' looking fuh somewhere tuh sleep. Now we got uh chance tuh git uh room at de hotel, where dey
got uh bath tub. Yuh can't live on de muck 'thout yuh take uh bath every day. Do
dat muck'll itch yuh lak ants. 'Tain't but one place round heah wid uh bath tub.
'Tain't nowhere near enough rooms."

"Whut we gointuh do round heah?"

"All day Ah'm pickin' beans. All night Ah'm pickin' mah box and rollin' dice.
Between de beans and de dice Ah can't lose. Ah'm gone right now tuh pick me uh
job uh work wid de best man on de muck. Before de rest of 'em gits heah. You can
always git jobs round heah in de season, but not wid de right folks."

"When do de job open up, Tea Cake? Everybody round here look lak dey
waitin' too."

"Dat's right. De big men haves uh certain time tuh open de season jus' lak in
everything else. Mah boss-man didn't get sufficient seed. He's out huntin' up uh
few mo' bushels. Den we'se gointuh plantin'."

"Bushels?"

"Yeah, bushels. Dis ain't no game fuh pennies. Po' man ain't got no business at
de show."

The very next day he burst into the room in high excitement. "Boss done
bought out another man and want me down on de lake. He got houses fuh de first
ones dat git dere. Less go!"

They rattled nine miles in a borrowed car to the quarters that squatted so close
that only the dyke separated them from great, sprawling Okechobee. Janie fussed
around the shack making a home while Tea Cake planted beans. After hours they
fished. Every now and then they'd run across a party of Indians in their long, narrow dug-outs calmly winning their living in the trackless ways of the 'Glades.
Finally the beans were in. Nothing much to do but wait to pick them. Tea Cake
picked his box a great deal for Janie, but he still didn't have enough to do. No
need of gambling yet. The people who were pouring in were broke. They didn't
come bringing money, they were coming to make some.

"Tell yuh whut, Janie, less buy us some shootin' tools and go huntin' round heah."

"Dat would be fine, Tea Cake, exceptin' you know Ah can't shoot. But Ah'd
love tuh go wid *you*."

"Oh, you needs tuh learn how. 'Tain't no need uh you not knowin' how tuh
handle shootin' tools. Even if you didn't never find no game, it's always some
trashy rascal dat needs uh good killin'," he laughed. "Less go intuh Palm Beach
and spend some of our money."

Every day they were practising. Tea Cake made her shoot at little things just to
give her good aim. Pistol and shot gun and rifle. It got so the others stood around
and watched them. Some of the men would beg for a shot at the target themselves.
It was the most exciting thing on the muck. Better than the jook and the pool-room
unless some special band was playing for a dance. And the thing that got everybody
was the way Janie caught on. She got to the place she could shoot a hawk out
of a pine tree and not tear him up. Shoot his head off. She got to be a better shot
than Tea Cake. They'd go out any late afternoon and come back loaded down with
game. One night they got a boat and went out hunting alligators. Shining their

phosphorescent eyes and shooting them in the dark. They could sell the hides and teeth in Palm Beach besides having fun together till work got pressing.

Day by day now, the hordes of workers poured in. Some came limping in with their shoes and sore feet from walking. It's hard trying to follow your shoe instead of your shoe following you. They came in wagons from way up in Georgia and they came in truck loads from east, west, north and south. Permanent transients with no attachments and tired looking men with their families and dogs in flivvers. All night, all day, hurrying in to pick beans. Skillets, beds, patched up spare inner tubes all hanging and dangling from the ancient cars on the outside and hopeful humanity, herded and hovered on the inside, chugging on to the muck. People ugly from ignorance and broken from being poor.

All night now the jooks clanged and clamored. Pianos living three lifetimes in one. Blues made and used right on the spot. Dancing, fighting, singing, crying, laughing, winning and losing love every hour. Work all day for money, fight all night for love. The rich black earth clinging to bodies and biting the skin like ants.

Finally no more sleeping places. Men made big fires and fifty or sixty men slept around each fire. But they had to pay the man whose land they slept on. He ran the fire just like his boarding place—for pay. But nobody cared. They made good money, even to the children. So they spent good money. Next month and next year were other times. No need to mix them up with the present.

Tea Cake's house was a magnet, the unauthorized center of the "job." The way he would sit in the doorway and play his guitar made people stop and listen and maybe disappoint the jook for that night. He was always laughing and full of fun too. He kept everybody laughing in the bean field.

Janie stayed home and boiled big pots of blackeyed peas and rice. Sometimes baked big pans of navy beans with plenty of sugar and hunks of bacon laying on top. That was something Tea Cake loved so no matter if Janie had fixed beans two or three times during the week, they had baked beans again on Sunday. She always had some kind of dessert too, as Tea Cake said it give a man something to taper off on. Sometimes she'd straighten out the two-room house and take the rifle and have fried rabbit for supper when Tea Cake got home. She didn't leave him itching and scratching in his work clothes, either. The kettle of hot water was already waiting when he got in.

Then Tea Cake took to popping in at the kitchen door at odd hours. Between breakfast and dinner, sometimes. Then often around two o'clock he'd come home and tease and wrestle with her for a half hour and slip on back to work. So one day she asked him about it.

"Tea Cake, whut you doin' back in de quarters when everybody else is still workin'?"

"Come tuh see 'bout you. De boogerman liable tuh tote yuh off whilst Ah'm gone."

"'Tain't no boogerman got me tuh study 'bout. Maybe you think Ah ain't treatin' yuh right and you watchin' me."

"Naw, naw, Janie. Ah *know* better'n dat. But since you got dat in yo' head, Ah'll have tuh tell yuh de real truth, so yuh can know. Janie, Ah gits lonesome out dere all day 'thout yuh. After dis, you betta come git uh job uh work out dere lak de rest uh de women—so Ah won't be losin' time comin' home."

"Tea Cake, you'se uh mess! Can't do 'thout me dat lil time."

"'Tain't no lil time. It's near 'bout all day."

So the very next morning Janie got ready to pick beans along with Tea Cake. There was a suppressed murmur when she picked up a basket and went to work. She was already getting to be a special case on the muck. It was generally assumed that she thought herself too good to work like the rest of the women and that Tea Cake "pomped her up tuh dat." But all day long the romping and playing they carried on behind the boss's back made her popular right away. It got the whole field to playing off and on. Then Tea Cake would help get supper afterwards.

"You don't think Ah'm tryin' tuh git outa takin' keer uh yuh, do yuh, Janie, 'cause Ah ast yuh tuh work long side uh me?" Tea Cake asked her at the end of her first week in the field.

"Ah naw, honey. Ah laks it. It's mo' nicer than settin' round dese quarters all day. Clerkin' in dat store wuz hard, but heah, we ain't got nothin' tuh do but do our work and come home and love."

The house was full of people every night. That is, all around the doorstep was full. Some were there to hear Tea Cake pick the box; some came to talk and tell stories, but most of them came to get into whatever game was going on or might go on. Sometimes Tea Cake lost heavily, for there were several good gamblers on the lake. Sometimes he won and made Janie proud of his skill. But outside of the two jooks, everything on that job went on around those two.

Sometimes Janie would think of the old days in the big white house and the store and laugh to herself. What if Eatonville could see her now in her blue denim overalls and heavy shoes? The crowd of people around her and a dice game on her floor! She was sorry for her friends back there and scornful of the others. The men held big arguments here like they used to do on the store porch. Only here, she could listen and laugh and even talk some herself if she wanted to. She got so she could tell big stories herself from listening to the rest. Because she loved to hear it, and the men loved to hear themselves, they would "woof" and "booger-boo" around the games to the limit. No matter how rough it was, people seldom got mad, because everything was done for a laugh. Everybody loved to hear Ed Dockery, Bootyny, and Sop-de-Bottom in a skin game. Ed Dockery was dealing one night and he looked over at Sop-de-Bottom's card and he could tell Sop thought he was going to win. He hollered, "Ah'll break up *dat* settin' uh eggs." Sop looked and said, "Root de peg." Bootyny asked, "What are you goin' tuh do? Do do!" Everybody was watching that next card fall. Ed got ready to turn. "Ah'm gointuh sweep out hell and burn up de broom." He slammed down another dollar. "Don't oversport yourself, Ed," Bootyny challenged. "You gittin' too yaller." Ed caught hold of the corner of the card. Sop dropped a dollar. "Ah'm gointuh shoot in de hearse, don't keer how sad de funeral be." Ed said, "You see how this man is teasin' hell?" Tea Cake nudged Sop not to bet. "You gointuh git caught in uh bullet storm if you don't watch out." Sop said, "Aw 'tain't nothin' tuh dat bear but his curly hair. Ah can look through muddy water and see dry land." Ed turned off the card and hollered, "Zachariah, Ah says come down out dat sycamore tree.

You can't do no business." Nobody fell on that card. Everybody was scared of the next one. Ed looked around and saw Gabe standing behind his chair and hollered, "Move, from over me, Gabe! You too black. You draw heat! Sop, you wanta pick up dat bet whilst you got uh chance?" "Naw, man, Ah wish Ah had uh thousand-leg tuh put on it." "So yuh won't lissen, huh? Dumb niggers and free schools. Ah'm gointuh take and teach yuh. Ah'll main-line but Ah won't side-track." Ed flipped the next card and Sop fell and lost. Everybody hollered and laughed. Ed laughed and said, "Git off de muck! You ain't nothin'. Dat's all! Hot boilin' water won't help yuh none." Ed kept on laughing because he had been so scared before. "Sop, Bootyny, all y'all dat lemme win yo' money: Ah'm sending it straight off to Sears and Roebuck and buy me some clothes, and when Ah turn out Christmas day, it would take a doctor to tell me how near Ah is dressed tuh death."

Chapter 15

Janie learned what it felt like to be jealous. A little chunky girl took to picking a play out of Tea Cake in the fields and in the quarters. If he said anything at all, she'd take the opposite side and hit him or shove him and run away to make him chase her. Janie knew what she was up to—luring him away from the crowd. It kept up for two or three weeks with Nunkie getting bolder all the time. She'd hit Tea Cake playfully and the minute he so much as tapped her with his finger she'd fall against him or fall on the ground and have to be picked up. She'd be almost helpless. It took a good deal of handling to set her on her feet again. And another thing, Tea Cake didn't seem to be able to fend her off as promptly as Janie thought he ought to. She began to be snappish a little. A little seed of fear was growing into a tree. Maybe some day Tea Cake would weaken. Maybe he had already given secret encouragement and this was Nunkie's way of bragging about it. Other people began to notice too, and that put Janie more on a wonder.

One day they were working near where the beans ended and the sugar cane began. Janie had marched off a little from Tea Cake's side with another woman for a chat. When she glanced around Tea Cake was gone. Nunkie too. She knew because she looked.

"Where's Tea Cake?" she asked Sop-de-Bottom.

He waved his hand towards the cane field and hurried away. Janie never thought at all. She just acted on feelings. She rushed into the cane and about the fifth row down she found Tea Cake and Nunkie struggling. She was on them before either knew.

"Whut's de matter heah?" Janie asked in a cold rage. They sprang apart.

"Nothin'," Tea Cake told her, standing shame-faced.

"Well, whut you doin' in heah? How come you ain't out dere wid de rest?"

"She grabbed mah workin' tickets outa mah shirt pocket and Ah run tuh git 'em back," Tea Cake explained, showing the tickets, considerably mauled about in the struggle.

Janie made a move to seize Nunkie but the girl fled. So she took out behind her over the humped-up cane rows. But Nunkie did not mean to be caught. So Janie went on home. The sight of the fields and the other happy people was too much for her that day. She walked slowly and thoughtfully to the quarters. It wasn't long before Tea Cake found her there and tried to talk. She cut him short with a blow and they fought from one room to the other, Janie trying to beat him, and Tea Cake kept holding her wrists and wherever he could to keep her from going too far.

"Ah b'lieve you been messin' round her!" she panted furiously.

"No sich uh thing!" Tea Cake retorted.

"Ah b'lieve yuh did."

"Don't keer how big uh lie get told, somebody kin b'lieve it!"

They fought on. "You done hurt mah heart, now you come wid uh lie tuh bruise mah ears! Turn go mah hands!" Janie seethed. But Tea Cake never let go. They wrestled on until they were doped with their own fumes and emanations; till their clothes had been torn away; till he hurled her to the floor and held her there melting her resistance with the heat of his body, doing things with their bodies to express the inexpressible; kissed her until she arched her body to meet him and they fell asleep in sweet exhaustion.

The next morning Janie asked like a woman, "You still love ole Nunkie?"

"Naw, never did, and you know it too. Ah didn't want her."

"Yeah, you did." She didn't say this because she believed it. She wanted to hear his denial. She had to crow over the fallen Nunkie.

"Whut would Ah do wid dat lil chunk of a woman wid you around? She ain't good for nothin' exceptin' tuh set up in uh corner by de kitchen stove and break wood over her head. You'se something tuh make uh man forget tuh git old and forgit tuh die."

Chapter 16

The season closed and people went away like they had come—in droves. Tea Cake and Janie decided to stay since they wanted to make another season on the muck. There was nothing to do, after they had gathered several bushels of dried beans to save over and sell to the planters in the fall. So Janie began to look around and see people and things she hadn't noticed during the season.

For instance during the summer when she heard the subtle but compelling rhythms of the Bahaman drummers, she'd walk over and watch the dances. She did not laugh the "Saws" to scorn as she had heard the people doing in the season. She got to like it a lot and she and Tea Cake were on hand every night till the others teased them about it.

Janie came to know Mrs. Turner now. She had seen her several times during the season, but neither ever spoke. Now they got to be visiting friends.

Mrs. Turner was a milky sort of a woman that belonged to child-bed. Her shoulders rounded a little, and she must have been conscious of her pelvis because she kept it stuck out in front of her so she could always see it. Tea Cake made a lot of fun about Mrs. Turner's shape behind her back. He claimed that she had been shaped up by a cow kicking her from behind. She was an ironing board with things throwed at it. Then that same cow took and stepped in her mouth when she was a baby and left it wide and flat with her chin and nose almost meeting.

But Mrs. Turner's shape and features were entirely approved by Mrs. Turner. Her nose was slightly pointed and she was proud. Her thin lips were an ever delight to her eyes. Even her buttocks in bas-relief were a source of pride. To her way of thinking all these things set her aside from Negroes. That was why she sought out Janie to friend with. Janie's coffee-and-cream complexion and her luxurious hair made Mrs. Turner forgive her for wearing overalls like the other women who worked in the fields. She didn't forgive her for marrying a man as dark as Tea Cake, but she felt that she could remedy that. That was what her brother was born for. She seldom stayed long when she found Tea Cake at home, but when she happened to drop in and catch Janie alone, she'd spend hours chatting away. Her disfavorite subject was Negroes.

"Mis' Woods, Ah have often said to mah husband, Ah don't see how uh lady like Mis' Woods can stand all them common niggers round her place all de time."

"They don't worry me atall, Mis' Turner. Fact about de thing is, they tickles me wid they talk."

"You got mo' nerve than me. When somebody talked mah husband intuh comin' down heah tuh open up uh eatin' place Ah never dreamt so many different kins uh black folks could colleck in one place. Did Ah never woulda come. Ah ain't useter 'ssociatin' wid black folks. Mah son claims dey draws lightnin'." They laughed a little and after many of these talks Mrs. Turner said, "Yo' husband musta had plenty money when y'all got married."

"Whut make you think dat, Mis' Turner?"

"Tuh git hold of uh woman lak you. You got mo' nerve than me. Ah jus' couldn't see mahself married to no black man. It's too many black folks already. We oughta lighten up de race."

"Naw, mah husband didn't had nothin' but hisself. He's easy tuh love if you mess round 'im. Ah loves 'im."

"Why you, Mis' Woods! Ah don't b'lieve it. You'se jus' sorter hypnotized, dat's all."

"Naw, it's real. Ah couldn't stand it if he wuz tuh quit me. Don't know whut Ah'd do. He kin take most any lil thing and make summertime out of it when times is dull. Then we lives offa dat happiness he made till some mo' happiness come along."

"You'se different from me. Ah can't stand black niggers. Ah don't blame de white folks from hatin' 'em 'cause Ah can't stand 'em mahself. 'Nother thing, Ah hates tuh see folks lak me and you mixed up wid 'em. Us oughta class off."

"Us can't *do* it. We'se uh mingled people and all of us got black kinfolks as well as yaller kinfolks. How come you so against black?"

"And dey makes me tired. Always laughin'! Dey laughs too much and dey laughs too loud. Always singin' ol' nigger songs! Always cuttin' de monkey for white folks. If it wuzn't for so many black folks it wouldn't be no race problem. De white folks would take us in wid dem. De black ones is holdin' us back."

"You reckon? 'course Ah ain't never thought about it too much. But Ah don't figger dey even gointuh want us for comp'ny. We'se too poor."

"'Tain't de poorness, it's de color and de features. Who want any lil ole black baby layin' up in de baby buggy lookin' lak uh fly in buttermilk? Who wants to be mixed up wid uh rusty black man, and uh black woman goin' down de street in all dem loud colors, and whoopin' and hollerin' and laughin' over nothin'? Ah don't know. Don't bring me no nigger doctor tuh hang over mah sick-bed. Ah done had six chillun—wuzn't lucky enough tuh raise but dat one—and ain't never had uh nigger tuh even feel mah pulse. White doctors always gits mah money. Ah don't go in no nigger store tuh buy nothin' neither. Colored folks don't know nothin' 'bout no business. Deliver me!"

Mrs. Turner was almost screaming in fanatical earnestness by now. Janie was dumb and bewildered before and she clucked sympathetically and wished she knew what to say. It was so evident that Mrs. Turner took black folk as a personal affront to herself.

"Look at me! Ah ain't got no flat nose and liver lips. Ah'm uh featured woman. Ah got white folks' features in mah face. Still and all Ah got tuh be lumped in wid all de rest. It ain't fair. Even if dey don't take us in wid de whites, dey oughta make us uh class tuh ourselves."

"It don't worry me atall, but Ah reckon Ah ain't got no real head fur thinkin'."

"You oughta meet mah brother. He's real smart. Got dead straight hair. Dey made him uh delegate tuh de Sunday School Convention and he read uh paper on Booker T. Washington and tore him tuh pieces!"

"Booker T.? He wuz a great big man, wusn't he?"

"'Sposed tuh be. All he ever done was cut de monkey for white folks. So dey pomped him up. But you know whut de ole folks say 'de higher de monkey climbs de mo' he show his behind' so dat's de way it wuz wid Booker T. Mah brother hit 'im every time dey give 'im chance tuh speak."

"Ah was raised on de notion dat he wuz uh great big man," was all that Janie knew to say.

"He didn't do nothin' but hold us back—talkin' 'bout work when de race ain't never done nothin' else. He wuz uh enemy tuh us, dat's whut. He wuz uh white folks' nigger."

According to all Janie had been taught this was sacrilege so she sat without speaking at all. But Mrs. Turner went on.

"Ah done sent fuh mah brother tuh come down and spend uh while wid us. He's sorter outa work now. Ah wants yuh tuh meet him mo' special. You and him would make up uh swell couple if you wuzn't already married. He's uh fine carpenter, when he kin git anything tuh do."

"Yeah, maybe so. But Ah *is* married now, so 'tain't no use in considerin'."

Mrs. Turner finally rose to go after being very firm about several other viewpoints of either herself, her son or her brother. She begged Janie to drop in on her anytime, but never once mentioning Tea Cake. Finally she was gone and Janie hurried to her kitchen to put on supper and found Tea Cake sitting in there with his head between his hands.

"Tea Cake! Ah didn't know you wuz home."

"Ah know yuh didn't. Ah been heah uh long time listenin' to dat heifer run me down tuh de dawgs uh try tuh tole you off from me."

"So dat whut she wuz up to? Ah didn't know."

"'Course she is. She got some no-count brother she wants yuh tuh hook up wid and take keer of Ah reckon."

"Shucks! If dat's her notion she's barkin' up de wrong tree. Mah hands is full already."

"Thanky Ma'am. Ah hates dat woman lak poison. Keep her from round dis house. Her look lak uh white woman! Wid dat meriny skin and hair jus' as close tuh her head as ninety-nine is tuh uh hundred! Since she hate black folks so, she don't need our money in her ol' eatin' place. Ah'll pass de word along. We kin go tuh dat white man's place and git good treatment. Her and dat whittled-down husband uh hers! And dat son! He's jus' uh dirty trick her womb played on her. Ah'm telling her husband tuh keep her home. Ah don't want her round dis house."

One day Tea Cake met Turner and his son on the street. He was a vanishing-looking kind of a man as if there used to be parts about him that stuck out individually but now he hadn't a thing about him that wasn't dwindled and blurred. Just like he had been sand-papered down to a long oval mass. Tea Cake felt sorry for him without knowing why. So he didn't blurt out the insults he had intended. But he couldn't hold in everything. They talked about the prospects for the coming season for a moment, then Tea Cake said, "Yo' wife don't seem tuh have nothin' much tuh do, so she kin visit uh lot. Mine got too much tuh do tuh go visitin' and too much tuh spend time talkin' tuh folks dat visit her."

"Mah wife takes time fuh whatever she wants tuh do. Real strong headed dat way. Yes indeed." He laughed a high lungless laugh. "De chillun don't keep her in no mo' so she visits when she chooses."

"De chillun?" Tea Cake asked him in surprise. "You got any smaller than him?" He indicated the son who seemed around twenty or so. "Ah ain't seen yo' others."

"Ah reckon you ain't 'cause dey all passed on befo' dis one wuz born. We ain't had no luck atall wid our chillun. We lucky to raise him. He's de last stroke of exhausted nature."

He gave his powerless laugh again and Tea Cake and the boy joined in with him. Then Tea Cake walked on off and went home to Janie.

"Her husband can't do nothin' wid dat butt-headed woman. All you can do is treat her cold whenever she come round here."

Janie tried that, but short of telling Mrs. Turner bluntly, there was nothing she could do to discourage her completely. She felt honored by Janie's acquaintance and she quickly forgave and forgot snubs in order to keep it. Anyone who looked more white folkish than herself was better than she was in her criteria, therefore it was right that they should be cruel to her at times, just as she was cruel to those more negroid than herself in direct ratio to their negroness. Like the pecking-order in a chicken yard. Insensate cruelty to those you can whip, and groveling submission to those you can't. Once having set up her idols and built altars to them it was inevitable that she would worship there. It was inevitable that she should accept any inconsistency and cruelty from her deity as all good worshippers do from theirs. All gods who receive homage are cruel. All gods dispense suffering without reason. Otherwise they would not be worshipped. Through indiscriminate suffering men know fear and fear is the most divine emotion. It is the stones for altars and the beginning of wisdom. Half gods are worshipped in wine and flowers. Real gods require blood.

Mrs. Turner, like all other believers had built an altar to the unattainable—Caucasian characteristics for all. Her god would smite her, would hurl her from pinnacles and lose her in deserts, but she would not forsake his altars. Behind her crude words was a belief that somehow she and others through worship could attain her paradise—a heaven of straight-haired, thin-lipped, high-nose-boned white seraphs. The physical impossibilities in no way injured faith. That was the mystery and mysteries are the chores of gods. Beyond her faith was a fanaticism to defend the altars of her god. It was distressing to emerge from her inner temple and find these black desecrators howling with laughter before the door. Oh, for an army, terrible with banners *and swords!*

So she didn't cling to Janie Woods the woman. She paid homage to Janie's Caucasian characteristics as such. And when she was with Janie she had a feeling of transmutation, as if she herself had become whiter and with straighter hair, and she hated Tea Cake first for his defilement of divinity and next for his telling mockery of her. If she only knew something she could do about it! But she didn't. Once she was complaining about the carryings-on at the jook and Tea Cake snapped, "Aw, don't make God look so foolish—findin' fault wid everything He made."

So Mrs. Turner frowned most of the time. She had so much to disapprove of. It didn't affect Tea Cake and Janie too much. It just gave them something to talk about in the summertime when everything was dull on the muck. Otherwise they made little trips to Palm Beach, Fort Myers and Fort Lauderdale for their fun. Before they realized it the sun was cooler and the crowds came pouring onto the muck again.

Chapter 17

A great deal of the old crowd were back. But there were lots of new ones too. Some of these men made passes at Janie, and women who didn't know took out after Tea Cake. Didn't take them long to be put right, however. Still and all, jealousies arose now and then on both sides. When Mrs. Turner's brother came and she brought him over to be introduced, Tea Cake had a brainstorm. Before the week was over he had whipped Janie. Not because her behavior justified his jealousy, but it relieved that awful fear inside him. Being able to whip her reassured him in possession. No brutal beating at all. He just slapped her around a bit to show he was boss. Everybody talked about it next day in the fields. It aroused a sort of envy in both men and women. The way he petted and pampered her as if those two or three face slaps had nearly killed her made the women see visions and the helpless way she hung on him made men dream dreams.

"Tea Cake, you sho is a lucky man," Sop-de-Bottom told him. "Uh person can see every place you hit her. Ah bet she never raised her hand tuh hit yuh back, neither. Take some uh dese ol' rusty black women and dey would fight yuh all night long and next day nobody couldn't tell you ever hit 'em. Dat's de reason Ah done quit beatin' mah woman. You can't make no mark on 'em at all. Lawd! wouldn't Ah love tuh whip uh tender woman lak Janie! Ah bet she don't even holler. She jus' cries, eh Tea Cake?"

"Dat's right."

"See dat! Mah woman would spread her lungs all over Palm Beach County, let alone knock out mah jaw teeth. You don't know dat woman uh mine. She got ninety-nine rows uh jaw teeth and git her good and mad, she'll wade through solid rock up to her hip pockets."

"Mah Janie is uh high time woman and useter things. Ah didn't git her outa de middle uh de road. Ah got her outa uh big fine house. Right now she got money enough in de bank tuh buy up dese ziggaboos and give 'em away."

"Hush yo' mouf! And she down heah on de muck lak anybody else!"

"Janie is wherever *Ah* wants tuh be. Dat's de kind uh wife she is and Ah love her for it. Ah wouldn't be knockin' her around. Ah didn't wants whup her last night, but ol' Mis' Turner done sent for her brother tuh come tuh bait Janie in and take her way from me. Ah didn't whup Janie 'cause *she* done nothin'. Ah beat her tuh show dem Turners who is boss. Ah set in de kitchen one day and heard dat woman tell mah wife Ah'm too black fuh her. She don't see how Janie can stand me."

"Tell her husband on her."

"Shucks! Ah b'lieve he's skeered of her."

"Knock her teeth down her throat."

"Dat would look like she had some influence when she ain't. Ah jus' let her see dat Ah got control."

"So she live offa our money and don't lak black folks, huh? O.K. we'll have her gone from here befo' two weeks is up. Ah'm goin' right off tuh all de men and drop rocks aginst her."

"Ah ain't mad wid her for whut she done, 'cause she ain't done me nothin' yet. Ah'm mad at her for thinkin'. Her and her gang got tuh go."

"Us is wid yuh, Tea Cake. You know dat already. Dat Turner woman is real smart, accordin' tuh her notions. Reckon she done heard 'bout dat money yo' wife got in de bank and she's bound tuh rope her in tuh her family one way or another."

"Sop, Ah don't think it's half de money as it is de looks. She's color-struck. She ain't got de kind of uh mind you meet every day. She ain't a fact and neither do she make a good story when you tell about her."

"Ah yeah, she's too smart tuh stay round heah. She figgers we'se jus' uh bunch uh dumb niggers so she think she'll grow horns. But dat's uh lie. She'll die butt-headed."

Saturday afternoon when the work tickets were turned into cash everybody began to buy coon-dick and get drunk. By dusk dark Belle Glade was full of loud-talking, staggering men. Plenty women had gotten their knots charged too. The police chief in his speedy Ford was rushing from jook to jook and eating house trying to keep order, but making few arrests. Not enough jail-space for all the drunks so why bother with a few? All he could do to keep down fights and get the white men out of colored town by nine o'clock. Dick Sterrett and Coodemay seemed to be the worst off. Their likker told them to go from place to place pushing and shoving and loud-talking and they were doing it.

Way after a while they arrived at Mrs. Turner's eating house and found the place full to the limit. Tea Cake, Stew Beef, Sop-de-Bottom, Bootyny, Motor Boat and all the familiar crowd was there. Coodemay straightened up as if in surprise and asked, "Say, whut y'all doin' in heah?"

"Eatin'," Stew Beef told him. "Dey got beef stew, so you *know* Ah'd be heah."

"We all laks tuh take uh rest from our women folks' cookin' once in uh while, so us all eatin' way from home tuhnight. Anyhow Mis' Turner got de best ole grub in town."

Mrs. Turner back and forth in the dining room heard Sop when he said this and beamed.

"Ah speck you two last ones tuh come in is gointuh have tuh wait for uh seat. Ah'm all full up now."

"Dat's all right," Sterrett objected. "You fry me some fish. Ah kin eat dat standin' up. Cuppa coffee on de side."

"Sling me up uh plate uh dat stew beef wid some coffee too, please ma'am. Sterrett is jus' ez drunk ez Ah is; and if he kin eat standin' up, Ah kin do de same." Coodemay leaned drunkenly against the wall and everybody laughed.

Pretty soon the girl that was waiting table for Mrs. Turner brought in the order and Sterrett took his fish and coffee in his hands and stood there. Coodemay wouldn't take his off the tray like he should have.

"Naw, you hold it fuh me, baby, and lemme eat," he told the waitress. He took the fork and started to eat off the tray.

"Nobody ain't got no time tuh hold yo' grub up in front uh yo' face," she told Coodemay. "Heah, take it yo'self."

"You'se right," Coodemay told her. "Gimme it heah. Sop kin gimme his chear."

"You'se uh lie," Sop retorted. "Ah ain't through and Ah ain't ready tuh git up."

Coodemay tried to shove Sop out of the chair and Sop resisted. That brought on a whole lot of shoving and scrambling and coffee got spilt on Sop. So he aimed at Coodemay with a saucer and hit Bootyny. Bootyny threw his thick coffee cup at Coodemay and just missed Stew Beef. So it got to be a big fight. Mrs. Turner came running in out of the kitchen. Then Tea Cake got up and caught hold of Coodemay by the collar.

"Looka heah, y'all, don't come in heah and raise no disturbance in de place. Mis' Turner is too nice uh woman fuh dat. In fact, she's more nicer than anybody else on de muck." Mrs. Turner beamed on Tea Cake.

"Ah knows dat. All of us knows it. But Ah don't give uh damn how nice she is, Ah got tuh have some place tuh set down and eat. Sop ain't gointuh bluff me, neither. Let 'im fight lak a man. Take yo' hands off me, Tea Cake."

"Naw, Ah won't neither. You comin' on outa de place."

"Who gointuh make me come out?"

"Me, dat's who. Ah'm in heah, ain't Ah? If you don't want tuh respect nice people lak Mrs. Turner, God knows you gointuh respect me! Come on outa heah, Coodemay."

"Turn him loose, Tea Cake!" Sterrett shouted. "Dat's *mah* buddy. Us come in heah together and he ain't goin' nowhere until Ah go mahself."

"Well, both of yuh is goin'!" Tea Cake shouted and fastened down on Coodemay. Dockery grabbed Sterrett and they wrassled all over the place. Some more joined in and dishes and tables began to crash.

Mrs. Turner saw with dismay that Tea Cake's taking them out was worse than letting them stay in. She ran out in the back somewhere and got her husband to put a stop to things. He came in, took a look and squinched down into a chair in an off corner and didn't open his mouth. So Mrs. Turner struggled into the mass and caught Tea Cake by the arm.

"Dat's all right, Tea Cake, Ah 'preciate yo' help, but leave 'em alone."

"Naw suh, Mis' Turner, Ah'm gointuh show 'em dey can't come runnin' over nice people and loud-talk no place whilst Ah'm around. Dey goin' outa heah!"

By that time everybody in and around the place was taking sides. Somehow or other Mrs. Turner fell down and nobody knew she was down there under all the fighting, and broken dishes and crippled up tables and broken-off chair legs and window panes and such things. It got so that the floor was knee-deep with something no matter where you put your foot down. But Tea Cake kept right on until Coodemay told him, "Ah'm wrong. Ah'm wrong! Y'all tried tuh tell me right and Ah wouldn't lissen. Ah ain't mad wid nobody. Just tuh show y'all Ah ain't mad, me and Sterrett gointuh buy everybody somethin' tuh drink. Ole man Vickers got some good coon-dick over round Pahokee. Come on everybody. Let's go git our knots charged." Everybody got in a good humor and left.

Mrs. Turner got up off the floor hollering for the police. Look at her place! How come nobody didn't call the police? Then she found out that one of her hands was all stepped on and her fingers were bleeding pretty peart. Two or three people who were not there during the fracas poked their heads in at the door to sympathize but that made Mrs. Turner madder. She told them where to go in a hurry. Then she saw her husband sitting over there in the corner with his long bony legs all crossed up smoking his pipe.

"What kinda man is *you*, Turner? You see dese no count niggers come in heah and break up mah place! How kin you set and see yo' wife all trompled on? You ain't no kinda man at all. You seen dat Tea Cake shove me down! Yes you did! You ain't raised yo' hand tuh do nothin' about it."

Turner removed his pipe and answered: "Yeah, and you see how Ah did swell up too, didn't yuh? You tell Tea Cake he better be keerful Ah don't swell up again." At that Turner crossed his legs the other way and kept right on smoking his pipe.

Mrs. Turner hit at him the best she could with her hurt hand and then spoke her mind for half an hour.

"It's a good thing mah brother wuzn't round heah when it happened do he would uh kilt somebody. Mah son too. Dey got some manhood about 'em. We'se goin' back tuh Miami where folks is civilized."

Nobody told her right away that her son and brother were already on their way after pointed warnings outside the café. No time for fooling around. They were hurrying into Palm Beach. She'd find out about that later on.

Monday morning Coodemay and Sterrett stopped by and begged her pardon profusely and gave her five dollars apiece. Then Coodemay said, "Dey tell me Ah wuz drunk Sat'day night and clownin' down. Ah don't 'member uh thing 'bout it. But when Ah git tuh peepin' through mah likker, dey tell me Ah'm uh mess."

Chapter 18

Since Tea Cake and Janie had friended with the Bahaman workers in the 'Glades, they, the "Saws," had been gradually drawn into the American crowd. They quit hiding out to hold their dances when they found that their American friends didn't laugh at them as they feared. Many of the Americans learned to jump and liked it as much as the "Saws." So they began to hold dances night after night in the quarters, usually behind Tea Cake's house. Often now, Tea Cake and Janie stayed up so late at the fire dances that Tea Cake would not let her go with him to the field. He wanted her to get her rest.

So she was home by herself one afternoon when she saw a band of Seminoles passing by. The men walking in front and the laden, stolid women following them like burros. She had seen Indians several times in the 'Glades, in twos and threes, but this was a large party. They were headed towards the Palm Beach road and kept moving steadily. About an hour later another party appeared and went the same way. Then another just before sundown. This time she asked where they were all going and at last one of the men answered her.

"Going to high ground. Saw-grass bloom. Hurricane coming."

Everybody was talking about it that night. But nobody was worried. The fire dance kept up till nearly dawn. The next day, more Indians moved east, unhurried but steady. Still a blue sky and fair weather. Beans running fine and prices good, so the Indians could be, *must* be, wrong. You couldn't have a hurricane when you're making seven and eight dollars a day picking beans. Indians are dumb anyhow, always were. Another night of Stew Beef making dynamic subtleties with his drum and living, sculptural, grotesques in the dance. Next day, no Indians passed at all. It was hot and sultry and Janie left the field and went home.

Morning came without motion. The winds, to the tiniest, lisping baby breath had left the earth. Even before the sun gave light, dead day was creeping from bush to bush watching man.

Some rabbits scurried through the quarters going east. Some possums slunk by and their route was definite. One or two at a time, then more. By the time the people left the fields the procession was constant. Snakes, rattlesnakes began to cross the quarters. The men killed a few, but they could not be missed from the crawling horde. People stayed indoors until daylight. Several times during the night Janie heard the snort of big animals like deer. Once the muted voice of a panther. Going east and east. That night the palm and banana trees began that long distance talk with rain. Several people took fright and picked up and went in to Palm Beach anyway. A thousand buzzards held a flying meet and then went above the clouds and stayed.

One of the Bahaman boys stopped by Tea Cake's house in a car and hollered. Tea Cake came out throwin' laughter over his shoulder into the house.

"Hello Tea Cake."

"Hello 'Lias. You leavin', Ah see."

"Yeah man. You and Janie wanta go? Ah wouldn't give nobody else uh chawnce at uh seat till Ah found out if you all had anyway tuh go."

"Thank yuh ever so much, 'Lias. But we 'bout decided tuh stay."

"De crow gahn up, man."

"Dat ain't nothin'. You ain't seen de bossman go up, is yuh? Well all right now. Man, de money's too good on the muck. It's liable tuh fair off by tuhmorrer. Ah wouldn't leave if Ah wuz you."

"Mah uncle come for me. He say hurricane warning out in Palm Beach. Not so bad dere, but man, dis muck is too low and dat big lake is liable tuh bust."

"Ah naw, man. Some boys in dere now talkin' 'bout it. Some of 'em been in de 'Glades fuh years. 'Tain't nothin' but uh lil blow. You'll lose de whole day tuh-morrer tryin' tuh git back out heah."

"De Indians gahn east, man. It's dangerous."

"Dey don't always know. Indians don't know much uh nothin', tuh tell de truth. Else dey'd own dis country still. De white folks ain't gone nowhere. Dey oughta know if it's dangerous. You better stay heah, man. Big jumpin' dance tuhnight right heah, when it fair off."

'Lias hesitated and started to climb out, but his uncle wouldn't let him. "Dis time tuhmorrer you gointuh wish you follow crow," he snorted and drove off. 'Lias waved back to them gaily.

"If Ah never see you no mo' on earth, Ah'll meet you in Africa."

Others hurried east like the Indians and rabbits and snakes and coons. But the majority sat around laughing and waiting for the sun to get friendly again.

Several men collected at Tea Cake's house and sat around stuffing courage into each other's ears. Janie baked a big pan of beans and something she called sweet biscuits and they all managed to he happy enough.

Most of the great flame-throwers were there and naturally, handling Big John de Conquer and his works. How he had done everything big on earth, then went up tuh heben without dying atall. Went up there picking a guitar and got all de angels doing the ring-shout round and round de throne. Then everybody but God and Old Peter flew off on a flying race to Jericho and back and John de Conquer won the race; went on down to hell, beat the old devil and passed out ice water to everybody down there. Somebody tried to say that it was a mouth organ harp that John was playing, but the rest of them would not hear that. Don't care how good anybody could play a harp, God would rather to hear a guitar. That brought them back to Tea Cake. How come he couldn't hit that box a lick or two? Well, all right now, make us know it.

When it got good to everybody, Muck-Boy woke up and began to chant with the rhythm and everybody bore down on the last word of the line:

Yo' mama don't wear no *Draws*
Ah seen her when she took 'em *Off*
She soaked 'em in alco*Hol*
She sold 'em tuh de Santy *Claus*
He told her 'twas aginst de *Law*
To wear dem dirty *Draws*

Then Muck-Boy went crazy through the feet and danced himself and everybody else crazy. When he finished he sat back down on the floor and went to sleep again. Then they got to playing Florida flip and coon-can. Then it was dice. Not for money. This was a show-off game. Everybody posing his fancy shots. As always it broiled down to Tea Cake and Motor Boat. Tea Cake with his shy grin and Motor Boat with his face like a little black cherubim just from a church tower doing amazing things with anybody's dice. The others forgot the work and the weather watching them throw. It was art. A thousand dollars a throw in Madison Square Garden wouldn't have gotten any more breathless suspense. It would have just been more people holding in.

After a while somebody looked out and said, "It ain't gitting no fairer out dere. B'lieve Ah'll git on over tuh mah shack." Motor Boat and Tea Cake were still playing so everybody left them at it.

Sometime that night the winds came back. Everything in the world had a strong rattle, sharp and short like Stew Beef vibrating the drum head near the edge with his fingers. By morning Gabriel was playing the deep tones in the center of the drum. So when Janie looked out of her door she saw the drifting mists gathered in the west—that cloud field of the sky—to arm themselves with thunder and march forth against the world. Louder and higher and lower and wider the sound and motion spread, mounting, sinking, darking.

It woke up old Okechobee and the monster began to roll in his bed. Began to roll and complain like a peevish world on a grumble. The folks in the quarters and the people in the big houses further around the shore heard the big lake and wondered. The people felt uncomfortable but safe because there were the seawalls to chain the senseless monster in his bed. The folks let the people do the thinking. If the castles thought themselves secure, the cabins needn't worry. Their decision was already made as always. Chink up your cracks, shiver in your wet beds and wait on the mercy of the Lord. The bossman might have the thing stopped before morning anyway. It is so easy to be hopeful in the day time when you can see the things you wish on. But it was night, it stayed night. Night was striding across nothingness with the whole round world in his hands.

A big burst of thunder and lightning that trampled over the roof of the house. So Tea Cake and Motor stopped playing. Motor looked up in his angel-looking way and said, "Big Massa draw him chair upstairs."

"Ah'm glad y'all stop dat crap-shootin' even if it wasn't for money," Janie said. "Ole Massa is doin' *His* work now. Us oughta keep quiet."

They huddled closer and stared at the door. They just didn't use another part of their bodies, and they didn't look at anything but the door. The time was past for asking the white folks what to look for through that door. Six eyes were questioning *God*.

Through the screaming wind they heard things crashing and things hurtling and dashing with unbelievable velocity. A baby rabbit, terror ridden, squirmed through a hole in the floor and squatted off there in the shadows against the wall, seeming to know that nobody wanted its flesh at such a time. And the lake got madder and madder with only its dikes between them and him.

In a little wind-lull, Tea Cake touched Janie and said, "Ah reckon you wish now you had of stayed in yo' big house 'way from such as dis, don't yuh?"

"Naw."

"Naw?"

"Yeah, naw. People don't die till dey time come nohow, don't keer where you at. Ah'm wid mah husband in uh storm, dat's all."

"Thanky, Ma'am. But 'sposing you wuz tuh die, now. You wouldn't git mad at me for draggin' yuh heah?"

"Naw. We been tuhgether round two years. If you kin see de light at daybreak, you don't keer if you die at dusk. It's so many people never seen de light at all. Ah wuz fumblin' round and God opened de door."

He dropped to the floor and put his head in her lap. "Well then, Janie, you meant whut you didn't say, 'cause Ah never *knowed* you wuz so satisfied wid me lak dat. Ah kinda thought—"

The wind came back with triple fury, and put out the light for the last time. They sat in company with the others in other shanties, their eyes straining against crude walls and their souls asking if He meant to measure their puny might against His. They seemed to be staring at the dark, but their eyes were watching God.

As soon as Tea Cake went out pushing wind in front of him, he saw that the wind and water had given life to lots of things that folks think of as dead and given death to so much that had been living things. Water everywhere. Stray fish swimming in the yard. Three inches more and the water would be in the house. Already in some. He decided to try to find a car to take them out of the 'Glades before worse things happened. He turned back to tell Janie about it so she could be ready to go.

"Git our insurance papers tuhgether, Janie. Ah'll tote mah box mahself and things lak dat."

"You got all de money out de dresser drawer, already?"

"Naw, git it quick and cut up piece off de table-cloth tuh wrap it up in. Us liable tuh git wet tuh our necks. Cut uh piece uh dat oilcloth quick fuh our papers. We got tuh go, if it ain't too late. De dish can't bear it out no longer."

He snatched the oilcloth off the table and took out his knife. Janie held it straight while he slashed off a strip.

"But Tea Cake, it's too awful out dere. Maybe it's better tuh stay heah in de wet than it is tuh try tuh—"

He stunned the argument with half a word. "Fix," he said and fought his way outside. He had seen more than Janie had.

Janie took a big needle and ran up a longish sack. Found some newspaper and wrapped up the paper money and papers and thrust them in and whipped over the open end with her needle. Before she could get it thoroughly hidden in the pocket of her overalls, Tea Cake burst in again.

"'Tain't no cars, Janie."

"Ah thought not! Whut we gointuh do now?"

"We got tuh walk."

"In all dis weather, Tea Cake? Ah don't b'lieve Ah could make it out de quarters."

"Oh yeah you kin. Me and you and Motor Boat kin all lock arms and hold one 'nother down. Eh, Motor?"

"He's sleep on de bed in yonder," Janie said. Tea Cake called without moving.

"Motor Boat! You better git up from dere! Hell done broke loose in Georgy. Dis minute! How kin you sleep at uh time lak dis? Water knee deep in de yard."

They stepped out in water almost to their buttocks and managed to turn east. Tea Cake had to throw his box away, and Janie saw how it hurt him. Dodging flying missiles, floating dangers, avoiding stepping in holes and warmed on the wind now at their backs until they gained comparatively dry land. They had to fight to keep from being pushed the wrong way and to hold together. They saw other people like themselves struggling along. A house down, here and there, frightened cattle. But above all the drive of the wind and the water. And the lake. Under its multiplied roar could be heard a mighty sound of grinding rock and timber and a wail. They looked back. Saw people trying to run in raging waters and screaming when they found they couldn't. A huge barrier of the makings of the dike to which the cabins had been added was rolling and tumbling forward. Ten feet higher and as far as they could see the muttering wall advanced before the braced-up waters like a road crusher on a cosmic scale. The monstropolous beast had left his bed. The two hundred miles an hour wind had loosed his chains. He seized hold of his dikes and ran forward until he met the quarters; uprooted them like grass and rushed on after his supposed-to-be conquerors, rolling the dikes, rolling the houses, rolling the people in the houses along with other timbers. The sea was walking the earth with a heavy heel.

"De lake is comin'!" Tea Cake gasped.

"De lake!" In amazed horror from Motor Boat, "De lake!"

"It's comin' behind us!" Janie shuddered. "Us can't fly."

"But we still kin run," Tea Cake shouted and they ran. The gushing water ran faster. The great body was held back, but rivers spouted through fissures in the rolling wall and broke like day. The three fugitives ran past another line of shanties that topped a slight rise and gained a little. They cried out as best they could, "De lake is comin'!" and barred doors flew open and others joined them in flight crying the same as they went. "De lake is comin'!" and the pursuing waters growled and shouted ahead, "Yes, Ah'm comin'!", and those who could fled on.

They made it to a tall house on a hump of ground and Janie said, "Less stop heah. Ah can't make it no further. Ah'm done give out."

"All of us is done give out," Tea Cake corrected. "We'se goin' inside out dis weather, kill or cure." He knocked with the handle of his knife, while they leaned their faces and shoulders against the wall. He knocked once more then he and Motor Boat went round to the back and forced a door. Nobody there.

"Dese people had mo' sense than Ah did," Tea Cake said as they dropped to the floor and lay there panting. "Us oughta went on wid 'Lias lak he ast me."

"You didn't know," Janie contended. "And when yuh don't know, yuh just don't know. De storms might not of come sho nuff."

They went to sleep promptly but Janie woke up first. She heard the sound of rushing water and sat up.

"Tea Cake! Motor Boat! De lake is comin'!"

The lake *was* coming on. Slower and wider, but coming. It had trampled on most of its supporting wall and lowered its front by spreading. But it came muttering and grumbling onward like a tired mammoth just the same.

"Dis is uh high tall house. Maybe it won't reach heah at all," Janie counseled. "And if it do, maybe it won't reach tuh de upstairs part."

"Janie, Lake Okechobee is forty miles wide and sixty miles long. Dat's uh whole heap uh water. If dis wind is shovin' dat whole lake disa way, dis house ain't nothin' tuh swaller. Us better go. Motor Boat!"

"Whut you want, man?"

"De lake is comin'!"

"Aw, naw it 'tain't."

"Yes, it is *so* comin'! Listen! You kin hear it way off."

"It kin jus' come on. Ah'll wait right here."

"Aw, get up, Motor Boat! Less make it tuh de Palm Beach road. Dat's on uh fill. We'se pretty safe dere."

"Ah'm safe here, man. Go ahead if yuh wants to. Ah'm sleepy."

"Whut you gointuh do if de lake reach heah?"

"Go upstairs."

"S'posing it come up dere?"

"Swim, man. Dat's all."

"Well, uh, Good bye, Motor Boat. Everything is pretty bad, yuh know. Us might git missed of one 'nother. You sho is a grand friend fuh uh man tuh have."

"Good bye, Tea Cake. Y'all oughta stay here and sleep, man. No use in goin' off and leavin' me lak dis."

"We don't wanta. Come on wid us. It might be night time when de water hem you up in heah. Dat's how come Ah won't stay. Come on, man."

"Tea Cake, Ah got tuh have mah sleep. Definitely."

"Good bye, then, Motor. Ah wish you all de luck. Goin' over tuh Nassau fuh dat visit widja when all dis is over."

"Definitely, Tea Cake. Mah mama's house is yours."

Tea Cake and Janie were some distance from the house before they struck serious water. Then they had to swim a distance, and Janie could not hold up more than a few strokes at a time, so Tea Cake bore her up till finally they hit a ridge that led on towards the fill. It seemed to him the wind was weakening a little so he kept looking for a place to rest and catch his breath. His wind was gone. Janie was tired and limping, but she had not had to do that hard swimming in the turbulent waters, so Tea Cake was much worse off. But they couldn't stop. Gaining the fill was something but it was no guarantee. The lake was coming. They had to reach the six-mile bridge. It was high and safe perhaps.

Everybody was walking the fill. Hurrying, dragging, falling, crying, calling out names hopefully and hopelessly. Wind and rain beating on old folks and beating on babies. Tea Cake stumbled once or twice in his weariness and Janie held him up. So they reached the bridge at Six Mile Bend and thought to rest.

But it was crowded. White people had preempted that point of elevation and there was no more room. They could climb up one of its high sides and down the other, that was all. Miles further on, still no rest.

They passed a dead man in a sitting position on a hummock, entirely surrounded by wild animals and snakes. Common danger made common friends. Nothing sought a conquest over the other.

Another man clung to a cypress tree on a tiny island. A tin roof of a building hung from the branches by electric wires and the wind swung it back and forth like a mighty ax. The man dared not move a step to his right lest this crushing blade split him open. He dared not step left for a large rattlesnake was stretched full length with his head in the wind. There was a strip of water between the island and the fill, and the man clung to the tree and cried for help.

"De snake won't bite yuh," Tea Cake yelled to him. "He skeered tuh go intuh uh coil. Skeered he'll be blowed away. Step round dat side and swim off!"

Soon after that Tea Cake felt he couldn't walk anymore. Not right away. So he stretched long side of the road to rest. Janie spread herself between him and the wind and he closed his eyes and let the tiredness seep out of his limbs. On each side of the fill was a great expanse of water like lakes—water full of things living and dead. Things that didn't belong in water. As far as the eye could reach, water and wind playing upon it in fury. A large piece of tar-paper roofing sailed through the air and scudded along the fill until it hung against a tree. Janie saw it with joy. That was the very thing to cover Tea Cake with. She could lean against it and hold it down. The wind wasn't quite so bad as it was anyway. The very thing. Poor Tea Cake!

She crept on hands and knees to the piece of roofing and caught hold of it by either side. Immediately the wind lifted both of them and she saw herself sailing off the fill to the right, out and out over the lashing water. She screamed terribly and released the roofing which sailed away as she plunged downward into the water.

"Tea Cake!" He heard her and sprang up. Janie was trying to swim but fighting water too hard. He saw a cow swimming slowly towards the fill in an oblique line. A massive built dog was sitting on her shoulders and shivering and growling. The cow was approaching Janie. A few strokes would bring her there.

"Make it tuh de cow and grab hold of her tail! Don't use yo' feet. Jus' yo' hands is enough. Dat's right, come on!"

Janie achieved the tail of the cow and lifted her head up along the cow's rump, as far as she could above water. The cow sunk a little with the added load and thrashed a moment in terror. Thought she was being pulled down by a gator. Then she continued on. The dog stood up and growled like a lion, stiff-standing hackles, stiff muscles, teeth uncovered as he lashed up his fury for the charge. Tea Cake split the water like an otter, opening his knife as he dived. The dog raced down the back-bone of the cow to the attack and Janie screamed and slipped far back on the tail of the cow, just out of reach of the dog's angry jaws. He wanted to plunge in after her but dreaded the water, somehow. Tea Cake rose out of the water at the cow's rump and seized the dog by the neck. But he was a powerful dog and Tea Cake was over-tired. So he didn't kill the dog with one stroke as he had intended. But the dog couldn't free himself either. They fought and somehow he managed to bite Tea Cake high up on his cheek-bone once. Then Tea Cake finished him and sent him to the bottom to stay there. The cow relieved of a great weight was landing on the fill with Janie before Tea Cake stroked in and crawled weakly upon the fill again.

Janie began to fuss around his face where the dog had bitten him but he said it didn't amount to anything. "He'd uh raised hell though if he had uh grabbed me uh inch higher and bit me in mah eye. Yuh can't buy eyes in de store, yuh know." He flopped to the edge of the fill as if the storm wasn't going on at all. "Lemme rest awhile, then us got tuh make it on intuh town somehow."

It was next day by the sun and the clock when they reached Palm Beach. It was years later by their bodies. Winters and winters of hardship and suffering. The wheel kept turning round and round. Hope, hopelessness and despair. But the storm blew itself out as they approached the city of refuge.

Havoc was there with her mouth wide open. Back in the Everglades the wind had romped among lakes and trees. In the city it had raged among houses and men. Tea Cake and Janie stood on the edge of things and looked over the desolation.

"How kin Ah find uh doctor fuh yo' face in all dis mess?" Janie wailed.

"Ain't got de damn doctor tuh study 'bout. Us needs uh place tuh rest."

A great deal of their money and perseverance and they found a place to sleep. It was just that. No place to live at all. Just sleep. Tea Cake looked all around and sat heavily on the side of the bed.

"Well," he said humbly, "reckon you never 'spected tuh come tuh dis when you took up wid me, didja?"

"Once upon uh time, Ah never 'spected nothin', Tea Cake, but bein' dead from the standin' still and tryin' tuh laugh. But you come 'long and made somethin' outa me. So Ah'm thankful fuh anything we come through together."

"Thanky, Ma'am."

"You was twice noble tuh save me from dat dawg. Tea Cake, Ah don't speck you seen his eyes lak Ah did. He didn't aim tuh jus' bite me, Tea Cake. He aimed tuh kill me stone dead. Ah'm never tuh fuhgit dem eyes. He wuzn't nothin' all over but pure hate. Wonder where he come from?"

"Yeah, Ah did see 'im too. It wuz frightenin'. Ah didn't mean tuh take his hate neither. He had tuh die uh me one. Mah switch blade said it wuz him."

"Po' me, he'd tore me tuh pieces, if it wuzn't fuh you, honey."

"You don't have tuh say, if it wuzn't fuh me, baby, cause Ah'm *heah*, and then Ah want yuh tuh know it's uh man heah."

Chapter 19

And then again Him-with-the-square-toes had gone back to his house. He stood once more and again in his high flat house without sides to it and without a roof with his soulless sword standing upright in his hand. His pale white horse had galloped over waters, and thundered over land. The time of dying was over. It was time to bury the dead.

"Janie, us been in dis dirty, slouchy place two days now, and dat's too much. Us got tuh git outa dis house and outa dis man's town. Ah never did lak round heah."

"Where we goin', Tea Cake? Dat we don't know."

"Maybe, we could go back up de state, if yuh want tuh go."

"Ah didn't say dat, but if dat is whut you—"

"Naw, Ah ain't said nothin' uh de kind. Ah wuz tryin' not tuh keep you outa yo' comfortable no longer'n you wanted tuh stay."

"If Ah'm in yo' way—"

"Will you lissen at dis woman? Me 'bout tuh bust mah britches tryin' tuh stay wid her and she heah—she oughta be shot wid tacks!"

"All right then, you name somethin' and we'll do it. We kin give it uh poor man's trial anyhow."

"Anyhow Ah done got rested up and de bed bugs is done got too bold round heah. Ah didn't notice when mah rest wuz broke. Ah'm goin' out and look around and see whut we kin do. Ah'll give *any*thing uh common trial."

"You better stay inside dis house and git some rest. 'Tain't nothin' tuh find out dere nohow."

"But Ah wants tuh look and see, Janie. Maybe it's some kinda work fuh me tuh help do."

"Whut dey want you tuh help do, you ain't gointuh like it. Dey's grabbin' all de menfolks dey kin git dey hands on and makin' 'em help bury de dead. Dey claims dey's after de unemployed, but dey ain't bein' too particular about whether you'se employed or not. You stay in dis house. De Red Cross is doin' all dat kin be done otherwise fuh de sick and de 'fflicted."

"Ah got money on me, Janie. Dey can't bother me. Anyhow Ah wants tuh go see how things is sho nuff. Ah wants tuh see if Ah kin hear anything 'bout de boys from de 'Glades. Maybe dey all come through all right. Maybe not."

Tea Cake went out and wandered around. Saw the hand of horror on everything. Houses without roofs, and roofs without houses. Steel and stone all crushed and crumbled like wood. The mother of malice had trifled with men.

While Tea Cake was standing and looking he saw two men coming towards him with rifles on their shoulders. Two white men, so he thought about what Janie had told him and flexed his knees to run. But in a moment he saw that wouldn't do him any good. They had already seen him and they were too close to miss him if they shot. Maybe they would pass on by. Maybe when they saw he had money they would realize he was not a tramp.

"Hello, there, Jim," the tallest one called out. "We been lookin' fuh you."

"Mah name ain't no Jim," Tea Cake said watchfully. "Whut you been lookin' fuh *me* fuh? Ah ain't done nothin'."

"Dat's whut we want yuh fuh—not doin' nothin'. Come on less go bury some uh dese heah dead folks. Dey ain't gittin' buried fast enough."

Tea Cake hung back defensively. "Whut Ah got tuh do wid dat? Ah'm uh workin' man wid money in mah pocket. Jus' got blowed outa de 'Glades by de storm."

The short man made a quick move with his rifle. "Git on down de road dere, suh! Don't look out somebody'll be buryin' *you!* G'wan in front uh me, suh!"

Tea Cake found that he was part of a small army that had been pressed into service to clear the wreckage in public places and bury the dead. Bodies had to be searched out, carried to certain gathering places and buried. Corpses were not just found in wrecked houses. They were under houses, tangled in shrubbery, floating in water, hanging in trees, drifting under wreckage.

Trucks lined with drag kept rolling in from the 'Glades and other outlying parts, each with its load of twenty-five bodies. Some bodies fully dressed, some naked and some in all degrees of dishevelment. Some bodies with calm faces and satisfied hands. Some dead with fighting faces and eyes flung wide open in wonder. Death had found them watching, trying to see beyond seeing.

Miserable, sullen men, black and white under guard had to keep on searching for bodies and digging graves. A huge ditch was dug across the white cemetery and a big ditch was opened across the black graveyard. Plenty quick-lime on hand to throw over the bodies as soon as they were received. They had already been unburied too long. The men were making every effort to get them covered up as quickly as possible. But the guards stopped them. They had received orders to be carried out.

"Hey, dere, y'all! Don't dump dem bodies in de hole lak dat! Examine every last one of 'em and find out if they's white or black."

"Us got tuh handle 'em slow lak dat? God have mussy! In de condition they's in got tuh examine 'em? Whut difference do it make 'bout de color? Dey all needs buryin' in uh hurry."

"Got orders from headquarters. They makin' coffins fuh all de white folks. 'Tain't nothin' but cheap pine, but dat's better'n nothin'. Don't dump no white folks in de hole jus' so."

"Whut tuh do 'bout de colored folks? Got boxes fuh dem too?"

"Nope. They cain't find enough of 'em tuh go 'round. Jus' sprinkle plenty quick-lime over 'em and cover 'em up."

"Shucks! Nobody can't tell nothin' 'bout some uh dese bodies, de shape dey's in. Can't tell whether dey's white or black."

The guards had a long conference over that. After a while they came back and told the men, "Look at they hair, when you cain't tell no other way. And don't lemme ketch none uh y'all dumpin' white folks, and don't be wastin' no boxes on colored. They's too hard tuh git holt of right now."

"They's mighty particular how dese dead folks goes tuh judgment," Tea Cake observed to the man working next to him. "Look lak dey think God don't know nothin' 'bout de Jim Crow law."

Tea Cake had been working several hours when the thought of Janie worrying about him made him desperate. So when a truck drove up to be unloaded he bolted and ran. He was ordered to halt on pain of being shot at, but he kept right on and got away. He found Janie sad and crying just as he had thought. They calmed each other about his absence then Tea Cake brought up another matter.

"Janie, us got tuh git outa dis house and outa dis man's town. Ah don't mean tuh work lak dat no mo'."

"Naw, naw, Tea Cake. Less stay right in heah until it's all over. If dey can't see yuh, dey can't bother yuh."

"Aw naw. S'posin' dey come round searchin'? Less git outa heah tuhnight."

"Where us goin', Tea Cake?"

"De quickest place is de 'Glades. Less make it on back down dere. Dis town is full uh trouble and compellment."

"But, Tea Cake, de hurricane wuz down in de 'Glades too. It'll be dead folks tuh be buried down dere too."

"Yeah, Ah know, Janie, but it couldn't never be lak it 'tis heah. In de first place dey been bringin' bodies outa dere all day so it can't be but so many mo' tuh find. And then again it never wuz as many dere as it wuz heah. And then too, Janie, de white folks down dere knows us. It's bad bein' strange niggers wid white folks. Everybody is aginst yuh."

"Dat sho is de truth. De ones de white man know is nice colored folks. De ones he don't know is bad niggers." Janie said this and laughed and Tea Cake laughed with her.

"Janie, Ah done watched it time and time again; each and every white man think he know all de GOOD darkies already. He don't need tuh know no mo'. So far as he's concerned, all dem he don't know oughta be tried and sentenced tuh six months behind de United States privy house at hard smellin'."

"How come de United States privy house, Tea Cake?"

"Well, you know Old Uncle Sam always do have de biggest and de best uh everything. So de white man figger dat anything less than de Uncle Sam's consolidated water closet would be too easy. So Ah means tuh go where de white folks know me. Ah feels lak uh motherless chile round heah."

They got things together and stole out of the house and away. The next morning they were back on the muck. They worked hard all day fixing up a house to live in so that Tea Cake could go out looking for something to do the next day. He got out soon next morning more out of curiosity than eagerness to work. Stayed off all day. That night he came in beaming out with light.

"Who you reckon Ah seen, Janie? Bet you can't guess."

"Ah'll betcha uh fat man you seen Sop-de-Bottom."

"Yeah Ah seen him and Stew Beef and Dockery and 'Lias, and Coodemay and Bootyny. Guess who else!"

"Lawd knows. Is it Sterrett?"

"Naw, he got caught in the rush. 'Lias help bury him in Palm Beach. Guess who else?"

"Ah g'wan tell me, Tea Cake. Ah don't know. It can't be Motor Boat."

"Dat's jus' who it is. Ole Motor! De son of a gun laid up in dat house and slept and de lake come moved de house way off somewhere and Motor didn't know nothin' 'bout it till de storm wuz 'bout over."

"Naw!"

"Yeah man. Heah we nelly kill our fool selves runnin' way from danger and him lay up dere and sleep and float on off!"

"Well, you know dey say luck is uh fortune."

"Dat's right too. Look, Ah got uh job uh work. Help clearin' up things in general, and then dey goin' build dat dike sho nuff. Dat ground got to be cleared off too. Plenty work. Dey needs mo' men even."

So Tea Cake made three hearty weeks. He bought another rifle and a pistol and he and Janie bucked each other as to who was the best shot with Janie ranking him always with the rifle. She could knock the head off of a chicken-hawk sitting up a pine tree. Tea Cake was a little jealous, but proud of his pupil.

About the middle of the fourth week Tea Cake came home early one afternoon complaining of his head. Sick headache that made him lie down for a while. He woke up hungry. Janie had his supper ready but by the time he walked from the bedroom to the table, he said he didn't b'lieve he wanted a thing.

"Thought you tole me you wuz hongry!" Janie wailed.

"Ah thought so too," Tea Cake said very quietly and dropped his head in his hands.

"But Ah done baked yuh uh pan uh beans."

"Ah knows dey's good all right but Ah don't choose nothin' now, Ah thank yuh, Janie."

He went back to bed. Way in the midnight he woke Janie up in his nightmarish struggle with an enemy that was at his throat. Janie struck a light and quieted him.

"Whut's de matter, honey?" She soothed and soothed. "You got tuh tell me so Ah kin feel widja. Lemme bear de pain 'long widja, baby. Where hurt yuh, sugar?"

"Somethin' got after me in mah sleep, Janie." He all but cried, "Tried tuh choke me tuh death. Hadn't been fuh *you* Ah'd be dead."

"You sho wuz strainin' wid it. But you'se all right, honey. Ah'm heah."

He went on back to sleep, but there was no getting around it. He was sick in the morning. He tried to make it but Janie wouldn't hear of his going out at all.

"If Ah kin jus' make out de week," Tea Cake said.

"Folks wuz makin' weeks befo' you wuz born and they gointuh be makin' 'em after you'se gone. Lay back down, Tea Cake. Ah'm goin' git de doctor tuh come see 'bout yuh."

"Aw ain't dat bad, Janie. Looka heah! Ah kin walk all over de place."

"But you'se too sick tuh play wid. Plenty fever round heah since de storm."

"Gimme uh drink uh water befo' you leave, then."

Janie dipped up a glass of water and brought it to the bed. Tea Cake took it and filled his mouth then gagged horribly, disgorged that which was in his mouth and threw the glass upon the floor. Janie was frantic with alarm.

"Whut make you ack lak dat wid yo' drinkin' water, Tea Cake? You ast me tuh give it tuh yuh."

"Dat water is somethin' wrong wid it. It nelly choke me tuh death. Ah tole yuh somethin' jumped on me heah last night and choked me. You come makin' out ah wuz dreamin'."

"Maybe it wuz uh witch ridin' yuh, honey. Ah'll see can't Ah find some mustard seed whilst Ah's out. But Ah'm sho tuh fetch de doctor when Ah'm come."

Tea Cake didn't say anything against it and Janie herself hurried off. This sickness to her was worse than the storm. As soon as she was well out of sight, Tea Cake got up and dumped the water bucket and washed it clean. Then he struggled to the irrigation pump and filled it again. He was not accusing Janie of malice and design. He was accusing her of carelessness. She ought to realize that water buckets needed washing like everything else. He'd tell her about it good and proper when she got back. What was she thinking about nohow? He found himself very angry about it. He eased the bucket on the table and sat down to rest before taking a drink.

Finally he dipped up a drink. It was so good and cool! Come to think about it, he hadn't had a drink since yesterday. That was what he needed to give him an appetite for his beans. He found himself wanting it very much, so he threw back his head as he rushed the glass to his lips. But the demon was there before him, strangling, killing him quickly. It was a great relief to expel the water from his mouth. He sprawled on the bed again and lay there shivering until Janie and the doctor arrived. The white doctor who had been around so long that he was part of the muck. Who told the workmen stories with brawny sweaty words in them. He came into the house quickly, hat sitting on the left back corner of his head.

"Hi there, Tea Cake. What de hell's de matter with *you?*"

"Wisht Ah knowed, Doctah Simmons. But Ah sho is sick."

"Ah, naw Tea Cake. 'Tain't a thing wrong that a quart of coon-dick wouldn't cure. You haven't been gettin' yo' right likker lately, eh?" He slapped Tea Cake lustily across his back and Tea Cake tried to smile as he was expected to do. But it was hard. The doctor opened up his bag and went to work.

"You do look a little peaked, Tea Cake. You got a temperature and yo' pulse is kinda off. What you been doin' here lately?"

"Nothin' 'cept workin' and gamin' uh little, doctah. But look lak water done turn't aginst me."

"Water? How do you mean?"

"Can't keep it on mah stomach, at all."

"What else?"

Janie came around the bed full of concern.

"Doctah, Tea Cake ain't tellin' yuh everything lak he oughta. We wuz caught in dat hurricane out heah, and Tea Cake over-strained hisself swimmin' such uh long time and holdin' me up too, and walkin' all dem miles in de storm and then befo' he could git his rest he had tuh come git me out de water agin and fightin' wid dat big ole dawg and de dawg bitin' 'im in de face and everything. Ah been spectin' him tuh be sick befo' now."

"Dawg bit 'im, did you say?"

"Aw twudn't nothin' much, doctah. It wuz all healed over in two three days," Tea Cake said impatiently. "Dat been over uh month ago, nohow. Dis is somethin' new, doctah. Ah figgers de water is yet bad. It's bound tuh be. Too many dead folks been in it fuh it tuh be good tuh drink fuh uh long time. Dat's de way Ah figgers it anyhow."

"All right, Tea Cake, Ah'll send you some medicine and tell Janie how tuh take care of you. Anyhow, I want you in a bed by yo' self until you hear from me. Just you keep Janie out of yo' bed for awhile, hear? Come on out to the car with me, Janie. I want to send Tea Cake some pills to take right away."

Outside he fumbled in his bag and gave Janie a tiny bottle with a few pellets inside.

"Give him one of these every hour to keep him quiet, Janie, and stay out of his way when he gets in one of his fits of gagging and choking."

"How you know he's havin' 'em, doctah? Dat's jus' what Ah come out heah tuh tell yuh."

"Janie, I'm pretty sure that was a mad dawg bit yo' husband. It's too late to get hold of de dawg's head. But de symptoms is all there. It's mighty bad dat it's gone on so long. Some shots right after it happened would have fixed him right up."

"You mean he's liable tuh die, doctah?"

"Sho is. But de worst thing is he's liable tuh suffer somethin' awful befo' he goes."

"Doctor, Ah loves him fit tuh kill. Tell me anything tuh do and Ah'll do it."

"'Bout de only thing you can do, Janie, is to put him in the County Hospital where they can tie him down and look after him."

"But he don't like no hospital at all. He'd think Ah wuz tired uh doin' fuh 'im, when God knows Ah ain't. Ah can't stand de idea us tyin' Tea Cake lak he wuz uh mad dawg."

"It almost amounts to dat, Janie. He's got almost no chance to pull through and he's liable to bite somebody else, specially you, and then you'll be in the same fix he's in. It's mighty bad."

"Can't nothin' be done fuh his case, doctah? Us got plenty money in de bank in Orlandah, doctah. See can't yuh do somethin' special tuh save him. Anything it cost, doctah, Ah don't keer, but please, doctah."

"Do what I can. Ah'll phone into Palm Beach right away for the serum which he should have had three weeks ago. I'll do all I can to save him, Janie. But it looks too late. People in his condition can't swallow water, you know, and in other ways it's terrible."

Janie fooled around outside awhile to try and think it wasn't so. If she didn't see the sickness in his face she could imagine it wasn't really happening. Well, she thought, that big old dawg with the hatred in his eyes had killed her after all. She wished she had slipped off that cow-tail and drowned then and there and been done. But to kill her through Tea Cake was too much to bear. Tea Cake, the son of Evening Sun, had to die for loving her. She looked hard at the sky for a long time. Somewhere up there beyond blue ether's bosom sat He. Was He noticing what was going on around here? He must be because He knew everything. Did He *mean* to do this thing to Tea Cake and her? It wasn't anything she could fight. She could only ache and wait. Maybe it was some big tease and when He saw it had gone far enough He'd give her a sign. She looked hard for something up there to move for a sign. A star in the daytime, maybe, or the sun to shout, or even a mutter of thunder. Her arms went up in a desperate supplication for a minute. It wasn't exactly pleading, it was asking questions. The sky stayed hard looking and quiet so she went inside the house. God would do less than He had in His heart.

Tea Cake was lying with his eyes closed and Janie hoped he was asleep. He wasn't. A great fear had took hold of him. What was this thing that set his brains afire and grabbed at his throat with iron fingers? Where did it come from and why did it hang around him? He hoped it would stop before Janie noticed anything. He wanted to try to drink water again but he didn't want her to see him fail. As soon as she got out of the kitchen he meant to go to the bucket and drink right quick before anything had time to stop him. No need to worry Janie, until he couldn't help it. He heard her cleaning out the stove and saw her go out back to empty the ashes. He leaped at the bucket at once. But this time the sight of the water was enough. He was on the kitchen floor in great agony when she returned. She petted him, soothed him, and got him back to bed. She made up her mind to go see about that medicine from Palm Beach. Maybe she could find somebody to drive over there for it.

"Feel better now, Tea Cake, baby chile?"

"Uh huh, uh little."

"Well, b'lieve Ah'll rake up de front yard. De mens is got cane chewin's and peanut hulls all over de place. Don't want de doctah tuh come back heah and find it still de same."

"Don't take too long, Janie. Don't lak tuh be by mahself when Ah'm sick."

She ran down the road just as fast as she could. Halfway to town she met Sop-de-Bottom and Dockery coming towards her.

"Hello, Janie, how's Tea Cake?"

"Pretty bad off. Ah'm gointuh see 'bout medicine fuh 'im right now."

"Doctor told somebody he wuz sick so us come tuh see. Thought somethin' he never come tuh work."

"Y'all set wid 'im till Ah git back. He need de company right long in heah."

She fanned on down the road to town and found Dr. Simmons. Yes, he had had an answer. They didn't have any serum but they had wired Miami to send it. She needn't worry. It would be there early the next morning if not before. People didn't fool around in a case like that. No, it wouldn't do for her to hire no car to go after it. Just go home and wait. That was all. When she reached home the visitors rose to go.

When they were alone Tea Cake wanted to put his head in Janie's lap and tell her how he felt and let her mama him in her sweet way. But something Sop had told him made his tongue lie cold and heavy like a dead lizard between his jaws. Mrs. Turner's brother was back on the muck and now he had this mysterious sickness. People didn't just take sick like this for nothing.

"Janie, whut is dat Turner woman's brother doin' back on de muck?"

"Ah don't know, Tea Cake. Didn't even knowed he wuz back."

"Accordin' tuh mah notion, you did. Whut you slip off from me just now for?"

"Tea Cake, Ah don't lak you astin' me no sich question. Dat shows how sick you is sho nuff. You'se jealous 'thout me givin' you cause."

"Well, whut didja slip off from de house 'thout tellin' me you wuz goin'. You ain't never done dat befo'."

"Dat wuz cause Ah wuz tryin' not tuh let yuh worry 'bout yo' condition. De doctah sent after some mo' medicine and Ah went tuh see if it come."

Tea Cake began to cry and Janie hovered him in her arms like a child. She sat on the side of the bed and sort of rocked him back to peace.

"Tea Cake, 'tain't no use in you bein' jealous uh me. In de first place Ah couldn't love nobody but yuh. And in de second place, Ah jus' uh ole woman dat nobody don't want but you."

"Naw, you ain't neither. You only sound ole when you tell folks when you wuz born, but wid de eye you'se young enough tuh suit most any man. Dat ain't no lie. Ah knows plenty mo' men would take yuh and work hard fuh de privilege. Ah done heard 'em talk."

"Maybe so, Tea Cake, Ah ain't never tried tuh find out. Ah jus' know dat God snatched me out de fire through you. And Ah loves yuh and feel glad."

"Thank yuh, ma'am, but don't say you'se ole. You'se uh lil girl baby all de time. God made it so you spent yo' ole age first wid somebody else, and saved up yo' young girl days to spend wid me."

"Ah feel dat uh way too, Tea Cake, and Ah thank yuh fuh sayin' it."

"'Tain't no trouble tuh say whut's already so. You'se uh pretty woman outside uh bein' nice."

"Aw, Tea Cake."

"Yeah you is too. Everytime Ah see uh patch uh roses uh somethin' over sportin' they selves makin' out they pretty, Ah tell 'em 'Ah want yuh tuh see mah Janie sometime.' You must let de flowers see yuh sometimes, heah, Janie?"

"You keep dat up, Tea Cake, Ah'll b'lieve yuh after while," Janie said archly and fixed him back in bed. It was then she felt the pistol under the pillow. It gave her a quick ugly throb, but she didn't ask him about it since he didn't say. Never had Tea Cake slept with a pistol under his head before. "Neb' mind 'bout all dat cleanin' round de front yard," he told her as she straightened up from fixing the bed. "You stay where Ah kin see yuh."

"All right, Tea Cake, jus' as you say."

"And if Mis' Turner's lap-legged brother come prowlin' by heah you kin tell 'im Ah got him stopped wid four wheel brakes. 'Tain't no need of him standin' 'round watchin' de job."

"Ah won't be tellin' 'im nothin' 'cause Ah don't expect tuh see 'im."

Tea Cake had two bad attacks that night. Janie saw a changing look come in his face. Tea Cake was gone. Something else was looking out of his face. She made up her mind to be off after the doctor with the first glow of day. So she was up and dressed when Tea Cake awoke from the fitful sleep that had come to him just before day. He almost snarled when he saw her dressed to go.

"Where are you goin', Janie?"

"After de doctor, Tea Cake. You'se too sick tuh be heah in dis house 'thout de doctah. Maybe we oughta git yuh tuh de hospital."

"Ah ain't goin' tuh no hospital no where. Put dat in yo' pipe and smoke it. Guess you tired uh waitin' on me and doing fuh me. Dat ain't de way Ah been wid *you*. Ah never is been able tuh do enough fuh yuh."

"Tea Cake, you'se sick. You'se takin' everything in de way Ah don't mean it. Ah couldn't never be tired uh waitin' on you. Ah'm just skeered you'se too sick fuh me tuh handle. Ah wants yuh tuh git well, honey. Dat's all."

He gave her a look full of black ferocity and gurgled in his throat. She saw him sitting up in bed and moving about so that he could watch her every move. And she was beginning to feel fear of this strange thing in Tea Cake's body. So when he went out to the outhouse she rushed to see if the pistol was loaded. It was a six shooter and three of the chambers were full. She started to unload it but she feared he might break it and find out she knew. That might urge his disordered mind to action. If that medicine would only come! She whirled the cylinder so that if he even did draw the gun on her it would snap three times before it would fire. She would at least have warning. She could either run or try to take it away before it was too late. Anyway Tea Cake wouldn't hurt *her*. He was jealous and wanted to scare her. She'd just be in the kitchen as usual and never let on. They'd laugh over it when he got well. She found the box of cartridges, however, and emptied it. Just as well to take the rifle from back of the head of the bed. She broke it and put the shell in her apron pocket and put it in a corner in the kitchen almost behind the stove where it was hard to see. She could outrun his knife if it came to that. Of course she was too fussy, but it did no harm to play safe. She ought not to let poor sick Tea Cake do something that would run him crazy when he found out what he had done.

She saw him coming from the outhouse with a queer loping gait, swinging his head from side to side and his jaws clenched in a funny way. This was too awful! Where was Dr. Simmons with that medicine? She was glad she was here to look after him. Folks would do such mean things to her Tea Cake if they saw him in such a fix. Treat Tea Cake like he was some mad dog when nobody in the world had more kindness about them. All he needed was for the doctor to come on with that medicine. He came back into the house without speaking, in fact, he did not seem to notice she was there and fell heavily into the bed and slept. Janie was standing by the stove washing up the dishes when he spoke to her in a queer cold voice.

"Janie, how come you can't sleep in de same bed wid me no mo'?"

"De doctah told you tuh sleep by yo'self, Tea Cake. Don't yuh remember him tellin' you dat yistiddy?"

"How come you ruther sleep on uh pallet than tuh sleep in de bed wid me?" Janie saw then that he had the gun in his hand that was hanging to his side. "Answer me when Ah speak."

"Tea Cake, Tea Cake, honey! Go lay down! Ah'll be too glad tuh be in dere wid yuh de minute de doctor say so. Go lay back down. He'll be heah wid some new medicine right away."

"Janie, Ah done went through everything tuh be good tuh you and it hurt me tuh mah heart tuh be ill treated lak Ah is."

The gun came up unsteadily but quickly and leveled at Janie's breast. She noted that even in his delirium he took good aim. Maybe he would point to scare her, that was all.

The pistol snapped once. Instinctively Janie's hand flew behind her on the rifle and brought it around. Most likely this would scare him off. If only the doctor would come! If anybody at all would come! She broke the rifle deftly and shoved in the shell as the second click told her that Tea Cake's suffering brain was urging him on to kill.

"Tea Cake, put down dat gun and go back tuh bed!" Janie yelled at him as the gun wavered weakly in his hand.

He steadied himself against the jamb of the door and Janie thought to run into him and grab his arm, but she saw the quick motion of taking aim and heard the click. Saw the ferocious look in his eyes and went mad with fear as she had done in the water that time. She threw up the barrel of the rifle in frenzied hope and fear. Hope that he'd see it and run, desperate fear for her life. But if Tea Cake could have counted costs he would not have been there with the pistol in his hands. No knowledge of fear nor rifles nor anything else was there. He paid no more attention to the pointing gun than if it were Janie's dog finger. She saw him stiffen himself all over as he leveled and took aim. The fiend in him must kill and Janie was the only thing living he saw.

The pistol and the rifle rang out almost together. The pistol just enough after the rifle to seem its echo. Tea Cake crumpled as his bullet buried itself in the joist over Janie's head. Janie saw the look on his face and leaped forward as he crashed forward in her arms. She was trying to hover him as he closed his teeth in the flesh of her forearm. They came down heavily like that. Janie struggled to a sitting position and pried the dead Tea Cake's teeth from her arm.

It was the meanest moment of eternity. A minute before she was just a scared human being fighting for its life. Now she was her sacrificing self with Tea Cake's head in her lap. She had wanted him to live so much and he was dead. No hour is ever eternity, but it has its right to weep. Janie held his head tightly to her breast and wept and thanked him wordlessly for giving her the chance for loving service. She had to hug him tight for soon he would be gone, and she had to tell him for the last time. Then the grief of outer darkness descended.

So that same day of Janie's great sorrow she was in jail. And when the doctor told the sheriff and the judge how it was, they all said she must be tried that same day. No need to punish her in jail by waiting. Three hours in jail and then they set the court for her case. The time was short and everything, but sufficient people were there. Plenty of white people came to look on this strangeness. And all the Negroes for miles around. Who was it didn't know about the love between Tea Cake and Janie?

The court set and Janie saw the judge who had put on a great robe to listen about her and Tea Cake. And twelve more white men had stopped whatever they were doing to listen and pass on what happened between Janie and Tea Cake Woods, and as to whether things were done right or not. That was funny too. Twelve strange men who didn't know a thing about people like Tea Cake and her were going to sit on the thing. Eight or ten white women had come to look at her too. They wore good clothes and had the pinky color that comes of good food. They were nobody's poor white folks. What need had *they* to leave their richness to come look on Janie in her overalls? But they didn't seem too mad, Janie thought. It would be nice if she could make *them* know how it was instead of those menfolks. Oh, and she hoped that undertaker was fixing Tea Cake up fine. They ought to let her go see about it. Yes, and there was Mr. Prescott that she knew right well and he was going to tell the twelve men to kill her for shooting Tea Cake. And a strange man from Palm Beach who was going to ask them not to kill her, and none of them knew.

Then she saw all of the colored people standing up in the back of the courtroom. Packed tight like a case of celery, only much darker than that. They were all against her, she could see. So many were there against her that a light slap from each one of them would have beat her to death. She felt them pelting her with dirty thoughts. They were there with their tongues cocked and loaded, the only real weapon left to weak folks. The only killing tool they are allowed to use in the presence of white folks.

So it was all ready after a while and they wanted people to talk so that they could know what was right to do about Janie Woods, the relic of Tea Cake's Janie. The white part of the room got calmer the more serious it got, but a tongue storm struck the Negroes like wind among palm trees. They talked all of a sudden and all together like a choir and the top parts of their bodies moved on the rhythm of it. They sent word by the bailiff to Mr. Prescott they wanted to testify in the case. Tea Cake was a good boy. He had been good to that woman. No nigger woman ain't never been treated no better. Naw suh! He worked like a dog for her and nearly killed himself saving her in the storm, then soon as he got a little fever from the water, she had took up with another man. Sent for him to come there from way off. Hanging was too good. All they wanted was a chance to testify. The bailiff went up and the sheriff and the judge, and the police chief, and the lawyers all came together to listen for a few minutes, then they parted again and the sheriff took the stand and told how Janie had come to his house with the doctor and how he found things when he drove out to hers.

Then they called Dr. Simmons and he told about Tea Cake's sickness and how dangerous it was to Janie and the whole town, and how he was scared for her and thought to have Tea Cake locked up in the jail, but seeing Janie's care he neglected to do it. And how he found Janie all bit in the arm, sitting on the floor and petting Tea Cake's head when he got there. And the pistol right by his hand on the floor. Then he stepped down.

"Any further evidence to present, Mr. Prescott?" the judge asked.

"No, Your Honor. The State rests."

The palm tree dance began again among the Negroes in the back. They had come to talk. The State couldn't rest until it heard.

"Mistah Prescott, Ah got somethin' tuh say," Sop-de-Bottom spoke out anonymously from the anonymous herd.

The courtroom swung round on itself to look.

"If you know what's good for you, you better shut your mouth up until somebody calls you," Mr. Prescott told him coldly.

"Yassuh, Mr. Prescott."

"We are handling this case. Another word out of *you*, out of any of you niggers back there, and I'll bind you over to the big court."

"Yassuh."

The white women made a little applause and Mr. Prescott glared at the back of the house and stepped down. Then the strange white man that was going to talk for her got up there. He whispered a little with the clerk and then called on Janie to take the stand and talk. After a few little questions he told her to tell just how it happened and to speak the truth, the whole truth and nothing but the truth. So help her God.

They all leaned over to listen while she talked. First thing she had to remember was she was not at home. She was in the courthouse fighting something and it wasn't death. It was worse than that. It was lying thoughts. She had to go way back to let them know how she and Tea Cake had been with one another so they could see she could never shoot Tea Cake out of malice.

She tried to make them see how terrible it was that things were fixed so that Tea Cake couldn't come back to himself until he had got rid of that mad dog that was in him and he couldn't get rid of the dog and live. He had to die to get rid of the dog. But she hadn't wanted to kill him. A man is up against a hard game when he must die to beat it. She made them see how she couldn't ever want to be rid of him. She didn't plead to anybody. She just sat there and told and when she was through she hushed. She had been through for some time before the judge and the lawyer and the rest seemed to know it. But she sat on in that trial chair until the lawyer told her she could come down.

"The defense rests," her lawyer said. Then he and Prescott whispered together and both of them talked to the judge in secret up high there where he sat. Then they both sat down.

"Gentlemen of the jury, it is for you to decide whether the defendant has committed a cold blooded murder or whether she is a poor broken creature, a devoted wife trapped by unfortunate circumstances who really in firing a rifle bullet into the heart of her late husband did a great act of mercy. If you find her a wanton killer you must bring in a verdict of first degree murder. If the evidence does not justify that then you must set her free. There is no middle course."

The jury filed out and the courtroom began to drone with talk, a few people got up and moved about. And Janie sat like a lump and waited. It was not death she feared. It was misunderstanding. If they made a verdict that she didn't want Tea Cake and wanted him dead, then that was a real sin and a shame. It was worse than murder. Then the jury was back again. Out five minutes by the courthouse clock.

"We find the death of Vergible Woods to be entirely accidental and justifiable, and that no blame should rest upon the defendant Janie Woods."

So she was free and the judge and everybody up there smiled with her and shook her hand. And the white women cried and stood around her like a protecting wall and the Negroes, with heads hung down, shuffled out and away. The sun was almost down and Janie had seen the sun rise on her troubled love and then she had shot Tea Cake and had been in jail and had been tried for her life and now she was free. Nothing to do with the little that was left of the day but to visit the kind white friends who had realized her feelings and thank them. So the sun went down.

She took a room at the boarding house for the night and heard the men talking around the front.

"Aw you know dem white mens wuzn't gointuh do nothin' tuh no woman dat look lak her."

"She didn't kill no white man, did she? Well, long as she don't shoot no white man she kin kill jus' as many niggers as she please."

"Yeah, de nigger women kin kill up all de mens dey wants tuh, but you bet' not kill one uh dem. De white folks will sho hang yuh if yuh do."

"Well, you know whut dey say 'uh white man and uh nigger woman is de freest thing on earth.' Dey do as dey please."

Janie buried Tea Cake in Palm Beach. She knew he loved the 'Glades but it was too low for him to lie with water maybe washing over him with every heavy rain. Anyway, the 'Glades and its waters had killed him. She wanted him out of the way of storms, so she had a strong vault built in the cemetery at West Palm Beach. Janie had wired to Orlando for money to put him away. Tea Cake was the son of Evening Sun, and nothing was too good. The Undertaker did a handsome job and Tea Cake slept royally on his white silken couch among the roses she had bought. He looked almost ready to grin. Janie bought him a brand new guitar and put it in his hands. He would be thinking up new songs to play to her when she got there.

Sop and his friends had tried to hurt her but she knew it was because they loved Tea Cake and didn't understand. So she sent Sop word and to all the others through him. So the day of the funeral they came with shame and apology in their faces. They wanted her quick forgetfulness. So they filled up and overflowed the ten sedans that Janie had hired and added others to the line. Then the band played, and Tea Cake rode like a Pharaoh to his tomb. No expensive veils and robes for Janie this time. She went on in her overalls. She was too busy feeling grief to dress like grief.

Chapter 20

Because they really loved Janie just a little less than they had loved Tea Cake, and because they wanted to think well of themselves, they wanted their hostile attitude forgotten. So they blamed it all on Mrs. Turner's brother and ran him off the muck again. They'd show him about coming back there posing like he was good looking and putting himself where men's wives could look at him. Even if they didn't look it wasn't his fault, he had put himself in the way.

"Naw, Ah ain't mad wid Janie," Sop went around explaining. "Tea Cake had done gone crazy. You can't blame her for puhtectin' herself. She wuz crazy 'bout 'im. Look at de way she put him away. Ah ain't got anything in mah heart aginst her. And Ah never woulda thought uh thing, but de very first day dat lap-legged nigger come back heah makin' out he wuz lookin' fuh work, he come astin' me 'bout how wuz Mr. and Mrs. Woods makin' out. Dat goes tuh show yuh he wuz up tuh somethin'."

"So when Stew Beef and Bootyny and some of de rest of 'em got behind 'im he come runnin' tuh me tuh save 'im. Ah told 'im, don't come tuh *me* wid yo' hair blowin' back, 'cause, Ah'm gointuh send yuh, and Ah sho did. De bitch's baby!" That was enough, they eased their feelings by beating him and running him off. Anyway, their anger against Janie had lasted two whole days and that was too long to keep remembering anything. Too much of a strain.

They had begged Janie to stay on with them and she had stayed a few weeks to keep them from feeling bad. But the muck meant Tea Cake and Tea Cake wasn't there. So it was just a great expanse of black mud. She had given away everything in their little house except a package of garden seed that Tea Cake had bought to plant. The planting never got done because he had been waiting for the right time of the moon when his sickness overtook him. The seeds reminded Janie of Tea Cake more than anything else because he was always planting things. She had noticed them on the kitchen shelf when she came home from the funeral and had put them in her breast pocket. Now that she was home, she meant to plant them for remembrance.

Janie stirred her strong feet in the pan of water. The tiredness was gone so she dried them off on the towel.

"Now, dat's how everything wuz, Pheoby, jus' lak Ah told yuh. So Ah'm back home agin and Ah'm satisfied tuh be heah. Ah done been tuh de horizon and back and now Ah kin set heah in mah house and live by comparisons. Dis house ain't so absent of things lak it used tuh be befo' Tea Cake come along. It's full uh thoughts, 'specially dat bedroom.

"Ah know all dem sitters-and-talkers gointuh worry they guts into fiddle strings till dey find out whut we been talkin' 'bout. Dat's all right, Pheoby, tell 'em. Dey gointuh make 'miration 'cause mah love didn't work lak they love, if dey ever had any. Then you must tell 'em dat love ain't somethin' lak uh grind-stone dat's de same thing everywhere and do de same thing tuh everything it touch. Love is lak de sea. It's uh movin' thing, but still and all, it takes its shape from de shore it meets, and it's different with every shore."

"Lawd!" Pheoby breathed out heavily, "Ah done growed ten feet higher from jus' listenin' tuh you, Janie. Ah ain't satisfied wid mahself no mo'. Ah means tuh make Sam take me fishin' wid him after this. Nobody better not criticize yuh in mah hearin'."

"Now, Pheoby, don't feel too mean wid de rest of 'em 'cause dey's parched up from not knowin' things. Dem meatskins is *got* tuh rattle tuh make out they's alive. Let 'em consolate theyselves wid talk. 'Course, talkin' don't mount tuh uh hill uh beans when yuh can't do nothin' else. And listenin' tuh dat kind uh talk is jus' lak openin' yo' mouth and lettin' de moon shine down yo' throat. It's uh known fact, Pheoby, you got tuh *go* there tuh *know* there. Yo' papa and yo' mama and nobody else can't tell yuh and show yuh. Two things everybody's got tuh do fuh theyselves. They got tuh go tuh God, and they got tuh find out about livin' fuh theyselves."

There was a finished silence after that so that for the first time they could hear the wind picking at the pine trees. It made Pheoby think of Sam waiting for her and getting fretful. It made Janie think about that room upstairs—her bedroom. Pheoby hugged Janie real hard and cut the darkness in flight.

Soon everything around downstairs was shut and fastened. Janie mounted the stairs with her lamp. The light in her hand was like a spark of sun-stuff washing her face in fire. Her shadow behind fell black and headlong down the stairs. Now, in her room, the place tasted fresh again. The wind through the open windows had broomed out all the fetid feeling of absence and nothingness. She closed in and sat down. Combing road-dust out of her hair. Thinking.

The day of the gun, and the bloody body, and the courthouse came and commenced to sing a sobbing sigh out of every corner in the room; out of each and every chair and thing. Commenced to sing, commenced to sob and sigh, singing and sobbing. Then Tea Cake came prancing around her where she was and the song of the sigh flew out of the window and lit in the top of the pine trees. Tea Cake, with the sun for a shawl. Of course he wasn't dead. He could never be dead until she herself had finished feeling and thinking. The kiss of his memory made pictures of love and light against the wall. Here was peace. She pulled in her horizon like a great fish-net. Pulled it from around the waist of the world and draped it over her shoulder. So much of life in its meshes! She called in her soul to come and see.

How It Feels to Be Colored Me (1928)

I am colored but I offer nothing in the way of extenuating circumstances except the fact that I am the only Negro in the United States whose grandfather on the mother's side was *not* an Indian chief.

I remember the very day that I became colored. Up to my thirteenth year I lived in the little Negro town of Eatonville, Florida. It is exclusively a colored town. The only white people I knew passed through the town going to or coming from Orlando. The native whites rode dusty horses, the Northern tourists chugged down the sandy village road in automobiles. The town knew the Southerners and never stopped cane chewing when they passed. But the Northerners were something else again. They were peered at cautiously behind curtains by the timid. The more venturesome would come out on the porch to watch them go past and got just as much pleasure out of the tourists as the tourists got out of the village.

The front porch might seem a daring place for the rest of the town, but it was a gallery seat to me. My favorite place was atop the gate-post. Proscenium box for a born first-nighter. Not only did I enjoy the show, but I didn't mind the actors knowing that I liked it. I actually spoke to them in passing. I'd wave at them and when they returned my salute, I would say something like this: "Howdy-do-well-I-thank-you-where-you-goin'?" Usually automobile or the horse paused at this, and after a queer exchange of compliments, I would probably "go a piece of the way" with them, as we say in farthest Florida. If one of my family happened to come to the front in time to see me, of course negotiations would be rudely broken off. But even so, it is clear that I was the first "welcome-to-our-state" Floridian, and I hope the Miami Chamber of Commerce will please take notice.

During this period, white people differed from colored to me only in that they rode through town and never lived there. They liked to hear me "speak pieces" and sing and wanted to see me dance the parse-me-la, and gave me generously of their small silver for doing these things, which seemed strange to me for I wanted to do them so much that I needed bribing to stop. Only they didn't know it. The colored people gave no dimes. They deplored any joyful tendencies in me, but I was their Zora nevertheless. I belonged to them, to the nearby hotels, to the county—everybody's Zora.

But changes came in the family when I was thirteen, and I was sent to school in Jacksonville. I left Eatonville, the town of the oleanders, as Zora. When I disembarked from the riverboat at Jacksonville, she was no more. It seemed that I had suffered a sea change. I was not Zora of Orange County any more, I was now a little colored girl. I found it out in certain ways. In my heart as well as in the mirror, I became a fast brown—warranted not to rub nor run.

But I am not tragically colored. There is no great sorrow dammed up in my soul, nor lurking behind my eyes. I do not mind at all. I do not belong to the sobbing school of Negrohood who hold that nature somehow has given them a low-down dirty deal and whose feelings are all hurt about it. Even in the helter-skelter skirmish that is my life, I have seen that the world is to the strong regardless of a little pigmentation more or less. No, I do not weep at the world—I am too busy sharpening my oyster knife.

Someone is always at my elbow reminding me that I am the grand-daughter of slaves. It fails to register depression with me. Slavery is sixty years in the past. The operation was successful and the patient is doing well, thank you. The terrible struggle that made me an American out of a potential slave said "On the line!" The Reconstruction said "Get set!"; and the generation before said "Go!" I am off to a flying start and I must not halt in the stretch to look behind and weep. Slavery is the price I paid for civilization, and the choice was not with me. It is a bully adventure and worth all that I have paid through my ancestors for it. No one on earth ever had a greater chance for glory. The world to be won and nothing to be lost. It is thrilling to think—to know that for any act of mine, I shall get twice as much praise or twice as much blame. It is quite exciting to hold the center of the national stage, with spectators not knowing whether to laugh or to weep.

The position of my white neighbor is much more difficult. No brown specter pulls up a chair beside me when I sit down to eat. No dark ghost thrusts its leg against mine in bed. The game of keeping what one has is never so exciting as the game of getting.

I do not always feel colored. Even now I often achieve the unconscious Zora of Eatonville before the Hegira. I feel most colored when I am thrown against a sharp white background.

For instance at Barnard. "Beside the waters of the Hudson" I feel my race. Among the thousand white persons, I am a dark rock surged upon, overswept by a creamy sea. I am surged upon and overswept, but through it all, I remain myself. When covered by the waters, I am; and the ebb but reveals me again.

Sometimes it is the other way around. A white person is set down in our midst, but the contrast is just as sharp for me. For instance, when I sit in the drafty basement that is The New World Cabaret with a white person, my color comes. We enter chatting about any little nothing that we have in common and are seated by the jazz waiters. In the abrupt way that jazz orchestras have, this one plunges into a number. It loses no time in circumlocutions, but gets right down to business. It constricts the thorax and splits the heart with its tempo and narcotic harmonies. This orchestra grows rambunctious, rears on its hind legs and attacks the tonal veil with primitive fury, rending it, clawing it until it breaks through to the jungle beyond. I follow those heathen—follow them exultingly. I dance wildly inside myself; I yell within, I whoop; I shake my assegai above my head, I hurl it true to the mark *yeeeeooww!* I am in the jungle and living in the jungle way. My face is painted red and yellow, and my body is painted blue. My pulse is throbbing like a war drum. I want to slaughter something—give pain, give death to what, I do not know. But the piece ends. The men of the orchestra wipe their lips and rest their fingers. I creep back slowly to the veneer we call civilization with the last tone and find the white friend sitting motionless in his seat, smoking calmly.

"Good music they have here," he remarks, drumming the table with his fingertips.

Music! The great blobs of purple and red emotion have not touched him. He has only heard what I felt. He is far away and I see him but dimly across the ocean and the continent that have fallen between us. He is so pale with his whiteness then and I am *so* colored.

At certain times I have no race, I am *me*. When I set my hat at a certain angle and saunter down Seventh Avenue, Harlem City, feeling as snooty as the lions in front of the Forty-Second Street Library, for instance. So far as my feelings are concerned, Peggy Hopkins Joyce on the Boule Mich with her gorgeous raiment, stately carriage, knees knocking together in a most aristocratic manner, has nothing on me. The cosmic Zora emerges. I belong to no race nor time, I am the eternal feminine with its string of beads.

I have no separate feeling about being an American citizen and colored. I am merely a fragment of the Great Soul that surges within the boundaries. My country, right or wrong.

Sometimes, I feel discriminated against, but it does not make me angry. It merely astonishes me. How *can* any deny themselves the pleasure of my company! It's beyond me.

But in the main, I feel like a brown bag of miscellany propped against a wall. Against a wall in company with other bags, white, red and yellow. Pour out the contents, and there is discovered a jumble of small things priceless and worthless. A first-water diamond, an empty spool, bits of broken glass, lengths of string, a key to a door long since crumbled away, a rusty knife-blade, old shoes saved for a road that never was and never will be, a nail bent under the weight of things too heavy for any nail, a dried flower or two, still a little fragrant. In your hand is the brown bag. On the ground before you is the jumble it held—so much like the jumble in the bags, could they be emptied, that all might be dumped in a single heap and the bags refilled without altering the content of any greatly. A bit of colored glass more or less would not matter. Perhaps that is how the Great Stuffer of Bags filled them in the first place—who knows?

◈ JEAN TOOMER (1894–1967)

Originally from Washington, D.C., Jean Toomer was the grandson of P. B. S. Pinchback, a powerful Southern politician. After attending several colleges, Toomer decided to pursue a writing career in New York City. By 1920, he had moved from New York to Georgia as a teacher. His immersion into the rural, agrarian South and the culture of Southern blacks helped fuel his masterpiece, Cane *(1923), a collection of poems and stories that analyzed the lives of African Americans desirous of living in a world without racism. A year later, Toomer studied the philosophical ideas of mystic George Gurdjieff. Toomer married twice in his life. He first wed Margery Latimer, but she died during childbirth. Later he wed Marjorie Content, and the two relocated to Pennsylvania. Toomer adopted the teachings of the Quakers around 1940. He died in 1967 of arteriosclerosis.*

From Cane (1923)

Bona and Paul

1

On the school gymnasium floor, young men and women are drilling. They are going to be teachers, and go out into the world . . . thud, thud . . . and give precision to the movements of sick people who all their lives have been drilling. One man is out of step. In step. The teacher glares at him. A girl in bloomers, seated on a mat in the corner because she has told the director that she is sick, sees that the footfalls of the men are rhythmical and syncopated. The dance of his blue-trousered limbs thrills her.

Bona: He is a candle that dances in a grove swung with pale balloons.

Columns of the drillers thud towards her. He is in the front row. He is in no row at all. Bona can look close at him. His red-brown face—

Bona: He is a harvest moon. He is an autumn leaf. He is a nigger. Bona! But dont all the dorm girls say so? And dont you, when you are sane, say so? Thats why I love—Oh, nonsense. You have never loved a man who didnt first love you. Besides—

Columns thud away from her. Come to a halt in line formation. Rigid. The period bell rings, and the teacher dismisses them.

A group collects around Paul. They are choosing sides for basket-ball. Girls against boys. Paul has his. He is limbering up beneath the basket. Bona runs to the girl captain and asks to be chosen. The girls fuss. The director comes to quiet them. He hears what Bona wants.

"But, Miss Hale, you were excused—"

"So I was, Mr. Boynton, but—"

"—you can play basket-ball, but you are too sick to drill."

"If you wish to put it that way."

She swings away from him to the girl captain.

"Helen, I want to play, and you must let me. This is the first time I've asked and I dont see why—"

"Thats just it, Bona. We have our team."

"Well, team or no team, I want to play and thats all there is to it."

She snatches the ball from Helen's hands, and charges down the floor.

Helen shrugs. One of the weaker girls says that she'll drop out. Helen accepts this: The team is formed. The whistle blows. The game starts. Bona, in center, is jumping against Paul. He plays with her. Out-jumps her, makes a quick pass, gets a quick return, and shoots a goal from the middle of the floor. Bona burns crimson. She fights, and tries to guard him. One of her team-mates advises her not to play so hard. Paul shoots his second goal.

Bona begins to feel a little dizzy and all in. She drives on. Almost hugs Paul to guard him. Near the basket, he attempts to shoot, and Bona lunges into his body and tries to beat his arms. His elbow, going up, gives her a sharp crack on the jaw. She whirls. He catches her. Her body stiffens. Then becomes strangely vibrant, and bursts to a swift life within her anger. He is about to give way before her hatred when a new passion flares at him and makes his stomach fall. Bona squeezes him. He suddenly feels stifled, and wonders why in hell the ring of silly gaping faces that's caked about him doesnt make way and give him air. He has a swift illusion that it is himself who has been struck. He looks at Bona. Whir. Whir. They seem to be human distortions spinning tensely in a fog. Spinning . . . dizzy . . . spinning. . . . Bona jerks herself free, flushes a startling crimson, breaks through the bewildered teams, and rushes from the hall.

2

Paul is in his room of two windows.

Outside, the South-Side L track cuts them in two.

Bona is one window. One window, Paul.

Hurtling Loop-jammed L trains throw them in swift shadow.

Paul goes to his. Gray slanting roofs of houses are tinted lavender in the setting sun. Paul follows the sun, over the stock-yards where a fresh stench is just arising, across wheat lands that are still waving above their stubble, into the sun. Paul follows the sun to a pine-matted hillock in Georgia. He sees the slanting roofs of gray unpainted cabins tinted lavender. A Negress chants a lullaby beneath the mate-eyes of a southern planter. Her breasts are ample for the suckling of a song. She weans it, and sends it, curiously weaving, among lush melodies of cane and corn. Paul follows the sun into himself in Chicago.

He is at Bona's window.

With his own glow he looks through a dark pane.

Paul's room-mate comes in.

"Say, Paul, I've got a date for you. Come on. Shake a leg, will you?"

His blonde hair is combed slick. His vest is snug about him.

He is like the electric light which he snaps on.

"Whatdoysay, Paul? Get a wiggle on. Come on. We havent got much time by the time we eat and dress and everything."

His bustling concentrates on the brushing of his hair.

Art: What in hell's getting into Paul of late, anyway? Christ, but he's getting moony. Its his blood. Dark blood: moony. Doesnt get anywhere unless you boost it. You've got to keep it going—

"Say, Paul!"

—or it'll go to sleep on you. Dark blood; nigger? Thats what those jealous she-hens say. Not Bona though, or she . . . from the South . . . wouldnt want me to fix a date for him and her. Hell of a thing, that Paul's dark: you've got to always be answering questions.

"Say, Paul, for Christ's sake leave that window, cant you?"

"Whats it, Art?"

"Hell, I've told you about fifty times. Got a date for you. Come on."

"With who?"

Art: He didnt use to ask; now he does. Getting up in the air. Getting funny.

"Heres your hat. Want a smoke? Paul! Here. I've got a match. Now come on and I'll tell you all about it on the way to supper."

Paul: He's going to Life this time. No doubt of that. Quit your kidding. Some day, dear Art, I'm going to kick the living slats out of you, and you wont know what I've done it for. And your slats will bring forth Life . . . beautiful woman. . . .

Pure Food Restaurant

"Bring me some soup with a lot of crackers, understand? And then a roast-beef dinner. Same for you, eh, Paul? Now as I was saying, you've got a swell chance with her. And she's game. Best proof: she dont give a damn what the dorm girls say about you and her in the gym, or about the funny looks that Boynton gives her, or about what they say about, well, hell, you know, Paul. And say, Paul, she's a sweetheart. Tall, not puffy and pretty, more serious and deep—the kind you like these days. And they say she's got a car. And say, she's on fire. But you know all about that. She got Helen to fix it up with me. The four of us—remember the last party? Crimson Gardens! Boy!"

Paul's eyes take on a light that Art can settle in.

3

Art has on his patent-leather pumps and fancy vest. A loose fall coat is swung across his arm. His face has been massaged, and over a close shave, powdered. It is a healthy pink the blue of evening tints a purple pallor. Art is happy and confident in the good looks that his mirror gave him. Bubbling over with a joy he must spend now if the night is to contain it all. His bubbles, too, are curiously tinted purple as Paul watches them. Paul, contrary to what he had thought he would be like, is cool like the dusk, and like the dusk, detached. His dark face is a floating shade in evening's shadow. He sees Art, curiously. Art is a purple fluid, carbon-charged, that effervesces besides him. He loves Art. But is it not queer, this pale purple facsimile of a red-blooded Norwegian friend of his? Perhaps for some reason, white skins are not supposed to live at night. Surely, enough nights would transform them fantastically, or kill them. And their red passion? Night paled that too, and made it moony. Moony. Thats what Art thought of him. Bona didnt, even in the daytime. Bona, would she be pale? Impossible. Not that red glow. But the conviction did not set his emotion flowing.

"Come right in, wont you? The young ladies will be right down. Oh, Mr. Carlstrom, do play something for us while you are waiting. We just love to listen to your music. You play so well."

Houses, and dorm sitting-rooms are places where white faces seclude themselves at night. There is a reason. . . .

Art sat on the piano and simply tore it down. Jazz. The picture of Our Poets hung perilously.

Paul: I've got to get the kid to play that stuff for me in the daytime. Might be different. More himself. More nigger. Different? There is. Curious, though.

The girls come in. Art stops playing, and almost immediately takes up a petty quarrel, where he had last left it, with Helen.

Bona, black-hair curled staccato, sharply contrasting with Helen's puffy yellow, holds Paul's hand. She squeezes it. Her own emotion supplements the return pressure. And then, for no tangible reason, her spirits drop. Without them, she is nervous, and slightly afraid. She resents this. Paul's eyes are critical. She resents Paul. She flares at him. She flares to poise and security.

"Shall we be on our way?"

"Yes, Bona, certainly."

The Boulevard is sleek in asphalt, and, with arc-lights and limousines, aglow. Dry leaves scamper behind the whir of cars. The scent of exploded gasoline that mingles with them is faintly sweet. Mellow stone mansions overshadow clapboard homes which now resemble Negro shanties in some southern alley. Bona and Paul, and Art and Helen, move along an island-like, far-stretching strip of leaf-soft ground. Above them, worlds of shadow-planes and solids, silently moving. As if on one of these, Paul looks down on Bona. No doubt of it: her face is pale. She is talking. Her words have no feel to them. One sees them. They are pink petals that fall upon velvet cloth. Bona is soft, and pale, and beautiful.

"Paul, tell me something about yourself—or would you rather wait?"

"I'll tell you anything you'd like to know."

"Not what I want to know, Paul; what you want to tell me."

"You have the beauty of a gem fathoms under sea."

"I feel that, but I dont want to be. I want to be near you. Perhaps I will be if I tell you something. Paul, I love you."

The sea casts up its jewel into his hands, and burns them furiously. To tuck her arm under his and hold her hand will ease the burn.

"What can I say to you, brave dear woman—I cant talk love. Love is a dry grain in my mouth unless it is wet with kisses."

"You would dare? right here on the Boulevard? before Arthur and Helen?"

"Before myself? I dare."

"Here then."

Bona, in the slim shadow of a tree trunk, pulls Paul to her. Suddenly she stiffens. Stops.

"But you have not said you love me."

"I cant—yet—Bona."

"Ach, you never will. Youre cold. Cold."

Bona: Colored; cold. Wrong somewhere.

She hurries and catches up with Art and Helen.

4

Crimson Gardens. Hurrah! So one feels. People . . . University of Chicago students, members of the stock exchange, a large Negro in crimson uniform who guards the door . . . had watched them enter. Had leaned towards each other over ash-smeared tablecloths and highballs and whispered: What is he, a Spaniard, an Indian, an Italian, a Mexican, a Hindu, or a Japanese? Art had at first fidgeted under their stares . . . what are *you* looking at, you godam pack of owl-eyed hyenas? . . . but soon settled into his fuss with Helen, and forgot them. A strange thing happened to Paul. Suddenly he knew that he was apart from the people around him. Apart from the pain which they had unconsciously caused. Suddenly he knew that people saw, not attractiveness in his dark skin, but difference. Their stares, giving him to himself, filled something long empty within him, and were like green blades sprouting in his consciousness. There was fullness, and strength and peace about it all. He saw himself, cloudy, but real. He saw the faces of the people at the tables round him. White lights, or as now, the pink lights of the Crimson Gardens gave a glow and immediacy to white faces. The pleasure of it, equal to that of love or dream, of seeing this. Art and Bona and Helen? He'd look. They were wonderfully flushed and beautiful. Not for himself; because they were. Distantly. Who were they, anyway? God, if he knew them. He'd come in with them. Of that he was sure. Come where? Into life? Yes. No.

Into the Crimson Gardens. A part of life. A carbon bubble. Would it look purple if he went out into the night and looked at it? His sudden starting to rise almost upset the table.

"What in hell—pardon—whats the matter, Paul?"

"I forgot my cigarettes—"

"Youre smoking one."

"So I am. Pardon me."

The waiter straightens them out. Takes their order.

Art: What in hell's eating Paul? Moony aint the word for it. From bad to worse. And those godam people staring so. Paul's a queer fish. Doesnt seem to mind. . . . He's my pal, let me tell you, you horn-rimmed owl-eyed hyena at that table, and a lot better than you whoever you are. . . . Queer about him. I could stick up for him if he'd only come out, one way or the other, and tell a feller. Besides, a room-mate has a right to know. Thinks I wont understand. Said so. He's got a swell head when it comes to brains, all right. God, he's a good straight feller, though. Only, moony. Nut. Nuttish. Nuttery. Nutmeg. . . . "What'd you say, Helen?"

"I was talking to Bona, thank you."

"Well, its nothing to get spiffy about."

"What? Oh, of course not. Please lets dont start some silly argument all over again."

"Well."

"Well."

"Now thats enough. Say, waiter, whats the matter with our order? Make it snappy, will you?"

Crimson Gardens. Hurrah! So one feels. The drinks come. Four highballs. Art passes cigarettes. A girl dressed like a bare-back rider in flaming pink, makes her way through tables to the dance floor. All lights are dimmed till they seem a lush afterglow of crimson. Spotlights the girl. She sings. "Liza, Little Liza Jane."

Paul is rosy before his window.

He moves, slightly, towards Bona.

With his own glow, he seeks to penetrate a dark pane.

Paul: From the South. What does that mean, precisely, except that you'll love or hate a nigger? Thats a lot. What does it mean except that in Chicago you'll have the courage to neither love or hate. A priori. But it would seem that you have. Queer words, arent these, for a man who wears blue pants on a gym floor in the daytime. Well, never matter. You matter. I'd like to know you whom I look at. Know, not love. Not that knowing is a greater pleasure; but that I have just found the joy of it. You came just a month too late. Even this afternoon I dreamed. To-night, along the Boulevard, you found me cold. Paul Johnson, cold! Thats a good one, eh, Art, you fine old stupid fellow, you! But I feel good! The color and the music and the song. . . . A Negress chants a lullaby beneath the mate-eyes of a southern planter. O song! . . . And those flushed faces. Eager brilliant eyes. Hard to imagine them as unawakened. Your own. Oh, they're awake all right. "And you know it too, dont you Bona?"

"What, Paul?"

"The truth of what I was thinking."

"I'd like to know I know—something of you."

"You will—before the evening's over. I promise it."

Crimson Gardens. Hurrah! So one feels. The bare-back rider balances agilely on the applause which is the tail of her song. Orchestral instruments warm up for jazz. The flute is a cat that ripples its fur against the deep-purring saxophone. The drum throws sticks. The cat jumps on the piano keyboard. Hi diddle, hi diddle, the cat and the fiddle. Crimson Gardens . . . hurrah! . . . jumps over the moon. Crimson Gardens! Helen . . . O Eliza . . . rabbit-eyes sparkling, plays up to, and tries to placate what she considers to be Paul's contempt. She always does that . . . Little Liza Jane. . . . Once home, she burns with the thought of what she's done. She says all manner of snidy things about him, and swears that she'll never go out again when he is along. She tries to get Art to break with him, saying, that if Paul, whom the whole dormitory calls a nigger, is more to him than she is, well, she's through. She does not break with Art. She goes out as often as she can with Art and Paul. She explains this to herself by a piece of information which a friend of hers had given her: men like him (Paul) can fascinate. One is not responsible for fascination. Not one girl had really loved Paul; he fascinated them. Bona didnt; only thought she did. Time would tell. And of course, *she* didnt. Liza. . . . She plays up to, and tries to placate, Paul.

"Paul is so deep these days, and I'm so glad he's found some one to interest him."

"I dont believe I do."

The thought escapes from Bona just a moment before her anger at having said it.

Bona: You little puffy cat, I do. I do!

Dont I, Paul? her eyes ask.

Her answer is a crash of jazz from the palm-hidden orchestra. Crimson Gardens is a body whose blood flows to a clot upon the dance floor. Art and Helen clot. Soon, Bona and Paul. Paul finds her a little stiff, and his mind, wandering to Helen (silly little kid who wants every highball spoon her hands touch, for a souvenir), supple, perfect little dancer, wishes for the next dance when he and Art will exchange.

Bona knows that she must win him to herself.

"Since when have men like you grown cold?"

"The first philosopher."

"I thought you were a poet—or a gym director."

"Hence, your failure to make love."

Bona's eyes flare. Water. Grow red about the rims. She would like to tear away from him and dash across the clotted floor.

"What do you mean?"

"Mental concepts rule you. If they were flush with mine—good. I dont believe they are."

"How do you know, Mr. Philosopher?"

"Mostly a priori."

"You talk well for a gym director."

"And you—"

"I hate you. Ou!"

She presses away. Paul, conscious of the convention in it, pulls her to him. Her body close. Her head still strains away. He nearly crushes her. She tries to pinch him. Then sees people staring, and lets her arms fall. Their eyes meet. Both, contemptuous. The dance takes blood from their minds and packs it, tingling, in the torsos of their swaying bodies. Passionate blood leaps back into their eyes. They are a dizzy blood clot on a gyrating floor. They know that the pink-faced people have no part in what they feel. Their instinct leads them away from Art and Helen, and towards the big uniformed black man who opens and closes the gilded exit door. The cloak-room girl is tolerant of their impatience over such trivial things as wraps. And slightly superior. As the black man swings the door for them, his eyes are knowing. Too many couples have passed out, flushed and fidgety, for him not to know. The chill air is a shock to Paul. A strange thing happens. He sees the Gardens purple, as if he were way off. And a spot is in the purple. The spot comes furiously towards him. Face of the black man. It leers. It smiles sweetly like a child's. Paul leaves Bona and darts back so quickly that he doesnt give the door-man a chance to open. He swings in. Stops. Before the huge bulk of the Negro.

"Youre wrong."

"Yassur."

"Brother, youre wrong.

"I came back to tell you, to shake your hand, and tell you that you are wrong. That something beautiful is going to happen. That the Gardens are purple like a bed of roses would be at dusk. That I came into the Gardens, into life in the Gardens with one whom I did not know. That I danced with her, and did not know her. That I felt passion, contempt and passion for her whom I did not know. That I thought of her. That my thoughts were matches thrown into a dark window. And all the while the Gardens were purple like a bed of roses would be at dusk. I came back to tell you, brother, that white faces are petals of roses. That dark faces are petals of dusk. That I am going out and gather petals. That I am going out and know her whom I brought here with me to these Gardens which are purple like a bed of roses would be at dusk."

Paul and the black man shook hands.

When he reached the spot where they had been standing, Bona was gone.

✿ ALICE RUTH MOORE DUNBAR-NELSON
(1875–1935)

Although her first husband, Paul Laurence Dunbar, is more widely known to readers, Alice Ruth Moore Dunbar-Nelson has received new attention from feminist scholars and specialists in African American literature. Dunbar-Nelson, a native of New Orleans, published her first volume, Violet and Other Tales, *in 1895. The collection incorporates a multiplicity of genres, including poems, stories, and essays.* The Goodness of St. Rocque and Other Stories *appeared to critical acclaim in 1899. Dunbar's stories focus on the lives of people living in Louisiana who have Cajun and Creole backgrounds, including their rituals, beliefs, and distinctive lifestyles and languages. She was a skilled short-story writer, and her talent with verse is reflected in poems such as "I Sit and Sew." Her poetry reveals a feminist strain in her analysis of gender roles and marriage in America in the late nineteenth and early twentieth centuries. Much of her early poetry appeared in publications such as* A. M. E. Review *and* The Crisis.

Dunbar-Nelson, a highly educated woman, earned a degree from Dillard University in 1892. She also attended Cornell University and the University of Pennsylvania. By 1898, she had married poet Paul Laurence Dunbar after a courtship largely via correspondence. The two artists, however, were unhappily married, and they separated around 1902, four years before Dunbar's death. In 1916, she married Robert Nelson, and the two edited a newspaper called The Wilmington Advocate *between 1920 and 1922. Dunbar-Nelson also worked as a schoolteacher, at schools such as Delaware's Industrial School for Colored Girls, and she was a member of the NAACP and the National Federation of Colored Women's Clubs. She died in 1935 after a distinguished life as a writer, editor, and activist, calling for the eradication of racial, gender, and class prejudices.*

I Sit and Sew (1920)

I sit and sew—a useless task it seems,
My hands grown tired, my head weighed down with dreams—
The panoply of war, the martial tred of men,
Grim-faced, stern-eyed, gazing beyond the ken
Of lesser souls, whose eyes have not seen Death,   5
Nor learned to hold their lives but as a breath—
But—I must sit and sew.

I sit and sew—my heart aches with desire
That pageant terrible, that fiercely pouring fire
On wasted fields, and writhing grotesque things   10
Once men. My soul in pity flings
Appealing cries, yearning only to go
There in that holocaust of hell, those fields of woe—
But—I must sit and sew.

The little useless seam, the idle patch;   15
Why dream I here beneath my homely thatch,
When there they lie in sodden mud and rain,
Pitifully calling me, the quick ones and the slain?
You need me, Christ! It is no roseate dream
That beckons me—this pretty futile seam,   20
It stifles me—God, must I sit and sew?

Violets (1917)

I had not thought of violets of late,
The wild, shy kind that springs beneath your feet
In wistful April days, when lovers mate
And wander through the fields in raptures sweet.
And thought of violets meant florists' shops,⁣   5
And bows and pins, and perfumed paper fine;
And garish lights, and mincing little fops
And cabarets and songs, and deadening wine.
So far from sweet real things my thoughts had strayed,
I had forgot wide fields, and clear brown streams;   10
The perfect loveliness that God has made—
Wild violets shy and heaven-mounting dreams.
And now—unwittingly, you've made me dream
Of violets, and my soul's forgotten gleam.

NELLA LARSEN (1891–1964)

Because of her provocative and insightful portrayals of African American women during the early twentieth century, Nella Larsen has emerged as one of the most important figures of the Harlem Renaissance era. Born to a white Danish mother and a black father in Chicago, Larsen moved to Tennessee to pursue studies at Fisk University from 1907 to 1908. She later studied at the University of Copenhagen. Her experiences in Copenhagen may have served as a backdrop for her novel Quicksand *(1928), which partly takes place in Denmark and chronicles the life of a racially mixed young black woman in quest of identity. After her stint in Europe, Larsen came back to America and studied nursing at the Lincoln School for Nurses in New York City, graduating in 1915. She worked at Tuskegee University's nursing school in 1916 but departed a year later. She held a supervisory position at Lincoln Hospital in New York and later worked at the Board of Health. She also studied library science and worked as a librarian in New York City in the early 1920s.*

Her novels Quicksand *(1928) and* Passing *(1929) focus on African American women attempting to negotiate race, class, and gender prejudice in America. Larsen married Elmer Imes, a black college professor, but the marriage was fraught with problems; by 1933 the two had divorced. She never again received the acclaim she had earned during the heyday of the Harlem Renaissance. Personal problems and a charge of plagiarism for her story "Sanctuary" (1930) may have contributed to her lack of literary output. In 1964, she died of heart failure in New York City, where she had been working as a nurse.*

From Quicksand (1928)

1

Helga Crane sat alone in her room, which at that hour, eight in the evening, was in soft gloom. Only a single reading lamp, dimmed by a great black and red shade, made a pool of light on the blue Chinese carpet, on the bright covers of the books which she had taken down from their long shelves, on the white pages of the opened one selected, on the shining brass bowl crowded with many-colored nasturtiums beside her on the low table, and on the oriental silk which covered the stool at her slim feet. It was a comfortable room, furnished with rare and intensely personal taste, flooded with Southern sun in the day, but shadowy just then with the drawn curtains and single shaded light. Large, too. So large that the spot where Helga sat was a small oasis in a desert of darkness. And eerily quiet. But that was what she liked after her taxing day's work, after the hard classes, in which she gave willingly and unsparingly of herself with no apparent return. She loved this tranquillity, this quiet, following the fret and strain of the long hours spent among fellow members of a carelessly unkind and gossiping faculty, following the strenuous rigidity of conduct required in this huge educational community of which she was an insignificant part. This was her rest, this intentional isolation for a short while in the evening, this little time in her own attractive room with her own books. To the rapping of other teachers, bearing fresh scandals, or seeking information, or other more concrete favors, or merely talk, at that hour Helga Crane never opened her door.

An observer would have thought her well fitted to that framing of light and shade. A slight girl of twenty-two years, with narrow, sloping shoulders and delicate, but well-turned, arms and legs, she had, none the less, an air of radiant, careless health. In vivid green and gold negligee and glistening brocaded mules, deep sunk in the big high-backed chair, against whose dark tapestry her sharply cut face, with skin like yellow satin, was distinctly outlined, she was—to use a hackneyed word—attractive. Black, very broad brows over soft, yet penetrating, dark eyes, and a pretty mouth, whose sensitive and sensuous lips had a slight questioning petulance and a tiny dissatisfied droop, were the features on which the observer's attention would fasten; though her nose was good, her ears delicately chiseled, and her curly blue-black hair plentiful and always straying in a little wayward, delightful way. Just then it was tumbled, falling unrestrained about her face and on to her shoulders.

Helga Crane tried not to think of her work and the school as she sat there. Ever since her arrival in Naxos[1] she had striven to keep these ends of the days from the intrusion of irritating thoughts and worries. Usually she was successful. But not this evening. Of the books which she had taken from their places she had decided on Marmaduke Pickthall's *Säid the Fisherman*. She wanted forgetfulness, complete mental relaxation, rest from thought of any kind. For the day had been more than usually crowded with distasteful encounters and stupid perversities. The sultry hot Southern spring had left her strangely tired, and a little unnerved.

---

[1] a fictional Southern town.

And annoying beyond all other happenings had been that affair of the noon period, now again thrusting itself on her already irritated mind.

She had counted on a few spare minutes in which to indulge in the sweet pleasure of a bath and a fresh, cool change of clothing. And instead her luncheon time had been shortened, as had that of everyone else, and immediately after the hurried gulping down of a heavy hot meal the hundreds of students and teachers had been herded into the sun-baked chapel to listen to the banal, the patronizing, and even the insulting remarks of one of the renowned white preachers of the state.

Helga shuddered a little as she recalled some of the statements made by that holy white man of God to the black folk sitting so respectfully before him.

This was, he had told them with obvious sectional pride, the finest school for Negroes anywhere in the country, north or south; in fact, it was better even than a great many schools for white children. And he had dared any Northerner to come south and after looking upon this great institution to say that the Southerner mistreated the Negro. And he had said that if all Negroes would only take a leaf out of the book of Naxos and conduct themselves in the manner of the Naxos products, there would be no race problem, because Naxos Negroes knew what was expected of them. They had good sense and they had good taste. They knew enough to stay in their places and that, said the preacher, showed good taste. He spoke of his great admiration for the Negro race, no other race in so short a time had made so much progress, but he had urgently besought them to know when and where to stop. He hoped, he sincerely hoped, that they wouldn't become avaricious and grasping, thinking only of adding to their earthly goods, for that would be a sin in the sight of Almighty God. And then he had spoken of contentment, embellishing his words with scriptural quotations and pointing out to them that it was their duty to be satisfied in the estate to which they had been called, hewers of wood and drawers of water. And then he had prayed.

Sitting there in her room, long hours after, Helga again felt a surge of hot anger and seething resentment. And again it subsided in amazement at the memory of the considerable applause which had greeted the speaker just before he had asked his God's blessing upon them.

The South. Naxos. Negro education. Suddenly she hated them all. Strange, too, for this was the thing which she had ardently desired to share in, to be a part of this monument to one man's genius and vision. She pinned a scrap of paper about the bulb under the lamp's shade, for, having discarded her book, in the certainty that in such a mood even *Saïd* and his audacious villainy could not charm her, she wanted an even more soothing darkness. She wished it were vacation, so that she might get away for a time.

"No, forever!" she said aloud.

The minutes gathered into hours, but still she sat motionless, a disdainful smile or an angry frown passing now and then across her face. Somewhere in the room a little clock ticked time away. Somewhere outside, a whippoorwill wailed. Evening died. A sweet smell of early Southern flowers rushed in on a newly-risen breeze which suddenly parted the thin silk curtains at the opened windows. A slender, frail glass vase fell from the sill with a tingling crash, but Helga Crane did not shift her position. And the night grew cooler, and older.

At last she stirred, uncertainly, but with an overpowering desire for action of some sort. A second she hesitated, then rose abruptly and pressed the electric switch with determined firmness, flooding suddenly the shadowy room with a white glare of light. Next she made a quick nervous tour to the end of the long room, paused a moment before the old bow-legged secretary that held with almost articulate protest her school-teacher paraphernalia of drab books and papers. Frantically Helga Crane clutched at the lot and then flung them violently, scornfully toward the wastebasket. It received a part, allowing the rest to spill untidily over the floor. The girl smiled ironically, seeing in the mess a simile of her own earnest endeavor to inculcate knowledge into her indifferent classes.

Yes, it was like that; a few of the ideas which she tried to put into the minds behind those baffling ebony, bronze, and gold faces reached their destination. The others were left scattered about. And, like the gay, indifferent wastebasket, it wasn't their fault. No, it wasn't the fault of those minds back of the diverse colored faces. It was, rather, the fault of the method, the general idea behind the system. Like her own hurried shot at the basket, the aim was bad, the material drab and badly prepared for its purpose.

This great community, she thought, was no longer a school. It had grown into a machine. It was now a show place in the black belt, exemplification of the white man's magnanimity, refutation of the black man's inefficiency. Life had died out of it. It was, Helga decided, now only a big knife with cruelly sharp edges ruthlessly cutting all to a pattern, the white man's pattern. Teachers as well as students were subjected to the paring process, for it tolerated no innovations, no individualisms. Ideas it rejected, and looked with open hostility on one and all who had the temerity to offer a suggestion or ever so mildly express a disapproval. Enthusiasm, spontaneity, if not actually suppressed, were at least openly regretted as unladylike or ungentlemanly qualities. The place was smug and fat with self-satisfaction.

A peculiar characteristic trait, cold, slowly accumulated unreason in which all values were distorted or else ceased to exist, had with surprising ferociousness shaken the bulwarks of that self-restraint which was also, curiously, a part of her nature. And now that it had waned as quickly as it had risen, she smiled again, and this time the smile held a faint amusement, which wiped away the little hardness which had congealed her lovely face. Nevertheless she was soothed by the impetuous discharge of violence, and a sigh of relief came from her.

She said aloud, quietly, dispassionately: "Well, I'm through with that," and, shutting off the hard, bright blaze of the overhead lights, went back to her chair and settled down with an odd gesture of sudden soft collapse, like a person who had been for months fighting the devil and then unexpectedly had turned round and agreed to do his bidding.

Helga Crane had taught in Naxos for almost two years, at first with the keen joy and zest of those immature people who have dreamed dreams of doing good to their fellow men. But gradually this zest was blotted out, giving place to a deep hatred for the trivial hypocrisies and careless cruelties which were, unintentionally perhaps, a part of the Naxos policy of uplift. Yet she had continued to try not only to teach, but to befriend those happy singing children, whose charm and distinctiveness the school was so surely ready to destroy. Instinctively Helga was aware that their smiling submissiveness covered many poignant heartaches and perhaps much secret contempt for their instructors. But she was powerless. In Naxos between teacher and student, between condescending authority and smoldering resentment, the gulf was too great, and too few had tried to cross it. It couldn't be spanned by one sympathetic teacher. It was useless to offer her atom of friendship, which under the existing conditions was neither wanted nor understood.

Nor was the general atmosphere of Naxos, its air of self-righteousness and intolerant dislike of difference, the best of mediums for a pretty, solitary girl with no family connections. Helga's essentially likable and charming personality was smudged out. She had felt this for a long time. Now she faced with determination that other truth which she had refused to formulate in her thoughts, the fact that she was utterly unfitted for teaching, even for mere existence, in Naxos. She was a failure here. She had, she conceded now, been silly, obstinate, to persist for so long. A failure. Therefore, no need, no use, to stay longer. Suddenly she longed for immediate departure. How good, she thought, to go now, tonight!—and frowned to remember how impossible that would be. "The dignitaries," she said, "are not in their offices, and there will be yards and yards of red tape to unwind, gigantic, impressive spools of it."

And there was James Vayle to be told, and much-needed money to be got. James, she decided, had better be told at once. She looked at the clock racing indifferently on. No, too late. It would have to be tomorrow.

She hated to admit that money was the most serious difficulty. Knowing full well that it was important, she nevertheless rebelled at the unalterable truth that it could influence her actions, block her desires. A sordid necessity to be grappled with. With Helga it was almost a superstition that to concede to money its importance magnified its power. Still, in spite of her reluctance and distaste, her financial situation would have to be faced, and plans made, if she were to get away from Naxos with anything like the haste she now so ardently desired.

Most of her earnings had gone into clothes, into books, into the furnishings of the room which held her. All her life Helga Crane had loved and longed for nice things. Indeed, it was this craving, this urge for beauty which had helped to bring her into disfavor in Naxos—"pride" and "vanity" her detractors called it.

The sum owing to her by the school would just a little more than buy her ticket back to Chicago. It was too near the end of the school term to hope to get teaching-work anywhere. If she couldn't find something else, she would have to ask Uncle Peter for a loan. Uncle Peter was, she knew, the one relative who thought kindly, or even calmly, of her. Her stepfather, her step-brothers and sisters, and the numerous cousins, aunts, and other uncles could not be even remotely considered. She laughed a little, scornfully, reflecting that the antagonism was mutual, or, perhaps, just a trifle keener on her side than on theirs. They feared and hated her. She pitied and despised them. Uncle Peter was different. In his contemptuous way he was fond of her. Her beautiful, unhappy mother had been his favorite sister. Even so, Helga Crane knew that he would be more likely to help her because her need would strengthen his oft-repeated conviction that because of her Negro blood she would never amount to anything, than from motives of affection or loving memory. This knowledge, in its present aspect of truth, irritated her to an astonishing degree. She regarded Uncle Peter almost vindictively, although always he had been extraordinarily generous with her and she fully intended to ask his assistance. "A beggar," she thought ruefully, "cannot expect to choose."

Returning to James Vayle, her thoughts took on the frigidity of complete determination. Her resolution to end her stay in Naxos would of course inevitably end her engagement to James. She had been engaged to him since her first semester there, when both had been new workers, and both were lonely. Together they had discussed their work and problems in adjustment, and had drifted into a closer relationship. Bitterly she reflected that James had speedily and with entire ease fitted into his niche. He was now completely "naturalized," as they used laughingly to call it. Helga, on the other hand, had never quite achieved the unmistakable Naxos mold, would never achieve it, in spite of much trying. She could neither conform, nor be happy in her unconformity. This she saw clearly now, and with cold anger at all the past futile effort. What a waste! How pathetically she had struggled in those first months and with what small success. A lack somewhere. Always she had considered it a lack of understanding on the part of the community, but in her present new revolt she realized that the fault had been partly hers. A lack of acquiescence. She hadn't really wanted to be made over. This thought bred a sense of shame, a feeling of ironical disillusion. Evidently there were parts of her she couldn't be proud of. The revealing picture of her past striving was too humiliating. It was as if she had deliberately planned to steal an ugly thing, for which she had no desire, and had been found out.

Ironically she visualized the discomfort of James Vayle. How her maladjustment had bothered him! She had a faint notion that it was behind his ready assent to her suggestion anent a longer engagement than, originally, they had planned. He was liked and approved of in Naxos and loathed the idea that the girl he was to marry couldn't manage to win liking and approval also. Instinctively Helga had known that secretly he had placed the blame upon her. How right he had been! Certainly his attitude had gradually changed, though he still gave her his attentions. Naxos pleased him and he had become content with life as it was lived there. No longer lonely, he was now one of the community and so beyond the need or the desire to discuss its affairs and its failings with an outsider. She was, she knew, in a queer indefinite way, a disturbing factor. She knew too that a something held him, a something against which he was powerless. The idea that she was in but one nameless way necessary to him filled her with a sensation amounting almost to shame. And yet his mute helplessness against that ancient appeal by which she held him pleased her and fed her vanity—gave her a feeling of power. At the same time she shrank away from it, subtly aware of possibilities she herself couldn't predict.

Helga's own feelings defeated inquiry, but honestly confronted, all pretense brushed aside, the dominant one, she suspected, was relief. At least, she felt no regret that tomorrow would mark the end of any claim she had upon him. The surety that the meeting would be a clash annoyed her, for she had no talent for quarreling—when possible she preferred to flee. That was all.

The family of James Vayle, in near-by Atlanta, would be glad. They had never liked the engagement, had never liked Helga Crane. Her own lack of family disconcerted them. No family. That was the crux of the whole matter. For Helga, it accounted for everything, her failure here in Naxos, her former loneliness in Nashville. It even accounted for her engagement to James. Negro society, she had learned, was as complicated and as rigid in its ramifications as the highest strata of white society. If you couldn't prove your ancestry and connections, you were tolerated, but you didn't "belong." You could be queer, or even attractive, or bad, or brilliant, or even love beauty and such nonsense if you were a Rankin, or a Leslie, or a Scoville; in other words, if you had a family. But if you were just plain Helga Crane, of whom nobody had ever heard, it was presumptuous of you to be anything but inconspicuous and conformable.

To relinquish James Vayle would most certainly be social suicide, for the Vayles were people of consequence. The fact that they were a "first family" had been one of James's attractions for the obscure Helga. She had wanted social background, but—she had not imagined that it could be so stuffy.

She made a quick movement of impatience and stood up. As she did so, the room whirled about her in an impish, hateful way. Familiar objects seemed suddenly unhappily distant. Faintness closed about her like a vise. She swayed, her small, slender hands gripping the chair arms for support. In a moment the faintness receded, leaving in its wake a sharp resentment at the trick which her strained nerves had played upon her. And after a moment's rest she got hurriedly into bed, leaving her room disorderly for the first time.

Books and papers scattered about the floor, fragile stockings and underthings and the startling green and gold negligee dripping about on chairs and stool, met the encounter of the amazed eyes of the girl who came in the morning to awaken Helga Crane.

ALAIN LOCKE (1886–1954)

A native of Philadelphia, Alain Locke was the son of teachers. He earned a degree from Harvard University in 1907. With the distinction of being the first African American to be named a Rhodes Scholar, he studied at Oxford University and the University of Berlin. He accepted a position at Howard University in 1912, and he was awarded a Ph.D. by Harvard in 1918. The New Negro: An Interpretation *(1925), an anthology, was his contribution to the Harlem Renaissance; it promotes the idea of artistic freedom for African Americans. The anthology addresses the contributions of black artists to American culture and calls for a reassessment of the black experience in America.*

From The New Negro (1925)

In the last decade something beyond the watch and guard of statistics has happened in the life of the American Negro and the three norns[1] who have traditionally presided over the Negro problem have a changeling in their laps. The Sociologist, the Philanthropist, the Race-leader are not unaware of the New Negro, but they are at a loss to account for him. He simply cannot be swathed in their formulæ. For the younger generation is vibrant with a new psychology; the new spirit is awake in the masses, and under the very eyes of the professional observers is transforming what has been a perennial problem into the progressive phases of contemporary Negro life.

Could such a metamorphosis have taken place as suddenly as it has appeared to? The answer is no; not because the New Negro is not here, but because the Old Negro had long become more of a myth than a man. The Old Negro, we must remember, was a creature of moral debate and historical controversy. His has been a stock figure perpetuated as an historical fiction partly in innocent sentimentalism, partly in deliberate reactionism. The Negro himself has contributed his share to this through a sort of protective social mimicry forced upon him by the adverse circumstances of dependence. So for generations in the mind of America, the Negro has been more of a formula than a human being—a something to be argued about, condemned or defended, to be "kept down," or "in his place," or "helped up," to be worried with or worried over, harassed or patronized, a social bogey or a social burden. The thinking Negro even has been induced to share this same general attitude, to focus his attention on controversial issues, to see himself in the distorted perspective of a social problem. His shadow, so to speak, has been more real to him than his personality. Through having had to appeal from the unjust stereotypes of his oppressors and traducers to those of his liberators, friends and benefactors he has had to subscribe to the traditional positions from which his case has been viewed. Little true social or self-understanding has or could come from such a situation.

But while the minds of most of us, black and white, have thus burrowed in the trenches of the Civil War and Reconstruction, the actual march of development has simply flanked these positions, necessitating a sudden reorientation of view. We have not been watching in the right direction; set North and South on a sectional axis, we have not noticed the East till the sun has us blinking.

Recall how suddenly the Negro spirituals revealed themselves; suppressed for generations under the stereotypes of Wesleyan hymn harmony, secretive, half-ashamed, until the courage of being natural brought them out—and behold, there was folk-music. Similarly the mind of the Negro seems suddenly to have slipped from under the tyranny of social intimidation and to be shaking off the psychology of imitation and implied inferiority. By shedding the old chrysalis of the Negro problem we are achieving something like a spiritual emancipation. Until recently, lacking self-understanding, we have been almost as much of a problem to ourselves as we still are to others. But the decade that found us with

---

[1]A Norn is a Norse goddess of fate.

a problem has left us with only a task. The multitude perhaps feels as yet only a strange relief and a new vague urge, but the thinking few know that in the reaction the vital inner grip of prejudice has been broken.

With this renewed self-respect and self-dependence, the life of the Negro community is bound to enter a new dynamic phase, the buoyancy from within compensating for whatever pressure there may be of conditions from without. The migrant masses, shifting from countryside to city, hurdle several generations of experience at a leap, but more important, the same thing happens spiritually in the life-attitudes and self-expression of the Young Negro, in his poetry, his art, his education and his new outlook, with the additional advantage, of course, of the poise and greater certainty of knowing what it is all about. From this comes the promise and warrant of a new leadership. As one of them has discerningly put it:

> We have tomorrow
> Bright before us
> Like a flame.
>
> Yesterday, a night-gone thing
> A sun-down name.
>
> And dawn today
> Broad arch above the road we came.
> We march!

This is what, even more than any "most creditable record of fifty years of freedom," requires that the Negro of to-day be seen through other than the dusty spectacles of past controversy. The day of "aunties," "uncles" and "mammies" is equally gone. Uncle Tom and Sambo have passed on, and even the "Colonel" and "George" play barnstorm rôles from which they escape with relief when the public spotlight is off. The popular melodrama has about played itself out, and it is time to scrap the fictions, garret the bogeys and settle down to a realistic facing of facts.

First we must observe some of the changes which since the traditional lines of opinion were drawn have rendered these quite obsolete. A main change has been, of course, that shifting of the Negro population which has made the Negro problem no longer exclusively or even predominantly Southern. Why should our minds remain sectionalized, when the problem itself no longer is? Then the trend of migration has not only been toward the North and the Central Midwest, but city-ward and to the great centers of industry—the problems of adjustment are new, practical, local and not peculiarly racial. Rather they are an integral part of the large industrial and social problems of our present-day democracy. And finally, with the Negro rapidly in process of class differentiation, if it ever was warrantable to regard and treat the Negro *en masse* it is becoming with every day less possible, more unjust and more ridiculous.

In the very process of being transplanted, the Negro is becoming transformed.

The tide of Negro migration, northward and city-ward, is not to be fully explained as a blind flood started by the demands of war industry coupled with the shutting off of foreign migration, or by the pressure of poor crops coupled with increased social terrorism in certain sections of the South and Southwest. Neither labor demand, the boll-weevil nor the Ku Klux Klan is a basic factor, however contributory any or all of them may have been. The wash and rush of this human tide on the beach line of the northern city centers is to be explained primarily in terms of a new vision of opportunity, of social and economic freedom, of a spirit to seize, even in the face of an extortionate and heavy toll, a chance for the improvement of conditions. With each successive wave of it, the movement of the Negro becomes more and more a mass movement toward the larger and the more democratic chance—in the Negro's case a deliberate flight not only from countryside to city, but from medieval America to modern.

Take Harlem as an instance of this. Here in Manhattan is not merely the largest Negro community in the world, but the first concentration in history of so many diverse elements of Negro life. It has attracted the African, the West Indian, the Negro American; has brought together the Negro of the North and the Negro of the South; the man from the city and the man from the town and village; the peasant, the student, the business man, the professional man, artist, poet, musician, adventurer and worker, preacher and criminal, exploiter and social outcast. Each group has come with its own separate motives and for its own special ends, but their greatest experience has been the finding of one another. Proscription and prejudice have thrown these dissimilar elements into a common area of contact and interaction. Within this area, race sympathy and unity have determined a further fusing of sentiment and experience. So what began in terms of segregation becomes more and more, as its elements mix and react, the laboratory of a great race-welding. Hitherto, it must be admitted that American Negroes have been a race more in name than in fact, or to be exact, more in sentiment than in experience. The chief bond between them has been that of a common condition rather than a common consciousness; a problem in common rather than a life in common. In Harlem, Negro life is seizing upon its first chances for group expression and self-determination. It is—or promises at least to be—a race capital. That is why our comparison is taken with those nascent centers of folk-expression and self-determination which are playing a creative part in the world to-day. Without pretense to their political significance, Harlem has the same rôle to play for the New Negro as Dublin has had for the New Ireland or Prague for the New Czechoslovakia.

Harlem, I grant you, isn't typical—but it is significant, it is prophetic. No sane observer, however sympathetic to the new trend, would contend that the great masses are articulate as yet, but they stir, they move, they are more than physically restless. The challenge of the new intellectuals among them is clear enough—the "race radicals" and realists who have broken with the old epoch of philanthropic guidance, sentimental appeal and protest. But are we after all only reading into the stirrings of a sleeping giant the dreams of an agitator? The answer is in the migrating peasant. It is the "man farthest down" who is most active in getting up. One of the most characteristic symptoms of this is the professional man, himself migrating to recapture his constituency after a vain effort to maintain in some Southern corner what for years back seemed an established living and clientele. The clergyman following his errant flock, the physician or lawyer trailing his clients, supply the true clues. In a real sense it is the rank and

file who are leading, and the leaders who are following. A transformed and transforming psychology permeates the masses.

When the racial leaders of twenty years ago spoke of developing race-pride and
stimulating race-consciousness, and of the desirability of race solidarity, they could
not in any accurate degree have anticipated the abrupt feeling that has surged up
and now pervades the awakened centers. Some of the recognized Negro leaders
and a powerful section of white opinion identified with "race work" of the older
order have indeed attempted to discount this feeling as a "passing phase," an attack
of "race nerves" so to speak, an "aftermath of the war," and the like. It has not
abated, however, if we are to gauge by the present tone and temper of the Negro
press, or by the shift in popular support from the officially recognized and orthodox spokesmen to those of the independent, popular, and often radical type who
are unmistakable symptoms of a new order. It is a social disservice to blunt the fact
that the Negro of the Northern centers has reached a stage where tutelage, even
of the most interested and well-intentioned sort, must give place to new relationships, where positive self-direction must be reckoned with in ever increasing measure. The American mind must reckon with a fundamentally changed Negro.

The Negro too, for his part, has idols of the tribe to smash. If on the one hand
the white man has erred in making the Negro appear to be that which would
excuse or extenuate his treatment of him, the Negro, in turn, has too often unnecessarily excused himself because of the way he has been treated. The intelligent
Negro of to-day is resolved not to make discrimination an extenuation for his
shortcomings in performance, individual or collective; he is trying to hold himself at par, neither inflated by sentimental allowances nor depreciated by current
social discounts. For this he must know himself and be known for precisely what
he is, and for that reason he welcomes the new scientific rather than the old sentimental interest. Sentimental interest in the Negro has ebbed. We used to lament
this as the falling off of our friends; now we rejoice and pray to be delivered both
from self-pity and condescension. The mind of each racial group has had a bitter
weaning, apathy or hatred on one side matching disillusion or resentment on
the other; but they face each other to-day with the possibility at least of entirely
new mutual attitudes.

It does not follow that if the Negro were better known, he would be better
liked or better treated. But mutual understanding is basic for any subsequent
coöperation and adjustment. The effort toward this will at least have the effect of
remedying in large part what has been the most unsatisfactory feature of our
present stage of race relationships in America, namely the fact that the more intelligent and representative elements of the two race groups have at so many points
got quite out of vital touch with one another.

The fiction is that the life of the races is separate, and increasingly so. The fact
is that they have touched too closely at the unfavorable and too lightly at the
favorable levels.

While inter-racial councils have sprung up in the South, drawing on forward
elements of both races, in the Northern cities manual laborers may brush elbows
in their everyday work, but the community and business leaders have experienced
no such interplay or far too little of it. These segments must achieve contact or

the race situation in America becomes desperate. Fortunately this is happening. There is a growing realization that in social effort the co-operative basis must supplant long-distance philanthropy, and that the only safeguard for mass relations in the future must be provided in the carefully maintained contacts of the enlightened minorities of both race groups. In the intellectual realm a renewed and keen curiosity is replacing the recent apathy; the Negro is being carefully studied, not just talked about and discussed. In art and letters, instead of being wholly caricatured, he is being seriously portrayed and painted.

To all of this the New Negro is keenly responsive as an augury of a new democracy in American culture. He is contributing his share to the new social understanding. But the desire to be understood would never in itself have been sufficient to have opened so completely the protectively closed portals of the thinking Negro's mind. There is still too much possibility of being snubbed or patronized for that. It was rather the necessity for fuller, truer self-expression, the realization of the unwisdom of allowing social discrimination to segregate him mentally, and a counter-attitude to cramp and fetter his own living—and so the "spite-wall" that the intellectuals built over the "color-line" has happily been taken down. Much of this reopening of intellectual contacts has centered in New York and has been richly fruitful not merely in the enlarging of personal experience, but in the definite enrichment of American art and letters and in the clarifying of our common vision of the social tasks ahead.

The particular significance in the re-establishment of contact between the more advanced and representative classes is that it promises to offset some of the unfavorable reactions of the past, or at least to re-surface race contacts somewhat for the future. Subtly the conditions that are molding a New Negro are molding a new American attitude.

However, this new phase of things is delicate; it will call for less charity but more justice; less help, but infinitely closer understanding. This is indeed a critical stage of race relationships because of the likelihood, if the new temper is not understood, of engendering sharp group antagonism and a second crop of more calculated prejudice. In some quarters, it has already done so. Having weaned the Negro, public opinion cannot continue to paternalize. The Negro to-day is inevitably moving forward under the control largely of his own objectives. What are these objectives? Those of his outer life are happily already well and finally formulated, for they are none other than the ideals of American institutions and democracy. Those of his inner life are yet in process of formation, for the new psychology at present is more of a consensus of feeling than of opinion, of attitude rather than of program. Still some points seem to have crystallized.

Up to the present one may adequately describe the Negro's "inner objectives" as an attempt to repair a damaged group psychology and reshape a warped social perspective. Their realization has required a new mentality for the American Negro. And as it matures we begin to see its effects; at first, negative, iconoclastic, and then positive and constructive. In this new group psychology we note the lapse of sentimental appeal, then the development of a more positive self-respect and self-reliance; the repudiation of social dependence, and then the gradual recovery from hyper-sensitiveness and "touchy" nerves, the repudiation of the double standard of judgment with its special philanthropic allowances and then the sturdier desire for objective and scientific appraisal; and finally the rise from social disillusionment to race pride, from the sense of social debt to the responsibilities of social contribution, and offsetting the necessary working and common-sense acceptance of restricted conditions, the belief in ultimate esteem and recognition. Therefore the Negro to-day wishes to be known for what he is, even in his faults and shortcomings, and scorns a craven and precarious survival at the price of seeming to be what he is not. He resents being spoken of as a social ward or minor, even by his own, and to being regarded a chronic patient for the sociological clinic, the sick man of American Democracy. For the same reasons, he himself is through with those social nostrums and panaceas, the so-called "solutions" of his "problem," with which he and the country have been so liberally dosed in the past. Religion, freedom, education, money—in turn, he has ardently hoped for and peculiarly trusted these things; he still believes in them, but not in blind trust that they alone will solve his life-problem.

Each generation, however, will have its creed, and that of the present is the belief in the efficacy of collective effort, in race co-operation. This deep feeling of race is at present the mainspring of Negro life. It seems to be the outcome of the reaction to proscription and prejudice; an attempt, fairly successful on the whole, to convert a defensive into an offensive position, a handicap into an incentive. It is radical in tone, but not in purpose and only the most stupid forms of opposition, misunderstanding or persecution could make it otherwise. Of course, the thinking Negro has shifted a little toward the left with the world-trend, and there is an increasing group who affiliate with radical and liberal movements. But fundamentally for the present the Negro is radical on race matters, conservative on others, in other words, a "forced radical," a social protestant rather than a genuine radical. Yet under further pressure and injustice iconoclastic thought and motives will inevitably increase. Harlem's quixotic radicalisms call for their ounce of democracy to-day lest to-morrow they be beyond cure.

The Negro mind reaches out as yet to nothing but American wants, American ideas. But this forced attempt to build his Americanism on race values is a unique social experiment, and its ultimate success is impossible except through the fullest sharing of American culture and institutions. There should be no delusion about this. American nerves in sections unstrung with race hysteria are often fed the opiate that the trend of Negro advance is wholly separatist, and that the effect of its operation will be to encyst the Negro as a benign foreign body in the body politic. This cannot be—even if it were desirable. The racialism of the Negro is no limitation or reservation with respect to American life; it is only a constructive effort to build the obstructions in the stream of his progress into an efficient dam of social energy and power. Democracy itself is obstructed and stagnated to the extent that any of its channels are closed. Indeed they cannot be selectively closed. So the choice is not between one way for the Negro and another way for the rest, but between American institutions frustrated on the one hand and American ideals progressively fulfilled and realized on the other.

There is, of course, a warrantably comfortable feeling in being on the right side of the country's professed ideals. We realize that we cannot be undone without

America's undoing. It is within the gamut of this attitude that the thinking Negro faces America, but with variations of mood that are if anything more significant than the attitude itself. Sometimes we have it taken with the defiant ironic challenge of McKay:

> Mine is the future grinding down to-day
> Like a great landslip moving to the sea,
> Bearing its freight of débris far away
> Where the green hungry waters restlessly
> Heave mammoth pyramids, and break and roar
> Their eerie challenge to the crumbling shore.

Sometimes, perhaps more frequently as yet, it is taken in the fervent and almost filial appeal and counsel of Weldon Johnson's:

> O Southland, dear Southland!
> Then why do you still cling
> To an idle age and a musty page,
> To a dead and useless thing?

But between defiance and appeal, midway almost between cynicism and hope, the prevailing mind stands in the mood of the same author's *To America*, an attitude of sober query and stoical challenge:

> How would you have us, as we are?
>   Or sinking 'neath the load we bear,
> Our eyes fixed forward on a star,
>   Or gazing empty at despair?
>
> Rising or falling? Men or things?
>   With dragging pace or footsteps fleet?
> Strong, willing sinews in your wings,
>   Or tightening chains about your feet?

More and more, however, an intelligent realization of the great discrepancy between the American social creed and the American social practice forces upon the Negro the taking of the moral advantage that is his. Only the steadying and sobering effect of a truly characteristic gentleness of spirit prevents the rapid rise of a definite cynicism and counter-hate and a defiant superiority feeling. Human as this reaction would be, the majority still deprecate its advent, and would gladly see it forestalled by the speedy amelioration of its causes. We wish our race pride to be a healthier, more positive achievement than a feeling based upon a realization of the shortcomings of others. But all paths toward the attainment of a sound social attitude have been difficult; only a relatively few enlightened minds have been able as the phrase puts it "to rise above" prejudice. The ordinary man has had until recently only a hard choice between the alternatives of supine and humiliating submission and stimulating but hurtful counter-prejudice. Fortunately from some inner, desperate resourcefulness has recently sprung up the simple expedient of fighting prejudice by mental passive resistance, in other words by trying to ignore it. For the few, this manna may perhaps be effective, but the masses cannot thrive upon it.

Fortunately there are constructive channels opening out into which the balked social feelings of the American Negro can flow freely.

Without them there would be much more pressure and danger than there is. These compensating interests are racial but in a new and enlarged way. One is the consciousness of acting as the advance-guard of the African peoples in their contact with Twentieth Century civilization; the other, the sense of a mission of rehabilitating the race in world esteem from that loss of prestige for which the fate and conditions of slavery have so largely been responsible. Harlem, as we shall see, is the center of both these movements; she is the home of the Negro's "Zionism." The pulse of the Negro world has begun to beat in Harlem. A Negro newspaper carrying news material in English, French and Spanish, gathered from all quarters of America, the West Indies and Africa has maintained itself in Harlem for over five years. Two important magazines, both edited from New York, maintain their news and circulation consistently on a cosmopolitan scale. Under American auspices and backing, three pan-African congresses have been held abroad for the discussion of common interests, colonial questions and the future co-operative development of Africa. In terms of the race question as a world problem, the Negro mind has leapt, so to speak, upon the parapets of prejudice and extended its cramped horizons. In so doing it has linked up with the growing group consciousness of the dark-peoples and is gradually learning their common interests. As one of our writers has recently put it: "It is imperative that we understand the white world in its relations to the non-white world." As with the Jew, persecution is making the Negro international.

As a world phenomenon this wider race consciousness is a different thing from the much asserted rising tide of color. Its inevitable causes are not of our making. The consequences are not necessarily damaging to the best interests of civilization. Whether it actually brings into being new Armadas of conflict or argosies of cultural exchange and enlightenment can only be decided by the attitude of the dominant races in an era of critical change. With the American Negro, his new internationalism is primarily an effort to recapture contact with the scattered peoples of African derivation. Garveyism[2] may be a transient, if spectacular, phenomenon, but the possible rôle of the American Negro in the future development of Africa is one of the most constructive and universally helpful missions that any modern people can lay claim to.

Constructive participation in such causes cannot help giving the Negro valuable group incentives, as well as increased prestige at home and abroad. Our greatest rehabilitation may possibly come through such channels, but for the present, more immediate hope rests in the revaluation by white and black alike of the Negro in terms of his artistic endowments and cultural contributions, past and prospective. It must be increasingly recognized that the Negro has already made very

---

[2]Garveyism derives from Marcus Garvey (1887–1940), who encouraged blacks to relocate to Africa ("Back to Africa" Movement) to achieve racial and social equality.

substantial contributions, not only in his folk-art, music especially, which has always found appreciation, but in larger, though humbler and less acknowledged ways. For generations the Negro has been the peasant matrix of that section of America which has most undervalued him, and here he has contributed not only materially in labor and in social patience, but spiritually as well. The South has unconsciously absorbed the gift of his folk-temperament. In less than half a generation it will be easier to recognize this, but the fact remains that a leaven of humor, sentiment, imagination and tropic nonchalance has gone into the making of the South from a humble, unacknowledged source. A second crop of the Negro's gifts promises still more largely. He now becomes a conscious contributor and lays aside the status of a beneficiary and ward for that of a collaborator and participant in American civilization. The great social gain in this is the releasing of our talented group from the arid fields of controversy and debate to the productive fields of creative expression. The especially cultural recognition they win should in turn prove the key to that revaluation of the Negro which must precede or accompany any considerable further betterment of race relationships. But whatever the general effect, the present generation will have added the motives of self-expression and spiritual development to the old and still unfinished task of making material headway and progress. No one who understandingly faces the situation with its substantial accomplishment or views the new scene with its still more abundant promise can be entirely without hope. And certainly, if in our lifetime the Negro should not be able to celebrate his full initiation into American democracy, he can at least, on the warrant of these things, celebrate the attainment of a significant and satisfying new phase of group development, and with it a spiritual Coming of Age.

WALLACE THURMAN (1902–1934)

Originally from Salt Lake City, Wallace Thurman studied at the University of Utah from 1920 to 1922. After suffering a nervous breakdown, he ceased his studies, but later he took classes for two years at the University of Southern California. By 1925, Thurman had left for Harlem to begin a writing career. While in New York City, he founded two publications: Harlem *and* Fire. *His two novels,* The Blacker the Berry *(1929) and* Infants of the Spring *(1932), examine color consciousness, class prejudice, and the role of the black artist. His fiction often focuses on characters who feel enslaved by an oppressive society.*

From The Blacker the Berry (1929)

II

Harlem

Emma Lou turned her face away from the wall, and quizzically squinted her dark, pea-like eyes at the recently closed door. Then, sitting upright, she strained her ears, trying to hear the familiar squeak of the impudent floor boards, as John tip-toed down the narrow hallway toward the outside door. Finally, after she had heard the closing click of the double-barreled police lock, she climbed out of the bed, picked up a brush from the bureau and attempted to smooth the sensuous disorder of her hair. She had just recently had it bobbed, boyishly bobbed, because she thought this style narrowed and enhanced the fulsome lines of her facial features. She was always trying to emphasize those things about her that seemed, somehow, to atone for her despised darkness, and she never faced the mirror without speculating upon how good-looking she might have been had she not been so black.

Mechanically, she continued the brushing of her hair, stopping every once in a while to give it an affectionate caress. She was intensely in love with her hair, in love with its electric vibrancy and its unruly buoyance. Yet, this morning, she was irritated because it seemed so determined to remain disordered, so determined to remain a stubborn and unnecessary reminder of the night before. Why, she wondered, should one's physical properties always insist upon appearing awry after a night of stolen or forbidden pleasure? But not being anxious to find an answer, she dismissed the question from her mind, put on a stocking-cap, and jumped back into the bed.

She began to think about John, poor John who felt so hurt because she had told him that he could not spend any more days or nights with her. She wondered if she should pity him, for she was certain that he would miss the nights more than he would the days. Yet, she must not be too harsh in her conclusions, for, after all, there had only been two nights, which, she smiled to herself, was a pretty good record for a newcomer to Harlem. She had been in New York now for five weeks, and it seemed like, well, just a few days. Five weeks—thirty-five days and thirty-five nights, and of these nights John had had two. And now he sulked because she would not promise him another; because she had, in fact, boldly told him that there could be no more between them. Mischievously, she wished now that she could have seen the expression on his face, when, after seeming moments of mutual ecstasy, she had made this cold, manifesto-like announcement. But the room had been dark, and so was John. Ugh!

She had only written home twice. This, of course, seemed quite all right to her. She was not concerned about any one there except her Uncle Joe, and she reasoned that since he was preparing to marry again, he would be far too busy to think much about her. All that worried her was the pitiful spectacle of her mother, her uncle, and her cousin trying to make up lies to tell inquiring friends. Well, she would write today, that is, if she did not start to work, and she must get up at eight o'clock—was the alarm set?—and hie herself to an employment agency. She had only thirty-five dollars left in the bank, and, unless it was replenished, she might have to rescind her avowals to John in order to get her room rent paid.

She must go to sleep for another hour, for she wished to look "pert" when she applied for a job, especially the kind of job she wanted, and she must get the kind of job she wanted in order to show those people in Boise and Los Angeles that she had been perfectly justified in leaving school, home, and all, to come to New York. They all wondered why she had come. So did she, now that she was here.

But at the moment of leaving she would have gone any place to escape having to remain in that hateful Southern California college, or having to face the more dreaded alternative of returning home. Home? It had never been a home.

It did seem strange, this being in Harlem when only a few weeks before she had been over three thousand miles away. Time and distance—strange things, immutable, yet conquerable. But was time conquerable? Hadn't she read or heard somewhere that all things were subject to time, even God? Yet, once she was there and now she was here. But even at that she hadn't conquered time. What was that line in Cullen's verse, "I run, but Time's abreast with me?" She had only traversed space and defied distance. This suggested a more banal, if a less arduous thought tangent. She had defied more than distance, she had defied parental restraint—still there hadn't been much of that—friendly concern—there had been still less of that, and malicious, meddlesome gossip, of which there had been plenty. And she still found herself unable to understand why two sets of people in two entirely different communities should seemingly become almost hysterically excited because she, a woman of twenty-one, with three years' college training and ample sophistication in the ways of sex and self-support, had decided to take a job as an actress' maid in order to get to New York. They had never seemed interested in her before.

Now she wondered why had she been so painfully anxious to come to New York. She had given as a consoling reason to inquisitive friends and relatives, school. But she knew too well that she had no intentions of ever re-entering school. She had had enough of *that* school in Los Angeles, and her experiences there, more than anything else, had caused this foolhardy hegira to Harlem. She had been desperately driven to escape, and had she not escaped in this manner she might have done something else much more mad.

Emma Lou closed her eyes once more, and tried to sublimate her mental reverie into a sleep-inducing lullaby. Most of all, she wanted to sleep. One had to look "pert" when one sought a job, and she wondered if eight o'clock would find her looking any more "pert" than she did at this present moment. What had caused her to urge John to spend what she knew would be his last night with her when she was so determined to be at her best the following morning! O, what the hell was the use? She was going to sleep.

The alarm had not yet rung, but Emma Lou was awakened gradually by the sizzling and smell of fried and warmed-over breakfast, by the raucous early morning wranglings and window to window greetings, and by the almost constant squeak of those impudent hall floor boards as the various people in her apartment raced one another to the kitchen or to the bathroom or to the front door. How could Harlem be so happily busy, so alive and merry at eight o'clock. Eight o'clock? The alarm rang. Emma Lou scuttled out of the bed and put on her clothes.

An hour later, looking as "pert" as possible, she entered the first employment agency she came to on 135th Street, between Lenox and Seventh Avenues. It was her first visit to such an establishment and she was particularly eager to experience this phase of a working girl's life. Her first four weeks in Harlem had convinced her that jobs were easy to find, for she had noticed that there were three or four employment agencies to every block in business Harlem. Assuring herself in this way that she would experience little difficulty in obtaining a permanent and tasty position, Emma Lou had abruptly informed Mazelle Lindsay that she was leaving her employ.

"But, child," her employer had objected, "I feel responsible for you. Your— your mother! Don't be preposterous. How can you remain in New York alone?"

Emma Lou had smiled, asked for her money once more, closed her ears to all protest, bid the chagrined woman good-bye, and joyously loafed for a week.

Now, with only thirty-five dollars left in the bank, she thought that she had best find a job—find a job and then finish seeing New York. Of course she had seen much already. She had seen John—and he—oh, damn John, she wanted a job.

"What can I do for you?" the harassed woman at the desk was trying to be polite.

"I—I want a job." R-r-ring. The telephone insistently petitioned for attention, giving Emma Lou a moment of respite, while the machine-like woman wearily shouted monosyllabic answers into the instrument, and, at the same time, tried to hush the many loud-mouthed men and women in the room, all, it seemed, trying to out-talk one another. While waiting, Emma Lou surveyed her fellow job-seekers. Seedy lot, was her verdict. Perhaps I should have gone to a more high-toned place. Well, this will do for the moment.

"What kinda job d'ye want?"

"I prefer," Emma Lou had rehearsed these lines for a week, "a stenographic position in some colored business or professional office."

"'Ny experience?"

"No, but I took two courses in business college, during school vacations. I have a certificate of competency."

"'Ny reference?"

"No New York ones."

"Where'd ya work before?"

"I—I just came to the city."

"Where'd ya come . . . ?" R-r-ring. The telephone mercifully reiterated its insistent blare, and, for a moment, kept that pesky woman from droning out more insulting queries.

"Now," she had finished again, "where'd ya come from?"

"Los Angeles."

"Ummm. What other kind of work would ya take?"

"Anything congenial."

"Waal, what is that, dishwashing, day work, nurse girl?"

Didn't this damn woman know what congenial meant? And why should a Jewish woman be in charge of a Negro employment agency in Harlem?

"Waal, girlie, others waiting."

"I'll consider anything you may have on hand, if stenographic work is not available."

"Wanta work part-time?"

"I'd rather not."

"Awright. Sit down. I'll call you in a moment."

"What can I do for you, young man?" Emma Lou was dismissed.

She looked for a place to sit down, and, finding none, walked across the narrow room to the window, hoping to get a breath of fresh air, and at the same time an advantageous position from which to watch the drama of some one else playing the rôle of a job-seeker.

"R-r-ring."

"Whadda want? Wait a minute. Oh, Sadie."

A heavy set, dark-brown-skinned woman, with full, flopping breasts, and extra wide buttocks, squirmed off a too narrow chair, and bashfully wobbled up to the desk.

"Wanta' go to a place on West End Avenue? Part-time cleaning, fifty cents an hour, nine rooms, yeah? All right? Hello, gotta girl on the way. 'Bye. Two and a half, Sadie. Here's the address. Run along now, don't idle."

R-r-ring. "'Lo, yes. What? Come down to the office. I can't sell jobs over the wire."

Emma Lou began to see the humor in this sordid situation, began to see something extremely comic in all these plaintive, pitiful-appearing colored folk, some greasy, some neat, some fat, some slim, some brown, some black (why was there only one mulatto in this crowd?), boys and men, girls and women, all single-filing up to the desk, laconically answering laconic questions, impertinently put, showing thanks or sorrow or indifference, as their cases warranted, paying off promptly, or else seeking credit, the while the Jewish overseer of the dirty, dingy office asserted and reasserted her superiority.

Some one on the outside pushed hard on the warped door. Protestingly it came open, and the small stuffy room was filled with the odor and presence of a stout, black lady dressed in a greasy gingham housedress, still damp in the front from splashing dishwater. On her head was a tight turban, too round for the rather long outlines of her head. Beneath this turban could be seen short and wiry strands of recently straightened hair. And her face! Emma Lou sought to observe it more closely, sought to fathom how so much grease could gather on one woman's face. But her head reeled. The room was vile with noise and heat and body-smells, and this woman—

"Hy, Rosie, Yer late. Got a job for ya."

The greasy-faced black woman grinned broadly, licked her pork chop lips and, with a flourish, sat down in an empty chair beside the desk. Emma Lou stumbled over three pairs of number ten shoes, pulled open the door and fled into the street.

She walked hurriedly for about twenty-five yards, then slowed down and tried to collect her wits. Telephone bells echoed in her ears. Sour smells infested her nostrils. She looked up and discovered that she had paused in front of two garbage cans, waiting on the curbstone for the scavenger's truck.

Irritated, she turned around and retraced her steps. There were few people on the street. The early morning work crowds had already been swallowed by the subway kiosks on Lenox Avenue, and it was too early for the afternoon idlers. Yet there was much activity, much passing to and fro. One Hundred and Thirty-Fifth Street, Emma Lou mumbled to herself as she strolled along. How she had longed to see it, and what a different thoroughfare she had imagined it to be! Her eyes sought the opposite side of the street and blinked at a line of monotonously regular fire-escape decorated tenement buildings. She thanked whoever might be responsible for the architectural difference of the Y. M. C. A., for the streaming bit of Seventh Avenue near by, and for the arresting corner of the newly constructed teachers' college building, which dominated the hill three blocks away, and cast its shadows on the verdure of the terraced park beneath.

But she was looking for a job. Sour smells assailed her nostrils once more. Rasping voices. Pleading voices. Tired voices. Domineering voices. And the insistent ring of the telephone bell all re-echoed in her head and beat against her eardrums. She must have staggered, for a passing youth eyed her curiously, and shouted to no one in particular, "oh, *no*, now." Some one else laughed. They thought she was drunk. Tears blurred her eyes. She wanted to run, but resolutely she kept her steady, slow pace, lifted her head a little higher, and, seeing another employment agency, faltered for a moment, then went in.

This agency, like the first, occupied the ground floor front of a tenement house, three-quarters of the way between Lenox and Seventh Avenue. It was cagey and crowded, and there was a great conversational hubbub as Emma Lou entered. In the rear of the room was a door marked "private," to the left of this door was a desk, littered with papers and index cards, before which was a swivel chair. The rest of the room was lined with a miscellaneous assortment of chairs, three rows of them, tied together and trying to be precise despite their varying sizes and shapes. A single window looked out upon the street, and the Y. M. C. A. building opposite.

All of the chairs were occupied and three people stood lined up by the desk. Emma Lou fell in at the end of this line. There was nothing else to do. In fact, it was all she could do after entering. Not another person could have been squeezed into that room from the outside. This office too was noisy and hot and pregnant with clashing body smells. The buzzing electric fan, in a corner over the desk, with all its whirring, could not stir up a breeze.

The rear door opened. A slender, light-brown-skinned boy, his high cheekbones decorated with blackheads, his slender form accentuated by a tight fitting jazz suit of the high-waistline, one-button coat, bell-bottom trouser variety, emerged smiling broadly, cap in one hand, a slip of pink paper in the other. He elbowed his way to the outside door and was gone.

"Musta got a job," somebody commented. "It's about time," came from some one else, "he said he'd been sittin' here a week."

The rear door opened again and a lady with a youthful brown face and iron-gray hair sauntered in and sat down in the swivel chair before the desk. Immediately all talk in the outer office ceased. An air of anticipation seemed to pervade the room. All eyes were turned toward her.

For a moment she fingered a pack of red index cards, then, as if remembering something, turned around in her chair and called out:

"Mrs. Blake says for all elevator men to stick around."

There was a shuffling of feet and a settling back into chairs. Noticing this, Emma Lou counted six elevator men and wondered if she was right. Again the brown aristocrat with the tired voice spoke up:

"Day workers come back at one-thirty. Won't be nothing doin' 'til then."

Four women, all carrying newspaper packages, got out of their chairs, and edged their way toward the door, murmuring to one another as they went, "I ain't fixin' to come back."

"Ah, she keeps you hyar."

They were gone.

Two of the people standing in line sat down, the third approached the desk, Emma Lou close behind.

"I wantsa—"

"What kind of job do you want?"

Couldn't people ever finish what they had to say?

"Porter or dishwashing, lady."

"Are you registered with us?"

"No'm."

"Have a seat. I'll call you in a moment."

The boy looked frightened, but he found a seat and slid into it gratefully. Emma Lou approached the desk. The woman's cold eyes appraised her. She must have been pleased with what she saw for her eyes softened and her smile re-appeared. Emma Lou smiled, too. Maybe she was "pert" after all. The tailored blue suit—

"What can I do for you?"

The voice with the smile wins. Emma Lou was encouraged.

"I would like stenographic work."

"Experienced?"

"Yes." It was so much easier to say than "no."

"Good."

Emma Lou held tightly to her under-arm bag.

"We have something that would just about suit you. Just a minute, and I'll let you see Mrs. Blake."

The chair squeaked and was eased of its burden. Emma Lou thought she heard a telephone ringing somewhere in the distance, or perhaps it was the clang of the street car that had just passed, heading for Seventh Avenue. The people in the room began talking again.

"Dat last job." "Boy, she was dressed right down to the bricks."

"And I told him. . . ." "Yeah, we went to see 'Flesh and the Devil'." "Some par-teee." "I just been here a week."

Emma Lou's mind became jumbled with incoherent wisps of thought. Her left foot beat a nervous tattoo upon a sagging floor board. The door opened. The gray-haired lady with the smile in her voice beckoned, and Emma Lou walked into the private office of Mrs. Blake.

Four people in the room. The only window facing a brick wall on the out-side. Two telephones, both busy. A good-looking young man, fingering papers in a filing cabinet, while he talked over one of the telephones. The lady from the outer office. Another lady, short and brown, like butterscotch, talking over a desk telephone and motioning for Emma Lou to sit down. Blur of high pow-ered electric lights, brighter than daylight. The butterscotch lady hanging up the receiver.

"I'm through with you young man." Crisp tones. Metal, warm in spite of itself.

"Well, I ain't through with you." The fourth person was speaking. Emma Lou had hardly noticed him before. Sullen face. Dull black eyes in watery sockets. The nose flat, the lips thick and pouting. One hand clutching a derby, the other clenched, bearing down on the corner of the desk.

"I have no intention of arguing with you. I've said my say. Go on outside. When a cook's job comes in, you can have it. That's all I can do."

"No, it ain't all you can do."

"Well, I'm not going to give you your fee back."

The lady from the outside office returns to her post. The good-looking young man is at the telephone again.

"Why not, I'm entitled to it."

"No, you're not. I send you on a job, the man asks you to do something, you walk out, Mister Big I-am. Then, show up here two days later and want your fee back. No siree."

"I didn't walk out."

"The man says you did."

"Aw, sure, he'd say anything. I told him I came there to be a cook, not a waiter. I—"

"It was your place to do as he said, then, if not satisfied, to come here and tell me so."

"I am here."

"All right now. I'm tired of this. Take either of two courses—go on outside and wait until a job comes in or else go down to the license bureau and tell them your story. They'll investigate. If I'm right—"

"You know you ain't right."

"Not according to you, no, but by law, yes. That's all."

Telephone ringing. Warm metal whipping words into it. The good-looking young man yawning. He looks like a Y. M. C. A. secretary. The butterscotch woman speaking to Emma Lou:

"You're a stenographer?"

"Yes."

"I have a job in a real estate office, nice firm, nice people. Fill out this card. Here's a pen."

"Mrs. Blake, you know you ain't doin' right."

Why didn't this man either shut up or get out?

"I told you what to do. Now please do one or the other. You've taken up enough of my time. The license bureau—"

"You know I ain't goin' down there. I'd rather you keep the fee, if you think it will do you any good."

"I only keep what belongs to me. I've found out that's the best policy."

Why should they want three people for reference? Where had she worked before? Lies. Los Angeles was far away.

"Then, if a job comes in you'll give it to me?"

"That's what I've been trying to tell you."

"Awright." And finally he went out.

Mrs. Blake grinned across the desk at Emma Lou. "Your folks won't do, honey."

"Do you have many like that?"

The card was made out. Mrs. Blake had it in her hand. Telephones ringing, both at once. Loud talking in the outer office. Lies. Los Angeles was far away. I can bluff. Mrs. Blake had finished reading over the card.

"Just came to New York, eh?"

"Yes."

"Like it better than Los Angeles?"

The good-looking young man turned around and stared at her coldly. Now he did resemble a Y. M. C. A. secretary. The lady from the outer office came in again. There was a triple criss-cross conversation carried on. It ended. The short bob-haired butterscotch boss gave Emma Lou instructions and information about her prospective position. She was half heard. Sixteen dollars a week. Is that all? Work from nine to five. Address on card. Corner of 139th Street, left side of the avenue. Dismissal. Smiles and good luck. Pay the lady outside five dollars. Awkward, flustered moments. Then the entrance door and 135th Street once more. Emma Lou was on her way to get a job.

She walked briskly to the corner, crossed the street and turned north on Seventh Avenue. Her hopes were high, her mind a medley of pleasing mental images. She visualized herself trim and pert in her blue tailored suit being secretary to some well-groomed Negro business man. There had not been many such in the West, and she was eager to know and admire one. There would be other girls in the office, too, girls who, like herself, were college trained and reared in cultured homes, and through these fellow workers she would meet still other girls and men, get in with the right sort of people.

She continued day-dreaming as she went her way, being practical only at such fleeting moments when she would wonder,—would she be able to take dictation at the required rate of speed?—would her fingers be nimble enough on the keyboard of the typewriter? Oh, bother. It wouldn't take her over one day to adapt herself to her new job.

A street crossing. Traffic delayed her and she was conscious of a man, a blurred tan image, speaking to her. He was ignored. Everything was to be ignored save the address digits on the buildings. Everything was secondary to the business at hand. Let traffic pass, let men aching for flirtations speak, let Seventh Avenue be spangled with forenoon sunshine and shadow, and polka-dotted with still or moving human forms. She was going to have a job. The rest of the world could go to hell.

Emma Lou turned into a four-story brick building and sped up one flight of stairs. The rooms were not numbered and directing signs in the hallway only served to confuse. But Emma Lou was not to be delayed. She rushed back and forth from door to door on the first floor, then to the second, until she finally found the office she was looking for.

Angus and Brown were an old Harlem real estate firm. They had begun business during the first decade of the century, handling property for a while in New York's far-famed San Juan Hill district. When the Negro population had begun to need more and better homes, Angus and Brown had led the way in buying real estate in what was to be Negro Harlem. *They had been fighters, unscrupulous and canny.* They had revealed a perverse delight in seeing white people rush pell-mell from the neighborhood in which they obtained homes for their colored clients. They had bought three six-story tenement buildings on 140th Street, and, when the white tenants had been slow in moving, had personally dispossessed them, and, in addition, had helped their incoming Negro tenants fight fistic battles in the streets and hallways, and legal battles in the court.

Now they were a substantial firm, grown fat and satisfied. Junior real estate men got their business for them. They held the whip. Their activities were many and varied. Politics and fraternal activities occupied more of their time than did real estate. They had had their hectic days. Now they sat back and took it easy.

Emma Lou opened the door to their office, consisting of one medium-sized outer room overlooking 139th Street and two cubby holes overlooking Seventh Avenue. There were two girls in the outer office. One was busy at a typewriter; the other was gazing over her desk through a window into the aristocratic tree-lined city lane of 139th Street. Both looked up expectantly. Emma Lou noticed the powdered smoothness of their fair skins and the marcelled waviness of their shingled brown hair. Were they sisters? Hardly, for their features were in no way similar. Yet that skin color and that brown hair—.

"Can I do something for you?" The idle one spoke, and the other ceased her peck-peck-pecking on the typewriter keys. Emma Lou was buoyant.

"I'm from Mrs. Blake's employment agency."

"Oh," from both. And they exchanged glances. Emma Lou thought she saw a quickly suppressed smile from the fairer of the two as she hastily resumed her typing. Then—

"Sit down a moment, won't you, please? Mr. Angus is out but I'll inform Mr. Brown that you are here." She picked a powder puff from an open side drawer in her desk, patted her nose and cheeks, then got up and crossed the office to enter cubby hole number one. Emma Lou observed that she, too, looked "pert" in a trim, blue suit and high-heeled patent leather oxfords—

"Mr. Brown?" She had opened the door.

"Come in Grace. What is it?" The door was closed.

Emma Lou felt nervous. Something in the pit of her stomach seemed to flutter. Her pulse raced. Her eyes gleamed and a smile of anticipation spread over her face, despite her efforts to appear dignified and suave. The typist continued her work. From the cubby hole came a murmur of voices, one feminine and affected, the other masculine and coarse. Through the open window came direct sounds and vagrant echoes of traffic noises from Seventh Avenue. Now the two in the cubby hole were laughing, and the girl at the typewriter seemed to be smiling to herself as she worked.

What did this mean? Nothing, silly. Don't be so sensitive. Emma Lou's eyes sought the pictures on the wall. There was an early twentieth century photographic bust-portrait, encased in a bevelled glass frame, of a heavy-set good-looking, brown-skinned man. She admired his mustache. Men didn't seem to take pride in such hirsute embellishments now. Mustaches these days were abbreviated and limp. They no longer were virile enough to dominate and make a man's face appear more strong. Rather, they were only insignificant patches weakly keeping the nostrils from merging with the upper lip.

Emma Lou wondered if that was Mr. Brown. He had a brown face and wore a brown suit. No, maybe that was Mr. Angus, and perhaps that was Mr. Brown on the other side of the room, in the square, enlarged kodak print, a slender yellow man, standing beside a motor car, looking as if he wished to say, "Yeah, this is me and this is my car." She hoped he was Mr. Angus. She didn't like his name and since she was to see Mr. Brown first, she hoped he was the more flatteringly portrayed.

The door to the cubby hole opened and the girl Mr. Brown had called Grace, came out. The expression on her face was too business-like to be natural. It seemed as if it had been placed there for a purpose.

She walked toward Emma Lou, who got up and stood like a child, waiting for punishment and hoping all the while that it will dissipate itself in threats. The typewriter was stilled and Emma Lou could feel an extra pair of eyes looking at her. The girl drew close then spoke:

"I'm sorry, Miss. Mr. Brown says he has some one else in view for the job. We'll call the agency. Thank you for coming in."

Thank her for coming in? What could she say? What should she say? The girl was smiling at her, but Emma Lou noticed that her fair skin was flushed and that her eyes danced nervously. Could she be hoping that Emma Lou would hurry and depart? The door was near. It opened easily. The steps were steep. One went down slowly. Seventh Avenue was still spangled with forenoon sunshine and shadow. Its pavement was hard and hot. The windows in the buildings facing it, gleaming reflectors of the mounting sun.

Emma Lou returned to the employment agency. It was still crowded and more stuffy than ever. The sun had advanced high into the sky and it seemed to be centering its rays on that solitary defenseless window. There was still much conversation. There were still people crowded around the desk, still people in all the chairs, people and talk and heat and smells.

"Mrs. Blake is waiting for you," the gray-haired lady with the young face was unflustered and cool. Emma Lou went into the inner office. Mrs. Blake looked up quickly and forced a smile. The good-looking young man, more than ever resembling a Y. M. C. A. secretary, turned his back and fumbled with the card files. Mrs. Blake suggested that he leave the room. He did, beaming benevolently at Emma Lou as he went.

"I'm sorry," Mrs. Blake was very kind and womanly. "Mr. Brown called me. I didn't know he had some one else in mind. He hadn't told me."

"That's all right," replied Emma Lou briskly. "Have you something else?"

"Not now. Er-er. Have you had luncheon? It's early yet, I know, but I generally go about this time. Come along, won't you, I'd like to talk to you. I'll be ready in about thirty minutes if you don't mind the wait."

Emma Lou warmed to the idea. At that moment, she would have warmed toward any suggestion of friendliness. Here, perhaps, was a chance to make a welcome contact. She was lonesome and disappointed, so she readily assented and felt elated and superior as she walked out of the office with the "boss."

They went to Eddie's for luncheon. Eddie's was an elbow-shaped combination lunch-counter and dining room that embraced a United Cigar Store on the northeast corner of 135th Street and Seventh Avenue. Following Mrs. Blake's lead, Emma Lou ordered a full noontime dinner, and, flattered by Mrs. Blake's interest and congeniality, began to talk about herself. She told of her birthplace and her home life. She told of her high school days, spoke proudly of the fact that she had been the only Negro student and how she had graduated cum laude. Asked about her college years, she talked less freely. Mrs. Blake sensed a cue.

"Didn't you like college?"

"For a little while, yes."

"What made you dislike it? Surely not the studies?"

"No." She didn't care to discuss this. "I was lonesome, I guess."

"Weren't there any other colored boys and girls? I thought. . . ."

Emma Lou spoke curtly. "Oh, yes, quite a number, but I suppose I didn't mix well."

The waiter came to take the order for dessert, and Emma Lou seized upon the fact that Mrs. Blake ordered sliced oranges to talk about California's orange groves, California's sunshine—anything but the California college she had attended and from which she had fled. In vain did Mrs. Blake try to maneuver the conversation back to Emma Lou's college experiences. She would have none of it and Mrs. Blake was finally forced to give it up.

When they were finished, Mrs. Blake insisted upon taking the check. This done, she began to talk about jobs.

"You know, Miss Morgan, good jobs are rare. It is seldom I have anything to offer outside of the domestic field. Most Negro business offices are family affairs. They either get their help from within their own family group or from among their friends. Then, too," Emma Lou noticed that Mrs. Blake did not look directly at her, "lots of our Negro business men have a definite type of girl in mind and will not hire any other."

Emma Lou wondered what it was Mrs. Blake seemed to be holding back. She began again:

"My advice to you is that you enter Teachers' College and if you *will* stay in New York, get a job in the public school system. You can easily take a light job of some kind to support you through your course. Maybe with three years' college you won't need to go to training school. Why don't you find out about that? Now, if I were you. . . ." Mrs. Blake talked on, putting much emphasis on every "If I were you."

Emma Lou grew listless and antagonistic. She didn't like this little sawed-off woman as she was now, being business like and giving advice. She was glad when they finally left Eddie's, and more than glad to escape after having been admonished not to oversleep. "But be in my office, and I'll see what I can do for you, dearie, early in the morning. There's sure to be something."

Left to herself, Emma Lou strolled south on the west side of Seventh Avenue to 134th Street, then crossed over to the east side and turned north. She didn't know what to do. It was too late to consider visiting another employment agency, and, furthermore, she didn't have enough money left to pay another fee. Let jobs go until tomorrow, then she would return to Mrs. Blake's, ask for a return of her fee, and find some other employment agency, a more imposing one, if possible. She had had enough of those on 135th Street.

She didn't want to go home, either. Her room had no outside vista. If she sat in the solitary chair by the solitary window, all she could see were other windows and brick walls and people either mysteriously or brazenly moving about in the apartments across the court. There was no privacy there, little fresh air, and no natural light after the sun began its downward course. Then the apartment always smelled of frying fish or of boiling cabbage. Her landlady seemed to alternate daily between these two foods. Fish smells and cabbage smells pervaded the long, dark hallway, swirled into the room when the door was opened and perfumed one's clothes disagreeably. Moreover, urinal and foecal smells surged upward from the garbage-littered bottom of the court which her window faced.

If she went home, the landlady would eye her suspiciously and ask, "Ain't you got a job yet?" then move away, shaking her head and dipping into her snuff box. Occasionally, in moments of excitement, she spat on the floor. And the little fat man who had the room next to Emma Lou's could be heard coughing suggestively—tapping on the wall, and talking to himself in terms of her. He had seen her slip John in last night. He might be more bold now. He might even try—oh no he wouldn't.

She was crossing 137th Street. She remembered this corner. John had told her that he could always be found there after work any spring or summer evening.

Emma Lou had met John on her first day in New York. He was employed as a porter in the theater where Mazelle Lindsay was scheduled to perform, and, seeing a new maid on the premises, had decided to "make" her. He had. Emma Lou had not liked him particularly, but he had seemed New Yorkish and genial. It was John who had found her her room. It was John who had taught her how to find her way up and down town on the subway and on the elevated. He had also conducted her on a Cook's tour of Harlem, had strolled up and down Seventh Avenue with her evenings after they had come uptown from the theater. He had pointed out for her the Y. W. C. A. with its imposing annex, the Emma Ranson House, and suggested that she get a room there later on. He had taken her on a Sunday to several of the Harlem motion picture and vaudeville theaters, and he had been as painstaking in pointing out the churches as he had been lax in pointing out the cabarets. Moreover, as they strolled Seventh Avenue, he had attempted to give her all the "inside dope" on Harlem, had told her of the "rent parties," of the "numbers," of "hot" men, of "sweetbacks," and other local phenomena.

Emma Lou was now passing a barber shop near 140th Street. A group of men were standing there beneath a huge white and black sign announcing, "Bobbing's, fifty cents; haircuts, twenty-five cents." They were whistling at three school girls, about fourteen or fifteen years of age, who were passing, doing much switching and giggling. Emma Lou curled her lips. Harlem streets presented many such scenes. She looked at the men significantly, forgetting for the moment that it was none of her business what they or the girls did. But they didn't notice her. They were too busy having fun with those fresh little chippies.

Emma Lou experienced a feeling of resentment, then, realizing how ridiculous it all was, smiled it away and began to think of John once more. She wondered why she had submitted herself to him. Was it cold-blooded payment for his kind chaperoning? Something like that. John wasn't her type. He was too pudgy and dark, too obviously an ex-cotton-picker from Georgia. He was unlettered and she couldn't stand for that, for she liked intelligent-looking, slender, light-brown-skinned men, like, well . . . like the one who was just passing. She admired him boldly. He looked at her, then over her, and passed on.

Seventh Avenue was becoming more crowded now. School children were out for their lunch hour, corner loafers and pool-hall loiterers were beginning to collect on their chosen spots. Knots of people, of no particular designation, also stood around talking, or just looking, and there were many pedestrians, either impressing one as being in a great hurry, or else seeming to have no place at all to go. Emma Lou was in this latter class. By now she had reached 142nd Street and had decided to cross over to the opposite side and walk south once more. Seventh Avenue was a wide, well-paved, busy thoroughfare, with a long, narrow, iron fenced-in parkway dividing the east side from the west. Emma Lou liked Seventh Avenue. It was so active and alive, so different from Central Avenue, the dingy main street of the black belt of Los Angeles. At night it was glorious! Where else could one see so many different types of Negroes? Where else would one view such a heterogeneous ensemble of mellow colors, glorified by the night?

People passing by. Children playing. Dogs on leashes. Stray cats crouching by the sides of buildings. Men standing in groups or alone. Black men. Yellow men. Brown men. Emma Lou eyed them. They eyed her. There were a few remarks passed. She thought she got their import even though she could not hear what they were saying. She quickened her step and held her head higher. Be yourself, Emma Lou. Do you want to start picking men up off of the street?

The heat became more intense. Brisk walking made her perspire. Her underclothes grew sticky. Harlem heat was so muggy. She could feel the shine on her nose and it made her self-conscious. She remembered how the "Grace" in the office of Angus and Brown had so carefully powdered her skin before confronting her employer, and, as she remembered this, she looked up, and sure enough, here she was in front of the building she had sought so eagerly earlier that morning. Emma Lou drew closer to the building. She must get that shine off of her nose. It was bad enough to be black, too black, without having a shiny face to boot. She stopped in front of the tailor shop directly beneath the office of Angus and Brown, and, turning her back to the street, proceeded to powder her shiny member. Three noisy lads passed by. They saw Emma Lou and her reflection in the sunlit show window. The one closest to her cleared his throat and crooned out, loud enough for her to hear, "There's a girl for you, 'Fats.'" "Fats" was the one in the middle. He had a rotund form and a coffee-colored face. He was in his shirt sleeves and carried his coat on his arm. Bell bottom trousers hid all save the tips of his shiny tan shoes. "Fats" was looking at Emma Lou, too, but as he passed, he turned his eyes from her and broadcast a withering look at the lad who had spoken:

"Man, you know I don't haul no coal." There was loud laughter and the trio merrily clicked their metal-cornered heels on the sun-baked pavement as they moved away.

❋ LANGSTON HUGHES (1902–1967)

Langston Hughes's incorporation of musical rhythms, his sensitive rendering of folk speech and dialect in his poems, and the protest element of his works left an important legacy in African American literature. A native of Joplin, Missouri, Hughes attended Columbia University for one year in 1921. He eventually returned to his college studies, attending Lincoln University from 1926 to 1929. By 1923, he had left the United States, and he spent two years traveling throughout Europe and West Africa. When he returned to the United States in 1925, he settled in New York City. The Weary Blues (1926) reflects Hughes's immersion into the jazz and blues musical culture of Harlem. In poems such as "I, Too," "Dream Boogie: Variation," and "Theme for English B," Hughes shows the irony of an America that was predicated upon the ideas of democracy, yet treated blacks as second-class citizens, preventing them from achieving freedom and equality. In addition to poetry, he penned autobiographies, including The Big Sea *(1940), in which he details his quest for selfhood and autonomy. Hughes died in 1967.*

Mother to Son (1922)

Well, son, I'll tell you:
Life for me ain't been no crystal stair.
It's had tacks in it,
And splinters,
And boards torn up,   5
And places with no carpet on the floor—
Bare.
But all the time
I'se been a-climbin' on,
And reachin' landin's,   10
And turnin' corners,
And sometimes goin' in the dark
Where there ain't been no light.
So boy, don't you turn back.
Don't you set down on the steps   15
'Cause you finds it's kinder hard.
Don't you fall now—
For I'se still goin', honey,
I'se still climbin',
And life for me ain't been no crystal stair.   20

Harlem [2] (1951)

What happens to a dream deferred?

    Does it dry up
    like a raisin in the sun?

Or fester like a sore—
And then run?   5
Does it stink like rotten meat?
Or crust and sugar over—
like a syrupy sweet?

Maybe it just sags
like a heavy load.   10

Or does it explode?

I, Too (1925)

I, too, sing America.

I am the darker brother.
They send me to eat in the kitchen
When company comes,
But I laugh,   5
And eat well,
And grow strong.

Tomorrow,
I'll be at the table
When company comes.   10
Nobody'll dare
Say to me,
"Eat in the kitchen,"
Then.

Besides,   15
They'll see how beautiful I am
And be ashamed—

I, too, am America.

Dream Boogie: Variation (1951)

Tinkling treble,
Rolling bass,
High noon teeth
In a midnight face,
Great long fingers   5
On great big hands,
Screaming pedals

Where his twelve-shoe lands,
Looks like his eyes
Are teasing pain,   10
A few minutes late
For the Freedom Train.

Theme for English B (1949)

The instructor said,

Go home and write
a page tonight.
And let that page come out of you—
Then, it will be true.   5

I wonder if it's that simple?
I am twenty-two, colored, born in Winston-Salem.
I went to school there, then Durham, then here
to this college on the hill above Harlem.
I am the only colored student in my class.   10
The steps from the hill lead down into Harlem,
through a park, then I cross St. Nicholas,
Eighth Avenue, Seventh, and I come to the Y,
the Harlem Branch Y, where I take the elevator
up to my room, sit down, and write this page: 15

It's not easy to know what is true for you or me
at twenty-two, my age. But I guess I'm what
I feel and see and hear, Harlem, I hear you:
hear you, hear me—we two—you, me, talk on this page.
(I hear New York, too.) Me—who?   20
Well, I like to eat, sleep, drink, and be in love.
I like to work, read, learn, and understand life.
I like a pipe for a Christmas present,
or records—Bessie, bop, or Bach.
I guess being colored doesn't make me *not* like   25
the same things other folks like who are other races.
So will my page be colored that I write?
Being me, it will not be white.
But it will be
a part of you, instructor.   30
You are white—
yet a part of me, as I am a part of you.
That's American.
Sometimes perhaps you don't want to be a part of me.

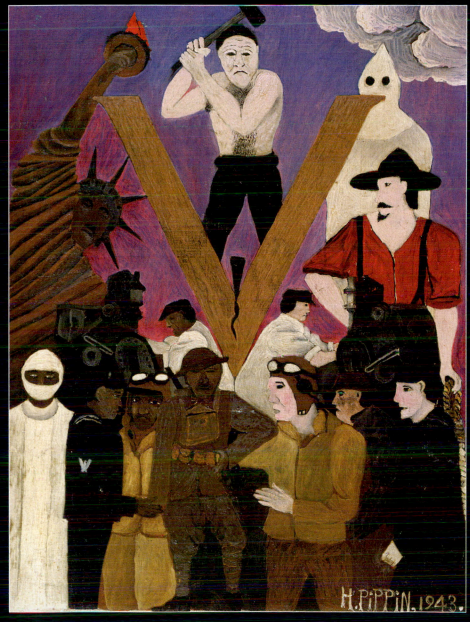

▲ Horace Pippin (American, 1888–1946), *Mr. Prejudice* (1943). Oil on canvas, 18" x 14". From the Philadelphia Museum of Art. Gift of Dr. and Mrs. Matthew T. Moore (1984.108.1). Photograph by Graydon Wood, 1995.

THE CRISIS

A RECORD OF THE DARKER RACES

Volume One   NOVEMBER, 1910   Number One

Edited by W. E. BURGHARDT DU BOIS, with the co-operation of Oswald Garrison Villard, J. Max Barber, Charles Edward Russell, Kelly Miller, W. S. Braithwaite and M. D. Maclean.

CONTENTS

PUBLISHED MONTHLY BY THE

National Association for the Advancement of Colored People

AT TWENTY VESEY STREET   NEW YORK CITY

ONE DOLLAR A YEAR   TEN CENTS A COPY

▲ The cover of the first issue of *The Crisis* (November 8, 1910), New York. The monthly magazine of the National Association for the Advancement of Colored People (NAACP), was first published in November, 1910. Its present editor, Henry Lee Moon, said in an interview, "It helped shape my own thinking and development and that of a whole group of Negroes of my generation who had any sort of intellectual aspirations." Corbis

▲ Red Jackson, *Gang Warfare in Harlem*/Gordon Parks Photography.

▲ *Harlem Newsboy,* **Washington D.C. (1943)/Gordon Parks/Corbis.**

▲ *Children with Doll* **(1942)/Gordon Parks/Corbis.**

Nor do I often want to be a part of you.　　35
But we are, that's true!
As I learn from you,
I guess you learn from me—
although you're older—and white—
and somewhat more free.　　40

This is my page for English B.

COUNTEE CULLEN (1903–1946)

Louisville, Kentucky, was his place of birth, but Countee Cullen was raised primarily in New York City after being adopted by Rev. Frederick Cullen, a Harlem minister. Cullen attended New York University. Shortly after he earned a degree, he published his first collection of poems, Color *(1925). He enrolled in the M.A. program at Harvard University and was awarded a degree in 1926. After being hired as an editor for* Opportunity, *he contributed to the artistic direction of the Harlem Renaissance with his column "The Dark Tower" by analyzing aesthetics. He continued to publish volumes of poetry, including* Copper Sun *(1927) and* Caroling Dusk *(1927), an anthology of African American poetry. Unlike Langston Hughes, who often used blues and jazz rhythms and a folk dialect in his poems, Cullen modeled his poetry after that of the British Romantics, such as Byron, Keats, and Shelley. His more formal approach contrasted sharply with his stringent critique of racial and class prejudice in poems such as "Incident" and "Heritage." The latter meditates on the meaning of Africa to African Americans, who are often centuries removed from their enslaved ancestors.*

Incident (1925)

For Eric Walrond

Once riding in old Baltimore,
　　Heart-filled, head-filled with glee,
I saw a Baltimorean
　　Keep looking straight at me.

Now I was eight and very small,　　5
　　And he was no whit bigger,
And so I smiled, but he poked out
　　His tongue, and called me, "Nigger."

I saw the whole of Baltimore
　　From May until December;　　10

Of all the things that happened there
　That's all that I remember.

Heritage (1925)

For Harold Jackman

What is Africa to me:
Copper sun or scarlet sea,
Jungle star or jungle track,
Strong bronzed men, or regal black
Women from whose loins I sprang   5
When the birds of Eden sang?
One three centuries removed
From the scenes his fathers loved,
Spicy grove, cinnamon tree,
What is Africa to me?   10

So I lie, who all day long
Want no sound except the song
Sung by wild barbaric birds
Goading massive jungle herds,
Juggernauts of flesh that pass   15
Trampling tall defiant grass
Where young forest lovers lie,
Plighting troth beneath the sky.
So I lie, who always hear,
Though I cram against my ear   20
Both my thumbs, and keep them there,
Great drums throbbing through the air.
So I lie, whose fount of pride,
Dear distress, and joy allied,
Is my somber flesh and skin,   25
With the dark blood dammed within
Like great pulsing tides of wine
That, I fear, must burst the fine
Channels of the chafing net
Where they surge and foam and fret.   30

Africa? A book one thumbs
Listlessly, till slumber comes.
Unremembered are her bats
Circling through the night, her cats
Crouching in the river reeds,   35
Stalking gentle flesh that feeds

By the river brink; no more
Does the bugle-throated roar
Cry that monarch claws have leapt
From the scabbards where they slept.   40
Silver snakes that once a year
Doff the lovely coats you wear,
Seek no covert in your fear
Lest a mortal eye should see;
What's your nakedness to me?   45
Here no leprous flowers rear
Fierce corollas in the air;
Here no bodies sleek and wet,
Dripping mingled rain and sweat,
Tread the savage measures of   50
Jungle boys and girls in love.
What is last year's snow to me,
Last year's anything? The tree
Budding yearly must forget
How its past arose or set—   55
Bough and blossom, flower, fruit,
Even what shy bird with mute
Wonder at her travail there,
Meekly labored in its hair.
One three centuries removed   60
From the scenes his fathers loved,
Spicy grove, cinnamon tree,
What is Africa to me?

So I lie, who find no peace
Night or day, no slight release   65
From the unremittant beat
Made by cruel padded feet
Walking through my body's street.
Up and down they go, and back,
Treading out a jungle track.   70
So I lie, who never quite
Safely sleep from rain at night—
I can never rest at all
When the rain begins to fall;
Like a soul gone mad with pain   75
I must match its weird refrain;
Ever must I twist and squirm,
Writhing like a baited worm,
While its primal measures drip
Through my body, crying, "Strip!   80
Doff this new exuberance.

Come and dance the Lover's Dance!"
In an old remembered way
Rain works on me night and day.

Quaint, outlandish heathen gods 85
Black men fashion out of rods,
Clay, and brittle bits of stone,
In a likeness like their own,
My conversion came high-priced;
I belong to Jesus Christ, 90
Preacher of humility;
Heathen gods are naught to me.

Father, Son, and Holy Ghost,
So I make an idle boast;
Jesus of the twice-turned cheek, 95
Lamb of God, although I speak
With my mouth thus, in my heart
Do I play a double part.
Ever at Thy glowing altar
Must my heart grow sick and falter, 100
Wishing He I served were black,
Thinking then it would not lack
Precedent of pain to guide it,
Let who would or might deride it;
Surely then this flesh would know 105
Yours had borne a kindred woe.
Lord, I fashion dark gods, too,
Daring even to give You
Dark despairing features where,
Crowned with dark rebellious hair, 110
Patience wavers just so much as
Mortal grief compels, while touches
Quick and hot, of anger, rise
To smitten cheek and weary eyes.
Lord, forgive me if my need 115
Sometimes shapes a human creed.

All day long and all night through,
One thing only must I do:
Quench my pride and cool my blood,
Lest I perish in the flood. 120
Lest a hidden ember set
Timber that I thought was wet
Burning like the dryest flax,
Melting like the merest wax,
Lest the grave restore its dead. 125

Not yet has my heart or head
In the least way realized
They and I are civilized.

Yet Do I Marvel (1925)

I doubt not God is good, well-meaning, kind,
And did He stoop to quibble could tell why
The little buried mole continues blind,
Why flesh that mirrors Him must some day die,
Make plain the reason tortured Tantalus   5
Is baited by the fickle fruit, declare
If merely brute caprice dooms Sisyphus
To struggle up a never-ending stair.
Inscrutable His ways are, and immune
To catechism by a mind too strewn   10
With petty cares to slightly understand
What awful brain compels His awful hand.
Yet do I marvel at this curious thing:
To make a poet black, and bid him sing!

To John Keats, Poet.
At Spring Time[1] (1925)

For Carl Van Vechten

I cannot hold my peace, John Keats;
There never was a spring like this;
It is an echo, that repeats
My last year's song and next year's bliss.
I know, in spite of all men say   5
Of Beauty, you have felt her most.
Yea, even in your grave her way
Is laid. Poor, troubled, lyric ghost,
Spring never was so fair and dear
As Beauty makes her seem this year.   10

I cannot hold my peace, John Keats,
I am as helpless in the toil
Of Spring as any lamb that bleats
To feel the solid earth recoil

[1]Spring 1924.

Beneath his puny legs. Spring beats   15
Her tocsin call to those who love her,
And lo! the dogwood petals cover
Her breast with drifts of snow, and sleek
White gulls fly screaming to her, and hover
About her shoulders, and kiss her cheek,   20
While white and purple lilacs muster
A strength that bears them to a cluster
Of color and odor; for her sake
All things that slept are now awake.

And you and I, shall we lie still,   25
John Keats, while Beauty summons us?
Somehow I feel your sensitive will
Is pulsing up some tremulous
Sap road of a maple tree, whose leaves
Grow music as they grow, since your   30
Wild voice is in them, a harp that grieves
For life that opens death's dark door.
Though dust, your fingers still can push
The Vision Splendid to a birth,
Though now they work as grass in the hush   35
Of the night on the broad sweet page of the earth.

"John Keats is dead," they say, but I
Who hear your full insistent cry
In bud and blossom, leaf and tree,
Know John Keats still writes poetry.   40
And while my head is earthward bowed
To read new life sprung from your shroud,
Folks seeing me must think it strange
That merely spring should so derange
My mind. They do not know that you,   45
John Keats, keep revel with me, too.

STERLING BROWN (1901–1989)

Originally from Washington, D.C., Sterling Brown earned a degree in 1922 from Williams College and an M.A. in 1923 from Harvard University. He immersed himself in African American folk culture and literature for several years after moving to the South to teach. Later he returned to Washington to teach at Howard University. His collection of poetry, Southern Road *(1932), testified to his interest in Southern folk culture and experience. Poems such as "Old Lem" reveal the depth of his commitment to rendering black folk dialect while protesting racial discrimination in America. In addition to creative work, he wrote textbooks on African American literature, such as* The Negro in

American Fiction (1937) and Negro Poetry and Drama *(1937). He also served as co-editor of* The Negro Caravan *(1941), an anthology of African American literature. In 1984, he was named poet laureate of Washington, D.C. He died of cancer in 1989.*

Odyssey of Big Boy (1927)

Lemme be wid Casey Jones,
 Lemme be wid Stagolee,
Lemme be wid such like men
 When Death takes hol' on me,
  When Death takes hol' on me. . . .   5

Done skinned as a boy in Kentucky hills,
 Druv steel dere as a man,
Done stripped tobacco in Virginia fiel's
 Alongst de River Dan,
  Alongst de River Dan;   10

Done mined de coal in West Virginia,
 Liked dat job jes' fine,
Till a load o' slate curved roun' my head,
 Won't work in no mo' mine,
  Won't work in no mo' mine;   15

Done shocked de corn in Marylan',
 In Georgia done cut cane,
Done planted rice in South Caline,
 But won't do dat again,
  Do dat no mo' again.   20

Been roustabout in Memphis,
 Dockhand in Baltimore,
Done smashed up freight on Norfolk wharves,
 A fust class stevedore,
  A fust class stevedore. . . .   25

Done slung hash yonder in de North
 On de ole Fall River Line,
Done busted suds in li'l New York,
 Which ain't no work o' mine—
  Lawd, ain't no work o' mine.   30

Done worked and loafed on such like jobs,
 Seen what dey is to see,
Done had my time wid a pint on my hip
 An' a sweet gal on my knee,
  Sweet mommer on my knee: 35

Had stovepipe blond in Macon,
  Yaller gal in Marylan',
In Richmond had a choklit brown,
  Called me huh monkey man—
    Huh big fool monkey man.   40

Had two fair browns in Arkansaw
  And three in Tennessee,
Had Creole gal in New Orleans,
  Sho Gawd did two time me—
    Lawd two time, fo' time me—   45

But best gal what I evah had
  Done put it over dem,
A gal in Southwest Washington
  At Four'n half and M—
    Four'n half and M. . . .   50

Done took my livin' as it came,
  Done grabbed my joy, done risked my life;
Train done caught me on de trestle,
  Man done caught me wid his wife,
    His doggone purty wife. . . .   55

I done had my women,
  I done had my fun;
Cain't do much complainin'
  When my jag is done,
    Lawd, Lawd, my jag is done.   60

An' all dat Big Boy axes
  When time comes fo' to go,
Lemme be wid John Henry, steel drivin' man,
  Lemme be wid old Jazzbo,
    Lemme be wid ole Jazzbo. . . .   65

Old Lem (1980)

I talked to old Lem
and old Lem said:
    "They weigh the cotton
    They store the corn
        We only good enough   5
        To work the rows;
    They run the commissary
    They keep the books
        We gotta be grateful
        For being cheated;   10

Whippersnapper clerks
Call us out of our name
    We got to say mister
    To spindling boys
They make our figgers   15
Turn somersets
We buck in the middle
    Say, "Thankyuh, sah."
        They don't come by ones
        They don't come by twos   20
        But they come by tens.

"They got the judges
They got the lawyers
They got the jury-rolls
They got the law   25
    They don't come by ones
They got the sheriffs
They got the deputies
        They don't come by twos
They got the shotguns   30
They got the rope
    We git the justice
    In the end
        And they come by tens.

"Their fists stay closed   35
Their eyes look straight
    Our hands stay open
    Our eyes must fall
        They don't come by ones
They got the manhood   40
They got the courage
        They don't come by twos
    We got to slink around
    Hangtailed hounds.
They burn us when we dogs   45
They burn us when we men
        They come by tens . . .

"I had a buddy
Six foot of man
Muscled up perfect   50
Game to the heart
        They don't come by ones
Outworked and outfought
Any man or two men

They don't come by twos   55
He spoke out of turn
At the commissary
They gave him a day
To git out the county
He didn't take it.   60
He said 'Come and get me.'
They came and got him
        And they came by tens.
He stayed in the county—
        He lays there dead.   65

They don't come by ones
They don't come by twos
But they come by tens."

Memphis Blues (1931)

1

Nineveh, Tyre,
Babylon,
Not much lef'
Of either one.
All dese cities   5
Ashes and rust,
De win' sing sperrichals
Through deir dus'. . . .
Was another Memphis
Mongst de olden days,   10
Done been destroyed
In many ways. . . .
Dis here Memphis
It may go;
Floods may drown it;   15
Tornado blow;
Mississippi wash it
Down to sea—
Like de other Memphis in
History.   20

2

Watcha gonna do when Memphis on fire,
   Memphis on fire, Mistah Preachin' Man?

Gonna pray to Jesus and nebber tire,
   Gonna pray to Jesus, loud as I can,
      Gonna pray to my Jesus, oh, my Lawd!   25

Watcha gonna do when de tall flames roar,
   Tall flames roar, Mistah Lovin' Man?
Gonna love my brownskin better'n before—
   Gonna love my baby lak a do right man,
      Gonna love my brown baby, oh, my Lawd!   30

Watcha gonna do when Memphis falls down,
   Memphis falls down, Mistah Music Man?
Gonna plunk on dat box as long as it soun',
   Gonna plunk dat box fo' to beat de ban',
      Gonna tickle dem ivories, oh, my Lawd!   35

Watcha gonna do in de hurricane,
   In de hurricane, Mistah Workin' Man?
Gonna put dem buildings up again,
   Gonna put em up dis time to stan',
      Gonna push a wicked wheelbarrow, oh, my Lawd!   40

Watcha gonna do when Memphis near gone,
   Memphis near gone, Mistah Drinkin' Man?
Gonna grab a pint bottle of Mountain Corn,
   Gonna keep de stopper in my han',
      Gonna get a mean jag on, oh, my Lawd!   45

Watcha gonna do when de flood roll fas',
   Flood roll fas', Mistah Gamblin' Man?
Gonna pick up my dice fo' one las' pass—
   Gonna fade my way to de lucky lan',
      Gonna throw my las' seven—oh, my Lawd!   50

3

Memphis go
By Flood or Flame;
Nigger won't worry
All de same—
Memphis go   55
Memphis come back,
Ain' no skin
Off de nigger's back.
All dese cities
Ashes, rust. . . .   60
De win' sing sperrichals
Through deir dus'.

❀ MARITA BONNER (1899–1971)

Like many of her female contemporaries in the Harlem Renaissance, such as Jessie Redmon Fauset, Nella Larsen, and Zora Neale Hurston, Bonner sought to examine the lives of black women in relation to race, class, and gender politics. A native of Boston, Bonner studied writing at Radcliffe College, where she earned a degree in 1922. Later, she relocated to Washington, D.C., to work as a teacher at Armstrong High School. Her essay "On Being Young—a Woman—and Colored" was published in a 1925 issue of The Crisis. *She was an accomplished playwright. Her works—such as* The Purple Flower *(1928)—reveal a proletarian aesthetic in her critique of racism, and she calls for a revolution to end racial oppression of blacks. Her work focuses on the fact that African Americans had not achieved freedom from racial discrimination in post-slavery America. Although she wrote less prolifically after marrying William Occomy in 1930 and having several children, she continued to write as a means of expression.*

The Purple Flower (1928)

TIME   *The Middle-of-Things-as-They-are.*

[Which means the End-of-Things for some of the characters and the Beginning-of-Things for others.]

PLACE   *Might be here, there or anywhere—or even nowhere.*

Characters

SUNDRY WHITE DEVILS.   *[They must be artful little things with soft wide eyes such as you would expect to find in an angel. Soft hair that flops around their horns. Their horns glow red all the time—now with blood—now with eternal fire—now with deceit—now with unholy desire. They have bones tied carefully across their tails to make them seem less like tails and more like mere decorations. They are artful little things full of artful movements and artful tricks. They are artful dancers too. You are amazed at their adroitness. Their steps are intricate. You almost lose your head following them. Sometimes they dance as if they were men—with dignity—erect. Sometimes they dance as if they were snakes. They are artful dancers on the Thin-Skin-of-Civilization.]*

THE US'S.   *[They can be as white as the White Devils, as brown as the earth, as black as the center of a poppy. They may look as if they were something or nothing.]*

SETTING   *The stage is divided horizontally into two sections, upper and lower, by a thin board. The main action takes place on the upper stage. The light is never quite clear on the lower stage; but it is bright enough for you to perceive that sometimes the action that takes place on the upper stage is duplicated on the lower. Sometimes the actors on the upper stage get too vociferous—too violent—and they crack through the boards and they lie twisted and curled in mounds. There are any number of mounds there, all twisted and broken. You look at them and you are not quite sure whether you see something or nothing; but you see by a curve that there might lie a human body. There is thrust out a white hand—a yellow one—one brown—a black. The Skin-of-Civilization must be very thin. A thought can drop you through it.*

SCENE *An open plain. It is bounded distantly on one side by Nowhere and faced by a high hill—Somewhere.*

ARGUMENT *The* WHITE DEVILS *live on the side of the hill. Somewhere. On top of the hill grows the purple Flower-of-Life-at-Its-Fullest. This flower is as tall as a pine and stands alone on top of the hill. The* US's *live in the valley that lies between Nowhere and Somewhere and spend their time trying to devise means of getting up the hill. The* WHITE DEVILS *live all over the sides of the hill and try every trick, known and unknown, to keep the* US's *from getting to the hill. For if the* US's *get up the hill, the Flower-of-Life-at-Its-Fullest will shed some of its perfume and then and there they will be Somewhere with the* WHITE DEVILS. *The* US's *started out by merely asking permission to go up. They tilled the valley, they cultivated it and made it as beautiful as it is. They built roads and houses even for the* WHITE DEVILS. *They let them build the houses and then they were knocked back down into the valley.*

SCENE *When the curtain rises, the evening sun is shining bravely on the valley and hillside alike.*

The US's *are having a siesta beside a brook that runs down the Middle of the valley. As usual they rest with their backs toward Nowhere and their faces toward Somewhere. The* WHITE DEVILS *are seen in the distance on the hillside. As you see them, a song is borne faintly to your ears from the hillside.*

The WHITE DEVILS *are saying:*

You stay where you are!
We don't want you up here!
If you come you'll be on par
With all we hold dear.
So stay—stay—stay—
Yes stay where you are!

(The song rolls full across the valley)

A LITTLE RUNTY US. Hear that, don't you?

ANOTHER US. *(lolling over on his back and chewing a piece of grass)* I ain't studying 'bout them devils. When I get ready to go up that hill—I'm going! *(he rolls over on his side and exposes a slender brown body to the sun)* Right now, I'm going to sleep. *(and he forthwith snores)*

OLD LADY. *(an old dark brown lady who has been lying down rises suddenly to her knees in the foreground. She gazes toward the hillside)* I'll never live to see the face of that flower! God knows I worked hard to get Somewhere though. I've washed the shirt off of every one of them White Devils' backs!

A YOUNG US. And you got a slap in the face for doing it.

OLD LADY. But that's what the Leader told us to do. "Work," he said. "Show them you know how." As if two hundred years of slavery had not showed them!

ANOTHER YOUNG US. Work doesn't do it. The Us who work for the White Devils get pushed in the face—down off of Somewhere every night. They don't even sleep up there.

OLD LADY. Something's got to be done though! The Us ain't got no business to sleep while the sun is shining. They'd ought to be up and working before the White Devils get to some other tricks.

YOUNG US. You just said work did not do you any good! What's the need of working if it doesn't get you anywhere? What's the use of boring around in the same hole like a worm? Making the hole bigger to stay in?

(There comes up the road a clatter of feet and four figures, a middle-aged well-browned man, a lighter-browned middle-aged woman, a medium light brown girl, beautiful as a browned peach and a slender, tall, bronzy brown youth who walks with his head high. He touches the ground with his feet as if it were a velvet rug and not sunbaked, jagged rocks)

OLD LADY. *(addressing the* OLDER MAN*)* Evenin', Average. I was just saying we ain't never going to make that hill.

AVERAGE. The Us will if they get the right leaders.

THE MIDDLE-AGED WOMAN—CORNERSTONE. Leaders! Leaders! They've had good ones looks like to me.

AVERAGE. But they ain't led us anywhere!

CORNERSTONE. But that is not their fault! If one of them gets up and says, "Do this," one of the Us will sneak up behind him and knock him down and stand up and holler, "Do that," and then he himself gets knocked down and we still sit in the valley and knock down and drag out!

A YOUNG US. *(aside)* Yeah! Drag Us out, but not White Devils.

OLD LADY. It's the truth Cornerstone. They say they going to meet this evening to talk about what we ought to do.

AVERAGE. What is the need of so much talking?

CORNERSTONE. Better than not talking! Somebody might say something after while.

THE YOUNG GIRL—SWEET. *(who just came up)* I want to talk too!

AVERAGE. What can you talk about?

SWEET. Things! Something, father!

THE YOUNG MAN—FINEST BLOOD. I'll speak too.

AVERAGE. Oh you all make me tired! Talk—talk—talk—talk! And the flower is still up on the hillside!

OLD LADY. Yes and the White Devils are still talking about keeping the Us away from it, too.

(A drum begins to beat in the distance. All the US *stand up and shake off their sleep. The drummer, a short, black, determined looking* US*, appears around the bushes beating the drum with strong, vigorous jabs that make the whole valley echo and re-echo with rhythm. Some of the* US *begin to dance in time to the music)*

AVERAGE. Look at that! Dancing!! The Us will never learn to be sensible!

CORNERSTONE. They dance well! Well!!

(The US *all congregate at the center front. Almost naturally, the* YOUNG US *range on one side, the* OLD US *on the other.* CORNERSTONE *sits her plump brown self comfortably in the center of the stage. An* OLD US *tottering with age and blind comes toward her)*

OLD US. What's it this time, chillun? Is it day yet? Can you see the road to that flower?

AVERAGE. Oh you know we ain't going to get up there! No use worrying!

CORNERSTONE. No, it's not day! It is still dark. It is night. *(for the sun has gone and purple blackness has lain across the Valley. Somehow, though, you can see the shape of the flower on top of Somewhere. Lights twinkle on the hill)*

OLD US. *(speaking as if to himself)* I'm blind from working—building for the White Devils in the heat of the noon-day sun and I'm weary!

CORNERSTONE. Lean against me so they won't crowd you.

(An OLD MAN rises in the back of the ranks; his beard reaches down to his knees but he springs upright. He speaks)

OLD MAN. I want to tell you all something! The Us can't get up the road unless we work! We want to hew and dig and toil!

A YOUNG US. You had better sit down before someone knocks you down! They told us that when your beard was sprouting.

CORNERSTONE. *(to* YOUTH*)* Do not be so stupid! Speak as if you had respect for that beard!

ANOTHER YOUNG US. We have! But we get tired of hearing "you must work" when we know the Old Us built practically every inch of that hill and are yet Nowhere.

FIRST YOUNG US. Yes, all they got was a rush down the hill—not a chance to take a step up!

CORNERSTONE. It was not time then.

OLD MAN. *(on the back row)* Here comes a Young Us who has been reading in the books! He'll tell us what the books say about getting Somewhere.

(A YOUNG MAN *pushes through the crowd. As soon as he reaches the center front, he throws a bundle of books)*

YOUNG MAN. I'm through! I do not need these things! They're no good!

OLD MAN. *(pushes up from the back and stands beside him)* You're through! Ain't you been reading in the books how to get Somewhere? Why don't you tell us how to get there?

YOUNG MAN. I'm through, I tell you! There isn't anything in one of these books that tells Black Us how to get around White Devils.

OLD MAN. *(softly—sadly)* I thought the books would tell us how!

YOUNG MAN. No! The White Devils wrote the books themselves. You know they aren't going to put anything like that in there!

YET ANOTHER OLD MAN. *(throwing back his head and calling into the air)* Lord! Why don't you come by here and tell us how to get Somewhere?

A YOUNG MAN. *(who had been idly chewing grass)* Aw, you ought to know by now that isn't the way to talk to God!

OLD MAN. It ain't! It ain't! It ain't! It ain't! Ain't I been talking to God just like that for seventy years? Three score and ten years—Amen!

THE GRASS CHEWER. Yes! Three score and ten years you been telling God to tell you what to do. Telling Him! And three score and ten years you been wearing your spine double sitting on the rocks in the valley too.

OLD US. He is all powerful! He will move in his own time!

YOUNG US. Well, if he is all powerful, God does not need you to tell Him what to do.

OLD US. Well, what's the need of me talkin' to Him then?

YOUNG US. Don't talk so much to Him! Give Him a chance! He might want to talk to you but you do so much yelling in His ears that He can't tell you anything.

(There is a commotion in the back stage. SWEET *comes running to* CORNERSTONE *crying)*

SWEET. Oh—oo—!

CORNERSTONE. What is it, Sweet?

SWEET. There's a White Devil sitting in the bushes in the dark over there! There's a White Devil sitting in the bushes over in the dark! And when I walked by—he pinched me!

FINEST BLOOD. *(catching a rock)* Where is he, sister? *(he starts toward the bushes)*

CORNERSTONE. *(screaming)* Don't go after him son! They will kill you if you hurt him!

FINEST BLOOD. I don't care if they do. Let them. I'd be out of this hole then!

AVERAGE. Listen to that young fool! Better stay safe and sound where he is! At least he got somewhere to eat and somewhere to lay his head.

FINEST BLOOD. Yes I can lay my head on the rocks of Nowhere.

(Up the center of the stage toils a new figure of a square set middle-aged US. *He walks heavily for in each hand he carries a heavy bag. As soon as he reaches the center front he throws the bags down groaning as he does so)*

AN OLD MAN. 'Smatter with you! Ain't them bags full of gold?

THE NEW COMER. Yes, they are full of gold!

OLD MAN. Well why ain't you smiling then? Them White Devils can't have anything no better!

THE NEW COMER. Yes they have! They have Somewhere! I tried to do what they said. I brought them money, but when I brought it to them they would not sell me even a spoonful of dirt from Somewhere! I'm through!

CORNERSTONE. Don't be through. The gold counts for something. It must!

(An OLD WOMAN *cries aloud in a quavering voice from the back)*

OLD LADY. Last night I had a dream.

A YOUNG US. Dreams? Excuse me! I know I'm going now! Dreams!!

OLD LADY. I dreamed that I saw a White Devil cut in six pieces—head there, *(pointing)* body here—one leg here—one there—an arm here—an arm there.

AN OLD MAN. Thank God! It's time then!

AVERAGE. Time for what? Time to eat? Sure ain't time to get Somewhere!

OLD MAN. *(walking forward)* It's time! It's time! Bring me an iron pot!

YOUNG US. Aw don't try any conjuring!

OLD MAN. *(louder)* Bring me a pot of iron. Get the pot from the fire in the valley.

CORNERSTONE. Give him the pot!

(Someone brings it up immediately)

OLD MAN. (*walking toward pot slowly*) Old Us! Do you hear me? Old Us that are here do you hear me?

ALL THE OLD US. (*cry in chorus*) Yes, Lord! We hear you! We hear you!

OLD MAN. (*crying louder and louder*) Old Us! Old Us! Old Us that are gone, Old Us that are dust do you hear me? (*his voice sounds strangely through the valley. Somewhere you think you hear—as if mouthed by ten million mouths through rocks and dust—"Yes!—Lord!—We hear you! We hear you!"*)

OLD MAN. And you hear me—give me a handful of dust! Give me a handful of dust! Dig down to the depths of the things you have made! The things you formed with your hands and give me a handful of dust!

(*An* OLD WOMAN *tottering with the weakness of old age crosses the stage and going to the pot, throws a handful of dust in. Just before she sits down again she throws back her head and shakes her cane in the air and laughs so that the entire valley echoes*)

A YOUNG US. What's the trouble? Choking on the dust?

OLD WOMAN. No child! Rejoicing!

YOUNG US. Rejoicing over a handful of dust?

OLD WOMAN. Yes. A handful of dust! Thanking God I could do something if it was nothing but make a handful of dust!

YOUNG US. Well, dust isn't much!

OLD MAN. (*at the pot*) Yes, it isn't much! You are dust yourself; but so is she. Like everything else, though, dust can be little or much, according to where it is.

(*The* YOUNG US *who spoke subsides. He subsides so completely that he crashes through the Thin-Skin-of-Civilization. Several of his group go too. They were thinking*)

OLD MAN. (*at the pot*) Bring me books! Bring me books!

YOUNG US. (*who threw books down*) Here! Take all these! I'll light the fire with them.

OLD MAN. No, put them in the pot. (YOUNG US *does so*) Bring me gold!

THE MAN OF THE GOLD BAGS. Here take this! It is just as well. Stew it up and make teething rings!! (*he pours it into the pot*)

OLD MAN. Now bring me blood! Blood from the eyes, the ears, the whole body! Drain it off and bring me blood! (*No one speaks or moves*) Ah hah, hah! I knew it! Not one of you willing to pour his blood in the pot!

YOUNG US. (*facetiously*) How you going to pour your own blood in there? You got to be pretty far gone to let your blood run in there. Somebody else would have to do the pouring.

OLD MAN. I mean red blood. Not yellow blood, thank you.

FINEST BLOOD. (*suddenly*) Take my blood! (*he walks toward the pot*)

CORNERSTONE. O no! Not my boy! Take me instead!

OLD MAN. Cornerstone we cannot stand without you!

AN OLD WOMAN. What you need blood for? What you doing anyhow? You ain't told us nothing yet. What's going on in that pot?

OLD MAN. I'm doing as I was told to do.

A YOUNG US. Who told you to do anything?

OLD MAN. God. I'm His servant.

Young Us. *(who spoke before)* God? I haven't heard God tell you anything.

Old Man. You couldn't hear. He told it to me alone.

Old Woman. I believe you. Don't pay any attention to that simpleton! What God told you to do?

Old Man. He told me take a handful of dust—dust from which all things came and put it in a hard iron pot. Put it in a hard iron pot. Things shape best in hard molds!! Put in books that Men learn by. Gold that Men live by. Blood that lets Men live.

Young Us. What you suppose to be shaping? A man?

Old Us. I'm the servant. I can do nothing. If I do this, God will shape a new man Himself.

Young Man. What's the things in the pot for?

Old Man. To show I can do what I'm told.

Old Woman. Why does He want blood?

Old Man. You got to give blood! Blood has to be let for births, to give life.

Old Woman. So the dust wasn't just nothing? Thank God!

Youth. Then the books were not just paper leaves? Thank God!

The Man of the Gold Bags. Can the gold mean something?

Old Man. Now I need the blood.

Finest Blood. I told you you could take mine.

Old Man. Yours!

Finest Blood. Where else could you get it? The New Man must be born. The night is already dark. We cannot stay here forever. Where else could blood come from?

Old Man. Think child. When God asked a faithful servant once to do sacrifice, even his only child, where did God put the real meat for sacrifice when the servant had the knife upon the son's throat?

Old Us. *(in a chorus)*

In the bushes, Lord!
In the bushes, Lord!
Jehovah put the ram
In the bushes!

Cornerstone. I understand!

Finest Blood. What do you mean?

Cornerstone. Where were you going a little while ago? Where were you going when your sister cried out?

Finest Blood. To the bushes! You want me to get the White Devil? *(he seizes the piece of rock and stands to his feet)*

Old Man. No! No! Not that way. The White Devils are full of tricks. You must go differently. Bring him gifts and offer them to him.

Finest Blood. What have I to give for a gift?

Old Man. There are the pipes of Pan that every Us is born with. Play on that. Soothe him—lure him—make him yearn for the pipe. Even a White Devil will soften at music. He'll come out, and he only comes to try to get the pipe from you.

FINEST BLOOD. And when he comes out, I'm to kill him in the dark before he sees me? That's a White Devil trick!

OLD MAN. An Old Us will never tell you to play White Devil's games! No! Do not kill him in the dark. Get him out of the bushes and say to him: "White Devil, God is using me for His instrument. You think that it is I who play on this pipe! You think that it is I who play upon this pipe so that you cannot stay in your bushes. So that you must come out of your bushes. But it is not I who play. It is not I, it is God who plays through me—to you. Will you hear what He says? Will you hear? He says it is almost day, White Devil. The night is far gone. A New Man must be born for the New Day. Blood is needed for birth. Blood is needed for the birth. Come out, White Devil. It may be your blood— it may be mine—but blood must be taken during the night to be given at the birth. It may be my blood—it may be your blood—but everything has been given. The Us toiled to give dust for the body, books to guide the body, gold to clothe the body. Now they need blood for birth so the New Man can live. You have taken blood. You must give blood. Come out! Give it." And then fight him!

FINEST BLOOD. I'll go! And if I kill him?

OLD MAN. Blood will be given!

FINEST BLOOD. And if he kills me?

OLD MAN. Blood will be given!

FINEST BLOOD. Can there be no other way—cannot this cup pass?

OLD MAN. No other way. It cannot pass. They always take blood. They built up half their land on our bones. They ripened crops of cotton, watering them with our blood. Finest Blood, this is God's decree: "You take blood—you give blood. Full measure—flooding full—over—over!"

FINEST BLOOD. I'll go. (*he goes quickly into the shadow. Far off soon you can hear him—his voice lifted, young, sweet, brave and strong*) White Devil! God speaks to you through me!—Hear Him!—Him! You have taken blood; there can be no other way. You will have to give blood! Blood!

(*All the* US *listen. All the valley listens. Nowhere listens. All the* WHITE DEVILS *listen. Somewhere listens.*

Let the curtain close leaving all the US*, the* WHITE DEVILS*, Nowhere, Somewhere, listening, listening. It is time?*)

CURTAIN

ARNA BONTEMPS (1902–1973)

Arna Bontemps was born in Alexandria, Louisiana, but his family moved to California about three years later. After earning a degree in 1923 from Pacific Union College, Bontemps accepted a position as a teacher in Harlem. By 1926, he had wed Alberta Johnson. His powerful poetry had attracted individuals such as W. E. B. Du Bois, gaining him acceptance in the community. God Sends Sunday, *a novel, was published in 1931, and shortly after, Bontemps accepted college teaching positions in the South and Midwest. He was awarded an M.A. in library science by the University of Chicago in 1945, and he worked in the Fisk University Library in Nashville, Tennessee, for the next twenty years. He died of complications from a heart attack in 1973.*

Bontemps promoted African American literature and history through works such as The Book of Negro Folklore *(1958), co-edited with Langston Hughes. In poems such as "A Black Man Talks of Reaping," he protests racial inequities in America and holds out the promise of a day when justice and equality for all will prevail. His legacy of social consciousness continues in the poetry of individuals such as Maya Angelou, Amiri Baraka, and Sonia Sanchez.*

A Black Man Talks of Reaping (1926)

I have sown beside all waters in my day.
I planted deep, within my heart the fear
That wind or fowl would take the grain away.
I planted safe against this stark, lean year.

I scattered seed enough to plant the land   5
In rows from Canada to Mexico,
But for my reaping only what the hand
Can hold at once is all that I can show.

Yet what I sowed and what the orchard yields
My brother's sons are gathering stalk and root,   10
Small wonder then my children glean in fields
They have not sown, and feed on bitter fruit.

Close Your Eyes! (1963)

Go through the gates with closed eyes.
Stand erect and let your black face front the west.
Drop the axe and leave the timber where it lies;
A woodman on the hill must have his rest.

Go where leaves are lying brown and wet.   5
Forget her warm arms and her breast who mothered you,
And every face you ever loved forget.
Close your eyes; walk bravely through.

THE HARLEM RENAISSANCE (1900–1940)

Topics for Research

1. Define the New Negro and address how writers in the Harlem Renaissance support this concept in their writing. Are there any works from the pre–Harlem Renaissance period that also illustrate the concept of the New Negro? If so, how and why do they connect with works of the Harlem Renaissance era?

2. The Harlem Renaissance represents a period of rapid migration and movement for blacks. Examine the theme of migration in these texts. The migration may be physical, artistic, emotional, or spiritual.

3. As African American writers sought to define their role in society, they often looked to Africa as a site of their heritage. Compare and contrast the use of Africa as a symbol for the theme of slavery versus freedom in literature of the Harlem Renaissance period.

4. The novel or story of passing functions as a vehicle for meditating on race relations in America—interracial and intraracial—during the Harlem Renaissance. Compare and contrast stories and/or novels of passing. How and why do these works examine intraracial and interracial race relations? Are the texts' examinations of race relevant to life today? Why? Why not?

5. Analyze the oral tradition in writing during the Harlem Renaissance period. How do the works in the oral tradition reflect key social, political, economic, or artistic aims of the Harlem Renaissance?

PART 5

THE PROTEST MOVEMENT
1940–1959

INTRODUCTION

AFRICAN AMERICAN LITERATURE HAS ALWAYS PROVIDED A FORUM for the concerns of African American people, commonly addressing the theme of slavery versus freedom. The central concern of this literature, if one can be identified, is to eliminate racism, an institution that has persisted over the years in different forms and to various degrees, depending on the historical period. African American writers since colonial times have used their voices in written and spoken form to protest racial discrimination—telling their stories to assert the only form of power they had. They used writing, a freedom previously denied them, to publish slave narratives, poetry, letters, essays, and speeches, attempting to convince primarily white audiences of the evils of slavery and of the high quality and unquestionable validity of black writing. Through the skillful employment of rhetorical strategies, African American writers have persuaded audiences with overt and covert protest—from the days of slavery to the Harlem Renaissance to the civil rights movement and beyond. Hence, African American protest literature is not limited to the selections included in this book.

Earlier African American literature paved the way for the protest literature published from 1940 to 1959—a period in which African American writers expanded on the authenticity established by their forerunners to give voice to racial protest. The political scene had much in common with the literary scene for African Americans. Economically, the country was trying to recuperate from the Depression, which devastated the lives of most Americans, especially African Americans, who experienced a much worse economic situation than whites. The economic can never be separated from the political and social, certainly not for African Americans at this, or any, time in history. Without economic support, African American writers had difficulty obtaining funds that would allow them to develop their writing careers. In large part, the reading public was still not ready to embrace literature that focused on the African American experience. Literature with protest as a purpose was especially distasteful to white readers who were not ready to face the realities of racism.

The racial issues of World War I remained issues in World War II. African Americans still fought in segregated units, and there was still tension and hostility between black soldiers and white soldiers; some white civilians also despised black soldiers. In spite of the racial conflicts, more than a million African Americans were drafted into the armed forces. For the first time, in World War II, African Americans could serve in the Marines, the Navy, and the Air Force. To protest segregation and discrimination in the armed forces, African Americans rioted for equal rights. A. Philip Randolph helped to bring about equal treatment in the military. He threatened President Roosevelt with a march on Washington if the needs of blacks were not met. To calm some of the protests, Roosevelt issued an Executive Order to end discrimination against African Americans in the military. Because the president acquiesced, Randolph did not go through with the march on Washington as planned.

Much of the protest of this period took the form of direct, but nonviolent, action such as sit-in demonstrations. The Congress of Racial Equality (CORE) was the organization behind these protests. Protests against racial injustices were also made by African American publications such the *Atlanta Daily World*, the Norfolk *Journal and Guide*, the *Pittsburgh Courier*, the *Chicago Defender*, and the *Baltimore Afro-American*. Articles in the African American press were instrumental in ending racial discrimination in the armed forces. Other publications helped to promote a climate of racial pride for African Americans. John H. Johnson, who started *Negro Digest*, *Ebony*, and *Jet*, in Chicago, presented positive images of black Americans in his publications.

African American literature published during this historical period embodies the racial concerns of the time—being closely linked to major events, movements, and people. In 1940, Marcus Garvey, head of the Universal Negro Improvement Association, leader of the Back to Africa campaign, and advocate of racial separatism, died. After his death, his movement began to decline. Garvey's rhetoric of separatism had widespread influence on the African American community, experiencing the strongest surge of support in the 1920s. The end of the Garvey movement led to more inclusive, less militant rhetoric by African American leaders and writers. Black authors at this time wrote about themes related to the African American experience, usually discussing slavery versus freedom; however, the underlying literary expression sent messages of desired freedom and equality. Garvey's separatist philosophy persisted in literature that focused on African American cultural expression and insisted on a place for black Americans in all aspects of United States citizenship, having all the rights and privileges of white Americans. African American writers were more concerned about how to live in this country with whites rather than moving to Africa to escape racism. The double consciousness identified by W. E. B. Du Bois in *The Souls of Black Folk* (pp. 168–181), written during the Harlem Renaissance, revealed the complexity of the African Americans' existence in the United States. One of the best-known quotations from his book explains what Du Bois meant by the term *double consciousness:* "One ever feels his two-ness,—an American, a Negro; two souls, two thoughts, two unreconciled strivings, two warring ideals in one dark body, whose dogged strength alone keeps it from being torn asunder". As the literature of protest shows, equality is often conditional, dependent on factors such as race, gender, and ethnicity.

With her poetry, Margaret Walker expresses pride in African American culture. She reveals the harsh realities of racial oppression against blacks and reinforces the sense of hope that has sustained the movement towards freedom. In "For My People" (1942) (pp. 473–475), one of her most noted poems, she explains the hardship African Americans have endured and offers praises and encouragement. Walker's poetry provides inspiration for racial protest.

Ann Petry's novel *The Street* (pp. 476–483) is a good example of literature as a vehicle of protest. Within the text, Petry reveals the problems of African American women in the inner city—a topic that black writers had not previously dealt with in depth. Lutie Johnson, the novel's protagonist, lives in a hostile environment in Harlem but struggles to overcome the obstacles she faces as an urban black mother. Racial tension divides the people in the Harlem community and causes them to commit criminal acts against each other. More than any other force, the environment is the antagonist for Lutie Johnson. Aspects of the environment work against her; not only does she suffer because of what is *not* available to her, but what *is* present makes her plight more difficult. Petry portrays a culture whose people lack support systems such as church, friends, and family. Yet black literature of the Harlem Renaissance and earlier shows that in spite of the difficulties caused by racism, black people relied on the support of other blacks, and their strong spiritual foundation helped them survive the storms. The dominant culture worked against black men by offering little support, preventing them from attaining economic advancement. However, social problems in the African American community, like poverty and broken homes, stemmed from racism more so than from troubled black men, such as Lutie's alcoholic father and unfaithful husband. Petry uses her experiences of living in Harlem and growing up in the only African American family in a small New England town to tell a story about negative environmental effects on a black mother. Petry's white characters help to show the effects of white power on black life.

Messages about racial inequality in protest literature of this period can be related to societal conditions of inequality, which persisted in the 1940s. The "separate but equal" policy had been established in the late nineteenth century with the *Plessy v. Ferguson* case. The NAACP was a strong working force that attempted to dismantle the Jim Crow structure and helped to overturn *Plessy v. Ferguson* by keeping the issue of segregation at the forefront of the political scene. *Plessy* was not declared unconstitutional until 1954, with the *Brown v. Board of Education of Topeka* case, which concluded that African American children lacked an equal opportunity to obtain a quality education because separate meant unequal. Thurgood Marshall, an attorney who later became the first African American justice on the Supreme Court, argued that segregation was discrimination and separate but equal was slavery; he was instrumental in winning the *Brown* case. The decision paved the way for integration of the public school system in the United States.

Richard Wright's literary contributions were also instrumental in the fight against racism. In contrast to Petry's black female protagonist, Wright's black men are controlled by their racist environments. Wright's upbringing in rural Mississippi did not include privilege; he grew up in extreme poverty, was abandoned by his father, and had a mother too ill to care for her children. He was sent to live with his grandmother in Jackson, Mississippi. Though he had little formal education, Wright wrote several novels and short stories that illustrated the way racism affected African American males. Wright's work protests the way black males are forced to act by a racist environment. In *Native Son* (pp. 483–492), published in 1940, the black male protagonist acts with murder provoked by fear and desperation—both emotions linked to his racial identity. These emotions are also stimuli for the actions of the protagonist of Wright's autobiography, *Black Boy* (pp. 528–543), which deals with his response to the cruelty of racist whites in the South. By revealing the emotions and actions of African American men controlled by their environments, Wright uses his writing to protest and persuade against racism, a form of slavery.

Ralph Ellison also deals with African American male identity in his best-known work, *Invisible Man* (pp. 553–559), published in 1952. He provides a close examination of the repression, degradation, and betrayal experienced by many black men during this time. He is a master of character development, often writing about the alienated black male engaged in a quest for self-identity. This theme is also found in *Shadow and Act* (1964), a collection of essays that presents Ellison's view of the importance of African American culture in the American experience. James Baldwin writes about African American male identity in similar ways. In *Go Tell It on the Mountain* (pp. 574–583), he presents African American male characters, showing how their experiences shape their identity. Among the topics explored in the text are the influence of religion on a young boy and the issues involved in a relationship between a son and his stepfather.

The 1950s were years of protest not only in literature but also in other aspects of society. In 1955, Rosa Parks, an NAACP officer, refused to give up her seat to a white man on a bus in Montgomery, Alabama. Her protest sparked a wave of reaction from other blacks, who responded to the racism of the era by boycotting the bus company and establishing the Montgomery Improvement Association (MIA). The U.S. Supreme Court found Montgomery's segregated public transit system unconstitutional. Martin Luther King, Jr., was elected president of the MIA, and in 1959 he formed the Southern Christian Leadership Conference (SCLC). In 1957, African American students set out to integrate Central High School in Little Rock, Arkansas. President Dwight D. Eisenhower sent soldiers to protect the black teenagers who enrolled in the school. Protests against inequality based on race, which were so much a part of society, were widely addressed in the black press of the time and in African American literature.

Poetry and drama were also vehicles for protest during this historical period. The two poets whose work is included in this section, Gwendolyn Brooks and Robert Hayden, were by no means the only poets during this time, but their work is known for its creative use of language and cultural themes. In fact, Brooks was the first black author to win a Pulitzer Prize. Like Petry, Brooks focuses on the experiences of inner-city African Americans—their ethical, racial, and economic struggles. Her poems, such as those in her 1949 volume, *Annie Allen*, often reveal the particular experiences of black women, as mothers, lovers, and friends, who are products of their environments of inequality and therefore poverty and despair. She also helps readers to understand the attitudes of inner-city blacks who attempt to gain status in the community through their street activities and tough demeanor. Like many other writers, Brooks turns to her own experiences, as a maid, in her only novel, *Maud Martha* (1953). However, she protests more strongly against racism and sexism in her poetry.

Hayden also uses his poetry to protest racism. "Middle Passage" (pp. 584–588) and "The Ballad of Nat Turner" (pp. 588–590) are two of Hayden's most renowned poems. Hayden's poetry gives readers a heavy dose of African American history. His political stance, however, is one of American, not African American, identity. Hayden wanted to be known as an American poet and not an African American poet. He attempted to use his works to bring human beings together, stressing unity of the races. However, in spite of his political views, Hayden's work contributed to African American protest writing because he dealt primarily with the black experience, from slavery to civil rights.

Likewise, Lorraine Hansberry protests racism in her 1959 play *A Raisin in the Sun* (pp. 594–657), a story about a struggling African American family. This was the first play by a black woman to be produced on Broadway. Much of the play is autobiographical; Hansberry's family, like the family in the play, moved to a predominantly white neighborhood in Chicago and endured racial harassment. Hansberry, like other African American protest writers, shows the negative effects of racism on blacks, whites, and the society at large. She especially shows how economic deprivation affects African Americans seeking the American Dream.

The African American oral tradition during this time expressed the despair of black citizens, who had little hope for the American Dream, with the blues. Some blues music emphasized the effects of racism by projecting negative emotions such as hopelessness. However, many blues singers sang about universal themes such as the downside of male-female relationships. Arthur "Big Boy" Crudup, a Mississippi Delta blues singer and one of the first blues artists to use an electric guitar, started rock and roll with "That's All Right, Mama." The opening lines of the song are the words of a man who is complaining about how his special woman treats him: "That's all right, Mama, / That's all right for you. / Treat me low down and dirty / Any old way you do." Elvis Presley was heavily influenced by Crudup and other black singers in and around Tupelo, Mississippi. The blues crossed racial barriers, appealing to a mixed audience. The African American experience is expressed through the blues; however, the music helped to bring the races together. Like black literature, the black music of this time countered racism.

𝔐 MARGARET WALKER ALEXANDER (1915–1998)

Margaret Walker Alexander was born in Birmingham, Alabama, and lived there until she was ten years old. Her family then moved to New Orleans, Louisiana, where she began writing. She earned a bachelor's degree from Northwestern University, in 1935, and both a Master of Arts degree (1940) and a Ph.D. in English (1965) from the University of Iowa. Walker (her married name, Alexander, is not generally used in her professional work) began her teaching career at Livingstone College in North Carolina in 1941 and was professor of English at Jackson State University in Jackson, Mississippi, from 1949 to 1979. While at Jackson State, Walker was director of the Institute for the Study of History, Life, and Culture of Black Peoples, an interdepartmental, interdisciplinary, and intercultural program established in 1968. The Institute sponsored many important seminars on African American literature, history, art, sociology, and anthropology.

Walker's first published book was a volume of poetry, For My People, *for which she won the Yale Series of Younger Poets Award for 1942. The title poem, "For My People," is one of the best known in the collection both nationally and internationally, and her novel,* Jubilee *(1966), was a best-seller. During her lifetime, Walker won many awards, including a Rosenthal fellowship (1944), a Ford fellowship for study at Yale (1954), a Houghton Mifflin Literary Fellowship (1966), a Fulbright fellowship (1971), and a fellowship from the National Endowment for the Humanities (1972). Walker's contributions to American literature have established her as a prominent literary artist and scholar. Her work embodies a celebration of African American culture, paying tribute to those who played a part in the struggle for racial equality. Other books published by Walker include* Prophets for a New Day *(1970),* October Journey *(1973),* Richard Wright, Daemonic Genius *(1988),* This Is My Century: New and Collected Poems by Margaret Walker *(1989), and* How I Wrote Jubilee *and Other Essays on Life and Literature (1990). In addition, she collaborated with Nikki Giovanni on* Poetic Equation: Conversations Between Nikki Giovanni and Margaret Walker *(1974).*

For My People (1942)

For my people everywhere singing their slave songs
    repeatedly: their dirges and their ditties and their blues
    and jubilees, praying their prayers nightly to an
    unknown god, bending their knees humbly to an
    unseen power;   5

For my people lending their strength to the years, to the
    gone years and the now years and the maybe years,
    washing ironing cooking scrubbing sewing mending
    hoeing plowing digging planting pruning patching
    dragging along never gaining never reaping never   10
    knowing and never understanding;

For my playmates in the clay and dust and sand of Alabama
    backyards playing baptizing and preaching and doctor

and jail and soldier and school and mama and cooking
and playhouse and concert and store and hair and Miss   15
Choomby and company;

For the cramped bewildered years we went to school to learn
to know the reasons why and the answers to and the
people who and the places where and the days when, in
memory of the bitter hours when we discovered we   20
were black and poor and small and different and nobody
cared and nobody wondered and nobody understood;

For the boys and girls who grew in spite of these things to
be man and woman, to laugh and dance and sing and
play and drink their wine and religion and success, to   25
marry their playmates and bear children and then die
of consumption and anemia and lynching;

For my people thronging 47th Street in Chicago and Lenox
Avenue in New York and Rampart Street in New
Orleans, lost disinherited dispossessed and happy   30
people filling the cabarets and taverns and other
people's pockets needing bread and shoes and milk and
land and money and something—something all our own;

For my people walking blindly spreading joy, losing time
being lazy, sleeping when hungry, shouting when   35
burdened, drinking when hopeless, tied, and shackled
and tangled among ourselves by the unseen creatures
who tower over us omnisciently and laugh;

For my people blundering and groping and floundering in
the dark of churches and schools and clubs and   40
societies, associations and councils and committees and
conventions, distressed and disturbed and deceived and
devoured by money-hungry glory-craving leeches,
preyed on by facile force of state and fad and novelty, by
false prophet and holy believer;   45

For my people standing staring trying to fashion a better way
from confusion, from hypocrisy and misunderstanding,
trying to fashion a world that will hold all the people,
all the faces, all the adams and eves and their countless
generations;   50

Let a new earth rise. Let another world be born. Let a
bloody peace be written in the sky. Let a second
generation full of courage issue forth; let a people
loving freedom come to growth. Let a beauty full of
healing and a strength of final clenching be the pulsing   55

in our spirits and our blood. Let the martial songs be
written, let the dirges disappear. Let a race of men now
rise and take control.

Ex-Slave (1942)

When I see you bending over something rare
   Like music, or a painting, or a book,
   And see within your eyes that vacant stare
   And halfway understand that pleading look;
   I cannot help but bitterly detest   5
   The age and men who made you what you are,
   Who robbed you of your all—your ample best—
   And left you seeking life across a hateful bar,
   And left you vainly searching for a star
   Your soul appreciates but cannot understand.   10

Lineage (1942)

My grandmothers were strong.
They followed plows and bent to toil.
They moved through fields sowing seed.
They touched earth and grain grew.
They were full of sturdiness and singing.   5
My grandmothers were strong.

My grandmothers are full of memories
Smelling of soap and onions and wet clay
With veins rolling roughly over quick hands
They have many clean words to say.   10
My grandmothers were strong.
Why am I not as they?

ANN PETRY (b. 1908)

At a time when African American writers were primarily writing about black characters, Ann Petry included white people in her writing, especially in her novel Country Place *(1947). She was born in Old Saybrook, Connecticut, so white people were an integral part of her world. She also depicted another world in her work: the urban ghetto of Harlem. After marrying George D. Petry in 1938, Petry moved to Harlem, where she worked as a journalist for the* Amsterdam News *and the* People's Voice. *The Harlem environment was a frequent topic in Petry's magazine articles. The social problems in Harlem disturbed Petry and stimulated her desire to study the effects of segregation on the children who were victims of inner-city life. The Street (1946) reflects Petry's experiences with racism and classism.*

After moving back to the middle-class New England town of her birth, she continued to deal with social influences in her writing. Petry wrote and published several other texts: The Narrows *(1953);* The Drugstore Cat *(1949), a children's book;* Harriet Tubman: Conductor on the Underground Railroad *(1955); and* Tituba of Salem Village *(1964), a book for young adults. Petry was one of the first successful African American women writers.*

From The Street (1946)

It was a cold, cheerless night. But in spite of the cold, the street was full of people. They stood on the corners talking, lounged half in and half out of hallways and on the stoops of the houses, looking at the street and talking. Some of them were coming home from work, from church meetings, from lodge meetings, and some of them were not coming from anywhere or going anywhere, they were merely deferring the moment when they would have to enter their small crowded rooms for the night.

In the middle of the block there was a sudden thrust of raw, brilliant light where the unshaded bulbs in the big poolroom reached out and pushed back the darkness. A group of men stood outside its windows watching the games going on inside. Their heads were silhouetted against the light.

Lutie, walking quickly through the block, glanced at them and then at the women coming toward her from Eighth Avenue. The women moved slowly. Their shoulders sagged from the weight of the heavy shopping bags they carried. And she thought, That's what's wrong. We don't have time enough or money enough to live like other people because the women have to work until they become drudges and the men stand by idle.

She made an impatient movement of her shoulders. She had no way of knowing that at fifty she wouldn't be misshapen, walking on the sides of her shoes because her feet hurt so badly; getting dressed up for church on Sunday and spending the rest of the week slaving in somebody's kitchen.

It could happen. Only she was going to stake out a piece of life for herself. She had come this far poor and black and shut out as though a door had been slammed in her face. Well, she would shove it open; she would beat and bang on it and push against it and use a chisel in order to get it open.

When she opened the street door of the apartment house, she was instantly aware of the silence that filled the hall. Mrs. Hedges had been quiet, too, for if she was sitting in her window she had given no indication of her presence.

There was no sound except for the steam hissing in the radiator. The silence and the dimly lit hallway and the smell of stale air depressed her. It was like a dead weight landing on her chest. She told herself that she mustn't put too much expectation in getting the singing job. Almost anything might happen to prevent it. Boots might change his mind.

She went up the stairs, thinking, But he can't. She wouldn't let him. It meant too much to her. It was a way out—the only way out of here and she and Bub had to get out.

On the third-floor landing she stopped. A man was standing in the hall. His back was turned toward her. She hesitated. It wasn't very late, but it was dark in the hall and she was alone.

He turned then and she saw that he had his arms wound tightly around a girl and he was pressed so close to her and was bending so far over her that they had given the effect of one figure. He wore a sailor's uniform and the collar of his jacket was turned high around his neck, for it was cold in the hall.

The girl looked to be about nineteen or twenty. She was very thin. Her black hair, thick with grease, gleamed in the dim light. There was an artificial white rose stuck in the center of the pompadour that mounted high above her small, dark face.

Lutie recognized her. It was Mary, one of the little girls who lived with Mrs. Hedges. The sailor gave Lutie a quick, appraising look and then turned back to the girl, blotting her out. The girl's thin arms went back around his neck.

'Mary,' Lutie said, and stopped right behind the sailor.

The girl's face appeared over the top of the sailor's shoulder.

'Hello,' she said sullenly.

'It's so cold out here,' Lutie said. 'Why don't you go inside?'

'Mis' Hedges won't let him come in no more,' Mary said. 'He's spent all his money. And she says she ain't in business for her health.'

'Can't you talk to him somewhere else? Isn't there a friend's house you could go to?'

'No, ma'am. Besides, it ain't no use, anyway. He's got to go back to his ship tonight.'

Lutie climbed the rest of the stairs fuming against Mrs. Hedges. The sailor would return to his ship carrying with him the memory of this dark narrow hallway and Mrs. Hedges and the thin resigned little girl. The street was full of young thin girls like this one with a note of resignation in their voices, with faces that contained no hope, no life. She shivered. She couldn't let Bub grow up in a place like this.

She put her key in the door quietly, trying to avoid the loud click of the lock being drawn back. She pushed the door open, mentally visualizing the trip across the living room to her bedroom. Once inside her room, she would close the door and put the light on and Bub wouldn't wake up. Then she saw that the lamp in the living room was lit and she shut the door noisily. He should have been asleep at least two hours ago, she thought, and walked toward the studio couch, her heels clicking on the congoleum rug.

Bub sat up and rubbed his eyes. For a moment she saw something frightened and fearful in his expression, but it disappeared when he looked at her.

'How come you're not in bed?' she demanded.

'I fell asleep.'

'With your clothes on?' she said, and then added: 'With the light on, too? You must be trying to make the bill bigger—' and she stopped abruptly. She was always talking to him about money. It wasn't good. He would be thinking about nothing else pretty soon. 'How was the movie?' she asked.

'It was swell,' he said eagerly. 'There was one guy who caught gangsters—'

'Skip it,' she interrupted, 'You get in bed in a hurry, Mister. I still don't know what you're doing up—' Her eyes fell on the ash tray on the blue-glass coffee table. It was filled with cigarette butts. That's funny. She had emptied all the trays when she washed the dinner dishes. She knew that she had. She looked closer at the cigarette ends. They were moist. Whoever had smoked them had held them, not between their lips, but far inside the mouth so that the paper got wet and the tobacco inside had stained and discolored it. She turned toward Bub.

'Supe was up.' Bub's eyes had followed hers. 'We played cards.'

'You mean he was in here?' she said sharply. And thought, Of course, dope, he didn't stand outside and throw his cigarette butts into the ash tray through a closed door.

'We played cards,' Bub said again.

'Let's get this straight once and for all.' She put her hands on his shoulders. 'When I'm not home, you're not to let anyone in here. Anyone. Understand?'

He nodded. 'Does that mean Supe, too?'

'Of course. Now you get in bed fast so you can get to school on time.'

While Bub undressed, she took the cover off the studio couch, smoothed the thin blanket and the sheets, pulled a pillowslip over one of the cushions. He seemed to be taking an awfully long time in the bathroom. 'Hey,' she said finally. 'Step on it. You can't get to heaven that way.'

She heard him giggle and smiled at the sound. Then her face sobered. She looked around the living room. One of these days he was going to have a real bed-room to himself instead of this shabby, sunless room. The plaid pattern of the blue congoleum rug was wearing off in front of the studio couch. It was scuffed down to the paper base at the door that led to the small hall. Everything in the room was worn and old—the lumpy studio couch, the overstuffed chair, the card table that served as desk, the bookcase filled with second-hand textbooks and old magazines. The blue-glass top on the coffee table was scratched and chipped. The small radio was scarred with cigarette burns. The first thing she would do would be to move and then she would get some decent furniture.

Bub got into bed, pulled the covers up under his chin. 'Good night, Mom,' he said.

He was almost asleep when she leaned over and kissed him on the forehead. She turned the light on in her bedroom, came back and switched the light off in the living room.

'Sleep tight!' she said. His only reply was a drowsy murmur—half laugh, half sigh.

She undressed, thinking of the Super sitting in the living room, of the time when she had come to look at the apartment and he had stood there in that room where Bub was now sleeping and how he had held the flashlight so that the beam of light from it was down at his feet. Now he had been back in there—sitting down, playing cards with Bub—making himself at home.

What had he talked to Bub about? The thought of his being friendly with Bub was frightening. Yet what could she do about it other than tell Bub not to let him into the apartment again? There was no telling what went on in the mind of a man like that—a man who had lived in basements and cellars, a man who had forever to stay within hailing distance of whatever building he was responsible for.

The last thing she thought before she finally went to sleep was that the Super was something less than human. He had been chained to buildings until he was like an animal.

She dreamed about him and woke up terrified, not certain that it was a dream and heard the wind sighing in the airshaft. And went back to sleep and dreamed about him again.

He and the dog had become one. He was still tall, gaunt, silent. The same man, but with the dog's wolfish mouth and the dog's teeth—white, sharp, pointed, in the redness of his mouth. His throat worked like the dog's throat. He made a whining noise deep inside it. He panted and strained to get free and run through the block, but the building was chained to his shoulders like an enormous doll's house made of brick. She could see the people moving around inside the building, drearily climbing the tiny stairs, sidling through the narrow halls. Mrs. Hedges sat on the first floor smiling at a cage full of young girls.

The building was so heavy he could hardly walk with it on his shoulders. It was a painful, slow, horrible crawl of a walk—hesitant, slowing down, now stopping completely and then starting again. He fawned on the people in the street, dragged himself close to them, stood in front of them, pointing to the building and to the chains. 'Unloose me! Unloose me!' he begged. His voice was cracked and hollow.

Min walked beside him repeating the same words. 'Unloose him! Unloose him!' and straining to reach up toward the lock that held the chains.

He thought she, Lutie, had the key. And he followed her through the street, whining in his throat, nuzzling in back of her with his sharp, pointed dog's face. She tried to walk faster and faster, but the shambling, slow, painful sound of his footsteps was always just behind her, the sound of his whining stayed close to her like someone talking in her ear.

She looked down at her hand and the key to the padlock that held the chains was there. She stopped, and there was a whole chorus of clamoring voices: 'Shame! Shame! She won't unloose him and she's got the key!'

Mrs. Hedges' window was suddenly in front of her. Mrs. Hedges nodded, 'If I was you, dearie, I'd unloose him. It's so easy, dearie. It's so easy, dearie. Easy—easy—easy—'

She reached out her hand toward the padlock and the long white fangs closed on her hand. Her hand and part of her arm were swallowed up inside his wolfish mouth. She watched in horror as more and more of her arm disappeared until there was only the shoulder left and then his jaws closed and she felt the sharp teeth sink in and in through her shoulder. The arm was gone and blood poured out.

She screamed and screamed and windows opened and the people poured out of the buildings—thousands of them, millions of them. She saw that they had turned to rats. The street was so full of them that she could hardly walk. They swarmed around her, jumping up and down. Each one had a building chained to its back, and they were all crying, 'Unloose me! Unloose me!'

She woke up and got out of bed. She couldn't shake loose the terror of the dream. She felt of her arm. It was still there and whole. Her mouth was wide open as though she had been screaming. It felt dry inside. She must have dreamed she was screaming, for Bub was still asleep—apparently she had made no sound. Yet she was so filled with fright from the nightmare memory of the dream that she stood motionless by the bed, unable to move for a long moment.

The air was cold. Finally she picked up the flannel robe at the foot of the bed and pulled it on. She sat down on the bed and tucked her feet under her, then carefully pulled the robe down over her feet, afraid to go back to sleep for fear of a recurrence of the dream.

The room was dark. Where the airshaft broke the wall there was a lighter quality to the darkness—a suggestion of dark blue space. Even in the dark like this her knowledge of the position of each piece of furniture made her aware of the smallness of the room. If she should get up quickly, she knew she would bump against the small chest and moving past it she might collide with the bureau.

Huddled there on the bed, her mind still clouded with the memory of the dream, her body chilled from the cold, she thought of the room, not with hatred, not with contempt, but with dread. In the darkness it seemed to close in on her until it became the sum total of all the things she was afraid of and she drew back nearer the wall because the room grew smaller and the pieces of furniture larger until she felt as though she were suffocating.

Suppose she got used to it, took it for granted, became resigned to it and all the things it represented. The thought set her to murmuring aloud, 'I mustn't get used to it. Not ever. I've got to keep on fighting to get away from here.'

All the responsibility for Bub was hers. It was up to her to keep him safe, to get him out of here so he would have a chance to grow up fine and strong. Because this street and the other streets just like it would, if he stayed in them long enough, do something terrible to him. Sooner or later they would do something equally as terrible to her. And as she sat there in the dark, she began to think about the things that she had seen on such streets as this one she lived in.

There was the afternoon last spring when she had got off the subway on Lenox Avenue. It was late afternoon. The spring sunlight was sharp and clear. The street was full of people taking advantage of the soft warm air after a winter of being shut away from the sun. They had peeled off their winter coats and sweaters and mufflers.

Kids on roller skates and kids precariously perched on home-made scooters whizzed unexpectedly through the groups of people clustered on the sidewalk. The sun was warm. It beamed on the boys and girls walking past arm in arm. It made their faces very soft and young and relaxed.

She had walked along slowly, thinking that the sun transformed everything it shone on. So that the people standing talking in front of the buildings, the push-cart men in the side streets, the peanut vendor, the sweet potato man, all had an unexpected graciousness in their faces and their postures. Even the drab brick of the buildings was altered to a deep rosy pinkness.

Thus she had come on the crowd suddenly, quite unaware that it was a crowd. She had walked past some of the people before she sensed some common impulse that had made this mass of people stand motionless and withdrawn in the middle of the block. She stopped, too. And she became sharply aware of a somber silence, a curious stillness that was all around her. She edged her way to the front of the crowd, squeezing past people, forcing her way toward whatever it was that held them in this strangely arrested silence.

There was a cleared space near the buildings and a handful of policemen and cameramen and reporters with pink cards stuck in their hatbands were standing in it looking down at something. She got as close to the cleared space as she could—so close that she was almost touching the policeman in front of her.

And she saw what they were looking at. Lying flat on the sidewalk was a man—thin, shabby, tall from the amount of sidewalk that his body occupied. There was blood on the sidewalk, and she saw that it was coming from somewhere under him. Part of his body and his face were covered with what looked to be a piece of white canvas.

But the thing she had never been able to forget were his shoes. Only the uppers were intact. They had once been black, but they were now a dark dull gray from long wear. The soles were worn out. They were mere flaps attached to the uppers. She could see the layers of wear. The first outer layer of leather was left near the edges, and then the great gaping holes in the center where the leather had worn out entirely, so that for weeks he must have walked practically barefooted on the pavement.

She had stared at the shoes, trying to figure out what it must have been like to walk barefooted on the city's concrete sidewalks. She wondered if he ever went downtown, and if he did, what did he think about when he passed store windows filled with sleek furs and fabulous food and clothing made of materials so fine you could tell by looking at them they would feel like sea foam under your hand?

How did he feel when the great long cars snorted past him as he waited for the lights to change or when he looked into a taxi and saw a delicate, soft, beautiful woman lifting her face toward an opulently dressed man? The woman's hair would gleam and shine, her mouth would be knowingly shaped with lip rouge. And the concrete would have been rough under this man's feet.

The people standing in back of her weren't moving. They weren't talking. They were simply standing there looking. She watched a cop touch one of the man's broken, grayish shoes with his foot. And she got a sick feeling because the cop's shoes were glossy with polish and the warm spring sunlight glinted on them.

One of the photographers and a newspaperman elbowed through the crowd. They had a thin, dark young girl by the arm. They walked her over to a man in a gray business suit. 'She thinks it's her brother,' the reporter said.

The man stared at the girl. 'What makes you think so?'

'He went out to get bread and he ain't home yet.'

'Look like his clothes?' He nodded toward the figure on the sidewalk.

'Yes.'

One of the cops reached down and rolled the canvas back from the man's face.

Lutie didn't look at the man's face. Instead, she looked at the girl and she saw something—some emotion that she couldn't name—flicker in the girl's face. It was as though for a fraction of a second something—hate or sorrow or surprise—had moved inside her and been reflected on her face. As quickly as it came, it was gone and it was replaced by a look of resignation, of complete acceptance. It was an expression that said the girl hoped for no more than this from life because other things that had happened to her had paved the way so that she had lost the ability to protest against anything—even death suddenly like this in the spring.

'I always thought it'd happen,' she said in a flat voice.

Why doesn't she scream? Lutie had thought angrily. Why does she stand there looking like that? Why doesn't she find out how it happened and yell her head off and hit out at people? The longer she looked at that still, resigned expression on the girl's face, the angrier she became.

Finally she had pushed her way to the back of the crowd. 'What happened to him?' she asked in a hard voice.

A woman with a bundle of newspapers under her arm answered her. She shifted the papers from one arm to the other. 'White man in the baker shop killed him with a bread knife.'

There was a silence, and then another voice added: 'He had the bread knife in him and he walked to the corner. The cops brought him back here and he died there where he's layin' now.'

'White man in the store claims he tried to hold him up.'

'If that bastard white man puts one foot out here, we'll kill him. Cops or no cops.'

She went home remembering, not the threat of violence in that silent, waiting crowd, but instead the man's ragged soleless shoes and the resigned look on the girl's face. She had never been able to forget either of them. The boy was so thin—painfully thin—and she kept thinking about his walking through the city barefooted. Both he and his sister were so young.

The next day's papers said that a 'burly Negro' had failed in his effort to hold up a bakery shop, for the proprietor had surprised him by resisting and stabbed him with a bread knife. She held the paper in her hand for a long time, trying to follow the reasoning by which that thin ragged boy had become in the eyes of a reporter a 'burly Negro.' And she decided that it all depended on where you sat how these things looked. If you looked at them from inside the framework of a fat weekly salary, and you thought of colored people as naturally criminal, then you didn't really see what any Negro looked like. You couldn't, because the Negro was never an individual. He was a threat, or an animal, or a curse, or a blight, or a joke.

It was like the Chandlers and their friends in Connecticut, who looked at her and didn't see her, but saw instead a wench with no morals who would be easy to come by. The reporter saw a dead Negro who had attempted to hold up a store, and so he couldn't really see what the man lying on the sidewalk looked like. He couldn't see the ragged shoes, the thin, starved body. He saw, instead, the picture he already had in his mind: a huge, brawny, blustering, ignorant, criminally disposed black man who had run amok with a knife on a spring afternoon in Harlem and who had in turn been knifed.

She had gone past the bakery shop again the next afternoon. The windows had been smashed, the front door had apparently been broken in, because it was boarded up. There were messages chalked on the sidewalk in front of the store. They all said the same thing: 'White man, don't come back.' She was surprised to see that there were men still standing around, on the nearest corners, across the street. Their faces were turned toward the store. They weren't talking. They were just standing with their hands in their pockets—waiting.

RICHARD WRIGHT (1908–1960)

Richard Wright was born in Natchez, Mississippi, where he was educated at a Seventh-Day Adventist school. As a young adult, he married and had two children. His career always involved writing, his passion. Starting in 1935, he worked with the Federal Writers' Project in Chicago. He also contributed to magazines such as Daily Worker *and* New Masses, *and he won a $50 prize for a story called "Uncle Tom's Children." For* Native Son *(1940) Wright won a Guggenheim Foundation fellowship. The novel was the first book by an African American to be selected as a Book-of-the-Month Club publication. Wright's* Black Boy *(1945), an autobiographical novel, was also selected for the Book-of-the-Month Club.*

In both Native Son *and* Black Boy, *Wright presents experiences of African American men in racially segregated environments. His novels illustrate the effects of racism on African Americans, particularly men. Wright writes about his own experiences as a black man in a racist society. His list of publications is impressive; he wrote both fiction and non-fiction and excelled as a writer.* Uncle Tom's Children *(1938) is a well-known text of memorable stories. Wright expanded his repertoire, becoming a successful Broadway producer and filmmaker.*

From Native Son (1940)

There was no day for him now, and there was no night; there was but a long stretch of time, a long stretch of time that was very short; and then—the end. Toward no one in the world did he feel any fear now, for he knew that fear was useless; and toward no one in the world did he feel any hate now, for he knew that hate would not help him.

Though they carried him from one police station to another, though they threatened him, persuaded him, bullied him, and stormed at him, he steadfastly refused to speak. Most of the time he sat with bowed head, staring at the floor; or he lay full length upon his stomach, his face buried in the crook of an elbow, just as he lay now upon a cot with the pale yellow sunshine of a February sky falling obliquely upon him through the cold steel bars of the Eleventh Street Police Station.

Food was brought to him upon trays and an hour later the trays were taken away, untouched. They gave him packages of cigarettes, but they lay on the floor, unopened. He would not even drink water. He simply lay or sat, saying nothing, not noticing when anyone entered or left his cell. When they wanted him to go from one place to another, they caught him by the wrist and led him; he went without resistance, walking always with dragging feet, head down. Even when they snatched him up by the collar, his weak body easily lending itself to be manhandled, he looked without hope or resentment, his eyes like two still pools of black ink in his flaccid face. No one had seen him save the officials and he had asked to see no one. Not once during the three days following his capture had an image of what he had done come into his mind. He had thrust the whole thing back of him, and there it lay, monstrous and horrible. He was not so much in a stupor, as in the grip of a deep physiological resolution not to react to anything.

Having been thrown by an accidental murder into a position where he had sensed a possible order and meaning in his relations with the people about him; having accepted the moral guilt and responsibility for that murder because it had made him feel free for the first time in his life; having felt in his heart some obscure need to be at home with people and having demanded ransom money to enable him to do it—having done all this and failed, he chose not to struggle any more. With a supreme act of will springing from the essence of his being, he turned away from his life and the long train of disastrous consequences that had flowed from it and looked wistfully upon the dark face of ancient waters upon which some spirit had breathed and created him, the dark face of the waters from which he had been first made in the image of a man with a man's obscure need and urge; feeling that he wanted to sink back into those waters and rest eternally.

And yet his desire to crush all faith in him was in itself built upon a sense of faith. The feelings of his body reasoned that if there could be no merging with the men and women about him, there should be a merging with some other part of the natural world in which he lived. Out of the mood of renunciation there sprang up in him again the will to kill. But this time it was not directed outward toward people, but inward, upon himself. Why not kill that wayward yearning within him that had led him to this end? He had reached out and killed and had not solved anything, so why not reach inward and kill that which had duped him? This feeling sprang up of itself, organically, automatically; like the rotted hull of a seed forming the soil in which it should grow again.

And, under and above it all, there was the fear of death before which he was naked and without defense; he had to go forward and meet his end like any other living thing upon the earth. And regulating his attitude toward death was the fact that he was black, unequal, and despised. Passively, he hungered for another orbit between two poles that would let him live again; for a new mode of life that would catch him up with the tension of hate and love. There would have to hover above him, like the stars in a full sky, a vast configuration of images and symbols whose magic and power could lift him up and make him live so intensely that the dread of being black and unequal would be forgotten; that even death would not matter, that it would be a victory. This would have to happen before he could look them in the face again: a new pride and a new humility would have to be born in him, a humility springing from a new identification with some part of the world in which he lived, and this identification forming the basis for a new hope that would function in him as pride and dignity.

But maybe it would never come; maybe there was no such thing for him; maybe he would have to go to his end just as he was, dumb, driven, with the shadow of emptiness in his eyes. Maybe this was all. Maybe the confused promptings, the excitement, the tingling, the elation—maybe they were false lights that led nowhere. Maybe they were right when they said that a black skin was bad, the covering of an apelike animal. Maybe he was just unlucky, a man born for dark doom, an obscene joke happening amid a colossal din of siren screams and white faces and circling lances of light under a cold and silken sky. But he could not feel that for long; just as soon as his feelings reached such a conclusion, the conviction that there was some way out surged back into him, strong and powerful, and, in his present state, condemning and paralyzing.

And then one morning a group of men came and caught him by the wrists and led him into a large room in the Cook County Morgue, in which there were many people. He blinked from the bright lights and heard loud and excited talking. The compact array of white faces and the constant flashing of bulbs for pictures made him stare in mounting amazement. His defense of indifference could protect him no longer. At first he thought that it was the trial that had begun, and he was prepared to sink back into his dream of nothingness. But it was not a court room. It was too informal for that. He felt crossing his feelings a sensation akin to the same one he had had when the reporters had first come into Mr. Dalton's basement with their hats on, smoking cigars and cigarettes, asking questions; only now it was much stronger. There was in the air a silent mockery that challenged him. It was not their hate he felt; it was something deeper than that. He sensed that in their attitude toward him they had gone beyond hate. He heard in the sound of their voices a patient certainty; he saw their eyes gazing at him with calm conviction. Though he could not have put it into words, he felt that not only had they resolved to put him to death, but that they were determined to make his death mean more than a mere punishment; that they regarded him as a figment of that black world which they feared and were anxious to keep under control. The atmosphere of the crowd told him that they were going to use his death as a bloody symbol of fear to wave before the eyes of that black world. And as he felt it, rebellion rose in him. He had sunk to the lowest point this side of death, but when he felt his life again threatened in a way that meant that he was to go down the dark road a helpless spectacle of sport for others, he sprang back into action, alive, contending.

He tried to move his hands and found that they were shackled by strong bands of cold steel to white wrists of policemen sitting to either side of him. He looked round; a policeman stood in front of him and one in back. He heard a sharp, metallic click and his hands were free. There was a rising murmur of voices and he sensed that it was caused by his movements. Then his eyes became riveted on a white face, tilted slightly upward. The skin had a quality of taut anxiety and around the oval of white face was a framework of whiter hair. It was Mrs. Dalton, sitting quietly, her frail, waxen hands folded in her lap. Bigger remembered as he looked at her that moment of stark terror when he had stood at the side of the bed in the dark blue room hearing his heart pound against his ribs with his fingers upon the pillow pressing down upon Mary's face to keep her from mumbling.

Sitting beside Mrs. Dalton was Mr. Dalton, looking straight before him with wide-open, unblinking eyes. Mr. Dalton turned slowly and looked at Bigger and Bigger's eyes fell.

He saw Jan: blond hair; blue eyes; a sturdy, kind face looking squarely into his own. Hot shame flooded him as the scene in the car came back; he felt again the pressure of Jan's fingers upon his hand. And then shame was replaced by guilty anger as he recalled Jan's confronting him upon the sidewalk in the snow.

He was getting tired; the more he came to himself, the more a sense of fatigue seeped into him. He looked down at his clothes; they were damp and crumpled and the sleeves of his coat were drawn halfway up his arms. His shirt was open and he could see the black skin of his chest. Suddenly, he felt the fingers of his right hand throb with pain. Two fingernails were torn off. He could not remember how it had happened. He tried to move his tongue and found it swollen. His lips were dry and cracked and he wanted water. He felt giddy. The lights and faces whirled slowly, like a merry-go-round. He was falling swiftly through space. . . .

When he opened his eyes he was stretched out upon a cot. A white face loomed above him. He tried to lift his body and was pushed back.

"Take it easy, boy. Here; drink this."

A glass touched his lips. Ought he to drink? But what difference did it make? He swallowed something warm; it was milk. When the glass was empty he lay upon his back and stared at the white ceiling; the memory of Bessie and the milk she had warmed for him came back strongly. Then the image of her death came and he closed his eyes, trying to forget. His stomach growled; he was feeling better. He heard a low drone of voices. He gripped the edge of the cot and sat up.

"Hey! How're you feeling, boy?"

"Hunh?" he grunted. It was the first time he had spoken since they had caught him.

"How're you feeling?"

He closed his eyes and turned his head away, sensing that they were white and he was black, that they were the captors and he the captive.

"He's coming out of it."

"Yeah. That crowd must've got 'im."

"Say, boy! You want something to eat?"

He did not answer.

"Get 'im something. He doesn't know what he wants."

"You better lie down, boy. You'll have to go back to the inquest this afternoon."

He felt their hands pushing him back onto the cot. The door closed; he looked round. He was alone. The room was quiet. He had come out into the world again. He had not tried to; it had just happened. He was being turned here and there by a surge of strange forces he could not understand. It was not to save his life that he had come out; he did not care what they did to him. They could place him in the electric chair right now, for all he cared. It was to save his pride that he had come. He did not want them to make sport of him. If they had killed him that night when they were dragging him down the steps, that would have been a deed born of their strength over him. But he felt they had no right to sit and watch him, to use him for whatever they wanted.

The door opened and a policeman brought in a tray of food, set it on a chair next to him and left. There was steak and fried potatoes and coffee. Gingerly, he cut a piece of steak and put it into his mouth. It tasted so good that he tried to swallow it before he chewed it. He sat on the edge of the cot and drew the chair forward so that he could reach the food. He ate so fast that his jaws ached. He stopped and held the food in his mouth, feeling the juices of his glands flowing round it. When he was through, he lit a cigarette, stretched out upon the cot and closed his eyes. He dozed off to an uneasy sleep.

Then suddenly he sat upright. He had not seen a newspaper in a long time. What were they saying now? He got up; he swayed and the room lurched. He was still weak and giddy. He leaned against the wall and walked slowly to the door. Cautiously, he turned the knob. The door swung in and he looked into the face of a policeman.

"What's the matter, boy?"

He saw a heavy gun sagging at the man's hip. The policeman caught him by the wrist and led him back to the cot.

"Here; take it easy."

"I want a paper," he said.

"Hunh? A paper?"

"I want to read the paper."

"Wait a minute. I'll see."

The policeman went out and presently returned with an armful of papers.

"Here you are, boy. You're in 'em all."

He did not turn to the papers until after the man had left the room. Then he spread out the *Tribune* and saw: NEGRO RAPIST FAINTS AT INQUEST. He understood now; it was the inquest he had been taken to. He had fainted and they had brought him here. He read:

Overwhelmed by the sight of his accusers, Bigger Thomas, Negro sex-slayer, fainted dramatically this morning at the inquest of Mary Dalton, millionaire Chicago heiress.

Emerging from a stupor for the first time since his capture last Monday night, the black killer sat cowed and fearful as hundreds sought to get a glimpse of him.

"He looks exactly like an ape!" exclaimed a terrified young white girl who watched the black slayer being loaded onto a stretcher after he had fainted.

Though the Negro killer's body does not seem compactly built, he gives the impression of possessing abnormal physical strength. He is about five feet, nine inches tall and his skin is exceedingly black. His lower jaw protrudes obnoxiously, reminding one of a jungle beast.

His arms are long, hanging in a dangling fashion to his knees. It is easy to imagine how this man, in the grip of a brain-numbing sex passion, overpowered little Mary Dalton, raped her, murdered her, beheaded her, then stuffed her body into a roaring furnace to destroy the evidence of his crime.

His shoulders are huge, muscular, and he keeps them hunched, as if about to spring upon you at any moment. He looks at the world with a strange, sullen, fixed-from-under stare, as though defying all efforts of compassion.

All in all, he seems a beast utterly untouched by the softening influences of modern civilization. In speech and manner he lacks the charm of the average, harmless, genial, grinning southern darky so beloved by the American people.

The moment the killer made his appearance at the inquest, there were shouts of "Lynch 'im! Kill 'im!"

But the brutish Negro seemed indifferent to his fate, as though inquests, trials, and even the looming certainty of the electric chair held no terror for him.

He acted like an earlier missing link in the human species. He seemed out of place in a white man's civilization.

An Irish police captain remarked with deep conviction: "I'm convinced that death is the only cure for the likes of him."

For three days the Negro has refused all nourishment. Police believe that he is either trying to starve himself to death and cheat the chair, or that he is trying to excite sympathy for himself.

From Jackson, Mississippi, came a report yesterday from Edward Robertson, editor of the *Jackson Daily Star*, regarding Bigger Thomas' boyhood there. The editor wired:

"Thomas comes of a poor darky family of a shiftless and immoral variety. He was raised here and is known to local residents as an irreformable sneak thief and liar. We were unable to send him to the chain gang because of his extreme youth.

"Our experience here in Dixie with such depraved types of Negroes has shown that only the death penalty, inflicted in a public and dramatic manner, has any influence upon their peculiar mentality. Had that nigger Thomas lived in Mississippi and committed such a crime, no power under Heaven could have saved him from death at the hands of indignant citizens.

"I think it but proper to inform you that in many quarters it is believed that Thomas, despite his dead-black complexion, may have a minor portion of white blood in his veins, a mixture which generally makes for a criminal and intractable nature.

"Down here in Dixie we keep Negroes firmly in their places and we make them know that if they so much as touch a white woman, good or bad, they cannot live.

"When Negroes become resentful over imagined wrongs, nothing brings them to their senses so quickly as when citizens take the law into their hands and make an example out of a trouble-making nigger.

"Crimes such as the Bigger Thomas murders could be lessened by segregating all Negroes in parks, playgrounds, cafés, theatres, and street cars. Residential segregation is imperative. Such measures tend to keep them as much as possible out of direct contact with white women and lessen their attacks against them.

"We of the South believe that the North encourages Negroes to get more education than they are organically capable of absorbing, with the result that northern Negroes are generally more unhappy and restless than those of the South. If separate schools were maintained, it would be fairly easy to limit the Negroes' education by regulating the appropriation of moneys through city, county, and state legislative bodies.

"Still another psychological deterrent can be attained by conditioning Negroes so that they have to pay deference to the white person with whom they come in contact. This is done by regulating their speech and actions. We have found that the injection of an element of constant fear has aided us greatly in handling the problem."

He lowered the paper; he could not read any more. Yes, of course; they were going to kill him; but they were having this sport with him before they did it. He held very still; he was trying to make a decision; not thinking, but feeling it out. Ought he to go back behind his wall? *Could* he go back now? He felt that he could not. But would not any effort he made now turn out like the others? Why go forward and meet more hate? He lay on the cot, feeling as he had felt that night when his fingers had gripped the icy edges of the water tank under the roving flares of light, knowing that men crouched below him with guns and tear gas, hearing the screams of sirens and shouts rising thirstily from ten thousand throats. . . .

Overcome with drowsiness, he closed his eyes; then opened them abruptly. The door swung in and he saw a black face. Who was this? A tall, well-dressed black man came forward and paused. Bigger pulled up and leaned on his elbow. The man came all the way to the cot and stretched forth a dingy palm, touching Bigger's hand.

"Mah po' boy! May the good Lawd have mercy on yuh."

He stared at the man's jet-black suit and remembered who he was: Reverend Hammond, the pastor of his mother's church. And at once he was on guard against the man. He shut his heart and tried to stifle all feeling in him. He feared that the preacher would make him feel remorseful. He wanted to tell him to go; but so closely associated in his mind was the man with his mother and what she stood for that he could not speak. In his feelings he could not tell the difference between what this man evoked in him and what he had read in the papers; the love of his own kind and the hate of others made him feel equally guilty now.

"How yuh feel, son?" the man asked; he did not answer and the man's voice hurried on: "Yo' ma ast me t' come 'n' see yuh. She wants t' come too."

The preacher knelt upon the concrete floor and closed his eyes. Bigger clamped his teeth and flexed his muscles; he knew what was coming.

"Lawd Jesus, turn Yo' eyes 'n' look inter the heart of this po' sinner! Yuh said mercy wuz awways Yo's 'n' ef we ast fer it on bended knee Yuh'd po' it out inter our hearts 'n' make our cups run over! We's astin' Yuh t' po' out Yo' mercy now, Lawd! Po' it out fer this po' sinner boy who stan's in deep need of it! Ef his sins be as scarlet, Lawd, wash 'em white as snow! Fergive 'im fer whutever he's done, Lawd! Let the light of Yo' love guide 'im th'u these dark days! 'N' he'p them who's a-tryin' to he'p 'im, Lawd! Enter inter they hearts 'n' breathe compassion on they sperits! We ast this in the nama Yo' Son Jesus who died on the cross 'n' gave us the mercy of Yo' love! Ahmen. . . ."

Bigger stared unblinkingly at the white wall before him as the preacher's words registered themselves in his consciousness. He knew without listening what they meant; it was the old voice of his mother telling of suffering, of hope, of love beyond this world. And he loathed it because it made him feel as condemned and guilty as the voice of those who hated him.

"Son. . . ."

Bigger glanced at the preacher, and then away.

"Fergit ever'thing but yo' soul, son. Take yo' mind off ever'thing but eternal life. Fergit whut the newspapers say. Fergit yuh's black. Gawd looks past yo' skin 'n' inter yo' soul, son. He's lookin' at the only parta yuh tha's *His*. He wants yuh 'n' He loves yuh. Give yo'se'f t' 'Im, son. Lissen, lemme tell yuh why yuh's here; lemme tell yuh a story tha'll make yo' heart glad. . . ."

Bigger sat very still, listening and not listening. If someone had afterwards asked him to repeat the preacher's words, he would not have been able to do so. But he felt and sensed their meaning. As the preacher talked there appeared before him a vast black silent void and the images of the preacher swam in that void, grew large and powerful; familiar images which his mother had given him when he was a child at her knee; images which in turn aroused impulses long dormant, impulses that he had suppressed and sought to shunt from his life. They were images which had once given him a reason for living, had explained the world. Now they sprawled before his eyes and seized his emotions in a spell of awe and wonder.

. . . an endless reach of deep murmuring waters upon whose face was darkness and there was no form no shape no sun no stars and no land and a voice came out of the darkness and the waters moved to obey and there emerged slowly a huge spinning ball and the voice said *let there be light* and there was light and it was good light and the voice said *let there be a firmament* and the waters parted and there was a vast space over the waters which formed into clouds stretching above the waters and like an echo the voice came from far away saying *let dry land appear* and with thundering rustling the waters drained off and mountain peaks reared into view and there were valleys and rivers and the voice called the dry land *earth* and the waters *seas* and the earth grew grass and trees and flowers that gave off seed that fell to the earth to grow again and the earth was lit by the light of a million stars and for the day there was a sun and for the night there was a moon and there were days and weeks and months and years and the voice called out of the twilight and moving creatures came forth out of the great waters whales and all kinds of living creeping things and on the land there were beasts and cattle and the voice said *let us make man in our own image* and from the dusty earth a man rose up and loomed against the day and the sun and after him a woman rose up and loomed against the night and the moon and they lived as one flesh and there was no Pain no Longing no Time no Death and Life was like the flowers that bloomed round them in the garden of earth and out of the clouds came a voice saying *eat not of the fruit of the tree in the midst of the garden, neither touch it, lest ye die.* . . .

The preacher's words ceased droning. Bigger looked at him out of the corners of his eyes. The preacher's face was black and sad and earnest and made him feel a sense of guilt deeper than that which even his murder of Mary had made him feel. He had killed within himself the preacher's haunting picture of life even before he had killed Mary; that had been his first murder. And now the preacher made it walk before his eyes like a ghost in the night, creating within him a sense of exclusion that was as cold as a block of ice. Why should this thing rise now to plague him after he had pressed a pillow of fear and hate over its face to smother it to death? To those who wanted to kill him he was not human, not included in that picture of Creation; and that was why he had killed it. To live, he had created a new world for himself, and for that he was to die.

Again the preacher's words seeped into his feelings:

"Son, yuh know whut tha' tree wuz? It wuz the tree of knowledge. It wuzn't enuff fer man t' be like Gawd, he wanted t' know *why*. 'N' all Gawd wanted 'im t' do wuz bloom like the flowers in the fiel's, live as chillun. Man wanted t' know why 'n' he fell from light t' darkness, from love t' damnation, from blessedness t' shame. 'N' Gawd cast 'em outa the garden 'n' tol' the man he had t' git his bread by the sweat of his brow 'n' tol' the woman she had t' bring fo'th her chillun in pain 'n' sorrow. The worl' turned ergin 'em 'n' they had t' fight the worl' fer life. . . .

. . . the man and the woman walked fearfully among trees their hands covering their nakedness and back of them high in the twilight against the clouds an angel waved a flaming sword driving them out of the garden into the wild night of cold wind and tears and pain and death and the man and woman took their food and burnt it to send smoke to the sky begging forgiveness. . . .

"Son, fer thousan's of years we been prayin' for Gawd t' take tha' cuss off us. Gawd heard our prayers 'n' said He'd show us a way back t' 'Im. His Son Jesus came down t' earth 'n' put on human flesh 'n' lived 'n' died t' show us the way. Jesus let men crucify 'Im; but His death wuz a victory. He showed us tha' t' live in this worl' wuz t' be crucified by it. This worl' ain' our home. Life ever' day is a crucifixion. There ain' but one way out, son, 'n' tha's Jesus' way, the way of love 'n' fergiveness. Be like Jesus. Don't resist. Thank Gawd tha' He done chose this way fer yuh t' come t' 'Im. It's love tha's gotta save yuh, son. Yuh gotta b'lieve tha' Gawd gives eternal life th'u the love of Jesus. Son, look at me. . . ."

Bigger's black face rested in his hands and he did not move.

"Son, promise me yuh'll stop hatin' long enuff fer Gawd's love t' come inter yo' heart."

Bigger said nothing.

"Won't yuh promise, son?"

Bigger covered his eyes with his hands.

"Jus' say yuh'll *try*, son."

Bigger felt that if the preacher kept asking he would leap up and strike him. How could he believe in that which he had killed? He was guilty. The preacher rose, sighed, and drew from his pocket a small wooden cross with a chain upon it.

"Look, son. Ah'm holdin' in mah hands a wooden cross taken from a tree. A tree is the worl', son. 'N' nailed t' this tree is a sufferin' man. Tha's whut life is, son. Sufferin'. How kin yuh keep from b'levin' the word of Gawd when Ah'm holdin' befo' yo' eyes the only thing tha' gives a meanin' t' yo' life? Here, lemme put it roun' yo' neck. When yuh git alone, look at this cross, son, 'n' b'lieve. . . ."

They were silent. The wooden cross hung next to the skin of Bigger's chest. He was feeling the words of the preacher, feeling that life was flesh nailed to the world, a longing spirit imprisoned in the days of the earth.

He glanced up, hearing the doorknob turn. The door opened and Jan stood framed in it, hesitating. Bigger sprang to his feet, galvanized by fear. The preacher also stood, took a step backward, bowed, and said,

"Good mawnin', suh."

Bigger wondered what Jan could want of him now. Was he not caught and ready for trial? Would not Jan get his revenge? Bigger stiffened as Jan walked to the middle of the floor and stood facing him. Then it suddenly occurred to Bigger that he need not be standing, that he had no reason to fear bodily harm from Jan here in jail. He sat and bowed his head; the room was quiet, so quiet that Bigger heard the preacher and Jan breathing. The white man upon whom he had tried to blame his crime stood before him and he sat waiting to hear angry words. Well, why didn't he speak? He lifted his eyes; Jan was looking straight at him and he looked away. But Jan's face was not angry. If he were not angry, then what did he want? He looked again and saw Jan's lips move to speak, but no words came. And when Jan did speak his voice was low and there were long pauses between the words; it seemed to Bigger that he was listening to a man talk to himself.

"Bigger, maybe I haven't the words to say what I want to say, but I'm going to try. . . . This thing hit me like a bomb. It t-t-took me all week to get myself together. They had me in jail and I couldn't for the life of me figure out what was happening. . . . I—I don't want to worry you, Bigger. I know you're in trouble. But there's something I just got to say. . . . You needn't talk to me unless you want to, Bigger. I think I know something of what you're feeling now. I'm not dumb, Bigger; I can understand, even if I didn't seem to understand that night. . . ." Jan paused, swallowed, and lit a cigarette. "Well, you jarred me. . . . I see now. I was kind of blind. I—I just wanted to come here and tell you that I'm not angry. . . . I'm not angry and I want you to let me help you. I don't hate you for trying to blame this thing on me. . . . Maybe you had good reasons. . . . I don't know. And maybe in a certain sense, I'm the one who's really guilty. . . ." Jan paused again and sucked long and hard at his cigarette, blew the smoke out slowly and nervously bit his lips. "Bigger, I've never done anything against you and your people in my life. But I'm a white man and it would be asking too much to ask you not to hate me, when every white man you see hates you. I—I know my . . . my face looks like theirs to you, even though I don't feel like they do. But I didn't know we were so far apart until that night. . . . I can understand now why you pulled that gun on me when I waited outside that house to talk to you. It was the only thing you could have done; but I didn't know my white face was making you feel guilty, condemning you. . . ." Jan's lips hung open, but no words came from them; his eyes searched the corners of the room.

Bigger sat silently, bewildered, feeling that he was on a vast blind wheel being turned by stray gusts of wind. The preacher came forward.

The Man Who Lived Underground (1944)

I've got to hide, he told himself. His chest heaved as he waited, crouching in a dark corner of the vestibule. He was tired of running and dodging. Either he had to find a place to hide, or he had to surrender. A police car swished by through the rain, its siren rising sharply. They're looking for me all over. . . . He crept to the door and squinted through the fogged plate glass. He stiffened as the siren rose and died in the distance. Yes, he had to hide, but where? He gritted his teeth. Then a sudden movement in the street caught his attention. A throng of tiny columns of water snaked into the air from the perforations of a manhole cover. The columns stopped abruptly, as though the perforations had become clogged; a gray spout of sewer water jutted up from underground and lifted the circular metal cover, juggled it for a moment, then let it fall with a clang.

He hatched a tentative plan: he would wait until the siren sounded far off, then he would go out. He smoked and waited, tense. At last the siren gave him his signal; it wailed, dying, going away from him. He stepped to the sidewalk, then paused and looked curiously at the open manhole, half expecting the cover to leap up again. He went to the center of the street and stooped and peered into the hole, but could see nothing. Water rustled in the black depths.

He started with terror; the siren sounded so near that he had the idea that he had been dreaming and had awakened to find the car upon him. He dropped instinctively to his knees and his hands grasped the rim of the manhole. The siren seemed to hoot directly above him and with a wild gasp of exertion he snatched the cover far enough off to admit his body. He swung his legs over the opening and lowered himself into watery darkness. He hung for an eternal moment to the rim by his finger tips, then he felt rough metal prongs and at once he knew that sewer workmen used these ridges to lower themselves into manholes. Fist over fist, he let his body sink until he could feel no more prongs. He swayed in dank space; the siren seemed to howl at the very rim of the manhole. He dropped and was washed violently into an ocean of warm, leaping water. His head was battered against a wall and he wondered if this were death. Frenziedly his fingers clawed and sank into a crevice. He steadied himself and measured the strength of the current with his own muscular tension. He stood slowly in water that dashed past his knees with fearful velocity.

He heard a prolonged scream of brakes and the siren broke off. Oh, God! They had found him! Looming above his head in the rain a white face hovered over the hole. "How did this damn thing get off?" he heard a policeman ask. He saw the steel cover move slowly until the hole looked like a quarter moon turned black. "Give me a hand here," someone called. The cover clanged into place, muffling the sights and sounds of the upper world. Knee-deep in the pulsing current, he breathed with aching chest, filling his lungs with the hot stench of yeasty rot.

From the perforations of the manhole cover, delicate lances of hazy violet sifted down and wove a mottled pattern upon the surface of the streaking current. His lips parted as a car swept past along the wet pavement overhead, its heavy rumble soon dying out, like the hum of a plane speeding through a dense cloud. He had never thought that cars could sound like that; everything seemed strange and unreal under here. He stood in darkness for a long time, knee-deep in rustling water, musing.

The odor of rot had become so general that he no longer smelled it. He got his cigarettes, but discovered that his matches were wet. He searched and found a dry folder in the pocket of his shirt and managed to strike one; it flared weirdly in the wet gloom, glowing greenishly, turning red, orange, then yellow. He lit a

crumpled cigarette; then, by the flickering light of the match, he looked for support so that he would not have to keep his muscles flexed against the pouring
water. His pupils narrowed and he saw to either side of him two steaming walls
that rose and curved inward some six feet above his head to form a dripping,
mouse-colored dome. The bottom of the sewer was a sloping V-trough. To the
left, the sewer vanished in ashen fog. To the right was a steep down-curve into
which water plunged.

He saw now that had he not regained his feet in time, he would have been swept
to death, or had he entered any other manhole he would have probably drowned.
Above the rush of the current he heard sharper juttings of water; tiny streams were
spewing into the sewer from smaller conduits. The match died; he struck another
and saw a mass of debris sweep past him and clog the throat of the down-curve. At
once the water began rising rapidly. Could he climb out before he drowned? A
long hiss sounded and the debris was sucked from sight; the current lowered. He
understood now what had made the water toss the manhole cover; the down-curve
had become temporarily obstructed and the perforations had become clogged.

He was in danger; he might slide into a down-curve; he might wander with a
lighted match into a pocket of gas and blow himself up; or he might contract some
horrible disease. . . . Though he wanted to leave, an irrational impulse held him
rooted. To the left, the convex ceiling swooped to a height of less than five feet.
With cigarette slanting from pursed lips, he waded with taut muscles, his feet
sloshing over the slimy bottom, his shoes sinking into spongy slop, the slate-
colored water cracking in creamy foam against his knees. Pressing his flat left
palm against the lowered ceiling, he struck another match and saw a metal pole
nestling in a niche of the wall. Yes, some sewer workman had left it. He reached
for it, then jerked his head away as a whisper of scurrying life whisked past and
was still. He held the match close and saw a huge rat, wet with slime, blinking
beady eyes and baring tiny fangs. The light blinded the rat and the frizzled head
moved aimlessly. He grabbed the pole and let it fly against the rat's soft body;
there was shrill piping and the grizzly body splashed into the dun-colored water
and was snatched out of sight, spinning in the scuttling stream.

He swallowed and pushed on, following the curve of the misty cavern, sounding the water with the pole. By the faint light of another manhole cover he saw,
amid loose wet brick, a hole with walls of damp earth leading into blackness.
Gingerly he poked the pole into it; it was hollow and went beyond the length of
the pole. He shoved the pole before him, hoisted himself upward, got to his hands
and knees, and crawled. After a few yards he paused, struck to wonderment by the
silence; it seemed that he had traveled a million miles away from the world. As he
inched forward again he could sense the bottom of the dirt tunnel becoming dry
and lowering slightly. Slowly he rose and to his astonishment he stood erect. He
could not hear the rustling of the water now and he felt confoundingly alone, yet
lured by the darkness and silence.

He crept a long way, then stopped, curious, afraid. He put his right foot forward and it dangled in space; he drew back in fear. He thrust the pole outward
and it swung in emptiness. He trembled, imagining the earth crumbling and
burying him alive. He scratched a match and saw that the dirt floor sheered away

steeply and widened into a sort of cave some five feet below him. An old sewer, he muttered. He cocked his head, hearing a feathery cadence which he could not identify. The match ceased to burn.

Using the pole as a kind of ladder, he slid down and stood in darkness. The air was a little fresher and he could still hear vague noises. Where was he? He felt suddenly that someone was standing near him and he turned sharply, but there was only darkness. He poked cautiously and felt a brick wall; he followed it and the strange sounds grew louder. He ought to get out of here. This was crazy. He could not remain here for any length of time; there was no food and no place to sleep. But the faint sounds tantalized him; they were strange but familiar. Was it a motor? A baby crying? Music? A siren? He groped on, and the sounds came so clearly that he could feel the pitch and timbre of human voices. Yes, singing! That was it! He listened with open mouth. It was a church service. Enchanted, he groped toward the waves of melody.

Jesus, take me to your home above
And fold me in the bosom of Thy love . . .

The singing was on the other side of a brick wall. Excited he wanted to watch the service without being seen. Whose church was it? He knew most of the churches in this area above ground, but the singing sounded too strange and detached for him to guess. He looked to the left, to the right down to the black dirt, then upward and was startled to see a bright sliver of light slicing the darkness like the blade of a razor. He struck one of his two remaining matches and saw rusty pipes running along an old concrete ceiling. Photographically he located the exact position of the pipes in his mind. The match flame sank and he sprang upward; his hands clutched a pipe. He swung his legs and tossed his body onto the bed of pipes and they creaked, swaying up and down; he thought that the tier was about to crash, but nothing happened. He edged to the crevice and saw a segment of black men and women, dressed in white robes, singing, holding tattered songbooks in their black palms. His first impulse was to laugh, but he checked himself.

What was he doing? He was crushed with a sense of guilt. Would God strike him dead for that? The singing swept on and he shook his head, disagreeing in spite of himself. They oughtn't to do that, he thought. But he could think of no reason *why* they should not do it. Just singing with the air of the sewer blowing in on them. . . . He felt that he was gazing upon something abysmally obscene, yet he could not bring himself to leave.

After a long time he grew numb and dropped to the dirt. Pain throbbed in his legs and a deeper pain, induced by the sight of those black people groveling and begging for something they could never get, churned in him. A vague conviction made him feel that those people should stand unrepentant and yield no quarter in singing and praying, yet *he* had run away from the police, had pleaded with them to believe in *his* innocence. He shook his head, bewildered.

How long had he been down here? He did not know. This was a new kind of living for him; the intensity of feelings he had experienced when looking at the church people sing made him certain that he had been down here a long time, but his mind told him that the time must have been short. In this darkness the only notion he had of time was when a match flared and measured time by its fleeting light. He groped back through the hole toward the sewer and the waves of song subsided and finally he could not hear them at all. He came to where the earth hole ended and he heard the noise of the current and time lived again for him, measuring the moments by the wash of water.

The rain must have slackened, for the flow of water had lessened and came only to his ankles. Ought he to go up into the streets and take his chances on hiding somewhere else? But they would surely catch him. The mere thought of dodging and running again from the police made him tense. No, he would stay and plot how to elude them. But what could he do down here? He walked forward into the sewer and came to another manhole cover; he stood beneath it, debating. Fine pencils of gold spilled suddenly from the little circles in the manhole cover and trembled on the surface of the current. Yes, street lamps. . . . It must be night. . . .

He went forward for about a quarter of an hour, wading aimlessly, poking the pole carefully before him. Then he stopped, his eyes fixed and intent. What's that? A strangely familiar image attracted and repelled him. Lit by the yellow stems from another manhole cover was a tiny nude body of a baby snagged by debris and half-submerged in water. Thinking that the baby was alive, he moved impulsively to save it, but his roused feelings told him that it was dead, cold, nothing, the same nothingness he had felt while watching the men and women singing in the church. Water blossomed about the tiny legs, the tiny arms, the tiny head, and rushed onward. The eyes were closed, as though in sleep; the fists were clenched, as though in protest; and the mouth gaped black in a soundless cry.

He straightened and drew in his breath, feeling that he had been staring for all eternity at the ripples of veined water skimming impersonally over the shriveled limbs. He felt as condemned as when the policemen had accused him. Involuntarily he lifted his hand to brush the vision away, but his arm fell listlessly to his side. Then he acted; he closed his eyes and reached forward slowly with the soggy shoe of his right foot and shoved the dead baby from where it had been lodged. He kept his eyes closed, seeing the little body twisting in the current as it floated from sight. He opened his eyes, shivered, placed his knuckles in the sockets, hearing the water speed in the somber shadows.

He tramped on, sensing at times a sudden quickening in the current as he passed some conduit whose waters were swelling the stream that slid by his feet. A few minutes later he was standing under another manhole cover, listening to the faint rumble of noises above ground. Streetcars and trucks, he mused. He looked down and saw a stagnant pool of gray-green sludge; at intervals a balloon pocket rose from the scum, glistening a bluish-purple, and burst. Then another. He turned, shook his head, and tramped back to the dirt cave by the church, his lips quivering.

Back in the cave, he sat and leaned his back against a dirt wall. His body was trembling slightly. Finally his senses quieted and he slept. When he awakened he felt stiff and cold. He had to leave this foul place, but leaving meant facing those policemen who had wrongly accused him. No, he could not go back aboveground. He remembered the beating they had given him and how he had signed his name to a confession, a confession which he had not even read. He had been too tired when they had shouted at him, demanding that he sign his name; he had signed it to end his pain.

He stood and groped about in the darkness. The church singing had stopped. How long had he slept? He did not know. But he felt refreshed and hungry. He doubled his fist nervously, realizing that he could not make a decision. As he walked about he stumbled over an old rusty iron pipe. He picked it up and felt a jagged edge. Yes, there was a brick wall and he could dig into it. What would he find? Smiling, he groped to the brick wall, sat, and began digging idly into damp cement. I can't make any noise, he cautioned himself. As time passed he grew thirsty, but there was no water. He had to kill time or go aboveground. The cement came out of the wall easily; he extracted four bricks and felt a soft draft blowing into his face. He stopped, afraid. What was beyond? He waited a long time and nothing happened; then he began digging again, soundlessly, slowly; he enlarged the hole and crawled through into a dark room and collided with another wall. He felt his way to the right; the wall ended and his fingers toyed in space, like the antennae of an insect.

He fumbled on and his feet struck something hollow, like wood. What's this? He felt with his fingers. Steps. . . . He stooped and pulled off his shoes and mounted the stairs and saw a yellow chink of light shining and heard a low voice speaking. He placed his eye to a keyhole and saw the nude waxen figure of a man stretched out upon a white table. The voice, low-pitched and vibrant, mumbled indistinguishable words, neither rising nor falling. He craned his neck and squinted to see the man who was talking, but he could not locate him. Above the naked figure was suspended a huge glass container filled with a blood-red liquid from which a white rubber tube dangled. He crouched closer to the door and saw the tip end of a black object lined with pink satin. A coffin, he breathed. This is an undertaker's establishment. . . . A fine-spun lace of ice covered his body and he shuddered. A throaty chuckle sounded in the depths of the yellow room.

He turned to leave. Three steps down it occurred to him that a light switch should be nearby; he felt along the wall, found an electric button, pressed it, and a blinding glare smote his pupils so hard that he was sightless, defenseless. His pupils contracted and he wrinkled his nostrils at a peculiar odor. At once he knew that he had been dimly aware of this odor in the darkness, but the light had brought it sharply to his attention. Some kind of stuff they use to embalm, he thought. He went down the steps and saw piles of lumber, coffins, and a long workbench. In one corner was a tool chest. Yes, he could use tools, could tunnel through walls with them. He lifted the lid of the chest and saw nails, a hammer, a crowbar, a screwdriver, a light bulb, and a long length of electric wire. Good! He would lug these back to his cave.

He was about to hoist the chest to his shoulders when he discovered a door behind the furnace. Where did it lead? He tried to open it and found it securely bolted. Using the crowbar so as to make no sound, he pried the door open; it swung on creaking hinges, outward. Fresh air came to his face and he caught the faint roar of faraway sound. Easy now, he told himself. He widened the door and a lump of coal rattled toward him. A coalbin. . . . Evidently the door led into another basement. The roaring noise was louder now, but he could not identify it. Where was he? He groped slowly over the coal pile, then ranged in darkness over a gritty floor. The roaring noise seemed to come from above him, then below. His fingers followed a wall until he touched a wooden ridge. A door, he breathed.

The noise died to a low pitch; he felt his skin prickle. It seemed that he was playing a game with an unseen person whose intelligence outstripped his. He put his ear to the flat surface of the door. Yes, voices. . . . Was this a prize fight stadium? The sound of the voices came near and sharp, but he could not tell if they were joyous or despairing. He twisted the knob until he heard a soft click and felt the springy weight of the door swinging toward him. He was afraid to open it, yet captured by curiosity and wonder. He jerked the door wide and saw on the far side of the basement a furnace glowing red. Ten feet away was still another door, half ajar. He crossed and peered through the door into an empty, high-ceilinged corridor that terminated in a dark complex of shadow. The belling voices rolled about him and his eagerness mounted. He stepped into the corridor and the voices swelled louder. He crept on and came to a narrow stairway leading circularly upward; there was no question but that he was going to ascend those stairs.

Mounting the spiraled staircase, he heard the voices roll in a steady wave, then leap to crescendo, only to die away, but always remaining audible. Ahead of him glowed red letters: E—X—I—T. At the top of the steps he paused in front of a black curtain that fluttered uncertainly. He parted the folds and looked into a convex depth that gleamed with clusters of shimmering lights. Sprawling below him was a stretch of human faces, tilted upward, chanting, whistling, screaming, laughing. Dangling before the faces, high upon a screen of silver, were jerking shadows. A movie, he said with slow laughter breaking from his lips.

He stood in a box in the reserved section of a movie house and the impulse he had had to tell the people in the church to stop their singing seized him. These people were laughing at their lives, he thought with amazement. They were shouting and yelling at the animated shadows of themselves. His compassion fired his imagination and he stepped out of the box, walked out upon thin air, walked on down to the audience; and, hovering in the air just above them, he stretched out his hand to touch them. . . . His tension snapped and he found himself back in the box, looking down into the sea of faces. No; it could not be done; he could not awaken them. He sighed. Yes, these people were children, sleeping in their living, awake in their dying.

He turned away, parted the black curtain, and looked out. He saw no one. He started down the white stone steps and when he reached the bottom he saw a man in trim blue uniform coming toward him. So used had he become to being underground that he thought that he could walk past the man, as though he were a ghost. But the man stopped. And he stopped.

"Looking for the men's room, sir?" the man asked, and, without waiting for an answer, he turned and pointed. "This way, sir. The first door to your right."

He watched the man turn and walk up the steps and go out of sight. Then he laughed. What a funny fellow! He went back to the basement and stood in the red darkness, watching the glowing embers in the furnace. He went to the sink and turned the faucet and the water flowed in a smooth silent stream that looked like a spout of blood. He brushed the mad image from his mind and began to wash his hands leisurely, looking about for the usual bar of soap. He found one and rubbed it in his palms until a rich lather bloomed in his cupped fingers, like a scarlet sponge. He scrubbed and rinsed his hands meticulously, then hunted for a towel; there was none. He shut off the water, pulled off his shirt, dried his hands on it; when he put it on again he was grateful for the cool dampness that came to his skin.

Yes, he was thirsty; he turned on the faucet again, bowled his fingers and when the water bubbled over the brim of his cupped palms, he drank in long, slow swallows. His bladder grew tight; he shut off the water, faced the wall, bent his head, and watched a red stream strike the floor. His nostrils wrinkled against acrid wisps of vapor; though he had tramped in the waters of the sewer, he stepped back from the wall so that his shoes, wet with sewer slime, would not touch his urine.

He heard footsteps and crawled quickly into the coalbin. Lumps rattled noisily. The footsteps came into the basement and stopped. Who was it? Had someone heard him and come down to investigate? He waited, crouching, sweating. For a long time there was silence, then he heard the clang of metal and a brighter glow lit the room. Somebody's tending the furnace, he thought. Footsteps came closer and he stiffened. Looming before him was a white face lined with coal dust, the face of an old man with watery blue eyes. Highlights spotted his gaunt cheekbones, and he held a huge shovel. There was a screechy scrape of metal against stone, and the old man lifted a shovelful of coal and went from sight.

The room dimmed momentarily, then a yellow glare came as coal flared at the furnace door. Six times the old man came to the bin and went to the furnace with shovels of coal, but not once did he lift his eyes. Finally he dropped the shovel, mopped his face with a dirty handkerchief, and sighed: "Wheeew!" He turned slowly and trudged out of the basement, his footsteps dying away.

He stood, and lumps of coal clattered down the pile. He stepped from the bin and was startled to see the shadowy outline of an electric bulb hanging above his head. Why had not the old man turned it on? Oh, yes. . . . He understood. The old man had worked here for so long that he had no need for light; he had learned a way of seeing in his dark world, like those sightless worms that inch along underground by a sense of touch.

His eyes fell upon a lunch pail and he was afraid to hope that it was full. He picked it up; it was heavy. He opened it. *Sandwiches!* He looked guiltily around; he was alone. He searched farther and found a folder of matches and a half-empty tin of tobacco; he put them eagerly into his pocket and clicked off the light. With the lunch pail under his arm, he went through the door, groped over the pile of coal, and stood again in the lighted basement of the undertaking establishment. I've got to get those tools, he told himself. And turn off that light. He tiptoed back up the steps and switched off the light; the invisible voice still droned on behind the door. He crept down and, seeing with his fingers, opened the lunch pail and tore off a piece of paper bag and brought out the tin and spilled grains of tobacco into the makeshift concave. He rolled it and wet it with spittle, then inserted one end into his mouth and lit it: he sucked smoke that bit his lungs. The nicotine reached his brain, went out along his arms to his finger tips, down to his stomach, and over all the tired nerves of his body.

He carted the tools to the hole he had made in the wall. Would the noise of the falling chest betray him? But he would have to take a chance; he had to have those tools. He lifted the chest and shoved it; it hit the dirt on the other side of the wall with a loud clatter. He waited, listening; nothing happened. Head first, he slithered through and stood in the cave. He grinned, filled with a cunning idea. Yes, he would now go back into the basement of the undertaking establishment and crouch behind the coal pile and dig another hole. Sure! Fumbling, he opened the tool chest and extracted a crowbar, a screwdriver, and a hammer; he fastened them securely about his person.

With another lumpish cigarette in his flexed lips, he crawled back through the hole and over the coal pile and sat, facing the brick wall. He jabbed with the crowbar and the cement sheered away; quicker than he thought, a brick came loose. He worked an hour; the other bricks did not come easily. He sighed, weak from effort. I ought to rest a little, he thought. I'm hungry. He felt his way back to the cave and stumbled along the wall till he came to the tool chest. He sat upon it, opened the lunch pail, and took out two thick sandwiches. He smelled them. Pork chops. . . . His mouth watered. He closed his eyes and devoured a sandwich, savoring the smooth rye bread and juicy meat. He ate rapidly, gulping down lumpy mouthfuls that made him long for water. He ate the other sandwich and found an apple and gobbled that up too, sucking the core till the last trace of flavor was drained from it. Then, like a dog, he ground the meat bones with his teeth, enjoying the salty, tangy marrow. He finished and stretched out full length on the ground and went to sleep. . . .

. . . His body was washed by cold water that gradually turned warm and he was buoyed upon a stream and swept out to sea where waves rolled gently and suddenly he found himself walking upon the water how strange and delightful to walk upon the water and he came upon a nude woman holding a nude baby in her arms and the woman was sinking into the water holding the baby above her head and screaming *help* and he ran over the water to the woman and he reached her just before she went down and he took the baby from her hands and stood watching the breaking bubbles where the woman sank and he called *lady* and still no answer yes dive down there and rescue that woman but he could not take this baby with him and he stooped and laid the baby tenderly upon the surface of the water expecting it to sink but it floated and he leaped into the water and held his breath and strained his eyes to see through the gloomy volume of water but there was no woman and he opened his mouth and called *lady* and the water bubbled and his chest ached and his arms were tired but he could not see the woman and he called again *lady lady* and his feet touched sand at the bottom of the sea and his chest felt as though it would burst and he bent his knees and propelled himself upward and water rushed past him and his head bobbed out and he breathed deeply and looked around where was the baby the baby was gone and he rushed over the water looking for the baby calling *where is it* and the empty sky and sea threw back his voice *where is it* and he began to doubt that he could stand upon the water and then he was sinking and as he struggled the water rushed him downward spinning dizzily and he opened his mouth to call for help and water surged into his lungs and he choked. . . .

He groaned and leaped erect in the dark, his eyes wide. The images of terror that thronged his brain would not let him sleep. He rose, made sure that the tools were hitched to his belt, and groped his way to the coal pile and found the rectangular gap from which he had taken the bricks. He took out the crowbar and hacked. Then dread paralyzed him. How long had he slept? Was it day or night now? He had to be careful. Someone might hear him if it were day. He hewed softly for hours at the cement, working silently. Faintly quivering in the air above him was the dim sound of yelling voices. Crazy people, he muttered. They're still there in that movie. . . .

Having rested, he found the digging much easier. He soon had a dozen bricks out. His spirits rose. He took out another brick and his fingers fluttered in space. Good! What lay ahead of him? Another basement? He made the hole larger, climbed through, walked over an uneven floor and felt a metal surface. He lighted a match and saw that he was standing behind a furnace in a basement; before him, on the far side of the room, was a door. He crossed and opened it; it was full of odds and ends. Daylight spilled from a window above his head.

Then he was aware of a soft, continuous tapping. What was it? A clock? No, it was louder than a clock and more irregular. He placed an old empty box beneath the window, stood upon it, and looked into an areaway. He eased the window up and crawled through; the sound of the tapping came clearly now. He glanced about; he was alone. Then he looked upward at a series of window ledges. The tapping identified itself. That's a typewriter, he said to himself. It seemed to be coming from just above. He grasped the ridges of a rain pipe and lifted himself upward; through a half-inch opening of window he saw a doorknob about three feet away. No, it was not a doorknob; it was a small circular disk made of stainless steel with many fine markings upon it. He held his breath; an eerie white hand, seemingly detached from its arm, touched the metal knob and whirled it, first to the left, then to the right. It's a safe! . . . Suddenly he could see the dial no more; a huge metal door swung slowly toward him and he was looking into a safe filled with green wads of paper money, rows of coins wrapped in brown paper, and glass jars and boxes of various sizes. His heart quickened. Good Lord! The white hand went in and out of the safe, taking wads of bills and cylinders of coins. The hand vanished and he heard the muffled click of the big door as it closed. Only the steel dial was visible now. The typewriter still tapped in his ears, but he could not see it. He blinked, wondering if what he had seen was real. There was more money in that safe than he had seen in all his life.

As he clung to the rain pipe, a daring idea came to him and he pulled the screwdriver from his belt. If the white hand twirled that dial again, he would be able to see how far to left and right it spun and he would have the combination! His blood tingled. I can scratch the numbers right here, he thought. Holding the pipe with one hand, he made the sharp edge of the screwdriver bite into the brick wall. Yes, he could do it. Now, he was set. Now, he had a reason for staying here in the underground. He waited for a long time, but the white hand did not return. Goddamn! Had he been more alert, he could have counted the twirls and he would have had the combination. He got down and stood in the areaway, sunk in reflection.

How could he get into that room? He climbed back into the basement and saw wooden steps leading upward. Was that the room where the safe stood? Fearing that the dial was now being twirled, he clambered through the window, hoisted himself up the rain pipe, and peered; he saw only the naked gleam of the steel dial. He got down and doubled his fists. Well, he would explore the basement. He returned to the basement room and mounted the steps to the door and squinted through the keyhole; all was dark, but the tapping was still somewhere near, still faint and directionless. He pushed the door in; along one wall of a room was a table piled with radios and electrical equipment. A radio shop, he muttered.

Well, he could rig up a radio in his cave. He found a sack, slid the radio into it, and slung it across his back. Closing the door, he went down the steps and stood again in the basement, disappointed. He had not solved the problem of the steel dial and he was irked. He set the radio on the floor and again hoisted himself through the window and up the rain pipe and squinted; the metal door was swinging shut. Goddamn! He's worked the combination again. If I had been patient, I'd have had it! How could he get into that room? He *had* to get into it. He could jimmy the window, but it would be much better if he could get in without any traces. To the right of him, he calculated, should be the basement of the building that held the safe; therefore, if he dug a hole right *here*, he ought to reach his goal.

He began a quiet scraping; it was hard work, for the bricks were not damp. He eventually got one out and lowered it softly to the floor. He had to be careful; perhaps people were beyond this wall. He extracted a second layer of brick and found still another. He gritted his teeth, ready to quit. I'll dig one more, he resolved. When the next brick came out he felt air blowing into his face. He waited to be challenged, but nothing happened.

He enlarged the hole and pulled himself through and stood in quiet darkness. He scratched a match to flame and saw steps; he mounted and peered through a keyhole: Darkness. . . . He strained to hear the typewriter, but there was only silence. Maybe the office had closed? He twisted the knob and swung the door in; a frigid blast made him shiver. In the shadows before him were halves and quarters of hogs and lambs and steers hanging from metal hooks on the low ceiling, red meat encased in folds of cold white fat. Fronting him was frost-coated glass from behind which came indistinguishable sounds. The odor of fresh raw meat sickened him and he backed away. A meat market, he whispered.

He ducked his head, suddenly blinded by light. He narrowed his eyes; the red-white rows of meat were drenched in yellow glare. A man wearing a crimson-spotted jacket came in and took down a bloody meat cleaver. He eased the door to, holding it ajar just enough to watch the man, hoping that the darkness in which he stood would keep him from being seen. The man took down a hunk of steer and placed it upon a bloody wooden block and bent forward and whacked with the cleaver. The man's face was hard, square, grim; a jet of mustache smudged his upper lip and a glistening cowlick of hair fell over his left eye. Each time he lifted the cleaver and brought it down upon the meat, he let out a short, deep-chested grunt. After he had cut the meat, he wiped blood off the wooden block with a sticky wad of gunny sack and hung the cleaver upon a hook. His face was proud as he placed the chunk of meat in the crook of his elbow and left.

The door slammed and the light went off; once more he stood in shadow. His tension ebbed. From behind the frosted glass he heard the man's voice:

"Forty-eight cents a pound, ma'am." He shuddered, feeling that there was some-thing he had to do. But what? He stared fixedly at the cleaver, then he sneezed and was terrified for fear that the man had heard him. But the door did not open. He took down the cleaver and examined the sharp edge smeared with cold blood. Behind the ice-coated glass a cash register rang with a vibrating, musical tinkle.

Absent-mindedly holding the meat cleaver, he rubbed the glass with his thumb and cleared a spot that enabled him to see into the front of the store. The shop was empty, save for the man who was now putting on his hat and coat. Beyond the front window a wan sun shone in the streets; people passed and now and then a fragment of laughter or the whir of a speeding auto came to him. He peered closer and saw on the right counter of the shop a mosquito netting covering pears, grapes, lemons, oranges, bananas, peaches, and plums. His stomach contracted.

The man clicked out the light and he gritted his teeth, muttering, Don't lock the icebox door. . . . The man went through the door of the shop and locked it from the outside. Thank God! Now, he would eat some more! He waited, trem-bling. The sun died and its rays lingered on in the sky, turning the streets to dusk. He opened the door and stepped inside the shop. In reverse letters across the front window was: NICK'S FRUITS AND MEATS. He laughed, picked up a soft ripe yellow pear and bit into it; juice squirted; his mouth ached as his saliva glands reacted to the acid of the fruit. He ate three pears, gobbled six bananas, and made away with several oranges, taking a bite out of their tops and holding them to his lips and squeezing them as he hungrily sucked the juice.

He found a faucet, turned it on, laid the cleaver aside, pursed his lips under the stream until his stomach felt about to burst. He straightened and belched, feeling satisfied for the first time since he had been underground. He sat upon the floor, rolled and lit a cigarette, his bloodshot eyes squinting against the film of drifting smoke. He watched a patch of sky turn red, then purple; night fell and he lit another cigarette, brooding. Some part of him was trying to remember the world he had left, and another part of him did not want to remember it. Sprawling before him in his mind was his wife, Mrs. Wooten for whom he worked, the three policemen who had picked him up. . . . He possessed them now more completely than he had ever possessed them when he had lived aboveground. How this had come about he could not say, but he had no desire to go back to them. He laughed, crushed the cigarette, and stood up.

He went to the front door and gazed out. Emotionally he hovered between the world aboveground and the world underground. He longed to go out, but sober judgment urged him to remain here. Then impulsively he pried the lock loose with one swift twist of the crowbar; the door swung outward. Through the twilight he saw a white man and a white woman coming toward him. He held himself tense, waiting for them to pass; but they came directly to the door and confronted him.

"I want to buy a pound of grapes," the woman said.

Terrified, he stepped back into the store. The white man stood to one side and the woman entered.

"Give me a pound of dark ones," the woman said.

The white man came slowly forward, blinking his eyes.

"Where's Nick?" the man asked.

"Were you just closing?" the woman asked.

"Yes, ma'am," he mumbled. For a second he did not breathe, then he mumbled again: "Yes, ma'am."

"I'm sorry," the woman said.

The street lamps came on, lighting the store somewhat. Ought he run? But that would raise an alarm. He moved slowly, dreamily, to a counter and lifted up a bunch of grapes and showed them to the woman.

"Fine," the woman said. "But isn't that more than a pound?"

He did not answer. The man was staring at him intently.

"Put them in a bag for me," the woman said, fumbling with her purse.

"Yes, ma'am."

He saw a pile of paper bags under a narrow ledge; he opened one and put the grapes in.

"Thanks," the woman said, taking the bag and placing a dime in his dark palm.

"Where's Nick?" the man asked again. "At supper?"

"Sir? Yes, sir," he breathed.

They left the store and he stood trembling in the doorway. When they were out of sight, he burst out laughing and crying. A trolley car rolled noisily past and he controlled himself quickly. He flung the dime to the pavement with a gesture of contempt and stepped into the warm night air. A few shy stars trembled above him. The look of things was beautiful, yet he felt a lurking threat. He went to an unattended newsstand and looked at a stack of papers. He saw a headline: HUNT NEGRO FOR MURDER.

He felt that someone had slipped up on him from behind and was stripping off his clothes; he looked about wildly, went quickly back into the store, picked up the meat cleaver where he had left it near the sink, then made his way through the icebox to the basement. He stood for a long time, breathing heavily. They know I didn't do anything, he muttered. But how could he prove it? He had signed a confession. Though innocent, he felt guilty, condemned. He struck a match and held it near the steel blade, fascinated and repelled by the dried blotches of blood. Then his fingers gripped the handle of the cleaver with all the strength of his body, he wanted to fling the cleaver from him, but he could not. The match flame wavered and fled; he struggled through the hole and put the cleaver in the sack with the radio. He was determined to keep it, for what purpose he did not know.

He was about to leave when he remembered the safe. Where was it? He wanted to give up, but felt that he ought to make one more try. Opposite the last hole he had dug, he tunneled again, plying the crowbar. Once he was so exhausted that he lay on the concrete floor and panted. Finally he made another hole. He wriggled through and his nostrils filled with the fresh smell of coal. He struck a match; yes, the usual steps led upward. He tiptoed to a door and eased it open. A fair-haired white girl stood in front of a steel cabinet, her blue eyes wide upon him. She turned chalky and gave a high-pitched scream. He bounded down the steps and raced to his hole and clambered through, replacing the bricks with nervous haste. He paused, hearing loud voices.

"What's the matter, Alice?"

"A man . . ."

"What man? Where?"

"A man was at that door . . ."

"Oh, nonsense!"

"He was looking at me through the door!"

"Aw, you're dreaming."

"I *did* see a man!"

The girl was crying now.

"There's nobody here."

Another man's voice sounded.

"What is it, Bob?"

"Alice says she saw a man in here, in that door!"

"Let's take a look."

He waited, poised for flight. Footsteps descended the stairs.

"There's nobody down here."

"The window's locked."

"And there's no door."

"You ought to fire that dame."

"Oh, I don't know. Women are that way."

"She's too hysterical."

The men laughed. Footsteps sounded again on the stairs. A door slammed. He sighed, relieved that he had escaped. But he had not done what he had set out to do; his glimpse of the room had been too brief to determine if the safe was there. He had to know. Boldly he groped through the hole once more; he reached the steps and pulled off his shoes and tiptoed up and peered through the keyhole. His head accidentally touched the door and it swung silently in a fraction of an inch; he saw the girl bent over the cabinet, her back to him. Beyond her was the safe. He crept back down the steps, thinking exultingly: I found it!

Now he had to get the combination. Even if the window in the areaway was locked and bolted, he could gain entrance when the office closed. He scoured through the holes he had dug and stood again in the basement where he had left the radio and the cleaver. Again he crawled out of the window and lifted himself up the rain pipe and peered. The steel dial showed lonely and bright, reflecting the yellow glow of an unseen light. Resigned to a long wait, he sat and leaned against a wall. From far off came the faint sounds of life aboveground; once he looked with a baffled expression at the dark sky. Frequently he rose and climbed the pipe to see the white hand spin the dial, but nothing happened. He bit his lip with impatience. It was not the money that was luring him, but the mere fact that he could get it with impunity. Was the hand now twirling the dial? He rose and looked, but the white hand was not in sight.

Perhaps it would be better to watch continuously? Yes; he clung to the pipe and watched the dial until his eyes thickened with tears. Exhausted, he stood again in the areaway. He heard a door being shut and he clawed up the pipe and looked. He jerked tense as a vague figure passed in front of him. He stared unblinkingly, hugging the pipe with one hand and holding the screwdriver with the other, ready to etch the combination upon the wall. His ears caught: *Dong . . . Dong . . . Dong*

. . . *Dong*. . . *Dong* . . . *Dong* . . . *Dong* . . . Seven o'clock, he whispered. Maybe they were closing now? What kind of a store would be open as late as this? he wondered. Did anyone live in the rear? Was there a night watchman? Perhaps the safe was *already* locked for the night! Goddamn! While he had been eating in that shop, they had locked up everything. . . . Then, just as he was about to give up, the white hand touched the dial and turned it once to the right and stopped at six. With quivering fingers, he etched 1—R—6 upon the brick wall with the tip of the screwdriver. The hand twirled the dial twice to the left and stopped at two, and he engraved 2—L—2 upon the wall. The dial was spun four times to the right and stopped at six again; he wrote 4—R—6. The dial rotated three times to the left and was centered straight up and down; he wrote 3—L—0. The door swung open and again he saw the piles of green money and the rows of wrapped coins. I got it, he said grimly.

Then he was stone still, astonished. There were two hands now. A right hand lifted a wad of green bills and deftly slipped it up the sleeve of a left arm. The hands trembled; again the right hand slipped a packet of bills up the left sleeve. He's stealing, he said to himself. He grew indignant, as if the money belonged to him. Though *he* had planned to steal the money, he despised and pitied the man. He felt that his stealing the money and the man's stealing were two entirely different things. He wanted to steal the money merely for the sensation involved in getting it, and he had no intention whatever of spending a penny of it; but he knew that the man who was now stealing it was going to spend it, perhaps for pleasure. The huge steel door closed with a soft click.

Though angry, he was somewhat satisfied. The office would close soon. I'll clean the place out, he mused. He imagined the entire office staff cringing with fear; the police would question everyone for a crime they had not committed, just as they had questioned him. And they would have no idea of how the money had been stolen until they discovered the holes he had tunneled in the walls of the basements. He lowered himself and laughed mischievously, with the abandoned glee of an adolescent.

He flattened himself against the wall as the window above him closed with rasping sound. He looked; somebody was bolting the window securely with a metal screen. That won't help you, he snickered to himself. He clung to the rain pipe until the yellow light in the office went out. He went back into the basement, picked up the sack containing the radio and cleaver, and crawled through the two holes he had dug and groped his way into the basement of the building that held the safe. He moved in slow motion, breathing softly. Be careful now, he told himself. There might be a night watchman. . . . In his memory was the combination written in bold white characters as upon a blackboard. Eel-like he squeezed through the last hole and crept up the steps and put his hand on the knob and pushed the door in about three inches. Then his courage ebbed; his imagination wove dangers for him.

Perhaps the night watchman was waiting in there, ready to shoot. He dangled his cap on a forefinger and poked it past the jamb of the door. If anyone fired, they would hit his cap; but nothing happened. He widened the door, holding the crowbar high above his head, ready to beat off an assailant. He stood like that for five minutes; the rumble of a streetcar brought him to himself. He entered the room. Moonlight floated in from a side window. He confronted the safe, then checked himself. Better take a look around first. . . . He stepped about and found a closed door. Was the night watchman in there? He opened it and saw a washbowl, a faucet, and a commode. To the left was still another door that opened into a huge dark room that seemed empty; on the far side of that room he made out the shadow of still another door. Nobody's here, he told himself.

He turned back to the safe and fingered the dial; it spun with ease. He laughed and twirled it just for fun. Get to work, he told himself. He turned the dial to the figures he saw on the blackboard of his memory; it was so easy that he felt that the safe had not been locked at all. The heavy door eased loose and he caught hold of the handle and pulled hard, but the door swung open with a slow momentum of its own. Breathless, he gaped at wads of green bills, rows of wrapped coins, curious glass jars full of white pellets, and many oblong green metal boxes. He glanced guiltily over his shoulder; it seemed impossible that someone should not call to him to stop.

They'll be surprised in the morning, he thought. He opened the top of the sack and lifted a wad of compactly tied bills; the money was crisp and new. He admired the smooth, clean-cut edges. The fellows in Washington sure know how to make this stuff, he mused. He rubbed the money with his fingers, as though expecting it to reveal hidden qualities. He lifted the wad to his nose and smelled the fresh odor of ink. Just like any other paper, he mumbled. He dropped the wad into the sack and picked up another. Holding the bag, he thought and laughed.

There was in him no sense of possessiveness; he was intrigued with the form and color of the money, with the manifold reactions which he knew that men aboveground held toward it. The sack was one-third full when it occurred to him to examine the denominations of the bills; without realizing it, he had put many wads of one-dollar bills into the sack. Aw, nuts, he said in disgust. Take the big ones. . . . He dumped the one-dollar bills onto the floor and swept all the hundred-dollars bills he could find into the sack, then he raked in rolls of coins with crooked fingers.

He walked to a desk upon which sat a typewriter, the same machine which the blond girl had used. He was fascinated by it; never in his life had he used one of them. It was a queer instrument of business, something beyond the rim of his life. Whenever he had been in an office where a girl was typing, he had almost always spoken in whispers. Remembering vaguely what he had seen others do, he inserted a sheet of paper into the machine; it went in lopsided and he did not know how to straighten it. Spelling in a soft diffident voice, he pecked out his name on the keys: *freddaniels*. He looked at it and laughed. He would learn to type correctly one of these days.

Yes, he would take the typewriter too. He lifted the machine and placed it atop the bulk of money in the sack. He did not feel that he was stealing, for the cleaver, the radio, the money, and the typewriter were all on the same level of value, all meant the same thing to him. They were the serious toys of the men who lived in the dead world of sunshine and rain he had left, the world that had condemned him, branded him guilty.

But what kind of a place is this? He wondered. What was in that dark room to his rear? He felt for his matches and found that he had only one left. He leaned the sack against the safe and groped forward into the room, encountering smooth, metallic objects that felt like machines. Baffled, he touched a wall and tried vainly to locate an electric switch. Well, he *had* to strike his last match. He knelt and struck it, cupping the flame near the floor with his palms. The place seemed to be a factory, with benches and tables. There were bulbs with green shades spaced about the tables; he turned on a light and twisted it low so that the glare was limited. He saw a half-filled packet of cigarettes and appropriated it. There were stools at the benches and he concluded that men worked here at some trade. He wandered and found a few half-used folders of matches. If only he could find more cigarettes! But there were none.

But what kind of a place was this? On a bench he saw a pad of paper captioned: PEER'S—MANUFACTURING JEWELERS. His lips formed an "O," then he snapped off the light and ran back to the safe and lifted one of the glass jars and stared at the tiny white pellets. Gingerly he picked up one and found that it was wrapped in tissue paper. He peeled the paper and saw a glittering stone that looked like glass, glinting white and blue sparks. Diamonds, he breathed.

Roughly he tore the paper from the pellets and soon his palm quivered with precious fire. Trembling, he took all four glass jars from the safe and put them into the sack. He grabbed one of the metal boxes, shook it, and heard a tinny rattle. He pried off the lid with the screwdriver. Rings! Hundreds of them. . . . Were they worth anything? He scooped up a handful and jets of fire shot fitfully from the stones. These are diamonds too, he said. He pried open another box. Watches! A chorus of soft, metallic ticking filled his ears. For a moment he could not move, then he dumped all the boxes into the sack.

He shut the safe door, then stood looking around, anxious not to overlook anything. Oh! He had seen a door in the room where the machines were. What was in there? More valuables? He re-entered the room, crossed the floor, and stood undecided before the door. He finally caught hold of the knob and pushed the door in; the room beyond was dark. He advanced cautiously inside and ran his fingers along the wall for the usual switch, then he was stark still. Something had moved in the room! What was it? Ought he to creep out, taking the rings and diamonds and money? Why risk what he already had? He waited and the ensuing silence gave him confidence to explore further. Dare he strike a match? Would not a match flame make him a good target? He tensed again as he heard a faint sigh; he was now convinced that there was something alive near him, something that lived and breathed. On tiptoe he felt slowly along the wall, hoping that he would not collide with anything. Luck was with him; he found the light switch.

No; don't turn the light on. . . . Then suddenly he realized that he did not know in what direction the door was. Goddamn! He had to turn the light on or strike a match. He fingered the switch for a long time, then thought of an idea. He knelt upon the floor, reached his arm up to the switch and flicked the button, hoping that if anyone shot, the bullet would go above his head. The moment the light came on he narrowed his eyes to see quickly. He sucked in his breath and his body gave a violent twitch and was still. In front of him, so close that it made him want to bound up and scream, was a human face.

He was afraid to move lest he touch the man. If the man had opened his eyes at that moment, there was no telling what he might have done. The man—long and rawboned—was stretched out on his back upon a little cot, sleeping in his clothes, his head cushioned by a dirty pillow; his face, clouded by a dark stubble of beard, looked straight up to the ceiling. The man sighed, and he grew tense to defend himself; the man mumbled and turned his face away from the light. I've got to turn off that light, he thought. Just as he was about to rise, he saw a gun and cartridge belt on the floor at the man's side. Yes, he would take the gun and cartridge belt, not to use them, but just to keep them, as one takes a memento from a country fair. He picked them up and was about to click off the light when his eyes fell upon a photograph perched upon a chair near the man's head; it was the picture of a woman, smiling, shown against a background of open fields; at the woman's side were two young children, a boy and a girl. He smiled indulgently; he could send a bullet into that man's brain and time would be over for him. . . .

He clicked off the light and crept silently back into the room where the safe stood; he fastened the cartridge belt about him and adjusted the holster at his right hip. He strutted about the room on tiptoe, lolling his head nonchalantly, then paused, abruptly pulled the gun, and pointed it with grim face toward an imaginary foe. "Boom!" he whispered fiercely. Then he bent forward with silent laughter. That's just like they do it in the movies, he said.

He contemplated his loot for a long time, then got a towel from the washroom and tied the sack securely. When he looked up he was momentarily frightened by his shadow looming on the wall before him. He lifted the sack, dragged it down the basement steps, lugged it across the basement, gasping for breath. After he had struggled through the hole, he clumsily replaced the bricks, then tussled with the sack until he got it to the cave. He stood in the dark, wet with sweat, brooding about the diamonds, the rings, the watches, the money; he remembered the singing in the church, the people yelling in the movie, the dead baby, the nude man stretched out upon the white table. . . . He saw these items hovering before his eyes and felt that some dim meaning linked them together, that some magical relationship made them kin. He stared with vacant eyes, convinced that all of these images, with their tongueless reality, were striving to tell him something. . . .

Later, seeing with his fingers, he untied the sack and set each item neatly upon the dirt floor. Exploring, he took the bulb, the socket, and the wire out of the tool chest; he was elated to find a double socket at one end of the wire. He crammed the stuff into his pockets and hoisted himself upon the rusty pipes and squinted into the church; it was dim and empty. Somewhere in this wall were live electric wires; but where? He lowered himself, groped and tapped the wall with the butt of the screwdriver, listening vainly for hollow sounds. I'll just take a chance and dig, he said.

For an hour he tried to dislodge a brick, and when he struck a match, he found that he had dug a depth of only an inch! No use in digging here, he sighed. By the flickering light of a match, he looked upward, then lowered his eyes, only to glance up again, startled. Directly above his head, beyond the pipes, was a wealth of electric wiring. I'll be damned, he snickered.

He got an old dull knife from the chest and, seeing again with his fingers, separated the two strands of wire and cut away the insulation. Twice he received a slight shock. He scraped the wiring clean and managed to join the two twin ends, then screwed in the bulb. The sudden illumination blinded him and he shut his lids to kill the pain in his eyeballs. I've got that much done, he thought jubilantly.

He placed the bulb on the dirt floor and the light cast a blatant glare on the bleak clay walls. Next he plugged one end of the wire that dangled from the radio into the light socket and bent down and switched on the button; almost at once there was the harsh sound of static, but no words or music. Why won't it work? he wondered. Had he damaged the mechanism in any way? Maybe it needed grounding? Yes. . . . He rummaged in the tool chest and found another length of wire, fastened it to the ground of the radio, and then tied the opposite end to a pipe. Rising and growing distinct, a slow strain of music entranced him with its measured sound. He sat upon the chest, deliriously happy.

Later he searched again in the chest and found a half-gallon can of glue; he opened it and smelled a sharp odor. Then he recalled that he had not even looked at the money. He took a wad of green bills and weighed it in his palm, then broke the seal and held one of the bills up to the light and studied it closely. *The United States of America will pay to the bearer on demand one hundred dollars,* he read in slow speech; then: *This note is legal tender for all debts, public and private. . . .* He broke into a musing laugh, feeling that he was reading of the doings of people who lived on some far-off planet. He turned the bill over and saw on the other side of it a delicately beautiful building gleaming with paint and set amidst green grass. He had no desire whatever to count the money; it was what it stood for—the various currents of life swirling aboveground—that captivated him. Next he opened the rolls of coins and let them slide from their paper wrappings to the ground; the bright, new gleaming pennies and nickles and dimes piled high at his feet, a glowing mound of shimmering copper and silver. He sifted them through his fingers, listening to their tinkle as they struck the conical heap.

Oh, yes! He had forgotten. He would now write his name on the typewriter. He inserted a piece of paper and poised his fingers to write. But what was his name? He stared, trying to remember. He stood and glared about the dirt cave, his name on the tip of his lips. But it would not come to him. Why was he here? Yes, he had been running away from the police. But why? His mind was blank. He bit his lips and sat again, feeling a vague terror. But why worry? He laughed, then pecked slowly: *itwasalonghotday.* He was determined to type the sentence without making any mistakes. How did one make capital letters? He experimented and luckily discovered how to lock the machine for capital letters and then shift it back to lower case. Next he discovered how to make spaces, then he wrote neatly and correctly: *It was a long hot day.* Just why he selected that sentence he did not know; it was merely the ritual of performing the thing that appealed to him. He took the sheet out of the machine and looked around with stiff neck and hard eyes and spoke to an imaginary person:

"Yes, I'll have the contracts ready tomorrow."

He laughed. That's just the way they talk, he said. He grew weary of the game and pushed the machine aside. His eyes fell upon the can of glue, and a mischievous idea bloomed in him, filling him with nervous eagerness. He leaped up and opened the can of glue, then broke the seals on all the wads of money. I'm going to have some wallpaper, he said with a luxurious, physical laugh that made him bend at the knees. He took the towel with which he had tied the sack and balled it into a swab and dipped it into the can of glue and dabbed glue onto the wall; then he pasted one green bill by the side of another. He stepped back and cocked his head. Jesus! That's funny. . . . He slapped his thighs and guffawed. He had triumphed over the world aboveground! He was free! If only people could see this! He wanted to run from this cave and yell his discovery to the world.

He swabbed all the dirt walls of the cave and pasted them with green bills; when he had finished the walls blazed with a yellow-green fire. Yes, this room would be his hide-out; between him and the world that had branded him guilty would stand this mocking symbol. He had not stolen the money; he had simply picked it up, just as a man would pick up firewood in a forest. And that was how the world aboveground now seemed to him, a wild forest filled with death.

The walls of money finally palled on him and he looked about for new interests to feed his emotions. The cleaver! He drove a nail into the wall and hung the bloody cleaver upon it. Still another idea welled up. He pried open the metal boxes and lined them side by side on the dirt floor. He grinned at the gold and fire. From one box he lifted up a fistful of ticking gold watches and dangled them by their gleaming chains. He stared with an idle smile, then began to wind them up; he did not attempt to set them at any given hour, for there was no time for him now. He took a fistful of nails and drove them into the papered walls and hung the watches upon them, letting them swing down by their glittering chains, trembling and ticking busily against the backdrop of green with the lemon sheen of the electric light shining upon the metal watch casings, converting the golden disks into blobs of liquid yellow. Hardly had he hung up the last watch than the idea extended itself; he took more nails from the chest and drove them into the green paper and took the boxes of rings and went from nail to nail and hung up the golden bands. The blue and white sparks from the stones filled the cave with brittle laughter, as though enjoying his hilarious secret. People certainly can do some funny things, he said to himself.

He sat upon the tool chest, alternately laughing and shaking his head soberly. Hours later he became conscious of the gun sagging at his hip and he pulled it from the holster. He had seen men fire guns in movies, but somehow his life had never led him into contact with firearms. A desire to feel the sensation others felt in firing came over him. But someone might hear. . . . Well, what if they did? They would not know where the shot had come from. Not in their wildest notions would they think that it had come from under the streets! He tightened his fingers on the trigger; there was a deafening report and it seemed that the entire underground had caved in upon his eardrums; and in the same instant there flashed an orange-blue spurt of flame that died quickly but lingered on as a vivid after-image. He smelled the acrid stench of burnt powder filling his lungs and he dropped the gun abruptly.

The intensity of his feelings died and he hung the gun and cartridge belt upon the wall. Next he lifted the jars of diamonds and turned them bottom upward, dumping the white pellets upon the ground. One by one he picked them up and peeled the tissue paper from them and piled them in a neat heap. He wiped his sweaty hands on his trousers, lit a cigarette, and commenced playing another game. He imagined that he was a rich man who lived aboveground in the obscene sunshine and he was strolling through a park of a summer morning, smiling, nodding to his neighbors, sucking an after-breakfast cigar. Many times he crossed the floor of the cave, avoiding the diamonds with his feet, yet subtly gauging his footsteps so that his shoes, wet with sewer slime, would strike the diamonds at some undetermined moment. After twenty minutes of sauntering, his right foot smashed into the heap and diamonds lay scattered in all directions, glinting with a million tiny chuckles of icy laughter. Oh, shucks, he mumbled in mock regret, intrigued by the damage he had wrought. He continued walking, ignoring the brittle fire. He felt that he had a glorious victory locked in his heart.

He stooped and flung the diamonds more evenly over the floor and they showered rich sparks, collaborating with him. He went over the floor and trampled the stones just deep enough for them to be faintly visible, as though they were set delicately in the prongs of a thousand rings. A ghostly light bathed the cave. He sat on the chest and frowned. Maybe *any*thing's right, he mumbled. Yes, if the world as men had made it was right, then anything else was right, any act a man took to satisfy himself, murder, theft, torture.

He straightened with a start. What was happening to him? He was drawn to these crazy thoughts, yet they made him feel vaguely guilty. He would stretch out upon the ground, then get up; he would want to crawl again through the holes he had dug, but would restrain himself; he would think of going again up into the streets, but fear would hold him still. He stood in the middle of the cave, surrounded by green walls and a laughing floor, trembling. He was going to do something, but what? Yes, he was afraid of himself, afraid of doing some nameless thing.

To control himself, he turned on the radio. A melancholy piece of music rose. Brooding over the diamonds on the floor was like looking up into a sky full of restless stars; then the illusion turned into its opposite: he was high up in the air looking down at the twinkling lights of a sprawling city. The music ended and a man recited news events. In the same attitude in which he had contemplated the city, so now, as he heard the cultivated tone, he looked down upon land and sea as men fought, as cities were razed, as planes scattered death upon open towns, as long lines of trenches wavered and broke. He heard the names of generals and the names of mountains and the names of countries and the names and numbers of divisions that were in action on different battle fronts. He saw black smoke billowing from the stacks of warships as they neared each other over wastes of water and he heard their huge guns thunder as red-hot shells screamed across the surface of night seas. He saw hundreds of planes wheeling and droning in the sky and heard the clatter of machine guns as they fought each other and he saw planes falling in plumes of smoke and blaze of fire. He saw steel tanks rumbling across fields of ripe wheat to meet other tanks and there was a loud clang of steel as numberless tanks collided. He saw troops with fixed bayonets charging in waves against other troops who held fixed bayonets and men groaned as steel ripped into their bodies and they went down to die. . . . The voice of the radio faded and he was staring at the diamonds on the floor at his feet.

He shut off the radio, fighting an irrational compulsion to act. He walked aimlessly about the cave, touching the walls with his finger tips. Suddenly he stood still. *What was the matter with him?* Yes, he knew. . . . It was these walls; these crazy walls were filling him with a wild urge to climb out into the dark sunshine aboveground. Quickly he doused the light to banish the shouting walls, then sat again upon the tool chest. Yes, he was trapped. His muscles were flexed taut and sweat ran down his face. He knew now that he could not stay here and he could not go out. He lit a cigarette with shaking fingers; the match flame revealed the green-papered walls with militant distinctness; the purple on the gun barrel glinted like a threat; the meat cleaver brooded with its eloquent splotches of blood; the mound of silver and copper smoldered angrily; the diamonds winked at him from the floor; and the gold watches ticked and trembled, crowning time the king of consciousness, defining the limits of living. . . . The match blaze died and he bolted from where he stood and collided brutally with the nails upon the walls. The spell was broken. He shuddered, feeling that, in spite of his fear, sooner or later he would go up into that dead sunshine and somehow say something to somebody about all this.

He sat again upon the tool chest. Fatigue weighed upon his forehead and eyes. Minutes passed and he relaxed. He dozed, but his imagination was alert. He saw himself rising, wading again in the sweeping water of the sewer; he came to a manhole and climbed out and was amazed to discover that he had hoisted himself into a room filled with armed policemen who were watching him intently. He jumped awake in the dark; he had not moved. He sighed, closed his eyes, and slept again; this time his imagination designed a scheme of protection for him. His dreaming made him feel that he was standing in a room watching over his own nude body lying stiff and cold upon a white table. At the far end of the room he saw a crowd of people huddled in a corner, afraid of his body. Though lying dead upon the table, he was standing in some mysterious way at his side, warding off the people, guarding his body, and laughing to himself as he observed the situation. *They're scared of me,* he thought.

He awakened with a start, leaped to his feet, and stood in the center of the black cave. It was a full minute before he moved again. He hovered between sleeping and waking, unprotected, a prey of wild fears. He could neither see nor hear. One part of him was asleep; his blood coursed slowly and his flesh was numb. On the other hand he was roused to a strange, high pitch of tension. He lifted his fingers to his face, as though about to weep. Gradually his hands lowered and he struck a match, looking about, expecting to see a door through which he could walk to safety; but there was no door, only the green walls and the moving floor. The match flame died and it was dark again.

Five minutes later he was still standing when the thought came to him that he had been asleep. Yes. . . . But he was not yet fully awake; he was still queerly blind and deaf. How long had he slept? Where was he? Then suddenly he recalled the green-papered walls of the cave and in the same instant he heard loud singing coming from the church beyond the wall. Yes, they woke me up, he muttered. He hoisted himself and lay atop the bed of pipes and brought his face to the narrow slit. Men and women stood here and there between pews. A song ended and a young black girl tossed back her head and closed her eyes and broke plaintively into another hymn:

Glad, glad, glad, oh, so glad
I got Jesus in my soul . . .

Those few words were all she sang, but what her words did not say, her emotions said as she repeated the lines, varying the mood and tempo, making her tone express meanings which her conscious mind did not know. Another woman melted her voice with the girl's, and then an old man's voice merged with that of the two women. Soon the entire congregation was singing:

Glad, glad, glad, oh, so glad
I got Jesus in my soul . . .

They're wrong, he whispered in the lyric darkness. He felt that their search for a happiness they could never find made them feel that they had committed some dreadful offense which they could not remember or understand. He was now in possession of the feeling that had gripped him when he had first come into the underground. It came to him in a series of questions: Why was this sense of guilt so seemingly innate, so easy to come by, to think, to feel, so verily physical? It seemed that when one felt this guilt one was retracing in one's feelings a faint pattern designed long before; it seemed that one was always trying to remember a gigantic shock that had left a haunting impression upon one's body which one could not forget or shake off, but which had been forgotten by the conscious mind, creating in one's life a state of eternal anxiety.

He had to tear himself away from this; he got down from the pipes. His nerves were so taut that he seemed to feel his brain pushing through his skull. He felt that he had to do something, but he could not figure out what it was. Yet he knew that if he stood here until he made up his mind, he would never move. He crawled through the hole he had made in the brick wall and the exertion afforded him respite from tension. When he entered the basement of the radio store, he stopped in fear, hearing loud voices.

"Come on, boy! Tell us what you did with the radio!"

"Mister, I didn't steal the radio! I swear!"

He heard a dull thumping sound and he imagined a boy being struck violently.

"Please, mister!"

"Did you take it to a pawn shop?"

"No, sir! I didn't steal the radio! I got a radio at home," the boy's voice pleaded hysterically. "Go to my home and look!"

There came to his ears the sound of another blow. It was so funny that he had to clap his hand over his mouth to keep from laughing out loud. They're beating some poor boy, he whispered to himself, shaking his head. He felt a sort of distant pity for the boy and wondered if he ought to bring back the radio and leave it in the basement. No. Perhaps it was a good thing that they were beating the boy; perhaps the beating would bring to the boy's attention, for the first time in his life, the secret of his existence, the guilt that he could never get rid of.

Smiling, he scampered over a coal pile and stood again in the basement of the building where he had stolen the money and jewelry. He lifted himself into the areaway, climbed the rain pipe, and squinted through a two-inch opening of window. The guilty familiarity of what he saw made his muscles tighten. Framed before him in a bright tableau of daylight was the night watchman sitting upon the edge of a chair, stripped to the waist, his head sagging forward, his eyes red and puffy. The watchman's face and shoulders were stippled with red and black welts. Back of the watchman stood the safe, the steel door wide open showing the empty vault. Yes, they think he did it, he mused.

Footsteps sounded in the room and a man in a blue suit passed in front of him, then another, then still another. Policemen, he breathed. Yes, they were trying to make the watchman confess, just as they had once made him confess to a crime he had not done. He stared into the room, trying to recall something. Oh. . . . Those were the same policemen who had beaten him, had made him sign that paper when he had been too tired and sick to care. Now, they were doing the same thing to the watchman. His heart pounded as he saw one of the policemen shake a finger into the watchman's face.

"Why don't you admit it's an inside job, Thompson?" the policeman said.

"I've told you all I know," the watchman mumbled through swollen lips.

"But nobody was here but you!" the policeman shouted.

"I was sleeping," the watchman said. "It was wrong, but I was sleeping all that night!"

"Stop telling us that lie!"

"It's the truth!"

"When did you get the combination?"

"I don't know how to open the safe," the watchman said.

He clung to the rain pipe, tense; he wanted to laugh, but he controlled himself. He felt a great sense of power; yes, he could go back to the cave, rip the money off the walls, pick up the diamonds and rings, and bring them here and write a note, telling them where to look for their foolish toys. No. . . . What good would that do? It was not worth the effort. The watchman was guilty; although he was not guilty of the crime of which he had been accused, he was guilty, had always been guilty. The only thing that worried him was that the man who had been really stealing was not being accused. But he consoled himself: they'll catch him sometime during his life.

He saw one of the policemen slap the watchman across the mouth.

"Come clean, you bastard!"

"I've told you all I know," the watchman mumbled like a child.

One of the police went to the rear of the watchman's chair and jerked it from under him; the watchman pitched forward upon his face.

"Get up!" a policeman said.

Trembling, the watchman pulled himself up and sat limply again in the chair.

"Now, are you going to talk?"

"I've told you all I know," the watchman gasped.

"Where did you hide the stuff?"

"I didn't take it!"

"Thompson, your brains are in your feet," one of the policemen said. "We're going to string you up and get them back into your skull."

He watched the policemen clamp handcuffs on the watchman's wrists and ankles; then they lifted the watchman and swung him upside-down and hoisted his feet to the edge of a door. The watchman hung, head down, his eyes bulging. They're crazy, he whispered to himself as he clung to the ridges of the pipe.

"You going to talk?" a policeman shouted into the watchman's ear.

He heard the watchman groan.

"We'll let you hang there till you talk, see?"

He saw the watchman close his eyes.

"Let's take 'im down. He passed out," a policeman said.

He grinned as he watched them take the body down and dump it carelessly upon the floor. The policeman took off the handcuffs.

"Let 'im come to. Let's get a smoke," a policeman said.

The three policemen left the scope of his vision. A door slammed. He had an impulse to yell to the watchman that he could escape through the hole in the basement and live with him in the cave. But he wouldn't understand, he told himself. After a moment he saw the watchman rise and stand, swaying from weakness. He stumbled across the room to a desk, opened a drawer, and took out a gun. He's going to kill himself, he thought, intent, eager, detached, yearning to see the end of the man's actions. As the watchman stared vaguely about he lifted the gun to his temple; he stood like that for some minutes, biting his lips until a line of blood etched its way down a corner of his chin. No, he oughtn't do that, he said to himself in a mood of pity.

"Don't!" he half whispered and half yelled.

The watchman looked wildly about; he had heard him. But it did not help; there was a loud report and the watchman's head jerked violently and he fell like a log and lay prone, the gun clattering over the floor.

The three policemen came running into the room with drawn guns. One of the policemen knelt and rolled the watchman's body over and stared at a ragged, scarlet hole in the temple.

"Our hunch was right," the kneeling policeman said. "He was guilty, all right."

"Well, this ends the case," another policeman said.

"He knew he was licked," the third one said with grim satisfaction.

He eased down the rain pipe, crawled back through the holes he had made, and went back into his cave. A fever burned in his bones. He had to act, yet he was afraid. His eyes stared in the darkness as though propped open by invisible hands, as though they had become lidless. His muscles were rigid and he stood for what seemed to him a thousand years.

When he moved again his actions were informed with precision, his muscular system reinforced from a reservoir of energy. He crawled through the hole of earth, dropped into the gray sewer current, and sloshed ahead. When his right foot went forward at a street intersection, he fell backward and shot down into water. In a spasm of terror his right hand grabbed the concrete ledge of a down-curve and he felt the streaking water tugging violently at his body. The current reached his neck and for a moment he was still. He knew that if he moved clumsily he would be sucked under. He held onto the ledge with both hands and slowly pulled himself up. He sighed, standing once more in the sweeping water, thankful that he had missed death.

He waded on through sludge, moving with care, until he came to a web of light sifting down from a manhole cover. He saw steel hooks running up the side of the sewer wall; he caught hold and lifted himself and put his shoulder to the cover and moved it an inch. A crash of sound came to him as he looked into a hot glare of sunshine through which blurred shapes moved. Fear scalded him and he dropped back into the pallid current and stood paralyzed in the shadows. A heavy car rumbled past overhead, jarring the pavement, warning him to stay in his world of dark light, knocking the cover back into place with an imperious clang.

He did not know how much fear he felt, for fear claimed him completely; yet it was not a fear of the police or of people, but a cold dread at the thought of the actions he knew he would perform if he went out into that cruel sunshine. His mind said no; his body said yes; and his mind could not understand his feelings. A low whine broke from him and he was in the act of uncoiling. He climbed upward and heard the faint honking of auto horns. Like a frantic cat clutching a rag, he clung to the steel prongs and heaved his shoulder against the cover and pushed it off halfway. For a split second his eyes were drowned in the terror of yellow light and he was in a deeper darkness than he had ever known in the underground.

Partly out of the hole, he blinked, regaining enough sight to make out meaningful forms. An odd thing was happening: No one was rushing forward to challenge him. He had imagined the moment of his emergence as a desperate tussle with men who wanted to cart him off to be killed; instead, life froze about him as the traffic stopped. He pushed the cover aside, stood, swaying in a world so fragile that he expected it to collapse and drop him into some deep void. But nobody seemed to pay him heed. The cars were now swerving to shun him and the gaping hole.

"Why in hell don't you put up a red light, dummy?" a raucous voice yelled.

He understood; they thought that he was a sewer workman. He walked toward the sidewalk, weaving unsteadily through the moving traffic.

"Look where you're going, nigger!"

"That's right! Stay there and get killed!"

"You blind, you bastard?"

"Go home and sleep your drunk off!"

A policeman stood at the curb, looking in the opposite direction. When he passed the policeman, he feared that he would be grabbed, but nothing happened. Where was he? Was this real? He wanted to look about to get his bearings, but felt that something awful would happen to him if he did. He wandered into a spacious doorway of a store that sold men's clothing and saw his reflection in a long mirror: his cheekbones protruded from a hairy black face; his greasy cap was perched askew upon his head and his eyes were red and glassy. His shirt and trousers were caked with mud and hung loosely. His hands were gummed with a black stickiness. He threw back his head and laughed so loudly that passers-by stopped and stared.

He ambled on down the sidewalk, not having the merest notion of where he was going. Yet, sleeping within him, was the drive to go somewhere and say something to somebody. Half an hour later his ears caught the sound of spirited singing.

The Lamb, the Lamb, the Lamb
  I hear thy voice a-calling
The Lamb, the Lamb, the Lamb
  I feel thy grace a-falling

A church! he exclaimed. He broke into a run and came to brick steps leading downward to a subbasement. This is it! The church into which he had peered. Yes, he was going in and tell them. What? He did not know; but, once face to face with them, he would think of what to say. Must be Sunday, he mused. He ran down the steps and jerked the door open; the church was crowded and a deluge of song swept over him.

The Lamb, the Lamb, the Lamb
  Tell me again your story
The Lamb, the Lamb, the Lamb
  Flood my soul with your glory

He stared at the singing faces with a trembling smile.
"Say!" he shouted.
Many turned to look at him, but the song rolled on. His arm was jerked violently.
"I'm sorry, Brother, but you can't do that in here," a man said.
"But, mister!"
"You can't act rowdy in God's house," the man said.
"He's filthy," another man said.
"But I want to tell 'em," he said loudly.
"He stinks," someone muttered.
The song had stopped, but at once another one began.

Oh, wondrous sight upon the cross
  Vision sweet and divine
Oh, wondrous sight upon the cross
  Full of such love sublime

He attempted to twist away, but other hands grabbed him and rushed him into the doorway.
"Let me alone!" he screamed, struggling.
"Get out!"
"He's drunk," somebody said. "He ought to be ashamed!"
"He acts crazy!"
He felt that he was failing and he grew frantic.
"But, mister, let me tell—"
"Get away from this door, or I'll call the police!"
He stared, his trembling smile fading in a sense of wonderment.
"The police," he repeated vacantly.

"Now, get!"

He was pushed toward the brick steps and the door banged shut. The waves of song came.

Oh, wondrous sight, wondrous sight
Lift my heavy heart above
Oh, wondrous sight, wondrous sight
Fill my weary soul with love

He was smiling again now. Yes, the police. . . . That was it! Why had he not thought of it before? The idea had been deep down in him, and only now did it assume supreme importance. He looked up and saw a street sign: COURT STREET—HARTSDALE AVENUE. He turned and walked northward, his mind filled with the image of the police station. Yes, that was where they had beaten him, accused him, and had made him sign a confession of his guilt. He would go there and clear up everything, make a statement. What statement? He did not know. He was the statement, and since it was all so clear to him, surely he would be able to make it clear to others.

He came to the corner of Hartsdale Avenue and turned westward. Yeah, there's the station. . . . A policeman came down the steps and walked past him without a glance. He mounted the stone steps and went through the door, paused; he was in a hallway where several policemen were standing, talking, smoking. One turned to him.

"What do you want, boy?"

He looked at the policeman and laughed.

"What in hell are you laughing about?" the policeman asked.

He stopped laughing and stared. His whole being was full of what he wanted to say to them, but he could not say it.

"Are you looking for the Desk Sergeant?"

"Yes, sir," he said quickly; then: "Oh, no, sir."

"Well, make up your mind, now."

Four policemen grouped themselves around him.

"I'm looking for the men," he said.

"What men?"

Peculiarly, at that moment he could not remember the names of the policemen; he recalled their beating him, the confession he had signed, and how he had run away from them. He saw the cave next to the church, the money on the walls, the guns, the rings, the cleaver, the watches, and the diamonds on the floor.

"They brought me here," he began.

"When?"

His mind flew back over the blur of the time lived in the underground blackness. He had no idea of how much time had elapsed, but the intensity of what had happened to him told him that it could not have transpired in a short space of time, yet his mind told him that time must have been brief.

"It was a long time ago." He spoke like a child relating a dimly remembered dream. "It was a long time," he repeated, following the promptings of his emotions. "They beat me . . . I was scared . . . I ran away."

A policeman raised a finger to his temple and made a derisive circle.

"Nuts," the policeman said.

"Do you know what place this is, boy?"

"Yes, sir. The police station," he answered sturdily, almost proudly.

"Well, who do you want to see?"

"The men," he said again, feeling that surely they knew the men. "You know the men," he said in a hurt tone.

"What's your name?"

He opened his lips to answer and no words came. He had forgotten. But what did it matter if he had? It was not important.

"Where do you live?"

Where did he live? It had been so long ago since he had lived up here in this strange world that he felt it was foolish even to try to remember. Then for a moment the old mood that had dominated him in the underground surged back. He leaned forward and spoke eagerly.

"They said I killed the woman."

"What woman?" a policeman asked.

"And I signed a paper that said I was guilty," he went on, ignoring their questions. "Then I ran off . . ."

"Did you run off from an institution?"

"No, sir," he said, blinking and shaking his head. "I came from under the ground. I pushed off the manhole cover and climbed out . . ."

"All right, now," a policeman said, placing an arm about his shoulder. "We'll send you to the psycho and you'll be taken care of."

"Maybe he's a Fifth Columnist!" a policeman shouted.

There was laughter and, despite his anxiety, he joined in. But the laughter lasted so long that it irked him.

"I got to find those men," he protested mildly.

"Say, boy, what have you been drinking?"

"Water," he said. "I got some water in a basement."

"Were the men you ran away from dressed in white, boy?"

"No, sir," he said brightly. "They were men like you."

An elderly policeman caught hold of his arm.

"Try and think hard. Where did they pick you up?"

He knitted his brows in an effort to remember, but he was blank inside. The policeman stood before him demanding logical answers and he could no longer think with his mind; he thought with his feelings and no words came.

"I was guilty," he said. "Oh, no, sir. I wasn't then, I mean, mister!"

"Aw, talk sense. Now, where did they pick you up?"

He felt challenged and his mind began reconstructing events in reverse; his feelings ranged back over the long hours and he saw the cave, the sewer, the bloody room where it was said that a woman had been killed.

"Oh, yes, sir," he said, smiling. "I was coming from Mrs. Wooten's."

"Who is she?"

"I work for her."

"Where does she live?"

"Next door to Mrs. Peabody, the woman who was killed."

The policemen were very quiet now, looking at him intently.

"What do you know about Mrs. Peabody's death, boy?"

"Nothing, sir. But they said I killed her. But it doesn't make any difference. I'm guilty!"

"What are you talking about, boy?"

His smile faded and he was possessed with memories of the underground; he saw the cave next to the church and his lips moved to speak. But how could he say it? The distance between what he felt and what these men meant was vast. Something told him, as he stood there looking into their faces, that he would never be able to tell them, that they would never believe him even if he told them.

"All the people I saw was guilty," he began slowly.

"Aw, nuts," a policeman muttered.

"Say," another policeman said, "that Peabody woman was killed over on Winewood. That's Number Ten's beat."

"Where's Number Ten?" a policeman asked.

"Upstairs in the swing room," someone answered.

"Take this boy up, Sam," a policeman ordered.

"O.K. Come along, boy."

An elderly policeman caught hold of his arm and led him up a flight of wooden stairs, down a long hall, and to a door.

"Squad Ten!" the policeman called through the door.

"What?" a gruff voice answered.

"Someone to see you!"

"About what?"

The old policeman pushed the door in and then shoved him into the room.

He stared, his lips open, his heart barely beating. Before him were the three policemen who had picked him up and had beaten him to extract the confession. They were seated about a small table, playing cards. The air was blue with smoke and sunshine poured through a high window, lighting up fantastic smoke shapes. He saw one of the policemen look up; the policeman's face was tired and a cigarette dropped limply from one corner of his mouth and both of his fat, puffy eyes were squinting and his hands gripped his cards.

"Lawson!" the man exclaimed.

The moment the man's name sounded he remembered the names of all of them: Lawson, Murphy, and Johnson. How simple it was. He waited, smiling, wondering how they would react when they knew that he had come back.

"Looking for me?" the man who had been called Lawson mumbled, sorting his cards. "For what?"

So far only Murphy, the red-headed one, had recognized him.

"Don't you-all remember me?" he blurted, running to the table.

All three of the policemen were looking at him now. Lawson, who seemed the leader, jumped to his feet.

"Where in hell have you been?"

"Do you know 'im, Lawson?" the old policeman asked.

"Huh?" Lawson frowned. "Oh, yes. I'll handle 'im." The old policeman left the room and Lawson crossed to the door and turned the key in the lock. "Come here, boy," he ordered in a cold tone.

He did not move; he looked from face to face. Yes, he would tell them about his cave.

"He looks batty to me," Johnson said, the one who had not spoken before.

"Why in hell did you come back here?" Lawson said.

"I—I just didn't want to run away no more," he said. "I'm all right, now." He paused; the men's attitude puzzled him.

"You've been hiding, huh?" Lawson asked in a tone that denoted that he had not heard his previous words. "You told us you were sick, and when we left you in the room, you jumped out of the window and ran away."

Panic filled him. Yes, they were indifferent to what he would say! They were waiting for him to speak and they would laugh at him. He had to rescue himself from this bog; he had to force the reality of himself upon them.

"Mister, I took a sackful of money and pasted it on the walls . . ." he began.

"I'll be damned," Lawson said.

"Listen," said Murphy, "let me tell you something for your own good. We don't want you, see? You're free, free as air. Now go home and forget it. It was all a mistake. We caught the guy who did the Peabody job. He wasn't colored at all. He was an Eyetalian."

"Shut up!" Lawson yelled. "Have you no sense!"

"But I want to tell 'im," Murphy said.

"We can't let this crazy fool go," Lawson exploded. "He acts nuts, but this may be a stunt . . ."

"I was down in the basement," he began in a childlike tone, as though repeating a lesson learned by heart; "and I went into a movie. . . ." His voice failed. He was getting ahead of his story. First, he ought to tell them about the singing in the church, but what words could he use? He looked at them appealingly. "I went into a shop and took a sackful of money and diamonds and watches and rings. . . . I didn't steal 'em; I'll give 'em all back. I just took 'em to play with. . . ." He paused, stunned by their disbelieving eyes.

Lawson lit a cigarette and looked at him coldly.

"What did you do with the money?" he asked in a quiet, waiting voice.

"I pasted the hundred-dollar bills on the walls."

"What walls?" Lawson asked.

"The walls of the dirt room," he said, smiling, "the room next to the church. I hung up the rings and the watches and I stamped the diamonds into the dirt. . . ." He saw that they were not understanding what he was saying. He grew frantic to make them believe, his voice tumbled on eagerly. "I saw a dead baby and a dead man . . ."

"Aw, you're nuts," Lawson snarled, shoving him into a chair.

"But, mister . . ."

"Johnson, where's the paper he signed?" Lawson asked.

"What paper?"

"The confession, fool!"

Johnson pulled out his billfold and extracted a crumpled piece of paper.

"Yes, sir, mister," he said, stretching forth his hand. "That's the paper I signed . . ."

Lawson slapped him and he would have toppled had his chair not struck a wall behind him. Lawson scratched a match and held the paper over the flame; the confession burned down to Lawson's fingertips.

He stared, thunderstruck; the sun of the underground was fleeing and the terrible darkness of the day stood before him. They did not believe him, but he *had* to make them believe him!

"But, mister . . ."

"It's going to be all right, boy," Lawson said with a quiet, soothing laugh. "I've burned your confession, see? You didn't sign anything." Lawson came close to him with the black ashes cupped in his palm. "You don't remember a thing about this, do you?"

"Don't you-all be scared of me," he pleaded, sensing their uneasiness. "I'll sign another paper, if you want me to. I'll show you the cave."

"What's your game, boy?" Lawson asked suddenly.

"What are you trying to find out?" Johnson asked.

"Who sent you here?" Murphy demanded.

"Nobody sent me, mister," he said. "I just want to show you the room . . ."

"Aw, he's plumb bats," Murphy said. "Let's ship 'im to the psycho."

"No," Lawson said. "He's playing a game and I wish to God I knew what it was."

There flashed through his mind a definite way to make them believe him; he rose from the chair with nervous excitement.

"Mister, I saw the night watchman blow his brains out because you accused him of stealing," he told them. "But he didn't steal the money and diamonds. I took 'em."

Tigerishly Lawson grabbed his collar and lifted him bodily.

"Who told you about that?"

"Don't get excited, Lawson," Johnson said. "He read about it in the papers."

Lawson flung him away.

"He couldn't have," Lawson said, pulling papers from his pocket. "I haven't turned in the reports yet."

"Then how *did* he find out?" Murphy asked.

"Let's get out of here," Lawson said with quick resolution. "Listen, boy, we're going to take you to a nice, quiet place, see?"

"Yes, sir," he said. "And I'll show you the underground."

"Goddamn," Lawson muttered, fastening the gun at his hip. He narrowed his eyes at Johnson and Murphy. "Listen," he spoke just above a whisper, "say nothing about this, you hear?"

"O.K.," Johnson said.

"Sure," Murphy said.

Lawson unlocked the door and Johnson and Murphy led him down the stairs. The hallway was crowded with policemen.

"What have you got there, Lawson?"

"What did he do, Lawson?"

"He's psycho, ain't he, Lawson?"

Lawson did not answer; Johnson and Murphy led him to the car parked at the curb, pushed him into the back seat. Lawson got behind the steering wheel and the car rolled forward.

"What's up, Lawson?" Murphy asked.

"Listen," Lawson began slowly, "we tell the papers that he spilled about the Peabody job, then he escapes. The Wop is caught and we tell the papers that we steered them wrong to trap the real guy, see? Now this dope shows up and acts nuts. If we let him go, he'll squeal that we framed him, see?"

"I'm all right, mister," he said, feeling Murphy's and Johnson's arm locked rigidly into his. "I'm guilty. . . . I'll show you everything in the underground. I laughed and laughed . . ."

"Shut that fool up!" Lawson ordered.

Johnson tapped him across the head with a blackjack and he fell back against the seat cushion, dazed.

"Yes, sir," he mumbled. "I'm all right."

The car sped along Hartsdale Avenue, then swung onto Pine Street and rolled to State Street, then turned south. It slowed to a stop, turned in the middle of a block, and headed north again.

"You're going around in circles, Lawson," Murphy said.

Lawson did not answer; he was hunched over the steering wheel. Finally he pulled the car to a stop at a curb.

"Say, boy, tell us the truth," Lawson asked quietly. "Where did you hide?"

"I didn't hide, mister."

The three policemen were staring at him now; he felt that for the first time they were willing to understand him.

"Then what happened?"

"Mister, when I looked through all of those holes and saw how people were living, I loved 'em . . ."

"Cut out that crazy talk!" Lawson snapped. "Who sent you back here?"

"Nobody, mister."

"Maybe he's talking straight," Johnson ventured.

"All right," Lawson said. "Nobody hid you. Now, tell us *where* you hid."

"I went underground . . ."

"What goddamn underground do you keep talking about?"

"I just went. . . ." He paused and looked into the street, then pointed to a manhole cover. "I went down in there and stayed."

"In the *sewer?*"

"Yes, sir."

The policemen burst into a sudden laugh and ended quickly. Lawson swung the car around and drive to Woodside Avenue; he brought the car to a stop in front of a tall apartment building.

"What're we going to do, Lawson?" Murphy asked.

"I'm taking him up to my place," Lawson said. "We've got to wait until night. There's nothing we can do now."

They took him out of the car and led him into a vestibule.

"Take the steps," Lawson muttered.

They led him up four flights of stairs and into the living room of a small apartment. Johnson and Murphy let go of his arms and he stood uncertainly in the middle of the room.

"Now, listen, boy," Lawson began, "forget those wild lies you've been telling us. Where did you hide?"

"I just went underground, like I told you."

The room rocked with laughter. Lawson went to a cabinet and got a bottle of whisky; he placed glasses for Johnson and Murphy. The three of them drank.

He felt that he could not explain himself to them. He tried to muster all the sprawling images that floated in him; the images stood out sharply in his mind, but he could not make them have the meaning for others that they had for him. He felt so helpless that he began to cry.

"He's nuts, all right," Johnson said. "All nuts cry like that."

Murphy crossed the room and slapped him.

"Stop that raving!"

A sense of excitement flooded him; he ran to Murphy and grabbed his arm.

"Let me show you the cave," he said. "Come on, and you'll see!"

Before he knew it a sharp blow had clipped him on the chin; darkness covered his eyes. He dimly felt himself being lifted and laid out on the sofa. He heard low voices and struggled to rise, but hard hands held him down. His brain was clearing now. He pulled to a sitting posture and stared with glazed eyes. It had grown dark. How long had he been out?

"Say, boy," Lawson said soothingly, "will you show us the underground?"

His eyes shone and his heart swelled with gratitude. Lawson believed him! He rose, glad; he grabbed Lawson's arm, making the policeman spill whisky from the glass to his shirt.

"Take it easy, goddammit," Lawson said.

"Yes, sir."

"O.K. We'll take you down. But you'd better be telling us the truth, you hear?"

He clapped his hands in wild joy.

"I'll show you everything!"

He had triumphed at last! He would now do what he had felt was compelling him all along. At last he would be free of his burden.

"Take 'im down," Lawson ordered.

They led him down to the vestibule; when he reached the sidewalk he saw that it was night and a fine rain was falling.

"It's just like when I went down," he told them.

"What?" Lawson asked.

"The rain," he said, sweeping his arm in a wide arc. "It was raining when I went down. The rain made the water rise and lift the cover off."

"Cut it out," Lawson snapped.

They did not believe him now, but they would. A mood of high selflessness throbbed in him. He could barely contain his rising spirits. They would see what he had seen; they would feel what he had felt. He would lead them through all the holes he had dug and. . . . He wanted to make a hymn, prance about in physical ecstasy, throw his arm about the policemen in fellowship.

"Get into the car," Lawson ordered.

He climbed in and Johnson and Murphy sat at either side of him; Lawson slid behind the steering wheel and started the motor.

"Now, tell us where to go," Lawson said.

"It's right around the corner from where the lady was killed," he said.

The car rolled slowly and he closed his eyes, remembering the song he had heard in the church, the song that had wrought him to such a high pitch of terror and pity. He sang softly, lolling his head:

Glad, glad, glad, oh, so glad
I got Jesus in my soul . . .

"Mister," he said, stopping his song, "you ought to see how funny the rings look on the wall." He giggled. "I fired a pistol, too. Just once, to see how it felt."

"What do you suppose he's suffering from?" Johnson asked.

"Delusions of grandeur, maybe," Murphy said.

"Maybe it's because he lives in a white man's world," Lawson said.

"Say, boy, what did you eat down there?" Murphy asked, prodding Johnson anticipatorily with his elbow.

"Pears, oranges, bananas, and pork chops," he said.

The car filled with laughter.

"You didn't eat any watermelon?" Lawson asked, smiling.

"No, sir," he answered calmly. "I didn't see any."

The three policemen roared harder and louder.

"Boy, you're sure some case," Murphy said, shaking his head in wonder.

The car pulled to a curb.

"All right, boy," Lawson said. "Tell us where to go."

He peered through the rain and saw where he had gone down. The streets, save for a few dim lamps glowing softly through the rain, were dark and empty.

"Right there, mister," he said, pointing.

"Come on; let's take a look," Lawson said.

"Well, suppose he did hide down there," Johnson said, "what is that supposed to prove?"

"I don't believe he hid down there," Murphy said.

"It won't hurt to look," Lawson said. "Leave things to me."

Lawson got out of the car and looked up and down the street.

He was eager to show them the cave now. If he could show them what he had seen, then they would feel what he had felt and they in turn would show it to others and those others would feel as they had felt, and soon everybody would be governed by the same impulse of pity.

"Take 'im out," Lawson ordered.

Johnson and Murphy opened the door and pushed him out; he stood trembling in the rain, smiling. Again Lawson looked up and down the street; no one was in sight. The rain came down hard, slanting like black wires across the wind-swept air.

"All right," Lawson said. "Show us."

He walked to the center of the street, stopped and inserted a finger in one of the tiny holes of the cover and tugged, but he was too weak to budge it.

"Did you really go down in there, boy?" Lawson asked; there was a doubt in his voice.

"Yes, sir. Just a minute. I'll show you."

"Help 'im get that damn thing off," Lawson said.

Johnson stepped forward and lifted the cover; it clanged against the wet pavement. The hole gaped round and black.

"I went down in there," he announced with pride.

Lawson gazed at him for a long time without speaking, then he reached his right hand to his holster and drew his gun.

"Mister, I got a gun just like that down there," he said, laughing and looking into Lawson's face. "I fired it once then hung it on the wall. I'll show you."

"Show us how you went down," Lawson said quietly.

"I'll go down first, mister, and then you-all can come after me, hear?" he spoke like a little boy playing a game.

"Sure, sure," Lawson said soothingly. "Go ahead. We'll come."

He looked brightly at the policemen; he was bursting with happiness. He bent down and placed his hands on the rim of the hole and sat on the edge, his feet dangling into watery darkness. He heard the familiar drone of the gray current. He lowered his body and hung for a moment by his fingers, then he went downward on the steel prongs, hand over hand, until he reached the last rung. He dropped and his feet hit the water and he felt the stiff current trying to suck him away. He balanced himself quickly and looked back upward at the policemen.

"Come on, you-all!" he yelled, casting his voice above the rustling at his feet.

The vague forms that towered above him in the rain did not move. He laughed, feeling that they doubted him. But, once they saw the things he had done, they would never doubt again.

"Come on! The cave isn't far!" he yelled. "But be careful when your feet hit the water, because the current's pretty rough down here!"

Lawson still held the gun. Murphy and Johnson looked at Lawson quizzically.

"What are we going to do, Lawson?" Murphy asked.

"We are not going to follow that crazy nigger down into that sewer, are we?" Johnson asked.

"Come on, you-all!" he begged in a shout.

He saw Lawson raise the gun and point it directly at him. Lawson's face twitched, as though he were hesitating.

Then there was a thunderous report and a streak of fire ripped through his chest. He was hurled into the water, flat on his back. He looked in amazement at the blurred white faces looming above him. They shot me, he said to himself. The water flowed past him, blossoming in foam about his arms, his legs, and his head. His jaw sagged and his mouth gaped soundless. A vast pain gripped his head and gradually squeezed out consciousness. As from a great distance he heard hollow voices.

"What did you shoot him for, Lawson?"

"I had to."

"Why?

"You've got to shoot his kind. They'd wreck things."

As though in a deep dream, he heard a metallic clank; they had replaced the manhole cover, shutting out forever the sound of wind and rain. From overhead came the muffled roar of a powerful motor and the swish of a speeding car. He felt the strong tide pushing him slowly into the middle of the sewer, turning him about. For a split second there hovered before his eyes the glittering cave, the shouting walls, and the laughing floor. . . . Then his mouth was full of thick, bitter water. The current spun him around. He sighed and closed his eyes, a whirling object rushing alone in the darkness, veering, tossing, lost in the heart of the earth.

From Black Boy (1945)

Chapter 3

Having grown taller and older, I now associated with older boys and I had to pay for my admittance into their company by subscribing to certain racial sentiments. The touchstone of fraternity was my feeling toward white people, how much hostility I held toward them, what degrees of value and honor I assigned to race. None of this was premeditated, but sprang spontaneously out of the talk of black boys who met at the crossroads.

It was degrading to play with girls and in our talk we relegated them to a remote island of life. We had somehow caught the spirit of the role of our sex and we flocked together for common moral schooling. We spoke boastfully in bass voices; we used the word "nigger" to prove the tough fiber of our feelings; we spouted excessive profanity as a sign of our coming manhood; we pretended callousness toward the injunctions of our parents; and we strove to convince one another that our decisions stemmed from ourselves and ourselves alone. Yet we frantically concealed how dependent we were upon one another.

Of an afternoon when school had let out I would saunter down the street, idly kicking an empty tin can, or knocking a stick against the palings of a wooden fence, or whistling, until I would stumble upon one or more of the gang loitering at a corner, standing in a field, or sitting upon the steps of somebody's house.

"Hey." Timidly.

"You eat yet?" Uneasily trying to make conversation.

"Yeah, man. I done really fed my face." Casually.

"I had cabbage and potatoes." Confidently.

"I had buttermilk and black-eyed peas." Meekly informational.

"Hell, I ain't gonna stand near you, nigger!" Pronouncement.

"How come?" Feigned innocence.

"'Cause you gonna smell up this air in a minute!" A shouted accusation.

Laughter runs through the crowd.

"Nigger, your mind's in a ditch." Amusingly moralistic.

"Ditch, nothing! Nigger, you going to break wind any minute now!" Triumphant pronouncement creating suspense.

"Yeah, when them black-eyed peas tell that buttermilk to move over, that buttermilk ain't gonna wanna move and there's gonna be war in your guts and your stomach's gonna swell up and bust!" Climax.

The crowd laughs loud and long.

"Man, them white folks oughta catch you and send you to the zoo and keep you for the next war!" Throwing the subject into a wider field.

"Then when that fighting starts, they oughta feed you on buttermilk and black-eyed peas and let you break wind!" The subject is accepted and extended.

"You'd win the war with a new kind of poison gas!" A shouted climax.

There is high laughter that simmers down slowly.

"Maybe poison gas is something good to have." The subject of white folks is associationally swept into the orbit of talk.

"Yeah, if they hava race riot round here, I'm gonna kill all the white folks with my poison." Bitter pride.

Gleeful laughter. Then silence, each waiting for the other to contribute something.

"Them white folks sure scared of us, though." Sober statement of an old problem.

"Yeah, they send you to war, make you lick them Germans, teach you how to fight and when you come back they scared of you, want to kill you." Half boastful and half complaining.

"My mama says that old white woman where she works talked 'bout slapping her and Ma said: 'Miz Green, if you slaps me, I'll kill you and go to hell and pay for it!'" Extension, development, sacrificial boasting.

"Hell, I woulda just killed her if she hada said that to me." An angry grunt of supreme racial assertion.

Silence.

"Man, them white folks sure is mean." Complaining.

"That's how come so many colored folks leaving the South." Informational.

"And, man, they sure hate for you to leave." Pride of personal and racial worth implied.

"Yeah. They wanna keep you here and work you to death."

"The first white sonofabitch that bothers me is gonna get a hole knocked in his head!" Naïve rebellion.

"That ain't gonna do you no good. Hell, they'll catch you." Rejection of naïve rebellion.

"Ha-ha-ha. . . . Yeah, goddammit, they really catch you, now." Appreciation of the thoroughness of white militancy.

"Yeah, white folks set on their white asses day and night, but leta nigger do something, and they get every bloodhound that was ever born and put 'em on his trail." Bitter pride in realizing what it costs to defeat them.

"Man, you reckon these white folks is ever gonna change?" Timid, questioning hope.

"Hell, no! They just born that way." Rejecting hope for fear that it could never come true.

"Shucks, man. I'm going north when I get grown." Rebelling against futile hope and embracing flight.

"A colored man's all right up north." Justifying flight.

"They say a white man hit a colored man up north and that colored man hit that white man, knocked him cold, and nobody did a damn thing!" Urgent wish to believe in flight.

"Man for man up there." Begging to believe in justice.

Silence.

"Listen, you reckon them buildings up north is as tall as they say they is?" Leaping by association to something concrete and trying to make belief real.

"They say they gotta building in New York forty stories high!" A thing too incredible for belief.

"Man, I'd be scareda them buildings!" Ready to abandon the now suppressed idea of flight.

"You know, they say that them buildings sway and rock in the wind." Stating a miracle.

"Naw, nigger!" Utter astonishment and rejection.

"Yeah, they say they do." Insisting upon the miracle.

"You reckon that could be?" Questioning hope.

"Hell, naw! If a building swayed and rocked in the wind, hell, it'd fall! Any fool knows that! Don't let people maka fool outta you, telling you them things!" Moving body agitatedly, stomping feet impatiently, and scurrying back to safe reality.

Silence. Somebody would pick up a stone and toss it across a field.

"Man, what makes white folks so mean?" Returning to grapple with the old problem.

"Whenever I see one I spit." Emotional rejection of whites.

"Man, ain't they ugly?" Increased emotional rejection.

"Man, you ever get right close to a white man, close enough to smell 'im?" Anticipation of statement.

"They say we stink. But my ma says white folks smell like dead folks." Wishing the enemy was dead.

"Niggers smell from sweat. But white folks smell *all* the time." The enemy is an animal to be killed on sight.

And the talk would weave, roll, surge, spurt, veer, swell, having no specific aim or direction, touching vast areas of life, expressing the tentative impulses of childhood. Money, God, race, sex, color, war, planes, machines, trains, swimming, boxing, anything. . . . The culture of one black household was thus transmitted to another black household, and folk tradition was handed from group to group. Our attitudes were made, defined, set, or corrected; our ideas were discovered, discarded, enlarged, torn apart, and accepted. Night would fall. Bats would zip through the air. Crickets would cry from the grass. Frogs would croak. The stars would come out. Dew would dampen the earth. Yellow squares of light would glow in the distance as kerosene lamps were lit in our homes. Finally, from across the fields or down the road a long slow yell would come:

"Youuuuuuuu, Daaaaaaaavee!"

Easy laughter among the boys, but no reply.

"Calling the hogs."

"Go home, pig."

Laughter again. A boy would slowly detach himself from the gang.

"Youuuuuuu, Daaaaaaaavee!"

He would not answer his mother's call, for that would have been a sign of dependence.

"I'll do you-all like the farmer did the potato," the boy would say.

"How's that?"

"Plant you now and dig you later!"

The boy would trot home slowly and there would be more easy laughter. More talk. One by one we would be called home to fetch water from the hydrant in the back yard, to go to the store and buy greens and meal for tomorrow, to split wood for kindling.

On Sundays, if our clothes were presentable, my mother would take me and my brother to Sunday school. We did not object, for church was not where we learned of God or His ways, but where we met our school friends and continued our long, rambling talks. Some of the Bible stories were interesting in themselves, but we always twisted them, secularized them to the level of our street life, rejecting all meanings that did not fit into our environment. And we did the same to the beautiful hymns. When the preacher intoned:

Amazing grace, how sweet it sounds

we would wink at one another and hum under our breath:

A bulldog ran my grandma down

We were now large enough for the white boys to fear us and both of us, the white boys and the black boys, began to play our traditional racial roles as though we had been born to them, as though it was in our blood, as though we were being guided by instinct. All the frightful descriptions we had heard about each other, all the violent expressions of hate and hostility that had seeped into us from our surroundings, came now to the surface to guide our actions. The roundhouse was the racial boundary of the neighborhood, and it had been tacitly agreed between the white boys and the black boys that the whites were to keep to the far side of the roundhouse and we blacks were to keep to our side. Whenever we caught a white boy on our side we stoned him; if we strayed to their side, they stoned us.

Our battles were real and bloody; we threw rocks, cinders, coal, sticks, pieces of iron, and broken bottles, and while we threw them we longed for even deadlier weapons. If we were hurt, we took it quietly; there was no crying or whimpering. If our wounds were not truly serious, we hid them from our parents. We did not want to be beaten for fighting. Once, in a battle with a gang of white boys, I was struck behind the ear with a piece of broken bottle; the cut was deep and bled profusely. I tried to stem the flow of blood by dabbing at the cut with a rag and when my mother came from work I was forced to tell her that I was hurt, for I needed medical attention. She rushed me to a doctor who stitched my scalp; but when she took me home she beat me, telling me that I must never fight white boys again, that I might be killed by them, that she had to work and had no time to worry about my fights. Her words did not sink in, for they conflicted with the code of the streets. I promised my mother that I would not fight, but I knew that if I kept my word I would lose my standing in the gang, and the gang's life was my life.

My mother became too ill to work and I began to do chores in the neighborhood. My first job was carrying lunches to the men who worked in the roundhouse, for which I received twenty-five cents a week. When the men did not finish their lunches, I would salvage what few crumbs remained. Later I obtained a job in a small café carting wood in my arms to keep the big stove going and taking trays of food to passengers when trains stopped for a half hour or so in a near-by station. I received a dollar a week for this work, but I was too young and too small to perform the duties; one morning while trying to take a heavily loaded tray up the steps of a train, I fell and dashed the tray of food to the ground.

Inability to pay rent forced us to move into a house perched atop high logs in a section of the town where flood waters came. My brother and I had great fun running up and down the tall, shaky steps.

Again paying rent became a problem and we moved nearer the center of town, where I found a job in a pressing shop, delivering clothes to hotels, sweeping floors, and listening to Negro men boast of their sex lives.

Yet again we moved, this time to the outskirts of town, near a wide stretch of railroad tracks to which, each morning before school, I would take a sack and gather coal to heat our frame house, dodging in and out between the huge, black, puffing engines.

My mother, her health failing rapidly, spoke constantly now of Granny's home, of how ardently she wanted to see us grow up before she died. Already there had crept into her speech a halting, lisping quality that, though I did not know it, was the shadow of her future. I was more conscious of my mother now than I had ever been and I was already able to feel what being completely without her would mean. A slowly rising dread stole into me and I would look at my mother for long moments, but when she would look at me I would look away. Then real fear came as her illness recurred at shorter intervals. Time stood still. My brother and I waited, hungry and afraid.

One morning a shouting voice awakened me.

"Richard! Richard!"

I rolled out of bed. My brother came running into the room.

"Richard, you better come and see Mama. She's very sick," he said.

I ran into my mother's room and saw her lying upon her bed, dressed, her eyes open, her mouth gaped. She was very still.

"Mama!" I called.

She did not answer or turn her head. I reached forward to shake her, but drew back, afraid that she was dead.

"Mama!" I called again, my mind unable to grasp that she could not answer.

Finally I went to her and shook her. She moved slightly and groaned. My brother and I called her repeatedly, but she did not speak. Was she dying? It seemed unthinkable. My brother and I looked at each other; we did not know what to do.

"We better get somebody," I said.

I ran into the hallway and called a neighbor. A tall, black woman bustled out of a door.

"Please, won't you come and see my mama? She won't talk. We can't wake her up. She's terribly sick," I told her.

She followed me into our flat.

"Mrs. Wright!" she called to my mother.

My mother lay still, unseeing, silent. The woman felt my mother's hands.

"She ain't dead," she said. "But she's sick, all right. I better get some more of the neighbors."

Five or six of the women came and my brother and I waited in the hallway while they undressed my mother and put her to bed. When we were allowed back in the room, a woman said:

"Looks like a stroke to me."

"Just like paralysis," said another.

"And she's so young," someone else said.

My brother and I stood against a wall while the bustling women worked frantically over my mother. A stroke? Paralysis? What were those things? Would she die? One of the women asked me if there was any money in the house; I did not know. They searched through the dresser and found a dollar or two and sent for a doctor. The doctor arrived. Yes, he told us, my mother had suffered a stroke of paralysis. She was in a serious condition. She needed someone with her day and night; she needed medicine. Where was her husband? I told him the story and he shook his head.

"She'll need all the help that she can get," the doctor said. "Her entire left side is paralyzed. She cannot talk and she will have to be fed."

Later that day I rummaged through drawers and found Granny's address; I wrote to her, pleading with her to come and help us. The neighbors nursed my mother day and night, fed us and washed our clothes. I went through the days with a stunned consciousness, unable to believe what had happened. Suppose Granny did not come? I tried not to think of it. She *had* to come. The utter loneliness was now terrifying. I had been suddenly thrown emotionally upon my own. Within an hour the half-friendly world that I had known had turned cold and hostile. I was too frightened to weep. I was glad that my mother was not dead, but there was the fact that she would be sick for a long, long time, perhaps for the balance of her life. I became morose. Though I was a child, I could no longer feel as a child, could no longer react as a child. The desire for play was gone and I brooded, wondering if Granny would come and help us. I tried not to think of a tomorrow that was neither real nor wanted, for all tomorrows held questions that I could not answer.

When the neighbors offered me food, I refused, already ashamed that so often in my life I had to be fed by strangers. And after I had been prevailed upon to eat I would eat as little as possible, feeling that some of the shame of charity would be taken away. It pained me to think that other children were wondering if I were hungry, and whenever they asked me if I wanted food, I would say no, even though I was starving. I was tense during the days I waited for Granny, and when she came

I gave up, letting her handle things, answering questions automatically, obeying, knowing that somehow I had to face things alone. I withdrew into myself.

I wrote letters that Granny dictated to her eight children—there were nine of them, including my mother—in all parts of the country, asking for money with which "to take Ella and her two little children to our home." Money came and again there were days of packing household effects. My mother was taken to the train in an ambulance and put on board upon a stretcher. We rode to Jackson in silence and my mother was put abed upstairs. Aunt Maggie came from Detroit to help nurse and clean. The big house was quiet. We spoke in lowered voices. We walked with soft tread. The odor of medicine hung in the air. Doctors came and went. Night and day I could hear my mother groaning. We thought that she would die at any moment.

Aunt Cleo came from Chicago. Uncle Clark came from Greenwood, Mississippi. Uncle Edward came from Carters, Mississippi. Uncle Charles from Mobile, Alabama. Aunt Addie from a religious school in Huntsville, Alabama. Uncle Thomas from Hazlehurst, Mississippi. The house had an expectant air and I caught whispered talk of "what is to become of her children?" I felt dread, knowing that others—strangers even though they were relatives—were debating my destiny. I had never seen my mother's brothers and sisters before and their presence made live again in me my old shyness. One day Uncle Edward called me to him and he felt my skinny arms and legs.

"He needs more flesh on him," he commented impersonally, addressing himself to his brothers and sisters.

I was horribly embarrassed, feeling that my life had somehow been full of nameless wrong, an unatonable guilt.

"Food will make him pick up in weight," Granny said.

Out of the family conferences it was decided that my brother and I would be separated, that it was too much of a burden for any one aunt or uncle to assume the support of both of us. Where was I to go? Who would take me? I became more anxious than ever. When an aunt or an uncle would come into my presence, I could not look at them. I was always reminding myself that I must not do anything that would make any of them feel they would not want me in their homes.

At night my sleep was filled with wild dreams. Sometimes I would wake up screaming in terror. The grownups would come running and I would stare at them, as though they were figures out of my nightmare, then go back to sleep. One night I found myself standing in the back yard. The moon was shining bright as day. Silence surrounded me. Suddenly I felt that someone was holding my hand. I looked and saw an uncle. He was speaking to me in a low, gentle voice.

"What's the matter, son?"

I stared at him, trying to understand what he was saying. I seemed to be wrapped in a kind of mist.

"Richard, what are you doing?"

I could not answer. It seemed that I could not wake up. He shook me. I came to myself and stared about at the moon-drenched yard.

"Where are we going?" I asked him.

"You were walking in your sleep," he said.

Granny gave me fuller meals and made me take naps in the afternoon and gradually my sleepwalking passed. The uneasy days and nights made me resolve to leave Granny's home as soon as I was old enough to support myself. It was not that they were unkind, but I knew that they did not have money enough to feed me and my brother. I avoided going into my mother's room now; merely to look at her was painful. She had grown very thin; she was still speechless, staring, quiet as stone.

One evening my brother and I were called into the front room where a conference of aunts and uncles was being held.

"Richard," said an uncle, "you know how sick your mother is?"

"Yes, sir."

"Well, Granny's not strong enough to take care of you two boys," he continued.

"Yes, sir," I said, waiting for his decision.

"Well, Aunt Maggie's going to take your brother to Detroit and send him to school."

I waited. Who was going to take me? I had wanted to be with Aunt Maggie, but I did not dare contest the decision.

"Now, where would you like to go?" I was asked.

The question caught me by surprise; I had been waiting for a fiat, and now a choice lay before me. But I did not have the courage to presume that anyone wanted me.

"Anywhere," I said.

"Any of us are willing to take you," he said.

Quickly I calculated which of them lived nearest to Jackson. Uncle Clark lived in Greenwood, which was but a few miles distant.

"I'd like to live with Uncle Clark, since he's close to the home here," I said.

"Is that what you really want?"

"Yes, sir."

Uncle Clark came to me and placed his hand upon my head.

"All right. I'll take you back with me and send you to school. Tomorrow we'll go and buy clothes."

My tension eased somewhat, but stayed with me. My brother was happy. He was going north. I wanted to go, but I said nothing.

A train ride and I was in yet another little southern town. Home in Greenwood was a four-room bungalow, comprising half of a double house that sat on a quiet shady road. Aunt Jody, a medium-sized, neat, silent, mulatto girl, had a hot supper waiting on the table. She baffled me with her serious, reserved manner; she seemed to be acting in conformity with a code unknown to me, and I assumed that she regarded me as a "wrong one," a boy who for some reason did not have a home; I felt that in her mind she would push me to the outskirts of life and I was awkward and self-conscious in her presence. Both Uncle Clark and Aunt Jody talked to me as though I were a grownup and I wondered if I could do what was expected of me. I had always felt a certain warmth with my mother, even when we had lived in squalor; but I felt none here. Perhaps I was too apprehensive to feel any.

During supper it was decided that I was to be placed in school the next day. Uncle Clark and Aunt Jody both had jobs and I was told that at noon I would find lunch on the stove.

"Now, Richard, this is your new home," Uncle Clark said.

"Yes, sir."

"After school, bring in wood and coal for the fireplaces."

"Yes, sir."

"Split kindling and lay a fire in the kitchen stove."

"Yes, sir."

"Bring in a bucket of water from the yard so that Jody can cook in the mornings."

"Yes, sir."

"After your chores are done, you may spend the afternoon studying."

"Yes, sir."

I had never been assigned definite tasks before and I went to bed a little frightened. I lay sleepless, wondering if I should have come, feeling the dark night holding strange people, strange houses, strange streets. What would happen to me here? How would I get along? What kind of woman was Aunt Jody? How ought I act around here? Would Uncle Clark let me make friends with other boys? I awakened the next morning to see the sun shining into my room; I felt more at ease.

"Richard!" my uncle was calling me.

I washed, dressed, and went into the kitchen and sat wordlessly at the table.

"Good morning, Richard," Aunt Jody said.

"Oh, good morning," I mumbled, wishing that I had thought to say it first.

"Don't people say good morning where you come from?" she asked.

"Yes, ma'am."

"I thought they did," she said pointedly.

Aunt Jody and Uncle Clark began to question me about my life and I grew so self-conscious that my hunger left me. After breakfast, Uncle Clark took me to school, introduced me to the principal. The first half of the school day passed without incident. I sat looking at the strange reading book, following the lessons. The subjects seemed simple and I felt that I could keep up. My anxiety was still in me; I was wondering how I would get on with the boys. Each new school meant a new area of life to be conquered. Were the boys tough? How hard did they fight? I took it for granted that they fought.

At noon recess I went into the school grounds and a group of boys sauntered up to me, looked at me from my head to my feet, whispering among themselves. I leaned against a wall, trying to conceal my uneasiness.

"Where you from?" a boy asked abruptly.

"Jackson," I answered.

"How come they make you people so ugly in Jackson?" he demanded.

There was loud laughter.

"You're not any too good-looking yourself," I countered instantly.

"Oh!"

"Aw!"

"You hear what he told 'im?"

"You think you're smart, don't you?" the boy asked, sneering.

"Listen, I ain't picking a fight," I said. "But if you want to fight, I'll fight."

"Hunh, hard guy, ain't you?"

"As hard as you."

"Do you know who you can tell that to?" he asked me.

"And you know who you can tell it back to?" I asked.

"Are you talking about my mama?" he asked, edging forward.

"If you want it that way," I said.

This was my test. If I failed now, I would have failed at school, for the first trial came not in books, but in how one's fellows took one, what value they placed upon one's willingness to fight.

"Take back what you said," the boy challenged me.

"Make me," I said.

The crowd howled, sensing a fight. The boy hesitated, weighing his chances of beating me.

"You ain't gonna take what that new boy said, is you?" someone taunted the boy.

The boy came close. I stood my ground. Our faces were four inches apart.

"You think I'm scared of you, don't you?" he asked.

"I told you what I think," I said.

Somebody, eager and afraid that we would not fight, pushed the boy and he bumped into me. I shoved him away violently.

"Don't push me!" the boy said.

"Then keep off me!" I said.

He was pushed again and I struck out with my right and caught him in the mouth. The crowd yelled, milled, surging so close that I could barely lift my arm to land a blow. When either of us tried to strike the other, we would be thrown off balance by the screaming boys. Every blow landed elicited shouts of delight. Knowing that if I did not win or make a good showing I would have to fight a new boy each day, I fought tigerishly, trying to leave a scar, seeking to draw blood as proof that I was not a coward, that I could take care of myself. The bell rang and the crowd pulled us apart. The fight seemed a draw.

"I ain't through with you!" the boy shouted.

"Go to hell!" I answered.

In the classroom the boys asked me questions about myself; I was someone worth knowing. When the bell rang for school to be dismissed, I was set to fight again; but the boy was not in sight.

On my way home I found a cheap ring in the streets and at once I knew what I was going to do with it. The ring had a red stone held by tiny prongs which I loosened, took the stone out, leaving the sharp tiny prongs jutting up. I slid the ring on to my finger and shadow boxed. Now, by God, let a goddamn bully come and I would show him how to fight; I would leave a crimson streak on his face with every blow.

But I never had to use the ring. After I had exhibited my new weapon at school, a description of it spread among the boys. I challenged my enemy to another fight, but he would not respond. Fighting was not now necessary. I had been accepted.

No sooner had I won my right to the school grounds than a new dread arose. One evening, before bedtime, I was sitting in the front room, reading, studying.

Uncle Clark, who was a contracting carpenter, was at his drawing table, drafting models of houses. Aunt Jody was darning. Suddenly the doorbell rang and Aunt Jody admitted the next-door neighbor, the owner of the house in which we lived and its former occupant. His name was Burden; he was a tall, brown, stooped man and when I was introduced to him I rose and shook his hand.

"Well, son," Mr. Burden told me, "it's certainly a comfort to see another boy in this house."

"Is there another boy here?" I asked eagerly.

"My son was here," Mr. Burden said, shaking his head. "But he's gone now."

"How old is he?" I asked.

"He was about your age," Mr. Burden mumbled sadly.

"Where did he go?" I asked stupidly.

"He's dead," Mr. Burden said.

"Oh," I said.

I had not understood him. There was a long silence. Mr. Burden looked at me wistfully.

"Do you sleep in there?" he asked, pointing to my room.

"Yes, sir."

"That's where my boy slept," he said.

"In *there?*" I asked, just to make sure.

"Yes, right in there."

"On *that* bed?" I asked.

"Yes, that was his bed. When I heard that you were coming, I gave your uncle that bed for you," he explained.

I saw Uncle Clark shaking his head vigorously at Mr. Burden, but he was too late. At once my imagination began to weave ghosts. I did not actually believe in ghosts, but I had been taught that there was a God and I had given a kind of uneasy assent to His existence, and if there was a God, then surely there must be ghosts. In a moment I built up an intense loathing for sleeping in the room where the boy had died. Rationally I knew that the dead boy could not bother me, but he had become alive for me in a way that I could not dismiss. After Mr. Burden had gone, I went timidly to Uncle Clark.

"I'm scared to sleep in there," I told him.

"Why? Because a boy died in there?"

"Yes, sir."

"But, son, that's nothing to be afraid of."

"I know. But I am scared."

"We all must die someday. So why be afraid?"

I had no answer for that.

"When you die, do you want people to be afraid of *you?*"

I could not answer that either.

"This is nonsense," Uncle Clark went on.

"But I'm scared," I told him.

"You'll get over it."

"Can't I sleep somewhere else?"

"There's nowhere else for you to sleep."

"Can I sleep here on the sofa?" I asked.

"*May* I sleep here on the sofa?" Aunt Jody corrected me in a mocking tone.

"May I sleep here on the sofa?" I repeated after her.

"No," Aunt Jody said.

I groped into the dark room and fumbled for the bed; I had the illusion that if I touched it I would encounter the dead boy. I trembled. Finally I jumped roughly into the bed and jerked the covers over my face. I did not sleep that night and my eyes were red and puffy the next morning.

"Didn't you sleep well?" Uncle Clark asked me.

"I can't sleep in that room," I said.

"You slept in it before you heard of that boy who died in there, didn't you?" Aunt Jody asked me.

"Yes, ma'am."

"Then why can't you sleep in it now?"

"I'm just scared."

"You stop being a baby," she told me.

The next night was the same; fear kept me from sleeping. After Uncle Clark and Aunt Jody had gone to bed, I rose and crept into the front room and slept in a tight ball on the sofa, without any cover. I awakened the next morning to find Uncle Clark shaking me.

"Why are you doing this?" he asked.

"I'm scared to sleep in there," I said.

"You go back into that room and sleep tonight," he told me. "You've got to get over this thing."

I spent another sleepless, shivering night in the dead boy's room—it was not my room any longer—and I was so frightened that I sweated. Each creak of the house made my heart stand still. In school the next day I was dull. I came home and spent another long night of wakefulness and the following day I went to sleep in the classroom. When questioned by the teacher, I could give no answer. Unable to free myself from my terror, I began to long for home. A week of sleeplessness brought me near the edge of nervous collapse.

Sunday came and I refused to go to church and Uncle Clark and Aunt Jody were astonished. They did not understand that my refusal to go to church was my way of silently begging them to let me sleep somewhere else. They left me alone in the house and I spent the entire day sitting on the front steps; I did not have enough courage to go into the kitchen to eat. When I became thirsty, I went around the house and drank water from the hydrant in the back yard rather than venture into the house. Desperation made me raise the issue of the room again at bedtime.

"Please, let me sleep on the sofa in the front room," I pleaded.

"You've got to get out of that fear," my uncle said.

I made up my mind to ask to be sent home. I went to Uncle Clark, knowing that he had incurred expense in bringing me here, that he had thought he was helping me, that he had bought my clothes and books.

"Uncle Clark, send me back to Jackson," I said.

He was bent over a little table and he straightened and stared at me.

"You're not happy here?" he asked.

"No, sir," I answered truthfully, fearing that the ceiling would crash down upon my head.

"And you really want to go back?"

"Yes, sir."

"Things will not be as easy for you at home as here," he said. "There's not much money for food and things."

"I want to be where my mother is," I said, trying to strengthen my plea.

"It's really about the room?"

"Yes, sir."

"Well, we tried to make you happy here," my uncle said, sighing. "Maybe we didn't know how. But if you want to go back, then you may go."

"When?" I asked eagerly.

"As soon as school term has ended."

"But I want to go now!" I cried.

"But you'll break up your year's schooling," he said.

"I don't mind."

"You will, in the future. You've never had a single year of steady schooling," he said.

"I want to go home," I said.

"Have you felt this way a long time?" he asked.

"Yes, sir."

"I'll write Granny tonight," he said, his eyes lit with surprise.

Daily I asked him if he had heard from Granny only to learn that there had been no word. My sleeplessness made me feel that my days were a hot, wild dream and my studies suffered at school. I had been making high marks and now I made low ones and finally began to fail altogether. I was fretful, living from moment to moment.

One evening, in doing my chores, I took the water pail to the hydrant in the back yard to fill it. I was half asleep, tired, tense, all but swaying on my feet. I balanced the handle of the pail on the jutting tip of the metal faucet and waited for it to fill; the pail slipped and water drenched my pants and shoes and stockings.

"That goddamn lousy bastard sonofabitching bucket!" I spoke in a whisper of hate and despair.

"Richard!" Aunt Jody's amazed voice sounded in the darkness behind me.

I turned. Aunt Jody was standing on the back steps. She came into the yard.

"What did you say, boy?" she asked.

"Nothing," I mumbled, looking contritely at the ground.

"Repeat what you said!" she demanded.

I did not answer. I stooped and picked up the pail. She snatched it from me.

"What did you say?" she asked again.

I still kept my head down, vaguely wondering if she were intimidating me or if she really wanted me to repeat my curses.

"I'm going to tell your uncle on you," she said at last.

I hated her then. I thought that hanging my head and looking mutely at the ground was a kind of confession and a petition for forgiveness, but she had not accepted it as such.

"I don't care," I said.

She gave me the pail, which I filled with water and carried to the house. She followed me.

"Richard, you are a very bad, bad boy," she said.

"I don't care," I repeated.

I avoided her and went to the front porch and sat. I had had no intention of letting her hear me curse, but since she had heard me and since there was no way to appease her, I decided to let things develop as they would. I would go home. But where was home? Yes, I would run away.

Uncle Clark came and called me into the front room.

"Jody says that you've been using bad language," he said.

"Yes, sir."

"You admit it?"

"Yes, sir."

"Why did you do it?"

"I don't know."

"I'm going to whip you. Pull off your shirt."

Wordlessly I bared my back and he lashed me with a strap. I gritted my teeth and did not cry.

"Are you going to use that language again?" he asked me.

"I want to go home," I said.

"Put on your shirt."

I obeyed.

"I want to go home," I said again.

"But this is your home."

"I want to go to Jackson."

"You have no home in Jackson."

"I want to go to my mother."

"All right," he relented. "I'll send you home Saturday." He looked at me with baffled eyes. "Tell me, where did you learn those words Jody heard you say?"

I looked at him and did not answer; there flashed through my mind a quick, running picture of all the squalid hovels in which I had lived and it made me feel more than ever a stranger as I stood before him. How could I have told him that I had learned to curse before I had learned to read? How could I have told him that I had been a drunkard at the age of six?

When he took me to the train that Saturday morning, I felt guilty and did not want to look at him. He gave me my ticket and I climbed hastily aboard the train. I waved a stiff good-bye to him through the window as the train pulled out. When I could see his face no longer, I wilted, relaxing. Tears blurred my vision. I leaned back and closed my eyes and slept all the way.

I was glad to see my mother. She was much better, though still abed. Another operation had been advised by the doctor and there was hope for recovery. But I was anxious. Why another operation? A victim myself of too many hopes that had never led anywhere, I was for letting my mother remain as she was. My feelings were governed by fear and I spoke to no one about them. I had already begun to sense that my feelings varied too far from those of the people around me for me to blab about what I felt.

I did not re-enter school. Instead, I played alone in the back yard, bouncing a rubber ball off the fence, drawing figures in the soft clay with an old knife, or reading what books I found about the house. I ached to be of an age to take care of myself.

Uncle Edward arrived from Carters to take my mother to Clarksdale for the operation; at the last moment I insisted upon being taken with them. I dressed hurriedly and we went to the station. Throughout the journey I sat brooding, afraid to look at my mother, wanting to return home and yet wanting to go on. We reached Clarksdale and hired a taxi to the doctor's office. My mother was jolly, brave, smiling, but I knew that she was as doubtful as I was. When we reached the doctor's waiting room the conviction settled in me that my mother would never be well again. Finally the doctor came out in his white coat and shook hands with me, then took my mother inside. Uncle Edward left to make arrangements for a room and a nurse. I felt crushed. I waited. Hours later the doctor came to the door.

"How's my mother?"

"Fine!" he said.

"Will she be all right?"

"Everything'll clear up in a few days."

"Can I see her now?"

"No, not now."

Later Uncle Edward returned with an ambulance and two men who carried a stretcher. They entered the doctor's office and brought out my mother; she lay with closed eyes, her body swathed in white. I wanted to run to the stretcher and touch her, but I could not move.

"Why are they taking mama that way?" I asked Uncle Edward.

"There are no hospital facilities for colored, and this is the way we have to do it," he said.

I watched the men take the stretcher down the steps; then I stood on the sidewalk and watched them lift my mother into the ambulance and drive away. I knew that my mother had gone out of my life; I could feel it.

Uncle Edward and I stayed at a boardinghouse; each morning he went to the rooming house to inquire about my mother and each time he returned gloomy and silent. Finally he told me that he was taking my mother back home.

"What chance has mama, really?" I asked him.

"She's very sick," he said.

We left Clarksdale; my mother rode on a stretcher in the baggage car with Uncle Edward attending her. Back home, she lay for days, groaning, her eyes vacant. Doctors visited her and left without making any comment. Granny grew frantic. Uncle Edward, who had gone home, returned and still more doctors were called in. They told us that a blod clot had formed on my mother's brain and that another paralytic stroke had set in.

Once, in the night, my mother called me to her bed and told me that she could not endure the pain, that she wanted to die. I held her hand and begged her to be quiet. That night I ceased to react to my mother; my feelings were frozen. I merely waited upon her, knowing that she was suffering. She remained abed ten years, gradually growing better, but never completely recovering, relapsing periodically into her paralytic state. The family had stripped itself of money to fight my mother's illness and there was no more forthcoming. Her illness gradually became an accepted thing in the house, something that could not be stopped or helped.

My mother's suffering grew into a symbol in my mind, gathering to itself all the poverty, the ignorance, the helplessness; the painful, baffling, hunger-ridden days and hours; the restless moving, the futile seeking, the uncertainty, the fear, the dread; the meaningless pain and the endless suffering. Her life set the emotional tone of my life, colored the men and women I was to meet in the future, conditioned my relation to events that had not yet happened, determined my attitude to situations and circumstances I had yet to face. A somberness of spirit that I was never to lose settled over me during the slow years of my mother's unrelieved suffering, a somberness that was to make me stand apart and look upon excessive joy with suspicion, that was to make me self-conscious, that was to make me keep forever on the move, as though to escape a nameless fate seeking to overtake me.

At the age of twelve, before I had had one full year of formal schooling, I had a conception of life that no experience would ever erase, a predilection for what was real that no argument could ever gainsay, a sense of the world that was mine and mine alone, a notion as to what life meant that no education could ever alter, a conviction that the meaning of living came only when one was struggling to wring a meaning out of meaningless suffering.

At the age of twelve I had an attitude toward life that was to endure, that was to make me seek those areas of living that would keep it alive, that was to make me skeptical of everything while seeking everything, tolerant of all and yet critical. The spirit I had caught gave me insight into the sufferings of others, made me gravitate toward those whose feelings were like my own, made me sit for hours while others told me of their lives, made me strangely tender and cruel, violent and peaceful.

It made me want to drive coldly to the heart of every question and lay it open to the core of suffering I knew I would find there. It made me love burrowing into psychology, into realistic and naturalistic fiction and art, into those whirlpools of politics that had the power to claim the whole of men's souls. It directed my loyalties to the side of men in rebellion; it made me love talk that sought answers to questions that could help nobody, that could only keep alive in me that enthralling sense of wonder and awe in the face of the drama of human feeling which is hidden by the external drama of life.

The Man Who Was Almost a Man (1960)

Dave struck out across the fields, looking homeward through paling light. Whut's the use talkin wid em niggers in the field? Anyhow, his mother was putting supper on the table. Them niggers can't understan nothing. One of these days he was going to get a gun and practice shooting, then they couldn't talk to him as though he were a little boy. He slowed, looking at the ground. Shucks, Ah ain scareda them even ef they are biggern me! Aw, Ah know whut Ahma do. Ahm going by ol Joe's sto n git that Sears Roebuck catlog n look at them guns. Mebbe Ma will lemme buy one when she gits mah pay from ol man Hawkins. Ahma beg her t gimme some money. Ahm ol ernough to hava gun. Ahm seventeen. Almost a man. He strode, feeling his long loose-jointed limbs. Shucks, a man oughta hava little gun aftah he done worked hard all day.

He came in sight of Joe's store. A yellow lantern glowed on the front porch. He mounted steps and went through the screen door, hearing it bang behind him. There was a strong smell of coal oil and mackerel fish. He felt very confident until he saw fat Joe walk in through the rear door, then his courage began to ooze.

"Howdy, Dave! Whutcha want?"

"How yuh, Mistah Joe? Aw, Ah don wanna buy nothing. Ah jus wanted t see ef yuhd lemme look at tha catlog erwhile."

"Sure! You wanna see it here?"

"Nawsuh. Ah wans t take it home wid me. Ah'll bring it back termorrow when Ah come in from the fiels."

"You plannin on buying something?"

"Yessuh."

"Your ma lettin you have your own money now?"

"Shucks. Mistah Joe, Ahm gittin t be a man like anybody else!"

Joe laughed and wiped his greasy white face with a red bandanna.

"Whut you plannin on buyin?"

Dave looked at the floor, scratched his head, scratched his thigh, and smiled. Then he looked up shyly.

"Ah'll tell yuh, Mistah Joe, ef yuh promise yuh won't tell."

"I promise."

"Waal, Ahma buy a gun."

"A gun? Whut you want with a gun?"

"Ah wanna keep it."

"You ain't nothing but a boy. You don't need a gun."

"Aw, lemme have the catlog, Mistah Joe. Ah'll bring it back."

Joe walked through the rear door. Dave was elated. He looked around at barrels of sugar and flour. He heard Joe coming back. He craned his neck to see if he were bringing the book. Yeah, he's got it. Gawddog, he's got it!

"Here, but be sure you bring it back. It's the only one I got."

"Sho, Mistah Joe."

"Say, if you wanna buy a gun, why don't you buy one from me? I gotta gun to sell."

"Will it shoot?"

"Sure it'll shoot."

"Whut kind is it?"

"Oh, it's kinda old . . . a left-hand Wheeler. A pistol. A big one."

"Is it got bullets in it?"

"It's loaded."

"Kin Ah see it?"

"Where's your money?"

"Whut yuh wan fer it?"

"I'll let you have it for two dollars."

"Just two dollahs? Shucks, Ah could buy tha when Ah git mah pay."

"I'll have it here when you want it."

"Awright, suh. Ah be in fer it."

He went through the door, hearing it slam again behind him. Ahma git some money from Ma n buy me a gun! Only two dollahs! He tucked the thick catalogue under his arm and hurried.

"Where yuh been, boy?" His mother held a steaming dish of black-eyed peas.

"Aw, Ma, Ah jus stopped down the road t talk wid the boys."

"Yuh know bettah t keep suppah waitin."

He sat down, resting the catalogue on the edge of the table.

"Yuh git up from there and git to the well n wash yosef! Ah ain feedin no hogs in mah house!"

She grabbed his shoulder and pushed him. He stumbled out of the room, then came back to get the catalogue.

"Whut this?"

"Aw, Ma, it's jusa catlog."

"Who yuh git it from?"

"From Joe, down at the sto."

"Waal, thas good. We kin use it in the outhouse."

"Naw, Ma." He grabbed for it. "Gimme ma catlog, Ma."

She held onto it and glared at him.

"Quit hollerin at me! Whut's wrong wid yuh? Yuh crazy?"

"But Ma, please. It ain mine! It's Joe's! He tol me t bring it back t im termorrow."

She gave up the book. He stumbled down the back steps, hugging the thick book under his arm. When he had splashed water on his face and hands, he groped back to the kitchen and fumbled in a corner for the towel. He bumped into a chair; it clattered to the floor. The catalogue sprawled at his feet. When he had dried his eyes he snatched up the book and held it again under his arm. His mother stood watching him.

"Now, ef yuh gonna act a fool over that ol book, Ah'll take it n burn it up."

"Naw, Ma, please."

"Waal, set down n be still!"

He sat down and drew the oil lamp close. He thumbed page after page, unaware of the food his mother set on the table. His father came in. Then his small brother.

"Whutcha got there, Dave?" his father asked.

"Jusa catlog," he answered, not looking up.

"Yeah, herc they is!" His eyes glowed at blue-and-black revolvers. He glanced up, feeling sudden guilt. His father was watching him. He eased the book under the table and rested it on his knees. After the blessing was asked, he ate. He scooped up peas and swallowed fat meat without chewing. Buttermilk helped to wash it down. He did not want to mention money before his father. He would do much better by cornering his mother when she was alone. He looked at his father uneasily out of the edge of his eye.

"Boy, how come yuh don quit foolin wid tha book n eat yo suppah?"

"Yessuh."

"How you n ol man Hawkins gitten erlong?"

"Suh?"

"Can't yuh hear? Why don yuh lissen? Ah ast yu how wuz yuh n ol man Hawkins gittin erlong?"

"Oh, swell, Pa. Ah plows mo lan than anybody over there."

"Waal, yuh oughta keep yo mind on whut yuh doin."

"Yessuh."

He poured his plate full of molasses and sopped it up slowly with a chunk of cornbread. When his father and brother had left the kitchen, he still sat and looked again at the guns in the catalogue, longing to muster courage enough to present his case to his mother. Lawd, ef Ah only had tha pretty one! He could almost feel the slickness of the weapon with his fingers. If he had a gun like that he would polish it and keep it shining so it would never rust. N Ah'd keep it loaded, by Gawd!

"Ma?" His voice was hesitant.

"Hunh?"

"Ol man Hawkins give yuh mah money yit?"

"Yeah, but ain no usa yuh thinking bout throwin nona it erway. Ahm keepin tha money sos yuh kin have cloes t go to school this winter."

He rose and went to her side with the open catalogue in his palms. She was washing dishes, her head bent low over a pan. Shyly he raised the book. When he spoke, his voice was husky, faint.

"Ma, Gawd knows Ah wans one of these."

"One of whut?" she asked, not raising her eyes.

"One of these," he said again, not daring even to point. She glanced up at the page, then at him with wide eyes.

"Nigger, is yuh gone plumb crazy?"

"Aw, Ma—"

"Git outta here! Don yuh talk t me bout no gun! Yuh a fool!"

"Ma, Ah kin buy one fer two dollahs."

"Not ef Ah knows it, yuh ain!"

"But yuh promised me one—"

"Ah don care whut Ah promised! Yuh ain nothing but a boy yit!"

"Ma, ef yuh lemme buy one Ah'll *never* ast yuh fer nothing no mo."

"Ah tol yuh t git outta here! Yuh ain gonna toucha penny of tha money fer no gun! Thas how come Ah has Mistah Hawkins t pay yo wages t me, cause Ah knows yuh ain got no sense."

"But, Ma, we needa gun. Pa ain got no gun. We needa gun in the house. Yuh kin never tell whut might happen."

"Now don yuh try to maka fool outta me, boy! Ef we did hava gun, yuh wouldn't have it!"

He laid the catalogue down and slipped his arm around her waist.

"Aw, Ma, Ah done worked hard alla summer n ain ast yuh fer nothin, is Ah, now?"

"Thas whut yuh spose t do!"

"But Ma, Ah wans a gun. Yuh kin lemme have two dollahs outta mah money. Please, Ma. I kin give it to Pa. . . . Please, Ma! Ah loves yuh, Ma."

When she spoke her voice came soft and low.

"Whut yu wan wida gun, Dave? Yuh don need no gun. Yuh'll git in trouble. N ef yo pa jus thought Ah let yuh have money t buy a gun he'd hava fit."

"Ah'll hide it, Ma. It ain but two dollahs."

"Lawd, chil, whut's wrong wid yuh?"

"Ain nothin wrong, Ma. Ahm almos a man now. Ah wans a gun."

"Who gonna sell yuh a gun?"

"Ol Joe at the sto."

"N it don cos but two dollahs?"

"Thas all, Ma. Jus two dollahs. Please, Ma."

She was stacking the plates away; her hands moved slowly, reflectively. Dave kept an anxious silence. Finally, she turned to him.

"Ah'll let yuh git tha gun ef yuh promise me one thing."

"Whut's tha, Ma?"

"Yuh bring it straight back t me, yuh hear? It be fer Pa."

"Yessum! Lemme go now, Ma."

She stooped, turned slightly to one side, raised the hem of her dress, rolled down the top of her stocking, and came up with a slender wad of bills.

"Here," she said. "Lawd knows yuh don need no gun. But yer pa does. Yuh bring it right back t me, yuh hear? Ahma put it up. Now ef yuh don, Ahma have yuh pa lick yuh so hard yuh won fergit it."

"Yessum."

He took the money, ran down the steps, and across the yard.

"Dave! Yuuuuuh Daaaaave!"

He heard, but he was not going to stop now. "Naw, Lawd!"

The first movement he made the following morning was to reach under his pillow for the gun. In the gray light of dawn he held it loosely, feeling a sense of power. Could kill a man with a gun like this. Kill anybody, black or white. And if he were holding his gun in his hand, nobody could run over him; they would have to respect him. It was a big gun, with a long barrel and a heavy handle. He raised and lowered it in his hand, marveling at its weight.

He had not come straight home with it as his mother had asked; instead he had stayed out in the fields, holding the weapon in his hand, aiming it now and then at some imaginary foe. But he had not fired it; he had been afraid that his father might hear. Also he was not sure he knew how to fire it.

To avoid surrendering the pistol he had not come into the house until he knew that they were all asleep. When his mother had tiptoed to his bedside late that night and demanded the gun, he had first played possum; then he had told her that the gun was hidden outdoors, that he would bring it to her in the morning. Now he lay turning it slowly in his hands. He broke it, took out the cartridges, felt them, and then put them back.

He slid out of bed, got a long strip of old flannel from a trunk, wrapped the gun in it, and tied it to his naked thigh while it was still loaded. He did not go in to breakfast. Even though it was not yet daylight, he started for Jim Hawkins' plantation. Just as the sun was rising he reached the barns where the mules and plows were kept.

"Hey! That you, Dave?"

He turned. Jim Hawkins stood eying him suspiciously.

"What're yuh doing here so early?"

"Ah didn't know Ah wuz gittin up so early, Mistah Hawkins. Ah wuz fixin t hitch up ol Jenny n take her t the fiels."

"Good. Since you're so early, how about plowing that stretch down by the woods?"

"Suits me, Mistah Hawkins."

"O.K. Go to it!"

He hitched Jenny to a plow and started across the fields. Hot dog! This was just what he wanted. If he could get down by the woods, he could shoot his gun and nobody would hear. He walked behind the plow, hearing the traces creaking, feeling the gun tied tight to his thigh.

When he reached the woods, he plowed two whole rows before he decided to take out the gun. Finally, he stopped, looked in all directions, then untied the gun and held it in his hand. He turned to the mule and smiled.

"Know whut this is, Jenny? Naw, yuh wouldn know! Yuhs jusa ol mule! Anyhow, this is a gun, n it kin shoot, by Gawd!"

He held the gun at arm's length. Whut t hell, Ahma shoot this thing! He looked at Jenny again.

"Lissen here, Jenny! When Ah pull this ol trigger, Ah don wan yuh t run n acka fool now!"

Jenny stood with head down, her short ears pricked straight. Dave walked off about twenty feet, held the gun far out from him at arm's length, and turned his head. Hell, he told himself, Ah ain afraid. The gun felt loose in his fingers; he waved it wildly for a moment. Then he shut his eyes and tightened his forefinger. Bloom! A report half deafened him and he thought his right hand was torn from his arm. He heard Jenny whinnying and galloping over the field, and he found himself on his knees, squeezing his fingers hard between his legs. His hand was numb; he jammed it into his mouth, trying to warm it, trying to stop the pain. The gun lay at his feet. He did not quite know what had happened. He stood up and stared at the gun as though it were a living thing. He gritted his teeth and kicked the gun. Yuh almos broke mah arm! He turned to look for Jenny; she was far over the fields, tossing her head and kicking wildly.

"Hol on there, ol mule!"

When he caught up with her she stood trembling, walling her big white eyes at him. The plow was far away; the traces had broken. Then Dave stopped short, looking, not believing. Jenny was bleeding. Her left side was red and wet with blood. He went closer. Lawd, have mercy! Wondah did Ah shoot this mule? He grabbed for Jenny's mane. She flinched, snorted, whirled, tossing her head.

"Hol on now! Hol on."

Then he saw the hole in Jenny's side, right between the ribs. It was round, wet, red. A crimson stream streaked down the front leg, flowing fast. Good Gawd! Ah wuzn't shootin at tha mule. He felt panic. He knew he had to stop that blood, or Jenny would bleed to death. He had never seen so much blood in all his life. He chased the mule for half a mile, trying to catch her. Finally she stopped, breathing hard, stumpy tail half arched. He caught her mane and led her back to where the plow and gun lay. Then he stooped and grabbed handfuls of damp black earth and tried to plug the bullet hole. Jenny shuddered, whinnied, and broke from him.

"Hol on! Hol on now!"

He tried to plug it again, but blood came anyhow. His fingers were hot and sticky. He rubbed dirt into his palms, trying to dry them. Then again he attempted to plug the bullet hole, but Jenny shied away, kicking her heels high. He stood helpless. He had to do something. He ran at Jenny; she dodged him. He watched a red stream of blood flow down Jenny's leg and form a bright pool at her feet.

"Jenny . . . Jenny," he called weakly.

His lips trembled. She's bleeding t death! He looked in the direction of home, wanting to go back, wanting to get help. But he saw the pistol lying in the damp black clay. He had a queer feeling that if he only did something, this would not be; Jenny would not be there bleeding to death.

When he went to her this time, she did not move. She stood with sleepy, dreamy eyes; and when he touched her she gave a low-pitched whinny and knelt to the ground, her front knees slopping in blood.

"Jenny . . . Jenny . . ." he whispered.

For a long time she held her neck erect; then her head sank, slowly. Her ribs swelled with a mighty heave and she went over.

Dave's stomach felt empty, very empty. He picked up the gun and held it gingerly between his thumb and forefinger. He buried it at the foot of a tree. He took a stick and tried to cover the pool of blood with dirt—but what was the use? There was Jenny lying with her mouth open and her eyes walled and glassy. He could not tell Jim Hawkins he had shot his mule. But he had to tell something. Yeah, Ah'll tell em Jenny started gittin wil n fell on the joint of the plow. . . . But that would hardly happen to a mule. He walked across the field slowly, head down.

It was sunset. Two of Jim Hawkins' men were over near the edge of the woods digging a hole in which to bury Jenny. Dave was surrounded by a knot of people, all of whom were looking down at the dead mule.

"I don't see how in the world it happened," said Jim Hawkins for the tenth time.

The crowd parted and Dave's mother, father, and small brother pushed into the center.

"Where Dave?" his mother called.

"There he is," said Jim Hawkins.

His mother grabbed him.

"Whut happened, Dave? Whut yuh done?"

"Nothin."

"C mon, boy, talk," his father said.

Dave took a deep breath and told the story he knew nobody believed.

"Waal," he drawled. "Ah brung ol Jenny down here sos Ah could do mah plowin. Ah plowed bout two rows, just like yuh see." He stopped and pointed at the long rows of upturned earth. "Then somethin musta been wrong wid ol Jenny. She wouldn ack right a-tall. She started snortin n kickin her heels. Ah tried t hol her, but she pulled erway, rearin n goin in. Then when the point of the plow was stickin up in the air, she swung erroun n twisted herself back on it. . . . She stuck herself n started t bleed. N fo Ah could do anything, she wuz dead."

"Did you ever hear of anything like that in all your life?" asked Jim Hawkins.

There were white and black standing in the crowd. They murmured. Dave's mother came close to him and looked hard into his face. "Tell the truth, Dave," she said.

"Looks like a bullet hole to me," said one man.

"Dave, whut yuh do wid the gun?" his mother asked.

The crowd surged in, looking at him. He jammed his hands into his pockets, shook his head slowly from left to right, and backed away. His eyes were wide and painful.

"Did he hava gun?" asked Jim Hawkins.

"By Gawd, Ah tol yuh tha wuz a gun wound," said a man, slapping his thigh.

His father caught his shoulders and shook him till his teeth rattled.

"Tell whut happened, yuh rascal! Tell whut . . ."

Dave looked at Jenny's stiff legs and began to cry.

"Whut yuh do wid tha gun?" his mother asked.

"Whut wuz he doin wida gun?" his father asked.

"Come on and tell the truth," said Hawkins. "Ain't nobody going to hurt you . . ."

His mother crowded close to him.

"Did yuh shoot tha mule, Dave?"

Dave cried, seeing blurred white and black faces.

"Ahh ddinn gggo tt sshooot hher . . . Ah sssswear ffo Gawd Ahh ddin. . . . Ah wuz a-tryin t sssee ef the old gggun would sshoot—"

"Where yuh git the gun from?" his father asked.

"Ah got it from Joe, at the sto."

"Where yuh git the money?"

"Ma give it t me."

"He kept worryin me, Bob. Ah had t. Ah tol im t bring the gun right back t me. . . . It was fer yuh, the gun."

"But how yuh happen to shoot that mule?" asked Jim Hawkins.

"Ah wuzn shootin at the mule, Mistah Hawkins. The gun jumped when Ah pulled the trigger. . . . N fo Ah knowed anythin Jenny was there a-bleedin."

Somebody in the crowd laughed. Jim Hawkins walked close to Dave and looked into his face.

"Well, looks like you have bought you a mule, Dave."

"Ah swear fo Gawd, Ah didn go t kill the mule, Mistah Hawkins!"

"But you killed her!"

All the crowd was laughing now. They stood on tiptoe and poked heads over one another's shoulders.

"Well, boy, looks like yuh done bought a dead mule! Hahaha!"

"Ain tha ershame."

"Hohohohoho."

Dave stood, head down, twisting his feet in the dirt.

"Well, you needn't worry about it, Bob," said Jim Hawkins to Dave's father. "Just let the boy keep on working and pay me two dollars a month."

"Whut yuh wan fer yo mule, Mistah Hawkins?"

Jim Hawkins screwed up his eyes.

"Fifty dollars."

"Whut yuh do wid tha gun?" Dave's father demanded.

Dave said nothing.

"Yuh wan me t take a tree n beat yuh till yuh talk!"

"Nawsuh!"

"Whut yuh do wid it?"

"Ah throwed it erway."

"Where?"

"Ah . . . Ah throwed it in the creek."

"Waal, c mon home. N firs thing in the mawnin git to tha creek n fin tha gun."

"Yessuh."

"Whut yuh pay fer it?"

"Two dollahs."

"Take tha gun n git yo money back n carry it t Mistah Hawkins, yuh hear? N don fergit Ahma lam you black bottom good fer this! Now march yosef on home, suh!"

Dave turned and walked slowly. He heard people laughing. Dave glared, his eyes welling with tears. Hot anger bubbled in him. Then he swallowed and stumbled on.

That night Dave did not sleep. He was glad that he had gotten out of killing the mule so easily, but he was hurt. Something hot seemed to turn over inside him each time he remembered how they had laughed. He tossed on his bed, feeling his hard pillow. N Pa says he's gonna beat me. . . . He remembered other beatings, and his back quivered. Naw, naw, Ah sho don wan im t beat me tha way no mo. Dam em all! Nobody ever gave him anything. All he did was work. They treat me like a mule, n then they beat me. He gritted his teeth. N Ma had t tell on me.

Well, if he had to, he would take old man Hawkins that two dollars. But that meant selling the gun. And he wanted to keep that gun. Fifty dollars for a dead mule.

He turned over, thinking how he had fired the gun. He had an itch to fire it again. Ef other men kin shoota gun, by Gawd, Ah kin! He was still, listening. Mebbe they all sleepin now. The house was still. He heard the soft breathing of his brother. Yes, now! He would go down and get that gun and see if he could fire it! He eased out of bed and slipped into overalls.

The moon was bright. He ran almost all the way to the edge of the woods. He stumbled over the ground, looking for the spot where he had buried the gun. Yeah, here it is. Like a hungry dog scratching for a bone, he pawed it up. He puffed his black cheeks and blew dirt from the trigger and barrel. He broke it and found four cartridges unshot. He looked around; the fields were filled with silence and moonlight. He clutched the gun stiff and hard in his fingers. But, as soon as he wanted to pull the trigger, he shut his eyes and turned his head. Naw, Ah can't shoot wid mah eyes closed n mah head turned. With effort he held his eyes open; then he squeezed. *Blooooom!* He was stiff, not breathing. The gun was still in his hands. Dammit, he'd done it! He fired again. *Blooooom!* He smiled. *Blooooom! Blooooom! Click, click.* There! It was empty. If anybody could shoot a gun, he could. He put the gun into his hip pocket and started across the fields.

When he reached the top of a ridge he stood straight and proud in the moonlight, looking at Jim Hawkins' big white house, feeling the gun sagging in his pocket. Lawd, ef Ah had just one mo bullet Ah'd taka shot at tha house. Ah'd like t scare ol man Hawkins jusa little. . . . Jusa enough t let im know Dave Saunders is a man.

To his left the road curved, running to the tracks of the Illinois Central. He jerked his head, listening. From far off came a faint *hoooof-hoooof; hoooof-hoooof; hoooof-hoooof.* . . . He stood rigid. Two dollahs a mont. Les see now . . . Tha means it'll take bout two years. Shucks! Ah'll be dam!

He started down the road, toward the tracks. Yeah, here she comes! He stood beside the track and held himself stiffly. Here she comes, erroun the ben. . . . C mon, yuh slow poke! C mon! He had his hand on his gun; something quivered in his stomach. Then the train thundered past, the gray and brown box cars rumbling and clinking. He gripped the gun tightly; then he jerked his hand out of his pocket. Ah betcha Bill wouldn't do it! Ah betcha. . . . The cars slid past, steel grinding upon steel. Ahm ridin yuh ternight, so hep me Gawd! He was hot all over. He hesitated just a moment; then he grabbed, pulled atop of a car, and lay flat. He felt his pocket; the gun was still there. Ahead the long rails were glinting in the moonlight, stretching away, away to somewhere, somewhere where he could be a man . . .

✺ RALPH ELLISON (1914–1994)

Ralph Waldo Ellison, born in Oklahoma City, Oklahoma, was a novelist, an essayist, and a lecturer. After winning a college scholarship, he pursued an undergraduate education in music from Tuskegee Institute from 1933 to 1936. Ellison left Tuskegee and went to New York City, where he met Richard Wright and participated in the New York City Federal Writers' Project. At New York University, Columbia, Princeton, and many other institutions of higher learning, Ellison lectured on black culture, including folklore, and taught creative writing. He was awarded several honorary doctoral degrees from institutions such as Rutgers University and the University of Michigan.

Invisible Man (1952) earned Ellison many awards, including a National Book Award in 1953, the National Newspaper Publication Award in 1954, and an Arts and Letters Award Fellowship in Rome in 1955. Ellison also wrote nonfiction: Shadow and Act *(1964) and* Going to the Territory *(1986). Although* Invisible Man *has been criticized for not being racially militant enough to help in the movement for civil rights, the novel contains an implied argument for racial equality.*

From Invisible Man (1952)

Prologue

I am an invisible man. No, I am not a spook like those who haunted Edgar Allan Poe; nor am I one of your Hollywood-movie ectoplasms. I am a man of substance, of flesh and bone, fiber and liquids—and I might even be said to possess a mind. I am invisible, understand, simply because people refuse to see me. Like the bodiless heads you see sometimes in circus sideshows, it is as though I have been surrounded by mirrors of hard, distorting glass. When they approach me they see only my surroundings, themselves, or figments of their imagination—indeed, everything and anything except me.

Nor is my invisibility exactly a matter of a biochemical accident to my epidermis. That invisibility to which I refer occurs because of a peculiar disposition of the eyes of those with whom I come in contact. A matter of the construction of their *inner* eyes, those eyes with which they look through their physical eyes upon reality. I am not complaining, nor am I protesting either. It is sometimes advantageous to be unseen, although it is most often rather wearing on the nerves. Then too, you're constantly being bumped against by those of poor vision. Or again, you often doubt if you really exist. You wonder whether you aren't simply a phantom in other people's minds. Say, a figure in a nightmare which the sleeper tries with all his strength to destroy. It's when you feel like this that, out of resentment, you begin to bump people back. And, let me confess, you feel that way most of the time. You ache with the need to convince yourself that you do exist in the real world, that you're a part of all the sound and anguish, and you strike out with your fists, you curse and you swear to make them recognize you. And, alas, it's seldom successful.

One night I accidentally bumped into a man, and perhaps because of the near darkness he saw me and called me an insulting name. I sprang at him, seized his coat lapels and demanded that he apologize. He was a tall blond man, and as my face came close to his he looked insolently out of his blue eyes and cursed me, his breath hot in my face as he struggled. I pulled his chin down sharp upon the crown of my head, butting him as I had seen the West Indians do, and I felt his flesh tear and the blood gush out, and I yelled, "Apologize! Apologize!" But he continued to curse and struggle, and I butted him again and again until he went down heavily, on his knees, profusely bleeding. I kicked him repeatedly, in a frenzy because he still uttered insults though his lips were frothy with blood. Oh yes, I kicked him! And in my outrage I got out my knife and prepared to slit his throat, right there beneath the lamplight in the deserted street, holding him in the collar with one hand, and opening the knife with my teeth—when it occurred to me that the man had not *seen* me, actually; that he, as far as he knew, was in the midst of a walking nightmare! And I stopped the blade, slicing the air as I pushed him away, letting him fall back to the street. I stared at him hard as the lights of a car stabbed through the darkness. He lay there, moaning on the asphalt; a man almost killed by a phantom. It unnerved me. I was both disgusted and ashamed. I was like a drunken man myself, wavering about on weakened legs. Then I was amused:

Something in this man's thick head had sprang out and beaten him within an inch of his life. I began to laugh at this crazy discovery. Would he have awakened at the point of death? Would Death himself have freed him for wakeful living? But I didn't linger. I ran away into the dark, laughing so hard I feared I might rupture myself. The next day I saw his picture in the *Daily News*, beneath a caption stating that he had been "mugged." Poor fool, poor blind fool, I thought with sincere compassion, mugged by an invisible man!

Most of the time (although I do not choose as I once did to deny the violence of my days by ignoring it) I am not so overtly violent. I remember that I am invisible and walk softly so as not to awaken the sleeping ones. Sometimes it is best not to awaken them; there are few things in the world as dangerous as sleepwalkers. I learned in time though that it is possible to carry on a fight against them without their realizing it. For instance, I have been carrying on a fight with Monopolated Light & Power for some time now. I use their service and pay them nothing at all, and they don't know it. Oh, they suspect that power is being drained off, but they don't know where. All they know is that according to the master meter back there in their power station a hell of a lot of free current is disappearing somewhere into the jungle of Harlem. The joke, of course, is that I don't live in Harlem but in a border area. Several years ago (before I discovered the advantages of being invisible) I went through the routine process of buying service and paying their outrageous rates. But no more. I gave up all that, along with my apartment, and my old way of life: That way based upon the fallacious assumption that I, like other men, was visible. Now, aware of my invisibility, I live rent-free in a building rented strictly to whites, in a section of the basement that was shut off and forgotten during the nineteenth century, which I discovered when I was trying to escape in the night from Ras the Destroyer. But that's getting too far ahead of the story, almost to the end, although the end is in the beginning and lies far ahead.

The point now is that I found a home—or a hole in the ground, as you will. Now don't jump to the conclusion that because I call my home a "hole" it is damp and cold like a grave; there are cold holes and warm holes. Mine is a warm hole. And remember, a bear retires to his hole for the winter and lives until spring; then he comes strolling out like the Easter chick breaking from its shell. I say all this to assure you that it is incorrect to assume that, because I'm invisible and live in a hole, I am dead. I am neither dead nor in a state of suspended animation. Call me Jack-the-Bear, for I am in a state of hibernation.

My hole is warm and full of light. Yes, *full* of light. I doubt if there is a brighter spot in all New York than this hole of mine, and I do not exclude Broadway. Or the Empire State Building on a photographer's dream night. But that is taking advantage of you. Those two spots are among the darkest of our whole civilization—pardon me, our whole *culture* (an important distinction, I've heard)—which might sound like a hoax, or a contradiction, but that (by contradiction, I mean) is how the world moves: Not like an arrow, but a boomerang. (Beware of those who speak of the *spiral* of history; they are preparing a boomerang. Keep a steel helmet handy.) I know; I have been boomeranged across my head so much that I now can see the darkness of lightness. And I love light. Perhaps you'll think it strange that an invisible man should need light, desire light, love light. But maybe it is exactly because I *am* invisible. Light confirms my reality, gives birth to my form. A beautiful girl once told me of a recurring nightmare in which she lay in the center of a large dark room and felt her face expand until it filled the whole room, becoming a formless mass while her eyes ran in bilious jelly up the chimney. And so it is with me. Without light I am not only invisible, but formless as well; and to be unaware of one's form is to live a death. I myself, after existing some twenty years, did not become alive until I discovered my invisibility.

That is why I fight my battle with Monopolated Light & Power. The deeper reason, I mean: It allows me to feel my vital aliveness. I also fight them for taking so much of my money before I learned to protect myself. In my hole in the basement there are exactly 1,369 lights. I've wired the entire ceiling, every inch of it. And not with fluorescent bulbs, but with the older, more-expensive-to-operate kind, the filament type. An act of sabotage, you know. I've already begun to wire the wall. A junk man I know, a man of vision, has supplied me with wire and sockets. Nothing, storm or flood, must get in the way of our need for light and ever more and brighter light. The truth is the light and light is the truth. When I finish all four walls, then I'll start on the floor. Just how that will go, I don't know. Yet when you have lived invisible as long as I have you develop a certain ingenuity. I'll solve the problem. And maybe I'll invent a gadget to place my coffee pot on the fire while I lie in bed, and even invent a gadget to warm my bed—like the fellow I saw in one of the picture magazines who made himself a gadget to warm his shoes! Though invisible, I am in the great American tradition of tinkers. That makes me kin to Ford, Edison and Franklin. Call me, since I have a theory and a concept, a "thinker-tinker." Yes, I'll warm my shoes; they need it, they're usually full of holes. I'll do that and more.

Now I have one radio-phonograph; I plan to have five. There is a certain acoustical deadness in my hole, and when I have music I want to *feel* its vibration, not only with my ear but with my whole body. I'd like to hear five recordings of Louis Armstrong playing and singing "What Did I Do to Be So Black and Blue"— all at the same time. Sometimes now I listen to Louis while I have my favorite dessert of vanilla ice cream and sloe gin. I pour the red liquid over the white mound, watching it glisten and the vapor rising as Louis bends that military instrument into a beam of lyrical sound. Perhaps I like Louis Armstrong because he's made poetry out of being invisible. I think it must be because he's unaware that he *is* invisible. And my own grasp of invisibility aids me to understand his music. Once when I asked for a cigarette, some jokers gave me a reefer, which I lighted when I got home and sat listening to my phonograph. It was a strange evening. Invisibility, let me explain, gives one a slightly different sense of time, you're never quite on the beat. Sometimes you're ahead and sometimes behind. Instead of the swift and imperceptible flowing of time, you are aware of its nodes, those points where time stands still or from which it leaps ahead. And you slip into the breaks and look around. That's what you hear vaguely in Louis' music.

Once I saw a prizefighter boxing a yokel. The fighter was swift and amazingly scientific. His body was one violent flow of rapid rhythmic action. He hit the yokel a hundred times while the yokel held up his arms in stunned surprise. But suddenly the yokel, rolling about in the gale of boxing gloves, struck one blow and knocked science, speed and footwork as cold as a well-digger's posterior. The smart money hit the canvas. The long shot got the nod. The yokel had simply stepped inside of his opponent's sense of time. So under the spell of the reefer I discovered a new analytical way of listening to music. The unheard sounds came through, and each melodic line existed of itself, stood out clearly from all the rest, said its piece, and waited patiently for the other voices to speak. That night I found myself hearing not only in time, but in space as well. I not only entered the music but descended, like Dante, into its depths. And *beneath the swiftness of the hot tempo there was a slower tempo and a cave and I entered it and looked around and heard an old woman singing a spiritual as full of Weltschmerz as flamenco, and beneath that lay a still lower level on which I saw a beautiful girl the color of ivory pleading in a voice like my mother's as she stood before a group of slaveowners who bid for her naked body, and below that I found a lower level and a more rapid tempo and I heard someone shout:*

"Brothers and sisters, my text this morning is the 'Blackness of Blackness.'"

And a congregation of voices answered: "That blackness is most black, brother, most black . . ."

"In the beginning . . ."

"At the very start," they cried.

". . . there was blackness . . ."

"Preach it . . ."

". . . and the sun . . ."

"The sun, Lawd . . ."

". . . was bloody red . . ."

"Red . . ."

"Now black is . . ." the preacher shouted.

"Bloody . . ."

"I said black is . . ."

"Preach it, brother . . ."

" . . . an' black ain't . . ."

"Red, Lawd, red: He said it's red!"

"Amen, brother . . ."

"Black will git you . . ."

"Yes, it will . . ."

"Yes, it will . . ."

". . . an' black won't . . ."

"Naw, it won't!"

"It do . . ."

"It do, Lawd . . ."

". . . an' it don't."

"Halleluiah . . ."

". . . It'll put you, glory, glory, Oh my Lawd, in the WHALE'S BELLY.*"*

"Preach it, dear brother . . ."

". . . an' make you tempt . . ."

"Good God a-mighty!"

"Old Aunt Nelly!"

"Black will make you . . ."

"Black . . ."

". . . or black will un-make you."

"Ain't it the truth, Lawd?"

And at that point a voice of trombone timbre screamed at me, "Git out of here, you fool! Is you ready to commit treason?"

And I tore myself away, hearing the old singer of spirituals moaning, "Go curse your God, boy, and die."

I stopped and questioned her, asked her what was wrong.

"I dearly loved my master, son," she said.

"You should have hated him," I said.

"He gave me several sons," she said, "and because I loved my sons I learned to love their father though I hated him too."

"I too have become acquainted with ambivalence," I said. "That's why I'm here."

"What's that?"

"Nothing, a word that doesn't explain it. Why do you moan?"

"I moan this way 'cause he's dead," she said.

"Then tell me, who is that laughing upstairs?"

"Them's my sons. They glad."

"Yes, I can understand that too," I said.

"I laughs too, but I moans too. He promised to set us free but he never could bring his-self to do it. Still I loved him . . ."

"Loved him? You mean . . . ?"

"Oh yes, but I loved something else even more."

"What more?"

"Freedom."

"Freedom," I said. "Maybe freedom lies in hating."

"Naw, son, it's in loving. I loved him and give him the poison and he withered away like a frost-bit apple. Them boys woulda tore him to pieces with they homemade knives."

"A mistake was made somewhere," I said, "I'm confused." And I wished to say other things, but the laughter upstairs became too loud and moan-like for me and I tried to break out of it, but I couldn't. Just as I was leaving I felt an urgent desire to ask her what freedom was and went back. She sat with her head in her hands, moaning softly; her leather-brown face was filled with sadness.

"Old woman, what is this freedom you love so well?" I asked around a corner of my mind.

She looked surprised, then thoughtful, then baffled. "I done forgot, son. It's all mixed up. First I think it's one thing, then I think it's another. It gits my head to spinning. I guess now it ain't nothing but knowing how to say what I got up in my head. But it's a hard job, son. Too much is done happen to me in too short a time. Hit's like I have a fever. Ever' time I starts to walk my head gits to swirling and I falls down. Or if it ain't that, it's the boys; they gits to laughing and wants to kill up the white folks. They's bitter, that's what they is . . ."

"But what about freedom?"

"Leave me 'lone, boy; my head aches!"

I left her, feeling dizzy myself. I didn't get far.

Suddenly one of the sons, a big fellow six feet tall, appeared out of nowhere and struck me with his fist.

"What's the matter, man?" I cried.

"You made Ma cry!"

"But how?" I said, dodging a blow.

"Askin' her them questions, that's how. Git outa here and stay, and next time you got questions like that, ask yourself!"

He held me in a grip like cold stone, his fingers fastening upon my windpipe until I thought I would suffocate before he finally allowed me to go. I stumbled about dazed, the music beating hysterically in my ears. It was dark. My head cleared and I wandered down a dark narrow passage, thinking I heard his footsteps hurrying behind me. I was sore, and into my being had come a profound craving for tranquillity, for peace and quiet, a state I felt I could never achieve. For one thing, the trumpet was blaring and the rhythm was too hectic. A tom-tom beating like heart-thuds began drowning out the trumpet, filling my ears. I longed for water and I heard it rushing through the cold mains my fingers touched as I felt my way, but I couldn't stop to search because of the footsteps behind me.

"Hey, Ras," I called. "Is it you, Destroyer? Rinehart?"

No answer, only the rhythmic footsteps behind me. Once I tried crossing the road, but a speeding machine struck me, scraping the skin from my leg as it roared past.

Then somehow I came out of it, ascending hastily from this underworld of sound to hear Louis Armstrong innocently asking,

What did I do
To be so black
And blue?

At first I was afraid; this familiar music had demanded action, the kind of which I was incapable, and yet had I lingered there beneath the surface I might have attempted to act. Nevertheless, I know now that few really listen to this music. I sat on the chair's edge in a soaking sweat, as though each of my 1,369 bulbs had everyone become a klieg light in an individual setting for a third degree with Ras and Rinehart in charge. It was exhausting—as though I had held my breath continuously for an hour under the terrifying serenity that comes from days of intense hunger. And yet, it was a strangely satisfying experience for an invisible man to hear the silence of sound. I had discovered unrecognized compulsions of my being—even though I could not answer "yes" to their promptings. I haven't smoked a reefer since, however; not because they're illegal, but because to *see* around corners is enough (that is not unusual when you are invisible). But to hear around them is too much; it inhibits action. And despite Brother Jack and all that sad, lost period of the Brotherhood, I believe in nothing if not in action.

Please, a definition: A hibernation is a covert preparation for a more overt action.

Besides, the drug destroys one's sense of time completely. If that happened, I might forget to dodge some bright morning and some cluck would run me down with an orange and yellow street car, or a bilious bus! Or I might forget to leave my hole when the moment for action presents itself.

Meanwhile I enjoy my life with the compliments of Monopolated Light & Power. Since you never recognize me even when in closest contact with me, and since, no doubt, you'll hardly believe that I exist, it won't matter if you know that

I tapped a power line leading into the building and ran it into my hole in the ground. Before that I lived in the darkness into which I was chased, but now I see. I've illuminated the blackness of my invisibility—and vice versa. And so I play the invisible music of my isolation. The last statement doesn't seem just right, does it? But it is; you hear this music simply because music is heard and seldom seen, except by musicians. Could this compulsion to put invisibility down in black and white be thus an urge to make music of invisibility? But I am an orator, a rabble rouser—Am? I *was*, and perhaps shall be again. Who knows? All sickness is not unto death, neither is invisibility.

I can hear you say, "What a horrible, irresponsible bastard!" And you're right. I leap to agree with you. I am one of the most irresponsible beings that ever lived. Irresponsibility is part of my invisibility; any way you face it, it is a denial. But to whom can I be responsible, and why should I be, when you refuse to see me? And wait until I reveal how truly irresponsible I am. Responsibility rests upon recognition, and recognition is a form of agreement. Take the man whom I almost killed: Who was responsible for that near murder—I? I don't think so, and I refuse it. I won't buy it. You can't give it to me. *He* bumped *me*, *he* insulted *me*. Shouldn't he, for his own personal safety, have recognized my hysteria, my "danger potential"? He, let us say, was lost in a dream world. But didn't *he* control that dream world—which, alas, is only too real!—and didn't *he* rule me out of it? And if he had yelled for a policeman, wouldn't *I* have been taken for the offending one? Yes, yes, yes! Let me agree with you, I was the irresponsible one; for I should have used my knife to protect the higher interests of society. Some day that kind of foolishness will cause us tragic trouble. All dreamers and sleepwalkers must pay the price, and even the invisible victim is responsible for the fate of all. But I shirked that responsibility; I became too snarled in the incompatible notions that buzzed within my brain. I was a coward . . .

But what did *I* do to be so blue? Bear with me.

"Welcome Home" Rally Speech

Paul Robeson

This speech by Paul Robeson was originally published in pamphlet form by the Council of African Affairs and reprinted in Paul Robeson Speaks: Writings, Speeches, Interviews, 1918–1974. *Robeson delivered the address in New York City, responding to negative reactions against his controversial political views, among them a belief in Soviet Union socialism as a way to achieve peace and freedom in the United States.*

Thanks for the welcome home. I have traveled many lands and I have sung and talked to many peoples. Wherever I appeared, whether in professional concert, at peace meetings, in the factories, at trade union gatherings, at the mining pits, at assemblies of representative colonial students from all over the world, always the greeting came: "Take back our affection, our love, our strength to the Negro people and to the members of the progressive movement of America."

It is especially moving to be here in this particular auditorium in Harlem. Way back in 1918, I came here to this very hall from a football game at the Polo Grounds between Rutgers and Syracuse. There was a basketball game between St. Christopher and Alpha. Later I played here for St. Christopher against the Alphas, against the Spartans, and the Brooklyn YMCA, time and time again. This was a home of mine. It is still my home.

I was then, through my athletics and my university record, trying to hold up the prestige of my people; trying in the only way I knew to ease the path for future Negro boys and girls. And I am still in there slugging, yes, at another level, and you can bet your life that I shall battle every step of the way until conditions around these corners change and conditions change for the Negro people all up and down this land.

The road has been long. The road has been hard. It began about as tough as I ever had it—in Princeton, New Jersey, a college town of Southern aristocrats, who from Revolutionary time transferred Georgia to New Jersey. My brothers couldn't go to high school in Princeton. They had to go to Trenton, ten miles away. That's right—Trenton, of the "Trenton Six." My brother or I could have been one of the "Trenton Six."

Almost every Negro in Princeton lived off the college and accepted the social status that went with it. We lived for all intents and purposes on a Southern plantation. And with no more dignity than that suggests—all the bowing and scraping to the drunken rich, all the vile names, all the Uncle Tomming to earn enough to lead miserable lives.

My father was of slave origin. He reached as honorable a position as a Negro could under these circumstances, but soon after I was born he lost his church and poverty was my beginning. Relatives from my father's North Carolina family took me in, a motherless orphan, while my father went to new fields to begin again in a corner grocery store. I slept four in a bed, ate the nourishing greens and corn-bread. I was and am forever thankful to my honest, intelligent, courageous, generous aunts, uncles and cousins, not long divorced from the cotton and tobacco fields of eastern North Carolina.

During the [Henry A.] Wallace [presidential] campaign [of 1948], I stood on the very soil on which my father was a slave, where some of my cousins are share-croppers and unemployed tobacco workers. I reflected upon the wealth bled from my near relatives alone, and of the very basic wealth of all this America, beaten out of millions of the Negro people, enslaved, freed, newly enslaved until this very day.

And I defied—and today I defy—any part of an insolent, dominating America, however powerful; I defy any errand boys, Uncle Toms of the Negro people, to challenge my Americanism, because by word and deed I challenge this vicious system to the death; because I refuse to let my personal success, as part of a fraction of one percent of the Negro people, explain away the injustices to fourteen million of my people; because with all the energy at my command, I fight for the right of the Negro people and other oppressed labor-driven Americans to have decent homes, decent jobs, and the dignity that belongs to every human being!

Somewhere in my childhood these feelings were planted. Perhaps when I resented being pushed off the sidewalk, when I saw my women being insulted, and especially when I saw my elder brother answer each insult with blows that sent would-be slave masters crashing to the stone sidewalks, even though jail was his constant reward. He never said it, but he told me day after day: "Listen to me, kid." (He loved me very dearly.) "Don't you ever take it, as long as you live."

I realized years after how grateful I was for that example. I've never accepted any inferior role because of my race or color. *And, by God, I never will!*

That explains my life. I'm looking for freedom, *full freedom*, not an inferior brand. That explains my attitude to different people, to Africa, the continent from which we came. I know much about Africa, and I'm not ashamed of my African origin. I'm *proud* of it. The rich culture of that continent, its magnificent potential gives me plenty of cause for pride. This was true of the deep stirrings that took place within me when I visited the West Indies in January. This explains my feeling toward the Soviet Union, where in 1934 I for the first time walked this earth in complete human dignity, a dignity denied me at the Columbia University of Medina, denied me everywhere in my native land, despite all the protestations about freedom, equality, constitutional rights, and the sanctity of the individual.

And I say to the *New York Times* that personal success can be no answer. It can no longer be a question of an Anderson, a Carver, a Robinson, a Jackson, or a Robeson. It must be a question of the well-being and opportunities not of a few but for *all* of this great Negro people of which I am a part.

There, in my childhood, I saw my father choose allies. To him, it was the Taylor Pineses of the Wall Street millionaires. They helped the church. They spread around a little manna now and then—that was an age of philanthropy. But I recall that my father could never think of attacking these men for the conditions of those times. Always one had to bend and bow.

That was forty years ago. These present-day sycophants of big business, these supposed champions of Negro rights, can't grow up to the knowledge that the world has gone forward. Millions and millions of people have wrung their freedom from these same Taylor Pineses, these same Wall Street operators, these traders in the lives of millions for their greedy profits. There is no more Eastern Europe to bleed; no more Russia, one-sixth of the earth's surface, to enslave; no more China at their disposal.

They can't imagine that our people, the Negro people—40 millions in the Caribbean and Latin America, 150 millions in Africa, and 14 million here, today, up and down this America of ours—are also determined to stop being industrial and agricultural serfs. They do not understand that a new reconstruction is here, and that this time we will not be betrayed by any coalition of Northern big finance barons and Southern bourbon plantation owners. They do not realize that the Negro people, with their allies, other oppressed groups, the progressive sections of labor, millions of the Jewish and foreign-born of former white indentured labor, north, south, east and west, in this day and time of ours are determined to see some basic change.

Roosevelt foreshadowed it. We are going to realize it! We were fooled in 1948. We aren't going to be fooled in 1949, 1950, and '51 and '52. We are going to fight for jobs and security at home, and we are going to join the forces of friendship and cooperation with advanced peoples and move on to build a decent world.

And you stooges try to do the work of your white bourbon masters, work they have not the courage to do. You try to play the role of cowardly labor leaders who are attempting to do the same job in the ranks of labor. Try it, but the Negro people will give you your answer! They'll drive you from public life! The Negro people know when they're being sold down the river. They've been watching a long, long time. It's good the challenge has come. Keep on, and you'll have no magazines in which to publish your viciousness. You'll not have many more opportunities to sell into a new slavery our cousins in Liberia, our relatives in South Africa, our brothers in the West Indies. You'll get your answer—and soon! The Negro people are smoldering. They're not afraid of their radicals who point out the awful, indefensible truth of our degradation and exploitation.

What a travesty is this supposed leadership of a great people! And in this historic time, when their people need them most. How Sojourner Truth, Harriet Tubman, Fred Douglass must be turning in their graves at this spectacle of a craven, fawning, despicable leadership, able to be naught but errand boys, and—at the lowest level—stooges and cowardly renegades, a disgrace to the Negro people and to the real and true America of which they so glibly talk. Let them get their crumbs from their Wall Street masters. Let them snatch their bit of cheese and go scampering rat-like into their holes, where, by heaven, the Negro people will keep them, left to their dirty consciences, if any they have.

Now, let's get out the record. In 1946, I declared in St. Louis on the picket line against segregation of Negro people that I would give up my professional career, then at its height, to devote my time and energy to the struggle for the liberation of the Negro people. I appeared everywhere, north, south, east, and west, for Negro colleges, churches, organizations.

I led an anti-lynch crusade to Washington. There I heard our president declare that it was not politically expedient to take any federal action against lynching. You may remember that I said that perhaps the Negro people would have to do something about it themselves. But a committee stepped in—one of those committees to stop the militant Negro struggle. And [the] lynch law is still in committee, while Negroes continue being lynched.

I entered the struggle for peace and freedom with Wallace in 1948, talking at street corner meetings four and five times a day. Without that struggle of the Progressive party the issues before the people would not have been clarified, and we might now be at war. Wallace made a tremendous contribution time and again to the cause of peace, to Negro freedom, and to American freedom. He said peace was the issue. *Peace was, and is, the issue.* He said a war economy was an economy of scarcity and unemployment. *That it was, and is.* He said it meant the loss of civil liberties, the loss of the freedom of European countries. *It has meant just that.* He said it meant slavery for colonial people. *That it is fast becoming.* He said it meant domestic fascism. *That is just around the corner.*

Negroes rallied to Wallace's banner, the banner of their freedom. Then their trusted leaders stepped in to confuse and to frighten them. They sold them a hollow bill of goods in the Democratic party, and a nominee that even these leaders did not trust. Remember, they wanted Eisenhower. But they were afraid of any militant struggle for our people. Where is the civil rights program? Are we still subject to terror? Ask Mrs. Mallard, ask the boys in Virginia, ask the Trenton Six: "Where are our liberties?"

As a consequence of my activities for Negro freedom, I had eighty-six concerts cancelled out of eighty-six. Of course, these were very special concerts. I don't blame auto barons in Detroit for not wanting to pay to hear me when I was in Cadillac Square fighting for the auto workers. I don't blame the iron-ore owners of the Michigan and Minnesota iron-ore ranges for not wanting to hear me when I was on picket lines for the steel workers in these regions. And so with the packinghouse owners of Chicago, or the ship owners of the east and west coasts, or the sugar plantation owners of Hawaii.

Well, they can have their concerts! I'll go back to their cities to sing for the people whom I love, for the Negro and white workers whose freedom will insure my freedom. I'll help, together with many other progressive artists, whenever I can get the time from freedom's struggle, to show how culture can be brought back to the people. We created it in the first place, and it's about time it came back to us!

Today the fight is still on for peace and freedom. Concerts must wait. There is a fierce political struggle which must be won. However, I decided to go to Europe to resume my professional concerts for a very short period, in order to make it perfectly clear that the world is wide and no few pressures could stop my career. Let's go to the record: Albert Hall (London) with its 8,000 seats sold out twice with a five dollar top; 10,000 in the Harringay Arena; thousands turned away all over Europe—the most successful concert tour of my career.

Why? Because I came to the English people from *progressive* America, from the America of Wallace and the Progressive party, from the America of the twelve great Communist leaders who are on trial for their devotion to the Negro people and to the American working class; because I came from Negro America whose struggle had become known to the English during the war when a folk saying grew up: "We love those American soldiers, the black and the brown ones."

I finished my professional tour at its height and announced that never again would I sing at a five dollar top, that I would sing at prices so that workers could come in comfort and dignity. I did this because I belonged to working people. I struggled as a boy in the brickyards, on the docks, in the hotels to get a living and an education. Ninety-five per cent of the Negro people are workers. So I said that my talents would henceforth belong to my people in their struggle. And I acted on this. Thousands and thousands came. That's my answer to the bourbons who think they can end my career!

Later I toured England in peace meetings for British-Soviet friendship, did a series of meetings on the issues of freedom for the peoples of Africa and the West Indies, and on the question of the right of colored seamen and colored technicians to get jobs in a land for which they had risked their lives. Ten thousand people turned out to a meeting in Liverpool on this latter issue.

I stood at the coal pits in Scotland and saw miners contribute from their earnings $1,500 to $2,000 for the benefit of African workers. I helped build up a substantial fund in England to help the cause of African freedom, saw this whole question of the relation of English and colonial peoples raised to a new level as English workers came to understand that if cheap labor could be obtained in Africa or the West Indies or in Southeast Asia, their living standards in England would suffer accordingly. This is a lesson white workers in America must increasingly learn. For the tentacles of American imperialism are stretched far and wide into colonial countries: Cuba, Haiti, Puerto Rico, Hawaii, Trinidad, Panama; down through Latin America; in the Philippines and some parts of the East; and all over the continent of Africa. White workers in America must be aware of this and watch it closely.

Then I moved into Scandinavia. Through a stroke of circumstance, I was booked through *Politiken*. This was an old liberal newspaper in years gone by, but the pressures of present-day American imperialism, exerted mainly through the

Marshall Plan, had caused all pretense of liberalism to vanish. I read an editorial of *Politiken* in England supporting the Atlantic Pact, attacking the eastern democracies and the Soviet Union. I immediately asked that my contracts be cancelled. I explained to the press that it was unthinkable that I could appear under the sponsorship of a paper which had allied itself with an imperialism which had enslaved my father and forefathers and was in the process of enslaving my brothers and sisters in Africa, Latin America, the West and East Indies, and which was trying to work up a war against the greatest champion of the rights of colonial and exploited peoples—the Union of Soviet Republics.

The contracts cancelled, I sang for the newspapers of the progressive and Communist forces of Scandinavia (papers like the *Daily Worker*). All the other press had gone the way of the Reuthers, Murrays, Careys, Townsends, et al., who have betrayed American workers and the Negro people to American, British, Dutch, French, Belgian and Japanese imperialists.

Thousands upon thousands in the Scandinavian countries turned out in support of peace and against the Atlantic Pact. These countries of Scandinavia had been freed by Soviet armies, had erected monuments to Soviet heroes. It was unthinkable that they would join the fascist elements of Western Germany and Vichy France against their natural friend and ally. It was clear from the meetings that the great majority of Scandinavian people did not support their governments. I am sure American imperialism is aware of this.

My role was in no sense personal. I represented to these people Progressive America, fighting for peace and freedom, and I bring back to you their love and affection, their promise of their strength to aid us, and their gratefulness for our struggles here. They beg us to send more progressive Americans—Wallace, Marcantonio, trade unionists Negro and white. And they all sent special messages to the Negro people, assuring them of their support of the liberation of Negro peoples everywhere.

Our allies stretch far and wide and they beg us for information and for collective united action. If the originators of the vicious Atlantic Pact can get in a huddle to plot joint action against us, one by one, let us get together to see that nobody can ever take us one by one, that they will have to engage us as a strong, unbending, united force for the peace and freedom of all oppressed peoples.

Why did I take this stand on the Atlantic Pact—the Arms Pact—and its forerunner, the Marshall Plan? Let us examine the results of the Marshall Plan. We don't need to guess and theorize. Western European countries have completely lost their freedom. This was honestly acknowledged everywhere. American big business tells all of Western Europe what to do, what it can produce, where it must buy, with whom it can trade. And finally, with the Atlantic Pact, the western Europeans are told that they must be ready to die to the last man in order to defend American Big Business.

The Eisler case illustrated the European people's revolt against American domination. For the English people decided this was too much. They still have

565

some respect for their judicial law, extending from Magna Charta days—different from us as yet here in America with our Foley Square travesties. The English people move from below—it was a mass movement which forced their government to retreat on Eisler and tell the United States, "Nothing doing." And the Communists of Great Britain started the defense which soon involved great sections of the British people—another important lesson for us. For British people knew that if Eisler was not freed, no longer could they themselves be protected under British law and the whole structure of British freedom would be in danger.

That is just as true here. If the twelve Communists are not freed, all Americans can say goodbye to their civil liberties. *Especially* will we Negro people be forced to say goodbye to any attempts to add to the few civil liberties we as yet have. Just as a mass movement in a few days won this tremendous victory for peace and freedom in London—I was there at the time—so we here in New York and America can do the same if we act with speed and courage in the cause of our freedoms, not just those of the "Twelve."

But beyond this strangling of Western Europe, the real meaning of the Marshall Plan is the complete enslavement of the colonies. For how can British, French and other Western European bankers repay Wall Street? Only in raw materials—in gold, copper, cocoa, rubber, uranium, manganese, iron ore, ground nuts, oils, fats, sugar, bananas. From where? Why, from South Africa, Nigeria, East Africa, French Africa, Belgian Congo, Trinidad, Jamaica, Cuba, Honduras, Guatemala, Viet Nam, Malaya. The Marshall Plan means enslavement of our people all over the earth, including here in the United States on the cotton and sugar plantations and in the mines of the North and South.

And the Atlantic Pact means legal sanction for sending guns and troops to the colonies to insure the enslavement and terrorization of our people. They will shoot our people down in Africa just as they lynch us in Mississippi. That's the other side of the same coin.

For who owns plantations in the South? Metropolitan Life—yes, the same Metropolitan Life Insurance Company that owns and won't let you live in the Stuyvesant Town flats in New York. It is such giant financial interests that are getting millions from the Marshall Plan. They enslave us, they enslave Western Europe, they enslave the colonies.

Many of our Negro leaders know this. But some of these so-called distinguished leaders are doing the dirty work for Stettinius, aiding his scheme for the exploitation of Liberia and its people, or are serving as errand boys for Forrestal's cartel interests, even though the chief has now departed. And there are a few others of these so-called Negro leaders who are too low and contemptible to give the courtesy of mention.

Are these financial big boys America? No! They are the former enemies of Roosevelt. They were the ones who were glad when Roosevelt died. They are the same ones who Roosevelt said were the core of American fascism. They are the allies of the remains of the Hitler entourage, that Hitler who burned up eight million of a great Jewish people and said he would like to burn up fourteen million of us. They are the friends of Franco, the living representatives of the Spanish Conquistadores who enslaved us and still enslave us in Latin America. They are the ones who hate American democracy as did the enemies of Jefferson and Lincoln before them. *They are no part of America!* They are the would-be preservers of world fascism and the enemies of progressive America!

And they are in the government, too—you saw them deny your civil rights on the floors of Congress; you saw them throw our promised civil rights right into our teeth, while our supposed chief defender enjoyed the sun down in Florida, a state that is the symbol, of course, of the freedom and equality of the Negro people.

And now this greedy section of democratic America, by corrupting our leaders, by shooting us as we attempt to vote, by terrorizing us as in the case of the "Trenton Six," has the gall to try to lure us into a war against countries where the freedoms that we so deeply desire are being realized, together with a rich and abundant life, the kind of life that should be ours also, because so much of America's wealth is realized from our blood and from our labor.

My last weeks abroad were spent in these countries to the East, Czechoslovakia, Poland, and finally the Soviet Union. Here thousands of people—men, women, children—cried to me to thank progressive America for sending one of its representatives, begged me so to take back their love, their heartfelt understanding of the suffering of their Negro brothers and sisters, that I wept time and time again. Whole nations of people gave me a welcome I can never forget—a welcome not for me, Paul Robeson, but in your name, the name of the Negro people of America, of the colonies; in the name of the progressive America of Wallace and the Progressive party; and in the name of the twelve Communist leaders. Outstanding people in the government treated me with the greatest respect and dignity because I represented you (but there were no calls from the American embassies).

Here in these countries are *the people*, their spokesmen are in the forefront of our struggle for liberation—on the floor of the United Nations, in the highest councils of world diplomacy. Here in the Soviet Union, in Czechoslovakia, in battered but gallant Warsaw with its brave saga of the ghetto, are the nations leading the battle for peace and freedom. They were busy building, reconstructing; and the very mention of war caused one to look at you as if you were insane.

I was in Stalingrad. I saw a letter from President Roosevelt—no equivocation there. It said that in Stalingrad came the turning point in the battle for civilization. I stood in the little rectangle where the heroic people of Stalingrad fought with their backs to the mighty Volga—and saved us—saved you and me from Hitler's wrath. We loved them then. What has happened to us? For they are the same, only braver. Midst their ruins, they sing and laugh and dance. Their factories are restored—fifty percent above prewar. I sang at their tractor factory and saw a tractor—*not a tank*—coming off the line every fifteen minutes. It was a factory built by Soviet hands, Soviet brains, Soviet know-how.

They want peace and an abundant life. Freedom is already theirs. The children cried, "Take back our love to the Negro children and the working class children." And they clasped and embraced me literally and symbolically for you. I love them.

Here is a whole one-sixth of the earth's surface, including millions of brown, yellow and black people who would be Negroes here in America and subject to the same awful race prejudice that haunts us. In this Soviet Union, the very term "backward country" is an insult, for in one generation former colonial peoples have been raised to unbelievable industrial and social levels. It is, indeed, a vast new concept of democracy. And these achievements make completely absurd the solemn pronouncements that it will take several generations, maybe hundreds of years, before we Negro people in the West Indies, Africa and America can have any real control over our own destiny.

Here is a whole nation which is now doing honor to our poet Pushkin—one of the greatest poets in history—the Soviet people's and our proud world possession. Could I find a monument to Pushkin in a public square of Birmingham or Atlanta or Memphis, as one stands in the center of Moscow? No. One perhaps to Goethe, but not to the dark-skinned Pushkin.

Yes, I love this Soviet people more than any other nation, because of their suffering and sacrifices for us, the Negro people, the progressive people, the people of the future in this world.

At the Paris Peace Conference I said it was unthinkable that the Negro people of America or elsewhere in the world could be drawn into war with the Soviet Union. I repeat it with hundredfold emphasis. THEY WILL NOT.

And don't ask a few intellectuals who are jealous of their comfort. Ask the sugar workers whom I saw starving in Louisiana, the workers in the cotton lands and the tobacco belts in the South. Ask the sugar workers in Jamaica. Ask the Africans in Malan's South Africa. Ask them if they will struggle for peace and friendship with the Soviet people, with the peoples of China and the new democracies, or if they will help their imperialist oppressors to return them to an even worse slavery. The answer lies there in the millions of my struggling people, not only the 14 million in America, but the 40 million in the Caribbean and Latin America and the 150 million in Africa. No wonder all the excitement! For one day this mighty mass will strike for freedom, and a new strength like that of gallant China will add its decisive weight to insuring a world where all men can be free and equal.

I am born and bred in this America of ours. I want to love it. I love a part of it. But it's up to the rest of America when I shall love it with the same intensity that I love the Negro people from whom I spring—in the way that I love progressives in the Caribbean, the black and Indian peoples of South and Central America, the peoples of China and Southeast Asia, yes suffering people the world over—and in the way that I deeply and intensely love the Soviet Union. That burden of proof rests upon America.

Now these peoples of the Soviet Union, of the new eastern democracies, of progressive Western Europe, and the representatives of the Chinese people whom I met in Prague and Moscow, were in great part Communists. They were the first to die for our freedom and for the freedom of all mankind. So I'm not afraid of Communists; no, far from that. I will defend them as they defended us, the Negro people. And I stand firm and immovable by the side of that great leader who has given his whole life to the struggle of the American working class, Bill Foster; by the side of Gene Dennis; by the side of my friend, Ben Davis; Johnny Gates, Henry Winston, Gus Hall, Gil Green, Jack Stachel, Carl Winter, Irving Potash, Bob Thompson, Johnny Williamson—twelve brave fighters for my freedom. Their struggle is *our* struggle.

But to fulfill our responsibilities as Americans, we must unite, especially we Negro people. We must know our strength. We are the decisive force. That's why they terrorize us. That's why they fear us. And if we unite in all our might, this world can fast be changed. Let us create that unity now. And this important, historic role of the Negro people our white allies here must fully comprehend. This means increasing understanding of the Negro, his tremendous struggle, his great contributions, his potential for leadership at all levels in the common task of liberation. It means courage to stand by our side whatever the consequences, as we the Negro people fulfill our historic duty in Freedom's struggle.

If we unite, we'll get our law against lynching, our right to vote and to labor. Let us march on Washington, representing 14,000,000 strong. Let us push aside the sycophants who tell us to be quiet.

The so-called western democracies—including our own, which so fiercely exploits us and daily denies us our simple constitutional guarantee—can find no answer before the bar of world justice for their treatment of the Negro people. Democracy, indeed! We must have the courage to shout at the top of our voices about our injustices and we must lay the blame where it belongs and where it has belonged for over three hundred years of slavery and misery: right here on our own doorstep—not in any far away place. This is the very time when we can win our struggle.

And we cannot win it by being lured into any kind of war with our closest friends and allies throughout the world. For any kind of decent life we need, we want, and *we demand* our constitutional right—RIGHT HERE IN AMERICA. We do not want to die in vain any more on foreign battlefields for Wall Street and the greedy supporters of domestic fascism. If we must die, let it be in Mississippi or Georgia! Let it be wherever we are lynched and deprived of our rights as human beings!

Let this be a final answer to the warmongers. Let them know that we will not help to enslave our brothers and sisters and eventually ourselves. Rather, we will help to insure peace in our time—the freedom and liberation of the Negro and other struggling peoples, and the building of a world where we can all walk in full equality and full human dignity.

✠ GWENDOLYN BROOKS (b. 1917)

Gwendolyn Brooks's poetry continues to make an impact on readers. Her poetry collections include the well-known A Street in Bronzeville *(1945);* Annie Allen *(1949), for which she won a Pulitzer Prize; and* The Bean Eaters *(1960). Brooks also wrote a novel,* Maud Martha *(1953). Brooks is known foremost for her poetry and secondly for her teaching. She has taught poetry workshops and other courses at Columbia College and Elmhurst College, both in Illinois. She eventually became distinguished professor of the arts at the City College of New York. Her poetry often deals with racial issues, not only interracial prejudice but intraracial prejudice as well. Like Ann Petry, she deals with social issues and reveals autobiographical experiences.*

Brooks published her autobiography, Report from Part One, *in 1972. In the 1970s and 1980s, Brooks aimed her writing at a young adult audience. She wrote* Primer for Blacks *(1981) to give advice to developing young poets. In her work, she presents experiences related to race, gender, and class. She is known as one of the best poets of the twentieth century.*

The Mother (1991)

Abortions will not let you forget.
You remember the children you got that you did not get,
The damp small pulps with a little or with no hair,
The singers and workers that never handled the air.
You will never neglect or beat   5
Them, or silence or buy with a sweet.
You will never wind up the sucking-thumb
Or scuttle off ghosts that come.
You will never leave them, controlling your luscious sigh,
Return for a snack of them, with gobbling mother-eye.   10

I have heard in the voices of the wind the voices of my
   dim killed children.
I have contracted. I have eased
My dim dears at the breasts they could never suck.
I have said, Sweets, if I sinned, if I seized
Your luck   15
And your lives from your unfinished reach,
If I stole your births and your names,
Your straight baby tears and your games,
Your stilted or lovely loves, your tumults, your marriages,
   aches, and your deaths,
If I poisoned the beginnings of your breaths,   20
Believe that even in my deliberateness I was not deliberate.
Though why should I whine,
Whine that the crime was other than mine?—

Since anyhow you are dead.
Or rather, or instead,   25
You were never made.

But that too, I am afraid,
Is faulty: oh, what shall I say, how is the truth to be
    said?
You were born, you had body, you died.
It is just that you never giggled or planned or cried.   30

Believe me, I loved you all.
Believe me, I knew you, though faintly, and I loved, I
    loved you
All.

The Rites for Cousin Vit (1949)

Carried her unprotesting out the door.
Kicked back the casket-stand. But it can't hold her,
That stuff and satin aiming to enfold her,
The lid's contrition nor the bolts before.
Oh oh. Too much. Too much. Even now, surmise,   5
She rises in the sunshine. There she goes,
Back to the bars she knew and the repose
In love-rooms and the things in people's eyes.
Too vital and too squeaking. Must emerge.
Even now she does the snake-hips with a hiss,   10
Slops the bad wine across her shantung, talks
Of pregnancy, guitars and bridgework, walks
In parks or alleys, comes haply on the verge
Of happiness, haply hysterics. Is.

What Shall I Give My Children? (1949)

What shall I give my children? who are poor,
Who are adjudged the leastwise of the land,
Who are my sweetest lepers, who demand
No velvet and no velvety velour;
But who have begged me for a brisk contour,   5
Crying that they are quasi, contraband
Because unfinished, graven by a hand
Less than angelic, admirable or sure.
My hand is stuffed with mode, design, device.
But I lack access to my proper stone.   10

And plenitude of plan shall not suffice
Nor grief nor love shall be enough alone
To ratify my little halves who bear
Across an autumn freezing everywhere.

The Sundays of Satin-Legs Smith (1945)

Inamoratas, with an approbation,
Bestowed his title. Blessed his inclination.

He wakes, unwinds, elaborately: a cat
Tawny, reluctant, royal. He is fat
And fine this morning. Definite. Reimbursed.   5

He waits a moment, he designs his reign,
That no performance may be plain or vain.
Then rises in a clear delirium.

He sheds, with his pajamas, shabby days.
And his desertedness, his intricate fear, the   10
Postponed resentments and the prim precautions.

Now, at his bath, would you deny him lavender
Or take away the power of his pine?
What smelly substitute, heady as wine,
Would you provide? life must be aromatic.   15
There must be scent, somehow there must be some.
Would you have flowers in his life? suggest
Asters? a Really Good geranium?
A white carnation? would you prescribe a Show
With the cold lilies, formal chrysanthemum   20
Magnificence, poinsettias, and emphatic
Red of prize roses? might his happiest
Alternative (you muse) be, after all,
A bit of gentle garden in the best
Of taste and straight tradition? Maybe so.   25
But you forget, or did you ever know,
His heritage of cabbage and pigtails,
Old intimacy with alleys, garbage pails,
Down in the deep (but always beautiful) South
Where roses blush their blithest (it is said)   30
And sweet magnolias put Chanel to shame.

No! He has not a flower to his name.
Except a feather one, for his lapel.
Apart from that, if he should think of flowers
It is in terms of dandelions or death.   35

Ah, there is little hope. You might as well—
Unless you care to set the world a-boil
And do a lot of equalizing things,
Remove a little ermine, say, from kings,
Shake hands with paupers and appoint them men,   40
For instance—certainly you might as well
Leave him his lotion, lavender and oil.

Let us proceed. Let us inspect, together
With his meticulous and serious love,
The innards of this closet. Which is a vault   45
Whose glory is not diamonds, not pearls,
Not silver plate with just enough dull shine.
But wonder-suits in yellow and in wine,
Sarcastic green and zebra-striped cobalt.
With shoulder padding that is wide   50
And cocky and determined as his pride;
Ballooning pants that taper off to ends
Scheduled to choke precisely.
                            Here are hats
Like bright umbrellas; and hysterical ties   55
Like narrow banners for some gathering war.

People are so in need, in need of help.
People want so much that they do not know.

Below the tinkling trade of little coins
The gold impulse not possible to show   60
Or spend. Promise piled over and betrayed.

These kneaded limbs receive the kiss of silk.
Then they receive the brave and beautiful
Embrace of some of that equivocal wool.
He looks into his mirror, loves himself—   65
The neat curve here; the angularity
That is appropriate at just its place;
The technique of a variegated grace.

Here is all his sculpture and his art
And all his architectural design.   70
Perhaps you would prefer to this a fine
Value of marble, complicated stone.
Would have him think with horror of baroque,
Rococo. You forget and you forget.

He dances down the hotel steps that keep   75
Remnants of last night's high life and distress.
As spat-out purchased kisses and spilled beer.
He swallows sunshine with a secret yelp.

Passes to coffee and a roll or two.
Has breakfasted. 80
     Out. Sounds about him smear,
Become a unit. He hears and does not hear
The alarm clock meddling in somebody's sleep;
Children's governed Sunday happiness;
The dry tone of a plane; a woman's oath; 85
Consumption's spiritless expectoration;
An indignant robin's resolute donation
Pinching a track through apathy and din;
Restaurant vendors weeping; and the L
That comes on like a slightly horrible thought. 90

Pictures, too, as usual, are blurred.
He sees and does not see the broken windows
Hiding their shame with newsprint; little girl
With ribbons decking wornness, little boy
Wearing the trousers with the decentest patch, 95
To honor Sunday; women on their way
From "service," temperate holiness arranged
Ably on asking faces; men estranged
From music and from wonder and from joy
But far familiar with the guiding awe 100
Of foodlessness.
    He loiters.
       Restaurant vendors
Weep, or out of them rolls a restless glee.
The Lonesome Blues, the Long-lost Blues, I Want A 105
Big Fat Mama. Down these sore avenues
Comes no Saint-Saëns, no piquant elusive Grieg,
And not Tschaikovsky's wayward eloquence
And not the shapely tender drift of Brahms.
But could he love them? Since a man must bring 110
To music what his mother spanked him for
When he was two: bits of forgotten hate,
Devotion: whether or not his mattress hurts:
The little dream his father humored: the thing
His sister did for money: what he ate 115
For breakfast—and for dinner twenty years
Ago last autumn: all his skipped desserts.

The pasts of his ancestors lean against
Him. Crowd him. Fog out his identity.
Hundreds of hungers mingle with his own, 120
Hundreds of voices advise so dexterously
He quite considers his reactions his,

Judges he walks most powerfully alone,
That everything is—simply what it is.

But movie-time approaches, time to boo   125
The hero's kiss, and boo the heroine
Whose ivory and yellow it is sin
For his eye to eat of. The Mickey Mouse,
However, is for everyone in the house.

Squires his lady to dinner at Joe's Eats.   130
His lady alters as to leg and eye,
Thickness and height, such minor points as these,
From Sunday to Sunday. But no matter what
Her name or body positively she's
In Queen Lace stockings with ambitious heels   135
That strain to kiss the calves, and vivid shoes
Frontless and backless, Chinese fingernails,
Earrings, three layers of lipstick, intense hat
Dripping with the most voluble of veils.
Her affable extremes are like sweet bombs   140
About him, whom no middle grace or good
Could gratify. He had no education
In quiet arts of compromise. He would
Not understand your counsels on control, nor
Thank you for your late trouble.   145
                                             At Joe's Eats
You get your fish or chicken on meat platters.
With coleslaw, macaroni, candied sweets,
Coffee and apple pie. You go out full.
(The end is—isn't it?—all that really matters.)   150

        And even and intrepid come
        The tender boots of night to home.

        Her body is like new brown bread
        Under the Woolworth mignonette.
        Her body is a honey bowl   155
        Whose waiting honey is deep and hot
        Her body is like summer earth,
        Receptive, soft, and absolute . . .

JAMES BALDWIN (1924–1987)

James Baldwin's literary career was substantial; he wrote novels, plays, and essays that deal with issues of race, gender, and sexual orientation. His voice in writing and in speeches attempted to explain what it was like to be black in America during the turbulent 1950s and 1960s. His first novel, Go Tell It On The Mountain *(1953), is one of his best-known works. Two of Baldwin's plays,* The Amen Corner *(1955) and* Blues for Mister Charlie *(1964), were successful Broadway productions. Baldwin's fiction and nonfiction texts often present his own religious experiences and struggles for equality. In* Giovanni's Room *(1956), Baldwin addresses the issue of homosexuality. At a time when homophobia was most overt, he included homosexual content in his literature.*

In "Everybody's Protest Novel," Baldwin attacks authors of protest fiction, but he used his forum as a writer and speaker to protest all forms of discrimination: embodied within his works are themes of protest, messages often presented in a covert fashion that still come through clearly. In the essay, Baldwin objects to fiction that tells rather than shows as it protests inequality. In contrast, he uses his texts to show the effects of racism and other societal problems. For example, If Beale Street Could Talk *(1974) shows the injustices inherent in the American judicial system for black citizens. Baldwin contributed significantly to the body of literature that illustrates the effects of discrimination.*

From Go Tell It on the Mountain

Part Three: The Threshing-Floor (1953)

Then said I, Woe is me! for I am undone;
because I am a man of unclean lips,
and I dwell in the midst of a people
of unclean lips; for mine eyes have
seen the King, the Lord of hosts.
Then I buckled up my shoes,
And I started.

He knew, without knowing how it had happened, that he lay on the floor, in the dusty space before the altar which he and Elisha had cleaned; and knew that above him burned the yellow light which he had himself switched on. Dust was in his nostrils, sharp and terrible, and the feet of the saints, shaking the floor beneath him, raised small clouds of dust that filmed his mouth. He heard their cries, so far, so high above him—he could never rise that far. He was like a rock, a dead man's body, a dying bird, fallen from an awful height; something that had no power of itself, any more, to turn.

And something moved in John's body which was not John. He was invaded, set at naught, possessed. This power had struck John, in the head or in the heart; and, in a moment, wholly, filling him with an anguish that he could never in his life have imagined, that he surely could not endure, that even now he could not believe, had opened him up; had cracked him open, as wood beneath the axe cracks down the middle, as rocks break up; had ripped him and felled him in a moment, so that John had not felt the wound, but only the agony, had not felt the fall, but only the fear; and lay here, now, helpless, screaming, at the very bottom of darkness.

He wanted to rise—a malicious, ironic voice insisted that he rise—and, at once, to leave this temple and go out into the world.

He wanted to obey the voice, which was the only voice that spoke to him; he tried to assure the voice that he would do his best to rise; he would only lie here a moment, after his dreadful fall, and catch his breath. It was at this moment, precisely, that he found he could not rise; something had happened to his arms, his legs, his feet—ah, something had happened to John! And he began to scream again in his great, bewildered terror, and felt himself, indeed, begin to move—not upward, toward the light, but down again, a sickness in his bowels, a tightening in his loin-strings; he felt himself turning, again and again, across the dusty floor, as though God's toe had touched him lightly. And the dust made him cough and retch; in his turning the center of the whole earth shifted, making of space a sheer void and a mockery of order, and balance, and time. Nothing remained: all was swallowed up in chaos. And: *Is this it?* John's terrified soul inquired—*What is it?*—to no purpose, receiving no answer. Only the ironic voice insisted yet once more that he rise from that filthy floor if he did not want to become like all the other niggers.

Then the anguish subsided for a moment, as water withdrawn briefly to dash itself once more against the rocks: he knew that it subsided only to return. And he coughed and sobbed in the dusty space before the altar, lying on his face. And still he was going down, farther and farther from the joy, the singing, and the light above him.

He tried, but in such despair!—the utter darkness does not present any point of departure, contains no beginning, and no end—to rediscover, and, as it were, to trap and hold tightly in the palm of his hand, the moment preceding his fall, his change. But that moment was also locked in darkness, was wordless, and would not come forth. He remembered only the cross: he had turned again to kneel at the altar, and had faced the golden cross. And the Holy Ghost was speaking—seeming to say, as John spelled out the so abruptly present and gigantic legend adorning the cross: *Jesus Saves.* He had stared at this, an awful bitterness in his heart, wanting to curse—and the Spirit spoke, and spoke in him. Yes: there was Elisha, speaking from the floor, and his father, silent, at his back. In his heart there was a sudden yearning tenderness for holy Elisha; desire, sharp and awful as a reflecting knife, to usurp the body of Elisha, and lie where Elisha lay; to speak in tongues, as Elisha spoke, and, with that authority, to confound his father. Yet this had not been the moment; it was as far back as he could go, but the secret, the turning, the abysmal drop was farther back, in darkness. As he cursed his father, as he loved Elisha, he had, even then, been weeping; he had already passed his moment, was already under the power, had been struck, and was going down.

Ah, down!—and to what purpose, where? To the bottom of the sea, the bowels of the earth, to the heart of the fiery furnace? Into a dungeon deeper than Hell, into a madness louder than the grave? What trumpet sound would awaken him, what hand would lift him up? For he knew, as he was struck again, and screamed again, his throat like burning ashes, and as he turned again, his body hanging from him like a useless weight, a heavy, rotting carcass, that if he were not lifted he would never rise.

His father, his mother, his aunt, Elisha—all were far above him, waiting, watching his torment in the pit. They hung over the golden barrier, singing behind them, light around their heads, weeping, perhaps, for John, struck down so early. And, no, they could not help him any more—nothing could help him any more. He struggled, struggled to rise up, and meet them—he wanted wings to fly upward and meet them in that morning, that morning where they were. But his struggles only thrust him downward, his cries did not go upward, but rang in his own skull.

Yet, though he scarcely saw their faces, he knew that they were there. He felt them move, every movement causing a trembling, an astonishment, a horror in the heart of darkness where he lay. He could not know if they wished him to come to them as passionately as he wished to rise. Perhaps they did not help him because they did not care—because they did not love him.

Then his father returned to him, in John's changed and low condition; and John thought, but for a moment only, that his father had come to help him. In the silence, then, that filled the void, John looked on his father. His father's face was black—like a sad, eternal night; yet in his father's face there burned a fire—a fire eternal in an eternal night. John trembled where he lay, feeling no warmth for him from this fire, trembled, and could not take his eyes away. A wind blew over him, saying: "Whosoever loveth and maketh a lie." And he knew that he had been thrust out of the holy, the joyful, the blood-washed community, that his father had thrust him out. His father's will was stronger than John's own. His power was greater because he belonged to God. Now, John felt no hatred, nothing, only a bitter, unbelieving despair: all prophecies were true, salvation was finished, damnation was real!

Then Death is real, John's soul said, and Death will have his moment.

"Set thine house in order," said his father, "for thou shalt die and not live."

And then the ironic voice spoke again, saying: "Get up, John. Get up, boy. Don't let him keep you here. You got everything your daddy got."

John tried to laugh—John thought that he was laughing—but found, instead, that his mouth was filled with salt, his ears were full of burning water. Whatever was happening in his distant body now, he could not change or stop; his chest heaved, his laughter rose and bubbled at his mouth, like blood.

And his father looked on him. His father's eyes looked down on him, and John began to scream. His father's eyes stripped him naked, and hated what they saw. And as he turned, screaming, in the dust again, trying to escape his father's eyes, those eyes, that face, and all their faces, and the far-off yellow light, all departed from his vision as though he had gone blind. He was going down again. There is, his soul cried out again, no bottom to the darkness!

He did not know where he was. There was silence everywhere—only a perpetual, distant, faint trembling far beneath him—the roaring, perhaps, of the fires of Hell, over which he was suspended, or the echo, persistent, invincible still, of the moving feet of the saints. He thought of the mountaintop, where he longed to be, where the sun would cover him like a cloth of gold, would cover his head like a crown of fire, and in his hands he would hold a living rod. But this was no mountain where John lay, here, no robe, no crown. And the living rod was uplifted in other hands.

"I'm going to beat sin out of him. I'm going to beat it out."

Yes, he had sinned, and his father was looking for him. Now, John did not make a sound, and did not move at all, hoping that his father would pass him by.

"Leave him be. Leave him alone. Let him pray to the Lord."

"Yes, Mama. I'm going to try to love the Lord."

"He done run off somewhere. I'm going to find him. I'm going to beat it out."

Yes, he had sinned: one morning, alone, in the dirty bathroom, in the square, dirt-gray cupboard room that was filled with the stink of his father. Sometimes, leaning over the cracked, "tattle-tale gray" bathtub, he scrubbed his father's back; and looked, as the accursed son of Noah had looked, on his father's hideous nakedness. It was secret, like sin, and slimy, like the serpent, and heavy, like the rod. Then he hated his father, and longed for the power to cut his father down.

Was this why he lay here, thrust out from all human or heavenly help tonight? This, and not that other, his deadly sin, having looked on his father's nakedness and mocked and cursed him in his heart? Ah, that son of Noah's had been cursed, down to the present groaning generation: *A servant of servants shall he be unto his brethren.*

Then the ironic voice, terrified, it seemed, of no depth, no darkness, demanded of John, scornfully, if he believed that he was cursed. All niggers had been cursed, the ironic voice reminded him, all niggers had come from this most undutiful of Noah's sons. How could John be cursed for having seen in a bathtub what another man—*if* that other man had ever lived—had seen ten thousand years ago, lying in an open tent? Could a curse come down so many ages? Did it live in time, or in the moment? But John found no answer for this voice, for he was in the moment, and out of time.

And his father approached. "I'm going to beat sin out of him. I'm going to beat it out." All the darkness rocked and wailed as his father's feet came closer; feet whose tread resounded like God's tread in the garden of Eden, searching the covered Adam and Eve. Then his father stood just above him, looking down. Then John knew that a curse was renewed from moment to moment, from father to son. Time was indifferent, like snow and ice; but the heart, crazed wanderer in the driving waste, carried the curse forever.

"John," said his father, "come with me."

Then they were in a straight street, a narrow, narrow way. They had been walking for many days. The street stretched before them, long, and silent, going down, and whiter than the snow. There was no one on the street, and John was frightened. The buildings on this street, so near that John could touch them on either side, were narrow, also, rising like spears into the sky, and they were made of beaten gold and silver. John knew that these buildings were not for him—not today—*no, nor tomorrow, either!* Then, coming up this straight and silent street, he saw a woman, very old and black, coming toward them, staggering on the crooked stones. She was drunk, and dirty, and very old, and her mouth was bigger than his mother's mouth, or his own; her mouth was loose and wet, and he had *never* seen anyone so black. His father was astonished to see her, and beside himself with anger; but John was glad. He clapped his hands and cried:

"See! She's uglier than Mama! She's uglier than me!"

"You mighty proud, ain't you," his father said, "to be the Devil's son?"

But John did not listen to his father. He turned to watch the woman pass. His father grabbed his arm.

"You see that? That's sin. That's what the Devil's son runs after."

"Whose son are you?" John asked.

His father slapped him. John laughed, and moved a little away.

"I seen it. I seen it. I ain't the Devil's son for nothing."

His father reached for him, but John was faster. He moved backward down the shining street, looking at his father—his father who moved toward him, one hand outstretched in fury.

"And I *heard* you—all the nighttime long. I know what you do in the dark, black man, when you think the Devil's son's asleep. I heard you, spitting, and groaning, and choking—and I *seen* you, riding up and down, and going in and out. I ain't the Devil's son for nothing."

The listening buildings, rising upward yet, leaned, closing out the sky. John's feet began to slip; tears and sweat were in his eyes; still moving backward before his father, he looked about him for deliverance; but there was no deliverance in this street for him.

"And I hate you. I hate you. I don't care about your golden crown. I don't care about your long white robe. I seen you under the robe, I seen you!"

Then his father was upon him; at his touch there was singing, and fire. John lay on his back in the narrow street, looking up at his father, that burning face beneath the burning towers.

"I'm going to beat it out of you. I'm going to beat it out."

His father raised his hand. The knife came down. John rolled away, down the white, descending street, screaming:

"Father! Father!"

These were the first words he uttered. In a moment there was silence, and his father was gone. Again, he felt the saints above him—and dust was in his mouth. There was singing somewhere; far away, above him; singing slow and mournful. He lay silent, racked beyond endurance, salt drying on his face, with nothing in him any more, no lust, no fear, no shame, no hope. And yet he knew that it would come again—the darkness was full of demons crouching, waiting to worry him with their teeth again.

Then I looked in the grave and I wondered.

Ah, down!—what was he searching here, all alone in darkness? But now he knew, for irony had left him, that he was searching something, hidden in the darkness, that must be found. He would die if it was not found; or, he was dead already, and would never again be joined to the living, if it was not found.

And the grave looked so sad and lonesome.

In the grave where he now wandered—he knew it was the grave, it was so cold and silent, and he moved in icy mist—he found his mother and his father, his mother dressed in scarlet, his father dressed in white. They did not see him: they looked backward, over their shoulders, at a cloud of witnesses. And there was his Aunt Florence, gold and silver flashing on her fingers, brazen earrings dangling from her ears; and there was another woman, whom he took to be that wife of his father's called Deborah—who had, as he had once believed, so much to tell him. But she, alone, of all that company, looked at him and signified that there was no speech in the grave. He was a stranger there—they did not see him pass, they did not know what he was looking for, they could not help him search. He wanted to find Elisha, who knew, perhaps, who would help him—but Elisha was not there. There was Roy: Roy also might have helped him, but he had been stabbed with a knife, and lay now, brown and silent, at his father's feet.

Then there began to flood John's soul the waters of despair. *Love is as strong as death, as deep as the grave.* But love, which had, perhaps, like a benevolent monarch, swelled the population of his neighboring kingdom, Death, had not himself descended: they owed him no allegiance here. Here there was no speech or language, and there was no love; no one to say: You are beautiful, John; no one to forgive him, no matter what his sin; no one to heal him, and lift him up. No one: father and mother looked backward, Roy was bloody, Elisha was not here.

Then the darkness began to murmur—a terrible sound—and John's ears trembled. In this murmur that filled the grave, like a thousand wings beating on the air, he recognized a sound that he had always heard. He began, for terror, to weep and moan—and this sound was swallowed up, and yet was magnified by the echoes that filled the darkness.

This sound had filled John's life, so it now seemed, from the moment he had first drawn breath. He had heard it everywhere, in prayer and in daily speech, and wherever the saints were gathered, and in the unbelieving streets. It was in his father's anger, and in his mother's calm insistence, and in the vehement mockery of his aunt; it had rung, so oddly, in Roy's voice this afternoon, and when Elisha played the piano it was there; it was in the beat and jangle of Sister McCandless's tambourine, it was in the very cadence of her testimony, and invested that testimony with a matchless, unimpeachable authority. Yes, he had heard it all his life, but it was only now that his ears were opened to this sound that came from darkness, that could only come from darkness, that yet bore such sure witness to the glory of the light. And now in his moaning, and so far from any help, he heard it in himself—it rose from his bleeding, his cracked-open heart. It was a sound of rage and weeping which filled the grave, rage and weeping from time set free, but bound now in eternity; rage that had no language, weeping with no voice—which yet spoke now, to John's startled soul, of boundless melancholy, of the bitterest patience, and the longest night; of the deepest water, the strongest chains, the most cruel lash; of humility most wretched, the dungeon most absolute, of love's bed defiled, and birth dishonored, and most bloody, unspeakable, sudden death. Yes, the darkness hummed with murder: the body in the water, the body in the fire, the body on the tree. John looked down the line of these armies of darkness, army upon army, and his soul whispered: *Who are these? Who are they?* And wondered: *Where shall I go?*

There was no answer. There was no help or healing in the grave, no answer in the darkness, no speech from all that company. They looked backward. And John looked back, seeing no deliverance.

I, John, saw the future, way up in the middle of the air.

Were the lash, the dungeon, and the night for him? And the sea for him? And the grave for him?

I, John, saw a number, way in the middle of the air.

And he struggled to flee—out of this darkness, out of this company—into the land of the living, so high, so far away. Fear was upon him, a more deadly fear than he had ever known, as he turned and turned in the darkness, as he moaned, and stumbled, and crawled through darkness, finding no hand, no voice, finding no door. *Who are these? Who are they?* They were the despised and rejected, the wretched and the spat upon, the earth's offscouring; and he was in their company, and they would swallow up his soul. The stripes they had endured would scar his back, their punishment would be his, their portion his, his their humiliation, anguish, chains, their dungeon his, their death his. *Thrice was I beaten with rods, once I was stoned, thrice I suffered shipwreck, a night and a day I have been in the deep.*

And their dread testimony would be his!

In journeyings often, in perils of waters, in perils of robbers, in perils by mine own countrymen, in perils by the heathen, in perils in the city, in perils in the wilderness, in perils in the sea, in perils among false brethren.

And their desolation, his:

In weariness and painfulness in watchings often, in hunger and thirst, in fastings often, in cold and nakedness.

And he began to shout for help, seeing before him the lash, the fire, and the depthless water, seeing his head bowed down forever, he, John, the lowest among these lowly. And he looked for his mother, but her eyes were fixed on this dark army—she was claimed by this army. And his father would not help him, his father did not see him, and Roy lay dead.

Then he whispered, not knowing that he whispered: "Oh, Lord, have mercy on me. Have mercy on me."

And a voice, for the first time in all his terrible journey, spoke to John, through the rage and weeping, and fire, and darkness, and flood:

"Yes," said the voice, "go through. Go through."

"Lift me up," whispered John, "lift me up. I can't go through."

"Go through," said the voice, "go through."

Then there was silence. The murmuring ceased. There was only this trembling beneath him. And he knew there was a light somewhere.

"Go through."

"Ask Him to take you through."

But he could never go through this darkness, through this fire and this wrath. He never could go through. His strength was finished, and he could not move. He belonged to the darkness—the darkness from which he had thought to flee had claimed him. And he moaned again, weeping, and lifted up his hands.

"Call on Him. Call on Him."

"Ask Him to take you through."

Dust rose again in his nostrils, sharp as the fumes of Hell. And he turned again in the darkness, trying to remember something he had heard, something he had read.

Jesus saves.

And he saw before him the fire, red and gold, and waiting for him—yellow, and red, and gold, and burning in a night eternal, and waiting for him. He must go through this fire, and into this night.

Jesus saves.

Call on Him.

Ask Him to take you through.

He could not call, for his tongue would not unlock, and his heart was silent, and great with fear. In the darkness, how to move?—with death's ten thousand jaws agape, and waiting in the darkness. On any turning whatsoever the beast may spring—to move in the darkness is to move into the waiting jaws of death. And yet, it came to him that he must move; for there was a light somewhere, and life, and joy, and singing—somewhere, somewhere above him.

And he moaned again: "Oh, Lord, have mercy. Have mercy, Lord."

There came to him again the communion service at which Elisha had knelt at his father's feet. Now this service was in a great, high room, a room made golden by the light of the sun; and the room was filled with a multitude of people, all in long, white robes, the women with covered heads. They sat at a long, bare, wooden table. They broke at this table flat, unsalted bread, which was the body of the Lord, and drank from a heavy silver cup the scarlet wine of His blood. Then he saw that they were barefoot, and that their feet were stained with this same blood. And a sound of weeping filled the room as they broke the bread and drank the wine.

Then they rose, to come together over a great basin filled with water. And they divided into four groups, two of women and two of men; and they began, woman before woman, and man before man, to wash each other's feet. But the blood would not wash off; many washings only turned the crystal water red; and someone cried: *"Have you been to the river?"*

Then John saw the river, and the multitude was there. And now they had undergone a change; their robes were ragged, and stained with the road they had traveled, and stained with unholy blood; the robes of some barely covered their nakedness; and some indeed were naked. And some stumbled on the smooth stones at the river's edge, for they were blind; and some crawled with a terrible wailing, for they were lame; some did not cease to pluck at their flesh, which was rotten with running sores. All struggled to get to the river, in a dreadful hardness of heart: the strong struck down the weak, the ragged spat on the naked, the naked cursed the blind, the blind crawled over the lame. And someone cried: *"Sinner, do you love my Lord?"*

Then John saw the Lord—for a moment only; and the darkness, for a moment only, was filled with a light he could not bear. Then, in a moment, he was set free; his tears sprang as from a fountain; his heart, like a fountain of waters, burst. Then he cried: "Oh, blessed Jesus! Oh, Lord Jesus! Take me through!"

Of tears there was, yes, a very fountain—springing from a depth never sounded before, from depths John had not known were in him. And he wanted to rise up, singing, singing in that great morning, the morning of his new life. Ah, how his tears ran down, how they blessed his soul!—as he felt himself, out of the darkness, and the fire, and the terrors of death, rising upward to meet the saints.

"Oh, yes!" cried the voice of Elisha. "Bless our God forever!"

And a sweetness filled John as he heard this voice, and heard the sound of singing: the singing was for him. For his drifting soul was anchored in the love of God; in the rock that endured forever. The light and the darkness had kissed each other, and were married now, forever, in the life and the vision of John's soul.

✥ ROBERT HAYDEN (1913–1982)

When he was born in a ghetto in Detroit, Michigan, Robert Hayden was given the name Asa Bundy Sheffey. He adopted the last name of his foster parents, Sue Ellen Westerfield Hayden and William Hayden, with whom he lived after his parents separated. Like Countee Cullen during the Harlem Renaissance, Robert Hayden wanted to be known as a poet, not a black poet. Hayden was an African American poet who sometimes imitated the poetry of well-known Euro-American poets such as Ezra Pound, William Carlos Williams, and Wallace Stevens. Hayden's poetry transcends race; therefore, it is enjoyed by a substantial reading audience. Hayden's "Middle Passage" is one of the best-known black history poems; it is a long poem divided into three sections that employ narrative, lyrical, and dramatic techniques.

While working for the Federal Writers' Project in Detroit, Hayden researched black culture and history. He later worked as a critic for a black weekly publication, the Michigan Chronicle, *whose editor founded Falcon Press and published Hayden's first book of poetry,* Heart-Shape in the Dust *(1940). After completing the requirements for a master's degree at the University of Michigan, Hayden was an instructor in the university's English department. From there, he took a job at Fisk University in Nashville, Tennessee.*

Middle Passage (1945)

I

Jesús Estrella, Esperanza, Mercy:

    Sails flashing to the wind like weapons,
    sharks following the moans the fever and the dying;
    horror the corposant and compass rose.

Middle Passage: 5
    voyage through death
        to life upon these shores.

"10 April 1800—
Blacks rebellious. Crew uneasy. Our linguist says
their moaning is a prayer for death,   10
ours and their own. Some try to starve themselves.
Lost three this morning leaped with crazy laughter
to the waiting sharks, sang as they went under."

Desire, Adventure, Tartar, Ann:

    Standing to America, bringing home   15
    black gold, black ivory, black seed.

        Deep in the festering hold thy father lies,
        of his bones New England pews are made,
        those are altar lights that were his eyes.

Jesus Saviour Pilot Me   20
Over Life's Tempestuous Sea

We pray that Thou wilt grant, O Lord,
safe passage to our vessels bringing
heathen souls unto Thy chastening.

Jesus Saviour   25

    "8 bells, I cannot sleep, for I am sick
with fear, but writing eases fear a little
since still my eyes can see these words take shape
upon the page & so I write, as one
would turn to exorcism. 4 days scudding,   30
but now the sea is calm again. Misfortune
follows in our wake like sharks (our grinning
tutelary gods). Which one of us
has killed an albatross? A plague among
our blacks—Ophthalmia: blindness—& we   35
have jettisoned the blind to no avail.
It spreads, the terrifying sickness spreads.
Its claws have scratched sight from the Capt.'s eyes
& there is blindness in the fo'c'sle
& we must sail 3 weeks before we come   40
to port."

       What port awaits us, Davy Jones'
       or home? I've heard of slavers drifting, drifting,
       playthings of wind and storm and chance, their crews
       gone blind, the jungle hatred   45
       crawling up on deck.

Thou Who Walked On Galilee

    "Deponent further sayeth *The Bella J*
left the Guinea Coast
with cargo of five hundred blacks and odd   50
for the barracoons of Florida:

    "That there was hardly room 'tween-decks for half
the sweltering cattle stowed spoon-fashion there;
that some went mad of thirst and tore their flesh
and sucked the blood: 55

    "That Crew and Captain lusted with the comeliest
of the savage girls kept naked in the cabins;
that there was one they called The Guinea Rose
and they cast lots and fought to lie with her:

    "That when the Bo's'n piped all hands, the flames   60
spreading from starboard already were beyond

control, the negroes howling and their chains
entangled with the flames:

"That the burning blacks could not be reached,
that the Crew abandoned ship,   65
leaving their shrieking negresses behind,
that the Captain perished drunken with the wenches:

"Further Deponent sayeth not."

Pilot Oh Pilot Me

II

Aye, lad, and I have seen those factories,   70
Gambia, Rio Pongo, Calabar;
have watched the artful mongos baiting traps
of war wherein the victor and the vanquished

Were caught as prizes for our barracoons.
Have seen the nigger kings whose vanity   75
and greed turned wild black hides of Fellatah,
Mandingo, Ibo, Kru to gold for us.

And there was one—King Anthracite we named him—
fetish face beneath French parasols
of brass and orange velvet, impudent mouth   80
whose cups were carven skulls of enemies:

He'd honor us with drum and feast and conjo
and palm-oil-glistening wenches deft in love,
and for tin crowns that shone with paste,
red calico and German-silver trinkets   85

Would have the drums talk war and send
his warriors to burn the sleeping villages
and kill the sick and old and lead the young
in coffles to our factories.

Twenty years a trader, twenty years,   90
for there was wealth aplenty to be harvested
from those black fields, and I'd be trading still
but for the fevers melting down my bones.

III

Shuttles in the rocking loom of history,
the dark ships move, the dark ships move,   95
their bright ironical names
like jests of kindness on a murderer's mouth;
plough through thrashing glister toward

fata morgana's lucent melting shore,
weave toward New World littorals that are   100
mirage and myth and actual shore.

Voyage through death,
                        voyage whose chartings are unlove.

A charnel stench, effluvium of living death
spreads outward from the hold,   105
where the living and the dead, the horribly dying,
lie interlocked, lie foul with blood and excrement.

> *Deep in the festering hold thy father lies,*
> *the corpse of mercy rots with him,*
> *rats eat love's rotten gelid eyes.*   110

> *But, oh, the living look at you*
> *with human eyes whose suffering accuses you,*
> *whose hatred reaches through the swill of dark*
> *to strike you like a leper's claw.*

> *You cannot stare that hatred down*   115
> *or chain the fear that stalks the watches*
> *and breathes on you its fetid scorching breath;*
> *cannot kill the deep immortal human wish,*
> *the timeless will.*

"But for the storm that flung up barriers   120
of wind and wave, *The Amistad,* señores,
would have reached the port of Principe in two,
three days at most; but for the storm we should
have been prepared for what befell.
Swift as the puma's leap it came. There was   125
that interval of moonless calm filled only
with the water's and the rigging's usual sounds,
then sudden movement, blows and snarling cries
and they had fallen on us with machete
and marlinspike. It was as though the very   130
air, the night itself were striking us.
Exhausted by the rigors of the storm,
we were no match for them. Our men went down
before the murderous Africans. Our loyal
Celestino ran from below with gun   135
and lantern and I saw, before the cane-
knife's wounding flash, Cinquez,
that surly brute who calls himself a prince,
directing, urging on the ghastly work.
He hacked the poor mulatto down, and then   140
he turned on me. The decks were slippery

when daylight finally came. It sickens me
to think of what I saw, of how these apes
threw overboard the butchered bodies of
our men, true Christians all, like so much jetsam.   145
Enough, enough. The rest is quickly told:
Cinquez was forced to spare the two of us
you see to steer the ship to Africa,
and we like phantoms doomed to rove the sea
voyaged east by day and west by night,   150
deceiving them, hoping for rescue,
prisoners on our own vessel, till
at length we drifted to the shores of this
your land, America, where we were freed
from our unspeakable misery. Now we   155
demand, good sirs, the extradition of
Cinquez and his accomplices to La
Havana. And it distresses us to know
there are so many here who seem inclined
to justify the mutiny of these blacks.   160
We find it paradoxical indeed
that you whose wealth, whose tree of liberty
are rooted in the labor of your slaves
should suffer the august John Quincy Adams
to speak with so much passion of the right   165
of chattel slaves to kill their lawful masters
and with his Roman rhetoric weave a hero's
garland for Cinquez. I tell you that
we are determined to return to Cuba
with our slaves and there see justice done. Cinquez—   170
or let us say 'the Prince'—Cinquez shall die."

The deep immortal human wish,
the timeless will:

   Cinquez its deathless primaveral image,
   life that transfigures many lives.   175

Voyage through death
        to life upon these shores.

The Ballad of Nat Turner (1962)

Then fled, O brethren, the wicked juba
  and wandered wandered far
from curfew joys in the Dismal's night.
  Fool of St. Elmo's fire

In scary night I wandered, praying,   5
   Lord God my harshener,
speak to me now or let me die;
   speak, Lord, to this mourner.

And came at length to livid trees
   where Ibo warriors   10
hung shadowless, turning in wind
   the moaned like Africa,

Their belltongue bodies dead, their eyes
   alive with the anger deep
in my own heart. Is this the sign,   15
   the sign forepromised me?

The spirits vanished. Afraid and lonely
   I wandered on in blackness.
Speak to me now or let me die.
   Die, whispered the blackness.   20

And wild things gasped and scuffled in
   the night; seething shapes
of evil frolicked upon the air.
   I reeled with fear, I prayed.

Sudden brightness clove the preying   25
   darkness, brightness that was
itself a golden darkness, brightness
   so bright that it was darkness.

And there were angels, their faces hidden
   from me, angels at war   30
with one another, angels in dazzling
   combat. And oh the splendor,

The fearful splendor of that warring.
   Hide me, I cried to rock and bramble.
Hide me, the rock, the bramble cried. . . .   35
   How tell you of that holy battle?

The shock of wing on wing and sword
   on sword was the tumult of
a taken city burning. I cannot
   say how long they strove,   40

For the wheel in a turning wheel which is time
   in eternity had ceased
its whirling, and owl and moccasin,
   panther and nameless beast

And I were held like creatures fixed   45
   in flaming, in fiery amber.
But I saw I saw oh many of
   those mighty beings waver,

Waver and fall, go streaking down
   into swamp water, and the water   50
hissed and steamed and bubbled and locked
   shuddering shuddering over

The fallen and soon was motionless.
   Then that massive light
began a-folding slowly in   55
   upon itself, and I

Beheld the conqueror faces and, lo,
   they were like mine, I saw
they were like mine and in joy and terror
   wept, praising praising Jehovah.   60

Oh praised my honer, harshener
   till a sleep came over me,
a sleep heavy as death. And when
   I awoke at last free

And purified, I rose and prayed   65
   and returned after a time
to the blazing fields, to the humbleness.
   And bided my time.

The Diver (1966)

Sank through easeful
azure. Flower
creatures flashed and
shimmered there—
lost images   5
fadingly remembered.
Swiftly descended
into canyon of cold
nightgreen emptiness.
Freefalling, weightless   10
as in dreams of
wingless flight,
plunged through infra-
space and came to

the dead ship,   15
carcass that swarmed with
voracious life.
Angelfish, their
lively blue and
yellow prised from   20
darkness by the
flashlight's beam,
thronged her portholes.
Moss of bryozoans
blurred, obscured her   25
metal. Snappers,
gold groupers explored her,
fearless of bubbling
manfish. I entered
the wreck, awed by her silence,   30
feeling more keenly
the iron cold.
With flashlight probing
fogs of water
saw the sad slow   35
dance of gilded
chairs, the ectoplasmic
swirl of garments,
drowned instruments
of buoyancy,   40
drunken shoes. Then
livid gesturings,
eldritch hide and
seek of laughing
faces. I yearned to   45
find those hidden
ones, to fling aside
the mask and call to them,
yield to rapturous
whisperings, have   50
done with self and
every dinning
vain complexity.
Yet in languid
frenzy strove, as   55
one freezing fights off
sleep desiring sleep;
strove against the
cancelling arms that
suddenly surrounded   60

me, fled the numbing
kisses that I craved.
Reflex of life-wish?
Respirator's brittle
belling? Swam from   65
the ship somehow;
somehow began the
measured rise.

We Shall Overcome

Sung by Zilphia Horton and others, this is a modern adaptation of the song that was used in the 1940s and 1950s on union picket lines and in other acts of political and racial protest. It is known as the Negro National Anthem, often sung at African American gatherings—religious, academic, and social.

We shall overcome, we shall overcome,
We shall overcome someday
Oh, deep in my heart (I know that) I do believe (oh)
We shall overcome someday.   4

We are not afraid, we are not afraid,
We are not afraid today.
Oh, deep in my heart, I do believe,
We shall overcome someday.   8

We are not alone, . . . (today)

The truth will make us free . . .

We'll walk hand in hand . . .

The Lord will see us through . . .

Black and white together (now) . . .

We shall all be free.

 LORRAINE HANSBERRY (1930–1965)

Lorraine Vivian Hansberry was born in Chicago, Illinois, to parents who were black activists. Her father was a member of the NAACP and the Urban League, and her mother, a former schoolteacher, worked on committees advocating racial equality. Her uncle William Leo Hansberry, a professor at Howard University, specialized in African history. During her upbringing, Hansberry was exposed to many accomplished African Americans, such as Paul Robeson, Duke Ellington, and Joe Louis. She was an active participant in movements for freedom and peace, often speaking and picketing for the cause.

    A Raisin in the Sun was published as a book and produced as a play in 1959; the screenplay came out in 1961. The play is Hansberry's best-known work; however, it has endured its share of contention. The question of whether the play was a black play was a point of controversy. For Hansberry, the play presented a black family dealing with some universal issues, but mostly with issues related to being African American in America. In addition to books and plays, she wrote articles for periodical publications, addressing issues of race and gender. The Drinking Gourd (1972) is based on family stories about slavery.

A Raisin in the Sun (1959)

Characters

RUTH YOUNGER
TRAVIS YOUNGER
WALTER LEE YOUNGER (BROTHER)
BENEATHA YOUNGER
LENA YOUNGER (MAMA)

JOSEPH ASAGAI
GEORGE MURCHISON
KARL LINDNER
BOBO
MOVING MEN

The action of the play is set in Chicago's Southside sometime between World War II and the present.

ACT 1

SCENE 1: *Friday morning.*
SCENE 2: *The following morning.*

ACT 2

SCENE 1: *Later, the same day.*
SCENE 2: *Friday night, a few weeks later.*
SCENE 3: *Moving day, one week later.*

ACT 3

An hour later.

ACT 1

SCENE 1

The YOUNGER living room would be a comfortable and well-ordered room if it were not for a number of indestructible contradictions to this state of being. Its furnishings are typical and undistinguished and their primary feature now is that they have clearly had to accommodate the living of too many people for too many years—and they are tired. Still, we can see that at some time, a time probably no longer remembered by the family (except perhaps for MAMA), the furnishings of this room were actually selected with care and love and even hope and brought to this apartment and arranged with taste and pride.

That was a long time ago. Now the once loved pattern of the couch upholstery has to fight to show itself from under acres of crocheted doilies and couch covers which have themselves finally come to be more important than the upholstery. And here a table or a chair has been moved to disguise the worn places in the carpet; but the carpet has fought back by showing its weariness, with depressing uniformity, elsewhere on its surface.

Weariness has, in fact, won in this room. Everything has been polished, washed, sat on, used, scrubbed too often. All pretenses but living itself have long since vanished from the very atmosphere of this room.

Moreover, a section of this room, for it is not really a room unto itself, though the landlord's lease would make it seem so, slopes backward to provide a small kitchen area, where the family prepares the meals that are eaten in the living room proper, which must also serve as dining room. The single window that has been provided for these "two" rooms is located in this kitchen area. The sole natural light the family may enjoy in the course of a day is only that which fights its way through this little window.

At Left, a door leads to a bedroom which is shared by MAMA *and her daughter,* BENEATHA. *At Right, opposite, is a second room (which in the beginning of the life of this apartment was probably a breakfast room) which serves as a bedroom for* WALTER *and his wife,* RUTH.

TIME:

Sometime between World War II and the present.

PLACE:

Chicago's Southside.

AT RISE:

It is morning dark in the living room. TRAVIS *is asleep on the make-down bed at Center. An* ALARM CLOCK *sounds from within the bedroom at Right, and presently* RUTH *enters from that room and closes the door behind her. She crosses sleepily toward the window. As she passes her sleeping son she reaches down and shakes him a little. At the window she raises the shade and a dusky Southside morning light comes in feebly. She fills a pot with water and puts it on to boil. She calls to the boy, between yawns, in a slightly muffled voice.*

RUTH *is about thirty. We can see that she was a pretty girl, even exceptionally so, but now it is apparent that life has been little that she expected, and disappointment has already begun to hang in her face. In a few years, before thirty-five even, she will be known among her people as a "settled woman."*

She crosses to her son and gives him a good, final, rousing shake.

RUTH. Come on now, boy, it's seven thirty!

(Her son sits up at last, in a stupor of sleepiness.)

I say hurry up, Travis! You ain't the only person in the world got to use a bathroom.

(The child, a sturdy, handsome little boy of ten or eleven, drags himself out of the bed and almost blindly takes his towels and "today's clothes" from drawers and a closet and goes out to the bathroom, which is in an outside hall and which is shared by another family or families on the same floor.)

*(*RUTH *crosses to the bedroom door at Right and opens it and calls in to her husband.)*

Walter Lee! . . . It's after seven thirty! Lemme see you do some waking up in there now! *(She waits.)* You better get up from there, man! It's after seven thirty I tell you. *(She waits again.)* All right, you just go ahead and lay there and next thing you know Travis be finished and Mr. Johnson'll be in there and you'll be fussing and cussing round here like a madman! And be late too! *(She waits, at the end of patience.)* Walter Lee—it's time for you to get up! *(She waits another second and then starts to go into the bedroom, but is apparently satisfied that her husband has begun to get up. She stops, pulls the door to, and returns to the kitchen area. She wipes her face with a moist cloth and runs her fingers through her sleep-disheveled hair in a vain effort and ties an apron around her housecoat.)*

(The bedroom door at Right opens and her husband stands in the doorway in his pajamas, which are rumpled and mis-mated. He is a lean, intense young man in his middle thirties, inclined to quick nervous movements and erratic speech habits—and always in his voice there is a quality of indictment.)

WALTER. Is he out yet?

RUTH. What do you mean *out*? He ain't hardly got in there good yet.

WALTER. *(Wandering in, still more oriented to sleep than to a new day.)* Well, what was you doing all that yelling for if I can't even get in there yet? *(Stopping and thinking.)* Check coming today?

RUTH. They *said* Saturday and this is just Friday and I hopes to God you ain't going to get up here first thing this morning and start talking to me 'bout no money—'cause I 'bout don't want to hear it.

WALTER. Something the matter with you this morning?

RUTH. No—I'm just sleepy as the devil. What kind of eggs you want?

WALTER. Not scrambled.

(RUTH starts to scramble eggs.)

Paper come?

(RUTH points impatiently to the rolled-up Tribune on the table, and he gets it and spreads it out and vaguely reads the front page.)

Set off another bomb yesterday.

RUTH. *(Maximum indifference.)* Did they?

WALTER. *(Looking up.)* What's the matter with you?

RUTH. Ain't nothing the matter with me. And don't keep asking me that this morning.

WALTER. Ain't nobody bothering you. *(Reading the news of the day absently again.)* Say Colonel McCormick is sick.

RUTH. *(Affecting tea-party interest.)* Is he now? Poor thing.

WALTER. *(Sighing and looking at his watch.)* Oh, me. *(He waits.)* Now what is that boy doing in that bathroom all this time? He just going to have to start getting up earlier. I can't be being late to work on account of him fooling around in there.

RUTH. *(Turning on him.)* Oh, no he ain't going to be getting up no earlier no such thing! It ain't his fault that he can't get to bed no earlier nights 'cause he got a bunch of crazy good-for-nothing clowns sitting up running their mouths in what is supposed to be his bedroom after ten o'clock at night. . . .

WALTER. That's what you mad about, ain't it? The things I want to talk about with my friends just couldn't be important in your mind, could they? (*He rises and finds a cigarette in her handbag on the table and crosses to the little window and looks out, smoking and deeply enjoying this first one.*)

RUTH. (*Almost matter of factly, a complaint too automatic to deserve emphasis.*) Why you always got to smoke before you eat in the morning?

WALTER. (*At the window.*) Just look at 'em down there . . . running and racing to work . . . (*He turns and faces his wife and watches her a moment at the stove, and then, suddenly.*) You look young this morning, baby.

RUTH. (*Indifferently.*) Yeah?

WALTER. Just for a second—stirring them eggs. It's gone now—just for a second it was—you looked real young again. (*Then, drily.*) It's gone now—you look like yourself again.

RUTH. Man, if you don't shut up and leave me alone.

WALTER. (*Looking out to the street again.*) First thing a man ought to learn in life is not to make love to no colored woman first thing in the morning. You all some evil people at eight o'clock in the morning.

(TRAVIS *appears in the hall doorway, almost fully dressed and quite wide awake now, his towels and pajamas across his shoulders. He opens the door and signals for his father to make the bathroom in a hurry.*)

TRAVIS. (*Watching the bathroom.*) Daddy, come on!

(WALTER *gets his bathroom utensils and flies out to the bathroom.*)

RUTH. Sit down and have your breakfast, Travis.

TRAVIS. Mama, this is Friday. (*Gleefully.*) Check coming tomorrow, huh?

RUTH. You get your mind off money and eat your breakfast.

TRAVIS. (*Eating.*) This is the morning we supposed to bring the fifty cents to school.

RUTH. Well, I ain't got no fifty cents this morning.

TRAVIS. Teacher say we have to.

RUTH. I don't care what teacher say. I ain't got it. Eat your breakfast, Travis.

TRAVIS. I *am* eating.

RUTH. Hush up now and just eat!

(*The boy gives her an exasperated look for her lack of understanding, and eats grudgingly.*)

TRAVIS. You think Grandmama would have it?

RUTH. No! And I want you to stop asking your grandmother for money, you hear me?

TRAVIS. (*Outraged.*) Gaaaleee! I don't ask her, she just gimme it sometimes!

RUTH. Travis Willard Younger—I got too much on me this morning to be—

TRAVIS. Maybe Daddy—

RUTH. TRAVIS!

(*The boy hushes abruptly. They are both quiet and tense for several seconds.*)

TRAVIS. (*Presently.*) Could I maybe go carry some groceries in front of the supermarket for a little while after school then?

RUTH. Just hush, I said.

(TRAVIS *jabs his spoon into his cereal bowl viciously, and rests his head in anger upon his fists.*)

If you through eating, you can get over there and make up your bed.

(*The boy obeys stiffly and crosses the room, almost mechanically, to the bed and more or less carefully folds the covering. He carries the bedding into his mother's room and returns with his books and cap.*)

TRAVIS. (*Sulking and standing apart from her unnaturally.*) I'm gone.

RUTH. (*Looking up from the stove to inspect him automatically.*) Come here. (*He crosses to her and she studies his head.*) If you don't take this comb and fix this here head, you better!

(TRAVIS *puts down his books with a great sigh of oppression, and crosses to the mirror. His mother mutters under her breath about his "slubbornness."*)

'Bout to march out of here with that head looking just like chickens slept in it! I just don't know where you get your slubborn ways. . . . And get your jacket, too. Looks chilly out this morning.

TRAVIS. (*With conspicuously brushed hair and jacket.*) I'm gone.

RUTH. Get carfare and milk money—(*Waving one finger.*)—and not a single penny for no caps, you hear me?

TRAVIS. (*With sullen politeness.*) Yes'm. (*He turns in outrage to leave.*)

(*His mother watches after him as in his frustration he approaches the door almost comically. When she speaks to him, her voice has become a very gentle tease.*)

RUTH. (*Mocking; as she thinks he would say it.*) Oh, Mama makes me so mad sometimes, I don't know what to do! (*She waits and continues to his back as he stands stock still in front of the door.*) I wouldn't kiss that woman good-bye for nothing in this world this morning!

(*The boy finally turns around and rolls his eyes at her, knowing the mood has changed and he is vindicated; he does not, however, move toward her yet.*)

Not for nothing in this world! (*She finally laughs aloud at him and holds out her arms to him and we see that it is a way between them, very old and practiced.*)

(*He crosses to her and allows her to embrace him warmly but keeps his face fixed with masculine rigidity. She holds him back from her presently and looks at him and runs her fingers over the features of his face.*)

(*With utter gentleness.*) Now—whose little old angry man are you?

TRAVIS. (*The masculinity and gruffness start to fade at last.*) Aw gaalee—Mama . . .

RUTH. (*Mimicking.*) Aw—gaaaaalleeeee, Mama! (*She pushes him, with rough playfulness and finality, toward the door.*) Get on out of here or you going to be late.

TRAVIS. (*In the face of love, new aggressiveness.*) Mama, could I *please* go carry groceries.

RUTH. Honey, it's starting to get so cold evenings.

WALTER. (*Coming in from the bathroom and drawing a make-believe gun from a make-believe holster and shooting at his son.*) What is it he wants to do?

RUTH. Go carry groceries after school at the supermarket.

WALTER. Well, let him go. . . .

TRAVIS. (*Quickly, to the ally.*) I *have* to—she won't gimme the fifty cents. . . .

WALTER. (*To his wife only.*) Why not?

RUTH. (*Simply, and with flavor.*) 'Cause we don't have it.

WALTER. (*To* RUTH *only.*) What you tell the boy things like that for? (*Reaching down into his pants with a rather important gesture.*) Here, son—(*He hands the boy the coin, but his eyes are directed to his wife's.*)

(TRAVIS *takes the money happily.*)

TRAVIS. Thanks, Daddy. (*He starts out.*)

(RUTH *watches both of them with murder in her eyes.* WALTER *stands and stares back at her with defiance, and suddenly reaches into his pocket again on an afterthought.*)

WALTER. (*Without even looking at his son, still staring hard at his wife.*) In fact, here's another fifty cents. . . . Buy yourself some fruit today—or take a taxicab to school or something!

TRAVIS. Whoopee—(*He leaps up and clasps his father around the middle with his legs, and they face each other in mutual appreciation.*)

(*Slowly* WALTER LEE *peeks around the boy to catch the violent rays from his wife's eyes and draws his head back as if shot.*)

WALTER. You better get down now—and get to school, man.

TRAVIS. (*At the door.*) O.K. Good-bye. (*He exits.*)

WALTER. (*After him, pointing with pride.*) That's *my* boy.

(*She looks at him in disgust and turns back to her work.*)

You know what I was thinking 'bout in the bathroom this morning?

RUTH. No.

WALTER. How come you always try to be so pleasant!

RUTH. What is there to be pleasant 'bout!

WALTER. You want to know what I was thinking 'bout in the bathroom or not!

RUTH. I know what you thinking 'bout.

WALTER. (*Ignoring her.*) 'Bout what me and Willy Harris was talking about last night.

RUTH. (*Immediately—a refrain.*) Willy Harris is a good-for-nothing loud mouth.

WALTER. Anybody who talks to me has got to be a good-for-nothing loud mouth, ain't he? And what you know about who is just a good-for-nothing loud mouth? Charlie Atkins was just a "good-for-nothing" loud mouth too, wasn't he! When he wanted me to go in the dry-cleaning business with him. And now—he's grossing a hundred thousand a year. A hundred thousand dollars a year! You still call *him* a loud mouth!

RUTH. (*Bitterly.*) Oh, Walter Lee. . . . (*She folds her head on her arms over the table.*)

WALTER. (*Rising and coming to her and standing over her.*) You tired, ain't you? Tired of everything. Me, the boy, the way we live—this beat-up hole—every-thing. Ain't you?

(*She doesn't look up, doesn't answer.*)

So tired—moaning and groaning all the time, but you wouldn't do nothing to help, would you? You couldn't be on my side that long for nothing, could you?

RUTH. Walter, please leave me alone.

WALTER. A man needs for a woman to back him up . . .

RUTH. Walter—

WALTER. Mama would listen to you. You know she listen to you more than she do me and Bennie. She think more of you. All you have to do is just sit down with her when you drinking your coffee one morning and talking 'bout things like you do and—(*He sits down beside her and demonstrates graphically what he thinks her methods and tone should be.*)—you just sip your coffee, see, and say easy like that you been thinking 'bout that deal Walter Lee is so interested in, 'bout the store and all, and sip some more coffee, like what you saying ain't really that important to you—and the next thing you know, she be listening good and asking you questions and when I come home—I can tell her the details. This ain't no fly-by-night proposition, baby. I mean we figured it out, me and Willy and Bobo.

RUTH. (*With a frown.*) Bobo?

WALTER. Yeah. You see, this little liquor store we got in mind cost seventy-five thousand and we figured the initial investment on the place be 'bout thirty thousand, see. That be ten thousand each. Course, there's a couple of hundred you got to pay so's you don't spend your life just waiting for them clowns to let your license get approved—

RUTH. You mean graft?

WALTER. (*Frowning impatiently.*) Don't call it that. See there, that just goes to show you what women understand about the world. Baby, don't *nothing* happen for you in this world 'less you pay *somebody* off!

RUTH. Walter, leave me alone! (*She raises her head and stares at him vigorously— then says, more quietly.*) Eat your eggs, they gonna be cold.

WALTER. (*Straightening up from her and looking off.*) That's it. There you are. Man say to his woman: I got me a dream. His woman say: Eat your eggs. (*Sadly, but gaining in power.*) Man say: I got to take hold of this here world, baby! And a woman will say: Eat your eggs and go to work. (*Passionately now.*) Man say: I got to change my life, I'm choking to death, baby! And his woman say—(*In utter anguish as he brings his fists down on his thighs.*)—Your eggs is getting cold!

RUTH. (*Softly.*) Walter, that ain't none of our money.

WALTER. (*Not listening at all or even looking at her.*) This morning, I was lookin' in the mirror and thinking about it . . . I'm thirty-five years old; I been married eleven years and I got a boy who sleeps in the living room—(*Very, very quietly.*)— and all I got to give him is stories about how rich white people live. . . .

RUTH. Eat your eggs, Walter.

WALTER. DAMN MY EGGS . . . DAMN ALL THE EGGS THAT EVER WAS!

RUTH. Then go to work.

WALTER. (*Looking up at her.*) See—I'm trying to talk to you 'bout myself— (*Shaking his head with the repetition.*)—and all you can say is eat them eggs and go to work.

RUTH. (*Wearily.*) Honey, you never say nothing new. I listen to you every day, every night and every morning, and you never say nothing new. (*Shrugging.*) So you would rather *be* Mr. Arnold than be his chauffeur. So—I would *rather* be living in Buckingham Palace.

WALTER. That is just what is wrong with the colored woman in this world . . . don't understand about building their men up and making 'em feel like they somebody. Like they can do something.

RUTH. (*Drily, but to hurt.*) There *are* colored men who do things.

WALTER. No thanks to the colored woman.

RUTH. Well, being a colored woman, I guess I can't help myself none. (*She rises and gets the ironing board and sets it up and attacks a huge pile of rough-dried clothes, sprinkling them in preparation for the ironing and then rolling them into tight fat balls.*)

WALTER. (*Mumbling.*) We one group of men tied to a race of women with small minds.

(*His sister* BENEATHA *enters. She is about twenty, as slim and intense as her brother. She is not as pretty as her sister-in-law, but her lean, almost intellectual face has a handsomeness of its own. She wears a bright-red flannel nightie, and her thick hair stands wildly about her head. Her speech is a mixture of many things; it is different from the rest of the family's in so far as education has permeated her sense of English— and perhaps the Midwest rather than the South has finally—at last—won out in her inflection; but not altogether, because over all of it is a soft slurring and transformed use of vowels which is the decided influence of the Southside. She passes through the room without looking at either* RUTH *or* WALTER *and goes to the outside door and looks, a little blindly, out to the bathroom. She sees that it has been lost to the Johnsons. She closes the door with a sleepy vengeance and crosses to the table and sits down a little defeated.*)

BENEATHA. I am going to start timing those people.

WALTER. You should get up earlier.

BENEATHA. (*Her face in her hands. She is still fighting the urge to go back to bed.*) Really—would you suggest dawn? Where's the paper?

WALTER. (*Pushing the paper across the table to her as he studies her almost clinically, as though he has never seen her before.*) You a horrible-looking chick at this hour.

BENEATHA. (*Drily.*) Good morning, everybody.

WALTER. (*Senselessly.*) How is school coming?

BENEATHA. (*In the same spirit.*) Lovely. Lovely. And you know, biology is the greatest. (*Looking up at him.*) I dissected something that looked just like you yesterday.

WALTER. I just wondered if you've made up your mind and everything.

BENEATHA. (*Gaining in sharpness and impatience.*) And what did I answer yesterday morning—and the day before that?

RUTH. (*From the ironing board, like someone disinterested and old.*) Don't be so nasty, Bennie.

BENEATHA. (*Still to her brother.*) And the day before that and the day before that!

WALTER. (*Defensively.*) I'm interested in you. Something wrong with that? Ain't many girls who decide—

WALTER *and* BENEATHA. (*In unison.*)—To be a doctor.

(Silence.)

WALTER. Have we figured out yet just exactly how much medical school is going to cost?

RUTH. Walter Lee, why don't you leave that girl alone and get out of here to work?

BENEATHA. *(Exits to the bathroom and bangs on the door.)* Come on out of there, please! *(She comes back into the room.)*

WALTER. *(Looking at his sister intently.)* You know the check is coming tomorrow.

BENEATHA. *(Turning on him with a sharpness all her own.)* That money belongs to Mama, Walter, and it's for her to decide how she wants to use it. I don't care if she wants to buy a house or a rocket ship or just nail it up somewhere and look at it. It's hers. Not ours—*hers.*

WALTER. *(Bitterly.)* Now ain't that fine! You just got your mother's interest at heart, ain't you, girl? You such a nice girl—but if Mama got that money she can always take a few thousand and help you through school too—can't she?

BENEATHA. I have never asked anyone around here to do anything for me!

WALTER. No! And the line between asking and just accepting when the time comes is big and wide—ain't it!

BENEATHA. *(With fury.)* What do you want from me, Brother—that I quit school or just drop dead, which!

WALTER. I don't want nothing but for you to stop acting holy 'round here. Me and Ruthie done made some sacrifices for you—why can't you do something for the family?

RUTH. Walter, don't be dragging me in it.

WALTER. You are in it—don't you get up and go to work in somebody's kitchen for the last three years to help put clothes on her back?

RUTH. Oh, Walter—that's not fair. . . .

WALTER. It ain't that nobody expects you to get on your knees and say thank you, Brother; thank you, Ruth; thank you, Mama—and thank you, Travis, for wearing the same pair of shoes for two semesters—

BENEATHA. *(Dropping to her knees.)* Well—I *do*—all right?—thank everybody . . . and forgive me for ever wanting to be anything at all . . . forgive me, forgive me!

RUTH. Please stop it! Your mama'll hear you.

WALTER. Who the hell told you you had to be a doctor? If you so crazy 'bout messing 'round with sick people—then go be a nurse like other women—or just get married and be quiet. . . .

BENEATHA. Well—you finally got it said. . . . It took you three years but you finally got it said. Walter, give up; leave me alone—it's Mama's money.

WALTER. HE WAS MY FATHER, TOO!

BENEATHA. So what? He was mine, too—and Travis' grandfather—but the insurance money belongs to Mama. Picking on me is not going to make her give it to you to invest in any liquor stores—*(Under breath, dropping into a chair.)*—and I for one say, God bless Mama for that!

WALTER. *(To* RUTH.*)* See—did you hear? Did you hear!

RUTH. Honey, please go to work.

WALTER. Nobody in this house is ever going to understand me.

BENEATHA. Because you're a nut.

WALTER. Who's a nut?

BENEATHA. You—you are a nut. Thee is mad, boy.

WALTER. (*Looking at his wife and sister from the door, very sadly.*) The world's most backward race of people, and that's a fact.

BENEATHA. (*Turning slowly in her chair.*) And then there are all those prophets who would lead us out of the wilderness—(WALTER *slams out of the house.*)—into the swamps!

RUTH. Bennie, why you always gotta be pickin' on your brother? Can't you be a little sweeter sometimes?

(*Door opens.* WALTER *walks in.*)

WALTER. (*To* RUTH.) I need some money for carfare.

RUTH. (*Looks at him, then warms; teasing, but tenderly.*) Fifty cents? (*She goes to her bag and gets money.*) Here, take a taxi.

(WALTER *exits.* MAMA *enters. She is a woman in her early sixties, full-bodied and strong. She is one of those women of a certain grace and beauty who wear it so unobtrusively that it takes a while to notice. Her dark-brown face is surrounded by the total whiteness of her hair, and, being a woman who has adjusted to many things in life and overcome many more, her face is full of strength. She has, we can see, wit and faith of a kind that keep her eyes lit and full of interest and expectancy. She is, in a word, a beautiful woman. Her bearing is perhaps most like the noble bearing of the women of the Hereros of Southwest Africa—rather as if she imagines that as she walks she still bears a basket or a vessel upon her head. Her speech, on the other hand, is as careless as her carriage is precise—she is inclined to slur everything—but her voice is perhaps not so much quiet as simply soft.*)

MAMA. Who that 'round here slamming doors at this hour? (*She crosses through the room, goes to the window, opens it, and brings in a feeble little plant growing doggedly in a small pot on the window sill. She feels the dirt and puts it back out.*)

RUTH. That was Walter Lee. He and Bennie was at it again.

MAMA. My children and they tempers. Lord, if this little old plant don't get more sun than it's been getting it ain't never going to see spring again. (*She turns from the window.*) What's the matter with you this morning, Ruth? You looks right peaked. You aiming to iron all them things? Leave some for me. I'll get to 'em this afternoon. Bennie honey, it's too drafty for you to be sitting 'round half dressed. Where's your robe?

BENEATHA. In the cleaners.

MAMA. Well, go get mine and put it on.

BENEATHA. I'm not cold, Mama, honest.

MAMA. I know—but you so thin. . . .

BENEATHA. (*Irritably.*) Mama, I'm not cold.

MAMA. (*Seeing the make-down bed as* TRAVIS *has left it.*) Lord have mercy, look at that poor bed. Bless his heart—he tries, don't he? (*She moves to the bed* TRAVIS *has sloppily made up.*)

RUTH. No—he don't half try at all 'cause he knows you going to come along behind him and fix everything. That's just how come he don't know how to do nothing right now—you done spoiled that boy so.

MAMA. Well—he's a little boy. Ain't supposed to know 'bout housekeeping. My baby, that's what he is. What you fix for his breakfast this morning?

RUTH. *(Angrily.)* I feed my son, Lena!

MAMA. I ain't meddling—*(Under breath; busy-bodyish.)* I just noticed all last week he had cold cereal, and when it starts getting this chilly in the fall a child ought to have some hot grits or something when he goes out in the cold—

RUTH. *(Furious.)* I gave him hot oats—is that all right!

MAMA. I ain't meddling. *(Pause.)* Put a lot of nice butter on it?

(RUTH shoots her an angry look and does not reply.)

He likes lots of butter.

RUTH. *(Exasperated.)* Lena—

MAMA. *(To* BENEATHA. MAMA *is inclined to wander conversationally sometimes.)* What was you and your brother fussing 'bout this morning?

BENEATHA. It's not important, Mama. *(She gets up and goes to look out at the bathroom, which is apparently free, and she picks up her towels and rushes out.)*

MAMA. What was they fighting about?

RUTH. Now you know as well as I do.

MAMA. *(Shaking her head.)* Brother still worrying hisself sick about that money?

RUTH. You know he is.

MAMA. You had breakfast?

RUTH. Some coffee.

MAMA. Girl, you better start eating and looking after yourself better. You almost thin as Travis.

RUTH. Lena—

MAMA. Un-hunh?

RUTH. What are you going to do with it?

MAMA. Now don't you start, child. It's too early in the morning to be talking about money. It ain't Christian.

RUTH. It's just that he got his heart set on that store—

MAMA. You mean that liquor store that Willy Harris want him to invest in?

RUTH. Yes—

MAMA. We ain't no business people, Ruth. We just plain working folks.

RUTH. Ain't nobody business people till they go into business. Walter Lee say colored people ain't never going to start getting ahead till they start gambling on some different kinds of things in the world—investments and things.

MAMA. What done got into you, girl? Walter Lee done finally sold you on investing.

RUTH. No. Mama, something is happening between Walter and me. I don't know what it is—but he needs something—something I can't give him any more. He needs this chance, Lena.

MAMA. *(Frowning deeply.)* But liquor, honey—

RUTH. Well—like Walter say—I 'spec' people going to always be drinking themselves some liquor.

MAMA. Well—whether they drinks it or not ain't none of my business. But whether I go into business selling it to 'em is, and I don't want that on my ledger this late in life. *(Stopping suddenly and studying her daughter-in-law.)* Ruth Younger, what's the matter with you today? You look like you could fall over right there.

RUTH. I'm tired.

MAMA. Then you better stay home from work today.

RUTH. I can't stay home. She'd be calling up the agency and screaming at them, "My girl didn't come in today—send me somebody! My girl didn't come in!" Oh, she just have a fit. . . .

MAMA. Well, let her have it. I'll just call her up and say you got the flu—

RUTH. *(Laughing.)* Why the flu?

MAMA. 'Cause it sounds respectable to 'em. Something white people get, too. They know 'bout the flu. Otherwise they think you been cut up or something when you tell 'em you sick.

RUTH. I got to go in. We need the money.

MAMA. Somebody would of thought my children done all but starved to death the way they talk about money here late. Child, we got a great big old check coming tomorrow.

RUTH. *(Sincerely, but also self-righteously.)* Now that's your money. It ain't got nothing to do with me. We all feel like that—Walter and Bennie and me—even Travis.

MAMA. *(Thoughtfully, and suddenly very far away.)* Ten thousand dollars—

RUTH. Sure is wonderful.

MAMA. Ten thousand dollars.

RUTH. You know what you should do, Miss Lena? You should take yourself a trip somewhere. To Europe or South America or someplace—

MAMA. *(Throwing up her hands at the thought.)* Oh, child!

RUTH. I'm serious. Just pack up and leave! Go on away and enjoy yourself some. Forget about the family and have yourself a ball for once in your life—

MAMA. *(Drily.)* You sound like I'm just about ready to die. Who'd go with me? What I look like wandering 'round Europe by myself?

RUTH. Shoot—these here rich white women do it all the time. They don't think nothing of packing up they suitcases and piling on one of them big steamships and—swoosh!—they gone, child.

MAMA. Something always told me I wasn't no rich white woman.

RUTH. Well—what are you going to do with it then?

MAMA. I ain't rightly decided. *(Thinking. She speaks now with emphasis.)* Some of it got to be put away for Beneatha and her schoolin'—and ain't nothing going to touch that part of it. Nothing. *(She waits several seconds, trying to make up her mind about something, and looks at* RUTH *a little tentatively before going on.)* Been thinking that we maybe could meet the notes on a little old two-story somewhere, with a yard where Travis could play in the summertime, if we use part of the insurance for a down payment and everybody kind of pitch in. I could maybe take on a little day work again, few days a week—

RUTH. *(Studying her mother-in-law furtively and concentrating on her ironing, anxious to encourage without seeming to.)* Well, Lord knows, we've put enough rent into this here rat trap to pay for four houses by now. . . .

MAMA. *(Looking up at the words "rat trap" and then looking around and leaning back and sighing, in a suddenly reflective mood.)* "Rat trap"—yes, that's all it is. *(Smiling.)* I remember just as well the day me and Big Walter moved in here. Hadn't been married but two weeks and wasn't planning on living here no more than a year. *(She shakes her head at the dissolved dream.)* We was going to set away, little by little, don't you know, and buy a little place out in Morgan Park. We had even picked out the house. *(Chuckling a little.)* Looks right dumpy today. But Lord, child, you should know all the dreams I had 'bout buying that house and fixing it up and making me a little garden in the back—*(She waits and stops smiling.)* And didn't none of it happen. *(Dropping her hands in a futile gesture.)*

RUTH. *(Keeps her head down, ironing.)* Yes, life can be a barrel of disappointments, sometimes.

MAMA. Honey, Big Walter would come in here some nights back then and slump down on that couch there and just look at the rug, and look at me and look at the rug and then back at me—and I'd know he was down then . . . really down. *(After a second very long and thoughtful pause; she is seeing back to times that only she can see.)* And then, Lord, when I lost that baby—little Claude—I almost thought I was going to lose Big Walter too. Oh, that man grieved hisself! He was one man to love his children.

RUTH. Ain't nothin' can tear at you like losin' your baby.

MAMA. I guess that's how come that man finally worked hisself to death like he done. Like he was fighting his own war with this here world that took his baby from him.

RUTH. He sure was a fine man, all right. I always liked Mr. Younger.

MAMA. Crazy 'bout his children! God knows there was plenty wrong with Walter Younger—hard-headed, mean, kind of wild with women—plenty wrong with him. But he sure loved his children. Always wanted them to have something—be something. That's where Brother gets all these notions, I reckon. Big Walter used to say, he'd get right wet in the eyes sometimes, lean his head back with the water standing in his eyes and say, "Seem like God don't see fit to give the black man nothing but dreams—but He did give us children to make them dreams seem worthwhile." *(She smiles.)* He could talk like that, don't you know.

RUTH. Yes, he sure could. He was a good man, Mr. Younger.

MAMA. Yes, a fine man—just couldn't never catch up with his dreams, that's all.

(BENEATHA comes in, brushing her hair and looking up at the ceiling, where the sound of a vacuum cleaner has started up.)

BENEATHA. What could be so dirty on that woman's rugs that she has to vacuum them every single day?

RUTH. I wish certain young women 'round here who I could name would take inspiration about certain rugs in a certain apartment I could also mention.

BENEATHA. *(Shrugging.)* How much cleaning can a house need, for Christ's sakes.

MAMA. *(Not liking the Lord's name used thus.)* Bennie!

RUTH. Just listen to her—just listen!

BENEATHA. Oh, God!

MAMA. If you use the Lord's name just one more time—

BENEATHA. *(A bit of a whine.)* Oh, Mama—

RUTH. Fresh—just fresh as salt, this girl!

BENEATHA. *(Drily.)* Well—if the salt loses its savor—

MAMA. Now that will do. I just ain't going to have you 'round here reciting the scriptures in vain—you hear me?

BENEATHA. How did I manage to get on everybody's wrong side by just walking into a room?

RUTH. If you weren't so fresh—

BENEATHA. Ruth, I'm twenty years old.

MAMA. What time you be home from school today?

BENEATHA. Kind of late. *(With enthusiasm.)* Madeline is going to start my guitar lessons today.

(MAMA and RUTH look up with the same expression.)

MAMA. Your *what* kind of lessons?

BENEATHA. Guitar.

RUTH. Oh, Father!

MAMA. How come you done taken it in your mind to learn to play the guitar?

BENEATHA. I just want to, that's all.

MAMA. *(Smiling.)* Lord, child, don't you know what to do with yourself? How long it going to be before you get tired of this now—like you got tired of that little play-acting group you joined last year? *(Looking at RUTH.)* And what was it the year before that?

RUTH. The horseback-riding club for which she bought that fifty-five-dollar riding habit that's been hanging in the closet ever since!

MAMA. *(To BENEATHA.)* Why you got to flit so from one thing to another, baby?

BENEATHA. *(Sharply.)* I just want to learn to play the guitar. Is there anything wrong with that?

MAMA. Ain't nobody trying to stop you. I just wonders sometimes why you has to flit so from one thing to another all the time. You ain't never done nothing with all that camera equipment you brought home—

BENEATHA. I don't flit! I—I experiment with different forms of expression—

RUTH. Like riding a horse?

BENEATHA. People have to express themselves one way or another.

MAMA. What is it you want to express?

BENEATHA. *(Angrily.)* Me!

(MAMA and RUTH look at each other and burst into raucous laughter.)

Don't worry—I don't expect you to understand.

MAMA. *(To change the subject.)* Who you going out with tomorrow night?

BENEATHA. *(With displeasure.)* George Murchison again.

MAMA. *(Pleased.)* Oh—you getting a little sweet on him?

RUTH. You ask me, this child ain't sweet on nobody but herself. *(Under breath.)* Express herself!

(They laugh.)

BENEATHA. Oh—I like George all right, Mama. I mean I like him enough to go out with him and stuff, but—

RUTH. *(For devilment.)* What does *and stuff* mean?

BENEATHA. Mind your own business.

MAMA. Stop picking at her now, Ruth. *(A thoughtful pause, and then a suspicious sudden look at her daughter as she turns in her chair for emphasis.)* What *does* it mean?

BENEATHA. *(Wearily.)* Oh, I just mean I couldn't ever really be serious about George. He's—he's so shallow.

RUTH. Shallow—what do you mean he's shallow? He's RICH!

MAMA. Hush, Ruth.

BENEATHA. I know he's rich. He knows he's rich, too.

RUTH. Well—what other qualities a man got to have to satisfy you, little girl?

BENEATHA. You wouldn't even begin to understand. Anybody who married Walter could not possibly understand.

MAMA. *(Outraged.)* What kind of way is that to talk about your brother?

BENEATHA. Brother is a flip—let's face it.

MAMA. *(To RUTH, helplessly.)* What's a flip?

RUTH. *(Glad to add kindling.)* She's saying he's crazy.

BENEATHA. Not crazy. Brother isn't really crazy yet—he—he's an elaborate neurotic.

MAMA. Hush your mouth!

BENEATHA. As for George. Well. George looks good—he's got a beautiful car and he takes me to nice places and, as my sister-in-law says, he is probably the richest boy I will ever get to know and I even like him sometimes—but if the Youngers are sitting around waiting to see if their little Bennie is going to tie up the family with the Murchisons, they are wasting their time.

RUTH. You mean you wouldn't marry George Murchison if he asked you someday? That pretty, rich thing? Honey, I knew you was odd—

BENEATHA. No I would not marry him if all I felt for him was what I feel now. Besides, George's family wouldn't really like it.

MAMA. Why not?

BENEATHA. Oh, Mama—the Murchisons are honest-to-God-real-*live*-rich colored people, and the only people in the world who are more snobbish than rich white people are rich colored people. I thought everybody knew that. I've met Mrs. Murchison. She's a scene!

MAMA. You must not dislike people 'cause they well off, honey.

BENEATHA. Why not? It makes just as much sense as disliking people 'cause they are poor, and lots of people do that.

RUTH. *(A wisdom-of-the-ages manner. To MAMA.)* Well, she'll get over some of this—

BENEATHA. Get over it? What are you talking about, Ruth? Listen, I'm going to be a doctor. I'm not worried about who I'm going to marry yet—if I ever get married.

MAMA *and* RUTH. IF!

MAMA. Now, Bennie—

BENEATHA. Oh, I probably will . . . but first I'm going to be a doctor, and George, for one, still thinks that's pretty funny. I couldn't be bothered with that. I am going to be a doctor and everybody around here better understand that!

MAMA. *(Kindly.)* 'Course you going to be a doctor, honey, God willing.

BENEATHA. *(Drily.)* God hasn't got a thing to do with it.

MAMA. Beneatha—that just wasn't necessary.

BENEATHA. Well—neither is God. I get sick of hearing about God.

MAMA. Beneatha!

BENEATHA. I mean it! I'm just tired of hearing about God all the time. What has He got to do with anything? Does he pay tuition?

MAMA. You 'bout to get your fresh little jaw slapped!

RUTH. That's just what she needs, all right!

BENEATHA. Why? Why can't I say what I want to around here, like everybody else?

MAMA. It don't sound nice for a young girl to say things like that—you wasn't brought up that way. Me and your father went to trouble to get you and Brother to church every Sunday.

BENEATHA. Mama, you don't understand. It's all a matter of ideas, and God is just one idea I don't accept. It's not important. I am not going out and be immoral or commit crimes because I don't believe in God. I don't even think about it. It's just that I get tired of Him getting credit for all the things the human race achieves through its own stubborn effort. There simply is no blasted God— there is only man and it is he who makes miracles!

(MAMA *absorbs this speech, studies her daughter and rises slowly and crosses to* BENEATHA *and slaps her powerfully across the face. After, there is only silence and the daughter drops her eyes from her mother's face, and* MAMA *is very tall before her.)*

MAMA. Now—you say after me, in my mother's house there is still God.

(*There is a long pause and* BENEATHA *stares at the floor wordlessly.* MAMA *repeats the phrase with precision and cool emotion.)*

In my mother's house there is still God.

BENEATHA. In my mother's house there is still God.

(*A long pause.)*

MAMA. *(Walking away from* BENEATHA, *too disturbed for triumphant posture. Stopping and turning back to her daughter.)* There are some ideas we ain't going to have in this house. Not long as I am at the head of this family.

BENEATHA. Yes, ma'am.

(MAMA *walks out of the room.)*

RUTH. *(Almost gently, with profound understanding.)* You think you a woman, Bennie—but you still a little girl. What you did was childish—so you got treated like a child.

BENEATHA. I see. *(Quietly.)* I also see that everybody thinks it's all right for Mama to be a tyrant. But all the tyranny in the world will never put a God in the heavens! *(She picks up her books and goes out.)*

RUTH. *(Goes to* MAMA's *door.)* She said she was sorry.

MAMA. *(Coming out, going to her plant.)* They frightens me, Ruth. My children.

RUTH. You got good children, Lena. They just a little off sometimes—but they're good.

MAMA. No—there's something come down between me and them that don't let us understand each other and I don't know what it is. One done almost lost his mind thinking 'bout money all the time and the other done commence to talk about things I can't seem to understand in no form or fashion. What is it that's changing, Ruth?

RUTH. *(Soothingly, older than her years.)* Now . . . you taking it all too seriously. You just got strong-willed children and it takes a strong woman like you to keep 'em in hand.

MAMA. *(Looking at her plant and sprinkling a little water on it.)* They spirited all right, my children. Got to admit they got spirit—Bennie and Walter. Like this little old plant that ain't never had enough sunshine or nothing—and look at it. . . .

(She has her back to RUTH, *who has had to stop ironing and lean against something and put the back of her hand to her forehead.)*

RUTH. *(Trying to keep* MAMA *from noticing.)* You . . . sure . . . loves that little old thing, don't you? . . .

MAMA. Well, I always wanted me a garden like I used to see sometimes at the back of the houses down home. This plant is close as I ever got to having one. *(She looks out of the window as she replaces the plant.)* Lord, ain't nothing as dreary as the view from this window on a dreary day, is there? Why ain't you singing this morning, Ruth? Sing that "No Ways Tired." That song always lifts me up so— *(She turns at last to see that* RUTH *has slipped quietly into a chair, in a state of semi-consciousness.)* Ruth! Ruth honey—what's the matter with you . . . Ruth!

CURTAIN

ACT 1

SCENE 2

It is the following morning; a Saturday morning, and house cleaning is in progress at the YOUNGERS. *Furniture has been shoved hither and yon and* MAMA *is giving the kitchen-area walls a washing down.* BENEATHA, *in dungarees, with a handkerchief tied around her face, is spraying insecticide into the cracks in the walls. As they work, the* RADIO *is on and a Southside disc-jockey program is inappropriately filling the house with a rather exotic saxophone blues.* TRAVIS, *the sole idle one, is leaning on his arms, looking out of the window.*

TRAVIS. Grandmama, that stuff Bennie is using smells awful. Can I go downstairs, please?

MAMA. Did you get all them chores done already? I ain't seen you doing much.

TRAVIS. Yes'm—finished early. Where did Mama go this morning?

MAMA. *(Looking at* BENEATHA.) She had to go on a little errand.

TRAVIS. Where?

MAMA. To tend to her business.

TRAVIS. Can I go outside then?

MAMA. Oh, I guess so. You better stay right in front of the house, though . . . and keep a good lookout for the postman.

TRAVIS. Yes'm. *(He starts out and decides to give his* AUNT BENEATHA *a good swat on the legs as he passes her.)* Leave them poor little old cockroaches alone, they ain't bothering you none. *(He runs as she swings the spray gun at him both viciously and playfully.)*

*(*WALTER *enters from the bedroom and goes to the phone.)*

MAMA. Look out there, girl, before you be spilling some of that stuff on that child!

TRAVIS. *(Teasing.)* That's right—look out now! *(He exits.)*

BENEATHA. *(Drily.)* I can't imagine that it would hurt him—it has never hurt the roaches.

MAMA. Well, little boys' hides ain't as tough as Southside roaches.

WALTER. *(Into phone.)* Hello—Let me talk to Willy Harris.

MAMA. You better get over there behind the bureau. I seen one marching out of there like Napoleon yesterday.

WALTER. Hello, Willy? It ain't come yet. It'll be here in a few minutes. Did the lawyer give you the papers?

BENEATHA. There's really only one way to get rid of them, Mama—

MAMA. How?

BENEATHA. Set fire to this building.

WALTER. Good. Good. I'll be right over.

BENEATHA. Where did Ruth go, Walter?

WALTER. I don't know. *(He exits abruptly.)*

BENEATHA. Mama, where did Ruth go?

MAMA. *(Looking at her with meaning.)* To the doctor, I think.

BENEATHA. The doctor? What's the matter? *(They exchange glances.)* You don't think—

MAMA. *(With her sense of drama.)* Now I ain't saying what I think. But I ain't never been wrong 'bout a woman neither.

(The phone rings.)

BENEATHA. *(At the phone.)* Hay-lo. . . . *(Pause, and a moment of recognition.)* Well— when did you get back! . . . And how was it? . . . Of course I've missed you— in my way. . . . This morning? No . . . house cleaning and all that and Mama hates it if I let people come over when the house is like this. . . . You *have?* Well, that's different . . . What is it—oh, what the hell, come on over. . . . Right, see you then. *(She hangs up.)*

MAMA. *(Who has listened vigorously, as is her habit.)* Who is that you inviting over here with this house looking like this? You ain't got the pride you was born with!

BENEATHA. Asagai doesn't care how houses look, Mama—he's an intellectual.

MAMA. WHO?

BENEATHA. Asagai—Joseph Asagai. He's an African boy I met on campus. He's been studying in Canada all summer.

MAMA. What's his name?

BENEATHA. Asagai, Joseph. Ah-sah-guy. . . . He's from Nigeria.

MAMA. Oh, that's the little country that was founded by slaves way back. . . .

BENEATHA. No, Mama—that's Liberia.

MAMA. I don't think I never met no African before.

BENEATHA. Well, do me a favor and don't ask him a whole lot of ignorant questions about Africans. I mean, do they wear clothes and all that—

MAMA. Well, now, I guess if you think we so ignorant 'round here maybe you shouldn't bring your friends here—

BENEATHA. It's just that people ask such crazy things. All anyone seems to know about when it comes to Africa is Tarzan—

MAMA. *(Indignantly.)* Why should I know anything about Africa?

BENEATHA. Why do you give money at church for the missionary work?

MAMA. Well, that's to help save people.

BENEATHA. You mean save them from *heathenism*—

MAMA. *(Innocently.)* Yes.

BENEATHA. I'm afraid they need more salvation from the British and the French.

(RUTH *comes in forlornly and pulls off her coat with dejection. They both turn to look at her.*)

RUTH. *(Dispiritedly.)* Well, I guess from all the happy faces—everybody knows.

BENEATHA. You pregnant?

MAMA. Lord have mercy, I sure hope it's a little old girl. Travis ought to have a sister.

(BENEATHA *and* RUTH *give her a hopeless look for this grandmotherly enthusiasm.*)

BENEATHA. How far along are you?

RUTH. Two months.

BENEATHA. Did you mean to? I mean did you plan it or was it an accident?

MAMA. What do you know about planning or not planning?

BENEATHA. Oh, Mama.

RUTH. *(Wearily.)* She's twenty years old, Lena.

BENEATHA. Did you plan it, Ruth?

RUTH. Mind your own business.

BENEATHA. It is my business—where is he going to live, on the *roof?*

(*There is silence following the remark as the three women react to the sense of it.*)

Gee—I didn't mean that, Ruth, honest. Gee, I don't feel like that at all. I—I think it is wonderful.

RUTH. *(Dully.)* Wonderful.

BENEATHA. Yes—really.

MAMA. *(Looking at* RUTH, *worried.)* Doctor say everything going to be all right?

RUTH. *(Far away.)* Yes—she says everything is going to be fine. . . .

MAMA. *(Immediately suspicious.)* "She"? What doctor you went to?

(RUTH *folds over, near hysteria.*)

MAMA. *(Worriedly hovering over* RUTH.) Ruth honey—what's the matter with you—you sick?

(RUTH *has her fists clenched on her thighs and is fighting hard to suppress a scream that seems to be rising in her.*)

BENEATHA. What's the matter with her, Mama?

MAMA. *(Working her fingers in* RUTH'S *shoulder to relax her.)* She be all right. Women gets right depressed sometimes when they get her way. *(Speaking softly, expertly, rapidly.)* Now you just relax. That's right . . . just lean back, don't think 'bout nothing at all . . . nothing at all—

RUTH. I'm all right. *(The glassy-eyed look melts and then she collapses into a fit of heavy sobbing.)*

(The BELL *rings.)*

BENEATHA. Oh, my God—that must be Asagai.

MAMA. *(To* RUTH.) Come on now, honey. You need to lie down and rest awhile . . . then have some nice hot food.

(They exit, RUTH'S *weight on her mother-in-law.* BENEATHA, *herself profoundly disturbed, opens the door to admit a rather dramatic-looking young man with a large package.)*

ASAGAI. Hello, Alaiyo—

BENEATHA. *(Holding the door open and regarding him with pleasure.)* Hello. . . . *(Long pause.)* Well—come in. And please excuse everything. My mother was very upset about my letting anyone come here with the place like this.

ASAGAI. *(Coming into the room.)* You look disturbed too. . . . Is something wrong?

BENEATHA. *(Still at the door, absently.)* Yes . . . we've all got acute ghetto-itus. *(She smiles and comes toward him, finding a cigarette and sitting.)* So—sit down! How was Canada?

ASAGAI. *(A sophisticate.)* Canadian.

BENEATHA. *(Looking at him.)* I'm very glad you are back.

ASAGAI. *(Looking back at her in turn.)* Are you really?

BENEATHA. Yes—very.

ASAGAI. Why—you were quite glad when I went away. What happened?

BENEATHA. You went away.

ASAGAI. Ahhhhhhhh.

BENEATHA. Before—you wanted to be so serious before there was time.

ASAGAI. How much time must there be before one knows what one feels?

BENEATHA. *(Stalling this particular conversation. Her hands pressed together, in a deliberately childish gesture.)* What did you bring me?

ASAGAI. *(Handing her the package.)* Open it and see.

BENEATHA. *(Eagerly opening the package and drawing out some records and the colorful robes of a Nigerian woman.)* Oh, Asagai! . . . You got them for me! . . . How beautiful . . . and the records too! *(She lifts out the robes and runs to the mirror with them and holds the drapery up in front of herself.)*

ASAGAI. *(Coming to her at the mirror.)* I shall have to teach you how to drape it properly. *(He flings the material about her for the moment and stands back to look at her.*) Ah—*Oh-pay-gay-day, oh-gbah-mu-shay.* (*A Yoruba exclamation for admiration.*) You wear it well . . . very well . . . mutilated hair and all.

BENEATHA. (*Turning suddenly.*) My hair—what's wrong with my hair?

ASAGAI. (*Shrugging.*) Were you born with it like that?

BENEATHA. (*Reaching up to touch it.*) No . . . of course not. (*She looks back to the mirror, disturbed.*)

ASAGAI. (*Smiling.*) How then?

BENEATHA. You know perfectly well how . . . as crinkly as yours . . . that's how.

ASAGAI. And it is ugly to you that way?

BENEATHA. (*Quickly.*) Oh, no—not ugly . . . (*More slowly, apologetically.*) but it's so hard to manage when it's, well—raw.

ASAGAI. And so to accommodate that—you mutilate it every week?

BENEATHA. It's not mutilation!

ASAGAI. (*Laughing aloud at her seriousness.*) Oh . . . please! I am only teasing you because you are so very serious about these things. (*He stands back from her and folds his arms across his chest as he watches her pulling at her hair and frowning in the mirror.*) Do you remember the first time you met me at school? . . . (*He laughs.*) You came up to me and you said—and I thought you were the most serious little thing I had ever seen—you said: (*He imitates her.*) "Mr. Asagai—I want very much to talk with you. About Africa. You see, Mr. Asagai, I am looking for my *identity!*" (*He laughs.*)

BENEATHA. (*Turning to him, not laughing.*) Yes—(*Her face is quizzical, profoundly disturbed.*)

ASAGAI. (*Still teasing and reaching out and taking her face in his hands and turning her profile to him.*) Well . . . it is true that this is not so much a profile of a Hollywood queen as perhaps a queen of the Nile—(*A mock dismissal of the importance of the question.*)—but what does it matter? Assimilationism is so popular in your country.

BENEATHA. (*Wheeling, passionately, sharply.*) I am not an assimilationist!

ASAGAI. (*The protest hangs in the room for a moment and* ASAGAI *studies her, his laughter fading.*) Such a serious one. (*There is a pause.*) So—you like the robes? You must take excellent care of them—they are from my sister's personal wardrobe.

BENEATHA. (*With incredulity.*) You—you sent all the way home—for me?

ASAGAI. (*With charm.*) For you—I would do much more. . . . Well, that is what I came for. I must go.

BENEATHA. Will you call me Monday?

ASAGAI. Yes . . . we have a great deal to talk about. I mean about identity and time and all that.

BENEATHA. Time?

ASAGAI. Yes. About how much time one needs to know what one feels.

BENEATHA. You never understood that there is more than one kind of feeling which can exist between a man and a woman—or, at least, there should be.

ASAGAI. (*Shaking his head negatively but gently.*) No. Between a man and a woman there need be only one kind of feeling. I have that for you . . . now even . . . right this moment . . .

BENEATHA. I know—and by itself—it won't do. I can find that anywhere.

ASAGAI. For a woman it should be enough.

BENEATHA. I know—because that's what it says in all the novels that men write. But it isn't. Go ahead and laugh—but I'm not interested in being someone's little episode in America or—(*With feminine vengeance.*)—one of them!

(ASAGAI *has burst into laughter again.*)

That's funny as hell, huh!

ASAGAI. It's just that every American girl I have known has said that to me. White—black—in this you are all the same. And the same speech, too!

BENEATHA. (*Angrily.*) Yuk, yuk, yuk!

ASAGAI. It's how you can be sure that the world's most liberated women are not liberated at all. You all talk about it too much!

(MAMA *enters and is immediately all social charm because of the presence of a guest.*)

BENEATHA. Oh—Mama—this is Mr. Asagai.

MAMA. How do you do?

ASAGAI. (*Total politeness to an elder.*) How do you do, Mrs. Younger. Please forgive me for coming at such an outrageous hour on a Saturday.

MAMA. Well, you are quite welcome. I just hope you understand that our house don't always look like this. (*Chatterish.*) You must come again. I would love to hear all about—(*Not sure of the name.*)—your country. I think it's so sad the way our American Negroes don't know nothing about Africa 'cept Tarzan and all that. And all that money they pour into these churches when they ought to be helping you people over there drive out them French and Englishmen done taken away your land. (*The mother flashes a slightly superior look at her daughter upon completion of the recitation.*)

ASAGAI. (*Taken aback by this sudden and acutely unrelated expression of sympathy.*) Yes . . . yes. . . .

MAMA. (*Smiling at him suddenly and relaxing and looking him over.*) How many miles is it from here to where you come from?

ASAGAI. Many thousands.

MAMA. (*Looking at him as she would* WALTER.) I bet you don't half look after yourself, being away from your mama either. I 'spec' you better come 'round here from time to time and get yourself some decent home-cooked meals. . . .

ASAGAI. (*Moved.*) Thank you. Thank you very much. (*They are all quiet, then—*) Well . . . I must go. I will call you Monday, Alaiyo.

MAMA. What's that he call you?

ASAGAI. Oh—"Alaiyo." I hope you don't mind. It is what you would call a nickname, I think. It is a Yoruba word. I am a Yoruba.

MAMA. (*Looking at* BENEATHA.) I—I thought he was from—

ASAGAI. (*Understanding.*) Nigeria is my country. Yoruba is my tribal origin—

BENEATHA. You didn't tell us what Alaiyo means . . . for all I know, you might be calling me Little Idiot or something. . . .

ASAGAI. Well . . . let me see . . . I do not know how just to explain it. . . . The sense of a thing can be so different when it changes languages.

BENEATHA. You're evading.

ASAGAI. No—really it is difficult. . . . *(Thinking.)* It means . . . it means One for Whom Bread—Food—Is Not Enough. *(He looks at her.)* Is that all right?

BENEATHA. *(Understanding, softly.)* Thank you.

MAMA. *(Looking from one to the other and not understanding any of it.)* Well . . . that's nice. . . . You must come see us again—Mr.—

ASAGAI. Ah-sah-guy.

MAMA. Yes . . . do come again.

ASAGAI. Good-bye. *(He exits.)*

MAMA. *(After him.)* Lord, that's a pretty thing just went out here! *(Insinuatingly, to her daughter.)* Yes, I guess I see why we done commence to get so interested in Africa 'round here. Missionaries my aunt Jenny! *(She exits.)*

BENEATHA. Oh, Mama! . . . *(She picks up the Nigerian dress and holds it up to her in front of the mirror again. She sets the headdress on haphazardly and then notices her hair again and clutches at it and then replaces the headdress and frowns at herself. Then she starts to wriggle in front of the mirror as she thinks a Nigerian woman might.)*

*(*TRAVIS *enters and regards her.)*

TRAVIS. You cracking up?

BENEATHA. Shut up. *(She pulls the headdress off and looks at herself in the mirror and clutches at her hair again and squinches her eyes as if trying to imagine something. Then, suddenly, she gets her raincoat and kerchief and hurriedly prepares for going out.)*

MAMA. *(Coming back into the room.)* She's resting now. Travis, baby, run next door and ask Miss Johnson to please let me have a little kitchen cleanser. This here can is empty as Jacob's kettle.

TRAVIS. I just came in.

MAMA. Do as you told. *(He exits and she looks at her daughter.)* Where are you going?

BENEATHA. *(Halting at the door.)* To become a queen of the Nile! *(She exits in a breathless blaze of glory.)*

*(*RUTH *appears in the bedroom doorway.)*

MAMA. Who told you to get up?

RUTH. Ain't nothing wrong with me to be lying in no bed for. Where did Bennie go?

MAMA. *(Drumming her fingers.)* Far as I could make out—to Egypt.

*(*RUTH *just looks at her.)*

What time is it getting to?

RUTH. Ten twenty. And the mailman going to ring that bell this morning just like he done every morning for the last umpteen years.

*(*TRAVIS *comes in with the cleanser can.)*

TRAVIS. She say to tell you that she don't have much.

MAMA. *(Angrily.)* Lord, some people I could name sure is tight-fisted! *(Directing her grandson.)* Mark two cans of cleanser down on the list there. If she that hard up for kitchen cleanser, I sure don't want to forget to get her none!

RUTH. Lena—maybe the woman is just short on cleanser—

MAMA. *(Not listening.)* Much baking powder as she done borrowed from me all these years, she could of done gone into the baking business!

(The BELL *sounds suddenly and sharply and all three are stunned—serious and silent—mid-speech. In spite of all the other conversations and distractions of the morning, this is what they have been waiting for, even* TRAVIS, *who looks helplessly from his mother to his grandmother.* RUTH *is the first to come to life again.)*

RUTH. *(To* TRAVIS.*)* GET DOWN THEM STEPS, BOY!

*(*TRAVIS *snaps to life and flies out to get the mail.)*

MAMA. *(Her eyes wide, her hand to her breast.)* You mean it done really come?

RUTH. *(Excited.)* Oh, Miss Lena!

MAMA. *(Collecting herself.)* Well . . . I don't know what we all so excited about 'round here. We known it was coming for months.

RUTH. That's a whole lot different from having it come and being able to hold it in your hands . . . a piece of paper worth ten thousand dollars. . . .

*(*TRAVIS *bursts back into the room. He holds the envelope high above his head, like a little dancer, his face is radiant and he is breathless. He moves to his grandmother with sudden slow ceremony and puts the envelope into her hands. She accepts it, and then merely holds it and looks at it.)*

Come on! Open it . . . Lord have mercy, I wish Walter Lee was here!

TRAVIS. Open it, Grandmama!

MAMA. *(Staring at it.)* Now you all be quiet. It's just a check.

RUTH. Open it. . . .

MAMA. *(Still staring at it.)* Now don't act silly. . . . We ain't never been no people to act silly 'bout no money—

RUTH. *(Swiftly.)* We ain't never had none before—OPEN IT!

*(*MAMA *finally makes a good strong tear and pulls out the thin blue slice of paper and inspects it closely. The boy and his mother study it raptly over* MAMA's *shoulders.)*

MAMA. TRAVIS! *(She is counting off with doubt.)* Is that the right number of zeros?

TRAVIS. Yes'm . . . ten thousand dollars. Gaalee, Grandmama, you rich.

MAMA. *(She holds the check away from her, still looking at it. Slowly her face sobers into a mask of unhappiness.)* Ten thousand dollars. *(She hands it to* RUTH.*)* Put it away somewhere, Ruth. *(She does not look at* RUTH; *her eyes seem to be seeing something somewhere very far off.)* Ten thousand dollars they give you. Ten thousand dollars.

TRAVIS. *(To his mother, sincerely.)* What's the matter with Grandmama—don't she want to be rich?

RUTH. *(Distractedly.)* You go on out and play now, baby.

*(*TRAVIS *exits.* MAMA *starts wiping dishes absently, humming intently to herself.)*

*(*RUTH *turns to her, with kind exasperation.)* You've gone and got yourself upset.

MAMA. *(Not looking at her.)* I 'spec' if it wasn't for you all . . . I would just put that money away or give it to the church or something.

RUTH. Now what kind of talk is that. Mr. Younger would just be plain mad if he could hear you talking foolish like that.

MAMA. *(Stopping and staring off.)* Yes . . . he sure would. *(Sighing.)* We got enough to do with that money, all right. *(She halts then, and turns and looks at her daughter-in-law hard;* RUTH *avoids her eyes and* MAMA *wipes her hands with finality and starts to speak firmly to* RUTH.*)* Where did you go today, girl?

RUTH. To the doctor.

MAMA. *(Impatiently.)* Now, Ruth . . . you know better than that. Old Doctor Jones is strange enough in his way but there ain't nothing 'bout him make somebody slip and call him "she"—like you done this morning.

RUTH. Well, that's what happened—my tongue slipped.

MAMA. You went to see that woman, didn't you?

RUTH. *(Defensively, giving herself away.)* What woman you talking about?

MAMA. *(Angrily.)* That woman who—

*(*WALTER *enters in great excitement.)*

WALTER. Did it come?

MAMA. *(Quietly.)* Can't you give people a Christian greeting before you start asking about money?

WALTER. *(To* RUTH.*)* Did it come?

*(*RUTH *unfolds the check and lays it quietly before him, watching him intently with thoughts of her own.)*

*(*WALTER *sits down and grasps it close and counts off the zeros.)* Ten thousand dollars. *(He turns suddenly, frantically to his mother and draws some papers out of his breast pocket.)* Mama—look. Old Willy Harris put everything on paper—

MAMA. Son—I think you ought to talk to your wife . . . I'll go on out and leave you alone if you want—

WALTER. I can talk to her later—Mama, look—

MAMA. Son—

WALTER. WILL SOMEBODY PLEASE LISTEN TO ME TODAY?

MAMA. *(Quietly.)* I don't 'low no yellin' in this house, Walter Lee, and you know it—

*(*WALTER *stares at them in frustration and starts to speak several times.)*

—and there ain't going to be no investing in no liquor stores. I don't aim to have to speak on that again.

(A long pause.)

WALTER. Oh—so you don't aim to have to speak on that again? So *you* have decided. . . . *(Crumpling his papers.)* Well, *you* tell that to my boy tonight when you put him to sleep on the living-room couch . . . *(Turning to* MAMA *and speaking directly to her.)* yeah—and tell it to my wife, Mama, tomorrow when she has to go out of here to look after somebody else's kids. And tell it to *me*, Mama, every time we need a new pair of curtains and I have to watch *you* go out and work in somebody's kitchen. Yeah, you tell me then! *(*WALTER *starts out.)*

RUTH. Where you going?

WALTER. I'm going out!

RUTH. Where?

WALTER. Just out of this house somewhere—

RUTH. *(Getting her coat.)* I'll come too.

WALTER. I don't want you to come!

RUTH. I got something to talk to you about, Walter.

WALTER. That's too bad.

MAMA. *(Still quietly.)* Walter Lee—*(She waits and he finally turns and looks at her)*—sit down.

WALTER. I'm a grown man, Mama.

MAMA. Ain't nobody said you wasn't grown. But you still in my house and my presence. And as long as you are—you'll talk to your wife civil. Now sit down.

RUTH. *(Suddenly.)* Oh, let him go on out and drink himself to death! He makes me sick to my stomach! *(She flings her coat against him.)*

WALTER. *(Violently.)* And you turn mine too, baby!

(RUTH goes into their bedroom and slams the door behind her.)

That was my greatest mistake—

MAMA. *(Still quietly.)* Walter, what is the matter with you?

WALTER. Matter with me? Ain't nothing the matter with *me!*

MAMA. Yes there is. Something eating you up like a crazy man. Something more than me not giving you this money. The past few years I been watching it happen to you. You get all nervous acting and kind of wild in the eyes—

(WALTER jumps up impatiently at her words.)

I said sit there now, I'm talking to you!—

WALTER. Mama—I don't need no nagging at me today.

MAMA. Seem like you getting to a place where you always tied up in some kind of knot about something. But if anybody ask you 'bout it you just yell at 'em and bust out the house and go out and drink somewheres. Walter Lee, people can't live with that. Ruth's a good, patient girl in her way—but you getting to be too much. Boy, don't make the mistake of driving that girl away from you.

WALTER. Why—what she do for me?

MAMA. She loves you.

WALTER. Mama—I'm going out. I want to go off somewhere and be by myself for a while.

MAMA. I'm sorry 'bout your liquor store, son. It just wasn't the thing for us to do. That's what I want to tell you about—

WALTER. I got to go out, Mama—*(He rises.)*

MAMA. It's dangerous, son.

WALTER. What's dangerous?

MAMA. When a man goes outside his home to look for peace.

WALTER. *(Beseechingly.)* Then why can't there never be no peace in this house then?

MAMA. You done found it in some other house?

WALTER. No—there ain't no woman! Why do women always think there's a woman somewhere when a man gets restless. *(Coming to her.)* Mama—Mama—I want so many things . . .

MAMA. Yes, son—

WALTER. I want so many things that they are driving me kind of crazy . . . Mama— look at me.

MAMA. I'm looking at you. You a good-looking boy. You got a job, a nice wife, a fine boy and—

WALTER. A job. *(Looks at her.)* Mama, a job? I open and close car doors all day long. I drive a man around in his limousine and I say, "Yes, sir; no, sir; very good, sir; shall I take the Drive, sir?" Mama, that ain't no kind of job . . . that ain't nothing at all. *(Very quietly.)* Mama, I don't know if I can make you understand.

MAMA. Understand what, baby?

WALTER. *(Quietly.)* Sometimes it's like I can see the future stretched out in front of me—just plain as day. The future, Mama. Hanging over there at the edge of my days. Just waiting for me—a big, looming blank space—full of *nothing*. Just waiting for *me*. *(Pause.)* Mama—sometimes when I'm downtown and I pass them cool, quiet-looking restaurants where them white boys are sitting back and talking 'bout things . . . sitting there turning deals worth millions of dollars . . . sometimes I see guys don't look much older than me—

MAMA. Son—how come you talk so much 'bout money?

WALTER. *(With immense passion.)* Because it is life, Mama!

MAMA. *(Quietly.)* Oh—*(Very quietly.)*—so now it's life. Money is life. Once upon a time freedom used to be life—now it's money. I guess the world really do change . . .

WALTER. No—it was always money, Mama. We just didn't know about it.

MAMA. No . . . something has changed. *(She looks at him.)* You something new, boy. In my time we was worried about not being lynched and getting to the North if we could and how to stay alive and still have a pinch of dignity too. . . . Now here come you and Beneatha—talking 'bout things we ain't never even thought about hardly, me and your daddy. You ain't satisfied or proud of nothing we done. I mean that you had a home; that we kept you out of trouble till you was grown; that you don't have to ride to work on the back of nobody's streetcar—you my children—but how different we done become.

WALTER. You just don't understand, Mama, you just don't understand.

MAMA. Son—do you know your wife is expecting another baby?

(WALTER stands, stunned, and absorbs what his mother has said.)

That's what she wanted to talk to you about.

(WALTER sinks down into a chair.)

This ain't for me to be telling—but you ought to know. *(She waits.)* I think Ruth is thinking 'bout getting rid of that child.

WALTER. *(Slowly understanding.)* No—no—Ruth wouldn't do that.

MAMA. When the world gets ugly enough—a woman will do anything for her family. *The part that's already living.*

WALTER. You don't know Ruth, Mama, if you think she would do that.

(RUTH opens the bedroom door and stands there a little limp.)

RUTH. *(Beaten.)* Yes I would too, Walter. *(Pause.)* I gave her a five-dollar down payment.

(There is total silence as the man stares at his wife and the mother stares at her son.)

MAMA. *(Presently.)* Well—*(Tightly.)*—well—son, I'm waiting to hear you say something . . . I'm waiting to hear how you be your father's son. Be the man he was. . . . *(Pause.)* Your wife say she going to destroy your child. And I'm waiting to hear you talk like him and say we a people who give children life, not who destroys them—*(She rises.)*—I'm waiting to see you stand up and look like your daddy and say we done give up one baby to poverty and that we ain't going to give up nary another one. . . . I'm waiting.

WALTER. Ruth—

MAMA. If you a son of mine, tell her!

(WALTER turns, looks at her and can say nothing.)

(She continues, bitterly.) You . . . you are a disgrace to your father's memory. Somebody get me my hat.

CURTAIN

ACT 2

SCENE 1

TIME:

Later the same day.

AT RISE:

RUTH *is ironing again. She has the* RADIO *going. Presently* BENEATHA's *bedroom door opens and* RUTH's *mouth falls and she puts down the iron in fascination.*

RUTH. What have we got on tonight!

BENEATHA. *(Emerging grandly from the doorway so that we can see her thoroughly robed in the costume Asagai brought.)* You are looking at what a well-dressed Nigerian woman wears—*(She parades for* RUTH, *her hair completely hidden by the headdress; she is coquettishly fanning herself with an ornate oriental fan, mistakenly more like Butterfly than any Nigerian that ever was.)*—isn't it beautiful? *(She promenades to the radio and, with an arrogant flourish, turns off the good loud blues that is playing.)* Enough of this assimilationist junk! *(*RUTH *follows her with her eyes as she goes to the phonograph and puts on a record and turns and waits ceremoniously for the music to come up. Then, with a shout—)* OCOMOGOSIAY!

*(*RUTH *jumps. The music comes up, a lovely Nigerian melody.* BENEATHA *listens, enraptured, her eyes far away—"back to the past." She begins to dance.* RUTH *is dumbfounded.)*

RUTH. What kind of dance is that?

BENEATHA. A folk dance.

RUTH. *(Pearl Bailey.)* What kind of folks do that, honey?

BENEATHA. It's from Nigeria. It's a dance of welcome.

RUTH. Who you welcoming?

BENEATHA. The men back to the village.

RUTH. Where they been?

BENEATHA. How should I know—out hunting or something. Anyway, they are coming back now. . . .

RUTH. Well, that's good.

BENEATHA. *(With the record.)*

> *Alundi, alundi*
> *Alundi alunya*
> *Jop pu a jeepua*
> *Ang gu sooooooooooo*

> *Ai yai yae . . .*
> *Ayehaye—alundi . . .*

(WALTER comes in during this performance; he has obviously been drinking. He leans against the door heavily and watches his sister, at first with distaste. Then his eyes look off—"back to the past"—as he lifts both his fists to the roof, screaming.)

WALTER. YEAH . . . AND ETHIOPIA STRETCH FORTH HER HANDS AGAIN! . . .

RUTH. *(Drily, looking at him.)* Yes—and Africa sure is claiming her own tonight. *(She gives them both up and starts ironing again.)*

WALTER. *(All in a drunken, dramatic shout.)* Shut up! . . . I'm digging them drums . . . them drums move me! . . . *(He makes his weaving way to his wife's face and leans in close to her.)* In my *heart of hearts*—(He thumps his chest.)—I am much warrior!

RUTH. *(Without even looking up.)* In your heart of hearts you are much drunkard.

WALTER. *(Coming away from her and starting to wander around the room, shouting.)* Me and Jomo . . . *(Intently, in his sister's face. She has stopped dancing to watch him in this unknown mood.)* that's my man, Kenyatta. *(Shouting and thumping his chest.)* FLAMING SPEAR! HOT DAMN! *(He is suddenly in possession of an imaginary spear and actively spearing enemies all over the room.)* OCOMOGOSIAY . . . THE LION IS WAKING . . . OWIMOWEH! *(He pulls his shirt open and leaps up on a table and gestures with his spear. The bell rings.* RUTH *goes to answer.)*

BENEATHA. *(To encourage* WALTER, *thoroughly caught up with this side of him.)* OCOMOGOSIAY, FLAMING SPEAR!

WALTER. *(On the table, very far gone, his eyes pure glass sheets. He sees what we cannot, that he is a leader of his people, a great chief, a descendant of Chaka, and that the hour to march has come.)* Listen, my black brothers—

BENEATHA. OCOMOGOSIAY!

WALTER. —Do you hear the waters rushing against the shores of the coastlands—

BENEATHA. OCOMOGOSIAY!

WALTER. —Do you hear the screeching of the cocks in yonder hills beyond where the chiefs meet in council for the coming of the mighty war—

BENEATHA. OCOMOGOSIAY!

WALTER. —Do you hear the beating of the wings of the birds flying low over the mountains and the low places of our land—

(RUTH *opens the door.* GEORGE MURCHISON *enters.*)

BENEATHA. OCOMOGOSIAY!

WALTER. —Do you hear the singing of the women, singing the war songs of our fathers to the babies in the great houses . . . singing the sweet war songs? OH, DO YOUR HEAR, MY BLACK BROTHERS!

BENEATHA. (*Completely gone.*) We hear you, Flaming Spear—

WALTER. Telling us to prepare for the greatness of the time—(*To* GEORGE.) Black Brother! (*He extends his hand for the fraternal clasp.*)

GEORGE. Black Brother, hell!

RUTH. (*Having had enough, and embarrassed for the family.*) Beneatha, you got company—what's the matter with you? Walter Lee Younger, get down off that table and stop acting like a fool . . .

(WALTER *comes down off the table suddenly and makes a quick exit to the bathroom.*)

RUTH. He's had a little to drink . . . I don't know what her excuse is.

GEORGE. (*To* BENEATHA.) Look honey, we're going *to* the theater—we're not going to be *in* it . . . so go change, huh?

RUTH. You expect this boy to go out with you looking like that?

BENEATHA. (*Looking at* GEORGE.) That's up to George. If he's ashamed of his heritage—

GEORGE. Oh, don't be so proud of yourself, Bennie—just because you look eccentric.

BENEATHA. How can something that's natural be eccentric?

GEORGE. That's what being eccentric means—being natural. Get dressed.

BENEATHA. I don't like that, George.

RUTH. Why must you and your brother make an argument out of everything people say?

BENEATHA. Because I hate assimilationist Negroes!

RUTH. Will somebody please tell me what assimila-whoever means!

GEORGE. Oh, it's just a college girl's way of calling people Uncle Toms—but that isn't what it means at all.

RUTH. Well, what does it mean?

BENEATHA. (*Cutting* GEORGE *off and staring at him as she replies to* RUTH.) It means someone who is willing to give up his own culture and submerge himself completely in the dominant, and in this case, *oppressive* culture!

GEORGE. Oh, dear, dear, dear! Here we go! A lecture on the African past! On our Great West African Heritage! In one second we will hear all about the great Ashanti empires; the great Songhay civilizations; and the great sculpture of Benin—and then some poetry in the Bantu—and the whole monologue will end with the word *heritage!* (*Nastily.*) Let's face it, baby, your heritage is nothing but a bunch of raggedy-assed spirituals and some grass huts!

BENEATHA. *Grass huts!*

(RUTH *crosses to her and forcibly pushes her toward the bedroom.*)

See there . . . you are standing there in your splendid ignorance talking about people who were the first to smelt iron on the face of the earth!

(RUTH *is pushing her through the door.*)

The Ashanti were performing surgical operations when the English—

(RUTH *pulls the door to, with* BENEATHA *on the other side, and smiles graciously at* GEORGE.)

(BENEATHA *opens the door and shouts the end of the sentence defiantly at* GEORGE.)— were still tattooing themselves with blue dragons. . . . (*She goes back inside.*)

RUTH. Have a seat, George. (*They both sit.* RUTH *folds her hands rather primly on her lap, determined to demonstrate the civilization of the family.*) Warm, ain't it? I mean for September. (*Pause.*) Just like they always say about Chicago weather: If it's too hot or cold for you, just wait a minute and it'll change. (*She smiles happily at this cliché of clichés.*) Everybody say it's got to do with them bombs and things they keep setting off. (*Pause.*) Would you like a nice cold beer?

GEORGE. No, thank you. I don't care for beer. (*He looks at his watch.*) I hope she hurries up.

RUTH. What time is the show?

GEORGE. It's an eight-thirty curtain. That's just Chicago, though. In New York standard curtain time is eight forty. (*He is rather proud of this knowledge.*)

RUTH. (*Properly appreciating it.*) You get to New York a lot?

GEORGE. (*Offhand.*) Few times a year.

RUTH. Oh—that's nice. I've never been to New York.

(WALTER *enters. We feel he has relieved himself, but the edge of unreality is still with him.*)

WALTER. New York ain't got nothing Chicago ain't. Just a bunch of hustling people all squeezed up together—being "Eastern." (*He turns his face into a screw of displeasure.*)

GEORGE. Oh—you've been?

WALTER. *Plenty* of times.

RUTH. (*Shocked at the lie.*) Walter Lee Younger!

WALTER. (*Staring her down.*) Plenty! (*Pause.*) What we got to drink in this house? Why don't you offer this man some refreshment. (*To* GEORGE.) They don't know how to entertain people in this house, man.

GEORGE. Thank you—I don't really care for anything.

WALTER. (*Feeling his head; sobriety coming.*) Where's Mama?

RUTH. She ain't come back yet.

WALTER. (*Looking* GEORGE *over from head to toe, scrutinizing his carefully casual tweed sports jacket over cashmere V-neck sweater over soft eyelet shirt and tie, and soft slacks, finished off with white buckskin shoes.*) Why all you college boys wear them fairy-ish-looking white shoes?

RUTH. Walter Lee!

(GEORGE *ignores the remark.*)

WALTER. (*To* RUTH.) Well, they look crazy as hell—white shoes, cold as it is.

RUTH. *(Crushed.)* You have to excuse him—

WALTER. No he don't! Excuse me for what? What you always excusing me for! I'll excuse myself when I needs to be excused! *(A pause.)* They look as funny as them black knee socks Beneatha wears out of here all the time.

RUTH. It's the college *style*, Walter.

WALTER. Style, hell. She looks like she got burnt legs or something!

RUTH. Oh, Walter—

WALTER. *(An irritable mimic.)* Oh, Walter! Oh, Walter! *(To* MURCHISON.*)* How's your old man making out? I understand you all going to buy that big hotel on the Drive? *(He finds a beer in the refrigerator, wanders over to* MURCHISON, *sipping and wiping his lips with the back of his hand, and straddling a chair backwards to talk to the other man.)* Shrewd move. Your old man is all right, man. *(Tapping his head and half winking for emphasis.)* I mean he knows how to operate. I mean he thinks *big*, you know what I mean, I mean for a *home*, you know? But I think he's kind of running out of ideas now. I'd like to talk to him. Listen, man, I got some plans that could turn this city upside down. I mean I think like he does. *Big*. Invest big, gamble big, hell, lose *big* if you have to, you know what I mean. It's hard to find a man on this whole Southside who understands my kind of thinking—you dig? *(He scrutinizes* MURCHISON *again, drinks his beer, squints his eyes and leans in close, confidential, man to man.)* Me and you ought to sit down and talk sometimes, man. Man, I got me some ideas. . . .

GEORGE. *(With boredom.)* Yeah—sometimes we'll have to do that, Walter.

WALTER. *(Understanding the indifference, and offended.)* Yeah—well, when you get the time, man. I know you a busy little boy.

RUTH. Walter, please—

WALTER. *(Bitterly, hurt.)* I know ain't nothing in this world as busy as you colored college boys with your fraternity pins and white shoes. . . .

RUTH. *(Covering her face with humiliation.)* Oh, Walter Lee—

WALTER. I see you all all the time—with the books tucked under your arms—going to your *(British A—a mimic.)* "clahsses." And for what! What the hell you learning over there? Filling up your heads—*(Counting off on his fingers.)*—with the sociology and the psychology—but they teaching you how to be a man? How to take over and run the world? They teaching you how to run a rubber plantation or a steel mill? Naw—just to talk proper and read books and wear white shoes. . . .

GEORGE. *(Looking at him with distaste, a little above it all.)* You're all wacked up with bitterness, man.

WALTER. *(Intently, almost quietly, between the teeth, glaring at the boy.)* And you—ain't you bitter, man? Ain't you just about had it yet? Don't you see no stars gleaming that you can't reach out and grab? You happy?—you contented son-of-a-bitch—you happy? You got it made? Bitter? Man, I'm a volcano. Bitter? Here I am a giant—surrounded by ants! Ants who can't even understand what it is the giant is talking about.

RUTH. *(Passionately and suddenly.)* Oh, Walter—ain't you with nobody!

WALTER. *(Violently.)* No! 'Cause ain't nobody with me! Not even my own mother!

RUTH. Walter, that's a terrible thing to say!

(BENEATHA enters, dressed for the evening in a cocktail dress and earrings.)

GEORGE. Well—hey, you look great.

BENEATHA. Let's go, George. See you all later.

RUTH. Have a nice time.

GEORGE. Thanks. Good night. *(To WALTER, sarcastically.)* Good night, *Prometheus.*

(BENEATHA and GEORGE exit.)

WALTER. *(To RUTH.)* Who is Prometheus?

RUTH. I don't know. Don't worry about it.

WALTER. *(In fury, pointing after GEORGE.)* See there—they get to a point where they can't insult you man to man—they got to go talk about something ain't nobody never heard of!

RUTH. How do you know it was an insult? *(To humor him.)* Maybe Prometheus is a nice fellow.

WALTER. Prometheus! I bet there ain't even no such thing! I bet that simple-minded clown—

RUTH. Walter—*(She stops what she is doing and looks at him.)*

WALTER. *(Yelling.)* Don't start!

RUTH. Start what?

WALTER. Your nagging! Where was I? Who was I with? How much money did I spend?

RUTH. *(Plaintively.)* Walter Lee—why don't we just try to talk about it. . . .

WALTER. *(Not listening.)* I been out talking with people who understand me. People who care about the things I got on my mind.

RUTH. *(Wearily.)* I guess that means people like Willy Harris.

WALTER. Yes, people like Willy Harris.

RUTH. *(With a sudden flash of impatience.)* Why don't you all just hurry up and go into the banking business and stop talking about it!

WALTER. Why? You want to know why? 'Cause we all tied up in a race of people that don't know how to do nothing but moan, pray and have babies! *(The line is too bitter even for him and he looks at her and sits down.)*

RUTH. Oh, Walter . . . *(Softly.)* honey, why can't you stop fighting me?

WALTER. *(Without thinking.)* Who's fighting you? Who even cares about you? *(This line begins the retardation of his mood.)*

RUTH. Well—*(She waits a long time, and then with resignation, starts to put away her things.)*—I guess I might as well go on to bed . . . *(More or less to herself.)* I don't know where we lost it . . . but we have . . . *(Then, to him.)* I—I'm sorry about this new baby, Walter. I guess maybe I better go on and do what I started . . . I guess I just didn't realize how bad things was with us . . . I guess I just didn't really realize—*(She starts out to the bedroom and stops.)*—you want some hot milk?

WALTER. Hot milk?

RUTH. Yes—hot milk.

WALTER. Why hot milk?

RUTH. 'Cause after all that liquor you come home with you ought to have something hot in your stomach.

WALTER. I don't want no milk.

RUTH. You want some coffee then?

WALTER. No, I don't want no coffee. I don't want nothing hot to drink. *(Almost plaintively.)* Why you always trying to give me something to eat?

RUTH. *(Standing and looking at him helplessly.)* What else can I give you, Walter Lee Younger? *(She stands and looks at him and presently turns to go out again.)*

(He lifts his head and watches her going away from him in a new mood which began to emerge when he asked her "Who cares about you?")

WALTER. It's been rough, ain't it, baby? *(She hears and stops but does not turn around and he continues to her back.)* I guess between two people there ain't never as much understood as folks generally thinks there is. I mean like between me and you—*(She turns to face him.)*—how we gets to the place where we scared to talk softness to each other. *(He waits, thinking hard himself.)* Why you think it got to be like that? *(He is thoughtful, almost as a child would be.)* Ruth, what is it gets into people ought to be close?

RUTH. I don't know, honey. I think about it a lot.

WALTER. On account of you and me, you mean? The way things are with us. The way something done come down between us.

RUTH. There ain't so much between us, Walter . . . not when you come to me and try to talk to me. Try to be with me . . . a little even.

WALTER. *(Total honesty.)* Sometimes . . . sometimes . . . I don't even know how to try.

RUTH. Walter—

WALTER. Yes?

RUTH. *(Coming to him, gently and with misgiving, but coming to him.)* Honey . . . life don't have to be like this. I mean sometimes people can do things so that things are better. . . . You remember how we used to talk when Travis was born . . . about the way we were going to live . . . the kind of house. . . . *(She is stroking his head.)* Well, it's all starting to slip away from us. . . .

(MAMA enters, and WALTER jumps up and shouts at her.)

WALTER. Mama, where have you been?

MAMA. My—them steps is longer than they used to be. Whew! *(She sits down and ignores him.)* How you feeling this evening, Ruth?

(RUTH shrugs, disturbed some at having been prematurely interrupted and watching her husband knowingly.)

WALTER. Mama, where you been all day?

MAMA. *(Still ignoring him and leaning on the table and changing to more comfortable shoes.)* Where's Travis?

RUTH. I let him go out earlier and he ain't come back yet. Boy, is he going to get it!

WALTER. Mama!

MAMA. *(As if she has heard him for the first time.)* Yes, son?

WALTER. Where did you go this afternoon?

MAMA. I went downtown to tend to some business that I had to tend to.

WALTER. What kind of business?

MAMA. You know better than to question me like a child, Brother.

WALTER. *(Rising and bending over the table.)* Where were you, Mama? *(Bringing his fists down and shouting.)* Mama, you didn't go do something with that insurance money, something crazy?

(The front door opens slowly, interrupting him, and TRAVIS *peeks his head in, less than hopefully.)*

TRAVIS. *(To his mother.)* Mama, I—

RUTH. "Mama I" nothing! You're going to get it, boy! Get on in that bedroom and get yourself ready!

TRAVIS. But I—

MAMA. Why don't you all never let the child explain hisself.

RUTH. Keep out of it now, Lena.

*(*MAMA *clamps her lips together, and* RUTH *advances toward her son menacingly.)*

RUTH. A thousand times I have told you not to go off like that—

MAMA. *(Holding out her arms to her grandson.)* Well—at least let me tell him something. I want him to be the first one to hear. . . . Come here, Travis.

(The boy obeys, gladly.)

Travis—*(She takes him by the shoulder and looks into his face.)*—you know that money we got in the mail this morning?

TRAVIS. Yes'm—

MAMA. Well—what do you think your grandmama gone and done with that money?

TRAVIS. I don't know, Grandmama.

MAMA. *(Putting her finger on his nose for emphasis.)* She went out and she bought you a house!

(The explosion comes from WALTER *at the end of the revelation and he jumps up and turns away from all of them in a fury.)*

*(*MAMA *continues, to* TRAVIS.*)* You glad about the house? It's going to be yours when you get to be a man.

TRAVIS. Yeah—I always wanted to live in a house.

MAMA. All right, gimme some sugar then—*(*TRAVIS *puts his arms around her neck as she watches her son over the boy's shoulder. Then, to* TRAVIS, *after the embrace.)*—now when you say your prayers tonight, you thank God and your grandfather—'cause it was him who give you the house—in his way.

RUTH. *(Taking the boy from* MAMA *and pushing him toward the bedroom.)* Now you get out of here and get ready for your beating.

TRAVIS. Aw, Mama—

RUTH. Get on in there. *(Closing the door behind him and turning radiantly to her mother-in-law.)* So you went and did it!

MAMA. *(Quietly, looking at her son with pain.)* Yes, I did.

RUTH. *(Raising both arms classically.)* PRAISE GOD! *(Looks at* WALTER *a moment, who says nothing. She crosses rapidly to her husband.)* Please, honey—let me be glad . . . you be glad too. (*She has laid her hands on his shoulders, but he shakes himself free of her roughly, without turning to face her.*) Oh, Walter . . . a home . . . a *home*. (*She comes back to* MAMA.) Well—where is it? How big is it? How much it going to cost?

MAMA. Well—

RUTH. When we moving?

MAMA. (*Smiling at her.*) First of the month.

RUTH. (*Throwing back her head with jubilance.*) PRAISE GOD!

MAMA. (*Tentatively, still looking at her son's back turned against her and* RUTH.) It's— it's a nice house too . . . (*She cannot help speaking directly to him. An imploring quality in her voice, her manner, makes her almost like a girl now.*) Three bed- rooms—nice big one for you and Ruth. . . . Me and Beneatha still have to share our room, but Travis have one of his own—and (*With difficulty.*) I figure if the—new baby—is a boy, we could get one of them double-decker out- fits. . . . And there's a yard with a little patch of dirt where I could maybe get to grow me a few flowers . . . and a nice big basement . . .

RUTH. Walter honey, be glad—

MAMA. (*Still to his back, fingering things on the table.*) 'Course I don't want to make it sound fancier than it is. . . . It's just a plain little old house—but it's made good and solid—and it will be *ours*. Walter Lee—it makes a difference in a man when he can walk on floors that belong to *him*. . . .

RUTH. Where is it?

MAMA. (*Frightened at this telling.*) Well—well—it's out there in Clybourne Park—

(RUTH's *radiance fades abruptly, and* WALTER *finally turns slowly to face his mother with incredulity and hostility.*)

RUTH. Where?

MAMA. (*Matter-of-factly.*) Four o six Clybourne Street, Clybourne Park.

RUTH. Clybourne Park? Mama, there ain't no colored people living in Clybourne Park.

MAMA. (*Almost idiotically.*) Well, I guess there's going to be some now.

WALTER. (*Bitterly.*) So that's the peace and comfort you went out and bought for us today!

MAMA. (*Raising her eyes to meet his finally.*) Son—I just tried to find the nicest place for the least amount of money for my family.

RUTH. (*Trying to recover from the shock.*) Well—well—'course I ain't one never been 'fraid of no crackers, mind you—but—well, wasn't there no other houses nowhere?

MAMA. Them houses they put up for colored in them areas way out all seem to cost twice as much as other houses. I did the best I could.

RUTH. (*Struck senseless with the news, in its various degrees of goodness and trouble, she sits a moment, her fists propping her chin in thought, and then she starts to rise, bring- ing her fists down with vigor, the radiance spreading from cheek to cheek again.*) Well—well!—All I can say is—if this is my time in life—*my time*—to say good-bye—(*And she builds with momentum as she starts to circle the room with an exuberant, almost tearfully happy release.*)—to these Goddamned cracking walls!—

(She pounds the walls.)—and these marching roaches!—*(She wipes at an imaginary army of marching roaches.)*—and this cramped little closet which ain't now or never was no kitchen! . . . then I say it loud and good, HALLELUJAH! AND GOOD-BYE MISERY . . . I DON'T NEVER WANT TO SEE YOUR UGLY FACE AGAIN! *(She laughs joyously, having practically destroyed the apartment, and flings her arms up and lets them come down happily, slowly, reflectively, over her abdomen, aware for the first time perhaps that the life therein pulses with happiness and not despair.)* Lena?

MAMA. *(Moved, watching her happiness.)* Yes, honey?

RUTH. *(Looking off.)* Is there—is there a whole lot of sunlight?

MAMA. *(Understanding.)* Yes, child, there's a whole lot of sunlight.

(Long pause.)

RUTH. *(Collecting herself and going to the door of the room* TRAVIS *is in.)* Well—I guess I better see 'bout Travis. *(To* MAMA.*)* Lord, I sure don't feel like whipping nobody today! *(She exits.)*

(The mother and son are left alone now and the mother waits a long time, considering deeply, before she speaks.)

MAMA. Son—you—you understand what I done, don't you?

*(*WALTER *is silent and sullen.)*

I—I just seen my family falling apart today . . . just falling to pieces in front of my eyes. . . . We couldn't of gone on like we was today. We was going backwards 'stead of forwards—talking 'bout killing babies and wishing each other was dead. . . . When it gets like that in life—you just got to do something different, push on out and do something bigger. . . . *(She waits.)* I wish you say something, son . . . I wish you'd say how deep inside you you think I done the right thing—

WALTER. *(Crossing slowly to his bedroom door and finally turning there and speaking measuredly.)* What you need me to say you done right for? *You* the head of this family. You run our lives like you want to. It was your money and you did what you wanted with it. So what you need for me to say it was all right for? *(Bitterly, to hurt her as deeply as he knows is possible.)* So you butchered up a dream of mine—you—who always talking 'bout your children's dreams . . .

MAMA. Walter Lee—

(He just closes the door behind him. MAMA *sits alone, thinking heavily.)*

CURTAIN

ACT 2

SCENE 2

TIME:

Friday night. A few weeks later.

AT RISE:

Packing crates mark the intention of the family to move. BENEATHA *and* GEORGE *come in, presumably from an evening out again.*

GEORGE. O.K. . . . O.K., whatever you say. . . .

(They both sit on the couch. He tries to kiss her. She moves away.)

Look, we've had a nice evening; let's not spoil it, huh? . . .

(He again turns her head and tries to nuzzle in and she turns away from him, not with distaste but with momentary lack of interest; in a mood to pursue what they were talking about.)

BENEATHA. I'm *trying* to talk to you.

GEORGE. We always talk.

BENEATHA. Yes—and I love to talk.

GEORGE. *(Exasperated; rising.)* I know it and I don't mind it sometimes . . . I want you to cut it out, see—the moody stuff, I mean. I don't like it. You're a nice-looking girl . . . all over. That's all you need, honey, forget the atmosphere. Guys aren't going to go for the atmosphere—they're going to go for what they see. Be glad for that. Drop the Garbo routine. It doesn't go with you. As for myself, I want a nice—*(Groping.)*—simple *(Thoughtfully.)*—sophisticated girl . . . not a poet—O.K.?

(She rebuffs him again and he starts to leave.)

BENEATHA. Why are you angry?

GEORGE. Because this is stupid! I don't go out with you to discuss the nature of "quiet desperation" or to hear all about your thoughts—because the world will go on thinking what it thinks regardless—

BENEATHA. Then why read books? Why go to school?

GEORGE. *(With artificial patience, counting on his fingers.)* It's simple. You read books—to learn facts—to get grades—to pass the course—to get a degree. That's all—it has nothing to do with thoughts.

(A long pause.)

BENEATHA. I see.

(A longer pause as she looks at him.)

Good night, George.

(GEORGE looks at her a little oddly, and starts to exit. He meets MAMA coming in.)

GEORGE. Oh—hello, Mrs. Younger.

MAMA. Hello, George, how you feeling?

GEORGE. Fine—fine, how are you?

MAMA. Oh, a little tired. You know them steps can get you after a day's work. You all have a nice time tonight?

GEORGE. Yes—a fine time. Well, good night.

MAMA. Good night.

(He exits.)

(MAMA closes the door behind her.) Hello, honey. What you sitting like that for?

BENEATHA. I'm just sitting.

MAMA. Didn't you have a nice time?

BENEATHA. No.

MAMA. No? What's the matter?

BENEATHA. Mama, George is a fool—honest. *(She rises.)*

MAMA. *(Hustling around unloading the packages she has entered with. She stops.)* Is he, baby?

BENEATHA. Yes. (BENEATHA *makes up* TRAVIS' *bed as she talks.*)

MAMA. You sure?

BENEATHA. Yes.

MAMA. Well—I guess you better not waste your time with no fools.

(BENEATHA *looks up at her mother, watching her put groceries in the refrigerator. Finally she gathers up her things and starts into the bedroom. At the door she stops and looks back at her mother.*)

BENEATHA. Mama—

MAMA. Yes, baby—

BENEATHA. Thank you.

MAMA. For what?

BENEATHA. For understanding me this time.

(*She exits quickly and the mother stands, smiling a little, looking at the place where* BENEATHA *just stood.* RUTH *enters.*)

RUTH. Now don't you fool with any of this stuff, Lena—

MAMA. Oh, I just thought I'd sort a few things out.

(*The phone rings.* RUTH *answers.*)

RUTH. *(At the phone.)* Hello—just a minute. *(Goes to the door.)* Walter, it's Mrs. Arnold. *(Waits. Goes back to the phone. Tense.)* Hello. Yes, this is his wife speaking . . . he's lying down now. Yes . . . well, he'll be in tomorrow. He's been very sick. Yes—I know we should have called, but we were so sure he'd be able to come in today. Yes—yes, I'm very sorry. Yes . . . thank you very much. *(She hangs up.)*

(WALTER *is standing in the doorway of the bedroom behind her.*)

That was Mrs. Arnold.

WALTER. *(Indifferently.)* Was it?

RUTH. She said if you don't come in tomorrow that they are getting a new man . . .

WALTER. Ain't that sad—ain't that crying sad.

RUTH. She said Mr. Arnold has had to take a cab for three days . . . Walter, you ain't been to work for three days! *(This is a revelation to her.)* Where you been, Walter Lee Younger?

(WALTER *looks at her and starts to laugh.*)

You're going to lose your job.

WALTER. That's right . . .

RUTH. Oh, Walter, and with your mother working like a dog every day—

WALTER. That's sad too—everything is sad.

MAMA. What you been doing for these three days, son?

WALTER. Mama—you don't know all the things a man what got leisure can find to do in this city. . . . What's this—Friday night? Well—Wednesday I borrowed Willy Harris' car and I went for a drive . . . just me and myself and I drove and drove . . . way out . . . way past South Chicago, and I parked the car and I sat and looked at the steel mills all day long. I just sat in the car and looked at them big black chimneys for hours. Then I drove back and I went to the Green Hat. *(Pause.)* And Thursday—Thursday I borrowed the car again and I got in and I pointed it the other way and I drove the other way—for hours—way, way up to Wisconsin, and I looked at the farms. I just drove and looked at the farms. Then I drove back and I went to the Green Hat. *(Pause.)* And today—today I didn't get the car. Today I just walked. All over the Southside. And I looked at the Negroes and they looked at me and finally I just sat down on the curb at Thirty-ninth and South Parkway and I just sat there and watched the Negroes go by. And then I went to the Green Hat. You all sad? You all depressed? And you know where I am going right now—

(RUTH *goes out quietly.*)

MAMA. Oh, Big Walter, is this the harvest of our days?

WALTER. You know what I like about the Green Hat? *(He turns the RADIO on and a steamy, deep blues pours into the room.)* I like this little cat they got there who blows a sax . . . he blows. He talks to me. He ain't but 'bout five feet tall and he's got a conked head and his eyes is always closed and he's all music—

MAMA. *(Rising and getting some papers out of her handbag.)* Walter—

WALTER. And there's this other guy who plays the piano . . . and they got a sound. I mean they can work on some music . . . they got the best little combo in the world in the Green Hat . . . you can just sit there and drink and listen to them three men play and you realize that don't nothing matter worth a damn, but just being there—

MAMA. I've helped do it to you, haven't I, son? Walter, I been wrong.

WALTER. Naw—you ain't never been wrong about nothing, Mama.

MAMA. Listen to me, now. I say I been wrong, son. That I been doing to you what the rest of the world been doing to you. *(She stops and he looks up slowly at her and she meets his eyes pleadingly.)* Walter—what you ain't never understood is that I ain't got nothing, don't own nothing, ain't never really wanted nothing that wasn't for you. There ain't nothing as precious to me. . . . There ain't nothing worth holding on to, money, dreams, nothing else—if it means—if it means it's going to destroy my boy. *(She puts her papers in front of him and he watches her without speaking or moving.)* I paid the man thirty-five hundred dollars down on the house. That leaves sixty-five hundred dollars. Monday morning I want you to take this money and take three thousand dollars and put it in a savings account for Beneatha's medical schooling. The rest you put in a checking account—with your name on it. And from now on any penny that come out of it or that go in it is for you to look after. For you to decide. *(She drops her hands a little helplessly.)* It ain't much, but it's all I got in this world and I'm putting it in your hands. I'm telling you to be the head of this family from now on like you supposed to be.

WALTER. *(Stares at the money.)* You trust me like that, Mama?

MAMA. I ain't never stop trusting you. Like I ain't never stop loving you.

(She goes out, and WALTER *sits looking at the money on the table as the* MUSIC *continues in its idiom, pulsing in the room. Finally, in a decisive gesture, he gets up, and, in mingled joy and desperation, picks up the money. At the same moment,* TRAVIS *enters for bed.)*

TRAVIS. What's the matter, Daddy? You drunk?

WALTER. *(Sweetly, more sweetly than we have ever known him.)* No, Daddy ain't drunk. Daddy ain't going to never be drunk again . . .

TRAVIS. Well, good night, Daddy.

(The father has come from behind the couch and leans over, embracing his son.)

WALTER. Son, I feel like talking to you tonight.

TRAVIS. About what?

WALTER. Oh, about a lot of things. About you and what kind of man you going to be when you grow up. . . . Son—son, what do you want to be when you grow up?

TRAVIS. A bus driver.

WALTER. *(Laughing a little.)* A what? Man, that ain't nothing to want to be!

TRAVIS. Why not?

WALTER. 'Cause, man—it ain't big enough—you know what I mean.

TRAVIS. I don't know then. I can't make up my mind. Sometimes Mama asks me that too. And sometimes when I tell her I want to be like you—she says she don't want me to be like that and sometimes she says she does. . . .

WALTER. *(Gathering him up in his arms.)* You know what, Travis? In seven years you going to be seventeen years old. And things is going to be very different with us in seven years, Travis. . . . One day when you are seventeen I'll come home—home from my office downtown somewhere—

TRAVIS. You don't work in no office, Daddy.

WALTER. No—but after tonight. After what your daddy gonna do tonight, there's going to be offices—a whole lot of offices. . . .

TRAVIS. What you gonna do tonight, Daddy?

WALTER. You wouldn't understand yet, son, but your daddy's gonna make a transaction . . . a business transaction that's going to change our lives. . . . That's how come one day when you 'bout seventeen years old I'll come home and I'll be pretty tired, you know what I mean, after a day of conferences and secretaries getting things wrong the way they do . . . 'cause an executive's life is hell, man—*(The more he talks the farther away he gets.)* And I'll pull the car up on the driveway . . . just a plain black Chrysler, I think, with white walls—no—black tires. More elegant. Rich people don't have to be flashy . . . though I'll have to get something a little sportier for Ruth—maybe a Cadillac convertible to do her shopping in. . . . And I'll come up the steps to the house and the gardener will be clipping away at the hedges and he'll say, "Good evening, Mr. Younger." And I'll say, "Hello, Jefferson, how are you this evening?" And I'll go inside and Ruth will come downstairs and meet me at the door and we'll kiss each other and she'll take my arm and we'll go up to your room to see you sitting on the floor with the catalogues of all the great schools in America around you. . . . All the great schools in the world! And—and I'll say, all right, son—it's your seventeenth birthday, what is it you've decided? . . . Just tell me where you want to go to school and you'll *go*. Just tell me, what it is you want to be—and you'll *be* it. . . . Whatever you want to be—Yessir! *(He holds his arms open for* TRAVIS.) You just name it, son . . .

*(*TRAVIS *leaps into them.)*

and I hand you the world! *(*WALTER'S *voice has risen in pitch and hysterical promise and on the last line he lifts* TRAVIS *high.)*

BLACKOUT

ACT 2

SCENE 3

TIME:

> *Saturday, moving day, one week later.*
>
> *Before the Curtain rises,* RUTH'S *VOICE, a strident, dramatic church alto, cuts through the silence.*
>
> *It is, in the darkness, a triumphant surge, a penetrating statement of expectation: "Oh, Lord, I don't feel no ways tired! Children, oh, glory hallelujah!"*
>
> *As the Curtain rises we see that* RUTH *is alone in the living room, finishing up the family's packing. It is moving day. She is nailing crates and tying cartons.* BENEATHA *enters, carrying a guitar case, and watches her exuberant sister-in-law.*

RUTH. Hey!

BENEATHA. *(Putting away the case.)* Hi.

RUTH. *(Pointing at a package.)* Honey—look in that package there and see what I found on sale this morning at the South Center. *(*RUTH *gets up and moves to the package and draws out some curtains.)* Lookahere—hand-turned hems!

BENEATHA. How do you know the window size out there?

RUTH. *(Who hadn't thought of that.)* Oh—well, they bound to fit something in the whole house. Anyhow, they was too good a bargain to pass up. *(*RUTH *slaps her head, suddenly remembering something.)* Oh, Bennie—I meant to put a special note on that carton over there. That's your mama's good china and she wants 'em to be very careful with it.

BENEATHA. I'll do it. *(*BENEATHA *finds a piece of paper and starts to draw large letters on it.)*

RUTH. You know what I'm going to do soon as I get in that new house?

BENEATHA. What?

RUTH. Honey—I'm going to run me a tub of water up to here . . . *(With her fingers practically up to her nostrils.)* and I'm going to get in it—and I am going to sit . . . and sit . . . and sit in that hot water and the first person who knocks to tell *me* to hurry up and come out—

BENEATHA. Gets shot at sunrise.

RUTH. *(Laughing happily.)* You said it, sister! *(Noticing how large* BENEATHA *is absent-mindedly making the note.)* Honey, they ain't going to read that from no airplane.

BENEATHA. *(Laughing herself.)* I guess I always think things have more emphasis if they are big, somehow.

RUTH. *(Looking up at her and smiling.)* You and your brother seem to have that as a philosophy of life. Lord, that man—done changed so 'round here. You know—you know what we did last night? Me and Walter Lee?

BENEATHA. What?

RUTH. *(Smiling to herself.)* We went to the movies. *(Looking at* BENEATHA *to see if she understands.)* We went to the movies. You know the last time me and Walter went to the movies together?

BENEATHA. No.

RUTH. Me neither. That's how long it been. *(Smiling again.)* But we went last night. The picture wasn't much good, but that didn't seem to matter. We went—and we held hands.

BENEATHA. Oh, Lord!

RUTH. We held hands—and you know what?

BENEATHA. What?

RUTH. When we come out of the show it was late and dark and all the stores and things was closed up . . . and it was kind of chilly and there wasn't many people on the streets . . . and we was still holding hands, me and Walter.

BENEATHA. You're killing me.

(WALTER enters with a large package. His happiness is deep in him; he cannot keep still with his new-found exuberance. He is singing and wiggling and snapping his fingers. He puts his package in a corner and puts a phonograph record, which he has brought in with him, on the record player. As the MUSIC comes up he dances over to RUTH and tries to get her to dance with him. She gives in at last to his raunchiness and in a fit of giggling, allows herself to be drawn into his mood and together they deliberately burlesque an old social dance of their youth.)

BENEATHA. *(Regarding them a long time as they dance, then drawing in her breath for a deeply exaggerated comment which she does not particularly mean.)* Talk about—oldddddddddd-fashioneddddddd—Negroes!

WALTER. *(Stopping momentarily.)* What kind of Negroes? *(He says this in fun. He is not angry with her today, nor with anyone. He starts to dance with his wife again.)*

BENEATHA. Old-fashioned.

WALTER. *(As he dances with* RUTH.*)* You know, when these *New Negroes* have their convention—*(Pointing at his sister.)*—that is going to be the chairman of the Committee on Unending Agitation. *(He goes on dancing, then stops.)* Race, race, race! . . . Girl, I do believe you are the first person in the history of the entire human race to successfully brainwash yourself. *(*BENEATHA *breaks up and he goes on dancing. He stops again, enjoying his tease.)* Damn, even the N double A C P takes a holiday sometimes!

*(*BENEATHA *and* RUTH *laugh.)*

(He dances with RUTH *some more and starts to laugh and stops and pantomimes someone over an operating table.)* I can just see that chick someday looking down at some poor cat on an operating table before she starts to slice him,

saying . . . (*Pulling his sleeves back maliciously.*) "By the way, what are your views on civil rights down there? . . ." (*He laughs at her again and starts to dance happily.*)

(*The* BELL *sounds.*)

BENEATHA. Sticks and stones may break my bones . . . but words will never hurt me! (BENEATHA *goes to the door and opens it as* WALTER *and* RUTH *go on with the clowning.* BENEATHA *is somewhat surprised to see a quiet-looking middle-aged* WHITE MAN *in a business suit holding his hat and a briefcase in his hand and consulting a small piece of paper.*)

MAN. Uh—how do you do, miss. I am looking for a Mrs.—(*He looks at the slip of paper.*) Mrs. Lena—Younger?

BENEATHA. (*Smoothing her hair with slight embarrassment.*) Oh—yes, that's my mother. Excuse me. (*She closes the door and turns to quiet the other two.*) Ruth! Brother! Somebody's here. (*Then she opens the door.*)

(*The* MAN *casts a curious glance at all of them.*)

Uh—come in please.

MAN. (*Coming in.*) Thank you.

BENEATHA. My mother isn't here just now. Is it business?

MAN. Yes . . . well, of a sort.

WALTER. (*Freely, the Man of the House.*) Have a seat. I'm Mrs. Younger's son. I look after most of her business matters.

(RUTH *and* BENEATHA *exchange amused glances.*)

MAN. (*Regarding* WALTER, *and sitting.*) Well—my name is Karl Lindner. . . .

WALTER. (*Stretching out his hand.*) Walter Younger. This is my wife—(RUTH *nods politely.*)—and my sister.

LINDNER. How do you do.

WALTER. (*Amiably, as he sits himself easily on a chair, leaning with interest forward on his knees and looking expectantly into the newcomer's face.*) What can we do for you, Mr. Lindner!

LINDNER. (*Some minor shuffling of the hat and briefcase on his knees.*) Well—I am a representative of the Clybourne Park Improvement Association—

WALTER. (*Pointing.*) Why don't you sit your things on the floor?

LINDNER. Oh—yes. Thank you. (*He slides the briefcase and hat under the chair.*) And as I was saying—I am from the Clybourne Park Improvement Association and we have had it brought to our attention at the last meeting that you people— or at least your mother—has bought a piece of residential property at—(*He digs for the slip of paper again.*)—four o six Clybourne Street. . . .

WALTER. That's right. Care for something to drink? Ruth, get Mr. Lindner a beer.

LINDNER. (*Upset for some reason.*) Oh—no, really. I mean thank you very much, but no thank you.

RUTH. (*Innocently.*) Some coffee?

LINDNER. Thank you, nothing at all.

(BENEATHA *is watching the man carefully.*)

LINDNER. Well, I don't know how much you folks know about our organization. *(He is a gentle man; thoughtful and somewhat labored in his manner.)* It is one of these community organizations set up to look after—oh, you know, things like block upkeep and special projects and we also have what we call our New Neighbors Orientation Committee. . . .

BENEATHA. *(Drily.)* Yes—and what do they do?

LINDNER. *(Turning a little to her and then returning the main force to* WALTER.*)* Well—it's what you might call a sort of welcoming committee, I guess. I mean they, we, I'm the chairman of the committee—go around and see the new people who move into the neighborhood and sort of give them the lowdown on the way we do things out in Clybourne Park.

BENEATHA. *(With appreciation of the two meanings, which escape* RUTH *and* WALTER.*)* Un-huh.

LINDNER. And we also have the category of what the association calls—*(He looks elsewhere.)*—uh—special community problems. . . .

BENEATHA. Yes—and what are some of those?

WALTER. Girl, let the man talk.

LINDNER. *(With understated relief.)* Thank you. I would sort of like to explain this thing in my own way. I mean I want to explain to you in a certain way.

WALTER. Go ahead.

LINDNER. Yes. Well. I'm going to try to get right to the point. I'm sure we'll all appreciate that in the long run.

BENEATHA. Yes.

WALTER. Be still now!

LINDNER. Well—

RUTH. *(Still innocently.)* Would you like another chair—you don't look comfortable.

LINDNER. *(More frustrated than annoyed.)* No, thank you very much. Please. Well— to get right to the point I—*(A great breath, and he is off at last.)*—I am sure you people must be aware of some of the incidents which have happened in various parts of the city when colored people have moved into certain areas—

(BENEATHA *exhales heavily and starts tossing a piece of fruit up and down in the air.)*

—well—because we have what I think is going to be a unique type of organization in American community life—not only do we deplore that kind of thing—but we are trying to do something about it.

(BENEATHA *stops tossing and turns with a new and quizzical interest to the man.)*

We feel—*(gaining confidence in his mission because of the interest in the faces of the people he is talking to.)*—we feel that most of the trouble in this world, when you come right down to it—*(He hits his knee for emphasis.)*—most of the trouble exists because people just don't sit down and talk to each other.

RUTH. *(Nodding as she might in church, pleased with the remark.)* You can say that again, mister.

LINDNER. *(More encouraged by such affirmation.)* That we don't try hard enough in this world to understand the other fellow's problem. The other guy's point of view.

RUTH. Now that's right.

(BENEATHA *and* WALTER *merely watch and listen with genuine interest.*)

LINDNER. Yes—that's the way we feel out in Clybourne Park. And that's why I was elected to come here this afternoon and talk to you people. Friendly like, you know, the way people should talk to each other and see if we couldn't find some way to work this thing out. As I say, the whole business is a matter of *caring* about the other fellow. Anybody can see that you are a nice family of folks, hard working and honest I'm sure.

(BENEATHA *frowns slightly, quizzically, her head tilted regarding him.*)

Today everybody knows what it means to be on the outside of *something*. And of course, there is always somebody who is out to take the advantage of people who don't always understand.

WALTER. What do you mean?

LINDNER. Well—you see our community is made up of people who've worked hard as the dickens for years to build up that little community. They're not rich and fancy people; just hard-working, honest people who don't really have much but those little homes and a dream of the kind of community they want to raise their children in. Now, I don't say we are perfect and there is a lot wrong in some of the things they want. But you've got to admit that a man, right or wrong, has the right to want to have the neighborhood he lives in a certain kind of way. And at the moment the overwhelming majority of our people out there feel that people get along better, take more of a common interest in the life of the community, when they share a common background. I want you to believe me when I tell you that race prejudice simply doesn't enter into it. It is a matter of the people of Clybourne Park believing, rightly or wrongly, as I say, that for the happiness of all concerned that our Negro families are happier when they live in their *own* communities.

BENEATHA. *(With a grand and bitter gesture.)* This, friends, is the Welcoming Committee!

WALTER. *(Dumbfounded, looking at* LINDNER.*)* Is this what you came marching all the way over here to tell us?

LINDNER. Well, now we've been having a fine conversation. I hope you'll hear me all the way through.

WALTER. *(Tightly.)* Go ahead, man.

LINDNER. You see—in the face of all things I have said, we are prepared to make your family a very generous offer. . . .

BENEATHA. Thirty pieces and not a coin less!

WALTER. Yeah?

LINDNER. *(Putting on his glasses and drawing a form out of the briefcase.)* Our association is prepared, through the collective effort of our people, to buy the house from you at a financial gain to your family.

RUTH. Lord have mercy, ain't this the living gall!

WALTER. All right, you through?

LINDNER. Well, I want to give you the exact terms of the financial arrangement—

WALTER. We don't want to hear no exact terms of no arrangements. I want to know if you got any more to tell us 'bout getting together?

LINDNER. *(Taking off his glasses.)* Well—I don't suppose that you feel . . .

WALTER. Never mind how I feel—you got any more to say 'bout how people ought to sit down and talk to each other? . . . Get out of my house, man. *(He turns his back and walks to the door.)*

LINDNER. *(Looking around at the hostile faces and reaching and assembling his hat and briefcase.)* Well—I don't understand why you people are reacting this way. What do you think you are going to gain by moving into a neighborhood where you just aren't wanted and where some elements—well—people can get awful worked up when they feel that their whole way of life and everything they've ever worked for is threatened.

WALTER. Get out.

LINDNER. *(At the door, holding a small card.)* Well—I'm sorry it went like this.

WALTER. Get out.

LINDNER. *(Almost sadly regarding WALTER.)* You just can't force people to change their hearts, son. *(He turns and puts his card on the table and exits.)*

(WALTER pushes the door to with stinging hatred, and stands looking at it. RUTH just sits and BENEATHA just stands. They say nothing. MAMA and TRAVIS enter.)

MAMA. Well—this all the packing got done since I left out of here this morning. I testify before God that my children got all the energy of the dead. What time the moving men due?

BENEATHA. Four o'clock. You had a caller, Mama. *(She is smiling, teasingly.)*

MAMA. Sure enough—who?

BENEATHA. *(Her arms folded saucily.)* The Welcoming Committee.

(WALTER and RUTH giggle.)

MAMA. *(Innocently.)* Who?

BENEATHA. The Welcoming Committee. They said they're sure going to be glad to see you when you get there.

WALTER. *(Devilishly.)* Yeah, they said they can't hardly wait to see your face.

(Laughter.)

MAMA. *(Sensing their facetiousness.)* What's the matter with you all?

WALTER. Ain't nothing the matter with us. We just telling you 'bout the gentleman who came to see you this afternoon. From the Clybourne Park Improvement Association.

MAMA. What he want?

RUTH. *(In the same mood as BENEATHA and WALTER.)* To welcome you, honey.

WALTER. He said they can't hardly wait. He said the one thing they don't have, that they just *dying* to have out there is a fine family of colored people! *(To RUTH and BENEATHA.)* Ain't that right!

RUTH and BENEATHA. *(Mockingly.)* Yeah! He left his card in case—

(They indicate the card, and MAMA picks it up and throws it on the floor—understanding and looking off as she draws her chair up to the table on which she has put her plant and some sticks and some cord.)

MAMA. Father, give us strength. (*Knowingly—and without fun.*) Did he threaten us?

BENEATHA. Oh—Mama—they don't do it like that anymore. He talked Brotherhood. He said everybody ought to learn how to sit down and hate each other with good Christian fellowship.

(*She and* WALTER *shake hands to ridicule the remark.*)

MAMA. (*Sadly.*) Lord, protect us. . . .

RUTH. You should hear the money those folks raised to buy the house from us. All we paid and then some.

BENEATHA. What they think we going to do—eat 'em?

RUTH. No, honey, marry 'em.

MAMA. (*Shaking her head.*) Lord, Lord, Lord . . .

RUTH. Well—that's the way the crackers crumble. Joke.

BENEATHA. (*Laughingly noticing what her mother is doing.*) Mama, what are you doing?

MAMA. Fixing my plant so it won't get hurt none on the way. . . .

BENEATHA. Mama, are you going to take *that* to the new house?

MAMA. Un-huh—

BENEATHA. That raggedy-looking old thing?

MAMA. (*Stopping and looking at her.*) It expresses *me*.

RUTH. (*With delight, to* BENEATHA.) So there, Miss Thing!

(WALTER *comes to* MAMA *suddenly and bends down behind her and squeezes her in his arms with all his strength. She is overwhelmed by the suddenness of it and, though delighted, her manner is like that of* RUTH *with* TRAVIS.)

MAMA. Look out now, boy! You make me mess up my thing here!

WALTER. (*His face lit, he slips down on his knees beside her, his arms still about her.*) Mama . . . you know what it means to climb up in the chariot?

MAMA. (*Gruffly, very happy.*) Get on away from me now. . . .

RUTH. (*Near the gift-wrapped package, trying to catch* WALTER's *eye.*) Psst—

WALTER. What the old song say, Mama . . .

RUTH. Walter—now? (*She is pointing at the package.*)

WALTER. (*Speaking the lines, sweetly, playfully, in his mother's face.*)

I got wings . . . you got wings . . .
All God's Children got wings . . .

MAMA. Boy—get out of my face and do some work. . . .

WALTER.

When I get to heaven gonna put on my wings,
Gonna fly all over God's heaven . . .

BENEATHA. (*Teasingly, from across the room.*) Everybody talking 'bout heaven ain't going there!

WALTER. (*To* RUTH, *who is carrying the box across to them.*) I don't know, you think we ought to give her that. . . . Seems to me she ain't been very appreciative around here.

MAMA. *(Eyeing the box, which is obviously a gift.)* What is that?

WALTER. *(Taking it from* RUTH *and planting it on the table in front of* MAMA.*)* Well—what you all think? Should we give it to her?

RUTH. Oh—she was pretty good today.

MAMA. I'll good you—*(She turns her eyes to the box again.)*

BENEATHA. Open it, Mama.

(She stands up, looks at it, turns and looks at all of them, and then presses her hands together and does not open the package.)

WALTER. *(Sweetly.)* Open it, Mama. It's for you.

*(*MAMA *looks in his eyes. It is the first present in her life without its being Christmas. Slowly she opens her package and lifts out, one by one, a brand-new sparkling set of gardening tools.)*

*(*WALTER *continues, prodding.)* Ruth made up the note—read it. . . .

MAMA. *(Picking up the card and adjusting her glasses.)* "To our own Mrs. Miniver—Love from Brother, Ruth and Beneatha." Ain't that lovely. . . .

TRAVIS. *(Tugging at his father's sleeve.)* Daddy, can I give her mine now?

WALTER. All right, son.

*(*TRAVIS *flies to get his gift.)*

Travis didn't want to go in with the rest of us, Mama. He got his own. *(Somewhat amused.)* We don't know what it is. . . .

TRAVIS. *(Racing back in the room with a large hatbox and putting it in front of his grandmother.)* Here!

MAMA. Lord have mercy, baby. You done gone and bought your grandmother a hat?

TRAVIS. *(Very proud.)* Open it!

(She does and lifts out an elaborate, but very elaborate, wide gardening hat, and all the adults break up at the sight of it.)

RUTH. Travis, honey, what is that?

TRAVIS. *(Who thinks it is beautiful and appropriate.)* It's a gardening hat! Like the ladies always have on in the magazines when they work in their gardens.

BENEATHA. *(Giggling fiercely.)* Travis—we were trying to make Mama Mrs. Miniver—not Scarlett O'Hara!

MAMA. *(Indignantly.)* What's the matter with you all! This here is a beautiful hat! *(Absurdly.)* I always wanted me one just like it! *(She pops it on her head to prove it to her grandson, and the hat is ludicrous and considerably oversized.)*

RUTH. Hot dog! Go, Mama!

WALTER. *(Doubled over with laughter.)* I'm sorry, Mama—but you look like you ready to go out and chop you some cotton sure enough!

(They all laugh except MAMA, *out of deference to* TRAVIS' *feelings.)*

MAMA. *(Gathering the boy up to her.)* Bless your heart—this is the prettiest hat I ever owned . . .

*(*WALTER, RUTH *and* BENEATHA *chime in—noisily, festively and insincerely congratulating* TRAVIS *on his gift.)*

What are we all standing around here for? We ain't finished packin' yet. Bennie, you ain't packed one book.

(The BELL *rings.)*

BENEATHA. That couldn't be the movers . . . it's not hardly two good yet— *(*BENEATHA *goes into her room.)*

*(*MAMA *starts for door.)*

WALTER. *(Turning, stiffening.)* Wait—wait—I'll get it. *(He stands and looks at the door.)*

MAMA. You expecting company, son?

WALTER. *(Just looking at the door.)* Yeah—yeah . . .

*(*MAMA *looks at* RUTH, *and they exchange innocent and unfrightened glances.)*

MAMA. *(Not understanding.)* Well, let them in, son.

BENEATHA. *(From her room.)* We need some more string.

MAMA. Travis—you run to the hardware and get me some string cord.

*(*MAMA *goes out and* WALTER *turns and looks at* RUTH. TRAVIS *goes to a dish for money.)*

RUTH. Why don't you answer the door, man?

WALTER. *(Suddenly bounding across the floor to her.)* 'Cause sometimes it hard to let the future begin! *(Stooping down in her face.)*

I got wings! You got wings!
All God's children got wings!

(He crosses to the door and throws it open. Standing there is a very slight little MAN *in a not too prosperous business suit and with haunted frightened eyes and a hat pulled down tightly, brim up, around his forehead.* TRAVIS *passes between the men and exits.)*

*(*WALTER *leans deep in the man's face, still in his jubilance.)*

When I get to heaven gonna put on my wings,
Gonna fly all over God's heaven . . .

(The little MAN *stares at him.)*

Heaven—

(Suddenly he stops and looks past the little man into the empty hallway.) Where's Willy, man?

BOBO. He ain't with me.

WALTER. *(Not disturbed.)* Oh—come on in. You know my wife.

BOBO. *(Dumbly, taking off his hat.)* Yes—h'you, Miss Ruth.

RUTH. *(Quietly, a mood apart from her husband already, seeing* BOBO.*)* Hello, Bobo.

WALTER. You right on time today . . . Right on time. That's the way! *(He slaps* BOBO *on his back.)* Sit down . . . lemme hear.

*(*RUTH *stands stiffly and quietly in back of them, as though somehow she senses death, her eyes fixed on her husband.)*

BOBO. *(His frightened eyes on the floor, his hat in his hands.)* Could I please get a drink of water, before I tell you about it, Walter Lee?

(WALTER does not take his eyes off the man. RUTH goes blindly to the tap and gets a glass of water and brings it to BOBO.)

WALTER. There ain't nothing wrong, is there?

BOBO. Lemme tell you—

WALTER. Man—didn't nothing go wrong?

BOBO. Lemme tell you—Walter Lee. *(Looking at RUTH and talking to her more than to WALTER.)* You know how it was. I got to tell you how it was. I mean first I got to tell you how it was all the way . . . I mean about the money I put in, Walter Lee. . . .

WALTER. *(With taut agitation now.)* What about the money you put in?

BOBO. Well—it wasn't much as we told you—me and Willy—*(He stops.)*—I'm sorry, Walter. I got a bad feeling about it. I got a real bad feeling about it. . . .

WALTER. Man, what you telling me about all this for? . . . Tell me what happened in Springfield. . . .

BOBO. Springfield.

RUTH. *(Like a dead woman.)* What was supposed to happen in Springfield?

BOBO. *(To her.)* This deal that me and Walter went into with Willy—me and Willy was going to go down to Springfield and spread some money 'round so's we wouldn't have to wait so long for the liquor license . . . that's what we were going to do. Everybody said that was the way you had to do, you understand, Miss Ruth?

WALTER. Man—what happened down there?

BOBO. *(A pitiful man, near tears.)* I'm trying to tell you, Walter.

WALTER. *(Screaming at him suddenly.)* THEN TELL ME, GODDAMMIT . . . WHAT'S THE MATTER WITH YOU?

BOBO. Man . . . I didn't go to no Springfield, yesterday.

WALTER. *(Halted, life hanging in the moment.)* Why not?

BOBO. *(The long way, the hard way to tell.)* 'Cause I didn't have no reasons to. . . .

WALTER. Man, what are you talking about!

BOBO. I'm talking about the fact that when I got to the train station yesterday morning—eight o'clock like we planned . . . man—*Willy didn't never show up.*

WALTER. Why . . . where was he . . . where is he?

BOBO. That's what I'm trying to tell you . . . I don't know . . . I waited six hours . . . I called his house . . . and I waited . . . six hours . . . I waited in that train station six hours. . . . *(Breaking into tears.)* That was all the extra money I had in the world. . . . *(Looking up at WALTER with the tears running down his face.)* Man, *Willy is gone.*

WALTER. Gone, what you mean Willy is gone? Gone where? You mean he went by himself. You mean he went off to Springfield by himself—to take care of getting the license—*(Turns and looks anxiously at RUTH.)* You mean maybe he didn't want too many people in on the business down there? *(Looks to RUTH again, as before.)* You know Willy got his own ways. *(Looks back to BOBO.)* Maybe you was late yesterday and he just went on down there without you. Maybe—

maybe—he's been callin' you at home tryin' to tell you what happened or something. Maybe—maybe—he just got sick. He's somewhere—he's got to be somewhere. We just got to find him—me and you got to find him. (*Grabs* BOBO *senselessly by the collar and starts to shake him.*) We got to!

BOBO. (*In sudden angry, frightened agony.*) What's the matter with you, Walter! WHEN A CAT TAKE OFF WITH YOUR MONEY HE DON'T LEAVE YOU NO MAPS!

WALTER. (*Turning madly, as though he is looking for* WILLY *in the very room.*) Willy! . . . Willy . . . don't do it . . . please don't do it . . . man, not with that money . . . man, please, not with that money . . . oh, God . . . don't let it be true. . . . (*He is wandering around, crying out for* WILLY *and looking for him or perhaps for help from God.*) Man . . . I trusted you . . . man, I put my life in your hands. . . . (*He starts to crumple down on the floor as* RUTH *just covers her face in horror.*)

(MAMA *opens the door and comes into the room, with* BENEATHA *behind her.*)

Man . . . (*He starts to pound the floor with his fists, sobbing wildly.*) THAT MONEY IS MADE OUT OF MY FATHER'S FLESH. . . .

BOBO. (*Standing over him helplessly.*) I'm sorry, Walter . . .

(*Only* WALTER'S *sobs reply.*)

(BOBO *puts on his hat.*) I had my life staked on this deal, too. . . . (*He exits.*)

MAMA. (*To* WALTER.) Son—(*She goes to him, bends down to him, talks to his bent head.*)—son . . . is it—gone? Son, I gave you sixty-five hundred dollars. Is it gone? All of it? Beneatha's money too!

WALTER. (*Lifting his head slowly.*) Mama . . . I never . . . went to the bank at all. . . .

MAMA. (*Not wanting to believe him.*) You mean . . . your sister's school money . . . you used that too . . . Walter? . . .

WALTER. Yessss! All of it . . . It's all gone . . .

(*There is total silence.* RUTH *stands with her face covered with her hands;* BENEATHA *leans forlornly against a wall, fingering a piece of red ribbon from the mother's gift.* MAMA *stops and looks at her son without recognition and then, quite without thinking about it, starts to beat him senselessly in the face.* BENEATHA *goes to them and stops it.*)

BENEATHA. Mama!

(MAMA *stops and looks at both of her children and rises slowly and wanders vaguely, aimlessly away from them.*)

MAMA. I seen . . . him . . . night after night . . . come in . . . and look at that rug . . . and then look at me . . . the red showing in his eyes . . . the veins moving in his head . . . I seen him grow thin and old before he was forty . . . working and working and working like somebody's old horse . . . killing himself . . . and you—you give it all away in a day. . . .

BENEATHA. Mama—

MAMA. Oh, God . . . (*She looks up to Him.*) Look down here—and show me the strength.

BENEATHA. Mama—

MAMA. (*Folding over.*) Strength . . .

BENEATHA. *(Plaintively.)* Mama . . .
MAMA. Strength!

CURTAIN

ACT 3

An hour later.

At Curtain there is a sullen light of gloom in the living room, gray light not unlike that which began the first scene of Act 1. At Left we can see WALTER *within his room, alone with himself. He is stretched out on the bed, his shirt out and open, his arms under his head. He does not smoke, he does not cry out, he merely lies there, looking up at the ceiling, much as if he were alone in the world.*

In the living room BENEATHA *sits at the table, still surrounded by the now almost ominous packing crates. She sits looking off. We feel that this is a mood struck perhaps an hour before, and it lingers now, full of the empty sound of profound disappointment. We see on a line from her brother's bedroom the sameness of their attitudes. Presently the* BELL *rings and* BENEATHA *rises without ambition or interest in answering. It is* ASAGAI, *smiling broadly, striding into the room with energy and happy expectation and conversation.*

ASAGAI. I came over . . . I had some free time. I thought I might help with the packing. Ah, I like the look of packing crates! A household in preparation for a journey! It depresses some people . . . but for me . . . it is another feeling. Something full of the flow of life, do you understand? Movement, progress . . . it makes me think of Africa.
BENEATHA. Africa!
ASAGAI. What kind of a mood is this? Have I told you how deeply you move me?
BENEATHA. He gave away the money, Asagai. . . .
ASAGAI. Who gave away what money?
BENEATHA. The insurance money. My brother gave it away.
ASAGAI. Gave it away?
BENEATHA. He made an investment! With a man even Travis wouldn't have trusted.
ASAGAI. And it's gone?
BENEATHA. Gone!
ASAGAI. I'm very sorry . . . And you, now?
BENEATHA. Me? . . . Me? . . . Me I'm nothing . . . me. When I was very small . . . we used to take our sleds out in the wintertime and the only hills we had were the ice-covered stone steps of some houses down the street. And we used to fill them in with snow and make them smooth and slide down them all day . . . and it was very dangerous you know . . . far too steep . . . and sure enough one day a kid named Rufus came down too fast and hit the sidewalk . . . and we saw his face just split open right there in front of us . . . and I remember standing there looking at his bloody open face thinking that was the end of Rufus. But the ambulance came and they took him to the hospital and they fixed the broken bones and they sewed it all up . . . and the next time I saw Rufus he just had a

little line down the middle of his face . . . I never got over that. . . .

(WALTER *sits up, listening on the bed. Throughout this scene it is important that we feel his reaction at all times, that he visibly respond to the words of his sister and* ASAGAI.)

ASAGAI. What?

BENEATHA. That that was what one person could do for another, fix him up—sew up the problem, make him all right again. That was the most marvelous thing in the world . . . I wanted to do that. I always thought it was the one concrete thing in the world that a human being could do. Fix up the sick, you know— and make them whole again. This was truly being God. . . .

ASAGAI. You wanted to be God?

BENEATHA. No—I wanted to cure. It used to be so important to me. I wanted to cure. It used to matter. I used to care. I mean about people and how their bodies hurt. . . .

ASAGAI. And you've stopped caring?

BENEATHA. Yes—I think so.

ASAGAI. Why?

(WALTER *rises, goes to the door of his room and is about to open it, then stops and stands listening, leaning on the door jamb.)*

BENEATHA. Because it doesn't seem deep enough, close enough to what ails mankind—I mean this thing of sewing up bodies or administering drugs. Don't you understand? It was a child's reaction to the world. I thought that doctors had the secret to all the hurts. . . . That's the way a child sees things—or an idealist.

ASAGAI. Children see things very well sometimes—and idealists even better.

BENEATHA. I know that's what you think. Because you are still where I left off— you still care. This is what you see for the world, for Africa. You with the dreams of the future will patch up all Africa—you are going to cure the Great Sore of colonialism with Independence—

ASAGAI. Yes!

BENEATHA. Yes—and you think that one word is the penicillin of the human spirit: "Independence!" But then what?

ASAGAI. That will be the problem for another time. First we must get there.

BENEATHA. And where does it end?

ASAGAI. End? Who even spoke of an end? To life? To living?

BENEATHA. An end to misery!

ASAGAI. *(Smiling.)* You sound like a French intellectual.

BENEATHA. No! I sound like a human being who just had her future taken right out of her hands! While I was sleeping in my bed in there, things were happening in this world that directly concerned me—and nobody asked me, consulted me—they just went out and did things—and changed my life. Don't you see there isn't any real progress, Asagai, there is only one large circle that we march in, around and around, each of us with our own little picture—in front of us—our own little mirage that we think is the future.

ASAGAI. That is the mistake.

BENEATHA. What?

ASAGAI. What you just said—about the circle. It isn't a circle—it is simply a long line—as in geometry, you know, one that reaches into infinity. And because we cannot see the end—we also cannot see how it changes. And it is very odd but those who see the changes are called "idealists"—and those who cannot, or refuse to think, they are the "realists." It is very strange, and amusing too, I think.

BENEATHA. You—you are almost religious.

ASAGAI. Yes . . . I think I have the religion of doing what is necessary in the world—and of worshipping man—because he is so marvelous, you see.

BENEATHA. Man is foul! And the human race deserves its misery!

ASAGAI. You see: *you* have become the religious one in the old sense. Already, and after such a small defeat, you are worshipping despair.

BENEATHA. From now on, I worship the truth—and the truth is that people are puny, small and selfish. . . .

ASAGAI. Truth? Why is it that you despairing ones always think that only you have the truth? I never thought to see *you* like that. You! Your brother made a stupid, childish mistake—and you are grateful to him. So that now you can give up the ailing human race on account of it. You talk about what good is struggle; what good is anything? Where are we all going? And why are we bothering?

BENEATHA. AND YOU CANNOT ANSWER IT! All your talk and dreams about Africa and Independence. Independence and then what? What about all the crooks and petty thieves and just plain idiots who will come into power to steal and plunder the same as before—only now they will be black and do it in the name of the new Independence— You cannot answer that.

ASAGAI. *(Shouting over her.)* I LIVE THE ANSWER! *(Pause.)* In my village at home it is the exceptional man who can even read a newspaper . . . or who ever *sees* a book at all. I will go home and much of what I will have to say will seem strange to the people of my village. . . . But I will teach and work and things will happen, slowly and swiftly. At times it will seem that nothing changes at all . . . and then again . . . the sudden dramatic events which make history leap into the future. And then quiet again. Retrogression even. Guns, murder, revolution. And I even will have moments when I wonder if the quiet was not better than all that death and hatred. But I will look about my village at the illiteracy and disease and ignorance and I will not wonder long. And perhaps . . . perhaps I will be a great man . . . I mean perhaps I will hold on to the substance of truth and find my way always with the right course . . . and perhaps for it I will be butchered in my bed some night by the servants of empire. . . .

BENEATHA. THE MARTYR!

ASAGAI. Or perhaps I shall live to be a very old man, respected and esteemed in my new nation . . . and perhaps I shall hold office and this is what I'm trying to tell you, Alaiyo; perhaps the things I believe now for my country will be wrong and outmoded, and I will not understand and do terrible things to have things my way or merely to keep my power. Don't you see that there will be young men and women, not British soldiers then, but my own black countrymen . . . to step out of the shadows some evening and slit my then useless throat? Don't you see they have always been there . . . that they always will be.

And that such a thing as my own death will be an advance? They who might kill me even . . . actually replenish me!

BENEATHA. Oh, Asagai, I know all that.

ASAGAI. Good! Then stop moaning and groaning and tell me what you plan to do.

BENEATHA. Do?

ASAGAI. I have a bit of a suggestion.

BENEATHA. What?

ASAGAI. *(Rather quietly for him.)* That when it is all over—that you come home with me—

BENEATHA. *(Slapping herself on the forehead with exasperation born of misunderstanding.)* Oh—Asagai—at this moment you decide to be romantic!

ASAGAI. *(Quickly understanding the misunderstanding.)* My dear, young creature of the New World—I do not mean across the city—I mean across the ocean; home—to Africa.

BENEATHA. *(Slowly understanding and turning to him with murmured amazement.)* To—to Nigeria?

ASAGAI. Yes! . . . *(Smiling and lifting his arms playfully.)* Three hundred years later the African Prince rose up out of the seas and swept the maiden back across the middle passage over which her ancestors had come—

BENEATHA. *(Unable to play.)* Nigeria?

ASAGAI. Nigeria. Home. *(Coming to her with genuine romantic flippancy.)* I will show you our mountains and our stars; and give you cool drinks from gourds and teach you the old songs and the ways of our people—and, in time, we will pretend that—*(Very softly.)*—you have only been away for a day—

(She turns her back to him, thinking. He swings her around and takes her full in his arms in a long embrace which proceeds to passion.)

BENEATHA. *(Pulling away.)* You're getting me all mixed up—

ASAGAI. Why?

BENEATHA. Too many things—too many things have happened today. I must sit down and think. I don't know what I feel about anything right this minute. *(She promptly sits down and props her chin on her fist.)*

ASAGAI. *(Charmed.)* All right, I shall leave you. No—don't get up. *(Touching her, gently, sweetly.)* Just sit awhile and think . . . never be afraid to sit awhile and think. *(He goes to door and looks at her.)* How often I have looked at you and said, "Ah—so this is what the New World hath finally wrought . . ." *(He exits.)*

(BENEATHA sits on alone. Presently WALTER enters from his room and starts to rummage through things, feverishly looking for something. She looks up and turns in her seat.)

BENEATHA. *(Hissingly.)* Yes—just look at what the New World hath wrought! . . . Just look! *(She gestures with bitter disgust.)* There he is! *Monsieur le petit bourgeois noir*—himself! There he is! Symbol of a Rising Class! Entrepreneur! Titan of the system!

(WALTER ignores her completely and continues frantically and destructively looking for something and hurling things to floor and tearing things out of their place in his search.)

(BENEATHA *ignores the eccentricity of his actions and goes on with the monologue of insult.*) Did you dream of yachts on Lake Michigan, Brother? Did you see yourself on that Great Day sitting down at the Conference Table, surrounded by all the mighty bald-headed men in America? All halted, waiting, breathless, waiting for your pronouncements on industry? Waiting for you—Chairman of the Board?

(WALTER *finds what he is looking for—a small piece of white paper—and pushes it in his pocket and puts on his coat and rushes out without ever having looked at her.*)

(*She shouts after him.*) I look at you and I see the final triumph of stupidity in the world!

(*The door slams and she returns to just sitting again.* RUTH *comes quickly out of* MAMA*'s room.*)

RUTH. Who was that?
BENEATHA. Your husband.
RUTH. Where did he go?
BENEATHA. Who knows—maybe he has an appointment at U.S. Steel.
RUTH. (*Anxiously, with frightened eyes.*) You didn't say nothing bad to him, did you?
BENEATHA. Bad? Say anything bad to him? No—I told him he was a sweet boy and full of dreams and everything is strictly peachy keen, as the ofay kids say!

(MAMA *enters from her bedroom. She is lost, vague, trying to catch hold, to make some sense of her former command of the world, but it still eludes her. A sense of waste overwhelms her gait; a measure of apology rides on her shoulders. She goes to her plant, which has remained on the table, looks at it, picks it up and takes it to the window sill and sits it outside, and she stands and looks at it a long moment. Then she closes the window, straightens her body with effort and turns around to her children.*)

MAMA. Well—ain't it a mess in here, though? (*A false cheerfulness, a beginning of something.*) I guess we all better stop moping around and get some work done. All this unpacking and everything we got to do.

(RUTH *raises her head slowly in response to the sense of the line; and* BENEATHA *in similar manner turns very slowly to look at her mother.*)

One of you all better call the moving people and tell 'em not to come.
RUTH. Tell 'em not to come?
MAMA. Of course, baby. Ain't no need in 'em coming all the way here and having to go back. They charges for that too. (*She sits down, fingers to her brow, thinking.*) Lord, ever since I was a little girl, I always remembers people saying, "Lena—Lena Eggleston, you aims too high all the time. You needs to slow down and see life a little more like it is. Just slow down some." That's what they always used to say down home—"Lord, that Lena Eggleston is a high-minded thing. She'll get her due one day!"
RUTH. No, Lena . . .
MAMA. Me and Big Walter just didn't never learn right.
RUTH. Lena, no! We gotta go. Bennie—tell her—(*She rises and crosses to* BENEATHA *with her arms outstretched.*)

(BENEATHA *doesn't respond.*)

—tell her we can still move . . . the notes ain't but a hundred and twenty-five a month. We got four grown people in this house—we can work. . . .

MAMA. *(To herself.)* Just aimed too high all the time—

RUTH. *(Turning and going to* MAMA *fast—the words pouring out with urgency and desperation.)* Lena—I'll work . . . I'll work twenty hours a day in all the kitchens in Chicago . . . I'll strap my baby on my back if I have to and scrub all the floors in America and wash all the sheets in America if I have to—but we got to move . . . We got to get out of here. . . .

(MAMA *reaches out absently and pats* RUTH's *hand.*)

MAMA. No—I sees things differently now. Been thinking 'bout some of the things we could do to fix this place up some. I seen a second-hand bureau over on Maxwell Street just the other day that could fit right there. *(She points to where the new furniture might go.)*

(RUTH *wanders away from her.*)

Would need some new handles on it and then a little varnish and then it look like something brand-new. And—we can put up them new curtains in the kitchen . . . why this place be looking fine. Cheer us all up so that we forget trouble ever came. . . . *(To* RUTH.*)* And you could get some nice screens to put up in your room round the baby's bassinet. . . . *(She looks at both of them, pleadingly.)* Sometimes you just got to know when to give up some things . . . and hold on to what you got.

(WALTER *enters from the outside, looking spent and leaning against the door, his coat hanging from him.*)

MAMA. Where you been, son?

WALTER. *(Breathing hard.)* Made a call.

MAMA. To who, son?

WALTER. To The Man.

MAMA. What man, baby?

WALTER. The Man, Mama. Don't you know who The Man is?

RUTH. Walter Lee?

WALTER. *The Man.* Like the guys in the streets say—The Man. Captain Boss— Mistuh Charley . . . Old Captain Please Mr. Bossman . . .

BENEATHA. *(Suddenly.)* Lindner!

WALTER. That's right! That's good. I told him to come right over.

BENEATHA. *(Fiercely, understanding.)* For what? What do you want to see him for?

WALTER. *(Looking at his sister.)* We going to do business with him.

MAMA. What you talking 'bout, son?

WALTER. Talking 'bout life, Mama. You all always telling me to see life like it is. Well—I laid in there on my back today . . . and I figured it out. Life just like it is. Who gets and who don't get. *(He sits down with his coat on and laughs.)* Mama, you know it's all divided up. Life is. Sure enough. Between the takers and the "tooken." *(He laughs.)* I've figured it out finally. *(He looks around at them.)* Yeah. Some of us always getting "tooken." *(He laughs.)* People like Willy Harris, they don't never get "tooken." And you know why the rest of us do? 'Cause we all mixed up. Mixed up bad. We get to looking 'round for the right and the wrong; and we worry about it and cry about it and stay up nights trying to figure out 'bout the wrong and the right of things all the time . . . and all the time, man, them takers is out there operating, just taking and taking. Willy Harris? Shoot—Willy Harris don't even count. He don't even count in the big scheme of things. But I'll say one thing for old Willy Harris . . . he's taught me some-thing. He's taught me to keep my eye on what counts in this world. Yeah— (*Shouting out a little.*)—thanks, Willy!

RUTH. What did you call that man for, Walter Lee?

WALTER. Called him to tell him to come on over to the show. Gonna put on a show for the man. Just what he wants to see. You see, Mama, the man came here today and he told us that them people out there where you want us to move—well they so upset they willing to pay us not to move out there. (*He laughs again.*) And—and oh, Mama—you would of been proud of the way me and Ruth and Bennie acted. We told him to get out. . . . Lord have mercy! We told the man to get out. Oh, we was some proud folks this afternoon, yeah. (*He lights a cigarette.*) We were still full of that old-time stuff. . . .

RUTH. (*Coming toward him slowly.*) You talking 'bout taking them people's money to keep us from moving in that house?

WALTER. I ain't just talking 'bout it, baby—I'm telling you that's what's going to happen.

BENEATHA. Oh, God! Where is the bottom! Where is the real honest-to-God bottom so he can't go any farther!

WALTER. See—that's the old stuff. You and that boy that was here today. You all want everybody to carry a flag and a spear and sing some marching songs, huh? You wanna spend your life looking into things and trying to find the right and the wrong part, huh? Yeah. You know what's going to happen to that boy some-day—he'll find himself sitting in a dungeon, locked in forever—and the takers will have the key! Forget it, baby! There ain't no causes—there ain't nothing but taking in this world, and he who takes most is smartest—and it don't make a damn bit of difference *how*.

MAMA. You making something inside me cry, son. Some awful pain inside me.

WALTER. Don't cry, Mama. Understand. That white man is going to walk in that door able to write checks for more money than we ever had. It's impor-tant to him and I'm going to help him . . . I'm going to put on the show, Mama.

MAMA. Son—I come from five generations of people who was slaves and share-croppers—but ain't nobody in my family never let nobody pay 'em no money that was a way of telling us we wanst' fit to walk the earth. We ain't never been that poor. (*Raising her eyes and looking at him.*) We ain't never been that dead inside.

BENEATHA. Well—we are dead now. All the talk about dreams and sunlight that goes on in this house. All dead.

WALTER. What's the matter with you all! I didn't make this world! It was give to me this way! Hell, yes, I want me some yachts someday! Yes, I want to hang some real pearls 'round my wife's neck. Ain't she supposed to wear no pearls? Somebody tell me—tell me, who decides which women is suppose to wear pearls in this world. I tell you I am a *man*—and I think my wife should wear some pearls in this world!

(This last line hangs a good while and WALTER *begins to move about the room. The word "Man" has penetrated his consciousness; he mumbles it to himself repeatedly between strange agitated pauses as he moves about.)*

MAMA. Baby, how you going to feel on the inside?

WALTER. Fine! . . . Going to feel fine . . . a man . . .

MAMA. You won't have nothing left then, Walter Lee.

WALTER. *(Coming to her.)* I'm going to feel fine, Mama. I'm going to look that son-of-a-bitch in the eyes and say—*(He falters.)*—and say, "All right, Mr. Lindner—*(He falters even more.)*—that's your neighborhood out there. You got the right to keep it like you want. You got the right to have it like you want. Just write the check and—the house is yours." And, and I am going to say—*(His voice almost breaks.)*—and you—you people just put the money in my hand and you won't have to live next to this bunch of stinking niggers! . . . *(He straightens up and moves away from his mother, walking around the room.)* Maybe—maybe I'll just get down on my black knees . . . *(He does so.)*

*(*RUTH *and* BENNIE *and* MAMA *watch him in frozen horror.)*

Captain, Mistuh, Bossman. *(He starts crying.)* A-hee-hee-hee! *(Wringing his hands in profoundly anguished imitation.)* Yasssssuh! Great White Father, just gi' ussen de money, fo' God's sake, and we's ain't gwine come out deh and dirty up yo' white folks neighborhood. . . . *(He breaks down completely, then gets up and goes into the bedroom.)*

BENEATHA. That is not a man. That is nothing but a toothless rat.

MAMA. Yes—death done come in this here house. *(She is nodding, slowly, reflectively.)* Done come walking in my house. On the lips of my children. You what supposed to be my beginning again. You—what supposed to be my harvest. *(To* BENEATHA.*)* You—you mourning your brother?

BENEATHA. He's no brother of mine.

MAMA. What you say?

BENEATHA. I said that that individual in that room is no brother of mine.

MAMA. That's what I thought you said. You feeling like you better than he is today?

*(*BENEATHA *does not answer.)*

Yes? What you tell him a minute ago? That he wasn't a man? Yes? You give him up for me? You done wrote his epitaph too—like the rest of the world? Well, who give you the privilege?

BENEATHA. Be on my side for once! You saw what he just did, Mama! You saw him—down on his knees. Wasn't it you who taught me—to despise any man who would do that. Do what he's going to do.

MAMA. Yes—I taught you that. Me and your daddy. But I thought I taught you something else too . . . I thought I taught you to love him.

BENEATHA. Love him? There is nothing left to love.

MAMA. There is always something left to love. And if you ain't learned that, you ain't learned nothing. *(Looking at her.)* Have you cried for that boy today? I don't mean for yourself and for the family 'cause we lost the money. I mean for him; what he been through and what it done to him. Child, when do you think is the time to love somebody the most; when they done good and made things easy for everybody? Well then, you ain't through learning—because that ain't the time at all. It's when he's at his lowest and can't believe in hisself 'cause the world done whipped him so. When you starts measuring somebody, measure him right, child, measure him right. Make sure you done taken into account what hills and valleys he come through before he got to wherever he is.

(TRAVIS bursts into the room at the end of the speech, leaving the door open.)

TRAVIS. Grandmama—the moving men are downstairs! The truck just pulled up.

MAMA. *(Turning and looking at him.)* Are they, baby? They downstairs? *(She sighs and sits.)*

(LINDNER appears in the doorway. He peers in and knocks lightly, to gain attention, and comes in. All turn to look at him.)

LINDNER. *(Hat and briefcase in hand.)* Uh-hello. . . .

(RUTH crosses mechanically to the bedroom door and opens it and lets it swing open freely and slowly as the lights come up on WALTER within, still in his coat, sitting at the far corner of the room. He looks up and out through the room to LINDNER.)

RUTH. He's here.

(A long minute passes and WALTER slowly gets up.)

LINDNER. *(Coming to the table with efficiency, putting his briefcase on the table and starting to unfold papers and unscrew fountain pens.)* Well, I certainly was glad to hear from you people.

(WALTER has begun the trek out of the room, slowly and awkwardly, rather like a small boy, passing the back of his sleeve across his mouth from time to time.)

Life can really be so much simpler than people let it be most of the time. Well—with whom do I negotiate? You, Mrs. Younger, or your son here?

(MAMA sits with her hands folded on her lap and her eyes closed as WALTER advances. TRAVIS gets closer to LINDNER and looks at the papers curiously.)

Just some official papers, sonny.

RUTH. Travis, you go downstairs.

MAMA. *(Opening her eyes and looking into WALTER's.)* No. Travis, you stay right here. And you make him understand what you doing, Walter Lee. You teach him good. Like Willy Harris taught you. You show where our five generations done come to. Go ahead, son—

WALTER. *(Looks down into his son's eyes.)*

(TRAVIS grins at him merrily and WALTER draws him beside him with his arm lightly around his shoulders.)

Well, Mr. Lindner.

(BENEATHA *turns away.*)

We called you—(*There is a profound, simple groping quality in his speech.*)—because, well, me and my family—(*He looks around and shifts from one foot to the other.*)—well—we are very plain people. . . .

LINDNER. Yes—

WALTER. I mean—I have worked as a chauffeur most of my life—and my wife here, she does domestic work in people's kitchens. So does my mother. I mean—we are plain people. . . .

LINDNER. Yes, Mr. Younger—

WALTER. (*Really like a small boy, looking down at his shoes and then up at the man.*) And—uh—well, my father, well, he was a laborer most of his life.

LINDNER. (*Absolutely confused.*) Uh, yes—

WALTER. (*Looking down at his toes once again.*) My father almost beat a man to death once because this man called him a bad name or something, you know what I mean?

LINDNER. No, I'm afraid I don't.

WALTER. (*Finally straightening up.*) Well, what I mean is that we come from people who had a lot of pride. I mean—we are very proud people. And that's my sister over there and she's going to be a doctor—and we are very proud—

LINDNER. Well—I am sure that is very nice, but—

WALTER. (*Starting to cry and facing the man eye to eye.*) What I am telling you is that we called you over here to tell you that we are very proud and that this is—this is my son, who makes the sixth generation of our family in this country, and that we have all thought about your offer and we have decided to move into our house because my father—my father—he earned it.

(MAMA *has her eyes closed and is rocking back and forth as though she were in church, with her head nodding the amen yes.*)

We don't want to make no trouble for nobody or fight no causes—but we will try to be good neighbors. That's all we got to say. (*He looks the man absolutely in the eyes.*) We don't want your money. (*He turns and walks away from the man.*)

LINDNER. (*Looking around at all of them.*) I take it then that you have decided to occupy.

BENEATHA. That's what the man said.

LINDNER. (*To* MAMA *in her reverie.*) Then I would like to appeal to you, Mrs. Younger. You are older and wiser and understand things better I am sure . . .

MAMA. (*Rising.*) I am afraid you don't understand. My son said we was going to move and there ain't nothing left for me to say. (*Shaking her head with double meaning.*) You know how these young folks is nowadays, mister. Can't do a thing with 'em. Good-bye.

LINDNER. (*Folding up his materials.*) Well—if you are that final about it . . . there is nothing left for me to say. (*He finishes. He is almost ignored by the family, who are concentrating on* WALTER LEE. *At the door* LINDNER *halts and looks around.*) I sure hope you people know what you're doing. (*He shakes his head and exits.*)

RUTH. (*Looking around and coming to life.*) Well, for God's sake—if the moving men are here—LET'S GET THE HELL OUT OF HERE!

MAMA. (*Into action.*) Ain't it the truth! Look at all this here mess. Ruth, put Travis' good jacket on him . . . Walter Lee, fix your tie and tuck your shirt in, you look just like somebody's hoodlum. Lord have mercy, where is my plant? (*She flies to get it amid the general bustling of the family, who are deliberately trying to ignore the nobility of the past moment.*) You all start on down . . . Travis child, don't go empty-handed . . . Ruth, where did I put that box with my skillets in it? I want to be in charge of it myself . . . I'm going to make us the biggest dinner we ever ate tonight . . . Beneatha, what's the matter with them stockings? Pull them things up, girl. . . .

(*The family starts to file out as* TWO MOVING MEN *appear and begin to carry out the heavier pieces of furniture, bumping into the family as they move about.*)

BENEATHA. Mama, Asagai asked me to marry him today and go to Africa—

MAMA. (*In the middle of her getting-ready activity.*) He did? You ain't old enough to marry nobody—(*Seeing the moving men lifting one of her chairs precariously.*)—darling, that ain't no bale of cotton, please handle it so we can sit in it again. I had that chair twenty-five years. . . .

(*The* MOVERS *sigh with exasperation and go on with their work.*)

BENEATHA. (*Girlishly and unreasonably trying to pursue the conversation.*) To go to Africa, Mama—be a doctor in Africa. . . .

MAMA. (*Distracted.*) Yes, baby—

WALTER. Africa! What he want you to go to Africa for?

BENEATHA. To practice there. . . .

WALTER. Girl, if you don't get all them silly ideas out your head! You better marry yourself a man with some loot. . . .

BENEATHA. (*Angrily, precisely as in the first scene of the play.*) What have you got to do with who I marry!

WALTER. Plenty. Now I think George Murchison—

(HE *and* BENEATHA *go out yelling at each other vigorously;* BENEATHA *is heard saying that she would not marry* GEORGE MURCHISON *if he were Adam and she were Eve, etc. The anger is loud and real till their voices diminish.* RUTH *stands at the door and turns to* MAMA *and smiles knowingly.*)

MAMA. (*Fixing her hat at last.*) Yeah—they something all right, my children. . . .

RUTH. Yeah—they're something. Let's go, Lena.

MAMA. (*Stalling, starting to look around at the house.*) Yes—I'm coming. Ruth—

RUTH. Yes?

MAMA. (*Quietly, woman to woman.*) He finally come into his manhood today, didn't he? Kind of like a rainbow after the rain. . . .

RUTH. (*Biting her lip lest her own pride explode in front of* MAMA.) Yes, Lena.

(WALTER's *voice calls for them raucously.*)

MAMA. (*Waving* RUTH *out vaguely.*) All right, honey—go on down. I be down directly.

(RUTH *hesitates, then exits.* MAMA *stands, at last alone in the living room, her plant on the table before her as the* LIGHTS *start to come down. She looks around at all the walls and ceilings and suddenly, despite herself, while the children call below, a great heaving thing rises in her and she puts her fist to her mouth, takes a final desperate look, pulls her coat about her, pats her hat and goes out. The* LIGHTS *dim down. The door opens and she comes back in, grabs her plant, and goes out for the last time.*)

CURTAIN

THE PROTEST MOVEMENT 1940–1959

Topics for Research

1. Compare written protest to oral protest by African Americans of the 1940s and 1950s. Is the nature of the protest the same in both forms? If not, what are some major differences?

2. What happened as a result of African American literary contributions during the 1940s and 1950s? How did this work help in the struggle for civil rights? Did it lead to direct action or attitude changes or both? Discuss both mental and physical effects.

3. How did the roles of women and men differ during this period of protest? Was sexism as prominent as racism? Discuss the gender hierarchy of African American protest literature.

4. Which genre did African American protest writers use most often? Why were some forms preferred over others?

5. How did earlier African American literature, from the Harlem Renaissance and before, influence black literature during the protest period?

6. Who was the primary audience for black protest literature produced in the 1940s and 1950s? How was the work received by the primary and secondary audiences? What influence, if any, did the audience have on content and style?

PART 6

BLACK AESTHETICS MOVEMENT
1960-1969

INTRODUCTION

LANGUAGE POWER WAS MORE IMPORTANT THAN FIST POWER IN THE black aesthetics movement. The civil rights movement, the black nationalist movement, and the women's movement were some of the defining social phenomena of this period. During a time when African Americans were asserting themselves with political force, black artists delivered their messages using a multiplicity of genres to promote change and transform society. Many African American authors were also strong political figures—for example, Martin Luther King, Jr. led a campaign of nonviolent resistance, and Malcolm X advocated the use of force, possibly violence, to fight racial injustices. Like Harlem Renaissance writers, African American writers in the 1960s protested in direct ways. Politics and writing were connected; in fact, political writing and literary writing were inseparable. This period was not a time for appreciating art for art's sake. Themes such as slavery versus freedom were geared toward the abolishment of slavery in any form and the promotion of freedom in its various manifestations. African American literature reached a larger audience than it had in previous years.

Imamu Amiri Baraka (formerly LeRoi Jones) played a crucial role in the founding of the black arts movement and black nationalism. Recognizing that white aesthetics excluded African American literature, Baraka helped to establish and define black aesthetics. For Baraka, there was something identifiably black about African American artistic creations, and his insistence on the projection of these ideas was a tool in the fight against racism. His writing is full of his own experiences; his poems, plays, and essays put forth his political agenda against imperialism and colonialism, creating a forum for black aesthetic, cultural, and political expression. He eventually converted from black nationalism to Marxism, focusing more on economics than race. *Dutchman* (1964), his first play to be produced professionally, focuses on a racial encounter between a black man and a white woman, showing the power of the white woman over the black man. Interestingly, Baraka married a white woman, whom he later divorced in his quest to establish a more intimate connection with his black roots. He also softened, to some extent, his belief that women should be submissive, advocating freedom for enslaved women and African Americans.

In groups such as the National Organization for Women (NOW), white women were working, often with black women, to eradicate sex discrimination. During the civil rights era, however, the women's movement was overshadowed by racial movements. In 1962, federal troops were called to protect James Meredith, who enrolled as the first black student at the University of Mississippi. The Congress of Racial Equality (CORE), the Student Nonviolent Coordinating Committee (SNCC), and the Southern Christian Leadership Conference (SCLC) also worked for black rights. Using nonviolent protests, these groups staged sit-in demonstrations against segregation in Southern eating establishments and used "freedom rides" to end segregation on public transportation.

In 1968, the year of Martin Luther King's assassination, violent protests erupted in urban ghettos, and a march was planned by the National Welfare Rights Organization. Black students were killed in race riots at various black colleges, including Jackson State University in Jackson, Mississippi. The women's movement did not address the numerous racial incidents but focused on male domination of the social system. Women's issues were ignored in the media except on a superficial level: "bra burning" was ridiculed. African American women also took a back seat in the male-dominated literary realm. The theme of the late 1960s was black power—black *male* power, symbolized by a closed fist. Black men, especially, struggled with powerlessness. They could not control their lives, provide for their families. As soldiers, African American men killed Vietnamese in the sevice of their government; however, when they returned from the war, they faced a grim reality: their own country was still ruled by racism. They returned to take a seat at the back of the bus and to be shut out by "Whites only" signs. They did not feel appreciated for their role in a long fight in which many lost their lives.

The African American literature of the 1960s was an important tool in the civil rights movement, a vehicle through which black Americans became empowered. Even though the writing expresses a variety of feelings, anger against racists and pride in African American culture are two of the strongest emotions in the literature of this period. The content or message embodied in the literature seemed to take precedence over form during the black aesthetics movement. However, the way the messages are expressed—the language used—is just as important as what is said. Form and content work together in the creation of black art. The speeches of Martin Luther King, Jr., illustrate how form and content work together in effective prose. King's "Letter from Birmingham Jail" (pp. 678–689) and his "I Have a Dream" speech have persuasion as their purpose. King was a master rhetorician, using metaphor, chiasmus, anaphora, isocolon, and other ways of presenting words to emphasize the message; African Americans and whites were persuaded by King's powerful language. Before he was assassinated in Memphis, Tennessee, in 1968, he gained widespread support from both races for his nonviolent political theory.

Some African American leaders, such as Malcolm X, created a rhetoric of exclusion. Malcolm X gave a major speech to black students at Tuskegee Institute in 1964. The students, for the most part, believed in nonviolence and integration; Malcolm X wanted to persuade them that integration was not the answer to the race problem and that the nonviolent approach left blacks with little power. After breaking away from Elijah Muhammad and the Nation of Islam, Malcolm X was assassinated in 1965 while speaking on behalf of an organization he had recently established—the Organization of Afro-American Unity.

Malcolm X uses some of the same rhetorical devices as King. King's writing draws attention to form, but the controversial views of both men overshadow their writing styles. Malcolm X's political agenda, expressed in speech and writing, included ideas that caused fear and resentment. Groups such as the Black Panthers subscribed to the "Violence is Necessary" motto of Malcolm X, but the majority of both African Americans and whites did not want to resolve conflict in this way. The Black Panther party was most concerned with police brutality against blacks. The party was supported by writers such as Angela Davis and Eldridge Cleaver, who agreed that African Americans should use self-defense if warranted. During the 1960s, African American militant groups tried more aggressive approaches to fight racism. The black nationalist perspective, which sought to give African Americans some control over their own lives, experienced a resurgence during this time, having started in the nineteenth century. This movement continued with Marcus Garvey's philosophy of separatism.

The poetry of Nikki Giovanni (pp. 692–693) and Sonia Sanchez (pp. 690–691) reflected the independence created by black nationalism, which moved African American writers away from white models of style toward art that used the content and form of black culture. Sanchez's commitment to black nationalism is evident: her poetry celebrates the distinct culture of African Americans. For example, Sanchez uses the black vernacular and incorporates African forms into her work, putting black aesthetic theory into practice. Her poetry, like that of Nikki Giovanni (pp. 691–692), is highly political; she addresses issues related to race, gender, poverty, and substance abuse. Giovanni's art reveals her views on the black liberation movement and deals with collective black experience and with her individual, personal life experiences as a black woman in relationships with black men. Her most racially charged poetry was included in her first two volumes—*Black Feeling, Black Talk* (1967) and *Black Judgment* (1968).

Alice Childress used drama to present her political views on race relations. Her work deals with themes such as segregation, white-black relationships, and lynching. She is well known for her children's book, banned in some schools, *A Hero Ain't Nothin' But a Sandwich* (1973)—controversial because it presents the experiences of a young boy trying to overcome drug addiction. During her writing career, which started with the production of her first play in 1949, Childress used her writing to deal with controversial topics. Her 1969 play *Wine in the Wilderness* (pp. 694–720) illustrates black aesthetics by dealing with black and white relationships and conflicts that stem from them. Childress was the first woman to receive the Obie Award, for a 1955 play, *Trouble in Mind*, that dealt with lynching.

Eldridge Cleaver, like Childress and other writers during the black arts movement, did not try to sugarcoat his prose. He wrote postprison writings and speeches while a fugitive in France, Cuba, and Algeria. His black art was straightforward and blatant; he fought vigorously against racial injustice, in the flesh and in his writing. His collection of essays *Soul on Ice* (pp. 729–738), published in 1968, presents his militant political agenda. Cleaver wrote most of the book while in prison, where he became a staunch follower of Malcolm X. After being released from prison, Cleaver participated actively in the Black Panther party as its minister of information. In 1968, Cleaver engaged in a gunfight between the Black Panthers and the San Francisco police and was charged with assault and attempted murder. Rather than face the charges and the possibility of more jail time, he left the country, going into exile.

The marriage of art and politics is illustrated also in the poetry of Haki R. Madhubuti, a black activist who played an important role in the black arts movement of the 1960s. He founded Third World Press in 1967 to publish the work of black writers. The titles of Madhubuti's books of poetry indicate their content: *Think Black* (1967) and *Don't Cry, Scream* (1969) are good examples. The poems included (pp. 739–741) exemplify his serious commitment to an exclusively black art form that addresses black issues. Like other writers in this period, Madhubuti's work is heavily influenced by black language and music.

Music contributed to the African American oral tradition in the 1960s in a major way. The Motown sound combined rock and roll with gospel music to create a new, more broadly popular form of rhythm and blues. Motown brought black music into mainstream society. In Detroit, Michigan, where the Motown Record Corporation was founded by Berry Gordy, Jr., the economy benefited from the success of recording artists such as Stevie Wonder, Diana Ross and the Supremes, Smokey Robinson, the Jackson Five, Marvin Gaye, and Gladys Knight and the Pips. Most of the music focused on the ups and downs of love. However, singers such as Marvin Gaye sang about the problematic state of the country, as in his "What's Going On?" White singers like Elvis Presley and Jerry Lee Lewis helped to make African American music, particularly rhythm and blues, acceptable to whites.

Also popular in the African American oral tradition of the 1960s were freedom songs such as "We Shall Overcome," which is considered the national anthem of the civil rights movement. In a nutshell, the song is about the hope of moving from slavery (racism) to freedom. The primary message in the song is that one day African Americans will be free from injustice. Another popular freedom song was "I'm On My Way to the Freedom Land."

The black power movement caused some African Americans to stop singing about freedom; they became impatient, wanting to abandon the passive approach and take any action necessary to make sure that their people would overcome racism. African American literature during the black aesthetics movement was often forceful, combining the political and the artistic. During this time, black activists used writing to voice anger and dissatisfaction. The civil rights movement was aided by the literature of these "militant" African American writers. The literature had a specific purpose independent of its value as art, in many instances to rebel against mainstream society. African American artists showed pride in art forms and traditions specific to the culture: jazz, rhythm and blues, and black English vernacular. During this time, African American literature was geared toward helping black Americans cope in society, suggesting that they take pride in the unique aspects of their culture.

AMIRI BARAKA (b. 1934)

Amiri Baraka (formerly known as LeRoi Jones) is a well-known poet, playwright, and revolutionary. Baraka was born Everett LeRoy Jones in Newark, New Jersey. He went from Rutgers University, attending for one year, to Howard University, then to the Air Force, and thereafter moved to New York City in 1957. His writing addresses racial and political issues. His controversial plays have brought him the most attention as a literary master. His first play to be produced, Dutchman *(1964), presents a confrontation between a black man and a white woman. Baraka uses drama to present the reality of racism in America, sometimes questioning the value of integration, as he did in two other plays,* The Slave *(1964) and* The Toilet *(1964).*

Later in his career, Baraka reevaluated his black nationalist stance; as a result, he adopted a Marxist philosophy that placed emphasis on economics instead of race. In 1979, he became a professor of African studies at the State University of New York at Stony Brook. He continues to write mostly about social concerns that affect the racial climate. His poetry reflects his view that literature should address political issues and should not simply be created for academic or entertainment purposes.

Black Bourgeoisie, (1969)

has a gold tooth, sits long hours
on a stool thinking about money.
sees white skin in a secret room
rummages his sense for sense
dreams about Lincoln(s)   5
conks his daughter's hair
sends his coon to school
works very hard
grins politely in restaurants
has a good word to say   10
never says it
does not hate ofays
hates, instead, him self
him black self

Poem for Half White College Students (1966)

Who are you, listening to me, who are you
listening to yourself? Are you white or
black, or does that have anything to do
with it? Can you pop your fingers to no
music, except those wild monkies go on   5

in your head, can you jerk, to no melody,
except finger poppers get it together
when you turn from starchecking to checking
yourself. How do you sound, your words, are they
yours? The ghost you see in the mirror, is it really   10
you, can you swear you are not an imitation greyboy,
can you look right next to you in that chair, and swear,
that the sister you have your hand on is not really
so full of Elizabeth Taylor, Richard Burton is
coming out of her ears. You may even have to be Richard   15
with a white shirt and face, and four million negroes
think you cute, you may have to be Elizabeth Taylor, old lady,
if you want to sit up in your crazy spot dreaming about dresses,
and the sway of certain porters' hips. Check yourself, learn who it is
speaking, when you make some ultrasophisticated point, check yourself,   20
when you find yourself gesturing like Steve McQueen, check it out, ask
in your black heart who it is you are, and is that image black or white,

you might be surprised right out the window, whistling dixie on the way in

The Pressures. (1964)

             (Love twists
the young man. Having seen it
only once. He expected it
to be, as the orange flower
leather of the poet's book.   5
He expected
less hurt, a lyric. And not
the slow effortless pain
as a new dripping sun pushes
up out of our river.)   10

             And
having seen it, refuses
to inhale. "It was a
green mist, seemed
to lift and choke   15
the town."

Return of the Native (1969)

Harlem is vicious
modernism. BangClash.

Vicious the way its made.
Can you stand such beauty?
So violent and transforming.   5
The trees blink naked, being
so few. The women stare
and are in love with them
selves. The sky sits awake
over us. Screaming   10
at us. No rain.
Sun, hot cleaning sun
drives us under it.

The place, and place
meant of   15
black people. Their heavy Egypt.
(Weird word!) Their minds, mine,
the black hope mine. In Time.
We slide along in pain or too
happy. So much love   20
for us. All over, so much of
what we need. Can you sing
yourself, your life, your place
on the warm planet earth.
And look at the stones   25

the hearts, the gentle hum
of meaning. Each thing, life
we have, or love, is meant
for us in a world like this.
Where we may see ourselves   30
all the time. And suffer
in joy, that our lives
are so familiar.

MALCOLM X (1925–1965)

*Born Malcolm Little in Omaha, Nebraska, Malcolm X was first recognized in the 1950s
for his role as spokesperson for the Nation of Islam, whose followers believe in racial separation. Alex Haley assisted him in writing* The Autobiography of Malcolm X *(1965),
in which Malcolm tells the story of his life, including his many religious and political
transformations. The autobiographical story was produced as a film by Spike Lee in 1992.*

*Malcolm's father was a Baptist minister who believed the separatist rhetoric of Marcus
Garvey, leader of the nationalist Universal Negro Improvement Association. While in
prison for a robbery—he was arrested in 1946 and sentenced to ten years—Malcolm*

began to study the tenets of Elijah Muhammad. When he was released in 1952, Malcolm became a minister for Muhammad; however, he eventually became disillusioned with the Nation of Islam and Muhammad and abandoned the sect. After visiting Mecca, Malcolm returned to the United States believing that race was not the only reason for American societal problems. He broadened his view of life, modifying his former belief that white people are inherently evil. He was assassinated in Harlem, allegedly by a member of the Nation of Islam. The Autobiography *and* Malcolm X Speaks *(1965), a collection of his speeches, were published after his death.*

From The Autobiography of Malcolm X (1965)

Chapter 4: Laura

Shorty would take me to groovy, frantic scenes in different chicks' and cats' pads, where with the lights and juke down mellow, everybody blew gage and juiced back and jumped. I met chicks who were fine as May wine, and cats who were hip to all happenings.

That paragraph is deliberate, of course; it's just to display a bit more of the slang that was used by everyone I respected as "hip" in those days. And in no time at all, I was talking the slang like a lifelong hipster.

Like hundreds of thousands of country-bred Negroes who had come to the Northern black ghetto before me, and have come since, I'd also acquired all the other fashionable ghetto adornments—the zoot suits and conk that I have described, liquor, cigarettes, then reefers—all to erase my embarrassing background. But I still harbored one secret humiliation: I couldn't dance.

I can't remember when it was that I actually learned how—that is to say, I can't recall the specific night or nights. But dancing was the chief action at those "pad parties," so I've no doubt about how and why my initiation into lindy-hopping came about. With alcohol or marijuana lightening my head, and that wild music wailing away on those portable record players, it didn't take long to loosen up the dancing instincts in my African heritage. All I remember is that during some party around this time, when nearly everyone but me was up dancing, some girl grabbed me—they often would take the initiative and grab a partner, for no girl at those parties ever would dream that anyone present couldn't dance—and there I was out on the floor.

I was up in the jostling crowd—and suddenly, unexpectedly, I got the idea. It was as though somebody had clicked on a light. My long-suppressed African instincts broke through, and loose.

Having spent so much time in Mason's white environment, I had always believed and feared that dancing involved a certain order or pattern of specific steps—as dancing *is* done by whites. But here among my own less-inhibited people, I discovered it was simply letting your feet, hands and body spontaneously act out whatever impulses were stirred by the music.

From then on, hardly a party took place without me turning up—inviting myself, if I had to—and lindy-hopping my head off.

I'd always been fast at picking up new things. I made up for lost time now so fast, that soon girls were asking me to dance with them. I worked my partners hard; that's why they liked me so much.

When I was at work, up in the Roseland men's room, I just couldn't keep still. My shine rag popped with the rhythm of those great bands rocking the ballroom. White customers on the shine stand, especially, would laugh to see my feet suddenly break loose on their own and cut a few steps. Whites are correct in thinking that black people are natural dancers. Even little kids are—except for those Negroes today who are so "integrated," as I had been, that their instincts are inhibited. You know those "dancing jigaboo" toys that you wind up? Well, I was like a live one—music just wound me up.

By the next dance for the Boston black folk—I remember that Lionel Hampton was coming in to play—I had given my notice to the Roseland's manager.

When I told Ella why I had quit, she laughed aloud: I told her I couldn't find time to shine shoes and dance, too. She was glad, because she had never liked the idea of my working at that no-prestige job. When I told Shorty, he said he'd known I'd soon outgrow it anyway.

Shorty could dance all right himself but, for his own reasons, he never cared about going to the big dances. He loved just the music-making end of it. He practiced his saxophone and listened to records. It astonished me that Shorty didn't care to go and hear the big bands play. He had his alto sax idol, Johnny Hodges, with Duke Ellington's band, but he said he thought too many young musicians were only carbon-copying the big-band names on the same instrument. Anyway, Shorty was really serious about nothing except his music, and about working for the day when he could start his own little group to gig around Boston.

The morning after I quit Roseland, I was down at the men's clothing store bright and early. The salesman checked and found that I'd missed only one weekly payment: I had "A-1" credit. I told him I'd just quit my job, but he said that didn't make any difference; I could miss paying them for a couple of weeks if I had to; he knew I'd get straight.

This time, I studied carefully everything in my size on the racks. And finally I picked out my second zoot. It was a sharkskin gray, with a big, long coat, and pants ballooning out at the knees and then tapering down to cuffs so narrow that I had to take off my shoes to get them on and off. With the salesman urging me on, I got another shirt, and a hat, and new shoes—the kind that were just coming into hipster style; dark orange colored, with paper-thin soles and knob style toes. It all added up to seventy or eighty dollars.

It was such a red-letter day that I even went and got my first barbershop conk. This time it didn't hurt so much, just as Shorty had predicted.

That night, I timed myself to hit Roseland as the thick of the crowd was coming in. In the thronging lobby, I saw some of the real Roxbury hipsters eyeing my zoot, and some fine women were giving me that look. I sauntered up to the men's room for a short drink from the pint in my inside coat-pocket. My replacement was there—a scared, narrow-faced, hungry-looking little brown-skinned fellow just in town from Kansas City. And when he recognized me, he couldn't keep down his admiration and wonder. I told him to "keep cool," that he'd soon catch on to the happenings. Everything felt right when I went into the ballroom.

Hamp's band was working, and that big, waxed floor was packed with people lindy-hopping like crazy. I grabbed some girl I'd never seen, and the next thing I knew we were out there lindying away and grinning at each other. It couldn't have been finer.

I'd been lindying previously only in cramped little apartment living rooms, and now I had room to maneuver. Once I really got myself warmed and loosened up, I was snatching partners from among the hundreds of unattached, free-lancing girls along the sidelines—almost every one of them could really dance—and I just about went wild! Hamp's band wailing. I was whirling girls so fast their skirts were snapping. Black girls, brownskins, high yellows, even a couple of the white girls there. Boosting them over my hips, my shoulders, into the air. Though I wasn't quite sixteen then, I was tall and rawboned and looked like twenty-one; I was also pretty strong for my age. Circling, tap-dancing, I was underneath them when they landed—doing the "flapping eagle," "the kangaroo" and the "split."

After that, I never missed a Roseland lindy-hop as long as I stayed in Boston.

The greatest lindy-dancing partner I had, everything considered, was a girl named Laura. I met her at my next job. When I quit shoeshining, Ella was so happy that she went around asking about a job for me—one she would approve. Just two blocks from her house, the Townsend Drug Store was about to replace its soda fountain clerk, a fellow who was leaving to go off to college.

When Ella told me, I didn't like it. She knew I couldn't stand those Hill characters. But speaking my mind right then would have made Ella mad. I didn't want that to happen, so I put on the white jacket and started serving up sodas, sundaes, splits, shakes and all the rest of that fountain stuff to those fancy-acting Negroes.

Every evening when I got off at eight and came home, Ella would keep saying, "I hope you'll meet some of these nice young people your age here in Roxbury." But those penny-ante squares who came in there putting on their millionaires' airs, the young ones and the old ones both, only annoyed me. People like the sleep-in maid for Beacon Hill white folks who used to come in with her "ooh, my deah" manners and order corn plasters in the Jew's drugstore for black folks. Or the hospital cafeteria-line serving woman sitting there on her day off with a cat fur around her neck, telling the proprietor she was a "dietitian"—both of them knowing she was lying. Even the young ones, my age, whom Ella was always talking about. The soda fountain was one of their hang-outs. They soon had me ready to quit, with their accents so phonied up that if you just heard them and didn't see them, you wouldn't even know they were Negroes. I couldn't wait for eight o'clock to get home to eat out of those soul-food pots of Ella's, then get dressed in my zoot and head for some of my friends' places in town, to lindy-hop and get high, or something, for relief from those Hill clowns.

Before long, I didn't see how I was going to be able to stick it out there eight hours a day; and I nearly didn't. I remember one night, I nearly quit because I had hit the numbers for ten cents—the first time I had ever hit—on one of the sideline bets that I'd made in the drugstore. (Yes, there were several runners on the Hill; even dignified Negroes played the numbers.) I won sixty dollars, and Shorty and I had a ball with it. I wished I had hit for the daily dollar that I played with my town man, paying him by the week. I would surely have quit the drugstore. I could have bought a car.

Anyway, Laura lived in a house that was catercorner across the street from the drugstore. After a while, as soon as I saw her coming in, I'd start making up a banana split. She was a real bug for them, and she came in late every afternoon—after school. I imagine I'd been shoving that ice cream dish under her nose for five or six weeks before somehow it began to sink in that she wasn't like the rest. She was certainly the only Hill girl that came in there and acted in any way friendly and natural.

She always had some book with her, and poring over it, she would make a thirty-minute job of that daily dish of banana split. I began to notice the books she read. They were pretty heavy school stuff—Latin, algebra, things like that. Watching her made me reflect that I hadn't read even a newspaper since leaving Mason.

Laura. I heard her name called by a few of the others who came in when she was there. But I could see they didn't know her too well; they said "hello"—that was about the extent of it. She kept to herself, and she never said more than "Thank you" to me. Nice voice. Soft. Quiet. Never another word. But no airs like the others, no black Bostonese. She was just herself.

I liked that. Before too long, I struck up a conversation. Just what subject I got off on I don't remember, but she readily opened up and began talking, and she was very friendly. I found out that she was a high school junior, an honor student. Her parents had split up when she was a baby, and she had been raised by her grandmother, an old lady on a pension, who was very strict and old-fashioned and religious. Laura had just one close friend, a girl who lived over in Cambridge, whom she had gone to school with. They talked on the telephone every day. Her grandmother scarcely ever let her go to the movies, let alone on dates.

But Laura really liked school. She said she wanted to go on to college. She was keen for algebra, and she planned to major in science. Laura never would have dreamed that she was a year older than I was. I gauged that indirectly. She looked up to me as though she felt I had a world of experience more than she did—which really was the truth. But sometimes, when she had gone, I felt let down, thinking how I had turned away from the books I used to like when I was back in Michigan.

I got to the point where I looked forward to her coming in every day after school. I stopped letting her pay, and gave her extra ice cream. And she wasn't hiding the fact that she liked me.

It wasn't long before she had stopped reading her books when she came in, and would just sit and eat and talk with me. And soon she began trying to get me to talk about myself. I was immediately sorry when I dropped that I had once thought about becoming a lawyer. She didn't want to let me rest about that. "Malcolm, there's no reason you can't pick up right where you are and become a lawyer." She had the idea that my sister Ella would help me as much as she could. And if Ella had ever thought that she could help any member of the Little family put up any kind of professional shingle—as a teacher, a foot-doctor, anything—why, you would have had to tie her down to keep her from taking in washing.

I never mentioned Laura to Shorty. I just knew she never would have understood him, or that crowd. And they wouldn't have understood her. She had never been touched, I'm certain she hadn't, or even had a drink, and she wouldn't even have known what a reefer was.

It was a great surprise to me when one afternoon Laura happened to let drop that she "just loved" lindy-hopping. I asked her how had she been able to go out dancing. She said she'd been introduced to lindy-hopping at a party given by the parents of some Negro friend just accepted by Harvard.

It was just about time to start closing down the soda fountain, and I said that Count Basie was playing the Roseland that weekend, and would she like to go?

Laura's eyes got wide. I thought I'd have to catch her, she was so excited. She said she'd never been there, she'd heard so much about it, she'd imagined what it was like, she'd just give anything—but her grandma would have a fit.

So I said maybe some other time.

But the afternoon before the dance, Laura came in full of excitement. She whispered that she'd never lied to her grandma before, but she had told her she had to attend some school function that evening. If I'd get her home early, she'd meet me—if I'd still take her.

I told her we'd have to go by for me to change clothes at the house. She hesitated, but said okay. Before we left, I telephoned Ella to say I'd be bringing a girl by on the way to the dance. Though I'd never before done anything like it, Ella covered up her surprise.

I laughed to myself a long time afterward about how Ella's mouth flew open when we showed up at the front door—me and a well-bred Hill girl. Laura, when I introduced her, was warm and sincere. And Ella, you would have thought she was closing in on her third husband.

While they sat and talked downstairs, I dressed upstairs in my room. I remember changing my mind about the wild sharkskin gray zoot I had planned to wear, and deciding instead to put on the first one I'd gotten, the blue zoot. I knew I should wear the most conservative thing I had.

They were like old friends when I came back down. Ella had even made tea. Ella's hawk-eye just about raked my zoot right off my back. But I'm sure she was grateful that I'd at least put on the blue one. Knowing Ella, I knew that she had already extracted Laura's entire life story—and all but had the wedding bells around my neck. I grinned all the way to the Roseland in the taxi, because I had showed Ella I could hang out with Hill girls if I wanted to.

Laura's eyes were so big. She said almost none of her acquaintances knew her grandmother, who never went anywhere but to church, so there wasn't much danger of it getting back to her. The only person she had told was her girl friend, who had shared her excitement.

Then, suddenly, we were in the Roseland's jostling lobby. And I was getting waves and smiles and greetings. They shouted "My man!" and "Hey, Red!" and I answered "Daddy-o."

She and I never before had danced together, but that certainly was no problem. Any two people who can lindy at all can lindy together. We just started out there on the floor among a lot of other couples.

It was maybe halfway in the number before I became aware of how she danced.

If you've ever lindy-hopped, you'll know what I'm talking about. With most girls, you kind of work opposite them, circling, side-stepping, leading. Whichever arm you lead with is half-bent out there, your hands are giving that little pull, that little push, touching her waist, her shoulders, her arms. She's in, out, turning, whirling, wherever you guide her. With poor partners, you feel their weight. They're slow and heavy. But with really good partners, all you need is just the push-pull suggestion. They guide nearly effortlessly, even off the floor and into the air, and your little solo maneuver is done on the floor before they land, when they join you, whirling, right in step.

I'd danced with plenty of good partners. But what I became suddenly aware of with Laura was that I'd never before felt so little weight! I'd nearly just *think* a maneuver, and she'd respond.

Anyway, as she danced up, down, under my arm, flinging out, while I felt her out and examined her style, I glimpsed her footwork. I can close my eyes right now and see it, like some blurring ballet—beautiful! And her lightness, like a shadow! My perfect partner, if somebody had asked me, would have been one who handled as lightly as Laura and who would have the strength to last through a long, tough showtime. But I knew that Laura wouldn't begin to be that strong.

In Harlem, years later, a friend of mine called "Sammy The Pimp" taught me something I wish I had known then to look for in Laura's face. It was what Sammy declared was his infallible clue for determining the "unconscious, true personality" of women. Considering all the women he had picked out of crowds and turned into prostitutes, Sammy qualified as an expert. Anyway, he swore that if a woman, any woman, gets really carried away while dancing, what she truly is—at least potentially—will surface and show on her face.

I'm not suggesting that a lady-of-easy-virtue look danced to the surface in Laura—although life did deal her cruel blows, starting with her meeting me. All I am saying is that it may be that if I had been equipped with Sammy's ability, I might have spotted in Laura then some of the subsurface potential, destined to become real, that would have shocked her grandma.

A third of the way or so through the evening the main vocalizing and instrumental stylings would come—and then showtime, when only the greatest lindy-hoppers would stay on the floor, to try and eliminate each other. All the other dancers would form a big "U" with the band at the open end.

The girls who intended to compete would slip over to the sidelines and change from high heels into low white sneakers. In competition, they never could survive in heels. And always among them were four or five unattached girls who would run around trying to hook up with some guy they knew could really lindy.

Now Count Basie turned on the showtime blast, and the other dancers moved off the floor, shifting for good watching positions, and began their hollering for their favorites. "All right now, Red!" they shouted to me, "Go get 'em, Red." And then a free-lancing lindy-girl I'd danced with before, Mamie Bevels, a waitress and a wild dancer ran up to me, with Laura standing right there. I wasn't sure what to do. But Laura started backing away toward the crowd, still looking at me.

The Count's band was wailing. I grabbed Mamie and we started to work. She was a big, rough, strong gal, and she lindied like a bucking horse. I remember the very night that she became known as one of the showtime favorites there at the Roseland. A band was screaming when she kicked off her shoes and got bare-footed, and shouted, and shook herself as if she were in some African jungle frenzy, and then she let loose with some dancing, shouting with every step, until the guy that was out there with her nearly had to fight her to control her. The crowd loved any way-out lindying style that made a colorful show like that. It was how Mamie had become known.

Anyway, I started driving her like a horse, the way she liked. When we came off the floor after the first number, we both were wringing wet with sweat, and people were shouting and pounding our backs.

I remember leaving early with Laura, to get her home in time. She was very quiet. And she didn't have much to say for the next week or so when she came into the drugstore. Even then, I had learned enough about women to know not to pressure them when they're thinking something out; they'll tell you when they're ready.

Every time I saw Ella, even brushing my teeth in the morning, she turned on the third degree. When was I seeing Laura again? Was I going to bring her by again? "What a nice girl she is!" Ella had picked her out for me.

But in that kind of way, I thought hardly anything about the girl. When it came to personal matters, my mind was strictly on getting "sharp" in my zoot as soon as I left work, and racing downtown to hang out with Shorty and the other guys—and with the girls they knew—a million miles away from the stuck-up Hill.

I wasn't even thinking about Laura when she came up to me in the drugstore and asked me to take her to the next Negro dance at the Roseland. Duke Ellington was going to play, and she was beside herself with excitement. I had no way to know what was going to happen.

She asked me to pick her up at her house this time. I didn't want any contact with the old grandma she had described, but I went. Grandma answered the door—an old-fashioned, wrinkled, black woman, with fuzzy gray hair. She just opened the door enough for me to get in, not even saying as much as "Come in, dog." I've faced armed detectives and gangsters less hostile than she was.

I remember the musty living room, full of those old Christ pictures, prayers woven into tapestries, statuettes of the crucifixion, other religious objects on the mantel, shelves, table tops, walls, everywhere.

Since the old lady wasn't speaking to me, I didn't speak to her, either. I completely sympathize with her now, of course. What could she have thought of me in my zoot and conk and orange shoes? She'd have done us all a favor if she had run screaming for the police. If something looked as I did then ever came knocking at my door today, asking to see one of my four daughters, I know I would explode.

When Laura rushed into the room, jerking on her coat, I could see that she was upset and angry and embarrassed. And in the taxi, she started crying. She had hated herself for lying before; she had decided to tell the truth about where she was going, and there had been a screaming battle with grandma. Laura had told the old lady that she was going to start going out when and where she wanted to, or she would quit school and get a job and move out on her own—and her grandma had pitched a fit. Laura just walked out.

When we got to the Roseland, we danced the early part of the evening with each other and with different partners. And finally the Duke kicked off showtime.

I knew, and Laura knew, that she couldn't match the veteran showtime girls, but she told me that she wanted to compete. And the next thing I knew, she was among those girls over on the sidelines changing into sneakers. I shook my head when a couple of the free-lancing girls ran up to me.

As always, the crowd clapped and shouted in time with the blasting band. "Go, Red, go!" Partly it was my reputation, and partly Laura's ballet style of dancing that helped to turn the spotlight—and the crowd's attention—to us. They never had seen the feather-lightness that she gave to lindying, a completely fresh style—and they were connoisseurs of styles. I turned up the steam, Laura's feet were flying; I had her in the air, down, sideways, around; backwards, up again, down, whirling. . . .

The spotlight was working mostly just us. I caught glimpses of the four or five other couples, the girls jungle-strong, animal-like, bucking and charging. But little Laura inspired me to drive to new heights. Her hair was all over her face, it was running sweat, and I couldn't believe her strength. The crowd was shouting and stomping. A new favorite was being discovered; there was a wall of noise around us. I felt her weakening, she was lindying like a fighter out on her feet, and we stumbled off to the sidelines. The band was still blasting. I had to half-carry her; she was gasping for air. Some of the men in the band applauded. And even Duke Ellington half raised up from his piano stool and bowed.

If a showtime crowd liked your performance, when you came off you were mobbed, mauled, grasped, and pummeled like the team that's just taken the series. One bunch of the crowd swarmed Laura; they had her clear up off her feet. And I was being pounded on the back . . . when I caught this fine blonde's eyes. . . . This one I'd never seen among the white girls who came to the Roseland black dances. She was eyeing me levelly.

Now at that time, in Roxbury, in any black ghetto in America, to have a white woman who wasn't a known, common whore was—for the average black man, at least—a status symbol of the first order. And this one, standing there, eyeing me, was almost too fine to believe. Shoulder-length hair, well built, and her clothes had cost somebody plenty.

It's shameful to admit, but I had just about forgotten Laura when she got loose from the mob and rushed up, big-eyed—and stopped. I guess she saw what there was to see in that girl's face—and mine—as we moved out to dance.

I'm going to call her Sophia.

She didn't dance well, at least not by Negro standards. But who cared? I could feel the staring eyes of other couples around us. We talked. I told her she was a good dancer, and asked her where she'd learned. I was trying to find out why she was there. Most white women came to the black dances for reasons I know, but you seldom saw her kind around there.

She had vague answers for everything. But in the space of that dance, we agreed that I would get Laura home early and rush back in a taxicab. And then she asked if I'd like to go for a drive later. I felt very lucky.

Laura was home and I was back at the Roseland in an hour flat. Sophia was waiting outside.

About five blocks down, she had a low convertible. She knew where she was going. Beyond Boston, she pulled off into a side road, and then off that into a deserted lane. And turned off everything but the radio.

For the next several months, Sophia would pick me up downtown, and I'd take her to dances, and to the bars around Roxbury. We drove all over. Sometimes it would be nearly daylight when she let me out in front of Ella's.

I paraded her. The Negro men loved her. And she just seemed to love all Negroes. Two or three nights a week, we would go out together. Sophia admitted that she also had dates with white fellows, "just for the looks of things," she said. She swore that a white man couldn't interest her.

I wondered for a long time, but I never did find out why she approached me so boldly that very first night. I always thought it was because of some earlier experience with another Negro, but I never asked, and she never said. Never ask a woman about other men. Either she'll tell you a lie, and you still won't know, or if she tells you the truth, you might not have wanted to hear it in the first place.

Anyway, she seemed entranced with me. I began to see less of Shorty. When I did see him and the gang, he would gibe, "Man, I had to comb the burrs out of my homeboy's head, and now he's got a Beacon Hill chick." But truly, because it was known that Shorty had "schooled" me, my having Sophia gave Shorty status. When I introduced her to him, she hugged him like a sister, and it just about finished Shorty off. His best had been white prostitutes and a few of those poor specimens that worked around in the mills and had "discovered" Negroes.

It was when I began to be seen around town with Sophia that I really began to mature into some real status in black downtown Roxbury. Up to then I had been just another among all of the conked and zooted youngsters. But now, with the best-looking white woman who ever walked in those bars and clubs, and with her giving me the money I spent, too, even the big, important black hustlers and "smart boys"—the club managers, name gamblers, numbers bankers, and others— were clapping me on the back, setting us up to drinks at special tables, and calling me "Red." Of course I knew their reason like I knew my own name: they wanted to steal my fine white woman away from me.

In the ghetto, as in suburbia, its the same status struggle to stand out in some envied way from the rest. At sixteen, I didn't have the money to buy a Cadillac, but she had her own fine "rubber," as we called a car in those days. And I had her, which was even better.

Laura never again came to the drugstore as long as I continued to work there. The next time I saw her, she was a wreck of a woman, notorious around black Roxbury, in and out of jail. She had finished high school, but by then she was already going the wrong way. Defying her grandmother, she had started going out late and drinking liquor. This led to dope, and that to selling herself to men. Learning to hate the men who bought her, she also became a Lesbian. One of the shames I have carried for years is that I blame myself for all of this. To have treated her as I did for a white woman made the blow doubly heavy. The only excuse I can offer is that like so many of my black brothers today, I was just deaf, dumb and blind.

In any case, it wasn't long after I met Sophia that Ella found out about it, and watching from the windows one early morning, saw me getting out of Sophia's car. Not surprisingly, Ella began treating me like a viper.

About then, Shorty's cousin finally moved in with the woman he was so crazy about, and Sophia financed me to take over half of the apartment with Shorty—and I quit the drugstore and soon found a new job.

I became a bus boy at the Parker House in Boston. I wore a starched white jacket out in the dining room, where the waiters would put the customers' dirty plates and silver on big aluminum trays which I would take back to the kitchen's dishwashers.

A few weeks later, one Sunday morning, I ran in to work expecting to get fired, I was so late. But the whole kitchen crew was too excited and upset to notice: Japanese planes had just bombed a place called Pearl Harbor.

What's Going On

Marvin Gaye

The song is by Motown recording artist Marvin Gaye. The lyrics call for love as a way to conquer hate and bring about understanding, leading to freedom from pain, including the pain caused by the slavery of racism.

Mother, mother
There's too many of you crying
Brother, brother, brother
There's far too many of you dying.
You know we've got to find a way   5
To bring some lovin' here today—Hey

Father, father, we don't need to escalate
You see, war is not the answer
For only love can conquer hate
You know we've got to find a way   10
To bring some lovin' here today.

Chorus 1:

Picket lines and picket signs
Don't punish me with brutality
Talk to me, so you can see
Oh, what's going on   15
What's going on
Yeah, what's going on
Ah, what's going on
Ahhh . . .
Right on brother   20
Right on baby
Right on

Mother, mother, everybody thinks we're wrong
Ah but who are they to judge us
Simply 'cos our hair is long   25
Ah you know we've got to find a way
To bring some understanding here today—Ohh

Chorus 2:

Picket lines and picket signs
Don't punish me with brutality

Come on talk to me 30
So you can see
What's going on
Yeah, what's going on
Tell me what's going on
I'll tell you what's going on—Uooo 35
Right on baby
Right on

Inner City Blues (Make Me Wanna Holler)

Marvin Gaye and James Nyx

Dah, dah, dah, dah
dah, dah, dah, dah, dah, dah, dah
Dah, dah, dah, dah
Dah, dah, dah, dah, dah, dah, dah
Dah, dah, dah 5
Rockets, moon shots
Spend it on the have nots
Money, we make it
Fore we see it you take it
Oh, make you wanna holler 10
The way they do my life
Make me wanna holler
The way they do my life
This ain't livin', This ain't livin'
No, no baby, this ain't livin' 15
No, no, no
Inflation no chance
To increase finance
Bills pile up sky high
Send that boy off to die 20
Oh, make me wanna holler
The way they do my life
Make me wanna holler
The way they do my life
Dah, dah, dah 25
Dah, dah, dah
Hang ups, let downs
Bad breaks, set backs
Natural fact is
I can't pay my taxes 30

Oh, make me wanna holler
And throw up both my hands
Yea, it makes me wanna holler
And throw up both my hands
Crime is increasing   35
Trigger happy policing
Panic is spreading
God knows where we're heading
Oh, make me wanna holler
They don't understand   40
Dah, dah, dah
Dah, dah, dah
Dah, dah, dah

Mother, mother
Everybody thinks we're wrong   45
Who are they to judge us
Simply cause we wear our hair long . . .

❊ MARTIN LUTHER KING, JR. (1929–1968)

Martin Luther King, Jr,. was perhaps the most influential African American leader of the civil rights movement of the 1960s. He used his speeches and essays to reveal the truth of racism and to advocate racial equality. King promoted a stance of nonviolent resistance. He believed in the Christian principles of love and forgiveness. He wrote a book about his role in the Montgomery, Alabama, boycott and desegregation attempts: Stride Toward Freedom: The Montgomery Story *(1958). King was assassinated on the balcony of a motel in Memphis, Tennessee; he was in Memphis to support a sanitation workers' strike.*

"Letter from Birmingham Jail" (1963) and "I Have a Dream" (1963) are two of King's best-known documents. He wrote the letter while imprisoned for participating in nonviolent demonstrations. In it he explains why he and others had the right to protest without violence. "I Have a Dream" is the most famous speech of the civil rights movement. The speech makes a plea to all American citizens to eliminate discrimination and prejudice, especially that based on race. In 1964, King was Time *magazine's first black "Man of the Year" and he was the twelfth American, the third black, and the youngest person (at age thirty-five) to win the Nobel Peace Prize. Martin Luther King Day, a national holiday since the mid-1980s, is celebrated to varying degrees across the nation.*

Letter from Birmingham Jail (1963)

April 16, 1963

My Dear Fellow Clergymen:[1]

While confined here in the Birmingham city jail, I came across your recent statement calling my present activities "unwise and untimely." Seldom do I pause to answer criticism of my work and ideas. If I sought to answer all the criticisms that cross my desk, my secretaries would have little time for anything other than such correspondence in the course of the day, and I would have no time for constructive work. But since I feel that you are men of genuine good will and that your criticisms are sincerely set forth, I want to try to answer your statement in what I hope will be patient and reasonable terms.

I think I should indicate why I am here in Birmingham, since you have been influenced by the view which argues against "outsiders coming in." I have the honor of serving as president of the Southern Christian Leadership Conference, an organization operating in every southern state, with headquarters in Atlanta, Georgia. We have some eighty-five affiliated organizations across the South, and one of them is the Alabama Christian Movement for Human Rights. Frequently we share staff, educational, and financial resources with our affiliates. Several months ago the affiliate here in Birmingham asked us to be on call to engage in a nonviolent direct-action program if such were deemed necessary. We readily consented, and when the hour came we lived up to our promise. So I, along with several members of my staff, am here because I was invited here. I am here because I have organizational ties here.

But more basically, I am in Birmingham because injustice is here. Just as the prophets of the eighth century B.C. left their villages and carried their "thus saith the Lord" far beyond the boundaries of their home towns, and just as the Apostle Paul left his village of Tarsus and carried the gospel of Jesus Christ to the far corners of the Greco-Roman world, so am I compelled to carry the gospel of freedom beyond my own home town. Like Paul, I must constantly respond to the Macedonian call for aid.

Moreover, I am cognizant of the interrelatedness of all communities and states. I cannot sit idly by in Atlanta and not be concerned about what happens in Birmingham. Injustice anywhere is a threat to justice everywhere. We are caught in an inescapable network of mutuality, tied in a single garment of destiny. Whatever affects one directly, affects all indirectly. Never again can we afford to live with the narrow, provincial, "outside agitator" idea. Anyone who lives inside the United States can never be considered an outsider anywhere within its bounds.

---

[1] This response to a published statement by eight fellow clergymen from Alabama (Bishop C. C. J. Carpenter, Bishop Joseph A. Durick, Rabbi Hilton L. Grafman, Bishop Paul Hardin, Bishop Holan B. Harmon, the Reverend George M. Murray, the Reverend Edward V. Ramage and the Reverend Earl Stallings) was composed under somewhat constricting circumstances. Begun on the margins of the newspaper in which the statement appeared while I was in jail, the letter continued on scraps of writing paper supplied by a friendly Negro trusty, and concluded on a pad my attorneys were eventually permitted to leave me. Although the text remains in substance unaltered, I have indulged in the author's prerogative of polishing it for publication. [King's note]

You deplore the demonstrations taking place in Birmingham. But your statement, I am sorry to say, fails to express a similar concern for the conditions that brought about the demonstrations. I am sure that none of you would want to rest content with the superficial kind of social analysis that deals merely with effects and does not grapple with underlying causes. It is unfortunate that demonstrations are taking place in Birmingham, but it is even more unfortunate that the city's white power structure left the Negro community with no alternative.

In any nonviolent campaign there are four basic steps: collection of the facts to determine whether injustices exist; negotiation; self-purification; and direct action. We have gone through all these steps in Birmingham. There can be no gainsaying the fact that racial injustice engulfs this community. Birmingham is probably the most thoroughly segregated city in the United States. Its ugly record of brutality is widely known. Negroes have experienced grossly unjust treatment in the courts. There have been more unsolved bombings of Negro homes and churches in Birmingham than in any other city in the nation. These are the hard brutal facts of the case. On the basis of these conditions, Negro leaders sought to negotiate with the city fathers. But the latter consistently refused to engage in good-faith negotiation.

Then, last September, came the opportunity to talk with leaders of Birmingham's economic community. In the course of the negotiations, certain promises were made by the merchants—for example, to remove the stores' humiliating racial signs. On the basis of these promises, the Reverend Fred Shuttlesworth and the leaders of the Alabama Christian Movement for Human Rights agreed to a moratorium on all demonstrations. As the weeks and months went by, we realized that we were the victims of a broken promise. A few signs, briefly removed, returned; the others remained.

As in so many past experiences, our hopes had been blasted, and the shadow of deep disappointment settled upon us. We had no alternative except to prepare for direct action, whereby we would present our very bodies as a means of laying our case before the conscience of the local and the national community. Mindful of the difficulties involved, we decided to undertake a process of self-purification. We began a series of workshops on nonviolence, and we repeatedly asked ourselves: "Are you able to accept blows without retaliating?" "Are you able to endure the ordeal of jail?" We decided to schedule our direct-action program for the Easter season, realizing that except for Christmas, this is the main shopping period of the year. Knowing that a strong economic-withdrawal program would be the by-product of direct action, we felt that this would be the best time to bring pressure to bear on the merchants for the needed change.

Then it occurred to us that Birmingham's mayoral election was coming up in March, and we speedily decided to postpone action until after election day. When we discovered that the Commissioner of Public Safety, Eugene "Bull" Connor, had piled up enough votes to be in the run-off, we decided again to postpone action until the day after the run-off so that the demonstrations could not be used to cloud the issues. Like many others, we waited to see Mr. Connor defeated, and to this end we endured postponement after postponement. Having aided in this community need, we felt that our direct-action program could be delayed no longer.

You may well ask, "Why direct action? Why sit-ins, marches, and so forth? Isn't negotiation a better path?" You are quite right in calling for negotiation. Indeed, this is the very purpose of direct action. Nonviolent direct action seeks to create such a crisis and foster such a tension that a community which has constantly refused to negotiate is forced to confront the issue. It seeks so to dramatize the issue that it can no longer be ignored. My citing the creation of tension as part of the work of the nonviolent resister may sound rather shocking. But I must confess that I am not afraid of the word "tension." I have earnestly opposed violent tension, but there is a type of constructive, nonviolent tension which is necessary for growth. Just as Socrates felt that it was necessary to create a tension in the mind so that individuals could rise from the bondage of myths and half truths to the unfettered realm of creative analysis and objective appraisal, so must we see the need for nonviolent gadflies to create the kind of tension in society that will help men rise from the dark depths of prejudice and racism to the majestic heights of understanding and brotherhood.

The purpose of our direct-action program is to create a situation so crisis-packed that it will inevitably open the door to negotiation. I therefore concur with you in your call for negotiation. Too long has our beloved Southland been bogged down in a tragic effort to live in monologue rather than dialogue.

One of the basic points in your statement is that the action that I and my associates have taken in Birmingham is untimely. Some have asked: "Why didn't you give the new city administration time to act?" The only answer that I can give to this query is that the new Birmingham administration must be prodded about as much as the outgoing one, before it will act. We are sadly mistaken if we feel that the election of Albert Boutwell as mayor will bring the millennium to Birmingham. While Mr. Boutwell is a much more gentle person than Mr. Connor, they are both segregationists, dedicated to maintenance of the status quo. I have hoped that Mr. Boutwell will be reasonable enough to see the futility of massive resistance to desegregation. But he will not see this without pressure from devotees of civil rights. My friends, I must say to you that we have not made a single gain in civil rights without determined legal and nonviolent pressure. Lamentably, it is an historical fact that privileged groups seldom give up their privileges voluntarily. Individuals may see the moral light and voluntarily give up their unjust posture; but, as Reinhold Niebuhr has reminded us, groups tend to be more immoral than individuals.

We know through painful experience that freedom is never voluntarily given by the oppressor; it must be demanded by the oppressed. Frankly, I have yet to engage in a direct-action campaign that was "well timed" in the view of those who have not suffered unduly from the disease of segregation. For years now I have heard the word "Wait!" It rings in the ear of every Negro with piercing familiarity. This "Wait" has almost always meant "Never." We must come to see, with one of our distinguished jurists, that "justice too long delayed is justice denied."

We have waited for more than 340 years for our constitutional and God-given rights. The nations of Asia and Africa are moving with jetlike speed toward gaining political independence, but we still creep at horse-and-buggy pace toward gaining a cup of coffee at a lunch counter. Perhaps it is easy for those who have never felt the stinging darts of segregation to say, "Wait." But when you have seen vicious mobs lynch your mothers and fathers at will and drown your sisters and brothers at whim; when you have seen hate-filled policemen curse, kick, and even kill your black brothers and sisters; when you see the vast majority of your twenty million Negro brothers smothering in an airtight cage of poverty in the midst of an affluent society; when you suddenly find your tongue twisted and your speech stammering as you seek to explain to your six-year-old daughter why she can't go to the public amusement park that has just been advertised on television, and see tears welling up in her eyes when she is told that Funtown is closed to colored children, and see ominous clouds of inferiority beginning to form in her little mental sky, and see her beginning to distort her personality by developing an unconscious bitterness toward white people; when you have to concoct an answer for a five-year-old son who is asking, "Daddy, why do white people treat colored people so mean?"; when you take a cross-country drive and find it necessary to sleep night after night in the uncomfortable corners of your automobile because no motel will accept you; when you are humiliated day in and day out by nagging signs reading "white" and "colored"; when your first name becomes "nigger," your middle name becomes "boy" (however old you are) and your last name becomes "John," and your wife and mother are never given the respected title "Mrs."; when you are harried by day and haunted by night by the fact that you are a Negro, living constantly at tiptoe stance, never quite knowing what to expect next, and are plagued with inner fears and outer resentments; when you are forever fighting a degenerating sense of "nobodi-ness"—then you will understand why we find it difficult to wait. There comes a time when the cup of endurance runs over, and men are no longer willing to be plunged into the abyss of despair. I hope, sirs, you can understand our legitimate and unavoidable impatience.

You express a great deal of anxiety over our willingness to break laws. This is certainly a legitimate concern. Since we so diligently urge people to obey the Supreme Court's decision of 1954 outlawing segregation in the public schools, at first glance it may seem rather paradoxical for us consciously to break laws. One may well ask: "How can you advocate breaking some laws and obeying others?" The answer lies in the fact that there are two types of laws: just and unjust. I would be the first to advocate obeying just laws. One has not only a legal but a moral responsibility to obey just laws. Conversely, one has a moral responsibility to disobey unjust laws. I would agree with St. Augustine that "an unjust law is no law at all."

Now, what is the difference between the two? How does one determine whether a law is just or unjust? A just law is a man-made code that squares with the moral law or the law of God. An unjust law is a code that is out of harmony with the moral law. To put it in the terms of St. Thomas Aquinas: An unjust law is a human law that is not rooted in eternal law and natural law. Any law that uplifts human personality is just. Any law that degrades human personality is unjust. All segregation statutes are unjust because segregation distorts the soul and damages the personality. It gives the segregator a false sense of superiority and the segregated a false sense of inferiority. Segregation, to use the terminology of the Jewish philosopher Martin Buber, substitutes an "I-it" relationship for an "I-thou" relationship and ends up relegating persons to the status of things. Hence segregation is not only politically, economically, and sociologically unsound, it is morally wrong and sinful. Paul Tillich has said that sin is separation. Is not segregation an existential expression of man's tragic separation, his awful estrangement, his terrible sinfulness? Thus it is that I can urge men to obey the 1954 decision of the Supreme Court, for it is morally right; and I can urge them to disobey segregation ordinances, for they are morally wrong.

Let us consider a more concrete example of just and unjust laws. An unjust law is a code that a numerical or power majority group compels a minority group to obey but does not make binding on itself. This is *difference* made legal. By the same token, a just law is a code that a majority compels a minority to follow and that it is willing to follow itself. This is *sameness* made legal.

Let me give another explanation. A law is unjust if it is inflicted on a minority that, as a result of being denied the right to vote, had no part in enacting or devising the law. Who can say that the legislature of Alabama which set up that state's segregation laws was democratically elected? Throughout Alabama all sorts of devious methods are used to prevent Negroes from becoming registered voters, and there are some counties in which, even though Negroes constitute a majority of the population, not a single Negro is registered. Can any law enacted under such circumstances be considered democratically structured?

Sometimes a law is just on its face and unjust in its application. For instance, I have been arrested on a charge of parading without a permit. Now, there is nothing wrong in having an ordinance which requires a permit for a parade. But such an ordinance becomes unjust when it is used to maintain segregation and to deny citizens the First Amendment privilege of peaceful assembly and protest.

I hope you are able to see the distinction I am trying to point out. In no sense do I advocate evading or defying the law, as would the rabid segregationist. That would lead to anarchy. One who breaks an unjust law must do so openly, lovingly, and with a willingness to accept the penalty. I submit that an individual who breaks a law that conscience tells him is unjust, and who willingly accepts the penalty of imprisonment in order to arouse the conscience of the community over its injustice, is in reality expressing the highest respect for law.

Of course, there is nothing new about this kind of civil disobedience. It was evidenced sublimely in the refusal of Shadrach, Meshach, and Abednego to obey the laws of Nebuchadnezzar, on the ground that a higher moral law was at stake. It was practiced superbly by the early Christians, who were willing to face hungry lions and the excruciating pain of chopping blocks rather than submit to certain unjust laws of the Roman Empire. To a degree, academic freedom is a reality today because Socrates practiced civil disobedience. In our own nation, the Boston Tea Party represented a massive act of civil disobedience.

We should never forget that everything Adolf Hitler did in Germany was "legal" and everything the Hungarian freedom fighters did in Hungary was "illegal." It was "illegal" to aid and comfort a Jew in Hitler's Germany. Even so, I am sure that, had I lived in Germany at the time, I would have aided and comforted my Jewish brothers. If today I lived in a Communist country where certain principles dear to the Christian faith are suppressed, I would openly advocate disobeying that country's antireligious laws.

I must make two honest confessions to you, my Christian and Jewish brothers. First, I must confess that over the past few years I have been gravely disappointed with the white moderate. I have almost reached the regrettable conclusion that the Negro's great stumbling block in his stride toward freedom is not the White Citizen's Counciler or the Ku Klux Klanner, but the white moderate, who is more devoted to "order" than to justice; who prefers a negative peace which is the absence of tension to a positive peace which is the presence of justice; who constantly says, "I agree with you in the goal you seek, but I cannot agree with your methods of direct action"; who paternalistically believes he can set the timetable for another man's freedom; who lives by a mythical concept of time and who constantly advises the Negro to wait for a "more convenient season." Shallow understanding from people of good will is more frustrating than absolute misunderstanding from people of ill will. Lukewarm acceptance is much more bewildering than outright rejection.

I had hoped that the white moderate would understand that law and order exist for the purpose of establishing justice and that when they fail in this purpose they become the dangerously structured dams that block the flow of social progress. I had hoped that the white moderate would understand that the present tension in the South is a necessary phase of the transition from an obnoxious negative peace, in which the Negro passively accepted his unjust plight, to a substantive and positive peace, in which all men will respect the dignity and worth of human personality. Actually, we who engage in nonviolent direct action are not the creators of tension. We merely bring to the surface the hidden tension that is already alive. We bring it out in the open, where it can be seen and dealt with. Like a boil that can never be cured so long as it is covered up but must be opened with all its ugliness to the natural medicines of air and light, injustice must be exposed, with all the tension its exposure creates, to the light of human conscience and the air of national opinion, before it can be cured.

In your statement you assert that our actions, even though peaceful, must be condemned because they precipitate violence. But is this a logical assertion? Isn't this like condemning a robbed man because his possession of money precipitated the evil act of robbery? Isn't this like condemning Socrates because his unswerving commitment to truth and his philosophical inquiries precipitated the act by the misguided populace in which they made him drink hemlock? Isn't this like condemning Jesus because his unique God-consciousness and never-ceasing devotion to God's will precipitated the evil act of crucifixion? We must come to see that, as the federal courts have consistently affirmed, it is wrong to urge an individual to cease his efforts to gain his basic constitutional rights because the quest may precipitate violence. Society must protect the robbed and punish the robber.

I had also hoped that the white moderate would reject the myth concerning time in relation to the struggle for freedom. I have just received a letter from a white brother in Texas. He writes: "All Christians know that the colored people will receive equal rights eventually, but it is possible that you are in too great a religious hurry. It had taken Christianity almost two thousand years to accomplish what it has. The teachings of Christ take time to come to earth." Such an attitude stems from a tragic misconception of time, from the strangely irrational notion that there is something in the very flow of time that will inevitably cure all ills. Actually, time itself is neutral; it can be used either destructively or constructively. More and more I feel that the people of ill will have used time much more effectively than have the people of good will. We will have to repent in this generation not merely for the hateful words and actions of the bad people, but for the appalling silence of the good people. Human progress never rolls in on wheels of inevitability; it comes through the tireless efforts of men willing to be co-workers with God, and without this hard work, time itself becomes an ally of the forces of social stagnation. We must use time creatively, in the knowledge that the time is always ripe to do right. Now is the time to make real the promise of democracy and transform our pending national elegy into a creative psalm of brotherhood. Now is the time to lift our national policy from the quicksand of racial injustice to the solid rock of human dignity.

You speak of our activity in Birmingham as extreme. At first I was rather disappointed that fellow clergymen would see my nonviolent efforts as those of an extremist. I began thinking about the fact that I stand in the middle of two opposing forces in the Negro community. One is a force of complacency, made up in part of Negroes who, as a result of long years of oppression, are so drained of self-respect and a sense of "somebodiness" that they have adjusted to segregation; and in part of a few middle-class Negroes who, because of a degree of academic and economic security and because in some ways they profit by segregation, have become insensitive to the problems of the masses. The other force is one of bitterness and hatred, and it comes perilously close to advocating violence. It is expressed in the various black nationalist groups that are springing up across the nation, the largest and best known being Elijah Muhammad's Muslim movement. Nourished by the Negro's frustration over the continued existence of racial discrimination, this movement is made up of people who have lost faith in America, who have absolutely repudiated Christianity, and who have concluded that the white man is an incorrigible "devil."

I have tried to stand between these two forces, saying that we need emulate neither the "do-nothingism" of the complacent nor the hatred and despair of the black nationalist. For there is the more excellent way of love and nonviolent protest. I am grateful to God that, through the influence of the Negro church, the way of nonviolence became an integral part of our struggle.

If this philosophy had not emerged, by now many streets of the South would, I am convinced, be flowing with blood. And I am further convinced that if our white brothers dismiss as "rabble-rousers" and "outside agitators" those of us who employ nonviolent direct action, and if they refuse to support our nonviolent efforts, millions of Negroes will, out of frustration and despair, seek solace and security in black nationalist ideologies—a development that would inevitably lead to a frightening racial nightmare.

Oppressed people cannot remain oppressed forever. The yearning for freedom eventually manifests itself, and that is what has happened to the American Negro. Something within has reminded him of his birthright of freedom, and something without has reminded him that it can be gained. Consciously or unconsciously, he has been caught up by the *Zeitgeist*, and with his black brothers of Africa and his brown and yellow brothers of Asia, South America, and the Caribbean, the United States Negro is moving with a sense of great urgency toward the promised land of racial justice. If one recognizes this vital urge that has engulfed the Negro community, one should readily understand why public demonstrations are taking place. The Negro has many pent-up resentments and latent frustrations, and he must release them. So let him march; let him make prayer pilgrimages to the city hall; let him go on freedom rides—and try to understand why he must do so. If his repressed emotions are not released in nonviolent ways, they will seek expression through violence; this is not a threat but a fact of history. So I have not said to my people, "Get rid of your discontent." Rather, I have tried to say that this normal and healthy discontent can be channeled into the creative outlet of nonviolent direct action. And now this approach is being termed extremist.

But though I was initially disappointed at being categorized as an extremist, as I continued to think about the matter I gradually gained a measure of satisfaction from the label. Was not Jesus an extremist for love: "Love your enemies, bless them that curse you, do good to them that hate you, and pray for them which despitefully use you, and persecute you." Was not Amos an extremist for justice: "Let justice roll down like waters and righteousness like an ever-flowing stream." Was not Paul an extremist for the Christian gospel: "I bear in my body the marks of the Lord Jesus." Was not Martin Luther an extremist: "Here I stand; I cannot do otherwise, so help me God." And John Bunyan: "I will stay in jail to the end of my days before I make a butchery of my conscience." And Abraham Lincoln: "This nation cannot survive half slave and half free." And Thomas Jefferson: "We hold these truths to be self-evident, that all men are created equal. . . ." So the question is not whether we will be extremists, but what kind of extremists we will be. Will we be extremists for hate or for love? Will we be extremists for the preservation of injustice or for the extension of justice? In that dramatic scene on Calvary's hill three men were crucified. We must never forget that all three were crucified for the same crime—the crime of extremism. Two were extremists for immorality, and thus fell below their environment. The other, Jesus Christ, was an extremist for love, truth, and goodness, and thereby rose above his environment. Perhaps the South, the nation, and the world are in dire need of creative extremists.

I had hoped that the white moderate would see this need. Perhaps I was too optimistic; perhaps I expected too much. I suppose I should have realized that few members of the oppressor race can understand the deep groans and passionate yearnings of the oppressed race, and still fewer have the vision to see that injustice must be rooted out by strong, persistent, and determined action. I am thankful, however, that some of our white brothers in the South have grasped the meaning of this social revolution and committed themselves to it. They are still all too few in quantity, but they are big in quality. Some—such as Ralph McGill, Lillian Smith, Harry Golden, James McBride Dabbs, Ann Braden, and Sarah Patton Boyle—have written about our struggle in eloquent and prophetic terms. Others have marched with us down nameless streets of the South. They have languished in filthy, roach-infested jails, suffering the abuse and brutality of policemen who view them as "dirty nigger-lovers." Unlike so many of their moderate brothers and sisters, they have recognized the urgency of the moment and sensed the need for powerful "action" antidotes to combat the disease of segregation.

Let me take note of my other major disappointment. I have been so greatly disappointed with the white church and its leadership. Of course, there are some notable exceptions. I am not unmindful of the fact that each of you has taken some significant stands on this issue. I commend you, Reverend Stallings, for your Christian stand on this past Sunday, in welcoming Negroes to your worship service on a nonsegregated basis. I commend the Catholic leaders of this state for integrating Spring Hill College several years ago.

But despite these notable exceptions, I must honestly reiterate that I have been disappointed with the church. I do not say this as one of those negative critics who can always find something wrong with the church. I say this as a minister of the gospel, who loves the church; who was nurtured in its bosom; who has been sustained by its spiritual blessings and who will remain true to it as long as the cord of life shall lengthen.

When I was suddenly catapulted into the leadership of the bus protest in Montgomery, Alabama, a few years ago, I felt we would be supported by the white church. I felt that the white ministers, priests, and rabbis of the South would be among our strongest allies. Instead, some have been outright opponents, refusing to understand the freedom movement and misrepresenting its leaders; all too many others have been more cautious than courageous and have remained silent behind the anesthetizing security of stained-glass windows.

In spite of my shattered dreams, I came to Birmingham with the hope that the white religious leadership of this community would see the justice of our cause and, with deep moral concern, would serve as the channel through which our just grievances could reach the power structure. I had hoped that each of you would understand. But again I have been disappointed. . . .

There was a time when the church was very powerful—in the time when the early Christians rejoiced at being deemed worthy to suffer for what they believed. In those days the church was not merely a thermometer that recorded the ideas and principles of popular opinion; it was a thermostat that transformed the mores of society. Whenever the early Christians entered a town, the people in power became disturbed and immediately sought to convict the Christians for being "disturbers of the peace" and "outside agitators." But the Christians pressed on, in the conviction that they were "a colony of heaven," called to obey God rather than man. Small in number, they were big in commitment. They were too God intoxicated to be "astronomically intimidated." By their effort and example they brought an end to such ancient evils as infanticide and gladiatorial contests.

Things are different now. So often the contemporary church is a weak, ineffectual voice with an uncertain sound. So often it is an arch-defender of the status quo. Far from being disturbed by the presence of the church, the power structure of the average community is consoled by the church's silent—and often even vocal—sanction of things as they are.

But the judgment of God is upon the church as never before. If today's church does not recapture the sacrificial spirit of the early church, it will lose its authenticity, forfeit the loyalty of millions, and be dismissed as an irrelevant social club with no meaning for the twentieth century. Every day I meet young people whose disappointment with the church has turned into outright disgust.

Perhaps I have once again been too optimistic. Is organized religion too inextricably bound to the status quo to save our nation and the world? Perhaps I must turn my faith to the inner spiritual church, the church within the church, as the true *ekklesia* and the hope of the world. But again I am thankful to God that some noble souls from the ranks of organized religion have broken loose from the paralyzing chains of conformity and joined us as active partners in the struggle for freedom. They have left their secure congregations and walked the streets of Albany, Georgia, with us. They have gone down the highways of the South on torturous rides for freedom. Yes, they have gone to jail with us. Some have been dismissed from their churches, have lost the support of their bishops and fellow ministers. But they have acted in the faith that right defeated is stronger than evil triumphant. Their witness has been the spiritual salt that has preserved the true meaning of the gospel in these troubled times. They have carved a tunnel of hope through the dark mountain of disappointment.

I hope the church as a whole will meet the challenge of this decisive hour. But even if the church does not come to the aid of justice, I have no despair about the future. I have no fear about the outcome of our struggle in Birmingham, even if our motives are at present misunderstood. We will reach the goal of freedom in Birmingham and all over the nation, because the goal of America is freedom. Abused and scorned though we may be, our destiny is tied up with America's destiny. Before the pilgrims landed at Plymouth, we were here. Before the pen of Jefferson etched the majestic words of the Declaration of Independence across the pages of history, we were here. For more than two centuries our forebears labored in this country without wages; they made cotton king; they built the homes of their masters while suffering gross injustice and shameful humiliation— and yet out of a bottomless vitality they continued to thrive and develop. If the inexpressible cruelties of slavery could not stop us, the opposition we now face will surely fail. We will win our freedom because the sacred heritage of our nation and the eternal will of God are embodied in our echoing demands.

Before closing I feel impelled to mention one other point in your statement that has troubled me profoundly. You warmly commended the Birmingham police force for keeping "order" and "preventing violence." I doubt that you would have so warmly commended the police force if you had seen its dogs sinking their teeth into unarmed, nonviolent Negroes. I doubt that you would so quickly commend the policemen if you were to observe their ugly and inhumane treatment of Negroes here in the city jail; if you were to watch them push and curse old Negro women and young Negro girls; if you were to see them slap and kick old Negro men and young boys; if you were to observe them, as they did on two occasions, refuse to give us food because we wanted to sing our grace together. I cannot join you in your praise of the Birmingham police department.

It is true that the police have exercised a degree of discipline in handling the demonstrators. In this sense they have conducted themselves rather "nonviolently" in public. But for what purpose? To preserve the evil system of segregation. Over the past few years I have consistently preached that nonviolence demands that the means we use must be as pure as the ends we seek. I have tried to make clear that it is wrong to use immoral means to attain moral ends. But now I must affirm that it is just as wrong, or perhaps even more so, to use moral means to preserve immoral ends. Perhaps Mr. Connor and his policemen have been rather nonviolent in public, as was Chief Pritchett in Albany, Georgia, but they have used the moral means of nonviolence to maintain the immoral end of racial injustice. As T. S. Eliot has said, "The last temptation is the greatest treason: To do the right deed for the wrong reason."

I wish you had commended the Negro sit-inners and demonstrators of Birmingham for their sublime courage, their willingness to suffer, and their amazing discipline in the midst of great provocation. One day the South will recognize its real heroes. They will be the James Merediths, with the noble sense of purpose that enables them to face jeering and hostile mobs, and with the agonizing loneliness that characterizes the life of the pioneer. They will be old, oppressed, battered Negro women, symbolized in a seventy-two-year-old woman in Montgomery, Alabama, who rose up with a sense of dignity and with her people decided not to ride segregated buses, and who responded with ungrammatical profundity to one who inquired about her weariness: "My feets is tired, but my soul is at rest." They will be the young high school and college students, the young ministers of the gospel and a host of their elders, courageously and nonviolently sitting in at lunch counters and willingly going to jail for conscience' sake. One day the South will know that when these disinherited children of God sat down at lunch counters, they were in reality standing up for what is best in the American dream and for the most sacred values in our Judaeo-Christian heritage, thereby bringing our nation back to those great wells of democracy which were dug deep by the founding fathers in their formulation of the Constitution and the Declaration of Independence.

Never before have I written so long a letter. I'm afraid it is much too long to take your precious time. I can assure you that it would have been much shorter if I had been writing from a comfortable desk, but what else can one do when he is alone in a narrow jail cell, other than write long letters, think long thoughts, and pray long prayers?

If I have said anything in this letter that overstates the truth and indicates an unreasonable impatience, I beg you to forgive me. If I have said anything that understates the truth and indicates my having a patience that allows me to settle for anything less than brotherhood, I beg God to forgive me.

I hope this letter finds you strong in the faith. I also hope that circumstances will soon make it possible for me to meet each of you, not as an integrationist or a civil rights leader but as a fellow clergyman and a Christian brother. Let us all hope that the dark clouds of racial prejudice will soon pass away and the deep fog of misunderstanding will be lifted from our fear-drenched communities, and in some not too distant tomorrow the radiant stars of love and brotherhood will shine over our great nation with all their scintillating beauty.

> Yours in the cause of
> Peace and Brotherhood,
> MARTIN LUTHER KING, JR.

〰 SONIA SANCHEZ (b. 1934)

Sonia Sanchez celebrates black culture in her poems, short stories, children's stories, and plays. In order to be true to realities of African American culture, in her writing she often uses the dialect of black people and portrays rituals such as playing the dozens (a word game that uses insults). Although she is best known for her poetry, Sanchez was active in the black liberation movement and started the first black studies program at the university level. She also taught at Temple University.

Sanchez's first book of poetry was Homecoming *(1969). Another volume of poetry,* We a BaddDDD People, *was published a year later. The poetry in these books deals with real-life issues such as drug abuse, race relations, and sexism. Sanchez was a member of the Nation of Islam for a short time; however, her feminist views clashed with the Muslim faith. Black feminist themes enter also into her drama and children's literature. The plays* Sister Son/ji *(1969) and* Uh Huh; But How Do It Free Us? *(1974) include some of her black feminist perspectives. She received the American Book Award in 1985 for* homegirls & handgrenades *(1984). One of her most recent publications is* Wounded in the House of a Friend *(1995).*

Poem at Thirty (1969)

it is midnight
no magical bewitching
hour for me
i know only that
i am here waiting   5
remembering that
once as a child
i walked two
miles in my sleep.
did i know   10
then where i
was going?
traveling. i'm
always traveling.
i want to tell   15
you about me
about nights on a
brown couch when
i wrapped my
bones in lint and   20
refused to move.
no one touches
me anymore.
father do not
send me out   25

among strangers.
you you black man
stretching scraping
the mold from your body.
here is my hand.　　　　　30
i am not afraid
of the night.

Summer Words of a Sistuh Addict　(1970)

the first day i shot dope
was on a sunday.
　　　　　i had just come
home from church
　　　　　got mad at my motha　　　　5
cuz she got mad at me.　u dig?
　　　　　went out.　shot up
behind a feelen against her.
　　　　　　it felt good.
gooder than dooing it.　yeah.　　　　10
　　　　　it was nice.
i did it.　uh huh.　i did it.　　uh. huh.
i want to do it again.　it felt so gooooood.
　　　　and as the sistuh
　　　　sits in her silent/　　　　　15
　　　　remembered/high
　　　　someone leans for
　　　　ward gently asks her:
　　　　　sistuh.
　　　　　did u　　　　　20
　　　　　finally
　　　　learn how to hold yo/mother?
and the music of the day
　　　　　drifts in the room
to mingle with the sistuh's young tears.　　　25
　　and we all sing.

NIKKI GIOVANNI　(b. 1943)

Nikki Giovanni is one of the most popular poets of the late twentieth century. She was born in Knoxville, Tennessee, and attended Fisk University, the University of Pennsylvania, and Columbia University. In 1967, she arranged a black arts festival in Cincinnati, Ohio, and was instrumental in the development of workshops on black theater and black history. She has taught creative writing at Livingston College, Rutgers University, and other colleges. At Wilberforce University, she earned a doctorate in humanities. She is a life member of the National Council of Negro Women and has received awards for outstanding achievement from magazines such as Mademoiselle *(1971) and* Ladies' Home Journal *(1973).*

Giovanni is a revolutionary writer who uses her fiction and nonfiction for political activism. She has contributed to the battle against societal ills with her volumes of poetry, including Black Feeling, Black Talk *(1967),* Black Judgment *(1968), and* Re-Creation *(1970). She has worked as an associate professor at Rutgers University and as a professor of English at Virginia Polytechnic Institute and Virginia State University. She continues to publish poems, some aimed at children.*

nikki-rosa (1968)

childhood remembrances are always a drag
if you're Black
you always remember things like living in Woodlawn
with no inside toilet
and if you become famous or something   5
they never talk about how happy you were to have
your mother
all to yourself and
how good the water felt when you got your bath
from one of those   10
big tubs that folk in chicago barbecue in
and somehow when you talk about home
it never gets across how much you
understood their feelings
as the whole family attended meetings about   15
Hollydale
and even though you remember
your biographers never understand
your father's pain as he sells his stock
and another dream goes   20
And though you're poor it isn't poverty that
concerns you
and though they fought a lot
it isn't your father's drinking that makes any
difference   25
but only that everybody is together and you
and your sister have happy birthdays and very good
Christmases
and I really hope no white person ever has cause
to write about me   30
because they never understand
Black love is Black wealth and they'll

probably talk about my hard childhood
and never understand that
all the while I was quite happy   35

Beautiful Black Men (1973)

(With compliments and apologies to all not mentioned by name)

i wanta say just gotta say something
bout those beautiful beautiful beautiful outasight
black men
with they afros
walking down the street   5
is the same ol danger
but a brand new pleasure

sitting on stoops, in bars, going to offices
running numbers, watching for their whores
preaching in churches, driving their hogs   10
walking their dogs, winking at me
in their fire red, lime green, burnt orange
royal blue tight tight pants that hug
what i like to hug

jerry butler, wilson pickett, the impressions   15
temptations, mighty mighty sly
don't have to do anything but walk
on stage
and i scream and stamp and shout
see new breed men in breed alls   20
dashiki suits with shirts that match
the lining that complements the ties
that smile at the sandals
where dirty toes peek at me
and i scream and stamp and shout   25
for more beautiful beautiful beautiful
black men with outasight afros

ALICE CHILDRESS (1920–1994)

Born in Charleston, South Carolina, Alice Childress was moved to Harlem, where she grew up, when she was five years old. She wrote and acted in plays and wrote fiction, screenplays, and articles for scholarly publications. Most of the critical attention to Childress's work applies to her contributions to theater; literary critics have rarely studied her short fiction, children's books, and novels. Her children's book A Hero Ain't Nothing But a Sandwich *(1973) was banned from many schools because of its subject: a young boy*

trying to beat a heroin addiction. However, for her play Trouble in Mind *(1955),
Childress received an Obie Award; the play deals with lynching.*

She continued her writing about racial issues with the play Wedding Band *(1966),
which explores interracial relationships.* Wine in the Wilderness *(1969) also provides a
social critique, using a riot as a primary event in the search for racial identity. Both plays
met a disapproving audience because of the controversial content they presented. Another of
Childress's best-known works is* Like One of the Family . . . conversations from a
domestic's life *(1956). Childress was not afraid to provide accurate portrayals of black life
and real-life societal problems. More interested in presenting realistic characters and plots,
she was less concerned about appealing to her audience than many other African American
writers.*

Wine in the Wilderness (1969)

Characters

BILL JAMESON
  an artist aged thirty-three
OLDTIMER
  an old roustabout
  character in his sixties
SONNY-MAN
  a writer aged twenty-seven

CYNTHIA
  a social worker aged twenty-five.
  She is SONNY-MAN's wife.
TOMMY
  a woman factory worker aged
  thirty

TIME: the summer of 1964. Night of a riot.
PLACE: Harlem, New York City, New York, U.S.A.

> SCENE: *A one room apartment in a Harlem tenement. It used to be a three room apart-
> ment but the tenant has broken out walls and is half finished with a redecorating job.
> The place is now only partly reminiscent of its past tawdry days, plaster broken away
> and lathing exposed right next to a new brick-faced portion of wall. The kitchen is now
> part of the room. There is a three-quarter bed covered with an African throw; a screen
> is placed at the foot of the bed to insure privacy when needed. The room is obviously black
> dominated, pieces of sculpture, wall hangings, paintings. An artist's easel is standing
> with a drapery thrown across it so the empty canvas beneath it is hidden. Two other can-
> vases the same size are next to it; they too are covered and conceal paintings. The place
> is in a beautiful, rather artistic state of disorder. The room also reflects an interest in
> other darker peoples of the world . . . A Chinese incense-burner Buddha, an American
> Indian feathered war helmet, a Mexican serape, a Japanese fan, a West Indian travel
> poster. There is a kitchen table, chairs, floor cushions, a couple of box crates, books, book-
> cases, plenty of artist's materials. There is a small raised platform for model posing. On
> the platform is a backless chair.*

> *The tail end of a riot is going on out in the street. Noise and screaming can be heard
> in the distance, . . . running feet, voices shouting over loudspeakers.*

OFFSTAGE VOICES. Offa the street! Into your homes! Clear the street! *(the whine
of a bullet is heard)* Cover that roof! It's from the roof!

(BILL *is seated on the floor with his back to the wall, drawing in a large sketch pad with charcoal pencil. He is very absorbed in his task but flinches as he hears the bullet sound, ducks and shields his head with upraised hand, . . . then resumes sketching. The telephone rings; he reaches for phone with caution, pulls it toward him by the cord in order to avoid going near window or standing up.*)

BILL. Hello? Yeah, my phone is on. How the hell I'm gonna be talkin' to you if it's not on? (*sound of glass breaking in the distance*) I could lose my damn life answerin' the phone. Sonny-man, what the hell you callin' me up for! I thought you and Cynthia might be downstairs dead, I banged on the floor and hollered down the air-shaft, no answer. No stuff! Thought yall was dead. I'm sittin' here drawin' a picture in your memory. In a bar! Yall sittin' in a bar? See there, you done blew the picture that's in your memory . . . No kiddin', they wouldn't let you in the block? Man, they can't keep you outta your own house. Found? You found who? Model? What model? Yeah, yeah, thanks, . . . but I like to find my own models. No! Don't bring nobody up here in the middle of a riot . . . Hey, Sonny-man! Hey!

(*sound of yelling and rushing footsteps in the hall*)

WOMAN'S VOICE. (*offstage*) Dammit, Bernice! The riot is over! What you hidin' in the hall for? I'm in the house, your father's in the house, . . . and you out there hidin' in the hall!

GIRL'S VOICE. (*offstage*) The house might burn down!

BILL. Sonny-man, I can't hear you!

WOMAN'S VOICE. (*offstage*) If it do burn down, what the hell you gon' do, run off and leave us to burn up by ourself? The riot is over. The police say it's over! Get back in the house!

(*sound of running feet and a knock on the door*)

BILL. They say it's over. Man, they oughta let you on your own block, in your own house . . . Yeah, we still standin', this seventy year old house got guts. Thank you, yeah, thanks but I like to pick my own models. You drunk? Can't you hear when I say not to . . . Okay, all right, bring her . . .

(*frantic knocking at the door*)

BILL. I gotta go. Yeah, yeah, bring her. I gotta go . . .

(BILL *hangs up phone and opens the door for* OLDTIMER. *The old man is carrying a haul of loot . . . two or three bottles of liquor, a ham, a salami and a suit with price tags attached.*)

BILL. What's this! Oh, no, no, no, Oldtimer, not here . . .

(*faint sound of a police whistle*)

BILL. The police after you? What you bring that stuff in here for?

OLDTIMER. (*runs past* BILL *to center as he looks for a place to hide the loot*) No, no they not really after me but . . . I was in the basement so I could stash this stuff, . . . but a fella told me they pokin' 'round down there . . . in the back yard pokin' 'round . . . the police doin' a lotta pokin' 'round.

BILL. If the cops are searchin' why you wanna dump your troubles on me?

OLDTIMER. I don't wanta go to jail. I'm too old to go to jail. What we gonna do?

BILL. We can throw it the hell outta the window. Didn't you think of just throwin' it away and not worry 'bout jail?

OLDTIMER. I can't do it. It's like . . . I'm Oldtimer but my hands and arms is some-body else that I don' know-a-tall.

(BILL *pulls stuff out of* OLDTIMER'*s arms and places loot on the kitchen table.* OLDTIMER'*s arms fall to his sides.*)

OLDTIMER. Thank you, son.

BILL. Stealin' ain't worth a bullet through your brain, is it? You wanna get shot down and drown in your own blood, . . . for what? A suit, a bottle of whiskey? Gonna throw your life away for a damn ham?

OLDTIMER. But I ain't really stole nothin', Bill, cause I ain't no thief. Them others, . . . they smash the windows, they run in the stores and grab and all. Me, I pick up what they left scatter in the street. Things they drop . . . things they trample underfoot. What's in the street ain't like stealin'. This is leavin's. What I'm gon' do if the police come?

BILL. (*starts to gather the things in the tablecloth that is on the table*) I'll throw it out the air-shaft window.

OLDTIMER. (*places himself squarely in front of the air-shaft window*) I be damn. Uh-uh, can't let you do it, Billy-Boy. (*grabs the liquor and holds on*)

BILL. (*wraps the suit, the ham and the salami in the tablecloth and ties the ends together in a knot*) Just for now, then you can go down and get it later.

OLDTIMER. (*getting belligerent*) I say I ain't gon' let you do it.

BILL. Sonny-man calls this "The people's revolution." A revolution should not be looting and stealing. Revolutions are for liberation.

(OLDTIMER *won't budge from before the window.*)

BILL. Okay, man, you win, it's all yours. (*walks away from* OLDTIMER *and prepares his easel for sketching*)

OLDTIMER. Don't be mad with me, Billy-Boy, I couldn't help myself.

BILL. (*at peace with the old man*) No hard feelin's.

OLDTIMER. (*as he uncorks bottle*) I don't blame you for bein' fed up with us, . . . fella like you oughta be fed up with your people sometime. Hey, Billy, let's you and me have a little taste together.

BILL. Yeah, why not.

OLDTIMER. (*at the table pouring drinks*) You mustn't be too hard on me. You see, you talented, you got somethin' on the ball, you gonna make it on past these white folk, . . . but not me, Billy-Boy, it's too late in the day for that. Time, time, time, . . . time done put me down. Father Time is a bad white cat. Whatcha been paintin' and drawin' lately? You can paint me again if you wanta, . . . no charge. Paint me 'cause that might be the only way I get to stay in the world after I'm dead and gone. Somebody'll look up at your paintin' and say, . . . "Who's that?" And you say, . . . "That's Oldtimer."

(BILL *joins* OLDTIMER *at table and takes one of the drinks.*)

OLDTIMER. Well, here's lookin' at you and goin' down me. (*gulps down drink*)

BILL. *(raising his glass)* Your health, Oldtimer.

OLDTIMER. My day we didn't have all this grants and scholarship like now. Whatcha been doin'?

BILL. I'm working on the third part of a triptych.

OLDTIMER. A what tick?

BILL. A triptych.

OLDTIMER. Hot-damn, that call for another drink. Here's to the trip-tick. Down the hatch. What is one-a-those?

BILL. It's three paintings that make one work . . . three paintings that make one subject.

OLDTIMER. Goes together like a new outfit . . . hat, shoes and suit.

BILL. Right. The title of my triptych is . . . "Wine in the Wilderness" . . . Three canvases on black womanhood . . .

OLDTIMER. *(eyes light up)* Are they naked pitchers?

BILL. *(crosses to paintings)* No, all fully clothed.

OLDTIMER. *(wishing it was a naked picture)* Man, ain' nothin' dirty 'bout naked pitchers. That's art. What you call artistic.

BILL. Right, right, right, but these are with clothes. That can be artistic too. *(uncovers one of the canvases and reveals painting of a charming little girl in Sunday dress and hair ribbon)* I call her . . . "Black Girlhood."

OLDTIMER. Awwwww, that's innocence! Don't know what it's all about. Ain't that the little child that live right down the street? Yeah. That call for another drink.

BILL. Slow down, Oldtimer, wait till you see this. *(He covers the painting of the little girl, then uncovers another canvas and reveals a beautiful woman, deep mahogany complexion; she is cold but utter perfection, draped in startling colors of African material, very "Vogue" looking. She wears a golden head-dress sparkling with brilliants and sequins applied over the paint.)* There she is . . . "Wine in the Wilderness" . . . Mother Africa, regal, black womanhood in her noblest form.

OLDTIMER. Hot damn. I'd die for her, no stuff, . . . Oh, man. "Wine in the Wilderness."

BILL. Once, a long time ago, a poet named Omar told us what a paradise life could be if a man had a loaf of bread, a jug of wine and . . , a woman singing to him in the wilderness. She is the woman; she is the bread; she is the wine; she is the singing. This Abyssinian maiden is paradise, . . . perfect black womanhood.

OLDTIMER. *(pours for BILL and himself)* To our Abyssinian maiden.

BILL. She's the Sudan, the Congo River, the Egyptian Pyramids . . . Her thighs are African mahogany . . . she speaks and her words pour forth sparkling clear as the waters . . . Victoria Falls.

OLDTIMER. Ow! Victoria Falls! She got a pretty name.

BILL. *(covers her up again)* Victoria Falls is a waterfall, not her name. Now, here's the one that calls for a drink. *(snatches cover from the empty canvas)*

OLDTIMER. *(stunned by the empty canvas)* Your . . . your pitcher is gone.

BILL. Not gone, . . . she's not painted yet. This will be the third part of the triptych. This is the unfinished third of "Wine in the Wilderness." She's gonna be the kinda chick that is grass roots, . . . no, not grass roots, . . . I mean she's underneath the grass roots. The lost woman, . . . what the society has made out of our women. She's as far from my African queen as a woman can get and still be female; she's as close to the bottom as you can get without crackin' up . . . She's ignorant, unfeminine, coarse, rude . . . vulgar . . . a poor, dumb chick that's had her behind kicked until it's numb . . . and the sad part is . . . she ain't together, you know . . . there's no hope for her.

OLDTIMER. Oh, man, you talkin' 'bout my first wife.

BILL. A chick that ain't fit for nothin' but to . . . to . . . just pass her by.

OLDTIMER. Yeah, later for her. When you see her, cross over to the other side of the street.

BILL. If you had to sum her up in one word it would be nothin'!

OLDTIMER. (*roars with laughter*) That call for a double!

BILL. (*beginning to slightly feel the drinks. He covers the canvas again.*) Yeah, that's a double! The kinda woman that grates on your damn nerves. And Sonny-man just called to say he found her runnin' 'round in the middle-a this riot; Sonny-man say she's the real thing from underneath them grass roots. A back-country chick right outta the wilds of Mississippi, . . . but she ain't never been near there. Born in Harlem, raised right here in Harlem, . . . but back country. Got the picture?

OLDTIMER. (*full of laughter*) When . . . when . . . when she get here let's us stomp her to death.

BILL. Not till after I paint her. Gonna put her right here on this canvas. (*pats the canvas, walks in a strut around the table*) When she gets put down on canvas, . . . then triptych will be finished.

OLDTIMER. (*joins him in the strut*) Trip-tick will be finish . . . trip-tick will be finish . . .

BILL. Then "Wine in the Wilderness" will go up against the wall to improve the view of some post office . . . or some library . . . or maybe a bank . . . and I'll win a prize . . . and the queen, my black queen will look down from the wall so the messed up chicks in the neighborhood can see what a woman oughta be . . . and the innocent child on the side of her and the messed up chick on the other side of her . . . MY STATEMENT.

OLDTIMER. (*turning the strut into a dance*) Wine in the wilderness . . . up against the wall . . . wine in the wilderness . . . up against the wall . . .

WOMAN FROM UPSTAIRS APT. (*offstage*) What's the matter! The house on fire?

BILL. (*calls upstairs through the air-shaft window*) No, baby! We down here paintin' pictures! (*sound of police siren in distance*)

WOMAN FROM UPSTAIRS APT. (*offstage*) So much-a damn noise! Cut out the noise! (*to her husband hysterically*) Percy! Percy! You hear a police siren! Percy! That a fire engine?!

BILL. Another messed up chick. (*gets a rope and ties it to* OLDTIMER'S *bundle*) Got an idea. We'll tie the rope to the bundle, . . . then . . . (*lowers bundle out the window*) lower the bundle outta the window . . . and tie it to this nail here behind the curtain. Now! Nobody can find it except you and me . . . Cops come, there's no loot. (*ties rope to nail under curtain*)

OLDTIMER. Yeah, yeah, loot long gone 'til I want it. (*makes sure window knot is secure*) It'll be swingin' in the breeze free and easy. (*There is knocking on the door.*)

SONNY-MAN. Open up! Open up! Sonny-man and company.

BILL. (*putting finishing touches on, securing knot to nail*) Wait, wait, hold on . . .

SONNY-MAN. And-a here we come!

(SONNY-MAN *pushes the door open. Enters room with his wife* CYNTHIA *and* TOMMY. SONNY-MAN *is in high spirits. He is in his late twenties; his wife* CYNTHIA *is a bit younger. She wears her hair in a natural style; her clothing is tweedy and in good, quiet taste.* SONNY-MAN *is wearing slacks and a dashiki over a shirt.* TOMMY *is dressed in a mis-matched shirt and sweater, wearing a wig that is not comical, but is wiggy. She has the habit of smoothing it every once in a while, patting to make sure it's in place. She wears sneakers and bobby sox, carries a brown paper sack.*)

CYNTHIA. You didn't think it was locked, did you?

BILL. Door not locked? (*looking over* TOMMY)

TOMMY. You oughta run him outta town, pushin' open people's door.

BILL. Come right on in.

SONNY-MAN. (*standing behind* TOMMY *and pointing down at her to draw* BILL'*s attention*) Yes, sireeeeee.

CYNTHIA. Bill, meet a friend-a ours . . . this is Miss Tommy Fields. Tommy, meet a friend-a ours . . . this is Bill Jameson . . . Bill, Tommy.

BILL. Tommy, if I may call you that . . .

TOMMY. (*likes him very much*) Help yourself, Bill. It's a pleasure. Bill Jameson, well, all right.

BILL. The pleasure is all mine. Another friend-a ours, Oldtimer.

TOMMY. (*with respect and warmth*) How are you, Mr. Timer?

BILL. (*laughs along with others,* OLDTIMER *included*) What you call him, baby?

TOMMY. Mr. Timer . . . ain't that what you say?

(*They all laugh expansively.*)

BILL. No, sugar pie, that's not his name, . . . we just say . . . "Oldtimer," that's what everybody call him.

OLDTIMER. Yeah, they all call me that . . . everybody say that . . . OLDTIMER.

TOMMY. That's cute, . . . but what's your name?

BILL. His name is . . . er . . . er . . . What is your name?

SONNY-MAN. Dog-bite, what's your name, man?

(*There is a significant moment of self-consciousness as* CYNTHIA, SONNY-MAN *and* BILL *realize they don't know* OLDTIMER'*s name.*)

OLDTIMER. Well, it's . . . Edmond L. Matthews.

TOMMY. Edmond L. Matthews. What's the L for?

OLDTIMER. Lorenzo, . . . Edmond Lorenzo Matthews.

BILL *and* SONNY-MAN. Edmond Lorenzo Matthews.

TOMMY. Pleased to meetcha, Mr. Matthews.

OLDTIMER. Nobody call me that in a long, long time.

TOMMY. I'll call you Oldtimer like the rest but I like to know who I'm meetin'.

(OLDTIMER *gives her a chair.*)

TOMMY. There you go. He's a gentleman too. Bet you can tell my feet hurt. I got one corn . . . and that one is enough. Oh, it'll ask you for somethin'.

(*general laughter.* BILL *indicates to* SONNY-MAN *that* TOMMY *seems right.* CYNTHIA *and* OLDTIMER *take seats near* TOMMY.)

BILL. You rest yourself, baby, er . . . er . . . Tommy. You did say Tommy.

TOMMY. I cut it to Tommy . . . Tommy-Marie; I use both of 'em sometime.

BILL. How 'bout some refreshment?

SONNY-MAN. Yeah, how 'bout that. (*pouring drinks*)

TOMMY. Don't yall carry me too fast, now.

BILL. (*indicating liquor bottles*) I got what you see and also some wine . . . couple-a cans-a beer.

TOMMY. I'll take the wine.

BILL. Yeah, I knew it.

TOMMY. Don't wanta start nothin' I can't keep up.

(OLDTIMER *slaps his thigh with pleasure.*)

BILL. That's all right, baby, you just a wine-o.

TOMMY. You the one that's got the wine, not me.

BILL. I use this for cookin'.

TOMMY. You like to get loaded while you cook?

(OLDTIMER *is having a ball.*)

BILL. (*as he pours wine for* TOMMY) Oh, baby, you too much.

OLDTIMER. (*admiring* TOMMY) Oh, Lord, I wish, I wish, I wish I was young again.

TOMMY. (*flirtatiously*) Lively as you are, . . . I don't know what we'd do with you if you got any younger.

OLDTIMER. Oh, hush now!

SONNY-MAN. (*whispering to* BILL *and pouring drinks*) Didn't I tell you! Know what I'm talkin' about. You dig? All the elements, man.

TOMMY. (*worried about what the whispering means*) Let's get somethin' straight. I didn't come bustin' in on the party, . . . I was asked. If you married and any wives or girl-friends round here . . . I'm innocent. Don't wanta get shot at, or jumped on. Cause I wasn't doin' a thing but mindin' my business! (*saying the last in loud tones to be heard in other rooms*)

OLDTIMER. Jus' us here, that's all.

BILL. I'm single, baby. Nobody wants a poor artist.

CYNTHIA. Oh, honey, we wouldn't walk you into a jealous wife or girl friend.

TOMMY. You paint all-a these pitchers?

(BILL *and* SONNY-MAN *hand out drinks.*)

BILL. Just about. Your health, baby, to you.

TOMMY. (*lifts her wine glass*) All right, and I got one for you . . . Like my grampaw used-ta say, . . . Here's to the men's collars and the women's skirts, . . . may they never meet.

(*general laughter*)

OLDTIMER. But they ain't got far to go before they do.

TOMMY. *(suddenly remembers her troubles)* Niggers, niggers . . . niggers . . . I'm sick-a niggers, ain't you? A nigger will mess up everytime . . . Lemmie tell you what the niggers done . . .

BILL. Tommy, baby, we don't use that word around here. We can talk about each other a little bit better than that.

CYNTHIA. Oh, she doesn't mean it.

TOMMY. What must I say?

BILL. Try Afro-Americans.

TOMMY. Well . . . the Afro-Americans burnt down my house.

OLDTIMER. Oh, no they didn't!

TOMMY. Oh, yes they did . . . it's almost burn down. Then the firemen nailed up my door . . . the door to my room, nailed up shut tight with all I got in the world.

OLDTIMER. Shame, what a shame.

TOMMY. A damn shame. My clothes . . . Everything gone. This riot blew my life. All I got is gone like it never was.

OLDTIMER. I know it.

TOMMY. My transistor radio . . . that's gone.

CYNTHIA. Ah, gee.

TOMMY. The transistor . . . and a brand new pair-a shoes I never had on one time . . . *(raises her right hand)* If I never move, that's the truth . . . new shoes gone.

OLDTIMER. Child, when hard luck fall it just keep fallin'.

TOMMY. And in my top dresser drawer I got a my-on-ase jar with forty-one dollars in it. The fireman would not let me in to get it . . . And it was a Afro-American fireman, don'tcha know.

OLDTIMER. And you ain't got no place to stay.

*(*BILL *is studying her for portrait possibilities.)*

TOMMY. *(rises and walks around room)* That's a lie. I always got some place to go. I don't wanta boast but I ain't never been no place that I can't go back the second time. Woman I use to work for say . . . "Tommy, any time, any time you want a sleep-in place you come right here to me." . . . And that's Park Avenue, my own private bath and T.V. set . . . But I don't want that . . . so I make it on out here to the dress factory. I got friends . . . not a lot of 'em . . . but a few good ones. I call my friend-girl and her mother . . . they say . . . "Tommy, you come here, bring yourself over here." So Tommy got a roof with no sweat. *(looks at torn wall)* Looks like the Afro-Americans got to you too. Breakin' up, breakin' down, . . . that's all they know.

BILL. No, Tommy, . . . I'm re-decorating the place . . .

TOMMY. You mean you did this to yourself?

CYNTHIA. It's gonna be wild . . . brick-face walls . . . wall to wall carpet.

SONNY-MAN. She was breakin' up everybody in the bar . . . had us all laughin' . . . crackin' us up. In the middle of a riot . . . she's gassin' everybody!

TOMMY. No need to cry, it's sad enough. They hollerin' whitey, whitey . . . but who they burn out? Me.

BILL. The brothers and sisters are tired, weary of the endless get-no-where struggle.

TOMMY. I'm standin' there in the bar . . . tellin' it like it is . . . next thing I know they talkin' 'bout bringin' me to meet you. But you know what I say? Can't nobody pick nobody for nobody else. It don't work. And I'm standin' there in a mis-match skirt and top and these sneaker-shoes. I just went to put my dresses in the cleaner . . . Oh, Lord, wonder if they burn down the cleaner. Well, no matter, when I got back it was all over . . . They went in the grocery store, rip out the shelves, pull out all the groceries . . . the hams . . . the . . . the . . . the can goods . . . everything . . . and then set fire . . . Now who you think live over the grocery? Me, that's who. I don't even go to the store lookin' this way . . . but this would be the time, when . . . folks got a fella they want me to meet.

BILL. *(suddenly self-conscious)* Tommy, they thought . . . they thought I'd like to paint you . . . that's why they asked you over.

TOMMY. *(pleased by the thought but she can't understand it)* Paint me? For what? If he was gonna paint somebody seems to me it'd be one of the pretty girls they show in the beer ads. They even got colored on television now, . . . brushin' their teeth and smokin' cigarettes, . . . some of the prettiest girls in the world. He could get them, . . . couldn't you?

BILL. Sonny-man and Cynthia were right. I want to paint you.

TOMMY. *(suspiciously)* Naked, with no clothes on?

BILL. No, baby, dressed just as you are now.

OLDTIMER. Wearin' clothes is also art.

TOMMY. In the cleaner I got a white dress with a orlon sweater to match it, maybe I can get it out tomorrow and pose in that.

(CYNTHIA, OLDTIMER *and* SONNY-MAN *are eager for her to agree.*)

BILL. No, I will paint you today, Tommy, just as you are, holding your brown paper bag.

TOMMY. Mmmmmm, me holdin' the damn bag; I don' know 'bout that.

BILL. Look at it this way, tonight has been a tragedy.

TOMMY. Sure in hell has.

BILL. And so I must paint you tonight, . . . Tommy in her moment of tragedy.

TOMMY. I'm tired.

BILL. Damn, baby, all you have to do is sit there and rest.

TOMMY. I'm hungry.

SONNY-MAN. While you're posin' Cynthia can run down to our house and fix you some eggs.

CYNTHIA. *(gives her husband a weary look)* Oh, Sonny, that's such a lovely idea.

SONNY-MAN. Thank you, darlin'; I'm in there, . . . on the beam.

TOMMY. *(ill at ease about posing)* I don't want no eggs. I'm goin' to find me some Chinese food.

BILL. I'll go. If you promise to stay here and let me paint you, . . . I'll get you anything you want.

TOMMY. *(brightening up)* Anything I want. Now, how he sound? All right, you comin' on mighty strong there. "Anything you want." When last you heard somebody say that? . . . I'm warnin' you, now, . . . I'm free, single and disengage, . . . so you better watch yourself.

BILL. *(keeping her away from ideas of romance)* Now this is the way the program will go down. First I'll feed you, then I'll paint you.

TOMMY. Okay, I'm game, I'm a good sport. First off, I want me some Chinese food.

CYNTHIA. Order up, Tommy, the treat's on him.

TOMMY. How come it is you never been married? All these girls runnin' 'round Harlem lookin' for husbands. *(to* CYNTHIA*)* I don't blame 'em, 'cause I'm lookin' for somebody myself.

BILL. I've been married, married and divorced; she divorced me, Tommy, so maybe I'm not much of a catch.

TOMMY. Look at it this-a-way. Some folks got bad taste. That woman had bad taste.

(All laugh except BILL *who pours another drink.)*

TOMMY. Watch it, Bill, you gonna rust the linin' of your stomach. Ain't this a shame? The riot done wipe me out and I'm sittin' here ballin'! *(as* BILL *refills her glass)* Hold it, that's enough. Likker ain' my problem.

OLDTIMER. I'm havin' me a good time.

TOMMY. Know what I say 'bout divorce. *(slaps her hands together in a final gesture)* Anybody don' wantcha, . . . later, let 'em go. That's bad taste for you.

BILL. Tommy, I don't wanta ever get married again. It's me and my work. I'm not gettin' serious about anybody . . .

TOMMY. He's spellin' at me, now. Nigger, . . . I mean Afro-American . . . I ain' ask you nothin'. You hinkty, I'm hinkty too. I'm independent as a hog on ice, . . . and a hog on ice is dead, cold, well-preserved . . . and don't need a mother-grabbin' thing.

(All laugh heartily except BILL *and* CYNTHIA.*)*

TOMMY. I know models get paid. I ain' no square but this is a special night and so this one'll be on the house. Show you my heart's in the right place.

BILL. I'll be glad to pay you, baby.

TOMMY. You don't really like me, do you? That's all right, sometime it happen that way. You can't pick for nobody. Friends get to matchin' up friends and they mess up everytime. Cynthia and Sonny-man done messed up.

BILL. I like you just fine and I'm glad and grateful that you came.

TOMMY. Good enough. *(extends her hand. They slap hands together.)* You'n me friends?

BILL. Friends, baby, friends. *(putting rock record on)*

TOMMY. *(trying out the model stand)* Okay, Dad! Let's see 'bout this anything I want jive. Want me a bucket-a Egg Foo Yong, and you get you a shrimp-fry rice, we split that and each have some-a both. Make him give you the soy sauce, the hot mustard and the duck sauce too.

BILL. Anything else, baby?

TOMMY. Since you ask, yes. If your money hold out, get me a double order egg roll. And a half order of the sweet and sour spare ribs.

BILL. *(to* OLDTIMER *and* SONNY-MAN*)* Come on, come on. I need some strong men to help me bring back your order, baby.

TOMMY. (*going into her dance . . . simply standing and going through some boo-ga-loo motions*) Better get it 'fore I think up some more to go 'long with it.

(*The men vanish out of the door. Steps heard descending stairs.*)

TOMMY. Turn that off. (CYNTHIA *turns off record player.*) How could I forget your name, good as you been to me this day. Thank you, Cynthia, thank you. I like him. Oh, I like him. But I don't wanta push him too fast. Oh, I got to play these cards right.

CYNTHIA. (*a bit uncomfortable*) Oh, Honey, . . . Tommy, you don't want a poor artist.

TOMMY. Tommy's not lookin' for a meal ticket. I been doin' for myself all my life. It takes two to make it in this high-price world. A black man see a hard way to go. The both of you gotta pull together. That way you accomplish.

CYNTHIA. I'm a social worker . . . and I see so many broken homes. Some of these men! Tommy, don't be in a rush about the marriage thing.

TOMMY. Keep it to yourself, . . . but I was thirty my last birthday and haven't ever been married. I coulda been. Oh, yes, indeed, coulda been. But I don't want any and everybody. What I want with a no-good piece-a nothin'? I'll never forget what the Reverend Martin Luther King said . . . "I have a dream." I liked him sayin' it 'cause truer words have never been spoke. (*straightening the room*) I have a dream, too. Mine is to find a man who'll treat me just half-way decent . . . just to meet me half-way is all I ask, to smile, be kind to me. Somebody in my corner. Not to wake up by myself in the mornin' and face this world all alone.

CYNTHIA. About Bill, it's best not to ever count on anything, anything at all, Tommy.

TOMMY. (*This remark bothers her for a split second but she shakes it off.*) Of course, Cynthia, that's one of the foremost rules of life. Don't count on nothin'!

CYNTHIA. Right, don't be too quick to put your trust in these men.

TOMMY. You put your trust in one and got yourself a husband.

CYNTHIA. Well, yes, but what I mean is . . . Oh, you know. A man is a man and Bill is also an artist and his work comes before all else and there are other factors . . .

TOMMY. (*sits facing* CYNTHIA) What's wrong with me?

CYNTHIA. I don't know what you mean.

TOMMY. Yes you do. You tryin' to tell me I'm aimin' too high by lookin' at Bill.

CYNTHIA. Oh, no, my dear.

TOMMY. Out there in the street, in the bar, you and your husband were so sure that he'd like me and want to paint my picture.

CYNTHIA. But he does want to paint you; he's very eager to . . .

TOMMY. But why? Somethin' don't fit right.

CYNTHIA. (*feeling sorry for* TOMMY) If you don't want to do it, just leave and that'll be that.

TOMMY. Walk out while he's buyin' me what I ask for, spendin' his money on me? That'd be too dirty. (*She looks at books and takes one from shelf.*) Books, books, books everywhere. "Afro-American History." I like that. What's wrong with me, Cynthia? Tell me, I won't get mad with you, I swear. If there's somethin' wrong that I can change, I'm ready to do it. Eight grade, that's all I had of school. You a social worker; I know that means college. I come from poor people. *(examining the book in her hand)* Talkin' 'bout poverty this and poverty that and studyin' it. When you in it you don' be studyin' 'bout it. Cynthia, I remember my mother tyin' up her stockin's with strips-a rag 'cause she didn't have no garters. When I get home from school she'd say, . . . "Nothin' much here to eat." Nothin' much might be grits, or bread and coffee. I got sick-a all that, got me a job. Later for school.

CYNTHIA. The Matriarchal Society.

TOMMY. What's that?

CYNTHIA. A Matriarchal Society is one in which the women rule . . . the women have the power . . . the women head the house.

TOMMY. We didn't have nothin' to rule over, not a pot nor a window. And my papa picked hisself up and ran off with some finger-poppin' woman and we never hear another word 'til ten, twelve years later when a undertaker call up and ask if Mama wanta claim his body. And don'cha know, Mama went on over and claim it. A woman need a man to claim, even if it's a dead one. What's wrong with me? Be honest.

CYNTHIA. You're a fine person . . .

TOMMY. Go on, I can take it.

CYNTHIA. You're too brash. You're too used to looking out for yourself. It makes us lose our femininity . . . It makes us hard . . . it makes us seem very hard. We do for ourselves too much.

TOMMY. If I don't, who's gonna do for me?

CYNTHIA. You have to let the black man have his manhood again. You have to give it back, Tommy.

TOMMY. I didn't take it from him, how I'm gonna give it back? What else is the matter with me? You had school, I didn't. I respect that.

CYNTHIA. Yes, I've had it, the degrees and the whole bit. For a time I thought I was about to move into another world, the so-called "integrated" world, a place where knowledge and know-how could set you free and open all the doors, but that's a lie. I turned away from that idea. The first thing I did was give up dating white fellas.

TOMMY. I never had none to give up. I'm not soundin' on you. White folks, nothin' happens when I look at 'em. I don't hate 'em, don't love 'em, . . . just nothin' shakes a-tall. The dullest people in the world. The way they talk . . . "Oh, hooty, hooty, hoo" . . . Break it down for me to A, B, C's. That Bill . . . I like him, with his black, uppity, high-handed ways. What do you do to get a man you want? A social worker oughta tell you things like that.

CYNTHIA. Don't chase him . . . at least don't let it look that way. Let him pursue you.

TOMMY. What if he won't? Men don't chase me much, not the kind I like.

CYNTHIA. *(rattles off instructions glibly)* Let him do the talking. Learn to listen. Stay in the background a little. Ask his opinion . . . "What do you think, Bill?"

TOMMY. Mmmmm, "Oh, hooty, hooty, hoo."

CYNTHIA. But why count on him? There are lots of other nice guys.

TOMMY. You don't think he'd go for me, do you?

CYNTHIA. *(trying to be diplomatic)* Perhaps you're not really his type.

TOMMY. Maybe not, but he's mine. I'm so lonesome . . . I'm lonesome . . . I want somebody to love. Somebody to say . . . "That's all-right when the World treats me mean."

CYNTHIA. Tommy, I think you're too good for Bill.

TOMMY. I don't wanta hear that. The last man that told me I was too good for him . . . was tryin' to get away. He's good enough for me. *(straightening room)*

CYNTHIA. Leave the room alone. What we need is a little more sex appeal and a little less washing, cooking and ironing.

(TOMMY *puts down the room straightening.*)

CYNTHIA. One more thing, . . . do you have to wear that wig?

TOMMY. *(a little sensitive)* I like how your hair looks. But some of the naturals I don't like. Can see all the lint caught up in the hair like it hasn't been combed since know not when. You a Muslim?

CYNTHIA. No.

TOMMY. I'm just sick-a hair, hair, hair. Do it this way, don't do it, leave it natural, straighten it, process, no process. I get sick-a hair and talkin' 'bout it and foolin' with it. That's why I wear the wig.

CYNTHIA. I'm sure your own must be just as nice or nicer than that.

TOMMY. It oughta be. I only paid nineteen ninety five for this.

CYNTHIA. You ought to go back to using your own.

TOMMY. *(tensely)* I'll be givin' that some thought.

CYNTHIA. You're pretty nice people just as you are. Soften up, Tommy. You might surprise yourself.

TOMMY. I'm listenin'.

CYNTHIA. Expect more. Learn to let men open doors for you . . .

TOMMY. What if I'm standin' there and they don't open it?

CYNTHIA. *(trying to level with her)* You're a fine person. He wants to paint you, that's all. He's doing a kind of mural thing and we thought he would enjoy painting you. I'd hate to see you expecting more out of the situation than what's there.

TOMMY. Forget it, sweetie-pie, don' nothin' that's not suppose to.

(*sound of laughter in the hall.* BILL, OLDTIMER *and* SONNY-MAN *enter.*)

BILL. No Chinese restaurant left, baby! It's wiped out. Gone with the revolution.

SONNY-MAN. *(to* CYNTHIA*)* Baby, let's move, split the scene, get on with it, time for home.

BILL. The revolution is here. Whatta you do with her? You paint her?

SONNY-MAN. You write her . . . you write the revolution into a novel nine hundred pages long.

BILL. Dance it! Sing it! "Down in the cornfield Hear dat mournful sound . . ."

(SONNY-MAN *and* OLDTIMER *harmonize.*)

BILL. Dear old Massa am-a sleepin'. A-sleepin' in the cold, cold ground. Now for "Wine in the Wilderness!" Triptych will be finished.

CYNTHIA. *(in* BILL's *face)* "Wine in the Wilderness," huh? Exploitation!

SONNY-MAN. Upstairs, all out, come on, Oldtimer. Folks can't create in a crowd. Cynthia, move it, baby.

OLDTIMER. *(starting toward the window)* My things! I got a package.

SONNY-MAN. *(heads him off)* Up and out. You don't have to go home, but you have to get outta here. Happy paintin', yall.

(One backward look and they all are gone.)

BILL. Whatta night, whatta night, whatta night, baby. It will be painted, written, sung and discussed for generations.

(TOMMY *notices nothing that looks like Chinese food.* BILL *is carrying a small bag and a container.)*

TOMMY. Where's the Foo-Yong?

BILL. They blew the restaurant, baby. All I could get was a couple-a franks and a orange drink from the stand.

TOMMY. *(tersely)* You brought me a frank-footer? That's what you think-a me, a frank-footer?

BILL. Nothin' to do with what I think. Place is closed.

TOMMY. *(quietly surly)* This is the damn City-a New York, any hour on the clock they sellin' the chicken in the basket, barbecue ribs, pizza pie, hot pastrami samitches; and you brought me a frank-footer?

BILL. Baby, don't break bad over somethin' to eat. The smart set, the jet set, the beautiful people, kings and queens eat frankfurters.

TOMMY. If a queen sent you out to buy her a bucket-a Foo-Yong, you wouldn't come back with no lonely-ass frank-footer.

BILL. Kill me 'bout it, baby! Go 'head and shoot me six times. That's the trouble with our women, yall always got your mind on food.

TOMMY. Is that our trouble? *(laughs)* Maybe you right. Only two things to do. Either eat the frank-footer or walk outta here. You got any mustard?

BILL. *(gets mustard from the refrigerator)* Let's face it, our folks are not together. The brothers and sisters have busted up Harlem, . . . no plan, no nothin'. There's your black revolution, heads whipped, hospital full and we still in the same old bag.

TOMMY. *(seated at the kitchen table)* Maybe what everybody need is somebody like you, who know how things oughta go, to get on out there and start some action.

BILL. You still mad about the frankfurter?

TOMMY. No. I keep seein' pitchers of what was in my room and how it all must be spoiled now. *(sips the orange drink)* A orange never been near this. Well, it's cold. *(looking at an incense burner)* What's that?

BILL. An incense burner, was given to me by the Chinese guy, Richard Lee. I'm sorry they blew his restaurant.

TOMMY. Does it help you to catch the number?

BILL. No, baby, I just burn incense sometime.

TOMMY. For what?

BILL. Just 'cause I feel like it. Baby, ain't you used to nothin'?

TOMMY. Ain't used to burnin' incent for nothin'.

BILL. *(laughs)* Burnin' what?

TOMMY. That stuff.

BILL. What did you call it?

TOMMY. Incent.

BILL. It's not incent, baby. It's incense.

TOMMY. Like the sense you got in your head. In-sense. Thank you. You're a very correctable person, ain't you.

BILL. Let's put you on canvas.

TOMMY. *(stubbornly)* I have to eat first.

BILL. That's another thing 'bout black women, they wanta eat 'fore they do anything else. Tommy, . . . Tommy, . . . I bet your name is Thomasina. You look like a Thomasina.

TOMMY. You could sit there and guess til your eyes pop out and you never would guess my first name. You might could guess the middle name but not the first one.

BILL. Tell it to me.

TOMMY. My name is Tomorrow.

BILL. How's that?

TOMMY. Tomorrow, . . . like yesterday and tomorrow, and the middle name is just plain Marie. That's what my father name me. Tomorrow Marie. My mother say he thought it had a pretty sound.

BILL. Crazy! I never met a girl named Tomorrow.

TOMMY. They got to callin' me Tommy for short, so I stick with that. Tomorrow Marie, . . . Sound like a promise that can never happen.

BILL. *(straightens chair on stand. He is very eager to start painting.)* That's what Shakespeare said, . . . "Tomorrow and tomorrow and tomorrow." Tomorrow, you will be on this canvas.

TOMMY. *(still uneasy about being painted)* What's the hurry? Rome wasn't built in a day, . . . that's another saying.

BILL. If I finish in time, I'll enter you in an exhibition.

TOMMY. *(loses interest in the food. She examines the room, and looks at portrait on the wall.)* He looks like somebody I know or maybe saw before.

BILL. That's Frederick Douglass. A man who used to be a slave. He escaped and spent his life trying to make us all free. He was a great man.

TOMMY. Thank you, Mr. Douglass. Who's the light colored man? *(indicates a frame next to the Douglass)*

BILL. He's white. That's John Brown. They killed him for tryin' to shoot the country outta the slavery bag. He dug us, you know. Old John said, "Hell no, slavery must go."

TOMMY. I heard all about him. Some folks say he was crazy.

BILL. If he had been shootin' at us they wouldn't have called him a nut.

TOMMY. School wasn't a great part-a my life.

BILL. If it was you wouldn't-a found out too much 'bout black history cause the books full-a nothin' but whitey, . . . all except the white ones who dug us, . . . they not there either. Tell me, . . . who was Elijah Lovejoy?

TOMMY. Elijah Lovejoy, . . . Mmmmmmm. I don't know. Have to do with the Bible?

BILL. No, that's another white fella, . . . Elijah had a printin' press and the main thing he printed was "Slavery got to go." Well the man moved in on him, smashed his press time after time . . . but he kept puttin' it back together and doin' his thing. So, one final day, they came in a mob and burned him to death.

TOMMY. *(blows her nose with sympathy as she fights tears)* That's dirty.

BILL. *(as TOMMY glances at titles in book case)* Who was Monroe Trotter?

TOMMY. Was he white?

BILL. No, soul brother. Spent his years tryin' to make it all right. Who was Harriet Tubman?

TOMMY. I heard-a her. But don't put me through no test, Billy. *(moving around studying pictures and books)* This room is full-a things I don' know nothin' about. How'll I get to know.

BILL. Read, go to the library, book stores, ask somebody.

TOMMY. Okay, I'm askin'. Teach me things.

BILL. Aw, baby, why torment yourself? Trouble with our women, . . . they all wanta be great brains. Leave somethin' for a man to do.

TOMMY. *(eager to impress him)* What you think-a Martin Luther King?

BILL. A great guy. But it's too late in the day for the singin' and prayin' now.

TOMMY. What about Malcolm X?

BILL. Great cat . . . but there again . . . Where's the program?

TOMMY. What about Adam Powell? I voted for him. That's one thing 'bout me. I vote. Maybe if everybody vote for the right people . . .

BILL. The ballot box. It would take me all my life to straighten you on that hype.

TOMMY. I got time.

BILL. You gonna wind up with a king size headache. The Matriarchy gotta go. Yall throw them suppers together, keep your husband happy, raise the kids.

TOMMY. I don't have a husband. Course, that could be fixed. *(leaving the unspoken proposal hanging in the air)*

BILL. You know the greatest thing you could do for your people? Sit up there and let me put you down on canvas.

TOMMY. Bein' married and havin' family might be good for your people as a race, but I was thinkin' 'bout myself a little.

BILL. Forget yourself sometime, sugar. On that canvas you'll be givin' and givin' and givin' . . . That's where you do your thing best. What you stallin' for?

TOMMY. *(returns to table and sits in chair)* I . . . I don't want to pose in this outfit.

BILL. *(patience wearing thin)* Why, baby, why?

TOMMY. I don't feel proud-a myself in this.

BILL. Art, baby, we talkin' art. Whatcha want . . . Ribbons? Lace? False eyelashes?

TOMMY. No, just my white dress with the orlon sweater, . . . or anything but this what I'm wearin'. You oughta see me in that dress with my pink linen shoes. Oh, hell, the shoes are gone, I forgot 'bout the fire . . .

BILL. Oh, stop fightin' me! Another thing . . . our women don't know a damn thing 'bout bein' feminine. Give in sometime. It won't kill you. You tellin' me how to paint? Maybe you oughta hang out your shingle and give art lessons! You too damn opinionated. You gonna pose or you not gonna pose? Say somethin'.

TOMMY. You makin' me nervous! Hollerin' at me. My mama never holler at me. Hollerin'.

BILL. I'll soon be too tired to pick up the brush, baby.

TOMMY. *(eye catches picture of white woman on the wall)* That's a white woman! Bet you never hollered at her and I bet she's your girlfriend . . . too, and when she posed for her pitcher I bet yall was laughin' . . . and you didn't buy her no frank-footer!

BILL. *(feels a bit smug about his male prowess)* Awww, come on, cut that out, baby. That's a little blonde, blue-eyed chick who used to pose for me. That ain't where it's at. This is a new day, the deal is goin' down different. This is the black moment, doll. Black, black, black is bee-yoo-tee-full. Got it? Black is beautiful.

TOMMY. Then how come it is that I don't feel beautiful when you talk to me?!!

BILL. That's your hang-up, not mine. You supposed to stretch forth your wings like Ethiopia, shake off them chains that been holdin' you down. Langston Hughes said let 'em see how beautiful you are. But you determined not to ever be beautiful. Okay, that's what makes you Tommy.

TOMMY. Do you have a girlfriend? And who is she?

BILL. *(now enjoying himself to the utmost)* Naw, naw, naw, doll. I know people, but none-a this "tie-you-up-and-I-own-you" jive. I ain't mistreatin' nobody and there's enough-a me to go around. That's another thing with our women, . . . they wanta latch on. Learn to play it by ear, roll with the punches, cut down on some-a this "got-you-to-the-grave" kinda relationship. Was today all right? Good, be glad, . . . take what's at hand because tomorrow never comes, it's always today.

(TOMMY begins to cry.)

BILL. Awwww, I didn't mean it that way . . . I forgot your name. *(He brushes her tears.)* You act like I belong to you. You're jealous of a picture?

TOMMY. That's how women are, always studyin' each other and wonderin' how they look up 'gainst the next person.

BILL. *(a bit smug)* That's human nature. Whatcha call healthy competition.

TOMMY. You think she's pretty?

BILL. She was, perhaps still is. Long, silky hair. She could sit on her hair.

TOMMY. *(with bitter arrogance)* Doesn't everybody?

BILL. You got a head like a rock and gonna have the last word if it kills you. Baby, I bet you could knock out Mohamud Ali in the first round, then rare back and scream like Tarzan . . . "Now, I am the greatest!" *(He is very close to her and is amazed to feel a great sense of physical attraction.)* What we arguin' 'bout ? *(looks her over as she looks away. He suddenly wants to put the conversation on a more intimate level. His eye is on the bed.)* Maybe tomorrow would be a better time for paintin'. Wanna freshen up, take a bath, baby? Water's nice n' hot.

TOMMY. *(knows the sound and turns to check on the look. She notices him watching the bed, and starts weeping.)* No, I don't. Nigger!

BILL. Was that nice? What the hell, let's paint the picture. Or are you gonna hold that back too?

TOMMY. I'm posin'. Shall I take off the wig?

BILL. No, it's part of your image, ain't it? You must have a reason for wearin' it.

(TOMMY *snatches up her orange drink and sits in the model's chair.*)

TOMMY. (*with defiance*) Yes, I wear it 'cause you and those like you go for long, silky hair, and this is the only way I can have some without burnin' my mother-grabbin brains out. Got it? (*She accidentally throws over container of orange drink in her lap.*) Hell, I can't wear this. I'm soaked through. I'm not gonna catch no double pneumonia sittin' up here wringin' wet while you paint and holler at me.

BILL. Bitch!

TOMMY. You must be talkin' 'bout your mama!

BILL. Shut up! Aw, shut-up! (*phone rings. He finds an African throw-cloth and hands it to her.*) Put this on. Relax, don't go way mad, and all the rest-a that jazz. Change, will you? I apologize. I'm sorry. (*He picks up phone.*) Hello, survivor of a riot speaking. Who's calling?

(TOMMY *retires behind the screen with the throw. During the conversation, she undresses and wraps the throw around her. We see* TOMMY *and* BILL, *but they can't see each other.*)

BILL. Sure, told you not to worry. I'll be ready for the exhibit. If you don't dig it, don't show it. Not time for you to see it yet. Yeah, yeah, next week. You just make sure your exhibition room is big enough to hold the crowds that's gonna congregate to see this fine chick I got here.

(TOMMY'S *ears perk up.*)

BILL. You oughta see her. The finest black woman in the world . . . No, . . . the finest any woman in the world . . . This gorgeous satin chick is . . . is . . . black velvet moonlight . . . an ebony queen of the universe . . .

(TOMMY *can hardly believe her ears.*)

BILL. One look at her and you go back to Spice Islands . . . She's Mother Africa . . . You flip, double flip. She has come through everything that has been put on her . . .

(*He unveils the gorgeous woman he has painted . . . "Wine in the Wilderness."* TOMMY *believes he is talking about her.*)

BILL. Regal . . . grand . . . magnificent, fantastic . . . You would vote her the woman you'd most like to meet on a desert island, or around the corner from anywhere. She's here with me now . . . and I don't know if I want to show her to you or anybody else . . . I'm beginnin' to have this deep attachment . . . She sparkles, man, Harriet Tubman, Queen of the Nile . . . sweetheart, wife, mother, sister, friend . . . The night . . . a black diamond . . . A dark, beautiful dream . . . A cloud with a silvery lining . . . Her wrath is a storm over the Bahamas. "Wine in the Wilderness" . . . The memory of Africa . . . The now of things . . . but best of all and most important . . . She's tomorrow . . . she's my tomorrow . . .

(TOMMY *is dressed in the African wrap. She is suddenly awakened to the feeling of being loved and admired. She removes the wig and fluffs her hair. Her hair under the wig must not be an accurate, well-cut Afro . . . but should be rather attractive natural hair. She studies herself in a mirror. We see her taller, more relaxed and sure of herself. Perhaps braided hair will go well with Afro robe.)*

BILL. Aw, man, later. You don't believe in nothin'! *(He covers "Wine in the Wilderness." He is now in a glowing mood.)* Baby, whenever you ready.

*(*TOMMY *emerges from behind the screen, dressed in the wrap, sans wig. He is astounded.)*

BILL. Baby, what . . . ? Where . . . where's the wig?

TOMMY. I don't think I want to wear it, Bill.

BILL. That is very becoming . . . the drape thing.

TOMMY. Thank you.

BILL. I don't know what to say.

TOMMY. It's time to paint. *(She steps up on the model stand and sits in the chair. She is now a queen, relaxed and smiling her appreciation for his last speech to the art dealer. Her feet are bare.)*

BILL. *(mystified by the change in her)* It is quite late.

TOMMY. Makes me no difference if it's all right with you.

BILL. *(wants to create the other image)* Could you put the wig back on?

TOMMY. You don't really like wigs, do you?

BILL. Well, no.

TOMMY. Then let's have things the way you like.

BILL. *(has no answer for this. He makes a haphazard line or two as he tries to remember the other image.)* Tell me something about yourself, . . . anything.

TOMMY. *(now on sure ground)* I was born in Baltimore, Maryland and raised here in Harlem. My favorite flower is "Four O'clocks," that's a bush flower. My wearin' flower, corsage flower, is pink roses. My mama raised me, mostly by herself, God rest the dead. Mama belonged to "The Eastern Star." Her father was a "Mason." If a man in the family is a "Mason" any woman related to him can be an "Eastern Star." My grandfather was a member of "The Prince Hall Lodge." I had a uncle who was an "Elk," . . . a member of "The Improved Benevolent Protective Order of Elks of the World": "The Henry Lincoln Johnson Lodge." You know, the white "Elks" are called "The Benevolent Protective Order of Elks" but black "Elks" are called "The Improved Benevolent Protective Order of Elks of the World." That's because the black "Elks" got copyright first but the white "Elks" took us to court about it to keep us from usin' the name. Over fifteen hundred black folk went to jail for wearin' the "Elk" emblem on their coat lapel. Years ago, . . . that's what you call history.

BILL. I didn't know about that.

TOMMY. Oh, it's understandable. Only way I heard about John Brown was because the black "Elks" bought his farmhouse where he trained his men to attack the government.

BILL. The black "Elks" bought the John Brown Farm? What did they do with it?

TOMMY. They built a outdoor theater an put a perpetual light in his memory, . . . and they buildin' cottages there, one named for each state in the union and . . .

BILL. How do you know about it?

TOMMY. Well, our "Elks" helped my cousin go through school with a scholarship. She won a speaking contest and wrote a composition titled "Onward and Upward, O, My Race." That's how she won the scholarship. Coreen knows all that Elk history.

BILL. (*seeing her with new eyes*) Tell me some more about you, Tomorrow Marie. I bet you go to church.

TOMMY. Not much as I used to. Early in life I pledged myself to the A. M. E. Zion Church.

BILL. (*studying her face, seeing her for the first time*) A. M. E.?

TOMMY. A. M. E. That's African Methodist Episcopal. We split off from the white Methodist Episcopal and started our own in the year 1796. We built our first buildin' in the year 1800. How 'bout that?

BILL. That right?

TOMMY. Oh, I'm just showin' off. I taught Sunday School for two years and you had to know the history of A. M. E. Zion . . . or else you couldn't teach. My great, great grandparents was slaves.

BILL. Guess everybody's was.

TOMMY. Mine was slaves in a place called Sweetwater Springs, Virginia. We tried to look it up one time but somebody at church told us that Sweetwater Springs had become a part of Norfolk . . . so we didn't carry it any further . . . As it would be a expense to have a lawyer trace your people.

BILL. (*throws charcoal pencil across room*) No good! It won't work! I can't work anymore.

TOMMY. Take a rest. Tell me about you.

BILL. (*sits on bed*) Everybody in my family worked for the Post Office. They bought a home in Jamaica, Long Island. Everybody on that block bought an aluminum screen door with a duck on it, . . . or was it a swan? I guess that makes my favorite flower crab grass and hedges. I have a lot of bad dreams.

(TOMMY *massages his temples and the back of his neck.*)

BILL. A dream like suffocating, dying of suffocation. The worst kinda dream. People are standing in a weird looking art gallery; they're looking and laughing at everything I've ever done. My work begins to fade off the canvas, right before my eyes. Everything I've ever done is laughed away.

TOMMY. Don't be so hard on yourself. If I was smart as you I'd wake up singin' every mornin'.

(*There is the sound of thunder. He kisses her.*)

TOMMY. When it thunders that's the angels in heaven playin', with their hoops, rollin' their hoops and bicycle wheels in the rain. My mama told me that.

BILL. I'm glad you're here. Black is beautiful, you're beautiful, A. M. E. Zion, Elks, pink roses, bush flower, . . . blooming out of the slavery of Sweetwater Springs, Virginia.

TOMMY. I'm gonna take a bath and let the riot and the hell of living go down the drain with the bath water.

BILL. Tommy, Tommy, Tomorrow Marie, let's save each other, let's be kind and good to each other while it rains and the angels roll those hoops and bicycle wheels.

(They embrace; after embrace and after rain music in as lights come down. As lights fade down to darkness, music comes in louder. There is a flash of lightning. We see TOMMY *and* BILL *in each other's arms. It is very dark, music up louder, then softer and down to very soft. Music is mixed with the sound of rain beating against the window. Music slowly fades as gray light of dawn shows at window. Lights go up gradually. The bed is rumpled and empty.* BILL *is in the bathroom.* TOMMY *is at the stove turning off the coffee pot. She sets table with cups, saucers, spoons.* TOMMY's *hair is natural; she wears another throw [African design] draped around her. She sings and hums a snatch of a joyous spiritual.)*

TOMMY. "Great day, Great day, the world's on fire, Great day . . ." *(calling out to* BILL *who is in the bath)* Honey, I found the coffee, and it's ready. Nothin' here to go with it but a cucumber and a Uneeda biscuit.

BILL. *(joyous yell from offstage)* Tomorrow and tomorrow and tomorrow! Good mornin', Tomorrow!

TOMMY. *(more to herself than to* BILL*)* "Tomorrow and tomorrow." That's Shakespeare. *(calls to* BILL*)* You say that was Shakespeare?

BILL. *(offstage)* Right, baby, right!

TOMMY. I bet Shakespeare was black! You know how we love poetry. That's what give him away. I bet he was passin'. *(laughs)*

BILL. *(offstage)* Just you wait, one hundred years from now all the honkeys gonna claim our poets just like they stole our blues. They gonna try to steal Paul Laurence Dunbar and LeRoi and Margaret Walker.

TOMMY. *(to herself)* God moves in a mysterious way, even in the middle of a riot.

(a knock on the door)

TOMMY. Great day, great day the world's on fire . . .

*(*TOMMY *opens the door.* OLDTIMER *enters. He is soaking wet. He does not recognize her right away.)*

OLDTIMER. 'Scuse me, I must be in the wrong place.

TOMMY. *(patting her hair)* This is me. Come on in, Edmond Lorenzo Matthews. I took off my hair-piece. This is me.

OLDTIMER. *(very distracted and worried)* Well, howdy-do and good mornin'. *(He has had a hard night of drinking and sleeplessness.)* Where Billy-Boy? It pourin' down some rain out there. *(makes his way to the window)*

TOMMY. What's the matter?

OLDTIMER. *(raises the window and starts pulling in the cord; the cord is weightless and he realizes there is nothing on the end of it.)* No, no, it can't be. Where is it? It's gone! *(looks out the window)*

TOMMY. You gonna catch your death. You wringin' wet.

OLDTIMER. Yall take my things in? It was a bag-a loot. A suit and some odds and ends. It was my loot. Yall took it in?

TOMMY. No. *(realizes his desperation. She calls to* BILL *through the closed bathroom door.)* Did you take in any loot that was outside the window?

BILL. *(offstage)* No.

TOMMY. He said "no."

OLDTIMER. *(yells out window)* Thieves, . . . dirty thieves . . . lotta good it'll do you . . .

TOMMY. *(leads him to a chair, dries his head with a towel)* Get outta the wet things. You smell just like a whiskey still. Why don't you take care of yourself. *(dries off his hands)*

OLDTIMER. Drinkin' with the boys. Likker was everywhere all night long.

TOMMY. You got to be better than this.

OLDTIMER. Everything I ever put my hand and mind to do, it turn out wrong, . . . Nothin' but mistakes . . . When you don' know, you don' know. I don' know nothin'. I'm ignorant.

TOMMY. Hush that talk . . . You know lotsa things, everybody does. *(helps him remove wet coat)*

OLDTIMER. Thanks. How's the trip-tick?

TOMMY. The what?

OLDTIMER. Trip-tick. That's a paintin'.

TOMMY. See there, you know more about art than I do. What's a trip-tick? Have some coffee and explain me a trip-tick.

OLDTIMER. *(proud of his knowledge)* Well, I tell you, . . . a trip-tick is a paintin' that's in three parts . . . but they all belong together to be looked at all at once. Now . . . this is the first one . . . a little innocent girl . . . *(unveils picture)*

TOMMY. She's sweet.

OLDTIMER. And this is "Wine in the Wilderness" . . . The Queen of the Universe . . . the finest chick in the world.

TOMMY. *(She is thoughtful as he unveils the second picture.)* That's not me.

OLDTIMER. No, you gonna be this here last one. The worst gal in town. A messed-up chick that—that—*(He unveils the third canvas and is face to face with the almost blank canvas, then realizes what he has said. He turns to see the stricken look on* TOMMY'S *face.)*

TOMMY. The messed-up chick, that's why they brought me here, ain't it? That's why he wanted to paint me! Say it!

OLDTIMER. No, I'm lyin', I didn't mean it. It's the society that messed her up. Awwwwww, Tommy, don't look that-a-way. It's art, . . . it's only art . . . He couldn't mean you . . . it's art . . .

(The door opens. CYNTHIA *and* SONNY-MAN *enter.)*

SONNY-MAN. Anybody want a ride down . . . down . . . down . . . downtown? What's wrong? Excuse me . . . *(starts back out)*

TOMMY. *(blocking the exit to* CYNTHIA *and* SONNY-MAN*)* No, come on in. Stay with it . . . "Brother" . . . "Sister." Tell 'em what a trip-tick is, Oldtimer.

CYNTHIA. *(very ashamed)* Oh, no.

TOMMY. You don't have to tell 'em. They already know. The messed-up chick! How come you didn't pose for that, my sister? The messed-up chick lost her home last night, . . . burnt out with no place to go. You and Sonny-man gave me comfort, you cheered me up and took me in, . . . took me in!

CYNTHIA. Tommy, we didn't know you, we didn't mean . . .

TOMMY. It's all right! I was lost but now I'm found! Yeah, the blind can see! *(She dashes behind the screen and puts on her clothing, sweater, skirt, etc.)*

OLDTIMER. *(goes to bathroom)* Billy, come out!

SONNY-MAN. Billy, step out here, please!

(BILL enters shirtless, wearing dungarees.)

SONNY-MAN. Oldtimer let it out 'bout the triptych.

BILL. The rest of you move on.

TOMMY. *(looking out from behind the screen)* No, don't go a step. You brought me here, see me out!

BILL. Tommy, let me explain it to you.

TOMMY. *(coming out from behind screen)* I gotta check out my apartment, and my clothes and money. Cynthia, . . . I can't wait for anybody to open the door or look out for me and all that kinda crap you talk. A bunch-a liars!

BILL. Oldtimer, why you . . .

TOMMY. Leave him the hell alone. He ain't said nothin' that ain' so!

SONNY-MAN. Explain to the sister that some mistakes have been made.

BILL. Mistakes have been made, baby. The mistakes were yesterday, this is today . . .

TOMMY. Yeah, and I'm Tomorrow, remember? Trouble is I was Tommy to you, to all of you, . . . "Oh, maybe they gon' like me." . . . I was your fool, thinkin' writers and painters know moren' I me, that maybe a little bit of you would rub off on me.

CYNTHIA. We are wrong. I knew it yesterday. Tommy, I told you not to expect anything out of this . . . this arrangement.

BILL. This is a relationship, not an arrangement.

SONNY-MAN. Cynthia, I tell you all the time, keep outta other people's business. What the hell you got to do with who's gonna get what outta what? You and Oldtimer, yakkin' and hakkin'. *(to OLDTIMER)* Man, your mouth gonna kill you.

BILL. It's me and Tommy. Clear the room.

TOMMY. Better not. I'll kill him! The "black people" this and the "Afro-American" . . . that . . . You ain't got no use for none-a us. Oldtimer, you their fool too. 'Til I got here they didn't even know your damn name. There's something inside-a me that says I ain' suppose to let nobody play me cheap. Don't care how much they know! *(She sweeps some of the books to the floor.)*

BILL. Don't you have any forgiveness in you? Would I be beggin' you if I didn't care? Can't you be generous enough . . .

TOMMY. Nigger, I been too damn generous with you already. All-a these people know I wasn't down here all night posin' for no pitcher, nigger!

BILL. Cut that out, Tommy, and you not going anywhere!

TOMMY. You wanna bet? Nigger!

BILL. Okay, you called it, baby, I did act like a low, degraded person . . .

TOMMY. *(combing out her wig with her fingers while holding it)* Didn't call you no low, degraded person. Nigger! *(to CYNTHIA who is handing her a comb)* "Do you have to wear a wig? Yes! To soften the blow when yall go up side-a my head with a baseball bat. (*going back to taunting* BILL *and ignoring* CYNTHIA'*s comb*) Nigger!

BILL. That's enough-a that. You right and you're wrong too.

TOMMY. Ain't a-one-a us you like that's alive and walkin' by you on the street . . . you don't like flesh and blood niggers.

BILL. Call me that, baby, but don't call yourself. That what you think of yourself?

TOMMY. If a black somebody is in a history book, or printed on a pitcher, or drawed on a paintin' . . . or if they're a statue, . . . dead, and outta the way, and can't talk back, then you dig 'em and full-a so much-a damn admiration and talk 'bout "our" history. But when you run into us livin' and breathin' ones, with the life's blood still pumpin' through us, . . . then you comin' on 'bout we ain' never together. You hate us, that's what! You hate black me!

BILL. (*stung to the heart, confused and saddened by the half truth which applies to himself*) I never hated you, I never will, no matter what you or any of the rest of you do to make me hate you. I won't! Hell, woman, why do you say that! Why would I hate you?

TOMMY. Maybe I look too much like the mother that give birth to you. Like the Ma and Pa that worked in the post office to buy you a house and a screen door with a damn duck on it. And you so ungrateful you didn't even like it.

BILL. No, I didn't, baby. I don't like screen doors with ducks on 'em.

TOMMY. You didn't like who was livin' behind them screen doors. Phoney Nigger!

BILL. That's all! Dammit! Don't go there no more!

TOMMY. Hit me, so I can tear this place down and scream bloody murder.

BILL. (*somewhere between laughter and tears*) Looka here, baby, I'm willin' to say I'm wrong, even in fronta the room fulla people . . .

TOMMY. (*through clinched teeth*) Nigger.

SONNY-MAN. The sister is upset.

TOMMY. And you stop callin' me "the" sister, . . . if you feelin' so brotherly why don't you say "my" sister? Ain't no we-ness in your talk. "The" Afro-American, "the" black man, there's no we-ness in you. Who you think you are?

SONNY-MAN. I was talkin' in general er . . . my sister, 'bout the masses.

TOMMY. There he go again. "The" masses. Tryin' to make out like we pitiful and you got it made. You the masses your damn self and don't even know it. (*another angry look at* BILL) Nigger.

BILL. (*pulls dictionary from shelf*) Let's get this ignorant "nigger" talk squared away. You can stand some education.

TOMMY. You treat me like a nigger, that's what. I'd rather be called one than treated that way.

BILL. (*questions* TOMMY) What is a nigger? (*talks as he is trying to find word*) A nigger is a low, degraded person, any low degraded person. I learned that from my teacher in the fifth grade.

TOMMY. Fifth grade is a liar! Don't pull that dictionary crap on me.

BILL. (*pointing to the book*) Webster's New World Dictionary of the American Language, College Edition.

TOMMY. I don't need to find out what no college white folks say nigger is.

BILL. I'm tellin' you it's a low, degraded person. Listen. *(reads from the book)* Nigger, N-i-g-g-e-r, . . . A Negro . . . A member of any dark-skinned people . . . Damn. *(amazed by dictionary description)*

SONNY-MAN. Brother Malcolm said that's what they meant . . . nigger is a Negro, Negro is a nigger.

BILL. *(slowly finishing his reading)* A vulgar, offensive term of hostility and contempt. Well, so much for the fifth grade teacher.

SONNY-MAN. No, they do not call low, degraded white folks niggers. Come to think of it, did you ever hear whitey call Hitler a nigger? Now if some whitey digs us, . . . the others might call him a nigger-lover, but they don't call him no nigger.

OLDTIMER. No, they don't.

TOMMY. *(near tears)* When they say "nigger," just dry-long-so, they mean educated you and uneducated me. They hate you and call you "nigger," I called you "nigger" but I love you. *(There is dead silence in the room for a split second.)*

SONNY-MAN. *(trying to establish peace)* There you go. There you go.

CYNTHIA. *(cautioning SONNY-MAN)* Now is not the time to talk, darlin'.

BILL. You love me? Tommy, that's the greatest compliment you could . . .

TOMMY. *(sorry she said it)* You must be runnin' a fever, nigger, I ain' said nothin' 'bout lovin' you.

BILL. *(in a great mood)* You did, yes, you did.

TOMMY. Well, you didn't say it to me.

BILL. Oh, Tommy, . . .

TOMMY. *(cuts him off abruptly)* And don't you dare say it now. I'm tellin' you, . . . it ain't to be said now. *(checks through her paper bag to see if she has everything. She starts to put on the wig, changes her mind, holds it to end of scene, turns to the others in the room.)* Oldtimer, . . . my brothers and my sister.

OLDTIMER. I wish I was a thousand miles away; I'm so sorry. *(He sits at the foot of the model stand.)*

TOMMY. I don't stay mad; it's here today and gone tomorrow. I'm sorry your feelin's got hurt, . . . but when I'm hurt I turn and hurt back. Somewhere, in the middle of last night, I thought the old me was gone, . . . lost forever, and gladly. But today was flippin' time, so back I flipped. Now it's "turn the other cheek" time. If I can go through life other-cheekin' the white folk, . . . guess yall can be other-cheeked too. But I'm going back to the nitty-gritty crowd, where the talk is we-ness and us-ness. I hate to do it but I have to thank you 'cause I'm walkin' out with much more than I brought in. *(goes over and looks at the queen in the "Wine in the Wilderness" painting)* Tomorrow-Marie had such a lovely yesterday.

(BILL takes her hand; she gently removes it from his grasp.)

TOMMY. Bill, I don't have to wait for anybody's by-your-leave to be a "Wine in the Wilderness" woman. I can be it if I wanta, . . . and I am. I am. I am. I'm not the one you made up and painted, the very pretty lady who can't talk back, . . . but I'm "Wine in the Wilderness." . . . alive and kickin', me . . . Tomorrow-Marie, cussin' and fightin' and lookin' out for my damn self 'cause ain' nobody else 'round to do it, dontcha know. And, Cynthia, if my hair is straight, or if it's natural, or if I wear a wig, or take it off, . . . that's all right; because wigs . . . shoes . . . hats . . . bags . . . and even this . . . *(She picks up the African throw she wore a few moments before . . . fingers it.)* They're just what . . . what you call . . . access . . . *(fishing for the word)* . . . like what you wear with your Easter outfit . . .

CYNTHIA. Accessories.

TOMMY. Thank you, my sister. Accessories. Somethin' you add on or take off. The real thing is takin' place on the inside . . . that's where the action is. That's "Wine in the Wilderness," . . . a woman that's a real one and a good one. And yall just better believe I'm it. *(She proceeds to the door.)*

BILL. Tommy.

(TOMMY turns. He takes the beautiful queen, "Wine in the Wilderness" from the easel.)

BILL. She's not it at all, Tommy. This chick on the canvas, . . . nothin' but accessories, a dream I drummed up outta the junk room of my mind. *(places the "queen" to one side)* You are and . . . *(points to OLDTIMER)* . . . Edmond Lorenzo Matthews . . . the real beautiful people, . . . Cynthia.

CYNTHIA. *(bewildered and unbelieving)* Who? Me?

BILL. Yeah, honey, you and Sonny-man, don't know how beautiful you are. *(indicates the other side of model stand)* Sit there.

SONNY-MAN. *(places cushions on the floor at the foot of the model stand)* Just sit here and be my beautiful self. *(to CYNTHIA)* Turn on, baby, we gonna get our picture took. *(CYNTHIA smiles.)*

BILL. Now there's Oldtimer, the guy who was here before there were scholarships and grants and stuff like that, the guy they kept outta the schools, the man the factories wouldn't hire; the union wouldn't let him join.

SONNY-MAN. Yeah, yeah, rap to me. Where you goin' with it, man? Rap on.

BILL. I'm makin' a triptych.

SONNY-MAN. Make it, man.

BILL. *(indicating CYNTHIA and SONNY-MAN)* On the other side, Young Man and Woman, workin' together to do our thing.

TOMMY. *(quietly)* I'm goin' now.

BILL. But you belong up there in the center, "Wine in the Wilderness" . . . that's who you are. *(moves the canvas of "the little girl" and places a sketch pad on the easel)* The nightmare, about all that I've done disappearing before my eyes. It was a good nightmare. I was painting in the dark, all head and no heart. I couldn't see until you came, baby. *(to CYNTHIA, SONNY-MAN and OLDTIMER)* Look at Tomorrow. She came through the biggest riot of all, . . . somethin' called "Slavery," and she's even comin' through the "now" scene, . . . folks laughin' at her, even her own folks laughin' at her. And look how . . . with her head high like she's poppin' her fingers at the world. *(takes up charcoal pencil and tears old page off sketch pad so he can make a fresh drawing)* Aw, let me put it down, Tommy. "Wine in the Wilderness," you gotta let me put it down so all the little boys and girls can look up and see you on the wall. And you know what they're gonna say? "Hey, don't she look like somebody we know?"

(TOMMY *slowly returns and takes her seat on the stand.* TOMMY *is holding the wig in her lap. Her hands are very graceful looking against the texture of the wig.*)

BILL. And they'll be right, you're somebody they know . . . *(He is sketching hastily. There is a sound of thunder and the patter of rain.)* Yeah, roll them hoops and bicycle wheels.

(Music in low; music up higher as BILL *continues to sketch.)*

CURTAIN

Learning from the 60s

Audre Lorde

Audre Lorde, an accomplished African American writer known for her poetry and her essays on black feminist and lesbian issues, delivered this speech in 1982 at a Harvard University Malcolm X celebration. In the text, she expresses an appreciation for the contributions of Malcolm X and others to the 1960s civil rights struggle.

Malcolm X is a distinct shape in a very pivotal period of my life. I stand here now—Black, Lesbian, Feminist—an inheritor of Malcolm and in his tradition, doing my work, and the ghost of his voice through my mouth asks each one of you here tonight: Are you doing yours?

There are no new ideas, just new ways of giving those ideas we cherish breath and power in our own living. I'm not going to pretend that the moment I first saw or heard Malcolm X he became my shining prince, because it wouldn't be true. In February 1965 I was raising two children and a husband in a three-room flat on 149th Street in Harlem. I had read about Malcolm X and the Black Muslims. I became more interested in Malcolm X after he left the Nation of Islam, when he was silenced by Elijah Muhammad for his comment, after Kennedy's assassination, to the effect that the chickens had come home to roost. Before this I had not given much thought to the Nation of Islam because of their attitude toward women as well as because of their nonactivist stance. I'd read Malcolm's autobiography, and I liked his style, and I thought he looked a lot like my father's people, but I was one of the ones who didn't really hear Malcolm's voice until it was amplified by death.

I had been guilty of what many of us are still guilty of—letting the media, and I don't mean only the white media—define the bearers of those messages most important to our lives.

When I read Malcolm X with careful attention, I found a man much closer to the complexities of real change than anything I had read before. Much of what I say here tonight was born from his words.

In the last year of his life, Malcolm X added a breadth to this essential vision that would have brought him, had he lived, into inevitable confrontation with the question of difference as a creative and necessary force for change. For as Malcolm X progressed from a position of resistance to, and analysis of, the racial status quo, to more active considerations of organizing for change, he began to reassess some of his earlier positions. One of the most basic Black survival skills is the ability to change, to metabolize experience, good or ill, into something that is useful, lasting, effective. Four hundred years of survival as an endangered species has taught most of us that if we intend to live, we had better become fast learners. Malcolm knew this. We do not have to live the same mistakes over again if we can look at them, learn from them, and build upon them.

Before he was killed, Malcolm had altered and broadened his opinions concerning the role of women in society and the revolution. He was beginning to speak with increasing respect of the connection between himself and Martin Luther King, Jr., whose policies of nonviolence appeared to be so opposite to his own. And he began to examine the societal conditions under which alliances and coalitions must indeed occur.

He had also begun to discuss those scars of oppression which lead us to war against ourselves in each other rather than against our enemies.

As Black people, if there is one thing we can learn from the 60s, it is how infinitely complex any move for liberation must be. For we must move against not only those forces which dehumanize us from the outside, but also against those oppressive values which we have been forced to take into ourselves. Through examining the combination of our triumphs and errors, we can examine the dangers of an incomplete vision. Not to condemn that vision but to alter it, construct templates for possible futures, and focus our rage for change upon our enemies rather than upon each other. In the 1960s, the awakened anger of the Black community was often expressed, not vertically against the corruption of power and true sources of control over our lives, but horizontally toward those closest to us who mirrored our own impotence.

We were poised for attack, not always in the most effective places. When we disagreed with one another about the solution to a particular problem, we were often far more vicious to each other than to the originators of our common problem. Historically, difference had been used so cruelly against us that as a people we were reluctant to tolerate any diversion from what was externally defined as Blackness. In the 60s, political correctness became not a guideline for living, but a new set of shackles. A small and vocal part of the Black community lost sight of the fact that unity does not mean unanimity—Black people are not some standardly digestible quantity. In order to work together we do not have to become a mix of indistinguishable particles resembling a vat of homogenized chocolate milk. Unity implies the coming together of elements which are, to begin with, varied and diverse in their particular natures. Our persistence in examining the tensions within diversity encourages growth toward our common goal. So often we either ignore the past or romanticize it, render the reason for unity useless or mythic. We forget that the necessary ingredient needed to make the past work for the future is our energy in the present, metabolizing one into the other. Continuity does not happen automatically, nor is it a passive process.

The 60s were characterized by a heady belief in instantaneous solutions. They were vital years of awakening, of pride, and of error. The civil rights and Black power movements rekindled possibilities for disenfranchised groups within this nation. Even though we fought common enemies, at times the lure of individual solutions made us careless of each other. Sometimes we could not bear the face of each other's differences because of what we feared those differences might say about ourselves. As if everybody can't eventually be too Black, too White, too man, too woman. But any future vision which can encompass all of us, by definition, must be complex and expanding, not easy to achieve. The answer to cold is heat, the answer to hunger is food. But there is no simple monolithic solution to racism, to sexism, to homophobia. There is only the conscious focusing within each of my days to move against them, wherever I come up against these particular manifestations of the same disease. By seeing who the we is, we learn to use our energies with greater precision against our enemies rather than against ourselves.

In the 60s, white america—racist and liberal alike—was more than pleased to sit back as spectator while Black militant fought Black Muslim, Black Nationalist badmouthed the non-violent, and Black women were told that our only useful position in the Black Power movement was prone. The existence of Black lesbian and gay people was not even allowed to cross the public consciousness of Black america. We know in the 1980s, from documents gained through the Freedom of Information Act, that the FBI and CIA used our intolerance of difference to foment confusion and tragedy in segment after segment of Black communities of the 60s. Black was beautiful, but still suspect, and too often our forums for debate became stages for playing who's-Blacker-than-who or who's-poorer-than-who games, ones in which there can be no winners.

The 60s for me was a time of promise and excitement, but the 60s was also a time of isolation and frustration from within. It often felt like I was working and raising my children in a vacuum, and that it was my own fault—if I was only Blacker, things would be fine. It was a time of much wasted energy, and I was often in a lot of pain. Either I denied or chose between various aspects of my identity, or my work and my Blackness would be unacceptable. As a Black lesbian mother in an interracial marriage, there was usually some part of me guaranteed to offend everybody's comfortable prejudices of who I should be. That is how I learned that if I didn't define myself for myself, I would be crunched into other people's fantasies for me and eaten alive. My poetry, my life, my work, my energies for struggle were not acceptable unless I pretended to match somebody else's norm. I learned that not only couldn't I succeed at that game, but the energy needed for that masquerade would be lost to my work. And there were babies to raise, students to teach. The Vietnam War was escalating, our cities were burning, more and more of our school kids were nodding out in the halls, junk was overtaking our streets. We needed articulate power, not conformity. There were other strong Black workers whose visions were racked and silenced upon some imagined grid of narrow Blackness. Nor were Black women immune. At a national meeting of Black women for political action, a young civil rights activist who had been beaten and imprisoned in Mississippi only a few years before, was trashed and silenced as suspect because of her white husband. Some of us made it and some of us were lost to the struggle. It was a time of great hope and great expectation; it was also a time of great waste. That is history. We do not need to repeat these mistakes in the 80s.

The raw energy of Black determination released in the 60s powered changes in Black awareness and self-concepts and expectations. This energy is still being felt in movements for change among women, other peoples of Color, gays, the handicapped—among all the disenfranchised peoples of this society. That is a legacy of the 60s to ourselves and to others. But we must recognize that many of our high expectations of rapid revolutionary change did not in fact occur. And many of the gains that did are even now being dismantled. This is not a reason for despair, nor for rejection of the importance of those years. But we must face with clarity and insight the lessons to be learned from the oversimplification of any struggle for self-awareness and liberation, or we will not rally the force we need to face the multidimensional threats to our survival in the 80s.

There is no such thing as a single-issue struggle because we do not live single-issue lives. Malcolm knew this. Martin Luther King, Jr. knew this. Our struggles are particular, but we are not alone. We are not perfect, but we are stronger and wiser than the sum of our errors. Black people have been here before us and survived. We can read their lives like signposts on the road and find, as Bernice Reagon says so poignantly, that each one of us is here because somebody before us did something to make it possible. To learn from their mistakes is not to lessen our debt to them, nor to the hard work of becoming ourselves, and effective.

We lose our history so easily, what is not predigested for us by the *New York Times*, or the *Amsterdam News*, or *Time* magazine. Maybe because we do not listen to our poets or to our fools, maybe because we do not listen to our mamas in ourselves. When I hear the deepest truths I speak coming out of my mouth sounding like my mother's, even remembering how I fought against her, I have to reassess both our relationship as well as the sources of my knowing. Which is not to say that I have to romanticize my mother in order to appreciate what she gave me—Woman, Black. We do not have to romanticize our past in order to be aware of how it seeds our present. We do not have to suffer the waste of an amnesia that robs us of the lessons of the past rather than permit us to read them with pride as well as deep understanding.

We know what it is to be lied to, and we know how important it is not to lie to ourselves.

We are powerful because we have survived, and that is what it is all about—survival and growth.

Within each one of us there is some piece of humanness that knows we are not being served by the machine which orchestrates crisis after crisis and is grinding all our futures into dust. If we are to keep the enormity of the forces aligned against us from establishing a false hierarchy of oppression, we must school ourselves to recognize that any attack against Blacks, any attack against women, is an attack against all of us who recognize that our interests are not being served by the systems we support. Each one of us here is a link in the connection between antipoor legislation, gay shootings, the burning of synagogues, street harassment, attacks against women, and resurgent violence against Black people. I ask myself as well as each one of you, exactly what alteration in the particular fabric of my everyday life does this connection call for? Survival is not a theory. In what way do I contribute to the subjugation of any part of those who I define as my people? Insight must illuminate the particulars of our lives: who labors to make the bread we waste, or the energy it takes to make nuclear poisons which will not biodegrade for one thousand years; or who goes blind assembling the microtransistors in our inexpensive calculators?

We are women trying to knit a future in a country where an Equal Rights Amendment was defeated as subversive legislation. We are Lesbians and gay men who, as the most obvious target of the New Right, are threatened with castration, imprisonment, and death in the streets. And we know that our erasure only paves the way for erasure of other people of Color, of the old, of the poor, of all of those who do not fit that mythic dehumanizing norm.

Can we really still afford to be fighting each other?

We are Black people living in a time when the consciousness of our intended slaughter is all around us. People of Color are increasingly expendable, our government's policy both here and abroad. We are functioning under a government ready to repeat in El Salvador and Nicaragua the tragedy of Vietnam, a government which stands on the wrong side of every single battle for liberation taking place upon this globe; a government which has invaded and conquered (as I edit this piece) the fifty-three square mile sovereign state of Grenada, under the pretext that her 110,000 people pose a threat to the U.S. Our papers are filled with supposed concern for human rights in white communist Poland while we sanction by acceptance and military supply the systematic genocide of apartheid in South Africa, of murder and torture in Haiti and El Salvador. American advisory teams bolster repressive governments across Central and South America, and in Haiti, while advisory is only a code name preceding military aid.

Decisions to cut aid for the terminally lit, for the elderly, for dependent children, for food stamps, even school lunches, are being made by men with full stomachs who live in comfortable houses with two cars and umpteen tax shelters. None of them go hungry to bed at night. Recently, it was suggested that senior citizens be hired to work in atomic plants because they are close to the end of their lives anyway.

Can any one of us here still afford to believe that efforts to reclaim the future can be private or individual? Can any one here still afford to believe that the pursuit of liberation can be the sole and particular province of any one particular race, or sex, or age, or religion, or sexuality, or class?

Revolution is not a one-time event. It is becoming always vigilant for the smallest opportunity to make a genuine change in established, outgrown responses; for instance, it is learning to address each other's difference with respect.

We share a common interest, survival, and it cannot be be pursued in isolation from others simply because their differences make us uncomfortable. We know what it is to be lied to. The 60s should teach us how important it is not to lie to ourselves. Not to believe that revolution is a one-time event, or something that happens around us rather than inside of us. Not to believe that freedom can belong to any one group of us without the others also being free. How important it is not to allow even our leaders to define us to ourselves, or to define our sources of power to us.

There is no Black person here who can afford to wait to be led into positive action for survival. Each one of us must look clearly and closely at the genuine particulars (conditions) of his or her life and decide where action and energy is needed and where it can be effective. Change is the immediate responsibility of each of us, wherever and however we are standing, in whatever arena we choose. For while we wait for another Malcolm, another Martin, another charismatic Black leader to validate our struggles, old Black people are freezing to death in tenements, Black children are being brutalized and slaughtered in the streets, or lobotomized by television, and the percentage of Black families living below the poverty line is higher today than in 1963.

And if we wait to put our future into the hands of some new messiah, what will happen when those leaders are shot, or discredited, or tried for murder, or called homosexual, or otherwise disempowered? Do we put our future on hold? What is that internalized and self-destructive barrier that keeps us from moving, that keeps us from coming together?

We who are Black are at an extraordinary point of choice within our lives. To refuse to participate in the shaping of our future is to give it up. Do not be misled into passivity either by false security (they don't mean me) or by despair (there's nothing we can do). Each of us must find our work and do it. Militancy no longer means guns at high noon, if it ever did. It means actively working for change, sometimes in the absence of any surety that change is coming. It means doing the unromantic and tedious work necessary to forge meaningful coalitions, and it means recognizing which coalitions are possible and which coalitions are not. It means knowing that coalition, like unity, means the coming together of whole, self-actualized human beings, focused and believing, not fragmented automatons marching to a prescribed step. It means fighting despair.

And in the university, that is certainly no easy task, for each one of you by virtue of your being here will be deluged by opportunities to misname yourselves, to forget who you are, to forget where your real interests lie. Make no mistake, you will be courted; and nothing neutralizes creativity quicker than tokenism, that false sense of security fed by a myth of individual solutions. To paraphrase Malcolm—a Black woman attorney driving a Mercedes through Avenue Z in Brooklyn is still a "nigger bitch," two words which never seem to go out of style.

You do not have to be me in order for us to fight alongside each other. I do not have to be you to recognize that our wars are the same. What we must do is commit ourselves to some future that can include each other and to work toward that future with the particular strengths of our individual identities. And in order to do this, we must allow each other our differences at the same time as we recognize our sameness.

If our history has taught us anything, it is that action for change directed only against the external conditions of our oppressions is not enough. In order to be whole, we must recognize the despair oppression plants within each of us—that thin persistent voice that says our efforts are useless, it will never change, so why bother, accept it. And we must fight that inserted piece of self-destruction that lives and flourishes like a poison inside of us, unexamined until it makes us turn upon ourselves in each other. But we can put our finger down upon that loathing buried deep within each one of us and see who it encourages us to despise, and we can lessen its potency by the knowledge of our real connectedness, arching across our differences.

Hopefully, we can learn from the 60s that we cannot afford to do our enemies' work by destroying each other.

What does it mean when an angry Black ballplayer—this happened in Illinois—curses a white heckler but pulls a knife on a Black one? What better way is there to police the streets of a minority community than to turn one generation against the other?

Referring to Black lesbians and gay men, the student president at Howard University says, on the occasion of a Gay Student Charter on campus, "The Black community has nothing to do with such filth—we will have to abandon these people." Abandon? Often without noticing, we absorb the racist belief that Black people are fitting targets for everybody's anger. We are closest to each other, and it is easier to vent fury upon each other than upon our enemies.

Of course, the young man at Howard was historically incorrect. As part of the Black community, he has a lot to do with "us." Some of our finest writers, organizers, artists and scholars in the 60s as well as today, have been lesbian and gay, and history will bear me out.

Over and over again in the 60s I was asked to justify my existence and my work, because I was a woman, because I was a Lesbian, because I was not a separatist, because some piece of me was not acceptable. Not because of my work but because of my identity. I had to learn to hold on to all the parts of me that served me, in spite of the pressure to express only one to the exclusion of all others. And I don't know what I'd say face to face with that young man at Howard University who says I'm filth because I identify women as my primary source of energy and support, except to say that it is my energy and the energy of other women very much like me which has contributed to his being where he is at this point. But I think he would not say it to my face because name-calling is always easiest when it is removed, academic. The move to render the presence of lesbians and gay men invisible in the intricate fabric of Black existence and survival is a move which contributes to fragmentation and weakness in the Black community.

In academic circles, as elsewhere, there is a kind of name-calling increasingly being used to keep young Black women in line. Often as soon as any young Black woman begins to recognize that she is oppressed as a woman as well as a Black, she is called a lesbian no matter how she identifies herself sexually. "What do you mean you don't want to make coffee take notes wash dishes go to bed with me, you a lesbian or something?" And at the threat of such a dreaded taint, all too often she falls meekly into line, however covertly. But the word lesbian is only threatening to those Black women who are intimidated by their sexuality, or who allow themselves to be defined by it and from outside themselves. Black women in struggle from our own perspective, speaking up for ourselves, sharing close ties with one another politically and emotionally, are not the enemies of Black men. We are Black women who seek our own definitions, recognizing diversity among ourselves with respect. We have been around within our communities for a very long time, and we have played pivotal parts in the survival of those communities: from Hat Shep Sut through Harriet Tubman to Daisy Bates and Fannie Lou Hamer to Lorraine Hansberry to your Aunt Maydine to some of you who sit before me now.

In the 60s Black people wasted a lot of our substance fighting each other. We cannot afford to do that in the 80s, when Washington, D.C., has the highest infant mortality rate of any U.S. city, 60 percent of the Black community under twenty is unemployed and more are becoming unemployable, lynchings are on the increase, and less than half the registered Black voters voted in the last election.

How are you practicing what you preach—whatever you preach, and who exactly is listening? As Malcolm stressed, we are not responsible for our oppression, but we must be responsible for our own liberation. It is not going to be easy, but we have what we have learned and what we have been given that is useful. We have the power those who came before us have given us, to move beyond the place where they were standing. We have the trees, and water, and sun, and our children. Malcolm X does not live in the dry texts of his words as we read them; he lives in the energy we generate and use to move along the visions we share with him. We are making the future as well as bonding to survive the enormous pressures of the present, and that is what it means to be a part of history.

❧ ELDRIDGE CLEAVER (1935–1998)

Eldridge Cleaver's contribution to African American writing is primarily in the essay genre. His essays present his philosophies and theories concerning issues of race and gender, forcefully expressing his "violence as necessary" political stance as a member of the Black Panther party. Soul on Ice (1968), a collection of essays, is perhaps his best-known text. In it, Cleaver attacks racial injustice in America in a militant fashion. He discusses racism and other societal problems, such as male-female relationships and the failure of blacks who have "made it" to help poor African Americans rise from low economic status. In one section of the book, he provides a long apology to black women from himself, a black man, and on behalf of all black men. His prose is forceful and ornate. Cleaver used Soul on Ice *to negotiate a release from prison. Therefore, his rhetoric is aimed at several different audiences and serves more than one purpose. His essay "Notes on a Native Son" appeals most to a scholarly audience of writers and academics.*

Cleaver was born in Wabbaseka, Arkansas, and during his childhood years, his family moved to Los Angeles. He allegedly committed many offenses, including robbery, rape, and murder. His parents' separation and the inner-city environment could have led him into the rough life-style. He was a rebel as a child and as an adult; his writing is full of his rebellion against oppressive systems in society.

From Soul on Ice

The White Race and Its Heroes (1968)

> White people cannot, in the generality, be taken as models of how to live. Rather, the white man is himself in sore need of new standards, which will release him from his confusion and place him once again in fruitful communion with the depths of his own being.
>
> —James Baldwin, *The Fire Next Time*

Right from the go, let me make one thing absolutely clear: I am not now, nor have I ever been, a white man. Nor, I hasten to add, am I now a Black Muslim—although I used to be. But I *am* an Ofay Watcher, a member of that unchartered, amorphous league which has members on all continents and the islands of the seas. Ofay Watchers Anonymous, we might be called, because we exist concealed in the shadows wherever colored people have known oppression by whites, by white enslavers, colonizers, imperialists, and neo-colonialists.

Did it irritate you, compatriot, for me to string those epithets out like that? Tolerate me. My intention was not necessarily to sprinkle salt over anyone's wounds. I did it primarily to relieve a certain pressure on my brain. Do you cop that? If not, then we're in trouble, because we Ofay Watchers have a pronounced tendency to slip into that mood. If it is bothersome to you, it is quite a task for me because not too long ago it was my way of life to preach, as ardently as I could, that the white race is a race of devils, created by their maker to do evil, and make evil appear as good; that the white race is the natural, unchangeable enemy of the black man, who is the original man, owner, maker, cream of the planet Earth; that the white race was soon to be destroyed by Allah, and that the black man would then inherit the earth, which has always, in fact, been his.

I have, so to speak, washed my hands in the blood of the martyr, Malcolm X, whose retreat from the precipice of madness created new room for others to turn about in, and I am now caught up in that tiny space, attempting a maneuver of my own. Having renounced the teachings of Elijah Muhammad, I find that a rebirth does not follow automatically, of its own accord, that a void is left in one's vision, and this void seeks constantly to obliterate itself by pulling one back to one's former outlook. I have tried a tentative compromise by adopting a select vocabulary, so that now when I see the whites of *their* eyes, instead of saying "devil" or "beast" I say "imperialist" or "colonialist," and everyone seems to be happier.

In silence, we have spent our years watching the ofays, trying to understand them, on the principle that you have a better chance coping with the known than with the unknown. Some of us have been, and some still are, interested in learning whether it is *ultimately* possible to live in the same territory with people who seem so disagreeable to live with; still others want to get as far away from ofays as possible. What we share in common is the desire to break the ofays' power over us.

At times of fundamental social change, such as the era in which we live, it is easy to be deceived by the onrush of events, beguiled by the craving for social stability into mistaking transitory phenomena for enduring reality. The strength and permanence of "white backlash" in America is just such an illusion. However much this rear-guard action might seem to grow in strength, the initiative, and the future, rest with those whites and blacks who have liberated themselves from the master/slave syndrome. And these are to be found mainly among the youth.

Over the past twelve years there has surfaced a political conflict between the generations that is deeper, even, than the struggle between the races. Its first dramatic manifestation was within the ranks of the Negro people, when college students in the South, fed up with Uncle Tom's hat-in-hand approach to revolution, threw off the yoke of the NAACP. When these students initiated the first sit-ins, their spirit spread like a raging fire across the nation, and the technique of non-violent direct action, constantly refined and honed into a sharp cutting tool, swiftly matured. The older Negro "leaders," who are now all die-hard advocates of this tactic, scolded the students for sitting-in. The students rained down contempt upon their hoary heads. In the pre-sit-in days, these conservative leaders had always succeeded in putting down insurgent elements among the Negro people. (A measure of their power, prior to the students' rebellion, is shown by their success in isolating such great black men as the late W. E. B. DuBois and Paul Robeson, when these stalwarts, refusing to bite their tongues, lost favor with the U.S. government by their unstinting efforts to link up the Negro revolution with national liberation movements around the world.)

The "Negro leaders," and the whites who depended upon them to control their people, were outraged by the impudence of the students. Calling for a moratorium on student initiative, they were greeted instead by an encore of sit-ins, and retired to their ivory towers to contemplate the new phenomenon. Others, less prudent because held on a tighter leash by the whites, had their careers brought to an abrupt end because they thought they could lead a black/white backlash against the students, only to find themselves in a kind of Bay of Pigs. Negro college presidents, who expelled students from all-Negro colleges in an attempt to quash the demonstrations, ended up losing their jobs; the victorious students would no longer allow them to preside over the campuses. The spontaneous protests on southern campuses over the repressive measures of their college administrations were an earnest of the Free Speech upheaval which years later was to shake the UC campus at Berkeley. In countless ways, the rebellion of the black students served as catalyst for the brewing revolt of the whites.

What has suddenly happened is that the white race has lost its heroes. Worse, its heroes have been revealed as villains and its greatest heroes as the arch-villains. The new generations of whites, appalled by the sanguine and despicable record carved over the face of the globe by their race in the last five hundred years, are rejecting the panoply of white heroes, whose heroism consisted in erecting the inglorious edifice of colonialism and imperialism; heroes whose careers rested on a system of foreign and domestic exploitation, rooted in the myth of white supremacy and the manifest destiny of the white race. The emerging shape of a new world order, and the requisites for survival in such a world, are fostering in young whites a new outlook. They recoil in shame from the spectacle of cowboys and pioneers—their heroic forefathers whose exploits filled earlier generations with pride—galloping across a movie screen shooting down Indians like Coke bottles. Even Winston Churchill, who is looked upon by older whites as perhaps the greatest hero of the twentieth century—even he, because of the system of which he was a creature and which he served, is an arch-villain in the eyes of the young white rebels.

At the close of World War Two, national liberation movements in the colonized world picked up new momentum and audacity, seeking to cash in on the democratic promises made by the Allies during the war. The Atlantic Charter, signed by President Roosevelt and Prime Minister Churchill in 1941, affirming "the right of all people to choose the form of government under which they may live," established the principle, although it took years of postwar struggle to give this piece of rhetoric even the appearance of reality. And just as world revolution has prompted the oppressed to re-evaluate their self-image in terms of the changing conditions, to slough off the servile attitudes inculcated by long years of subordination, the same dynamics of change have prompted the white people of the world to re-evaluate their self-image as well, to disabuse themselves of the Master Race psychology developed over centuries of imperial hegemony.

It is among the white youth of the world that the greatest change is taking place. It is they who are experiencing the great psychic pain of waking into consciousness to find their inherited heroes turned by events into villains. Communication and understanding between the older and younger generations of whites has entered a crisis. The elders, who, in the tradition of privileged classes or races, genuinely do not understand the youth, trapped by old ways of thinking and blind to the future, have only just begun to be vexed—because the youth have only just begun to rebel. So thoroughgoing is the revolution in the psyches of white youth that the traditional tolerance which every older generation has found it necessary to display is quickly exhausted, leaving a gulf of fear, hostility, mutual misunderstanding, and contempt.

The rebellion of the oppressed peoples of the world, along with the Negro revolution in America, have opened the way to a new evaluation of history, a re-examination of the role played by the white race since the beginning of European expansion. The positive achievements are also there in the record, and future generations will applaud them. But there can be no applause now, not while the master still holds the whip in his hand! Not even the master's own children can find it possible to applaud him—he cannot even applaud himself! The negative rings too loudly. Slave-catchers, slaveowners, murderers, butchers, invaders, oppressors—the white heroes have acquired new names. The great white statesmen whom school children are taught to revere are revealed as the architects of systems of human exploitation and slavery. Religious leaders are exposed as condoners and justifiers of all these evil deeds. Schoolteachers and college professors are seen as a clique of brainwashers and whitewashers.

The white youth of today are coming to see, intuitively, that to escape the onus of the history their fathers made they must face and admit the moral truth concerning the works of their fathers. That such venerated figures as George Washington and Thomas Jefferson owned hundreds of black slaves, that all of the Presidents up to Lincoln presided over a slave state, and that every President since Lincoln connived politically and cynically with the issues affecting the human rights and general welfare of the broad masses of the American people—these facts weigh heavily upon the hearts of these young people.

The elders do not like to give these youngsters credit for being able to understand what is going on and what has gone on. When speaking of juvenile delinquency, or the rebellious attitude of today's youth, the elders employ a glib rhetoric. They speak of the "alienation of youth," the desire of the young to be independent, the problems of "the father image" and "the mother image" and their effect upon growing children who lack sound models upon which to pattern themselves. But they consider it bad form to connect the problems of the youth with the central event of our era—the national liberation movements abroad and the Negro revolution at home. The foundations of authority have been blasted to bits in America because the whole society has been indicted, tried, and convicted of injustice. To the youth, the elders are Ugly Americans; to the elders, the youth have gone mad.

The rebellion of the white youth has gone through four broadly discernible stages. First there was an initial recoiling away, a rejection of the conformity which America expected, and had always received, sooner or later, from its youth. The disaffected youth were refusing to participate in the system, having discovered that America, far from helping the underdog, was up to its ears in the mud trying to hold the dog down. Because of the publicity and self-advertisements of the more vocal rebels, this period has come to be known as the beatnik era, although not all of the youth affected by these changes thought of themselves as beatniks. The howl of the beatniks and their scathing, outraged denunciation of the system—characterized by Ginsberg as Moloch, a bloodthirsty Semitic deity to which the ancient tribes sacrificed their firstborn children—was a serious, irrevocable declaration of war. It is revealing that the elders looked upon the beatniks as mere obscene misfits who were too lazy to take baths and too stingy to buy a haircut. The elders had eyes but couldn't see, ears but couldn't hear—not even when the message came through as clearly as in this remarkable passage from Jack Kerouac's *On the Road*:

At lilac evening I walked with every muscle aching among the lights of 27th and Welton in the Denver colored section, wishing I were a Negro, feeling that the best the white world had offered was not enough ecstasy for me, not enough life, joy, kicks, darkness, music, not enough night. I wished I were a Denver Mexican, or even a poor overworked Jap, anything but what I so drearily was, a "white man" disillusioned. All my life I'd had white ambitions. . . . I passed the dark porches of Mexican and Negro homes; soft voices were there, occasionally the dusky knee of some mysterious sensuous gal; the dark faces of the men behind rose arbors. Little children sat like sages in ancient rocking chairs.

The second stage arrived when these young people, having decided emphatically that the world, and particularly the U.S.A., was unacceptable to them in its present form, began an active search for roles they could play in changing the society. If many of these young people were content to lay up in their cool beat pads, smoking pot and listening to jazz in a perpetual orgy of esoteric bliss, there were others, less crushed by the system, who recognized the need for positive action. Moloch could not ask for anything more than to have its disaffected victims withdraw into safe, passive, apolitical little nonparticipatory islands, in an economy less and less able to provide jobs for the growing pool of unemployed. If all the unemployed had followed the lead of the beatniks, Moloch would gladly have legalized the use of euphoric drugs and marijuana, passed out free jazz albums and sleeping bags, to all those willing to sign affidavits promising to remain "beat." The non-beat disenchanted white youth were attracted magnetically to the Negro revolution, which had begun to take on a mass, insurrectionary tone. But they had difficulty understanding their relationship to the Negro, and what role "whites" could play in a "Negro revolution." For the time being they watched the Negro activists from afar.

The third stage, which is rapidly drawing to a close, emerged when white youth started joining Negro demonstrations in large numbers. The presence of whites among the demonstrators emboldened the Negro leaders and allowed them to use tactics they never would have been able to employ with all-black troops. The racist conscience of America is such that murder does not register as murder, really, unless the victim is white. And it was only when the newspapers and magazines started carrying pictures and stories of white demonstrators being beaten and maimed by mobs and police that the public began to protest. Negroes have become so used to this double standard that they, too, react differently to the death of a white. When white freedom riders were brutalized along with blacks, a sigh of relief went up from the black masses, because the blacks knew that white blood is the coin of freedom in a land where for four hundred years black blood has been shed unremarked and with impunity. America has never truly been outraged by the murder of a black man, woman, or child. White politicians may, if Negroes are aroused by a particular murder, say with their lips what they know with their minds they should feel with their hearts—but don't.

It is a measure of what the Negro feels that when the two white and one black civil rights workers were murdered in Mississippi in 1964, the event was welcomed by Negroes on a level of understanding beyond and deeper than the grief they felt for the victims and their families. This welcoming of violence and death to whites can almost be heard—indeed it can be heard—in the inevitable words, oft repeated by Negroes, that those whites, and blacks, do not die in vain. So it was with Mrs. Viola Liuzzo. And much of the anger which Negroes felt toward Martin Luther King during the Battle of Selma stemmed from the fact that he denied history a great moment, never to be recaptured, when he turned tail on the Edmund Pettus Bridge and refused to all those whites behind him what they had traveled thousands of miles to receive. If the police had turned them back by force, all those nuns, priests, rabbis, preachers, and distinguished ladies and gentlemen old and young—as they had done the Negroes a week earlier—the violence and brutality of the system would have been ruthlessly exposed. Or if, seeing King determined to lead them on to Montgomery, the troopers had stepped aside to avoid precisely the confrontation that Washington would not have tolerated, it would have signaled the capitulation of the militant white South. As it turned out, the March on Montgomery was a show of somewhat dim luster, stage-managed by the Establishment. But by this time the young whites were already active participants in the Negro revolution. In fact they had begun to transform it into something broader, with the potential of encompassing the whole of America in a radical reordering of society.

The fourth stage, now in its infancy, sees these white youth taking the initiative, using techniques learned in the Negro struggle to attack problems in the general society. The classic example of this new energy in action was the student battle on the UC campus at Berkeley, California—the Free Speech Movement. Leading the revolt were veterans of the civil rights movement, some of whom spent time on the firing line in the wilderness of Mississippi/Alabama. Flowing from the same momentum were student demonstrations against U.S. interference in the internal affairs of Vietnam, Cuba, the Dominican Republic, and the Congo and U.S. aid to apartheid in South Africa. The students even aroused the intellectual community to actions and positions unthinkable a few years ago: witness the teach-ins. But their revolt is deeper than single-issue protest. The characteristics of the white rebels which most alarm their elders—the long hair, the new dances, their love for Negro music, their use of marijuana, their mystical attitude toward sex—are all tools of their rebellion. They have turned these tools against the totalitarian fabric of American society—and they mean to change it.

From the beginning, America has been a schizophrenic nation. Its two conflicting images of itself were never reconciled, because never before has the survival of its most cherished myths made a reconciliation mandatory. Once before, during the bitter struggle between North and South climaxed by the Civil War, the two images of America came into conflict, although whites North and South scarcely understood it. The image of America held by its most alienated citizens was advanced neither by the North nor by the South; it was perhaps best expressed by Frederick Douglass, who was born into slavery in 1817, escaped to the North, and became the greatest leader-spokesman for the blacks of his era. In words that can still, years later, arouse an audience of black Americans, Frederick Douglass delivered, in 1852, a scorching indictment in his Fourth of July oration in Rochester:

> What to the American slave is your Fourth of July? I answer: a day that reveals to him, more than all other days in the year, the gross injustice and cruelty to which he is the constant victim. To him your celebration is a sham; your boasted liberty, an unholy licence; your national greatness, swelling vanity; your sounds

of rejoicing are empty and heartless; your denunciation of tyrants, brass-fronted impudence; your shouts of liberty and equality, hollow mockery; your prayers and hymns, your sermons and thanksgivings, with all your religious parade and solemnity, are, to him, more bombast, fraud, deception, impiety and hypocrisy— a thin veil to cover up crimes which would disgrace a nation of savages. . . .

You boast of your love of liberty, your superior civilization, and your pure Christianity, while the whole political power of the nation (as embodied in the two great political parties) is solemnly pledged to support and perpetuate the enslavement of three millions of your countrymen. You hurl your anathemas at the crown-headed tyrants of Russia and Austria and pride yourselves on your democratic institutions, while you yourselves consent to be the mere *tools* and *bodyguards* of the tyrants of Virginia and Carolina.

You invite to your shores fugitives of oppression from abroad, honor them with banquets, greet them with ovations, cheer them, toast them, salute them, protect them, and pour out your money to them like water; but the fugitive from your own land you advertise, hunt, arrest, shoot, and kill. You glory in your refinement and your universal education; yet you maintain a system as barbarous and dreadful as ever stained the character of a nation—a system begun in avarice, supported in pride, and perpetuated in cruelty.

You shed tears over fallen Hungary, and make the sad story of her wrongs the theme of your poets, statesmen and orators, till your gallant sons are ready to fly to arms to vindicate her cause against the oppressor; but, in regard to the ten thousand wrongs of the American slave, you would enforce the strictest silence, and would hail him as an enemy of the nation who dares to make these wrongs the subject of public discourse!

This most alienated view of America was preached by the Abolitionists, and by Harriet Beecher Stowe in her *Uncle Tom's Cabin*. But such a view of America was too distasteful to receive wide attention, and serious debate about America's image and her reality was engaged in only on the fringes of society. Even when confronted with overwhelming evidence to the contrary, most white Americans have found it possible, after steadying their rattled nerves, to settle comfortably back into their vaunted belief that America is dedicated to the proposition that all men are created equal and endowed by their Creator with certain inalienable rights—life, liberty and the pursuit of happiness. With the Constitution for a rudder and the Declaration of Independence as its guiding star, the ship of state is sailing always toward a brighter vision of freedom and justice for all.

Because there is no common ground between these two contradictory images of America, they had to be kept apart. But the moment the blacks were let into the white world—let out of the voiceless and faceless cages of their ghettos, singing, walking, talking, dancing, writing, and orating *their* image of America and of Americans—the white world was suddenly challenged to match its practice to its preachments. And this is why those whites who abandon the *white* image of America and adopt the *black* are greeted with such unmitigated hostility by their elders.

For all these years whites have been taught to believe in the myth they preached, while Negroes have had to face the bitter reality of what America practiced. But without the lies and distortions, white Americans would not have been able to do the things they have done. When whites are forced to look honestly upon the objective proof of their deeds, the cement of mendacity holding white society together swiftly disintegrates. On the other hand, the core of the black world's vision remains intact, and in fact begins to expand and spread into the psychological territory vacated by the non-viable white lies, i.e., into the minds of young whites. It is remarkable how the system worked for so many years, how the majority of whites remained effectively unaware of any contradiction between their view of the world and that world itself. The mechanism by which this was rendered possible requires examination at this point.

Let us recall that the white man, in order to justify slavery and, later on, to justify segregation, elaborated a complex, all-pervasive myth which at one time classified the black man as a subhuman beast of burden. The myth was progressively modified, gradually elevating the blacks on the scale of evolution, following their slowly changing status, until the plateau of separate-but-equal was reached at the close of the nineteenth century. During slavery, the black was seen as a mindless Supermasculine Menial. Forced to do the backbreaking work, he was conceived in terms of his ability to do such work—"field niggers," etc. The white man administered the plantation, doing all the thinking, exercising omnipotent power over the slaves. He had little difficulty dissociating himself from the black slaves, and he could not conceive of their positions being reversed or even reversible.

Blacks and whites being conceived as mutually exclusive types, those attributes imputed to the blacks could not also be imputed to the whites—at least not in equal degree—without blurring the line separating the races. These images were based upon the social function of the two races, the work they performed. The ideal white man was one who knew how to use his head, who knew how to manage and control things and get things done. Those whites who were not in a position to perform these functions nevertheless aspired to them. The ideal black man was one who did exactly as he was told, and did it efficiently and cheerfully. "Slaves," said Frederick Douglass, "are generally expected to sing as well as to work." As the black man's position and function became more varied, the images of white and black, having become stereotypes, lagged behind.

The separate-but-equal doctrine was promulgated by the Supreme Court in 1896. It had the same purpose domestically as the Open Door Policy toward China in the international arena: to stabilize a situation and subordinate a non-white population so that racist exploiters could manipulate those people according to their own selfish interests. These doctrines were foisted off as *the epitome of enlightened justice, the highest expression of morality.* Sanctified by religion, justified by philosophy and legalized by the Supreme Court, separate-but-equal was enforced by day by agencies of the law, and by the KKK & Co. under cover of night. Booker T. Washington, the Martin Luther King of his day, accepted separate-but-equal in the name of all Negroes. W. E. B. DuBois denounced it.

Separate-but-equal marked the last stage of the white man's flight into cultural neurosis, and the beginning of the black man's frantic striving to assert his humanity and equalize his position with the white. Blacks ventured into all fields of endeavor to which they could gain entrance. Their goal was to present in all fields a performance that would equal or surpass that of the whites. It was long axiomatic among blacks that a black had to be twice as competent as a white in any field in order to win grudging recognition from the whites. This produced a pathological motivation in the blacks to equal or surpass the whites, and a pathological motivation in the whites to maintain a distance from the blacks. This is the rack on which black and white Americans receive their delicious torture! At first there was the color bar, flatly denying the blacks entrance to certain spheres of activity. When this no longer worked, and blacks invaded sector after sector of American life and economy, the whites evolved other methods of keeping their distance. The illusion of the Negro's inferior nature had to be maintained.

One device evolved by the whites was to tab whatever the blacks did with the prefix "Negro." We had *Negro* literature, *Negro* athletes, *Negro* music, *Negro* doctors, *Negro* politicians, *Negro* workers. The malignant ingeniousness of this device is that although it accurately describes an objective biological fact—or, at least, a sociological fact in America—it concealed the paramount psychological fact: that to the white mind, prefixing anything with "Negro" automatically consigned it to an inferior category. A well-known example of the white necessity to deny due credit to blacks is in the realm of music. White musicians were famous for going to Harlem and other Negro cultural centers literally to steal the black man's music, carrying it back across the color line into the Great White World and passing off the watered-down loot as their own original creations. Blacks, meanwhile, were ridiculed as *Negro* musicians playing inferior coon music.

The Negro revolution at home and national liberation movements abroad have unceremoniously shattered the world of fantasy in which the whites have been living. It is painful that many do not yet see that their fantasy world has been rendered uninhabitable in the last half of the twentieth century. But it is away from this world that the white youth of today are turning. The "paper tiger" hero, James Bond, offering the whites a triumphant image of themselves, is saying what many whites want desperately to hear reaffirmed: *I am still the White Man, lord of the land, licensed to kill, and the world is still an empire at my feet.* James Bond feeds on that secret little anxiety, the psychological white backlash, felt in some degree by most whites alive. It is exasperating to see little brown men and little yellow men from the mysterious Orient, and the opaque black men of Africa (to say nothing of these impudent American Negroes!) who come to the UN and talk smart to us, who are scurrying all over *our* globe in their strange modes of dress— much as if they were new, unpleasant arrivals from another planet. Many whites believe in their ulcers that it is only a matter of time before the Marines get the signal to round up these truants and put them back securely in their cages. But it is away from this fantasy world that the white youth of today are turning.

In the world revolution now under way, the initiative rests with people of color. That growing numbers of white youth are repudiating their heritage of blood and taking people of color as their heroes and models is a tribute not only to their insight but to the resilience of the human spirit. For today the heroes of the initiative are people not usually thought of as white: Fidel Castro, Che Guevara, Kwame Nkrumah, Mao Tse-tung, Gamal Abdel Nasser, Robert F. Williams, Malcolm X, Ben Bella, John Lewis, Martin Luther King, Jr., Robert Parris Moses, Ho Chi Minh, Stokeley Carmichael, W. E. B. DuBois, James Forman, Chou En-lai.

The white youth of today have begun to react to the fact that the "American Way of Life" is a fossil of history. What do they care if their old baldheaded and crew-cut elders don't dig their caveman mops? They couldn't care less about the old, stiffassed honkies who don't like their new dances: Frug, Monkey, Jerk, Swim, Watusi. All they know is that it feels good to swing to way-out body-rhythms instead of dragassing across the dance floor like zombies to the dead beat of mind-smothered Mickey Mouse music. Is it any wonder that the youth have lost all respect for their elders, for law and order, when for as long as they can remember all they've witnessed is a monumental bickering over the Negro's place in American society and the right of people around the world to be left alone by out-side powers? They have witnessed the law, both domestic and international, being spat upon by those who do not like its terms. Is it any wonder, then, that they feel justified, by sitting-in and freedom riding, in breaking laws made by lawless men? Old funny-styled, zipper-mouthed political night riders know nothing but to haul out an investigating committee *to look into the disturbance* to find the cause of the unrest among the youth. Look into a mirror! The cause is you, Mr. and Mrs. Yesterday, you with your forked tongues.

A young white today cannot help but recoil from the base deeds of his people. On every side, on every continent, he sees racial arrogance, savage brutality toward the conquered and subjugated people, genocide; he sees the human cargo of the slave trade; he sees the systematic extermination of American Indians; he sees the civilized nations of Europe fighting in imperial depravity over the lands of other people—and over possession of the very people themselves. There seems to be no end to the ghastly deeds of which his people are guilty. GUILTY. The slaughter of the Jews by the Germans, the dropping of atomic bombs on the Japanese people—these deeds weigh heavily upon the prostrate souls and tumul-tuous consciences of the white youth. The white heroes, their hands dripping with blood, are dead.

The young whites know that the colored people of the world, Afro-Americans included, do not seek revenge for their suffering. They seek the same things the white rebel wants: an end to war and exploitation. Black and white, the young rebels are free people, free in a way that Americans have never been before in the history of their country. And they are outraged.

There is in America today a generation of white youth that is truly worthy of a black man's respect, and this is a rare event in the foul annals of American history. From the beginning of the contact between blacks and whites, there has been very little reason for a black man to respect a white, with such exceptions as John Brown and others lesser known. But respect commands itself and it can neither be given nor withheld when it is due. If a man like Malcolm X could change and repudiate racism, if I myself and other former Muslims can change, if young whites can change, then there is hope for America. It was certainly strange to find myself, while steeped in the doctrine that all whites were devils by nature, commanded by the heart to applaud and acknowledge respect for these young whites—despite the fact that they are descendants of the masters and I the descendant of slave. The sins of the fathers are visited upon the heads of the children—but only if the children continue in the evil deeds of the fathers.

HAKI R. MADHUBUTI (b. 1942)

Haki R. Madhubuti has contributed greatly to the black arts movement with his poetry. Madhubuti was born in Little Rock, Arkansas, and later moved to Detroit and then to Chicago, where he completed high school. He began to write poetry in the early 1960s. He changed his name from Don Luther Lee to a Swahili name. He started Third World Press to publish the works of black authors. Later in his writing career, he started to write essays about racial issues; however, he is best known for his poetry.

Madhubuti uses the language of African Americans and musical rhythms such as jazz in his poems, attempting to capture the essence of black American experience. Among his books of poetry are Think Black *(1967),* Don't Cry, Scream *(1969), and* We Walk the Way of the New World *(1970).*

Possibilities: Remembering Malcolm X (1967)

it was not that you were pure.
your contradictions were small wheels,
returning to the critical questions:
    what is good?
    what does it mean to be black?   5
    what is wise?
    what is beautiful?
    where are the women and men of honor?
    what is a moral-ethical consciousness?
    where will our tomorrows be?   10
    what does a people need to mature?

    it was your search and doings
    that separated you from puppets.
    "a man lives as a man does"

    if you lived among the committed   15
    this day how would you lead us?

    what would be your strength,
    the word, the example, both?

    would you style in thousand
    dollar suits and false eye glasses?   20

    would you kneel at the feet of arabs
    that raped your grandmother?

    would you surround yourself with
    zombies in bow ties, zombies with parrot tongues?

it was not that you were pure.   25
the integrity of your vision and pain,
the quality of your heart and decision
confirmed your caring for local people, and your
refusal to assassinate progressive thought
has carved your imprint on the serious.   30

Poet: What Ever Happened to Luther? (1967)

he was strange weather, this luther, he read books, mainly poetry and
    sometimes
long books about people in foreign places. for a young man he was too
    serious,
he never did smile, and the family still don't know if he had good teeth. he   5
    liked
music too, even tried to play the trumpet until he heard the young miles
    davis. He
then said that he'd try writing. the family didn't believe him because there
    ain't   10
never been no writers in this family, and everybody knows that whatever
    you end
up doing, it's gotta be in your blood. It's like loving women, it's in the
    blood, arteries
and brains. this family don't even write letters, they call everybody. thats   15
    why
the phone is off 6 months out of a year. Then again, his brother willie T.
    use to
write long, long letters from prison about the books he was reading by
    malcolm x,   20
frantz fanon, george jackson, richard wright and others. luther, unlike his
    brother,
didn't smoke or drink and he'd always be doing odd jobs to get money.
    even his
closest friends clyde and t. bone didn't fully understand him. while they be   25
    partying
all weekend, luther would be traveling. he would take his little money
    with a
bag full of food, mainly fruit, and a change of underwear and get on the
    greyhound   30
bus and go. he said he be visiting cities. yet, the real funny thing about
    luther was
his ideas. he was always talking about africa and black people. he was into
    that
black stuff and he was as light skin as a piece of golden corn on the cob.   35
    he'd be

calling himself black and african and upsetting everybody, especially white
    people.
they be calling him crazy but not to his face. anyway the family, mainly
    the educated   40
side, just left him alone. they would just be polite to him, and every child
    of god
knows that when family members act polite, that means that they don't
    want to be
around you. It didn't matter much because after his mother died he left the   45
    city
and went into the army. the last time we heard from him was in 1963.
    he got put
out the army for rioting. he disappeared somewhere between mississippi
    and   50
chicago. a third cousin, who family was also polite to, appeared one day
    and said
that luther had grown a beard, changed his name and stopped eating meat.
    She
said that he had been to africa and now lived in Chicago doing what he   55
    wanted to
do, writing books, she also said that he smiles a lot and kinda got good
teeth.

BLACK AESTHETICS MOVEMENT 1960–1969

Topics for Research

1. Examine the connections between political movements and African American literature during the 1960s. Was there a clear division, or did one reflect the other?

2. Compare the work of Martin Luther King, Jr. and Malcolm X, analyzing not only the content but also the writing style. What rhetorical strategies did the two writers employ, and for what purpose? What part did their writing play in the civil rights movement?

3. Define black aesthetics and white aesthetics. Use the work of writers during this period to help construct these definitions. Were the two art forms distinct, or was there some overlap?

4. Much African American literature during the black aesthetics movement focused on racial issues. Did any African American writers produce work with a different focus? If so, what was the purpose of their racially neutral writing?

5. What part did white artists play in the African American oral tradition of the 1960s? To what extent were African American musical forms, such as blues and jazz, used by whites?

PART 7

NEOREALISM MOVEMENT
1970–PRESENT

INTRODUCTION

T HE NEOREALISM MOVEMENT IN AFRICAN AMERICAN LITERATURE has elements in common with the European realism movement established in the nineteenth century as a response to or reaction against the idealization of the Romantic period. African American literature over the years has tended toward a realistic depiction of life. Written expression of the feelings and experiences of blacks started with slave narratives. In fact, autobiography is an important genre in African American writing because these works are closely based on the truth as the author experienced it. Every literary period represented in this book includes works of realism—an important aspect of most black writing. When African American writers were finally allowed to speak, they expressed themselves primarily through writing, and they used their voices to talk about the experience of being black in a world where racism saturates the society—in other words, to talk about slavery versus freedom. Therefore, neorealism in African American literature is new realism because it focuses on the real-life experiences of black people.

During the neorealism period, from 1970 to the present, American society changed in some ways and stayed the same in others. The protest aspect of African American literature has remained constant; however, the form of expressing the protest has moved from covert to more overt rhetorical strategies. Changes in audience account for the change in strategy. Earlier writers had to conceal some information, to avoid stating it directly, so as not to offend any readers. The intent of early African American writers was to convince by using example, metaphor, and other stylistic devices. During slavery, many whites did not believe that blacks actually suffered the brutality that they claimed; therefore, black writers told their stories of enslavement and the desire for freedom to evoke empathy and action from those who had the power to do something to improve conditions.

The creative freedom of African American literary artists is evident in the range of writing in this section. Elements of protest remain in late-twentieth-century African American literature—a theme that is present throughout the black artistic tradition. A balance exists between the importance of style and content; in contrast, the literature of black aesthetics had privileged the message. By no means does the balance suggest that late-twentieth-century black literature is of a higher quality than that of the other literary periods. The differences in focus over the years correspond to the political, economic, and social climate of the times. Neorealist literature depicts improved race relations, and African American writers are free to be artists foremost and activists to a lesser degree. Racism has always been a problem in our society; therefore, the tendency for black writers to persuade against it is a major aspect of African American literature. Similarly, the womanist movement, akin to the feminist movement but with the added element of the black race, has helped to provide a place for African American women's writing. More African Americans and women have been allowed into the canon of great literature, but the barriers of race, gender, class, and sexual preference still stand. Recent African American literature continues to elevate the status of the genre and seeks to dismantle the barriers which have been lowered but are still in place.

During the literary period from the 1970s to the present, African American literature has become an important part of most university curriculums. Education on all levels has recognized and acted on the need for multiculturalism, appreciating the value of the contributions from all people regardless of race, gender, or ethnicity. From children's books to college textbooks, a range of material represents all the people who live in this country.

To address the needs of African American students, the Oakland, California, school district adopted a resolution to train teachers in the characteristics of black English (also called Ebonics or black English vernacular). Teachers were to move children to Standard English—the language of the schools. This is not a new issue. A federal court in Ann Arbor, Michigan, ruled in 1979 that the city's public schools were denying black elementary school students their civil rights by failing to teach them to speak, read, and write standard American English. The teachers were unable to successfully teach African American students; unaware that black English vernacular is a language variety with rules, teachers had judged the students inferior because of their speech. Many teachers—even at the post-secondary level—have the same kind of unawareness today when they are faced with a classroom of students who come from primarily oral cultural backgrounds. African American literature gives students pride in their language and culture. Some African American literature uses black vernacular but is written primarily in Standard English.

The literary academy has made room for scholars of African American literature, many of whom have prestige because of their contributions to the genre—such as the authors in this neorealism section. Many of these authors are women who up until the 1970s were published but were not widely recognized as contributors to the canon of great literature. African American women's voices began to be heard more and more during this time as a result of the women's movement and the civil rights movement. Another movement that developed during this span of years provided African American literary criticism. African American writers realized that the critical theory that was available was not sufficient for application to African American literature.

Not only did African American writers need theory appropriate for the art, but musical artists desired the freedom to express themselves using their own language and themes. Rap music is a politically charged medium in which artists "rap" about their experiences. In African American communities, it is not uncommon to hear people—especially youngsters—rapping spontaneously without any prior preparation. Black youth often learn valuable lessons about life from rap music, music that employs the language of the black experience. Gangsta rap focuses on realities such as drug abuse, violence, drugs, sex, and teenage pregnancy. Rap music allows people into a world that they may not understand or know about. In the music, rappers "tell it like it is," using language from their environments. They are promoting pride in African American culture by glorifying, in a sense, what some would call a rough life. But rap music is usually realistic. Gospel music has also become more popular and often transcends race because of the universal spiritual element.

African American literature in the 1970s emphasized historical information about slavery and racism. Ernest Gaines uses history in literature in his novel *The Autobiography of Miss Jane Pittman* (pp. 747–760), published in 1971. The text provides a good example of literature that uses realism to persuade against the barriers of racism and sexism. Critics have recognized the realism created through the use of autobiographical elements in the novel. The construction of Jane Pittman's ethos is central in the persuasive appeal of the book. Gaines uses language to promote a political and moral agenda to reveal the nature and effects of racism on both African Americans and whites. His expression is clearly tied to the fictional and autobiographical traditions of African American writers. Gaines's novel serves a function similar to that of the African American autobiography (like Harriet Jacobs's *Incidents in the Life of a Slave Girl*). Gaines teaches us, through Miss Jane, the effects of racism and demonstrates how an African American woman was able to survive slavery and its aftermath with strength and dignity.

Post-1960s African American literature calls attention to the importance of the past on the lives of African Americans in contemporary society. Poets such as Audre Lorde, Maya Angelou, June Jordan, Rita Dove, and Michael Harper examine race, class, and gender in the present and the past in their works. Playwrights such as August Wilson, whose well-known plays include *The Piano Lesson* (pp. 838–898), explore in very provocative manners the quest for freedom, autonomy, and self-direction so prevalent in African American literature.

The voices of African American women poets express the politics of race, gender, and sexual orientation in profound ways. Lorde used her poetry to not only counter racism but also to promote feminism and gay rights. She published seven books of poetry, including *The Black Unicorn* (1978), which was boldly political in nature compared to some of her earlier work; among other topics, she discussed lesbian relationships. Her struggle with breast cancer prompted her to publish *The Cancer Journals* (1980). Jordan also produced politically charged verse, often addressing black-white relationships.

The first black poet laureate of the United States, Rita Dove, writes about racial issues to some extent, but she also writes about other issues of a more universal nature, such as mother-daughter relationships. She won a Pulitzer Prize for *Thomas and Beulah* (1986), a book of verse in narrative form.

Maya Angelou's poetry and prose are filled with inspiration and encouragement not only for African American women but for all people. Her self-confidence and her ability to survive difficulties in her life provide readers with tones of uplift, as demonstrated by her 1970 autobiography *I Know Why the Caged Bird Sings* (pp. 784–787). With "On the Pulse of Morning," a poem she delivered at President Clinton's first inauguration in 1993, she made history as the first woman and the first African American to make such a presentation. The poem stimulates conversation about content, form, and delivery. It also invites comparisons of its rhetorical strategies to those in Angelou's other works, such as her autobiographies.

Angelou brings a rich and varied vocabulary, a feeling for the rhythms of speech, and a fertile imagination to bear on her memories of childhood. Her use of metaphor and simile, which almost invariably communicates the richness of her family and community environment and the African American culture of which they were part, is especially engaging. Nevertheless, Angelou's control of imagery and metaphor does not make merely for stylish writing; it creates drama and force in her commentary on life. The lyric nature of her prose can be compared to that of Langston Hughes's autobiographies. Angelou has taken her skill with language to the big screen. She directed *Down in the Delta*, a 1999 film about African American family life.

African American women writers of the late twentieth century, like Maya Angelou, made their contributions at a time when university African American literature departments were flourishing and African American literary theory became a genre unto itself. Benefiting from struggles for civil rights for African Americans and women and an increased appreciation for diversity, black women are finally being heard: their voices emerge in writing, speech, and music. Many female rap artists, such as Queen Latifah, Salt 'n' Pepa, and MC Lyte have helped to elevate the status of women; their lyrics of independence demonstrate a freedom of expression that has increased over the years.

Within this realm of free expression, divisions have formed between African American men and women. African American women writers, such as Alice Walker and Gloria Naylor, have been criticized by African American men for what they perceive as negative portrayals of black men. Some readers perceive male characters who are abusive or absent as representative of all black men. Walker's *The Color Purple* (pp. 798–802) is a good example of a story that promotes this rift. On a positive note, black women writers in the neorealism movement are not afraid to use realistic male and female characters who have both positive and negative traits, to reflect society's diverse population of all types of people.

The diversity of African American literature during this period is evident. All genres are represented, and the themes and styles of writing cover a wide range. In a sense, Octavia Butler's science fiction novel *Kindred* (pp. 926–930) represents the newest type of realism. Science fiction is not a popular form for many African

American writers, yet Butler has been successful; she won three awards for her science fiction in 1985 alone.

Diversity can also be seen in the wide scope of texts, in several genres, produced by single authors throughout the neorealism movement. For example, Ishmael Reed started his career with the publication of a novel in 1967, and has also published poetry (pp. 899–901), plays, and essays. Michelle Cliff presents a story focused on female concerns in *Abeng* (pp. 920–926). She adds diversity to this group of writers because she is of Jamaican ancestry and writes about that culture. In *Let the Dead Bury Their Dead*, which was nominated for a National Book Critics Circle Award in 1992, Randall Kenan presents a series of stories about the culture of Tims Creek, North Carolina. Instead of focusing on racial issues, he writes about "people" issues, as in the story "Clarence and the Dead" (pp. 936–947). In 1999 Kenan's *Walking on Water: Black American Life at the Turn of the Twenty-First Century* was published. Also writing about culture, Yusef Komunyakaa writes poetry about his Vietnam War experiences (pp. 947–949).

There is something for all readers in the neorealism movement. The saying "There is nothing new under the sun" partly applies to African American literature. African American writers still use their work to present personal and political material. The past is part of the present in the canon of black literature. The changes over the years are obvious as well. African American women writers have more of a presence, and African American literary criticism is a necessary element of black literature that is growing in importance and quantity.

❦ ERNEST GAINES (b. 1933)

Ernest Gaines is best known for his 1971 novel that was produced as a television movie:
The Autobiography of Miss Jane Pittman. *The movie presents the life of Jane
Pittman as she moves from slavery toward freedom. People often assume that the movie
and novel are actual autobiographies of a black woman; however, they are in the genre of
fiction. Gaines endows Jane Pittman with qualities that make her endearing and realistic to readers. He helps the reader identify with the character by putting a story about race
into the larger context of universality. Gaines includes his experiences in Louisiana, where
he was raised, in much of his work.*

Gaines's work is beginning to gain more scholarly attention. His first novels, Catherine
Carmier *(1964) and* Of Love and Dust *(1967), were not popular when initially published.* A Gathering of Old Men *(1983) and* A Lesson Before Dying *(1993), have
been read and studied from the outset. In addition to novels, Gaines has written several
short-story collections, including* Bloodline *(1968). His works make major contributions
to American literature.*

From The Autobiography of Miss Jane Pittman (1971)

Soldiers

It was a day something like right now, dry, hot, and dusty dusty. It might 'a' been
a July, I'm not sure, but it was July or August. Burning up, I won't ever forget. The
Secesh Army, they came by first. The Officers on their horses, the Troops walking, some of them dragging the guns in the dust they was so tired. The Officers
rode up in the yard, and my mistress told them to get down and come in. The
colonel said he couldn't come in, he was going somewhere in a hurry, but he would
be glad to get down and stretch his legs if the good lady of the house would be so
gracious to let him. My mistress said she most graciously did, and after the colonel
had got down he told the others to get down too. The colonel was a little man with
a gun and a sable. The sable was so long it almost dragged on the ground. Looked
like the colonel was a little boy who had got somebody else's sable to play with. My
mistress told me stop standing there gaping, go out there in the road and give the
Troops some water. I had the water in a barrel under one of the chinaball trees. We
knowed the soldiers was coming that way—we had heard the gunfire the day
before, and somebody had already passed the house and told us if the soldiers came
by be prepared to help in every way we could; so they had put me to hauling water.
All morning long I hauled water to that barrel. Now I had to haul the water out
the barrel to the Troops out in the road. Buckets after buckets after buckets. I can't
remember how many buckets I hauled. The Troops was so tired and ragged they
didn't even see me. They took the gourd from me when I handed it to them, and
that was all. After they had drunk, they just let it hang there in their hands, and I
had to reach and get it so I could serve another one. But they didn't even see little

old black me. They couldn't tell if I was white or black, a boy or a girl. They didn't even care what I was. One was just griping. He didn't look too much older than me—face just as dirty as it could be. Just griping: "Just left to me I'll turn them niggers loose, just left to me." When I handed him the water he held the gourd a long time before he drank, then after he had drunk he let the gourd hang in his hand while he just sat there gazing down at the ground.

But these was the same ones, mind you, who had told their people they wouldn't be late for supper. That was before—when the war was just getting started—when they thought fighting a war was nothing but another day's work. "Don't put my food up," they said, "Don't put it up and don't give it away. I'm go'n kill me up a few Yankees and I'm coming right on back home. Who they think they is trying to destruck us way of living? We the nobles, not them. God put us here to live the way we want live, that's in the Bible." (I have asked people to find that in the Bible for me, but no one's found it yet.) "And He put niggers here to see us live that way—that's in the Bible, too. John, chapter so and so. Verse, right now I forget. Now, here them Yankees want come and destruck what the Good Lord done said we can have. Keep my supper warm, Mama, I'll be back before breakfast." These was the same ones griping out in the road right now.

Before all them had a chance to get some water, I looked up and saw another one coming down the road on a horse. He was hitting and kicking that horse fast as his arms and feet could move. Hollering far as you could hear him: "Colonel, Colonel, they coming. Colonel, Colonel, they coming." He went right by us, but the Troops was so tired some of them didn't even raise their head. Some of them even laid down on the ground when he went by. "How far?" the colonel asked him. "I don't know for sure," he said. "Maybe three, four miles back there. All I can see is that dust way up in the air." My mistress handed him two biscuits and a cup of water. He looked at that bread and water like he hadn't seen food or water in a long time and he kept bowing and saying, "Thank you, ma'am; thank you, ma'am; thank you, ma'am." The colonel hit his boots together and kissed my mistress on the hand, then he told the others to get on their horses. He hollered for them in the road to get to their feet, too. Some of them did like he said, but many of them just sat there gazing down at the ground. One of the Officers had to come out in the road and call them to attention. Even then they wasn't in any kind of hurry to get on their feet. They started down the road, and I could hear that same one that had been griping before: "Just left to me I'll turn them niggers loose, just left to me." One of the other Troops told him shut up before he got both of them shot. Him for complaining, and him for being his cousin. He told him shut up or cousin or no cousin he liable to shoot him himself. But till they got out hearing distance all I could hear was that little fellow griping: "Yankees want them, let the Yankees have them—just left to me."

After they had made the bend, I went back in the yard with the bucket and the gourd. My mistress was standing on the gallery watching the dust rising over the field, and just crying. "Sweet, precious blood of the South; sweet precious blood of the South." Just watching that dust, wringing her hands and crying. Then she saw me standing there looking up at her. "What you standing there for?" she said. "Go fill that barrel."

"What for, Mistress?" I said. "They gone now."

"Don't you think Yankees drink?" she said. "Go get that water."

"I got to haul water for old Yankees, too?" I said.

"Yes," she said. "You don't want them boiling you in oil and eating you, do you?"

"No, Mistress," I said.

"You better get that water then," she said. "A Yankee like nothing better than cooking a little nigger gal and chewing her up. Where the rest of them no 'count niggers at, I wonder?"

"They went hiding with Master in the swamps," I said, pointing toward the back.

"Stop that pointing," my mistress said. "You can't tell where a Yankee might be. And you watch your tongue when they get here, too. You say anything about your master and the silver, I'll have you skinned."

"Yes, Mistress," I said.

While I was standing there, one of the other slaves bust round the house and said: "Master say come ask that's all?"

"Where your master at?" my mistress asked him.

"Edge of the swamps there," he said. "Peeping round a tree."

"Go back and tell your master that ain't half of them yet," my mistress said.

The slave bust back round the house, running faster than he did coming there. My mistress told me stop standing there and go get that water.

The Yankees didn't show up till late that evening, so that little fellow who had spotted that dust in the air had a keen eye sight or a bad judge of distance. The Yankee Officers rode up in the yard just like the Secesh Officers did; the Yankee troops plopped down side the road just like the other Troops did. I got the bucket and the gourd and went out there to give them water.

"How many Rebs went by here?" one of the Troops asked me.

"I didn't see no Rebs, Master," I said.

"Come now," he said. "Who made all them tracks out there?"

"Just us niggers," I said.

"Wearing shoes?" he said. "Where your shoes?"

"I took mine off," I said. "They hurt my foot."

"Little girl, don't you know you not suppose to lie?" he said.

"I ain't lying, Master," I said.

"What's your name?" he asked me.

"Ticey, Master," I said.

"They ever beat you, Ticey?" he asked.

"No, Master," I said.

The Troop said, "I ain't a master, Ticey. You can be frank with me. They ever beat you?"

I looked back toward the house and I could see my mistress talking with the Officers on the gallery. I knowed she was too far to hear me and the Troop talking. I looked at him again. I waited for him to ask me the same question.

"They do beat you, don't they, Ticey?" he said.

I nodded.

"What they beat you with, Ticey?" he said.

"Cat-o'-nine-tails, Master," I said.

"We'll get them," the Troop said. "Ten'll die for every whipping you ever got."

"Ten houses will burn," another Troop said.

"Ten fields, too," another one said.

"One of y'all sitting there, take that bucket and go haul that water," the first Troop said.

"I better do it, Master," I said. "They whip me if I don't do my work."

"You rest," he said. "Troop Lewis, on your feet."

Troop Lewis got up real slow; he was tired just like all the rest. He was a little fellow and I felt sorry for him because he looked like the kind everybody was always picking on. He took the bucket from me and went in the yard talking to himself. The other Troop had to holler on him to get moving.

"What they whip you for, Ticey?" he asked me.

"I go to sleep when I look after Young Mistress children," I said.

"You nothing but a child yourself," he said. "How old is you right now?"

"I don't know, Master," I said.

"Would you say ten? 'leven?"

"Yes, Master," I said.

"I ain't a master, Ticey," he said. "I'm just a' old ordinary Yankee soldier come down here to beat them Rebs and set y'all free. You want to be free, don't you, Ticey?"

"Yes, Master," I said.

"And what you go'n do when you free?" he asked me.

"Just sleep, Master," I said.

"Ticey, you not the only one go'n just sleep," he said. "But stop calling me master. I'm Corporal Brown. Can you say corporal?"

"No, Master," I said.

"Try," he said,

I started grinning.

"Come on," he said. "Try."

"I can't say that, Master," I said.

"Can you say Brown?"

"Yes, Master."

"Well, just call me Mr. Brown," he said. "And I'm go'n call you something else 'sides Ticey. Ticey is a slave name, and I don't like slavery. I'm go'n call you Jane," he said. "That's right, I'll call you Jane. That's my girl name back there in Ohio. You like for me to call you that?"

I stood there grinning like a little fool. I rubbed my foot with my big toe and just stood there grinning. The other Troops was grinning at me, too.

"Yes," he said, "I think you do like that name. Well, from now on your name is Jane. Not Ticey no more. Jane. Jane Brown. Miss Jane Brown. When you get older you can change it to what else you want. But till then your name is Jane Brown."

I just stood there grinning, rubbing my foot with my big toe. It was the prettiest name I had ever heard.

"And if any of them ever hit you again, you catch up with me and let me know," he said. "I'll come back here and I'll burn down this place."

The Yankee Officers got on their horses and came out in the road and told the Troops let's go. They got to their feet and marched on. And soon as my mistress thought they couldn't hear her she started calling my name. I just stood there and watched the soldiers go down the road. One of them looked back and waved at me—not Troop Lewis: I reckoned he was still mad at me. I grinned and waved back. After they had made the bend, I stood there and watched the dust high over the field. I was still feeling good because of my new name. Then all of a sudden my mistress was out there and she had grabbed me by the shoulders.

"You little wench, didn't you hear me calling you?" she said. I raised my head high and looked her straight in the face and said: "You called me Ticey. My name ain't no Ticey no more, it's Miss Jane Brown. And Mr. Brown say catch him and tell him if you don't like it."

My mistress face got red, her eyes got wide, and for about half a minute she just stood there gaping at me. Then she gathered up her dress and started running for the house. That night when the master and the rest of them came in from the swamps she told my master I had sassed her in front of the Yankees. My master told two of the other slaves to hold me down. One took my arms, the other one took my legs. My master jecked up my dress and gived my mistress the whip and told her to teach me a lesson. Every time she hit me she asked me what I said my name was. I said Jane Brown. She hit me again: what I said my name was. I said Jane Brown.

My mistress got tired beating me and told my master to beat me some. He told her that was enough, I was already bleeding.

"Sell her," my mistress said.

"Who go'n buy her with them Yankees tramping all over the place?" my master said.

"Take her to the swamps and kill her," my mistress said. "Get her out my sight."

"Kill her?" my master said. "Brown come back here asking 'bout her, then what? I'll put her in the field and bring another one up here to look after them children."

They put me in the field when I was ten or 'leven. A year after that the Freedom come.

Freedom

We was in the field chopping cotton when we heard the bell ringing. We was scared to stop work—the sun was too high in the sky for us to go in yet. But the bell went on ringing and ringing; just ringing and ringing. The driver, a great big old black, round, oily-face nigger kept on looking back over his shoulders toward the house. Every time the bell rang he looked back. He told us to keep on working, he was going in to see what all the ringing was about. I watched him go up to the house, then I saw him coming back waving his arm. We swung our hoes on our shoulders and went across the field. The driver told us the master wanted us all at the house. We didn't ask what he wanted us for, we had no idea, we just went up there. The master was standing on the gallery with a sheet of paper.

"This all y'all?" he asked. "All them children in the quarters, too? I want every-body here who can stand up."

The people said this was all us.

"All right, I got news for y'all," the master said. "Y'all free. Proclamation papers just come to me and they say y'all free as I am. Y'all can stay and work on shares—because I can't pay you nothing, because I ain't got nothing myself since them Yankees went by here last time. Y'all can stay or y'all can go. If y'all stay I promise I'll be fair as I always been with y'all."

Old Mistress and Young Mistress was standing in the door crying, and right behind them the house niggers crying, too. For a while after the master got through reading the Proclamation the people didn't make a sound. Just standing there looking up at him like they was still listening to his words.

"Well, that's that," he said.

Then all a sudden somebody hollered, and everybody started singing. Just singing and dancing and clapping. Old people you didn't think could even walk started hopping round there like game roosters. This what the people was singing:

"We free, we free, we free
We free, we free, we free
We free, we free, we free
Oh, Lordy, we free."

Just singing and clapping, just singing and clapping. Just talking to each other, just patting each other on the back.

The driver he never got in the celebration him. Everybody else singing and clapping, he just standing there looking up at the master. Then he moved closer to the gallery and said: "Master, if we free to go, where is we to go?"

Before the master could open his mouth, I said: "Where North at? Point to it. I'll show y'all where to go."

The driver said: "Shut up. You ain't nothing but trouble. I ain't had nothing but trouble out you since you come in that field."

"If I ain't nothing but trouble, you ain't nothing but Nothing," I said.

And the next thing I knowed, my mouth was numb and I was laying down there on the ground. The master looked at me down there and said: "I can't do a thing about it. You free and don't belong to me no more. Got to fight your own battle best you can."

I jumped up from there and sunk my teeth in that nigger's hand. His hand was rough as 'cuda legs. He wrenched his hand out my mouth and numbed the side of my face. This time when I got up I grabbed that hoe I had brought out the field. An old man we all called Unc Isom stepped in front of me.

"Hold," he said.

"Hold nothing," I said. "Nigger, say your prayers. Maker, here you come."

"Didn't I say hold," Unc Isom said. "When I say hold, I mean just that: hold."

I eased the hoe to the ground, but I kept my eyes on the driver all the time. I touched my lips with my hand, but I couldn't feel a thing. Not bleeding, but numb as it could be.

When Unc Isom seen I wasn't go'n hit that nigger with that hoe, he turned to the master.

"The papers say we can go or we can stay, Master?" he asked him.

"No, they just say y'all free, Isom," the master said. "They don't care what y'all do, where y'all go. I'm the one who saying y'all can stay on if y'all want. If you stay, I got to work you on shares, and you work when you want. You don't have to work on Sundays less you want. Can go to church and stay there and sing all day if you want. You free as I am, Isom."

Unc Isom said, "Master, we can gather down the quarters and talk just between us?"

The master said, "What you go'n be talking 'bout down there, Isom?"

"Just if we ought to go or stay, Master," Unc Isom said.

"Sure, y'all free as I am," the master said. "Y'all can take all the time y'all want to decide. Long as you ain't deciding on burning down the place."

Unc Isom had to grin to himself. "Master, ain't nothing like that," he said.

"Give the children some apples before they go," the mistress said.

"And the men and women cider," the master said. "Celebrate y'all freedom."

"Hold," Unc Isom said. "Apples and cider later. Now, we go in the quarters and talk."

Unc Isom was a kind of advisor to us there in the quarters. Some people said he had been a witch doctor sometime back. I know he knowed a lot about roots and herbs, and the people was always going to him for something to cure colic or the bots or whatever they had. That's why they followed him when he spoke. The young people grumbled because they wanted the apples, but the old people followed him without a word. When we came up to his cabin he told everybody to kneel down and thank God for freedom. I didn't want kneel, I didn't know too much about the Lord then, but I knelt out of respect. When Unc Isom got through praying he stood up and looked at us again. He was an old man, black black, with long white hair. He could have been in his 80s, he could have been in his 90s—I have no idea how old he was.

"Now, I ask the question," he said. "What's we to do?"

"Slavery over, let's get moving," somebody said.

"Let's stay," somebody else said. "See if old Master go'n act different when it's freedom."

"Y'all do like y'all want," I said. "I'm headed North." I turned to leave, but I stopped. "Which way North?"

"Before y'all start out here heading anywhere, what y'all go'n eat?" Unc Isom said. "Where y'all go'n sleep? Who go'n protect you from the patrollers?"

"They got Yankees," I said.

"They got Yankees, they got Yankees," Unc Isom mocked me. I could see he didn't have a tooth in his mouth. "Yankee told you your name was Jane; soon as Old Mistress start beating on you, you can't find Yankee."

"They can't beat me no more," I said. "Them papers say I'm free, free like everybody else."

"They ain't go'n just beat you if they catch you, they kill you if they catch you now," Unc Isom said. "Before now they didn't kill you because you was somebody chattel. Now you ain't owned by nobody but fate. Nobody to protect you now, little Ticey."

"My name is Jane, Unc Isom," I said. "And I'm headed for Ohio. Soon as you point that way."

"I don't know too much 'bout Ohio," Unc Isom said, coming out in the road. "Where it at or where it s'pose to be, I ain't for sure." He turned toward the swamps, then he raised his hand and pointed. "North is that way. Sun on your right in the morning, your left in the evening. North Star point the way at night. If you stay in the swamps, the moss is on the north side of the tree root."

"I'm heading out," I said. "Soon as I get me few of them apples and my other dress. Anybody else going?"

The young people started moving out in the road, but the old people started crying and holding them back. I didn't have a mama or a daddy to cry and hold me back. My mama was killed when I was young and I had never knowed my daddy. He belong to another plantation. I never did know his name.

"Hold," Unc Isom said. He raised both of his hands like he was getting ready to wave us back. "This rejoicing time, not crying time. Ain't we done seen enough weeping? Ain't we done seen enough separation? Hold now."

"You telling us to stay here?" somebody young said.

"Them who want stay, stay," he said. "Then who must go, go. But this no time for weeping. Rejoice now."

"We leaving out," somebody young said. "If the old people want stay here, stay. We free, let's move."

"Amen," I said.

"You free from what?" Unc Isom said. "Free to do what—break more hearts?"

"Niggers hearts been broke ever since niggers been in this world," somebody young said. "I done seen babies jecked from mama titty. That was breaking hearts, too."

"That couldn't be helped," Unc Isom said. "This can be helped."

"This can't be helped," somebody young said. "They got blood on this place, and I done stepped all in it. I done waded in it to my waist. You can mend a broken heart, you can't wash blood off your body."

"Hold," Unc Isom said, raising his hands again. "When you talking 'bout mama and papa's heart, hold now."

"Mama and papa's heart can't be pained no more than they been pained already," somebody young said.

"Let's go," somebody else said. "All this arguing ain't putting us no closer North."

"Hold," Unc Isom said. "This wisdom I'm speaking from. Hold now."

"Give your wisdom to the ones staying here with you," somebody young said. "Rest of us moving out."

The boy who spoke to Unc Isom like that started up the quarters toward the big house. Unc Isom let him walk a little piece, then he hollered at him to stop. The boy wouldn't stop. Unc Isom hollered at him again. This time the boy looked back over his shoulder. Unc Isom didn't say a thing, he just stood there pointing his finger at the boy.

Me and some of the other people started toward the big house to get some apples, and one of the women said Unc Isom had put bad mark on the boy. Another woman said Unc Isom didn't have power to put bad mark on you no more, he was too old now. I didn't know how powerful Unc Isom was, so I just listened to the talking and didn't say nothing.

The master had put a barrel of potatoes side the barrel of apples, and he was sitting on the gallery watching the people coming back in the yard. He asked us what we had decided in the quarters. We told him some of us was going, some of us was staying. We asked him could the ones going take anything. He wanted to tell us no, but he nodded toward the barrel and told us to take what we needed and get out. We got all the apples and potatoes we could carry, then we went back to the quarters to get our clothes. In slavery you had two dresses and a pair of shoes and a coat. A man had an extra pair of pants and an extra shirt, a pair of shoes and a coat. We tied up the apples and potatoes in our extra clothes and started out.

Heading North

We didn't know a thing. We didn't know where we was going, we didn't know what we was go'n eat when the apples and potatoes ran out, we didn't know where we was go'n sleep that night. If we reached the North, we didn't know if we was go'n stay together or separate. We had never thought about nothing like that, because we had never thought we was go'n ever be free. Yes, we had heard about freedom, we had even talked about freedom, but we never thought we was go'n ever see that day. Even when we knowed the Yankees had come in the State, even when we saw them marching by the gate we still didn't feel we was go'n ever be free. That's why we hadn't got ourself ready. When the word came down that we was free, we dropped everything and started out.

It was hot. Must have been May or June. Probably June—but I'm not sure. We went across the cotton patch toward the swamps. The young men and boys started breaking down cotton stalks just to show Old Master what they thought of him and his old slavery. Somebody hollered that they better use their strength to get some corn, and we all shot out for the corn patch across the field.

Now, when we came up to the swamps nobody wanted to take the lead. Nobody wanted to be the one blamed for getting everybody else lost. All us just standing there fumbling round, waiting for somebody else to take charge.

Then somebody in the back said, "Move out the way." I looked, and that was Big Laura. She was big just like her name say, and she was tough as any man I ever seen. She could plow, chop wood, cut and load much cane as any man on the place. She had two children. One in her arms, a little girl; and she was leading Ned by the hand. Don't worry, I'll come to Ned later. Yes, Lord, I'll come to him later. But even with them two children she had the biggest bundle out there balanced on her head.

Big Laura took the lead and we started walking again. Walking fast, but staying quiet. Somebody said we ought to get sticks just in case of snakes, so we all hunted for a good green stick. Now everybody had a stick but Big Laura. She leading the way with that little girl in her arms and Ned by the hand. She had found us a good clean path and it was cool under the trees, and everybody was happy. We walked and walked and walked. Almost sundown before we stopped the first time.

"We headed toward Ohio?" I asked.

"You got somebody waiting for you in Ohio?" they asked me.

"Mr. Brown told me look him up," I said.

Nobody believed Mr. Brown had told me that, but they didn't say nothing.

"I want go to Ohio," I said.

"Go on to Ohio," one of them said. "Nobody holding you back."

"I don't know the way," I said.

"Then shut up," one of them said.

"Y'all just sorry y'all ain't got nobody waiting for y'all nowhere," I said.

Nobody said nothing. I was little, and they didn't feel they needed to argue with me.

We was in a thicket of sycamore trees, and it was quiet and clean here, and we had a little breeze, because way up in the top of the trees I could see the limbs sagging just a little. Everybody was tired from the long walk and we just sat there quiet, not saying a thing for a good while. Then somebody said: "My new name Abe Washington. Don't call me Buck no more." We must have been two dozens of us there, and now everybody started changing names like you change hats. Nobody was keeping the same name Old Master had gived them. This one would say, "My new name Cam Lincoln." That one would say, "My new name Ace Freeman." Another one, "My new name Sherman S. Sherman." "What that S for?" "My Title." Another one would say, "My new name Job." "Job what?" "Just Job." "Nigger, this ain't slavery no more. You got to have two names." "Job Lincoln, then." "Nigger, you ain't no kin to me. I'm Lincoln." "I don't care. I'm still Job Lincoln. Want fight?" Another one would say, "My name Neremiah King." Another one standing by a tree would say, "My new name Bill Moses. No more Rufus."

They went on and on like that. We had one slow-wit fellow there who kept on opening his mouth to say his new name, but before he could get it out somebody else had said a name. He was just opening and closing his mouth like a baby after his mama's titty. Then all a sudden when he had a little time to speak he said Brown. They had took all the other names from him, so he took Brown. I had been sitting there on the end of a log listening to them squabbling over new names, but I didn't have to get in the squabbling because I already had a new name. I had had mine for over a year now, and I had put up with a lot of trouble to hold on to it. But when I heard the slow-wit say his name was Brown I was ready to fight. I jumped up off that log and went for him.

"No, you don't," I said.

He said, "I, I, I, can be, be, be Brown if I want be, be, be Brown." He was picking on me because I was small and didn't have nobody there to stand up for me. "You not the on', on', only one ra, ra, round here that can be, be, be Brown," he said. "Me', me', mess round here wi', wi', with me, I ma', ma', make you, you, you change your name back to Ti', Ti', Ticey."

"I'll die first," I said.

"Go, go, go right on and di' di', die," he said. "Br', Br', Brown my name."

And I tried to crack his head open with that stick. But I didn't bit more hurt that loon than I would hurt that post at the end of my gallery. He came on me and I swung the stick and backed from him. He kept coming on me, and I kept hitting and backing back. Hitting and backing back. Then he jecked the stick out my hand and swung it away. I tried to get the stick, but I fell, and when I looked up, there he was right over me. He didn't look like a man now, he didn't even look like a loon, he looked more like a wild animal. Animal-like greed in his face. He grabbed me and started with me in the bushes. But we hadn't gone more than three, four steps when I started hearing this noise. *Whup, whup, whup.* I didn't know what the noise was. I was too busy trying to get away from that loon to think this noise had anything to do with me or him. I heard the noise again: *whup, whup, whup.* Every time it hit now I saw the hurt in the slow-wit's face. He was still heading with me in the bushes, but every time the noise hit I could see the hurt in his face. Then I saw the stick come down on his shoulder, and this time he swung around. Big Laura had the stick cocked back to hit him again.

"Drop her, you stud-dog," she said. "Drop her or I'll break your neck."

He let me slide out of his arms, just standing there looking at Big Laura like he was wondering why she had hit him. I tried to get the stick away from Big Laura so I could get another crack at him, but she pushed me to the side.

"Go back to that plantation," she said. "Go back there. That's where you do your stud-ing."

"No," he said.

"I say get out of here," she said, ready to hit him.

"No," he said. (Because he was a slow-wit, and he wouldn't know where to go by himself.)

Big Laura hit him in the side with the stick. She hit him twice in the side, but all he did was covered his head and cried. He was a slow-wit and couldn't look after himself. All he could do was do what you told him to do.

"You got just one more time to try your stud-ing round me," Big Laura told him. "Just one more time, and I'll kill you." She looked at everybody there. "That go for the rest of y'all," she said. "You free, then you go'n act like free men. If you want act like you did on that plantation, turn around now and go on back to that plantation."

Nobody said a thing. Most of them looked down at the ground. Big Laura went back to her children, and I went back and sat down on the log. The slow-wit stood over there crying and slobbering on himself.

The sun went down and we found the North Star. Big Laura put her bundle on her head, then she took that little girl in her arms and Ned by the hand and we started walking again. We walked and walked and walked and walked. Lord, we walked. I got so tired I wanted to drop. Some of the people started grumbling and hanging back, but they didn't know where else to turn and they soon caught up. Big Laura never stopped and never looked around to see who was following. That little girl clutched in her arms, Ned by the hand, she moved through them trees like she knowed exactly where she was going and wasn't go'n let nothing in the world get in her way.

We went on till way up in the night before we stopped to sleep. Big Laura dropped her bundle on the ground and sat the children side it. She took everything out the bundle and spread the dress out so the children could have a pallet to lay down on. Then she dug a hole in the ground and filled it with leaves and dry moss. She stuck a little piece of lint cotton under the moss and leaves and started scraping a piece of flint and iron together near the cotton. Soon she had made fire, and she covered the fire with green moss to get smoke. She sat down by the pallet and waved her hand over the children in case mosquitoes broke through the screen. The rest of the people closed in but stayed quiet. And you heard nothing but the swamps. Crickets, frogs, an owl in a tree somewhere.

"You can go to sleep," I told Big Laura. "I'll keep mosquitoes off the children."

"Sleep yourself," she said. "You go'n need all the strength you have to reach Ohio."

That was all I needed to hear. The next minute I was snoring.

Massacre

The next thing I knowed the sun was shining bright and somebody was hollering, "Patrollers."

Everybody jumped up and made it for the bushes. Big Laura hollered at me to grab Ned and run. I had already passed Ned, but I leaned back and grabbed him and almost jecked him up off the ground. Half the time I was carrying him, half the time I was dragging him. We crawled under a bush and I pressed his face to the ground and told him to stay quiet quiet. From the bush I could still see the spot where we had been. The big slow-wit was still out there. He didn't know where to run to or what to do. Like he wanted to go in every direction at the same time, but he didn't know where to go. I wanted to call him—but I was scared the patrollers might see him coming toward us. Then the patrollers came in on horses and mules. Patrollers was poor white trash that used to find the runaway slaves for the masters. Them and the soldiers from the Secesh Army was the ones who made up the Ku Klux Klans later on. Even that day they had Secesh soldiers mixed in there with them. I could tell the Secesh from the patrollers by the uniforms. The Secesh wore gray; the patrollers wore work clothes no better than what the slaves wore. They came in on horses and mules, and soon as they saw the slow-wit they surrounded him and started beating him with sticks of wood. Some of them had guns, but they would not waste a bullet. More satisfaction beating him with sticks. They beat him, he covered up, but they beat him till he was down. Then one of the patrollers slid off the mule, right cross his tail, and cracked the slow-wit in the head. I could hear his head crack like you hear dry wood break.

I wanted to jump up from there and run—but what about Ned? I couldn't leave him there—look what Big Laura had done for me just yesterday. I couldn't take him with me, either—they would see us. I stayed there, with my heart jumping, jumping, jumping.

The patrollers moved in the bushes to hunt for the rest of the people. They could tell from the camp there must have been lot of us there, and they knowed we was still close around. They moved in with sticks now to look for us. I could hear them hitting against the bushes and talking to each other. Then when they spotted somebody, a bunch of them would surround the person and beat him till they had knocked him unconscious or killed him. Then they would move somewhere else. First you would hear them hitting against the bushes lightly, then after they spotted somebody you would hear them hitting the bushes hard. Now, you heard screaming, begging; screaming, begging; screaming, begging—till it was quiet again.

I kept one hand on my bundle and one on the side of Ned's face holding him down. I was go'n stay there till I thought they had spotted me, then I was getting out of there fast. I told Ned be ready to run, but stay till I gived him the sign. I was pressing so hard on his face I doubt if he even heard me, but all my pressing he never made a sound. Small as he was he knowed death was only a few feet away.

After a while the patrollers left. They went right by us, and I could hear them talking. One was saying, "Goddamn, she was mean. Did you see her? Did you see her? Goddam, she could fight." Another one spit and said: "They ain't human. Gorilla, I say." The first one said: "Lord, did you see Gat's head? Made me sick." Another one: "Gat all right?" Another one: "Afraid not. Afraid he go'n die on us."

They passed right by us, and my heart jumping, jumping, jumping. I kept my hand on my bundle and I kept Ned quiet till the last one had passed. Then I relaxed a little bit. I took me a deep breath and looked up at the sky. It was quiet, quiet, not a sound. I mean you couldn't even hear a bird. Nothing but the sun— and the dust the men had raised thrashing in the bushes. I could see the sun streaking through the trees down to the ground like a long slide. Only one time, so they say, it refused to shine: when they nailed the Master to the cross.

I stood up and told Ned come on, and we went back to the place where we had camped. The slow-wit was dead, all right; his skull busted there like a coconut. One of his shirt sleeves was knocked clean off. I turned to Ned, but he was standing there just as calm as he could be.

I left the slow-wit, I wanted to find Big Laura and give Ned back to her. I saw somebody laying over in the bushes, but when I got closer I saw it was a man. He was dead like the slow-wit, and I went on looking for Big Laura. I had to give Ned back to her, and I needed her to show me how to reach Ohio.

I looked for her everywhere. Sometimes I made Ned stand side a tree while I went in the bushes looking for her. I saw people laying everywhere. All of them was dead or dying, or so broken up they wouldn't ever move on their own. I stood there a little while looking at them, but I didn't know what to do, and I moved back.

Then I saw Big Laura. She was laying on the ground with her baby still clutched in her arms. I made Ned stay back while I went closer. Even before I knelt down I saw that her and the baby was both dead.

I took the baby out her arms. I had to pull hard to get her free. I knowed I couldn't bury Big Laura—I didn't have a thing to dig with—but maybe I could bury her child. But when I looked back at Big Laura and saw how empty her arms was, I just laid the little baby right back down. I didn't cry, I couldn't cry. I had seen so much beating and suffering; I had heard about so much cruelty in those 'leven or twelve years of my life I hardly knowed how to cry. I went back to Ned and asked him if he wanted to go to Ohio with me. He nodded.

When I turned away I saw a patroller's cap laying on the ground covered with blood. I wondered if that was Gat's cap. Then I saw another one all busted up. So she had busted two of them in the head before they killed her and her baby.

Before we started out I thought we might as well take some of the grub that was left there. I got enough corn and potatoes to last us a week. I reckoned that in a week I ought to be in Ohio or close there. After I got the food, I got a few pieces of clothes for me and Ned to sleep on at night. Then I found the flint and iron Big Laura had used to light the fire with. Both of them looked like pieces of rock, so anytime anybody asked me what they was I just told them, "Two little rocks." I gived them to Ned and told him it was go'n be his job to see that they got to Ohio same time we did. After I had covered up Big Laura and the child with some clothes, I put the bundle on my head and we started out. Every now and then I asked Ned if he was tired. If he said no, we went on; if he said yes, we found a good place to sit down. Then I would take something out the bundle for us to eat. Ned would put the rocks on the ground while we ate. But soon as he was through eating he'd pick them up again.

We went on, staying in the bushes all the time. When Ned got tired, we stopped, nibbled on something, then after he had rested we started out again. When the sun went down and the stars came out we traveled by the North Star. We didn't stop that night till we came up to a river. But I could see it was too wide and too deep for us to cross, so we moved back in the swamps for the night. I dug a hole in the ground and built a little fire just like I saw Big Laura do the night before. While me and Ned sat there eating a raw potato, I put two more potatoes and two more yers of corn in the fire. When Ned got through eating, he went to sleep on the little pallet I had made for him on the ground.

I sat there looking at Ned, wondering what I was go'n do next. "I got this child to take care, I got that river to cross—and how many more rivers I got to cross before I reach Ohio?" I said to myself.

I looked at Ned laying there. He was snoring like he was in a little bed at home. I didn't hear any mosquitoes but I waved my hand over him like I saw Big Laura do the night before. After a while I laid down side him, and I didn't wake up till I felt the sun shining in my face.

The sky was more pretty and bluer than I had ever seen it before. I felt better than I had ever felt in my life. Birds was singing in every tree. I woke up Ned and told him look at the air and listen to the birds. But Ned wasn't much interested in this kind of stuff. He was probably thinking about his mama and his little sister. I was thinking about them, too; thinking about all the people; 'specially the slow-wit I had seen them kill; but I looked at it this way, we had to keep going. We couldn't let what happened yesterday stop us today.

I pulled the corn and potatoes out the hole. All of them good and done. We ate the potatoes for breakfast. I was go'n save the corn for me and Ned's dinner.

The Sky Is Gray (1968)

1

Go'n be coming in a few minutes. Coming round that bend down there full speed. And I'm go'n get out my handkerchief and wave it down, and we go'n get on it and go.

I keep on looking for it, but Mama don't look that way no more. She's looking down the road where we just come from. It's a long old road, and far 's you can see you don't see nothing but gravel. You got dry weeds on both sides, and you got trees on both sides, and fences on both sides, too. And you got cows in the pastures and they standing close together. And when we was coming out here to catch the bus I seen the smoke coming out of the cows's noses.

I look at my mama and I know what she's thinking. I been with Mama so much, just me and her, I know what she's thinking all the time. Right now it's home—Auntie and them. She's thinking if they got enough wood—if she left enough there to keep them warm till we get back. She's thinking if it go'n rain and if any of them go'n have to go out in the rain. She's thinking 'bout the hog—if he go'n get out, and if Ty and Val be able to get him back in. She always worry like that when she leaves the house. She don't worry too much if she leave me there with the smaller ones, 'cause she know I'm go'n look after them and look after Auntie and everything else. I'm the oldest and she say I'm the man.

I look at my mama and I love my mama. She's wearing that black coat and that black hat and she's looking sad. I love my mama and I want put my arm round her and tell her. But I'm not supposed to do that. She say that's weakness and that's crybaby stuff, and she don't want no crybaby round her. She don't want you to be scared, either. 'Cause Ty's scared of ghosts and she's always whipping him. I'm scared of the dark, too, but I make 'tend I ain't. I make 'tend I ain't 'cause I'm the oldest, and I got to set a good sample for the rest. I can't ever be scared and I can't ever cry. And that's why I never said nothing 'bout my teeth. It's been hurting me and hurting me close to a month now, but I never said it. I didn't say it 'cause I didn't want act like a crybaby, and 'cause I know we didn't have enough money to go have it pulled. But, Lord, it been hurting me. And look like it wouldn't start till at night when you was trying to get yourself little sleep. Then soon 's you shut your eyes—ummmummm, Lord, look like it go right down to your heartstring.

"Hurting, hanh?" Ty'd say.

I'd shake my head, but I wouldn't open my mouth for nothing. You open your mouth and let that wind in, and it almost kill you.

I'd just lay there and listen to them snore. Ty there, right 'side me, and Auntie and Val over by the fireplace. Val younger than me and Ty, and he sleeps with Auntie. Mama sleeps round the other side with Louis and Walker.

I'd just lay there and listen to them, and listen to that wind out there, and listen to that fire in the fireplace. Sometimes it'd stop long enough to let me get little rest. Sometimes it just hurt, hurt, hurt. Lord, have mercy.

2

Auntie knowed it was hurting me. I didn't tell nobody but Ty, 'cause we buddies and he ain't go'n tell nobody. But some kind of way Auntie found out. When she asked me, I told her no, nothing was wrong. But she knowed it all the time. She told me to mash up a piece of aspirin and wrap it in some cotton and jugg it down in that hole. I did it, but it didn't do no good. It stopped for a little while, and started right back again. Auntie wanted to tell Mama, but I told her, "Uh-uh." 'Cause I knowed we didn't have any money, and it just was go'n make her mad again. So Auntie told Monsieur Bayonne, and Monsieur Bayonne came over to the house and told me to kneel down 'side him on the fireplace. He put his finger in his mouth and made the Sign of the Cross on my jaw. The tip of Monsieur Bayonne's finger is some hard, 'cause he's always playing on that guitar. If we sit outside at night we can always hear Monsieur Bayonne playing on his guitar. Sometimes we leave him out there playing on the guitar.

Monsieur Bayonne made the Sign of the Cross over and over on my jaw, but that didn't do no good. Even when he prayed and told me to pray some, too, that tooth still hurt me.

"How you feeling?" he say.

"Same," I say.

He kept on praying and making the Sign of the Cross and I kept on praying, too.

"Still hurting?" he say.

"Yes, sir."

Monsieur Bayonne mashed harder and harder on my jaw. He mashed so hard he almost pushed me over on Ty. But then he stopped.

"What kind of prayers you praying, boy?" he say.

"Baptist," I say.

"Well, I'll be—no wonder that tooth still killing him. I'm going one way and he pulling the other. Boy, don't you know any Catholic prayers?"

"I know 'Hail Mary,'" I say.

"Then you better start saying it."

"Yes, sir."

He started mashing on my jaw again, and I could hear him praying at the same time. And, sure enough, after while it stopped hurting me.

Me and Ty went outside where Monsieur Bayonne's two hounds was and we started playing with them. "Let's go hunting," Ty say. "All right," I say; and we went on back in the pasture. Soon the hounds got on a trail, and me and Ty followed them all 'cross the pasture and then back in the woods, too. And then they cornered this little old rabbit and killed him, and me and Ty made them get back, and we picked up the rabbit and started on back home. But my tooth had started hurting me again. It was hurting me plenty now, but I wouldn't tell Monsieur Bayonne. That night I didn't sleep a bit, and first thing in the morning Auntie told me to go back and let Monsieur Bayonne pray over me some more. Monsieur Bayonne was in his kitchen making coffee when I got there. Soon 's he seen me he knowed what was wrong.

"All right, kneel down there 'side that stove," he say. "And this time make sure you pray Catholic. I don't know nothing 'bout that Baptist, and I don't want know nothing 'bout him."

3

Last night Mama say, "Tomorrow we going to town."

"It ain't hurting me no more," I say. "I can eat anything on it."

"Tomorrow we going to town," she say.

And after she finished eating, she got up and went to bed. She always go to bed early now. 'Fore Daddy went in the Army, she used to stay up late. All of us sitting out on the gallery or round the fire. But now, look like soon 's she finish eating she go to bed.

This morning when I woke up, her and Auntie was standing 'fore the fireplace. She say: "Enough to get there and get back. Dollar and a half to have it pulled. Twenty-five for me to go, twenty-five for him. Twenty-five for me to come back, twenty-five for him. Fifty cents left. Guess I get little piece of salt meat with that."

"Sure can use it," Auntie say. "White beans and no salt meat ain't white beans."

"I do the best I can," Mama say.

They was quiet after that, and I made 'tend I was still asleep.

"James, hit the floor," Auntie say.

I still made 'tend I was asleep. I didn't want them to know I was listening.

"All right," Auntie say, shaking me by the shoulder. "Come on. Today's the day."

I pushed the cover down to get out, and Ty grabbed it and pulled it back.

"You, too, Ty," Auntie say.

"I ain't getting no teef pulled," Ty say.

"Don't mean it ain't time to get up," Auntie say. "Hit it, Ty."

Ty got up grumbling.

"James, you hurry up and get in your clothes and eat your food," Auntie say. "What time y'all coming back?" she say to Mama.

"That 'leven o'clock bus," Mama say. "Got to get back in that field this evening."

"Get a move on you, James," Auntie say.

I went in the kitchen and washed my face, then I ate my breakfast. I was having bread and syrup. The bread was warm and hard and tasted good. And I tried to make it last a long time.

Ty came back there grumbling and mad at me.

"Got to get up," he say. "I ain't having no teefes pulled. What I got to be getting up for?"

Ty poured some syrup in his pan and got a piece of bread. He didn't wash his hands, neither his face, and I could see that white stuff in his eyes.

"You the one getting your teef pulled," he say. "What I got to get up for. I bet if I was getting a teef pulled, you wouldn't be getting up. Shucks; syrup again. I'm getting tired of this old syrup. Syrup, syrup, syrup. I'm go'n take with the sugar diabetes. I want me some bacon sometime."

"Go out in the field and work and you can have your bacon," Auntie say. She stood in the middle door looking at Ty. "You better be glad you got syrup. Some people ain't got that—hard 's time is."

"Shucks," Ty say. "How can I be strong."

"I don't know too much 'bout your strength," Auntie say; "but I know where you go'n be hot at, you keep that grumbling up. James, get a move on you; your mama waiting."

I ate my last piece of bread and went in the front room. Mama was standing 'fore the fireplace warming her hands. I put on my coat and my cap, and we left the house.

4

I look down there again, but it still ain't coming. I almost say, "It ain't coming yet," but I keep my mouth shut. 'Cause that's something else she don't like. She don't like for you to say something just for nothing. She can see it ain't coming, I can see it ain't coming, so why say it ain't coming. I don't say it, I turn and look at the river that's back of us. It's so cold the smoke's just raising up from the water. I see a bunch of pool-doos not too far out—just on the other side the lilies. I'm wondering if you can eat pool-doos. I ain't too sure, 'cause I ain't never ate none. But I done ate owls and blackbirds, and I done ate redbirds, too. I didn't want kill the redbirds, but she made me kill them. They had two of them back there. One in my trap, one in Ty's trap. Me and Ty was go'n play with them and let them go, but she made me kill them 'cause we needed the food.

"I can't," I say. "I can't."

"Here," she say. "Take it."

"I can't," I say. "I can't. I can't kill him, Mama, please."

"Here," she say. "Take this fork, James."

"Please, Mama, I can't kill him," I say.

I could tell she was go'n hit me. I jerked back, but I didn't jerk back soon enough.

"Take it," she say.

I took it and reached in for him, but he kept on hopping to the back.

"I can't, Mama," I say. The water just kept on running down my face. "I can't," I say.

"Get him out of there," she say.

I reached in for him and he kept on hopping to the back. Then I reached in farther, and he pecked me on the hand.

"I can't, Mama," I say.

She slapped me again.

I reached in again, but he kept on hopping out my way. Then he hopped to one side and I reached there. The fork got him on the leg and I heard his leg pop. I pulled my hand out 'cause I had hurt him.

"Give it here," she say, and jerked the fork out my hand.

She reached in and got the little bird right in the neck. I heard the fork go in his neck, and I heard it go in the ground. She brought him out and helt him right in front of me.

"That's one," she say. She shook him off and gived me the fork. "Get the other one."

"I can't, Mama," I say. "I'll do anything, but don't make me do that."

She went to the corner of the fence and broke the biggest switch over there she could find. I knelt 'side the trap, crying.

"Get him out of there," she say.

"I can't, Mama."

She started hitting me 'cross the back. I went down on the ground, crying.

"Get him," she say.

"Octavia?" Auntie say.

'Cause she had come out of the house and she was standing by the tree looking at us.

"Get him out of there," Mama say.

"Octavia," Auntie say, "explain to him. Explain to him. Just don't beat him. Explain to him."

But she hit me and hit me and hit me.

I'm still young—I ain't no more than eight; but I know now; I know why I had to do it. (They was so little, though. They was so little. I 'member how I picked the feathers off them and cleaned them and helt them over the fire. Then we all ate them. Ain't had but a little bitty piece each, but we all had a little bitty piece, and everybody just looked at me 'cause they was so proud.) Suppose she had to go away? That's why I had to do it. Suppose she had to go away like Daddy went away? Then who was go'n look after us? They had to be somebody left to carry on. I didn't know it then, but I know it now. Auntie and Monsieur Bayonne talked to me and made me see.

5

Time I see it I get out my handkerchief and start waving. It's still 'way down there, but I keep waving anyhow. Then it come up and stop and me and Mama get on. Mama tell me go sit in the back while she pay. I do like she say, and the people look at me. When I pass the little sign that say "White" and "Colored," I start looking for a seat. I just see one of them back there, but I don't take it, 'cause I want my mama to sit down herself. She comes in the back and sit down, and I lean on the seat. They got seats in the front, but I know I can't sit there, 'cause I have to sit back of the sign. Anyhow, I don't want sit there if my mama go'n sit back here.

They got a lady sitting 'side my mama and she looks at me and smiles little bit. I smile back, but I don't open my mouth, 'cause the wind'll get in and make that tooth ache. The lady take out a pack of gum and reach me a slice, but I shake my head. The lady just can't understand why a little boy'll turn down gum, and she reach me a slice again. This time I point to my jaw. The lady understands and smiles little bit, and I smile little bit, but I don't open my mouth, though.

They got a girl sitting 'cross from me. She got on a red overcoat and her hair's plaited in one big plait. First, I make 'tend I don't see her over there, but then I start looking at her little bit. She make 'tend she don't see me, either, but I catch her looking that way. She got a cold, and every now and then she h'ist that little handkerchief to her nose. She ought to blow it, but she don't. Must think she's too much a lady or something.

Every time she h'ist that little handkerchief, the lady 'side her say something in her ear. She shakes her head and lays her hands in her lap again. Then I catch her kind of looking where I'm at. I smile at her little bit. But think she'll smile back? Uh-uh. She just turn up her little old nose and turn her head. Well, I show her both of us can turn us head. I turn mine too and look out at the river.

The river is gray. The sky is gray. They have pool-doos on the water. The water is wavy, and the pool-doos go up and down. The bus go round a turn, and you got plenty trees hiding the river. Then the bus go round another turn, and I can see the river again.

I look toward the front where all the white people sitting. Then I look at that little old gal again. I don't look right at her, 'cause I don't want all them people to know I love her. I just look at her little bit, like I'm looking out that window over there. But she knows I'm looking that way, and she kind of look at me, too. The lady sitting 'side her catch her this time, and she leans over and says something in her ear.

"I don't love him nothing," that little old gal says out loud.

Everybody back there hear her mouth, and all of them look at us and laugh.

"I don't love you, either," I say. "So you don't have to turn up your nose, Miss."

"You the one looking," she say.

"I wasn't looking at you," I say. "I was looking out that window, there."

"Out that window, my foot," she say. "I seen you. Everytime I turned round you was looking at me."

"You must of been looking yourself if you seen me all them times," I say.

"Shucks," she say, "I got me all kind of boyfriends."

"I got girlfriends, too," I say.

"Well, I just don't want you getting your hopes up," she say.

I don't say no more to that little old gal 'cause I don't want have to bust her in the mouth. I lean on the seat where Mama sitting, and I don't even look that way no more. When we get to Bayonne, she jugg her little old tongue out at me. I make 'tend I'm go'n hit her, and she duck down 'side her mama. And all the people laugh at us again.

6

Me and Mama get off and start walking in town. Bayonne is a little bitty town. Baton Rouge is a hundred times bigger than Bayonne. I went to Baton Rouge once—me, Ty, Mama, and Daddy. But that was 'way back yonder, 'fore Daddy went in the Army. I wonder when we go'n see him again. I wonder when. Look like he ain't ever coming back home. . . . Even the pavement all cracked in Bayonne. Got grass shooting right out the sidewalk. Got weeds in the ditch, too; just like they got at home.

It's some cold in Bayonne. Look like it's colder than it is home. The wind blows in my face, and I feel that stuff running down my nose. I sniff. Mama says use that handkerchief. I blow my nose and put it back.

We pass a school and I see them white children playing in the yard. Big old red school, and them children just running and playing. Then we pass a café and I see a bunch of people in there eating. I wish I was in there 'cause I'm cold. Mama tells me keep my eyes in front where they belong.

We pass stores that's got dummies, and we pass another café, and then we pass a shoe shop, and that bald-head man in there fixing on a shoe. I look at him and I butt into that white lady, and Mama jerks me in front and tells me stay there.

We come up to the courthouse, and I see the flag waving there. This flag ain't like the one we got at school. This one here ain't got but a handful of stars. One at school got a big pile of stars—one for every state. We pass it and we turn and there it is—the dentist office. Me and Mama go in, and they got people sitting everywhere you look. They even got a little boy in there younger than me.

Me and Mama sit on that bench, and a white lady come in there and ask me what my name is. Mama tells her and the white lady goes on back. Then I hear somebody hollering in there. Soon 's that little boy hear him hollering, he starts hollering, too. His mama pats him and pats him, trying to make him hush up, but he ain't thinking 'bout his mama.

The man that was hollering in there comes out holding his jaw. He is a big old man and he's wearing overalls and a jumper.

"Got it, hanh?" another man asks him.

The man shakes his head—don't want open his mouth.

"Man, I thought they was killing you in there," the other man says. "Hollering like a pig under a gate."

The man don't say nothing. He just heads for the door, and the other man follows him.

"John Lee," the white lady says. "John Lee Williams."

The little boy juggs his head down in his mama's lap and holler more now. His mama tells him go with the nurse, but he ain't thinking 'bout his mama. His mama tells him again, but he don't even hear her. His mama picks him up and takes him in there, and even when the white lady shuts the door I can still hear little old John Lee.

"I often wonder why the Lord let a child like that suffer," a lady says to my mama. The lady's sitting right in front of us on another bench. She's got on a white dress and a black sweater. She must be a nurse or something herself, I reckon.

"Not us to question," a man says.

"Sometimes I don't know if we shouldn't," the lady says.

"I know definitely we shouldn't," the man says. The man looks like a preacher. He's big and fat and he's got on a black suit. He's got a gold chain, too.

"Why?" the lady says.

"Why anything?" the preacher says.

"Yes," the lady says. "Why anything?"

"Not us to question," the preacher says.

The lady looks at the preacher a little while and looks at Mama again.

"And look like it's the poor who suffers the most," she says. "I don't understand it."

"Best not to even try," the preacher says. "He works in mysterious ways—wonders to perform."

Right then little John Lee bust out hollering, and everybody turn they head to listen.

"He's not a good dentist," the lady says. "Dr. Robillard is much better. But more expensive. That's why most of the colored people come here. The white people go to Dr. Robillard. Y'all from Bayonne?"

"Down the river," my mama says. And that's all she go'n say, 'cause she don't talk much. But the lady keeps on looking at her, and so she says, "Near Morgan."

"I see," the lady says.

7

"That's the trouble with the black people in this country today," somebody else says. This one here's sitting on the same side me and Mama's sitting, and he is kind of sitting in front of that preacher. He looks like a teacher or somebody that goes to college. He's got on a suit, and he's got a book that he's been reading. "We don't question is exactly our problem," he says. "We should question and question and question—question everything."

The preacher just looks at him a long time. He done put a toothpick or something in his mouth, and he just keeps on turning it and turning it. You can see he don't like that boy with that book.

"Maybe you can explain what you mean," he says.

"I said what I meant," the boy says. "Question everything. Every stripe, every star, every word spoken. Everything."

"It 'pears to me that this young lady and I was talking 'bout God, young man," the preacher says.

"Question Him, too," the boy says.

"Wait," the preacher says. "Wait now."

"You heard me right," the boy says. "His existence as well as everything else. Everything."

The preacher just looks across the room at the boy. You can see he's getting madder and madder. But mad or no mad, the boy ain't thinking 'bout him. He looks at that preacher just 's hard 's the preacher looks at him.

"Is this what they coming to?" the preacher says. "Is this what we educating them for?"

"You're not educating me," the boy says. "I wash dishes at night so that I can go to school in the day. So even the words you spoke need questioning."

The preacher just looks at him and shakes his head.

"When I come in this room and seen you there with your book, I said to myself, 'There's an intelligent man.' How wrong a person can be."

"Show me one reason to believe in the existence of a God," the boy says.

"My heart tells me," the preacher says.

" 'My heart tells me,' " the boy says. " 'My heart tells me.' Sure, 'My heart tells me.' And as long as you listen to what your heart tells you, you will have only what the white man gives you and nothing more. Me, I don't listen to my heart. The purpose of the heart is to pump blood throughout the body, and nothing else."

"Who's your paw, boy?" the preacher says.

"Why?"

"Who is he?"

"He's dead."

"And your mom?"

"She's in Charity Hospital with pneumonia. Half killed herself, working for nothing."

"And 'cause he's dead and she's sick, you mad at the world?"

"I'm not mad at the world. I'm questioning the world. I'm questioning it with cold logic, sir. What do words like Freedom, Liberty, God, White, Colored mean? I want to know. That's why *you* are sending us to school, to read and to ask questions. And because we ask these questions, you call us mad. No sir, it is not us who are mad."

"You keep saying 'us'?"

"'Us.' Yes—us. I'm not alone."

The preacher just shakes his head. Then he looks at everybody in the room—everybody. Some of the people look down at the floor, keep from looking at him. I kind of look 'way myself, but soon 's I know he done turn his head, I look that way again.

"I'm sorry for you," he says to the boy.

"Why?" the boy says. "Why not be sorry for yourself? Why are you so much better off than I am? Why aren't you sorry for these other people in here? Why not be sorry for the lady who had to drag her child into the dentist office? Why not be sorry for the lady sitting on that bench over there? Be sorry for them. Not for me. Some way or the other I'm going to make it."

"No, I'm sorry for you," the preacher says.

"Of course, of course," the boy says, nodding his head. "You're sorry for me because I rock that pillar you're leaning on."

"You can't ever rock the pillar I'm leaning on, young man. It's stronger than anything man can ever do."

"You believe in God because a man told you to believe in God," the boy says. "A white man told you to believe in God. And why? To keep you ignorant so he can keep his feet on your neck."

"So now we the ignorant?" the preacher says.

"Yes," the boy says. "Yes." And he opens his book again.

The preacher just looks at him sitting there. The boy done forgot all about him. Everybody else make 'tend they done forgot the squabble, too.

Then I see that preacher getting up real slow. Preacher's a great big old man and he got to brace himself to get up. He comes over where the boy is sitting. He just stands there a little while looking down at him, but the boy don't raise his head.

"Get up, boy," preacher says.

The boy looks up at him, then he shuts his book real slow and stands up. Preacher just hauls back and hit him in the face. The boy falls back 'gainst the wall, but he straightens himself up and looks right back at that preacher.

"You forgot the other cheek," he says.

The preacher hauls back and hit him again on the other side. But this time the boy braces himself and don't fall.

"That hasn't changed a thing," he says.

The preacher just looks at the boy. The preacher's breathing real hard like he just run up a big hill. The boy sits down and opens his book again.

"I feel sorry for you," the preacher says. "I never felt so sorry for a man before."

The boy makes 'tend he don't even hear that preacher. He keeps on reading his book. The preacher goes back and gets his hat off the chair.

"Excuse me," he says to us. "I'll come back some other time. Y'all, please excuse me."

And he looks at the boy and goes out the room. The boy h'ist his hand up to his mouth one time to wipe 'way some blood. All the rest of the time he keeps on reading. And nobody else in there say a word.

8

Little John Lee and his mama come out the dentist office, and the nurse calls somebody else in. Then little bit later they come out, and the nurse calls another name. But fast 's she calls somebody in there, somebody else comes in the place where we sitting, and the room stays full.

The people coming in now, all of them wearing big coats. One of them says something 'bout sleeting, another one says he hope not. Another one says he think it ain't nothing but rain. 'Cause, he says, rain can get awful cold this time of year.

All round the room they talking. Some of them talking to people right by them, some of them talking to people clear 'cross the room, some of them talking to anybody'll listen. It's a little bitty room, no bigger than us kitchen, and I can see everybody in there. The little old room's full of smoke, 'cause you got two old men smoking pipes over by that side door. I think I feel my tooth thumping me some, and I hold my breath and wait. I wait and wait, but it don't thump me no more. Thank God for that.

I feel like going to sleep, and I lean back 'gainst the wall. But I'm scared to go to sleep. Scared 'cause the nurse might call my name and I won't hear her. And Mama might go to sleep, too, and she'll be mad if neither one of us heard the nurse.

I look up at Mama. I love my mama. I love my mama. And when cotton come I'm go'n get her a new coat. And I ain't go'n get a black one, either. I think I'm go'n get her a red one.

"They got some books over there," I say. "Want read one of them?"

Mama looks at the books, but she don't answer me.

"You got yourself a little man there," the lady says.

Mama don't say nothing to the lady, but she must've smiled, 'cause I seen the lady smiling back. The lady looks at me a little while, like she's feeling sorry for me.

"You sure got that preacher out here in a hurry," she says to that boy.

The boy looks up at her and looks in his book again. When I grow up I want be just like him. I want clothes like that and I want keep a book with me, too.

"You really don't believe in God?" the lady says.

"No," he says.

"But why?" the lady says.

"Because the wind is pink," he says.

"What?" the lady says.

The boy don't answer her no more. He just reads in his book.

"Talking 'bout the wind is pink," that old lady says. She's sitting on the same bench with the boy and she's trying to look in his face. The boy makes 'tend the old lady ain't even there. He just keeps on reading. "Wind is pink," she says again. "Eh, Lord, what children go'n be saying next?"

The lady 'cross from us bust out laughing.

"That's a good one," she says. "The wind is pink. Yes sir, that's a good one."

"Don't you believe the wind is pink?" the boys says. He keeps his head down in the book.

"Course I believe it, honey," the lady says. "Course I do." She looks at us and winks her eye. "And what color is grass, honey?"

"Grass? Grass is black."

She bust out laughing again. The boy looks at her.

"Don't you believe grass is black?" he says.

The lady quits her laughing and looks at him. Everybody else looking at him, too. The place quiet, quiet.

"Grass is green, honey," the lady says. "It was green yesterday, it's green today, and it's go'n be green tomorrow."

"How do you know it's green?"

"I know because I know."

"You don't know it's green," the boy says. "You believe it's green because someone told you it was green. If someone had told you it was black you'd believe it was black."

"It's green," the lady says. "I know green when I see green."

"Prove it's green," the boy says.

"Sure, now," the lady says. "Don't tell me it's coming to that."

"It's coming to just that," the boy says. "Words mean nothing. One means no more than the other."

"That's what it all coming to?" that old lady says. That old lady got on a turban and she got on two sweaters. She got a green sweater under a black sweater. I can see the green sweater 'cause some of the buttons on the other sweater's missing.

"Yes ma'am," the boy says. "Words mean nothing. Action is the only thing. Doing. That's the only thing."

"Other words, you want the Lord to come down here and show Hisself to you?" she says.

"Exactly, ma'am," he says.

"You don't mean that, I'm sure?" she says.

"I do, ma'am," he says.

"Done, Jesus," the old lady says, shaking her head.

"I didn't go 'long with that preacher at first," the other lady says; "but now—I don't know. When a person say the grass is black, he's either a lunatic or something's wrong."

"Prove to me that it's green," the boy says.

"It's green because the people say it's green."

"Those same people say we're citizens of these United States," the boy says.

"I think I'm a citizen," the lady says.

"Citizens have certain rights," the boy says. "Name me one right that you have. One right, granted by the Constitution, that you can exercise in Bayonne."

The lady don't answer him. She just looks at him like she don't know what he's talking 'bout. I know I don't.

"Things changing," she says.

"Things are changing because some black men have begun to think with their brains and not their hearts," the boy says.

"You trying to say these people don't believe in God?"

"I'm sure some of them do. Maybe most of them do. But they don't believe that God is going to touch these white people's hearts and change things tomorrow. Things change through action. By no other way."

Everybody sit quiet and look at the boy. Nobody says a thing. Then the lady 'cross the room from me and Mama just shakes her head.

"Let's hope that not all your generation feel the same way you do," she says.

"Think what you please, it doesn't matter," the boy says. "But it will be men who listen to their heads and not their hearts who will see that your children have a better chance than you had."

"Let's hope they ain't all like you, though," the old lady says. "Done forgot the heart absolutely."

"Yes ma'am, I hope they aren't all like me," the boy says. "Unfortunately, I was born too late to believe in your God. Let's hope that the ones who come after will have your faith—if not in your God, then in something else, something definitely that they can lean on. I haven't anything. For me, the wind is pink, the grass is black."

9

The nurse comes in the room where we all sitting and waiting and says the doctor won't take no more patients till one o'clock this evening. My mama jumps up off the bench and goes up to the white lady.

"Nurse, I have to go back in the field this evening," she says.

"The doctor is treating his last patient now," the nurse says. "One o'clock this evening."

"Can I at least speak to the doctor?" my mama asks.

"I'm his nurse," the lady says.

"My little boy's sick," my mama says. "Right now his tooth almost killing him."

The nurse looks at me. She's trying to make up her mind if to let me come in. I look at her real pitiful. The tooth ain't hurting me at all, but Mama say it is, so I make 'tend for her sake.

"This evening," the nurse says, and goes on back in the office.

"Don't feel 'jected, honey," the lady says to Mama. "I been round them a long time—they take you when they want to. If you was white, that's something else; but we the wrong color."

Mama don't say nothing to the lady, and me and her go outside and stand 'gainst the wall. It's cold out there. I can feel that wind going through my coat. Some of the other people come out of the room and go up the street. Me and Mama stand there a little while and we start walking. I don't know where we going. When we come to the other street we just stand there.

"You don't have to make water, do you?" Mama says.

"No, ma'am," I say.

We go on up the street. Walking real slow. I can tell Mama don't know where she's going. When we come to a store we stand there and look at the dummies. I look at a little boy wearing a brown overcoat. He's got on brown shoes, too. I look at my old shoes and look at his'n again. You wait till summer, I say.

Me and Mama walk away. We come up to another store and we stop and look at them dummies, too. Then we go on again. We pass a café where the white people in there eating. Mama tells me keep my eyes in front where they belong, but I can't help from seeing them people eat. My stomach starts to growling 'cause I'm hungry. When I see people eating, I get hungry; when I see a coat, I get cold.

A man whistles at my mama when we go by a filling station. She makes 'tend she don't even see him. I look back and I feel like hitting him in the mouth. If I was bigger, I say; if I was bigger, you'd see.

We keep on going. I'm getting colder and colder, but I don't say nothing. I feel that stuff running down my nose and I sniff.

"That rag," Mama says.

I get it out and wipe my nose. I'm getting cold all over now—my face, my hands, my feet, everything. We pass another little café, but this'n for white people, too, and we can't go in there, either. So we just walk. I'm so cold now I'm 'bout ready to say it. If I knowed where we was going I wouldn't be so cold, but I don't know where we going. We go, we go, we go. We walk clean out of Bayonne. Then we cross the street and we come back. Same thing I seen when I got off the bus this morning. Same old trees, same old walk, same old weeds, same old cracked pave—same old everything.

I sniff again.

"That rag," Mama says.

I wipe my nose real fast and jugg that handkerchief back in my pocket 'fore my hand gets too cold. I raise my head and I can see David's hardware store. When we come up to it, we go in. I don't know why, but I'm glad.

It's warm in there. It's so warm in there you don't ever want to leave. I look for the heater, and I see it over by them barrels. Three white men standing round the heater talking in Creole. One of them comes over to see what my mama want.

"Got any axe handles?" she says.

Me, Mama and the white man start to the back, but Mama stops me when we come up to the heater. She and the white man go on. I hold my hands over the heater and look at them. They go all the way to the back, and I see the white man pointing to the axe handles 'gainst the wall. Mama takes one of them and shakes it like she's trying to figure how much it weighs. Then she rubs her hand over it from one end to the other end. She turns it over and looks at the other side, then she shakes it again, and shakes her head and puts it back. She gets another one and she does it just like she did the first one, then she shakes her head. Then she gets a brown one and do it that, too. But she don't like this one, either. Then she gets another one, but 'fore she shakes it or anything, she looks at me. Look like she's trying to say something to me, but I don't know what it is. All I know is I done got warm now and I'm feeling right smart better. Mama shakes this axe handle just like she did the others, and shakes her head and says something to the white man. The white man just looks at his pile of axe handles, and when Mama pass him to come to the front, the white man just scratch his head and follows her. She tells me come on and we go on out and start walking again.

We walk and walk, and no time at all I'm cold again. Look like I'm colder now 'cause I can still remember how good it was back there. My stomach growls and I suck it in to keep Mama from hearing it. She's walking right 'side me, and it growls so loud you can hear it a mile. But Mama don't say a word.

10

When we come up to the courthouse, I look at the clock. It's got quarter to twelve. Mean we got another hour and a quarter to be out here in the cold. We go and stand 'side a building. Something hits my cap and I look up at the sky. Sleet's falling.

I look at Mama standing there. I want stand close 'side her, but she don't like that. She say that's crybaby stuff. She say you got to stand for yourself, by yourself.

"Let's go back to that office," she says.

We cross the street. When we get to the dentist office I try to open the door, but I can't. I twist and twist, but I can't. Mama pushes me to the side and she twist the knob, but she can't open the door, either. She turns 'way from the door. I look at her, but I don't move and I don't say nothing. I done seen her like this before and I'm scared of her.

"You hungry?" she says. She says it like she's mad at me, like I'm the cause of everything.

"No, ma'am," I say.

"You want eat and walk back, or you rather don't eat and ride?"

"I ain't hungry," I say.

I ain't just hungry, but I'm cold, too. I'm so hungry and cold I want to cry. And look like I'm getting colder and colder. My feet done got numb. I try to work my toes, but I don't even feel them. Look like I'm go'n die. Look like I'm go'n stand right here and freeze to death. I think 'bout home. I think 'bout Val and Auntie and Ty and Louis and Walker. It's 'bout twelve o'clock and I know they eating dinner now. I can hear Ty making jokes. He done forgot 'bout getting up early this morning and right now he's probably making jokes. Always trying to make somebody laugh. I wish I was right there listening to him. Give anything in the world if I was home round the fire.

"Come on," Mama says

We start walking again. My feet so numb I can't hardly feel them. We turn the corner and go on back up the street. The clock on the courthouse starts hitting for twelve.

The sleet's coming down plenty now. They hit the pave and bounce like rice. Oh, Lord; oh, Lord, I pray. Don't let me die, don't let me die, don't let me die, Lord.

11

Now I know where we going. We going back of town where the colored people eat. I don't care if I don't eat. I been hungry before. I can stand it. But I can't stand the cold.

I can see we go'n have a long walk. It's 'bout a mile down there. But I don't mind. I know when I get there I'm go'n warm myself. I think I can hold out. My hands numb in my pockets and my feet numb, too, but if I keep moving I can hold out. Just don't stop no more, that's all.

The sky's gray. The sleet keeps on falling. Falling like rain now—plenty, plenty. You can hear it hitting the pave. You can see it bouncing. Sometimes it bounces two times 'fore it settles.

We keep on going. We don't say nothing. We just keep on going, keep on going.

I wonder what Mama's thinking. I hope she ain't mad at me. When summer come I'm go'n pick plenty cotton and get her a coat. I'm go'n get her a red one.

I hope they'd make it summer all the time. I'd be glad if it was summer all the time—but it ain't. We got to have winter, too. Lord, I hate the winter. I guess everybody hate the winter.

I don't sniff this time. I get out my handkerchief and wipe my nose. My hands's so cold I can hardly hold the handkerchief.

I think we getting close, but we ain't there yet. I wonder where everybody is. Can't see a soul but us. Look like we the only two people moving round today. Must be too cold for the rest of the people to move round in.

I can hear my teeth. I hope they don't knock together too hard and make that bad one hurt. Lord, that's all I need, for that bad one to start off.

I hear a church bell somewhere. But today ain't Sunday. They must be ringing for a funeral or something.

I wonder what they doing at home. They must be eating. Monsieur Bayonne might be there with his guitar. One day Ty played with Monsieur Bayonne's guitar and broke one of the strings. Monsieur Bayonne was some mad with Ty. He say Ty wasn't go'n ever 'mount to nothing. Ty can go just like Monsieur Bayonne when he ain't there. Ty can make everybody laugh when he starts to mocking Monsieur Bayonne.

I used to like to be with Mama and Daddy. We used to be happy. But they took him in the Army. Now, nobody happy no more. . . . I be glad when Daddy comes home.

Monsieur Bayonne say it wasn't fair for them to take Daddy and give Mama nothing and give us nothing. Auntie say, "Shhh, Etienne. Don't let them hear you talk like that." Monsieur Bayonne say, "It's God truth. What they giving his children? They have to walk three and a half miles to school hot or cold. That's anything to give for a paw? She's got to work in the field rain or shine just to make ends meet. That's anything to give for a husband?" Auntie say, "Shhh, Etienne, shhh." "Yes, you right," Monsieur Bayonne say. "Best don't say it in front of them now. But one day they go'n find out. One day." "Yes, I suppose so," Auntie say. "Then what, Rose Mary?" Monsieur Bayonne say. "I don't know, Etienne," Auntie say. "All we can do is us job, and leave everything else in His hand . . ."

We getting closer, now. We getting closer. I can even see the railroad tracks.

We cross the tracks, and now I see the café. Just to get in there, I say. Just to get in there. Already I'm starting to feel little better.

12

We go in. Ahh, it's good. I look for the heater; there 'gainst the wall. One of them little brown ones. I just stand there and hold my hands over it. I can't open my hands too wide 'cause they almost froze.

Mama's standing right 'side me. She done unbuttoned her coat. Smoke rises out of the coat, and the coat smells like a wet dog.

I move to the side so Mama can have more room. She opens out her hands and rubs them together. I rub mine together, too, 'cause this keep them from hurting. If you let them warm too fast, they hurt you sure. But if you let them warm just little bit at a time, and you keep rubbing them, they be all right every time.

They got just two more people in the café. A lady back of the counter, and a man on this side the counter. They been watching us ever since we come in.

Mama gets out the handkerchief and count up the money. Both of us know how much money she's got there. Three dollars. No, she ain't got three dollars, 'cause she had to pay us way up here. She ain't got but two dollars and a half left. Dollar and a half to get my tooth pulled, and fifty cents for us to go back on, and fifty cents worth of salt meat.

She stirs the money round with her finger. Most of the money is change 'cause I can hear it rubbing together. She stirs it and stirs it. Then she looks at the door. It's still sleeting. I can hear it hitting 'gainst the wall like rice.

"I ain't hungry, Mama," I say.

"Got to pay them something for they heat," she says.

She takes a quarter out the handkerchief and ties the handkerchief up again. She looks over her shoulder at the people, but she still don't move. I hope she don't spend the money. I don't want her spending it on me. I'm hungry, I'm almost starving I'm so hungry, but I don't want her spending the money on me.

She flips the quarter over like she's thinking. She's must be thinking 'bout us walking back home. Lord, I sure don't want walk home. If I thought it'd do any good to say something, I'd say it. But Mama makes up her own mind 'bout things.

She turns 'way from the heater right fast, like she better hurry up and spend the quarter 'fore she change her mind. I watch her go toward the counter. The man and the lady look at her, too. She tells the lady something and the lady walks away. The man keeps on looking at her. Her back's turned to the man, and she don't even know he's standing there.

The lady puts some cakes and a glass of milk on the counter. Then she pours up a cup of coffee and sets it 'side the other stuff. Mama pays her for the things and comes on back where I'm standing. She tells me sit down at the table 'gainst the wall.

The milk and the cakes's for me; the coffee's for Mama. I eat slow and I look at her. She's looking outside at the sleet. She's looking real sad. I say to myself, I'm go'n make all this up one day. You see, one day, I'm go'n make all this up. I want say it now; I want tell her how I feel right now; but Mama don't like for us to talk like that.

"I can't eat all this," I say.

They ain't got but just three little old cakes there. I'm so hungry right now, the Lord knows I can eat a hundred times three, but I want my mama to have one.

Mama don't even look my way. She knows I'm hungry, she knows I want it. I let it stay there a little while, then I get it and eat it. I eat just on my front teeth, though, 'cause if cake touch that back tooth I know what'll happen. Thank God it ain't hurt me at all today.

After I finish eating I see the man go to the juke box. He drops a nickel in it, then he just stand there a little while looking at the record. Mama tells me keep my eyes in front where they belong. I turn my head like she say, but then I hear the man coming toward us.

"Dance, pretty?" he says.

Mama gets up to dance with him. But 'fore you know it, she done grabbed the little man in the collar and done heaved him 'side the wall. He hit the wall so hard he stop the juke box from playing.

"Some pimp," the lady back of the counter says. "Some pimp."

The little man jumps up off the floor and starts toward my mama. 'Fore you know it, Mama done sprung open her knife and she's waiting for him.

"Come on," she says. "Come on. I'll gut you from your neighbo to your throat. Come on."

I go up to the little man to hit him, but Mama makes me come and stand 'side her. The little man looks at me and Mama and goes on back to the counter.

"Some pimp," the lady back of the counter says. "Some pimp." She starts laughing and pointing at the little man. "Yes sir, you a pimp, all right. Yes sir-ree."

13

"Fasten that coat, let's go," Mama says.

"You don't have to leave," the lady says.

Mama don't answer the lady, and we right out in the cold again. I'm warm right now—my hands, my ears, my feet—but I know this ain't go'n last too long. It done sleet so much now you got ice everywhere you look.

We cross the railroad tracks, and soon's we do, I get cold. That wind goes through this little old coat like it ain't even there. I got on a shirt and a sweater under the coat, but that wind don't pay them no mind. I look up and I can see we got a long way to go. I wonder if we go'n make it 'fore I get too cold.

We cross over to walk on the sidewalk. They got just one sidewalk back here, and it's over there.

After we go just a little piece, I smell bread cooking. I look, then I see a baker shop. When we get closer, I can smell it more better. I shut my eyes and make 'tend I'm eating. But I keep them shut too long and I butt up 'gainst a telephone post. Mama grabs me and see if I'm hurt. I ain't bleeding or nothing and she turns me loose.

I can feel I'm getting colder and colder, and I look up to see how far we still got to go. Uptown is 'way up yonder. A half mile more, I reckon. I try to think of something. They say think and you won't get cold. I think of that poem, "Annabel Lee." I ain't been to school in so long—this bad weather—I reckon they done passed "Annabel Lee" by now. But passed it or not, I'm sure Miss Walker go'n make me recite it when I get there. That woman don't never forget nothing. I ain't never seen nobody like that in my life.

I'm still getting cold. "Annabel Lee" or no "Annabel Lee," I'm still getting cold. But I can see we getting closer. We getting there gradually.

Soon 's we turn the corner, I see a little old white lady up in front of us. She's the only lady on the street. She's all in black and she's got a long black rag over her head.

"Stop," she says.

Me and Mama stop and look at her. She must be crazy to be out in all this bad weather. Ain't got but a few other people out there, and all of them's men.

"Y'all done ate?" she says.

"Just finish," Mama says.

"Y'all must be cold then?" she says.

"We headed for the dentist," Mama says. "We'll warm up when we get there."

"What dentist?" the old lady says. "Mr. Bassett?"

"Yes, ma'am," Mama says.

"Come on in," the old lady says. "I'll telephone him and tell him y'all coming."

Me and Mama follow the old lady in the store. It's a little bitty store, and it don't have much in there. The old lady takes off her head rag and folds it up.

"Helena?" somebody calls from the back.

"Yes, Alnest?" the old lady says.

"Did you see them?"

"They're here. Standing beside me."

"Good. Now you can stay inside."

The old lady looks at Mama. Mama's waiting to hear what she brought us in here for. I'm waiting for that, too.

"I saw y'all each time you went by," she says. "I came out to catch you, but you were gone."

"We went back of town," Mama says.

"Did you eat?"

"Yes, ma'am."

The old lady looks at Mama a long time, like she's thinking Mama might be just saying that. Mama looks right back at her. The old lady looks at me to see what I have to say. I don't say nothing. I sure ain't going 'gainst my mama.

"There's food in the kitchen," she says to Mama. "I've been keeping it warm."

Mama turns right around and starts for the door.

"Just a minute," the old lady says. Mama stops. "The boy'll have to work for it. It isn't free."

"We don't take no handout," Mama says.

"I'm not handing out anything," the old lady says. "I need my garbage moved to the front. Ernest has a bad cold and can't go out there."

"James'll move it for you," Mama says.

"Not unless you eat," the old lady says. "I'm old, but I have my pride, too, you know."

Mama can see she ain't go'n beat this old lady down, so she just shakes her head.

"All right," the old lady says. "Come into the kitchen."

She leads the way with that rag in her hand. The kitchen is a little bitty little old thing, too. The table and the stove just 'bout fill it up. They got a little room to the side. Somebody in there laying 'cross the bed—'cause I can see one of his feet. Must be the person she was talking to: Ernest or Alnest—something like that.

"Sit down," the old lady says to Mama. "Not you," she says to me. "You have to move the cans."

"Helena?" the man says in the other room.

"Yes, Alnest?" the old lady says.

"Are you going out there again?"

"I must show the boy where the garbage is, Alnest," the old lady says.

"Keep that shawl over your head," the old man says.

"You don't have to remind me, Alnest. Come, boy," the old lady says.

We go out in the yard. Little old back yard ain't no bigger than the store or the kitchen. But it can sleet here just like it can sleet in any big back yard. And 'fore you know it, I'm trembling.

"There," the old lady says, pointing to the cans. I pick up one of the cans and set it right back down. The can's so light, I'm go'n see what's inside of it.

"Here," the old lady says. "Leave that can alone."

I look back at her standing there in the door. She's got that black rag wrapped round her shoulders, and she's pointing one of her little old fingers at me.

"Pick it up and carry it to the front," she says. I go by her with the can, and she's looking at me all the time. I'm sure the can's empty. I'm sure she could've carried it herself—maybe both of them at the same time. "Set it on the sidewalk by the door and come back for the other one," she says.

I go and come back, and Mama looks at me when I pass her. I get the other can and take it to the front. It don't feel a bit heavier than that first one. I tell myself I ain't go'n be nobody's fool, and I'm go'n look inside this can to see just what I been hauling. First, I look up the street, then down the street. Nobody coming. Then I look over my shoulder toward the door. That little old lady done slipped up there quiet 's mouse, watching me again. Look like she knowed what I was go'n do.

"Ehh, Lord," she says. "Children, children. Come in here, boy, and go wash your hands."

I follow her in the kitchen. She points toward the bathroom, and I go in there and wash up. Little bitty old bathroom, but it's clean, clean. I don't use any of her towels; I wipe my hands on my pants legs.

When I come back in the kitchen, the old lady done dished up the food. Rice, gravy, meat—and she even got some lettuce and tomato in a saucer. She even got a glass of milk and a piece of cake there, too. It looks so good, I almost start eating 'fore I say my blessing.

"Helena?" the old man says.

"Yes, Alnest?"

"Are they eating?"

"Yes," she says.

"Good," he says. "Now you'll stay inside."

The old lady goes in there where he is and I can hear them talking. I look at Mama. She's eating slow like she's thinking. I wonder what's the matter now. I reckon she's thinking 'bout home.

The old lady comes back in the kitchen.

"I talked to Dr. Bassett's nurse," she says. "Dr. Bassett will take you as soon as you get there."

"Thank you, ma'am," Mama says.

"Perfectly all right," the old lady says. "Which one is it?"

Mama nods toward me. The old lady looks at me real sad. I look sad, too.

"You're not afraid, are you?" she says.

"No, ma'am," I say.

"That's a good boy," the old lady says. "Nothing to be afraid of. Dr. Bassett will not hurt you."

When me and Mama get through eating, we thank the old lady again.

"Helena, are they leaving?" the old man says.

"Yes, Alnest."

"Tell them I say good-bye."

"They can hear you, Alnest."

"Good-bye both mother and son," the old man says. "And may God be with you."

Me and Mama tell the old man good-bye, and we follow the old lady in the front room. Mama opens the door to go out, but she stops and comes back in the store.

"You sell salt meat?" she says.

"Yes."

"Give me two bits worth."

"That isn't very much salt meat," the old lady says.

"That's all I have," Mama says.

The old lady goes back of the counter and cuts a big piece off the chunk. Then she wraps it up and puts it in a paper bag.

"Two bits," she says.

"That looks like awful lot of meat for a quarter," Mama says.

"Two bits," the old lady says. "I've been selling salt meat behind this counter twenty-five years. I think I know what I'm doing."

"You got a scale there," Mama says.

"What?" the old lady says.

"Weigh it," Mama says.

"What?" the old lady says. "Are you telling me how to run my business?"

"Thanks very much for the food," Mama says.

"Just a minute," the old lady says.

"James," Mama says to me. I move toward the door.

"Just one minute, I said," the old lady says.

Me and Mama stop again and look at her. The old lady takes the meat out of the bag and unwraps it and cuts 'bout half of it off. Then she wraps it up again and juggs it back in the bag and gives the bag to Mama. Mama lays the quarter on the counter.

"Your kindness will never be forgotten," she says. "James," she says to me.

We go out, and the old lady comes to the door to look at us. After we go a little piece I look back, and she's still there watching us.

The sleet's coming down heavy, heavy now, and I turn up my coat collar to keep my neck warm. My mama tells me turn it right back down.

"You not a bum," she says. "You a man."

The Revolution Will Not Be Televised

Gil Scott Heron

In this 1975 song, Gil Scott Heron raps about a race revolution that will over-shadow all other aspects of life in American society. The lyrics emphasize the intensity of the struggle for racial equality.

You will not be able to stay home brother
you will not be able to plug in, turn on and drop out
you will not be able to lose yourself on skag and skip
skip out for beer during commercials
Because the revolution will not be televised   5
The revolution will not be televised
The revolution will not be brought to you by xerox
in 4 parts without commercial interruption
The revolution will not show you pictures of Nixon
blowing a bugle and leading a charge by John   10
Mitchell, General Abrams and Spiro Agnew to eat
hog moss confiscated from a Harlem sanctuary
The revolution will not be televised
The revolution will not be brought to you by the
Schaefer Award Theatre and will not star Natalie   15
Wood and Steve McQueen or Bullwinkle and Julia
The revolution will not give your mouth sex appeal
The revolution will not get rid of the nubs
The revolution will not make you look five pounds
thinner because The revolution will not be televised brother   20
There will be no pictures of you and Willie Mays
pushing that cart down the block on the
dead run
or trying to slide that color television into a stolen
ambulance   25
NBC will not be able to predict the winner at 8:32
or the count from 29 districts
The revolution will not be televised
There will be no pictures of pigs shooting down
brothers in the instant replay   30
There will be no pictures of young being
run out of Harlem a rail with a brand new process
There will be no slow motion or still life of Roy

Wilkens strolling through Watts in a red, black and
green liberation jumpsuit that he had been saving   35
for just the right occasion
Green Acres, The Beverly Hillbillies and Hooterville
Junction will no longer be so damned relevant and
women will not care if Dick finally gets down with
Jane on Search for Tomorrow because black people   40
will be in the street looking for a brighter day
The revolution will not be televised
there will be no highlights on the eleven o'clock
news and no pictures of hairy armed women
liberationists and Jackie Onassis blowing her nose   45
The theme song will not be written by Jim Webb,
Francis Scott Key nor sung by Glen Campbell, Tom
Jones, Johnny Cash, Engelbert Humperdinck or The
Rare Earth
The revolution will not be televised   50
The revolution will not be right back after a message
about a white tornado, white lightning, or white people
You will not have to worry about a germ in your
bedroom, the tiger in your tank, or the giant in you
toilet bowl   55
The revolution will not go better with Coke
The revolution will not fight germs that can cause
bad breath
The revolution WILL put you in the driver's
seat   60
The revolution will not be televised, will not be televised
will not be televised
The revolution will be no re-run brothers
The revolution will be live

MAYA ANGELOU (b. 1928)

*I Know Why the Caged Bird Sings (1969), Maya Angelou's first and best-known
autobiography, was nominated for a National Book Award. Angelou has written a series
of autobiographical texts that take her from childhood, depicted in the first autobiography,
to her experiences as a visitor to Ghana in* All God's Children Need Traveling Shoes

(1986). Her other autobiographies include Gather Together in My Name *(1974) and* The Heart of a Woman *(1981).*

In addition to her autobiographical works, Angelou has written several volumes of poetry, including And Still I Rise *(1976) and* Just Give Me a Cool Drink of Water 'fore I Diiie *(1971); the latter was nominated for a Pulitzer Prize. Angelou was the first woman and first African American to write and present a poem for a presidential inauguration: she read "On the Pulse of Morning" at President Bill Clinton's first inauguration in 1993.*

Maya Angelou was born Marguerite Johnson in St. Louis, Missouri, and grew up in Arkansas. Besides autobiographies and poetry, she has written plays and biographies. She has also been a dancer, singer, and actress, traveling through Europe as a member of the cast of Porgy and Bess. *In 1999, she added movie directing to her list of accomplishments. She directed* Down in the Delta, *a drama about an African American family.*

From I Know Why the Caged Bird Sings (1969)

13

In the hospital, Bailey told me that I had to tell who did that to me, or the man would hurt another little girl. When I explained that I couldn't tell because the man would kill him, Bailey said knowingly, "He can't kill me. I won't let him." And of course I believed him. Bailey didn't lie to me. So I told him.

Bailey cried at the side of my bed until I started to cry too. Almost fifteen years passed before I saw my brother cry again.

Using the old brain he was born with (those were his words later on that day) he gave his information to Grandmother Baxter, and Mr. Freeman was arrested and was spared the awful wrath of my pistol-whipping uncles.

I would have liked to stay in the hospital the rest of my life. Mother brought flowers and candy. Grandmother came with fruit and my uncles clumped around and around my bed, snorting like wild horses. When they were able to sneak Bailey in, he read to me for hours.

The saying that people who have nothing to do become busybodies is not the only truth. Excitement is a drug, and people whose lives are filled with violence are always wondering where the next "fix" is coming from.

The court was filled. Some people even stood behind the churchlike benches in the rear. Overhead fans moved with the detachment of old men. Grandmother Baxter's clients were there in gay and flippant array. The gamblers in pin-striped suits and their makeup-deep women whispered to me out of blood-red mouths that now I knew as much as they did. I was eight, and grown. Even the nurses in the hospital had told me that now I had nothing to fear. "The worst is over for you," they had said. So I put the words in all the smirking mouths.

I sat with my family (Bailey couldn't come) and they rested still on the seats like solid, cold gray tombstones. Thick and forevermore unmoving.

Poor Mr. Freeman twisted in his chair to look empty threats over to me. He didn't know that he couldn't kill Bailey . . . and Bailey didn't lie . . . to me.

"What was the defendant wearing?" That was Mr. Freeman's lawyer.

"I don't know."

"You mean to say this man raped you and you don't know what he was wearing?" He snickered as if I had raped Mr. Freeman. "Do you know if you were raped?"

A sound pushed in the air of the court (I was sure it was laughter). I was glad that Mother had let me wear the navy-blue winter coat with brass buttons. Although it was too short and the weather was typical St. Louis hot, the coat was a friend that I hugged to me in the strange and unfriendly place.

"Was that the first time the accused touched you?" The question stopped me. Mr. Freeman had surely done something very wrong, but I was convinced that I had helped him to do it. I didn't want to lie, but the lawyer wouldn't let me think, so I used silence as a retreat.

"Did the accused try to touch you before the time he or rather you say he raped you?"

I couldn't say yes and tell them how he had loved me once for a few minutes and how he had held me close before he thought I had peed in my bed. My uncles would kill me and Grandmother Baxter would stop speaking, as she often did when she was angry. And all those people in the court would stone me as they had stoned the harlot in the Bible. And Mother, who thought I was such a good girl, would be so disappointed. But most important, there was Bailey. I had kept a big secret from him.

"Marguerite, answer the question. Did the accused touch you before the occasion on which you claim he raped you?"

Everyone in the court knew that the answer had to be No. Everyone except Mr. Freeman and me. I looked at his heavy face trying to look as if he would have liked me to say No. I said No.

The lie lumped in my throat and I couldn't get air. How I despised the man for making me lie. Old, mean, nasty thing. Old, black, nasty thing. The tears didn't soothe my heart as they usually did. I screamed, "Ole, mean, dirty thing, you. Dirty old thing." Our lawyer brought me off the stand and to my mother's arms. The fact that I had arrived at my desired destination by lies made it less appealing to me.

Mr. Freeman was given one year and one day, but he never got a chance to do his time. His lawyer (or someone) got him released that very afternoon.

In the living room, where the shades were drawn for coolness, Bailey and I played Monopoly on the floor. I played a bad game because I was thinking how I would be able to tell Bailey how I had lied and, even worse for our relationship, kept a secret from him. Bailey answered the doorbell, because Grandmother was in the kitchen. A tall white policeman asked for Mrs. Baxter. Had they found out about the lie? Maybe the policeman was coming to put me in jail because I had sworn on the Bible that everything I said would be the truth, the whole truth, so help me, God. The man in our living room was taller than the sky and whiter than my image of God. He just didn't have the beard.

"Mrs. Baxter, I thought you ought to know. Freeman's been found dead on the lot behind the slaughterhouse."

Softly, as if she was discussing a church program, she said, "Poor man." She wiped her hands on the dishtowel and just as softly asked, "Do they know who did it?"

The policeman said, "Seems like he was dropped there. Some say he was kicked to death."

Grandmother's color only rose a little. "Tom, thanks for telling me. Poor man. Well, maybe it's better this way. He *was* a mad dog. Would you like a glass of lemonade? Or some beer?"

Although he looked harmless, I knew he was a dreadful angel counting out my many sins.

"No, thanks, Mrs. Baxter. I'm on duty. Gotta be getting back."

"Well, tell your ma that I'll be over when I take up my beer and remind her to save some kraut for me."

And the recording angel was gone. He was gone, and a man was dead because I lied. Where was the balance in that? One lie surely wouldn't be worth a man's life. Bailey could have explained it all to me, but I didn't dare ask him. Obviously I had forfeited my place in heaven forever, and I was as gutless as the doll I had ripped to pieces ages ago. Even Christ Himself turned His back on Satan. Wouldn't He turn His back on me? I could feel the evilness flowing through my body and waiting, pent up, to rush off my tongue if I tried to open my mouth. I clamped my teeth shut, I'd hold it in. If it escaped, wouldn't it flood the world and all the innocent people?

Grandmother Baxter said, "Ritie and Junior, you didn't hear a thing. I never want to hear this situation nor that evil man's name mentioned in my house again. I mean that." She went back into the kitchen to make apple strudel for my celebration.

Even Bailey was frightened. He sat all to himself, looking at a man's death—a kitten looking at a wolf. Not quite understanding it but frightened all the same.

In those moments I decided that although Bailey loved me he couldn't help. I had sold myself to the Devil and there could be no escape. The only thing I could do was to stop talking to people other than Bailey. Instinctively, or somehow, I knew that because I loved him so much I'd never hurt him, but if I talked to anyone else that person might die too. Just my breath, carrying my words out, might poison people and they'd curl up and die like the black fat slugs that only pretended.

I had to stop talking.

I discovered that to achieve perfect personal silence all I had to do was to attach myself leechlike to sound. I began to listen to everything. I probably hoped that after I had heard all the sounds, really heard them and packed them down, deep in my ears, the world would be quiet around me. I walked into rooms where people were laughing, their voices hitting the walls like stones, and I simply stood still—in the midst of the riot of sound. After a minute or two, silence would rush into the room from its hiding place because I had eaten up all the sounds.

In the first weeks my family accepted my behavior as a post-rape, post-hospital affliction. (Neither the term nor the experience was mentioned in Grandmother's house, where Bailey and I were again staying.) They understood that I could talk to Bailey, but to no one else.

Then came the last visit from the visiting nurse, and the doctor said I was healed. That meant that I should be back on the sidewalks playing handball or enjoying the games I had been given when I was sick. When I refused to be the child they knew and accepted me to be, I was called impudent and my muteness sullenness.

For a while I was punished for being so uppity that I wouldn't speak; and then came the thrashings, given by any relative who felt himself offended.

We were on the train going back to Stamps, and this time it was I who had to console Bailey. He cried his heart out down the aisles of the coach, and pressed his little-boy body against the window pane looking for a last glimpse of his Mother Dear.

I have never known if Momma sent for us, or if the St. Louis family just got fed up with my grim presence. There is nothing more appalling than a constantly morose child.

I cared less about the trip than about the fact that Bailey was unhappy, and had no more thought of our destination than if I had simply been heading for the toilet.

AUDRE LORDE (1934–1992)

Audre Lorde, like many other writers, used her forum to fight racism and sexism. She was born in New York City and grew up in Manhattan. She worked as a librarian for several years before starting her teaching career. In 1968, she was awarded a grant by the National Endowment for the Arts and began working at Tougaloo College as poet in residence. She was poet laureate of New York State in 1991. Sometimes published as Rey Domini, Lorde wrote as a proponent of feminist and homosexual issues.

Her books of poetry include The First Cities *(1968),* Cables to Rage *(1970), and* The Black Unicorn *(1978). She also published an autobiographical piece,* The Cancer Journals *(1980), and a novel,* Zami: A New Spelling of My Name *(1982).*

Coal (1962)

I
is the total black, being spoken
from the earth's inside.
There are many kinds of open
how a diamond comes into a knot of flame   5
how sound comes into a word, colored
by who pays what for speaking.

Some words are open like a diamond
on glass windows
singing out within the passing crash of sun   10
Then there are words like stapled wagers

in a perforated book—buy and sign and tear apart—
and come whatever wills all chances
the stub remains
an ill-pulled tooth with a ragged edge.   15
Some words live in my throat
breeding like adders. Others know sun
seeking like gypsies over my tongue
to explode through my lips
like young sparrows bursting from shell.   20
Some words
bedevil me.

Love is a word, another kind of open.
As the diamond comes into a knot of flame
I am Black because I come from the earth's inside   25
now take my word for jewel in the open light.

Black Mother Woman (1971)

I cannot recall you gentle
yet through your heavy love
I have become
an image of your once delicate flesh
split with deceitful longings.   5

When strangers come and compliment me
your aged spirit takes a bow
jingling with pride
but once you hid that secret
in the center of furies   10
hanging me
with deep breasts and wiry hair
with your own split flesh
and long suffering eyes
buried in myths of little worth.   15

But I have peeled away your anger
down to the core of love
and look mother
I Am
a dark temple where your true spirit rises   20
beautiful
and tough as chestnut
stanchion against your nightmare of weakness
and if my eyes conceal
a squadron of conflicting rebellions   25

I learned from you
to define myself
through your denials.

ALICE WALKER (b. 1944)

Alice Walker—a novelist, short-story writer, poet, and teacher born in Eatonton, Georgia—has received many honors for her work. Among them are a National Institute of Arts and Letters award in 1973 for In Love and Trouble, *a short-story collection; the Lillian Smith Award in the same year for* Revolutionary Petunias, *a poetry collection; a Guggenheim Fellowship in 1978; and the National Book Award and the Pulitzer Prize for fiction for the novel* The Color Purple *(1982), which was made into a movie.*

The women in Walker's fiction are often on a quest for identity. Her stories often advocate gender and racial equality. Her first book was The Third Life of Grange Copeland *(1970), and her second,* Meridian *(1976). In* The Temple of My Familiar *(1989) and* Possessing the Secret of Joy *(1992), Walker writes about African culture. Walker's* By the Light of My Father's Smile *was published in 1998.*

To Hell with Dying (1973)

"To hell with dying," my father would say. "These children want Mr. Sweet!"

Mr. Sweet was a diabetic and an alcoholic and a guitar player and lived down the road from us on a neglected cotton farm. My older brothers and sisters got the most benefit from Mr. Sweet for when they were growing up he had quite a few years ahead of him and so was capable of being called back from the brink of death any number of times—whenever the voice of my father reached him as he lay expiring. "To hell with dying, man," my father would say, pushing the wife away from the bedside (in tears although she knew the death was not necessarily the last one unless Mr. Sweet really wanted it to be). "These children want Mr. Sweet!" And they did want him, for at a signal from Father they would come crowding around the bed and throw themselves on the covers, and whoever was the smallest at the time would kiss him all over his wrinkled brown face and begin to tickle him so that he would laugh all down in his stomach, and his moustache, which was long and sort of straggly, would shake like Spanish moss and was also that color.

Mr. Sweet had been ambitious as a boy, wanted to be a doctor or lawyer or sailor, only to find that black men fare better if they are not. Since he could become none of these things he turned to fishing as his only earnest career and playing the guitar as his only claim to doing anything extraordinarily well. His son, the only one that he and his wife, Miss Mary, had, was shiftless as the day is long and spent money as if he were trying to see the bottom of the mint, which Mr. Sweet would tell him was the clean brown palm of his hand. Miss Mary loved her "baby," however, and worked hard to get him the "li'l necessaries" of life, which turned out mostly to be women.

Mr. Sweet was a tall, thinnish man with thick kinky hair going dead white. He was dark brown, his eyes were very squinty and sort of bluish, and he chewed Brown Mule tobacco. He was constantly on the verge of being blind drunk, for he brewed his own liquor and was not in the least a stingy sort of man, and was always very melancholy and sad, though frequently when he was "feelin' good" he'd dance around the yard with us, usually keeling over just as my mother came to see what the commotion was.

Toward all of us children he was very kind, and had the grace to be shy with us, which is unusual in grown-ups. He had great respect for my mother for she never held his drunkenness against him and would let us play with him even when he was about to fall in the fireplace from drink. Although Mr. Sweet would sometimes lose complete or nearly complete control of his head and neck so that he would loll in his chair, his mind remained strangely acute and his speech not too affected. His ability to be drunk and sober at the same time made him an ideal playmate, for he was as weak as we were and we could usually best him in wrestling, all the while keeping a fairly coherent conversation going.

We never felt anything of Mr. Sweet's age when we played with him. We loved his wrinkles and would draw some on our brows to be like him, and his white hair was my special treasure and he knew it and would never come to visit us just after he had had his hair cut off at the barbershop. Once he came to our house for something, probably to see my father about fertilizer for his crops because, although he never paid the slightest attention to his crops, he liked to know what things would be best to use on them if he ever did. Anyhow, he had not come with his hair since he had just had it shaved off at the barbershop. He wore a huge straw hat to keep off the sun and also to keep his head away from me. But as soon as I saw him I ran up and demanded that he take me up and kiss me with his funny beard which smelled so strongly of tobacco. Looking forward to burying my small fingers into his woolly hair I threw away his hat only to find he had done something to his hair, that it was no longer there! I let out a squall which made my mother think that Mr. Sweet had finally dropped me in the well or something and from that day I've been wary of men in hats. However, not long after, Mr. Sweet showed up with his hair grown out and just as white and kinky and impenetrable as it ever was.

Mr. Sweet used to call me his princess, and I believed it. He made me feel pretty at five and six, and simply outrageously devastating at the blazing age of eight and a half. When he came to our house with his guitar the whole family would stop whatever they were doing to sit around him and listen to him play. He liked to play "Sweet Georgia Brown," that was what he called me sometimes, and also he liked to play "Caldonia" and all sorts of sweet, sad, wonderful songs which he sometimes made up. It was from one of these songs that I learned that he had had to marry Miss Mary when he had in fact loved somebody else (now living in Chi-ca-go, or De-stroy, Michigan). He was not sure that Joe Lee, her "baby," was also his baby. Sometimes he would cry and that was an indication that he was about to die again. And so we would all get prepared, for we were sure to be called upon.

I was seven the first time I remember actually participating in one of Mr. Sweet's "revivals"—my parents told me I had participated before, I had been the one chosen to kiss him and tickle him long before I knew the rite of Mr. Sweet's rehabilitation. He had come to our house, it was a few years after his wife's death, and was very sad, and also, typically, very drunk. He sat on the floor next to me and my older brother, the rest of the children were grown up and lived elsewhere, and began to play his guitar and cry. I held his woolly head in my arms and wished I could have been old enough to have been the woman he loved so much and that I had not been lost years and years ago.

When he was leaving, my mother said to us that we'd better sleep light that night for we'd probably have to go over to Mr. Sweet's before daylight. And we did. For soon after we had gone to bed one of the neighbors knocked on our door and called my father and said that Mr. Sweet was sinking fast and if he wanted to get in a word before the crossover he'd better shake a leg and get over to Mr. Sweet's house. All the neighbors knew to come to our house if something was wrong with Mr. Sweet, but they did not know how we always managed to make him well, or at least stop him from dying, when he was often so near death. As soon as we heard the cry we got up, my brother and I and my mother and father, and put on our clothes. We hurried out of the house and down the road for we were always afraid that we might someday be too late and Mr. Sweet would get tired of dallying.

When we got to the house, a very poor shack really, we found the front room full of neighbors and relatives and someone met us at the door and said that it was all very sad that old Mr. Sweet Little (for Little was his family name, although we mostly ignored it) was about to kick the bucket. My parents were advised not to take my brother and me into the "death room," seeing we were so young and all, but we were so much more accustomed to the death room than he that we ignored him and dashed in without giving his warning a second thought. I was almost in tears, for these deaths upset me fearfully, and the thought of how much depended on me and my brother (who was such a ham most of the time) made me very nervous.

The doctor was bending over the bed and turned back to tell us for at least the tenth time in the history of my family that, alas, old Mr. Sweet Little was dying and that the children had best not see the face of implacable death (I didn't know what "implacable" was, but whatever it was, Mr. Sweet was not!). My father pushed him rather abruptly out of the way saying, as he always did and very loudly for he was saying it to Mr. Sweet, "To hell with dying, man, these children want Mr. Sweet"—which was my cue to throw myself upon the bed and kiss Mr. Sweet all around the whiskers and under the eyes and around the collar of his nightshirt where he smelled so strongly of all sorts of things, mostly liniment.

I was very good at bringing him around, for as soon as I saw that he was struggling to open his eyes I knew he was going to be all right, and so could finish my revival sure of success. As soon as his eyes were open he would begin to smile and that way I knew that I had surely won. Once, though, I got a tremendous scare, for he could not open his eyes and later I learned that he had had a stroke and that one side of his face was stiff and hard to get into motion. When he began to smile I could tickle him in earnest because I was sure that nothing would get in the way of his laughter, although once he began to cough so hard that he almost threw me off his stomach, but that was when I was very small, little more than a baby, and my bushy hair had gotten in his nose.

When we were sure he would listen to us we would ask him why he was in bed and when he was coming to see us again and could we play with his guitar, which more than likely would be leaning against the bed. His eyes would get all misty and he would sometimes cry out loud, but we never let it embarrass us, for he knew that we loved him and that we sometimes cried too for no reason. My parents would leave the room to just the three of us; Mr. Sweet, by that time, would be propped up in bed with a number of pillows behind his head and with me sitting and lying on his shoulder and along his chest. Even when he had trouble breathing he would not ask me to get down. Looking into my eyes he would shake his white head and run a scratchy old finger all around my hairline, which was rather low down, nearly to my eyebrows, and made some people say I looked like a baby monkey.

My brother was very generous in all this, he let me do all the revivaling—he had done it for years before I was born and so was glad to be able to pass it on to someone new. What he would do while I talked to Mr. Sweet was pretend to play the guitar, in fact pretend that he was a young version of Mr. Sweet, and it always made Mr. Sweet glad to think that someone wanted to be like him—of course, we did not know this then, we played the thing by ear, and whatever he seemed to like, we did. We were desperately afraid that he was just going to take off one day and leave us.

It did not occur to us that we were doing anything special; we had not learned that death was final when it did come. We thought nothing of triumphing over it so many times, and in fact became a trifle contemptuous of people who let themselves be carried away. It did not occur to us that if our own father had been dying we could not have stopped it, that Mr. Sweet was the only person over whom we had power.

When Mr. Sweet was in his eighties I was studying in the university many miles from home. I saw him whenever I went home, but he was never on the verge of dying that I could tell and I began to feel that my anxiety for his health and psychological well-being was unnecessary. By this time he not only had a moustache but a long flowing snow-white beard, which I loved and combed and braided for hours. He was very peaceful, fragile, gentle, and the only jarring note about him was his old steel guitar, which he still played in the old sad, sweet, down-home blues way.

On Mr. Sweet's ninetieth birthday I was finishing my doctorate in Massachusetts and had been making arrangements to go home for several weeks' rest. That morning I got a telegram telling me that Mr. Sweet was dying again and could I please drop everything and come home. Of course I could. My dissertation could wait and my teachers would understand when I explained to them when I got back. I ran to the phone, called the airport, and within four hours I was speeding along the dusty road to Mr. Sweet's.

The house was more dilapidated than when I was last there, barely a shack, but it was overgrown with yellow roses which my family had planted many years ago. The air was heavy and sweet and very peaceful. I felt strange walking through the gate and up the old rickety steps. But the strangeness left me as I caught sight of the long white beard I loved so well flowing down the thin body over the familiar quilt coverlet. Mr. Sweet!

His eyes were closed tight and his hands, crossed over his stomach, were thin and delicate, no longer scratchy. I remembered how always before I had run and jumped up on him just anywhere; now I knew he would not be able to support my weight. I looked around at my parents, and was surprised to see that my father and mother also looked old and frail. My father, his own hair very gray, leaned over the quietly sleeping old man, who, incidentally, smelled still of wine and tobacco, and said, as he'd done so many times, "To hell with dying, man! My daughter is home to see Mr. Sweet!" My brother had not been able to come as he was in the war in Asia. I bent down and gently stroked the closed eyes and gradually they began to open. The closed, wine-stained lips twitched a little, then parted in a warm, slightly embarrassed smile. Mr. Sweet could see me and he recognized me and his eyes looked very spry and twinkly for a moment. I put my head down on the pillow next to his and we just looked at each other for a long time. Then he began to trace my peculiar hairline with a thin, smooth finger. I closed my eyes when his finger halted above my ear (he used to rejoice at the dirt in my ears when I was little), his hand stayed cupped around my cheek. When I opened my eyes, sure that I had reached him in time, his were closed.

Even at twenty-four how could I believe that I had failed? that Mr. Sweet was really gone? He had never gone before. But when I looked up at my parents I saw that they were holding back tears. They had loved him dearly. He was like a piece of rare and delicate china which was always being saved from breaking and which finally fell. I looked long at the old face, the wrinkled forehead, the red lips, the hands that still reached out to me. Soon I felt my father pushing something cool into my hands. It was Mr. Sweet's guitar. He had asked them months before to give it to me; he had known that even if I came next time he would not be able to respond in the old way. He did not want me to feel that my trip had been for nothing.

The old guitar! I plucked the strings, hummed "Sweet Georgia Brown." The magic of Mr. Sweet lingered still in the cool steel box. Through the window I could catch the fragrant delicate scent of tender yellow roses. The man on the high old-fashioned bed with the quilt coverlet and the flowing white beard had been my first love.

Strong Horse Tea (1973)

Rannie Toomer's little baby boy Snooks was dying from double pneumonia and whooping cough. She sat away from him, gazing into the low fire, her long crusty bottom lip hanging. She was not married. Was not pretty. Was not anybody much. And he was all she had.

"Lawd, why don't that doctor come on here?" she moaned, tears sliding from her sticky eyes. She had not washed since Snooks took sick five days ago and a long row of whitish snail tracks laced her ashen face.

"What you ought to try is some of the old home remedies," Sarah urged. She was an old neighboring lady who wore magic leaves round her neck sewed up in possumskin next to a dried lizard's foot. She knew how magic came about, and could do magic herself, people said.

"We going to have us a doctor," Rannie Toomer said fiercely, walking over to shoo a fat winter fly from her child's forehead. "I don't believe in none of that swamp magic. All the old home remedies I took when I was a child come just short of killing me."

Snooks, under a pile of faded quilts, made a small gravelike mound in the bed. His head was like a ball of black putty wedged between the thin covers and the dingy yellow pillow. His little eyes were partly open, as if he were peeping out of his hard wasted skull at the chilly room, and the forceful pulse of his breathing caused a faint rustling in the sheets near his mouth like the wind pushing damp papers in a shallow ditch.

"What time you reckon that doctor'll git here?" asked Sarah, not expecting Rannie Toomer to answer her. She sat with her knees wide apart under many aprons and long dark skirts heavy with stains. From time to time she reached long cracked fingers down to sweep her damp skirts away from the live coals. It was almost spring, but the winter cold still clung to her bones and she had to almost sit in the fireplace to be warm. Her deep sharp eyes set in the rough leather of her face had aged a moist hesitant blue that gave her a quick dull stare like a hawk's. Now she gazed coolly at Rannie Toomer and rapped the hearthstones with her stick.

"White mailman, white doctor," she chanted skeptically, under her breath, as if to banish spirits.

"They gotta come see 'bout this baby," Rannie Toomer said wistfully. "Who'd go and ignore a little sick baby like my Snooks?"

"Some folks we don't know so well as we thinks we do might," the old lady replied. "What you want to give that boy of yours is one or two of the old home remedies; arrowsroot or sassyfras and cloves, or a sugar tit soaked in cat's blood."

Rannie Toomer's face went tight.

"We don't need none of your witch's remedies," she cried, grasping her baby by his shrouded toes, trying to knead life into him as she kneaded limberness into flour dough.

"We going to git some of them shots that makes peoples well, cures 'em of all they ails, cleans 'em out and makes 'em strong all at the same time."

She spoke upward from her son's feet as if he were an altar. "Doctor'll be here soon, baby," she whispered to him, then rose to look out the grimy window. "I done sent the mailman." She rubbed her face against the glass, her flat nose more flattened as she peered out into the rain.

"Howdy, Rannie Mae," the red-faced mailman had said pleasantly as he always did when she stood by the car waiting to ask him something. Usually she wanted to ask what certain circulars meant that showed pretty pictures of things she needed. Did the circulars mean that somebody was coming around later and would give her hats and suitcases and shoes and sweaters and rubbing alcohol and a heater for the house and a fur bonnet for her baby? Or, why did he always give her the pictures if she couldn't have what was in them? Or, what did the words say . . . especially the big word written in red: "S-A-L-E!"?

He would explain shortly to her that the only way she could get the goods pictured on the circulars was to buy them in town and that town stores did their advertising by sending out pictures of their goods. She would listen with her mouth hanging open until he finished. Then she would exclaim in a dull amazed way that *she* never *had* any money and he could ask anybody. *She* couldn't ever buy any of the things in the pictures—so why did the stores keep sending them to her?

He tried to explain to her that *everybody* got the circulars, whether they had any money to buy with or not. That this was one of the laws of advertising and he could do nothing about it. He was sure she never understood what he tried to teach her about advertising, for one day she asked him for any extra circulars he had and when he asked what she wanted them for—since she couldn't afford to buy any of the items advertised—she said she needed them to paper the inside of her house to keep out the wind.

Today he thought she looked more ignorant than usual as she stuck her dripping head inside his car. He recoiled from her breath and gave little attention to what she was saying about her sick baby as he mopped up the water she dripped on the plastic door handle of the car.

"Well, never *can* keep 'em dry, I mean *warm* enough, in rainy weather like this here," he mumbled absently, stuffing a wad of circulars advertising hair driers and cold creams into her hands. He wished she would stand back from his car so he could get going. But she clung to the side gabbing away about "Snooks" and "NEWmonia" and "shots" and how she wanted a "REAL doctor."

"That right?" he injected sympathetically from time to time, and from time to time he sneezed, for she was letting in wetness and damp, and he felt he was coming down with a cold. Black people as black as Rannie Mae always made him uneasy, especially when they didn't smell good, and when you could tell they didn't right away. Rannie Mae, leaning in over him out of the rain, smelt like a wet goat. Her dark dirty eyes clinging to his face with such hungry desperation made him nervous.

Why did colored folks always want you to do something for them?

Now he cleared his throat and made a motion forward as if to roll up his window. "Well, ah, *mighty* sorry to hear 'bout that little fella," he said, groping for the window crank. "We'll see what we can do!" He gave her what he hoped was a big friendly smile. God! He didn't want to hurt her feelings! She looked so pitiful hanging there in the rain. Suddenly he had an idea.

"Whyn't you try some of old Aunt Sarah's home remedies?" he suggested brightly, still smiling. He half believed with everybody else in the county that the old blue-eyed black woman possessed magic. Magic that if it didn't work on whites probably would on blacks. But Rannie Mae almost turned the car over shaking her head and body with an emphatic "NO!" She reached in a wet crusted hand to grasp his shoulder.

"We wants a doctor, a real doctor!" she screamed. She had begun to cry and drop her tears on him. "You git us a doctor from town," she bellowed, shaking the solid shoulder that bulged under his new tweed coat.

"Like I say," he drawled lamely although beginning to be furious with her, "we'll do what we can!" And he hurriedly rolled up the window and sped down the road, cringing from the thought that she had put her hands on him.

"Old home remedies! Old home remedies!" Rannie Toomer cursed the words while she licked at the hot tears that ran down her face, the only warmth about her. She turned back to the trail that led to her house, trampling the wet circulars under her feet. Under the fence she went and was in a pasture, surrounded by dozens of fat white folks' cows and an old gray horse and a mule or two. Animals lived there in the pasture all around her house, and she and Snooks lived in it.

It was less than an hour after she had talked to the mailman that she looked up expecting the doctor and saw old Sarah tramping through the grass on her walking stick. She couldn't pretend she wasn't home with the smoke climbing out the chimney, so she let her in, making her leave her bag of tricks on the front porch.

Old woman old as that ought to forget trying to cure other people with her nigger magic . . . ought to use some of it on herself, she thought. She would not let her lay a finger on Snooks and warned her if she tried she would knock her over the head with her own cane.

"He coming all right," Rannie Toomer said firmly, looking, straining her eyes to see through the rain.

"Let me tell you, child," the old woman said almost gently, "he ain't." She was sipping something hot from a dish. When would this one know, she wondered, that she could only depend on those who would come.

"But I *told* you," Rannie Toomer said in exasperation, as if explaining something to a backward child. "I asked the mailman to bring a doctor for my Snooks!"

Cold wind was shooting all around her from the cracks in the window framing, faded circulars blew inward from the walls. The old woman's gloomy prediction made her tremble.

"He done fetched the doctor," Sarah said, rubbing her dish with her hand. "What you reckon brung me over here in this here flood? Wasn't no desire to see no rainbows, I can tell you."

Rannie Toomer paled.

"I's the doctor, child." Sarah turned to Rannie with dull wise eyes. "That there mailman didn't git no further with that message than the road in front of my house. Lucky he got good lungs—deef as I is I had myself a time trying to make out what he was yellin'."

Rannie began to cry, moaning.

Suddenly the breathing of Snooks from the bed seemed to drown out the noise of the downpour outside. Rannie Toomer could feel his pulse making the whole house tremble.

"Here," she cried, snatching up the baby and handing him to Sarah. "Make him well. *O my lawd*, make him well!"

Sarah rose from her seat by the fire and took the tiny baby, already turning a purplish blue around the eyes and mouth.

"Let's not upset this little fella unnessarylike," she said, placing the baby back on the bed. Gently she began to examine him, all the while moaning and humming some thin pagan tune that pushed against the sound of the wind and rain with its own melancholy power. She stripped him of all his clothes, poked at his fibreless baby ribs, blew against his chest. Along his tiny flat back she ran her soft old fingers. The child hung on in deep rasping sleep, and his small glazed eyes neither opened fully nor fully closed.

Rannie Toomer swayed over the bed watching the old woman touching the baby. She thought of the time she had wasted waiting for the real doctor. Her feeling of guilt was a stone.

"I'll do anything you say do, Aunt Sarah," she cried, mopping at her nose with her dress. "Anything. Just, please God, make him git better!"

Old Sarah dressed the baby again and sat down in front of the fire. She stayed deep in thought for several moments. Rannie Toomer gazed first into her silent face and then at the baby, whose breathing seemed to have eased since Sarah picked him up.

Do something quick, she urged Sarah in her mind, wanting to believe in her powers completely. Do something that'll make him rise up and call his mama!

"The child's dying," said Sarah bluntly, staking out beforehand some limitation to her skill. "But there still might be something we can do. . . ."

"What, Aunt Sarah, what?" Rannie Toomer was on her knees before the old woman's chair, wringing her hands and crying. She fastened hungry eyes on Sarah's lips.

"What can I *do?*" she urged fiercely, hearing the faint labored breathing from the bed.

It's going to take a strong stomach," said Sarah slowly. "A *mighty* strong stomach. And most you young peoples these days don't have 'em."

"Snooks got a strong stomach," said Rannie Toomer, looking anxiously into the old serious face.

"It ain't him that's got to have the strong stomach," Sarah said, glancing down at Rannie Toomer. "*You* the one got to have a strong stomach . . . he won't know *what* it is he's drinking."

Rannie Toomer began to tremble way down deep in her stomach. It sure was weak, she thought. Trembling like that. But what could she mean her Snooks to drink? Not cat's blood—! And not some of the messes with bat's wings she'd heard Sarah mixed for people sick in the head?

"What is it?" she whispered, bringing her head close to Sarah's knee. Sarah leaned down and put her toothless mouth to her ear.

"The only thing that can save this child now is some good strong horse tea," she said, keeping her eyes on the girl's face. "The *only* thing. And if you wants him out of that bed you better make tracks to git some."

Rannie Toomer took up her wet coat and stepped across the porch into the pasture. The rain fell against her face with the force of small hailstones. She started walking in the direction of the trees where she could see the bulky lightish shapes of cows. Her thin plastic shoes were sucked at by the mud, but she pushed herself forward in search of the lone gray mare.

All the animals shifted ground and rolled big dark eyes at Rannie Toomer. She made as little noise as she could and leaned against a tree to wait.

Thunder rose from the side of the sky like tires of a big truck rumbling over rough dirt road. Then it stood a split second in the middle of the sky before it exploded like a giant firecracker, then rolled away again like an empty keg. Lightning streaked across the sky, setting the air white and charged.

Rannie Toomer stood dripping under her tree, hoping not to be struck. She kept her eyes carefully on the behind of the gray mare, who, after nearly an hour, began nonchalantly to spread her muddy knees.

At that moment Rannie Toomer realized that she had brought nothing to catch the precious tea in. Lightning struck something not far off and caused a crackling and groaning in the woods that frightened the animals away from their shelter. Rannie Toomer slipped down in the mud trying to take off one of her plastic shoes to catch the tea. And the gray mare, trickling some, broke for a clump of cedars yards away.

Rannie Toomer was close enough to catch the tea if she could keep up with the mare while she ran. So alternately holding her breath and gasping for air she started after her. Mud from her fall clung to her elbows and streaked her frizzy hair. Slipping and sliding in the mud she raced after the mare, holding out, as if for alms, her plastic shoe.

In the house Sarah sat, her shawls and sweaters tight around her, rubbing her knees and muttering under her breath. She heard the thunder, saw the lightning that lit up the dingy room and turned her waiting face to the bed. Hobbling over on stiff legs she could hear no sound; the frail breathing had stopped with the thunder, not to come again.

Across the mud-washed pasture Rannie Toomer stumbled, holding out her plastic shoe for the gray mare to fill. In spurts and splashes mixed with rainwater she gathered her tea. In parting, the old mare snorted and threw up one big leg, knocking her back into the mud. She rose, trembling and crying, holding the shoe, spilling none over the top but realizing a leak, a tiny crack at her shoe's front. Quickly she stuck her mouth there, over the crack, and ankle deep in the slippery mud of the pasture and freezing in her shabby wet coat, she ran home to give the still warm horse tea to her baby Snooks.

From The Color Purple (1982)

Dear God,

Shug Avery is coming to town! She coming with her orkestra. She going to sing in the Lucky Star out on Coalman road. Mr. _____ going to hear her. He dress all up in front the glass, look at himself, then undress and dress all over again. He slick back his hair with pomade, then wash it out again. He been spitting on his shoes and hitting it with a quick rag.

He tell me, Wash this. Iron that. Look for this. Look for that. Find this. Find that. He groan over holes in his sock.

I move round darning and ironing, finding hanskers. Anything happening? I ast.

What you mean? he say, like he mad. Just trying to git some of the hick farmer off myself. Any other woman be glad.

I'm is glad, I say.

What you mean? he ast.

You looks nice, I say. Any woman be proud.

You think so? he say.

First time he ast me. I'm so surprise, by time I say Yeah, he out on the porch, trying to shave where the light better.

I walk round all day with the announcement burning a hole in my pocket. It pink. The trees tween the turn off to our road and the store is lit up with them. He got bout five dozen in his trunk.

Shug Avery standing upside a piano, elbow crook, hand on her hip. She wearing a hat like Indian Chiefs. Her mouth open showing all her teef and don't nothing seem to be troubling her mind. Come one, come all, it say. The Queen Honeybee is back in town.

Lord, I wants to go so bad. Not to dance. Not to drink. Not to play card. Not even to hear Shug Avery sing. I just be thankful to lay eyes on her.

. . .

Dear Celie,

Guess what? Samuel thought the children were mine too! That is why he urged me to come to Africa with them. When I showed up at their house he thought I was following my children, and, soft-hearted as he is, didn't have the heart to turn me away.

If they are not yours, he said, whose are they?

But I had some questions for him, first.

Where did you get them? I asked. And Celie, he told me a story that made my hair stand on end. I hope you, poor thing, are ready for it.

Once upon a time, there was a well-to-do farmer who owned his own property near town. Our town, Celie. And as he did so well farming and everything he turned his hand to prospered, he decided to open a store, and try his luck selling dry goods as well. Well, his store did so well that he talked two of his brothers into helping him run it, and, as the months went by, they were doing better and better. Then the white merchants began to get together and complain that this store was taking all the black business away from them, and the man's blacksmith shop that he set up behind the store, was taking some of the white. This would not do. And so, one night, the man's store was burned down, his smithy destroyed, and the man and his two brothers dragged out of their homes in the middle of the night and hanged.

The man had a wife whom he adored, and they had a little girl, barely two years old. She was also pregnant with another child. When the neighbors brought her husband's body home, it had been mutilated and burnt. The sight of it nearly killed her, and her second baby, also a girl, was born at this time. Although the widow's body recovered, her mind was never the same. She continued to fix her husband's plate at mealtimes just as she'd always done and was always full of talk about the plans she and her husband had made. The neighbors, though not always intending to, shunned her more and more, partly because the plans she talked about were grander than anything they could even conceive of for colored people, and partly because her attachment to the past was so pitiful. She was a good-looking woman, though, and still owned land, but there was no one to work it for her, and she didn't know how herself; besides she kept waiting for her husband to finish the meal she'd cooked for him and go to the fields himself. Soon there was nothing to eat that the neighbors did not bring, and she and her small children grubbed around in the yard as best they could.

While the second child was still a baby, a stranger appeared in the community, and lavished all his attention on the widow and her children; in a short while, they were married. Almost at once she was pregnant a third time, though her mental health was no better. Every year thereafter, she was pregnant, every year she became weaker and more mentally unstable, until, many years after she married the stranger, she died.

Two years before she died she had a baby girl that she was too sick to keep. Then a baby boy. These children were named Olivia and Adam.

This is Samuel's story, almost word for word.

The stranger who married the widow was someone Samuel had run with long before he found Christ. When the man showed up at Samuel's house with first Olivia and then Adam, Samuel felt not only unable to refuse the children, but as if God had answered his and Corrine's prayers.

He never told Corrine about the man or about the children's "mother" because he hadn't wanted any sadness to cloud her happiness.

But then, out of nowhere, I appeared. He put two and two together, remembered that his old running buddy had always been a scamp, and took me in without any questions. Which, to tell the truth, had always puzzled me, but I put it down to Christian charity. Corrine had asked me once whether I was running away from home. But I explained I was a big girl now, my family back home very large and poor, and it was time for me to get out and earn my own living.

Tears had soaked my blouse when Samuel finished telling me all this. I couldn't begin, then, to tell him the truth. But Celie, I can tell you. And I pray with all my heart that you will get this letter, if none of the others.

Pa is not our pa!

Your devoted Sister,

Nettie

. . .

Dearest Nettie,

The man us knowed as Pa is dead.

How come you still call him Pa? Shug ast me the other day.

But, too late to call him Alphonso. I never even remember Ma calling him by his name. She always said, Your Pa. I reckon to make us believe it better. Anyhow, his little wife, Daisy, call me up on the telephone in the middle of the night.

Miss Celie, she say, I got bad news. Alphonso dead.

Who? I ast.

Alphonso, she say. Your stepdaddy.

How he die? I ast. I think of killing, being hit by a truck, struck by lightening, lingering disease. But she say, Naw, he died in his sleep. Well, not quite in his sleep, she say. Us was spending a little time in bed together, you know, before us drop off.

Well, I say, you have my sympathy.

Yes ma'am, she say, and I thought I had this house too, but look like it belong to your sister Nettie and you.

Say what? I ast.

Your stepdaddy been dead over a week, she say. When us went to town to hear the will read yesterday, you could have knock me over with a feather. Your real daddy owned the land and the house and the store. He left it to your mama. When your mama died, it passed on to you and your sister Nettie. I don't know why Alphonso never told you that.

Well, I say, anything coming from him, I don't want it.

I hear Daisy suck in her breath. How about your sister Nettie, she say. You think she feel the same way?

I wake up a little bit then. By the time Shug roll over and ast me who it is, I'm beginning to see the light.

Don't be a fool, Shug say, nudging me with her foot. You got your own house now. Your daddy and mama left it for you. That dog of a stepdaddy just a bad odor passing through.

But I never had no house, I say. Just to think about having my own house enough to scare me. Plus, this house I'm gitting is bigger than Shug's, got more land around it. And, it come with a store.

My God, I say to Shug. Me and Nettie own a drygood store. What us gon sell?

How bout pants? she say.

So us hung up the phone and rush down home again to look at the property.

About a mile before us got to town us come up on the entrance to the colored cemetery. Shug was sound asleep, but something told me I ought to drive in. Pretty soon I see something look like a short skyscraper and I stop the car and go up to it. Sure enough it's got Alphonso's name on it. Got a lot of other stuff on it too. Member of this and that. Leading businessman and farmer. Upright husband and father. Kind to the poor and helpless. He been dead two weeks but fresh flowers still blooming on his grave.

Shug git out the car and come stand by me.

Finally she yawn loud and stretch herself. The son of a bitch still dead, she say.

Daisy try to act like she glad to see us, but she not. She got two children and look pregnant with one more. But she got nice clothes, a car, and Alphonso left her all his money. Plus, I think she manage to set her folks up while she live with him.

She say, Celie, the old house you remember was torn down so Alphonso could build this one. He got an Atlanta architect to design it, and these tiles come all the way from New York. We was standing in the kitchen at the time. But he put tiles everywhere. Kitchen, toilet, back porch. All around the fireplaces in back and front parlour. But this the house go with the place, right on, she say. Of course I did take the furniture, because Alphonso bought it special for me.

Fine with me, I say. I can't get over having a house. Soon as Daisy leave me with the keys I run from one room to another like I'm crazy. Look at this, I say to Shug. Look at that! She look, she grin. She hug me whenever she git the chance and I stand still.

You doin' all right, Miss Celie, she say. God know where you live.

Then she took some cedar sticks out of her bag and lit them and gave one of them to me. Us started at the very top of the house in the attic, and us smoked it all the way down to the basement, chasing out all the evil and making a place for good.

Oh, Nettie, us have a house! A house big enough for us and our children, for your husband and Shug. Now you can come home cause you have a home to come to!

Your Loving Sister,

Celie

 TONI CADE BAMBARA (1939–1995)

At birth, in New York City, Toni Cade Bambara was named Toni Cade. She changed her name to include Bambara after seeing the name in one of her great-grandmother's books. Her colorful career was filled with various jobs. She reviewed films, plays, and books; she worked as the director of recreation in a hospital psychiatric department; she was a social worker, a freelance writer, and a professor of English.

Bambara is most noted for her short-story collections, including Gorilla, My Love *(1972) and* The Sea Birds Are Still Alive *(1977). Her first novel,* The Salt Eaters *(1980), explores racial and ethnic divisions. In addition, she wrote other novels and screenplays.*

The Lesson (1972)

Back in the days when everyone was old and stupid or young and foolish and me and Sugar were the only ones just right, this lady moved on our block with nappy hair and proper speech and no makeup. And quite naturally we laughed at her, laughed the way we did at the junk man who went about his business like he was some big-time president and his sorry-ass horse his secretary. And we kinda hated her too, hated the way we did the winos who cluttered up our parks and pissed on our handball walls and stank up our hallways and stairs so you couldn't halfway play hide-and-seek without a goddamn gas mask. Miss Moore was her name. The only woman on the block with no first name. And she was black as hell, cept for her feet, which were fish-white and spooky. And she was always planning these boring-ass things for us to do, us being my cousin, mostly, who lived on the block cause we all moved North the same time and to the same apartment then spread out gradual to breathe. And our parents would yank our heads into some kinda shape and crisp up our clothes so we'd be presentable for travel with Miss Moore, who always looked like she was going to church, though she never did. Which is just one of the things the grownups talked about when they talked behind her back like a dog. But when she came calling with some sachet she'd sewed up or some gingerbread she'd made or some book, why then they'd all be too embarrassed to turn her down and we'd get handed over all spruced up. She'd been to college and said it was only right that she should take responsibility for the young ones' education, and she not even related by marriage or blood. So they'd go for it. Specially Aunt Gretchen. She was the main gofer in the family. You got some ole dumb shit foolishness you want somebody to go for, you send for Aunt Gretchen. She been screwed into the go-along for so long, it's a blood-deep natural thing with her. Which is how she got saddled with me and Sugar and Junior in the first place while our mothers were in a la-de-da apartment up the block having a good ole time.

So this one day Miss Moore rounds us all up at the mailbox and it's purdee hot and she's knockin herself out about arithmetic. And school suppose to let up in summer I heard, but she don't never let up. And the starch in my pinafore scratching the shit outta me and I'm really hating this nappy-head bitch and her goddamn college degree. I'd much rather go to the pool or to the show where it's cool. So me and Sugar leaning on the mailbox being surly, which is a Miss Moore word. And Flyboy checking out what everybody brought for lunch. And Fat Butt already wasting his peanut-butter-and-jelly sandwich like the pig he is. And Junebug punchin on Q.T.'s arm for potato chips. And Rosie Giraffe shifting from one hip to the other waiting for somebody to step on her foot or ask her if she from Georgia so she can kick ass, preferably Mercedes'. And Miss Moore asking us do we know what money is, like we a bunch of retards. I mean real money, she say, like it's only poker chips or monopoly papers we lay on the grocer. So right away I'm tired of this and say so. And would much rather snatch Sugar and go to the Sunset and terrorize the West Indian kids and take their hair ribbons and their money too. And Miss Moore files that remark away for next week's lesson on brotherhood, I can tell. And finally I say we oughta get to the subway cause it's cooler and besides we might meet some cute boys. Sugar done swiped her mama's lipstick, so we ready.

So we heading down the street and she's boring us silly about what things cost and what our parents make and how much goes for rent and how money ain't divided up right in this country. And then she gets to the part about we all poor and live in the slums, which I don't feature. And I'm ready to speak on that, but she steps out in the street and hails two cabs just like that. Then she hustles half the crew in with her and hands me a five-dollar bill and tells me to calculate 10 percent tip for the driver. And we're off. Me and Sugar and Junebug and Flyboy hangin out the window and hollering to everybody, putting lipstick on each other cause Flyboy a faggot anyway, and making farts with our sweaty armpits. But I'm mostly trying to figure how to spend this money. But they all fascinated with the meter ticking and Junebug starts laying bets as to how much it'll read when Flyboy can't hold his breath no more. Then Sugar lays bets as to how much it'll be when we get there. So I'm stuck. Don't nobody want to go for my plan, which is to jump out at the next light and run off to the first bar-b-que we can find. Then the driver tells us to get the hell out cause we there already. And the meter reads eighty-five cents. And I'm stalling to figure out the tip and Sugar say give him a dime. And I decide he don't need it bad as I do, so later for him. But then he tries to take off with Junebug foot still in the door so we talk about his mama something ferocious. Then we check out that we on Fifth Avenue and everybody dressed up in stockings. One lady in a fur coat, hot as it is. White folks crazy.

"This is the place," Miss Moore say, presenting it to us in the voice she uses at the museum. "Let's look in the windows before we go in."

"Can we steal?" Sugar asks very serious like she's getting the ground rules squared away before she plays. "I beg your pardon," say Miss Moore, and we fall out. So she leads us around the windows of the toy store and me and Sugar screamin, "This is mine, that's mine, I gotta have that, that was made for me, I was born for that," till Big Butt drowns us out.

"Hey, I'm goin to buy that there."

"That there? You don't even know what it is, stupid."

"I do so," he say punchin on Rosie Giraffe. "It's a microscope."

"Whatcha gonna do with a microscope, fool?"

"Look at things."

"Like what, Ronald?" ask Miss Moore. And Big Butt ain't got the first notion. So here go Miss Moore gabbing about the thousands of bacteria in a drop of water and the somethinorother in a speck of blood and the million and one living things in the air around us is invisible to the naked eye. And what she say that for? Junebug go to town on that "naked" and we rolling. Then Miss Moore ask what it cost. So we all jam into the window smudgin it up and the price tag say $300. So then she ask how long'd take for Big Butt and Junebug to save up their allowances. "Too long," I said. "Yeh," adds Sugar, "outgrown it by that time." And Miss Moore say no, you never outgrow learning instruments. "Why, even medical students and interns and," blah, blah, blah. And we ready to choke Big Butt for bringing it up in the first damn place.

"This here costs four hundred eighty dollars," say Rosie Giraffe. So we pile up all over her to see what she pointin out. My eyes tell me it's a chunk of glass cracked with something heavy and different-color inks dripped into the splits, then the whole thing put into a oven or something. But for $480 it don't make sense.

"That's a paperweight made of semi-precious stones fused together under tremendous pressure," she explains slowly, with her hands doing the mining and all the factory work.

"So what's a paperweight?" asks Rosie Giraffe.

"To weigh paper with, dumbbell," say Flyboy, the wise man from the East.

"Not exactly," say Miss Moore, which is what she say when you warm or way off too. "It's to weigh paper down so it won't scatter and make your desk untidy." So right away me and Sugar curtsy to each other and then to Mercedes who is more the tidy type.

"We don't keep paper on top of the desk in my class," say Junebug, figuring Miss Moore crazy or lyin one.

"At home, then," she say. "Don't you have a calendar and a pencil case and a blotter and a letter-opener on your desk at home where you do your homework?"

And she know damn well what our homes look like cause she nosys around in them every chance she gets.

"I don't even have a desk," say Junebug. "Do we?"

"No. And I don't get no homework neither," say Big Butt.

"And I don't even have a home," say Flyboy like he do at school to keep the white folks off his back and sorry for him. Send this poor kid to camp posters, is his specialty.

"I do," say Mercedes. "I have a box of stationery on my desk and a picture of my cat. My godmother bought the stationery and the desk. There's a big rose on each sheet and the envelopes smell like roses."

"Who wants to know about your smelly-ass stationery," say Rosie Giraffe fore I can get my two cents in.

"It's important to have a work area all your own so that . . ."

"Will you look at this sailboat, please," say Flyboy, cuttin her off and pointin to the thing like it was his. So once again we tumble all over each other to gaze at this magnificent thing in the toy store which is just big enough to maybe sail two kittens across the pond if you strap them to the posts tight. We all start reciting the price tag like we in assembly. "Handcrafted sailboat of fiberglass at one thousand one hundred ninety-five dollars."

"Unbelievable," I hear myself say and am really stunned. I read it again for myself just in case the group recitation put me in a trance. Same thing. For some reason this pisses me off. We look at Miss Moore and she lookin at us, waiting for I dunno what.

Who'd pay all that when you can buy a sailboat set for a quarter at Pop's, a tube of glue for a dime, and a ball of string for eight cents? "It must have a motor and a whole lot else besides," I say. "My sailboat cost me about fifty cents."

"But will it take water?" say Mercedes with her smart ass.

"Took mine to Alley Pond Park once," say Flyboy. "String broke. Lost it. Pity."

"Sailed mine in Central Park and it keeled over and sank. Had to ask my father for another dollar."

"And you got the strap," laugh Big Butt. "The jerk didn't even have a string on it. My old man wailed on his behind."

Little Q.T. was staring hard at the sailboat and you could see he wanted it bad. But he too little and somebody'd just take it from him. So what the hell. "This boat for kids, Miss Moore?"

"Parents silly to buy something like that just to get all broke up," say Rosie Giraffe.

"That much money it should last forever," I figure.

"My father'd buy it for me if I wanted it."

"Your father, my ass," say Rosie Giraffe getting a chance to finally push Mercedes.

"Must be rich people shop here," say Q.T.

"You are a very bright boy," say Flyboy. "What was your first clue?" And he rap him on the head with the back of his knuckles, since Q.T. the only one he could get away with. Though Q.T. liable to come up behind you years later and get his licks in when you half expect it.

"What I want to know is," I say to Miss Moore though I never talk to her, I wouldn't give the bitch that satisfaction, "is how much a real boat costs? I figure a thousand'd get you a yacht any day."

"Why don't you check that out," she say, "and report back to the group?" Which really pains my ass. If you gonna mess up a perfectly good swim day least you could do is have some answers. "Let's go in," she say like she got something up her sleeve. Only she don't lead the way. So me and Sugar turn the corner to where the entrance is, but when we get there I kinda hang back. Not that I'm scared, what's there to be afraid of, just a toy store. But I feel funny, shame. But what I got to be shamed about? Got as much right to go in as anybody. But somehow I can't seem to get hold of the door, so I step away for Sugar to lead. But she hangs back too. And I look at her and she looks at me and this is ridiculous. I mean, damn, I have never ever been shy about doing nothing or going nowhere. But then Mercedes steps up and then Rosie Giraffe and Big Butt crowd in behind and shove, and next thing we all stuffed into the doorway with only Mercedes squeezing past us, smoothing out her jumper and walking right down the aisle. Then the rest of us tumble in like a glued-together jigsaw done all wrong. And people lookin at us. And it's like the time me and Sugar crashed into the Catholic church on a dare. But once we got in there and everything so hushed and holy and the candles and the bowin and the handkerchiefs on all the drooping heads, I just couldn't go through with the plan. Which was for me to run up to the altar and do a tap dance while Sugar played the nose flute and messed around in the holy water. And Sugar kept givin me the elbow. Then later teased me so bad I tied her up in the shower and turned it on and locked her in. And she'd be there till this day if Aunt Gretchen hadn't finally figured I was lyin about the boarder takin a shower.

Same thing in the store. We all walkin on tiptoe and hardly touchin the games and puzzles and things. And I watched Miss Moore who is steady watchin us like she waitin for a sign. Like Mama Drewery watches the sky and sniffs the air and takes note of just how much slant is in the bird formation. Then me and Sugar bump smack into each other, so busy gazing at the toys, 'specially the sailboat. But we don't laugh and go into our fat-lady bump-stomach routine. We just stare at that price tag. Then Sugar run a finger over the whole boat. And I'm jealous and want to hit her. Maybe not her, but I sure want to punch somebody in the mouth.

"Watcha bring us here for, Miss Moore?"

"You sound angry, Sylvia. Are you mad about something?" Givin me one of them grins like she tellin a grown-up joke that never turns out to be funny. And she's lookin very closely at me like maybe she plannin to do my portrait from memory. I'm mad, but I won't give her that satisfaction. So I slouch around the store being very bored and say, "Let's go."

Me and Sugar at the back of the train watchin the tracks whizzin by large then small then gettin gobbled up in the dark. I'm thinkin about this tricky toy I saw in the store. A clown that somersaults on a bar then does chin-ups just cause you yank lightly at his leg. Cost $35. I could see me askin my mother for a $35 birthday clown. "You wanna who that costs what?" she'd say, cocking her head to the side to get a better view of the hole in my head. Thirty-five dollars could buy new bunk beds for Junior and Gretchen's boy. Thirty-five dollars and the whole

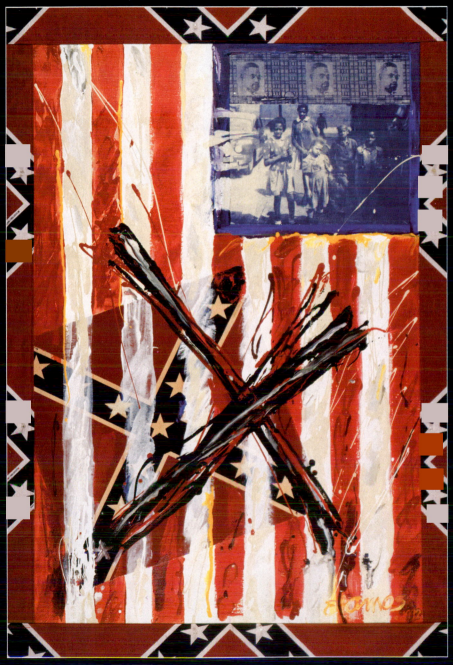

▲ "X Flag," Emma Amos, 1993, acrylic, photo transfer, Confederate Flag on linen, Confederate Flag borders and backed with African fabric, 58" x 40". Collection, Alice Zimmerman. Photograph by Becket Logan.

▲ *What You Lookn At*/Pat Ward Williams.

▲ *Christ the Teacher/*
Painted in the traditional
art form of the Byzantine
era of the Orthodox
Christian Church by
modern day iconographer
Rev. Mark C.E. Dukes,
AOC. The Greek inscrip-
tion *IC IX* is the abbrevi-
ation of "Jesus Christ."
W.O.N. is the abbrevia-
tion of the name of God,
presented to Moses on
Mt. Sinai, "I Am That I
Am." St. John's Cathedral
African Orthodox Church.

IC XC

I am That
Bread
of Life,
if any
Man eat

of This
Bread
he shall
Live
for ever!

▲ *Man and Child*/John Eddie Jones.

▲ *Woman in Crowd*/John Eddie Jones.

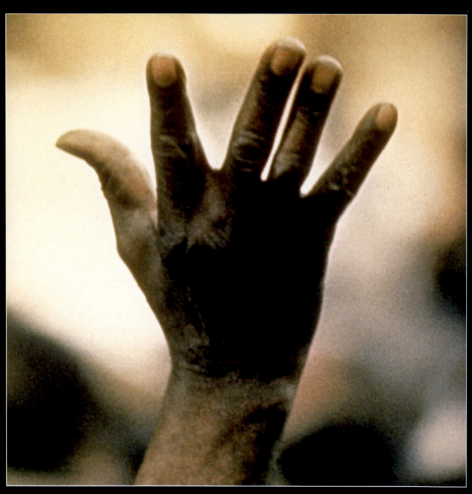

▲ *Hand, Black Militant Rally*, New York City (1963)/Gordon Parks Photography.

household could go visit Granddaddy Nelson in the country. Thirty-five dollars would pay for the rent and the piano bill too. Who are these people that spend that much for performing clowns and $1,000 for toy sailboats? What kinda work they do and how they live and how come we ain't in on it? Where we are is who we are, Miss Moore always pointin out. But it don't necessarily have to be that way, she always adds then waits for somebody to say that poor people have to wake up and demand their share of the pie and don't none of us know what kind of pie she talkin about in the first damn place. But she ain't so smart cause I still got her four dollars from the taxi and she sure ain't gettin it. Messin up my day with this shit. Sugar nudges me in my pocket and winks.

Miss Moore lines us up in front of the mailbox where we started from, seem like years ago, and I got a headache for thinkin so hard. And we lean all over each other so we can hold up under the draggy-ass lecture she always finishes us off with at the end before we thank her for borin us to tears. But she just looks at us like she readin tea leaves. Finally she say, "Well, what did you think of F.A.O. Schwarz?"

Rosie Giraffe mumbles, "White folks crazy."

"I'd like to go there again when I get my birthday money," says Mercedes, and we shove her out the pack so she has to lean on the mailbox by herself.

"I'd like a shower. Tiring day," said Flyboy.

Then Sugar surprises me by sayin, "You know, Miss Moore, I don't think all of us here put together eat in a year what that sailboat costs." And Miss Moore lights up like somebody goosed her. "And?" she say, urging Sugar on. Only I'm standin on her foot so she don't continue.

"Imagine for a minute what kind of society it is in which some people can spend on a toy what it would cost to feed a family of six or seven. What do you think?"

"I think," say Sugar pushing me off her feet like she never done before, cause I whip her ass in a minute, "that this is not much of a democracy if you ask me. Equal chance to pursue happiness means an equal crack at the dough, don't it?" Miss Moore is besides herself and I am disgusted with Sugar's treachery. So I stand on her foot one more time to see if she'll shove me. She shuts up, and Miss Moore looks at me, sorrowfully I'm thinkin. And somethin weird is goin on, I can feel it in my chest.

"Anybody else learn anything today?" lookin dead at me. I walk away and Sugar has to run to catch up and don't even seem to notice when I shrug her arm off my shoulder.

"Well, we got four dollars anyway," she said.

"Uh hunh."

"We could go to Hascombs and get half a chocolate layer and then go to the Sunset and still have plenty money for potato chips and ice-cream sodas."

"Uh hunh."

"Race you to Hascombs," she say.

We start down the block and she gets ahead which is O.K. by me cause I'm goin to the West End and then over to the Drive to think this day through. She can run if she want to and even run faster. But ain't nobody gonna beat me at nuthin.

🔶 CHARLES JOHNSON (b. 1948)

Charles Johnson, novelist, teacher, and editorial cartoonist, was born in Evanston, Illinois. He is a professor of English at the University of Washington in Seattle, where he eventually became director of the school's creative writing program. In 1990, he won the National Book Award for Middle Passage, *a novel that deals with incidents, such as a revolt, on an illegal American slave ship in 1830. His first and second novels,* Faith and the Good Thing *(1974) and* Oxherding Tale *(1982), received critical praise. In 1988, he published a collection of stories, including "Popper's Disease," which was honored with the Callaloo Creative Writing Award in 1983. He also wrote* Being and Race: Black Writing Since 1970 *(1988).*

From Middle Passage (1990)

Entry, the eighth

August 1, 1830

Visiting the village of the Allmuseri, the Spanish explorer Rafael García was driven mad. I now knew why. I glimpsed the creature, coal black and squatting on stubbly legs, as you might see objects through clouded glass. This blistering vision licked itself clean, as cats do, and had other beings, whole cultures of them, living parasitically on its body. Do I exaggerate? Not at all. It stood before me mute as a mountain, preferring not to speak, I suspected, because to say anything was to fall short of ever saying enough. (Within its contours my father's incarnation was trapped like a ship in a bottle, contained in a silence where all was possibility, perfection, pre-formed.) It was top-heavy. All head. Luscious hair fell past protruding eyes and a nose broad as a mallet, and framed a grin stretched in hysterical laughter, bunching skin on its cheeks into a hundred mirthful folds: a ceremonial mask from Gambia, I guessed, but it's safe to say I was hardly in my right mind. Nausea plummeted from my belly straight down to my balls, drawing tight the skin along my scrotum. I came within a hair's-breadth of collapsing, for this god, or devil, had dressed itself in the flesh of my father. That is what I mostly saw, and for the life of me I could no more separate the two, deserting father and divine monster, than I could sort wave from sea. Nor something more phantasmal that forever confused my lineage as a marginalized American colored man. To wit, his gradual unfoldment before me, a seriality of images I could not stare at straight on but only take in furtive glimpses, because the god, like a griot asked one item of tribal history, which he could only recite by reeling forth the entire story of his people, could not bring forth this one man's life without delivering as well the *complete* content of the antecedent universe to which my father, as a single thread, belonged.

All my life I'd hated him because he had cut and run like hundreds of field hands before him. He was a dark man and fiercely handsome, to hear Jackson tell it, and even when he was tired after a day's work he could whip a guitar like nobody's business and sing until it made grown women cry. They liked him, the womenfolks, but Da wasn't so popular with the men who sometimes found his old, wired shoes next to their pallets. A couple tried to kill him, said Jackson, and lost because Da was big through his chest and could lift a cow his damnself, then afterward he'd bring stump whiskey to whomever he'd whooped, saying he was sorry for all the bedswerving and scrapping and gambling he did—that he couldn't help it, and besides, it wasn't really *his* fault he acted thataway, was it? "Looka how we livin'," he'd say. "Looka what they done to us." You couldn't rightly blame a colored man for acting like a child, could you—stealing and sloughing off work when people like Peleg Chandler took the profits, and on top of that so much of their dignity he couldn't look his wife Ruby in the face when they made love without seeing how much she hated him for being powerless, even with their own children, who had no respect for a man they had seen whipped more than once by an overseer and knew in this world his word was no better than theirs. Each time Da talked like this, checking off cankers and cancer spots of slavery on his porch in the quarters, the other men listened, even those who hated him for pestering their wives, their eyes rage-kindled and drifting away to old angers of their own. "We was kings once," he would say, scrawling with one finger on the dusty porch a crude map of an African village he remembered vaguely (and neglecting to add that in his tribe his own family was not royalty but instead the equivalent of Russian serfs or Chinese coolies). "We lost a war—naw, a battle. So now we's prisoners. And the way I see it we supposed to keep on fightin'."

Most of the time Da did fight. Never Reverend Chandler, though. Rather, he fought his family and others in the fields, chafing under the constraints of bondage, and every other constraint as well: marriage and religion, as white men imposed these on Africans. Finally, in the light of my slush lamp, I beheld his benighted history and misspent manhood turn toward the night he plotted his escape to the Promised Land. It was New Year's Eve, *anno* 1811. For good luck he took with him a little of the fresh greens and peas Chandler's slaves cooked at year's end (greens for "greenbacks" and peas for "change"), then took himself to the stable, saddled one of the horses, and, since he had never ventured more than ten miles from home, wherefore lost his way, was quickly captured by padderolls and quietly put to death, the bullet entering through his left eye, exiting through his right ear, leaving him forever eight and twenty, an Eternal Object, pure essence rotting in a fetid stretch of Missouri swamp. But even in death he seemed to be *doing* something, or perhaps should I say he squeezed out one final cry wherethrough I heard a cross wind of sounds just below his breathing. A thousand soft undervoices that jumped my jangling senses from his last, weakly syllabled wind to a mosaic of voices within voices, each one immanent in the other, none his but all strangely his, the result being that as the loathsome creature, this deity from the dim beginnings of the black past, folded my father back into the broader, shifting field—as waves vanish into water—his breathing blurred in a dissolution of sounds and I could only feel that identity was imagined; I had to listen harder to isolate him from the We that swelled each particle and pore of him, as if the (black) self was the greatest of all fictions; and then I could not find him at all. He seemed everywhere, his presence, and that of countless others, in me as well as the chamber, which had subtly changed. Suddenly I knew the god's name: Rutherford. And the *feel* of the ship beneath the wafer-thin soles of my boots was different. Not like any physical surface I knew, but rather as if every molecule of matter in her vibrated gently, almost imperceptibly, and the effect of all this was that from bowsprit to stern she seemed to *sing* like the fabled *Argo*.

Then I fainted.

Or died.

Whatever.

A long, long interval passed in the most unimaginable quietude. Silence as deep, as pervading as the depths of the sea. There was stillness, the sweet smell of growing things, then their stench. I heard screaming, felt it barreling out of my bones. I was thrashing and two Josiah Squibbs were holding me down in the fo'c's'le—my sight was distorted, I saw everything in doubles—mopping my brow with his kerchief. Apparently he had been feeding me from a bucket by his left elbow. Feeding me the choicest cut of medium-raw *steak*, unless the meat on the fork in his right hand was a product of my prolonged fever. Once he saw me awake, Squibb set down his fork and began fooling with my arm.

"Lie back now, bucko. Yuh need to bleed," said he. "And pray."

Beside him were instruments of venesection that made me cringe: fleams, thumb lances, and a copper bleeding bowl. I was not, I should mention, an advocate of bleeding, cupping, or leeches, though these medical practices still lingered on ship when all other methods had failed. I wondered: Was this necessary? And, more to the point, was Squibb capable of carrying it off without killing me? Nay, I was not eager for this, but I knew the cook, so tired, was ready to try everything he'd seen to save us. Squibb's cold hands rubbed my right arm vigorously; he consulted astrological charts to confirm that the hour was right for an incision and tightened a rag just below my elbow to enlarge the vein.

"Josiah, half a moment—"

"Don't talk. Ain't nothin' to say." The cook's face was pale as a scrubbed hammock, his eyes as red as a pigeon's. He shoved a stick into my hand and demanded I squeeze it. "This'll balance the humors, though Gawd knows I don't know what happened to yuh. We pulled yuh hup from below. Yuh been out of yer head fer a long time. Christ, lad, yer hair's sugah white."

"How long?"

"Three days full. Ever since yuh went below. But lissen. We spotted a *ship* this mornin', boy!"

"Whereaway?"

"Two miles to leeward in the southeast corner."

"Her flag?"

"None. Leastways none I kin see, but I think she's American. She's been following us hank fer hank, tryin' to eat our wind. I think her skipper knows we're in trouble. If she's British, we're sunk. They'll search us and charge you 'n' me with murder!"

"Peter hailed her, then?"

Squibb stiffened, shipped a long face, then looked at the bucket from which he'd fed me. "Yuh had Mr. Cringle fer supper, m'boy. We all did. Now, lie back, dammit! This was what he wanted. I was sittin' with him toward the end, which he knew was comin'. Yuh know, when a body goes the bladder 'n' bowels fly open—I seen it happen a hundred times—and yer mates have to clean yuh hup and all. He wanted to spare us that, so he asked the blacks to he'p him to the head. After he was done, he had a few mates gather round him. By that time we was eatin' our shoes, barnacles, 'n' the buttons off our shirts. The women and children had chewed every shred of leather off the pumps. So Cringle says, in a voice as calm as a chaplain's, 'My friends, I have no inheritance to leave my family in America. They'll not miss me, I'm sure, but I wish to leave you something, for no man could ask for better shipmates than thee. You're brave lads. The lasses have given their full share as bluejackets too, and methinks 'tis scandalous how some writers such as Amasa Delano have slandered black rebels in their tales. Of course, I fear you'll get ptomaine if you put me into a pot, but I've nothing else to give. I hope this will help. Please, leave me a moment to pray. . . .'

"He took mebbe fifteen minutes. After that he called me in and give me his knife. Cringle closed me fingers round the handle. He instructed me that if I preferred not to kill him face to face, he'd turn his back to me. Don't you know he told me to cover his mouth, plunge the knife between his shoulder blades, then pull it free and cut his throat from behind. If that was too difficult for me, he said I should stab into the soft flesh behind his ear, pokin' straight through the brain. If not that method, then I was to grip the blade with both hands and strike just below his collarbone, workin' the knife back and forth so it wouldn't break when I withdrew it. He told me we was down to only four or five knives, so I couldn't afford to have this one snap off inside him when his body pitched forward.

"At first I couldn't do it, Illinois. I started to ask if it wouldn't be better fer us to die like men, but I checked meself before sayin' a thing so foolish, 'cause what could I mean? What was the limit of bein' human? How much could yuh take away and still *be* a man? In a kind of daze I done what he wanted, standin' back from meself, then unstringin' him, and it was in a daze that I lay back, short-winded and watchin' the Africans cut away Cringle's head, hands, feet, and bowels, and throw 'em overboard. Next, they quartered him. They skinned him and cut the meat into spareribs, fatback, bacon, and ham. It was then I reckon it hit me, that I'd killed a man." Squibb's eyes darted toward the cabin door, as if the mate's ghost might be standing there. "I can't sink no lower, laddie, and I 'spect Mr. Cringle's won his wings. After what he done, I don't plan to lose yuh. Yuh kin count on that. . . ."

Cringle's death silenced me. By any measure, he had been the best mate among us, the most magnanimous and gentle during our ordeal, the most generous in the face of hopelessness—in fact, a sailor who gave hope, steadied the ladder for others, and solved more problems than he created. I could not long straddle the thought that Providence had taken him so brutally. I wanted Squibb to deny it, but as I watched him work I saw, as he could not, how thoroughly his own life had been altered by our voyage. As our mates perished, Squibb was pressed into service not only as the ship's cook but also as our surgeon, and was often obliged to search his rum-pickled memory for nautical knowledge when a helmsman was needed. More than anyone, I think I knew how these demands and duties, all in the face of probable death, tested him. Now, what I am about to say must go no farther than the pages of this logbook. Five or maybe six days after the mutiny Cringle caught Josiah Squibb stealing rations reserved for the children. He was that hungry. That afraid. When the mate called him on the carpet he cried. His parrot too. It behooves me to explain how great a crime this, more than murder and man-eating, seemed to him. Until those days of sin, the darkest for him in the calendar of our cruise, he had believed the Almighty would safely deliver us to shore. But no longer. Distinctly, I remembered the Old Man saying, "A ship is a society, if you get my drift. A commonwealth, Mr. Calhoun," and Squibb, after snatching food from the mouths of infants, felt too ashamed to speak to me or anyone for a few days after Cringle caught him stealing. What was the use? Every day since leaving the fort we had lost something. Now there was nothing more to lose. Being that far down he was no longer afraid to fall. In this new condition, the concepts of good and evil, sinner and saved, even of life and death, falsified the only question of significance aboard ship, which was this: What must he do next? If asked to double-breech the lower decks or batten hatchways, he quietly did so, lifting himself above likes and dislikes, dwelling on the smallest details of his chores to deflect his mind from brooding—a Way, perhaps, to solder that deep schism Falcon believed bifurcated Mind. When someone had to fit a strap around the main topmasthead, it was Squibb who swung the block, a coil of halyards, and a marlinespike round his neck and, oblivious to the ship's swinging hard to starboard, to the fact that he had a bad foot and might fall from the crosstrees, climbed aloft and finished the job in Bristol fashion. Whatever was needful he did, including the learning of a little conversational Allmuseri when Diamelo demanded his former captors ease back from English. It would have been helpful to know if he still sought perfection in women who looked like his late wife. . . . Don't care about that? Okay, we shall push on. . . .

The result of Squibb's sea change was that his touch, as he worked the lancet, reminded me of Ngonyama's (or that of a thief), as if he could anticipate my pain before I felt it and therefore move the other way. His breathing even resembled that of the Allmuseri, the proportion of inhalation, retention, and exhalation being something like 1:4:2, like oil slowly flowing from one vessel to another. I felt perfectly balanced crosscurrents of culture in him, each a pool of possibilities from which he was unconsciously drawing, moment by moment, to solve whatever problem was at hand.

"Josiah, that ship . . ."

"Ah was the one signaled her. I cried, 'Ho there, the ship, ahoy,' then Diamelo stopped me with a cat. He's afraid she's a man-o'-war that'll put the blacks back in irons. Things are bad. I have to tell yuh that. Ngonyama can't help us now. He's pissin' blood, bleedin' inside, I figure, so I don't give him much time. I don't give *any* of us much time. We're comin' into dirty weather again. The ship won't wear. This boat's mebbe our only chance to get home. Diamelo wants to fire on her, then abandon this tub—and us—fer that one. Y'know, I'd say that boy's a li'l slack in the stays . . ."

"No question, but has he convinced the others to become corsairs too?"

The cook sighed. The lines of his face were all vertical, those on his forehead flat, like currents. "Can't say. It's all touch 'n' go from heah, Illinois."

"Josiah—"

Squibb shushed me. The telling of this left him looking squally and shivering so badly, like a man lost in snow, that he took himself duckfooting from the room, splashing through water, after removing the tourniquet from my arm, and I cannot say I heard him rightly through the natter and babble of voices in my head. More weakened than before from bleeding—he had drawn a pint of purplish blood—I could only rest quietly, thinking of the ship that might be our savior, my heart whamming away like a drum as our own boat convulsed.

I slept. Deeply at first, then in pools of my own milky perspiration. Slept through the passing of light and patches of darkness in the portal above my head, and came awake into a conscious nightmare. Never ill a day in my life, thanks to Master Chandler's Saturday morning doses of castor oil, I now found that my gums were bleeding. I could not stop the flow. Rags of bedclothing stained with blood began to pile up beneath the berth where I lay. Crisp pain coursed through all parts of my body—stomach, head—and I would have felt pain in my spleen and pancreas too, but I wasn't exactly sure where they were. There came a knock at my door. Twice, I think, but I was unable to answer. The catch was turned. The door eased open. Someone looked in, saying nothing, then passed on. In the cavity of my chest a fire burned like camphor. I lay sprawled in purging fever. A quivering mass of jelly. My eyes felt filmy, and so I tried to keep them closed, sleeping again and shivering violently, though, as I say, I felt that I was on fire.

When I opened my eyes again—I do not know the day—the cabin had a twisted feel, the surface of objects warped, the planes and lines of the room falling away to a point in the corner millions of leagues away. I closed my eyes, only to experience a vertigo like the vortices that suck ships to the bottom of the briny. Slowly I pulled myself to the floor, feeling nothing under my feet, though I knew well enough I must be standing, feeling, in fact, no physical tie to the other objects in the room at all. Then I gave at the knees and keeled over.

How long I lay at the foot of the berth I cannot say. Again, daylight burned from ruby to blue in the portal, then shaded down into night. I wobbled to the door, intending to call for help, sideswiped a table, which caused me astounding pain, and fumbled with friction matches to light the lantern, burning myself several times, I could see, but I felt nothing in my fingers. I stumbled into my trousers, then made my way outside onto the deck, a slight paralysis pinching my left side, so that I dragged that leg a little, then stumbled down to the orlop, its tainted air filled with buzzing insects like floating plankton, burning my lungs. As I squatted there, my head swung into this cesspool of swishing fecal matter, I brought up black clumps I can only liken to an afterbirth or a living thing aborted from the body—something foul and shaped like the African god, as if its homunculus had been growing inside me—and voiding this was so violent a thing I was too weakened to rise again, and lay jackknifed for a long time with my face flat against the splintery hollow rind of the hull, listening to the swash and purl of waters below me.

Then, as before, I desperately dreamed of home. I'm sure the Allmuseri did the same, but home was a clear, positive image to them as they worked on the ship. As *I* remembered home, it was a battlefield, a boiling cauldron. It created white rascals like Ebenezer Falcon, black ones like Zeringue, uppity Creoles, hundreds of slave lords, bondmen crippled and caricatured by the disfiguring hand of servitude. Nay, the States were hardly the sort of place a Negro would pine for, but pine for them I did. Even for *that* I was ready now after months at sea, for the strangeness and mystery of black life, even for the endless round of social obstacles and challenges and trials colored men faced every blessed day of their lives, for there were indeed triumphs, I remembered, that balanced the suffering on shore, small yet enduring things, very deep, that Isadora often pointed out to me during our evening walks. If this weird, upside-down caricature of a country called America, if this land of refugees and former indentured servants, religious heretics and half-breeds, whoresons and fugitives—this cauldron of mongrels from all points on the compass—was all I could rightly call *home*, then aye: I was of it. There, as I lay weakened from bleeding, was where I wanted to be. Do I sound like a patriot? Brother, I put it to you: What Negro, in his heart (if he's not a hypocrite), is not?

I was lying where I had fallen when Baleka came below, saw me, then rolled me upon my back like a beetle. She was speaking, I knew that much, but my ears were stopped completely. Her face seemed fathoms away, or perhaps it was that my own eyes had shrunk back into my head, receding inward to some smoking corner of the brain. Try as I might, I could not remember my full name. She and one other I did not know lifted me up the gangway to the deck, and dropped me back on the bed in the fo'c's'le. I tried to sit. The room spun. I fell back again, lying half off the bed, and wept at my helplessness. I had not known before that everything, within and without, could break down so thoroughly. For all I knew I had already lived through many afflictions and survived them, too busy at ship's business to know I was afflicted. And then they were gone. No, they did not walk out. One second they stood beside me, then they dematerialized like phantoms. All that day and night I lay in a dissolving, diseased world, unable to find a position comfortable enough to remain in. My bowels ran black. The pain was quick. Everywhere at once. Then, at some point in this river of sickness, I saw Ngonyama crack open the cabin door. He was alone, his eyes like sea mist, a breath of ice in his matted hair.

For a moment he stood above me, keeping his own counsel. He cupped my hands together in his to warm them. He was feverish too. A blue tinge stained his lips. And, more's the pity, he could not straighten out the fingers on his right hand or stop shivering, as if someone stood upon his grave. He was in pain, but tried not to show this, because he was disassociating himself from the misfortunes of his body, as he'd done when the Old Man put a brand to his backside, going out to meet his suffering, you might say, as a proud African king meets a king. With him sitting hard by, I could not help but remember the practice his people had of setting aside one day each month for giving up a deep-rooted, selfish desire; the Allmuseri made this day a celebration, a festive holiday so colorful, with dancing and music and clowning magicians everywhere, that even their children were eager for the Day of Renunciation, as they called it, to arrive. Would such a four-dimensional culture perish with him and the others? During all this time I tried to speak, but felt my throat to be phlegmed, my lips soldered together, a crusty material caking my mouth. Ngonyama put his hand on my chest, urging me to lie back, and I did, feeling another flicker of panic. Even though we had come through much together—mutiny, storms, meetings with gods—my friends could help me no more than a man who falls overboard during a gale, the sea taking him instantly. I gave myself up for lost. Even as he watched me, I sank farther away, his face dislimning, the room fading in a frightening way that made me realize how dependent its appearance was upon the workings of my own nervous system, how in this sickness my faculties that gave it shape were loosened, shut down, switched off, and for all purposes nothing in my sight could sustain itself without me, how *I* was responsible for *all* of it, the beauty and ugliness; and I thought of how the mate was righter than he knew, and of Blake, a poet Master Chandler had me read, his beguiling, Berkeleyesque words, "I see the windmill before me; I blink my eyes, it goes away," and so did the cabin, and so did the world. In the black space behind my eyelids I saw nothing, and knew I was dying, no doubt about that, and I did not care for myself anymore, only that my mates should survive.

At six bells Ngonyama left, and I lay, as in a chrysalis, until I could hear no longer, then fell again through leagues and leagues of darkness, the paralysis of my legs spreading upward toward my groin, deadening and numbing as it went. There came tremors, as if I were bursting or splitting apart. For a few seconds I was blind. Huge, frosty waves pitched the *Republic*, rolling her so prodigiously the floor shook and the cabin walls panted. Thrown open by deckwash blue as flood-water, the cabin door banged loudly against the wall. The storm outside, for certainly it was that, changed pressure inside the cabin and further troubled my breathing. I lay eager to question Ngonyama again, and lifted my head when I heard footsteps enter the room.

"Ngonyama," I said too quickly, for it was not him but Squibb, looming over me, knee-deep in water, his face pooled in wet hair.

"Kin yuh stand, Illinois?"

I pushed myself up. "Help me get dressed."

"No time fer modesty. We've got to use this storm as cover till we gets a boat over the side."

"How many are left?"

"Twelve, countin' us. I've already got the gel in one of the longboats. Smack it about now, 'less yuh plan to follow this bastard into the briny!"

Furniture was floating as high as Squibb's hams. He guided me through the door, but no sooner did we reach the deck than an explosion rocked the ship: I was stunned, thrown back against a bulkhead, Squibb falling beneath me. The ceiling caved in, raining planks and boards that buried us and broke the cook's left arm. Somehow, with a strength I cannot explain, he shoved them aside and, upon gaining the deck again, stepping over a body I recognized as Diamelo's, we found the foreyard broken in its slings, the larboard railings torn away, and the orlop deck fallen into the hold. From what I could tell, clinging to the remains of the masthead, Diamelo had gone the wrong side of the buoy by popping off one of the cannons, unattended for weeks, and with unstable powder. The ball ignited but failed to fire, and moments later when it eventually blew, spraying the deck with bricks and burning metal, not a man, African or American, in the line of fire was left standing. Smoke was burning my face, blinding me again, but I was able to make out Ngonyama at the wheel. There on the flaming bridge he seemed preposterously alone, black flesh and wood so blended—he had lashed himself to the wheel and now could not break free—it was impossible to tell where ship ended and sailor began or, for that matter, to clearly distinguish what was ship, what sailor, and what sea, for in this chaosmos of roily water and fire, formless mist and men flying everywhere, the sea and all within it seemed a churning field that threw out forms indistinctly. I tried to make my way to the helm and add my hands, weak as they were, but Squibb restrained me. The wind was high. I could not hear his voice, but knew he was saying the ship was hogged, falling to pieces around our heads. The mizzenmast had snapped. The ship began bilging at her center, a heart-stopping grind of timber as her waist broke in half, the decks opened, her beams gave way, her topsides broke from the floor heads, and heavy sea swamped all the forward compartments. With a knife Squibb cut off his boots, stripped away his stockings, shirt, trousers, and, naked as a fish, pushed me toward a jolly boat where he had earlier sent three of the children. Judging this to be their last hour on earth, the little ones wailed. Every new wave lifted the ship, which again dropped so low water combed forward, then aft, dragging yet another hand away. And it was as I fought to keep the children in the boat that I felt the deck slam upward suddenly, pitching all of us into the sky, then dashing us into a feather-white sea.

You cannot know the feeling, nor words deliver the fact, of how I felt once flung into the Cupboard. My eyes were logged, full of freezing water. Still, I was able to make out the ship rolling onto her beam ends. Her stern sank foremost. I slipped underwater, the sea filling my throat, ballooning my lungs—it was a feeling of inversion, as if I'd mistakenly touched a harmless-looking wall, thinking it solid, then tripped, falling through into a shadowy realm of mist and specters on the netherside. Drowning, I saw my past spool by me, a most unsettling experience, there being in my case precious little of value to review. My lungs were bursting. I found myself following the broken ship; she was clearly before me, only ten cables below, her carcass suspended like an antique bark hung from a museum's ceiling, as were my shipmates, their lips bubbling ribbons of air. I batted my hands frantically to get back, my fingers scratching at the bottomside of the Atlantic and, surfacing, shaking water from my eyes, I saw chests, water casks, and debris crowded with quaking bilge rats floating near me and threw myself upon a hammock lashed in the orthodox way, with seven hitches. Likewise, some of the Allmuseri were gripping loose deckboards, furniture, and shrouds awaft round the hulk of the *Republic*. But not for long. The speed of the ship's descent quick dragged them down at the rate of knots. Husbands, fighting to keep afloat, called their wives, but in the black bowl of sky, and blacker sea, no one could identify another, and soon their chins flipped up and disappeared in a sparge of foam.

In principle, the hammock should have kept me floating for a full day. It did not. During the night, the shipwrecked went under, one by one. Who lived, I could not say, for the hammock beneath me grew heavy and at last, filling with salt water, surrendered its weight and mine into the Atlantic's dancing, lemon-colored lights.

GLORIA NAYLOR (b. 1950)

Gloria Naylor was born in New York City. She writes extensively about African American female experiences. In 1983, she won the American Book Award for her well-known novel The Women of Brewster Place *(1982), which was made into a television movie in 1989. In the novel, Naylor writes about bonding between women and about the obstacles that they face because of gender, race, or sexual orientation.* Linden Hills *(1985) is also a novel about black women's issues. The focus on experiences unique to African American women, such as the search for identity, is also embodied in* Mama Day *(1988) and* Bailey's Café *(1992). With her novels, Naylor has made an important contribution to African American women's literature.*

From Linden Hills (1985)

There had been a dispute for years over the exact location of Linden Hills. Everyone associated with Wayne County had taken part in it: the U.S. Post Office, census takers, city surveyors, real estate brokers, and the menagerie of blacks and whites who had lived along its fringes for a hundred and sixty years. The original 1820 surveys that Luther Nedeed kept locked in his safe-deposit box stated that it was a V-shaped section of land with the boundaries running south for one and a half miles from the stream that bordered Putney Wayne's high grazing fields down a steep, rocky incline of brier bush and linden trees before curving through the town's burial ground and ending in a sharp point at the road in front of Patterson's apple orchard. It wasn't a set of hills, or even a whole hill— just the worthless northern face of a rich plateau. But it patiently bore the designation of Linden Hills as its boundaries contracted and expanded over the years to include no one, and then practically everyone in Wayne County.

The fact never disputed by anyone was that the Nedeeds have always lived there. Luther's double great-grandfather bought the entire northern face of the plateau, descending from what is now First Crescent Drive to Tupelo Drive— which is really the last three of a series of eight curved roads that ring themselves around the hill. But Luther's double great-grandfather, coming from Tupelo, Mississippi, where it was rumored that he'd actually sold his octoroon wife and six children for the money that he used to come North and obtain the hilly land, named that section Tupelo Drive. And at the time none of the white farmers gave a flying squat what he called it, 'cause if some crazy nigger wanted to lay out solid gold eagles for hard sod only good enough to support linden trees that barely got you ten cents on the dollar for a cord of oak or birch—let him. And the entire bottom of the land is hemmed in by the town cemetery. Had to be half-witted— who'd want to own land near a graveyard, especially a darky who is known to be scared pantless of haints and such? They pocketed Nedeed's money and had a good laugh: first full moon on All Hallows would send them spirits walking and him running to beg them to buy the property back. That is, if he didn't starve to death first. Couldn't eat linden trees, and Lord knows he wasn't gonna raise spit on that land. Would raise a lot of sand, though. Knees were slapped and throats choked on tobacco juice. Yup, he'd raise plenty of sand while trying to get a team and wagon down through that bush to fetch supplies.

But Nedeed didn't try to farm Linden Hills. He built a two-room cabin at the bottom of the slope—dead center—with its door and windows facing the steep incline. After the cabin was finished, they could see him sitting in front of it for an hour at dawn, high noon, and dusk—his dark, immobile face rotating slowly amid the lime tombstones, the tangled brier, and the high stretch of murky forest. He sat there every day for exactly seven days—his thick, puffed lids raising, lowering, and narrowing over eyes that seemed to be measuring precisely the depth and length of light that the sun allowed his wedge of their world.

"Guess he's trying to *think* a living out of that land." But their victory had been replaced by a question as they watched Nedeed watching the path of the sun. No one admitted that they lacked the courage just to walk over and demand to know what he was doing. There was something in Luther Nedeed's short, squat body that stopped those men from treating him like a nigger—and something in his eyes that soon stopped them from even thinking the word. It was said that his protruding eyes could change color at will, and over the course of his life, they would be assigned every color except red. They were actually dark brown—a flat brown—but since no man ever had the moral stamina to do more than glance at his face, because those huge, bottomless globes could spell out a starer's midnight thoughts, black men looked at his feet or hands and white men looked over his shoulder at the horizon.

As the sun disappeared on the seventh day of his vigil, Luther Nedeed closed his eyes slowly and smiled. Patterson said he was hauling his apples away from the field and the sight of Nedeed sitting there grinning like one of them heathen E-jip mummies scared him out of a year's growth, and when he got home, all the bushels facing Nedeed's side of the road had fruit worms in them. He claimed that as the justification for the eight-foot fence he erected on the northern border of his orchard. It might have been closer to the truth to admit that he just couldn't stomach the sight of Nedeed dragging all those dead bodies into his yard. Because the day after Patterson's alleged plague of worms, Nedeed went and bought a team of horses, a box-shaped wagon, and began an undertaker's business in the back room of his cabin. His proximity to the town cemetery put little strain on the horses and funeral hearse, and Nedeed knew that, unlike the South, the North didn't care if blacks and whites were buried together so long as they didn't live together. Appalled by the reports of the evils that lay below the Mason-Dixon and the cry that "the only good nigger is a dead nigger," Wayne County let it be known that any of their sable brothers who were good and dead were welcome to a Christian burial right next to a white person—Tuesdays, Thursdays, and Saturdays, the days assigned for colored funerals.

Nedeed then built wooden shacks up on the hill, from what is now First Crescent Drive down to Fifth Crescent Drive, and rented them out to local blacks who were too poor to farm and earned their living from the sawmills or tar pit. He also wanted to rent out shacks along Tupelo Drive, but no one wanted any part of the cemetery land. It was bad enough they were down on their luck and had to resort to living in the hills, but they didn't have to live near that strange Nedeed by a graveyard. News that someone had moved into the hills was always rebuffed: They lived *up* from Linden Hills; only Nedeed lived down on Linden Hills. And the white farmer who owned the grazing land over the stream at the crest of the hill would fight over being told that he had land in Linden Hills: That was coon town and he didn't have a blade of grass there; he was *across* from Linden Hills.

The fact that no one wanted to be associated with his land didn't bother Luther Nedeed. The nature of things being what they are, his business thrived. And over the years he was able to build a large, white clapboard house with a full veranda and a concrete morgue in the basement. He went away for a while in the spring of 1837 and brought back an octoroon wife. Rumor had it that he had returned to Mississippi and bought back the wife he had sold to a Cajun saloonkeeper. But the girl who set up housekeeping in the undertaker's home couldn't have been more than twenty years old, and Nedeed had owned Linden Hills for almost seventeen years by then. She gave him a son the following winter—short, squat, dark, and with an immobile face, even from birth. He grew up to carry his father's first name, broad chest, and bowlegs. Big frog and little frog, the town whispered behind their backs.

Luther left his land and business to this only son, who everyone was betting would sell it before the old man was cold, since little Luther had been sent to one of them fancy boarding schools and surely had more sense than old crazy Luther to hold on to worthless hill land. But the son came back to the land and the undertaking business and carried the butt of the jokes about his father's property on his quiet back. It seemed that when old Luther died in 1879, he hadn't died at all, especially when they spoke to his son and especially when they glanced at those puffed eyelids and around those bottomless eyes. He, too, brought an octoroon woman into his home who gave him only one son—another Luther Nedeed.

Nothing was changing in the white clapboard house at the bottom of Linden Hills. There was another generation of big frog and little frog going through the hills together every first of the month to collect rent. What was changing slowly—very slowly—was the face of Wayne County. Farms were dwindling and small townships were growing in the place of cornfields and fruit groves. Putney Wayne's son had sold a quarter of his pasture to a shoe factory and the smoky cinders blew over the entire field, settling in the sheep's wool and turning the grass an ashy blue. This caused Wayne's grandson to think that the price a Welsh developer offered him for the land was a miracle, and he grabbed the money and headed for New York City at the miraculous speed of thirty-five mph on the new railroad lines and never came back. The second wealthiest man in Wayne County bought a curved-dash Oldsmobile, proudly announcing that he now had the power of three horses that he could feed for a tenth the cost of grain.

But the wealthiest man in Wayne County sat at the bottom of Linden Hills and still carried wooden coffins to the cemetery with a horse and wagon. Old Luther's son had sent away to England for the circulars from a new locomotive company called Rolls-Royce that was willing to custom design and ship him a funeral hearse with a mahogany dashboard and pure silver handles. He locked the circulars up in his desk, went to the second wealthiest man, and bought his team of

Cleveland Bays at an incredibly low price. Nedeed knew he would have to wait until almost the poorest white family in Wayne County owned an automobile before even dead blacks rode in mahogany and silver.

Old Luther's son was finally able to rent shacks along Tupelo Drive. These tenants didn't seem to mind that they were surrounded by a cemetery. Talk had it that they had been murderers, root doctors, carpetbaggers, and bootleg preachers who were thrown out of the South and needed the short memory of the dead and the long shadows of the lindens for their left-of-center carryings-on. Nedeed didn't care how they were able to pay their rent so long as they did it promptly on the first of the month. When the area within five acres of his funeral home became populated, he constructed an artificial lake (really a moat), a full twenty yards across, totally around his house and grounds. He filled it with marsh weeds, catfish, and ducks. Now the only entrance to his veranda was at the back, through a wood-and-brick drawbridge that he always kept down, but his neighbors saw the pulleys on the bridge and took immediate offense. Seemed as if he wanted to make out he was better than other folks—yeah, separate himself from the scum. Well, everybody knew that he'd been able to make them fancy changes on his house—building extra rooms and a *third* level—'cause years ago he'd financed gunrunners to the Confederacy. A rebel-loving nigger and now he was putting on airs with his blood money. They secretly nicknamed the lake Wart's Pond—a fitting place for him and his frog-eyed son to squat on.

But they kept paying him rent and letting him bury their dead. And as the faces on the hill changed and the old town became a young city as the last farmlands gave way to housing developments, Nedeed sat on his porch swing and watched the sun move as it always had over his world. He remembered his father and was thankful that he had lived long enough to watch his words engraved in the scarred landscape of the county: Let 'em think as they want; let 'em say as they want—black or white. Just sit right here and they'll make you a rich man through the two things they'll all *have* to do: live and die. Nedeed watched the sun, the twentieth century, and the value of his hard, sod hill creep upward as slowly and concretely as the last laugh from a dead man's grave.

The young municipal government soon took an interest in Linden Hills and tried to buy it from old Luther's son, who was now very old himself. His refusal to sell provided months of employment for title searchers, city surveyors, and public works assessors. The location of Linden Hills made confiscation for the purpose of a bridge, tunnel, or some other "public good" ludicrous. Nedeed told the assessors that if they could come up with a blueprint for any type of municipal project, he'd *give* them the land—root to leaf. But set one brick on his property for some high-blown private development and—he pointed a gnarled finger at the squat carbon copy beside him—he would personally drag Wayne County all the way to the Supreme Court. The title searchers and surveyors were then sent to unearth crumbling state statutes and fading deeds, looking for some clause that either invalidated or whittled down Nedeed's claim to the hill. Finally, an ambitious young lawyer found a seventeenth-century mandate forbidding Negroes to own, lease, or transfer property in Wayne County—regrettably, the same law that prohibited Hebrews, Catholics, and Devil worshipers from holding public office. Mayor Kilpatrick called an emergency meeting of the city council and they voted six to nothing to revoke the mandate. The mayor thanked them for convening on such short notice; then, after strongly advising the young lawyer to seek employment outside of Wayne County, he decided to let the matter of Linden Hills rest.

Nedeed, seeing that the government and real estate developers wanted his land so badly, decided to insure that they'd never be able to get their hands on it. So he went throughout the hill with his son beside him and, starting with First Crescent Drive all the way down through Fifth Crescent Drive, sold the land practically for air to the blacks who were shacking there. He gave them a thousand-year-and-a-day lease—provided only that they passed their property on to their children. And if they wanted to sell it, they had to sell it to another black family or the rights would revert back to the Nedeeds. And it seemed as if there were always going to be Nedeeds, because his son's pale-skinned bride was bloated with child. It surprised no one when the baby was male and had the father's complexion, protruding eyes, and first name—by now it had come to be expected.

Nedeed gave the same thousand-year-and-a-day option to the tenants who rented along Tupelo Drive, but he didn't have to worry about them. They couldn't move because only he would tolerate them on his land. Linden Hills was puzzled over Nedeed's behavior. Why was he up and being so nice to colored folks when his daddy had been a slave dealer and he himself had sold guns to the Confederacy? Probably trying to make good with his kind before the Lord called him home. "God bless you," an old woman breathed over her parchment of paper. Let him bless *you*—you'll need it, Nedeed thought as he stonily turned his back.

Like his father, he saw where the future of Wayne County—the future of America—was heading. It was going to be white: white money backing wars for white power because the very earth was white—look at it—white gold, white silver, white coal running white railroads and steamships, white oil fueling white automotives. Under the earth—across the earth—and one day, *over* the earth. Yes, the very sky would be white. He didn't know exactly how, but it was the only place left to go. And when they got there, they weren't taking anyone black with them—and why should they? These people, his people, were always out of step, a step behind or a step ahead, still griping and crying about slavery, hanging up portraits of Abraham Lincoln in those lousy shacks. They couldn't do nothing because they *were* slaves or because they *will be* in heaven. Praying and singing about what lay beyond the sky—"God bless you"—open your damned Bible, woman, and you'll see that even the pictures of your god are white. Well, keep trying to make your peace with that white god, keep moaning and giving the Nedeeds over half a year's wages to send a hunk of rotting flesh off to heaven in style instead of putting that money into bonds or land or even the bank at one-and-a-half-percent interest. Yes, make your peace with that white god who lived beyond the sky—he was going to deal with the white god who would one day *own* that sky. And you and yours would help him.

Sure, they thought him a fool—look at the fools that he had to claim as his own. When they laughed at them, they laughed at him. Well, he would show them. This wedge of earth was his—he couldn't rule but he sure as hell could ruin.

He could be a fly in that ointment, a spot on that bleached sheet, and Linden Hills would prove it. He had given his people some of the most expensive property in the county. They had the land for a millennium. Now just let them sit on it and do what they do best: digging another man's coal, cleaning another man's home, rocking another man's baby. And let them learn to count enough to keep paying monthly insurance, because they could read enough to believe that heaven was still waiting while they wrote just enough to sign those insurance premiums over to him. Nedeed's last vision when he closed his puffy eyelids, with his image bending over him, was of Wayne County forced to drive past Linden Hills and being waved at by the maids, mammies, and mules who were bringing the price of that sweat back to his land and his hands. A wad of spit—a beautiful, black wad of spit right in the white eye of America.

But Nedeed hadn't foreseen the Great Depression that his grandson was to live through. Those years brought another pale-skinned bride to the clapboard house, the construction of a separate mortuary and chapel, a triple garage, and the first set of automated hearses. They also brought a wave of rumors that Nedeed managed to come through so well because he'd sold all his stocks and bonds just a day before Black Friday and kept his money in a coffin, where it grew like a dead man's toenails because he sprinkled it with the dust he gathered from the graves of babies.

Luther Nedeed didn't care where Linden Hills thought he had gotten his money, but he spent several years deciding where it should go. Watching America's nervous breakdown during the thirties, he realized that nothing was closer to the spleen and guts of the country than success. The Sunday papers now told him what the sun had told his dead fathers about the cycles of men: Life is in the material—anything high, wide, deep. Success is being able to stick an "er" on it. And death is watching someone else have it. His grandfather's dream was still possible—the fact that they had this land was a blister to the community, but to make that sore fester and pus over, Linden Hills had to be a showcase. He had to turn it into a jewel—an ebony jewel that reflected the soul of Wayne County but reflected it black. Let them see the marble and brick, the fast and sleek, yes, and all those crumbs of power they uniformed their sons to die for, magnified tenfold and shining bright—so bright that it would spawn dreams of dark kings with dark counselors leading dark armies against the white god and toward a retribution all feared would not be just, but long overdue. Yes, a brilliance that would force a waking nightmare of what the Nedeeds were capable. And the fools would never realize—he looked down at his son playing with a toy dragon—that it was nothing but light from a hill of carbon paper dolls.

There would be no problem in financing his vision. It took exactly three phone calls and one letter to acquire the state charter the new Tupelo Realty Corporation needed to finance, construct, and sell private developments. Nedeed never doubted that he'd be able to build the houses; the real problem was deciding who in Linden Hills should own them. This was something that he couldn't leave to his lawyers, so with his son beside him Luther Nedeed visited every shack on the hill and talked to his tenants. He walked through Linden Hills as it would be—along smooth curved roads, up long sloping lawns and manicured meridians.

He stood under the door fronts of imitation Swiss chalets, British Tudors, and Georgian town houses flanked by arbors choked with morning glories, wisteria, and honeysuckle. Driveways were lined with mimosas, and gazebos sat in the shadow of elms and tulip oaks while lavender and marigolds outlined the bases of marble fountains and aviaries. He trod quietly amid his vision, knowing that he must take extreme care to weed out anyone who threatened to produce seeds that would block the light from his community. And empty goblets let through the most light, Nedeed thought as he began knocking on doors down along Tupelo Drive.

He started with the ones who would be the most eager to work with him on the future of Linden Hills. The children of the parasites and outcasts from the South, who could find a welcome only from the dead that bordered their homes, wanted nothing better than a way to forget and make the world forget their past. Many had already taken the ample income from their families and built frame houses on their land, with wire fences surrounding the neat front yards and back-yard gardens. Beyond the money they had received from their parents, they had no use for the clouded inheritance of incense, blood, and distilled alcohol that had built the walls which they were constantly painting and whitewashing as if to remove a stench. Yes, they would gladly match dollar for dollar the investment from the Tupelo Realty Corporation to build up a community for their children to be proud of. So when their grandchildren thought back, it would be to Linden Hills. When they needed to journey back, it would be to the brick and marble they would erect with this man's help. Strong, solid walls and heavy, marble steps—the finest in the new community—strong enough, solid enough to bury permanently any outside reflections about other beginnings. The Tupelo Realty Corporation offered them all this, and a memory was a small price to pay.

Nedeed's work was done quickly in Tupelo Drive, but now he had to tread more carefully as he made his way up the rest of the slope. Most of these people were proud of the lousy quarters and dimes, damp with their parents' sweat, that had been invested in their thousand-year-and-a-day leases. The painted walls, additional bedrooms, and raked dirt yards were the labor of people who had hopes of building on, not over, their past. These were the fools who could do the most damage if he let them stay. There were some up there who had rooted themselves in the beliefs that Africa could be more than a word; slavery hadn't run its course; there was salvation in Jesus and salve in the blues. Sure, Nedeed could tell them that you spelled real progress in white capital letters, but their parents hadn't been able to read and here they sat as living proof that you could survive anyway. No, people like that looked back a millennium, and if they could sit on Linden Hills for a millennium they'd produce children who would dream of a true black power that spread beyond the Nedeeds; children who would take this wedge of earth and try to turn it into a real weapon against the white god. He'd cultivate no madmen like Nat Turner or Marcus Garvey in Linden Hills—that would only get them all crushed back into the dust.

He knew how to stop that before it began. Even a goblet filled with the darkest liquid will let through light—if it's diluted enough, Nedeed thought as he carefully dressed himself and his son before they visited the rest of Linden Hills.

As he placed his polished wing-tip shoes on their sagging front porches, he watched them watching the crisp lines in his linen suit, counting the links in his gold watch chain, and measuring the grade of his son's gabardine knickers. He made a note of the eyes that returned to his dark face carrying respect and not suspicion, and silently chose the ones who then found some pretense to make their playing children come up from the road or out of the house to stand quietly and listen while he talked about everything from the weather to the price of soap. He could now safely tell these about the Tupelo Realty Corporation with its low-interest mortgage and scholarship funds to Fisk and Howard, because he knew they were calling their children to watch a wizard: Come, look, listen and perhaps you will learn how to turn the memory of our iron chains into gold chains. The cotton fields that broke your grandparents' backs can cover yours in gabardine. See, the road to salvation can be walked in leather shoes and sung about in linen choir robes. Nedeed almost smiled at their simplicity. Yes, they would invest their past and apprentice their children to the future of Linden Hills, forgetting that a magician's supreme art is not in transformation but in making things disappear.

Nedeed got rid of the unwanted tenants by either buying or tricking them out of their leases. He finally managed to clear out most of the upper slope, but when he reached First Crescent Drive, he ran into a problem with Grandma Tilson.

"I used to fish with your daddy down in that there pond, Luther, and he gave me this land and I ain't giving it up. So take your frog-eyed self and your frog-eyed son out of here. And I know your evil ways—all of you. So if you plan to try something like burning my house down while I just happen to be in it, I got this here deed *and* my will registered at the courthouse. Your daddy weren't no fool and he didn't fish with fools either."

Mamie Tilson's grown children hadn't made her a grandmother yet, but she had carried that nickname from a young girl because she was born with an old face, the color of oiled cheesecloth. Her clear skin allowed people to see the firmness of character that it covered. She had never minded staring down a Nedeed, because she liked what she read about herself in their bottomless eyes. So when Nedeed put his foot up on the top step of her porch and in a slow whisper asked if she wanted to think her position over, she paused for a moment and then sent a wad of tobacco spit near his wing-tips. That said she had thought it over and hoped he finally understood her answer.

Nedeed took his son's hand and left her yard. Let the hateful old hag just sit up there and rot. She'd die one day and then his son would deal with her children. The Tupelo Realty Corporation would build around her, and even over her if need be. He'd bury that one flaw deep in the middle of his jewel and no one would know the difference.

Nedeed didn't live long enough to have the pleasure of actually burying Grandma Tilson, who shuffled past his grave for ten winters. But he did see the outlines of his dream crystallize into a zoned district of eight circular drives that held some of the finest homes—and eventually the wealthiest black families—in the county. When the city first zoned its districts, the grazing land that once belonged to the sheep farmer, Putney Wayne, became Wayne Avenue. And after two white children drowned in the stream that separated Linden Hills from the avenue, a marble banister was erected along both its sides. The eight circular roads that curved around the three faces of the plateau were designated as First Crescent Drive, Second Crescent Drive, Third Crescent Drive, and the city commissioner wanted to continue it all the way down to Eighth Crescent Drive. But the families in the newly slated Sixth, Seventh, and Eighth Crescent drives of the Linden Hills section went to the commissioner and protested. Their area had always been known as Tupelo Drive and should stay that way, and besides, the old town cemetery cut them off from the other side of the plateau, so he didn't have eight whole crescents anyway. The city commissioner reared back in his tweed swivel chair and told them in so many words that he was keeping it just like it was and if they didn't like it, they could go to hell. They went to Nedeed, instead, who went to Washington, D.C., and had the town cemetery and Tupelo Drive designated as a historical landmark.

News of this sent the Wayne County Citizens Alliance, headed by Patterson's great-granddaughter, to the commissioner's office, to question why their side of the plateau wasn't a historical landmark as well. Their families had owned land there long before the Nedeeds. Patterson even dragged in her family Bible with dates and names that went back to the Revolutionary War. The disgruntled commissioner told them that there was nothing he could do. It seemed that Washington thought the site where some ex-slave's cabin had been more American than the sheep dung that had sat on her parents' land. And as long as that socialist with his nigger-loving wife was in office, that was the way it had to be. And no, they could *not* start calling their foot of the plateau Tupelo Drive. Weren't his street plans messed up enough already?

That didn't stop the white families on the other side of the plateau from telling stray tourists that, of course, they lived in Linden Hills—the *real* Linden Hills. And even after both Nedeed and Grandma Tilson had died, some of them were still putting LINDEN HILLS on their mail. This only added to the confusion of the post office that had to deal with the poor black families across Wayne Avenue in the Putney Wayne section who were also addressing their mail LNDEN HILLS. The Putney Wayne residents were telling census takers, school superintendents, and anyone else who cared to listen, that since Linden Road ran up the side of Linden Hills, crossed Wayne Avenue, and continued northward for three miles through *their* neighborhood, they lived in Linden Hills too. Weren't both areas full of nothing but black folks? And trying to call their section Putney Wayne was just another example of the way all those lousy racists in Wayne County tried to keep black people down.

Because the cemetery stopped Linden Road at Fifth Crescent Drive, Tupelo Drive could only be entered through the center of Fifth Crescent, and the Tupelo residents built a private road with a flower-trimmed meridian headed by two twelve-foot brick pillars. They then put up a bronze plaque on the pillars and had the words LINDEN HILLS engraved in deep Roman type. This caused the residents on First through Fifth Crescent drives immediately to erect a wooden sign—WELCOME TO LINDEN HILLS—behind the marble banister and the stream, separating them from the avenue. They didn't know what those people down in

Tupelo Drive were trying to pull; maybe their homes weren't as large and fancy as those down there, but they definitely knew that they also lived in Linden Hills. They had the papers—actual deeds—that said this land was theirs as long as they sat on it, and sit they would.

So now practically every black in Wayne County wanted to be a part of Linden Hills. While it did have homes that had brought a photographer out from *Life* magazine for pictures of the Japanese gardens and marble swimming pools on Tupelo Drive, that wasn't the only reason they wanted to live there. There were other black communities with showcase homes, but somehow making it into Linden Hills meant "making it." The Tupelo Realty Corporation was terribly selective about the types of families who received its mortgages. Entrance obviously didn't depend upon your profession, because there was a high school janitor living right next to a municipal judge on Third Crescent Drive. And even your income wasn't a problem, because didn't the realty corporation subsidize that family of Jamaicans on Tupelo Drive who were practically starving to put two of their kids through Harvard? No, only "certain" people got to live in Linden Hills, and the blacks in Wayne County didn't know what that certain something was that qualified them, but they kept sending in applications to the Tupelo Realty Corporation—and hoping. Hoping for the moment they could move in, because then it was possible to move down toward Tupelo Drive and Luther Nedeed.

Yes, Linden Hills. The name had spread beyond Wayne County, and applicants were coming from all over the country and even the Caribbean. Linden Hills—a place where people had worked hard, fought hard, and saved hard for the privilege to rest in the soft shadows of those heart-shaped trees. In Linden Hills they could forget that the world said you spelled black with a capital nothing. Well, they were something and there was everything around them to show it. The world hadn't given them anything but the chance to fail—and they hadn't failed, because they were in Linden Hills. They had a thousand years and a day to sit right there and forget what it meant to be black, because it meant working yourself to death just to stand still. Well, they had the chance to move down in Linden Hills—as far as Luther Nedeed, sitting at the foot of the hill behind a lake and a whole line of men who had shown Wayne County what it was possible to do with a little patience and a lot of work. They wanted what Luther Nedeed had, and he had shown them how to get it: Just stay right here; you step outside Linden Hills and you've stepped into history—someone else's history about what you couldn't ever do. The Nedeeds had made a history there and it spoke loudly of what blacks could do. They were never leaving Linden Hills. There was so much to be gotten. Surely, in a millennium their children could move down or even marry down the hill toward Tupelo Drive and Luther Nedeed.

Tupelo Drive and Luther Nedeed: it became one cry of dark victory for blacks outside or inside Linden Hills. And the ultimate dark victor sat in front of his home and behind his lake and looked up at the Nedeed dream. It had finally crystallized into that jewel, but he wore it like a weighted stone around his neck. Something had gone terribly wrong with Linden Hills. He knew what his dead fathers had wanted to do with this land and the people who lived on it. These people were to reflect the Nedeeds in a hundred facets and then the Nedeeds could take those splintered mirrors and form a mirage of power to torment a world that dared think them stupid—or worse, totally impotent. But there was no torment in Linden Hills for the white god his fathers had shaken their fists at, because there was no white god, and there never had been.

They looked at the earth, the sea, and the sky, Luther thought sadly, and mistook those who were owned by it as the owners. They looked only at the products and thought they saw God—they should have looked at the process. If they could have sat with him in front of a television that now spanned their tiny planet and universe to universes beyond the sun and moments that had guided their hand, they would have known the futility of their vengeance. Because when men begin to claw men for the rights to a vacuum that stretches into eternity, then it becomes so painfully clear that the omnipresent, omnipotent, Almighty Divine is simply the *will* to possess. It had chained the earth to the names of a few and it would chain the cosmos as well.

A white god? Luther shook his head. How could it be any color when it stripped the skin, sex, and soul of any who offered themselves at its altar before it decided to bless? His fathers had made a fatal mistake: they had given Linden Hills the will to possess and so had lost it to the very god they sought to defy. How could these people ever reflect the Nedeeds? Linden Hills wasn't black; it was successful. The shining surface of their careers, brass railings, and cars hurt his eyes because it only reflected the bright nothing that was inside of them. Of course Wayne County had lived in peace with Linden Hills for the last two decades, since it now understood that they were both serving the same god. Wayne County had watched his wedge of earth become practically invisible—indistinguishable from their own pathetic souls.

The only ones who didn't seem to know what was happening in Linden Hills were the thousands of blacks who sent him applications every year. And since there was nowhere left to go with his land and nothing left to build, he would just let the fools keep coming. Let them think that he held some ultimate prize down there. Let them think that they were proving something to the world, to themselves, or to him about their worth. Unlike his fathers, he welcomed those who thought they had personal convictions and deep ties to their past, because then he had the pleasure of watching their bewilderment as it all melted away the farther they came down. Applications from any future Baptist ministers, political activists, and Ivy League graduates were now given first priority, since their kind seemed to reach the bottom faster than the others, leaving more room at the top, And whenever anyone reached the Tupelo area, they eventually disappeared. Finally, devoured by their own drives, there just wasn't enough humanity left to fill the rooms of a real home, and the property went up for sale. Luther often wondered why none of the applicants ever questioned the fact that there was always space in Linden Hills.

But they were too busy to question—they were so busy coming. And the one consuming purpose in Luther's life was to keep them doing that. Get them in, give them their deeds, and watch them come down. The plans and visions of his fathers might have been misdirected, but the Nedeeds could still live as a force to be reckoned with—if only within Linden Hills. His dark face at the bottom of the hill served as a beacon to draw the blacks needed as fuel for that continually dying dream. And it could go on forever through his son. But whenever Luther was forced to look at his son, his heart tightened.

Luther had not followed the pattern of his fathers and married a pale-skinned woman. He knew those wives had been chosen for the color of their spirits, not their faces. They had been brought to Tupelo Drive to fade against the white-washed boards of the Nedeed home after conceiving and giving over a son to the stamp and will of the father. He actually had to pause a moment in order to remember his mother's first name, because everyone—including his father—had called her nothing but Mrs. Nedeed. And that's all she had called herself. Luther's wife was better than pale—a dull, brown shadow who had given him a son, but a white son. The same squat bowlegs, the same protruding eyes and puffed lips, but a ghostly presence that mocked everything his fathers had built. How could Luther die and leave this with the future of Linden Hills? He looked at this whiteness and saw the destruction of five generations. The child went unnamed and avoided by his father for the first five years of his life and Luther tried to discover what had brought such havoc into his home.

He took out the journals and charts that were locked in the ancient rolltop desk in his den. Weeks were spent tracing the dates and times of penetrations, conceptions, and births for every Nedeed in Linden Hills. He then matched all of this with the position of the stars and the earth's axis at those moments and it all verified what had been passed down to him about the facts of life: "There must be five days of penetration at the appearance of Aries, and the son is born when the sun has died."

Luther slammed the journals shut. He had done that—it was followed to the word. Like every Nedeed before him, his seed was only released at the vernal equinox so the child would come during the Sign of the Goat when the winter's light was the weakest. It had been infallible for generations, so what was wrong now? He then bore the humiliation of seeing a doctor to be sure that there was nothing abnormal with his reproductive organs. When the medical reports returned positive and healthy, Luther held the written evidence for what he had felt all along in his heart: there was no way that this child could be his son.

And as the child faded to him against the clapboards of Tupelo Drive, Luther's eyes rested on the shadow floating through the carpeted rooms. It began to take form in front of his face. He noticed when it bent over and walked and sat down. He heard the lilt in the voice when it spoke. He distinguished between the colors that hung from the short frame and smelled the perfumed talc as it passed him. He could see the amber flecks in the heavily lashed eyes, the tiny scar on the right side of the lips. The long neck, small breasts, thick waist. Woman. She became a constant irritant to Luther, who now turned her presence over in his mind several times a day. Somewhere inside of her must be a deep flaw or she wouldn't have been capable of such treachery. Everything she owned he had given her—even her name—and she had thanked him with this? The irritation began to fester in his mind and he knew he had to remove it or go insane. He could throw her out tomorrow; there wasn't a court in this country that would deny him that right, but no one in his family had ever gotten divorced. And she had to learn why she was brought to Tupelo Drive. Obviously, he had allowed a whore into his home but he would turn her into a wife.

It was then that Luther reopened the old morgue in his basement. He worked alone and in a methodical fury, connecting plumbing and lighting, stacking trunks and boxes against the damp walls. A grimy sweat stung his eyes as he erected metal shelving and wired an intercom. He brought down clumsy cartons of powdered milk and dry cereal, and finally, trembling from exhaustion, he dragged two small cots down the twelve concrete steps. He stood in the middle of the basement and surveyed his work.

Now, let her stay down here with her bastard and think about what she'd done. Think about who she was playing with. He climbed the steps and checked the iron bolt on the door. Did she really think she could pass her lie off as his son? His fathers slaved to build Linden Hills and the very home she had tried to destroy. It took over a hundred and fifty years to build what he now had and it would be a cold day in hell before he saw some woman tear it down.

It was cold. In fact, it was the coldest week of the year when White Willie and Shit slapped five on Wayne Avenue and began their journey down Linden Hills.

⚜ JOHN EDGAR WIDEMAN (b. 1941)

John Edgar Wideman is an accomplished writer of novels and short stories. He was born in Washington, D.C., but he often writes about the inner-city ghetto of Pittsburgh, Pennsylvania. He earned his bachelor's degree from the University of Pennsylvania in 1963, and he directed the Afro-American studies program there from 1967. Wideman's training was enhanced by his experience as a Rhodes Scholar at Oxford University.

A Glance Away (1967), Wideman's first novel, deals with the struggles of a recovering drug addict. Wideman also wrote the novels Hurry Home *(1970),* The Lynchers *(1973),* Hiding Place *(1981),* Sent for You Yesterday *(1983),* Philadelphia Fire *(1990), which won the PEN/Faulkner Award, and* Fatheralong: A Meditation on Fathers and Sons, Race and Society *(1995). He also published a short-story collection,* Damballah *(1981).*

From Damballah (1981)

Hazel

> "Don't worry bout what hates you. What loves you's what you got to worry bout."
>
> —Bess

The day it happened Hazel dreamed of steps. The black steps her brother Faun had pushed her down. The white steps clinging to the side of the house she would not leave till she died. Down the steep black stairwell you always fell faster and faster. In the first few moments of the dream you could count the steps as parts of your body cracked on each sharp, wooden edge. But soon you were falling so fast your body trailed behind you, a broken, rattling noise like tin cans tied to a wedding car. The white steps were up. You mounted them patiently at first. The sun made them gleam and printed their shadow black against the blank, clapboard wall. If you looked up you could see a pattern repeated endlessly to the sky. A narrow, slanted ladder of nine steps, a landing, another bank of bare, bone white railings and steps leaning toward the next landing. Patiently at first, step by step, but then each landing only leads you to another flight of steps and you have been climbing forever and the ground is too far away to see but you are not getting any closer to the top of the building. The sun dazzles you when you stop to catch your breath. You are dizzy, exposed. You must hurry on to the next landing. You realize you cannot stop. You understand suddenly that you are falling up and this dream is worse than your brother's hands flinging you down into the black pit.

"Eat your peas now, honey." Her mother was busy halving peas into neat green hemispheres so Hazel wiggled her tongue at the ones prepared for her, the ones her mother had shoved with the edge of her knife into a mound in one compartment of her plate. They're good and juicy her mother said as she speared another pea. Can hardly catch them, she said as she sliced the pea and its two halves disappeared in the gray soup covering the bottom of the plate's largest section. Her mother boiled everything and always splashed water from pan to plate when she portioned Hazel's meals into the thick, trisected platter. If my food had those little wings like fish it could swim to me, Hazel thought. I'd put my lips on my plate and open my mouth wide like the whale swallowing Jonah and my food just swim to me like that.

"Here's the rest now. You eat up now." The knife squeaked through the flood, driving split peas before it, tumbling them over the divider so the section nearest Hazel was as green as she remembered spring.

"Have a nice breast of lamb cooking. By the time you finish these, it'll be ready, darling."

So green she wanted to cry. Hazel wished she knew why her tears came so easily, so suddenly over nothing. She hated peas. Her mother boiled them till the skins were loose and wrinkled. Pure mush when you bit into them. And who ever heard of cutting peas in half. *So you don't choke, darling. Mama doesn't want to lose her baby. Can't be too careful.* She had screwed up her face and stuck out her tongue at the peas just a moment before when her mother wasn't looking but now she felt like crying. Mushy and wrinkled and wet didn't matter at all. She didn't want to disturb the carpet of green. Didn't want to stick her fork in it. It was too beautiful, too green. A corner of spring in the drab room she would never leave.

Her mother never gets any older. She's slim, dainty, perfect as she rises and crosses to the stove, a young girl from the back, her trim hips betraying no sign of the three children they've borne. The long, straight hair they say she inherited from her mother Maggie is twisted and pinned into a bun on top of her head. A picture of Maggie they say when she lets it down and gathers it in her hands and pulls it forward and lets it fall over one shoulder the way Maggie always wore hers. Grandmother Maggie in the oval photograph on the mantelpiece. That's your grandmother, Hazel. Looks like a white lady, don't she? She could sit on her hair. Black and straight as any white woman's. Liked to let it hang like it is in the picture. She'd sit and play with it. Curl the end round her fingers. *That's your grandmother. It's a shame she didn't live long enough for you to see her. But she was too delicate, too beautiful. God didn't make her for living long in this world.*

Not one gray hair in the black mass when her mother swept it over her shoulder, two handfuls thick when her mother Gaybrella pulled and smoothed the dark river of hair down across her breast. Like a river or the wide, proud tail of a horse.

If her mother was not getting older, then she must be getting younger, Hazel thought, because nobody stood still. Hazel knew no one could stand still, not even a person who lives in a chair, a person who is helpless as a little baby, a person who never leaves the house. Even if you become Hazel, a person like that, you can't stand still. Some days took a week to pass. Some nights she'd awaken from her dreams and the darkness would stun her, would strike her across her mouth like a blow from a man's fist and she'd sink down into a stupor, not awake and not asleep for dull years at a time. She knew it hurt to have children, that women sweated and shrieked to wring life out of their bodies. That's why they called that hard, killing work *labor*, called it a woman's bed of pain. She knew it hurt to have a child dragged from your loins but it couldn't be any worse than those nights which were years and years ripped away from the numb cave of nothingness which began at her waist.

You couldn't stand still. You got older and more like a stone each day you sat in that chair, the chair which had been waiting at the foot of the stairs your brother pushed you down. So her mother was growing younger, was a girl again in her grace, in her slim body crossing to the stove and raising the lid to check the boiling breast of lamb.

"It's getting good and tender. It's almost done." Lamb smell filled the room, the shriveled pea halves were already cold to the touch. Hazel mashed one under her finger. As she wiped the mush on the napkin beside her plate she wondered what God used to clean his hands. How He got her off his thumb after he had squashed her in the darkness at the bottom of the steps.

The day it happened she dreamed of steps and thought of swallowing peas and chewing the lamb her mother Gaybrella had boiled to tastelessness. Until the day it roared beside her Hazel had never seen death. Death to her was that special look in her mother's eyes, a sneaky, frightened look which was not really something in the eyes but something missing, the eyes themselves missing from her mother's face. Death was her mother's eyes hiding, hiding for a whole morning, a whole afternoon, avoiding any encounter with Hazel's. Someone had knocked at the door early and Hazel had heard voices in her sleep. Her mother had shushed whoever it was and by the time Hazel was awake enough to listen the whispering on the other side of the door had stopped. Then the outside door was shut and bolted, a woman's footsteps had clattered down the three flights of outside steps and a strange something had emptied her mother's eyes. Hazel hadn't asked who had arrived at dawn, or asked what news the visitor had carried. She hadn't asked because there was no one to ask. Sometimes their three rooms at the top floor of Mr. Gray's house seemed smaller than a dress mother and daughter were struggling to wear at the same time. But the day of the empty eyes her mother found a million places in the tiny rooms to hide. Hazel had hummed all the songs she knew to keep herself company. By two o'clock her nervousness, the constant alert she forced herself to maintain had drained her. She was ready to cry or scream and did both when her mother had appeared from the bedroom in her long black coat. Her mother never left the house alone. Once or twice a year on Ferd's arm she might venture down into the Homewood streets but never alone. With her head tied in a scarf and her body wrapped from ankles to chin in the column of black she had faced Hazel for the first time that day. Her mother Gaybrella had looked like a child bundled up for an outing on a winter day. A child whose wide eyes were full of good-bye.

She's leaving me. She's going away. The words were too terrible to say. They were unthinkable but Hazel couldn't think anything else as she had stared at the pale girl woman who had once been her mother, who was too young now to be her mother, at the child who was going away forever.

"It's John French, sugar." Her mother's eyes had gone again. There was no one to ask why, or how long, no one but her own pitiful, crippled self in the room she would never leave. John French was a big, loud, gentle man who brought her candy and fruit. Her mother smiled at him in a way Hazel had never seen her smile before. Those kisses he planted on Hazel's forehead each time he left smelled of wine and tobacco. Coming and going he'd rattle the three flights of stairs which climbed the outside of Mr. Gray's clapboard house.

"You don't come on down outa here like you got good sense, Gay, I'ma come up and get you one day. Drag you if I have to. Fine woman like you cooped up here don't even see the light of day. I'ma come up here and grab you sure enough."

John French who was an uncle or an in-law or whatever you were to somebody when he married your mother's niece. Cousin Freeda who was Gert's girl. Aunt Gert and Aunt Aida and Aunt Bess your mother's sisters. John French had daughters who would be relatives too. Nice girls he said. *I'ma get those hussies come to see you some time.* How many years had it been since he said that. How many years before Lizabeth knocked on Sunday morning. She said it was Sunday and said she was just stopping by on her way home from church. And said her Daddy said hello. And said he's not doing so well. Heart and all and won't listen to the doctor. My Daddy's hardheaded, stubborn as a mule, she said. How many years ago and Lizabeth still coming, still dropping by on Sundays to say hello. That's how you know it's a Sunday. Lizabeth knocking in her Sunday clothes and, Hi, how you all doing? That's how you know Sunday still comes and comes in winter when she wears a big coat and in summer when she's sweating under her Sunday clothes. She'll take off the little hats she wears and set them on the table. In spring they look like Easter baskets. Girl, it's hot out there. Phew, she'll say and stretch out her legs. Ain't fit for a dog out there. Aunt Gay, she'll say. You should have heard Miss Lewis this morning. She can still sing, Aunt Gay. Old as she is she can still get that whole church shouting. You ought to come the next time she's singing. She always does a solo with the Gospel Chorus and they're on every third Sunday. You ought to come and I'll stay here with Hazel. Or Hazel could come too. We could get somebody to help her down the steps. We could get a wheelchair and somebody would give us a ride. Why don't both you'all come next third Sunday?

John French in Lizabeth's face. His high cheekbones and long jaw. White like her Daddy and his French eyes and the good French hair he used to have and she still does. Lizabeth is like John French always worrying them to come down into the world. A girl then a woman. The years pretty on her. Lizabeth can get up when she's finished with her tea in winter or her lemonade in summer, get up and walk away on two strong legs so the years do not pile up on her. She does not lose them by the fistful in the middle of the night and wake up years older in the morning. Lizabeth is not a thousand years old, she is not a stone heavy with too many years to count.

It's John French, sugar. Her mother had never said more than that. Just stood there in her long black coat, in the body of that child she was becoming again. Stood there a moment to see if her silence, her lost eyes might do what she knew words couldn't. But silence and eyes staring through her, around her, hadn't checked Hazel's sobs so Gaybrella left and tiptoed down the three flights of steps and returned in two hours, tiptoeing again, easing the door open and shut again, saying nothing as she shed the black coat and washed her hands and started water boiling for dinner.

Death was that something missing in her mother Gaybrella's eyes. Death was her mother leaving to go to John French, leaving without a word, without any explanation but Hazel knowing exactly where she was going, and why and knowing if her mother ever leaves that way again it will be death again. It will be Aunt Aida or Aunt Bess if she leaves again, if there is anyone else who can make her tip down the steps, make her lose her eyes the way John French did.

The day it happened (the *it* still unthinkable, unsayable as it was when her mother stood draped in black on the threshold) began with Bess *yoo-hooing* from the yard behind Mr. Gray's house.

"Yoo-hoo. Yoo-hoo, Gay." Little Aunt Bess yodeling up from the yard. That made it Tuesday because that's when Aunt Bess came to do the wash. First the dream of steps, of black steps and white steps, then the day beginning with Aunt Bess hollering "*Yoo-hoo.* What you got today? it's Tuesday. What you got for me?"

Her mother hated to drop the bundle of laundry into the yard but short-legged Bess hated all those steps and since she was the one doing the favor she'd yoo-hoo till she got her sister's attention and got her on the landing and got the bundle sailing down to her feet.

"Oww. Look at that dust. Look at that dust lapping at my things. If they weren't dirty before, they're dirty now.

"You wouldn't be dropping them down here if they wasn't dirty in the first place. I know you're the cleaningest woman in the world sister Gaybrella, but you still get things dirty."

"Let's not have a conversation about my laundry out here in public."

"Ain't no public to it. Ain't nobody here but us chickens. This all you got for me, Gay?"

"I can do the rest."

"Just throw it all down here. Don't make no sense for you to be doing no rest."

"You know I can't do that. You know I don't let anybody touch the rest."

"You can be downright insultin sometimes. Holding on to them few little things like you don't trust your own sister or something. And me bending over your wash every week."

"If it's too much trouble, I'll do it all myself. Just bring it back up here and I'll do it all myself."

"Shut up, woman. I've been doing it all these years. What makes you think I'ma stop today?"

"Then you know I can't give you everything. You know I have to do our private things myself."

"Suit yourself. Mize well run my head against a brick wall as try to change your ways. If you got sheets in here I'll have to hang them on this line. Won't have room on mine today."

"Go ahead. You know I dry the little business I have right up here."

"Say hello to that sweet angel, Hazel. Yoo-hoo, Hazel. You hear me girl?"

"She hears you, Bess. The whole neighborhood hears you."

"What I care about some neighborhood, I'm saying hello to my angel and anybody don't like it can kiss my behind."

"Please Bess."

"Don't be pleasing me. Just throw the rest of your dirty clothes down here so I can go on my way. Don't you be washing today. Don't do it today."

"I'm going inside now. Thank you."

"And don't you be thanking me. Just listen to me for once and don't be washing youall's underwear and hanging it over that stove."

"Good-bye."

And the door slams over Bess's head. She yells again. *Don't wash today*, but not loud enough to carry up the three flights of steps. She is bending over and pulling the drawstrings of the laundry bundle tighter so there is enough cord to sling the sack over her back. She is a short, sturdy-legged, reddish-yellow woman. Her skin is pocked with freckles. No one would guess she is the sister of the ivory woman who dropped the bundle from the landing. Bess hefts the sack over her shoulder and cuts catty-corner through the backyards toward the intersection of Albion and Tioga and her washing machine.

It happened on a Tuesday because her mother slammed the door and came in muttering about that Bess, that uncouth Bess. Her tongue's going to be the death of that woman. She married below her color but that's where her mouth always wanted to be anyway. Out in the street with those roughnecks and field-hands and their country nigger ways. Her mother Gaybrella just fussing and scolding and not knowing what to do with her hands till she opened the wicker basket in the bathroom where she stored their soiled private things and ran the sink full of water and started to wash them out. That calmed her. In a few moments Hazel could hear her humming to herself. Hear the gentle lapping of the water and the silk plunged in again and again. Smell the perfumed soap and hear the rasp of her mother's knuckles as she scrubbed their underthings against the washboard.

A warm breeze had entered the room while her mother stood outside on the landing talking to Bess. A spring, summer breeze green as peas. It spread like the sunlight into every corner of the room. Hazel could see it touching the curtains, feel it stirring the hair at the nape of her neck. In the chair she never left except when her mother lifted her into bed each night Hazel tried to remember the wind. If she shut her eyes and held her palms over her ears she could hear it.

Pulled close to the window she could watch it bend trees, or scatter leaves or see snowflakes whirl sideways and up in the wind's grasp. But hearing it or watching it play were not enough. She wanted to remember how the wind felt when you ran into it, or it ran into you and pasted your clothes to your skin, and tangled your hair into a mad streaming wake and took your breath away. Once she held her cupped hands very close to her face and blew into them, blew with all her might till her jaws ached and tears came. But it wasn't wind. Couldn't bring back the sensation she wanted to remember.

"Mama." Her mother is stringing a line above the stove. Their underthings have been cleaned and wrung into tight cylinders which are stacked in the basin her mother set on the sideboard.

"Bess never did listen to Mama. She was always the wild one. A hard head. She did her share of digging Mama an early grave. Mama never could do anything with her. Had a mind of her own while she was still in the cradle. I don't know how many times I've explained to her. There are certain things you wear close to your body you just can't let anybody touch. She knows that. And knows better than to be putting people's business in the street."

"Mama."

"What's that honey?"

"Could you set me on the landing for a while?"

"Honey I don't trust those stairs. I never did trust them. As long as we've been here I've been begging Mister Gray to shore them up. They sway and creak so bad. Think you're walking on a ship sometimes. I just don't trust them. The last time I went down with Ferdinand I just knew they wouldn't hold us both. I made him go first and held on to his coattail so we both wouldn't have to be on the same step at the same time. Still was scared to death the whole way down. Creaking and groaning like they do. Wouldn't trust my baby out there a minute."

"Is it warm?"

"In the sun, baby."

"I won't fall."

"Don't be worrying your mama now. You see I got these things to hang. And this place to clean. And I want to clean myself up and wash my hair this morning. Don't want to be looking like an old witch when Bess comes back this afternoon with the laundry. We can't slip, darling. We have to keep ourselves neat and clean no matter what. Doesn't matter what people see or don't see. What they never see are the places we have to be most careful of. But you know that. You're my good girl and you know that."

"If the sun's still out when you finish, maybe . . ."

"Don't worry me. I have enough to do without you picking at me. You just keep me company awhile. Or nap if you're tired."

Hazel watched as piece by piece her mother unrolled and pinned their under-clothes on the line stretched above the stove. The back burners were lit. Steam rose off the lace-frilled step-ins and combinations.

"I have a feeling Ferdinand will come by today. He said last time he was here he was being fitted for a new suit and if I know my son it won't be long before he has to come up here to his mama and show off what he's bought. He's a good son.

Never lost a night's sleep worrying over Ferdinand. If all mothers' sons were sweet as that boy, bearing children wouldn't be the burden it surely is. It's a trial. I can tell you it's a trial. When I look at you sitting in that chair and think of the terrible guilt on your other brother's shoulders, I can't tell you what a trial it is. Then I think sometimes, there's my little girl and she's going to miss a lot but then again she's blessed too because there's a whole lot she'll never have to suffer. The filth and dirt of this world. The lies of men, their nasty hands. What they put in you and what they turn you into. Having their way, having their babies. And worst of all expecting you to like it. Expecting you to say *thank you* and bow down like they're kings of the world. So I cry for you, precious. But you're blessed too. And it makes my heart feel good to know you'll always be neat and clean and pure."

It was always "your other brother" when her mother spoke of Faun. She had named him and then just as carefully unnamed him after he pushed his sister down the stairs. Her mother was the one who blamed him, who couldn't forgive, who hadn't said his name in fifteen years. There was Ferdinand and "your other brother." Hazel had always shortened her brother's names. To her they had been Ferd and Faun from the time she could speak. Her mother said every syllable distinctly and cut her eyes at people who didn't say *Fauntleroy* and *Ferdinand*. I gave my sons names. Real names. All niggers have nick-names. They get them every-where and anywhere. White folks. Children. Hoodlums and ignorant darkies. All of them will baptize you in a minute. But I chose real names for my boys. Good, strong names. Names from their mother and that's who they'll be in my mouth as long as I live. But she was wrong. Fauntleroy became "your other brother." Faun had forced his mother to break her promise to herself.

Ferd was a timid, little man, a man almost dandified in his dress and manner-isms. He was nearly as picky as their mother. He couldn't stand dust on his shoes. His watch chain and the gold eagle head of his cane always shone as if freshly pol-ished. A neat, slit-eyed man who pursed his lips to smile. When he sat with them he never looked his sister in the eye. He'd cross his leg and gossip with his mother and drink his tea from the special porcelain cups, never set out for anyone but him. Hazel knew he didn't like their mother. Never adored her the way she and Faun always did. To him Gaybrella was never a fairy princess. As a child he made fun of her strange ways. Once he had pursed his lips and asked them: If she's so good, if she's so perfect, why did Daddy leave her? But daddies had nothing to do with fairy princesses and they giggled at the silliness of his question. Then, like their father, Faun had run away or been run away, and ever since in Ferd's voice as he sat sipping tea and bringing news of the world, Hazel could hear the sneer, the taunt, the same mocking question he had asked about their father, asked about the absent brother. Hazel knew her mother also heard the question and that her mother saw the dislike in Ferd's distant eyes but instead of ordering him from the room, instead of punishing him the way she punished Faun for the least offense, she doted on Ferdinand. His was the only arm she'd accept, the only arm she'd allow to lead her down into the streets of Homewood.

Faun was like the wind. There were days when Hazel said his name over and over to herself. Never Fauntleroy but *Faun*. Faun. She'd close her eyes and try to picture him. The sound of his name was warm; it could lull her to sleep, to daydreaming of the times they ran together and talked together and shared a thousand secrets. He was her brother and the only man she had ever loved. Even as a girl she had understood that any other man who came into her life would be measured against Faun. Six days a week he killed animals. He always changed his clothes at work but Hazel believed she could smell the slaughterhouse blood, could feel the killing strength in his hands when he pinched her cheek and teased her about getting prettier every day. Her big brother who was like the wind. Changeable as the wind. But his mood didn't matter; just staying close to him mattered. That's why they fought. Why they raged at each other and stood inseparable against the world. So when he was twenty and full of himself and full of his power over other women and she was seventeen and learning what parts of him she must let go and learning her own woman powers as he rejected them in her and sought them in others, when they rubbed and chafed daily, growing too close and too far apart at once, the fight in the kitchen was no different than a hundred others, except his slaughterhouse hands on her shoulders pushed harder than he meant to, and her stumbling, lurching recoil from a blow she really didn't feel much at all, was carried too far and she lost her balance and tumbled through the kitchen door someone had left unlocked and pitched down the dark steep stairwell to Mr. Gray's second floor where the chair was waiting from which she would never rise.

"I expect him up those stairs anytime." Her mother had let her hair down. It dangled to her waist, flouncing like the broad, proud tail of a horse as she swept the kitchen floor.

Then it happened. So fast Hazel could not say what came first or second or third. Just that it happened. The unspeakable, the unsayable acted out before her eyes.

A smell of something burning. Almost like lamb. Flames crackling above the stove. Curling ash dropping down. Her mother shouting something. Words or a name. A panicked look back over her shoulders at the chair. Hazel forever in the chair. Then flames like wings shooting up her mother's back. Her mother wheeling, twisting slim and graceful as a girl. Her mother Gaybrella grabbing the river of her hair and whipping it forward over her shoulders, and the river on fire, blazing in her fists. Did her mother scream then or had she been screaming all along? Was it really hair in her hands or the burning housecoat she was trying to tear from her back? And as she rushed past Hazel like a roaring, hot wind, what was she saying, who was she begging for help? When her mother burst through the door and crashed through the railing into thin air who was she going to meet, who was making her leave without a word, without an explanation.

Fifteen years after the day it happened, fourteen years after Hazel too, had died, Lizabeth rode in the ambulance which was rushing with sirens blaring to Allegheny County Hospital. She was there because Faun was Gaybrella's son and Hazel's brother and she had stopped by all those Sundays and was one of the few who remembered the whole story. She had heard Faun had returned to Homewood but hadn't seen him till one of the church sisters who also possessed a long memory asked her if she knew her cousin was sick. So Lizabeth had visited him in the old people's home. And held his hand. And watched the torment of his slow dying, watched his silent agony because the disease had struck him dumb. She didn't know if he recognized her but she visited him as often as she could. A nurse called the ambulance when his eyes rolled to the top of his head and his mouth began to foam. Lizabeth rode with Faun in the screaming ambulance so she was there when he bolted upright and spoke for the first time in the two months she had been visiting him. "I'm sorry . . . I'm so sorry," was what he said. She heard that plainly and then he began to fail for the last time, tottering, exhausting the last bit of his strength to resist the hands of the attendants who were trying to push him back down on the stretcher. She thought he said, *Forgive me,* she thought those were Faun's last words but they sputtered through the bubbling froth of his lips and were uttered with the last of his fading strength so she couldn't be sure.

AUGUST WILSON (b. 1945)

August Wilson, a playwright who grew up in Philadelphia, Pennsylvania, was awarded the Pulitzer Prize twice—for Fences *(1985) and for* The Piano Lesson *(1990). Much of Wilson's work, like these prizewinning plays, presents black family issues. In addition to the Pulitzer Prize, he has won the Tony Award, and his play* Ma Rainey's Black Bottom *(1981) was named Best Play of the Year by the New York Drama Critics Circle. With this play, Wilson brought Ma Rainey, a 1920s blues singer, back to life. It was produced on Broadway in 1984, as was* Two Trains Running *(1990) in 1992. Wilson became active in the theater while in his teens, and in 1968 he founded Black Horizons Theatre Company in Minnesota.*

The Piano Lesson (1990)

THE SETTING:

The action of the play takes place in the kitchen and parlor of the house where DOAKER CHARLES lives with his niece, BERNIECE, and her eleven-year-old daughter, MARETHA. The house is sparsely furnished, and although there is evidence of a woman's touch, there is a lack of warmth and vigor. BERNIECE and MARETHA occupy the upstairs rooms. DOAKER'S room is prominent and opens onto the kitchen. Dominating the parlor is an old upright piano. On the legs of the piano, carved in the manner of African sculpture, are mask-like figures resembling totems. The carvings are rendered with a grace and power of invention that lifts them out of the realm of craftsmanship and into the realm of art. At left is a staircase leading to the upstairs.

ACT 1

SCENE 1

(The lights come up on the Charles household. It is five o'clock in the morning. The dawn is beginning to announce itself, but there is something in the air that belongs to the night. A stillness that is a portent, a gathering, a coming together of something akin to a storm. There is a loud knock at the door.)

BOY WILLIE. *(Off stage, calling.)* Hey, Doaker . . . Doaker!

(He knocks again and calls.)

Hey, Doaker! Hey, Berniece! Berniece!

(DOAKER enters from his room. He is a tall, thin man of forty-seven, with severe features, who has for all intents and purposes retired from the world though he works full-time as a railroad cook.)

DOAKER. Who is it?

BOY WILLIE. Open the door, nigger! It's me . . . Boy Willie!

DOAKER. Who?

BOY WILLIE. Boy Willie! Open the door!

(DOAKER opens the door and BOY WILLIE and LYMON enter. BOY WILLIE is thirty years old. He has an infectious grin and a boyishness that is apt for his name. He is brash and impulsive, talkative and somewhat crude in speech and manner. LYMON is twenty-nine. BOY WILLIE's partner, he talks little, and then with a straightforwardness that is often disarming.)

DOAKER. What you doing up here?

BOY WILLIE. I told you, Lymon. Lymon talking about you might be sleep. This is Lymon. You remember Lymon Jackson from down home? This my Uncle Doaker.

DOAKER. What you doing up here? I couldn't figure out who that was. I thought you was still down in Mississippi.

BOY WILLIE. Me and Lymon selling watermelons. We got a truck out there. Got a whole truckload of watermelons. We brought them up here to sell. Where's Berniece?

(Calls.)

Hey, Berniece!

DOAKER. Berniece up there sleep.

BOY WILLIE. Well, let her get up.

(Calls.)

Hey, Berniece!

DOAKER. She got to go to work in the morning.

BOY WILLIE. Well she can get up and say hi. It's been three years since I seen her.

(Calls.)

Hey, Berniece! It's me . . . Boy Willie.

DOAKER. Berniece don't like all that hollering now. She got to work in the morning.

BOY WILLIE. She can go on back to bed. Me and Lymon been riding two days in that truck . . . the least she can do is get up and say hi.

DOAKER. *(Looking out the window.)* Where you all get that truck from?

BOY WILLIE. It's Lymon's. I told him let's get a load of watermelons and bring them up here.

LYMON. Boy Willie say he going back, but I'm gonna stay. See what it's like up here.

BOY WILLIE. You gonna carry me down there first.

LYMON. I told you I ain't going back down there and take a chance on that truck breaking down again. You can take the train. Hey, tell him Doaker, he can take the train back. After we sell them watermelons he have enough money he can buy him a whole railroad car.

DOAKER. You got all them watermelons stacked up there no wonder the truck broke down. I'm surprised you made it this far with a load like that. Where you break down at?

BOY WILLIE. We broke down three times! It took us two and a half days to get here. It's a good thing we picked them watermelons fresh.

LYMON. We broke down twice in West Virginia. The first time was just as soon as we got out of Sunflower. About forty miles out she broke down. We got it going and got all the way to West Virginia before she broke down again.

BOY WILLIE. We had to walk about five miles for some water.

LYMON. It got a hole in the radiator but it runs pretty good. You have to pump the brakes sometime before they catch. Boy Willie have his door open and be ready to jump when that happens.

BOY WILLIE. Lymon think that's funny. I told the nigger I give him ten dollars to get the brakes fixed. But he thinks that funny.

LYMON. They don't need fixing. All you got to do is pump them till they catch.

(BERNIECE enters on the stairs. Thirty-five years old, with an eleven-year-old daughter, she is still in mourning for her husband after three years.)

BERNIECE. What you doing all that hollering for?

BOY WILLIE. Hey, Berniece. Doaker said you was sleep. I said at least you could get up and say hi.

BERNIECE. It's five o'clock in the morning and you come in here with all this noise. You can't come like normal folks. You got to bring all that noise with you.

BOY WILLIE. Hell, I ain't done nothing but come in and say hi. I ain't got in the house good.

BERNIECE. That's what I'm talking about. You start all that hollering and carry on as soon as you hit the door.

BOY WILLIE. Aw hell, woman, I was glad to see Doaker. You ain't had to come down if you didn't want to. I come eighteen hundred miles to see my sister I figure she might want to get up and say hi. Other than that you can go back upstairs. What you got, Doaker? Where your bottle? Me and Lymon want a drink.

(To BERNIECE.)

This is Lymon. You remember Lymon Jackson from down home.

LYMON. How you doing, Berniece. You look just like I thought you looked.

BERNIECE. Why you all got to come in hollering and carrying on? Waking the neighbors with all that noise.

BOY WILLIE. They can come over and join the party. We fixing to have a party. Doaker, where your bottle? Me and Lymon celebrating. The Ghosts of the Yellow Dog got Sutter.

BERNIECE. Say what?

BOY WILLIE. Ask Lymon, they found him the next morning. Say he drowned in his well.

DOAKER. When this happen, Boy Willie?

BOY WILLIE. About three weeks ago. Me and Lymon was over in Stoner County when we heard about it. We laughed. We thought it was funny. A great big old three-hundred-and-forty-pound man gonna fall down his well.

LYMON. It remind me of Humpty Dumpty.

BOY WILLIE. Everybody say the Ghosts of the Yellow Dog pushed him.

BERNIECE. I don't want to hear that nonsense. Somebody down there pushing them people in their wells.

DOAKER. What was you and Lymon doing over in Stoner County?

BOY WILLIE. We was down there working. Lymon got some people down there.

LYMON. My cousin got some land down there. We was helping him.

BOY WILLIE. Got near about a hundred acres. He got it set up real nice. Me and Lymon was down there chopping down trees. We was using Lymon's truck to haul the wood. Me and Lymon used to haul wood all around them parts.

(*To* BERNIECE.)

Me and Lymon got a truckload of watermelons out there.

(BERNIECE *crosses to the window to the parlor.*)

Doaker, where your bottle? I know you got a bottle stuck up in your room. Come on, me and Lymon want a drink.

(DOAKER *exits into his room.*)

BERNIECE. Where you all get that truck from?

BOY WILLIE. I told you it's Lymon's.

BERNIECE. Where you get the truck from, Lymon?

LYMON. I bought it.

BERNIECE. Where he get that truck from, Boy Willie?

BOY WILLIE. He told you he bought it. Bought it for a hundred and twenty dollars. I can't say where he got that hundred and twenty dollars from . . . but he bought that old piece of truck from Henry Porter. (*To* LYMON.) Where you get that hundred and twenty dollars from, nigger?

LYMON. I got it like you get yours. I know how to take care of money.

(DOAKER *brings a bottle and sets it on the table.*)

BOY WILLIE. Aw hell, Doaker got some of that good whiskey. Don't give Lymon none of that. He ain't used to good whiskey. He liable to get sick.

LYMON. I done had good whiskey before.

BOY WILLIE. Lymon bought that truck so he have him a place to sleep. He down there wasn't doing no work or nothing. Sheriff looking for him. He bought that truck to keep away from the sheriff. Got Stovall looking for him too. He down there sleeping in that truck ducking and dodging both of them. I told him come on let's go up and see my sister.

BERNIECE. What the sheriff looking for you for, Lymon?

BOY WILLIE. The man don't want you to know all his business. He's my company. He ain't asking you no questions.

LYMON. It wasn't nothing. It was just a misunderstanding.

BERNIECE. He in my house. You say the sheriff looking for him, I wanna know what he looking for him for. Otherwise you all can go back out there and be where nobody don't have to ask you nothing.

LYMON. It was just a misunderstanding. Sometimes me and the sheriff we don't think alike. So we just got crossed on each other.

BERNIECE. Might be looking for him about that truck. He might have stole that truck.

BOY WILLIE. We ain't stole no truck, woman. I told you Lymon bought it.

DOAKER. Boy Willie and Lymon got more sense than to ride all the way up here in a stolen truck with a load of watermelons. Now they might have stole them watermelons, but I don't believe they stole that truck.

BOY WILLIE. You don't even know the man good and you calling him a thief. And we ain't stole them watermelons either. Them old man Pitterford's watermelons. He give me and Lymon all we could load for ten dollars.

DOAKER. No wonder you got them stacked up out there. You must have five hundred watermelons stacked up out there.

BERNIECE. Boy Willie, when you and Lymon planning on going back?

BOY WILLIE. Lymon say he staying. As soon as we sell them watermelons I'm going on back.

BERNIECE. (Starts to exit up the stairs.) That's what you need to do. And you need to do it quick. Come in here disrupting the house. I don't want all that loud carrying on around here. I'm surprised you ain't woke Maretha up.

BOY WILLIE. I was fixing to get her now.

(Calls.)

Hey, Maretha!

DOAKER. Berniece don't like all that hollering now.

BERNIECE. Don't you wake that child up!

BOY WILLIE. You going up there . . . wake her up and tell her her uncle's here. I ain't seen her in three years. Wake her up and send her down here. She can go back to bed.

BERNIECE. I ain't waking that child up . . . and don't you be making all that noise. You and Lymon need to sell them watermelons and go on back.

(BERNIECE exits up the stairs.)

BOY WILLIE. I see Berniece still try to be stuck up.

DOAKER. Berniece alright. She don't want you making all that noise. Maretha up there sleep. Let her sleep until she get up. She can see you then.

BOY WILLIE. I ain't thinking about Berniece. You hear from Wining Boy? You know Cleotha died?

DOAKER. Yeah, I heard that. He come by here about a year ago. Had a whole sack of money. He stayed here about two weeks. Ain't offered nothing. Berniece asked him for three dollars to buy some food and he got mad and left.

LYMON. Who's Wining Boy?

BOY WILLIE. That's my uncle. That's Doaker's brother. You heard me talk about Wining Boy. He play piano. He done made some records and everything. He still doing that, Doaker?

DOAKER. He made one or two records a long time ago. That's the only ones I ever known him to make. If you let him tell it he a big recording star.

BOY WILLIE. He stopped down home about two years ago. That's what I hear. I don't know. Me and Lymon was up on Parchman Farm doing them three years.

DOAKER. He don't never stay in one place. Now, he been here about eight months ago. Back in the winter. Now, you subject not to see him for another two years. It's liable to be that long before he stop by.

BOY WILLIE. If he had a whole sack of money you liable never to see him. You ain't gonna see him until he get broke. Just as soon as that sack of money is gone you look up and he be on your doorstep.

LYMON. *(Noticing the piano.)* Is that the piano?

BOY WILLIE. Yeah . . . look here, Lymon. See how it got all those carvings on it. See, that's what I was talking about. See how it's carved up real nice and polished and everything? You never find you another piano like that.

LYMON. Yeah, that look real nice.

BOY WILLIE. I told you. See how it's polished? My mama used to polish it every day. See all them pictures carved on it? That's what I was talking about. You can get a nice price for that piano.

LYMON. That's all Boy Willie talked about the whole trip up here. I got tired of hearing him talk about the piano.

BOY WILLIE. All you want to talk about is women. You ought to hear this nigger, Doaker. Talking about all the women he gonna get when he get up here. He ain't had none down there but he gonna get a hundred when he get up here.

DOAKER. How your people doing down there, Lymon?

LYMON. They alright. They still there. I come up here to see what it's like up here. Boy Willie trying to get me to go back and farm with him.

BOY WILLIE. Sutter's brother selling the land. He say he gonna sell it to me. That's why I come up here. I got one part of it. Sell them watermelons and get me another part. Get Berniece to sell that piano and I'll have the third part.

DOAKER. Berniece ain't gonna sell that piano.

BOY WILLIE. I'm gonna talk to her. When she see I got a chance to get Sutter's land she'll come around.

DOAKER. You can put that thought out your mind. Berniece ain't gonna sell that piano.

BOY WILLIE. I'm gonna talk to her. She been playing on it?

DOAKER. You know she won't touch that piano. I ain't never known her to touch it since Mama Ola died. That's over seven years now. She say it got blood on it. She got Maretha playing on it though. Say Maretha can go on and do everything she can't do. Got her in an extra school down at the Irene Kaufman Settlement House. She want Maretha to grow up and be a schoolteacher. Say she good enough she can teach on the piano.

BOY WILLIE. Maretha don't need to be playing on no piano. She can play on the guitar.

DOAKER. How much land Sutter got left?

BOY WILLIE. Got a hundred acres. Good land. He done sold it piece by piece, he kept the good part for himself. Now he got to give that up. His brother come down from Chicago for the funeral . . . he up there in Chicago got some kind of business with soda fountain equipment. He anxious to sell the land, Doaker. He don't want to be bothered with it. He called me to him and said cause of how long our families done known each other and how we been good friends and all, say he wanted to sell the land to me. Say he'd rather see me with it than Jim Stovall. Told me he'd let me have it for two thousand dollars cash money. He don't know I found out the most Stovall would give him for it was fifteen hundred dollars. He trying to get that extra five hundred out of me telling me he doing me a favor. I thanked him just as nice. Told him what a good man Sutter was and how he had my sympathy and all. Told him to give me two weeks. He said he'd wait on me. That's why I come up here. Sell them watermelons. Get Berniece to sell that piano. Put them two parts with the part I done saved. Walk in there. Tip my hat. Lay my money down on the table. Get my deed and walk on out. This time I get to keep all the cotton. Hire me some men to work it for me. Gin my cotton. Get my seed. And I'll see you again next year. Might even plant some tobacco or some oats.

DOAKER. You gonna have a hard time trying to get Berniece to sell that piano. You know Avery Brown from down there don't you? He up here now. He followed Berniece up here trying to get her to marry him after Crawley got killed. He been up here about two years. He call himself a preacher now.

BOY WILLIE. I know Avery. I know him from when he used to work on the Willshaw place. Lymon know him too.

DOAKER. He after Berniece to marry him. She keep telling him no but he won't give up. He keep pressing her on it.

BOY WILLIE. Avery think all white men is bigshots. He don't know there some white men ain't got as much as he got.

DOAKER. He supposed to come past here this morning. Berniece going down to the bank with him to see if he can get a loan to start his church. That's why I know Berniece ain't gonna sell that piano. He tried to get her to sell it to help him start his church. Sent the man around and everything.

BOY WILLIE. What man?

DOAKER. Some white fellow was going around to all the colored people's houses looking to buy up musical instruments. He'd buy anything. Drums. Guitars. Harmonicas. Pianos. Avery sent him past here. He looked at the piano and got excited. Offered her a nice price. She turned him down and got on Avery for sending him past. The man kept on her about two weeks. He seen where she wasn't gonna sell it, he gave her his number and told her if she ever wanted to sell it to call him first. Say he'd go one better than what anybody else would give her for it.

BOY WILLIE. How much he offer her for it?

DOAKER. Now you know me. She didn't say and I didn't ask. I just know it was a nice price.

LYMON. All you got to do is find out who he is and tell him somebody else wanna buy it from you. Tell him you can't make up your mind who to sell it to, and if he like Doaker say, he'll give you anything you want for it.

BOY WILLIE. That's what I'm gonna do. I'm gonna find out who he is from Avery.

DOAKER. It ain't gonna do you no good. Berniece ain't gonna sell that piano.

BOY WILLIE. She ain't got to sell it. I'm gonna sell it. I own just as much of it as she does.

BERNIECE. *(Offstage, hollers.)* Doaker! Go on get away. Doaker!

DOAKER. *(Calling.)* Berniece?

(DOAKER *and* BOY WILLIE *rush to the stairs,* BOY WILLIE *runs up the stairs, passing* BERNIECE *as she enters, running.)*

DOAKER. Berniece, what's the matter? You alright? What's the matter?

(BERNIECE *tries to catch her breath. She is unable to speak.)*

DOAKER. That's alright. Take your time. You alright. What's the matter?

(He calls.)

Hey, Boy Willie?

BOY WILLIE. *(Offstage.)* Ain't nobody up here.

BERNIECE. Sutter . . . Sutter's standing at the top of the steps.

DOAKER. *(Calls.)* Boy Willie!

(LYMON *crosses to the stairs and looks up.* BOY WILLIE *enters from the stairs.)*

BOY WILLIE. Hey Doaker, what's wrong with her? Berniece, what's wrong? Who was you talking to?

DOAKER. She say she seen Sutter's ghost standing at the top of the stairs.

BOY WILLIE. Seen what? Sutter? She ain't seen no Sutter.

BERNIECE. He was standing right up there.

BOY WILLIE. *(Entering on the stairs.)* That's all in Berniece's head. Ain't nobody up there. Go on up there, Doaker.

DOAKER. I'll take your word for it. Berniece talking about what she seen. She say Sutter's ghost standing at the top of the steps. She ain't just make all that up.

BOY WILLIE. She up there dreaming. She ain't seen no ghost.

LYMON. You want a glass of water, Berniece? Get her a glass of water, Boy Willie.

BOY WILLIE. She don't need no water. She ain't seen nothing. Go on up there and look. Ain't nobody up there but Maretha.

DOAKER. Let Berniece tell it.

BOY WILLIE. I ain't stopping her from telling it.

DOAKER. What happened, Berniece?

BERNIECE. I come out my room to come back down here and Sutter was standing there in the hall.

BOY WILLIE. What he look like?

BERNIECE. He look like Sutter. He look like he always look.

BOY WILLIE. Sutter couldn't find his way from Big Sandy to Little Sandy. How he gonna find his way all the way up here to Pittsburgh? Sutter ain't never even heard of Pittsburgh.

DOAKER. Go on, Berniece.

BERNIECE. Just standing there with the blue suit on.

BOY WILLIE. The man ain't never left Marlin County when he was living . . . and he's gonna come all the way up here now that he's dead?

DOAKER. Let her finish. I want to hear what she got to say.

BOY WILLIE. I'll tell you this. If Berniece had seen him like she think she seen him she'd still be running.

DOAKER. Go on, Berniece. Don't pay Boy Willie no mind.

BERNIECE. He was standing there . . . had his hand on top of his head. Look like he might have thought if he took his hand down his head might have fallen off.

LYMON. Did he have on a hat?

BERNIECE. Just had on that blue suit . . . I told him to go away and he just stood there looking at me . . . calling Boy Willie's name.

BOY WILLIE. What he calling my name for?

BERNIECE. I believe you pushed him in the well.

BOY WILLIE. Now what kind of sense that make? You telling me I'm gonna go out there and hide in the weeds with all them dogs and things he got around there . . . I'm gonna hide and wait till I catch him looking down his well just right . . . then I'm gonna run over and push him in. A great big old three-hundred-and-forty-pound man.

BERNIECE. Well, what he calling your name for?

BOY WILLIE. He bending over looking down his well, woman . . . how he know who pushed him? It could have been anybody. Where was you when Sutter fell in his well? Where was Doaker? Me and Lymon was over in Stoner County. Tell her, Lymon. The Ghosts of the Yellow Dog got Sutter. That's what happened to him.

BERNIECE. You can talk all that Ghosts of the Yellow Dog stuff if you want. I know better.

LYMON. The Ghosts of the Yellow Dog pushed him. That's what the people say. They found him in his well and all the people say it must be the Ghosts of the Yellow Dog. Just like all them other men.

BOY WILLIE. Come talking about he looking for me. What he come all the way up here for? If he looking for me all he got to do is wait. He could have saved himself a trip if he looking for me. That ain't nothing but in Berniece's head. Ain't no telling what she liable to come up with next.

BERNIECE. Boy Willie, I want you and Lymon to go ahead and leave my house. Just go on somewhere. You don't do nothing but bring trouble with you everywhere you go. If it wasn't for you Crawley would still be alive.

BOY WILLIE. Crawley what? I ain't had nothing to do with Crawley getting killed. Crawley three time seven. He had his own mind.

BERNIECE. Just go on and leave. Let Sutter go somewhere else looking for you.

BOY WILLIE. I'm leaving. Soon as we sell them watermelons. Other than that I ain't going nowhere. Hell, I just got here. Talking about Sutter looking for me. Sutter was looking for that piano. That's what he was looking for. He had to die to find out where that piano was at. . . . If I was you I'd get rid of it. That's the way to get rid of Sutter's ghost. Get rid of that piano.

BERNIECE. I want you and Lymon to go on and take all this confusion out of my house!

BOY WILLIE. Hey, tell her, Doaker. What kind of sense that make? I told you, Lymon, as soon as Berniece see me she was gonna start something. Didn't I tell you that? Now she done made up that story about Sutter just so she could tell me to leave her house. Well, hell, I ain't going nowhere till I sell them watermelons.

BERNIECE. Well why don't you go out there and sell them! Sell them and go on back!

BOY WILLIE. We waiting till the people get up.

LYMON. Boy Willie say if you get out there too early and wake the people up they get mad at you and won't buy nothing from you.

DOAKER. You won't be waiting long. You done let the sun catch up with you. This the time everybody be getting up around here.

BERNIECE. Come on, Doaker, walk up here with me. Let me get Maretha up and get her started. I got to get ready myself. Boy Willie, just go on out there and sell them watermelons and you and Lymon leave my house.

(BERNIECE *and* DOAKER *exit up the stairs.*)

BOY WILLIE. (*Calling after them.*) If you see Sutter up there . . . tell him I'm down here waiting on him.

LYMON. What if she see him again?

BOY WILLIE. That's all in her head. There ain't no ghost up there.

(*Calls.*)

Hey, Doaker . . . I told you ain't nothing up there.

LYMON. I'm glad he didn't say he was looking for me.

BOY WILLIE. I wish I would see Sutter's ghost. Give me a chance to put a whupping on him.

LYMON. You ought to stay up here with me. You be down there working his land . . . he might come looking for you all the time.

BOY WILLIE. I ain't thinking about Sutter. And I ain't thinking about staying up here. You stay up here. I'm going back and get Sutter's land. You think you ain't got to work up here. You think this the land of milk and honey. But I ain't scared of work. I'm going back and farm every acre of that land.

(DOAKER *enters from the stairs.*)

I told you there ain't nothing up there, Doaker. Berniece dreaming all that.

DOAKER. I believe Berniece seen something. Berniece level-headed. She ain't just made all that up. She say Sutter had on a suit. I don't believe she ever seen Sutter in a suit. I believe that's what he was buried in, and that's what Berniece saw.

BOY WILLIE. Well, let her keep on seeing him then. As long as he don't mess with me.

(DOAKER *starts to cook his breakfast.*)

I heard about you, Doaker. They say you got all the women looking out for you down home. They be looking to see you coming. Say you got a different one every two weeks. Say they be fighting one another for you to stay with them.

(To LYMON.*)*

Look at him, Lymon. He know it's true.

DOAKER. I ain't thinking about no women. They never get me tied up with them. After Coreen I ain't got no use for them. I stay up on Jack Slattery's place when I be down there. All them women want is somebody with a steady payday.

BOY WILLIE. That ain't what I hear. I hear every two weeks the women all put on their dresses and line up at the railroad station.

DOAKER. I don't get down there but once a month. I used to go down there every two weeks but they keep switching me around. They keep switching all the fellows around.

BOY WILLIE. Doaker can't turn that railroad loose. He was working the railroad when I was walking around crying for sugartit. My mama used to brag on him.

DOAKER. I'm cooking now, but I used to line track. I pieced together the Yellow Dog stitch by stitch. Rail by rail. Line track all up around there. I lined track all up around Sunflower and Clarksdale. Wining Boy worked with me. He helped put in some of that track. He'd work it for six months and quit. Go back to playing piano and gambling.

BOY WILLIE. How long you been with the railroad now?

DOAKER. Twenty-seven years. Now, I'll tell you something about the railroad. What I done learned after twenty-seven years. See, you got North. You got West. You look over here you got South. Over there you got East. Now, you can start from anywhere. Don't care where you at. You got to go one of them four ways. And whichever way you decide to go they got a railroad that will take you there. Now, that's something simple. You think anybody would be able to understand that. But you'd be surprised how many people trying to go North get on a train going West. They think the train's supposed to go where they going rather than where it's going.

Now, why people going? Their sister's sick. They leaving before they kill somebody . . . and they sitting across from somebody who's leaving to keep from getting killed. They leaving cause they can't get satisfied. They going to meet someone. I wish I had a dollar for every time that someone wasn't at the station to meet them. I done seen that a lot. In between the time they sent the telegram and the time the person get there . . . they done forgot all about them.

They got so many trains out there they have a hard time keeping them from running into each other. Got trains going every whichaway. Got people on all of them. Somebody going where somebody just left. If everybody stay in one place I believe this would be a better world. Now what I done learned after twenty-seven years of railroading is this . . . if the train stays on the track . . . it's going to get where it's going. It might not be where you going. If it ain't, then all you got to do is sit and wait cause the train's coming back to get you. The train don't never stop. It'll come back every time. Now I'll tell you another thing . . .

BOY WILLIE. What you cooking over there, Doaker? Me and Lymon's hungry.

DOAKER. Go on down there to Wylie and Kirkpatrick to Eddie's restaurant. Coffee cost a nickel and you can get two eggs, sausage, and grits for fifteen cents. He even give you a biscuit with it.

BOY WILLIE. That look good what you got. Give me a little piece of that grilled bread.

DOAKER. Here . . . go on take the whole piece.

BOY WILLIE. Here you go, Lymon . . . you want a piece?

(He gives LYMON *a piece of toast.* MARETHA *enters from the stairs.)*

BOY WILLIE. Hey, sugar. Come here and give me a hug. Come on give Uncle Boy Willie a hug. Don't be shy. Look at her, Doaker. She done got bigger. Ain't she got big?

DOAKER. Yeah, she getting up there.

BOY WILLIE. How you doing, sugar?

MARETHA. Fine.

BOY WILLIE. You was just a little old thing last time I seen you. You remember me, don't you? This your Uncle Boy Willie from down South. That there's Lymon. He my friend. We come up here to sell watermelons. You like watermelons?

*(*MARETHA *nods.)*

We got a whole truckload out front. You can have as many as you want. What you been doing?

MARETHA. Nothing.

BOY WILLIE. Don't be shy now. Look at you getting all big. How old is you?

MARETHA. Eleven. I'm gonna be twelve soon.

BOY WILLIE. You like it up here? You like the North?

MARETHA. It's alright.

BOY WILLIE. That there's Lymon. Did you say hi to Lymon?

MARETHA. Hi.

LYMON. How you doing? You look just like your mama. I remember you when you was wearing diapers.

BOY WILLIE. You gonna come down South and see me? Uncle Boy Willie gonna get him a farm. Gonna get a great big old farm. Come down there and I'll teach you how to ride a mule. Teach you how to kill a chicken, too.

MARETHA. I seen my mama do that.

BOY WILLIE. Ain't nothing to it. You just grab him by his neck and twist it. Get you a real good grip and then you just wring his neck and throw him in the pot. Cook him up. Then you got some good eating. What you like to eat? What kind of food you like?

MARETHA. I like everything . . . except I don't like no black-eyed peas.

BOY WILLIE. Uncle Doaker tell me your mama got you playing that piano. Come on play something for me.

*(*BOY WILLIE *crosses over to the piano followed by* MARETHA.*)*

Show me what you can do. Come on now. Here . . . Uncle Boy Willie give you a dime . . . show me what you can do. Don't be bashful now. That dime say you can't be bashful.

*(*MARETHA *plays. It is something any beginner first learns.)*

Here, let me show you something.

(BOY WILLIE *sits and plays a simple boogie-woogie.*)

See that? See what I'm doing? That's what you call the boogie-woogie. See now . . . you can get up and dance to that. That's how good it sound. It sound like you wanna dance. You can dance to that. It'll hold you up. Whatever kind of dance you wanna do you can dance to that right there. See that? See how it go? Ain't nothing to it. Go on you do it.

MARETHA. I got to read it on the paper.

BOY WILLIE. You don't need no paper. Go on. Do just like that there.

BERNIECE. Maretha! You get up here and get ready to go so you be on time. Ain't no need you trying to take advantage of company.

MARETHA. I got to go.

BOY WILLIE. Uncle Boy Willie gonna get you a guitar. Let Uncle Doaker teach you how to play that. You don't need to read no paper to play the guitar. Your mama told you about that piano? You know how them pictures got on there?

MARETHA. She say it just always been like that since she got it.

BOY WILLIE. You hear that, Doaker? And you sitting up here in the house with Berniece.

DOAKER. I ain't got nothing to do with that. I don't get in the way of Berniece's raising her.

BOY WILLIE. You tell your mama to tell you about that piano. You ask her how them pictures got on there. If she don't tell you I'll tell you.

BERNIECE. Maretha!

MARETHA. I got to get ready to go.

BOY WILLIE. She getting big, Doaker. You remember her, Lymon?

LYMON. She used to be real little.

(*There is a knock on the door.* DOAKER *goes to answer it.* AVERY *enters. Thirty-eight years old, honest and ambitious, he has taken to the city like a fish to water, finding in it opportunities for growth and advancement that did not exist for him in the rural South. He is dressed in a suit and tie with a gold cross around his neck. He carries a small Bible.*)

DOAKER. Hey, Avery, come on in. Berniece upstairs.

BOY WILLIE. Look at him . . . look at him . . . he don't know what to say. He wasn't expecting to see me.

AVERY. Hey, Boy Willie. What you doing up here?

BOY WILLIE. Look at him, Lymon.

AVERY. Is that Lymon? Lymon Jackson?

BOY WILLIE. Yeah, you know Lymon.

DOAKER. Berniece be ready in a minute, Avery.

BOY WILLIE. Doaker say you a preacher now. What . . . we supposed to call you Reverend? You used to be plain old Avery. When you get to be a preacher, nigger?

LYMON. Avery say he gonna be a preacher so he don't have to work.

BOY WILLIE. I remember when you was down there on the Willshaw place planting cotton. You wasn't thinking about no Reverend then.

AVERY. That must be your truck out there. I saw that truck with them watermelons, I was trying to figure out what it was doing in front of the house.

BOY WILLIE. Yeah, me and Lymon selling watermelons. That's Lymon's truck.

DOAKER. Berniece say you all going down to the bank.

AVERY. Yeah, they give me a half day off work. I got an appointment to talk to the bank about getting a loan to start my church.

BOY WILLIE. Lymon say preachers don't have to work. Where you working at, nigger?

DOAKER. Avery got him one of them good jobs. He working at one of them skyscrapers downtown.

AVERY. I'm working down there at the Gulf Building running an elevator. Got a pension and everything. They even give you a turkey on Thanksgiving.

LYMON. How you know the rope ain't gonna break? Ain't you scared the rope's gonna break?

AVERY. That's steel. They got steel cables hold it up. It take a whole lot of breaking to break that steel. Naw, I ain't worried about nothing like that. It ain't nothing but a little old elevator. Now, I wouldn't get in none of them airplanes. You couldn't pay me to do nothing like that.

LYMON. That be fun. I'd rather do that than ride in one of them elevators.

BOY WILLIE. How many of them watermelons you wanna buy?

AVERY. I thought you was gonna give me one seeing as how you got a whole truck full.

BOY WILLIE. You can get one, get two. I'll give you two for a dollar.

AVERY. I can't eat but one. How much are they?

BOY WILLIE. Aw, nigger, you know I'll give you a watermelon. Go on, take as many as you want. Just leave some for me and Lymon to sell.

AVERY. I don't want but one.

BOY WILLIE. How you get to be a preacher, Avery? I might want to be a preacher one day. Have everybody call me Reverend Boy Willie.

AVERY. It come to me in a dream. God called me and told me he wanted me to be a shepherd for his flock. That's what I'm gonna call my church . . . The Good Shepherd Church of God in Christ.

DOAKER. Tell him what you told me. Tell him about the three hobos.

AVERY. Boy Willie don't want to hear all that.

LYMON. I do. Lots a people say your dreams can come true.

AVERY. Naw. You don't want to hear all that.

DOAKER. Go on. I told him you was a preacher. He didn't want to believe me. Tell him about the three hobos.

AVERY. Well, it come to me in a dream. See . . . I was sitting out in this railroad yard watching the trains go by. The train stopped and these three hobos got off. They told me they had come from Nazareth and was on their way to Jerusalem. They had three candles. They gave me one and told me to light it . . . but to be careful that it didn't go out. Next thing I knew I was standing in front of this house. Something told me to go knock on the door. This old woman opened the door and said they had been waiting on me. Then she led me into this room. It was a big room and it was full of all kinds of different people. They looked like anybody else except they all had sheep heads and was making noise like sheep make. I heard somebody call my name. I looked around and there was these same three hobos. They told me to take off my clothes and they give me a blue robe with gold thread. They washed my feet and combed my hair. Then they showed me these three doors and told me to pick one.

I went through one of them doors and that flame leapt off that candle and it seemed like my whole head caught fire. I looked around and there was four or five other men standing there with these same blue robes on. Then we heard a voice tell us to look out across this valley. We looked out and saw the valley was full of wolves. The voice told us that these sheep people that I had seen in the other room had to go over to the other side of this valley and somebody had to take them. Then I heard another voice say, "Who shall I send?" Next thing I knew I said, "Here I am. Send me." That's when I met Jesus. He say, "If you go, I'll go with you." Something told me to say, "Come on. Let's go." That's when I woke up. My head still felt like it was on fire . . . but I had a peace about myself that was hard to explain. I knew right then that I had been filled with the Holy Ghost and called to be a servant of the Lord. It took me a while before I could accept that. But then a lot of little ways God showed me that it was true. So I became a preacher.

LYMON. I see why you gonna call it the Good Shepherd Church. You dreaming about them sheep people. I can see that easy.

BOY WILLIE. Doaker say you sent some white man past the house to look at that piano. Say he was going around to all the colored people's houses looking to buy up musical instruments.

AVERY. Yeah, but Berniece didn't want to sell that piano. After she told me about it . . . I could see why she didn't want to sell it.

BOY WILLIE. What's this man's name?

AVERY. Oh, that's a while back now. I done forgot his name. He give Berniece a card with his name and telephone number on it, but I believe she throwed it away.

(BERNIECE *and* MARETHA *enter from the stairs.*)

BERNIECE. Maretha, run back upstairs and get my pocketbook. And wipe that hair grease off your forehead. Go ahead, hurry up.

(MARETHA *exits up the stairs.*)

How you doing, Avery? You done got all dressed up. You look nice. Boy Willie, I thought you and Lymon was going to sell them watermelons.

BOY WILLIE. Lymon done got sleepy. We liable to get some sleep first.

LYMON. I ain't sleepy.

DOAKER. As many watermelons as you got stacked up on that truck out there, you ought to have been gone.

BOY WILLIE. We gonna go in a minute. We going.

BERNIECE. Doaker, I'm gonna stop down there on Logan Street. You want anything?

DOAKER. You can pick up some ham hocks if you going down there. See if you can get the smoked ones. If they ain't got that get the fresh ones. Don't get the ones that got all that fat under the skin. Look for the long ones. They nice and lean.

(He gives her a dollar.)

Don't get the short ones lessen they smoked. If you got to get the fresh ones make sure that they the long ones. If they ain't got them smoked then go ahead and get the short ones.

(Pause.)

You may as well get some turnip greens while you down there. I got some buttermilk . . . if you pick up some cornmeal I'll make me some cornbread and cook up them turnip greens.

(MARETHA enters from the stairs.)

MARETHA. We gonna take the streetcar?

BERNIECE. Me and Avery gonna drop you off at the settlement house. You mind them people down there. Don't be going down there showing your color. Boy Willie, I done told you what to do. I'll see you later, Doaker.

AVERY. I'll be seeing you again, Boy Willie.

BOY WILLIE. Hey, Berniece . . . what's the name of that man Avery sent past say he want to buy the piano?

BERNIECE. I knew it. I knew it when I first seen you. I knew you was up to something.

BOY WILLIE. Sutter's brother say he selling the land to me. He waiting on me now. Told me he'd give me two weeks. I got one part. Sell them watermelons get me another part. Then we can sell that piano and I'll have the third part.

BERNIECE. I ain't selling that piano, Boy Willie. If that's why you come up here you can just forget about it.

(To DOAKER.)

Doaker, I'll see you later. Boy Willie ain't nothing but a whole lot of mouth. I ain't paying him no mind. If he come up here thinking he gonna sell that piano then he done come up here for nothing.

(BERNIECE, AVERY, and MARETHA exit the front door.)

BOY WILLIE. Hey, Lymon! You ready to go sell these watermelons.

(BOY WILLIE and LYMON start to exit. At the door BOY WILLIE turns to DOAKER.)

Hey, Doaker . . . if Berniece don't want to sell that piano . . . I'm gonna cut it in half and go on and sell my half.

(BOY WILLIE and LYMON exit.)

(The lights go down on the scene.)

SCENE 2

(The lights come up on the kitchen. It is three days later. WINING BOY sits at the kitchen table. There is a half-empty pint bottle on the table. DOAKER busies himself washing pots. WINING BOY is fifty-six years old. DOAKER's older brother, he tries to present the image of a successful musician and gambler, but his music, his clothes, and even his manner of presentation are old. He is a man who looking back over his life continues to live it with an odd mixture of zest and sorrow.)

WINING BOY. So the Ghosts of the Yellow Dog got Sutter. That just go to show you I believe I always lived right. They say every dog gonna have his day and time it go around it sure come back to you. I done seen that a thousand times. I know the truth of that. But I'll tell you outright . . . if I see Sutter's ghost I'll be on the first thing I find that got wheels on it.

(DOAKER *enters from his room.*)

DOAKER. Wining Boy!

WINING BOY. And I'll tell you another thing . . . Berniece ain't gonna sell that piano.

DOAKER. That's what she told him. He say he gonna cut it in half and go on and sell his half. They been around here three days trying to sell them watermelons. They trying to get out to where the white folks live but the truck keep breaking down. They go a block or two and it break down again. They trying to get out to Squirrel Hill and can't get around the corner. He say soon as he can get that truck empty to where he can set the piano up in there he gonna take it out of here and go sell it.

WINING BOY. What about them boys Sutter got? How come they ain't farming that land?

DOAKER. One of them going to school. He left down there and come North to school. The other one ain't got as much sense as that frying pan over yonder. That is the dumbest white man I ever seen. He'd stand in the river and watch it rise till it drown him.

WINING BOY. Other than seeing Sutter's ghost how's Berniece doing?

DOAKER. She doing alright. She still got Crawley on her mind. He been dead three years but she still holding on to him. She need to go out here and let one of these fellows grab a whole handful of whatever she got. She act like it done got precious.

WINING BOY. They always told me any fish will bite if you got good bait.

DOAKER. She stuck up on it. She think it's better than she is. I believe she messing around with Avery. They got something going. He a preacher now. If you let him tell it the Holy Ghost sat on his head and heaven opened up with thunder and lightning and God was calling his name. Told him to go out and preach and tend to his flock. That's what he gonna call his church. The Good Shepherd Church.

WINING BOY. They had that joker down in Spear walking around talking about he Jesus Christ. He gonna live the life of Christ. Went through the Last Supper and everything. Rented him a mule on Palm Sunday and rode through the town. Did everything . . . talking about he Christ. He did everything until they got up to that crucifixion part. Got up to that part and told everybody to go home and quit pretending. He got up to the crucifixion part and changed his mind. Had a whole bunch of folks come down there to see him get nailed to the cross. I don't know who's the worse fool. Him or them. Had all them folks come down there . . . even carried the cross up this little hill. People standing around waiting to see him get nailed to the cross and he stop everything and preach a little sermon and told everybody to go home. Had enough nerve to tell them to come to church on Easter Sunday to celebrate his resurrection.

DOAKER. I'm surprised Avery ain't thought about that. He trying every little thing to get him a congregation together. They meeting over at his house till he get him a church.

WINING BOY. Ain't nothing wrong with being a preacher. You got the preacher on one hand and the gambler on the other. Sometimes there ain't too much difference in them.

DOAKER. How long you been in Kansas City?

WINING BOY. Since I left here. I got tied up with some old gal down there.

(Pause.)

You know Cleotha died.

DOAKER. Yeah, I heard that last time I was down there. I was sorry to hear that.

WINING BOY. One of her friends wrote and told me. I got the letter right here.

(He takes the letter out of his pocket.)

I was down in Kansas City and she wrote and told me Cleotha had died. Name of Willa Bryant. She say she know cousin Rupert.

(He opens the letter and reads.)

Dear Wining Boy. I am writing this letter to let you know Miss Cleotha Holman passed on Saturday the first of May she departed this world in the loving arms of her sister Miss Alberta Samuels. I know you would want to know this and am writing as a friend of Cleotha. There have been many hardships since last you seen her but she survived them all and to the end was a good woman whom I hope have God's grace and is in His Paradise. Your cousin Rupert Bates is my friend also and he give me your address and I pray this reaches you about Cleotha. Miss Willa Bryant. A friend.

(He folds the letter and returns it to his pocket.)

They was nailing her coffin shut by the time I heard about it. I never knew she was sick. I believe it was that yellow jaundice. That's what killed her mama.

DOAKER. Cleotha wasn't but forty-some.

WINING BOY. She was forty-six. I got ten years on her. I met her when she was sixteen. You remember I used to run around there. Couldn't nothing keep me still. Much as I loved Cleotha I loved to ramble. Couldn't nothing keep me still. We got married and we used to fight about it all the time. Then one day she asked me to leave. Told me she loved me before I left. Told me, Wining Boy, you got a home as long as I got mine. And I believe in my heart I always felt that and that kept me safe.

DOAKER. Cleotha always did have a nice way about her.

WINING BOY. Man that woman was something. I used to thank the Lord. Many a night I sat up and looked out over my life. Said, well, I had Cleotha. When it didn't look like there was nothing else for me, I said, thank God, at least I had that. If ever I go anywhere in this life I done known a good woman. And that used to hold me till the next morning.

(Pause.)

What you got? Give me a little nip. I know you got something stuck up in your room.

DOAKER. I ain't seen you walk in here and put nothing on the table. You done sat there and drank up your whiskey. Now you talking about what you got.

WINING BOY. I got plenty money. Give me a little nip.

(DOAKER *carries a glass into his room and returns with it half-filled. He sets it on the table in front of* WINING BOY.)

WINING BOY. You hear from Coreen?

DOAKER. She up in New York. I let her go from my mind.

WINING BOY. She was something back then. She wasn't too pretty but she had a way of looking at you made you know there was a whole lot of woman there. You got married and snatched her out from under us and we all got mad at you.

DOAKER. She up in New York City. That's what I hear.

(*The door opens and* BOY WILLIE *and* LYMON *enter.*)

BOY WILLIE. Aw hell . . . look here! We was just talking about you. Doaker say you left out of here with a whole sack of money. I told him we wasn't going see you till you got broke.

WINING BOY. What you mean broke? I got a whole pocketful of money.

DOAKER. Did you all get that truck fixed?

BOY WILLIE. We got it running and got halfway out there on Centre and it broke down again. Lymon went out there and messed it up some more. Fellow told us we got to wait till tomorrow to get it fixed. Say he have it running like new. Lymon going back down there and sleep in the truck so the people don't take the watermelons.

LYMON. Lymon nothing. You go down there and sleep in it.

BOY WILLIE. You was sleeping in it down home, nigger! I don't know nothing about sleeping in no truck.

LYMON. I ain't sleeping in no truck.

BOY WILLIE. They can take all the watermelons. I don't care. Wining Boy, where you coming from? Where you been?

WINING BOY. I been down in Kansas City.

BOY WILLIE. You remember Lymon? Lymon Jackson.

WINING BOY. Yeah, I used to know his daddy.

BOY WILLIE. Doaker say you don't never leave no address with nobody. Say he got to depend on your whim. See when it strike you to pay a visit.

WINING BOY. I got four or five addresses.

BOY WILLIE. Doaker say Berniece asked you for three dollars and you got mad and left.

WINING BOY. Berniece try and rule over you too much for me. That's why I left. It wasn't about no three dollars.

BOY WILLIE. Where you getting all these sacks of money from? I need to be with you. Doaker say you had a whole sack of money . . . turn some of it loose.

WINING BOY. I was just fixing to ask you for five dollars.

BOY WILLIE. I ain't got no money. I'm trying to get some. Doaker tell you about Sutter? The Ghosts of the Yellow Dog got him about three weeks ago. Berniece done seen his ghost and everything. He right upstairs.

(Calls.)

Hey Sutter! Wining Boy's here. Come on, get a drink!

WINING BOY. How many that make the Ghosts of the Yellow Dog done got?

BOY WILLIE. Must be about nine or ten, eleven or twelve. I don't know.

DOAKER. You got Ed Saunders. Howard Peterson. Charlie Webb.

WINING BOY. Robert Smith. That fellow that shot Becky's boy . . . say he was stealing peaches . . .

DOAKER. You talking about Bob Mallory.

BOY WILLIE. Berniece say she don't believe all that about the Ghosts of the Yellow Dog.

WINING BOY. She ain't got to believe. You go ask them white folks in Sunflower County if they believe. You go ask Sutter if he believe. I don't care if Berniece believe or not. I done been to where the Southern cross the Yellow Dog and called out their names. They talk back to you, too.

LYMON. What they sound like? The wind or something?

BOY WILLIE. You done been there for real, Wining Boy?

WINING BOY. Nineteen thirty. July of nineteen thirty I stood right there on that spot. It didn't look like nothing was going right in my life. I said everything can't go wrong all the time . . . let me go down there and call on the Ghosts of the Yellow Dog, see if they can help me. I went down there and right there where them two railroads cross each other . . . I stood right there on that spot and called out their names. They talk back to you, too.

LYMON. People say you can ask them questions. They talk to you like that?

WINING BOY. A lot of things you got to find out on your own. I can't say how they talked to nobody else. But to me it just filled me up in a strange sort of way to be standing there on that spot. I didn't want to leave. It felt like the longer I stood there the bigger I got. I seen the train coming and it seem like I was bigger than the train. I started not to move. But something told me to go ahead and get on out the way. The train passed and I started to go back up there and stand some more. But something told me not to do it. I walked away from there feeling like a king. Went on and had a stroke of luck that run on for three years. So I don't care if Berniece believe or not. Berniece ain't got to believe. I know cause I been there. Now Doaker'll tell you about the Ghosts of the Yellow Dog.

DOAKER. I don't try and talk that stuff with Berniece. Avery got her all tied up in that church. She just think it's a whole lot of nonsense.

BOY WILLIE. Berniece don't believe in nothing. She just think she believe. She believe in anything if it's convenient for her to believe. But when that convenience run out then she ain't got nothing to stand on.

WINING BOY. Let's not get on Berniece now. Doaker tell me you talking about selling that piano.

BOY WILLIE. Yeah . . . hey, Doaker, I got the name of that man Avery was talking about. The man what's fixing the truck gave me his name. Everybody know him. Say he buy up anything you can make music with. I got his name and his telephone number. Hey, Wining Boy, Sutter's brother say he selling the land to me.

I got one part. Sell them watermelons get me the second part. Then . . . soon as I get them watermelons out that truck I'm gonna take and sell that piano and get the third part.

DOAKER. That land ain't worth nothing no more. The smart white man's up here in these cities. He cut the land loose and step back and watch you and the dumb white man argue over it.

WINING BOY. How you know Sutter's brother ain't sold it already? You talking about selling the piano and the man's liable to sold the land two or three times.

BOY WILLIE. He say he waiting on me. He say he give me two weeks. That's two weeks from Friday. Say if I ain't back by then he might gonna sell it to somebody else. He say he wanna see me with it.

WINING BOY. You know as well as I know the man gonna sell the land to the first one walk up and hand him the money.

BOY WILLIE. That's just who I'm gonna be. Look, you ain't gotta know he waiting on me. I know. Okay. I know what the man told me. Stoval already done tried to buy the land from him and he told him no. The man say he waiting on me . . . he waiting on me. Hey, Doaker . . . give me a drink. I see Wining Boy got his glass.

(DOAKER *exits into his room.*)

Wining Boy, what you doing in Kansas City? What they got down there?

LYMON. I hear they got some nice-looking women in Kansas City. I sure like to go down there and find out.

WINING BOY. Man, the women down there is something else.

(DOAKER *enters with a bottle of whiskey. He sets it on the table with some glasses.*)

DOAKER. You wanna sit up here and drink up my whiskey, leave a dollar on the table when you get up.

BOY WILLIE. You ain't doing nothing but showing your hospitality. I know we ain't got to pay for your hospitality.

WINING BOY. Doaker say they had you and Lymon down on the Parchman Farm. Had you on my old stomping grounds.

BOY WILLIE. Me and Lymon was down there hauling wood for Jim Miller and keeping us a little bit to sell. Some white fellows tried to run us off of it. That's when Crawley got killed. They put me and Lymon in the penitentiary.

LYMON. They ambushed us right there where that road dip down and around that bend in the creek. Crawley tried to fight them. Me and Boy Willie got away but the sheriff got us. Say we was stealing wood. They shot me in my stomach.

BOY WILLIE. They looking for Lymon down there now. They rounded him up and put him in jail for not working.

LYMON. Fined me a hundred dollars. Mr. Stovall come and paid my hundred dollars and the judge say I got to work for him to pay him back his hundred dollars. I told them I'd rather take my thirty days but they wouldn't let me do that.

BOY WILLIE. As soon as Stovall turned his back, Lymon was gone. He down there living in that truck dodging the sheriff and Stovall. He got both of them looking for him. So I brought him up here.

LYMON. I told Boy Willie I'm gonna stay up here. I ain't going back with him.

BOY WILLIE. Ain't nobody twisting your arm to make you go back. You can do what you want to do.

WINING BOY. I'll go back with you. I'm on my way down there. You gonna take the train? I'm gonna take the train.

LYMON. They treat you better up here.

BOY WILLIE. I ain't worried about nobody mistreating me. They treat you like you let them treat you. They mistreat me I mistreat them right back. Ain't no difference in me and the white man.

WINING BOY. Ain't no difference as far as how somebody supposed to treat you. I agree with that. But I'll tell you the difference between the colored man and the white man. Alright. Now you take and eat some berries. They taste real good to you. So you say I'm gonna go out and get me a whole pot of these berries and cook them up to make a pie or whatever. But you ain't looked to see them berries is sitting in the white fellow's yard. Ain't got no fence around them. You figure anybody want something they'd fence it in. Alright. Now the white man come along and say that's my land. Therefore everything that grow on it belong to me. He tell the sheriff, "I want you to put this nigger in jail as a warning to all the other niggers. Otherwise first thing you know these niggers have everything that belong to us."

BOY WILLIE. I'd come back at night and haul off his whole patch while he was sleep.

WINING BOY. Alright. Now Mr. So and So, he sell the land to you. And he come to you and say, "John, you own the land. It's all yours now. But them is my berries. And come time to pick them I'm gonna send my boys over. You got the land . . . but them berries, I'm gonna keep them. They mine." And he go and fix it with the law that them is his berries. Now that's the difference between the colored man and the white man. The colored man can't fix nothing with the law.

BOY WILLIE. I don't go by what the law say. The law's liable to say anything. I go by if it's right or not. It don't matter to me what the law say. I take and look at it for myself.

LYMON. That's why you gonna end up back down there on the Parchman Farm.

BOY WILLIE. I ain't thinking about no Parchman Farm. You liable to go back before me.

LYMON. They work you too hard down there. All that weeding and hoeing and chopping down trees. I didn't like all that.

WINING BOY. You ain't got to like your job on Parchman. Hey, tell him, Doaker, the only one got to like his job is the waterboy.

DOAKER. If he don't like his job he need to set that bucket down.

BOY WILLIE. That's what they told Lymon. They had Lymon on water and everybody got mad at him cause he was lazy.

LYMON. That water was heavy.

BOY WILLIE. They had Lymon down there singing. (*Sings.*)

O Lord Berta Berta O Lord gal oh-ah
O Lord Berta Berta O Lord gal well

(LYMON *and* WINING BOY *join in.*)

Go 'head marry don't you wait on me oh-ah
Go 'head marry don't you wait on me well
Might not want you when I go free oh-ah
Might not want you when I go free well

BOY WILLIE. Come on, Doaker. Doaker know this one.

(*As* DOAKER *joins in the men stamp and clap to keep time. They sing in harmony with great fervor and style.*)

O Lord Berta Berta O Lord gal oh-ah
O Lord Berta Berta O Lord gal well

Raise them up higher, let them drop on down oh-ah
Raise them up higher, let them drop on down well
Don't know the difference when the sun go down oh-ah
Don't know the difference when the sun go down well

Berta in Meridan and she living at ease oh-ah
Berta in Meridan and she living at ease well
I'm on old Parchman, got to work or leave oh-ah
I'm on old Parchman, got to work or leave well

O Alberta, Berta, O Lord gal oh-ah
O Alberta, Berta, O Lord gal well

When you marry, don't marry no farming man oh-ah
When you marry, don't marry no farming man well
Everyday Monday, hoe handle in your hand oh-ah
Everyday Monday, hoe handle in your hand well

When you marry, marry a railroad man, oh-ah
When you marry, marry a railroad man, well
Everyday Sunday, dollar in your hand oh-ah
Everyday Sunday, dollar in your hand well

O Alberta, Berta, O Lord gal oh-ah
O Alberta, Berta, O Lord gal well

BOY WILLIE. Doaker like that part. He like that railroad part.
LYMON. Doaker sound like Tangleye. He can't sing a lick.
BOY WILLIE. Hey, Doaker, they still talk about you down on Parchman. They ask me, "You Doaker Boy's nephew?" I say, "Yeah, me and him is family." They treated me alright soon as I told them that. Say, "Yeah, he my uncle."
DOAKER. I don't never want to see none of them niggers no more.
BOY WILLIE. I don't want to see them either. Hey, Wining Boy, come on play some piano. You a piano player, play some piano. Lymon wanna hear you.
WINING BOY. I give that piano up. That was the best thing that ever happened to me, getting rid of that piano. That piano got so big and I'm carrying it around on my back. I don't wish that on nobody. See, you think it's all fun being a

recording star. Got to carrying that piano around and man did I get slow. Got just like molasses. The world just slipping by me and I'm walking around with that piano. Alright. Now, there ain't but so many places you can go. Only so many road wide enough for you and that piano. And that piano get heavier and heavier. Go to a place and they find out you play piano, the first thing they want to do is give you a drink, find you a piano, and sit you right down. And that's where you gonna be for the next eight hours. They ain't gonna let you get up! Now, the first three or four years of that is fun. You can't get enough whiskey and you can't get enough women and you don't never get tired of playing that piano. But that only last so long. You look up one day and you hate the whiskey, and you hate the women, and you hate the piano. But that's all you got. You can't do nothing else. All you know how to do is play that piano. Now, who am I? Am I me? Or am I the piano player? Sometime it seem like the only thing to do is shoot the piano player cause he the cause of all the trouble I'm having.

DOAKER. What you gonna do when your troubles get like mine?

LYMON. If I knew how to play it, I'd play it. That's a nice piano.

BOY WILLIE. Whoever playing better play quick. Sutter's brother say he waiting on me. I sell them watermelons. Get Berniece to sell that piano. Put them two parts with the part I done saved . . .

WINING BOY. Berniece ain't gonna sell that piano. I don't see why you don't know that.

BOY WILLIE. What she gonna do with it? She ain't doing nothing but letting it sit up there and rot. That piano ain't doing nobody no good.

LYMON. That's a nice piano. If I had it I'd sell it. Unless I knew how to play like Wining Boy. You can get a nice price for that piano.

DOAKER. Now I'm gonna tell you something, Lymon don't know this . . . but I'm gonna tell you why me and Wining Boy say Berniece ain't gonna sell that piano.

BOY WILLIE. She ain't got to sell it! I'm gonna sell it! Berniece ain't got no more rights to that piano than I do.

DOAKER. I'm talking to the man . . . let me talk to the man. See, now . . . to understand why we say that . . . to understand about that piano . . . you got to go back to slavery time. See, our family was owned by a fellow named Robert Sutter. That was Sutter's grandfather. Alright. The piano was owned by a fellow named Joel Nolander. He was one of the Nolander brothers from down in Georgia. It was coming up on Sutter's wedding anniversary and he was looking to buy his wife . . . Miss Ophelia was her name . . . he was looking to buy her an anniversary present. Only thing with him . . . he ain't had no money. But he had some niggers. So he asked Mr. Nolander to see if maybe he could trade off some of his niggers for that piano. Told him he would give him one and a half niggers for it. That's the way he told him. Say he could have one full grown and one half grown. Mr. Nolander agreed only he say he had to pick them. He didn't want Sutter to give him just any old nigger. He say he wanted to have the pick of the litter. So Sutter lined up his niggers, and Mr. Nolander looked them over and out of the whole bunch he picked my grandmother . . . her name was Berniece . . . same like Berniece . . . and he picked my daddy when he wasn't nothing but a little boy nine years old. They made the trade off and Miss Ophelia was so happy with that piano that it got to be just about all she would do was play on that piano.

WINING BOY. Just get up in the morning, get all dressed up and sit down and play on that piano.

DOAKER. Alright. Time go along. Time go along. Miss Ophelia got to missing my grandmother . . . the way she would cook and clean the house and talk to her and what not. And she missed having my daddy around the house to fetch things for her. So she asked to see if maybe she could trade back that piano and get her niggers back. Mr. Nolander said no. Said a deal was a deal. Him and Sutter had a big falling out about it and Miss Ophelia took sick to the bed. Wouldn't get out of the bed in the morning. She just lay there. The doctor said she was wasting away.

WINING BOY. That's when Sutter called our granddaddy up to the house.

DOAKER. Now, our granddaddy's name was Boy Willie. That's who Boy Willie's named after . . . only they called him Willie Boy. Now, he was a worker of wood. He could make you anything you wanted out of wood. He'd make you a desk. A table. A lamp. Anything you wanted. Them white fellows around there used to come up to Mr. Sutter and get him to make all kinds of things for them. Then they'd pay Mr. Sutter a nice price. See, everything my granddaddy made Mr. Sutter owned cause he owned him. That's why when Mr. Nolander offered to buy him to keep the family together Mr. Sutter wouldn't sell him. Told Mr. Nolander he didn't have enough money to buy him. Now . . . am I telling it right, Wining Boy?

WINING BOY. You telling it.

DOAKER. Sutter called him up to the house and told him to carve my grandmother and my daddy's picture on the piano for Miss Ophelia. And he took and carved this . . .

(DOAKER *crosses over to the piano.*)

See that right there? That's my grandmother, Berniece. She looked just like that. And he put a picture of my daddy when he wasn't nothing but a little boy the way he remembered him. He made them up out of his memory. Only thing . . . he didn't stop there. He carved all this. He got a picture of his mama . . . Mama Esther . . . and his daddy, Boy Charles.

WINING BOY. That was the first Boy Charles.

DOAKER. Then he put on the side here all kinds of things. See that? That's when him and Mama Berniece got married. They called it jumping the broom. That's how you got married in them days. Then he got here when my daddy was born . . . and here he got Mama Esther's funeral . . . and down here he got Mr. Nolander taking Mama Berniece and my daddy away down to his place in Georgia. He got all kinds of things what happened with our family. When Mr. Sutter seen the piano with all them carvings on it he got mad. He didn't ask for all that. But see . . . there wasn't nothing he could do about it. When Miss Ophelia seen it . . . she got excited. Now she had her piano and her niggers too. She took back to playing it and played on it right up till the day she died. Alright . . . now see, our brother Boy Charles . . . that's Berniece and Boy Willie's daddy . . . he was the oldest of us three boys. He's dead now. But he would have been fifty-seven if he had lived. He died in 1911 when he was thirty-one years old. Boy Charles used to talk about that piano all the time. He never could get it off his mind. Two or three months go by and he be talking about it again. He be talking about taking it out of Sutter's house. Say it was the story of our whole family and as long as Sutter had it . . . he had us. Say we was still in slavery. Me and Wining Boy tried to talk him out of it but it wouldn't do any good. Soon as he quiet down about it he'd start up again. We seen where he wasn't gonna get it off his mind . . . so, on the Fourth of July, 1911 . . . when Sutter was at the picnic what the county give every year . . . me and Wining Boy went on down there with him and took that piano out of Sutter's house. We put it on a wagon and me and Wining Boy carried it over into the next county with Mama Ola's people. Boy Charles decided to stay around there and wait until Sutter got home to make it look like business as usual.

Now, I don't know what happened when Sutter came home and found that piano gone. But somebody went up to Boy Charles's house and set it on fire. But he wasn't in there. He must have seen them coming cause he went down and caught the 3:57 Yellow Dog. He didn't know they was gonna come down and stop the train. Stopped the train and found Boy Charles in the boxcar with four of them hobos. Must have got mad when they couldn't find the piano cause they set the boxcar afire and killed everybody. Now, nobody know who done that. Some people say it was Sutter cause it was his piano. Some people say it was Sheriff Carter. Some people say it was Robert Smith and Ed Saunders. But don't nobody know for sure. It was about two months after that that Ed Saunders fell down his well. Just upped and fell down his well for no reason. People say it was the ghost of them men who burned up in the boxcar that pushed him in his well. They started calling them the Ghosts of the Yellow Dog. Now, that's how all that got started and that why we say Berniece ain't gonna sell that piano. Cause her daddy died over it.

BOY WILLIE. All that's in the past. If my daddy had seen where he could have traded that piano in for some land of his own, it wouldn't be sitting up here now. He spent his whole life farming on somebody else's land. I ain't gonna do that. See, he couldn't do no better. When he come along he ain't had nothing he could build on. His daddy ain't had nothing to give him. The only thing my daddy had to give me was that piano. And he died over giving me that. I ain't gonna let it sit up there and rot without trying to do something with it. If Berniece can't see that, then I'm gonna go ahead and sell my half. And you and Wining Boy know I'm right.

DOAKER. Ain't nobody said nothing about who's right and who's wrong. I was just telling the man about the piano. I was telling him why we say Berniece ain't gonna sell it.

LYMON. Yeah, I can see why you say that now. I told Boy Willie he ought to stay up here with me.

BOY WILLIE. You stay! I'm going back! That's what I'm gonna do with my life! Why I got to come up here and learn to do something I don't know how to do when I already know how to farm? You stay up here and make your own way if that's what you want to do. I'm going back and live my life the way I want to live it.

(WINING BOY *gets up and crosses to the piano.*)

WINING BOY. Let's see what we got here. I ain't played on this thing for a while.

DOAKER. You can stop telling that. You was playing on it the last time you was through here. We couldn't get you off of it. Go on and play something.

(WINING BOY *sits down at the piano and plays and sings. The song is one which has put many dimes and quarters in his pocket, long ago, in dimly remembered towns and way stations. He plays badly, without hesitation, and sings in a forceful voice.*)

WINING BOY. *(Singing.)*

I am a rambling gambling man
I gambled in many towns
I rambled this wide world over
I rambled this world around
I had my ups and downs in life
And bitter times I saw
But I never knew what misery was
Till I lit on old Arkansas.

I started out one morning
to meet that early train
He said, "You better work for me
I have some land to drain.
I'll give you fifty cents a day,
Your washing, board and all
And you shall be a different man
In the state of Arkansas."

I worked six months for the rascal
Joe Herrin was his name
He fed me old corn dodgers
They was hard as any rock
My tooth is all got loosened
And my knees begin to knock
That was the kind of hash I got
In the state of Arkansas.

Traveling man
I've traveled all around this world
Traveling man
I've traveled from land to land
Traveling man

I've traveled all around this world
Well it ain't no use
writing no news
I'm a traveling man.

(*The door opens and* BERNIECE *enters with* MARETHA.)

BERNIECE. Is that . . . Lord, I know that ain't Wining Boy sitting there.

WINING BOY. Hey, Berniece.

BERNIECE. You all had this planned. You and Boy Willie had this planned.

WINING BOY. I didn't know he was gonna be here. I'm on my way down home. I stopped by to see you and Doaker first.

DOAKER. I told the nigger he left out of here with that sack of money, we thought we might never see him again. Boy Willie say he wasn't gonna see him till he got broke. I looked up and seen him sitting on the doorstep asking for two dollars. Look at him laughing. He know it's the truth.

BERNIECE. Boy Willie, I didn't see that truck out there. I thought you was out selling watermelons.

BOY WILLIE. We done sold them all. Sold the truck too.

BERNIECE. I don't want to go through none of your stuff. I done told you to go back where you belong.

BOY WILLIE. I was just teasing you, woman. You can't take no teasing?

BERNIECE. Wining Boy, when you get here?

WINING BOY. A little while ago. I took the train from Kansas City.

BERNIECE. Let me go upstairs and change and then I'll cook you something to eat.

BOY WILLIE. You ain't cooked me nothing when I come.

BERNIECE. Boy Willie, go on and leave me alone. Come on, Maretha, get up here and change your clothes before you get them dirty.

(BERNIECE *exits up the stairs, followed by* MARETHA.)

WINING BOY. Maretha sure getting big, ain't she, Doaker. And just as pretty as she want to be. I didn't know Crawley had it in him.

(BOY WILLIE *crosses to the piano.*)

BOY WILLIE. Hey, Lymon . . . get up on the other side of this piano and let me see something.

WINING BOY. Boy Willie, what is you doing?

BOY WILLIE. I'm seeing how heavy this piano is. Get up over there, Lymon.

WINING BOY. Go on and leave that piano alone. You ain't taking that piano out of here and selling it.

BOY WILLIE. Just as soon as I get them watermelons out that truck.

WINING BOY. Well, I got something to say about that.

BOY WILLIE. This my daddy's piano.

WINING BOY. He ain't took it by himself. Me and Doaker helped him.

BOY WILLIE. He died by himself. Where was you and Doaker at then? Don't come telling me nothing about this piano. This is me and Berniece's piano. Am I right, Doaker?

DOAKER. Yeah, you right.

BOY WILLIE. Let's see if we can lift it up, Lymon. Get a good grip on it and pick it up on your end. Ready? Lift!

(As they start to move the piano, the sound of SUTTER'S GHOST *is heard.* DOAKER *is the only one to hear it. With difficulty they move the piano a little bit so it is out of place.)*

BOY WILLIE. What you think?

LYMON. It's heavy . . . but you can move it. Only it ain't gonna be easy.

BOY WILLIE. It wasn't that heavy to me. Okay, let's put it back.

(The sound of SUTTER'S GHOST *is heard again. They all hear it as* BERNIECE *enters on the stairs.)*

BERNIECE. Boy Willie . . . you gonna play around with me one too many times. And then God's gonna bless you and West is gonna dress you. Now set that piano back over there. I done told you a hundred times I ain't selling that piano.

BOY WILLIE. I'm trying to get me some land, woman. I need that piano to get me some money so I can buy Sutter's land.

BERNIECE. Money can't buy what that piano cost. You can't sell your soul for money. It won't go with the buyer. It'll shrivel and shrink to know that you ain't taken on to it. But it won't go with the buyer.

BOY WILLIE. I ain't talking about all that, woman. I ain't talking about selling my soul. I'm talking about trading that piece of wood for some land. Get something under your feet. Land the only thing God ain't making no more of. You can always get you another piano. I'm talking about some land. What you get something out the ground from. That's what I'm talking about. You can't do nothing with that piano but sit up there and look at it.

BERNIECE. That's just what I'm gonna do. Wining Boy, you want me to fry you some pork chops?

BOY WILLIE. Now, I'm gonna tell you the way I see it. The only thing that make that piano worth something is them carvings Papa Willie Boy put on there. That's what make it worth something. That was my great-grandaddy. Papa Boy Charles brought that piano into the house. Now, I'm supposed to build on what they left me. You can't do nothing with that piano sitting up here in the house. That's just like if I let them watermelons sit out there and rot. I'd be a fool. Alright now, if you say to me, Boy Willie, I'm using that piano. I give out lessons on it and that help me make my rent or whatever. Then that be something else. I'd have to go on and say, well, Berniece using that piano. She building on it. Let her go on and use it. I got to find another way to get Sutter's land. But Doaker say you ain't touched that piano the whole time it's been up here. So why you wanna stand in my way? See, you just looking at the sentimental value. See, that's good. That's alright. I take my hat off whenever somebody say my daddy's name. But I ain't gonna be no fool about no sentimental value. You can sit up here and look at the piano for the next hundred years and it's just gonna be a piano. You can't make more than that. Now I want to get Sutter's land with that piano. I get Sutter's land and I can go down and cash in the crop and get my seed. As long as I got the land and the seed then I'm alright. I can always get me a little something else. Cause that land give back to you. I can make me another crop and cash that in. I still got the land and the seed. But that piano don't put out nothing else. You ain't got nothing working for you. Now, the kind of man my daddy was he would have understood that. I'm sorry you can't see it that way. But that's why I'm gonna take that piano out of here and sell it.

BERNIECE. You ain't taking that piano out of my house.

(She crosses to the piano.)

Look at this piano. Look at it. Mama Ola polished this piano with her tears for seventeen years. For seventeen years she rubbed on it till her hands bled. Then she rubbed the blood in . . . mixed it up with the rest of the blood on it. Every day that God breathed life into her body she rubbed and cleaned and polished and prayed over it. "Play something for me, Berniece. Play something for me, Berniece." Every day. "I cleaned it up for you, play something for me, Berniece." You always talking about your daddy but you ain't never stopped to look at what his foolishness cost your mama. Seventeen years' worth of cold nights and an empty bed. For what? For a piano? For a piece of wood? To get even with somebody? I look at you and you're all the same. You, Papa Boy Charles, Wining Boy, Doaker, Crawley . . . you're all alike. All this thieving and killing and thieving and killing. And what it ever lead to? More killing and more thieving. I ain't never seen it come to nothing. People getting burned up. People getting shot. People falling down their wells. It don't never stop.

DOAKER. Come on now, Berniece, ain't no need in getting upset.

BOY WILLIE. I done a little bit of stealing here and there, but I ain't never killed nobody. I can't be speaking for nobody else. You all got to speak for yourself, but I ain't never killed nobody.

BERNIECE. You killed Crawley just as sure as if you pulled the trigger.

BOY WILLIE. See, that's ignorant. That's downright foolish for you to say something like that. You ain't doing nothing but showing your ignorance. If the nigger was here I'd whup his ass for getting me and Lymon shot at.

BERNIECE. Crawley ain't knew about the wood.

BOY WILLIE. We told the man about the wood. Ask Lymon. He knew all about the wood. He seen we was sneaking it. Why else we gonna be out there at night? Don't come telling me Crawley ain't knew about the wood. Them fellows come up on us and Crawley tried to bully them. Me and Lymon seen the sheriff with them and give in. Wasn't no sense in getting killed over fifty dollars' worth of wood.

BERNIECE. Crawley ain't knew you stole that wood.

BOY WILLIE. We ain't stole no wood. Me and Lymon was hauling wood for Jim Miller and keeping us a little bit on the side. We dumped our little bit down there by the creek till we had enough to make a load. Some fellows seen us and we figured we better get it before they did. We come up there and got Crawley to help us load it. Figured we'd cut him in. Crawley trying to keep the wolf from his door . . . we was trying to help him.

LYMON. Me and Boy Willie told him about the wood. We told him some fellows might be trying to beat us to it. He say let me go back and get my thirty-eight. That's what caused all the trouble.

BOY WILLIE. If Crawley ain't had the gun he'd be alive today.

LYMON. We had it about half loaded when they come up on us. We seen the sheriff with them and we tried to get away. We ducked around near the bend in the creek . . . but they was down there too. Boy Willie say let's give in. But Crawley pulled out his gun and started shooting. That's when they started shooting back.

BERNIECE. All I know is Crawley would be alive if you hadn't come up there and got him.

BOY WILLIE. I ain't had nothing to do with Crawley getting killed. That was his own fault.

BERNIECE. Crawley's dead and in the ground and you still walking around here eating. That's all I know. He went off to load some wood with you and ain't never come back.

BOY WILLIE. I told you, woman . . . I ain't had nothing to do with . . .

BERNIECE. He ain't here, is he? He ain't here!

(BERNIECE *hits* BOY WILLIE.)

I said he ain't here. Is he?

(BERNIECE *continues to hit* BOY WILLIE, *who doesn't move to defend himself, other than back up and turning his head so that most of the blows fall on his chest and arms.*)

DOAKER. (*Grabbing* BERNIECE.) Come on, Berniece . . . let it go, it ain't his fault.

BERNIECE. He ain't here, is he? Is he?

BOY WILLIE. I told you I ain't responsible for Crawley.

BERNIECE. He ain't here.

BOY WILLIE. Come on now, Berniece . . . don't do this now. Doaker, get her. I ain't had nothing to do with Crawley . . .

BERNIECE. You come up there and got him!

BOY WILLIE. I done told you now. Doaker, get her. I ain't playing.

DOAKER. Come on. Berniece.

(MARETHA *is heard screaming upstairs. It is a scream of stark terror.*)

MARETHA. Mama! . . . Mama!

(*The lights go down to black. End of Act 1.*)

ACT 2

SCENE 1

(*The lights come up on the kitchen. It is the following morning.* DOAKER *is ironing the pants to his uniform. He has a pot cooking on the stove at the same time. He is singing a song. The song provides him with the rhythm for his work and he moves about the kitchen with the ease born of many years as a railroad cook.*)

DOAKER.

Gonna leave Jackson Mississippi
and go to Memphis

and double back to Jackson
Come on down to Hattiesburg
Change cars on the Y.D.
coming through the territory to
Meridian
and Meridian to Greenville
and Greenville to Memphis
I'm on my way and I know where

Change cars on the Katy
Leaving Jackson
and going through Clarksdale
Hello Winona!
Courtland!
Bateville!
Como!
Senatobia!
Lewisberg!
Sunflower!
Glendora!
Sharkey!
And double back to Jackson
Hello Greenwood
I'm on my way Memphis
Clarksdale
Moorhead
Indianola
Can a highball pass through?
Highball on through sir
Grand Carson!
Thirty First Street Depot
Fourth Street Depot
Memphis!

(WINING BOY *enters carrying a suit of clothes.*)

DOAKER. I thought you took that suit to the pawnshop?

WINING BOY. I went down there and the man tell me the suit is too old. Look at this suit. This is one hundred percent silk! How a silk suit gonna get too old? I know what it was he just didn't want to give me five dollars for it. Best he wanna give me is three dollars. I figure a silk suit is worth five dollars all over the world. I wasn't gonna part with it for no three dollars so I brought it back.

DOAKER. They got another pawnshop up on Wylie.

WINING BOY. I carried it up there. He say he don't take no clothes. Only thing he take is guns and radios. Maybe a guitar or two. Where's Berniece?

DOAKER. Berniece still at work. Boy Willie went down there to meet Lymon this morning. I guess they got that truck fixed, they been out there all day and ain't come back yet. Maretha scared to sleep up there now. Berniece don't know, but I seen Sutter before she did.

WINING BOY. Say what?

DOAKER. About three weeks ago. I had just come back from down there. Sutter couldn't have been dead more than three days. He was sitting over there at the piano. I come out to go to work . . . and he was sitting right there. Had his hand on top of his head just like Berniece said. I believe he broke his neck when he fell in the well. I kept quiet about it. I didn't see no reason to upset Berniece.

WINING BOY. Did he say anything? Did he say he was looking for Boy Willie?

DOAKER. He was just sitting there. He ain't said nothing. I went on out the door and left him sitting there. I figure as long as he was on the other side of the room everything be alright. I don't know what I would have done if he had started walking toward me.

WINING BOY. Berniece say he was calling Boy Willie's name.

DOAKER. I ain't heard him say nothing. He was just sitting there when I seen him. But I don't believe Boy Willie pushed him in the well. Sutter here cause of that piano. I heard him playing on it one time. I thought it was Berniece but then she don't play that kind of music. I come out here and ain't seen nobody, but them piano keys was moving a mile a minute. Berniece need to go on and get rid of it. It ain't done nothing but cause trouble.

WINING BOY. I agree with Berniece. Boy Charles ain't took it to give it back. He took it cause he figure he had more right to it than Sutter did. If Sutter can't understand that . . . then that's just the way that go. Sutter dead and in the ground . . . don't care where his ghost is. He can hover around and play on the piano all he want. I want to see him carry it out the house. That's what I want to see. What time Berniece get home? I don't see how I let her get away from me this morning.

DOAKER. You up there sleep. Berniece leave out of here early in the morning. She out there in Squirrel Hill cleaning house for some bigshot down there at the steel mill. They don't like you to come late. You come late they won't give you your carfare. What kind of business you got with Berniece?

WINING BOY. My business. I ain't asked you what kind of business you got.

DOAKER. Berniece ain't got no money. If that's why you was trying to catch her. She having a hard enough time trying to get by as it is. If she go ahead and marry Avery . . . he working every day . . . she go ahead and marry him they could do alright for themselves. But as it stands she ain't got no money.

WINING BOY. Well, let me have five dollars.

DOAKER. I just give you a dollar before you left out of here. You ain't gonna take my five dollars out there and gamble and drink it up.

WINING BOY. Aw, nigger, give me five dollars. I'll give it back to you.

DOAKER. You wasn't looking to give me five dollars when you had that sack of money. You wasn't looking to throw nothing my way. Now you wanna come in here and borrow five dollars. If you going back with Boy Willie you need to be trying to figure out how you gonna get train fare.

WINING BOY. That's why I need the five dollars. If I had five dollars I could get me some money.

(DOAKER *goes into his pocket.*)

Make it seven.

DOAKER. You take this five dollars . . . and you bring my money back here too.

(BOY WILLIE *and* LYMON *enter. They are happy and excited. They have money in all of their pockets and are anxious to count it.*)

DOAKER. How'd you do out there?

BOY WILLIE. They was lining up for them.

LYMON. Me and Boy Willie couldn't sell them fast enough. Time we got one sold we'd sell another.

BOY WILLIE. I seen what was happening and told Lymon to up the price on them.

LYMON. Boy Willie say charge them a quarter more. They didn't care. A couple of people give me a dollar and told me to keep the change.

BOY WILLIE. One fellow bought five. I say now what he gonna do with five watermelons? He can't eat them all. I sold him the five and asked him did he want to buy five more.

LYMON. I ain't never seen nobody snatch a dollar fast as Boy Willie.

BOY WILLIE. One lady asked me say, "Is they sweet?" I told her say, "Lady, where we grow these watermelons we put sugar in the ground." You know, she believed me. Talking about she had never heard of that before. Lymon was laughing his head off. I told her, "Oh, yeah, we put the sugar right in the ground with the seed." She say, "Well, give me another one." Them white folks is something else . . . ain't they, Lymon?

LYMON. Soon as you holler watermelons they come right out their door. Then they go and get their neighbors. Look like they having a contest to see who can buy the most.

WINING BOY. I got something for Lymon.

(WINING BOY *goes to get his suit.* BOY WILLIE *and* LYMON *continue to count their money.*)

BOY WILLIE. I know you got more than that. You ain't sold all them watermelons for that little bit of money.

LYMON. I'm still looking. That ain't all you got either. Where's all them quarters?

BOY WILLIE. You let me worry about the quarters. Just put the money on the table.

WINING BOY. (*Entering with his suit.*) Look here, Lymon . . . see this? Look at his eyes getting big. He ain't never seen a suit like this. This is one hundred percent silk. Go ahead . . . put it on. See if it fit you.

(LYMON *tries the suit coat on.*)

Look at that. Feel it. That's one hundred percent genuine silk. I got that in Chicago. You can't get clothes like that nowhere but New York and Chicago. You can't get clothes like that in Pittsburgh. These folks in Pittsburgh ain't never seen clothes like that.

LYMON. This is nice, feel real nice and smooth.

WINING BOY. That's a fifty-five-dollar suit. That's the kind of suit the bigshots wear. You need a pistol and a pocketful of money to wear that suit. I'll let you have it for three dollars. The women will fall out their windows they see you in a suit like that. Give me three dollars and go on and wear it down the street and get you a woman.

BOY WILLIE. That looks nice, Lymon. Put the pants on. Let me see it with the pants.

(LYMON *begins to try on the pants.*)

WINING BOY. Look at that . . . see how it fits you? Give me three dollars and go on and take it. Look at that, Doaker . . . don't he look nice?

DOAKER. Yeah . . . that's a nice suit.

WINING BOY. Got a shirt to go with it. Cost you an extra dollar. Four dollars you got the whole deal.

LYMON. How this look, Boy Willie?

BOY WILLIE. That look nice . . . if you like that kind of thing. I don't like them dress-up kind of clothes. If you like it, look real nice.

WINING BOY. That's the kind of suit you need for up here in the North.

LYMON. Four dollars for everything? The suit and the shirt?

WINING BOY. That's cheap. I should be charging you twenty dollars. I give you a break cause you a homeboy. That's the only way I let you have it for four dollars.

LYMON. (*Going into his pocket.*) Okay . . . here go the four dollars.

WINING BOY. You got some shoes? What size you wear?

LYMON. Size nine.

WINING BOY. That's what size I got! Size nine. I let you have them for three dollars.

LYMON. Where they at? Let me see them.

WINING BOY. They real nice shoes, too. Got a nice tip to them. Got pointy toe just like you want.

(WINING BOY *goes to get his shoes.*)

LYMON. Come on, Boy Willie, let's go out tonight. I wanna see what it looks like up here. Maybe we go to a picture show. Hey, Doaker, they got picture shows up here?

DOAKER. The Rhumba Theater. Right down there on Fullerton Street. Can't miss it. Got the speakers outside on the sidewalk. You can hear it a block away. Boy Willie know where it's at.

(DOAKER *exits into his room.*)

LYMON. Let's go to the picture show, Boy Willie. Let's go find some women.

BOY WILLIE. Hey, Lymon, how many of them watermelons would you say we got left? We got just under a half a load . . . right?

LYMON. About that much. Maybe a little more.

BOY WILLIE. You think that piano will fit up in there?

LYMON. If we stack them watermelons you can sit it up in the front there.

BOY WILLIE. I'm gonna call that man tomorrow.

WINING BOY. (*Returns with his shoes.*) Here you go . . . size nine. Put them on. Cost you three dollars. That's a Florsheim shoe. That's the kind Staggerlee wore.

LYMON. (*Trying on the shoes.*) You sure these size nine?

WINING BOY. You can look at my feet and see we wear the same size. Man, you put on that suit and them shoes and you got something there. You ready for whatever's out there. But is they ready for you? With them shoes on you be the King of the Walk. Have everybody stop to look at your shoes. Wishing they had a pair. I'll give you a break. Go on and take them for two dollars.

(LYMON *pays* WINING BOY *two dollars.*)

LYMON. Come on, Boy Willie . . . let's go find some women. I'm gonna go upstairs and get ready. I'll be ready to go in a minute. Ain't you gonna get dressed?

BOY WILLIE. I'm gonna wear what I got on. I ain't dressing up for these city niggers.

(LYMON *exits up the stairs.*)

That's all Lymon think about is women.

WINING BOY. His daddy was the same way. I used to run around with him. I know his mama too. Two strokes back and I would have been his daddy! His daddy's dead now . . . but I got the nigger out of jail one time. They was fixing to name him Daniel and walk him through the Lion's Den. He got in a tussle with one of them white fellows and the sheriff lit on him like white on rice. That's how the whole thing come about between me and Lymon's mama. She knew me and his daddy used to run together and he got in jail and she went down there and took the sheriff a hundred dollars. Don't get me to lying about where she got it from. I don't know. The sheriff looked at that hundred dollars and turned his nose up. Told her, say, "That ain't gonna do him no good. You got to put another hundred on top of that." She come up there and got me where I was playing at this saloon . . . said she had all but fifty dollars and asked me if I could help. Now the way I figured it . . . without that fifty dollars the sheriff was gonna turn him over to Parchman. The sheriff turn him over to Parchman it be three years before anybody see him again. Now I'm gonna say it right . . . I will give anybody fifty dollars to keep them out of jail for three years. I give her the fifty dollars and she told me to come over to the house. I ain't asked her. I figure if she was nice enough to invite me I ought to go. I ain't had to say a word. She invited me over just as nice. Say, "Why don't you come over to the house?" She ain't had to say nothing else. Them words rolled off her tongue just as nice. I went on down there and sat about three hours. Started to leave and changed my mind. She grabbed hold to me and say, "Baby, it's all night long." That was one of the shortest nights I have ever spent on this earth! I could have used another eight hours. Lymon's daddy didn't even say nothing to me when he got out. He just looked at me funny. He had a good notion something had happened between me an' her. L. D. Jackson. That was one bad-luck nigger. Got killed at some dance. Fellow walked in and shot him thinking he was somebody else.

(DOAKER *enters from his room.*)

Hey, Doaker, you remember L. D. Jackson?

DOAKER. That's Lymon's daddy. That was one bad-luck nigger.

BOY WILLIE. Look like you ready to railroad some.

DOAKER. Yeah, I got to make that run.

(LYMON enters from the stairs. He is dressed in his new suit and shoes, to which he has added a cheap straw hat.)

LYMON. How I look?

WINING BOY. You look like a million dollars. Don't he look good, Doaker? Come on, let's play some cards. You wanna play some cards?

BOY WILLIE. We ain't gonna play no cards with you. Me and Lymon gonna find some women. Hey, Lymon, don't play no cards with Wining Boy. He'll take all your money.

WINING BOY. *(To* LYMON.*)* You got a magic suit there. You can get you a woman easy with that suit . . . but you got to know the magic words. You know the magic words to get you a woman?

LYMON. I just talk to them to see if I like them and they like me.

WINING BOY. You just walk right up to them and say, "If you got the harbor I got the ship." If that don't work ask them if you can put them in your pocket. The first thing they gonna say is, "It's too small." That's when you look them dead in the eye and say, "Baby, ain't nothing small about me." If that don't work then you move on to another one. Am I telling him right, Doaker?

DOAKER. That man don't need you to tell him nothing about no women. These women these days ain't gonna fall for that kind of stuff. You got to buy them a present. That's what they looking for these days.

BOY WILLIE. Come on, I'm ready. You ready, Lymon? Come on, let's go find some women.

WINING BOY. Here, let me walk out with you. I wanna see the women fall out their window when they see Lymon.

(They all exit and the lights go down on the scene.)

SCENE 2

(The lights come up on the kitchen. It is late evening of the same day. BERNIECE *has set a tub for her bath in the kitchen. She is heating up water on the stove. There is a knock at the door.)*

BERNIECE. Who is it?

AVERY. It's me, Avery.

*(*BERNIECE *opens the door and lets him in.)*

BERNIECE. Avery, come on in. I was just fixing to take my bath.

AVERY. Where Boy Willie? I see that truck out there almost empty. They done sold almost all them watermelons.

BERNIECE. They was gone when I come home. I don't know where they went off to. Boy Willie around here about to drive me crazy.

AVERY. They sell them watermelons . . . he'll be gone soon.

BERNIECE. What Mr. Cohen say about letting you have the place?

AVERY. He say he'll let me have it for thirty dollars a month. I talked him out of thirty-five and he say he'll let me have it for thirty.

BERNIECE. That's a nice spot next to Benny Diamond's store.

AVERY. Berniece . . . I be at home and I get to thinking you up here an' I'm down there. I get to thinking how that look to have a preacher that ain't married. It makes for a better congregation if the preacher was settled down and married.

BERNIECE. Avery . . . not now. I was fixing to take my bath.

AVERY. You know how I feel about you, Berniece. Now . . . I done got the place from Mr. Cohen. I get the money from the bank and I can fix it up real nice. They give me a ten cents a hour raise down there on the job . . . now Berniece, I ain't got much in the way of comforts. I got a hole in my pockets near about as far as money is concerned. I ain't never found no way through life to a woman I care about like I care about you. I need that. I need somebody on my bond side. I need a woman that fits in my hand.

BERNIECE. Avery, I ain't ready to get married now.

AVERY. You too young a woman to close up, Berniece.

BERNIECE. I ain't said nothing about closing up. I got a lot of woman left in me.

AVERY. Where's it at? When's the last time you looked at it?

BERNIECE. (*Stunned by his remark.*) That's a nasty thing to say. And you call yourself a preacher.

AVERY. Anytime I get anywhere near you . . . you push me away.

BERNIECE. I got enough on my hands with Maretha. I got enough people to love and take care of.

AVERY. Who you got to love you? Can't nobody get close enough to you. Doaker can't half say nothing to you. You jump all over Boy Willie. Who you got to love you, Berniece?

BERNIECE. You trying to tell me a woman can't be nothing without a man. But you alright, huh? You can just walk out of here without me—without a woman— and still be a man. That's alright. Ain't nobody gonna ask you, "Avery, who you got to love you?" That's alright for you. But everybody gonna be worried about Berniece. "How Berniece gonna take care of herself? How she gonna raise that child without a man? Wonder what she do with herself. How she gonna live like that?" Everybody got all kinds of questions for Berniece. Everybody telling me I can't be a woman unless I got a man. Well, you tell me, Avery—you know—how much woman am I?

AVERY. It wasn't me, Berniece. You can't blame me for nobody else. I'll own up to my own shortcomings. But you can't blame me for Crawley or nobody else.

BERNIECE. I ain't blaming nobody for nothing. I'm just stating the facts.

AVERY. How long you gonna carry Crawley with you, Berniece? It's been over three years. At some point you got to let go and go on. Life's got all kinds of twists and turns. That don't mean you stop living. That don't mean you cut yourself off from life. You can't go through life carrying Crawley's ghost with you. Crawley's been dead three years. Three years, Berniece.

BERNIECE. I know how long Crawley's been dead. You ain't got to tell me that. I just ain't ready to get married right now.

AVERY. What is you ready for, Berniece? You just gonna drift along from day to day. Life is more than making it from one day to another. You gonna look up one day and it's all gonna be past you. Life's gonna be gone out of your hands—there won't be enough to make nothing with. I'm standing here now, Berniece—but I don't know how much longer I'm gonna be standing here waiting on you.

BERNIECE. Avery, I told you . . . when you get your church we'll sit down and talk about this. I got too many other things to deal with right now. Boy Willie and the piano . . . and Sutter's ghost. I thought I might have been seeing things, but Maretha done seen Sutter's ghost, too.

AVERY. When this happen, Berniece?

BERNIECE. Right after I came home yesterday. Me and Boy Willie was arguing about the piano and Sutter's ghost was standing at the top of the stairs. Maretha scared to sleep up there now. Maybe if you bless the house he'll go away.

AVERY. I don't know, Berniece. I don't know if I should fool around with something like that.

BERNIECE. I can't have Maretha scared to go to sleep up there. Seem like if you bless the house he would go away.

AVERY. You might have to be a special kind of preacher to do something like that.

BERNIECE. I keep telling myself when Boy Willie leave he'll go on and leave with him. I believe Boy Willie pushed him in the well.

AVERY. That's been going on down there a long time. The Ghosts of the Yellow Dog been pushing people in their wells long before Boy Willie got grown.

BERNIECE. Somebody down there pushing them people in their wells. They ain't just upped and fell. Ain't no wind pushed nobody in their well.

AVERY. Oh, I don't know. God works in mysterious ways.

BERNIECE. He ain't pushed nobody in their wells.

AVERY. He caused it to happen. God is the Great Causer. He can do anything. He parted the Red Sea. He say I will smite my enemies. Reverend Thompson used to preach on the Ghosts of the Yellow Dog as the hand of God.

BERNIECE. I don't care who preached what. Somebody down there pushing them people in their wells. Somebody like Boy Willie. I can see him doing something like that. You ain't gonna tell me that Sutter just upped and fell in his well. I believe Boy Willie pushed him so he could get his land.

AVERY. What Doaker say about Boy Willie selling the piano?

BERNIECE. Doaker don't want no part of that piano. He ain't never wanted no part of it. He blames himself for not staying behind with Papa Boy Charles. He washed his hands of that piano a long time ago. He didn't want me to bring it up here—but I wasn't gonna leave it down there.

AVERY. Well, it seems to me somebody ought to be able to talk to Boy Willie.

BERNIECE. You can't talk to Boy Willie. He been that way all his life. Mama Ola had her hands full trying to talk to him. He don't listen to nobody. He just like my daddy. He get his mind fixed on something and can't nobody turn him from it.

AVERY. You ought to start a choir at the church. Maybe if he seen you was doing something with it—if you told him you was gonna put it in my church—maybe he'd see it different. You ought to put it down in the church and start a choir. The Bible say "Make a joyful noise unto the Lord." Maybe if Boy Willie see you was doing something with it he'd see it different.

BERNIECE. I done told you I don't play on that piano. Ain't no need in you to keep talking this choir stuff. When my mama died I shut the top on that piano and

I ain't never opened it since. I was only playing it for her. When my daddy died seem like all her life went into that piano. She used to have me playing on it . . . had Miss Eula come in and teach me . . . say when I played it she could hear my daddy talking to her. I used to think them pictures came alive and walked through the house. Sometime late at night I could hear my mama talking to them. I said that wasn't gonna happen to me. I don't play that piano cause I don't want to wake them spirits. They never be walking around in this house.

AVERY. You got to put all that behind you, Berniece.

BERNIECE. I got Maretha playing on it. She don't know nothing about it. Let her go on and be a schoolteacher or something. She don't have to carry all of that with her. She got a chance I didn't have. I ain't gonna burden her with that piano.

AVERY. You got to put all of that behind you, Berniece. That's the same thing like Crawley. Everybody got stones in their passway. You got to step over them or walk around them. You picking them up and carrying them with you. All you got to do is set them down by the side of the road. You ain't got to carry them with you. You can walk over there right now and play that piano. You can walk over there right now and God will walk over there with you. Right now you can set that sack of stones down by the side of the road and walk away from it. You don't have to carry it with you. You can do it right now.

(AVERY *crosses over to the piano and raises the lid.*)

Come on, Berniece . . . set it down and walk away from it. Come on, play "Old Ship of Zion." Walk over here and claim it as an instrument of the Lord. You can walk over here right now and make it into a celebration.

(BERNIECE *moves toward the piano.*)

BERNIECE. Avery . . . I done told you I don't want to play that piano. Now or no other time.

AVERY. The Bible say, "The Lord is my refuge . . . and my strength!" With the strength of God you can put the past behind you, Berniece. With the strength of God you can do anything! God got a bright tomorrow. God don't ask what you done . . . God ask what you gonna do. The strength of God can move mountains! God's got a bright tomorrow for you . . . all you got to do is walk over here and claim it.

BERNIECE. Avery, just go on and let me finish my bath. I'll see you tomorrow.

AVERY. Okay, Berniece. I'm gonna go home. I'm gonna go home and read up on my Bible. And tomorrow . . . if the good Lord give me strength tomor- row . . . I'm gonna come by and bless the house . . . and show you the power of the Lord.

(AVERY *crosses to the door.*)

It's gonna be alright, Berniece. God say he will soothe the troubled waters. I'll come by tomorrow and bless the house.

(*The lights go down to black.*)

SCENE 3

(Several hours later. The house is dark. BERNIECE *has retired for the night.* BOY WILLIE *enters the darkened house with* GRACE.*)*

BOY WILLIE. Come on in. This my sister's house. My sister live here. Come on, I ain't gonna bite you.

GRACE. Put some light on. I can't see.

BOY WILLIE. You don't need to see nothing, baby. This here is all you need to see. All you need to do is see me. If you can't see me you can feel me in the dark. How's that, sugar?

(He attempts to kiss her.)

GRACE. Go on now . . . wait!

BOY WILLIE. Just give me one little old kiss.

GRACE. *(Pushing him away.)* Come on, now. Where I'm gonna sleep at?

BOY WILLIE. We got to sleep out here on the couch. Come on, my sister don't mind. Lymon come back he just got to sleep on the floor. He run off with Dolly somewhere he better stay there. Come on, sugar.

GRACE. Wait now . . . you ain't told me nothing about no couch. I thought you had a bed. Both of us can't sleep on that little old couch.

BOY WILLIE. It don't make no difference. We can sleep on the floor. Let Lymon sleep on the couch.

GRACE. You ain't told me nothing about no couch.

BOY WILLIE. What difference it make? You just wanna be with me.

GRACE. I don't want to be with you on no couch. Ain't you got no bed?

BOY WILLIE. You don't need no bed, woman. My granddaddy used to take women on the backs of horses. What you need a bed for? You just want to be with me.

GRACE. You sure is country. I didn't know you was this country.

BOY WILLIE. There's a lot of things you don't know about me. Come on, let me show you what this country boy can do.

GRACE. Let's go to my place. I got a room with a bed if Leroy don't come back there.

BOY WILLIE. Who's Leroy? You ain't said nothing about no Leroy.

GRACE. He used to be my man. He ain't coming back. He gone off with some other gal.

BOY WILLIE. You let him have your key?

GRACE. He ain't coming back.

BOY WILLIE. Did you let him have your key?

GRACE. He got a key but he ain't coming back. He took off with some other gal.

BOY WILLIE. I don't wanna go nowhere he might come. Let's stay here. Come on, sugar.

(He pulls her over to the couch.)

Let me heist your hood and check your oil. See if your battery needs charged.

(He pulls her to him. They kiss and tug at each other's clothing. In their anxiety they knock over a lamp.)

BERNIECE. Who's that . . . Wining Boy?

BOY WILLIE. It's me . . . Boy Willie. Go on back to sleep. Everything's alright.

(To GRACE.*)*

That's my sister. Everything's alright, Berniece. Go on back to sleep.

BERNIECE. What you doing down there? What you done knocked over?

BOY WILLIE. It wasn't nothing. Everything's alright. Go on back to sleep.

(To GRACE.*)*

That's my sister. We alright. She gone back to sleep.

(They begin to kiss. BERNIECE *enters from the stairs dressed in a nightgown. She cuts on the light.)*

BERNIECE. Boy Willie, what you doing down here?

BOY WILLIE. It was just that there lamp. It ain't broke. It's okay. Everything's alright. Go on back to bed.

BERNIECE. Boy Willie, I don't allow that in my house. You gonna have to take your company someplace else.

BOY WILLIE. It's alright. We ain't doing nothing. We just sitting here talking. This here is Grace. That's my sister Berniece.

BERNIECE. You know I don't allow that kind of stuff in my house.

BOY WILLIE. Allow what? We just sitting here talking.

BERNIECE. Well, your company gonna have to leave. Come back and talk in the morning.

BOY WILLIE. Go on back upstairs now.

BERNIECE. I got an eleven-year-old girl upstairs. I can't allow that around here.

BOY WILLIE. Ain't nobody said nothing about that. I told you we just talking.

GRACE. Come on . . . let's go to my place. Ain't nobody got to tell me to leave but once.

BOY WILLIE. You ain't got to be like that, Berniece.

BERNIECE. I'm sorry, Miss. But he know I don't allow that in here.

GRACE. You ain't got to tell me but once. I don't stay nowhere I ain't wanted.

BOY WILLIE. I don't know why you want to embarrass me in front of my company.

GRACE. Come on, take me home.

BERNIECE. Go on, Boy Willie. Just go on with your company.

*(*BOY WILLIE *and* GRACE *exit.* BERNIECE *puts the light on in the kitchen and puts on the teakettle. Presently there is a knock at the door.* BERNIECE *goes to answer it.* BERNIECE *opens the door.* LYMON *enters.)*

LYMON. How you doing, Berniece? I thought you'd be asleep. Boy Willie been back here?

BERNIECE. He just left out of here a minute ago.

LYMON. I went out to see a picture show and never got there. We always end up doing something else. I was with this woman she just wanted to drink up all my money. So I left her there and came back looking for Boy Willie.

BERNIECE. You just missed him. He just left out of here.

LYMON. They got some nice-looking women in this city. I'm gonna like it up here real good. I like seeing them with their dresses on. Got them high heels. I like that. Make them look like they real precious. Boy Willie met a real nice one today. I wish I had met her before he did.

BERNIECE. He come by here with some woman a little while ago. I told him to go on and take all that out of my house.

LYMON. What she look like, the woman he was with? Was she a brown-skinned woman about this high? Nice and healthy? Got nice hips on her?

BERNIECE. She had on a red dress.

LYMON. That's her! That's Grace. She real nice. Laugh a lot. Lot of fun to be with. She don't be trying to put on. Some of these women act like they the Queen of Sheba. I don't like them kind. Grace ain't like that. She real nice with herself.

BERNIECE. I don't know what she was like. He come in here all drunk knocking over the lamp, and making all kind of noise. I told them to take that somewhere else. I can't really say what she was like.

LYMON. She real nice. I seen her before he did. I was trying not to act like I seen her. I wanted to look at her a while before I said something. She seen me when I come into the saloon. I tried to act like I didn't see her. Time I looked around Boy Willie was talking to her. She was talking to him kept looking at me. That's when her friend Dolly came. I asked her if she wanted to go to the picture show. She told me to buy her a drink while she thought about it. Next thing I knew she done had three drinks talking about she too tired to go. I bought her another drink, then I left. Boy Willie was gone and I thought he might have come back here. Doaker gone, huh? He say he had to make a trip.

BERNIECE. Yeah, he gone on his trip. This is when I can usually get me some peace and quiet, Maretha asleep.

LYMON. She look just like you. Got them big eyes. I remember her when she was in diapers.

BERNIECE. Time just keep on. It go on with or without you. She going on twelve.

LYMON. She sure is pretty. I like kids.

BERNIECE. Boy Willie say you staying . . . what you gonna do up here in this big city? You thought about that?

LYMON. They never get me back down there. The sheriff looking for me. All because they gonna try and make me work for somebody when I don't want to. They gonna try and make me work for Stovall when he don't pay nothing. It ain't like that up here. Up here you more or less do what you want to. I figure I find me a job and try to get set up and then see what the year brings. I tried to do that two or three times down there . . . but it never would work out. I was always in the wrong place.

BERNIECE. This ain't a bad city once you get to know your way around.

LYMON. Up here is different. I'm gonna get me a job unloading boxcars or something. One fellow told me say he know a place. I'm gonna go over there with him next week. Me and Boy Willie finish selling them watermelons I'll have enough money to hold me for a while. But I'm gonna go over there and see what kind of jobs they have.

BERNIECE. You shouldn't have too much trouble finding a job. It's all in how you present yourself. See now, Boy Willie couldn't get no job up here. Somebody hire him they got a pack of trouble on their hands. Soon as they find that out they fire him. He don't want to do nothing unless he do it his way.

LYMON. I know. I told him let's go to the picture show first and see if there was any women down there. They might get tired of sitting at home and walk down to the picture show. He say he wanna look around first. We never did get down there. We tried a couple of places and then we went to this saloon where he met Grace. I tried to meet her before he did but he beat me to her. We left Wining Boy sitting down there running his mouth. He told me if I wear this suit I'd find me a woman. He was almost right.

BERNIECE. You don't need to be out there in them saloons. Ain't no telling what you liable to run into out there. This one liable to cut you as quick as that one shoot you. You don't need to be out there. You start out that fast life you can't keep it up. It makes you old quick. I don't know what them women out there be thinking about.

LYMON. Mostly they be lonely and looking for somebody to spend the night with them. Sometimes it matters who it is and sometimes it don't. I used to be the same way. Now it got to matter. That's why I'm here now. Dolly liable not to even recognize me if she sees me again. I don't like women like that. I like my women to be with me in a nice and easy way. That way we can both enjoy ourselves. The way I see it we the only two people like us in the world. We got to see how we fit together. A woman that don't want to take the time to do that I don't bother with. Used to. Used to bother with all of them. Then I woke up one time with this woman and I didn't know who she was. She was the prettiest woman I had ever seen in my life. I spent the whole night with her and didn't even know it. I had never taken the time to look at her. I guess she kinda knew I ain't never really looked at her. She must have known that cause she ain't wanted to see me no more. If she had wanted to see me I believe we might have got married. How come you ain't married? It seem like to me you would be married. I remember Avery from down home. I used to call him plain old Avery. Now he Reverend Avery. That's kinda funny about him becoming a preacher. I like when he told about how that come to him in a dream about them sheep people and them hobos. Nothing ever come to me in a dream like that. I just dream about women. Can't never seem to find the right one.

BERNIECE. She out there somewhere. You just got to get yourself ready to meet her. That's what I'm trying to do. Avery's alright. I ain't really got nobody in mind.

LYMON. I get me a job and a little place and get set up to where I can make a woman comfortable I might get married. Avery's nice. You ought to go ahead and get married. You be a preacher's wife you won't have to work. I hate living by myself. I didn't want to be no strain on my mama so I left home when I was about sixteen. Everything I tried seem like it just didn't work out. Now I'm trying this.

BERNIECE. You keep trying it'll work out for you.

LYMON. You ever go down there to the picture show?

BERNIECE. I don't go in for all that.

LYMON. Ain't nothing wrong with it. It ain't like gambling and sinning. I went to one down in Jackson once. It was fun.

BERNIECE. I just stay home most of the time. Take care of Maretha.

LYMON. It's getting kind of late. I don't know where Boy Willie went off to. He's liable not to come back. I'm gonna take off these shoes. My feet hurt. Was you in bed? I don't mean to be keeping you up.

BERNIECE. You ain't keeping me up. I couldn't sleep after that Boy Willie woke me up.

LYMON. You got on that nightgown. I likes women when they wear them fancy nightclothes and all. It makes their skin look real pretty.

BERNIECE. I got this at the five-and-ten-cents store. It ain't so fancy.

LYMON. I don't too often get to see a woman dressed like that.

(There is a long pause. LYMON takes off his suit coat.)

Well, I'm gonna sleep here on the couch. I'm supposed to sleep on the floor but I don't reckon Boy Willie's coming back tonight. Wining Boy sold me this suit. Told me it was a magic suit. I'm gonna put it on again tomorrow. Maybe it bring me a woman like he say.

(He goes into his coat pocket and takes out a small bottle of perfume.)

I almost forgot I had this. Some man sold me this for a dollar. Say it come from Paris. This is the same kind of perfume the Queen of France wear. That's what he told me. I don't know if it's true or not. I smelled it. It smelled good to me. Here . . . smell it see if you like it. I was gonna give it to Dolly. But I didn't like her too much.

BERNIECE. *(Takes the bottle.)* It smells nice.

LYMON. I was gonna give it to Dolly if she had went to the picture with me. Go on, you take it.

BERNIECE. I can't take it. Here . . . go on you keep it. You'll find somebody to give it to.

LYMON. I wanna give it to you. Make you smell nice.

(He takes the bottle and puts perfume behind BERNIECE's ear.)

They tell me you supposed to put it right here behind your ear. Say if you put it there you smell nice all day.

(BERNIECE stiffens at his touch. LYMON bends down to smell her.)

There . . . you smell real good now.

(He kisses her neck.)

You smell real good for Lymon.

(He kisses her again. BERNIECE returns the kiss, then breaks the embrace and crosses to the stairs. She turns and they look silently at each other. LYMON hands her the bottle of perfume. BERNIECE exits up the stairs. LYMON picks up his suit coat and strokes it lovingly with the full knowledge that it is indeed a magic suit. The lights go down on the scene.)

SCENE 4

(It is late the next morning. The lights come up on the parlor. LYMON is asleep on the sofa. BOY WILLIE enters the front door.)

BOY WILLIE. Hey, Lymon! Lymon, come on get up.

LYMON. Leave me alone.

BOY WILLIE. Come on, get up, nigger! Wake up, Lymon.

LYMON. What you want?

BOY WILLIE. Come on, let's go. I done called the man about the piano.

LYMON. What piano?

BOY WILLIE. (*Dumps* LYMON *on the floor.*) Come on, get up!

LYMON. Why you leave, I looked around and you was gone.

BOY WILLIE. I come back here with Grace, then I went looking for you. I figured you'd be with Dolly.

LYMON. She just want to drink and spend up your money. I come on back here looking for you to see if you wanted to go to the picture show.

BOY WILLIE. I been up at Grace's house. Some nigger named Leroy come by but I had a chair up against the door. He got mad when he couldn't get in. He went off somewhere and I got out of there before he could come back. Berniece got mad when we came here.

LYMON. She say you was knocking over the lamp busting up the place.

BOY WILLIE. That was Grace doing all that.

LYMON. Wining Boy seen Sutter's ghost last night.

BOY WILLIE. Wining Boy's liable to see anything. I'm surprised he found the right house. Come on, I done called the man about the piano.

LYMON. What he say?

BOY WILLIE. He say to bring it on out. I told him I was calling for my sister, Miss Berniece Charles. I told him some man wanted to buy it for eleven hundred dollars and asked him if he would go any better. He said yeah, he would give me eleven hundred and fifty dollars for it if it was the same piano. I described it to him again and he told me to bring it out.

LYMON. Why didn't you tell him to come and pick it up?

BOY WILLIE. I didn't want to have no problem with Berniece. This way we just take it on out there and it be out the way. He want to charge twenty-five dollars to pick it up.

LYMON. You should have told him the man was gonna give you twelve hundred for it.

BOY WILLIE. I figure I was taking a chance with that eleven hundred. If I had told him twelve hundred he might have run off. Now I wish I had told him twelve-fifty. It's hard to figure out white folks sometimes.

LYMON. You might have been able to tell him anything. White folks got a lot of money.

BOY WILLIE. Come on, let's get it loaded before Berniece come back. Get that end over there. All you got to do is pick it up on that side. Don't worry about this side. You wanna stretch you' back for a minute?

LYMON. I'm ready.

BOY WILLIE. Get a real good grip on it now.

(*The sound of* SUTTER'S GHOST *is heard. They do not hear it.*)

LYMON. I got this end. You get that end.

BOY WILLIE. Wait till I say ready now. Alright. You got it good? You got a grip on it?

LYMON. Yeah, I got it. You lift up on that end.

BOY WILLIE. Ready? Lift!

(The piano will not budge.)

LYMON. Man, this piano is heavy! It's gonna take more than me and you to move this piano.

BOY WILLIE. We can do it. Come on—we did it before.

LYMON. Nigger—you crazy! That piano weighs five hundred pounds!

BOY WILLIE. I got three hundred pounds of it! I know you can carry two hundred pounds! You be lifting them cotton sacks! Come on lift this piano!

(They try to move the piano again without success.)

LYMON. It's stuck. Something holding it.

BOY WILLIE. How the piano gonna be stuck? We just moved it. Slide you' end out.

LYMON. Naw—we gonna need two or three more people. How this big old piano get in the house?

BOY WILLIE. I don't know how it got in the house. I know how it's going out though! You get on this end. I'll carry three hundred and fifty pounds of it. All you got to do is slide your end out. Ready?

(They switch sides and try again without success. DOAKER *enters from his room as they try to push and shove it.)*

LYMON. Hey, Doaker . . . how this piano get in the house?

DOAKER. Boy Willie, what you doing?

BOY WILLIE. I'm carrying this piano out the house. What it look like I'm doing? Come on, Lymon, let's try again.

DOAKER. Go on let the piano sit there till Berniece come home.

BOY WILLIE. You ain't got nothing to do with this, Doaker. This my business.

DOAKER. This is my house, nigger! I ain't gonna let you or nobody else carry nothing out of it. You ain't gonna carry nothing out of here without my permission!

BOY WILLIE. This is my piano. I don't need your permission to carry my belongings out of your house. This is mine. This ain't got nothing to do with you.

DOAKER. I say leave it over there till Berniece come home. She got part of it too. Leave it set there till you see what she say.

BOY WILLIE. I don't care what Berniece say. Come on, Lymon. I got this side.

DOAKER. Go on and cut it half in two if you want to. Just leave Berniece's half sitting over there. I can't tell you what to do with your piano. But I can't let you take her half out of here.

BOY WILLIE. Go on, Doaker. You ain't got nothing to do with this. I don't want you starting nothing now. Just go on and leave me alone. Come on, Lymon. I got this end.

*(*DOAKER *goes into his room.* BOY WILLIE *and* LYMON *prepare to move the piano.)*

LYMON. How we gonna get it in the truck?

BOY WILLIE. Don't worry about how we gonna get it on the truck. You got to get it out the house first.

LYMON. It's gonna take more than me and you to move this piano.

BOY WILLIE. Just lift up on that end, nigger!

(DOAKER *comes to the doorway of his room and stands.*)

DOAKER. (*Quietly with authority.*) Leave that piano set over there till Berniece come back. I don't care what you do with it then. But you gonna leave it sit over there right now.

BOY WILLIE. Alright . . . I'm gonna tell you this, Doaker. I'm going out of here . . . I'm gonna get me some rope . . . find me a plank and some wheels . . . and I'm coming back. Then I'm gonna carry that piano out of here . . . sell it and give Berniece half the money. See . . . now that's what I'm gonna do. And you . . . or nobody else is gonna stop me. Come on, Lymon . . . let's go get some rope and stuff. I'll be back, Doaker.

(BOY WILLIE *and* LYMON *exit. The lights go down on the scene.*)

SCENE 5

(*The lights come up.* BOY WILLIE *sits on the sofa, screwing casters on a wooden plank.* MARETHA *is sitting on the piano stool.* DOAKER *sits at the table playing solitaire.*)

BOY WILLIE. (*To* MARETHA.) Then after that them white folks down around there started falling down their wells. You ever seen a well? A well got a wall around it. It's hard to fall down a well. You got to be leaning way over. Couldn't nobody figure out too much what was making these fellows fall down their well . . . so everybody says the Ghosts of the Yellow Dog must have pushed them. That's what everybody called them four men what got burned up in the boxcar.

MARETHA. Why they call them that?

BOY WILLIE. Cause the Yazoo Delta railroad got yellow boxcars. Sometime the way the whistle blow sound like an old dog howling so the people call it the Yellow Dog.

MARETHA. Anybody ever see the Ghosts?

BOY WILLIE. I told you they like the wind. Can you see the wind?

MARETHA. No.

BOY WILLIE. They like the wind you can't see them. But sometimes you be in trouble they might be around to help you. They say if you go where the Southern cross the Yellow Dog . . . you go to where them two railroads cross each other . . . and call out their names . . . they say they talk back to you. I don't know, I ain't never done that. But Uncle Wining Boy he say he been down there and talked to them. You have to ask him about that part.

(BERNIECE *has entered from the front door.*)

BERNIECE. Maretha, you go on and get ready for me to do your hair.

(MARETHA *crosses to the steps.*)

Boy Willie, I done told you to leave my house.

(*To* MARETHA.)

Go on, Maretha.

(MARETHA *is hesitant about going up the stairs.*)

BOY WILLIE. Don't be scared. Here, I'll go up there with you. If we see Sutter's ghost I'll put a whupping on him. Come on, Uncle Boy Willie going with you.

(BOY WILLIE *and* MARETHA *exit up the stairs.*)

BERNIECE. Doaker—what is going on here?

DOAKER. I come home and him and Lymon was moving the piano. I told them to leave it over there till you got home. He went out and got that board and them wheels. He say he gonna take that piano out of here and ain't nobody gonna stop him.

BERNIECE. I ain't playing with Boy Willie. I got Crawley's gun upstairs. He don't know but I'm through with it. Where Lymon go?

DOAKER. Boy Willie sent him for some rope just before you come in.

BERNIECE. I ain't studying Boy Willie or Lymon—or the rope. Boy Willie ain't taking that piano out this house. That's all there is to it.

(BOY WILLIE *and* MARETHA *enter on the stairs.* MARETHA *carries a hot comb and a can of hair grease.* BOY WILLIE *crosses over and continues to screw the wheels on the board.*)

MARETHA. Mama, all the hair grease is gone. There ain't but this little bit left.

BERNIECE. (*Gives her a dollar.*) Here . . . run across the street and get another can. You come straight back, too. Don't you be playing around out there. And watch the cars. Be careful when you cross the street.

(MARETHA *exits out the front door.*)

Boy Willie, I done told you to leave my house.

BOY WILLIE. I ain't in you' house. I'm in Doaker's house. If he ask me to leave then I'll go on and leave. But consider me done left your part.

BERNIECE. Doaker, tell him to leave. Tell him to go on.

DOAKER. Boy Willie ain't done nothing for me to put him out of the house. I told you if you can't get along just go on and don't have nothing to do with each other.

BOY WILLIE. I ain't thinking about Berniece.

(*He gets up and draws a line across the floor with his foot.*)

There! Now I'm out of your part of the house. Consider me done left your part. Soon as Lymon come back with that rope. I'm gonna take that piano out of here and sell it.

BERNIECE. You ain't gonna touch that piano.

BOY WILLIE. Carry it out of here just as big and bold. Do like my daddy would have done come time to get Sutter's land.

BERNIECE. I got something to make you leave it over there.

BOY WILLIE. It's got to come better than this thirty-two-twenty.

DOAKER. Why don't you stop all that! Boy Willie, go on and leave her alone. You know how Berniece get. Why you wanna sit there and pick with her?

BOY WILLIE. I ain't picking with her. I told her the truth. She the one talking about what she got. I just told her what she better have.

BERNIECE. That's alright, Doaker. Leave him alone.

BOY WILLIE. She trying to scare me. Hell, I ain't scared of dying. I look around and see people dying every day. You got to die to make room for somebody else. I had a dog that died. Wasn't nothing but a puppy. I picked it up and put it in a bag and carried it up there to Reverend C. L. Thompson's church. I carried it up there and prayed and asked Jesus to make it live like he did the man in the Bible. I prayed real hard. Knelt down and everything. Say ask in Jesus' name. Well, I must have called Jesus' name two hundred times. I called his name till my mouth got sore. I got up and looked in the bag and the dog still dead. It ain't moved a muscle! I say, "Well, ain't nothing precious." And then I went out and killed me a cat. That's when I discovered the power of death. See, a nigger that ain't afraid to die is the worse kind of nigger for the white man. He can't hold that power over you. That's what I learned when I killed that cat. I got the power of death too. I can command him. I can call him up. The white man don't like to see that. He don't like for you to stand up and look him square in the eye and say, "I got it too." Then he got to deal with you square up.

BERNIECE. That's why I don't talk to him, Doaker. You try and talk to him and that's the only kind of stuff that comes out his mouth.

DOAKER. You say Avery went home to get his Bible?

BOY WILLIE. What Avery gonna do? Avery can't do nothing with me. I wish Avery would say something to me about this piano.

DOAKER. Berniece ain't said about that. Avery went home to get his Bible. He coming by to bless the house see if he can get rid of Sutter's ghost.

BOY WILLIE. Ain't nothing but a house full of ghosts down there at the church. What Avery look like chasing away somebody's ghost?

(MARETHA *enters the front door.*)

BERNIECE. Light that stove and set that comb over there to get hot. Get something to put around your shoulders.

BOY WILLIE. The Bible say an eye for an eye, a tooth for a tooth, and a life for a life. Tit for tat. But you and Avery don't want to believe that. You gonna pass up that part and pretend it ain't in there. Everything else you gonna agree with. But if you gonna agree with part of it you got to agree with all of it. You can't do nothing halfway. You gonna go at the Bible halfway. You gonna act like that part ain't in there. But you pull out the Bible and open it and see what it say. Ask Avery. He a preacher. He'll tell you it's in there. He the Good Shepherd. Unless he gonna shepherd you to heaven with half the Bible.

BERNIECE. Maretha, bring me that comb. Make sure it's hot.

(MARETHA *brings the comb.* BERNIECE *begins to do her hair.*)

BOY WILLIE. I will say this for Avery. He done figured out a path to go through life. I don't agree with it. But he done fixed it so he can go right through it real smooth. Hell, he liable to end up with a million dollars that he done got from selling bread and wine.

MARETHA. OWWWWWW!

BERNIECE. Be still, Maretha. If you was a boy I wouldn't be going through this.

BOY WILLIE. Don't you tell that girl that. Why you wanna tell her that?

BERNIECE. You ain't got nothing to do with this child.

BOY WILLIE. Telling her you wished she was a boy. How's that gonna make her feel?

BERNIECE. Boy Willie, go on and leave me alone.

DOAKER. Why don't you leave her alone? What you got to pick with her for? Why don't you go on out and see what's out there in the streets? Have something to tell the fellows down home.

BOY WILLIE. I'm waiting on Lymon to get back with that truck. Why don't you go on out and see what's out there in the streets? You ain't got to work tomorrow. Talking about me . . . why don't you go out there? It's Friday night.

DOAKER. I got to stay around here and keep you all from killing one another.

BOY WILLIE. You ain't got to worry about me. I'm gonna be here just as long as it takes Lymon to get back here with that truck. You ought to be talking to Berniece. Sitting up there telling Maretha she wished she was a boy. What kind of thing is that to tell a child? If you want to tell her something tell her about that piano. You ain't even told her about that piano. Like that's something to be ashamed of. Like she supposed to go off and hide somewhere about that piano. You ought to mark down on the calendar the day that Papa Boy Charles brought that piano into the house. You ought to mark that day down and draw a circle around it . . . and every year when it come up throw a party. Have a celebration. If you did that she wouldn't have no problem in life. She could walk around here with her head held high. I'm talking about a big party!

Invite everybody! Mark that day down with a special meaning. That way she know where she at in the world. You got her going out here thinking she wrong in the world. Like there ain't no part of it belong to her.

BERNIECE. Let me take care of my child. When you get one of your own then you can teach it what you want to teach it.

(DOAKER *exits into his room.*)

BOY WILLIE. What I want to bring a child into this world for? Why I wanna bring somebody else into all this for? I'll tell you this . . . If I was Rockefeller I'd have forty or fifty. I'd make one every day. Cause they gonna start out in life with all the advantages. I ain't got no advantages to offer nobody. Many is the time I looked at my daddy and seen him staring off at his hands. I got a little older I know what he was thinking. He sitting there saying, "I got these big old hands but what I'm gonna do with them? Best I can do is make a fifty-acre crop for Mr. Stovall. Got these big old hands capable of doing anything. I can take and build something with these hands. But where's the tools? All I got is these hands. Unless I go out here and kill me somebody and take what they got . . . it's a long row to hoe for me to get something of my own. So what I'm gonna do with these big old hands? What would you do?"

See now . . . if he had his own land he wouldn't have felt that way. If he had something under his feet that belonged to him he could stand up taller. That's what I'm talking about. Hell, the land is there for everybody. All you got to do is figure out how to get you a piece. Ain't no mystery to life. You just got to go out and meet it square on. If you got a piece of land you'll find everything else fall right into place. You can stand right up next to the white man and talk about the price of cotton . . . the weather, and anything else you want to talk about. If you teach that girl that she living at the bottom of life, she's gonna grow up and hate you.

BERNIECE. I'm gonna teach her the truth. That's just where she living. Only she ain't got to stay there.

(*To* MARETHA.)

Turn you' head over to the other side.

BOY WILLIE. This might be your bottom but it ain't mine. I'm living at the top of life. I ain't gonna just take my life and throw it away at the bottom. I'm in the world like everybody else. The way I see it everybody else got to come up a little taste to be where I am.

BERNIECE. You right at the bottom with the rest of us.

BOY WILLIE. I'll tell you this . . . and ain't a living soul can put a come back on it. If you believe that's where you at then you gonna act that way. If you act that way then that's where you gonna be. It's as simple as that. Ain't no mystery to life. I don't know how you come to believe that stuff. Crawley didn't think like that. He wasn't living at the bottom of life. Papa Boy Charles and Mama Ola wasn't living at the bottom of life. You ain't never heard them say nothing like that. They would have taken a strap to you if they heard you say something like that.

(DOAKER *enters from his room.*)

Hey, Doaker . . . Berniece say the colored folks is living at the bottom of life. I tried to tell her if she think that . . . that's where she gonna be. You think you living at the bottom of life? Is that how you see yourself?

DOAKER. I'm just living the best way I know how. I ain't thinking about no top or no bottom.

BOY WILLIE. That's what I tried to tell Berniece. I don't know where she got that from. That sound like something Avery would say. Avery think cause the white man give him a turkey for Thanksgiving that makes him better than everybody else. That's gonna raise him out of the bottom of life. I don't need nobody to give me a turkey. I can get my own turkey. All you have to do is get out my way. I'll get me two or three turkeys.

BERNIECE. You can't even get a chicken let alone two or three turkeys. Talking about get out your way. Ain't nobody in your way.

(*To* MARETHA.)

Straighten your head, Maretha! Don't be bending down like that. Hold your head up!

(*To* BOY WILLIE.)

All you got going for you is talk. You' whole life that's all you ever had going for you.

BOY WILLIE. See now . . . I'll tell you something about me. I done strung along and strung along. Going this way and that. Whatever way would lead me to a moment of peace. That's all I want. To be as easy with everything. But I wasn't born to that. I was born to a time of fire.

The world ain't wanted no part of me. I could see that since I was about seven. The world say it's better off without me. See, Berniece accept that. She trying to come up to where she can prove something to the world. Hell, the world a better place cause of me. I don't see it like Berniece. I got a heart that beats here and it beats just as loud as the next fellow's. Don't care if he black or white. Sometime it beats louder. When it beats louder, then everybody can hear it. Some people get scared of that. Like Berniece. Some people get scared to hear a nigger's heart beating. They think you ought to lay low with that heart. Make it beat quiet and go along with everything the way it is. But my mama ain't birthed me for nothing. So what I got to do? I got to mark my passing on the road. Just like you write on a tree, "Boy Willie was here."

That's all I'm trying to do with that piano. Trying to put my mark on the road. Like my daddy done. My heart say for me to sell that piano and get me some land so I can make a life for myself to live in my own way. Other than that I ain't thinking about nothing Berniece got to say.

(There is a knock at the door. BOY WILLIE *crosses to it and yanks it open thinking it is* LYMON. AVERY *enters. He carries a Bible.)*

BOY WILLIE. Where you been, nigger? Aw . . . I thought you was Lymon. Hey, Berniece, look who's here.

BERNIECE. Come on in, Avery. Don't you pay Boy Willie no mind.

BOY WILLIE. Hey . . . Hey, Avery . . . tell me this . . . can you get to heaven with half the Bible?

BERNIECE. Boy Willie . . . I done told you to leave me alone.

BOY WILLIE. I just ask the man a question. He can answer. He don't need you to speak for him. Avery . . . if you only believe on half the Bible and don't want to accept the other half . . . you think God let you in heaven? Or do you got to have the whole Bible? Tell Berniece . . . if you only believe in part of it . . . when you see God he gonna ask you why you ain't believed in the other part . . . then he gonna send you straight to Hell.

AVERY. You got to be born again. Jesus say unless a man be born again he cannot come unto the Father and who so ever heareth my words and believeth them not shall be cast into a fiery pit.

BOY WILLIE. That's what I was trying to tell Berniece. You got to believe in it all. You can't go at nothing halfway. She think she going to heaven with half the Bible.

(To BERNIECE.*)*

You hear that . . . Jesus say you got to believe in it all.

BERNIECE. You keep messing with me.

BOY WILLIE. I ain't thinking about you.

DOAKER. Come on in, Avery, and have a seat. Don't pay neither one of them no mind. They been arguing all day.

BERNIECE. Come on in, Avery.

AVERY. How's everybody in here?

BERNIECE. Here, set this comb back over there on that stove.

(*To* AVERY.)

Don't pay Boy Willie no mind. He been around here bothering me since I come home from work.

BOY WILLIE. Boy Willie ain't bothering you. Boy Willie ain't bothering nobody. I'm just waiting on Lymon to get back. I ain't thinking about you. You heard the man say I was right and you still don't want to believe it. You just wanna go and make up anythin'. Well there's Avery . . . there's the preacher . . . go on and ask him.

AVERY. Berniece believe in the Bible. She been baptized.

BOY WILLIE. What about that part that say an eye for an eye a tooth for a tooth and a life for a life? Ain't that in there?

DOAKER. What they say down there at the bank, Avery?

AVERY. Oh, they talked to me real nice. I told Berniece . . . they say maybe they let me borrow the money. They done talked to my boss down at work and everything.

DOAKER. That's what I told Berniece. You working every day you ought to be able to borrow some money.

AVERY. I'm getting more people in my congregation every day. Berniece says she gonna be the Deaconess. I get me my church I can get married and settled down. That's what I told Berniece.

DOAKER. That be nice. You all ought to go ahead and get married. Berniece don't need to be by herself. I tell her that all the time.

BERNIECE. I ain't said nothing about getting married. I said I was thinking about it.

DOAKER. Avery get him his church you all can make it nice.

(*To* AVERY.)

Berniece said you was coming by to bless the house.

AVERY. Yeah, I done read up on my Bible. She asked me to come by and see if I can get rid of Sutter's ghost.

BOY WILLIE. Ain't no ghost in this house. That's all in Berniece's head. Go on up there and see if you see him. I'll give you a hundred dollars if you see him. That's all in her imagination.

DOAKER. Well, let her find that out then. If Avery blessing the house is gonna make her feel better . . . what you got to do with it?

AVERY. Berniece say Maretha seen him too. I don't know, but I found a part in the Bible to bless the house. If he is here then that ought to make him go.

BOY WILLIE. You worse than Berniece believing all that stuff. Talking about . . . if he here. Go on up there and find out. I been up there I ain't seen him. If you reading from that Bible gonna make him leave out of Berniece imagination, well, you might be right. But if you talking about . . .

DOAKER. Boy Willie, why don't you just be quiet? Getting all up in the man's business. This ain't got nothing to do with you. Let him go ahead and do what he gonna do.

BOY WILLIE. I ain't stopping him. Avery ain't got no power to do nothing.

AVERY. Oh, I ain't got no power. God got the power! God got power over every-thing in His creation. God can do anything. God say, "As I commandeth so it shall be." God said, "Let there be light," and there was light. He made the world in six days and rested on the seventh. God's got a wonderful power. He got power over life and death. Jesus raised Lazareth from the dead. They was getting ready to bury him and Jesus told him say, "Rise up and walk." He got up and walked and the people made great rejoicing at the power of God. I ain't worried about him chasing away a little old ghost!

(There is a knock at the door. BOY WILLIE *goes to answer it.* LYMON *enters carrying a coil of rope.)*

BOY WILLIE. Where you been? I been waiting on you and you run off somewhere.

LYMON. I ran into Grace. I stopped and bought her drink. She say she gonna go to the picture show with me.

BOY WILLIE. I ain't thinking about no Grace nothing.

LYMON. Hi, Berniece.

BOY WILLIE. Give me that rope and get up on this side of the piano.

DOAKER. Boy Willie, don't start nothing now. Leave the piano alone.

BOY WILLIE. Get that board there, Lymon. Stay out of this, Doaker.

*(BERNIECE *exits up the stairs.)*

DOAKER. You just can't take the piano. How you gonna take the piano? Berniece ain't said nothing about selling that piano.

BOY WILLIE. She ain't got to say nothing. Come on, Lymon. We got to lift one end at a time up on the board. You got to watch so that the board don't slide up under there.

LYMON. What we gonna do with the rope?

BOY WILLIE. Let me worry about the rope. You just get up on this side over here with me.

*(BERNIECE *enters from the stairs. She has her hand in her pocket where she has Crawley's gun.)*

AVERY. Boy Willie . . . Berniece . . . why don't you all sit down and talk this out now?

BERNIECE. Ain't nothing to talk out.

BOY WILLIE. I'm through talking to Berniece. You can talk to Berniece till you get blue in the face, and it don't make no difference. Get up on that side, Lymon. Throw that rope around there and tie it to the leg.

LYMON. Wait a minute . . . wait a minute, Boy Willie. Berniece got to say. Hey, Berniece . . . did you tell Boy Willie he could take this piano?

BERNIECE. Boy Willie ain't taking nothing out of my house but himself. Now you let him go ahead and try.

BOY WILLIE. Come on, Lymon, get up on this side with me.

*(LYMON *stands undecided.)*

Come on, nigger! What you standing there for?

LYMON. Maybe Berniece is right, Boy Willie. Maybe you shouldn't sell it.

AVERY. You all ought to sit down and talk it out. See if you can come to an agreement.

DOAKER. That's what I been trying to tell them. Seem like one of them ought to respect the other one's wishes.

BERNIECE. I wish Boy Willie would go on and leave my house. That's what I wish. Now, he can respect that. Cause he's leaving here one way or another.

BOY WILLIE. What you mean one way or another? What's that supposed to mean? I ain't scared of no gun.

DOAKER. Come on, Berniece, leave him alone with that.

BOY WILLIE. I don't care what Berniece say. I'm selling my half. I can't help it if her half got to go along with it. It ain't like I'm trying to cheat her out of her half. Come on, Lymon.

LYMON. Berniece . . . I got to do this . . . Boy Willie say he gonna give you half of the money . . . say he want to get Sutter's land.

BERNIECE. Go on, Lymon. Just go on . . . I done told Boy Willie what to do.

BOY WILLIE. Here, Lymon . . . put that rope up over there.

LYMON. Boy Willie, you sure you want to do this? The way I figure it . . . I might be wrong . . . but I figure she gonna shoot you first.

BOY WILLIE. She just gonna have to shoot me.

BERNIECE. Maretha, get on out the way. Get her out the way, Doaker.

DOAKER. Go on, do what your mama told you.

BERNIECE. Put her in your room.

(MARETHA *exits to* DOAKER'*s room.* BOY WILLIE *and* LYMON *try to lift the piano. The door opens and* WINING BOY *enters. He has been drinking.*)

WINING BOY. Man, these niggers around here! I stopped down there at Seefus. . . . These folks standing around talking about Patchneck Red's coming. They jumping back and getting off the sidewalk talking about Patchneck Red this and Patchneck Red that. Come to find out . . . you know who they was talking about? Old John D. from up around Tyler! Used to run around with Otis Smith. He got everybody scared of him. Calling him Patchneck Red. They don't know I whupped the nigger's head in one time.

BOY WILLIE. Just make sure that board don't slide, Lymon.

LYMON. I got this side. You watch that side.

WINING BOY. Hey, Boy Willie, what you got? I know you got a pint stuck up in your coat.

BOY WILLIE. Wining Boy, get out the way!

WINING BOY. Hey, Doaker. What you got? Gimme a drink. I want a drink.

DOAKER. It look like you had enough of whatever it was. Come talking about "What you got?" You ought to be trying to find somewhere to lay down.

WINING BOY. I ain't worried about no place to lay down. I can always find me a place to lay down in Berniece's house. Ain't that right, Berniece?

BERNIECE. Wining Boy, sit down somewhere. You been out there drinking all day. Come in here smelling like an old polecat. Sit on down there, you don't need nothing to drink.

DOAKER. You know Berniece don't like all that drinking.

WINING BOY. I ain't disrespecting Berniece. Berniece, am I disrespecting you? I'm just trying to be nice. I been with strangers all day and they treated me like family. I come in here to family and you treat me like a stranger. I don't need your whiskey. I can buy my own. I wanted your company, not your whiskey.

DOAKER. Nigger, why don't you go upstairs and lay down? You don't need nothing to drink.

WINING BOY. I ain't thinking about no laying down. Me and Boy Willie fixing to party. Ain't that right, Boy Willie? Tell him. I'm fixing to play me some piano. Watch this.

(WINING BOY *sits down at the piano.*)

BOY WILLIE. Come on, Wining Boy! Me and Lymon fixing to move the piano.

WINING BOY. Wait a minute . . . wait a minute. This a song I wrote for Cleotha. I wrote this song in memory of Cleotha.

(*He begins to play and sing.*)

Hey little woman what's the matter with you now
Had a storm last night and blowed the line all down

Tell me how long
Is I got to wait
Can I get it now
Or must I hesitate

It takes a hesitating stocking in her hesitating shoe
It takes a hesitating woman wanna sing the blues

Tell me how long
Is I got to wait
Can I kiss you now
Or must I hesitate.

BOY WILLIE. Come on, Wining Boy, get up! Get up, Wining Boy! Me and Lymon's fixing to move the piano.

WINING BOY. Naw . . . Naw . . . you ain't gonna move this piano!

BOY WILLIE. Get out the way, Wining Boy.

(WINING BOY, *his back to the piano, spreads his arms out over the piano.*)

WINING BOY. You ain't taking this piano out the house. You got to take me with it!

BOY WILLIE. Get on out the way, Wining Boy! Doaker get him!

(*There is a knock on the door.*)

BERNIECE. I got him, Doaker. Come on, Wining Boy. I done told Boy Willie he ain't taking the piano.

(BERNIECE *tries to take* WINING BOY *away from the piano.*)

WINING BOY. He got to take me with it!

(DOAKER *goes to answer the door.* GRACE *enters.*)

GRACE. Is Lymon here?

DOAKER. Lymon.

WINING BOY. He ain't taking that piano.

BERNIECE. I ain't gonna let him take it.

GRACE. I thought you was coming back. I ain't gonna sit in that truck all day.

LYMON. I told you I was coming back.

GRACE. (*Sees* BOY WILLIE.) Oh, hi, Boy Willie. Lymon told me you was gone back down South.

LYMON. I said he was going back. I didn't say he had left already.

GRACE. That's what you told me.

BERNIECE. Lymon, you got to take your company someplace else.

LYMON. Berniece, this is Grace. That there is Berniece. That's Boy Willie's sister.

GRACE. Nice to meet you.

(*To* LYMON.)

I ain't gonna sit out in that truck all day. You told me you was gonna take me to the movie.

LYMON. I told you I had something to do first. You supposed to wait on me.

BERNIECE. Lymon, just go on and leave. Take Grace or whoever with you. Just go on get out my house.

BOY WILLIE. You gonna help me move this piano first, nigger!

LYMON. (*To* GRACE.) I got to help Boy Willie move the piano first.

(*Everybody but* GRACE *suddenly senses* SUTTER'*s presence.*)

GRACE. I ain't waiting on you. Told me you was coming right back. Now you got to move a piano. You just like all the other men.

(GRACE *now senses something.*)

Something ain't right here. I knew I shouldn't have come back up in this house.

(GRACE *exits.*)

LYMON. Hey, Grace! I'll be right back, Boy Willie.

BOY WILLIE. Where you going, nigger?

LYMON. I'll be back. I got to take Grace home.

BOY WILLIE. Come on, let's move the piano first!

LYMON. I got to take Grace home. I told you I'll be back.

(LYMON *exits.* BOY WILLIE *exits and calls after him.*)

BOY WILLIE. Come on, Lymon! Hey . . . Lymon! Lymon . . . come on!

(*Again, the presence of* SUTTER *is felt.*)

WINING BOY. Hey, Doaker, did you feel that? Hey, Berniece . . . did you get cold? Hey, Doaker . . .

DOAKER. What you calling me for?

WINING BOY. I believe that's Sutter.

DOAKER. Well, let him stay up there. As long as he don't mess with me.

BERNIECE. Avery, go on and bless the house.

DOAKER. You need to bless that piano. That's what you need to bless. It ain't done nothing but cause trouble. If you gonna bless anything go on and bless that.

WINING BOY. Hey, Doaker, if he gonna bless something let him bless everything. The kitchen . . . the upstairs. Go on and bless it all.

BOY WILLIE. Ain't no ghost in this house. He need to bless Berniece's head. That's what he need to bless.

AVERY. Seem like that piano's causing all the trouble. I can bless that. Berniece, put me some water in that bottle.

(AVERY *takes a small bottle from his pocket and hands it to* BERNIECE, *who goes into the kitchen to get water.* AVERY *takes a candle from his pocket and lights it. He gives it to* BERNIECE *as she gives him the water.*)

Hold this candle. Whatever you do make sure it don't go out.

O Holy Father we gather here this evening in the Holy Name to cast out the spirit of one James Sutter. May this vial of water be empowered with thy spirit. May each drop of it be a weapon and a shield against the presence of all evil and may it be a cleansing and blessing of this humble abode.

Just as Our Father taught us how to pray so He say, "I will prepare a table for you in the midst of mine enemies," and in His hands we place ourselves to come unto his presence. Where there is Good so shall it cause Evil to scatter to the Four Winds.

(*He throws water at the piano at each commandment.*)

AVERY. Get thee behind me, Satan! Get thee behind the face of Righteousness as we Glorify His Holy Name! Get thee behind the Hammer of Truth that breaketh down the Wall of Falsehood! Father. Father. Praise. Praise. We ask in Jesus' name and call forth the power of the Holy Spirit as it is written. . . .

(*He opens the Bible and reads from it.*)

I will sprinkle clean water upon thee and ye shall be clean.

BOY WILLIE. All this old preaching stuff. Hell, just tell him to leave.

(AVERY *continues reading throughout* BOY WILLIE'*s outburst.*)

AVERY. I will sprinkle clean water upon you and you shall be clean: from all your uncleanliness, and from all your idols, will I cleanse you. A new heart also will I give you, and a new spirit will I put within you: and I will take out of your flesh the heart of stone, and I will give you a heart of flesh. And I will put my spirit within you, and cause you to walk in my statutes, and ye shall keep my judgments, and do them.

(BOY WILLIE *grabs a pot of water from the stove and begins to fling it around the room.*)

BOY WILLIE. Hey Sutter! Sutter! Get your ass out this house! Sutter! Come on and get some of this water! You done drowned in the well, come on and get some more of this water!

(BOY WILLIE *is working himself into a frenzy as he runs around the room throwing water and calling* SUTTER'*s name.* AVERY *continues reading.*)

BOY WILLIE. Come on, Sutter!

(He starts up the stairs.)

Come on, get some water! Come on, Sutter!

(The sound of SUTTER's GHOST *is heard. As* BOY WILLIE *approaches the steps he is suddenly thrown back by the unseen force, which is choking him. As he struggles he frees himself, then dashes up the stairs.)*

BOY WILLIE. Come on, Sutter!

AVERY. *(Continuing.)* A new heart also will I give you and a new spirit will I put within you: and I will take out of your flesh the heart of stone, and I will give you a heart of flesh. And I will put my spirit within you, and cause you to walk in my statutes, and ye shall keep my judgments, and do them.

(There are loud sounds heard from upstairs as BOY WILLIE *begins to wrestle with* SUTTER's GHOST. *It is a life-and-death struggle fraught with perils and faultless terror.* BOY WILLIE *is thrown down the stairs.* AVERY *is stunned into silence.* BOY WILLIE *picks himself up and dashes back upstairs.)*

AVERY. Berniece, I can't do it.

(There are more sounds heard from upstairs. DOAKER *and* WINING BOY *stare at one another in stunned disbelief. It is in this moment, from somewhere old, that* BERNIECE *realizes what she must do. She crosses to the piano. She begins to play. The song is found piece by piece. It is an old urge to song that is both a commandment and a plea. With each repetition it gains in strength. It is intended as an exorcism and a dressing for battle. A rustle of wind blowing across two continents.)*

BERNIECE. *(Singing.)*

I want you to help me
I want you to help me
I want you to help me
I want you to help me
I want you to help me
I want you to help me
Mama Berniece
I want you to help me
Mama Esther
I want you to help me
Papa Boy Charles
I want you to help me
Mama Ola
I want you to help me

I want you to help me
I want you to help me
I want you to help me
I want you to help me
I want you to help me

I want you to help me
I want you to help me
I want you to help me

(The sound of a train approaching is heard. The noise upstairs subsides.)

BOY WILLIE. Come on, Sutter! Come back, Sutter!

(BERNIECE begins to chant:)

BERNIECE.

Thank you.
Thank you.
Thank you.

(A calm comes over the house. MARETHA enters from DOAKER's room. BOY WILLIE enters on the stairs. He pauses a moment to watch BERNIECE at the piano.)

BERNIECE.

Thank you.
Thank you.

BOY WILLIE. Wining Boy, you ready to go back down home? Hey, Doaker, what time the train leave?

DOAKER. You still got time to make it.

(MARETHA crosses and embraces BOY WILLIE.)

BOY WILLIE. Hey Berniece . . . if you and Maretha don't keep playing on that piano . . . ain't no telling . . . me and Sutter both liable to be back.

(He exits.)

BERNIECE. Thank you.

(The lights go down to black.)

✹ ISHMAEL REED (b. 1938)

Ishmael Reed, who was born in Chattanooga, Tennessee, is a well-known, highly published novelist and poet. He has co-founded several publications, including the East Village Other *in 1965 and a Newark community newspaper,* Advance, *in the same year. In 1971, he became the editorial director for Yardbird Publishing Company, which he co-founded. He also co-founded Reed, Cannon & Johnson Communications. Among other places, Reed has taught at the University of California, Berkeley, and the University of Washington in Seattle. His novels include* Yellow Back Radio Broke-Down *(1969),* Mumbo Jumbo *(1972),* Flight to Canada *(1976), and* Japanese by Spring *(1993). His books of poetry include* Conjure *(1972),* Calafia: The California Poetry *(1977), and* New and Collected Poems *(1988). He has also written several essay collections. His work is characterized by his use of black dialect and satire.*

I am a Cowboy in the Boat of Ra (1988)

'The devil must be forced to reveal any such physical evil
(potions, charms, fetishes, etc.) still outside the body
and these must be burned.'

(Rituale Romanum, *published 1947, endorsed by the coat-of-arms*
and introductory letter from Francis cardinal Spellman)

I am a cowboy in the boat of Ra,
sidewinders in the saloons of fools
bit my forehead   like   O
the untrustworthiness of Egyptologists
who do not know their trips. Who was that   5
dog-faced man? they asked, the day I rode
from town.

School marms with halitosis cannot see
the Nefertiti fake chipped on the run by slick
germans, the hawk behind Sonny Rollins' head or   10
the ritual beard of his axe; a longhorn winding
its bells thru the Field of Reeds.

I am a cowboy in the boat of Ra. I bedded
down with Isis, Lady of the Boogaloo, dove
down deep in her horny, stuck up her Wells-Far-ago   15
in daring midday getaway. 'Start grabbing the
blue,' I said from top of my double crown.

I am a cowboy in the boat of Ra. Ezzard Charles
of the Chisholm Trail. Took up the bass but they
blew off my thumb. Alchemist in ringmanship but a   20
sucker for the right cross.

I am a cowboy in the boat of Ra. Vamoosed from
the temple i bide my time. The price on the wanted
poster was a-going down, outlaw alias copped my stance
and moody greenhorns were making me dance;   25
   while my mouth's
shooting iron got its chambers jammed.

I am a cowboy in the boat of Ra. Boning-up in
the ol West i bide my time. You should see
me pick off these tin cans whippersnappers. I   30
write the motown long plays for the comeback of
Osiris. Make them up when stars stare at sleeping
steer out here near the campfire. Women arrive
on the backs of goats and throw themselves on
my Bowie.   35

I am a cowboy in the boat of Ra. Lord of the lash,
the Loup Garou Kid. Half breed son of Pisces and
Aquarius. I hold the souls of men in my pot. I do
the dirty boogie with scorpions. I make the bulls
keep still and was the first swinger to grape the taste.   40

I am a cowboy in his boat. Pope Joan of the
Ptah Ra. C/mere a minute willya doll?
Be a good girl and
bring me my Buffalo horn of black powder
bring me my headdress of black feathers   45
bring me my bones of Ju-Ju snake
go get my eyelids of red paint.
Hand me my shadow

I'm going into town after Set

I am a cowboy in the boat of Ra   50

look out Set   here i come Set
to get Set   to sunset Set
to unseat Set   to Set down Set

                    usurper of the Royal couch
                    —imposter RAdio of Moses' bush   55
                    party pooper O hater of dance
                    vampire outlaw of the milky way

Oakland Blues (1988)

Well it's six o'clock in Oakland
and the sun is full of wine
I say, it's six o'clock in Oakland
and the sun is red with wine
We buried you this morning, baby   5
in the shadow of a vine

Well, they told you of the sickness
almost eighteen months ago
Yes, they told you of the sickness
almost eighteen months ago   10
You went down fighting, daddy. Yes
You fought Death toe to toe

O, the egrets fly over Lake Merritt
and the blackbirds roost in trees
O, the egrets fly over Lake Merritt   15
and the blackbirds roost in trees

Without you little papa
what O, what will become of me

O, it's hard to come home, baby
To a house that's still and stark   20
O, it's hard to come home, baby
To a house that's still and stark
All I hear is myself
thinking
and footsteps in the dark   25

JUNE JORDAN (b. 1936)

June Jordan is known for her forceful poetry that boldly addresses racial issues. She was born in Harlem and has used the pseudonym June Meyer for some of her work. Like many other African American writers, Jordan uses her writer forum politically to speak out against injustice. Jordan's first book of poetry was Some Changes *(1971). Her second was* New Days: Poems of Exile and Return *(1974). Toni Morrison edited* Things That I Do in the Dark *(1977), in which Jordan presents not only her feelings about race in general but also her personal experiences within the context of race. Walt Whitman, William Butler Yeats, and Phillis Wheatley are some of the models for Jordan's poetic style. For example, Yeats and Wheatley influenced Jordan's* Naming Our Destiny: New and Selected Poems *(1989). Jordan has also written children's books. In 1989, she began teaching African American studies and women's studies at the University of California, Berkeley.*

Independence Day in the U.S.A. (1985)

I wanted to tell you about July 4th
in northamerica and the lights computerized
shrapnel in white
or red or fast-fuse blue
to celebrate the only revolution   5
that was legitimate
in human history

I wanted to tell you about the baby
screaming this afternoon where the park
and the music of thousands who eat   10
food and stay hungry or homicidal
on the subways or the windowsills of the city
came together loud

like the original cannon shots
from that only legitimate revolution   15
in human history

I wanted to tell you about my Spanish
how it starts like a word aggravating the beat
of my heart then rushes up to my head
where my eyes dream Carribean   20
flowers and my mouth waters
around black beans
or coffee that lets me forget
the hours before morning

But I am living inside the outcome   25
of the only legitimate revolution
in human history
and the operator will not place my call to Cuba
the mailman will not carry my letters to Managua
the State Department will not okay my visa   30
for a short-wave conversation
and you do not speak English

and I can dig it

Song of the Law Abiding Citizen (1985)

so hot so hot so hot so what
so hot so what so hot so hot

They made a mistake
I got more than I usually take
I got food stamps food stamps I got   5
so many stamps in the mail
I thought maybe I should put them on sale
How lucky I am
I got food stamps: Hot damn!
I made up my mind   10
to be decent and kind
to let my upright character shine
I sent 10,000 food stamps
back to the President (and his beautiful wife)
and I can't pay the rent   15
but I sent 10,000 food stamps
back to the President (and his beautiful wife)
how lucky I am

hot damn
They made a mistake 20
for Chrissake
And I gave it away to the President
I thought that was legal I thought that was kind
and I can't pay the rent
but I sent 10,000 food stamps 25
back back back to the President

so hot so hot so hot so what
so hot so what so hot so hot

Trucks cruisin' down the avenue
carrying nuclear garbage right next to you 30
and it's legal
it's radioaction ridin' like a regal
load of jewels
past the bars the cruel
school house and the church and if 35
the trucks wipeout or crash
or even lurch too hard around a corner
we will just be goners
and it's legal
it's radioaction ridin' regal 40
through the skittery city street
and don't be jittery
because it's legal
radioaction ridin' the road

Avenue A Avenue B Avenue C Avenue D 45
Avenue of the Americas

so hot so hot so hot so what
so hot so what so hot so hot
so hot so hot so hot so what

Relativity (1985)

It's 5 after 4 a.m. and nothing but my own
motion stirs throughout the waiting air
the rain completely purged earlier and all
day long. I could call
you now but that would join you to this 5
restless lying down and getting up to list
still another act I must commit

tomorrow if I ever sleep if I ever stop
sleeping long enough to act upon the space
between this comatose commotion   10
and the next time I can look into your
face. I hope you're laughing at the cans
of soup the house to clean the kitchen curtains
I will wash and iron
like so many other promises I make   15
myself: to sweep the stairs down
to the front door
and to answer every letter down to no
thanks.
    My own motion   20
does not satisfy tonight and later
in the daylight I'll be speeding through the streets
a secret messenger a wakeup agent walking
backwards maybe walking sideways
but for damn sure headed possibly southeast   25
as well as every other whichway
in your absolute
direction

� MICHAEL S. HARPER (b. 1938)

Michael S. Harper was born in Brooklyn, New York. He has established himself as an important American poet. After being discouraged by a teacher while attending a college medical program, because he was black, Harper started to write poetry, joining the Iowa Writers' Workshop in 1961. Harper's poetry advocates unity among the races. His first book of poetry, Dear John, Dear Coltrane *(1970), was nominated for a National Book Award in 1971. Some of his other collections are* History Is Your Own Heartbeat: Poems *(1971),* Song: I Want a Witness *(1972), and* Images of Kin: New and Selected Poems *(1977), which was also nominated for a National Book Award. Harper became I. J. Kapstein Professor of English at Brown University in 1983 and became poet laureate of Rhode Island in 1988.*

American History (1970)

Those four black girls blown up
in that Alabama church
remind me of five hundred
middle passage blacks,
in a net, under water   5

in Charleston harbor
so *redcoats* wouldn't find them.
Can't find what you can't see
can you?

for John Callahan

Black Study (1970)

No one's been told
that black men
went first to the moon
the dark side
for dark brothers   5
without space ship
gravity complex
in our computer centers
government campuses
instant play and replay   10
white mice and pig-guineas
in concentric digital rows.

Someone has been
pulling brother's curls
into fancy barbed wire,   15
measuring his forelegs,
caressing his dense innards
into formaldehyde
pruning the jellied marrow:
a certain formula is appearing: 20
someone has been studying you.

Village Blues (1970)

(After a Story by John O. Stewart)

The birds flit
in the blue palms,
the cane workers wait,
the man hangs
twenty feet above;   5
he must come down;
they wait for the priest.
The flies ride on the carcass
which sways like cork in a circle.
The easter light pulls him west.   10

The priest comes, a man
sunken with rum,
his face sandpapered
into a rouge of split
and broken capillaries.   15
His duty is the cutting
down of this fruit
of this quiet village
and he staggers slowly, coming.

Address to the Democratic National Convention

Jesse Jackson

Jesse Jackson delivered this speech at the 1984 Democratic National Convention in San Francisco. He was the second African American, after Shirley Chisholm much earlier, to seek the Democratic nomination for president of the United States. He received significant support from African Americans, women, the poor, and others who form the Rainbow Coalition, the name Jackson uses to describe his political coalition.

Tonight we come together, bound by our faith in a mighty God, with genuine respect and love for our country, and inheriting the legacy of a great party—the Democratic party—which is the best hope for redirecting our nation on a more humane, just, and peaceful course. This is not a perfect party. We are not a perfect people. Yet we are called to a perfect mission: to feed the hungry, to clothe the naked, to house the homeless, to teach the illiterate, to provide jobs for the jobless, and to choose the human race over the nuclear race. We are gathered here this week to nominate a candidate and write a platform which will expand, unify, direct, and inspire our party and the nation to fulfill this mission.

My constituency is the damned, the disinherited, the disrespected, and the despised. They are restless and seek relief. They've voted in record numbers. They have invested faith, hope, and trust in us. The Democratic party must send them a signal that we care. I pledge my best not to let them down.

Leadership must heed the call of conscience—redemption, expansion, healing, and unity—for they are the keys to achieving our mission. Time is neutral and does not change things. With courage and initiative, leaders change things. No generation can choose the age or circumstances in which it is born, but through leadership it can choose to make the age in which it is born an age of enlightenment—an age of jobs, peace, and justice. Only leadership—that intangible combination of gifts, discipline, information, circumstance, courage, timing, will, and divine inspiration—can lead us out of the crisis in which we find ourselves. Leadership can mitigate the misery of our nation. Leadership can part the waters and lead our nation in the direction of the Promised Land. Leadership can lift the boats stuck at the bottom.

I have had the rare opportunity to watch seven men, and then two, pour out their souls, offer their service, and heed the call of duty to direct the course of our nation. There is a proper season for everything. There is a time to sow, and a time to reap. There is a time to compete, and a time to cooperate. I ask for your vote on the first ballot as a vote for a new direction for this party and this nation—a vote of conscience and conviction. But I will be proud to support the nominee of this convention for the presidency of the United States. I have watched the leadership of our party grow and develop. My respect for both Mr. Mondale and Mr. Hart is great. I have watched them struggle with the crosswinds and cross fires of being visible public servants, and I believe that they will both continue to try to serve us faithfully. I am elated by the knowledge that, for the first time in our history, a woman, Geraldine Ferraro, will be recommended to share our ticket.

Throughout this campaign, I have tried to offer leadership to the Democratic party and the nation. If, in my high moments, I have done some good, offered some service, shed some light, healed some wounds, rekindled some hope, stirred someone from apathy and indifference, or in any way helped someone along the way, then this campaign has not been in vain. For friends who loved and cared for me, for a God who spared me, and for a family who understood me, I am eternally grateful.

If, in my low moments, in word, deed, or attitude, through some error of temper, taste, or tone, I have caused anyone discomfort, created pain, or revived someone's fears, that was not my truest self. If there were occasions when my grape turned into a raisin and my joy bell lost its resonance, please forgive me. Charge it to my head and not to my heart. My head is so limited in its finitude, but my heart is boundless in its love for the human family. I am not a perfect servant. I am a public servant, doing my best against the odds. As I grow, develop, and serve, be patient. God is not finished with me yet.

This campaign has taught me much: that leaders must be tough enough to fight, tender enough to cry, human enough to make mistakes, humble enough to admit them, strong enough to absorb the pain, and resilient enough to bounce back. For leaders, the pain is often intense. But you must smile through tears and keep moving with the faith that there is a brighter side somewhere.

I went to see Hubert Humphrey three days before he died. He had just called Richard Nixon from his dying bed, and many people wondered why. I asked him. He said, "Jesse, from this vantage point, with the sun setting in my life, all of the speeches, the political conventions, the crowds, and the great fights are behind me now. At a time like this, you are forced to deal with your irreducible essence, forced to grapple with that which is really important to you. What I have concluded is this: when all is said and done, we must forgive each other, redeem each other, and move on."

Our party is emerging from one of its most hard-fought battles for the Democratic party's presidential nomination in our history. But our healthy competition should make us better, not bitter. We must use the insight, wisdom, and experience of the late Hubert Humphrey as a balm to heal the wounds in our party, this nation, and the world. We must forgive each other, redeem each other, regroup, and move on.

Our flag is red, white, and blue, but our nation is a rainbow—red, yellow, brown, black, and white—and all are precious in God's sight. America is not like a blanket, one piece of unbroken cloth—the same color, the same texture, the same size. It is more like a quilt—many patches, many pieces, many colors, many sizes, all woven and held together by a common thread. The white, the Hispanic, the black, the Arab, the Jew, the woman, the Native American, the small farmer, the businessperson, the environmentalist, the peace activist, the young, the old, the lesbian, the gay, and the disabled make up the American quilt. Even in our fractured state, all of us count and fit in somewhere. We have proven that we can survive without each other. But we have not proven that we can win or make progress without each other. We must come together.

From Fannie Lou Hamer in Atlantic City in 1964 to the Rainbow Coalition in San Francisco today, from the Atlantic to the Pacific, we have experienced pain, but progress, as we obtained open housing; as young people got the right to vote; as we lost Malcolm, Martin, Medgar, Bobby, John, and Viola. The team that got us here must be expanded, not abandoned. Twenty years ago, tears welled up in our eyes as the bodies of Schwerner, Goodman, and Chaney were dredged from the depths of a river in Mississippi. Twenty years later, our communities, black and Jewish, are in anguish, anger, and pain. Feelings have been hurt on both sides. There is a crisis in communications. Confusion is in the air, but we cannot afford to lose our way. We may agree to agree, or agree to disagree on issues, but we must bring back civility to the tensions. We are copartners in a long and rich religious history—the Judeo-Christian traditions. Many blacks and Jews have a shared passion for social justice at home and peace abroad. We must seek a revival of the spirit, inspired by a new vision and new possibilities. We must return to higher ground. We are bound by Moses and Jesus, but also connected with Islam and Muhammad. We are bound by Dr. Martin Luther King, Jr., and Rabbi Abraham Heschel crying out from their graves for us to reach common ground. We are bound by shared blood and shared sacrifices. We are much too intelligent; much too bound by our Judeo-Christian heritage; much too victimized by racism, sexism, militarism, and anti-Semitism; much too threatened as historical scapegoats to go on divided one from another. We must turn from finger-pointing to clasped hands. We must share our burdens and our joys with each other once again. We must turn to each other and not on each other.

Twenty years later, we cannot be satisfied by just restoring the old coalition. Old wineskins must make room for new wine. We must heal and expand. The Rainbow Coalition is making room for Arab Americans. They too know the pain and hurt of racial and religious rejection. They must not continue to be made pariahs. The Rainbow Coalition is making room for Hispanic Americans who this very night are living under the threat of the Simpson-Mazzoli immigration bill and farm workers in Ohio who are fighting the Campbell Soup Company with a boycott to achieve legitimate worker rights.

The Rainbow is making room for the Native Americans, the most exploited people of all and a people with the greatest moral claim among us. We support them as they seek to preserve their ancestral homelands and the beauty of a land that once was all theirs. They can never receive a fair share for all that they have given, but they must finally have a fair chance to develop their great resources and to preserve their people and their culture.

The Rainbow includes Asian Americans, now being killed in our streets—scapegoats for the failures of corporate, industrial, and economic policies. The Rainbow is making room for young Americans. Twenty years ago, our young people were dying in a war for which they could not even vote. Twenty years later, young America has the power to stop a war in Central America and the responsibility to vote in great numbers. Young America must be politically active in 1984. The choice is war or peace. We must make room for young America.

The Rainbow includes disabled Americans. The color "chrome" fits in the rainbow. The disabled have their handicap revealed and their genius concealed, while the able-bodied have their genius revealed and their disability concealed. But ultimately we must judge people by their values and their contribution. Don't leave anybody out. I would rather have Roosevelt in a wheelchair than Reagan on a horse.

The Rainbow is making room for small farmers. They have suffered tremendously under the Reagan regime. They will either receive ninety percent parity or one hundred percent charity. We must address their concerns and make room for them. The Rainbow includes lesbians and gays. No American citizen ought to be denied equal protection under the law.

We must be unusually committed and caring as we expand our family to include new members. All of us must be tolerant and understanding as the fears and anxieties of the rejected and of the party leadership express themselves in so many different ways. Too often what we call hate—as if it were deeply rooted in some philosophy or strategy—is simply ignorance, anxiety, paranoia, fear, and insecurity. We must be long-suffering as we seek to right the wrongs of our party and our nation. We must expand our party, heal our party, and unify our party. That is the means to our mission in 1984.

We are often reminded that we live in a great nation—and we do. But it can be greater still. The Rainbow is mandating a new definition of greatness. We must not measure greatness from the mansion down but from the manger up. Jesus said that we should not be judged by the bark we wear but by the fruit we bear. Jesus said that we must measure greatness by how we treat the least of these.

President Reagan says the nation is in recovery. Those ninety thousand corporations that made a profit last year but paid no federal taxes are recovering. The thirty-seven thousand military contractors who have benefited from Reagan's more than doubling the military budget in peacetime are surely recovering. The big corporations and rich individuals who received the bulk of the three-year multi-billion-dollar tax cut from Mr. Reagan are recovering. But no such comparable recovery is under way for the least of these. Rising tides don't lift all boats, particularly those stuck on the bottom.

For the boats stuck at the bottom, there is a rising misery index. This administration has made life for the poor miserable. Its attitude toward poor people has been contemptuous. Its policies and programs have been cruel and unfair to working people. It must be held accountable in November for an increasing infant-mortality rate among the poor. In Detroit, one of the great cities of the Western world, babies are dying at the same rate as in Honduras, the most underdeveloped nation in our hemisphere. This administration must be held accountable for policies that contribute to the growing poverty in America. Under President Reagan, there are eight million more people in poverty. Currently fifteen percent of our nation is in poverty, thirty-four million people. Of the thirty-four million poor people, twenty-three million are white, eleven million are black, Hispanic, Asian, and others. More and more of the poor are children. By the end of this year, there will be forty-one million people in poverty—more people than at any time since the inadequate War on Poverty program began in 1965. We cannot stand by idly. We must fight for change, now.

Under President Reagan, the misery index has increased.

Social Security. The 1981 budget cuts included 9 permanent Social Security benefit cuts totaling 20 billion dollars over five years. Now he says we may need more.

Small Businesses. Approximately 98 percent of all businesses in America can be considered "small"—employing fewer than 500 workers. Yet under the Reagan tax cuts, only 18 percent of total business tax cuts went to them—82 percent went to big business.

Health Care. Reagan sharply cut funding for screening children for lead poisoning—which can lead to retardation, behavioral difficulties, and learning disabilities—from 9.1 million dollars in 1981 to 5.8 million dollars in 1983. Estimates for 24 states indicate that the number of children screened dropped from 1.1 million to 600,000.

Education. He cut real spending for education by 6 billion dollars, or 25 percent. Four million three hundred thousand handicapped children are receiving delayed or reduced services. One hundred twenty-four thousand fewer college students receive Pell Grant assistance from the federal government.

Women. There are now 9.7 million female-headed families. They represent 16 percent of all families, but half of all poor families. Seventy percent of all poor children live in a household headed by a woman. Working women make less than men in every job category, at every educational level, yet Mr. Reagan sees no need for the Equal Rights Amendment.

Environmental Protection. This administration has cleaned up only 6 of 546 priority toxic-waste dumps in 3 years.

Farmers. In 1983, real net farm income was only about half its level of 1979 and was lower than at any time since the Great Depression.

Many say that the race in November will be decided in the South. President Reagan is depending on the conservative South to return him to office. But the South, I tell you, is unnaturally conservative. The South is the nation's poorest region and therefore has the least to conserve. In his appeal to the South, Mr. Reagan is trying to substitute flags and prayer clauses for jobs, food, clothing, education, health care, and housing. But apparently President Reagan is not even familiar with the structure of a prayer. We must watch false prophecy. He has cut energy assistance to the poor, he has cut food stamps, children's breakfast and lunch programs, the Women, Infants, and Children (WIC) program for pregnant mothers and infants, and job training for children; and then says, "Let us pray." In a prayer, you are supposed to thank God for the food you are about to receive, not for the food that just left. I take prayer very seriously—I've come this way by the power of prayer. So we need to pray. But we need to pray to remove the man that removed the food. We need a change in November.

Poor people and working people—black, white, and brown—all across America, but especially in the South, must resist the temptation to go for Mr. Reagan's social placebo as a substitute for jobs and economic justice. Cotton candy may taste good, it may even go down smoothly, but it has no substance and it's not good for you.

Under President Reagan, the misery index has increased dramatically for the poor, but the danger index for everyone has escalated. The military budget has been doubled to protect us from the Russians, yet today Soviet submarines are closer to our shores, and their missiles are more accurate. Tonight we live in a world that is more miserable and dangerous.

The Reagan administration has failed to achieve any agreed-upon nuclear arms reductions whatsoever. The Reagan administration's attempts to regain military superiority, to achieve a first-strike capability, its plans and preparations to launch and win a limited nuclear war, and its commitment to "Star Wars" have left the world a much more unstable and dangerous place in which to live. We are at a nuclear standoff in Europe. We are mining the harbors of Nicaragua and attempting to covertly overthrow a legitimate government there—actions which have been condemned by many of our allies and by the World Court. Under this administration we have been at war and lost the lives of American boys in Lebanon, Honduras, and Grenada. Under this administration, one-third of America's children have come to believe that they will die in a nuclear war. The danger index for everybody is increasing—and it is frightening.

But it is not enough simply to react to the effects—a growing misery and danger index. We must dig deeper and comprehend the underlying cause of the growing misery and danger index—Reaganomics. We must distinguish between Mr. Reagan's political appeal and his economic deal. Mr. Reagan's economic program is a combination of cyanide and Kool-Aid, jelly beans and poison. It may taste good, but the results are disastrous. We must distinguish between Reaganism and Reaganomics.

While Reaganism is largely subjective, supply-side economics is more objective. Reaganism was used to impose Reaganomics. Reaganism is the perception. Reaganomics is the reality. We are fatter now, but less secure. Many who were once basking in the sun of Reaganism have now been burned to a crisp with Reaganomics. In 1980 many thought they saw a light at the end of the tunnel in Reaganism. But in 1984 we now know it was not sunshine, but a train coming this way.

In 1980 then-candidate George Bush called Mr. Reagan's economic plan to get America back on track "voodoo economics." Third-party candidate John Anderson said that the combination of massive military spending, tax cuts, and a balanced budget by 1984 could only be accomplished with blue smoke and mirrors. We now know they were both right.

President Reagan declares that we are having a dynamic economic recovery. And we are having a recovery of sorts. After three and a half years, unemployment has inched just below where it was when he took office in 1981. But there are still 8.1 million people officially unemployed, and 11 million working only part-time jobs. Make no mistake about it, inflation has come down, but let's examine how and at whose expense this was achieved—and how long it is likely to last.

President Reagan's 1984 economic recovery has come after the deepest and longest recession since the Great Depression. President Reagan curbed inflation by cutting consumer demand. He cut consumer demand with conscious and callous fiscal and monetary policies. He used the federal budget deliberately to induce unemployment and curb social spending. He then urged and supported the tight monetary policies of the Federal Reserve Board deliberately to drive up interest rates—again to curb consumer demand created through borrowing.

Unemployment reached 10.7 percent; we experienced skyrocketing interest rates; our dollar inflated abroad; there were record bank failures, record farm foreclosures, record business bankruptcies, record budget deficits, record trade deficits, and more. President Reagan brought inflation down by destabilizing our economy, disrupting family life, and wreaking havoc on the poor.

Remember President Reagan's central promise of the 1980 campaign—to balance the budget by 1984? Instead of balancing the budget, in 1984 we are having record budget deficits and looking at record budget deficits for as far as the eye can see. Under President Reagan, the cumulative budget deficits for just his four years in office will be virtually equal to the total budget deficits from George Washington to Jimmy Carter—equal to all past presidents' budget deficits combined. I tell you, we need a change. Reagan's economic recovery is being financed by deficit spending—nearly $200 billion a year. Yet military spending, a major cause of the deficit, is projected over the next five years to be nearly $2 trillion and will cost about $40,000 for every taxpaying family.

When the government borrows $200 billion annually to finance the deficit, this encourages the private sector to make money off of interest rates rather than investing in economic development and growth. Even worse, we don't have enough domestically to finance the debt, so we are borrowing money abroad from foreign banks, governments, and financial institutions—$40 billion in 1983; $70 to $80 billion in 1984 (40 percent of our total); over $100 billion in 1985 (50 percent of the total); and rising. By 1989, it is projected that 50 percent of all individual income taxes will be going just to pay for the interest on the debt. The U.S. used to be the largest exporter of capital, but under President Reagan we soon will become the largest debtor nation. About two weeks ago, on July 4, we celebrated our Declaration of Independence and our freedom. Yet every day supply-side economics is making our nation more economically dependent and less economically free. Five to six percent of our gross national product is now being eaten up with President Reagan's budget deficit.

To depend on foreign military powers to protect our national security would be foolish and make us less secure. Yet Reaganomics is increasingly making us more dependent. By increasing our economic dependency, Reaganomics decreases our ability to control our own economic future and destiny, decreases our security, and decreases our self-respect. A great nation must be measured by its ability to produce, not just its ability to consume. We are negotiating away our independence. Freedom and independence are the result of self-determination, self-reliance, self-discipline, and self-respect. Under President Reagan, America is less economically free and more dependent.

President Reagan's consumer-led, but deficit-financed, recovery is unbalanced, artificial, and will be short-lived. President Reagan's recovery is an economic "quick fix" that is based on foreign borrowing and will end in another recession. The boom of '84 will become a boomerang. If we continue down the road of supply-side—with a "dead-end" sign in front of us, with no brakes, and a cliff behind the sign—we will deserve our inevitable fate.

Reaganomics is economic opium that is destroying us from within. President Reagan's recovery is like Santa Claus's wish list at Christmas time—buy now and pay later. President Reagan's recovery may bring the joy of Christmas morning in 1984, but there will be sadness, sacrifice, and suffering when the generation of your children, and your children's children, have to pay for it. Our adult generation should not be so selfish and self-centered as to burden our children with our indulgent and short-lived behavior. It is short-term pleasure, but it's leading to long-term pain.

Yet an artificial recovery is merely the beginning of our problems. The record Reagan budget deficits drive up interest rates. High interest rates overvalue the dollar abroad. Because of an overvalued dollar, our prices have increased relative to all of our competitors by about thirty-five percent over the last three years. We cannot give our competitors a thirty-five-percent subsidy, or give ourselves a thirty-five-percent tax, and remain competitive in the world market. An overvalued dollar is good for the American consumer because it subsidizes imports, but it is bad for American exports (farm products and machinery in particular) because it taxes Americans out of jobs and competition. The trade imbalance this year is projected to be close to $120 billion. For every $1 billion of trade imbalance, it costs Americans about 25,000 jobs. Thus President Reagan's record trade imbalance alone will cost Americans nearly 3 million jobs. We need a balance of trade, because another four years of Reaganomics will bring on the greatest tide of protectionism in American history.

Record budget deficits, high interest rates, and an overvalued dollar are contributing to the international debt crisis in the Third World. The greatest threat to our national security in Central America is not the East-West conflict. It is the international debt crisis, created principally by President Reagan's record budget deficits. They are threatening to destabilize the world economy, including the U.S. economy. In light of the international debt crisis, the International Monetary Fund and the big multinational banks are imposing austerity programs on the developing nations. Some developing nations cannot even pay the interest on their debt. These governments are unable to meet the basic needs of their citizens, and the people are rebelling. The buildup of our large interventionary forces is mainly for the purpose of putting down these economic and social rebellions in the name of stopping communism, but it is largely of our own making— and heightened under Reaganomics.

Democracy guarantees opportunity; it does not guarantee success. Democracy guarantees the right to participate; it does not give a license to either a majority or a minority to dominate. The victory for the Rainbow Coalition in the platform debates today was not whether we won or lost the vote but that we raised the right issues. We could afford to lose the vote. Issues are negotiable. We could not afford to avoid raising the right questions. Our self-respect and our moral integrity were at stake. Our heads are perhaps bloody but unbowed. Our backs are straight, and our vision is clear. We can go home and face our people. And when we think, in this journey from slave ship to championship, that we have gone from the planks of the boardwalk in Atlantic City in 1964 to fighting to help to write the planks in the Democratic party platform in San Francisco in 1984, there is a deep and abiding sense of joy in our soul, in spite of the tears in our eyes. Although there are missing planks, there is a solid foundation upon which we can build.

The real challenge to our individual and collective Democratic leadership is to do three things: (1) provide hope, which will inspire people to struggle and achieve, (2) provide a plan that shows the people a way out of our dilemma, and (3) courageously lead the way out.

There is a way out. Justice. The requirement for rebuilding America is justice. The linchpin of progressive politics in America is not new programs in the North but new power in the South. That is why I argue over and over again, that from Lynchburg, Virginia, around to Texas, there is only one black congressperson out of 115. Nineteen years after passage of the Voting Rights Act, we're locked out of the House, the Senate, and the governor's mansion. The key to unlocking Southern power is getting the Voting Rights Act enforced and ending the new forms of political disenfranchisement.

The key to a Democratic victory in 1984 is enfranchisement of the progressive wing of the Democratic party. They are the ones who have been devastated by Reaganomics, and, therefore, it is in their self-interest to vote in record numbers to oust their oppressor. Those already poor and those who are being impoverished do not simply want a change in leaders, they want a change in direction. The poor are not looking to be embellished, they have a need to be empowered. The key to political enfranchisement is enforcement of the Voting Rights Act. Gerrymandering, annexations, at-large elections, inaccessible registrars, roll purges, dual registrations, and second primaries—these are the schemes that continue to disenfranchise the locked-out. Why do I fight these impediments? Because you cannot hold someone in the ditch without lingering there with them. If the Voting Rights Act is enforced, we'll get twelve to twenty black, Hispanic, female, and progressive congresspersons from the South. We can save the cotton, but we've got to fight the boll weevils. We've got to make a judgment.

It's not enough to hope ERA will pass. How can we pass ERA? If blacks vote in great numbers, progressive whites win. It's the only way progressive whites win. If blacks vote in great numbers, Hispanics win. If blacks, Hispanics, and progressive whites vote, women win. When women win, children win. When women and children win, workers win. We must all come up together. We must come up together I tell you, with all of our joy and excitement, we must not save the world and lose our souls. We should never short-circuit enforcement of the Voting Rights Act at every level. If one of us rises, all of us must rise. Justice is the way out.

There is a way out. Peace. The only way we can have jobs at home is to have peace abroad. We should not act as if nuclear weaponry is negotiable and debatable. In 1984, other nations have nuclear weapons too. Now if we drop the bomb, six to eight minutes later, we, too, will be destroyed. The issue now is not about dropping the bomb on somebody; it's about dropping the bomb on everybody. We must choose developed minds over guided missiles and think our way out, not fight it out. We must develop a coherent strategic nuclear strategy. We used nuclear weapons once before on Japan. But we must declare that never again will we be the ones to engage in the "first use" of nuclear weapons. Our real security is in developed minds, not guided missiles.

Our foreign policy must be demilitarized. We must choose mutual respect, talk, negotiations, diplomacy, trade, and aid, and measure human rights by one yardstick as the way of resolving international conflicts. We should support a legitimate Solidarity labor movement and oppose martial law in Poland. But then we cannot become the number-one trading partner with South Africa when they impose martial law and violently crush a black solidarity labor movement—especially while they are developing a nuclear capability. The U.S. must apply a new formula in assisting South African liberation—enfranchisement, investment; disenfranchisement, disinvestment. Our present relationship with South Africa is a moral disgrace.

Beyond the liberation of South Africa, we must fight for trade and aid for development in all of Africa, as well as in Europe and the Middle East. We must be as concerned about the preservation of democracy in Africa as we are in Europe. We've turned our heads and our backs when democracy has been dealt blows in Africa. This indifference must not be allowed to happen in the future.

Our present formula for peace in the Middle East is inadequate and will not work. There are twenty-two nations in the Middle East, and we must be able to talk, act, influence, and reconcile all of them. Currently we have too many interests and too few friends. We must have a mutual recognition policy, built on the Camp David agreement, which was a good first step, and measure human rights by one yardstick.

We should not be mining the harbors of Nicaragua and trying to covertly overthrow that government. Military aid and military advisors (who will give military advice) should be withdrawn from El Salvador. We should use our strength to get FDR-FMLN and President Duarte to agree to a cease-fire and negotiations. We should not be establishing military bases in Honduras and militarizing the nation of Costa Rica. It was wrong for our nation to invade tiny Grenada. And if we can have diplomatic relations with the Soviet Union and China, as we should, we can have diplomatic relations with Cuba. Just this week, we have seen progress as a result of our moral appeal. In addition to the Americans returned, the political prisoners released (and more to be released), negotiations, at this very moment, are being conducted over the Mariel prisoners, a Cuban family-reunification program, and President Castro has agreed to exchange ambassadors without preconditions. Let's give peace a chance.

There is a way out. Jobs. If we enforce the Voting Rights Act as a way of achieving justice; and if we achieve peace through cutting the defense budget without cutting our defense, respect other nations of the world, and resolve conflicts through negotiations instead of confrontations; then we will have enough power and money to rebuild America. We can use the money we are currently squandering on the arms race to save the human race. We can use that money to build millions of new houses, to build hospitals, to train and pay our teachers and educate our young people, to provide health care and health-care training, to rebuild our cities and end rural poverty; use that money to rebuild two hundred and fifty thousand bridges, rebuild our railroads, and build mass-transit systems; use that money to put steelworkers back to work; use that money to rebuild the infrastructure of our country: repair our roads, our ports, our riverbeds, our sewer systems, and stop soil erosion; use that money to clean up our environment: our land, our water, and our air; use that money to make "America the Beautiful." We could put America back to work.

Ronald Reagan claims the votes of the South. I say to you this night that the soil is too rich and the people are too poor for Ronald Reagan to have the votes of the South. The South is going to rise up and move from racial battlegrounds to economic common ground and moral higher ground. We love our God, and we love our country too, but we want moral values with material substance. Black and white together, men and women, we will take the South.

We have fought hard to build our Rainbow Coalition of the rejected over the last eight months. We have fought hard for party justice and for our minority planks because we believe that expanding our party to include the locked-out is the key to victory in November and to developing the progressive politics of the future.

What this campaign has shown above all else is that the key to our liberation is in our own hands and in our dream and vision of a better world. It is the vision

917

that allows us to reach out to each other and to redeem each other. It is the dream that sustains us through the dark times and the dark realities. It is our hope that gives us a why for living when we do not see how to live.

In the final analysis, however, we must be driven not by a negative—the fear of Reagan—but by the positive leadership and programs of the Democratic party. It is not enough motivation just to vote against Reagan, we must inspire our constituency to vote for us. We must offer our people the vision of a just society and the dream of a peaceful world. We must inspire the American people with hope. We must put forth the vision of a government that cares for all of its people, the vision of a people at work rebuilding its nation. We must not be forced to choose between the two valid principles of seniority and affirmative action. We must put all of America back to work.

With courage and conscience, conviction and vision, we can win. If we don't raise the issues, if the truth is locked away, the people won't get excited. But when the truth is lifted up, they'll come running. Across lines of race and sex, they'll come running to vote for us. If we lift up before this nation a plan to wipe out cheese and bread lines, to feed our hungry and malnourished people, they'll come running. If we lift up a plan to house the homeless and educate the illiterate, they'll come running. If we reach out to the Vietnam veteran, to the disabled, to the poor, to the widow, to the orphan, and tell them that help is on the way, they'll come running.

When I was a child in Greenville, South Carolina, the Reverend James Hall used to preach a sermon, every so often, about Jesus. He would quote Jesus as saying, "If I be lifted up, I'll draw all men unto me." When I was a child I didn't quite understand what he meant. But I understand it a little better now. If you raise up truth, it's magnetic. It has a way of drawing people. With all this confusion in the convention—bright lights, parties, and big fun—we must raise up a simple proposition: feed the hungry, and the poor will come running; study war no more, and our youth will come running. If we lift up a program to put America back to work as an alternative to welfare and despair, the unemployed will come running. If we cut the military budget without cutting our defense and use that money to rebuild bridges and put steelworkers back to work; use that money to provide jobs for our citizens; use that money to build schools and train teachers and educate our children; use that money to build hospitals and train doctors and nurses—the whole nation will come running to us.

As I lived in the ghettos, in barrios, on reservations, and in the slums, I had a message for our youth. Young America, I know you face a cutback in jobs, large reductions in housing and food, inferior health care and education, and a general environment that tries to break your spirit. But don't put dope in your veins; put hope in your brains. Don't let them break your spirit. There is a way out. Our party must not only have the courage and the conscience to expose the slummy side. We must have the conviction and vision to show America the sunny side, the way out. When I see urban decay I see a sunny side and a slummy side. A broken window is the slummy side. Train that youth to be a carpenter. That's the sunny side. A missing brick? That's the slummy side. Train that youth to be a brick mason. That's the sunny side. The hieroglyphics of destitution on the walls? That's the slummy side. Train that youth to be a painter or an artist. That's the sunny side. Then unions must open up, embrace, and train our youth so they can help to rebuild America.

I am more convinced than ever that we can win. We'll vault up the rough side of the mountain—we can win. But I just want the youth of America to do me one favor: Exercise the right to dream. You must face reality—that which is. But then dream of the reality that ought to be, that must be. Live beyond the pain of reality with the dream of a bright tomorrow. Use hope and imagination as weapons of survival and progress. Use love to motivate you and obligate you to serve the human family.

Young people, dream of peace. Choose the human race over the nuclear race. We must bury the weapons and not burn the people. We are the first generation that will either freeze the weapons or burn the people and freeze the planet.

Young people, dream of a new value system. Dream of teachers, but teachers who will teach for life, not just for a living. Dream of doctors, but doctors who are more concerned with public health than personal wealth. Dream of lawyers, but lawyers who are more concerned with justice than a judgeship. Dream of artists, but artists who will convey music and message, rhythm, rhyme, and reason. Dream of priests and preachers, but priests and preachers who will prophesy and not profiteer. Dream of writers, but writers who will ascribe, describe, prescribe, not just scribble. Dream of authentic leaders who will mold public opinion against a headwind, not just ride the tailwinds of opinion polls. Dream of a world where we measure character by how much we share and care, not by how much we take and consume. Preach and dream. Our time has come.

We must measure character by how we treat the least of these, by who feeds the most hungry people, by who educates the most uneducated people, by who cares and loves the most, by who fights for the needy and seeks to save the greedy. We must dream and choose the laws of sacrifice, which lead to greatness, and not the laws of convenience, which lead to collapse.

In your dreaming you must know that unearned suffering is redemptive. Water cannot wash away the blood of martyrs. Blood is thicker than water. Water makes grass and flowers grow, but blood makes sons and daughters of liberation grow. No matter how difficult the days and dark the nights, there is a brighter side somewhere. In Angola, Mozambique, Nicaragua, El Salvador, South Africa, Greenville, South Carolina, and Harlem, there is a brighter side.

Jesus was rejected from the inn and born in the slum. But just because you were born in the slum does not mean that the slum was born in you. With a made-up mind, which is the most powerful instrument in the world, you can rise above your circumstances. No mountain is too high, and no valley is too low; no forest is too dense, and no water is too deep—if your mind is made up. With eyesight, you may see misery. But with insight, you can see the brighter side.

Suffering breeds character, character breeds faith, and in the end faith will not disappoint. Faith, hope, and dreams will prevail. Weeping may endure for a night, but joy is coming in the morning. Troubles won't last always. Our time has come. No graves can hold our bodies down. Our time has come. No lie can live forever. Our time has come. We must leave our racial battlegrounds, come to economic common ground, and rise to moral higher ground. America, our time has come. Give me your tired, your poor, your huddled masses yearning to breathe free. And come November, there will be a change, because our time has come.

MICHELLE CLIFF (b. 1946)

Michelle Cliff, now a United States citizen, was born in Kingston, Jamaica. She is a novelist and poet who uses her writing to address both social and political issues. Cliff's novel Abeng *(1984) deals with skin color issues within the black race. In* No Telephone to Heaven *(1987) and* Free Enterprise *(1993), Cliff addresses the influence of African culture on African American culture, among other themes. Both* The Land of Look Behind *(1985) and* Claiming an Identity They Taught Me to Despise *(1980) are compilations of her poetry. She has also published a book of short stories,* Bodies of Water *(1990).*

From Abeng (1984)

Chapter 1

The island rose and sank. Twice. During periods in which history was recorded by indentations on rock and shell.

This is a book about the time which followed on that time. As the island became a place where people lived. Indians. Africans. Europeans.

It was a Sunday morning at the height of the height of the mango season. High July—and hot. No rain probably until October—at least no rain of any consequence.

There was a splendid profusion of fruit. The slender cylinders of St. Juliennes hung from a grafted branch of a common mango tree in a backyard in town. Round and pink Bombays seemed to be everywhere—brimming calabashes in the middle of dining tables, pouring out of crates and tumbling onto sidewalks. Small and orange number elevens filled the market baskets at Crossroads, the baskets carried on the heads of women traveling to town from country. Green and spotted Black mangoes dotted the ground at bus stops, schoolyards, country stores—these were only to be gathered, not sold. The fruit was all over and each variety was unto itself—with its own taste, its own distinction of shade and highlight, its own occasion and use. In the yards around town and on the hills in the country, spots of yellow, pink, red, orange, black, and green appeared between the almost-blue elongated leaves of the fat and laden trees—and created a confusion underneath.

The Savages—father, mother, and two daughters—were getting ready for church, the first service of the day. "This is the day the Lord has made. Let us rejoice and be glad in it." Mr. Savage chanted as he shaved. The girls were bickering over something or other in the room they shared, and at the same time filling their small plastic purses with a shilling for collection, clean handkerchief with SUNDAY embroidered in the corner, and a ripe number eleven.

It seemed to many people that all the children on the island were carrying pieces of the fruit with them. Khaki pockets bulged out of shape with roundness and in defiance—just one slip on the pavement could release juice or sap, and there would be hell to pay. Mouths everywhere burned from the sap and tingled from the juice; teeth caught the hairs from the seed and tightened around the yellow and gold fibers—even though there was bounty, it was important to reach every last bit of flesh—to complete the mango, and move on to the next.

It was as if the island was host to some ripe sweet plague. Because of the visitation, peppermint and chocolate sales had dropped off, so had paradise plums, bullah cakes—and the Fudgie men who peddled popsicles from wooden boxes on the backs of their bicycles noticed fewer responses to their cry of FUDGEEEE. The new-to-the-island soft custard stand on the Halfway Tree Road reported that they were not doing very well, but expected sales to pick up in the heat of August, when the mangoes would be finished and the avocado would be in season.

Mangotime was not usually such a business, but this was 1958 and the biggest crop in recent memory—as the *Daily Gleaner* itself reported. The paper ran an editorial which spoke of God's Gift to Jamaica, and concluded by telling all inhabitants to be hospitable to the tourists.

Some of the mystery and wonder of mangotime may have been in the fact that this was a wild fruit. Jamaicans did not cultivate it for export to America or England—like citrus, cane, bananas. So much was this so, that when walking through Harlem or Notting Hill Gate, Brooklyn or Ladbroke Grove, island people were genuinely shocked to see a Bombay, half-ripe usually ("Picked much too young"), nesting in a bed of green excelsior, showing through a display window, priced out of reach ("Lord, have mercy, we use them to stone dogs back home"), and they wondered where the mango had come from. Someone somewhere else must be exporting the fruit. For them, the mango was to be kept an island secret.

They did not cultivate the mango, but they made occasional efforts to change the course of its development. These efforts were usually few and far between and carried out with care and discretion. A branch was sliced from a common mango tree and replaced with a branch from a St. Julienne—the former could withstand all manner of disease or weather; the latter was fragile. But the Jamaican taste was growing for the St. Julienne, which was judged to be consistently full and deep in its sweetness, while the common mango was termed unpredictable, with a sweetness that could be thin and might leave an aftertaste. That was as far as cultivation went in 1958, though—a few grafts here and there—they did not tamper further.

There were other wild fruit on the island—the bush of Jamaica had long been written about as one of the most naturally fruitful places on earth—but the mango was supreme among all other growing things—the paragon: "Mother Sugar herself."

It was a surprising fruit—sometimes remaining hidden for years behind vines and underbrush—saving its sweetness for wild pigs and wild birds.

In 1958 Jamaica had two rulers: a white queen and a white governor. Independence-in-practically-name-only was four years away. The portrait of the white queen hung in banks, department stores, grocery stores, schools, government buildings, and homes—from countryside shanties to the split-levels on the hills above Kingston Harbor. A rather plain little white woman decked in medals and other regalia—wearing, of course, a crown. Our-lady-of-the-colonies. The whitest woman in the world. Elizabeth II, great-granddaughter of Victoria, for whom the downtown crafts market—where women came from the countryside to sell their baskets and Rastafarians sold their brooms and old Black men sold their wood-carvings to the passengers of cruise ships and Pan-American Clippers—was named.

The monetary system of the island was based on the pounds/shillings/pence of the "mother" country. The coins and notes were similar to those struck and printed for Great Britain itself. The coins came from the Royal Mint and the notes from the Bank of England, popularly called the Old Lady of Threadneedle Street. There were two basic differences: Jamaican money bore the word JAMAICA, and the sovereign crest of the island—an Arawak Indian and a white conqueror: only one of these existed in 1958.

The population of the island was primarily Black ("overwhelmingly," some sources said), with gradations of shading reaching into the top strata of the society. Africans were mixed with Sephardic Jews, Chinese, Syrians, Lebanese, East Indians—but the large working class, and class of poor people, was Black.

It was the Sunday custom of the Savages to attend their first church service at the John Knox Memorial Church at Constant Spring. Of light brown stucco, the long low building had mahogany louvers running the length of the two far aisles—the louvers were turned down against the sun. The pews were also mahogany, and were divided down the middle by one single center aisle. The church was spare and clean in its design—the only decoration, if that is what it could be called, was a large cross behind the pulpit, carved of Godwood—the original tree—the tree of Eden. Commonly known as the birch gum.

There was no church choir at John Knox; a Scottish schoolteacher played Presbyterian hymns at a harpsichord, which had been shipped to Jamaica in a box and was reassembled by the minister. The instrument had never adjusted to the climate. The schoolteacher explained to the congregation that a harpsichord had to be tuned each time it was to be played; even so, tuning upon tuning never made the instrument sound quite right. There was a gravelly tinkle in its voice, far more than a harpsichord is supposed to have, and it was easily drowned out by the passing traffic, the voices of the congregation, the pair of croaking lizards who lived behind the cross of Godwood, sounding a double bass in the wrong tempo, as the schoolteacher tinkled out the prelude, when the congregation entered, and the postlude, when they left the church. Although they were not able to say so, most of the congregation felt that the harpsichord had been a mistake—not meant even in the most perfect of climatic conditions to accompany a hundred voices. It seemed that English people must sing softer—or not at all—and that the climate of that place—damp and dreary—surpassed the clear light and deep warmth of Jamaica. They had always thought their island climate a gift; the harpsichord told them different. The schoolteacher advised the congregation to tone down their singing, to consider the nuances of harmony and quiet—but this didn't work.

The minister of the church was a red-faced Englishman, who preached plainly and briefly, and had been a major in the King's Household Cavalry during the last war. He had emigrated to Jamaica in 1949, and since then had spent his afternoons at the bar of the South Camp Hotel, where he drank beer and played skittles with English soldiers and merchant seamen. On special days he led the congregation in "God Save the Queen"—during the Suez Crisis of 1956 they had stood and sung it every Sunday for a month. On other, more ordinary Sundays, they sang the standards—"Onward Christian Soldiers, Marching as to War"; "Faith of Our Fathers, Living Still, in Spite of Dungeon, Fire and Sword"; "Fairest Lord Jesus, Ruler of All Nature"; "Fling Out the Banner, Let It Float, Skyward and Seaward, High and Wide"—in which the banner of righteousness carried by the Christian soldiers mingled with the Union Jack.

The congregation at John Knox was Black and white—Jamaican and English and American. Mostly of the middle class. The church was Mr. Savage's choice for worship.

In 1958, and for some time before, the two most socially prestigious churches in Kingston were Holy Cross, the cathedral at Halfway Tree, and the Kingston Parish Church, downtown on King Street, near King's Parade, founded in 1692.

Holy Cross Cathedral was the church of the island's wealthy Catholics—most of them Lebanese and Syrian and Chinese, some Spanish. These were the same people who sent their daughters to the Convent of the Immaculate Conception, a group of pink-stucco Spanish-tiled-roof villas, set back on green lawns next to a golf course. The Protestants sent their daughters to St. Catherine's, a red-brick girls' school, which was less grand but more severe than Immaculate Conception.

The Parish Church was High Anglican—it was the church of attendance of the white governor, and members of the royal family stopped there when the queen's yacht, *H. M. S. Britannia*, docked in Kingston Harbor. A very large stone edifice, it was foursquare and had been built to last. A rood screen had been imported from a church in Canterbury; a choir loft had been carved by a team of local craftsmen—in 1820, before the slaves were freed.

In 1958, while digging near the churchyard during some renovations to the building, workers uncovered a coffin of heavy metal—a coffin of huge proportions.

Not the shape of a coffin at all—shaped like a monstrous packing case, made of lead and welded shut. A brass plate which had been affixed to the coffin and etched with an inscription informed the vicar that the coffin contained the remains of a hundred plague victims, part of a shipload of slaves from the Gold Coast, who had contracted the plague from the rats on the vessel which brought them to Jamaica. Others, many others, would have died onboard and their bodies dropped in the sea along the Middle Passage—the route across the Atlantic from Africa—or the Windward Passage—the route from the Atlantic to the islands of the Caribbean Sea. The people in the coffin had died in a *barracoon* in Kingston— a holding pen—a stockade.

The coffin should be opened on no account, the plaque said, as the plague might still be viable. The vicar commissioned an American navy warship in port to take the coffin twenty miles out and sink it in the sea.

After the morning service, the Savages left Constant Spring and drove to their house on Dunbarton Crescent, where Dorothy, the Black woman who worked for them, prepared Sunday dinner. When the family had eaten, and she had cleaned up, she caught the bus to Trench Town, where her three-year-old daughter lived with Dorothy's mother. The Savages left also, for their weekly seabath at Tumbleover, a rocky and wild beach, unsheltered by cove or harbor, opposite the mangrove swamps on the Palisadoes Road, between Kingston Airport and the Gypsum factory at Rock Fort—a fort built by the Spanish, with the cannon still in place.

There was a wicked undertow at Tumbleover, and huge waves unbroken by a reef. Underneath the water was smooth rock covered with slippery sealife, and no foothold to be had. Once in the waves, a swimmer had to relax and ride the breakers—far out and then in. The beach was usually deserted, with only the water's force as background noise, and occasional planes circling to land at Palisadoes.

A Sunday afternoon not long before this Sunday afternoon, Clare, the elder Savage daughter, who was twelve years old, found a trilobite fossil embedded in the rocks under the water, and Mr. Savage had explained in great detail how old the world was, and how insignificant was man.

"Clare, if you took a broomstick; or if you took an obelisk from ancient Egypt, like Cleopatra's Needle, and made a pinprick at the tip—that would represent the history of mankind; the rest all came before us. Think about it. Consider it."

Clare's relationship with her father took the form of what she imagined a son would have, if there had been a son. Mr. Savage took his daughter to a mountaintop to prove to her that the island had exploded from the sea. True to his theory—she was his daughter; she assumed the idea belonged to him—there were fragments of seashells and pieces of coral on top. He explained to her how the entire chain of the West Indies had once been underwater. He spoke of mountain-folding, the process by which flat rock becomes peaks and slopes. While this process usually took thousands of years, Mr. Savage preferred to believe that Jamaican mountains had been created in cataclysm. All of a sudden.

Perhaps, he said to his daughter, the islands of the West Indies—particularly the Greater Antilles, which were said once to have been joined—were the remains of Atlantis, the floating continent Plato had written about in the *Timaeus*, that sank under the sea. It had been an ideal place, too good for this world. "But then there was a great and powerful earthquake, and the continent came back up again—and was first joined in a chain and then was split apart into islands." He stopped; then thought further. "Or maybe the islands were an undersea mountain range, and emerged when Atlantis went under the Mediterranean. When the volcano erupted in Crete." He paused again.

"Some say that Crete and Atlantis were one," still trying to forge some connection between the pieces of knowledge he possessed, and how he wanted things to be.

Mr. Savage was fascinated by myth and natural disaster. He collected books on Stonehenge, the Pyramids, the Great Wall of China—he knew the details of each ancient structure and was convinced that all were connected to some magical source—some "divine plan," he said. Nothing, to him, was ever what it seemed to be. Nothing was an achievement of human labor. Devising arch and circle; creating brick from straw and mud and hauling stones to the site of construction. Mr. Savage was a believer in extraterrestrial life—in a mythic piece of machinery found in a bed of coal: part of a spaceship, he concluded; proof that we had been visited by beings from another planet, who might be observing us even now. Most people thought him focused out, most of the time, while they were focused in, or down. "Down to earth," was what they called his wife—sometimes his complement, sometimes his opposite. To pass the time until his deliverance, he went to the racetrack, courted women on the sly, drank rum and water, and moved from job to job, while his wife kept her faith, saved her own money from her job in a downtown hotel, spoke sometimes with her relatives, and prayed for a better day.

Clare's father was no commonplace dreamer, one whose visions were only slightly distorted by rum; he didn't have dreams anywhere near the realm of accomplishment. His visions—which included the second coming, the end of the world, Armageddon—would be achieved only by waiting; only through intervention from the outside—when God judged the time was right. In the meanwhile he tried to pass these ideals on to his elder daughter—calling her an Aztec princess, golden in the sun. "Clare, you would have certainly been a choice for sacrifice—you know the Aztecs slaughtered their most beautiful virgins and drank their blood." It did not occur to Clare to question her father's reading of history—a worldview in which she would have been chosen for divine slaughter.

Most often, she became his defender. When he talked about his notions of space and time and magic to her mother's family, they only laughed at him. Telling him the planets were but dust. Illusions created by God to speak of his glory. Dust and shadow was the rest of the universe. Earth was the one concrete reality. And this life, life on Earth, just a gateway to the life everlasting. Which was the one true realm of existence. Many of them only waited to pass into that realm.

This particular afternoon, Mr. Savage had just stepped into the water, when he came running and screaming out again—"Shark! Shark!" He was howling and shaking and pale. He claimed a shark had swum up right beside his thigh and touched him. Mrs. Savage went into the water to prove it was safe now, and the girls, Clare and Jennie, who was seven, followed her. But it was no use. "As God is my judge," Mr. Savage vowed, "I am never going into the sea again—never."

In later weeks, the family moved from Tumbleover to Cable Hut, a beach sheltered by reef and cove, but Mr. Savage only disappeared into the shed where they sold rum, and reappeared when one of the girls was sent to get him, and they were ready to leave for home.

✵ OCTAVIA BUTLER (b. 1947)

Octavia Butler is an accomplished science fiction writer. She was born in Pasadena, California, and attended Pasadena City College and other colleges in Southern California. She has worked with the Writers Guild of America and received a MacArthur Foundation grant in 1995. Butler published a five-part novel sequence, starting with Patternmaster *in 1976, followed by* Mind of My Mind *(1977),* Survivor *(1978),* Wild Seed *(1980), and* Clay's Ark *(1984). Heroic female characters are evident in her writing, such as Lauren Oya in* Parable of the Sower *(1993). Butler's novelette* Bloodchild *(1985) won three prestigious science fiction awards: the Locus, Hugo, and Nebula Awards. She published her best-known book,* Kindred, *in 1988.*

From Kindred (1988)

The River

The trouble began long before June 9, 1976, when I became aware of it, but June 9 is the day I remember. It was my twenty-sixth birthday. It was also the day I met Rufus—the day he called me to him for the first time.

Kevin and I had not planned to do anything to celebrate my birthday. We were both too tired for that. On the day before, we had moved from our apartment in Los Angeles to a house of our own a few miles away in Altadena. The moving was celebration enough for me. We were still unpacking—or rather, I was still unpacking. Kevin had stopped when he got his office in order. Now he was closeted there either loafing or thinking because I didn't hear his typewriter. Finally, he came out to the living room where I was sorting books into one of the big bookcases. Fiction only. We had so many books, we had to try to keep them in some kind of order.

"What's the matter?" I asked him.

"Nothing." He sat down on the floor near where I was working. "Just struggling with my own perversity. You know, I had half-a-dozen ideas for that Christmas story yesterday during the moving."

"And none now when there's time to write them down."

"Not a one." He picked up a book, opened it, and turned a few pages. I picked up another book and tapped him on the shoulder with it. When he looked up, surprised, I put a stack of nonfiction down in front of him. He stared at it unhappily.

"Hell, why'd I come out here?"

"To get more ideas. After all, they come to you when you're busy."

He gave me a look that I knew wasn't as malevolent as it seemed. He had the kind of pale, almost colorless eyes that made him seem distant and angry whether he was or not. He used them to intimidate people. Strangers. I grinned at him and went back to work. After a moment, he took the nonfiction to another bookcase and began shelving it.

I bent to push him another box full, then straightened quickly as I began to feel dizzy, nauseated. The room seemed to blur and darken around me. I stayed on my feet for a moment holding on to a bookcase and wondering what was wrong, then finally, I collapsed to my knees. I heard Kevin make a wordless sound of surprise, heard him ask, "What happened?"

I raised my head and discovered that I could not focus on him. "Something is wrong with me," I gasped.

I heard him move toward me, saw a blur of gray pants and blue shirt. Then, just before he would have touched me, he vanished.

The house, the books, everything vanished. Suddenly, I was outdoors kneeling on the ground beneath trees. I was in a green place. I was at the edge of a woods. Before me was a wide tranquil river, and near the middle of that river was a child splashing, screaming . . .

Drowning!

I reacted to the child in trouble. Later I could ask questions, try to find out where I was, what had happened. Now I went to help the child.

I ran down to the river, waded into the water fully clothed, and swam quickly to the child. He was unconscious by the time I reached him—a small red-haired boy floating, face down. I turned him over, got a good hold on him so that his head was above water, and towed him in. There was a red-haired woman waiting for us on the shore now. Or rather, she was running back and forth crying on the shore. The moment she saw that I was wading, she ran out, took the boy from me and carried him the rest of the way, feeling and examining him as she did.

"He's not breathing!" she screamed.

Artificial respiration. I had seen it done, been told about it, but I had never done it. Now was the time to try. The woman was in no condition to do anything useful, and there was no one else in sight. As we reached shore, I snatched the child from her. He was no more than four or five years old, and not very big.

I put him down on his back, tilted his head back, and began mouth-to-mouth resuscitation. I saw his chest move as I breathed into him. Then, suddenly, the woman began beating me.

"You killed my baby!" she screamed. "You killed him!"

I turned and managed to catch her pounding fists. "Stop it!" I shouted, putting all the authority I could into my voice. "He's alive!" Was he? I couldn't tell. Please God, let him be alive. "The boy's alive. Now let me help him." I pushed her away, glad she was a little smaller than I was, and turned my attention back to her son. Between breaths, I saw her staring at me blankly. Then she dropped to her knees beside me, crying.

Moments later, the boy began breathing on his own—breathing and coughing and choking and throwing up and crying for his mother. If he could do all that, he was all right. I sat back from him, feeling light-headed, relieved. I had done it!

"He's alive!" cried the woman. She grabbed him and nearly smothered him. "Oh, Rufus, baby . . ."

Rufus. Ugly name to inflict on a reasonably nice-looking little kid.

When Rufus saw that it was his mother who held him, he clung to her, screaming as loudly as he could. There was nothing wrong with his voice, anyway. Then, suddenly, there was another voice.

"What the devil's going on here?" A man's voice, angry and demanding.

I turned, startled, and found myself looking down the barrel of the longest rifle I had ever seen. I heard a metallic click, and I froze, thinking I was going to be shot for saving the boy's life. I was going to die.

I tried to speak, but my voice was suddenly gone. I felt sick and dizzy. My vision blurred so badly I could not distinguish the gun or the face of the man behind it. I heard the woman speak sharply, but I was too far gone into sickness and panic to understand what she said.

Then the man, the woman, the boy, the gun all vanished.

I was kneeling in the living room of my own house again several feet from where I had fallen minutes before. I was back at home—wet and muddy, but intact. Across the room, Kevin stood frozen, staring at the spot where I had been. How long had he been there?

"Kevin?"

He spun around to face me. "What the hell . . . how did you get over there?" he whispered.

"I don't know."

"Dana, you . . ." He came over to me, touched me tentatively as though he wasn't sure I was real. Then he grabbed me by the shoulders and held me tightly. "What happened?"

I reached up to loosen his grip, but he wouldn't let go. He dropped to his knees beside me.

"Tell me!" he demanded.

"I would if I knew what to tell you. Stop hurting me."

He let me go, finally, stared at me as though he'd just recognized me. "Are you all right?"

"No." I lowered my head and closed my eyes for a moment. I was shaking with fear, with residual terror that took all the strength out of me. I folded forward, hugging myself, trying to be still. The threat was gone, but it was all I could do to keep my teeth from chattering.

Kevin got up and went away for a moment. He came back with a large towel and wrapped it around my shoulders. It comforted me somehow, and I pulled it tighter. There was an ache in my back and shoulders where Rufus's mother had pounded with her fists. She had hit harder than I'd realized, and Kevin hadn't helped.

We sat there together on the floor, me wrapped in the towel and Kevin with his arm around me calming me just by being there. After a while, I stopped shaking.

"Tell me now," said Kevin.

"What?"

"Everything. What happened to you? How did you . . . how did you move like that?"

I sat mute, trying to gather my thoughts, seeing the rifle again leveled at my head. I had never in my life panicked that way—never felt so close to death.

"Dana." He spoke softly. The sound of his voice seemed to put distance between me and the memory. But still . . .

"I don't know what to tell you," I said. "It's all crazy."

"Tell me how you got wet," he said. "Start with that."

I nodded. "There was a river," I said. "Woods with a river running through. And there was a boy drowning. I saved him. That's how I got wet." I hesitated, trying to think, to make sense. Not that what had happened to me made sense, but at least I could tell it coherently.

I looked at Kevin, saw that he held his expression carefully neutral. He waited. More composed, I went back to the beginning, to the first dizziness, and remembered it all for him—relived it all in detail. I even recalled things that I hadn't realized I'd noticed. The trees I'd been near, for instance, were pine trees, tall and straight with branches and needles mostly at the top. I had noticed that much somehow in the instant before I had seen Rufus. And I remembered something extra about Rufus's mother. Her clothing. She had worn a long dark dress that covered her from neck to feet. A silly thing to be wearing on a muddy riverbank. And she had spoken with an accent—a southern accent. Then there was the unforgettable gun, long and deadly.

Kevin listened without interrupting. When I was finished, he took the edge of the towel and wiped a little of the mud from my leg. "This stuff had to come from somewhere," he said.

"You don't believe me?"

He stared at the mud for a moment, then faced me. "You know how long you were gone?"

"A few minutes. Not long."

"A few seconds. There were no more than ten or fifteen seconds between the time you went and the time you called my name."

"Oh, no . . ." I shook my head slowly. "All that couldn't have happened in just seconds."

He said nothing.

"But it was real! I was there!" I caught myself, took a deep breath, and slowed down. "All right. If you told me a story like this, I probably wouldn't believe it either, but like you said, this mud came from somewhere."

"Yes."

"Look, what did you see? What do you think happened?"

He frowned a little, shook his head. "You vanished." He seemed to have to force the words out. "You were here until my hand was just a couple of inches from you. Then, suddenly, you were gone. I couldn't believe it. I just stood there. Then you were back again and on the other side of the room."

"Do you believe it yet?"

He shrugged. "It happened. I saw it. You vanished and you reappeared. Facts."

"I reappeared wet, muddy, and scared to death."

"Yes."

"And I know what I saw, and what I did—my facts. They're no crazier than yours."

"I don't know what to think."

"I'm not sure it matters what we think."

"What do you mean?"

"Well . . . it happened once. What if it happens again?"

"No. No, I don't think . . ."

"You don't know!" I was starting to shake again. "Whatever it was, I've had enough of it! It almost killed me!"

"Take it easy," he said. "Whatever happens, it's not going to do you any good to panic yourself again."

I moved uncomfortably, looked around. "I feel like it could happen again—like it could happen anytime. I don't feel secure here."

"You're just scaring yourself."

"No!" I turned to glare at him, and he looked so worried I turned away again. I wondered bitterly whether he was worried about my vanishing again or worried about my sanity. I still didn't think he believed my story. "Maybe you're right," I said. "I hope you are. Maybe I'm just like a victim of robbery or rape or something—a victim who survives, but who doesn't feel safe any more." I shrugged. "I don't have a name for the thing that happened to me, but I don't feel safe any more."

He made his voice very gentle. "If it happens again, and if it's real, the boy's father will know he owes you thanks. He won't hurt you."

"You don't know that. You don't know what could happen." I stood up unsteadily. "Hell, I don't blame you for humoring me." I paused to give him a chance to deny it, but he didn't. "I'm beginning to feel as though I'm humoring myself."

"What do you mean?"

"I don't know. As real as the whole episode was, as real as I know it was, it's beginning to recede from me somehow. It's becoming like something I saw on television or read about—like something I got second hand."

"Or like a . . . a dream?"

I looked down at him. "You mean a hallucination."

"All right."

"No! I know what I'm doing. I can see. I'm pulling away from it because it scares me so. But it was real."

"Let yourself pull away from it." He got up and took the muddy towel from me. "That sounds like the best thing you can do, whether it was real or not. Let go of it."

☘ RITA DOVE (b. 1952)

Known foremost for her poetry, Rita Dove has also written novels and short stories. She was born in Akron, Ohio; her father was the first black chemist to work in the tire and rubber industry. She graduated with honors from Miami University of Ohio in 1973. In 1977, she finished a master of fine arts degree at the Iowa Writers' Workshop.

Dove won a Pulitzer Prize in poetry for her well-known book Thomas and Beulah *(1986). She has published several other books of poetry, including* The Yellow House on the Corner *(1980),* Museum *(1983),* Grace Notes *(1989), and* Mother Love *(1995). Her poetry often deals with her own history and the history of the world. Among other works, Dove has written a novel,* Through the Ivory Gate *(1992), and a short-story collection,* Fifth Sunday *(1985). She has taught at Arizona State University and the University of Virginia. She was named poet laureate of the United States in 1993— the first African American to hold this title.*

Gospel (1986)

Swing low so I
can step inside—
a humming ship of voices
big with all

the wrongs done   5
done them.
No sound this generous
could fail:

ride joy until
it cracks like an egg,   10
make sorrow
seethe and whisper.

From a fortress
of animal misery
soars the chill voice   15
of the tenor, enraptured

with sacrifice.
What do I see,
he complains, notes
brightly rising   20

towards a sky
blank with promise.
Yet how healthy
the single contralto

settling deeper   25
into her watery furs!
Carry me home,
she cajoles, bearing

down. Candelabras
brim. But he slips   30
through God's net and swims
heavenward, warbling.

Obedience (1986)

That smokestack, for instance,
in the vacant lot across the street:
if she could order it down and watch
it float in lapse-time over buckled tar and macadam
it would stop an inch or two perhaps   5
before her patent leather shoes.

Her body's no longer tender, but her mind is free.
She can think up a twilight, sulfur
flicking orange then black
as the tip of a flamingo's wing, the white   10
picket fence marching up the hill . . .

but she would never create such puny stars.
The house, shut up like a pocket watch,
those tight hearts breathing inside—
she could never invent them.   15

Variation on Pain (1986)

Two strings, one pierced cry.
So many ways to imitate
The ringing in his ears.

He lay on the bunk, mandolin
In his arms. Two strings   5
For each note and seventeen
Frets; ridged sound
Humming beneath calloused
Fingertips.

There was a needle   10
In his head but nothing

Fit through it. Sound quivered
Like a rope stretched clear
To land, tensed and brimming,
A man gurgling air.   15

Two greased strings
For each pierced lobe:
So is the past forgiven.

❊ WALTER MOSLEY (b. 1952)

Walter Mosley is known for his detective novels that feature the adventures of Easy Rawlins, a black detective in Los Angeles. Devil in a Blue Dress *(1990) is perhaps Mosley's best-known novel. The novel, set in 1948, won a Shamus Award from the Private Eye Writers of America and received a nomination for an Edgar Award from the Mystery Writers of America. It was also made into a popular movie. Mosley has written several other novels about the life of Easy, including* A Red Death *(1991),* White Butterfly *(1992), and* Betty Black *(1994).*

From Devil in a Blue Dress (1990)

1

I was surprised to see a white man walk into Joppy's bar. It's not just that he was white but he wore an off-white linen suit and shirt with a Panama straw hat and bone shoes over flashing white silk socks. His skin was smooth and pale with just a few freckles. One lick of strawberry-blond hair escaped the band of his hat. He stopped in the doorway, filling it with his large frame, and surveyed the room with pale eyes; not a color I'd ever seen in a man's eyes. When he looked at me I felt a thrill of fear, but that went away quickly because I was used to white people by 1948.

I had spent five years with white men, and women, from Africa to Italy, through Paris, and into the Fatherland itself. I ate with them and slept with them, and I killed enough blue-eyed young men to know that they were just as afraid to die as I was.

The white man smiled at me, then he walked to the bar where Joppy was running a filthy rag over the marble top. They shook hands and exchanged greetings like old friends.

The second thing that surprised me was that he made Joppy nervous. Joppy was a tough ex-heavyweight who was comfortable brawling in the ring or in the street, but he ducked his head and smiled at that white man just like a salesman whose luck had gone bad.

I put a dollar down on the bar and made to leave, but before I was off the stool Joppy turned my way and waved me toward them.

"Com'on over here, Easy. This here's somebody I want ya t'meet."

I could feel those pale eyes on me.

"This here's a ole friend'a mines, Easy. Mr. Albright."

"You can call me DeWitt, Easy," the white man said. His grip was strong but slithery, like a snake coiling around my hand.

"Hello," I said.

"Yeah, Easy," Joppy went on, bowing and grinning. "Mr. Albright and me go way back. You know he prob'ly my oldest friend from L.A. Yeah, we go ways back."

"That's right," Albright smiled. "It must've been 1935 when I met Jop. What is it now? Must be thirteen years. That was back before the war, before every farmer, and his brother's wife, wanted to come to L.A."

Joppy guffawed at the joke; I smiled politely. I was wondering what kind of business Joppy had with that man and, along with that, I wondered what kind of business that man could have with me.

"Where you from, Easy?" Mr. Albright asked.

"Houston."

"Houston, now that's a nice town. I go down there sometimes, on business." He smiled for a moment. He had all the time in the world. "What kind of work you do up here?"

Up close his eyes were the color of robins' eggs; matte and dull.

"He worked at Champion Aircraft up to two days ago," Joppy said when I didn't answer. "They laid him off."

Mr. Albright twisted his pink lips, showing his distaste. "That's too bad. You know these big companies don't give a damn about you. The budget doesn't balance just right and they let ten family men go. You have a family, Easy?" He had a light drawl like a well-to-do southern gentleman.

"No, just me, that's all," I said.

"But they don't know that. For all they know you could have ten kids and one on the way but they let you go just the same."

"That's right!" Joppy shouted. His voice sounded like a regiment of men marching through a gravel pit. "Them people own them big companies don't never even come in to work, they just get on the telephone to find out how they money is. And you know they better get a good answer or some heads gonna roll."

Mr. Albright laughed and slapped Joppy on the arm. "Why don't you get us some drinks, Joppy? I'll have scotch. What's your pleasure, Easy?"

"Usual?" Joppy asked me.

"Sure."

When Joppy moved away from us Mr. Albright turned to look around the room. He did that every few minutes, turning slightly, checking to see if anything had changed. There wasn't much to see though. Joppy's was a small bar on the second floor of a butchers' warehouse. His only usual customers were the Negro butchers and it was early enough in the afternoon that they were still hard at work.

The odor of rotted meat filled every corner of the building; there were few people, other than butchers, who could stomach sitting in Joppy's bar.

Joppy brought Mr. Albright's scotch and a bourbon on the rocks for me. He put them both down and said, "Mr. Albright lookin' for a man to do a lil job, Easy. I told him you outta work an' got a mortgage t'pay too."

"That's hard." Mr. Albright shook his head again. "Men in big business don't even notice or care when a working man wants to try to make something out of himself."

"And you know Easy always tryin' t'be better. He just got his high school papers from night school and he been threatenin' on some college." Joppy wiped the marble bar as he spoke. "And he's a war hero, Mr. Albright. Easy went in with Patton. Volunteered! You know he seen him some blood."

"That a fact?" Albright said. He wasn't impressed. "Why don't we go have a chair, Easy? Over there by the window."

Joppy's windows were so dingy that you couldn't see out onto 103rd Street. But if you sat at a small cherry table next to them, at least you had the benefit of the dull glow of daylight.

"You got a mortgage to meet, eh, Easy? The only thing that's worse than a big company is the bank. They want their money on the first and if you miss the payment, they will have the marshal knocking down your door on the second."

"What's my business got to do with you, Mr. Albright? I don't wanna be rude, but I just met you five minutes ago and now you want to know all my business."

"Well, I thought that Joppy said you needed to get work or you were going to lose your house."

"What's that got to do with you?"

"I just might need a bright pair of eyes and ears to do a little job for me, Easy."

"And what kind of work is it that you do?" I asked. I should have gotten up and walked out of there, but he was right about my mortgage. He was right about the banks too.

"I used to be a lawyer when I lived in Georgia. But now I'm just another fella who does favors for friends, and for friends of friends."

"What kind of favors?"

"I don't know, Easy." He shrugged his great white shoulders. "Whatever somebody might need. Let's say that you need to get a message to someone but it's not, um, convenient for you to do it in person; well, then you call me and I take the job. You see I always do the job I'm asked to do, everybody knows that, so I always have lots of work. And sometimes I need a little helper to get the job done. That's where you come in."

"And how's that?" I asked. While he talked it dawned on me that Albright was a lot like a friend I had back in Texas—Raymond Alexander was his name but we called him Mouse. Just thinking about Mouse set my teeth on edge.

"I need to find somebody and I might need a little help looking."

"And who is it you want to—"

"Easy," he interrupted. "I can see that you're a smart man with a lot of very good questions. And I'd like to talk more about it, but not here." From his shirt pocket he produced a white card and a white enameled fountain pen. He scrawled on the card and then handed it to me.

"Talk to Joppy about me and then, if you want to try it out, come to my office any time after seven tonight."

He downed the shot, smiled at me again, and stood up, straightening his cuffs. He tilted the Panama hat on his head and saluted Joppy, who grinned and waved from behind the bar. Then Mr. DeWitt Albright strolled out of Joppy's place like a regular customer going home after his afternoon snort.

The card had his name printed on it in flourished letters. Below that was the address he'd scribbled. It was a downtown address; a long drive from Watts.

I noted that Mr. DeWitt Albright didn't pay for the drinks he ordered. Joppy didn't seem in a hurry to ask for his money though.

RANDALL KENAN (b. 1963)

Randall Kenan, a brilliant writer and an extraordinary teacher, was born in Brooklyn, New York, and raised in Chinquapin, North Carolina. Kenan has published two acclaimed books of literature: A Visitation of Spirits *(1989) and* Let the Dead Bury Their Dead *(1991). The first is a novel, the second a collection of short stories centered around a uni-fying theme. In his stories, he writes about everyday life—interactions between people, animals, and nature—with an element of magic realism. He creates a mysterious world that he explores in his stories. He captures readers with his ability to explain the human condition so well. His work is based in large part on African American cultural experiences; however, his characters, and the issues they face, transcend race into the realm of universal identification. He has taught creative writing at Sarah Lawrence College and at Columbia University. Recently, he served as John Grisham Writer-in-Residence at the University of Mississippi in Oxford, where he taught writing workshops.*

Clarence and the Dead (1991)

(And What Do They Tell You, Clarence? And the Dead Speak to Clarence)

On the day Clarence Pickett died, Wilma Jones's hog Francis stopped talking. Now of course no one else had ever heard the swine utter word the first, but Wilma swore up and down that the creature had first said to her "Jesus wept" on a sunny day in June. But the peculiar thing was that Wilma had not known of Clarence's death when she declared the hog's final hushing up; and oddly enough it was on the exact day of Clarence's birth, five years before, that Wilma had com-menced preaching that the hog could talk.

They say that day the sun shone while the rain poured—the old folk say that's when the devil beats his wife—the day Estelle Pickett died giving birth to Clarence. Her mama was out in the cucumber patch when Estelle went into labor and we came to get her—Miss Eunice, not being an excitable woman, asked if the midwife had been sent for and when we said yeah, she insisted on topping off her bushel before heading home. Estelle's papa, Mr. George Edward, was away in Wilmington that day looking for a new tractor since he was sick and tired of his old Farmall breaking down every other row and needing more oil than gasoline.

We never knew if Miss Eunice blamed herself, cause she never admitted to it, one, and two we never saw much sign that she did. We all arrived at the Pickett place at the same time as the midwife. We walked in on one of the most hideous sights we can remember seeing or hearing tell of: there lay Estelle on the bed, her legs apart, her eyes rolled back in her head, her body kind of twisted to the side in a pool so deep red it could have been a maroon sheet she was sitting on instead of white; and on the floor squalling like a stuck pig was Clarence, a twitching, pitiful little thing, in a soup of blood and purple mess and shit. There wont no caul to worry about being over his face as people came to gossip. Just not so. The caul seemed to be everywhere else though, on his head, on his hands, on his belly like a raw liver, quivery and oozy, him coated in a mucky white paste like snot. A nasty enough mess to make you lose your breakfast. Miss Eunice went to fix him up straightaway and the midwife looked to Estelle.

"She's gone, child. Poor thing," she said.

"Well . . ." Miss Eunice didn't say anything else, but that "Well . . ." seemed to say everything and nothing. She handed the baby to the midwife to cut and tuck his stem. (Folk who said he didn't have a belly button just don't know what they're talking about, cause we saw it knotted.)

That summer turned out to be a mild one—only a few days over a hundred. And ever since that day back in June folk had been wondering if we should take it upon ourselves to have Wilma committed and her talking hog butchered proper, seeing as she didn't have any children to see after her. But we left her alone, saying that all that meanness she had had all her life and all that insurance money she'd collected from two husbands and all that land they left her had come back to visit her in the form of a hallucination about a talking hog which she'd collar folk to come hear, only to be met by an occasional grunt or squeal, them scratching their noggins and casting sideways glances at Wilma, feeling a little sorry for her but not daring to say a word since she may well of kicked them out of their houses or called in mortgages they owed her. So when she took the damn thing into her house, making it a canopy bed with frills and ruffles, feeding it topshelf Purina Hog Chow, along with Spanish omelettes and tuna casserole (she forbore to give it pork cause that would be cannibalism, of course), we didn't say a thing other than "Oh that's nice, Wilma," and rolled our eyes.

Nothing much happened to point out that Clarence was different, not until that summer three years later when he began to talk, the day Ed Phelps found him out in his cow pasture surrounded by buzzards and talking in complete sentences. Of course folk said they knew of strange thises and thats to have occurred in hindsight, but we didn't believe none of it cause we hadn't heard tell of any of it at the time; we didn't believe anything except what happened after he turned three and commenced to talk, which we did believe cause we were witness to most of it—unlikely though it seems.

But Ed Phelps found him that day—some claim it was the exact same day of Clarence's third birthday, but we couldn't seem to come to an agreement after the fact, seeing as nobody had thought to note it down—after Miss Eunice and Mr. George Edward had like to gone crazy looking for the boy. They were already perturbed, understandably, over the child since, at near on three years, he hadn't yet said a blessed word, and neither Miss Eunice, nor Mr. George Edward for that matter, was too keen on having a retarded heir, seeing as Estelle had been their last living child—Henry, the oldest, died in Korea, and Frederick, who called himself Long John, had died in a shoot-out in Detroit. So when the child disappeared, its leave-taking allowed them to give vent to a whole slew of emotions these normally buttoned-down folk kept under their hats. About six hours after they'd searched and called and hollered, having the whole town in a fit to find the child, Ed drove up into Miss Eunice and Mr. George Edward's yard with Clarence in his arms. The toddler ran to Miss Eunice and hollered, "Miss Eunice, Miss Eunice." She just looked at the boy, her eyes big as Mr. George Edward's, who asked Ed where he found the boy. Ed said he'd come out on his porch after his after-dinner catnap and heard this awful fuss coming from the side of the house. He went to investigate, he said, and came to see seven or eight buzzards playing— that was the word he used—playing with little Clarence Pickett. All the cows were at the other end of the pasture avoiding the birds. Said he went and got his shot-gun and fired but the scavengers didn't pay him no notice, so he shot one of them through the neck—had to shoot the damn thing again to kill it—and the others took off hopping and tripping and stumbling into the air.

When they asked Clarence what he was doing in the cow pasture and how he got there and a whole other passel of questions, he just smiled and grinned possum-like. And just as Ed Phelps was about to leave, Clarence turned to Miss Eunice with all the innocence and seriousness you're apt to see on the face of a three-year-old and asked: "Why'd he kill it, Miss Eunice?" Of course she didn't answer him; of course she didn't know how to answer him. The look on her face seemed only to ask for peace.

Yet it seemed the end of peace in that house. Even though Clarence still sucked on his bottle he could and would talk to Miss Eunice and Mr. George Edward like an adult. We had to admire the two of them cause where it would of spooked some into their graves they took it all in stride. But people will accept some pretty outrageous behavior from their own blood, and after all it was just talking. But it wont the talking itself that caused the problem: it was what he said.

One time Emma Chaney stopped by to say hey to Miss Eunice and Mr. George Edward and just before she left Clarence walked into the room and said: "Your mama says Joe Hattan is stepping out on you with that strumpet Viola Stokes." Well, everybody was shocked and embarrassed and Mr. George Edward took a switch to Clarence telling him he shouldn't say such things to grownfolks, and all the while Clarence yelled through his tears: "But Miss Ruella told me to tell her." "Boy, quit your lying," Mr. George Edward said through his teeth. "Miss Ruella been dead." Mr. George Edward gave Clarence a few extra licks for lying, all the while wondering how on earth the boy'd come to know about a woman long dead before Clarence was even thought about.

Well, come to find out—seems Emma's curiosity was piqued and she followed Hattan on the sly—that her husband *was* cheating on her with that low-down Viola Stokes. Emma had a bullwhip of her daddy's and went into the house right on the spot and lashed the both of them good-fashioned. Viola got out her pistol and—not being a good shot—got Hattan in the hind parts.

Emma went straight back to Mr. George Edward and Miss Eunice wanting to know how the boy knew, and when he said Miss Ruella told him Mr. George Edward took the switch to him again.

Of course it didn't stop there. Clarence would tell people who happened by the Pickett place that this or that person was out to get them; that this woman was going to have twins; that that man had prostate cancer; that that woman's husband intended to give her a cruise for their wedding anniversary. He was good for getting up in the morning and announcing: "Such and such a person's going to die today," or "Such and such a person died last night." He told one person where they put an old insurance policy they'd lost, another where they mislaid their keys. Most folk came to avoid going by Miss Eunice and Mr. George Edward's house if they could, and prayed they wouldn't bring along Clarence when they came a-calling.

One green May day Mabel Pearsall stopped by to give Miss Eunice a mess of mustard greens. As they sat gossiping over a glass of lemonade in the kitchen, Clarence walked in clutching his soldier-doll. "Mr. Joe Allen wants a apple pie tonight," he said to Mabel the way an old woman coaches a new bride. "He been wanting one for months. You ought to make it for him."

Mabel laughed nervous-like and looked to Miss Eunice for help, who shooed Clarence away with a broom, presently turning to admit to Mabel: "I just don't know what to do with that boy." Mabel left not long after that.

On the way home Mabel stopped by McTarr's Grocery Store and got fixings for a pie—she said she wont paying any mind to that crazy boy, just had a craving for one, she said; but who could believe her? She baked the pie and her husband Joe Allen ate it without a word; and Mabel *harrumphed* and washed the dishes and went to bed laughing at herself and that strange boy, thinking she should tell Miss Eunice to be harder on him in the future. But that night, she said, she had a dream, and in the dream she dreamt that Joe Allen had come home and she hadn't baked the pie and in the middle of supper they had an argument and Joe Allen up and left her that very night. Mabel said she woke up from that dream in the wee hours of the morning powerfully afeared since the dream had the taste and feel of real life. She went back to sleep, to be waked up not by the rooster but by Joe Allen rocking on top of her, singing in her ear. (She admitted to some of us that he hadn't touched her in a year; though we suspect it had been closer to five, considering Mabel.)

Soon the boy seemed to get more outlandish in his testaments—as if what he'd said before wont outlandish enough. He told Sarah Phillips to stop fretting, that her husband forgave her for the time she tried to stab him with that hunting knife; he told Cleavon Simpson his mama despised him for tricking her to sign all of her property over to him and for putting her in a nursing home; he told Sealey Richards her daddy apologized for the times he tried to have his way with her.

Clarence told people things a four-year-old boy ain't had no business knowing the language for, let alone the circumstances around them. All from people dead five, six, ten, twenty, and more years. Secrets people had shared with no living person, much less a boy who could do well to stand and walk at the same time and who refused to give up his bottle. Miss Eunice and Mr. George Edward tried as hard as they could to ignore the boy, to shrug off his testimonials from the grave, but you could see that it preyed on their minds heavily, and it's a wonder they could get to sleep at night in the same house with him. God only knows what all went on in the dark in that old house.

Wilma soon started throwing parties for the Holy Hog Francis (as she'd taken to calling him in mixed company "My Holy Hog"). She'd invite all the little children (except Clarence) and they had ice cream and cake and orange and grape and strawberry soda and little hats, and Francis sat at the head of the table with a hat on, making a mess of his German chocolate cake, and the parties were a great success, and one boy, Perry Mitchell, came away and somebody asked if he heard the pig talk, and everybody was amazed cause he said yes, kind of offhanded-like and unimpressed, and they asked what did the pig say, and the boy said: "Oink, oink."

When Clarence was four and a half, folk started seeing things. Ben Stokes was driving down the road and saw a white shepherd come up to Clarence in Miss Eunice and Mr. George Edward's yard—and he said he didn't think much of it at first but he backed up and looked again and he said he could swear it was Rickie Jones's ole dog Sweetpea that got hit by a truck a year back, and he said the dog had the same ole red collar on. Ab Batts said he drove by one day and saw Clarence sitting up in a walnut tree with crows all on the limbs like black fruit, caw-cawing to beat the band. Hettie Mae Carr said she saw him swinging in a porch swing with a woman she swore had to be Mr. George Edward's mother, Miss Maybelle, dead now on twenty-seven years. G. W. Gillespie said he came to visit one day and as he knocked at the door he heard a whole bunch of menfolk talking. He knocked again and Mr. George Edward came from the side of the house. "You having a party inside, Mr. George Edward?" "No," said Mr. George Edward. "Ain't nobody in there but Clarence." When they opened the door, he said, they both could hear men's voices in the kitchen. Mr. George Edward called out and the voices stopped. They went into the kitchen and saw six hands of cards set in midgame of poker, with Clarence sitting at the head of the table holding a hand. A flush. Mr. George Edward didn't ask for explanation, just fussed about Clarence knowing better than to mess with his playing cards and collected them and put them on a high shelf out of the boy's reach. G. W. left right soon after that.

But it was around the time Wilma decided Francis needed to attend regular church services, and argued down the Reverend Barden that the hog should and could attend First Baptist. That's when all hell—or whatever you've a mind to call it—really broke loose.

Seems one day things just didn't want to go right at the Pickett place: Miss Eunice couldn't seem to find her car keys; the refrigerator broke down; the hens didn't lay egg one; the water pump lost pressure; the fuse box blew; plates fell out of the cabinet and broke. But the most curious thing had to do with Clarence. He acted like he was scared to death, Miss Eunice said. He'd cling to Mr. George

Edward's leg like he might to be gobbled up any minute. Mr. George Edward and Miss Eunice were so distracted and annoyed by all those other fixes that they were just more bothered by the boy and just didn't think to put two and two together.

Mr. George Edward took Clarence with him to disk the old field over the branch, and riding on the dusty tractor Clarence kept looking back like they were being followed; but when Mr. George Edward would ask what the matter was the boy'd just look at him, not saying a word.

Now after Mr. George Edward had disked up one piece of land—he recollected later that the five-year-new tractor was suddenly giving him the devil with stalling and the hydraulic lifts just wouldn't lift without coaxing—he got tired of Clarence sitting in his lap and put him down at the end of a row and told him to sit out a couple of turns.

The boy pitched a fit, but Mr. George Edward had no intention of giving in, and as he headed back to the tractor Clarence started talking.

"He says he's gone get you, Granddaddy. He says you's a dead man!"

Mr. George Edward turned around, a little spooked. "Who, boy? Who you talking bout?"

"Fitzhugh Oxendine. Fitzhugh Oxendine! He say he gone fix you good, Granddaddy!"

Mr. George Edward was doubly spooked now. Specially seeing as how the five-year-old boy had no way heard tell of ole Fitzhugh Oxendine. Seems when he was a young turk, Mr. George Edward worked laying new track for the railroad all along the southeast of the state. Now among the boys he worked with there was a fellow by the name of Fitzhugh Oxendine from Lumberton, who was just plain bad news. Well, the long and the short of it is that one payday while enjoying the end of the week them boys got themselves into a piece of trouble with a bunch of white sailors in Wilmington. A white boy got bad-off hurt, and Fitzhugh went on the lam. The law was giving them colored boys hell to find Fitzhugh and finally Mr. George Edward broke down and told them where they'd find him. Fitzhugh went to jail and from then on went in and out of the state penitentiary like it had a revolving door. Mr. George Edward said he always did regret doing what he done.

But that day Mr. George Edward just shook his head and tried to put that hollering boy and his queer knowledge out of his mind and looked onto the lower back field, which he wanted to finish before dinnertime. He climbed up on the tractor and put it in gear.

Now a ole John Deere tractor—which is the kind Mr. George Edward had—if you play the clutch and the gas and the brake just right, will rear up its front part just like a horse. Boys round Tims Creek use to do it all the time to impress folk, pretending they were in the wild wild west. It's not too likely it'll rear up like that with a cultivator attached to the back; but it happens. Well, that's what Mr. George Edward's tractor done that day, he said, and it went higher than he could ever recollect one going without flipping over—which happens too—and he fell slam off his seat, onto the ground, and the tractor kept going and the cultivator went right over his hand. It didn't slice clean off, but seeing how he'd just got the cultivator new it was sharp as the devil and cut into the bone deep. What done the true damage was the dragging since he couldn't well get aloose.

The most curious thing happened next. Mr. George Edward said amidst his agony and yelling for help he saw through all the tears and dust in his eyes a woman hop up on the tractor and jerk it to a stop. Wilma Jones leapt down and pulled Mr. George Edward free. He said he could hear the bone crack as she got him loose. He said he couldn't verify for true as he was so overcome by the pain and the sight of his blood-muddy mangled hand, but he heard what he thought was Clarence screaming, and as Wilma got him to his feet and begun walking him to her station wagon he could tell it wasn't Clarence at all: it was Francis, cater-wauling and squealing and rolling about and biting in the dirt, like it was fighting with something or somebody. Mr. George Edward said this brought to his mind the scene from the Good Book when our Lord cast the demon from the man and sent it into the swine. Soon the dust was so thick you couldn't see the hog, only hear it; and after a while the thing came trotting out with a look like contentment about its face.

"How . . . ?" was about all Mr. George Edward could utter. Wilma had tied off the hand with her apron to keep him from bleeding to death.

"Just rest easy now, Mr. George Edward. You gone be all right. You'll be at York General before you know it. I can drive this ole Bessie when I got to. Francis took care of everything else."

Mr. George Edward said he passed out then with the hog staring at him with them beady eyes, its great big head stuck over the front seat staring at him, its frothy slobber drooling on his overalls. When he come to he found Miss Eunice humming "At the Cross" and saw that them know-nothing doctors had left him with a stump instead of a left hand. But all he could think about was them gray eyes. "Eunice, that hog got eyes like a human person's."

"Go on back to sleep, George Edward. All hogs do."

We found out a few weeks later that the day before all this happened Fitzhugh Oxendine had died in Central Prison.

Well, after that episode if you think folk avoided Miss Eunice and Mr. George Edward and their grandbaby before, you should of seen how they stayed away now. From Wilma too, for that matter. And her sacred hog. When she told them the pig had told her Fitzhugh Oxendine was after Mr. George Edward and up to evil business, people whispered a little louder about calling the folks at Dorothea Dix. But after all, she did save Mr. George Edward from his tractor. How did she know? Probably just happened by, we said. Paying no mind to the fact that you didn't "just happen by" a field a mile off a secondary road.

Of course we all hear and all have heard tell about children born with a sixth sense or clairvoyance or ESP or some such, out of the mouths of babes and all that, but, we being good, commonsensical, level-headed, churchgoing folk, we didn't have no truck with such nonsense and third-hand tales. But the evidence kept accumulating and accumulating till you'd have to be deaf, dumb, blind, and stupid to whistle, nod your head, and turn away. But that's exactly what most of us did anyhow. Ain't it strange how people behave?

Some folk didn't ignore it though. Those full of the Holy Ghost preached against the boy, and at a Pentecostal revival meeting one preacher, after a round of prayers for the souls of Mr. George Edward and Miss Eunice, said the boy ought to be bound to a stake and burnt or left on a dry riverbed for the devil to claim his own. (Oddly, he didn't mention the hog Francis, who was at that moment attending prayer meeting at First Baptist.) Dead chickens and blood on the doorpost became regular morning greetings at the Pickett place.

Now there were a few who saw opportunity in the boy; just as there'll always be scheming rascals who see opportunity in other folks' misery. But they soon learned their lesson. One woman came to see if she had a prosperous future. Clarence told her she'd die at forty-nine of heartbreak and sugar diabetes. One man came to get in touch with his dead grandmother—we later found out rumor had it that she'd buried gold somewhere on her property. Clarence just told him: "Wont no gold, Jimmy, you damn fool. Why don't you quit looking for get-rich-quick and learn to work for what you want in life?" The man stormed out after cussing Mr. George Edward good-fashioned. In two weeks the man and his family just went, left everything, without a word. Finally come back that the man had moved to Oregon to get as far away from Tims Creek as he could. Said, according to what we heard, strange things commenced to happening in the house, which was his grandma's in the first place: doors slamming, lights coming on and going off, footsteps, you know, the usual. We just laughed and said, some people . . .

Nobody looking for profit much bothered Clarence after that.

The summer before Clarence was about to begin school—Wilma had set out to start a church for Francis, seems the Deacon Board and the Board of Trustees at First Baptist finally put their foot down about cleaning up hog droppings after service—well, Clarence met Ellsworth Batts. Miss Eunice had taken Clarence with her to do the Saturday shopping at McTarr's, and Ellsworth had just been dropped off there after helping Ab Batts clean out his turkey house. Ellsworth didn't show his face much in Tims Creek but he was a good and hard worker who did an odd job now and again for beer money. Miss Eunice said they passed Ellsworth on the way to the car, him not smelling or looking too pretty after a hot morning of shoveling turkey manure. She gave her most courteous hey, not being one to discourage hard and decent work, and kept going, but Clarence stopped and went back to Ellsworth.

"Clarence, come back here."

She said Clarence reached out for the man's hand but didn't touch it and said: "She says she grieves for your pain, but you were wrong to give it all up for her . . ."

"What? Who?" Miss Eunice said Ellsworth's eyes looked madder than she'd ever seen them look and he commenced to quake and tremble.

"Mildred. She says she wants you to return to the living folk. She says you have eternity to be dead. You love too much, she says. There's more to life than love."

"Mildred? Mildred. Mildred!"

Well, Miss Eunice said she grabbed Clarence by the hand and ran to the car cause Ellsworth put the fear of God in her and after she had thrown the groceries in the backseat and rolled the windows up and locked the door, Ellsworth kept calling: "Mildred, Mildred," crying and pounding on the door. She said he had the look of a wild bear on his face with all his beard and hair. Fearing for herself and the boy, Miss Eunice slowly pulled the car out and started down the road, leaving Ellsworth running behind in the dust hollering: "Mildred, Mildred, Mildred."

Mildred had been his childhood sweetheart, a fresh cocoa-brown gal with the biggest, brightest eyes and the prettiest smile. Even before they were married Ellsworth was crazy with love for her, once almost beating a boy to death who he claimed looked too long at her. Sweethearts since childhood, they'd agreed to marry after he got out of the army. He'd see Mildred as often as he could, writing her once a day, sometimes more, and dreaming of that little house and children and nice supper after a hard day's work and all the foolishness young boys have in their heads that marriage is all about and ain't.

Well, when he got out they got married at First Baptist Church and set up a home so nice and pretty it'd make you sick—in a house owned by Wilma Jones's first husband, by the way. Nobody's sure exactly what caused the fire; Ellsworth always blamed Wilma's husband for faulty wiring—but three months after their honeymoon at Myrtle Beach, the house caught afire. They couldn't even show Mildred's body at her funeral.

They say Ellsworth cried every day for a month and after that just seemed to give up. Seems he didn't have any other dreams than that one with Mildred and didn't see the use in conjuring up any more to replace it the way folk have to do sometime. When his mama died and the house started to fall apart from plain ole neglect, Ellsworth took to living in a broken-down bus shell one of his brothers bought for him at a junkyard.

He let his hair grow wild, his teeth go bad, his clothes get ragged and tattered. His brothers tried to help, but he refused more than an occasional meal and pocket change now and again, and made it clear he wanted to be left alone. We just shrugged and accepted his crazy behavior as one of those things that happen. And the memory of why he'd come to live like he did just faded in our minds the way colors in a hand-me-down quilt wash out after time.

Clarence had set off something deep in Ellsworth. The next day, first thing in the morning, he presented himself at the Pickett place and asked Mr. George Edward if he could talk to the boy.

"I don't want no trouble now, Ellsworth. You hear me? You like to scared Miss Eunice clear to death. You shoulda heard—"

"I beg you and Miss Eunice's pardon, Mr. George Edward. But if I . . ."

Clarence came out and he and Ellsworth talked for about half an hour, sitting in the swing on the front porch. Mr. George Edward said he couldn't remember what all was said, but he could testify to a change coming over Ellsworth. First he cried and the boy admonished him stern-like, Mr. George Edward said, saying the time for tears had long passed. They talked and talked and directly Ellsworth and the boy laughed and giggled and after a while Mr. George Edward, who said he was coming to feel a touch uneasy, said he figured it was time for Ellsworth to be on his way. Ellsworth stood to go, Mr. George Edward said, and the look on his face made Mr. George Edward worried. Tweren't the sort of look a grown man shows to a five-year-old boy.

The next day Ellsworth came at dusk dark, and lo and behold, said Miss Eunice, he'd fixed himself up, washed and trimmed his hair, and had on a nice clean set of clothes—God knows where he got them from—looking in a spirit she hadn't seen him in since he went off to the army. Not knowing what to do, after a spell she invited Ellsworth in to supper and they all ate listening to the boy talk to Ellsworth about what Mildred had said. At one point, forgetting himself, Ellsworth grasped the boy's hand. Mr. George Edward had to clear his throat to reacquaint Ellsworth with the impropriety of doing what he was doing. Right then and there, Miss Eunice said, she knew this was going to be nothing but trouble but could see no way to put a peaceable end to it.

Every day for a week Ellsworth showed up to see Clarence and every day Miss Eunice and Mr. George Edward would exchange weary glances and shrugs, while one would stand guard over what begun to look more and more like courting and sparking. Ellsworth brought candy and then flowers, which Miss Eunice took from Clarence straightaway and finally said to Mr. George Edward: "This has just got to stop." And Mr. George Edward said: "I know. I know. I'll talk to him."

Nothing like talk of crimes against nature gets people all riled up and speculating and conjecturing and postulating the way they did when word got out about Ellsworth Batts's "unnatural affection" for Clarence Pickett. The likelihood of him conversing with his dead Mildred through the boy paled next to the idea of him fermenting depraved intentions for young and tender boys. Imaginations sparked like lightning in a dry August wood, and folk took to shunning poor Ellsworth and keeping an extra eye on their womenfolk and children and locking doors after dark.

Thrice Ellsworth tried to get to Clarence, who seemed about as indifferent to his grandparents' commands as he was to Ellsworth's advances. Once Ellsworth motioned to him from under a sweetgum tree and embraced and kissed him in the shade; Clarence didn't say a mumbling word. When Mr. George Edward saw it he hollered and ran to get his gun but lost Ellsworth after chasing him and missing him—Mr. George Edward had been a good shot but the lack of a hand hindered him something awful—after missing him four times in the thick of the woods.

The second time, Ellsworth snuck into the house after twelve midnight and had the nerve to slip under the covers with the boy. Miss Eunice heard noises and woke Mr. George Edward. He had the gun this time when he found him, but he missed again and Ellsworth was covered by the night. He left his shoes.

By this time folk were on the lookout for Ellsworth Batts, figuring he was a true menace. They staked out his bus and had his brothers come to town to take charge of him but they found no Ellsworth.

About a week later—and we still can't believe that he did—Ellsworth snuck into the house again and tried to take the boy away. It was soon in the morning and everybody had just got out of bed. Mr. George Edward had only his long drawers on and Miss Eunice was out in the chicken coop collecting eggs. Ellsworth had the boy up in his arms when Mr. George Edward came out of the bathroom.

"You can't keep us apart. We were meant to be together."

"You one crazy son of a bitch is what you is, Ellsworth Batts."

Miss Eunice saw him running out the back door and tackled him, breaking all her eggs. Mr. George Edward had his gun by now, and having learned how to aim the gun with his stump finally shot Ellsworth in the foot. Running as best he could Ellsworth got a lead in the woods, but by now Mr. George Edward was joined by seven men who'd heard the shotgun and were ready.

They chased Ellsworth Batts for a good hour, figuring this time they had him. Cleavon Simpson and G. W. Gillespie had their bloodhounds on the trail now. They finally spotted him on the Chinquapin River bridge and he tried to double back but they had him trapped on both sides. Ellsworth Batts didn't look, they said, he just jumped. The Chinquapin was at its lowest, so it was pretty easy to find the body with the broken neck.

We were all mostly relieved seeing what we considered a threat to our peace and loved ones done away with; a few of us—the ones who dared put one iota of stock in believing in Clarence and his talking dead folk—figured it to be a kind of happy ending, seeing as Ellsworth would now be reunited with his beloved beyond the pale. But the most of us thought such talk a load of horse hockey, reckoning if that was the answer why didn't he just kill himself in the first place and leave us off from the trouble?

Some of us entertained fancies about the type of stories we'd begin hearing when Clarence got to school. But we never got to hear any such tales. Just before he was to start kindergarten, he took sick and died. Doctors say it was a bad case of the flu on top of a weak heart we'd never heard tell of. We figured there was more to it than that, something our imaginations were too timid to draw up, something to do with living and dying that we, so wound up in harvesting corn, cleaning house, minding chickenpox, building houses, getting our hair done, getting our cars fixed, getting good loving, fishing, drinking, sleeping, and minding other people's business, really didn't care about or have time or space to know. Why mess in such matters?—matters we didn't really believe in in the first place, and of which the memory grows dimmer and dimmer every time the sun sets.

At his funeral Miss Eunice and Mr. George Edward looked neither relieved nor sad. Just worn out; like two old people who did what their Lord had asked of them, and who, like Job, bore the tiresome effort unhappily but faithfully. Robins and sparrows perched on the tombstones near the grave as the dust-to-dust was said and the dirt began to rain down on the too-short coffin, and as we walked away from the Pickett cemetery we noted a herd of deer congregating at the edge of the wood. Of course we put this all out of our minds, eager to forget. And life in Tims Creek went on as normal after he died: folk went on propagating, copulating, and castigating, folk loved, folk hated, folk debauched, got lonely and died. No one talks about Clarence, and God only knows what lies they'd tell if they did.

As for Francis, oddly enough Wilma Jones stopped proclaiming the hog's oracular powers and eventually butchered him. But at the last minute, with the poor thing roasting over a pit, Wilma had a crisis of conscience and couldn't eat it; so she gave it a semi-Christian burial with a graveside choir and a minister and pallbearers, all made hungry by the scent of barbecue. Finally Wilma stopped raising hogs altogether. She opened a shoe store with her cousin Joceline in Crosstown.

YUSEF KOMUNYAKAA (b. 1947)

Yusef Komunyakaa writes strikingly about his Vietnam experiences. His poetry is filled with images of the war; he takes readers into that world with realism and rhythm. Audiences are mesmerized, emotionally affected, at his poetry readings because he gives so much of himself through his poetry. After serving in Vietnam, he worked as a newspaper editor and an English professor at Indiana University. He has written several volumes of poetry, including Dien Cai Dau *(1988),* Thieves of Paradise *(1998), and* Neon Vernacular *(1993), for which he won a Pulitzer Prize. Currently, Komunyakaa holds a creative writing professorship at Princeton University.*

The Deck (1998)

I have almost nailed my left thumb to the 2 x 4 brace that holds the deck together. This Saturday morning in June, I have sawed 2 x 6s, T-squared and levelled everything with three bubbles sealed in green glass, and now the sweat on my tongue tastes like what I am. I know I'm alone, using leverage to swing the long boards into place, but at times it seems as if   5
there are two of us working side by side like old lovers guessing each other's moves.

This hammer is the only thing I own of yours, and it makes me feel I have carpentered for years. Even the crooked nails are going in straight. The handsaw glides through grease. The toenailed stubs hold. The deck has   10
risen up around me, and now it's strong enough to support my weight, to not sway with this old, silly, wrong-footed dance I'm about to throw my whole body into.

Plumbed from sky to ground, this morning's work can take nearly any-thing! With so much uproar and punishment, footwork and euphoria, I'm   15
almost happy this Saturday.

I walk back inside and here you are. Plain and simple as the sunlight on the tools outside. Daddy, if you'd come back a week ago, or day before yester-day, I would have been ready to sit down and have a long talk with you. There were things I wanted to say. So many questions I wanted to ask, but   20
now they've been answered with as much salt and truth as we can expect from the living.

Rhythm Method (1998)

If you were sealed inside a box
within a box deep in a forest,
with no birdsongs, no crickets
rubbing legs together, no leaves
letting go of mottled branches,   5
you'd still hear the rhythm
of your heart. A red tide
of beached fish oscillates in sand,
copulating beneath a full moon,
& we can call this the first   10
rhythm because sex is what
nudged the tongue awake
& taught the hand to hit
drums & embrace reed flutes
before they were worked   15
from wood & myth. Up
& down, in & out, the piston
drives a dream home. Water
drips till it sculpts a cup
into a slab of stone.   20
At first, no bigger
than a thimble, it holds
joy, but grows to measure
the rhythm of loneliness
that melts sugar in tea.   25
There's a season for snakes
to shed rainbows on the grass,
for locust to chant out of the dunghill.
Oh yes, oh yes, oh yes, oh yes
is a confirmation the skin   30
sings to hands. The Mantra
of spring rain opens the rose
& spider lily into shadow,
& someone plays the bones
till they rise & live   35
again. We know the whole weight
depends on small silences
we fit ourselves into.
High heels at daybreak
is the saddest refrain.   40
If you can see blues
in the ocean, light & dark,
can feel worms ease through
a subterranean path

beneath each footstep,   45
Baby, you got rhythm.

"You and I Are Disappearing" (1988)

—Björn Håkansson

The cry I bring down from the hills
belongs to a girl still burning
inside my head. At daybreak
    she burns like a piece of paper.
She burns like foxfire   5
in a thigh-shaped valley.
A skirt of flames
dances around her
at dusk.
      We stand with our hands   10
hanging at our sides,
while she burns
    like a sack of dry ice.
She burns like oil on water.
She burns like a cattail torch   15
dipped in gasoline.
She glows like the fat tip
of a banker's cigar,
    silent as quicksilver.
A tiger under a rainbow   20
  at nightfall.
She burns like a shot glass of vodka.
She burns like a field of poppies
at the edge of a rain forest.
She rises like dragonsmoke   25
  to my nostrils.
She burns like a burning bush
driven by a godawful wind.

NEOREALISM MOVEMENT 1970–PRESENT

Topics for Research

1. Define the neorealism movement in African American literature. Analyze
   African American writing produced from the 1970s to the present, focusing on
   patterns in content and form. Use these findings to divide or unify the work.
   How do factors such as gender and point of view influence patterns of commonality and discontinuity during this time?

2. To what extent do African American writers during this period use Ebonics or black dialect? Examine the use of language from the 1970s to the present, formulating main ideas to explain connections between politics and art.

3. Trace the progression of African American women's writing during the neorealism period. What did African American women write about? What form did they use to present their writing? How was it received?

4. Who are the best writers of the African American neorealism movement? What criteria are necessary to make this judgment? What criteria have critics used to decide what is good African American literature? How do these criteria compare to the standards used to judge white American literature?

5. How does the African American literature of the neorealism movement illustrate the theme of this anthology—slavery versus freedom? Compare the state of race relations in American society to representations of race in the literature to determine literal and figurative instances of slavery and freedom. Draw conclusions based on your findings.

AFRICAN AMERICAN LITERARY CRITICISM

INTRODUCTION

T HE LITERARY CRITICISM IN THIS SECTION HELPS TO CONTEXTUALIZE the material in this anthology within a theoretical framework. The following selections define African American literature from various critical perspectives; examine the racial, social, and political concerns of African American writers; and provide examples of the slavery versus freedom theme. Each literary period of African American writing has had its theorists and critics—within and outside the race. Henry Louis Gates, Jr., made a major contribution to African American literary criticism with his 1988 book *The Signifying Monkey: A Theory of Afro-American Literary Criticism*. (An excerpt from his 1992 work, *Loose Canons: Notes on the Culture Wars*, which focuses on the question of what constitutes "black" literature, appears on pp. 1044–1052.) For years, scholars had used critical methods developed by white writers to analyze and evaluate African American literature. Gates presented a theory based on African American culture, particularly the use of language. Even though black English vernacular had been identified in the 1970s with the Ann Arbor case that recognized it as a language (see p. 743), the language was not being applied to the study of African American literature. The debate over whether or not this variety of English is a dialect or a language, whether it should be encouraged or discarded in the schools, came to a climax in 1996 when the school board in Oakland, California, voted to accept Ebonics as a language and to discover ways for teachers to help students move from black English to Standard English. Going back to African roots, Gates explains the origins of black language, with its rituals and distinct characteristics, and analyzes how it differs from white language. He proves that in order to critique African American literature, the reader must have specific knowledge about the culture and must understand the way black authors use language.

Various theories developed by white scholars have been applied to African American texts: structuralism, deconstruction, romanticism, realism, naturalism, and modernism. These applications have produced interesting readings and some valid interpretations; in fact, this anthology uses the term *neorealism* in discussion of

African American literature from the 1970s to the present. *Neo* suggests the black difference (to use Gates's language). Earlier critics of African American literature focused on historical, political, and social aspects of the works and neglected the ways in which they engage in a dialogue with other texts by both black and white authors.

During the black aesthetics movement, African American writers concerned themselves with defining an exclusively black art form—by, for, and about African Americans. The primary theoretical approach was the black aesthetic, which was defined in various ways by black writers. Essays published in Addison Gayle, Jr.'s collection *The Black Aesthetic* (1971) are included in this section because they express the concerns of African American writers of the time. The critical selections define African American literature from various perspectives and examine the racial, social, and political concerns of black writers.

Creative writers as well as academic critics study literary elements and the historical, social, cultural, and political contexts of literature, using a variety of critical approaches. Alice Walker, Henry Louis Gates, Jr., and Hazel Carby chart the progress of African American literature from the colonial period to the twentieth century. Amiri Baraka, Addison Gayle, Jr., and Larry Neal discuss the literature of the black arts movement and the political issues that influenced it. Langston Hughes, Richard Wright, and Zora Neale Hurston develop an African American literary aesthetic by addressing the role of the African American artist. The critical selections included here are merely representative of literary criticism about African American literature; they provide a catalyst for discussion, a starting point for research, a source of relevant material for writing.

Influential black thinkers in the late nineteenth and early twentieth centuries made important contributions to African American literary criticism. The theories of writers such as W. E. B. Du Bois, Alain Locke, and James Weldon Johnson still influence the theoretical underpinnings of black writing. Du Bois helped to define black literature and the role of the writer. He focused on how African American history and the scientific study of racism would help to eliminate the ignorance that caused racial conflicts. Du Bois believed that writers should use their forum to argue for social equality as he did in his 1903 essay collection *The Souls of Black Folk* (pp. 168–181). Du Bois explains the black experience with his idea of double consciousness—the situation of being black and American, the two being in contrast with each other for African Americans. African American literature reflects the two elements because most of it deals with the effects of racism on black people.

African American writers, according to Alain Locke, should use their writing to record and cultivate their African heritage. Locke drew critical attention to black literature with his 1925 anthology *The New Negro: An Interpretation* (pp. 422–430). The first of its kind, the anthology demonstrated the quality of African American literature and therefore stimulated the interest of literary critics. Locke's belief in the supremacy of the collective over the individual in the African American community is a theme found in much of black literature. Another aspect of black experience was promoted by James Weldon Johnson, who believed that black dialect should be used by African American writers to show pride in their heritage. He recognized the importance of satisfying his white audience, but he also wanted to use the language of his people. He was criticized for his use of black dialect and eventually ceased to use it in his work. This issue of whether or not to employ the language and other attributes of black culture in African American literature is still part of scholarly discussions among literary critics and writers.

Langston Hughes agreed with Johnson's desire to let the literature mirror the culture. In "The Negro Artist and the Racial Mountain" (pp. 955–958), published in the *Nation* in 1926, Hughes addresses important aspects of being an African American artist. In the essay, Hughes encourages black writers to produce art that reflects the unique qualities of the African American experience (exercising freedom) and to overcome the racial mountain—an urge to conform to white standards of artistic presentation (perpetuating slavery). According to Hughes, instead of allowing the racial mountain to destroy individuality, African American artists should let their work reveal the distinct characteristics of black language and culture.

Benjamin Brawley writes about the portrayal of African Americans in novels and short stories in "The Negro in American Fiction" (959–965). According to Brawley, fiction writers should not write about only the past; they should also address issues of future concern and present ways to resolve past concerns. He encourages writers to move from African American stereotypes to a more realistic, balanced view of African Americans—to abandon Uncle Remus and Uncle Tom and bring in new characters who demonstrate the multifaceted nature of African American experience. Brawley wants the literature to reflect the continuous journey from slavery to freedom.

In "Blueprint for Negro Writing" (pp. 965–973), Richard Wright attempts to bridge the gap between African American writers and African American people. Like Hughes, he defines the role of African American writing as a vehicle for racial uplift and racial consciousness, stressing the need for a redefining of audience. According to Wright in this essay, which was published in *New Challenge* in 1937, the primary audience for African American writing should not be bourgeois blacks or whites but working-class blacks.

Zora Neale Hurston argues for a greater representation of middle-class black life in "What White Publishers Won't Print" (pp. 973–976), which originally appeared in *Negro Digest* in April 1950. Much of African American literature presents stereotypical portrayals of black people, according to Hurston, who advocates a more accurate reflection of African Americans. This essay provides a juxtaposition to Wright's essay, suggesting a different perspective on promoting racial uplift through African American literature, challenging the white publishing audience.

In his collection of essays *The Black Aesthetic*, Addison Gayle, Jr., defines the role of African American literature, specifically the black arts movement of the 1960s. Like Hughes, Gayle believes that black literature should address the concerns of black people, providing accurate representations of African American struggle. Amiri Baraka argues for the same themes in black theatre. Baraka's "The Revolutionary Theatre" (pp. 984–987) and Larry Neal's "The Black Arts Movement" (pp. 992–1003) also help to establish what has become known as African American literature.

Alice Walker pays tribute to the contributions of African American women writers in "In Search of Our Mothers' Gardens" (pp. 1003–1010), originally printed in *Ms.* Magazine in May 1974. Walker examines the repression of black women's artistic talent and traces her own creativity to her mother. Her mother produced magnificent flower gardens; Walker creates powerful literature. African American women were suppressed artistically; they expressed themselves in covert ways. Walker traces this long tradition of African American female creativity as it has evolved into more overt expression.

In *Reconstructing Womanhood* (1987), Hazel Carby traces the development of African American women's writing from the slave narrative tradition to the literature of the Harlem Renaissance. She provides a feminist/Marxist theory of African American women's writing that challenges traditional notions of race, class, and gender.

African American literature, as the works in this anthology illustrate, frequently embodies the theme of slavery versus freedom. Critics of the literature frequently examine racial themes and discuss aspects such as purpose and meaning in their writing. The critical analyses take readers beyond surface features of the writings, revealing specifics about not only what is written but the way it is written, who it was written for, and why it was written, among other issues. African literary criticism provides an ongoing discussion of the issues surrounding and within African American literature.

⊞ LANGSTON HUGHES

For a brief biography about Langston Hughes, see page 444.

The Negro Artist and the Racial Mountain (1926)

One of the most promising of the young Negro poets said to me once, "I want to be a poet—not a Negro poet," meaning, I believe, "I want to write like a white poet"; meaning subconsciously "I would like to be a white poet"; meaning behind that, "I would like to be white." And I was sorry the young man said that, for no great poet has ever been afraid of being himself. And I doubted then that, with his desire to run away spiritually from his race, this boy would ever be a great poet. But this is the mountain standing in the way of any true Negro art in America— this urge within the race toward whiteness, the desire to pour racial individuality into the mold of American standardization, and to be as little Negro and as much American as possible.

But let us look at the immediate background of this young poet. His family is of what I suppose one would call the Negro middle class: people who are by no means rich yet never uncomfortable nor hungry—smug, contented, respectable folk, members of the Baptist church. The father goes to work every morning. He is a chief steward at a large white club. The mother sometimes does fancy sewing or supervises parties for the rich families of the town. The children go to a mixed school. In the home they read white papers and magazines. And the mother often says "Don't be like niggers" when the children are bad. A frequent phrase from the father is, "Look how well a white man does things." And so the word white comes to be unconsciously a symbol of all the virtues. It holds for the children beauty, morality, and money. The whisper of "I want to be white" runs silently through their minds. This young poet's home is, I believe, a fairly typical home of the colored middle class. One sees immediately how difficult it would be for an artist born in such a home to interest himself in interpreting the beauty of his own people. He is never taught to see that beauty. He is taught rather not to see it, or if he does, to be ashamed of it when it is not according to Caucasian patterns.

For racial culture the home of a self-styled "high-class" Negro has nothing better to offer. Instead there will perhaps be more aping of things white than in a less cultured or less wealthy home. The father is perhaps a doctor, lawyer, landowner, or politician. The mother may be a social worker, or a teacher, or she may do nothing and have a maid. Father is often dark but he has usually married the lightest woman he could find. The family attend a fashionable church where few really colored faces are to be found. And they themselves draw a color line. In the North they go to white theaters and white movies. And in the South they have at least two cars and a house "like white folks." Nordic manners, Nordic faces, Nordic hair, Nordic art (if any), and an Episcopal heaven. A very high mountain indeed for the would-be racial artist to climb in order to discover himself and his people.

But then there are the low-down folks, the so-called common element, and they are the majority—may the Lord be praised! The people who have their nip of gin on Saturday nights and are not too important to themselves or the community, or too well fed, or too learned to watch the lazy world go round. They live on Seventh Street in Washington or State Street in Chicago and they do not particularly care whether they are like white folks or anybody else. Their joy runs, bang! into ecstasy. Their religion soars to a shout. Work maybe a little today, rest a little tomorrow. Play awhile. Sing awhile. O, let's dance! These common people are not afraid of spirituals, as for a long time their more intellectual brethren were, and jazz is their child. They furnish a wealth of colorful, distinctive material for any artist because they still hold their own individuality in the face of American standardizations. And perhaps these common people will give to the world its truly great Negro artist, the one who is not afraid to be himself. Whereas the better-class Negro would tell the artist what to do, the people at least let him alone when he does appear. And they are not ashamed of him—if they know he exists at all. And they accept what beauty is their own without question.

Certainly there is, for the American Negro artist who can escape the restrictions the more advanced among his own group would put upon him, a great field of unused material ready for his art. Without going outside his race, and even among the better classes with their "white" culture and conscious American manners, but still Negro enough to be different, there is sufficient matter to furnish a black artist with a lifetime of creative work. And when he chooses to touch on the relations between Negroes and whites in this country with their innumerable overtones and undertones, surely, and especially for literature and the drama, there is an inexhaustible supply of themes at hand. To these the Negro artist can give his racial individuality, his heritage of rhythm and warmth, and his incongruous humor that so often, as in the Blues, becomes ironic laughter mixed with tears. But let us look again at the mountain.

A prominent Negro clubwoman in Philadelphia paid eleven dollars to hear Raquel Meller sing Andalusian popular songs. But she told me a few weeks before she would not think of going to hear "that woman," Clara Smith, a great black artist, sing Negro folksongs. And many an upper-class Negro church, even now, would not dream of employing a spiritual in its services. The drab melodies in white folks' hymnbooks are much to be preferred. "We want to worship the Lord correctly and quietly. We don't believe in 'shouting.' Let's be dull like the Nordics," they say, in effect.

The road for the serious black artist, then, who would produce a racial art is most certainly rocky and the mountain is high. Until recently he received almost no encouragement for his work from either white or colored people. The fine novels of Chesnutt go out of print with neither race noticing their passing. The quaint charm and humor of Dunbar's dialect verse brought to him, in his day, largely the same kind of encouragement one would give a sideshow freak (A colored man writing poetry! How odd!) or a clown (How amusing!).

The present vogue in things Negro, although it may do as much harm as good for the budding colored artist, has at least done this: it has brought him forcibly to the attention of his own people among whom for so long, unless the other race had noticed him beforehand, he was a prophet with little honor. I understand that Charles Gilpin acted for years in Negro theaters without any special acclaim from his own, but when Broadway gave him eight curtain calls, Negroes, too, began to beat a tin pan in his honor. I know a young colored writer, a manual worker by day, who had been writing well for the colored magazines for some years, but it was not until he recently broke into the white publications and his first book was accepted by a prominent New York publisher that the "best" Negroes in his city took the trouble to discover that he lived there. Then almost immediately they decided to give a grand dinner for him. But the society ladies were careful to whisper to his mother that perhaps she'd better not come. They were not sure she would have an evening gown.

The Negro artist works against an undertow of sharp criticism and misunderstanding from his own group and unintentional bribes from the whites. "Oh, be respectable, write about nice people, show how good we are," say the Negroes. "Be stereotyped, don't go too far, don't shatter our illusions about you, don't amuse us too seriously. We will pay you," say the whites. Both would have told Jean Toomer not to write *Cane*. The colored people did not praise it. The white people did not buy it. Most of the colored people who did read *Cane* hate it. They are afraid of it. Although the critics gave it good reviews the public remained indifferent. Yet (excepting the work of DuBois) *Cane* contains the finest prose written by a Negro in America. And like the singing of Robeson, it is truly racial.

But in spite of the Nordicized Negro intelligentsia and the desires of some white editors we have an honest American Negro literature already with us. Now I await the rise of the Negro theater. Our folk music, having achieved world-wide fame, offers itself to the genius of the great individual American Negro composer who is to come. And within the next decade I expect to see the work of a growing school of colored artists who paint and model the beauty of dark faces and create with new technique the expression of their own soul-world. And the Negro dancers who will dance like flame and the singers who will continue to carry our songs to all who listen—they will be with us in even greater numbers tomorrow.

Most of my own poems are racial in theme and treatment, derived from the life I know. In many of them I try to grasp and hold some of the meanings and rhythms of jazz. I am as sincere as I know how to be in these poems and yet after every reading I answer questions like these from my own people: Do you think Negroes should always write about Negroes? I wish you wouldn't read some of your poems to white folks. How do you find anything interesting in a place like a cabaret? Why do you write about black people? You aren't black. What makes you do so many jazz poems?

But jazz to me is one of the inherent expressions of Negro life in America: the eternal tom-tom beating in the Negro soul—the tom-tom of revolt against weariness in a white world, a world of subway trains, and work, work, work; the tom-tom of joy and laughter, and pain swallowed in a smile. Yet the Philadelphia clubwoman is ashamed to say that her race created it and she does not like me to write about it. The old subconscious "white is best" runs through her mind. Years of study under white teachers, a lifetime of white books, pictures, and papers, and white manners, morals, and Puritan standards made her dislike the spirituals. And now she turns up her nose at jazz and all its manifestations—likewise almost everything else distinctly racial. She doesn't care for the Winold Reiss portraits of

Negroes because they are "too Negro." She does not want a true picture of herself from anybody. She wants the artist to flatter her, to make the white world believe that all Negroes are as smug and as near white in soul as she wants to be. But, to my mind, it is the duty of the younger Negro artist, if he accepts any duties at all from outsiders, to change through the force of his art that old whispering "I want to be white," hidden in the aspirations of his people, to "Why should I want to be white? I am a Negro—and beautiful!"

So I am ashamed for the black poet who says, "I want to be a poet, not a Negro poet," as though his own racial world were not as interesting as any other world. I am ashamed, too, for the colored artist who runs from the painting of Negro faces to the painting of sunsets after the manner of the academicians because he fears the strange unwhiteness of his own features. An artist must be free to choose what he does, certainly, but he must also never be afraid to do what he might choose.

Let the blare of Negro jazz bands and the bellowing voice of Bessie Smith singing Blues penetrate the closed ears of the colored near-intellectuals until they listen and perhaps understand. Let Paul Robeson singing "Water Boy," and Rudolph Fisher writing about the streets of Harlem, and Jean Toomer holding the heart of Georgia in his hands, and Aaron Douglas drawing strange black fantasies cause the smug Negro middle class to turn from their white, respectable, ordinary books and papers to catch a glimmer of their own beauty. We younger Negro artists who create now intend to express our individual dark-skinned selves without fear or shame. If white people are pleased we are glad. If they are not, it doesn't matter. We know we are beautiful. And ugly too. The tom-tom cries and the tom-tom laughs. If colored people are pleased we are glad. If they are not, their displeasure doesn't matter either. We build our temples for tomorrow, strong as we know how, and we stand on top of the mountain, free within ourselves.

BENJAMIN BRAWLEY (1882–1939)

Born in Washington, D.C., Benjamin Griffith Brawley was a poet, a literary and social historian, and an English professor. He was educated at Morehouse College, the University of Chicago, and Harvard University. He worked as a professor of English at Morehouse College, Shaw University, and Howard University. He was ordained as a Baptist minister in 1921.

Brawley's The Negro in Literature and Art in the United States *(1918) and* New Survey of English Literature *(1925) have been used as college texts. In 1937, Brawley published two short biographies—*The Negro Genius *and* Negro Builders and Heroes—*that survey noted African Americans. He wrote many other nonfiction texts, such as* History of Morehouse College *(1917) and* Early Negro American Writers *(1935).*

The Negro in American Fiction (1930)

Ever since Sydney Smith sneered at American books a hundred years ago, honest critics have asked themselves if the literature of the United States was not really open to the charge of provincialism. Within the last year or two the argument has been very much revived; and an English critic, Mr. Edward Garnett, writing in *The Atlantic Monthly*, has pointed out that with our predigested ideas and made-to-order fiction we not only discourage individual genius, but make it possible for the multitude to think only such thoughts as have passed through a sieve. Our most popular novelists, and sometimes our most respectable writers, see only the sensation that is uppermost for the moment in the mind of the crowd—divorce, graft, tainted meat or money—and they proceed to cut the cloth of their fiction accordingly. Mr. Owen Wister, a "regular practitioner" of the novelist's art, in substance admitting the weight of these charges, lays the blame on our crass democracy which utterly refuses to do its own thinking and which is satisfied only with the tinsel and gewgaws and hobbyhorses of literature. And no theme has suffered so much from the coarseness of the mob-spirit in literature as that of the Negro.

As a matter of fact, the Negro in his problems and strivings offers to American writers the greatest opportunity that could possibly be given to them to-day. It is commonly agreed that only one other large question, that of the relations of capital and labor, is of as much interest to the American public; and even this great issue fails to possess quite the appeal offered by the Negro from the social standpoint. One can only imagine what a Victor Hugo, detached and philosophical, would have done with such a theme in a novel. When we see what actually has been done—how often in the guise of fiction a writer has preached a sermon or shouted a political creed, or vented his spleen—we are not exactly proud of the art of novel-writing as it has been developed in the United States of America. Here was opportunity for tragedy, for comedy, for the subtle portrayal of all the relations of man with his fellow man, for faith and hope and love and sorrow. And yet, with the Civil War fifty years in the distance, not one novel or one short story of the first rank has found its inspiration in this great theme. Instead of such work we have consistently had traditional tales, political tracts, and lurid melodramas.

Let us see who have approached the theme, and just what they have done with it, for the present leaving out of account all efforts put forth by Negro writers themselves.

The name of four exponents of Southern life come at once to mind—George W. Cable, Joel Chandler Harris, Thomas Nelson Page, and Thomas Dixon; and at once, in their outlook and method of work, the first two become separate from the last two. Cable and Harris have looked toward the past, and have embalmed vanished or vanishing types. Mr. Page and Mr. Dixon, with their thought on the present (though for the most part they portray the recent past), have used the novel as a vehicle for political propaganda.

It was in 1879 that "Old Creole Days" evidenced the advent of a new force in American literature; and on the basis of this work, and of "The Grandissimes" which followed, Mr. Cable at once took his place as the foremost portrayer of life in old New Orleans. By birth, by temperament, and by training he was thoroughly fitted for the task to which he set himself. His mother was from New England, his father of the stock of colonial Virginia; and the stern Puritanism of the North was mellowed by the gentler influences of the South. Moreover, from his long apprenticeship in newspaper work in New Orleans he had received abundantly the knowledge and training necessary for his work. Setting himself to a study of the Negro of the old régime, he made a specialty of the famous—and infamous—quadroon society of Louisiana of the third and fourth decades of the last century. And excellent as was his work, turning his face to the past in manner as well as in matter, from the very first he raised the question propounded by this paper. In his earliest volume there was a story entitled "'Tite Poulette," the heroine of which was a girl amazingly fair, the supposed daughter of one Madame John. A young Dutchman fell in love with 'Tite Poulette, championed her cause at all times, suffered a beating and stabbing for her, and was by her nursed back to life and love. In the midst of his perplexity about joining himself to a member of another race, came the word from Madame John that the girl was not her daughter, but the child of yellow fever patients whom she had nursed until they died, leaving their infant in her care. Immediately upon the publication of this story, the author received a letter from a young woman who had actually lived in very much the same situation as that portrayed in "'Tite Poulette," telling him that his story was not true to life and that he knew it was not, for Madame John really *was* the mother of the heroine. Accepting the criticism, Mr. Cable set about the composition of "Madame Delphine," in which the situation is somewhat similar, but in which at the end the mother tamely makes a confession to a priest. What is the trouble? The artist is so bound by circumstances and hemmed in by tradition that he simply has not the courage to launch out into the deep and work out his human problems for himself. Take a representative portrait from "The Grandissimes":

> Clemence had come through ages of African savagery, through fires that do not refine, but that blunt and blast and blacken and char; starvation, gluttony, drunkenness, thirst, drowning, nakedness, dirt, fetichism, debauchery, slaughter, pestilence, and the rest—she was their heiress; they left her the cinders of human feelings. . . . She had had children of assorted colors—had one with her now, the black boy that brought the basil to Joseph; the others were here and there, some in the Grandissime households or field-gangs, some elsewhere within occasional sight, some dead, some not accounted for. Husbands—like the Samaritan woman's. We know she was a constant singer and laugher.

Very brilliant of course; and yet Clemence is a relic, not a prophecy.

Still more of a relic is Uncle Remus. For decades now, this charming old Negro has been held up to the children of the South as the perfect expression of the beauty of life in the glorious times "befo' de wah," when every Southern gentleman was suckled at the bosom of a "black mammy." Why should we not occasionally attempt to paint the Negro of the new day—intelligent, ambitious, thrifty, manly? Perhaps he is not so poetic; but certainly the human element is greater.

To the school of Cable and Harris belong also of course Miss Grace King and Mrs. Ruth McEnery Stuart, a thoroughly representative piece of work being Mrs. Stuart's "Uncle 'Riah's Christmas Eve." Other more popular writers of the day, Miss Mary Johnston and Miss Ellen Glasgow for instance, attempt no special analysis of the Negro. They simply take him for granted as an institution that always has existed and always will exist, as a hewer of wood and drawer of water, from the first flush of creation to the sounding of the trump of doom.

But more serious is the tone when we come to Thomas Nelson Page and Thomas Dixon. We might tarry for a few minutes with Mr. Page to listen to more such tales as those of Uncle Remus; but we must turn to living issues. Times have changed. The grandson of Uncle Remus does not feel that he must stand with his hat in his hand when he is in our presence, and he even presumes to help us in the running of our government. This will never do; so in "Red Rock" and "The Leopard's Spots" it must be shown that he should never have been allowed to vote anyway, and those honorable gentlemen in the Congress of the United States in the year 1865 did not know at all what they were about. Though we are given the characters and setting of a novel, the real business is to show that the Negro has been the "sentimental pet" of the nation all too long. By all means let us have an innocent white girl, a burly Negro, and a burning at the stake, or the story would be incomplete.

We have the same thing in "The Clansman,"[1] a "drama of fierce revenge." But here we are concerned very largely with the blackening of a man's character. Stoneman (Thaddeus Stevens very thinly disguised) is himself the whole Congress of the United States. He is a gambler, and "spends a part of almost every night at Hall & Pemberton's Faro Place on Pennsylvania Avenue." He is hysterical, "drunk with the joy of a triumphant vengeance." "The South is conquered soil," he says to the President (a mere figure-head, by the way), "I mean to blot it from the map." Further: "It is but the justice and wisdom of heaven that the Negro shall rule the land of his bondage. It is the only solution of the race problem. Wait until I put a ballot in the hand of every Negro, and a bayonet at the breast of every white man from the James to the Rio Grande." Stoneman, moreover, has a mistress, a mulatto woman, a "yellow vampire" who dominates him completely. "Senators, representatives, politicians of low and high degree, artists, correspondents, foreign ministers, and cabinet officers hurried to acknowledge their fealty to the uncrowned king, and hail the strange brown woman who held the keys of his house as the first lady of the land." This, let us remember, was for some months the best-selling book in the United States. A slightly altered version of it has very recently commanded such prices as were never before paid for seats at a moving-picture entertainment; and with "The Traitor" and "The Southerner" it represents our most popular treatment of the gravest social question in American life! "The Clansman" is to American literature exactly what a Louisiana mob is to American democracy. Only too frequently, of course, the mob represents us all too well.

Turning from the longer works of fiction to the short story, I have been interested to see how the matter has been dealt with here. For purposes of comparison I have selected from ten representative periodicals as many distinct stories, no one

---

[1] *The Clansman: A Historical Romance of the Ku Klux Klan* by Thomas Dixon was published in 1905.

of which was published more than ten years ago; and as these are in almost every case those stories that first strike the eye in a periodical index, we may assume that they are thoroughly typical. The ten are: "Shadow," by Harry Stillwell Edwards, in the *Century* (December, 1906); "Callum's Co'tin': A Plantation Idyl," by Frank H. Sweet, in the *Craftsman* (March, 1907); "His Excellency the Governor," by L. M. Cooke, in *Putnam's* (February, 1908); "The Black Drop," by Margaret Deland in *Collier's Weekly* (May 2 and 9, 1908); "Jungle Blood," by Elmore Elliott Peake, in *McClure's* (September, 1908); "The Race-Rioter," by Harris Merton Lyon, in the *American* (February, 1910); "Shadow," by Grace MacGowan Cooke and Alice MacGowan, in *Everybody's* (March, 1910); "Abram's Freedom," by Edna Turpin, in the *Atlantic* (September, 1912); "A Hypothetical Case," by Norman Duncan, in *Harper's* (June, 1915); and "The Chalk Game," by L. B. Yates, in the *Saturday Evening Post* (June 5, 1915). For high standards of fiction I think we may safely say that, all in all, the periodicals here mentioned are representative of the best that America has to offer. In some cases the story cited is the only one on the Negro question that a magazine has published within the decade.

"Shadow" (in the *Century*) is the story of a Negro convict who for a robbery committed at the age of fourteen was sentenced to twenty years of hard labor in the mines of Alabama. An accident disabled him, however, and prevented his doing the regular work for the full period of his imprisonment. At twenty he was a hostler, looking forward in despair to the fourteen years of confinement still waiting for him. But the three little girls of the prison commissioner visit the prison. Shadow performs many little acts of kindness for them, and their hearts go out to him. They storm the governor and the judge for his pardon, and present the Negro with his freedom as a Christmas gift. The story is not long, but it strikes a note of genuine pathos.

"Callum's Co'tin'" is concerned with a hardworking Negro, a blacksmith, nearly forty, who goes courting the girl who called at his shop to get a trinket mended for her mistress. At first he makes himself ridiculous by his finery; later he makes the mistake of coming to a crowd of merrymakers in his working clothes. More and more, however, he storms the heart of the girl, who eventually capitulates. From the standpoint simply of craftsmanship, the story is an excellent piece of work.

"His Excellency the Governor" deals with the custom on Southern plantations of having, in imitation of the white people, a Negro "governor" whose duty it was to settle minor disputes. At the death of old Uncle Caleb, who for years had held this position of responsibility, his son Jubal should have been the next in order. He was likely to be superseded, however, by loud-mouthed Sambo, though urged to assert himself by Maria, his wife, an old house-servant who had no desire whatever to be defeated for the place of honor among the women by Sue, a former field-hand. At the meeting where all was to be decided, however, Jubal with the aid of his fiddle completely confounded his rival and won. There are some excellent touches in the story; but, on the whole, the composition is hardly more than fair in literary quality.

"The Black Drop," throughout which we see the hand of an experienced writer, analyzes the heart of a white boy who is in love with a girl who is almost white, and who when the test confronts him suffers the tradition that binds him to get the better of his heart. "But you will still believe that I love you?" he asks, ill at ease as they separate. "No, of course I can not believe that," replies the girl.

"Jungle Blood" is the story of a simple-minded, simple-hearted Negro of gigantic size who in a moment of fury kills his pretty wife and the white man who has seduced her. The tone of the whole may be gleaned from the description of Moss Harper's father: "An old darky sat drowsing on the stoop. There was something ape-like about his long arms, his flat, wide-nostriled nose, and the mat of gray wool which crept down his forehead to within two inches of his eyebrows."

"The Race-Rioter" sets forth the stand of a brave young sheriff to protect his prisoner, a Negro boy, accused of the assault and murder of a little white girl. Hank Egge tries by every possible subterfuge to defeat the plans of a lynching party, and finally dies riddled with bullets as he is defending his prisoner. The story is especially remarkable for the strong and sympathetic characterization of such contrasting figures as young Egge and old Dikeson, the father of the dead girl.

"Shadow" (in *Everybody's*) is a story that depends for its force very largely upon incident. It studies the friendship of a white boy, Ranny, and a black boy, Shadow, a relationship that is opposed by both the Northern white mother and the ambitious and independent Negro mother. In a fight, Shad breaks a collar-bone for Ranny; later he saves him from drowning. In the face of Ranny's white friends, all the harsher side of the problem is seen; and yet the human element is strong beneath it all. The story, not without considerable merit as it is, would have been infinitely stronger if the friendship of the two boys had been pitched on a higher plane. As it is, Shad is very much like a dog following his master.

"Abram's Freedom" is at the same time one of the most clever and one of the most provoking stories with which we have to deal. It is a perfect example of how one may walk directly up to the light and then deliberately turn his back upon it. The story is set just before the Civil War. It deals with the love of the slave Abram for a free young woman, Emmeline. "All his life he had heard and used the phrase 'free nigger' as a term of contempt. What, then, was this vague feeling, not definite enough yet to be a wish or even a longing?" So far, so good. Emmeline inspires within her lover the highest ideals of manhood, and he becomes a hostler in a livery-stable, paying to his master so much a year for his freedom. Then comes the astounding and forced conclusion. At the very moment when, after years of effort, Emmeline has helped her husband to gain his freedom (and when all the slaves are free as a matter of fact by virtue of the Emancipation Proclamation), Emmeline, whose husband has special reason to be grateful to his former master, says to the lady of the house: "Me an' Abram ain't got nothin' to do in dis worl' but to wait on you an' master."

In "A Hypothetical Case" we again see the hand of a master-craftsman. Is a white boy justified in shooting a Negro who has offended him? The white father is not quite at ease, quibbles a good deal, but finally says Yes. The story, however, makes it clear that the Negro did not strike the boy. He was a hermit living on the Florida coast and perfectly abased when he met Mercer and his two companions. When the three boys pursued him and finally overtook him, the Negro simply held the hands of Mercer until the boy had recovered his temper. Mercer in his rage really struck himself.

"The Chalk Game" is the story of a little Negro jockey who wins a race in Louisville only to be drugged and robbed by some "flashlight" Negroes who send him to Chicago. There he recovers his fortunes by giving to a group of gamblers the correct "tip" on another race, and he makes his way back to Louisville much richer by his visit. Throughout the story emphasis is placed upon the superstitious element in the Negro race, an element readily considered by men who believe in luck.

Of these ten stories, only five strike out with even the slightest degree of independence. "Shadow" (in the *Century*) is not a powerful piece of work, but it is written in tender and beautiful spirit. "The Black Drop" is a bold handling of a strong situation. "The Race-Rioter" also rings true, and in spite of the tragedy there is optimism in this story of a man who is not afraid to do his duty. "Shadow" (in *Everybody's*) awakens all sorts of discussion, but at least attempts to deal honestly with a situation that might arise in any neighborhood at any time. "A Hypothetical Case" is the most tense and independent story in the list.

On the other hand, "Callum's Co'tin'" and "His Excellency the Governor," bright comedy though they are, belong, after all, to the school of Uncle Remus. "Jungle Blood" and "The Chalk Game" belong to the class that always regards the Negro as an animal, a minor, a plaything—but never as a man. "Abram's Freedom," exceedingly well written for two-thirds of the way, falls down hopelessly at the end. Many old Negroes after the Civil War preferred to remain with their former masters; but certainly no young woman of the type of Emmeline would sell her birthright for a mess of pottage.

Just there is the point. That the Negro is ever to be taken seriously is incomprehensible to some people. It is the story of "The Man that Laughs" over again. The more Gwynplaine protests, the more outlandish he becomes to the House of Lords.

We are simply asking that those writers of fiction who deal with the Negro shall be thoroughly honest with themselves, and not remain forever content to embalm old types and work over outworn ideas. Rather should they sift the present and forecast the future. But of course the editors must be considered. The editors must give their readers what the readers want; and when we consider the populace, of course we have to reckon with the mob. And the mob does not find anything very attractive about a Negro who is intelligent, cultured, manly, and who does not smile. It will be observed that in no one of the ten stories above mentioned, not even in one of the five remarked most favorably, is there a Negro of this type. Yet he is obliged to come. America has yet to reckon with him. The day of Uncle Remus as well as of Uncle Tom is over.

Even now, however, there are signs of better things. Such an artist as Mr. Howells, for instance, has once or twice dealt with the problem in excellent spirit. Then there is the work of the Negro writers themselves. The numerous attempts in fiction made by them have most frequently been open to the charge of crassness already considered; but Paul Laurence Dunbar, Charles W. Chesnutt, and W. E. Burghardt DuBois have risen above the crowd. Mr. Dunbar, of course, was better in poetry than in prose. Such a short story as "Jimsella," however, exhibited considerable technique. "The Uncalled" used a living topic treated with only partial success. But for the most part, Mr. Dunbar's work looked toward the past. Somewhat stronger in prose is Mr. Chesnutt. "The Marrow of Tradition" is not much more than a political tract, and "The Colonel's Dream" contains a good deal of preaching; but "The House Behind the Cedars" is a real novel. Among his short stories, "The Bouquet" may be remarked for technical excellence, and "The Wife of His Youth" for a situation of unusual power. Dr. DuBois's "The Quest of the Silver Fleece" contains at least one strong dramatic situation, that in which Bles probes the heart of Zora; but the author is a sociologist and essayist rather than a novelist. The grand epic of the race is yet to be produced.

Some day we shall work out the problems of our great country. Some day we shall not have a state government set at defiance, and the massacre of Ludlow.[2] Some day our little children will not slave in mines and mills, but will have some chance at the glory of God's creation; and some day the Negro will cease to be a problem and become a human being. Then, in truth, we shall have the Promised Land. But until that day comes let those who mold our ideals and set the standards of our art in fiction at least be honest with themselves and independent. Ignorance we may for a time forgive; but a man has only himself to blame if he insists on not seeing the sunrise in the new day.

RICHARD WRIGHT

For a brief biography of Richard Wright, see page 483.

Blueprint for Negro Writing (1937)

The Role of Negro Writing: Two Definitions

Generally speaking, Negro writing in the past has been confined to humble novels, poems, and plays, prim and decorous ambassadors who went a-begging to white America. They entered the Court of American Public Opinion dressed in the knee-pants of servility, curtsying to show that the Negro was not inferior, that he was human, and that he had a life comparable to that of other people. For the most part these artistic ambassadors were received as though they were French poodles who do clever tricks.

White America never offered these Negro writers any serious criticism. The mere fact that a Negro could write was astonishing. Nor was there any deep concern on the part of white America with the role Negro writing should play in American culture; and the role it did play grew out of accident rather than intent or design. Either it crept in through the kitchen in the form of jokes; or it was the fruits of that foul soil which was the result of a liaison between inferiority-complexed Negro "geniuses" and burnt-out white Bohemians with money.

On the other hand, these often technically brilliant performances by Negro writers were looked upon by the majority of literate Negroes as something to be proud of. At best, Negro writing has been something external to the lives of educated

[2]The Massacre of Ludlow happened during a coal strike in Colorado in 1914. John D. Rockefeller was part owner of Colorado Fuel & Iron, and John D. Rockefeller, Jr., was a member of its staff. The Rockefellers opposed unionization along with other company officials, inciting a war in which at least twenty-four people were killed.

Negroes themselves. That the productions of their writers should have been something of a guide in their daily living is a matter which seems never to have been raised seriously.

Under these conditions Negro writing assumed two general aspects: (1) It became a sort of conspicuous ornamentation, the hallmark of "achievement." (2) It became the voice of the educated Negro pleading with white America for justice.

Rarely was the best of this writing addressed to the Negro himself, his needs, his sufferings, his aspirations. Through misdirection, Negro writers have been far better to others than they have been to themselves. And the mere recognition of this places the whole question of Negro writing in a new light and raises a doubt as to the validity of its present direction.

The Minority Outlook

Somewhere in his writings Lenin makes the observation that oppressed minorities often reflect the techniques of the bourgeoisie more brilliantly than some sections of the bourgeoisie themselves. The psychological importance of this becomes meaningful when it is recalled that oppressed minorities, and especially the petty bourgeois sections of oppressed minorities, strive to assimilate the virtues of the bourgeoisie in the assumption that by doing so they can lift themselves into a higher social sphere. But not only among the oppressed petty bourgeoisie does this occur. The workers of a minority people, chafing under exploitation, forge organizational forms of struggle to better their lot. Lacking the handicaps of false ambition and property, they have access to a wide social vision and a deep social consciousness. They display a greater freedom and initiative in pushing their claims upon civilization than even do the petty bourgeoisie. Their organizations show greater strength, adaptability, and efficiency than any other group or class in society.

That Negro workers, propelled by the harsh conditions of their lives, have demonstrated this consciousness and mobility for economic and political action there can be no doubt. But has this consciousness been reflected in the work of Negro writers to the same degree as it has in the Negro workers' struggle to free Herndon[1] and the Scottsboro Boys,[2] in the drive toward unionism, in the fight against lynching? Have they as creative writers taken advantage of their unique minority position?

The answer decidedly is *no*. Negro writers have lagged sadly, and as time passes the gap widens between them and their people.

How can this hiatus be bridged? How can the enervating effects of this long-standing split be eliminated?

---

[1]Angelo Herndon was a political activist in the 1930s, a member of the Communist party. He worked for the Scottsboro Trials, for the unionization of miners in Alabama and Tennessee, and for longshoremen striking in New Orleans. In 1932, he was arrested for leading a march of unemployed blacks and whites in Fulton County, Georgia.

[2]The Scottsboro Boys were a group of African American males who were convicted of rape in 1931, based on the testimony of two white women. The young men allegedly raped them after a fight broke out on a train car going from Chattanooga to Memphis, in which the young black men fought young white men. It is commonly believed that since the black males won the fight, the white males pressured the white females, who may have been prostitutes, to say that they had been raped.

In presenting questions of this sort an attitude of self-consciousness and self-criticism is far more likely to be a fruitful point of departure than a mere recounting of past achievements. An emphasis upon tendency and experiment, a view of society as something becoming rather than as something fixed and admired is the one which points the way for Negro writers to stand shoulder to shoulder with Negro workers in mood and outlook.

A Whole Culture

There is, however, a culture of the Negro which is his and has been addressed to him; a culture which has, for good or ill, helped to clarify his consciousness and create emotional attitudes which are conducive to action. This culture has stemmed mainly from two sources: (1) the Negro church; and (2) the folklore of the Negro people.

It was through the portals of the church that the American Negro first entered the shrine of western culture. Living under slave conditions of life, bereft of his African heritage, the Negroes' struggle for religion on the plantations between 1820–1860 assumed the form of a struggle for human rights. It remained a relatively revolutionary struggle until religion began to serve as an antidote for suffering and denial. But even today there are millions of American Negroes whose only sense of a whole universe, whose only relation to society and man, and whose only guide to personal dignity comes through the archaic morphology of Christian salvation.

It was, however, in a folklore molded out of rigorous and inhuman conditions of life that the Negro achieved his most indigenous and complete expression. Blues, spirituals, and folk tales recounted from mouth to mouth; the whispered words of a black mother to her black daughter on the ways of men, to confidential wisdom of a black father to his black son; the swapping of sex experiences on street corners from boy to boy in the deepest vernacular; work songs sung under blazing suns—all these formed the channels through which the racial wisdom flowed.

One would have thought that Negro writers in the last century of striving at expression would have continued and deepened this folk tradition, would have tried to create a more intimate and yet a more profoundly social system of artistic communication between them and their people. But the illusion that they could escape through individual achievement the harsh lot of their race swung Negro writers away from any such path. Two separate cultures sprang up: one for the Negro masses, unwritten and unrecognized; and the other for the sons and daughters of a rising Negro bourgeoisie, parasitic and mannered.

Today the question is: Shall Negro writing be for the Negro masses, molding the lives and consciousness of those masses toward new goals, or shall it continue begging the question of the Negroes' humanity?

The Problem of Nationalism in Negro Writing

In stressing the difference between the role Negro writing failed to play in the lives of the Negro people, and the role it should play in the future if it is to serve its historic function; in pointing out the fact that Negro writing has been addressed in the main to a small white audience rather than to a Negro one, it should be stated that no attempt is being made here to propagate a specious and blatant nationalism. Yet the nationalist character of the Negro people is unmistakable. Psychologically, this nationalism is reflected in the whole of Negro culture, and especially in folklore.

In the absence of fixed and nourishing forms of culture, the Negro has a folklore which embodies the memories and hopes of his struggle for freedom. Not yet caught in paint or stone, and as yet but feebly depicted in the poem and novel, the Negroes' most powerful images of hope and despair still remains in the fluid state of daily speech. How many John Henrys have lived and died on the lips of these black people? How many mythical heroes in embryo have been allowed to perish for lack of husbanding by alert intelligence?

Negro folklore contains, in a measure that puts to shame more deliberate forms of Negro expression, the collective sense of Negro life in America. Let those who shy at the nationalist implications of Negro life look at this body of folklore, living and powerful, which rose out of a unified sense of a common life and a common fate. Here are those vital beginnings of a recognition of value in life as it is *lived*, a recognition that marks the emergence of a new culture in the shell of the old. And at the moment this process starts, at the moment when a people begin to realize a *meaning* in their suffering, the civilization that engenders that suffering is doomed.

The nationalist aspects of Negro life are as sharply manifest in the social institutions of Negro people as in folklore. There is a Negro church, a Negro press, a Negro social world, a Negro sporting world, a Negro business world, a Negro school system, Negro professions; in short, a Negro way of life in America. The Negro people did not ask for this, and deep down, though they express themselves through their institutions and adhere to this special way of life, they do not want it now. This special existence was forced upon them from without by lynch rope, bayonet and mob rule. They accepted these negative conditions with the inevitability of a tree which must live or perish in whatever soil it finds itself.

The few crumbs of American civilization which the Negro has got from the tables of capitalism have been through these segregated channels. Many Negro institutions are cowardly and incompetent; but they are all that the Negro has. And, in the main, any move, whether for progress or reaction, must come through these institutions for the simple reason that all other channels are closed. Negro writers who seek to mold or influence the consciousness of the Negro people must address their messages to them through the ideologies and attitudes fostered in this warping way of life.

The Basis and Meaning of Nationalism in Negro Writing

The social institutions of the Negro are imprisoned in the Jim Crow political system of the South, and this Jim Crow political system is in turn built upon a plantation-feudal economy. Hence, it can be seen that the emotional expression of group-feeling which puzzles so many whites and leads them to deplore what they call "black chauvinism" is not a morbidly inherent trait of the Negro, but rather the reflex expression of a life whose roots are imbedded deeply in Southern soil.

Negro writers must accept the nationalist implications of their lives, not in order to encourage them, but in order to change and transcend them. They must accept the concept of nationalism because, in order to transcend it, they must *possess* and *understand* it. And a nationalist spirit in Negro writing means a nationalism carrying the highest possible pitch of social consciousness. It means a nationalism that knows its origins, its limitations; that is aware of the dangers of its position; that knows its ultimate aims are unrealizable within the framework of capitalist America; a nationalism whose reason for being lies in the simple fact of self-possession and in the consciousness of the interdependence of people in modern society.

For purposes of creative expression it means that the Negro writer must realize within the area of his own personal experience those impulses which, when prefigured in terms of broad social movements, constitute the stuff of nationalism.

For Negro writers even more so than for Negro politicians, nationalism is a bewildering and vexing question, the full ramifications of which cannot be dealt with here. But among Negro workers and the Negro middle class the spirit of nationalism is rife in a hundred devious forms; and a simple literary realism which seeks to depict the lives of these people devoid of wider social connotations, devoid of the revolutionary significance of these nationalist tendencies, must of necessity do a rank injustice to the Negro people and alienate their possible allies in the struggle for freedom.

Social Consciousness and Responsibility

The Negro writer who seeks to function within his race as a purposeful agent has a serious responsibility. In order to do justice to his subject matter, in order to depict Negro life in all of its manifold and intricate relationships, a deep, informed, and complex consciousness is necessary; a consciousness which draws for its strength upon the fluid lore of a great people, and molds this lore with the concepts that move and direct the forces of history today.

With the gradual decline of the moral authority of the Negro church, and with the increasing irresolution which is paralyzing Negro middle class leadership, a new role is devolving upon the Negro writer. He is being called upon to do no less than create values by which his race is to struggle, live and die.

By his ability to fuse and make articulate the experiences of men, because his writing possesses the potential cunning to steal into the inmost recesses of the human heart, because he can create the myths and symbols that inspire a faith in life, he may expect either to be consigned to oblivion, or to be recognized for the valued agent he is.

This raises the question of the personality of the writer. It means that in the lives of Negro writers must be found those materials and experiences which will create a meaningful picture of the world today. Many young writers have grown to believe that a Marxist analysis of society presents such a picture. It creates a picture which, when placed before the eyes of the writer, should unify his personality, organize his emotions, buttress him with a tense and obdurate will to change the world.

And, in turn, this changed world will dialectically change the writer. Hence, it is through a Marxist conception of reality and society that the maximum degree of freedom in thought and feeling can be gained for the Negro writer. Further, this dramatic Marxist vision, when consciously grasped, endows the writer with a sense of dignity which no other vision can give. Ultimately, it restores to the writer his lost heritage, that is, his role as a creator of the world in which he lives, and as a creator of himself.

Yet, for the Negro writer, Marxism is but the starting point. No theory of life can take the place of life. After Marxism has laid bare the skeleton of society, there remains the task of the writer to plant flesh upon those bones out of his will to live. He may, with disgust and revulsion, say *no* and depict the horrors of capitalism encroaching upon the human being. Or he may, with hope and passion, say *yes* and depict the faint stirrings of a new and emerging life. But in whatever social voice he chooses to speak, whether positive or negative, there should always be heard or *over*-heard his faith, his necessity, his judgement.

His vision need not be simple or rendered in primer-like terms; for the life of the Negro people is not simple. The presentation of their lives should be simple, yes; but all the complexity, the strangeness, the magic wonder of life that plays like a bright sheen over the most sordid existence, should be there. To borrow a phrase from the Russians, it should have a *complex simplicity*. Eliot, Stein, Joyce, Proust, Hemingway, and Anderson; Gorky, Barbusse, Nexo, and Jack London no less than the folklore of the Negro himself should form the heritage of the Negro writer. Every iota of gain in human thought and sensibility should be ready grist for his mill, no matter how farfetched they may seem in their immediate implications.

The Problem of Perspective

What vision must Negro writers have before their eyes in order to feel the impelling necessity for an about-face? What angle of vision can show them all the forces of modern society in process, all the lines of economic development converging toward a distant point of hope? Must they believe in some "ism"?

They may feel that only dupes believe in "isms"; they feel with some measure of justification that another commitment means only another disillusionment. But anyone destitute of a theory about the meaning, structure and direction of modern society is a lost victim in a world he cannot understand or control.

But even if Negro writers found themselves through some "ism," how would that influence their writing? Are they being called upon to "preach"? To be "salesmen"? To "prostitute" their writing? Must they "sully" themselves? Must they write "propaganda"?

No; it is a question of awareness, of consciousness; it is, above all, a question of perspective.

Perspective is that part of a poem, novel, or play which a writer never puts directly upon paper. It is that fixed point in intellectual space where a writer stands to view the struggles, hopes, and sufferings of his people. There are times when he may stand too close and the result is a blurred vision. Or he may stand too far away and the result is a neglect of important things.

Of all the problems faced by writers who as a whole have never allied themselves with world movements, perspective is the most difficult of achievement. At its best, perspective is a preconscious assumption, something which a writer takes for granted, something which he wins through his living.

A Spanish writer recently spoke of living in the heights of one's time. Surely, perspective means just *that*.

It means that a Negro writer must learn to view the life of a Negro living in New York's Harlem or Chicago's South Side with the consciousness that one-sixth of the earth surface belongs to the working class. It means that a Negro writer must create in his readers' minds a relationship between a Negro woman hoeing cotton in the South and the men who loll in swivel chairs in Wall Street and take the fruits of her toil.

Perspective for Negro writers will come when they have looked and brooded so hard and long upon the harsh lot of their race and compared it with the hopes and struggles of minority peoples everywhere that the cold facts have begun to tell them something.

The Problem of Theme

This does not mean that a Negro writer's sole concern must be with rendering the social scene; but if his conception of the life of his people is broad and deep enough, if the sense of the *whole* life he is seeking is vivid and strong in him, then his writing will embrace all those social, political, and economic forms under which the life of his people is manifest.

In speaking of theme one must necessarily be general and abstract; the temperament of each writer molds and colors the world he sees. Negro life may be approached from a thousand angles, with no limit to technical and stylistic freedom.

Negro writers spring from a family, a clan, a class, and a nation; and the social units in which they are bound have a story, a record. Sense of theme will emerge in Negro writing when Negro writers try to fix this story about some pole of meaning, remembering as they do so that in the creative process meaning proceeds *equally* as much from the contemplation of the subject matter as from the hopes and apprehensions that rage in the heart of the writer.

Reduced to its simplest and most general terms, theme for Negro writers will rise from understanding the meaning of their being transplanted from a "savage" to a "civilized" culture in all of its social, political, economic, and emotional implications. It means that Negro writers must have in their consciousness the foreshortened picture of the *whole*, nourishing culture from which they were torn in Africa, and of the long, complex (and for the most part, unconscious) struggle to regain in some form and under alien conditions of life a *whole* culture again.

It is not only this picture they must have, but also a knowledge of the social and emotional milieu that gives it tone and solidity of detail. Theme for Negro writers will emerge when they have begun to feel the meaning of the history of their race as though they in one life time had lived it themselves throughout all the long centuries.

Autonomy of Craft

For the Negro writer to depict this new reality requires a greater discipline and consciousness than was necessary for the so-called Harlem school of expression. Not only is the subject matter dealt with far more meaningful and complex, but the new role of the writer is qualitatively different. The Negro writers' new position demands a sharper definition of the status of his craft, and a sharper emphasis upon its functional autonomy.

Negro writers should seek through the medium of their craft to play as meaningful a role in the affairs of men as do other professionals. But if their writing is demanded to perform the social office of other professions, then the autonomy of craft is lost and writing detrimentally fused with other interests. The limitations of the craft constitute some of its greatest virtues. If the sensory vehicle of imaginative writing is required to carry too great a load of didactic material, the artistic sense is submerged.

The relationship between reality and the artistic image is not always direct and simple. The imaginative conception of a historical period will not be a carbon copy of reality. Image and emotion possess a logic of their own. A vulgarized simplicity constitutes the greatest danger in tracing the reciprocal interplay between the writer and his environment.

Writing has its professional autonomy; it should complement other professions, but it should not supplant them or be swamped by them.

The Necessity for Collective Work

It goes without saying that these things cannot be gained by Negro writers if their present mode of isolated writing and living continues. This isolation exists *among* Negro writers as well as *between* Negro and white writers. The Negro writers' lack of thorough integration with the American scene, their lack of a clear realization among themselves of their possible role, have bred generation after generation of embittered and defeated literati.

Barred for decades from the theater and publishing houses, Negro writers have been *made* to feel a sense of difference. So deep has this white-hot iron of exclusion been burnt into their hearts that thousands have all but lost the desire to become identified with American civilization. The Negro writers' acceptance of this enforced isolation and their attempt to justify it is but a defense-reflex of the whole special way of life which has been rammed down their throats.

This problem, by its very nature, is one which must be approached contemporaneously from *two* points of view. The ideological unity of Negro writers and the alliance of that unity with all the progressive ideas of our day is the primary prerequisite for collective work. On the shoulders of white writers and Negro writers alike rest the responsibility of ending this mistrust and isolation.

By placing cultural health above narrow sectional prejudices, liberal writers of all races can help to break the stony soil of aggrandizement out of which the stunted plants of Negro nationalism grow. And, simultaneously, Negro writers can help to weed out these choking growths of reactionary nationalism and replace them with hardier and sturdier types.

These tasks are imperative in light of the fact that we live in a time when the majority of the most basic assumptions of life can no longer be taken for granted. Tradition is no longer a guide. The world has grown huge and cold. Surely this is the moment to ask questions, to theorize, to speculate, to wonder out of what materials can a human world be built.

Each step along this unknown path should be taken with thought, care, self-consciousness, and deliberation. When Negro writers think they have arrived at something which smacks of truth, humanity, they should want to test it with others, feel it with a degree of passion and strength that will enable them to communicate it to millions who are groping like themselves.

Writers faced with such tasks can have no possible time for malice or jealousy. The conditions for the growth of each writer depend too much upon the good work of other writers. Every first-rate novel, poem, or play lifts the level of consciousness higher.

ZORA NEALE HURSTON

For a brief biography of Zora Neale Hurston, see page 301.

What White Publishers Won't Print (1950)

I have been amazed by the Anglo-Saxon's lack of curiosity about the internal lives and emotions of the Negroes, and for that matter, any non-Anglo-Saxon peoples within our borders, above the class of unskilled labor.

This lack of interest is much more important than it seems at first glance. It is even more important at this time than it was in the past. The internal affairs of the nation have bearings on the international stress and strain, and this gap in the national literature now has tremendous weight in world affairs. National coherence and solidarity is implicit in a thorough understanding of the various groups within a nation, and this lack of knowledge about the internal emotions and behavior of the minorities cannot fail to bar out understanding. Man, like all the other animals fears and is repelled by that which he does not understand, and mere difference is apt to connote something malign.

The fact that there is no demand for incisive and full-dress stories around Negroes above the servant class is indicative of something of vast importance to this nation. This blank is NOT filled by the fiction built around upperclass Negroes exploiting the race problem. Rather, it tends to point it up. A college-bred Negro still is not a person like other folks, but an interesting problem, more or less. It calls to mind a story of slavery time. In this story, a master with more intellectual curiosity than usual, set out to see how much he could teach a particularly bright slave of his. When he had gotten him up to higher mathematics and to be a fluent reader of Latin, he called in a neighbor to show off his brilliant slave, and to argue that Negroes had brains just like the slave-owners had, and given the same opportunities, would turn out the same.

The visiting master of slaves looked and listened, tried to trap the literate slave in Algebra and Latin, and failing to do so in both, turned to his neighbor and said:

"Yes, he certainly knows his higher mathematics, and he can read Latin better than many white men I know, but I cannot bring myself to believe that he understands a thing that he is doing. It is all an aping of our culture. All on the outside. You are crazy if you think that it has changed him inside in the least. Turn him loose, and he will revert at once to the jungle. He is still a savage, and no amount of translating Virgil and Ovid is going to change him. In fact, all you have done is to turn a useful savage into a dangerous beast."

That was in slavery time, yes, and we have come a long, long way since then, but the troubling thing is that there are still too many who refuse to believe in the ingestion and digestion of western culture as yet. Hence the lack of literature about the higher emotions and love life of upperclass Negroes and the minorities in general.

Publishers and producers are cool to the idea. Now, do not leap to the conclusion that editors and producers constitute a special class of unbelievers. That is far from true. Publishing houses and theatrical promoters are in business to make money. They will sponsor anything that they believe will sell. They shy away from romantic stories about Negroes and Jews because they feel that they know the public indifference to such works, unless the story or play involves racial tension. It can then be offered as a study in Sociology, with the romantic side subdued. They know the skepticism in general about the complicated emotions in the minorities. The average American just cannot conceive of it, and would be apt to reject the notion, and publishers and producers take the stand that they are not in business to educate, but to make money. Sympathetic as they might be, they cannot afford to be crusaders.

In proof of this, you can note various publishers and producers edging forward a little, and ready to go even further when the trial balloons show that the public is ready for it. This public lack of interest is the nut of the matter.

The question naturally arises as to the why of this indifference, not to say skepticism, to the internal life of educated minorities.

The answer lies in what we may call THE AMERICAN MUSEUM OF UNNATURAL HISTORY. This is an intangible built on folk belief. It is assumed that all non-Anglo-Saxons are uncomplicated stereotypes. Everybody knows all about them. They are lay figures mounted in the museum where all may take them in at a glance. They are made of bent wires without insides at all. So how could anybody write a book about the nonexistent?

The American Indian is a contraption of copper wires in an eternal war-bonnet, with no equipment for laughter, expressionless face and that says "How" when spoken to. His only activity is treachery leading to massacres. Who is so dumb as not to know all about Indians, even if they have never seen one, nor talked with anyone who ever knew one?

The American Negro exhibit is a group of two. Both of these mechanical toys are built so that their feet eternally shuffle, and their eyes pop and roll. Shuffling feet and those popping, rolling eyes denote the Negro, and no characterization is genuine without this monotony. One is seated on a stump picking away on his banjo and singing and laughing. The other is a most amoral character before a sharecropper's shack mumbling about injustice. Doing this makes him out to be a Negro "intellectual." It is as simple as all that.

The whole museum is dedicated to the convenient "typical." In there is the "typical" Oriental, Jew, Yankee, Westerner, Southerner, Latin, and even out-of-favor Nordics like the German. The Englishman "I say old chappie," and the gesticulating Frenchman. The least observant American can know them all at a glance. However, the public willingly accepts the untypical in Nordics, but feels cheated if the untypical is portrayed in others. The author of *Scarlet Sister Mary* complained to me that her neighbors objected to her book on the grounds that she had the characters thinking, "and everybody know that Nigras don't think."

But for the national welfare, it is urgent to realize that the minorities do think, and think about something other than the race problem. That they are very human and internally, according to natural endowment, are just like everybody else. So long as this is not conceived, there must remain that feeling of unsurmountable difference, and difference to the average man means something bad. If people were made right, they would be just like him.

The trouble with the purely problem arguments is that they leave too much unknown. Argue all you will or may about injustice, but as long as the majority cannot conceive of a Negro or a Jew feeling and reacting inside just as they do, the majority will keep right on believing that people who do not look like them cannot possibly feel as they do, and conform to the established pattern. It is well known that there must be a body of waived matter, let us say, things accepted and taken for granted by all in a community before there can be that commonality of feeling. The usual phrase is having things in common. Until this is thoroughly established in respect to Negroes in America, as well as of other minorities, it will remain impossible for the majority to conceive of a Negro experiencing a deep and abiding love and not just the passion of sex. That a great mass of Negroes can be stirred by the pageants of Spring and Fall; the extravaganza of summer, and the majesty of winter. That they can and do experience discovery of the numerous subtle faces as a foundation for a great and selfless love, and the diverse nuances that go to destroy that love as with others. As it is now, this capacity, this evidence of high and complicated emotions, is ruled out. Hence the lack of interest in a romance uncomplicated by the race struggle has so little appeal.

This insistence on defeat in a story where upperclass Negroes are portrayed, perhaps says something from the subconscious of the majority. Involved in western culture, the hero or the heroine, or both, must appear frustrated and go down to defeat, somehow. Our literature reeks with it. Is it the same as saying, "You can translate Virgil, and fumble with the differential calculus, but can you really comprehend it? Can you cope with our subtleties?"

That brings us to the folklore of "reversion to type." This curious doctrine has such wide acceptance that it is tragic. One has only to examine the huge literature on it to be convinced. No matter how high we may *seem* to climb, put us under strain and we revert to type, that is, to the bush. Under a superficial layer of western culture, the jungle drums throb in our veins.

This ridiculous notion makes it possible for that majority who accept it to conceive of even a man like the suave and scholarly Dr. Charles S. Johnson to hide a black cat's bone on his person, and indulge in a midnight voodoo ceremony, complete with leopard skin and drums if threatened with the loss of the presidency of Fisk University, or the love of his wife. "Under the skin . . . better to deal with them in business, etc., but otherwise keep them at a safe distance and under control. I tell you, Carl Van Vechten, think as you like, but they are just not like us."

The extent and extravagance of this notion reaches the ultimate in nonsense in the widespread belief that the Chinese have bizarre genitals, because of that eye-fold that makes their eyes seem to slant. In spite of the fact that no biology has ever mentioned any such difference in reproductive organs makes no matter. Millions of people believe it. "Did you know that a Chinese has. . . ." Consequently, their quiet contemplative manner is interpreted as a sign of slyness and a treacherous inclination.

But the opening wedge for better understanding has been thrust into the crack. Though many Negroes denounced Carl Van Vechten's *Nigger Heaven* because of the title, and without ever reading it, the book, written in the deepest sincerity, revealed Negroes of wealth and culture to the white public. It created curiosity even when it aroused skepticism. It made folks want to know. Worth Tuttle Hedden's *The Other Room* has definitely widened the opening. Neither of these well-written works take a romance of upperclass Negro life as the central theme, but the atmosphere and the background is there. These works should be followed up by some incisive and intimate stories from the inside.

The realistic story around a Negro insurance official, dentist, general practitioner, undertaker and the like would be most revealing. Thinly disguised fiction around the well known Negro names is not the answer, either. The "exceptional" as well as the Ol' Man Rivers has been exploited all out of context already. Everybody is already resigned to the "exceptional" Negro, and willing to be entertained by the "quaint." To grasp the penetration of western civilization in a minority, it is necessary to know how the average behaves and lives. Books that deal with people like in Sinclair Lewis' *Main Street* is the necessary métier. For various reasons, the average, struggling, nonmorbid Negro is the best-kept secret in America. His revelation to the public is the thing needed to do away with that feeling of difference which inspires fear, and which ever expresses itself in dislike.

It is inevitable that this knowledge will destroy many illusions and romantic traditions which America probably likes to have around. But then, we have no record of anybody sinking into a lingering death on finding out that there was no Santa Claus. The old world will take it in its stride. The realization that Negroes are no better nor no worse, and at times just as boring as everybody else, will hardly kill off the population of the nation.

Outside of racial attitudes, there is still another reason why this literature should exist. Literature and other arts are supposed to hold up the mirror to nature. With only the fractional "exceptional" and the "quaint" portrayed, a true picture of Negro life in America cannot be. A great principle of national art has been violated.

These are the things that publishers and producers, as the accredited representatives of the American people, have not as yet taken into consideration sufficiently. Let there be light!

ADDISON GAYLE, JR. (1932–1991)

Addison Gayle, Jr., an editor, teacher, critic, and essayist, was born in Newport News, Virginia. He was educated at the City College of New York and the University of California and worked as a lecturer and a professor of literature and creative writing. He was a consultant for minority writers for Doubleday and Random House, and he was on the editorial staff of the magazines Amistad *and* Black Lines *and for Third World Press. He wrote many nonfiction texts, including* The Black Aesthetic *(1971), a book of essays that define black art and analyze the experience of the black writer in America. He also wrote biographies of Paul Laurence Dunbar and Claude McKay. Gayle, with others, created a prominent space for African American art.*

The Function of Black Literature at the Present Time (1970)

"One of the most promising of the young Negro poets once said to me," Langston Hughes related in "The Negro Artist and the Racial Mountain," "'I want to be a poet—not a Negro poet,' meaning, I believe, 'I want to write like a white poet'; meaning subconsciously 'I would like to be a white poet'; meaning behind that, 'I would like to be white.' . . . This is the mountain standing in the way of any true Negro art in America—this urge within the race toward whiteness, the desire to pour racial individuality into the mold of American standardization, and to be as little Negro and as much American as possible."

We, too, have our literary assimilationists in the 1970s. More sophisticated than their counterparts of yesteryear, they declaim in the language of the academic scholars. The black writer, they argue, must "join the American mainstream"; he must "make his work more universal," and, instead of "writing about Negroes all the time, he must write about people." "Your book" (*The Black Situation*), remarked a black colleague, "is interesting; but you should've included more universal experiences."

"Black-Writing—The Other Side" (*Dissent*, May-June 1968), by Jervis Anderson, is a case in point. One supposes that Anderson is an honest man and should not be held accountable for the unsavory company he keeps. Afro-Americans, however, do not publish in *Dissent*, edited by Irving Howe—a racist *par excellence*—unless they are content to play the role of Friday to Irving Howe's Crusoe.

Apparently, Anderson has few compunctions about playing such a role. As a prelude to his major thesis, he quotes William Melvin Kelley: "There's no basic reason why we should talk to white people. Dostoyevsky did not talk to the Germans but to the Russians. . . . And we have to talk to our own people." The voice of the rebuttal is that of Anderson; the theme, tone, and contempt belong to "Father" Howe, who, one supposes, smiles approvingly over the shoulder of his young protégé: "Dostoyevsky's importance in the tradition of Western writing rests as much on the fact that he made a *great and universal art* (italics mine) out of Russian experiences as on the fact that diverse peoples of diverse life styles were able to find in his work images of their own situation. Obviously, black separatist writing has not left itself open to such accomplishments."

The "urge . . . toward whiteness" in the race, as evidenced by Fridays, past and present, has prevented the creation of a nationalistic art. Moreover, because of it, black writers have postulated an imaginary dichotomy between art and function that has made much of the writing of black authors irrelevant to the lives of black people. In an attempt to curry favor with the Crusoes of America, such writers, like Anderson, negate the idea of a unique group experience, and deny that black people, but for the accident of history and geography, would constitute a separate nation.

When put forward by black people, the thesis of a separate nation is dismissed as an absurdity. Yet, the same thesis, argued by white men of the nineteenth century, is catalogued in American history texts as "sound, patriotic, idealism." The poet Philip Freneau was one of the most vociferous advocates of a break with the cultural traditions of Europe—he was only slightly more militant than his contemporaries Ralph Waldo Emerson, John Trumbull, and Noah Webster.

Another of his contemporaries was the black poetess Phillis Wheatley. Like Freneau, she borrowed extensively from the poetical forms of the English neoclassicists. However, unlike Freneau, she failed to use these forms to call a new nation into being. Oblivious of the lot of her fellow blacks, she sang not of a separate nation, but of a Christian Eden. She wrote, as Richard Wright so aptly put it, "as a Negro reacting not as a Negro."

In the main, black writers have traveled the road of Phillis Wheatley. They have negated or falsified their racial experiences in an attempt to transform the pragmatics of their everyday lives into abstract formulas and theorems. They believe, with Margaret Just Butcher and Hugh Gloster, that there is a universal condition that transcends race and nationality, and that this condition is relevant to men of all colors. In this analysis, the function of the artist is to depict the unique manner in which each man reacts to his condition. Therefore, Eric Jones, of *Another Country*, is a more universal character than Rufus Scott, because he copes with his condition (homosexuality) in a way in which Rufus cannot cope with his (blackness).

The degree of similarity between the conditions under which blacks and whites live has been exaggerated. This exaggeration results from the tendency to regard American slavery as an economical, political, and legal institution, capable of being legislated out of existence by the thirteenth, fourteenth, and fifteenth amendments. However, under the creative aegis of the Americans, slavery assumed a uniqueness heretofore unsurpassed in the annals of slave institutions. Men were separated, not only in terms of laws and economics, but also in terms of basic human qualities. For Quaker and southern plantation owner alike, the black man was a subhuman being whose condition could be alleviated—if at all—only by divine intervention.

He was not an American, nor was his condition analogous to that of Americans. To be an American was not to be censured with Benedict Spinoza: "Let him be accursed by day, and accursed by night; let him be accursed in his lying down, and accursed in his rising up; accursed in going out and accursed in coming in. May the lord never more pardon or acknowledge him; may the wrath and displeasure of the lord burn henceforth against this man, load him with all the curses written in the book of the law, and blot his name from under the sky. . . ." The criteria for defining an American went beyond accidents of birth, acts of immigration, or legal statutes erected during periods of national frenzy.

Nevertheless, with more zeal than whites, Blacks continue to flaunt their Americanism. Like Don Quixote, they insist that this earthly hell can be transformed into a heavenly paradise through the sheer effort of will power. No one is more culpable in this respect than the black writer. He attempts to gain recognition as an American by arguing that there are no separate cultural streams dividing the two races. There is, he supposes, only one giant cultural ocean, in which white and black experiences have been churned into one. The result of such assimilationism is the transformation of black men into carbon copies of white men.

Nowhere is this attempt at cultural assimilation more readily apparent than in the Afro-American novel, of which the works of William Wells Brown are early examples. The first Afro-American novelist and playwright as well as one of the first historians, Brown was also an eloquent speaker, ranking—with Frederick Douglass, Charles Remond, and Henry Highland Garnet—among the giants of the Afro-American oratorical tradition. Yet, Brown the abolitionist orator differs noticeably from Brown the novelist.

The orator dealt with the American society in uncompromising terms, pointing out, in the vein of Douglass, the manifest differences in a nation composed of masters and slaves. However, in his novels—and the second, *Miralda; or The Beautiful Quadroon*, is a better example than the first, *Clotel, or The President's Daughter*—he attempted to convince his white reading audience that Blacks and whites, with few exceptions, were indistinguishable in terms of cultural artifacts. *Miralda* was written to prove that Blacks were willing to deal with their experience in terms of the American experience.

The function of the novel as delineated by Brown has survived the years. His ideas of cultural assimilation have been adopted and refined by writers more sophisticated—if not more talented—than he, and his thesis is restated in the twentieth century in three works that are considered among the best literary efforts by Afro-Americans: *The Autobiography of an Ex-Coloured Man*, by James Weldon Johnson; *Go Tell It on the Mountain*, by James Baldwin; and *Invisible Man*, by Ralph Ellison.

The Autobiography of an Ex-Coloured Man presents a portrait of the Afro-American artist as a young man. The child of a white father and a black mother, the protagonist is forced to choose between two worlds—one black, the other white. A man with no ethnic ties, he symbolizes what James Baldwin has called the "blood relationship" that exists between Blacks and whites in the American society.

The world of art is also delineated in terms of black and white. Black art is to be found in the spirituals, in the surviving African cultural artifacts, and in jazz. White art is depicted in Bach and Beethoven, the paintings of Michelangelo, and the Chartres Cathedral. The protagonist, a concert pianist, makes a pilgrimage to Europe, where he plays the works of European composers.

His objective is to merge the two worlds into one, to saturate the white artistic world with the black idiom. Like Dvořák, who synthesized symphonic music, spirituals, and jazz in the *New World Symphony*, the narrator will also attempt to assimilate the two in the hope of producing a new American product. How far we are from Stephen in Joyce's *Portrait of the Artist as a Young Man!* Stephen wanted to cultivate and hold on to the artifacts of his Irish heritage; Johnson's narrator wants to debase his by fusing it with another. After spending time in both worlds, the protagonist finds his identity in the white world. In so doing, he fails as artist and as man; for although he realizes the richness of his African heritage, he cannot allow himself to think of his culture as unique and distinct—he can accept it only as a submerged entity within a larger cultural sphere.

The theme of identity, so prevalent in the works of Brown, Baldwin, and Ellison, is presented in *The Autobiography of an Ex-Coloured Man* in terms of its varied dimensions. Forced to choose between a white world and a black world, between a white culture and a black culture, the narrator opts for the former. With the exception of Ellison's protagonist, who, by the end of the novel, is content to remain faceless, formless, and rootless as he hangs midway between heaven and hell, each protagonist chooses cultural sameness instead of cultural diversity, and surrenders his racial identity to the American Mephistopheles for a pittance that Faust would have labeled demeaning.

"One writes out of one thing only—one's own experiences," notes James Baldwin in *Notes of a Native Son*. For the serious black writer, this means writing from a group experience, for, in the American society, the individual experiences of the Afro-American, unless he is quite fair or quite lucky, is indistinguishable from that of the group.

John Grimes of *Go Tell It on the Mountain*, however, is ashamed of his group (read racial) experiences and attempts to transcend them by negating his racial identity. On two occasions in the novel, he is confronted with the problem of choosing between the two worlds offered him by his creator.

The initial, and most important, confrontation takes place on the mountaintop—a hill in Central Park overlooking New York City. Young Grimes is tempted by Satan, who offers him "the pottage" of the world in exchange for his birthright: ". . . the gigantic towers, the people in their dark grey clothes: and Broadway. The way that led to death was broad, and many could be found thereon; but narrow was the way that led to life eternal; and few there were who found it."

There is this difference between the worlds: the white leads to death and decay; the black, to life and vitality. Nevertheless, Grimes ". . . did not long for the narrow way, where all his people walked; where the houses did not rise, piercing, as it seemed, the unchanging clouds, . . . where the streets and the hallways and rooms were dark."

Baldwin prefers light to darkness, life to death. The dilemma confronting his protagonist is the same as that confronting Johnson's: to what world am I morally and culturally bound? Like Johnson's narrator, John Grimes has also "been down to the valley" and received the message of the anointed: ". . . they move with an authority which I shall never have; . . . they have made the modern world, in effect, even if they do not know it. The most illiterate among them is related in a way that I am not to

Dante, Shakespeare, Michelangelo, Aeschylus, Da Vinci, Rembrandt and Racine. . . . Out of their hymns and dances come Beethoven and Bach. Go back a few centuries and they are in their full glory—but I am in Africa, watching the conquerors arrive."

These are the words of John's creator in the essay "Stranger in the Village." The tone of assimilation, the obsession with fusing the black and white cultures—even at the risk of destroying the black—is as pervasive in the novel as it is in the essay. At the outset, John will settle for nothing less than a colorless world. Unable to bring this about, eventually he will sell "his birthright for a mess of pottage."

On the first reading, *Invisible Man,* by Ralph Ellison, does not appear to be a novel in the assimilationist tradition. Ellison is a student of black literature and history, and his novel illustrates a remarkable grasp of the Afro-American's historical past. No other writer has presented so well, in fiction, the vicissitudes of "The Age of Booker T. Washington"—an age that is fundamental to an understanding of black nationalism.

Ellison's knowledge of black culture might have enabled him, with Joyce, to "forge in the smithy of [his] soul the uncreated conscious of [his] race." However, the assimilationist aspirations are as strong in Ralph Ellison as in black writers of the past: "When I began writing in earnest," he relates in *Shadow and Act,* "I was forced, thus, to relate myself consciously and imaginatively to my mixed background as American, as Negro American, and as Negro from what in its own belated way was a pioneer background." In addition, there was "the necessity of determining my true relationship to that body of American literature to which I was most attracted and through which, aided by what I could learn from the literatures of Europe, I would find my own voice, and to which I was challenged by way of achieving, myself, to make some small contribution, and to whose composite picture of reality I was obliged to offer some necessary modification."

We are again with James Baldwin, and the Chartres Cathedral stands before us, dazzling in its ancient beauty, striking in its reminder of the genius, mastery, and artistic superiority of white, Western man. Although Ellison's journey was only spiritual, like Baldwin, after the pilgrimage to Gethsemane, he, too, was able to stare "down the deadly and hypnotic temptation to interpret the world and all its devices in terms of race."

"It is quite possible," he writes after the baptism, "that much potential fiction by Negro Americans fails precisely at this point: through the writers' refusal (often through provincialism or lack of courage or opportunism) to achieve a vision of life and a resourcefulness of craft commensurate with the complexity of their actual situation. Too often they fear to leave the uneasy sanctuary of race to take their chances in the world of art."

Such statements do little justice to Brown, Johnson, and Baldwin, who, like Ellison, have not only refused to use race as a sanctuary, but instead have attempted to negate race either by integrating the racial idiom with that of whites, or by obliterating racial characteristics altogether. The narrator of *Invisible Man* is a good example. He is—to be sure—a Rinehart, the identity he assumes near the end of the novel. A man without a distinctive identity, he is all things to all men, and after the excursion through the black world, he retreats to his dungeon to await the coming millennium, when race will have become irrelevant.

"Dr. Johnson," T. S. Eliot wrote of Samuel Johnson, "is a dangerous man to disagree with." The same may be said of Ralph Ellison. For this reason, among others, academic critics have been reluctant to meet the author of *Invisible Man* on his own terms. Ellison traces his literary lineage to the "comic tradition inherent in American literature"—one critic has called him "the Negro Mark Twain"—irrespective of the fact that there is no comic tradition in American literature. There is what can be labeled, at best, a tradition of minstrelsy, slapstick, and buffoonery. In terms of the comic tradition, therefore, it is in Europe, not in America, that Ellison's predecessors must be found; and *Invisible Man*, to get a fair hearing in the court of "mainstream criticism," must be evaluated in light of the comic tradition handed down from Aristophanes through Cervantes to Fielding, Thackery, Dickens, and Meredith.

Dickens, Thackery, and Meredith, England's nineteenth-century masters of the comic tradition, postulated no dichotomy between art and fiction. The Preface to *Joseph Andrews*, by Henry Fielding, is as nationalistic a tract as there is to be found in literature, surpassed, perhaps, only by sections of *The Republic*, and the Preface to *Lyrical Ballads*. The English novelists did not use the novel form to negate their identity as Englishmen. The pride in English cities, churches, and towns, the love for England's cultural past, and the sense of the Englishman as different from other Europeans led Dickens to create his people and his cities.

As a result of English nationalism, a comic tradition was continued and a comic theory was enunciated—a theory to which American writers have only in part been attuned. "Comedy," writes George Meredith, "is an interpretation of the general mind. . . . The comic poet is in the narrow field, or enclosed square of the society he depicts; and he addresses the still narrow enclosure of man's intellect, with references to the operation of the social world upon their characters. . . . To understand his work and value it, you must have a sober liking of your kind, and a sober estimate of our civilized qualities."

The function of comedy—"the perceptive or governing spirit"—is to awaken and give "aim to the powers of laughter." Laughter is, then, the cathartic instrument, capable of deflating egos, of forcing the individual to laugh at himself, and by so doing, force him to relate to others. On this level, comedy is the saving grace—the *deus ex machina* for man and society alike. Instead of laughing themselves to death, men will laugh themselves into greater unity with their fellows.

Meredith, the Englishman, spoke to other Englishmen. His faith in his countrymen led him to believe that they were endowed with that "sensitiveness to the comic laugh [which] is a step in civilization. . . ." "We know," he argues at one point, "the degree of refinement in men by the matter they will laugh at; but we know likewise that the larger natures are distinguished by the breadth of their laughter. . . ." Such statements have little relevance in America, where historical racism occasions—in the majority group—contempt instead of understanding, barbarity instead of refinement, and an animosity toward the minority group that renders the term "civilized" obscure and irrelevant.

The lack of an American comic tradition "which feeds upon civilized and sensitive natures" makes Bret Harte so unreadable, Joel Chandler Harris so contemptible, and Mark Twain such a sentimentalist and buffoon. America is the last place to which one would go to find laughter. For instead of being transformed by the comic spirit, Americans, when gazing at the reflection of their egotistical selves, are more likely to be inflated than deflated. Richard Wright knew this very well, and thus there is no laughter in his fiction.

"If my work fails," writes Ellison, "it fails on artistic grounds alone." When *Invisible Man*, like its American mainstream predecessors, is evaluated by the criteria established by England's comic artists, the verdict that Ellison demands can then be rendered. There is, however, an Afro-American comic tradition, as manifested in the works of George Moses Horton, the best of Paul Laurence Dunbar, Langston Hughes, George Schuyler, Wallace Thurman, and Ishmael Reed. In this tradition, despite its assimilationist denouncement, *Invisible Man* ranks high indeed. This will bring little satisfaction to Ellison, who, like Brown, Johnson, and Baldwin, remains wedded to the concept of assimilation at a time when such a concept has ceased to be the preoccupation of the black writer.

"Season it as you will," writes Saunders Redding, "the thought that the Negro American is different from other Americans is still unpalatable to most Negroes. Nevertheless, the Negro is different. An iron ring of historical circumstance has made him so." This difference is manifested in our cultural and social institutions. Although most black institutions are photographic copies of white ones, each has its own uniqueness—white form with black content. An example is the Afro-American church, which though white in form—Methodist, Episcopalian, Baptist—differs in ritual and message.

Black artists of the past expropriated and remodeled the forms of white America to fit the needs of black people. Nowhere is this more evident than in the letters, speeches, and essays of David Walker, Henry Highland Garnet, Charles Remond, and Frederick Douglass. But not all was expropriation! The earliest Afro-American artists—the creators of the spirituals—constructed new forms with which to deal with their racial experiences. Not having been seduced by the scholastic Merlins, they were free from the myth that black manhood was attainable only if one transcended his race and group experiences. ". . . the nationalistic character of the Negro people," wrote Richard Wright, in 1937, "is unmistakable. Psychologically, this nationalism is reflected in the whole of Negro culture, and especially in folklore. . . . Let those who shy at the nationalistic implications of Negro life look at this body of folklore, living and powerful, which rose out of a unified sense of common life and a common fate."

The black writer at the present time must forgo the assimilationist tradition and redirect his art to the strivings within the race—those strivings that have become so pronounced, here, in the latter half of the twentieth century. To do so, he must write for and speak to the majority of black people; not to a sophisticated elite fashioned out of the programmed computers of America's largest universities.

For here we stand, acknowledging those truths we would not admit at the beginning of the twentieth century: that the problem of the color line is insoluble, that the idea of an egalitarian America belongs to the trash basket of history, and that the concept of an American melting pot is one to which sane men no longer adhere. In light of such realities, the literature of assimilationism belongs to the period of the dinosaur and the mastodon.

To return to Richard Wright: "The Negro writer who seeks to function within his race as a purposeful agent has a serious responsibility. In order to do justice to his subject matter, in order to depict Negro life in all of its manifold and intricate relationships, a deep, informed, and complex consciousness is necessary; a consciousness which draws for its strength upon the fluid lore of a great people, and molds this lore with the concepts that move and direct the forces of history today. . . . A new role is devolving upon the Negro writer. He is being called upon to do no less than create values by which his race is to struggle, live and die. . . ." This is no easy task. To create such values, the writer must undergo a baptism in thought and spirit. He must descend into the pit of the mountain and rise to the top with a clearer vision than before; he must have a greater understanding of the task that lies before him; and above all, if he is to function effectively as a black writer, he must believe with Don L. Lee[1]: "Black. Poet. Black poet am I. This should leave little doubt in the minds of anyone as to which is first. Black art will elevate and enlighten our people and lead them towards an awareness of self, i.e., their blackness. It will show them mirrors. Beautiful symbols. And will aid in the destruction of anything nasty and detrimental to our advancement as a people."

❦ AMIRI BARAKA (b. 1934)

For a brief biography of Amiri Baraka (formerly LeRoi Jones), see page 663.

The Revolutionary Theatre (1966)

The Revolutionary Theatre should force change; it should be change. (All their faces turned into the lights and you work on them black nigger magic, and cleanse them at having seen the ugliness. And if the beautiful see themselves, they will love themselves.) We are preaching virtue again, but by that to mean NOW, toward what seems the most constructive use of the world.

The Revolutionary Theatre must EXPOSE! Show up the insides of these humans, look into black skulls. White men will cower before this theatre because it hates them. Because they themselves have been trained to hate. The Revolutionary Theatre must hate them for hating. For presuming with their technology to deny the supremacy of the Spirit. They will all die because of this.

The Revolutionary Theatre must teach them their deaths. It must crack their faces open to the mad cries of the poor. It must teach them about silence and the truths lodged there. It must kill any God anyone names except Common Sense. The Revolutionary Theatre should flush the fags and murders out of Lincoln's face.

It should stagger through our universe correcting, insulting, preaching, spitting craziness—but a craziness taught to us in our most rational moments. People must be taught to trust true scientists (knowers, diggers, oddballs) and that the

---

[1]Don L. Lee is Haki R. Madhubuti's birth name.

holiness of life is the constant possibility of widening the consciousness. And they must be incited to strike back against *any* agency that attempts to prevent this widening.

The Revolutionary Theatre must Accuse and Attack anything that can be accused and attacked. It must Accuse and Attack because it is a theatre of Victims. It looks at the sky with the victims' eyes, and moves the victims to look at the strength in their minds and their bodies.

Clay, in *Dutchman*, Ray in *The Toilet*, Walker in *The Slave*, are all victims. In the Western sense they could be heroes. But the Revolutionary Theatre, even if it is Western, must be anti-Western. It must show horrible coming attractions of *The Crumbling of the West*. Even as Artaud designed *The Conquest of Mexico*, so we must design *The Conquest of White Eye*, and show the missionaries and wiggly Liberals dying under blasts of concrete. For sound effects, wild screams of joy, from all the peoples of the world.

The Revolutionary Theatre must take dreams and give them a reality. It must isolate the ritual and historical cycles of reality. But it must be food for all those who need food, and daring propaganda for the beauty of the Human Mind. It is a political theatre, a weapon to help in the slaughter of these dim-witted fatbellied white guys who somehow believe that the rest of the world is here for them to slobber on.

This should be a theatre of World Spirit. Where the spirit can be shown to be the most competent force in the world. Force. Spirit. Feeling. The language will be anybody's, but tightened by the poet's backbone. And even the language must show what the facts are in this consciousness epic, what's happening. We will talk about the world, and the preciseness with which we are able to summon the world will be our art. Art is method. And art, "like any ashtray or senator," remains in the world. Wittgenstein said ethics and aesthetics are one. I believe this. So the Broadway theatre is a theatre of reaction whose ethics, like its aesthetics, reflect the spiritual values of this unholy society, which sends young crackers all over the world blowing off colored people's heads. (In some of these flippy Southern towns they even shoot up the immigrants' Favorite Son, be it Michael Schwerner or JFKennedy.)

The Revolutionary Theatre is shaped by the world, and moves to reshape the world, using as its force the natural force and perpetual vibrations of the mind in the world. We are history and desire, what we are, and what any experience can make us.

It is a social theatre, but all theatre is social theatre. But we will change the drawing rooms into places where real things can be said about a real world, or into smoky rooms where the destruction of Washington can be plotted. The Revolutionary Theatre must function like an incendiary pencil planted in Curtis Lemay's cap. So that when the final curtain goes down brains are splattered over the seats and the floor, and bleeding nuns must wire SOS's to Belgians with gold teeth.

Our theatre will show victims so that their brothers in the audience will be better able to understand that they are the brothers of victims, and that they themselves are victims if they are blood brothers. And what we show must cause the blood to rush, so that pre-revolutionary temperaments will be bathed in this blood, and it will cause their deepest souls to move, and they will find themselves tensed and clenched, even ready to die, at what the soul has been taught. We will scream and cry, murder, run through the streets in agony, if it means some soul will be moved, moved to actual life understanding of what the world is, and what it ought to be. We are preaching virtue and feeling, and a natural sense of the self in the world. All men live in the world, and the world ought to be a place for them to live.

What is called the imagination (from image, magi, magic, magician, etc.) is a practical vector from the soul. It stores all data, and can be called on to solve all our "problems." The imagination is the projection of ourselves past our sense of ourselves as "things." Imagination (Image) is all possibility, because from the image, the initial circumscribed energy, any use (idea) is possible. And so begins that image's use in the world. Possibility is what moves us.

The popular white man's theatre like the popular white man's novel shows tired white lives, and the problems of eating white sugar, or else it herds bigca-boosed blondes onto huge stages in rhinestones and makes believe they are danc-ing or singing. WHITE BUSINESSMEN OF THE WORLD, DO YOU WANT TO SEE PEOPLE REALLY DANCING AND SINGING??? ALL OF YOU GO UP TO HARLEM AND GET YOURSELF KILLED. THERE WILL BE DANCING AND SINGING, THEN, FOR REAL!! (In *The Slave*, Walker Vessels, the black revolutionary, wears an armband, which is the insignia of the attacking army—a big red-lipped minstrel, grinning like crazy.)

The liberal white man's objection to the theatre of the revolution (if he is "hip" enough) will be on aesthetic grounds. Most white Western artists do not need to be "political," since usually, whether they know it or not, they are in complete sympathy with the most repressive social forces in the world today. There are more junior birdmen fascists running around the West today disguised as Artists than there are disguised as fascists. (But then, that word, *Fascist*, and with it, *Fascism*, has been made obsolete by the words *America*, and *Americanism*.) The American Artist usually turns out to be just a super-Bourgeois, because, finally, all he has to show for his sojourn through the world is "better taste" than the Bourgeois—many times not even that.

Americans will hate the Revolutionary Theatre because it will be out to destroy them and whatever they believe is real. American cops will try to close the the-atres where such nakedness of the human spirit is paraded. American producers will say the revolutionary plays are filth, usually because they will treat human life as if it were actually happening. American directors will say that the white guys in the plays are too abstract and cowardly ("don't get me wrong . . . I mean aesthet-ically . . .") and they will be right.

The force we want is of twenty million spooks storming America with furious cries and unstoppable weapons. We want actual explosions and actual brutality: AN EPIC IS CRUMBLING and we must give it the space and hugeness of its actual demise. The Revolutionary Theatre, which is now peopled with victims, will soon begin to be peopled with new kinds of heroes—not the weak Hamlets debating whether or not they are ready to die for what's on their minds, but men and women (and minds) digging out from under a thousand years of "high art" and weak-faced dalliance. We must make an art that will function so as to call down the actual wrath of world spirit. We are witch doctors and assassins, but we will open a place for the true scientists to expand our consciousness. This is a theatre of assault. The play that will split the heavens for us will be called THE DESTRUCTION OF AMERICA. The heroes will be Crazy Horse, Denmark Vesey, Patrice Lumumba, and not history, not memory, not sad sentimental groping for a warmth in our despair; these will be new men, new heroes, and their enemies most of you who are reading this.

A Challenge To Artists

Lorraine Hansberry

Lorraine Hansberry, noted African American playwright, delivered this speech in 1963. In the address, she expresses her beliefs that the role of an artist is not confined to the creative arena; an artist is also responsible for addressing political concerns.

I am afraid that I haven't made a speech for a very long time, and there is a significance in that fact, which is part of what I should like to talk about this evening.

A week or so ago I was at my typewriter working on a scene in a play of mine in which one character, a German novelist, is trying to explain to another character, an American intellectual, something about what led the greater portion of the German intelligentsia to acquiesce to Nazism. He says this: "They [the Nazis] permitted us to feel, in return for our silence, that we were nonparticipants— merely irrelevant if inwardly agonized observers who had nothing whatsoever to do with that which was being committed in our names."

Just as I put the period after that sentence, my own telephone rang and I was confronted with the voice of Dr. Otto Nathan, asking this particular American writer if she would be of this decade and this nation and appear at this rally this evening and join a very necessary denunciation of a lingering *American* kind of travesty.

It is the sort of moment of truth that dramatists dearly love to put on the stage but find as uncomfortable as everyone else in life. To make it short, however, I am here.

I mean to say that one can become detached in this world of ours; we can get to a place where we read only the theater or photography or music pages of our newspapers. And then we wake up one day and find that the better people of our nation are still where they were when we last noted them: in the courts defending *our* Constitutional rights for us.

This makes me feel that it might be interesting to talk about where are our artists in the contemporary struggles. Some of them, of course, are being heard and felt. Some of the more serious actresses such as Shelley Winters and Julie Harris and a very thoughtful comedian such as Steve Allen have associated themselves with some aspect of the peace movement and Sidney Poitier and Harry Belafonte have made significant contributions to the Negro struggle. But the vast majority—where are they?

Well, I am afraid that they are primarily where the ruling powers have always wished the artist to be and to stay: in their studios. They are consumed, in the main, with what they consider to be larger issues—such as "the meaning of life," et-cetera. I personally consider that part of this detachment is the direct and indirect result of many years of things like the House Committee and concurrent years of McCarthyism in all its forms. I mean to suggest that the climate of fear, which we were once told, as I was coming along, by wise men, would bear a bitter harvest in the culture of our civilization, has in fact come to pass. In the contemporary arts, the rejection of this particular world is no longer a mere grotesque threat, but a fact.

Among my contemporaries and colleagues in the arts the search for the roots of war, the exploitation of man, of poverty and of despair itself, is sought in any arena other than the one which has shaped these artists. Having discovered that the world is incoherent, they have—some of them—also come to the conclusion that it is also unreal and, in any case, beyond the corrective powers of human energy. Having determined that life is in fact an absurdity, they have not yet decided that the task of the thoughtful is to try and help impose purposefulness on that absurdity. They don't yet agree, by and large, that simply being against life as it is is not enough; that simply *not* being a "rhinoceros" is not enough. That, moreover, replacing phony utopianism of one kind with vulgar and cheap little philosophies of accommodation is also not enough. In a word, they do not yet agree that it is perhaps the task, I should think certainly the joy, of the artist to chisel out some expression of what life can conceivably be.

The fact is that this unwitting capitulation really does aim to be a revolt; really does aim to indict—*something*. Really does aim to be partisan in saying no to a world which it generally characterizes as a "brothel." I am thinking now, mainly, of course, of writers of my generation. It is they, upon whom we must depend so heavily for the refinement and articulation of the aspiration of man, who do not yet agree that if the world is a brothel, then someone has built the edifice; and that if it was the hand of man, then the hand of man can reconstruct it—that whatever man renders, creates, imagines, he can render afresh, re-create and even more gloriously re-imagine. But, I must repeat, that anyone who can even think so these days is held to be an example of unparalleled simple-mindedness.

Why? For this is what is cogent to our meeting tonight; the writers that I am presently thinking of come mainly from my generation. That is to say that they come from a generation which was betrayed in the late forties and fifties by the domination of McCarthyism. We were ceaselessly told, after all, to be everything which mutilates youth: to be silent, to be ignorant, to be without unsanctioned opinions, to be compliant and, above all else, obedient to all the ideas which are in fact the dregs of an age. We were taught that agitational activity in behalf of changing this world was nothing but an expression, among other things, of our "neurotic compulsions" about our own self-dissatisfactions because our mothers dominated our fathers or some such as that. We were told in an age of celebrated liberations of repressions that the repression of the urge to protest against war was surely the only respectable repression left in the universe.

As for those who went directly into science or industry it was all even less oblique than any of that. If you went to the wrong debates on campus, signed the wrong petitions, you simply didn't get the job you wanted and you were forewarned of this early in your college career.

And, of course, things are a little different than in my parents' times—I mean, with regard to the candor with which young people have been made to think in terms of money. It is the only single purpose which has been put before them. That which Shakespeare offered as a curse, "Put money in thy purse," is now a boast. What makes me think of that in connection with what we are speaking of tonight? Well, I hope that I am wise enough to determine the nature of a circle. If, after all, the ambition in life is merely to be rich, then all which might threaten that possibility is much to be avoided, is it not? This means, therefore, not incurring the disfavor of employers. It means that one will not protest war if one expects to draw one's livelihood from, say, the aircraft industry if one is an engineer. Or, in the arts, how can one write plays which have either implicit or explicit in them a quality of the detestation of commerciality, if in fact one is beholden to the commerciality of the professional theatre? How can one protest the criminal persecution of political dissenters if one has already discovered at nineteen that to do so is to risk a profession? If all one's morality is wedded to the opportunistic, the expedient in life, how can one have the deepest, most profound moral outrage about the fact of the condition of the Negro people in the United States? Particularly, thinking of expediency, when one has it dinned into one's ears day after day that the only reason why, perhaps, that troublesome and provocative group of people must some day be permitted to buy a cup of coffee or rent an apartment or get a job—is *not* because of the recognition of the universal humanity of the human race, but because it happens to be extremely expedient international politics to now *think* of granting these things!

As I stand here I know perfectly well that such institutions as the House Committee, and all the other little committees, have dragged on their particular obscene theatrics for all these years not to expose "Communists" or do anything really in connection with the "security" of the United States, but merely to create an atmosphere where, in the first place, I should be afraid to come here tonight at all and, secondly, to absolutely guarantee that I will not say what I am going to say, which is this:

I think that my government is wrong. I would like to see them turn back our ships from the Caribbean. The Cuban people, to my mind, and I speak only for myself, have chosen their destiny and I cannot believe that it is the place of the descendants of those who did not ask the monarchists of the eighteenth century for permission to make the United States a republic, to interfere with the twentieth-century choice of another sovereign people.

I will go further, speaking as a Negro in America, and impose a little of what Negroes say all the time to each other on what I am saying to you. And that is that it would be a great thing if they would not only turn back the ships from the

Caribbean but turn to the affairs of our country that need righting. For one thing, empty the legislative and judicial chambers of the victims of political persecution so we know why that lamp is burning out there in the Brooklyn waters. And, while they are at it, go on and help fulfill the American dream and empty the Southern jails of the genuine heroes, practically the last vestige of dignity that we have to boast about at this moment in our history; those students whose imprisonment for trying to insure what is already on the book is our national disgrace at this moment.

And I would go so far—perhaps with an over sense of drama, but I don't think so—to say that maybe without waiting for another two men to die, that we send those troops to finish the Reconstruction in Alabama, Georgia, Mississippi, and every place else where the fact of our federal flag flying creates the false notion that what happened at the end of the Civil War was the defeat of the slavocracy at the political as well as the military level. And I say this not merely in behalf of the black and oppressed but, for a change—and more and more thoughtful Negroes must begin to make this point—also for the white and disinherited of the South, those poor whites who, by the millions, have been made the tragic and befuddled instruments of their own oppression at the hand of the most sinister political apparatus in our country. I think perhaps that if our government would do that it would not have to compete in any wishful way for the respect of the new black and brown nations of the world.

Finally, I think that all of us who are thinking such things, who wish to exercise these rights that we are here defending tonight, must really exercise them. Speaking to my fellow artists in particular, I think that we must paint them, sing them, write about them. All these matters which are not currently fashionable. Otherwise, I think, as I have put into the mouth of my German novelist, we are indulging in a luxurious complicity—and no other thing.

I personally agree with those who say that from here on in, if we are to survive, we, the people—still an excellent phrase—we the people of the world must oblige the heads of all governments to become responsible to us. I personally do not feel that it matters if it be the government of China presently engaging in incomprehensible and insane antics at the border of India or my President, John F. Kennedy, dismissing what he knows to be in the hearts of the American people and engaging in overt provocation with our sister people to the South. I think that it is imperative to say "No" to all of it—"No" to war of any kind, anywhere. And I think, therefore, and it is my reason for being here tonight, that it is imperative to remove from the American fabric any and all such institutions or agencies as the House Committee on Un-American Activities which are designed expressly to keep us from saying "No!"

✺ LARRY NEAL (1937–1981)

Larry Neal, an influential anthologist, editor, critic, and activist, was born in Atlanta, Georgia, and educated at Lincoln University and the University of Pennsylvania. From 1964 to 1966 he was arts editor for The Cricket *&* Journal of Black Poetry. *He taught at the City College of New York, served as writer in residence at Wesleyan University, and was named a Yale University Fellow. With LeRoi Jones, he co-edited* Black Fire: An Anthology of Afro-American Writings *(1968). He also wrote nonfiction texts such as* Hoodoo Hollerin' Bebop Ghosts *(1971) and* Analytical Study of Afro-American Culture *(1972). Neal worked with LeRoi Jones to bring about the black arts movement and was educational director for the New York Black Panther party.*

The Black Arts Movement (1968)

1

The Black Arts Movement is radically opposed to any concept of the artist that alienates him from his community. Black Art is the aesthetic and spiritual sister of the Black Power concept. As such, it envisions an art that speaks directly to the needs and aspirations of Black America. In order to perform this task, the Black Arts Movement proposes a radical reordering of the Western cultural aesthetic. It proposes a separate symbolism, mythology, critique, and iconology. The Black Arts and the Black Power concept both relate broadly to the Afro-American's desire for self-determination and nationhood. Both concepts are nationalistic. One is concerned with the relationship between art and politics; the other with the art of politics.

Recently, these two movements have begun to merge: the political values inherent in the Black Power concept are now finding concrete expression in the aesthetics of Afro-American dramatists, poets, choreographers, musicians, and novelists. A main tenet of Black Power is the necessity for Black people to define the world in their own terms. The Black artist has made the same point in the context of aesthetics. The two movements postulate that there are in fact and in spirit two Americas—one black, one white. The Black artist takes this to mean that his primary duty is to speak to the spiritual and cultural needs of Black people. Therefore, the main thrust of this new breed of contemporary writers is to confront the contradictions arising out of the Black man's experience in the racist West. Currently, these writers are reevaluating Western aesthetics, the traditional role of the writer, and the social function of art. Implicit in this reevaluation is the need to develop a "Black aesthetic." It is the opinion of many Black writers, I among them, that the Western aesthetic has run its course: it is impossible to construct anything meaningful within its decaying structure. We advocate a cultural revolution in art and ideas. The cultural values inherent in Western history must either be radicalized or destroyed, and we will probably find that even radicalization is impossible. In fact, what is needed is a whole new system of ideas. Poet Don L. Lee expresses it:

> . . . We must destroy Faulkner, dick, jane, and other perpetuators of evil. It's time for DuBois, Nat Turner, and Kwame Nkrumah. As Frantz Fanon points out: destroy the culture and you destroy the people. This must not happen. Black artists are culture stabilizers; bringing back old values, and introducing new ones. Black Art will talk to the people and with the will of the people stop impending "protective custody."

The Black Arts Movement eschews "protest" literature. It speaks directly to Black people. Implicit in the concept of "protest" literature, as Brother Knight has made clear, is an appeal to white morality:

> Now any Black man who masters the technique of his particular art form, who adheres to the white aesthetic, and who directs his work toward a white audience is, in one sense, protesting. And implicit in the act of protest is the belief that a change will be forthcoming once the masters are aware of the protestor's "grievance" (the very word connotes begging, supplications to the gods). Only when that belief has faded and protestings end, will Black art begin.

Brother Knight also has some interesting statements about the development of a "Black aesthetic":

> Unless the Black artist establishes a "Black aesthetic" he will have no future at all. To accept the white aesthetic is to accept and validate a society that will not allow him to live. The Black artist must create new forms and new values, sing new songs (or purify old ones); and along with other Black authorities, he must create a new history, new symbols, myths and legends (and purify old ones by fire). And the Black artist, in creating his own aesthetic, must be accountable for it only to the Black people. Further, he must hasten his own dissolution as an individual (in the Western sense)—painful though the process may be, having been breast-fed the poison of "individual experience."

When we speak of a "Black aesthetic" several things are meant. First, we assume that there is already in existence the basis for such an aesthetic. Essentially, it consists of an African-American cultural tradition. But this aesthetic is finally, by implication, broader than that tradition. It encompasses most of the useable elements of Third World culture. The motive behind the Black aesthetic is the destruction of the white thing, the destruction of white ideas, and white ways of looking at the world. The new aesthetic is mostly predicated on an Ethics which asks the question: whose vision of the world is finally more meaningful, ours or the white oppressors'? What is truth? Or more precisely, whose truth shall we express, that of the oppressed or of the oppressors? These are basic questions. Black intellectuals of previous decades failed to ask them. Further, national and international affairs demand that we appraise the world in terms of our own interests. It is clear that the question of human survival is at the core of contemporary experience. The Black artist must address himself to this reality in the strongest terms possible. In a context of world upheaval, ethics and aesthetics must interact positively and be consistent with the demands for a more spiritual world. Consequently, the Black Arts Movement is an ethical movement. Ethical, that is, from the viewpoint of the oppressed. And much of the oppression confronting the Third World and Black America is directly traceable to the Euro-American cultural sensibility. This sensibility, anti-human in nature, has, until recently, dominated the psyches of most Black artists and intellectuals; it must be destroyed before the Black creative artist can have a meaningful role in the transformation of society.

It is this natural reaction to an alien sensibility that informs the cultural attitudes of the Black Arts and the Black Power movement. It is a profound ethical sense that makes a Black artist question a society in which art is one thing and the actions of men another. The Black Arts Movement believes that your ethics and your aesthetics are one. That the contradictions between ethics and aesthetics in Western society is symptomatic of a dying culture.

The term "Black Arts" is of ancient origin, but it was first used in a positive sense by LeRoi Jones:

We are unfair
And unfair
We are black magicians
Black arts we make
in black labs of the heart

The fair are fair
and deathly white

The day will not save them
And we own the night

There is also a section of the poem "Black Dada Nihilismus" that carries the same motif. But a fuller amplification of the nature of the new aesthetics appears in the poem "Black Art":

Poems are bullshit unless they are
teeth or trees or lemons piled
on a step. Or black ladies dying
of men leaving nickel hearts
beating them down. Fuck poems
and they are useful, would they shoot
come at you, love what you are,
breathe like wrestlers, or shudder
strangely after peeing. We want live
words of the hip world, live flesh &
coursing blood. Hearts and Brains
Souls splintering fire. We want poems
like fists beating niggers out of Jocks
or dagger poems in the slimy bellies
of the owner-jews . . .

Poetry is a concrete function, an action. No more abstractions. Poems are physical entities: fists, daggers, airplane poems, and poems that shoot guns. Poems are transformed from physical objects into personal forces:

> . . . Put it on him poem. Strip him naked
> to the world. Another bad poem cracking
> steel knuckles in a jewlady's mouth
> Poem scream poison gas on breasts in green berets . . .

Then the poem affirms the integral relationship between Black Art and Black people:

> . . . Let Black people understand
> that they are the lovers and the sons
> of lovers and warriors and sons
> of warriors Are poems & poets &
> all the loveliness here in the world

It ends with the following lines, a central assertion in both the Black Arts Movement and the philosophy of Black Power:

> We want a black poem. And a
> Black World.
> Let the world be a Black Poem
> And let All Black People Speak This Poem
> Silently
> Or LOUD

The poem comes to stand for the collective conscious and unconscious of Black America—the real impulse in back of the Black Power movement, which is the will toward self-determination and nationhood, a radical reordering of the nature and function of both art and the artist.

2

In the spring of 1964, LeRoi Jones, Charles Patterson, William Patterson, Clarence Reed, Johnny Moore, and a number of other Black artists opened the Black Arts Repertoire Theatre School. They produced a number of plays including Jones' *Experimental Death Unit # One, Black Mass, Jello,* and *Dutchman.* They also initiated a series of poetry readings and concerts. These activities represented the most advanced tendencies in the movement and were of excellent artistic quality. The Black Arts School came under immediate attack by the New York power structure. The Establishment, fearing Black creativity, did exactly what it was expected to do—it attacked the theatre and all of its values. In the meantime, the school was granted funds by OEO[1] through HARYOU-ACT[2].

---

[1]OEO is an acronym for Office of Economic Opportunity.

[2]Congressman Adam Clayton Powell started HARYOU, an anti-poverty campaign directed by Kenneth Clark. In 1960, Dr. John Henrik Clarke, black historian and educator, directed the HARYOU-ACT (anti-poverty act) African Heritage Program of Harlem.

Lacking a cultural program itself, HARYOU turned to the only organization which addressed itself to the needs of the community. In keeping with its "revolutionary" cultural ideas, the Black Arts Theatre took its programs into the streets of Harlem. For three months, the theatre presented plays, concerts, and poetry readings to the people of the community. Plays that shattered the illusions of the American body politic, and awakened Black people to the meaning of their lives.

Then the hawks from the OEO moved in and chopped off the funds. Again, this should have been expected. The Black Acts Theatre stood in radical opposition to the feeble attitudes about culture of the "War On Poverty" bureaucrats. And later, because of internal problems, the theatre was forced to close. But the Black Arts group proved that the community could be served by a valid and dynamic art. It also proved that there was a definite need for a cultural revolution in the Black community.

With the closing of the Black Arts Theatre, the implications of what Brother Jones and his colleagues were trying to do took on even more significance. Black Art groups sprang up on the West Coast and the idea spread to Detroit, Philadelphia, Jersey City, New Orleans, and Washington, D.C. Black Arts movements began on the campuses of San Francisco State College, Fisk University, Lincoln University, Hunter College in the Bronx, Columbia University, and Oberlin College. In Watts, after the rebellion, Maulana Karenga welded the Black Arts Movement into a cohesive cultural ideology which owed much to the work of LeRoi Jones. Karenga sees culture as the most important element in the struggle for self-determination:

> Culture is the basis of all ideas, images and actions. To move is to move culturally, i.e. by a set of values given to you by your culture.
>
> Without a culture Negroes are only a set of reactions to white people.
>
> The seven criteria for culture are:
> 1. Mythology
> 2. History
> 3. Social Organization
> 4. Political Organization
> 5. Economic Organization
> 6. Creative Motif
> 7. Ethos

In drama, LeRoi Jones represents the most advanced aspects of the movement. He is its prime mover and chief designer. In a poetic essay entitled "The Revolutionary Theatre," he outlines the iconology of the movement:

> The Revolutionary Theatre should force change: it should be change. (All their faces turned into the lights and you work on them black nigger magic, and cleanse them at having seen the ugliness. And if the beautiful see themselves, they will love themselves.) We are preaching virtue again, but by that to mean NOW, toward what seems the most constructive use of the word.

The theatre that Jones proposes is inextricably linked to the Afro-American political dynamic. And such a link is perfectly consistent with Black America's contemporary demands. For theatre is potentially the most social of all of the arts. It is an integral part of the socializing process. It exists in direct relationship to the audience it claims to serve. The decadence and inanity of the contemporary American theatre is an accurate reflection of the state of American society. Albee's *Who's Afraid of Virginia Woolf?* is very American: sick white lives in a homosexual hell hole. The theatre of white America is escapist, refusing to confront concrete reality. Into this cultural emptiness come the musicals, an up-tempo version of the same stale lives. And the use of Negroes in such plays as *Hello Dolly* and *Hallelujah Baby* does not alert their nature; it compounds the problem. These plays are simply hipper versions of the minstrel show. They present Negroes acting out the hang-ups of middle-class white America. Consequently, the American theatre is a palliative prescribed to bourgeois patients who refuse to see the world as it is. Or, more crucially, as the world sees them. It is no accident, therefore, that the most "important" plays come from Europe—Brecht, Weiss, and Ghelderode. And even these have begun to run dry.

The Black Arts theatre, the theatre of LeRoi Jones, is a radical alternative to the sterility of the American theatre. It is primarily a theatre of the Spirit, confronting the Black man in his interaction with his brothers and with the white thing.

> Our theatre will show victims so that their brothers in the audience will be better able to understand that they are brothers of victims, and that they themselves are blood brothers. And what we show must cause the blood to rush, so that prerevolutionary temperaments will be bathed in this blood, and it will cause their deepest souls to move, and they will find themselves tensed and clenched, even ready to die, at what the soul has been taught. We will scream and cry, murder, run through the streets in agony, if it means some soul will be moved, moved to actual life understanding of what the world is, and what it ought to be. We are preaching virtue and feeling, and a natural sense of the self in the world. All men live in the world, and the world ought to be a place for them to live.

The victims in the world of Jones' early plays are Clay, murdered by the white bitch-goddess in *Dutchman*, and Walker Vessels, the revolutionary in *The Slave*. Both of these plays present Black men in transition. Clay, the middle-class Negro trying to get himself a little action from Lula, digs himself and his own truth only to get murdered after telling her like it really is:

> Just let me bleed you, you loud whore, and one poem vanished. A whole people neurotics, struggling to keep from being sane. And the only thing that would cure the neurosis would be your murder. Simple as that. I mean if I murdered you, then other white people would understand me. You understand? No, I guess not. If Bessie Smith had killed some white people she wouldn't needed that music. She could have talked very straight and plain about the world. Just straight two and two are four. Money. Power. Luxury. Like that. All of them. Crazy niggers turning their back on sanity. When all it needs is that simple act. Just murder. Would make us all sane.

But Lula understands, and she kills Clay first. In a perverse way it is Clay's nascent knowledge of himself that threatens the existence of Lula's idea of the world. Symbolically, and in fact, the relationship between Clay (Black America) and Lula (white America) is rooted in the historical castration of black manhood. And in the twisted psyche of white America, the Black man is both an object of love and hate. Analogous attitudes exist in most Black Americans, but for decidedly different reasons. Clay is doomed when he allows himself to participate in Lula's "fantasy" in the first place. It is the fantasy to which Frantz Fanon alludes in *The Wretched of the Earth* and *Black Skins, White Mask:* the native's belief that he can acquire the oppressor's power by acquiring his symbols, one of which is the white woman. When Clay finally digs himself it is too late.

Walker Vessels, in *The Slave*, is Clay reincarnated as the revolutionary confronting problems inherited from his contact with white culture. He returns to the home of his ex-wife, a white woman, and her husband, a literary critic. The play is essentially about Walker's attempt to destroy his white past. For it is the past, with all of its painful memories, that is really the enemy of the revolutionary. It is impossible to move until history is either recreated or comprehended. Unlike Todd, in Ralph Ellison's *Invisible Man*, Walker cannot fall outside history. Instead, Walker demands a confrontation with history, a final shattering of bullshit illusions. His only salvation lies in confronting the physical and psychological forces that have made him and his people powerless. Therefore, he comes to understand that the world must be restructured along spiritual imperatives. But in the interim it is basically a question of *who* has power:

> *Easley.* You're so wrong about everything. So terribly, sickeningly wrong. What can you change? What do you hope to change? Do you think Negroes are better people than whites . . . that they can govern a society *better* than whites? That they'll be more judicious or more tolerant? Do you think they'll make fewer mistakes? I mean really, if the Western white man has proved one thing . . . it's the futility of modern society. So the have-not peoples become the haves. Even so, will that change the essential functions of the world? Will there be more love or beauty in the world . . . more knowledge . . . because of it?
>
> *Walker.* Probably. Probably there will be more . . . if more people have a chance to understand what it is. But that's not even the point. It comes down to baser human endeavor than any social-political thinking. What does it matter if there's more love or beauty? Who the fuck cares? Is that what the Western ofay thought while he was ruling . . . that his rule somehow brought more love and beauty into the world? Oh, he might have thought that concomitantly, while sipping a gin rickey and scratching his ass . . . but that was not ever the point. Not even on the Crusades. The point is that you had your chance, darling, now these other folks have theirs. *Quietly.* Now they have theirs.
>
> *Easley:* God, what an ugly idea.

This confrontation between the black radical and the white liberal is symbolic of larger confrontations occurring between the Third World and Western society. It is a confrontation between the colonizer and the colonized, the slavemaster and the slave. Implicit in Easley's remarks is the belief that the white man is culturally and politically superior to the Black Man. Even though Western society has been traditionally violent in its relation with the Third World, it sanctimoniously deplores violence or self-assertion on the part of the enslaved. And the Western mind, with clever rationalizations, equates the violence of the oppressed with the violence of the oppressor. So that when the native preaches self-determination, the Western white man cleverly misconstrues it to mean hate of *all* white men. When the Black political radical warns his people not to trust white politicians of the left and the right, but instead to organize separately on the basis of power, the white man cries: "racism in reverse." Or he will say, as many of them do today: "We deplore both white and black racism." As if the two could be equated.

There is a minor element in *The Slave* which assumes great importance in a later play entitled *Jello*. Here I refer to the emblem of Walker's army: a red-mouthed grinning field slave. The revolutionary army has taken one of the most hated symbols of the Afro-American past and radically altered its meaning. This is the supreme act of freedom, available only to those who have liberated themselves psychically. Jones amplifies this inversion of emblem and symbol in *Jello* by making Rochester (Ratfester) of the old Jack Benny (Penny) program into a revolutionary nationalist. Ratfester, ordinarily the supreme embodiment of the Uncle Tom Clown, surprises Jack Penny by turning on the other side of the nature of the Black man. He skillfully, and with an evasive black humor, robs Penny of all of his money. But Ratfester's actions are "moral." That is to say, Ratfester is getting his back pay; payment of a long overdue debt to the Black man. Ratfester's sensibilities are different from Walker's. He is *blues people* smiling and shuffling while trying to figure out how to destroy the white thing. And like the blues man, he is the master of the understatement. Or in the Afro-American folk tradition, he is the Signifying Monkey, Shine, and Stagolee all rolled into one. There are no stereotypes any more. History has killed Uncle Tom. Because even Uncle Tom has a breaking point beyond which he will not be pushed. Cut deeply enough into the most docile Negro, and you will find a conscious murderer. Behind the lyrics of the blues and the shuffling porter looms visions of white throats being cut and cities burning.

Jones' particular power as a playwright does not rest solely on his revolutionary vision, but is instead derived from his deep lyricism and spiritual outlook. In many ways, he is fundamentally more a poet than a playwright. And it is his lyricism that gives body to his plays. Two important plays in this regard are *Black Mass* and *Slave Ship*. *Black Mass* is based on the Muslim myth of Yacub. According to this myth, Yacub, a Black scientist, developed the means of grafting different colors of the Original Black Nation until a White Devil was created. In *Black Mass*, Yacub's experiments produce a raving White Beast who is condemned to the coldest regions of the North. The other magicians implore Yacub to cease his experiments. But he insists on claiming the primacy of scientific knowledge over spiritual knowledge. The sensibility of the White Devil is alien, informed by lust and sensuality. The Beast is the consummate embodiment of evil, the beginning of the historical subjugation of the spiritual world.

Black Mass takes place in some prehistorical time. In fact, the concept of time, we learn, is the creation of an alien sensibility, that of the Beast. This is a deeply weighted play, a colloquy on the nature of man, and the relationship between legitimate spiritual knowledge and scientific knowledge. It is LeRoi Jones' most important play mainly because it is informed by a mythology that is wholly the creation of the Afro-American sensibility.

Further, Yacub's creation is not merely a scientific exercise. More fundamentally, it is the aesthetic impulse gone astray. The Beast is created merely for the sake of creation. Some artists assert a similar claim about the nature of art. They argue that art need not have a function. It is against this decadent attitude toward art—ramified throughout most of Western society—that the play militates. Yacub's real crime, therefore, is the introduction of a meaningless evil into a harmonious universe. The evil of the Beast is pervasive, corrupting everything and everyone it touches. What was beautiful is twisted into an ugly screaming thing. The play ends with destruction of the holy place of the Black Magicians. Now the Beast and his descendants roam the earth. An offstage voice chants a call for the Jihad to begin. It is then that myth merges into legitimate history, and we, the audience, come to understand that all history is merely someone's version of mythology.

Slave Ship presents a more immediate confrontation with history. In a series of expressionistic tableaux it depicts the horrors and the madness of the Middle Passage. It then moves through the period of slavery, early attempts at revolt, tendencies toward Uncle Tom–like reconciliation and betrayal, and the final act of liberation. There is no definite plot (LeRoi calls it a pageant), just a continuous rush of sound, groans, screams, and souls wailing for freedom and relief from suffering. This work has special affinities with the New Music of Sun Ra, John Coltrane, Albert Ayler, and Ornette Coleman. Events are blurred, rising and falling in a stream of sound. Almost cinematically, the images flicker and fade against a heavy backdrop of rhythm. The language is spare, stripped to the essential. It is a play which almost totally eliminates the need for a text. It functions on the basis of movement and energy—the dramatic equivalent of the New Music.

3

LeRoi Jones is the best known and the most advanced playwright of the movement, but he is not alone. There are other excellent playwrights who express the general mood of the Black Arts ideology. Among them are Ron Milner, Ed Bullins, Ben Caldwell, Jimmy Stewart, Joe White, Charles Patterson, Charles Fuller, Aisha Hughes, Carol Freeman, and Jimmy Garrett.

Ron Milner's *Who's Got His Own* is of particular importance. It strips bare the clashing attitudes of a contemporary Afro-American family. Milner's concern is with legitimate manhood and morality. The family in *Who's Got His Own* is in search of its conscience, or more precisely its own definition of life. On the day of his father's death, Tim and his family are forced to examine the inner fabric of their lives; the lies, self-deceits, and sense of powerlessness in a white world. The basic conflict, however, is internal. It is rooted in the historical search for black manhood. Tim's mother is representative of a generation of Christian Black women who have implicitly understood the brooding violence lurking in their men. And with this understanding, they have interposed themselves between their men and the object of that violence—the white man. Thus unable to direct his violence against the oppressor, the Black man becomes more frustrated and the sense of powerlessness deepens. Lacking the strength to be a man in the white world, he turns against his family So the oppressed, as Fanon explains, constantly dreams violence against his oppressor, while killing his brother on fast weekends.

Tim's sister represents the Negro woman's attempt to acquire what Eldridge Cleaver calls "ultrafemininity." That is, the attributes of her white upper-class counterpart. Involved here is a rejection of the body-oriented life of the working class Black man, symbolized by the mother's traditional religion. The sister has an affair with a white upper-class liberal, ending in abortion. There are hints of lesbianism, i.e. a further rejection of the body. The sister's life is a pivotal factor in the play. Much of the stripping away of falsehood initiated by Tim is directed at her life, which they have carefully kept hidden from the mother.

Tim is the product of the new Afro-American sensibility, informed by the psychological revolution now operative within Black America. He is a combination ghetto soul brother and militant intellectual, very hip and slightly flawed himself. He would change the world, but without comprehending the particular history that produced his "tyrannical" father. And he cannot be the man his father was—not until he truly understands his father. He must understand why his father allowed himself to be insulted daily by the "honky" types on the job; why he took a demeaning job in the "shit-house"; and why he spent on his family the violence that he should have directed against the white man. In short, Tim must confront the history of his family. And that is exactly what happens. Each character tells his story, exposing his falsehood to the other until a balance is reached

Who's Got His Own is not the work of an alienated mind. Milner's main thrust is directed toward unifying the family around basic moral principles, toward bridging the "generation gap." Other Black playwrights, Jimmy Garrett for example, see the gap as unbridgeable.

Garrett's *We Own the Night* takes place during an armed insurrection. As the play opens we see the central characters defending a section of the city against attacks by white police. Johnny, the protagonist, is wounded. Some of his Brothers intermittently fire at attacking forces, while others look for medical help. A doctor arrives, forced at gun point. The wounded boy's mother also comes. She is a female Uncle Tom who berates the Brothers and their cause. She tries to get Johnny to leave. She is hysterical. The whole idea of Black people fighting white people is totally outside of her orientation. Johnny begins a vicious attack on his mother, accusing her of emasculating his father—a recurring theme in the sociology of the Black community. In Afro-American literature of previous decades the strong Black mother was the object of awe and respect. But in the new literature her status is ambivalent and laced with tension. Historically, Afro-American women have had to be the economic mainstays of the family. The oppressor allowed them to have jobs while at the same time limiting the economic mobility of the Black man. Very often, therefore, the woman's aspirations and values are closely tied to those of the white power structure and not to those of her man. Since he cannot provide for his family the way white men do, she despises his weakness, tearing into him at every opportunity until, very often, there is nothing left but a shell.

The only way out of this dilemma is through revolution. It either must be an actual blood revolution, or one that psychically redirects the energy of the oppressed. Milner is fundamentally concerned with the latter and Garrett with the former. Communication between Johnny and his mother breaks down. The revolutionary imperative demands that men step outside the legal framework. It is a question of erecting *another* morality. The old constructs do not hold up, because adhering to them means consigning oneself to the oppressive reality. Johnny's mother is involved in the old constructs. Manliness is equated with white morality. And even though she claims to love her family (her men), the overall design of her ideas are against black manhood. In Garrett's play the mother's morality manifests itself in a deep-seated hatred of Black men; while in Milner's work the mother understands, but holds her men back.

The mothers that Garrett and Milner see represent the Old Spirituality—the Faith of the Fathers of which DuBois spoke. Johnny and Tim represent the New Spirituality. They appear to be a type produced by the upheavals of the colonial world of which Black America is a part. Johnny's assertion that he is a criminal is remarkably similar to the rebel's comments in Aimé Césaire's play, *Les Armes Miraculeuses (The Miraculous Weapons)*. In that play the rebel, speaking to his mother, proclaims: "My name—an offense; my Christian name—humiliation; my status—a rebel; my age—the stone age." To which the mother replies: "My race— the human race. My religion—brotherhood." The Old Spirituality is generalized. It seeks to recognize Universal Humanity. The New Spirituality is specific. It begins by seeing the world from the concise point-of-view of the colonialized. Where the Old Spirituality would live with oppression while ascribing to the oppressors an innate goodness, the New Spirituality demands a radical shift in point-of-view. The colonialized native, the oppressed must, of necessity, subscribe to a *separate* morality. One that will liberate him and his people.

The assault against the Old Spirituality can sometimes be humorous. In Ben Caldwell's play, *The Militant Preacher*, a burglar is seen slipping into the home of a wealthy minister. The preacher comes in and the burglar ducks behind a large chair. The preacher, acting out the role of the supplicant minister begins to moan, praying to De Lawd for understanding.

In the context of today's politics, the minister is an Uncle Tom, mouthing platitudes against self-defense. The preacher drones in a self-pitying monologue about the folly of protecting oneself against brutal policeman. Then the burglar begins to speak. The preacher is startled, taking the burglar's voice for the voice of God. The burglar begins to play on the preacher's old time religion. He *becomes* the voice of God insulting and goading the preacher on until the preacher's attitudes about protective violence change. The next day the preacher emerges militant, gun in hand, sounding like Reverend Cleage in Detroit. He now preaches a new gospel—the gospel of the gun, an eye for an eye. The gospel is preached in the rhythmic cadences of the old Black church. But the content is radical. Just as Jones inverted the symbols in *Jello*, Caldwell twists the rhythms of the Uncle Tom preacher into the language of the new militancy.

These plays are directed at problems within Black America. They begin with the premise that there is a well defined Afro-American audience. An audience that must see itself and the world in terms of its own interests. These plays, along with many others, constitute the basis for a viable movement in the theatre—a movement which takes as its task a profound reevaluation of the Black man's presence in America. The Black Arts Movement represents the flowering of a cultural nationalism that has been suppressed since the 1920s. I mean the "Harlem Renaissance"—which was essentially a failure. It did not address itself to the mythology and the lifestyles of the Black community. It failed to take roots, to link itself concretely to the struggles of that community, to become its voice and spirit. Implicit in the Black Arts Movement is the idea that Black people, however dispersed, constitute a *nation* within the belly of white America. This is not a new idea. Garvey said it and the Honorable Elijah Muhammad says it now. And it is on this idea that the concept of Black Power is predicated.

Afro-American life and history is full of creative possibilities, and the movement is just beginning to perceive them. Just beginning to understand that the most meaningful statements about the nature of Western society must come from the Third World of which Black America is a part. The thematic material is broad, ranging from folk heroes like Shine and Stagolee to historical figures like Marcus Garvey and Malcolm X. And then there is the struggle for Black survival, the coming confrontation between white America and Black America. If art is the harbinger of future possibilities, what does the future of Black America portend?

ALICE WALKER

For a brief biography of Alice Walker, see page 789.

In Search of Our Mothers' Gardens (1972)

> *I described her own nature and temperament. Told how they needed a larger life for their expression. . . . I pointed out that in lieu of proper channels, her emotions had overflowed into paths that dissipated them. I talked, beautifully I thought, about an art that would be born, an art that would open the way for women the likes of her. I asked her to hope, and build up an inner life against the coming of that day. . . . I sang, with a strange quiver in my voice, a promise song.*
>
> —*Jean Toomer, "Avey," Cane*

The poet speaking to a prostitute who falls asleep while he's talking—

When the poet Jean Toomer walked through the South in the early twenties, he discovered a curious thing: black women whose spirituality was so intense, so deep, so *unconscious*, that they were themselves unaware of the richness they held. They stumbled blindly through their lives: creatures so abused and mutilated in body, so dimmed and confused by pain, that they considered themselves unworthy even of hope. In the selfless abstractions their bodies became to the men who used them, they became more than "sexual objects," more even than mere women: they became "Saints." Instead of being perceived as whole persons, their bodies became shrines: what was thought to be their minds became temples suitable for worship. These crazy Saints stared out at the world, wildly, like lunatics—or quietly, like suicides; and the "God" that was in their gaze was as mute as a great stone.

Who were these Saints? These crazy, loony, pitiful women?

Some of them, without a doubt, were our mothers and grandmothers.

In the still heat of the post-Reconstruction South, this is how they seemed to Jean Toomer: exquisite butterflies trapped in an evil honey, toiling away their lives in an era, a century, that did not acknowledge them, except as "the *mule* of the world." They dreamed dreams that no one knew—not even themselves, in any coherent fashion—and saw visions no one could understand. They wandered or sat about the countryside crooning lullabies to ghosts, and drawing the mother of Christ in charcoal on courthouse walls.

They forced their minds to desert their bodies and their striving spirits sought to rise, like frail whirlwinds from the hard red clay. And when those frail whirlwinds fell, in scattered particles, upon the ground, no one mourned. Instead, men lit candles to celebrate the emptiness that remained, as people do who enter a beautiful but vacant space to resurrect a God.

Our mothers and grandmothers, some of them: moving to music not yet written. And they waited.

They waited for a day when the unknown thing that was in them would be made known; but guessed, somehow in their darkness, that on the day of their revelation they would be long dead. Therefore to Toomer they walked, and even ran, in slow motion. For they were going nowhere immediate, and the future was not yet within their grasp. And men took our mothers and grandmothers, "but got no pleasure from it." So complex was their passion and their calm.

To Toomer, they lay vacant and fallow as autumn fields, with harvest time never in sight: and he saw them enter loveless marriages, without joy; and become prostitutes, without resistance; and become mothers of children, without fulfillment.

For these grandmothers and mothers of ours were not Saints, but Artists; driven to a numb and bleeding madness by the springs of creativity in them for which there was no release. They were Creators, who lived lives of spiritual waste, because they were so rich in spirituality—which is the basis of Art—that the strain of enduring their unused and unwanted talent drove them insane. Throwing away this spirituality was their pathetic attempt to lighten the soul to a weight their work-worn, sexually abused bodies could bear.

What did it mean for a black woman to be an artist in our grandmothers' time? In our great-grandmothers' day? It is a question with an answer cruel enough to stop the blood.

Did you have a genius of a great-great-grandmother who died under some ignorant and depraved white overseer's lash? Or was she required to bake biscuits for a lazy backwater tramp, when she cried out in her soul to paint watercolors of sunsets, or the rain falling on the green and peaceful pasturelands? Or was her body broken and forced to bear children (who were more often than not sold away from her)—eight, ten, fifteen, twenty children—when her one joy was the thought of modeling heroic figures of rebellion, in stone or clay?

How was the creativity of the black woman kept alive, year after year and century after century, when for most of the years black people have been in America, it was a punishable crime for a black person to read or write? And the freedom to paint, to sculpt, to expand the mind with action did not exist. Consider, if you can bear to imagine it, what might have been the result if singing, too, had been forbidden by law. Listen to the voices of Bessie Smith, Billie Holiday, Nina Simone, Roberta Flack, and Aretha Franklin, among others, and imagine those voices muzzled for life. Then you may begin to comprehend the lives of our "crazy," "Sainted" mothers and grandmothers. The agony of the lives of women who might have been Poets, Novelists, Essayists, and Short-Story Writers (over a period of centuries), who died with their real gifts stifled within them.

And, if this were the end of the story, we would have cause to cry out in my paraphrase of Okot p'Bitek's great poem:

O, my clanswomen
Let us all cry together!
Come,
Let us mourn the death of our mother,
The death of a Queen
The ash that was produced
By a great fire!
O, this homestead is utterly dead
Close the gates
With *lacari* thorns,
For our mother
The creator of the Stool is lost!
And all the young women
Have perished in the wilderness!

But this is not the end of the story, for all the young women—our mothers and grandmothers, *ourselves*—have not perished in the wilderness. And if we ask ourselves why, and search for and find the answer, we will know beyond all efforts to erase it from our minds, just exactly who, and of what, we black American women are.

One example, perhaps the most pathetic, most misunderstood one, can provide a backdrop for our mothers' work: Phillis Wheatley, a slave in the 1700s.

Virginia Woolf, in her book *A Room of One's Own*, wrote that in order for a woman to write fiction she must have two things, certainly: a room of her own (with key and lock) and enough money to support herself.

What then are we to make of Phillis Wheatley, a slave, who owned not even herself? This sickly, frail black girl who required a servant of her own at times—her health was so precarious—and who, had she been white, would have been easily considered the intellectual superior of all the women and most of the men in the society of her day.

Virginia Woolf wrote further, speaking of course not of our Phillis, that "any woman born with a great gift in the sixteenth century [insert "eighteenth century," insert "black woman," insert "born or made a slave"] would certainly have gone crazed, shot herself, or ended her days in some lonely cottage outside the village, half witch, half wizard [insert "Saint"], feared and mocked at. For it needs little skill and psychology to be sure that a highly gifted girl who had tried to use her gift for poetry would have been so thwarted and hindered by contrary instincts [add "chains, guns, the lash, the ownership of one's body by someone else, submission to an alien religion"), that she must have lost her health and sanity to a certainty."

The key words, as they relate to Phillis, are "contrary instincts." For when we read the poetry of Phillis Wheatley—as when we read the novels of Nella Larsen or the oddly false-sounding autobiography of that freest of all black women writers, Zora Hurston—evidence of "contrary instincts" is everywhere. Her loyalties were completely divided, as was, without question, her mind.

But how could this be otherwise? Captured at seven, a slave of wealthy, doting whites who instilled in her the "savagery" of the Africa they "rescued" her from, one wonders if she was even able to remember her homeland as she had known it, or as it really was.

Yet, because she did try to use her gift for poetry in a world that made her a slave, she was "so thwarted and hindered by . . . contrary instincts, that she . . . lost her health. . . ." In the last years of her brief life, burdened not only with the need to express her gift but also with a penniless, friendless "freedom" and several small children for whom she was forced to do strenuous work to feed, she lost her health, certainly. Suffering from malnutrition and neglect and who knows what mental agonies, Phillis Wheatley died.

So torn by "contrary instincts" was black, kidnapped, enslaved Phillis that her description of "the Goddess"—as she poetically called the Liberty she did not have—is ironically, cruelly humorous. And, in fact, has held Phillis up to ridicule for more than a century. It is usually read prior to hanging Phillis's memory as that of a fool. She wrote:

> The Goddess comes, she moves divinely fair,
> Olive and laurel binds her *golden* hair.
> Wherever shines this native of the skies,
> Unnumber'd charms and recent graces rise. [My italics]

It is obvious that Phillis, the slave, combed the "Goddess's" hair every morning; prior, perhaps, to bringing in the milk, or fixing her mistress's lunch. She took her imagery from the one thing she saw elevated above all others.

With the benefit of hindsight we ask, "How could she?"

But at last, Phillis, we understand. No more snickering when your stiff, struggling, ambivalent lines are forced on us. We know now that you were not an idiot or a traitor; only a sickly little black girl, snatched from your home and country and made a slave; a woman who still struggled to sing the song that was your gift, although in a land of barbarians who praised you for your bewildered tongue. It is not so much what you sang, as that you kept alive, in so many of our ancestors, *the notion of song.*

Black women are called, in the folklore that so aptly identifies one's status in society, "the *mule* of the world," because we have been handed the burdens that everyone else—*everyone* else—refused to carry. We have also been called "Matriarchs," "Superwomen," and "Mean and Evil Bitches." Not to mention "Castraters" and "Sapphire's Mama." When we have pleaded for understanding, our character has been distorted; when we have asked for simple caring, we have been handed empty inspirational appellations, then stuck in the farthest corner. When we have asked for love, we have been given children. In short, even our plainer gifts, our labors of fidelity and love, have been knocked down our throats. To be an artist and a black woman, even today, lowers our status in many respects, rather than raises it: and yet, artists we will be.

Therefore we must fearlessly pull out of ourselves and look at and identify with our lives the living creativity some of our great-grandmothers were not allowed to know. I stress *some* of them because it is well known that the majority of our great-grandmothers knew, even without "knowing" it, the reality of their spirituality, even if they didn't recognize it beyond what happened in the singing at church—and they never had any intention of giving it up.

How they did it—those millions of black women who were not Phillis Wheatley, or Lucy Terry or Frances Harper or Zora Hurston or Nella Larsen or Bessie Smith; or Elizabeth Catlett, or Katherine Dunham, either—brings me to the title of this essay, "In Search of Our Mothers' Gardens," which is a personal account that is yet shared, in its theme and its meaning, by all of us. I found, while thinking about the far-reaching world of the creative black woman, that often the truest answer to a question that really matters can be found very close.

In the late 1920s my mother ran away from home to marry my father. Marriage, if not running away, was expected of seventeen-year-old girls. By the time she was twenty, she had two children and was pregnant with a third. Five children later, I was born. And this is how I came to know my mother: she seemed a large, soft, loving-eyed woman who was rarely impatient in our home. Her quick, violent temper was on view only a few times a year, when she battled with the white landlord who had the misfortune to suggest to her that her children did not need to go to school.

She made all the clothes we wore, even my brothers' overalls. She made all the towels and sheets we used. She spent the summers canning vegetables and fruits. She spent the winter evenings making quilts enough to cover all our beds.

During the "working" day, she labored beside—not behind—my father in the fields. Her day began before sunup, and did not end until late at night. There was never a moment for her to sit down, undisturbed, to unravel her own private thoughts; never a time free from interruption—by work or the noisy inquiries of her many children. And yet, it is to my mother—and all our mothers who were not famous—that I went in search of the secret of what has fed that muzzled and often mutilated, but vibrant, creative spirit that the black woman has inherited, and that pops out in wild and unlikely places to this day.

But when, you will ask, did my overworked mother have time to know or care about feeding the creative spirit?

The answer is so simple that many of us have spent years discovering it. We have constantly looked high, when we should have looked high—and low.

For example: in the Smithsonian Institution in Washington, D.C., there hangs a quilt unlike any other in the world. In fanciful, inspired, and yet simple and identifiable figures, it portrays the story of the Crucifixion. It is considered rare, beyond price. Though it follows no known pattern of quiltmaking, and though it is made of bits and pieces of worthless rags, it is obviously the work of a person of powerful imagination and deep spiritual feeling. Below this quilt I saw a note that says it was made by "an anonymous Black woman in Alabama, a hundred years ago."

If we could locate this "anonymous" black woman from Alabama, she would turn out to be one of our grandmothers—an artist who left her mark in the only materials she could afford, and in the only medium her position in society allowed her to use.

As Virginia Woolf wrote further, in *A Room of One's Own*:

> Yet genius of a sort must have existed among women as it must have existed among the working class. [Change this to "slaves" and "the wives and daughters of sharecroppers."] Now and again an Emily Brontë or a Robert Burns [change this to "a Zora Hurston or a Richard Wright"] blazes out and proves its presence. But certainly it never got itself on to paper. When, however, one reads of a witch being ducked, of a woman possessed by devils [or "Sainthood"], of a wise woman selling herbs [our root workers], or even a very remarkable man who had a mother, then I think we are on the track of a lost novelist, a suppressed poet, of some mute and inglorious Jane Austen. . . . Indeed, I would venture to guess that Anon, who wrote so many poems without signing them, was often a woman. . . .

And so our mothers and grandmothers have, more often than not anonymously, handed on the creative spark, the seed of the flower they themselves never hoped to see: or like a sealed letter they could not plainly read.

And so it is, certainly, with my own mother. Unlike "Ma" Rainey's songs, which retained their creator's name even while blasting forth from Bessie Smith's mouth, no song or poem will bear my mother's name. Yet so many of the stories that I write, that we all write, are my mother's stories. Only recently did I fully realize this: that through years of listening to my mother's stories of her life, I have absorbed not only the stories themselves, but something of the manner in which she spoke, something of the urgency that involves the knowledge that her stories—like her life—must be recorded. It is probably for this reason that so much of what I have written is about characters whose counterparts in real life are so much older than I am.

But the telling of these stories, which came from my mother's lips as naturally as breathing, was not the only way my mother showed herself as an artist. For stories, too, were subject to being distracted, to dying without conclusion. Dinners must be started, and cotton must be gathered before the big rains. The artist that was and is my mother showed itself to me only after many years. This is what I finally noticed:

Like Mem, a character in *The Third Life of Grange Copeland,* my mother adorned with flowers whatever shabby house we were forced to live in. And not just your typical straggly country stand of zinnias, either. She planted ambitious gardens—and still does—with over fifty different varieties of plants that bloom profusely from early March until late November. Before she left home for the fields, she watered her flowers, chopped up the grass, and laid out new beds. When she returned from the fields she might divide clumps of bulbs, dig a cold pit, uproot and replant roses, or prune branches from her taller bushes or trees— until night came and it was too dark to see.

Whatever she planted grew as if by magic, and her fame as a grower of flowers spread over three counties. Because of her creativity with her flowers, even my memories of poverty are seen through a screen of blooms—sunflowers, petunias, roses, dahlias, forsythia, spirea, delphiniums, verbena . . . and on and on.

And I remember people coming to my mother's yard to be given cuttings from her flowers; I hear again the praise showered on her because whatever rocky soil she landed on, she turned into a garden. A garden so brilliant with colors, so original in its design, so magnificent with life and creativity, that to this day people drive by our house in Georgia—perfect strangers and imperfect strangers—and ask to stand or walk among my mother's art.

I notice that it is only when my mother is working in her flowers that she is radiant, almost to the point of being invisible—except as Creator: hand and eye. She is involved in work her soul must have. Ordering the universe in the image of her personal conception of Beauty.

Her face, as she prepares the Art that is her gift, is a legacy of respect she leaves to me, for all that illuminates and cherishes life. She has handed down respect for the possibilities—and the will to grasp them.

For her, so hindered and intruded upon in so many ways, being an artist has still been a daily part of her life. This ability to hold on, even in very simple ways, is work black women have done for a very long time.

This poem is not enough, but it is something, for the woman who literally covered the holes in our walls with sunflowers:

They were women then
My mama's generation
Husky of voice—Stout of
Step
With fists as well as
Hands
How they battered down
Doors
And ironed
Starched white
Shirts
How they led
Armies
Headragged Generals

Across mined
Fields
Booby-trapped
Kitchens
To discover books
Desks
A place for us
How they knew what we
Must know
Without knowing a page
Of it
Themselves.

Guided by my heritage of a love of beauty and a respect for strength—in search of my mother's garden, I found my own.

And perhaps in Africa over two hundred years ago, there was just such a mother; perhaps she painted vivid and daring decorations in oranges and yellows and greens on the walls of her hut; perhaps she sang—in a voice like Roberta Flack's—*sweetly* over the compounds of her village; perhaps she wove the most stunning mats or told the most ingenious stories of all the village storytellers. Perhaps she was herself a poet—though only her daughter's name is signed to the poems that we know.

Perhaps Phillis Wheatley's mother was also an artist.

Perhaps in more than Phillis Wheatley's biological life is her mother's signature made clear.

BARBARA SMITH (b. 1946)

Barbara Smith has made a name for herself as a black feminist critic. Her focus on African American women's issues is reflected in an anthology she edited with Patricia Bell Scott and Gloria T. Hull: All the Women Are White, All the Blacks Are Men, But Some of Us Are Brave *(1982). "Toward a Black Feminist Criticism" is one of Smith's most important essays, in which she deals with black feminism and black female sexuality as they relate to the study of literature. Her work has helped to give black lesbian feminists a voice.* Home Girls: A Black Feminist Anthology *(1983) and* Conditions: Five, The Black Women's Issue *(1979) are two of her most important texts.*

Toward a Black Feminist Criticism (1977)

For all my sisters, especially Beverly and Demita

I do not know where to begin. Long before I tried to write this I realized that I was attempting something unprecedented, something dangerous merely by writing about black women writers from a feminist perspective and about black lesbian writers from any perspective at all. These things have not been done. Not by white male critics, expectedly. Not by black male critics. Not by white women critics who think of themselves as feminists. And most crucially not by black women critics who, although they pay the most attention to black women writers as a group, seldom use a consistent feminist analysis or write about black lesbian literature. All segments of the literary world—whether establishment, progressive, black, female, or lesbian—do not know, or at least act as if they do not know, that black women writers and black lesbian writers exist.

For whites, this specialized lack of knowledge is inextricably connected to their not knowing in any concrete or politically transforming way that black women of any description dwell in this place. Black women's existence, experience and culture, and the brutally complex systems of oppression which shape these, are in the "real world" of white and/or male consciousness beneath consideration, invisible, unknown.

This invisibility, which goes beyond anything that either black men or white women experience and tell about in their writing, is one reason it is so difficult for me to know where to start. It seems overwhelming to break such a massive silence. Even more numbing, however, is the realization that so many of the women who will read this have not yet noticed us missing either from their reading matter, their politics or their lives. It is galling that ostensible feminists and acknowledged lesbians have been so blinded to the implications of any womanhood that is not white womanhood and that they have yet to struggle with the deep racism in themselves that is at the source of this blindness.

I think of the thousands and thousands of books, magazines and articles which have been devoted, by this time, to the subject of women's writing and I am filled with rage at the fraction of those pages that mention black and other Third World women. I finally do not know how to begin because in 1977 I want to be writing this for a black feminist publication, for black women who know and love these writers as I do and who, if they do not yet know their names, have at least profoundly felt the pain of their absence.

The conditions that coalesce into the impossibilities of this essay have as much to do with politics as with the practice of literature. Any discussion of Afro-American writers can rightfully begin with the fact that for most of the time we have been in this country we have been categorically denied not only literacy, but the most minimal possibility of a decent human life. In her landmark essay "In Search of Our Mothers' Gardens," Alice Walker discloses how the political, economic and social restrictions of slavery and racism have historically stunted the creative lives of black women.

At the present time I feel that the politics of feminism have a direct relationship to the state of black women's literature. A viable, autonomous black feminist movement in this country would open up the space needed for the exploration of black women's lives and the creation of consciously black woman-identified art. At the same time a redefinition of the goals and strategies of the white feminist movement would lead to much needed change in the focus and content of what is now generally accepted as women's culture.

I want to make in this essay some connections between the politics of black women's lives, what we write about and our situation as artists. In order to do this I will look at how black women have been viewed critically by outsiders, demonstrate the necessity for black feminist criticism, and try to understand what the existence or nonexistence of black lesbian writing reveals about the state of black women's culture and the intensity of *all* black women's oppression.

The role that criticism plays in making a body of literature recognizable and real hardly needs to be explained here. The necessity for nonhostile and perceptive analysis of works written by persons outside the mainstream of white/male cultural rule has been proven by the black cultural resurgence of the 1960s and 1970s and by the even more recent growth of feminist literary scholarship. For books to be real and remembered they have to be talked about. For books to be understood they must be examined in such a way that the basic intentions of the writers are at least considered. Because of racism, black literature has usually been viewed as a discrete subcategory of American literature and there have been black critics of black literature who did much to keep it alive long before it caught the attention of whites. Before the advent of specifically feminist criticism in this decade, books by white women, on the other hand, were not clearly perceived as the cultural manifestation of an oppressed people. It took the surfacing of the second wave of the North American feminist movement to expose the fact that these works contain a stunningly accurate record of the impact of patriarchal values and practice upon the lives of women and more significantly that literature by women provides essential insights into female experience.

In speaking about the current situation of black women writers, it is important to remember that the existence of a feminist movement was an essential precondition to the growth of feminist literature, criticism and women's studies, which focused at the beginning almost entirely upon investigations of literature. The fact that a parallel black feminist movement has been much slower in evolving cannot help but have impact upon the situation of black women writers and artists and explains in part why during this very same period we have been so ignored.

There is no political movement to give power or support to those who want to examine black women's experience through studying our history, literature and culture. There is no political presence that demands a minimal level of consciousness and respect from those who write or talk about our lives. Finally, there is not a developed body of black feminist political theory whose assumptions could be used in the study of black women's art. When black women's books are dealt with at all, it is usually in the context of black literature which largely ignores the implications of sexual politics. When white women look at black women's works they are of course ill-equipped to deal with the subtleties of racial politics. A black feminist approach to literature that embodies the realization that the politics of sex as well as the politics of race and class are crucially interlocking factors in the works of black women writers is an absolute necessity. Until a black feminist criticism exists we will not even know what these writers mean. The citations from a variety of critics which follow prove that without a black feminist critical perspective not only are books by black women misunderstood, they are destroyed in the process.

Jerry H. Bryant, the *Nation*'s white male reviewer of Alice Walker's *In Love and Trouble: Stories of Black Women*, wrote in 1973: "The subtitle of the collection, 'Stories of Black Women,' is probably an attempt by the publisher to exploit not only black subjects but feminine ones. There is nothing feminist about these stories, however." Blackness and feminism are to his mind mutually exclusive and peripheral to the act of writing fiction. Bryant of course does not consider that Walker might have titled the work herself, nor did he apparently read the book which unequivocally reveals the author's feminist consciousness.

In *The Negro Novel in America*, a book that black critics recognize as one of the worst examples of white racist pseudoscholarship, Robert Bone cavalierly dismisses Ann Petry's classic, *The Street*. He perceives it to be "a superficial social analysis" of how slums victimize their black inhabitants. He further objects that:

> It is an attempt to interpret slum life in terms of *Negro* experience, when a larger frame of reference is required. As Alain Locke has observed, *"Knock on Any Door* is superior to *The Street* because it designates class and environment, rather than mere race and environment, as its antagonist."

Neither Robert Bone nor Alain Locke, the black male critic he cites, can recognize that *The Street* is one of the best delineations in literature of how sex, race *and* class interact to oppress black women.

In her review of Toni Morrison's *Sula* for *The New York Times Book Review* in 1973, putative feminist Sara Blackburn makes similarly racist comments. She writes:

> Toni Morrison is far too talented to remain only a marvelous recorder of the black side of provincial American life. If she is to maintain the large and serious audience she deserves, she is going to have to address a riskier contemporary reality than this beautiful but nevertheless distanced novel. *And if she does this, it seems to me that she might easily transcend that early and unintentionally limiting classification "black woman writer" and take her place among the most serious, important and talented American novelists now working.* [Italics mine]

Recognizing Morrison's exquisite gift, Blackburn unashamedly asserts that Morrison is "too talented" to deal with mere black folk, particularly those double nonentities, black women. In order to be accepted as "serious," "important," "talented" and "American," she must obviously focus her efforts upon chronicling the doings of white men.

The mishandling of black women writers by whites is paralleled more often by their not being handled at all, particularly in feminist criticism. Although Elaine Showalter in her review essay on literary criticism for *Signs* states that: "The best work being produced today [in feminist criticism] is exacting and cosmopolitan," her essay is neither. If it were, she would not have failed to mention a single black or Third World woman writer, whether "major" or "minor," to cite her questionable categories. That she also does not even hint that lesbian writers of any color exist renders her purported overview virtually meaningless. Showalter obviously thinks that the identities of being black and female are mutually exclusive, as this statement illustrates: "Furthermore, there are other literary subcultures (black American novelists, for example) whose history offers a precedent for feminist scholarship to use." The idea of critics like Showalter *using* black literature is chilling, a case of barely disguised cultural imperialism. The final insult is that she footnotes the preceding remark by pointing readers to works on black literature by white males Robert Bone and Roger Rosenblatt.

Two recent works by white women, Ellen Moers's *Literary Women: The Great Writers* and Patricia Meyer Spacks's *The Female Imagination*, evidence the same racist flaw. Moers includes the names of four black and one Puertorriqueña writer in her seventy pages of bibliographical notes and does not deal at all with Third World women in the body of her book. Spacks refers to a comparison between Negroes (sic) and women in Mary Ellmann's *Thinking About Women* under the index entry, "blacks, women and." "Black Boy (Wright)" is the preceding entry. Nothing follows. Again there is absolutely no recognition that black and female identity ever coexist, specifically in a group of black women writers. Perhaps one can assume that these women do not know who black women writers are, that they have little opportunity like most Americans to learn about them. Perhaps. Their ignorance seems suspiciously selective, however, particularly in the light of the dozens of truly obscure white women writers they are able to unearth. Spacks was herself employed at Wellesley College at the same time that Alice Walker was there teaching one of the first courses on black women writers in the country.

I am not trying to encourage racist criticism of black women writers like that of Sara Blackburn, to cite only one example. As a beginning I would at least like to see in print white women's acknowledgment of the contradictions of who and what are being left out of their research and writing.

Black male critics can also act as if they do not know that black women writers exist and are, of course, hampered by an inability to comprehend black women's experience in sexual as well as racial terms. Unfortunately there are also those who are as virulently sexist in their treatment of black women writers as their white male counterparts. Darwin Turner's discussion of Zora Neale Hurston in his *In a Minor Chord: Three Afro-American Writers and Their Search for Identity* is a frightening example of the near assassination of a great black woman writer. His descriptions of her and her work as "artful," "coy," "irrational," "superficial" and "shallow" bear no relationship to the actual quality of her achievements. Turner is completely insensitive to the sexual political dynamics of Hurston's life and writing.

In a recent interview, the notoriously misogynist writer, Ishmael Reed, comments in this way upon the low sales of his newest novel:

> but the book only sold 8000 copies. I don't mind giving out the figure: 8000. Maybe if I was one of those young *female* Afro-American writers that are so hot now, I'd sell more. You know, fill my books with ghetto women who can *do no wrong*. . . . But come on, I think I could have sold 8000 copies by myself.

The politics of the situation of black women are glaringly illuminated by this statement. Neither Reed nor his white male interviewer has the slightest compunction about attacking black women in print. They need not fear widespread public denunciation since Reed's statement is in perfect agreement with the values of a society that hates black people, women and black women. Finally the two of them feel free to base their actions on the premise that black women are powerless to alter either their political or their cultural oppression.

In her introduction to "A Bibliography of Works Written by American Black Women" Ora Williams quotes some of the reactions of her colleagues toward her efforts to do research on black women. She writes:

> Others have reacted negatively with such statements as, "I really don't think you are going to find very much written." "Have 'they' written anything that is any good?" and "I wouldn't go overboard with this woman's lib thing." When discussions touched on the possibility of teaching a course in which emphasis would be on the literature by black women, one response was. "Ha, ha. That will certainly be the most nothing course ever offered!"

A remark by Alice Walker capsulizes what all the preceding examples indicate about the position of black women writers and the reasons for the damaging criticism about them. In response to her interviewer's question "Why do you think that the black woman writer has been so ignored in America? Does she have even more difficulty than the black male writer, who perhaps has just begun to gain recognition?" Walker replies:

> There are two reasons why the black woman writer is not taken as seriously as the black male writer. One is that she's a woman. Critics seem unusually ill-equipped to intelligently discuss and analyze the works of black women. Generally, they do not even make the attempt; they prefer, rather, to talk about the lives of black women writers, not about what they write. And, since black women writers are not—it would seem—very likable—until recently they were the least willing worshippers of male supremacy—comments about them tend to be cruel.

A convincing case for black feminist criticism can obviously be built solely upon the basis of the negativity of what already exists. It is far more gratifying, however, to demonstrate its necessity by showing how it can serve to reveal for the first time the profound subtleties of this particular body of literature.

Before suggesting how a black feminist approach might be used to examine a specific work I will outline some of the principles that I think a black feminist critic could use. Beginning with a primary commitment to exploring how both sexual and racial politics and black and female identity are inextricable elements in black women's writings, she would also work from the assumption that black women writers constitute an identifiable literary tradition. The breadth of her familiarity with these writers would have shown her that not only is theirs a verifiable historical tradition that parallels in time the tradition of black men and white women writing in this country, but that thematically, stylistically, aesthetically and conceptually black women writers manifest common approaches to the act of creating literature as a direct result of the specific political, social and economic experience they have been obliged to share. The way, for example, that Zora Neale Hurston, Margaret Walker, Toni Morrison and Alice Walker incorporate the traditional black female activities of rootworking, herbal medicine, conjure and midwifery into the fabric of their stories is not mere coincidence, nor is their use of specifically black female language to express their own and their characters' thoughts accidental. The use of black women's language and cultural experience in books *by* black women *about* black women results in a miraculously rich coalescing of form and content and also takes their writing far beyond the confines of white/male literary structures. The black feminist critic would find innumerable commonalities in works by black women.

Another principle which grows out of the concept of a tradition and which would also help to strengthen this tradition would be for the critic to look first for precedents and insights in interpretation within the works of other black women. In other words she would think and write out of her own identity and not try to graft the ideas or methodology of white/male literary thought upon the precious materials of black women's art. Black feminist criticism would by definition be highly innovative, embodying the daring spirit of the works themselves. The black feminist critic would be constantly aware of the political implications of her work and would assert the connections between it and the political situation of all black women. Logically developed, black feminist criticism would owe its existence to a black feminist movement while at the same time contributing ideas that women in the movement could use.

Black feminist criticism applied to a particular work can overturn previous assumptions about it and expose for the first time its actual dimensions. At the "Lesbians and Literature" discussion at the 1976 Modern Language Association convention Bertha Harris suggested that if in a woman writer's work a sentence refuses to do what it is supposed to do, if there are strong images of women and if there is a refusal to be linear, the result is innately lesbian literature. As usual, I wanted to see if these ideas might be applied to the black women writers that I know and quickly realized that many of their works were, in Harris's sense, lesbian. Not because women are lovers, but because they are the central figures, are positively portrayed and have pivotal relationships with one another. The form and language of these works are also nothing like what white patriarchal culture requires or expects.

I was particularly struck by the way in which Toni Morrison's novels *The Bluest Eye* and *Sula* could be explored from this new perspective. In both works the relationships between girls and women are essential, yet at the same time physical sexuality is overtly expressed only between men and women. Despite the apparent heterosexuality of the female characters, I discovered in re-reading *Sula* that it works as a lesbian novel not only because of the passionate friendship between Sula and Nel, but because of Morrison's consistently critical stance toward the heterosexual institutions of male/female relationships, marriage and the family. Consciously or not, Morrison's work poses both lesbian and feminist questions about black women's autonomy and their impact upon each other's lives.

Sula and Nel find each other in 1922 when each of them is 12, on the brink of puberty and the discovery of boys. Even as awakening sexuality "clotted their dreams," each girl desires "a someone" obviously female with whom to share her feelings. Morrison writes:

> for it was in dreams that the two girls had met. Long before Edna Finch's Mellow House opened, even before they marched through the chocolate halls of Garfield

Primary School . . . they had already made each other's acquaintance in the delirium of their noon dreams. They were solitary little girls whose loneliness was so profound it intoxicated them and sent them stumbling into Technicolored visions that always included a presence, a someone who, quite like the dreamer, shared the delight of the dream. When Nel, an only child, sat on the steps of her back porch surrounded by the high silence of her mother's incredibly orderly house, feeling the neatness pointing at her back, she studied the poplars and fell easily into a picture of herself lying on a flower bed, tangled in her own hair, waiting for some fiery prince. He approached but never quite arrived. But always, watching the dream along with her, were some smiling sympathetic eyes. Someone as interested as she herself in the flow of her imagined hair, the thickness of the mattress of flowers, the voile sleeves that closed below her elbows in gold-threaded cuffs.

Similarly, Sula, also an only child, but wedged into a household of throbbing disorder constantly awry with things, people, voices and the slamming of doors, spent hours in the attic behind a roll of linoleum galloping through her own mind on a gray-and-white horse tasting sugar and smelling roses in full view of someone who shared both the taste and the speed.

So when they met, first in those chocolate halls and next through the ropes of the swing, they felt the ease and comfort of old friends. Because each had discovered years before that they were neither white nor male, and that all freedom and triumph was forbidden to them, they had set about creating something else to be. Their meeting was fortunate, for it let them use each other to grow on. Daughters of distant mothers and incomprehensible fathers (Sula's because he was dead; Nel's because he wasn't), they found in each other's eyes the intimacy they were looking for.

As this beautiful passage shows, their relationship, from the very beginning, is suffused with an erotic romanticism. The dreams in which they are initially drawn to each other are actually complementary aspects of the same sensuous fairytale. Nel imagines a "fiery prince" who never quite arrives while Sula gallops like a prince "on a gray-and-white horse." The "real world" of patriarchy requires, however, that they channel this energy away from each other to the opposite sex. Lorraine Bethel explains this dynamic in her essay "Conversations with Ourselves: Black Female Relationships in Toni Cade Bambara's *Gorilla, My Love* and Toni Morrison's *Sula*." She writes:

I am not suggesting that Sula and Nel are being consciously sexual, or that their relationship has an overt lesbian nature. I am suggesting, however, that there is a certain sensuality in their interactions that is reinforced by the mirror-like nature of their relationship. Sexual exploration and coming of age is a natural part of adolescence. Sula and Nel discover men together, and though their flirtations with males are an important part of their sexual exploration, the sensuality that they experience in each other's company is equally important.

Sula and Nel must also struggle with the constrictions of racism upon their lives. The knowledge that "they were neither white nor male" is the inherent explanation of their need for each other. Morrison depicts in literature the necessary bonding that has always taken place between black women for the sake of barest survival. Together the two girls can find the courage to create themselves.

Their relationship is severed only when Nel marries Jude, an unexceptional young man who thinks of her as "the hem—the tuck and fold that hid his raveling edges." Sula's inventive wildness cannot overcome social pressure or the influence of Nel's parents who "had succeeded in rubbing down to a dull glow any sparkle or splutter she had." Nel falls prey to convention while Sula escapes it. Yet at the wedding which ends the first phase of their relationship, Nel's final action is to look past her husband toward Sula:

> a slim figure in blue, gliding, with just a hint of a strut, down the path towards the road. . . . Even from the rear Nel could tell that it was Sula and that she was smiling; that something deep down in that litheness was amused.

When Sula returns ten years later, her rebelliousness full-blown, a major source of the town's suspicion stems from the fact that although she is almost thirty, she is still unmarried. Sula's grandmother, Eva, does not hesitate to bring up the matter as soon as she arrives. She asks "When you gone to get married? You need to have some babies. It'll settle you. . . . Ain't no woman got no business floatin' around without no man." Sula replies: "I don't want to make somebody else. I want to make myself." Self-definition is a dangerous activity for any women to engage in, especially a black one, and it expectedly earns Sula pariah status in Medallion.

Morrison clearly points out that it is the fact that Sula has not been tamed or broken by the exigencies of heterosexual family life which most galls the others. She writes:

> Among the weighty evidence piling up was the fact that Sula did not look her age. She was near thirty and, unlike them, had lost no teeth, suffered no bruises, developed no ring of fat at the waist or pocket at the back of her neck.

In other words she is not a domestic serf, a woman run down by obligatory child-bearing or a victim of battering. Sula also sleeps with the husbands of the town once and then discards them, needing them even less than her own mother did, for sexual gratification and affection. The town reacts to her disavowal of patriarchal values by becoming fanatically serious about their own family obligations, as if in this way they might counteract Sula's radical criticism of their lives.

Sula's presence in her community functions much like the presence of lesbians everywhere to expose the contradictions of supposedly normal life. The opening paragraph of the essay "Woman Identified Woman" has amazing relevance as an explanation of Sula's position and character in the novel. It asks:

> What is a lesbian? A lesbian is the rage of all women condensed to the point of explosion. She is the woman who, often beginning at an extremely early age, acts in accordance with her inner compulsion to be a more complete and freer human being than her society—perhaps then, but certainly later—cares to allow her. These needs and actions, over a period of years, bring her into painful conflict with people, situations, the accepted ways of thinking, feeling and behaving, until

she is in a state of continual war with everything around her, and usually with herself. She may not be fully conscious of the political implications of what for her began as personal necessity, but on some level she has not been able to accept the limitations and oppression laid on her by the most basic role of her society—the female role.

The limitations of the *black* female role are even greater in a racist and sexist society as is the amount of courage it takes to challenge them. It is no wonder that the townspeople see Sula's independence as imminently dangerous.

Morrison is also careful to show the reader that despite their years of separation and their opposing paths, Nel and Sula's relationship retains its primacy for each of them. Nel feels transformed when Sula returns and thinks:

> It was like getting the use of an eye back, having a cataract removed. Her old friend had come home. Sula. Who made her laugh, who made her see old things with new eyes, in whose presence she felt clever, gentle and a littly raunchy.

Laughing together in the familiar "rib-scraping" way. Nel feels "new, soft and new." Morrison uses here the visual imagery which symbolizes the women's closeness throughout the novel.

Sula fractures this closeness, however, by sleeping with Nel's husband, an act of little import according to her system of values. Nel, of course, cannot understand. Sula thinks ruefully:

> Nel was the one person who had wanted nothing from her, who had accepted all aspects of her. Now she wanted everything, and all because of *that*. Nel was the first person who had been real to her, whose name she knew, who had seen as she had the slant of life that made it possible to stretch it to its limits. Now Nel was one of *them*.

Sula also thinks at the realization of losing Nel about how unsatisfactory her relationships with men have been and admits: "She had been looking all along for a friend, and it took her a while to discover that a lover was not a comrade and could never be—for a woman." The nearest that Sula comes to actually loving a man is in a brief affair with Ajax and what she values most about him is the intellectual companionship he provides, the brilliance he "allows" her to show.

Sula's feelings about sex with men are also consistent with a lesbian interpretation of the novel. Morrison writes:

> She went to bed with men as frequently as she could. It was the only place where she could find what she was looking for: *misery and the ability to feel deep sorrow*. . . . During the lovemaking she found and needed to find the cutting edge. When she left off cooperating with her body and began to assert herself in the act, particles of strength gathered in her like steel shavings drawn to a spacious magnetic center, forming a tight cluster that nothing, it seemed, could break. *And there was utmost irony and outrage in lying under someone, in a position of surrender, feeling her own abiding strength and limitless power*. . . . When her partner disengaged himself, she looked up at him in wonder trying to recall his

name . . . waiting impatiently for him to turn away . . . *leaving her to the postcoital privateness in which she met herself, welcomed herself and joined herself in matchless harmony.* [Italics mine]

Sula uses men for sex which results not in communion with them, but in her further delving into self.

Ultimately the deepest communion and communication in the novel occurs between two women who love each other. After their last painful meeting, which does not bring reconciliation, Sula thinks as Nel leaves her:

> "So she will walk on down that road, her back so straight in that old green coat . . . thinking how much I have cost her and never remember the days when we were two throats and one eye and we had no price."

It is difficult to imagine a more evocative metaphor for what women can be to each other, the "pricelessness" they achieve in refusing to sell themselves for male approval, the total worth that they can only find in each other's eyes.

Decades later the novel concludes with Nel's final comprehension of the source of the grief that has plagued her from the time her husband walked out. Morrison writes:

> "All that time, all that time, I thought I was missing Jude." And the loss pressed down on her chest and came up into her throat. "We was girls together," she said as though explaining something. "O Lord, Sula," she cried, "girl, girl, girlgirlgirl."
>
> It was a fine cry—loud and long—but it had no bottom and it had no top, just circles and circles of sorrow.

Again Morrison exquisitely conveys what women, black women, mean to each other. This final passage verifies the depth of Sula and Nel's relationship and its centrality to an accurate interpretation of the work.

Sula is an exceedingly lesbian novel in the emotions expressed, in the definition of female character, and in the way that the politics of heterosexuality are portrayed. The very meaning of lesbianism is being expanded in literature, just as it is being redefined through politics. The confusion that many readers have felt about *Sula* may well have a lesbian explanation. If one sees Sula's inexplicable "evil" and nonconformity as the evil of not being male-identified, many elements in the novel become clear. The work might be clearer still if Morrison had approached her subject with the consciousness that a lesbian relationship was at least a possibility for her characters. Obviously Morrison did not *intend* the reader to perceive Sula and Nel's relationship as inherently lesbian. However, this lack of intention only shows the way in which heterosexist assumptions can veil what may logically be expected to occur in a work. What I have tried to do here is not to prove that Morrison wrote something that she did not, but to point out how a black feminist critical perspective at least allows consideration of this level of the novel's meaning.

In her interview in *Conditions: One* Adrienne Rich talks about unconsummated relationships and the need to reevaluate the meaning of intense yet supposedly nonerotic connections between women. She asserts: "We need a lot more documentation about what actually happened: I think we can also imagine it, because we know it happened—we know it out of our own lives." Black women are still in the position of having to "imagine," discover and verify black lesbian literature because so little has been written from an avowedly lesbian perspective. The near nonexistence of black lesbian literature which other black lesbians and I so deeply feel has everything to do with the politics of our lives, the total suppression of identity that all black women, lesbian or not, must face. This literary silence is again intensified by the unavailability of an autonomous black feminist movement through which we could fight our oppression and also begin to name ourselves.

In a speech, "The Autonomy of Black Lesbian Women," Wilmette Brown comments upon the connection between our political reality and the literature we must invent:

> Because the isolation of Black lesbian women, given that we are superfreaks, given that our lesbianism defies both the sexual identity that capital gives us and the racial identity that capital gives us, the isolation of Black lesbian women from heterosexual Black women is very profound. Very profound. I have searched throughout Black history, Black literature, whatever, looking for some women that I could see were somehow lesbian. Now I know that in a certain sense they were all lesbian. But that was a very painful search.

Heterosexual privilege is usually the only privilege that black women have. None of us have racial or sexual privilege, almost none of us have class privilege, maintaining "straightness" is our last resort. Being out, particularly out in print, is the final renunciation of any claim to the crumbs of tolerance that nonthreatening ladylike black women are sometimes fed. I am convinced that it is our lack of privilege and power in every other sphere that allows so few black women to make the leap that many white women, particularly writers, have been able to make in this decade, not merely because they are white or have economic leverage, but because they have had the strength and support of a movement behind them.

As black lesbians we must be out not only in white society, but in the black community as well, which is at least as homophobic. That the sanctions against black lesbians are extremely high is well illustrated in this comment by black male writer Ishmael Reed. Speaking about the inroads that whites make into black culture, he asserts:

> In Manhattan you find people actively trying to impede intellectual debate among Afro-Americans. The powerful "liberal/radical/existentialist" influences of the Manhattan literary and drama establishment speak through tokens, like for example that ancient notion of the *one* black ideologue (who's usually a Communist), the *one* black poetess (who's usually a feminist lesbian).

To Reed, "feminist" and "lesbian" are the most pejorative terms he can hurl at a black woman and totally invalidate anything she might say, regardless of her actual politics or sexual identity. Such accusations are quite effective for keeping black women writers who are writing with integrity and strength from any conceivable perspective in line, but especially ones who are actually feminist and lesbian. Unfortunately Reed's reactionary attitude is all too typical. A community which has not confronted sexism, because a widespread black feminist movement has not required it to, has likewise not been challenged to examine its heterosexism. Even at this moment I am not convinced that one can write explicitly as a black lesbian and live to tell about it.

Yet there are a handful of black women who have risked everything for truth. Audre Lorde, Pat Parker and Ann Allen Shockley have at least broken ground in the vast wilderness of works that do not exist. Black feminist criticism will again have an essential role not only in creating a climate in which black lesbian writers can survive, but in undertaking the total reassessment of black literature and literary history needed to reveal the black woman-identified women that Wilmette Brown and so many of us are looking for.

Although I have concentrated here upon what does not exist and what needs to be done, a few black feminist critics have already begun this work. Gloria T. Hull at the University of Delaware has discovered in her research on black women poets of the Harlem Renaissance that many of the women who are considered minor writers of the period were in constant contact with each other and provided both intellectual stimulation and psychological support for each other's work. At least one of these writers, Angelina Weld Grimké, wrote many unpublished love poems to women. Lorraine Bethel, a recent graduate of Yale College, has done substantial work on black women writers, particularly in her senior essay, "This Infinity of Conscious Pain: Blues Lyricism and Hurston's Black Female Folk Aesthetic and Cultural Sensibility in *Their Eyes Were Watching God*," in which she brilliantly defines and uses the principles of black feminist criticism. Elaine Scott at the State University of New York at Old Westbury is also involved in highly creative and politically resonant research on Hurston and other writers.

The fact that these critics are young and, except for Hull, unpublished merely indicates the impediments we face. Undoubtedly there are other women working and writing whom I do not even know, simply because there is no place to read them. As Michele Wallace states in her article "A Black feminist's search for sisterhood":

> We exist as women who are Black who are feminists, each stranded for the moment, working independently because there is not yet an environment in this society remotely congenial to our struggle—[or our thoughts].

I only hope that this essay is one way of breaking our silence and our isolation, of helping us to know each other.

Just as I did not know where to start I am not sure how to end. I feel that I have tried to say too much and at the same time have left too much unsaid. What I want this essay to do is lead everyone who reads it to examine *everything* that they have ever thought and believed about feminist culture and to ask themselves how their thoughts connect to the reality of black women's writing and lives. I want to encourage in white women, as a first step, a sane accountability to all the women who write and live on this soil. I want most of all for black women and black lesbians somehow not to be so alone. This last will require the most expansive of revolutions as well as many new words to tell us how to make this revolution real. I finally want to express how much easier both my waking and my sleeping hours would be if there were one book in existence that would tell me something specific about my life. One book based in black feminist and black lesbian experience, fiction or nonfiction. Just one work to reflect the reality that I and the black women whom I love are trying to create. When such a book exists then each of us will not only know better how to live, but how to dream.

ROBERT B. STEPTO (b. 1945)

Robert Stepto is a critic of African American literature and has worked as an English professor. He was born in Chicago and was educated at Trinity College and Stanford University. In the late 1970s, he became associate professor of English and Afro-American studies and director of Afro-American graduate studies at Yale University. Stepto has published several nonfiction texts, including the widely read, highly esteemed From Behind the Veil: A Study of Afro-American Narrative *(1979).*

From From Behind the Veil: A Study of Afro-American Narrative (1979)

Chapter 1: I Rose and Found My Voice: Narration, Authentication, and Authorial Control in Four Slave Narratives

The strident, moral voice of the former slave recounting, exposing, appealing, apostrophizing, and above all *remembering* his ordeal in bondage is the single most impressive feature of a slave narrative. This voice is striking because of what it relates, but even more so because the slave's acquisition of that voice is quite possibly his only permanent achievement once he escapes and casts himself upon a new and larger landscape. In their most elementary form, slave narratives are full of other voices which are frequently just as responsible for articulating a narrative's tale and strategy. These other voices may belong to various "characters" in the "story," but mainly they appear in the appended documents written by slaveholders and abolitionists alike. These documents—and voices—may not always be smoothly integrated with the former slave's tale, but they are nevertheless parts of the narrative. Their primary function is, of course, to authenticate the former slave's account; in doing so, they are at least partially responsible for the narrative's acceptance as historical evidence. However, in literary terms, the documents collectively create something close to a dialogue—of forms as well as voices—which suggests that, in its primal state or first phase, the slave narrative is an *eclectic narrative* form. A "first phase" slave narrative that illustrates these points rather well is Henry Bibb's *Narrative of the Life and Adventures of Henry Bibb, an American Slave* (1849).

When the various forms (letters, prefaces, guarantees, tales) and their accompanying voices become integrated in the slave narrative text, we are presented with another type of basic narrative which I call an *integrated narrative*. This type of narrative represents the second phase of slave narrative narration; it usually yields a more sophisticated text, wherein most of the literary and rhetorical functions previously performed by several texts and voices (the appended prefaces, letters, and documents as well as the tale) are now rendered by a loosely unified single text and voice. In this second phase, the authenticating documents "come alive" in the former slave's tale as speech and even action; and the former slave—often while assuming a deferential posture toward his white friends, editors, and guarantors—carries much of the burden of introducing and authenticating his own tale. In short, as my remarks on Solomon Northup's *Twelve Years a Slave* (1854) will suggest, a "second phase" narrative is a more sophisticated narrative because the former slave's voice is responsible for much more than recounting the tale.

Because an integrated or second-phase narrative is less a collection of texts and more a unified narrative, we may say that, in terms of narration, the integrated narrative is in the process of becoming—irrespective of authorial intent—a generic narrative, by which I mean a narrative of discernible genre such as history, fiction, essay, or autobiography. This process is no simple "gourd vine" activity: an integrated narrative does not become a generic narrative overnight, and indeed, there are no assurances that in becoming a new type of narrative it is transformed automatically into a distinctive generic text. What we discover, then, is a third phase to slave narration wherein two developments may occur: the integrated narrative (phase II) may be dominated either by its tale or by its authenticating strategies. In the first instance, as we see in Frederick Douglass's *Narrative of the Life of Frederick Douglass, an American Slave, Written by Himself* (1845), the narrative and moral energies of the former slave's voice and tale so resolutely dominate the narrative's authenticating machinery (voices, documents, rhetorical strategies) that the narrative becomes, in thrust and purpose, far more metaphorical than rhetorical. When the integrated narrative becomes, in this way, a figurative account of action, landscape, and heroic self-transformation, it is so close generally to history, fiction, and autobiography that I term it a *generic narrative*.

In the second instance, as we see in William Wells Brown's *Narrative of the Life and Escape of William Wells Brown* (1852; appended to his novel *Clotel, or The President's Daughter*), the authenticating machinery either remains as important as the tale or actually becomes, usually for some purpose residing outside the text, the dominant and motivating feature of the narrative. Since this is also a sophisticated narrative phase, figurative presentations of action, landscape, and self may also occur; however, such developments are rare and always ancillary to the central thrust of the text. When the authenticating machinery dominates in this fashion, the integrated narrative becomes an *authenticating narrative*.

As these remarks suggest, one reason for investigating the phases of slave narrative narration is to gain a clearer view of how some slave narrative types become generic narratives, and how, in turn, generic narratives—once formed, shaped, and set in motion by certain distinctly Afro-American cultural imperatives—have roots in the slave narratives. All this is, of course, central to our discussion of Washington's *Up from Slavery*, DuBois's *The Souls of Black Folk*, Johnson's *The Autobiography of an Ex-Coloured Man*, Wright's *Black Boy*, and Ellison's *Invisible Man*. Moreover, it bears on our ability to distinguish between narrative modes and forms, and to describe what we see. When a historian or literary critic calls a slave narrative an autobiography, for example, what he or she sees most likely is a first-person narrative that possesses literary features to distinguish it from ordinary documents providing historical and sociological data. But a slave narrative is *not* necessarily an autobiography. We need to observe the finer shades between the more easily discernible categories of narration, and we must discover whether these stops arrange themselves in progressive, contrapuntal, or dialectic fashion—or if they possess any arrangement at all. As the scheme described above and diagrammed below suggests, I believe there are at least four identifiable modes of narration within the slave narratives, and that all four have a direct bearing on the development of subsequent Afro-American narrative forms.

The Three Phases of Narration

PHASE I: Basic Narrative (a) : "Eclectic Narrative"—authenticating documents and strategies (sometimes including one by the author of the tale) are *appended* to the tale

$\downarrow$

PHASE II: Basic Narrative (b) : "Integrated Narrative"—authenticating documents and strategies are *integrated* into the tale and formally become voices and/or characters in the tale

PHASE III:

(a) "Generic Narrative"—authenticating documents and strategies are totally *subsumed by the tale;* the slave narrative becomes an identifiable generic text, e.g., autobiography

(b) "Authenticating Narrative"—the tale is *subsumed by the authenticating strategy;* the slave narrative becomes an authenticating document for other, usually generic, texts, e.g., novels, histories

Phase I: Eclectic Narrative

Henry Bibb's *Narrative of the Life and Adventures of Henry Bibb, an American Slave,* begins with several introductory documents offering, collectively, what may be the most elaborate guarantee of authenticity found in the slave narrative canon. What is most revealing—in terms of eclectic narrative form, authenticating strategy, and race rituals along the color line—is the segregation of Bibb's own "Author's Preface" from the white-authored texts of the "Introduction." Bibb's "Author's Preface" is further removed from the preceding introductory texts by the fact that he does not address or acknowledge what has gone before. There is no exchange, no verbal bond, between the two major units of introductory material; this reflects not only the quality of Bibb's relations with his benefactors, but also his relatively modest degree of control over the text and event of the narrative itself.

The "Introduction" is basically a frame created by Bibb's publisher, Lucius Matlack, for the presentation of guarantees composed mostly by abolitionists in

Detroit (where, in freedom, Bibb chose to reside). Yet Matlack, as the publisher, also has his own authenticating duties to perform. He assures the reader that while he did indeed "examine" and "prepare" Bibb's manuscript, "The work of preparation . . . was that of orthography and punctuation merely, an arrangement of the chapters, and a table of contents—little more than falls to the lot of publishers generally." When Matlack tackles the issue of the tale's veracity, he mutes his own voice and offers instead those of various "authentic" documents gathered by the abolitionists. These gentlemen, all members of the Detroit Liberty Association, appear most sympathetic to Bibb, especially since he has spoken before their assemblies and lived an exemplary Christian life in their midst. To aid him—and their cause—they have interrogated Bibb (to which he submitted with "praiseworthy spirit") and have solicited letters from slaveholders, jailors, and Bibb's acquaintances, so that the truth of his tale might be established. No fewer than six of these letters plus the conclusion of the Association's report, all substantiating Bibb's story, appear in the "Introduction"; and, as if to "guarantee the guarantee," a note certifying the "friendly recommendation" of the abolitionists and verifying Bibb's "correct deportment" (composed, quite significantly, by a Detroit *judge*) is appended as well.

The elaborate authenticating strategy contained in Matlack's "Introduction" is typical of those found in the first-phase or eclectic narrative. The publisher or editor, far more than the former slave, assembles and manipulates the authenticating machinery, and seems to act on the premise that there is a direct correlation between the quantity of documents or texts assembled and the readership's acceptance of the narrative as a whole. I would like to suggest that Matlack's "Introduction" also constitutes a literary presentation of race rituals and cultural conditions, and that, as such, it functions as a kind of metaphor in the narrative.

To be sure, Matlack displays typical nineteenth-century American enthusiasm and superficiality when he writes of the literary merits of slave narratives: "Gushing fountains of poetic thought have started from beneath the rod of violence, that will long continue to slake the feverish thirst of humanity outraged, until swelling to a flood it shall rush with wasting violence over the ill-gotten heritage of the oppressor." However, the thrust of his "Introduction" is to guarantee the truth of a tale and, by extension, the *existence* of a man calling himself Henry Bibb. In his own aforementioned remarks regarding the preparation of Bibb's text for publication, Matlack appears to address the issue of the author's—Bibb's—credibility. However, the issue is really the audience's—white America's—credulity: their acceptance not so much of the former slave's escape and newfound freedom, but of his literacy. Many race rituals are enacted here, not the least of which is Matlack's "conversation" with white America across the text and figurative body of a silent former slave. The point we may glean from them all is that, insofar as Bibb must depend on his publisher to be an intermediary between his text and his audience, he relinquishes control of the narrative—which is, after all, the vehicle for the account of how he obtained his voice in freedom.

While we are impressed by the efforts of the Detroit Liberty Association's members to conduct an investigation of Bibb's tale, issue a report, and lend their names to the guarantee, we are still far more overwhelmed by the examples of the cultural disease with which they wrestle than by their desire to find a cure. That disease is, of course, cultural myopia, the badge and sore bestowed upon every nation mindlessly heedful of race ritual instead of morality: Henry Bibb is alive and well in Detroit, but by what miraculous stroke will he, as a man, be able to cast his shadow on this soil? The effort in the narrative's "Introduction" to prove that Bibb exists, and hence has a tale, goes far to explain why a prevailing metaphor in Afro-American letters is, in varying configurations, one of invisibility and translucence. Indirectly, and undoubtedly on a subconscious level, Matlack and the abolitionists confront the issue of Bibb's inability "to cast his shadow." But even in their case we may ask: Are they bolstering a cause, comforting a former slave, or recognizing a man?

The letters from the slaveholders and jailors Bibb knew while in bondage must not be overlooked here, for they help illuminate the history of the disease we are diagnosing. The letter from Silas Gatewood, whose father once owned Bibb, is designed solely to portray Bibb as "a notorious liar . . . and a rogue." Placed within the compendium of documents assembled by the abolitionists, the letter completes, through its nearly hysterical denunciation of Bibb, the "Introduction's" portrait of America at war with itself. The debate over Bibb's character, and, by extension, his right to a personal history bound to that of white Americans, is really nothing less than a literary omen of the Civil War. In this regard, the segregation of Bibb's "Author's Preface" from the introductory compendium of documents is, even more than his silence within the compendium, indicative of how the former slave's voice was kept muted and distant while the nation debated questions of slavery and the Negro's humanity.

Bibb's "Preface" reveals two features to his thinking, each of which helps us see how the former slave approached the task of composing a narrative. In answer to his own rhetorical question as to why he wrote the narrative, he replies, "in no place have I given orally the detail of my narrative; and some of the most interesting events of my life have never reached the public ear." This is not extraordinary except in that it reminds us of the oral techniques and traditions that lay behind most of the written narratives. The former slave's accomplishment of a written narrative should by no means be minimized, but we must also recognize the extent to which the abolitionist lecture circuit, whether in Michigan, Maine, or New York, gave former slaves an opportunity to structure, to embellish, and above all to polish an oral version of their tale—and to do so before the very audiences who would soon purchase hundreds, if not thousands, of copies of the written account. The former slave, not altogether unlike the semi-literate black preacher whose sermons were (and are) masterpieces of oral composition and rhetorical strategy, often had a fairly well developed version of his or her tale either memorized or (more likely) sufficiently *patterned* for effective presentation, even before the question of written composition was entertained. Certainly such was the case for Bibb, and this reminds us not to be too narrow when we call the basic slave narrative an eclectic narrative form. Oral as well as written forms are part of the eclectic whole.

The second revealing feature of Bibb's "Preface" returns us to a point on which his publisher, Matlack, began. Bibb appears extremely aware of the issue of his authorship when he writes:

> The reader will remember that I make no pretension to literature; for I can truly say, that I have been educated in the school of adversity, whips, and chains. Experience and observation have been my principal teachers, with the exception of three weeks schooling which I have had the good fortune to receive since my escape from the "grave yard of the mind," or the dark prison of human bondage.

That Bibb had only three weeks of formal schooling is astonishing; however, I am intrigued even more by the two metaphors for slavery with which he concludes. While both obviously suggest confinement—one of the mind, the other of his body—it seems significant that Bibb did not choose between the two (for reasons of style, if no other). Both images are offered *after* the act of writing his tale, possibly because Bibb is so terribly aware of both. His body is now free, his mind limber, his voice resonant; together they and his tale, if not his narrative, are his own.

On a certain level, we must study Matlack's "Introduction," with all its documents and guarantees, and Bibb's "Author's Preface" as a medley of voices, rather than as a loose conglomerate of discrete and even segregated texts. Together, both in what they do and do not say, these statements reflect the passions, politics, interpersonal relations, race rituals, and uses of language of a cross-section of America in the 1840's. But on another level, we must hold fast to what we have discovered regarding how Bibb's removal from the primary authenticating documents and strategy (that is, from the "Introduction") weakens his control of the narrative and, in my view, relegates him to a posture of partial literacy. Bibb's tale proves that he has acquired a voice, but his narrative shows that his voice does not yet control the imaginative forms which his personal history assumes in print.

In the Bibb narrative, the various texts within the "Introduction" guarantee Bibb and his tale; Bibb sustains this strategy of guarantee late in his tale by quoting letters and proclamations by many of the same figures who provided documents for the "Introduction." As we will discover in Solomon Northup's narrative, this use of authenticating documents within the text of the tale indicates the direction of more sophisticated slave narrative texts. Indeed, the question of whether the authenticating documents and strategies have been integrated into the central text (usually the tale) of the slave narrative is a major criterion by which we may judge author and narrative alike. The inclusion and manipulation of peripheral documents and voices suggests a remarkable level of literacy and self-assurance on the part of the former slave, and the reduction of many texts and strategies into one reflects a search, irrespective of authorial intent, for a more sophisticated written narrative form. Here, then, is a point of departure from which we may study the development of pregeneric narratives into generic and other sophisticated narrative types.

Phase II: Integrated Narrative

While I am not prepared to classify Solomon Northup's *Twelve Years a Slave* (1854) as an autobiography, it is certainly a more sophisticated text than Henry Bibb's, principally because its most important authenticating document is integrated into the tale as a voice and character. *Twelve Years a Slave* is, however, an integrated narrative unsure of itself. Ultimately, its authenticating strategy depends as much upon an appended set of authenticating texts as upon integrated documents and voices.

In comparison to the Bibb "Introduction," the Northup introductory materials appear purposely short and undeveloped. Northup's editor and amanuensis, a Mr. David Wilson, offers a one-page "Preface," not a full-blown "Introduction," and Northup's own introductory words are placed in the first chapter of his tale, rather than in a discrete entry written expressly for that purpose. Wilson's "Preface" is, predictably, an authenticating document, formulaically acknowledging whatever "faults of style and of expression" the narrative may contain while assuring the reader that he, the editor and a white man, is convinced of Northup's strict adherence to the truth. Northup's own contributions, like Bibb's, are not so much authenticating as they are reflective of what a slave may have been forced to consider while committing his tale to print.

Northup's first entry is simply and profoundly his signature—his proof of literacy writ large, with a bold, clear hand. It appears beneath a pen-and-ink frontispiece portrait entitled "Solomon in His Plantation Suit." His subsequent entries quite self-consciously place his narrative amid the antislavery literature of the era, in particular, with Harriet Beecher Stowe's *Uncle Tom's Cabin* (1852) and *Key to Uncle Tom's Cabin* (1853). If one wonders why Northup neither establishes his experience among those of other kidnapped and enslaved blacks nor positions his narrative with other narratives, the answer is provided in part by his dedicatory page. There, after quoting a passage from *Key to Uncle Tom's Cabin* which, in effect, verifies his account of slavery because it is said to "form a striking parallel" to Uncle Tom's, Northup respectfully dedicates his narrative to Miss Stowe, remarking that his tale affords "another *Key to Uncle Tom's Cabin.*"

This is no conventional dedication; it tells us much about the requisite act of authentication. While the Bibb narrative is authenticated by documents provided by the Detroit Liberty Association, the Northup narrative begins the process of authentication by assuming kinship with a popular antislavery novel. Audience, and the former slave's relationship to that audience, are the key issues here: authentication is, apparently, a rhetorical strategy designed not only for verification purposes, but also for the task of initiating and insuring a readership. No matter how efficacious it undoubtedly was for Northup (or his editor) to ride Miss Stowe's coattails and share in her immense notoriety, one cannot help wondering about the profound implications involved in authenticating personal history by binding it to historical fiction. In its way, this strategy says as much about a former slave's inability to confirm his existence and "cast his shadow" as does the more conventional strategy observed in the Bibb narrative, Apparently, a novel may authenticate a personal history, especially when the personal history is that of a former slave.

While not expressing the issue in these terms, Northup seems to have thought about the dilemma of authentication and that of slave narratives competing with fictions of both the pro- and antislavery variety. He writes:

> Since my return to liberty, I have not failed to perceive the increasing interest throughout the Northern states, in regard to the subject of Slavery. Works of fiction, professing to portray its features in their more pleasing as well as more repugnant aspects, have been circulated to an extent unprecedented, and, as I understand, have created a fruitful topic of comment and discussion.

> I can speak of Slavery only so far as it came under my own observation—only so far as I have known and experienced it in my own person. My object is, to give a candid and truthful statement of facts: to repeat the story of my life, without exaggeration, leaving it for others to determine, whether even the pages of fiction present a picture of more cruel wrong or a severer bondage.

Clearly, Northup felt that the authenticity of his tale would not be taken for granted, and that, on a certain peculiar but familiar level enforced by rituals along the color line, his narrative would be viewed as a fiction competing with other fictions. However, in this passage Northup also inaugurates a counter-strategy. His reference to his own observation of slavery may be a just and subtle dig at the "armchair sociologists" of North and South alike, who wrote of the slavery question amid the comforts of their libraries and verandas. But more important, in terms of plot as well as point of view, the remark establishes Northup's authorial posture as a "participant-observer" in the truest and (given his bondage) most regrettable sense of the phrase. In these terms, then, Northup contributes personally to the authentication of *Twelve Years a Slave:* he challenges the authenticity of the popular slavery fictions and their power of authenticating his own personal history by first exploiting the bond between them and his tale and then assuming the posture of an authenticator. One needn't delve far into the annals of American race relations for proof that Northup's rhetorical strategy is but a paradigm for the classic manipulation of the master by the slave.

As the first chapter of *Twelve Years a Slave* unfolds, Northup tells of his family's history and circumstances. His father, Mintus Northup, was a slave in Rhode Island and in Rensselaer County, New York, before gaining his freedom in 1803 upon the death of his master. Mintus quickly amassed property and gained suffrage; he came to expect the freedoms that accompany self-willed mobility and self-initiated employment, and gave his son, Solomon, the extraordinary advantage of being born a free man. As a result, Solomon writes of gaining "an education surpassing that ordinarily bestowed upon children in our condition," and he recollects leisure hours "employed over my books, or playing the violin." Solomon describes employment (such as lumber-rafting on Lake Champlain) that was not only profitable but also, in a way associated with the romance of the frontier, adventurous and even manly. When Solomon Northup married Anne Hampton on Christmas Day of 1829, they did not jump over a broomstick, as was the (reported) lot of most enslaved black Americans; rather, the two were married by a magistrate of the neighborhood, Timothy Eddy, Esq. Furthermore, their first home was neither a hovel nor a hut but the "Fort House," a residence "lately occupied by Captain Lathrop" and used in 1777 by General Burgoyne.

This saga of Solomon's heritage is full of interest, and it has its rhetorical and strategical properties as well. Northup has begun to establish his authorial posture removed from the condition of the black masses in slavery—a move which, as we have indicated, is as integral to the authenticating strategy as to the plot of his tale. In addition to portraying circumstances far more pleasant and fulfilling than those which he suffers in slavery, Northup's family history also yields some indication of his relations with whites in the district, especially the white Northups. Of course, these indications also advance both the plot and the authenticating strategy. One notes, for example, that while Mintus Northup did indeed migrate from the site of his enslavement once he was free, he retained the Northup surname and labored for a relative of his former master. Amid his new prosperity and mobility, Mintus maintained fairly amicable ties with his past; apparently this set the tone for relations between Northups, black and white. One should be wary of depicting New York north of Albany as an ideal or integrated area in the early 1800's, but the black Northups had bonds with whites—perhaps blood ties. To the end Solomon depends on these bonds for his escape from slavery and for the implicit verification of his tale.

In the first chapter of *Twelve Years a Slave*, Henry B. Northup, Esq., is mentioned only briefly as a relative of Mintus Northup's former master; in the context of Solomon's family history, he is but a looming branch of the (white) Northup family tree. However, as the tale concludes, Henry Northup becomes a voice and character in the narrative. He requests various legal documents essential to nullifying Solomon's sale into bondage; he inquires into Solomon's whereabouts in Bayou Boeuf, Louisiana; he presents the facts before lawyers, sheriffs, and Solomon's master, Edwin Epps; he pleads Solomon's case against his abductors before a District of Columbia court of law; and, most important, after the twelve years of assault on Solomon's sense of identity, Henry Northup utters, to Solomon's profound thanksgiving, Solomon's given name—not his slave name. In this way Henry Northup enters the narrative, and whatever linguistic authentication of the tale Solomon inaugurated by assuming the rather objective posture of the participant-observer-authenticator is concluded and confirmed, not by appended letter, but by Henry Northup's presence.

This strategy of authentication functions hand in hand with the narrative's strategy of reform. Like the carpenter, Bass, who jeopardizes his own safety by personally mailing Solomon's appeals for help to New York, Henry Northup embodies the spirit of reform in the narrative. In terms of reform strategy, Henry Northup and Bass—who, as a Canadian, represents a variation on the archetype of deliverance in Canada—are not only saviors but also models whose example might enlist other whites in the reform cause. Certainly abolitionists near and far could identify with these men, and that was important. Slave narratives were often most successful when they were as subtly pro-abolition as they were overtly antislavery—a consideration which could only have exacerbated the former slave's already sizeable problems with telling his tale in such a way that he, and not his editors or guarantors, controlled it.

But Henry Northup is a different kind of savior from Bass: he is an American descended from slaveowners, and he shares his surname with the kidnapped Solomon. Furthermore, his posture as a family friend is inextricably bound to his position in the tale as a lawyer. At the end of *Twelve Years a Slave*, Henry Northup appears in Louisiana as an embodiment of the law, as well as of Solomon Northup's past (in all its racial complexity) come to reclaim him. In this way, Solomon's *tale* assumes the properties of an integrated narrative—the authenticating texts (here, the words and actions of Henry Northup) are integrated into the former slave's tale. But in what follows after the tale, we see that Solomon's *narrative* ultimately retrogresses to the old strategies of a phase-one eclectic narrative. Whereas the Bibb narrative begins with a discrete set of authenticating texts, the Northup narrative ends with such a set—an "Appendix."

The Northup Appendix contains three types of documents. First comes the New York state law, passed May 14, 1840, employed by Henry Northup and others to reclaim Solomon Northup from bondage in Louisiana. There follows a petition to the Governor of New York from Solomon's wife, Ann Northup, replete with legal language that persists in terming her a "memorialist." The remaining documents are letters, mostly from the black Northups' white neighbors, authenticating Solomon's claim that he is a free Negro. Despite our initial disappointment upon finding such an orthodox authenticating strategy appended to what had heretofore been a refreshingly sophisticated slave narrative (the narrative does not need the Appendix to fulfill its form), the Appendix does have its points of interest. Taken as a whole, it portrays the unfolding of a law; the New York law with which it begins precipitates the texts that follow, notably, in chronological order. On one level, then, Northup's Appendix is, far more than Bibb's Introduction, a story in epistolary form that authenticates not only his tale but also those voices within the tale, such as Henry Northup's. On another level, however, the Appendix becomes a further dimension to the reform strategy subsumed within the narrative. Just as Bass and Henry Northup posture as model reformers, the narrative's Appendix functions as a primer, complete with illustrative documents, on how to use the law to retrieve kidnapped free Negroes. Thus, the Appendix, as much as the tale itself, can be seen (quite correctly) as an elaborate rhetorical strategy against the Fugitive Slave Law of 1850.

In the end, the Northup narrative reverts to primitive authenticating techniques, but that does not diminish the sophistication and achievement of the tale within the narrative. We must now ask: To what end does the immersion of authenticating documents and strategies within the texture of Northup's tale occur? Furthermore, is this goal literary or extraliterary? In answering these questions we come a little closer, I think, to an opinion on whether narratives like Northup's may be autobiographies.

Northup's conscious or unconscious integration and subsequent manipulation of authenticating voices advances his tale's plot and most certainly advances his narrative's validation and reform strategies. However, it does little to develop what Albert Stone has called a literary strategy of self-presentation. The narrative renders an extraordinary experience, but not a remarkable self. The two need not be exclusive, as Frederick Douglass's 1845 *Narrative* illustrates, but in the Northup book they appear to be distinct entities, principally because of the eye or "I" shaping and controlling the narration. Northup's eye and "I" are not so much introspective as they are inquisitive; even while in the pit of slavery in Louisiana, Northup takes time to inform us of various farming methods and of how they differ from practices in the North. Of course, this remarkable objective posture results directly from Northup assuming the role of a participant-observer for authentication purposes. But it all has a terrible price. Northup's tale is neither the history nor a metaphor for the history of his life; and because this is so, his tale cannot be called autobiographical.

Phase IIIa: Generic Narrative

In the first two phases of slave narrative narration we observe the former slave's ultimate lack of control over his own narrative, occasioned primarily by the demands
of audience and authentication. This dilemma is not unique to the authors of these
narratives; indeed, many modern black writers still do not control their personal
history once it assumes literary form. For this reason, Frederick Douglass's
Narrative of the Life of Frederick Douglass, an American Slave, Written by Himself
(1845) seems all the more a remarkable literary achievement. Because it contains
several segregated narrative texts—a preface, a prefatory letter, the tale, an appendix—it appears to be, in terms of the narrative phases, a rather primitive slave narrative. But each ancillary text is drawn to the tale by some sort of extraordinary
gravitational pull or magnetic attraction. There is, in short, a dynamic energy
between the tale and each supporting text that we do not discover in the Bibb or
Northup narratives, save perhaps in the relationship between Solomon Northup
and his guarantor-become-character, Henry Northup. The Douglass narrative is an
integrated narrative of a very special order. The integrating process does, in a small
way, pursue the conventional path found in Northup's narrative, creating characters
out of authenticating texts (William Lloyd Garrison silently enters Douglass's tale
at the very end); however, its new and major thrust is the creation of that aforementioned energy which binds the supporting texts to the tale, while at the same
time removing them from participation in the narrative's rhetorical and authenticating strategies. Douglass's tale dominates the narrative because it alone authenticates the narrative.

The introductory texts to the tale are two in number: a "Preface" by William
Lloyd Garrison, the famous abolitionist and editor of *The Liberator*; and a "Letter
from Wendell Phillips, Esq.," who was equally well known as an abolitionist, cru-
sading lawyer, and judge. In theory, each of these introductory documents should
be classic guarantees written almost exclusively for a white reading public, concerned primarily and ritualistically with the white validation of a newfound black
voice, and removed from the tale in such ways that the guarantee and tale vie
silently and surreptitiously for control of the narrative as a whole. But these entries
are not fashioned that way. To be sure, Garrison offers a conventional guarantee
when he writes, "MR. DOUGLASS has very properly chosen to write his own
Narrative, in his own style, and according to the best of his ability, rather than to
employ some one else. It is, therefore, entirely his own production; and . . . it is, in
my judgment, highly creditable to his head and heart." And Phillips, while addressing Douglass, most certainly offers a guarantee to "another" audience as well:

> Every one who has heard you speak has felt, and, I am confident, every one who
> read your book will feel, persuaded that you give them a fair specimen of the
> whole truth. No one-sided portrait,—no wholesale complaints,—but strict jus-
> tice done, whenever individual kindliness has neutralized, for a moment, the
> deadly system with which it was strangely allied.

But these passages dominate neither the tone nor the substance of their respective texts.

Garrison is far more interested in writing history (specifically, that of the 1841 Nantucket Anti-Slavery Convention, and the launching of Douglass's career as a lecture agent for various antislavery societies) and recording his own place in it. His declaration, "I shall never forget his [Douglass's] first speech at the convention," is followed within a paragraph by, "*I rose*, and declared that PATRICK HENRY, of revolutionary fame, never made a speech more eloquent in the cause of liberty . . . *I reminded* the audience of the peril which surrounded this self-emancipated young man . . . *I appealed* to them, whether they would ever allow him to be carried back into slavery,—law or no law, constitution or no constitution" (italics added). His "Preface" ends, not with a reference to Douglass or his tale, but with an apostrophe very much like one he would use to exhort and arouse an antislavery assembly. With the following cry Garrison hardly guarantees Douglass's tale, but enters and reenacts his own abolitionist career instead:

> Reader! are you with the man-stealers in sympathy and purpose, or on the side of their down-trodden victims? If with the former, then you are the foe of God and man. If with the latter, what are you prepared to do and dare in their behalf? Be faithful, be vigilant, be untiring in your efforts to break every yoke, and let the oppressed go free. Come what may—cost what may—inscribe on the banner which you unfurl to the breeze, as your religious and political motto—"NO COMPROMISE WITH SLAVERY! NO UNION WITH SLAVEHOLDERS!"

In the light of this closure, and (no matter how hard we try to ignore it) the friction that developed between Garrison and Douglass in later years, we might be tempted to see Garrison's "Preface" at war with Douglass's tale for authorial control of the narrative as a whole. Certainly there is a tension, but that tension is stunted by Garrison's enthusiasm for Douglass's tale. Garrison writes:

> This *Narrative* contains many affecting incidents, many *passages* of great eloquence and power; but I think the most thrilling one of them all is the *description* DOUGLASS gives of his feelings, as he stood soliloquizing respecting his fate, and the chances of his one day being a free man. . . . Who can read that *passage*, and be insensible to its pathos and sublimity? [Italics added.]

Here Garrison does, probably subconsciously, an unusual and extraordinary thing—he becomes the first guarantor we have seen in this study who not only directs the reader to the tale, but also acknowledges the tale's singular rhetorical power. Garrison enters the tale by being at the Nantucket convention with Douglass in 1841 (the same year Solomon Northup was kidnapped) and by, in effect, authenticating the impact, rather than the facts, of the tale. He fashions his own apostrophe, but finally he remains a member of Douglass's audience far more than he assumes the posture of a competing or superior voice. In this way Garrison's "Preface" stands outside Douglass's tale but is steadfastly bound to it.

Such is the case for Wendell Phillips's "Letter" as well. As I have indicated, it contains passages which seem addressed to credulous readers in need of a "visible" authority's guarantee, but by and large the "Letter" is directed to Frederick Douglass alone. It opens with "My Dear Friend," and there are many extraliterary reasons for wondering initially if the friend is actually Frederick. Shortly thereafter, however, Phillips declares, "I am glad the time has come when the 'lions write history,'" and it becomes clear that he both addresses Douglass and writes in response to the tale. These features, plus Phillips's specific references to how Douglass acquired his "A B C" and learned "where the 'white sails' of the Chesapeake were bound," serve to integrate Phillips's "Letter" into Douglass's tale.

Above all, we must understand in what terms the "Letter" is a cultural and linguistic event. Like the Garrison document, it presents its author as a member of Douglass's audience; but the act of letter-writing, of correspondence, implies a moral and linguistic parity between a white guarantor and black author which we haven't seen before—and which we do not always see in American literary history *after* 1845. The tone and posture initiated in Garrison's "Preface" are completed and confirmed in Phillips's "Letter"; while these documents are integrated into Douglass's tale, they remain segregated outside the tale in the all-important sense that they yield Douglass sufficient narrative and rhetorical space in which to render personal history in—and as—a literary form.

What marks Douglass's narration and control of his tale is his extraordinary ability to pursue several types of writing with ease and with a degree of simultaneity. The principal types of writing we discover in the tale are: syncretic phrasing, introspective analysis, internalized documentation, and participant observation. Of course, each of these types has its accompanying authorial posture, the result being that even the telling of the tale (as distinct from the content of the tale) yields a portrait of a complex individual marvelously facile with the tones, shapes, and dimensions of his voice.

Douglass's syncretic phrasing is often discussed; the passage most widely quoted is probably, "My feet have been so cracked with the frost, that the pen with which I am writing might be laid in the gashes." The remarkable clarity of this language needs no commentary, but what one admires as well is Douglass's ability to conjoin past and present, and to do so with images that not only stand for different periods in his personal history but also, in their fusion, speak of his evolution from slavery to freedom. The pen, symbolizing the quest for literacy fulfilled, actually measures the wounds of the past, and this measuring process becomes a metaphor in and of itself for the artful composition of travail transcended. While I admire this passage, I find even more intriguing the syncretic phrases that pursue a kind of acrid punning upon the names of Douglass's oppressors. A minor example appears early in the tale, when Douglass deftly sums up an overseer's character by writing, "Mr. Severe was rightly named: he was a cruel man." Here Douglass is content with "glossing" the name; but late in the tale, just before attempting to escape in 1835, he takes another oppressor's name and does not so much gloss it or play with it as *work upon* it—to such an extent that, riddled with irony, it is devoid of its original meaning: "At the close of the year 1834, Mr. Freeland again hired me of my master, for the year 1835. But, by this time, I began to want to live *upon free land* as well as *with Freeland*; and I was no longer content, therefore, to live with him or any other slaveholder." Of course, this is effective writing—far more effective than what is found in the average slave narrative. But my point is that Douglass seems to fashion these passages for both his readership and himself. Each example of his increasing facility and wit with language charts his ever-shortening path to literacy; thus, in their way, Douglass's syncretic phrases reveal his emerging comprehension of freedom and literacy, and are another introspective tool by which he may mark the progress of his personal history.

But the celebrated passages of introspective analysis are even more pithy and direct. In these, Douglass fashions language as finely honed and balanced as an aphorism or Popean couplet, and thereby orders his personal history with neat, distinct, and credible moments of transition. When Mr. Auld forbids Mrs. Auld from teaching Douglass the alphabet, for example, Douglass relates, "From that moment, I understood the pathway from slavery to freedom. . . . Whilst I was saddened by the thought of losing the aid of my kind mistress, I was gladdened by the invaluable instruction which, by the merest accident, I gained from my master." The clarity of Douglass's revelation is as unmistakable as it was remarkable. As rhetoric, the passage is successful because its nearly extravagant beginning is finally rendered quite acceptable by the masterly balance and internal rhyming of "saddened" and "gladdened," which is persuasive because it is pleasant and because it offers the illusion of a reasoned conclusion.

Balance is an important feature to two other equally celebrated passages which open and close Douglass's telling of his relations with Mr. Covey, an odd (because he *worked* in the fields alongside the slaves) but vicious overseer. At the beginning of the episode, in which Douglass finally fights back and draws Covey's blood, he writes: "You have seen how a man was made a slave; you shall see how a slave was made a man." And at the end of the episode, to bring matters linguistically as well as narratively full circle, Douglass declares: "I now resolved that, however long I might remain a slave in form, the day has passed forever when I could be a slave in fact. I did not hesitate to let it be known of me, that the white man who expected to succeed in whipping, must also succeed in killing me."

The sheer poetry of these statements is not lost on us, nor is the reason why the poetry was created in the first place. One might suppose that in another age Douglass's determination and rage would take a more effusive expression, but I cannot imagine that to be the case. In the first place, his linguistic model is obviously scriptural; and in the second, his goal, as Albert Stone has argued, is the presentation of a "*historical* self," not the record of temporary hysteria.

This latter point, to refer back to the Northup narrative, is one of the prime distinctions between Solomon Northup and Frederick Douglass—one which ultimately persuades me that Douglass is about the business of discovering how personal history may be transformed into autobiography, while Northup is not. Both narratives contain episodes in which the author finally stands up to and soundly beats his overseer, but while Douglass performs this task and reflects upon its place in his history, Northup resorts to effusion:

> As I stood there, feelings of unutterable agony overwhelmed me. I was conscious that I had subjected myself to unimaginable punishment. The reaction that followed my extreme ebullition of anger produced the most painful sensations of regret. An

unfriended, helpless slave—what could I *do*, what could I *say*, to justify, in the remotest manner, the heinous act I had committed . . . I tried to pray . . . but emotion choked my utterance, and I could only bow my head upon my hands and weep.

Passages such as these may finally link certain slave narratives with the popular sentimental literary forms of the nineteenth century, but Douglass's passages of introspective analysis create fresh space for themselves in the American literary canon.

Internal documentation in Douglass's tale is unusual in that, instead of reproducing letters and other documents written by white guarantors within the tale or transforming guarantees into characters, Douglass internalizes documents which, like the syncretic and introspective passages, order his personal history. Again a comparison of Douglass and Northup is useful, because while both authors present documents having only a secondary function in the authenticating process, their goals (and, perhaps one might say, their ambitions) seem quite different.

Northup, for example, documents slave songs in two major passages: first in the text of the tale, and then in a segregated text serving as a musical interlude between the tale and the Appendix. His discussion of the songs within the tale is one dimensional, by which I mean it merely reflects his limited comprehension and appreciation of the songs at a given moment in his life. Rather than establishing Northup within the slave community, remarks like "those unmeaning songs, composed rather for [their] adaptation to a certain tune or measure, than for the purpose of expressing any distinct idea" or "equally nonsensical, but full of melody" serve only to reinforce his displacement as a participant-observer. One might have assumed that Northup (who was, after all, kidnapped into slavery partly because of his musicianship) found music a bond between him and his enslaved brethren, and in passages such as these would relinquish or soften his objective posture. But apparently the demands of audience and authentication precluded such a shift.

In contrast, Douglass's discussion of slave songs begins with phrases such as "wild songs" and "unmeaning jargon" but concludes, quite typically for him, with a study of how he grew to "hear" the songs and how that hearing affords yet another illumination of his path from slavery to freedom:

> I did not, when a slave, understand the deep meaning of those rude and apparently incoherent songs. I was myself within the circle; so that I neither saw nor heard as those without might see and hear. They told a tale of woe which was then altogether beyond my feeble comprehension. . . . Every tone was a testimony against slavery, and a prayer to God for deliverance from chains. The hearing of those wild notes always depressed my spirit, and filled me with ineffable sadness. I have frequently found myself in tears while hearing them. The mere recurrence to those songs, even now, afflicts me; and while I am writing these lines, an expression of feeling has already found its way down my cheek.

The tears of the past and present interflow. Douglass not only documents his saga of enslavement but also, with typical recourse to syncretic phrasing and introspective analysis, advances his presentation of self.

Douglass's other internalized documents are employed with comparable efficiency, as we see in the episode where he attempts an escape in 1835. There the document reproduced is the pass or "protection" Douglass wrote for himself and his compatriots in the escape plan:

> This is to certify that I, the undersigned, have given the bearer, my servant, full liberty to go to Baltimore, and spend the Easter holidays. Written with mine own hand, &c., 1835.
>
> WILLIAM HAMILTON,
Near St. Michael's, in Talbot county, Maryland.

The protection exhibits Douglass's increasingly refined sense of how to manipulate language—he has indeed come a long way from that day when Mr. Auld halted his A B C lessons. But even more impressive, I believe, is the act of reproducing the document itself. We know from the tale that each slave managed to destroy his pass when the scheme was thwarted; Douglass is reproducing his language from memory, and there is no reason to doubt a single jot of his recollection. He can draw so easily from the wellsprings of memory because the protection is not a mere scrap of memorabilia, but a veritable roadsign on his path to freedom and literacy. In this sense, his protection assumes a place in Afro-American letters as an antedating trope for such documents as "The Voodoo of Hell's Half Acre" in Richard Wright's *Black Boy*, and the tale framed by the prologue and epilogue in Ralph Ellison's *Invisible Man*.

All of the types of narrative discourse discussed thus far reveal features of Douglass's particular posture as a participant-observer narrator, a posture that is as introspective as Solomon Northup's is inquisitive. But the syncretic phrases, introspective studies, and internalized documents only exhibit Douglass as a teller and doer, and part of the great effect of his tale depends upon what he does *not* tell, what he refuses to reenact in print. Late in the tale, at the beginning of the eleventh chapter, Douglass writes:

> I now come to that part of my life during which I planned, and finally succeeded in making, my escape from slavery. But before narrating any of the peculiar circumstances, I deem it proper to make known my intention not to state all the facts connected with the transaction . . . I deeply regret the necessity that impels me to suppress any thing of importance connected with my experience in slavery. It would afford me great pleasure indeed, as well as materially add to the interest of my narrative, were I at liberty to gratify a curiosity, which I know exists. . . . But I must deprive myself of this pleasure, and the curious gratification which such a statement would afford. I would allow myself to suffer under the greatest imputations which evil-minded men might suggest, rather than exculpate myself, and thereby run the hazard of closing the slightest avenue by which a brother slave might clear himself of the chains and fetters of slavery.

John Blassingame has argued, in *The Slave Community* (1972), that one way to test a slave narrative's authenticity is by gauging how much space the narrator gives to relating his escape, as opposed to describing the conditions of his captivity. If the adventure, excitement, and perils of the escape seem to be the *raison d'être* for the narrative's composition, then the narrative is quite possibly an exceedingly adulterated slave's tale or a bald fiction. The theory does not always work perfectly:

Henry "Box" Brown's narrative and that of William and Ellen Craft are predominantly recollections of extraordinary escapes; yet, as far as we can tell, these are authentic tales. But Blassingame's theory nevertheless has great merit, and I have often wondered to what extent it derives from the example of Douglass's tale and from his fulminations against those authors who unwittingly excavate the Underground Railroad and expose it to the morally thin mid-nineteenth-century American air. Douglass's tale is spectacularly free from suspicion because he never divulges a detail of his escape to New York. (That information is given ten years later, in *My Bondage and My Freedom* and other statements.) This marvelously rhetorical omission or silence both sophisticates and authenticates his posture as a participant-observer narrator. When a narrator wrests this kind of preeminent authorial control from the ancillary voices in the narrative, we may say that he controls the presentation of his personal history, and that his tale is becoming autobiographical. In this light, then, Douglass's last few sentences of the tale take on special meaning:

> But, while attending an anti-slavery convention at Nantucket, on the 11th of August, 1841, I felt strongly moved to speak. . . . It was a severe cross, and I took it up reluctantly. The truth was, I felt myself a slave, and the idea of speaking to white people weighed me down. I spoke but a few moments, when I felt a degree of freedom, and said what I desired with considerable ease. From that time until now, I have been engaged in pleading the case of my brethren—with what success, and what devotion, I leave those acquainted with my labors to decide.

With these words, the *narrative*, as Albert Stone has remarked, comes full circle. We are returned not to the beginning of the *tale*, but to Garrison's prefatory remarks on the convention and Douglass's first public address. This return may be pleasing in terms of the sense of symmetry it affords, but it is also a remarkable feat of rhetorical strategy: having traveled with Douglass through his account of his life, we arrive in Nantucket in 1841 to hear him speak. We become, along with Mr. Garrison, his audience. The final effect is that Douglass reinforces his posture as an articulate hero, while supplanting Garrison as the definitive historian of his past.

Even more important, I think, is Douglass's final image of a slave shedding his last fetter and becoming a man by first finding his voice and then, as surely as light follows dawn, speaking "with considerable ease." In one brilliant stroke, the quest for freedom and literacy, implied from the start even by the narrative's title, is resolutely consummated.

The final text of the narrative, the Appendix, differs from the one attached to the Northup narrative. It is not a series of letters and legal documents, but a discourse by Douglass on *his* view of Christianity and Christian practice, as opposed to what he exposed in his tale to be the bankrupt, immoral faith of slaveholders. As rhetorical strategy, the discourse is effective because it lends weight and substance to what passes for a conventional complaint of slave narrators, and because Douglass's exhibition of faith can only enhance his already considerable posture as an articulate hero. But more specifically, the discourse is most efficacious because at its heart lies a vitriolic poem written by a northern Methodist minister that Douglass introduces by writing: "I conclude these remarks by copying the following portrait of the religion of the south, (which is, by communion and fellowship, the religion of the north,) which I soberly affirm is 'true to life,' and without caricature or the slightest exaggeration." The poem is strong and imbued with considerable irony, but what we must appreciate here is the effect of the white Northerner's poem conjoined with Douglass's *authentication* of the poem. The tables are clearly reversed: Douglass has not only controlled his personal history, but also fulfilled the prophecy suggested by his implicit authentication of Garrison's "Preface" by explicitly authenticating what is conventionally a white Northerner's validating text. Douglass's narrative thus offers what is unquestionably our best portrait in Afro-American letters of the requisite act of assuming authorial control. An author can go no further than Douglass did without himself writing all the texts constituting the narrative.

Phase IIIb: Authenticating Narrative

In an authenticating narrative, represented here by William Wells Brown's *Narrative of the Life and Escape of William Wells Brown* (not to be confused with Brown's 1847 volume, *Narrative of William Wells Brown, a Fugitive Slave, Written by Himself*), the narrator exhibits considerable control of his narrative by becoming an editor of disparate texts for authentication purposes, far more than for the goal of recounting personal history. The texts Brown displays include passages from his speeches and other writings, but for the most part they are testimonials from antislavery groups in both America and England, excerpts from reviews of his travel book, *Three Years in Europe* (1852), selections from antislavery verse, and, quite significantly, letters to Brown's benefactors from his last master in slavery, Mr. Enoch Price of St. Louis. Brown's control of his narrative is comparable to Douglass's, but while Douglass gains control by improving upon the narrative failures of authors like Henry Bibb, Brown's control represents a refinement of the authenticating strategies used by publishers like Bibb's Lucius Matlack, who edited and deployed authenticating documents very much like those gathered by Brown. In this way, Brown's narrative is not so much a tale of personal history as it is a conceit upon the authorial mode of the white guarantor. Control and authentication are achieved, but at the enormous price of abandoning the quest to present personal history in and as literary form.

Brown's "Preface," written notably by himself and not by a white guarantor, is peculiar in that it introduces both his narrative and the text authenticated by the narrative, *Clotel; or, The President's Daughter*. By and large, the tone of the "Preface" is sophisticated and generally that of a self-assured writer. Unlike Bibb or Northup, Brown does not skirmish with other authenticators for authorial control of the text, nor is he anxious about competition from other literary quarters of the antislavery ranks. He scans briefly the history of slavery in North America and reasons, with the British (with whom he resides after passage of the 1850 Fugitive Slave Law), that they who controlled the American colonies when slavery was introduced should feel "a lively interest in its abolition." All this is done without resort to conventional apologia or the confession of verbal deficiencies; Brown is humble not so much in his rhetoric as in his goal: "If the incidents set forth in the following pages should add anything new to the information already given to the public through similar publications, and should thereby aid in bringing British influence to bear upon American slavery, the main object for which this work was written will have been accomplished." That Brown introduces a personal narrative and a somewhat fictive narrative *(Clotel)* with language and intentions commonly reserved for works of history and journalism constitutes his first admission of being motivated by extraliterary concerns. His second admission emerges from his persistent use of the term "memoir." In contrast to a confession or autobiography, a memoir refers specifically to an author's recollections of his public life, far more than to his rendering of personal history as literary form or metaphor. This former kind of portrait is, of course, exactly what Brown gives us in his narrative.

The narrative is, as I have indicated, bereft of authorship. Brown rarely renders in fresh language those incidents of which he has written elsewhere; he simply quotes himself. His posture as the editor and not the author of his tale disallows any true expression of intimacy with his personal past. This feature is reinforced by certain objectifying and distancing qualities created by third-person narration. Brown's 1847 narrative begins, "I was born in Lexington, Ky. The man who stole me as soon as I was born, recorded the births of all the infants which he claimed to be born his property, in a book which he kept for that purpose. . . ." Thus, it inaugurates the kind of personal voice and hardboiled prose which is Brown's contribution to early Afro-American letters. In contrast, the opening of the 1852 narrative is flat, without pith or strength: "William Wells Brown, the subject of this narrative, was born a slave in Lexington, Kentucky, not far from the residence of the late Hon. Henry Clay." These words do not constitute effective writing, but that is not Brown's goal. The goal is, rather, authentication, and the seemingly superfluous aside about Henry Clay—which in another narrative might very well generate the first ironic thrust against America's moral blindness—appears for the exclusive purpose of validation. In this way Brown commences an authentication strategy which he will pursue throughout the tale.

The tale or memoir is eclectic in its collection of disparate texts; however, very few of the collected texts merit discussion. I will simply list their types to suggest both their variety and their usefulness to Brown:

1. The scrap of verse, usually effusive, always saccharine, culled from antislavery poets known and unknown. The verse expresses high sentiment and deep emotion when the text requires it, engages the popular reading public, and suggests erudition and sensitivity.

2. Quotations from Brown's speeches at famous institutions like Exeter Hall and from "addresses" bestowed on him after such speeches. These advance the memoir, embellish Brown's résumé, and authenticate his claim that he was where he said he was.

3. Quotations from Brown's travel book, *Three Years in Europe*, and from the book's reviews. The passages of personal history advance the memoir and validate "The energy of the man," as well as call attention to the book. The reviews call further attention to the book, and authenticate Brown's literacy and good character.

4. Testimonies and testimonials from various abolitionist groups in the United States and England, white and colored. These texts profess the success of Brown's labors as a lecturing agent, "commend him to the hospitality and encouragement of all true friends of humanity," and, upon his departure for England, provide him with what Douglass would have termed a "protection" for his travels. These are, in short, recommending letters attached to Brown's résumé validating his character and the fact that he is a fugitive slave.

5. Two letters from a former master, Enoch Price of St. Louis, dated before and after the Fugitive Slave Law was passed in 1850.

The Enoch Price letters are undoubtedly the most interesting documents in Brown's compendium, and he makes good narrative use of them. While the other assembled documents merely serve the authenticating strategy, Price's letters, in their portrait of a slaveholder ironically invoking the dictates of fair play while vainly attempting to exact a bargain price for Brown from his benefactors, actually tell us something about Brown's circumstances. Despite the lionizing illustrated by the other documents, Brown is still not a free man. He is most aware of this, and for this reason the narrative concludes, not with another encomium, but with the second of Price's letters once again requesting payment—payment for lost property, payment for papers that will set Brown free. All Brown can do under the circumstances is refuse to acknowledge Price's supposed right to payment, and order his present condition by controlling not so much his tale, which is his past, as the authentication of himself, which is his present and possibly his future. As the editor of his résumé—his present circumstance—Brown must acknowledge slavery's looming presence in his life, but he can also attempt to bury it beneath a mountain of antislavery rhetoric and self-authenticating documentation. Through the act of self-authentication Brown may contextualize slavery and thereby control it. In these terms, then, the heroic proportions to Brown's editorial act of including and manipulating Enoch Price's letters become manifest.

Brown's personal narrative most certainly authenticates himself, but how does it also authenticate *Clotel*? The answer takes us back to Brown's "Preface," where he outlines the extraliterary goals of both narratives, and forward to the concluding chapter of *Clotel*, where he writes:

> My narrative has now come to a close. I may be asked, and no doubt shall, Are the various incidents and scenes related founded in truth? I answer, Yes. I have personally participated in many of those scenes. Some of the narratives I have derived from other sources; many from the lips of those who, like myself, have run away from the land of bondage. . . . To Mrs. Child, of New York, I am indebted for part of a short story. American Abolitionist journals are another source from whence some of the characters appearing in my narrative are taken. All these combined have made up my story.

Brown's personal narrative functions, then, as a successful rhetorical device, authenticating his *access* to the incidents, characters, scenes, and tales which collectively make up *Clotel*. In the end, we witness a dynamic interplay between the two narratives, established by the need of each for resolution and authentication within the other. Since *Clotel* is not fully formed as either a fiction or a slave narrative, it requires completion of some sort, and finds this when it is transformed into a fairly effective antislavery device through linkage with its prefatory authenticating text. Since Brown's personal narrative is not fully formed as either an autobiography or a slave narrative, it requires fulfillment as a literary form through intimacy with a larger, more developed but related text. *Clotel* is no more a novel than Brown's preceding personal narrative is autobiography, but together they represent a roughly hewn literary tool which is, despite its defects, a sophisticated departure from the primary phases of slave narration and authentication.

Brown's personal narrative is hardly an aesthetic work, but that is because Brown had other goals in mind. He is willing to forsake the goal of presenting personal history in literary form in order to promote his books and projects like the Manual Labor School for fugitive slaves in Canada, to authenticate *Clotel*, and to authenticate himself while on British soil. He is willing to abandon the goals of true authorship and to assume instead the duties of an editor in order to gain some measure of control over the present, as opposed to illuminating the past. Brown's narrative is present and future oriented: most of his anecdotes from the past are offered as testimony to the energy and character he will bring to bear on future tasks. In short, just as Douglass inaugurates the autobiographical mode in Afro-American letters, Brown establishes what curiously turns out to be the equally common mode of the authenticating narrative. To see the popularity and great effect of the Afro-American authenticating narrative—once it assumes a more sophisticated form—one need look no further than Booker T. Washington's *Up from Slavery*.

HENRY LOUIS GATES, JR. (b. 1950)

Henry Louis Gates, Jr., is a prominent critic and scholar of African American literature. He was born in Keyser, West Virginia, and grew up in Piedmont, West Virginia. He excelled, graduated with honors from Yale and entered Cambridge University in 1973. Gates started teaching in 1976 at Yale and in 1981 won a MacArthur Foundation Fellowship. In 1983, he published Our Nig; or, Sketches from the Life of a Free Black—*a nineteenth-century novel by Harriet E. Wilson that he discovered around 1981. In 1985, Gates became a professor of African studies and English at Cornell University. While at Cornell, he wrote two important works of African American literary criticism:* Figure in Black: Words, Signs, and the Racial Self *(1987) and* The Signifying Monkey: A Theory of Afro-American Literary Criticism *(1988), which won an American Book Award.*

Gates's career took him from Duke University to Harvard University in 1991. At Harvard he is W. E. B. Du Bois Professor of Humanities, director of the W. E. B. Du Bois Institute for Afro-American Research, and chair of African American studies. An excerpt from his 1992 work, Loose Canons: Notes on the Culture Wars, *appears here.*

From Loose Canons: Notes on the Culture Wars (1992)

"Tell Me, Sir, . . . What *Is* 'Black' Literature?"

In memory of James A. Snead

> . . . even today, it seems to me (possibly because I am black) very dangerous to model one's opposition to the arbitrary definition, the imposed ordeal. merely on the example supplied by one's oppressor.
>
> The object of one's hatred is never, alas, conveniently outside but is seated in one's lap, stirring in one's bowels and dictating the beat of one's heart. And if one does not know this, one risks becoming an imitation—and, therefore. a continuation—of principles one imagines oneself to despise.
>
> —James Baldwin, "Here Be Dragons"

For those of us who were students or professors of African or African-American literature in the late sixties or through the seventies, it is a thing of wonder to behold the various ways in which our specialties and the works we explicate and teach have moved, if not exactly from the margins to the center of the profession of literature, at least from defensive postures to a position of generally accepted validity. My own graduate students often greet with polite skepticism an anecdote I draw on in the introduction to my seminars. When I was a student at the University of Cambridge, Wole Soyinka, recently released from a two-year confinement in a Nigerian prison, was on campus to deliver a lecture series on African literature (collected and published by Cambridge in 1976 under the title *Myth, Literature, and the African World*). Soyinka had come to Cambridge in 1973 from Ghana, where he had been living in exile, ostensibly to assume a two-year lectureship in the faculty of English. To his astonishment, as he told me in our first supervision, the faculty of English apparently did not recognize African literature as a legitimate area of study within the "English" tripos, so he had been forced to accept an appointment in social anthropology, of all things! (Much later, the distinguished Nigerian literary scholar Emmanuel Obiechina related a similar tale when I asked him why he had taken his Cambridge doctorate in social anthropology.) Shortly after I heard Soyinka's story, I asked the tutor in English at Clare College, Cambridge, why Soyinka had been treated this way, explaining as politely as I could that I would very much like to write a doctoral thesis on "black literature." To which the tutor replied with great disdain, "Tell me, sir, . . . what *is* black literature?" When I responded with a veritable bibliography of texts written by authors who were black, his evident irritation informed me that I had taken as a serious request for information what he had intended as a rhetorical question.

Few, if any, students or scholars of African or African-American literature encounter the sort of hostility, skepticism, or suspicion that Soyinka, Obiechina, and I did at the University of Cambridge. (To be perfectly fair, I should add that I was later able to find professors who, confessing their ignorance of my topic, were quite willing to allow me to work with them and to write the Ph.D. thesis I chose.

The faculty of English there is even trying to fund a chair in "Commonwealth Literature.") At Oxford, meanwhile, a scholar of African-American literature is to deliver the Clarendon Lectures in the spring of 1992. At Oxford, Cambridge, Sussex, Birmingham, and Kent—to list just a few institutions—sophisticated and innovative work in "postcolonial" literary criticism is defining this branch of study. Many of the youngest scholars in the field are accepting teaching positions in Africa, India, Pakistan, and throughout the "Third World," attempting to wrestle control of pedagogy and scholarship from older conservative scholars, who are still under the spell of F. R. Leavis (whose influence on "Third World" literary pedagogy merits several doctoral dissertations) and who still believe in the possibility of a "pretheoretical" practical criticism.

In the United States, the status of black literatures within the academy has changed even more dramatically. Since 1985, according to the *MLA Job Information Lists*, few departments of English, for example, have not engaged in, or will not continue to engage in, searches for junior and senior professors of African-American, African, or postcolonial literatures. Because of the sharp increase in demand, along with the scarcity of Ph.D.'s in these fields, scholars of African-American literature commonly find themselves pursued by several departments competing to make imaginative job offers—especially at institutions that confuse the inclusion of black studies with affirmative action. Although non-minority job seekers in this area sometimes encounter difficulties reaching, or surviving, interviews at the MLA convention (if their ethnic identities have not been ascertained beforehand, often by phone calls to their referees) several of the major scholar-critics of African-American and African literature are white. (Last year, I wrote *forty-nine* letters of recommendation for one talented white job candidate in African literature; all forty-nine applications were unsuccessful.) Despite such exceptional instances, however, African-American and African literatures have never been more widely taught or analyzed in the academy than they are today. We have come a long way since the early twenties, when Charles Eaton Burch (1891–1941), as chairman of the department of English at Howard, introduced into the curriculum a course entitled Poetry and Prose of Negro Life, and a long way, too, from the mid-thirties, when James Weldon Johnson, then the Adam K. Spence Professor of Creative Literature and Writing at Fisk University, became the first scholar to teach black literature at a white institution, New York University, where he delivered an annual lecture series on "Negro Literature."

These larger changes, however, have yet to reach the high schools. As Arthur N. Applebee reports, Shakespeare, Steinbeck, Dickens, and Twain are the most frequently required authors, even in public schools with the highest proportion of minority students. In public schools overall, only Lorraine Hansberry and Richard Wright appear among the top fifty authors required in English classes between grades 7 and 12. In urban schools they rank twenty-fifth and thirty-seventh. In schools with a 50 percent or higher minority enrollment, they rank only fourteenth and seventeenth. (Wright's *Black Boy*, in contrast, is among the three books most frequently banned from public schools.) These figures are still more surprising when we recall the extraordinarily large sales of the novels of Toni Morrison, Alice Walker, and Gloria Naylor. Clearly the opening of the canon in traditional university literature departments has not yet affected the pedagogical practices of high school teachers.

What has happened within the profession of literature at the college level to elevate the status of African-American and other "minority" texts within the past decade and a half? It is difficult to be certain about the reasons for the heightened popularity of any area of study. Nevertheless, we can isolate several factors that, in retrospect, seem to bear directly both on the growth of student interest in these fields—an interest that has never been greater, if we can judge from the proliferation of titles being produced and the high sales figures—and on the vast increase in the number of teachers attempting to satisfy student demand.

One factor would seem to be the women's movement within African-American and African literature. Since 1970, when Toni Morrison published *The Bluest Eye,* Alice Walker published *The Third Life of Grange Copeland,* and Toni Cade Bambara published her anthology, *The Black Woman,* black women writers have produced a remarkable number of novels and books of poetry. Morrison alone has published five novels, Walker four, and Gloria Naylor three. The list of black women writers with first and second novels is a very long one. Walker, Morrison, Naylor, and, in poetry, Rita Dove have won Pulitzer Prizes and National and American Book Awards: before 1970, Ralph Ellison and Gwendolyn Brooks were the only black writers who had been accorded these honors. The works by black women novelists, especially Walker and Morrison, are selling in record-breaking numbers, in part because of an expanded market that includes white and black feminists as well as the general black studies readership. What has happened, clearly, is that the feminist movement, in the form of women's studies on campus and the abandonment of quotas for the admission of women to heretofore elite male institutions, has had a direct impact on what we might think of as black women's studies. Indeed, black studies and women's studies have met on the common terrain of black women's studies, ensuring a larger audience for black women authors than ever before.

Scholars of women's studies have accepted the work and lives of black women as their subject matter in a manner unprecedented in the American academy. Perhaps only the Anglo-American abolitionist movement was as cosmopolitan as the women's movement has been in its concern for the literature of blacks. Certainly, Richard Wright, Ralph Ellison, and James Baldwin did not become the subjects of essays, reviews, books, and dissertations as quickly as Morrison and Walker have. Hurston, of course, attracted her largest following only after 1975, precisely when other black women authors rose to prominence. The women's studies movement in the academy has given new life to African-American studies, broadly conceived.

Forecasts of the death of African-American studies abounded in 1975. Although the field had benefited from a great burst of interest in the late sixties, when student protests on its behalf were at their noisiest, it had begun to stagnate by the mid-seventies, as many ill-conceived, politically overt programs collapsed or were relegated to an even more marginal status than they had had before. American publishers, ever sensitive to their own predictions about market size, became reluctant to publish works in this field. Toni Morrison, however, herself an editor at Random House, continued to publish texts by black women and men, from Africa, the Caribbean, and the United States. The burgeoning sales of books by black women, for many of whom Morrison served as editor, began to reverse the trends that by 1975 had jeopardized the survival of black studies. Morrison's own novels, especially *Tar Baby* (1981), which led to a cover story in *Newsweek*, were pivotal in redefining the market for books in black studies. The popularity of—and the controversy surrounding—Michele Wallace's *Black Macho and the Myth of the Superwoman* (1978) and Ntozake Shange's *For Coloured Girls Who Have Considered Suicide* (1976) also generated a great amount of interest in the writings of black women.

Simultaneously, within the academy, scholars of black literature were undertaking important projects that would bear directly on the direction of their field. Whereas in the late sixties, when black studies formally entered the curriculum, history had been the predominant subject, a decade later, literary studies had become the "glamor" area of black studies. While the black arts movement of the mid-sixties had declared literature, and especially poetry, to be the cultural wing of the black power revolution, it had little effect on the curricula offered by traditional departments of English. As Kimberly Benston aptly characterizes the import of this movement, "the profound reorientation of energy and vision which took place among Afro-American thinkers, writers, performers, and their audiences during this period, centering on considerations of a nationalist, or *sui generis*, understanding of the 'black self,' took place through dynamic and complex *disputations* about the provenance, nature, and teleology of the sign of blackness." More than any other single factor, the black arts movement gave birth to the larger black studies movement, even if it did not have a direct impact on traditional university literature departments. This intervention would be dependent on the studies produced by a group of younger scholars—Donald Gibson, June Jordan, Houston A. Baker, Jr., Robert Stepto, Arnold Rampersad, Geneva Smitherman, Jerry Ward, Mary Helen Washington, Kimberly Benston, Addison Gayle, Werner Sollors, Stephen Henderson, Sherley Anne Williams, Carolyn Fowler, R. Baxter Miller, and others—many of whom had been trained by an older generation of African-Americanists. That generation included such literary critics as Charles Davis, Charles Nilon, Michael G. Cooke, Margaret Walker, Charles Nichols, Richard Barksdale, Blyden Jackson, Darwin Turner, and J. Saunders Redding, many of whom had been recruited to previously segregated schools in response to student demands for the creation of black studies, as well as Arthur P. Davis, Hugh Gloster, Sterling Brown, and others who remained at historically black colleges.

For a variety of reasons, and in a remarkable variety of ways, these scholars began to theorize about the nature and function of black literature and its criticism and, simultaneously, to train an even younger generation of students. While it is difficult, precisely, to characterize their concerns, it seems safe to say that they shared a concern with the "literariness" of African-American works, as they wrestled to make these texts a "proper" object of analysis within traditional departments of English. Whereas black literature had generally been taught and analyzed through an interdisciplinary methodology, in which sociology and history (and, for

African literature, anthropology) had virtually blocked out the "literariness" of the black text, these scholars, after 1975, began to argue for the explication of the formal properties of the writing. If the "blackness" of a text was to be found anywhere, they argued, it would be in the practical uses of language. So, at a time when theorists of European and Anglo-American literature were offering critiques of Anglo-American formalism, scholars of black literature, responding to the history of their own discipline, found it "radical" to teach formal methods of reading.

Of the several gestures that were of great importance to this movement, I can mention only three here. In chronological order, these are Dexter Fisher's *Minority Language and Literature* (1977), Dexter Fisher and Robert Stepto's *Afro-American Literature: The Reconstruction of Instruction* (1979), and Leslie Fiedler and Houston A. Baker, Jr.'s *Opening Up the Canon: Selected Papers from the English Institute, 1979* (1981). Conveniently, for my argument here, each of these anthologies, the published results of seminal conferences. expresses a different aspect of a larger movement.

The first two collections grew out of conferences sponsored by the Modern Language Association (MLA), while the third was sponsored by the English Institute. "In an effort to address the critical, philosophical, pedagogical, and curricular issues surrounding the teaching of minority literature." Dexter Fisher explains in her introduction to *Minority Language and Literature*, the MLA in 1972 formed the Commission on Minority Groups and the Study of Language and Literature. (Until the early seventies, black scholars did not find the MLA a welcoming institution; they formed instead the predominantly black College Language Association, which still thrives today. The commission's establishment was an attempt, in part, to redefine the MLA sufficiently to "open up" its membership to black and other minority professors.) Beginning in 1974, the commission, funded by the National Endowment for the Humanities (NEH), sponsored various colloquiums "to stimulate greater awareness and to encourage more equitable representation of minority literature in the mainstream of literary studies." Fisher's book stemmed directly from a conference held in 1976, at which forty-four scholars. publishers, and foundation program officers came together to consider "the relationship of minority literature to the mainstream of American literary tradition":

> One of the major issues raised repeatedly at Commission-sponsored meetings is the relationship of minority literature to the mainstream of American literary tradition. The question of the "place" of minority literature in American literature raises a deeper, and perhaps more controversial, question: "In what ways does minority literature share the values and assumptions of the dominant culture, and in what ways does it express divergent perspectives?" This question has implications not only for curriculum development and critical theory, but also, and even more important, for the role of the humanities in bringing about a truly plural system of education.

The conference's participants, including J. Lee Greene, Mary Helen Washington, Michael G. Cooke, Michael Harper, Geneva Smitherman, and Houston A. Baker, Jr., each a specialist in African-American literature, explored the relations between "principles of criticism" and social contexts. As Fisher puts it nicely:

> The emergence of the Black Aesthetics Movement in the 1960s focused attention on the dilemma faced by minority writers trying to reconcile cultural dualism. Willingly or otherwise, minority writers inherit certain tenets of Western civilization through American society, though they often live alienated from that society. At the same time, they may write out of a cultural and linguistic tradition that sharply departs from the mainstream. Not only does this present constant social, political, and literary choices to minority writers, but it also challenges certain aesthetic principles of evaluation for the critic. When the cultural gap between writer and critic is too great, new critical approaches are needed.

Above all else, the conference was concerned with "revising the canons of American literature," a matter that Fiedler and Baker would explore in even broader terms three years later at the English Institute.

In the same year that Fisher's volume appeared, she and Robert Stepto, a professor of English, American, and Afro-American studies at Yale, again with NEH funding, convened a two-week seminar at Yale entitled Afro-American Literature: From Critical Approach to Course Design. The five seminar leaders—Fisher, Stepto, Robert O'Meally, Sherley Anne Williams, and I—defined its purpose as "the reconstruction of instruction": "in this case," as Fisher and Stepto put it, "to design courses in, and to refine critical approaches to, Afro-American literature yielding a 'literary' understanding of the literature." The "literary," Stepto explains, is contrasted with the " sociological," the "ideological, etc." Noting that "many schools still do not teach Afro-American literature, while other institutions offering courses in the field seem to be caught in a lockstep of stale critical and pedagogical ideas, many of which are tattered hand-me-downs from disciplines other than literature," Stepto and his colleagues, with all the zeal of reformers, sought to redefine African-American literary study by introducing into its explication formalist and structuralist methods of reading and by providing a critique of the essentialism of black aesthetic criticism that had grown out of the black arts movement. These scholars were intent on defining a canon of both African-American literature and its attendant formal critical practices.

As bold and as controversial as the Fisher–Stepto volume was within African-American literary studies, the volume edited by Fiedler and Baker was perhaps even more daring, since it sought to explode the notion that English is, somehow—or could ever be, somehow—a neutral container for "world literature." Indeed, the institute's theme in 1979 was English as a World Language for Literature. The volume, featuring papers by Dennis Brutus and Edward Kamau Braithwaite on South African and Caribbean literature, respectively, carries a succinct yet seminal introduction by Baker that suggests something of the polemics generated by the notion that English might be anything but the most fertile and flexible language available to any writer for the fullest expression of literary sensibility. Baker's laconic remarks, made just a decade ago, suggest the heated responses of the institute's audiences to the participants' critique of the "neocolonialism" of traditional English studies and to Baker's observations that "the conception of English as a 'world language' is rooted in Western economic history" and that we must juxtapose "the economic ascendancy of English and the historical correlation between this academy and processes of modern thought." English literature, Baker concludes, is not what it appears to be:

> The fact that a Sotho writer claims that he has chosen English because it guarantees a wide audience and ensures access to the literary reproduction systems of a world market may be less important as a literary consideration than what the writer has actually made of the English language as a literary agency. One might want to ask, for example, what summits of experience inaccessible to occupants of the heartland have been incorporated into the world of English literature? What literary strategies have been employed by the Sotho writer to preserve and communicate culturally-specific meanings? What codes of analysis and evaluation must be articulated in order to render accurate explanations for a Sotho or a Tewa or a Yoruba literary work written in English?

These foundational volumes proved to be, each in its own way. enabling gestures for the growth of sophisticated theories and critical practices in African, Caribbean, and African-American literatures. In the past decade, scores of books and hundreds of essays, reflecting structuralists, poststructuralist, gay, lesbian, Marxist, and feminist theories and practices, have been devoted to the study of black literature. Even the essentialism of race itself, long thought to be a sacrosanct concept within African-American studies, has been extensively analyzed as a social construction rather than a thing. The black women's literary renaissance has found counterparts in Africa and the Caribbean. Since 1970 alone, fifty-six novels by black women have been published in the Caribbean. One scholar even declared recently that we are living in the age of the greatest African-American novelist (Morrison). Therefore the critical endeavor in black literary studies has a certain immediacy not found in other English studies. Derek Walcott's achievements in poetry and Soyinka's in the drama have had a similar effect on the study of Caribbean and African literature. That this generation of critics lives contemporaneousIy with the first black Nobel laureate is only one sign, albeit a large one, of the vibrancy and youth of the field today.

When the MLA's Executive Council and *PMLA*'s Editorial Board decided to introduce "special topics" into *PMLA*'s format, the unanimous choice for the first issue was African and African-American literature. Despite the great activity in the field, the journal had published only three essays in this area. And despite the large number of sessions devoted to such topics at the annual convention, membership in the African, black American, and ethnic divisions remained surprisingly low. While the black American division had grown by a remarkable 93.3 percent between 1985 and 1987, there were still only 319 members. We hoped that our announcement of this special topic would attract new members to these divisions.

We were not to be disappointed. Since 1987, when the first advertisement for this special topic appeared, memberships in the three divisions have grown dramatically.

And what is the current state of the field? While one can be encouraged by the important institutional interventions that are serving to integrate African and African-American literature into traditional literature departments and by the several editorial ventures that are making "lost" black texts available once again and generating sophisticated reference works and anthologies, black authors are still not well represented in many college curricula. (It is one of the paradoxes of pedagogic reform that the newfound prominence of black literature is still primarily a phenomenon of elite institutions.) Moreover, a large percentage of those who teach this literature are black, and such black scholars are themselves a diminishing presence in the profession. (In 1986, according to the National Research Council, blacks earned only seventy Ph.D.'s in all the humanities.) Thus we must conclude that the growth of the field within the academy depends in part on increasing the number of minority students in our graduate programs. The keen competition among literature departments for talented job candidates is based on scarcity; it is incumbent on the members of the MLA to develop viable recruitment mechanisms that will continue to diversify our graduate student population.

What, finally, can we say about the concerns of Africanists and African-Americanists? Virtually no one, it seems clear, believes that the texts written by black authors cohere into a tradition because the authors share certain innate characteristics. Opposing the essentialism of European "universality" with a dark essentialism—an approach that in various ways had characterized a large component of black literary criticism since the black arts movement—has given way to subtler questions. What is following the critique of the essentialist notions that cloaked the text in a mantle of "blackness," replete with the accretions of all sorts of sociological clichés, is a "postformal" resituation of texts, accounting for the social dynamism of subjection, incorporation, and marginalization in relation to the cultural dominant.

Black literature, recent critics seem to be saying, can no longer simply name the "margin." Close readings are increasingly naming the specificity of black-texts, revealing the depth and range of cultural details far beyond the economic exploitation of blacks by whites. This increased focus on the specificity of the text has enabled us to begin to chart the patterns of repetition and revision among texts by black authors. In *Notes of a Native Son* James Baldwin described his own obsession with "race" in his fiction: "I have not written about being a Negro at such length because I expect that to be my only subject, but only because it was the gate I had to unlock before I could hope to write about anything else." One must *learn* to be "black" in this society, precisely because "blackness" is a socially produced category. Accordingly, many black authors read and revise one another, address similar themes, and repeat the cultural and linguistic codes of a common symbolic geography. For these reasons, we can think of them as forming literary traditions.

We might think of the development of African-American criticism over the past two decades in four distinct stages, beginning with the black arts movement of the mid and late sixties. The black arts movement, whose leading theoreticians were Amiri Baraka and Larry Neal, was a reaction against the New Criticism's formalism. The readings these critics advanced were broadly cultural and richly contextualized; they aimed to be "holistic" and based formal literature firmly on black urban vernacular, expressive culture. Art was a fundamental part of "the people"; "art for art's sake" was seen to be a concept alien to a "pan-African" sensibility, a sensibility that was whole, organic, and, of course, quite ahistorical. What was identified as European or Western essentialism—masked under the rubric of "universality"—was attacked by asserting an oppositional black or "neo-African" essentialism. In place of formalist notions about art, these critics promoted a poetics rooted in a social realism, indeed, in a sort of mimeticism; the relation between black art and black life was a direct one.

In response to what we might think of as the social organicism of the black arts movement, a formalist organicism emerged in the mid-seventies. This movement was concerned with redirecting the critic's attention to the "literariness" of the black texts as autotelic artifacts, to their status as "acts of language" first and foremost. The use of formalist and structuralist theories and modes of reading characterized the criticism of this period. The formalists saw their work as a "corrective" to the social realism of the black arts critics.

In the third stage, critics of black literature began to retheorize social—and textual—boundaries. Drawing on poststructuralist theory as well as deriving theories from black expressive, vernacular culture, these critics were able to escape both the social organicism of the black arts movement and the formalist organicism of the "reconstructionists." Their work might be characterized as a "new black aesthetic" movement, though it problematizes the categories of both the "black" and the "aesthetic." An initial phase of theorizing has given way to the generation of close readings that attend to the "social text" as well. These critics use close readings to reveal cultural contradictions and the social aspects of literature, the larger dynamics of subjection and incorporation through which the subject is produced.

This aspect of contemporary African-American literary studies is related directly to recent changes in critical approaches to American studies generally. Black studies has functioned as a strategic site for autocritique within American studies itself. No longer, for example, are the concepts of "black" and "white" thought to be preconstituted; rather, they are mutually constitutive and socially produced. The theoretical work of feminist critics of African and African-American literature, moreover, has turned away from a naively additive notion of sexism and racism. Especially in this work, we have come to understand that critiques of "essentialism" are inadequate to explain the complex social dynamism of marginalized cultures.

Richard Wright once argued, polemically, that if white racism did not exist, then black literature would not exist, and he predicted the demise of the latter with the cessation of the former. It is difficult to deny that certain elements of African-American culture are the products of cross-cultural encounters with white racism. But black culture, these close readings reveal, is radically underdetermined by the social dynamism of white racism. While it is important to criticize nativistic essentialism, in doing so we can lose sight of the larger social dynamic, the things that make people come together into groups in the first place. Developments in African-American studies have helped to reveal the factitious nature of an "American" identity; that which had been systematically excluded has now been revoiced as a mainstream concern.

✸ TONI MORRISON (b. 1931)

Toni Morrison has become one of the major African American novelists of the twentieth century. Her works are often complex pieces of art that deal with human relationships. Her characters come to life because of her skillful use of language. Each of her texts presents a challenge to readers who must make connections and interpret meaning.

She was born in Lorain, Ohio and given the name Chloe Anthony Wofford. She changed her name to simplify it during her college years. She attended Howard University and later taught there. She also worked as a textbook editor for Random House. Her first novel, The Bluest Eye *(1969), provided a good start for her career as a novelist. The text presents a black female child's search for identity within the context of white society.* Sula *(1973) also deals with personal identity and family relations of black women.* Song of Solomon *(1977) explores black male issues; the text won the National Book Critics Circle Award and the American Academy of Arts and Letters Award. In 1981, she published* Tar Baby *and her novel* Beloved *(1987) won the Pulitzer Prize in 1988. She followed with* Jazz *(1992) and* Paradise *(1998). She received the Nobel Prize for literature in 1993.*

From Playing in the Dark: Whiteness and the Literary Imagination (1992)

Disturbing Nurses and the Kindness of Sharks

Race has become metaphorical—a way of referring to and disguising forces, events, classes, and expressions of social decay and economic division far more threatening to the body politic than biological "race" ever was. Expensively kept, economically unsound, a spurious and useless political asset in election campaigns, racism is as healthy today as it was during the Enlightenment. It seems that it has a utility far beyond economy, beyond the sequestering of classes from one another, and has assumed a metaphorical life so completely embedded in daily discourse that it is perhaps more necessary and more on display than ever before.

I am prepared to be corrected on this point insofar as it misrepresents the shelf life of racism in social and political behavior. But I remain convinced that the metaphorical and metaphysical uses of race occupy definitive places in American literature, in the "national" character, and ought to be a major concern of the literary scholarship that tries to know it.

. . . I wish to observe and trace the transformation of American Africanism from its simplistic, though menacing, purposes of establishing hierarchic difference to its surrogate properties as self-reflexive meditations on the loss of difference, to its lush and fully blossomed existence in the rhetoric of dread and desire.

My suggestion that Africanism has come to have a metaphysical necessity should in no way be understood to imply that it has lost its ideological utility. There is still much ill-gotten gain to reap from rationalizing power grabs and clutches with inferences of inferiority and the ranking of differences. There is still much national solace in continuing dreams of democratic egalitarianism available by hiding class conflict, rage, and impotence in figurations of race. And there is quite a lot of juice to be extracted from plummy reminiscences of "individualism" and "freedom" if the tree upon which such fruit hangs is a black population forced to serve as freedom's polar opposite: individualism is foregrounded (and believed in) when its background is stereotypified, enforced dependency. Freedom (to move, to earn, to learn, to be allied with a powerful center, to narrate the world) can be relished more deeply in a cheek-by-jowl existence with the bound and unfree, the economically oppressed, the marginalized, the silenced. The ideological dependence on racialism is intact and, like its metaphysical existence, offers in historical, political, and literary discourse a safe route into meditations on morality and ethics; a way of examining the mind-body dichotomy; a way of thinking about justice; a way of contemplating the modern world.

Surely, it will be said, white America has considered questions of morality and ethics, the supremacy of mind and the vulnerability of body, the blessings and liabilities of progress and modernity, without reference to the situation of its black population. After all, it will be argued, where does one find a fulsome record that such a referent was part of these deliberations? My answer to these questions is another: where is it not?

In what public discourse does the reference to black people not exist? It exists in every one of this nation's mightiest struggles. The presence of black people is not only a major referent in the framing of the Constitution, it is also in the battle over enfranchising unpropertied citizens, women, the illiterate. It is there in the construction of a free and public school system; the balancing of representation in legislative bodies; jurisprudence and legal definitions of justice. It is there in theological discourse; the memoranda of banking houses; the concept of manifest destiny and the preeminent narrative that accompanies (if it does not precede) the initiation of every immigrant into the community of American citizens. The presence of black people is inherent, along with gender and family ties, in the earliest lesson every child is taught regarding his or her distinctiveness. Africanism is inextricable from the definition of Americanness—from its origins on through its integrated or disintegrating twentieth-century self.

The literature of the United States, like its history, represents commentary on the transformations of biological, ideological, and metaphysical concepts of racial difference. But the literature has an additional concern and subject matter: the private imagination interacting with the external world it inhabits. Literature redistributes and mutates in figurative language the social conventions of Africanism. In minstrelsy, a layer of blackness applied to a white face released it from law. Just as entertainers, through or by association with blackface, could render permissible topics that otherwise would have been taboo, so American writers were able to employ an imagined Africanist persona to articulate and imaginatively act out the forbidden in American culture.

Encoded or explicit, indirect or overt, the linguistic responses to an Africanist presence complicate texts, sometimes contradicting them entirely. A writer's response to American Africanism often provides a subtext that either sabotages the surface text's expressed intentions or escapes them through a language that mystifies what it cannot bring itself to articulate but still attempts to register.

Linguistic responses to Africanism serve the text by further problematizing its matter with resonances and luminations. They can serve as allegorical fodder for the contemplation of Eden, expulsion, and the availability of grace. They provide paradox, ambiguity; they strategize omissions, repetitions, disruptions, polarities, reifications, violence. In other words, they give the text a deeper, richer, more complex life than the sanitized one commonly presented to us.

In his book on Faulkner, James Snead comments that racial divisions "show their flaws best in written form":

> Racism might be considered a normative recipe for domination created by speakers using rhetorical tactics. The characteristic figures of racial division repeat on the level of phoneme, sentence, and story: (1) The fear of merging, or loss of identity through synergistic union with the other, leads to the wish to use racial purification as a separating strategy against difference; (2) Marking, or supplying physically significant (usually visual) characteristics with internal value equivalents, sharpening, by visual antithesis, their conceptual utility; (3) Spatial and conceptual separation, often facilitated through unequal verbal substitutions that tend to omit and distance a subordinate class from realms of value and esteem; (4) Repetition, or pleonastic reinforcement of these antitheses in writing, storytelling, or hearsay; (5) Invective and threat, exemplified in random and unpredictable violence to punish real or imagined crimes; (6) Omission and concealment of the process by a sort of paralepsis that claims discrimination to be self-evidently valid and natural.

"Faulkner," he goes on to say, "counters these social figures with literary devices of his own."

Following Snead's helpful categories, it may be useful to list some of the common linguistic strategies employed in fiction to engage the serious consequences of blacks.

1. Economy of stereotype. This allows the writer a quick and easy image without the responsibility of specificity, accuracy, or even narratively useful description.

2. Metonymic displacement. This promises much but delivers little and counts on the reader's complicity in the dismissal. Color coding and other physical traits become metonyms that displace rather than signify the Africanist character.

3. Metaphysical condensation. This allows the writer to transform social and historical differences into universal differences. Collapsing persons into animals prevents human contact and exchange; equating speech with grunts or other animal sounds closes off the possibility of communication.

4. Fetishization. This is especially useful in evoking erotic fears or desires and establishing fixed and major difference where difference does not exist or is minimal. Blood, for example, is a pervasive fetish: black blood, white blood, the purity of blood; the purity of white female sexuality, the pollution of African blood and sex. Fetishization is a strategy often used to assert the categorical absolutism of civilization and savagery.

5. Dehistoricizing allegory. This produces foreclosure rather than disclosure. If difference is made so vast that the civilizing process becomes indefinite—

taking place across an unspecified infinite amount of time—history, as a process of becoming, is excluded from the literary encounter. Flannery O'Connor's "The Artificial Nigger" makes this point with reference to Mr. Head's triumphantly racist views in that brilliant story. Carson McCullers deploys allegory among her characters in *The Heart Is a Lonely Hunter*, to mourn the inevitability of closure and the fruitlessness of monologue. Melville uses allegorical formations—the white whale, the racially mixed crew, the black-white pairings of male couples, the questing, questioning white male captain who confronts impenetrable whiteness—to investigate and analyze hierarchic difference. Poe deploys allegorical mechanisms in *Pym* not to confront and explore, as Melville does, but to evade and simultaneously register the cul de sac, the estrangement, the non-sequitur that is entailed in racial difference. William Styron opens and closes *The Confessions of Nat Turner* with the sealed white structure that serves as an allegorical figuration of the defeat of the enterprise he is engaged in: penetration of the black-white barrier.

6. Patterns of explosive, disjointed, repetitive language. These indicate a loss of control in the text that is attributed to the objects of its attention rather than to the text's own dynamics.

I have gone on at some length about these linguistic strategies because I want to make use of them in a specific connection.

My interest in Ernest Hemingway becomes heightened when I consider how much apart his work is from African-Americans. That is, he has no need, desire, or awareness of them either as readers of his work or as people existing anywhere other than in his imaginative (and imaginatively lived) world. I find, therefore, his use of African-Americans much more artless and unselfconscious than Poe's, for example, where social unease required the servile black bodies in his work.

Hemingway's work could be described as innocent of nineteenth-century ideological agenda as well as free of what may be called recent, postmodernist sensitivity. With this in mind, a look at how Hemingway's fiction is affected by an Africanist presence—when it makes the writing belie itself, contradict itself, or depend on that presence for attempts at resolution—can be taken by way of a "pure" case to test some of the propositions I have been advancing.

I begin with the novel said by many to be intentionally political, *To Have and Have Not* (published in 1937). Harry Morgan, the central figure, seems to represent the classic American hero: a solitary man battling a government that would limit his freedom and his individuality. He is romantically and sentimentally respectful of the nature he destroys for a living (deep-sea fishing)—competent, street-wise, knowing, and impatient with those who are not. He is virile, risk-taking, risk-loving, and so righteous and guiltless in his evaluation of himself that it seems a shame to question or challenge it. Before I do challenge it, I want to examine how Hemingway shows the reader that Harry is knowing, virile, free, brave, and moral.

Only ten pages into the novel we encounter the Africanist presence. Harry includes a "nigger" in his crew, a man who, throughout all of part one, has no name. His appearance is signaled by the sentence, "Just then this nigger we had getting bait comes down the dock." The black man is not only nameless for five chapters, he is not even hired, just someone "we had getting bait"—a kind of trained response, not an agent possessing a job. His inclusion on the voyage, objected to by the white client, Johnson, is defended by Harry on the basis of the black man's skill: he "put on a nice bait and he was fast." The rest of the time, we are told, this nameless man sleeps and reads the papers.

Something very curious happens to this namelessness when, in part two, the author shifts voices. Part one is told in the first person, and whenever Harry thinks about this black man he thinks "nigger." In part two, where Hemingway uses the third-person point of view in narrating and representing Harry's speech, two formulations of the black man occur: he both remains nameless and stereotyped and becomes named and personalized.

Harry *says* "Wesley" when speaking to the black man in direct dialogue; Hemingway *writes* "nigger" when as narrator he refers to him. Needless to report, this black man is never identified as one (except in his own mind). Part two reserves and repeats the word "man" for Harry. The spatial and conceptual difference is marked by the shortcut that the term "nigger" allows, with all of its color and caste implications. The term occupies a territory between man and animal and thus withholds specificity even while marking it. This black character either does not speak (as a "nigger" he is silent) or speaks in very legislated and manipulated ways (as a " Wesley" his speech serves Harry's needs). Enforcing the silence of the "nigger" proves problematic in this action-narrative and requires of Hemingway some strenuous measures.

In part one, at a crucial moment during the fishing expedition, which has disappointed both the captain and his customer, the boat moves into promising waters. Harry is coaching Johnson; the black man is at the wheel. Earlier Harry assured us that the black man does nothing aside from cutting bait but read and sleep. But Hemingway realizes that Harry cannot be in two critical places at the same time, instructing the incompetent Johnson and guiding the vessel. It is important to remember that there is another person aboard, an alcoholic named Eddy, who is too unreliable to be given the responsibility of steering but who is given manhood and speech and a physical description. Eddy is white, and we know he is because nobody says so. Now, with Harry taking care of his customer and Eddy in a pleasant stupor, there is only the black man to tend the wheel.

When the sign heralding the promising waters arrives—the sighting of flying fish beyond the prow of the boat—the crewman facing forward ought to be the first to see them. In fact he is. The problem is how to acknowledge that first sighting and continue the muzzling of this "nigger" who, so far, has not said one word. The solution is a strangely awkward, oddly constructed sentence: "The nigger was still taking her out and I looked and saw he had seen a patch of flying fish burst out ahead." "Saw he had seen" is improbable in syntax, sense, and tense but, like other choices available to Hemingway, it is risked to avoid a speaking black. The problem this writer gives himself, then, is to say how one sees that someone else has already seen.

A better, certainly more graceful choice would be to have the black man cry out at the sighting. But the logic of the narrative's discrimination prevents a verbal initiative of importance to Harry's business coming from this nameless, sexless, nationless Africanist presence. It is the powerful one, the authoritative one, who sees. The power of looking is Harry's; the passive powerlessness is the black man's, though he himself does not speak of it. Silencing him, refusing him the opportunity of one important word, forces the author to abandon his search for transparency in the narrative act and to set up a curiously silent mate-captain relationship.

What would have been the cost, I wonder, of humanizing, genderizing, this character at the opening of the novel? For one thing, Harry would be positioned—set off, defined—very differently. He would have to be compared to a helpless alcoholic, a contemptible customer, and an individualized crew member with, at least by implication, an independent life. Harry would lack the juxtaposition and association with a vague presence suggesting sexual excitement, a possible threat to his virility and competence, violence under wraps. He would, finally, lack the complementarity of a figure who can be assumed to be in some way bound, fixed, unfree, and serviceable.

The proximity to violence is stressed at once in the novel, before the black crewman's entrance, by the shooting outside the café. The Cubans in this scene are separated not by nationality (all the people born in Cuba are Cubans) but as black and not black, Cubans and blacks. In this slaughter the blacks are singled out as the most gratuitously violent and savage. Hemingway writes:

> The nigger with the Tommy gun got his face almost into the street and gave the back of the wagon a burst from underneath and sure enough one came down . . . at ten feet the nigger shot him in the belly with the Tommy gun, with what must have been the last shot . . . old Pancho sat down hard and went over forwards. He was trying to come up, still holding onto the Luger, only he couldn't get his head up, when the nigger took the shotgun that was lying against the wheel of the car by the chauffeur and blew the side of his head off. Some nigger.

In part two, Harry and the black crewman do engage in dialogue, and the black man talks a great deal. The serviceability of the black man's speech, however, is transparent. What he says and when he says it are plotted to win admiration for Harry. Wesley's speech is restricted to grumbles and complaints and apologies for weakness. We hear the grumbles, the groans, the weakness as Wesley's responses to his gunshot wounds for three pages before we learn that Harry is also shot, and much worse than Wesley is. By contrast, Harry has not only not mentioned his own pain, he has taken Wesley's whining with compassion and done the difficult work of steering and tossing the contraband overboard in swift, stoic gestures of manliness. Information about Harry's more serious pain is deferred while we listen to Wesley:

> "I'm shot . . ."
> "You're just scared."
> "No, sir. I'm shot. And I'm hurting bad. I've been throbbing all night." . . .
> "I hurt," the nigger said. "I hurt worse all the time."
> "I'm sorry, Wesley," the man said. "But I got to steer."

"You treat a man no better than a dog," the nigger said. He was getting ugly now. But the man was still sorry for him.

Finally, our patience and Harry's exhausted, we get this exchange: "'Who the hell's shot worse?' he asked him. 'You or me?' 'You're shot worse,' the nigger said."

The choice and positioning of the naming process ("nigger," "Wesley," and, once, "negro") may seem arbitrary and confusing, but in fact it is carefully structured. Harry, in dialogue with a helpmate, cannot say "nigger" without offending the reader (if not the helpmate)—and losing his claim to compassionate behavior—so he uses a name. No such responsibility is taken on, however, by the legislating narrator, who always uses the generic and degrading term: "The nigger blubbered with his face against a sack. The man went on slowly lifting the sacked packages of liquor and dropping them over the side." Once Wesley has apologized, recognized, and accepted his inferiority, Harry can and does use "nigger," along with the proper name, in direct dialogue—in familiar camaraderie: "'Mr. Harry,' said the nigger, 'I'm sorry I couldn't help dump that stuff.' 'Hell,' said Harry, 'ain't no nigger any good when he's shot. You're a all right nigger, Wesley.'"

I mentioned two main categories of speech for the black man: grumbles and apology. But there is a third. Throughout the exchange, while the two men are suffering—one stoically, one whimperingly—the black man criticizes the white man in lapses between his whining and his terror. They are interesting lapses because they limn another Harry—a figure of antihuman negation and doom. Such lapses occur over and over again in Hemingway's fiction. Accusations of inhumanity, used as prophecies of doom, are repeatedly placed in the mouths of the blacks who people his work. "Ain't a man's life worth more than a load of liquor?" Wesley asks Harry. "Why don't people be honest and decent and make a decent honest living? . . . You don't care what happens to a man . . . You ain't hardly human." "'You ain't human,'" the nigger said. 'You ain't got human feelings.'"

The serviceability of the Africanist presence I have been describing becomes even more pronounced when Hemingway begins to describe male and female relationships. In this same novel, the last voice we hear is that of Harry's devoted wife, Marie, listing and celebrating the virtues, the virility and bravery, of her husband, who is now dead. The elements of her reverie can be schematically organized as follows: (1) virile, good, brave Harry; (2) racist views of Cuba; (3) black sexual invasion thwarted; (4) reification of whiteness.

Marie recalls him fondly as "snotty and strong and quick, and like some kind of expensive animal. It would always get me to just watch him move." Immediately following this encomium to sexuality and power and revered (expensive) brutality, she meditates on her hatred of Cubans (the Cubans killed Harry) and says they are "bad luck for Conchs" and "bad luck for anybody. They got too many niggers there too." This judgment is followed by her recollection of a trip she and Harry took to Havana when she was twenty-six years old. Harry had a lot of money then and while they walked in the park a "nigger" (as opposed to a Cuban, though the black man she is referring to is both black and Cuban), "said something" to Marie. Harry smacked him and threw his straw hat into the street where a taxi ran over it.

Marie remembers laughing so hard it made her belly ache. With nothing but a paragraph indention between them, the next reverie is a further association of Harry with sexuality, power, and protection. "That was the first time I ever made my hair blonde." The two anecdotes are connected in time and place and, significantly, by color as sexual coding. We do not know what the black man said, but the horror is that he said anything at all. It is enough that he spoke, claimed an intimacy perhaps, but certainly claimed a view and inserted his sexual self into their space and their consciousness. By initiating the remark, he was a speaking, therefore aggressive, presence. In Marie's recollection, sexuality, violence, class, and the retribution of an impartial machine are fused into an all-purpose black man.

The couple, Marie and Harry, is young and in love with obviously enough money to feel and be powerful in Cuba. Into that Eden comes the violating black male making impertinent remarks. The disrespect, with its sexual overtones, is punished at once by Harry's violence. He smacks the black man. Further, he picks up the fallen straw hat, violating the black man's property, just as the black man had sullied Harry's property—his wife. When the taxi, inhuman, onrushing, impartial machine, runs over the hat, it is as if the universe were rushing to participate in and validate Harry's response. It is this underscoring that makes Marie laugh—along with her obvious comfort in and adulation of this "strong and quick" husband of hers.

What follows in the beauty parlor is positioned as connected with and dependent on the episode of black invasion of privacy and intimation of sexuality from which Marie must be protected. The urgency to establish difference—a difference within the sexual context—is commanding. Marie tells us how she is transformed from black to white, from dark to blond. It is a painful and difficult process that turns out to be well worth the pain in its sexual, protective, differentiating payout: "They were working on it all afternoon and it was naturally so dark they didn't want to do it . . . but I kept telling them to see if they couldn't make it a little lighter . . . and all I'd say was, just see if you can't make it a little lighter."

When the bleaching and perming are done, Marie's satisfaction is decidedly sensual, if not explicitly sexual: "when I put my hand and touched it, and I couldn't believe it was me and I was so excited I was choked with it . . . I was so excited feeling all funny inside, sort of faint like." It is a genuine transformation. Marie becomes a self she can hardly believe, golden and soft and silky.

Her own sensual reaction to her whitening is echoed by Harry, who sees her and says, "Jesus, Marie, you're beautiful." And when she wants to hear more about her beauty, he tells her not to talk—just "Let's go to the hotel." This enhanced sexuality comes on the heels of a sexual intrusion by a black man.

What would have been the consequence if the insult to Marie had come from a white man? Would the bleaching have followed? If so, would it have been in such lush and sexually heightened language? What does establishing a difference from darkness to lightness accomplish for the concept of a self as sexually alive and potent? Or so powerful and coherent in the world?

These tourists in Havana meet a native of that city and have a privileged status because they are white. But to assure us that this status is both deserved and, by implication, potently generative, they encounter a molesting, physically inferior black male (his inferiority is designated by the fact that Harry does not use his fists, but slaps him) who represents the outlaw sexuality that, by comparison, spurs the narrative on to contemplation of a superior, legal, white counterpart.

Here we see Africanism used as a fundamental fictional technique by which to establish character. Within a milieu that threatens the dissolution of all distinctions of value—the milieu of the working poor, the unemployed, sinister Chinese, terrorist Cubans, violent but cowardly blacks, upper-class castrati, female predators—Harry and Marie (an ex-prostitute) gain potency, a generative sexuality. They solicit our admiration by the comparison that is struck between their claims to fully embodied humanity and a discredited Africanism. The voice of the text is complicit in these formulations: Africanism becomes not only a means of displaying authority but, in fact, constitutes its source.

The strategies that employ and distribute Africanism in *To Have and Have Not* become more sophisticated in the other work by Ernest Hemingway I will discuss here. In the posthumously published *The Garden of Eden* ideological Africanism is extended metaphorically to function as a systematic articulation, through an Africanist discursive practice and an Africanist mythology, of an entire aesthetics. Africanism—the fetishizing of color, the transference to blackness of the power of illicit sexuality, chaos, madness, impropriety, anarchy, strangeness, and helpless, hapless desire—provides a formidable field for a novel that works out the terms and maps a complete, if never formalized, aesthetics. Before describing this aesthetic field, I would like to mention one of the author's special concerns.

Hemingway's romantic attachment to a nurse is well documented in the fiction, in criticism, in biographical data, and more recently in the published recollection of the original nurse herself. The wounded soldier and the nurse is a familiar story and contains elements reliably poignant. To be in a difficult, even life-threatening position and to have someone dedicated to helping you, paid to help you, is soothing. And if you are bent on dramatic gestures of self-reliance, eager to prove that you can go it alone (without complaining), a nurse who chooses or is paid to take care of you does not violate your view of yourself as a brave, silent sufferer. Needfulness does not enter the picture; asking for help is always out of the question, and the benefits that derive from the attentive, expert care do not incur emotional debt.

Some of the other women in Hemingway's fiction who become objects of desire have the characteristics of nurses without the professional status. They are essentially the good wives or the good lovers, ministering, thoughtful, never needing to be told what the loved man needs. Such perfect nurses are rare, though important because they serve as a reference toward which the prose yearns. More common are the women who abandon or have difficulty sustaining their nursing abilities: women who destroy the silent sufferer, hurt him instead of nurturing him.

But in the exclusively male world that Hemingway usually prefers to inhabit, it would be missing something not to notice that there are nurse figures in the masculine domain as well. These characters are just as dedicated, thoughtful, and ministering of the narrator's needs as the few female nurses are. Some of these male nurses are explicitly, forthrightly tender helpers—with nothing to gain from their care but the most minimal wage or the pleasure of a satisfied patient. Other male nurses serve the narrator reluctantly, sullenly, but are excessively generous in the manner in which they serve the text. Cooperative or sullen, they are Tontos all, whose role is to do everything possible to serve the Lone Ranger without disturbing his indulgent delusion that he is indeed alone.

The reference is pertinent here, for not only is the Hemingway Ranger invariably accompanied but his Tontos, his nursemen, are almost always black. From the African bearers who tote the white man's burden in the hunting grounds of Africa, to the bait cutters aboard fishing boats, to loyal companions of decaying boxers, to ministering bartenders—the array of enabling black nursemen is impressive.

Along with their enabling properties are some disabling ones. They say— once their rank and status are signaled by the narrator and accepted by the black man—extraordinary things. Sam, the black man in "The Killers," tells Nick that "little boys always know what they want to do," scorning and dismissing what Nick takes on as his responsibility, commenting with derision on Nick's manhood. Wesley tells Harry Morgan, "You ain't hardly human." Bearers tell Francis Macomber that the lion is alive, and the buffalo too. Bugs in "The Battler" is described as a "gentle-voiced, crazy black man." According to Kenneth Lynn, Bugs "mothers" Ad, the ex-fighter deformed by his profession, "cooking him delicious fried ham and egg sandwiches and referring to him with unfailing politeness as Mister Francis. But the solicitous Negro is also a sadist, as the worn black leather on the blackjack he carries silently testifies. Master as well as slave, destroyer as well as caretaker, this black man is another of Hemingway's dark mother figures." Although this critic uses the label "mother," he is extrapolating not the biological relationship but the caretaking, nursing characteristic inherent in the term. When Ad gets unmanageable, Bugs smashes him with his blackjack. (Remember the slave Jupiter in Poe's "Gold-Bug" who has similar leave to whip his master.) Bugs has also been given the gift of prophecy: "He says he's never been crazy," Ad tells Bugs. Bugs replies, "He's got a lot coming to him." Lynn notes that, in the late 1950s, Hemingway would reveal to a friend "an astonishing touchiness about these ominous words, as though he considered them to be a prophecy fulfilled."

No matter if they are loyal or resistant nurses, nourishing *and* bashing the master's body, these black men articulate the narrator's doom and gainsay the protagonist-narrator's construction of himself. They modify his self-image; they violate the nurse's primary function of providing balm. In short, they disturb, in subtle and forceful ways, the narrator's construction of reality. We are left, as readers, wondering what to make of such prophecies, these slips of the pen, these clear and covert disturbances. And to wonder, as well, why they are placed so frequently in the mouths of black men.

It is as if the nurse were quite out of control. The other side of nursing, the opposite of the helping, healing hand, is the figure of destruction—the devouring predator whose inhuman and indifferent impulses pose immediate danger. Never still, always hungry, these figures are nevertheless seductive, elusive, and theatrical in their combination of power and deceit, love and death.

The devouring properties are given to women like Mrs. Macomber, women who slaughter their mates rather than see them in control and strongly independent. Hemingway describes the wife in "The Snows of Kilimanjaro" as "this kindly caretaker and destroyer of his talent." The black male nurses may verbalize destruction and doom, deny and contradict manliness, introduce and represent antagonism, but the Africanist codes keep them bound to their nursing function. The female nurses—as wives and lovers with caretaking as their primary role—give voice to and complete acts of destruction. They are predators, sharks, unnatural women who combine the signs of a nurse with those of the shark. This combination brings us back for a moment to *To Have and Have Not*.

During a passionate scene of lovemaking, when even the stump of Harry's arm is in sexual play, Marie asks her husband:

> "Listen, did you ever do it with a nigger wench?"
> "Sure."
> "What's it like?"
> "Like nurse shark."

This extraordinary remark is saved and savored for Hemingway's description of a black female. The strong notion here is that of a black female as the furthest thing from human, so far away as to be not even mammal but fish. The figure evokes a predatory, devouring eroticism and signals the antithesis to femininity, to nurturing, to nursing, to replenishment. In short, Harry's words mark something so brutal, contrary, and alien in its figuration that it does not belong to its own species and cannot be spoken of in language, in metaphor or metonym, evocative of anything resembling the woman to whom Harry is speaking—his wife Marie. The kindness he has done Marie is palpable. His projection of black female sexuality has provided her with solace, for which she is properly grateful. She responds to the kindness and giggles, "You're funny."

It would be irresponsible and unjustified to invest Hemingway with the thoughts of his characters. It is Harry who thinks a black woman is like a nurse shark, not Hemingway. An author is not personally accountable for the acts of his fictive creatures, although he is responsible for them. And there is no evidence I know of to persuade me that Hemingway shared Harry's views. In point of fact there is strong evidence to suggest the opposite.

In *The Garden of Eden* Catherine, the wife of the narrator/protagonist David Bourne, spends all her days tanning, and clearly requires this darkening process for complex reasons other than cosmetic. Early in the novel, David interrogates her about what appears to him, and to us, an obsession with the aesthetics of her body:

> "Why do you want to be so dark?"
> "I don't know. Why do you want anything? Right now it's the thing that I want most. That we don't have I mean. Doesn't it make you excited to have me getting so dark?"
> "Uh-huh. I love it."
> "Did you think I could ever be this dark?"

"No, because you're blond."

"I can because I'm lion color and they can go dark. But I want every part of me dark and it's getting that way and you'll be darker than an Indian and that takes us further away from other people. You see why it's important."

Catherine well understands the association of blackness with strangeness, with taboo—understands also that blackness is something one can "have" or appropriate; it's the one thing they lack, she tells him. Whiteness here is a deficiency. She comprehends how this acquisition of blackness "others" them and creates an ineffable bond between them—unifying them within the estrangement. When this lack is overcome, it is taken to be an assertion. The effect is heightened by Catherine's accompanying obsession with blonding her hair. Both of these coloring gestures—blackening up and whiting out—are codes Catherine imposes on David (inscribes on his body and places in his mind) to secure the sibling-twin emphasis that produces further sexual excitement.

The couple is not content with the brother-sister relationship; they require the further accent of twins, which the color coding, like the offprint of a negative, achieves. (This excitement of brother-sister incest is also the story the black man Bugs in "The Battler" tells Nick to explain why Ad went crazy: Ad's marriage dissolved after rumors that his wife was his sister.)

That story, acted out by a blacked-up couple in *The Garden of Eden*, is marked and stressed in its forbiddenness. Its voluptuous illegality is enforced by the associations constantly made between darkness and desire, darkness and irrationality, darkness and the thrill of evil. "Devil things," "night things," are Hemingway's descriptions of David and Catherine's appetites, and "Devil" becomes Catherine's nickname. "Just look at me," she says, after they have both had bleaching and haircuts, " That's how you are . . . And we're damned now. I was and now you are. Look at me and see how much you like it."

The remarkable and overt signs of brother-sister incest and of cross gender have occupied most of the published criticism of this novel. Unremarked is the Africanist field in which the drama is played out. Echoing Marie's tryst in the beauty parlor compelled by the specter of black sexuality she has just encountered, Catherine persuades herself that, while she needs regular hair whitening, she no longer needs tanning. "I don't really wear it," she says. "It's me. I really am this dark. The sun just develops it."

Catherine is both black and white, both male and female, and descends into madness once Marita appears, the "real" nurse, with dedicated, normal nursing functions. And it should be noted that Marita is naturally dark, with skin like the Javanese, a woman given to David by Catherine as a healing balm. The figurative gift that Harry gives Marie is analyzed and reformulated here: Catherine the shark gives David a dark nurse as an act of kindness. Her own nursing capabilities—her breasts—she calls her dowry. What is new and powerful and *hers* is the bleached white male-cut hair. It is a change Hemingway describes as "dark magic."

"When we go to Africa I want to be your African girl too," Catherine tells him. While we are not sure of exactly what this means to her, we are sure of what Africa means to him. Its availability as a blank, empty space into which he asserts himself, an uncreated void ready, waiting, and offering itself up for his artistic imagination, his work, his fiction, is unmistakable.

At the heart of *The Garden of Eden* is "Eden": the story David is writing about his adventures in Africa. It is a tale replete with male bonding, a father-son relationship, and even the elephant they track is loyal to his male companion. This fictional, Africanized Eden is sullied by the surrounding events of the larger Catherine-David Africanist Eden. Africa, imagined as innocent and under white control, is the inner story; Africanism, imagined as evil, chaotic, impenetrable, is the outer story.

The inner story Catherine despises and eventually destroys. She thinks it boring, irrelevant. David ought to be writing about her instead. The reader is made to understand and be repelled by her selfish narcissism. But in fact she is right. At least Hemingway thinks she is, for the story we are reading and the one he has written *is* about her. The African story David is struggling to write (and is able to write when Marita, the authentic dark nurse, takes over) is an old, familiar myth, Africa-as-Eden before and after its fall, where, as in "The Snows of Kilimanjaro," one goes to "work the fat off [one's] soul."

That story, which Catherine burns up, has value as a cherished masculine enclave of white domination and slaughter, complete with African servants who share David's "guilt and knowledge." But the narrative that encloses it, the blacked-up, Africanist one, comments thoroughly on an aestheticized blackness and a mythologized one. Both are fantastic. Both are pulled from fields of desire and need. Both are enabled by the discursive Africanism at the author's disposal.

I wish to close by saying that these deliberations are not about a particular author's attitudes toward race. That is another matter. Studies in American Africanism, in my view, should be investigations of the ways in which a nonwhite, Africanist presence and personae have been constructed—invented—in the United States, and of the literary uses this fabricated presence has served. In no way do I mean investigation of what might be called racist or nonracist literature, and I take no position, nor do I encourage one, on the quality of a work based on the attitudes of an author or whatever representations are made of some group. Such judgments can and are being formed, of course. Recent critical scholarship on Ezra Pound, Céline, T. S. Eliot, and Paul de Man comes to mind. But such concerns are not the intent of this exercise (although they fall within its reach). My project is an effort to avert the critical gaze from the racial object to the racial subject; from the described and imagined to the describers and imaginers; from the serving to the served.

Ernest Hemingway, who wrote so compellingly about what it was to be a white male American, could not help folding into his enterprise of American fiction its Africanist properties. But it would be a pity if the criticism of that literature continued to shellac those texts, immobilizing their complexities and power and luminations just below its tight, reflecting surface. All of us, readers and writers, are bereft when criticism remains too polite or too fearful to notice a disrupting darkness before its eyes.

Nobel Prize Acceptance Speech

Toni Morrison

Toni Morrison delivered the speech in response to receiving the Nobel Prize in 1993. In the Nobel lecture, she discusses and illustrates the power of language.

"Once upon a time there was an old woman. Blind but wise." Or was it an old man? A guru, perhaps. Or a griot soothing restless children. I have heard this story, or one exactly like it, in the lore of several cultures. "Once upon a time there was an old woman. Blind. Wise."

In the version I know the woman is the daughter of slaves, black American, and lives alone in a small house outside of town. Her reputation for wisdom is without peer and without question. Among her people she is both the law and its transgression. The honor she is paid and the awe in which she is held reach beyond her neighborhood to places far away; to the city where the intelligence of rural prophets is the source of much amusement.

One day the woman is visited by some young people who seem to be bent on disproving her clairvoyance and showing her up for the fraud they believe she is. Their plan is simple: they enter her house and ask the one question the answer to which rides solely on her difference from them, a difference they regard as a profound disability: her blindness. They stand before her, and one of them says, "Old woman, I hold in my hand a bird. Tell me whether it is living or dead."

She does not answer, and the question is repeated. "Is the bird I am holding living or dead?"

Still she doesn't answer. She is blind and cannot see her visitors, let alone what is in their hands. She does not know their color, gender or homeland. She only knows their motive.

The old woman's silence is so long, the young people have trouble holding their laughter.

Finally she speaks and her voice is soft but stern. "I don't know," she says. "I don't know whether the bird you are holding is dead or alive, but what I do know is that it is in your hands. It is in your hands."

Her answer can be taken to mean: if it is dead, you have either found it that way or you have killed it. If it is alive, you can still kill it. Whether it is to stay alive, it is your decision. Whatever the case, it is your responsibility.

For parading their power and her helplessness, the young visitors are reprimanded, told they are responsible not only for the act of mockery but also for the small bundle of life sacrificed to achieve its aims. The blind woman shifts attention away from assertions of power to the instrument through which that power is exercised.

Speculation on what (other than its own frail body) that bird-in-the-hand might signify has always been attractive to me, but especially so now, thinking as I have been, about the work I do that has brought me to this company. So I choose to read the bird as language and the woman as a practiced writer. She is worried about how the language she dreams in, given to her at birth, is handled, put into service, even withheld from her for certain nefarious purposes. Being a writer she thinks of language partly as a system, partly as a living thing over which one has control, but mostly as agency—as an act with consequences. So the question the children put to her: "Is it living or dead?" is not unreal because she thinks of language as susceptible to death, erasure; certainly imperiled and salvageable only by an effort of the will. She believes that if the bird in the hands of her visitors is dead the custodians are responsible for the corpse. For her a dead language is not only one no longer spoken or written, it is unyielding language content to admire its own paralysis. Like statist language, censored and censoring. Ruthless in its policing duties, it has no desire or purpose other than maintaining the free range of its own narcotic narcissism, its own exclusivity and dominance. However, moribund, it is not without effect for it actively thwarts the intellect, stalls conscience, suppresses human potential. Unreceptive to interrogation, it cannot form or tolerate new ideas, shape other thoughts, tell another story, fill baffling silences. Official language smitheryed to sanction ignorance and preserve privilege is a suit of armor, polished to shocking glitter, a husk from which the knight departed long ago. Yet there it is: dumb, predatory, sentimental. Exciting reverence in school-children, providing shelter for despots, summoning false memories of stability, harmony among the public.

She is convinced that when language dies, out of carelessness, disuse, and absence of esteem, indifference or killed by fiat, not only she herself, but all users and makers are accountable for its demise. In her country children have bitten their tongues off and use bullets instead to iterate the voice of speechlessness, of disabled and disabling language, of language adults have abandoned altogether as a device for grappling with meaning, providing guidance, or expressing love. But she knows tongue-suicide is not only the choice of children. It is common among the infantile heads of state and power merchants whose evacuated language leaves them with no access to what is left of their human instincts for they speak only to those who obey, or in order to force obedience.

The systematic looting of language can be recognized by the tendency of its users to forgo its nuanced, complex, mid-wifery properties for menace and subjugation. Oppressive language does more than represent violence; it is violence; does more than represent the limits of knowledge; it limits knowledge. Whether it is obscuring state language or the faux-language of mindless media; whether it is the proud but calcified language of the academy or the commodity driven language of science; whether it is the malign language of law-without-ethics, or language designed for the estrangement of minorities, hiding its racist plunder in its literary cheek—it must be rejected, altered and exposed. It is the language that drinks blood, laps vulnerabilities, tucks its fascist boots under crinolines of respectability and patriotism as it moves relentlessly toward the bottom line and the bottomed-out mind. Sexist language, racist language, theistic language—all are typical of the policing languages of mastery, and cannot, do not permit new knowledge or encourage the mutual exchange of ideas.

The old woman is keenly aware that no intellectual mercenary, nor insatiable dictator, no paid-for politician or demagogue; no counterfeit journalist would be persuaded by her thoughts. There is and will be rousing language to keep citizens armed and arming; slaughtered and slaughtering in the malls, courthouses, post offices, playgrounds, bedrooms and boulevards; stirring, memorializing language to mask the pity and waste of needless death. There will be more diplomatic language to countenance rape, torture, assassination. There is and will be more seductive, mutant language designed to throttle women, to pack their throats like paté-producing geese with their own unsayable, transgressive words; there will be more of the language of surveillance disguised as research; of politics and history calculated to render the suffering of millions mute; language glamorized to thrill the dissatisfied and bereft into assaulting their neighbors; arrogant pseudoempirical language crafted to lock creative people into cages of inferiority and hopelessness.

Underneath the eloquence, the glamour, the scholarly associations, however, stirring or seductive, the heart of such language is languishing, or perhaps not beating at all—if the bird is already dead.

She has thought about what could have been the intellectual history of any discipline if it had not insisted upon, or been forced into, the waste of time and life that rationalizations for and representations of dominance required—lethal discourses of exclusion blocking access to cognition for both the excluder and the excluded.

The conventional wisdom of the Tower of Babel story is that the collapse was a misfortune. That it was the distraction, or the weight of many languages that precipitated the tower's failed architecture. That one monolithic language would have expedited the building and heaven would have been reached. Whose heaven, she wonders? And what kind? Perhaps the achievement of Paradise was premature, a little hasty if no one could take the time to understand other languages, other views, other narratives. Had they, the heaven they imagined might have been found at their feet. Complicated, demanding yes, but a view of heaven as life; not heaven as postlife.

She would not want to leave her young visitors with the impression that language should be forced to stay alive merely to be. The vitality of language lies in its ability to limn the actual, imagined, and possible lives of its speakers, readers, writers. Although its poise is sometimes in displacing experience it is not a substitute for it. It arcs toward the place where meaning may lie. When a president of the United States thought about the graveyard his country had become, and said "The world will little note nor long remember what we say here. But it will never forget what they did here." His simple words are exhilarating in their life-sustaining properties because they refused to encapsulate the reality of six hundred thousand dead men in a cataclysmic race war. Refusing to monumentalize, disdaining the "final word," the precise "summing up," acknowledging their "poor power to add or detract," his words signal deference to the uncapturability of the life it mourns. It is the deference that moves her, that recognition that language can never live up to life once and for all. Nor should it. Language can never "pin down" slavery, genocide, war. Nor should it yearn for the arrogance to be able to do so. Its force, its felicity is in its reach toward the ineffable.

Be it grand or slender, burrowing, blasting, or refusing to sanctify; whether it laughs out loud or is a cry without an alphabet, the choice word, the chosen silence, unmolested language surges toward knowledge, not its destruction. But who does not know of literature banned because it is interrogative; discredited because it is critical; erased because alternative? And how many are outraged by the thought of a self-ravaged tongue?

Word-work is sublime, she thinks, because it is generative; it makes meaning that secures our difference, our human difference—the way in which we are like no other life.

We die. That may be the meaning of life. But we do language. That may be the measure of our lives.

"'Once upon a time, . . .'" visitors ask an old woman a question. Who are they, these children? What did they make of that encounter? What did they hear in those final words: "The bird is in your hands?" A sentence that gestures toward possibility or one that drops a latch? Perhaps what the children heard was "It's not my problem. I am old, female, black, blind. What wisdom I have now is in knowing I can not help you. The future of language is yours."

They stand there. Suppose nothing was in their hands? Suppose the visit was only a ruse, a trick to get to be spoken to, taken seriously as they have not been before? A chance to interrupt, to violate the adult world, its miasma of discourse about them, for them, but never to them? Urgent questions are at stake, including the one they have asked: "Is the bird we hold living or dead?" Perhaps the question meant: "Could someone tell us what is life? What is death?" No trick at all; no silliness. A straightforward question worthy of the attention of a wise one. An old one. And if the old and wise who have lived life and faced death cannot describe either, who can?

But she does not; she keeps her secret; her good opinion of herself; her gnomic pronouncements; her art without commitment. She keeps her distance, enforces it and retreats into the singularity of isolation, in sophisticated, privileged space.

Nothing, no word follows her declarations of transfer. That silence is deep, deeper than the meaning available in the words she has spoken. It shivers, this silence, and the children, annoyed, fill it with language invented on the spot.

"Is there no speech," they ask her, "no words you can give us that help us break through your dossier of failures? Through the education you have just given us that is no education at all because we are paying close attention to what you have done as well as to what you have said? To the barrier you have erected between generosity and wisdom?

"We have no bird in our hands, living or dead. We have only you and our important question. Is the nothing in our hands something you could not bear to contemplate, to even guess? Don't you remember being young when language was magic without meaning? When what you could say, could not mean? When the invisible was what imagination strove to see? When questions and demands for answers burned so brightly you trembled with fury at not knowing?

"Do we have to begin consciousness with a battle heroines and heroes like you have already fought and lost leaving us with nothing in our hands except what you have imagined is there? Your answer is artful, but its artiness embarrasses us and ought to embarrass you. Your answer is indecent in its self-congratulation. A made-for-television script that makes no sense if there is nothing in our hands.

"Why didn't you reach out, touch us with your soft fingers, delay the sound bite, the lesson, until you knew who we were? Did you so despise our trick, our *modus operandi* you could not see that we were baffled about how to get your attention? We are young. Unripe. We have heard all our short lives that we have to be responsible. What could that possibly mean in the catastrophe this world has become; where, as a poet said, "nothing needs to be exposed since it is already barefaced." Our inheritance is an affront. You want us to have your old, blank eyes and see only cruelty and mediocrity. Do you think we are stupid enough to perjure ourselves again and again with the fiction of nationhood? How dare you talk to us of duty when we stand waist deep in the toxin of your past?

"You trivialize us and trivialize the bird that is not in our hands. Is there no context for our lives? No song, no literature, no poem full of vitamins, no history connected to experience that you can pass along to help us start strong? You are an adult. The old one, the wise one. Stop thinking about saving your face. Think of our lives and tell us your particularized world. Make up a story. Narrative is radical, creating us at the very moment it is being created. We will not blame you if your reach exceeds your grasp; if love so ignites your words they go down in flames and nothing is left but their scald. Or if, with the reticence of a surgeon's hands, your words suture only the places where blood might flow. We know you can never do it properly—once and for all. Passion is never enough; neither is skill. But try. For our sake and yours forget your name in the street; tell us what the world has been to you in the dark places and in the light. Don't tell us what to believe, what to fear. Show us belief's wide skirt and the stitch that unravels fear's caul. You, old woman, blessed with blindness, can speak the language that tells us what only language can: how to see without pictures. Language alone protects us from the scariness of things with no names. Language alone is meditation.

"Tell us what it is to be a woman so that we may know what it is to be a man. What moves at the margin. What it is to have no home on this place. To be set adrift from the one you knew. What it is to live at the edge of towns that cannot bear your company.

"Tell us about ships turned away from shorelines at Easter, placenta in a field. Tell us about a wagonload of slaves, how they sang so softly their breath was indistinguishable from the falling snow. How they knew from the hunch of the nearest shoulder that the next stop would be their last. How, with hands prayered in their sex they thought of heat, then suns. Lifting their faces, as though it was there for the taking. Turning as though there for the taking. They stop at an inn. The driver and his mate go in with the lamp leaving them humming in the dark. The horse's void steams into the snow beneath its hooves and its hiss and melt is the envy of the freezing slaves.

"The inn door opens: a girl and a boy step away from its light. They climb into the wagon bed. The boy will have a gun in three years, but now he carries a lamp and a jug of warm cider. They pass it from mouth to mouth. The girl offers bread, pieces of meat and something more: a glance into the eyes of the one she serves. One helping for each man, two for each woman. And a look. They look back. The next stop will be their last. But not this one. This one is warmed."

It's quiet again when the children finish speaking, until the woman breaks into the silence.

"Finally," she says, "I trust you now. I trust you with the bird that is not in your hands because you have truly caught it. Look. How lovely it is, this thing we have done—together."

﷽ CORNEL WEST (b. 1953)

Cornel West is a philosopher, educator, writer, and social activist. He often speaks and writes about race and class issues. He received a scholarship from Harvard University after graduating from high school and is now a professor there. West is one of the foremost African American intellectual thinkers. He is articulate and knowledgeable in various disciplines, including religion, having served as professor of religion and philosophy at Yale Divinity School. Some of his texts include Keeping Faith: Philosophy and Race in America *(1993) and* Race Matters *(1993), in which he examines the role of black intellectuals and the black middle class.*

The Dilemma of the Black Intellectual (1993)

The peculiarities of the American social structure, and the position of the intellectual class within it, make the functional role of the negro intellectual a special one. The negro intellectual must deal intimately with the white power structure and cultural apparatus, and the inner realities of the black world at one and the same time. But in order to function successfully in this role, he has to be acutely aware of the nature of the American social dynamic and how it monitors the ingredients of class stratifications in American society. . . . Therefore the functional role of the negro intellectual demands that he *cannot* be absolutely separated from either the black or white world.

—Harold Cruse, *The Crisis of the Negro Intellectual*

The contemporary black intellectual faces a grim predicament. Caught between an insolent American society and an insouciant black community, the African American who takes seriously the life of the mind inhabits an isolated and insulated world. This condition has little to do with the motives and intentions of black intellectuals; rather it is an objective situation created by circumstances not of their own choosing. In this meditative essay, I will explore this dilemma of the black intellectual and suggest various ways of understanding and transforming it.

On Becoming a Black Intellectual

The choice of becoming a black intellectual is an act of self-imposed marginality; it assures a peripheral status in and to the black community. The quest for literacy indeed is a fundamental theme in African American history and a basic impulse in the black community. But for blacks, as with most Americans, the uses for literacy are usually perceived to be for more substantive pecuniary benefits than those of the writer, artist, teacher or professor. The reasons some black people choose to become serious intellectuals are diverse. But in most cases these reasons can be traced back to a common root: a conversionlike experience with a highly influential teacher or peer that convinced one to dedicate one's life to the activities of reading, writing and conversing for the purposes of individual pleasure, personal worth and political enhancement of black (and often other oppressed) people.

The way in which one becomes a black intellectual is highly problematic. This is so because the traditional roads others travel to become intellectuals in American society have only recently been opened to black people—and remain quite difficult. The main avenues are the academy or the literate subcultures of art, culture and politics. Prior to the acceptance of black undergraduate students to elite white universities and colleges in the late sixties, select black educational institutions served as the initial stimulus for potential black intellectuals. And in all honesty, there were relatively more and better black intellectuals then than now. After a decent grounding in a black college, where self-worth and self-confidence were affirmed, bright black students then matriculated to leading white institutions to be trained by liberal, sympathetic scholars, often of renowned stature. Stellar figures such as W. E. B. Du Bois, E. Franklin Frazier and John Hope Franklin were products of this system. For those black intellectuals-to-be who missed college opportunities for financial or personal reasons, there were literate subcultures—especially in the large urban centers—of writers, painters, musicians and politicos for unconventional educational enhancement. Major personages such as Richard Wright, Ralph Ellison and James Baldwin were products of this process.

Ironically, the present-day academy and contemporary literate subcultures present more obstacles for young blacks than those in decades past. This is so for three basic reasons. First, the attitudes of white scholars in the academy are quite different from those in the past. It is much more difficult for black students, especially graduate students, to be taken seriously as *potential scholars and intellectuals* owing to the managerial ethos of our universities and colleges (in which less time is spent with students) and to the vulgar (racist) perceptions fueled by affirmative action programs which pollute many black student–white professor relations.

Second, literate subcultures are less open to blacks now than they were three or four decades ago, not because white avant-garde journals or leftist groups are more racist today, but rather because heated political and cultural issues, such as the legacy of the Black Power movement, the Israeli-Palestinian conflict, the invisibility of Africa in American political discourse, have created rigid lines of demarcation and distance between black and white intellectuals. Needless to say, black presence in leading liberal journals like the *New York Review of Books* and the *New York Times Book Review* is negligible—nearly nonexistent. And more leftist periodicals such as *Dissent, Socialist Review,* the *Nation* and *Telos,* or avant-garde scholarly ones like *Diacritics, Salmagundi, Partisan Review* and *Raritan* do not do much better. Only *Monthly Review,* the *Massachusetts Review, Boundary 2* and *Social Text* make persistent efforts to cover black subject matter and have regular black contributors. The point here is not mere finger-pointing at negligent journals (though it would not hurt matters), but rather an attempt to highlight the racially separatist publishing patterns and practices of American intellectual life which are characteristic of the chasm between black and white intellectuals.

Third, the general politicization of American intellectual life (in the academy and outside), along with the rightward ideological drift, constitutes a hostile climate for the making of black intellectuals. To some extent, this has always been so, but the ideological capitulation of a significant segment of former left-liberals to the new-style conservatism and old-style imperialism has left black students and black professors with few allies in the academy and in influential periodicals. This hostile climate requires that black intellectuals fall back upon their own resources—institutions, journals and periodicals—which, in turn, reinforce the de facto racially separatist practices of American intellectual life.

The tragedy of black intellectual activity is that the black institutional support for such activity is in shambles. The quantity and quality of black intellectual exchange is at its worst since the Civil War. There is no major black academic journal; no major black intellectual magazine; no major black periodical of highbrow journalism; not even a major black newspaper of national scope. In short, the black infrastructure for intellectual discourse and dialogue is nearly nonexistent. This tragedy is, in part, the price for integration—which has yielded mere marginal black groups within the professional disciplines of a fragmented academic community. But this tragedy also has to do with the refusal of black intellectuals to establish and sustain their own institutional mechanisms of criticism and self-criticism, organized in such a way that people of whatever color would be able to contribute to them. This refusal over the past decade is significant in that it has lessened the appetite for, and the capacity to withstand, razor-sharp criticism among many black intellectuals whose formative years were passed in a kind of intellectual vacuum. So besides the external hostile climate, the tradition of serious black intellectual activity is also threatened from within.

The creation of an intelligentsia is a monumental task. Yet black churches and colleges, along with white support, served as resources for the first black intellectuals with formal training. The formation of high-quality habits of criticism and international networks of serious intellectual exchange among a relatively isolated and insulated intelligentsia is a gargantuan endeavor. Yet black intellectuals have little choice: either continued intellectual lethargy on the edges of the academy and literate subcultures unnoticed by the black community, or insurgent creative activity on the margins of the mainstream ensconced within bludgeoning new infrastructures.

Black Intellectuals and the Black Community

The paucity of black infrastructures for intellectual activity results, in part, from the inability of black intellectuals to gain respect and support from the black community—and especially the black middle class. In addition to the general anti-intellectual tenor of American society, there is a deep distrust and suspicion of black intellectuals within the black community. This distrust and suspicion stem not simply from the usual arrogant and haughty disposition of intellectuals toward ordinary folk, but, more importantly, from the widespread refusal of black intellectuals to remain, in some visible way, organically linked with African American cultural life. The relatively high rates of exogamous marriage, the abandonment of black institutions and the preoccupation with Euro-American intellectual products are often perceived by the black community as intentional efforts to escape the negative stigma of blackness or are viewed as symptoms of self-hatred. And the minimal immediate impact of black intellectual activity on the black community and American society reinforces common perceptions of the impotence, even uselessness, of black intellectuals. In good American fashion, the black community lauds those black intellectuals who excel as *political activists* and *cultural artists;* the life of the mind is viewed as neither possessing intrinsic virtues nor harboring emancipatory possibilities—solely short-term political gain and social status.

This truncated perception of intellectual activity is widely held by black intellectuals themselves. Given the constraints upon black upward social mobility and the pressures for status and affluence among middle-class peers, many black intellectuals principally seek material gain and cultural prestige. Since these intellectuals are members of an anxiety-ridden and status-hungry black middle class, their proclivities are understandable and, to some extent, justifiable. For most intellectuals are in search of recognition, status, power and often wealth. Yet for black intellectuals this search requires immersing oneself in and addressing oneself to the very culture and society which degrade and devalue the black community from whence one comes. And, to put it crudely, most black intellectuals tend to fall within the two camps created by this predicament: "successful" ones, distant from (and usually condescending toward) the black community, and "unsuccessful" ones, disdainful of the white intellectual world. But both camps remain marginal to the black community—dangling between two worlds with little or no black infrastructural bases. Therefore, the "successful" black intellectual capitulates, often uncritically, to the prevailing paradigms and research programs of the white bourgeois academy, and the "unsuccessful" black intellectual remains encapsulated within the parochial discourses of African American intellectual life. The alternatives of meretricious pseudo-cosmopolitanism and tendentious, cathartic provincialism loom large in the lives of black intellectuals. And the black community views both alternatives with distrust and disdain—and with good reason. Neither alternative has had a positive impact on the black community. The major black intellectuals from W. E. B. Du Bois and St. Clair Drake to Ralph Ellison and Toni Morrison have shunned both alternatives.

This situation has resulted in the major obstacle confronting black intellectuals: the inability to transmit and sustain the requisite institutional mechanisms for the persistence of a discernible intellectual tradition. The racism of American society, the relative lack of black community support, and hence the dangling status of black intellectuals have prevented the creation of a rich heritage of intellectual exchange, intercourse and dialogue. There indeed have been grand black intellectual achievements, but such achievements do not substitute for tradition.

I would suggest that there are two *organic* intellectual traditions in African American life: *the black Christian tradition of preaching* and *the black musical tradition of performance*. Both traditions, though undoubtedly linked to the life of the mind, are oral, improvisational and histrionic. Both traditions are rooted in black life and possess precisely what the literate forms of black intellectual activity lack: institutional matrices over time and space within which there are accepted rules of procedure, criteria for judgment, canons for assessing performance, models of past achievement and present emulation and an acknowledged succession and accumulation of superb accomplishments. The richness, diversity and vitality of the traditions of black preaching and black music stand in strong contrast to the paucity, even poverty, of black literate intellectual production. There simply have been no black literate intellectuals who have mastered their craft commensurate with the achievements of Louis Armstrong, Charlie Parker or Rev. Manuel Scott—just as there are no black literate intellectuals today comparable to Miles Davis, Sarah Vaughn or Rev. Gardner Taylor. This is so not because there have been or are no first-rate black literate intellectuals, but rather because without strong institutional channels to sustain traditions, great achievement is impossible. And, to be honest, black America has yet to produce a great literate intellectual with the exception of Toni Morrison. There indeed have been superb ones—Du Bois, Frazier, Ellison, Baldwin, Hurston—and many good ones. But none can compare to the heights achieved by black preachers and musicians.

What is most troubling about black literate intellectual activity is that as it slowly evolved out of the black Christian tradition and interacted more intimately with secular Euro-American styles and forms, it seemed as if by the latter part of the twentieth century maturation would set in. Yet, as we approach the last few years of this century, black literate intellectual activity has declined in both quantity and quality. As I noted earlier, this is so primarily because of relatively greater black integration into postindustrial capitalist America with its bureaucratized elite universities, dull middlebrow colleges and decaying high schools, which have little concern for or confidence in black students as potential intellectuals. Needless to say, the predicament of the black intellectual is inseparable from that of the black community—especially the black middle-class community—in American society. And only a fundamental transformation of American society can possibly change the situation of the black community and the black intellectual. And though my own Christian skepticism regarding human totalistic schemes for change chastens my deep socialist sentiments regarding radically democratic and libertarian socioeconomic and cultural arrangements, I shall forego these larger issues and focus on more specific ways to enhance the quantity and quality of black literate intellectual activity in the USA. This focus shall take the form of sketching four models for black intellectual activity, with the intent to promote the crystallization of infrastructures for such activity.

The Bourgeois Model: Black Intellectual as Humanist

For black intellectuals, the bourgeois model of intellectual activity is problematic. On the one hand, the racist heritage—aspects of the exclusionary and repressive effects of white academic institutions and humanistic scholarship—puts black intellectuals on the defensive: there is always the need to assert and defend the humanity of black people, including their ability and capacity to reason logically, think coherently and write lucidly. The weight of this inescapable burden for black students in the white academy has often determined the content and character of black intellectual activity. In fact, black intellectual life remains largely preoccupied with such defensiveness, with "successful" black intellectuals often proud of their white approval and "unsuccessful" ones usually scornful of their white rejection. This concern is especially acute among the first generation of black intellectuals accepted as teachers and scholars within elite white universities and colleges, largely a post-1968 phenomenon. Only with the publication of the intimate memoirs of these black intellectuals and their students will we have the gripping stories of how this defensiveness cut at much of the heart of their intellectual activity and creativity within white academic contexts. Yet, however personally painful such battles have been, they had to be fought, given the racist milieu of American intellectual and academic life. These battles will continue, but with far fewer negative consequences for the younger generation because of the struggles by the older black trailblazers.

On the other hand, the state of siege raging in the black community requires that black intellectuals accent the practical dimension of their work. And the prestige and status, as well as the skills and techniques provided by the white bourgeois academy, render it attractive for the task at hand. The accentuation of the practical dimension holds for most black intellectuals regardless of ideological persuasion—even more than for the stereotypical, pragmatic, American intellectual. This is so not simply because of the power-seeking lifestyles and statusoriented dispositions of many black intellectuals, but also because of their relatively small number, which forces them to play multiple roles vis-á-vis the black community and, in addition, intensifies their need for self-vindication—the attempt to justify to themselves that, given such unique opportunities and privileges, they are spending their time as they ought—which often results in activistic and pragmatic interests.

The linchpin of the bourgeois model is academic legitimation and placement. Without the proper certificate, degree and position, the bourgeois model loses its raison d'être. The influence and attractiveness of the bourgeois model permeate the American academic system; yet the effectiveness of the bourgeois model is credible for black intellectuals only if they possess sufficient legitimacy and placement. Such legitimacy and placement will give one access to select networks and contacts which may facilitate black impact on public policies. This seems to have been the aim of the first generation of blacks trained in elite white institutions (though not permitted to teach there), given their predominant interests in the social sciences.

The basic problem with the bourgeois model is that it is existentially and intellectually stultifying for black intellectuals. It is existentially debilitating because it not only generates anxieties of defensiveness on the part of black intellectuals; it also thrives on them. The need for hierarchical ranking and the deep-seated racism shot through bourgeois humanistic scholarship cannot provide black intellectuals with either the proper ethos or conceptual framework to overcome a defensive posture. And charges of intellectual inferiority can never be met upon the opponent's terrain—to try to do so only intensifies one's anxieties. Rather the terrain itself must be viewed as part and parcel of an antiquated form of life unworthy of setting the terms of contemporary discourse.

The bourgeois model sets intellectual limits, in that one is prone to adopt uncritically prevailing paradigms predominant in the bourgeois academy because of the pressures of practical tasks and deferential emulation. Every intellectual passes through some kind of apprenticeship stage in which s/he learns the language and style of the authorities, but when s/he is already viewed as marginally talented s/he may be either excessively encouraged or misleadingly discouraged to examine critically paradigms deemed marginal by the authorities. This hostile environment results in the suppression of one's critical analyses and in the limited use of one's skills in a manner considered legitimate and practical.

Despite its limitations, the bourgeois model is inescapable for most black intellectuals. This is so because most of the important and illuminating discourses in the country take place in white bourgeois academic institutions and because the more significant intellectuals teach in such places. Many of the elite white universities and colleges remain high-powered schools of education, learning and training principally due to large resources and civil traditions that provide the leisure time and atmosphere necessary for sustained and serious intellectual endeavor. So aside from the few serious autodidactic black intellectuals (who often have impressive scope but lack grounding and depth), black intellectuals must pass through the white bourgeois academy (or its black imitators).

Black academic legitimation and placement can provide a foothold in American intellectual life so that black infrastructures for intellectual anxiety can be created. At present, there is a small yet significant black presence within the white bourgeois academic organizations, and it is able to produce newsletters and small periodicals. The next step is to institutionalize more broadly black intellectual presence, as the Society of Black Philosophers of New York has done, by publishing journals anchored in a discipline (crucial for the careers of prospective professors) yet relevant to other disciplines. It should be noted that such a black infrastructure for intellectual activity should attract persons of whatever hue or color. Black literary critics and especially black psychologists are far ahead of other black intellectuals in this regard, with journals such as the *Black American Literature Forum*, the *College Language Association* and the *Journal of Black Psychology*.

Black academic legitimation and placement also can result in black control over a portion of, or significant participation within, the larger white infrastructures for intellectual activity. This has not yet occurred on a broad scale. More black representation is needed on the editorial boards of significant journals so that a larger black intellectual presence is permitted. This process is much slower and has less visibility, yet, given the hegemony of the bourgeois model, it must be pursued by those so inclined.

The bourgeois model is, in some fundamental and ultimate sense, more part of the problem than the solution in regard to black intellectuals. Yet, since we live our lives daily and penultimately within this system, those of us highly critical of the bourgeois model must try to subvert it, in part, from within the white bourgeois academy. For black intellectuals—in alliance with nonblack progressive intellectuals—this means creating and augmenting infrastructures for black intellectual activity.

The Marxist Model: Black Intellectual as Revolutionary

Among many black intellectuals, there is a knee-jerk reaction to the severe limitations of the bourgeois model (and capitalist society)—namely, to adopt the Marxist model. This adoption satisfies certain basic needs of the black intelligentsia: the need for social relevance, political engagement and organizational involvement. The Marxist model also provides entry into the least xenophobic white intellectual subculture available to black intellectuals.

The Marxist model privileges the activity of black intellectuals and promotes their prophetic role. As Harold Cruse has noted, such privileging is highly circumscribed and rarely accents the theoretical dimension of black intellectual activity. In short, the Marxist privileging of black intellectuals often reeks of condescension that confines black prophetic roles to spokespersons and organizers; only rarely are they allowed to function as creative thinkers who warrant serious critical attention. It is no accident that the relatively large numbers of black intellectuals attracted to Marxism over the past sixty years have yet to produce a major black Marxist theoretician with the exception of C. L. R. James. Only W. E. B. Du Bois's *Black Reconstruction* (1935), Oliver Cox's *Caste, Class and Race* (1948) and, to some degree, Harold Cruse's *The Crisis of the Negro Intellectual* (1967) are even candidates for such a designation. This is so not because of the absence of black intellectual talent in the Marxist camp but rather because of the absence of the kind of tradition and community (including intense critical exchange) that would allow such talent to flower.

In stark contrast to the bourgeois model, the Marxist model neither generates black intellectual defensiveness nor provides an adequate analytical apparatus for short-term public policies. Rather the Marxist model yields black intellectual self-satisfaction which often inhibits growth; it also highlights social structural constraints with little practical direction regarding conjunctural opportunities. This self-satisfaction results in either dogmatic submission to and upward mobility within sectarian party or preparty formations or marginal placement in the bourgeois academy equipped with cantankerous Marxist rhetoric and sometimes insightful analysis utterly divorced from the integral dynamics, concrete realities and progressive possibilities of the black community. The preoccupation with social structural constraints tends to produce either preposterous chiliastic projections or paralyzing pessimistic pronouncements. Such projections and pronouncements have as much to do with the self-image of black Marxist intellectuals as with the prognosis for black liberation.

It is often claimed "that Marxism is the false consciousness of the radicalized, bourgeois intelligentsia." For black intellectuals, the Marxist model functions in a more complex manner than this glib formulation permits. On the one hand, the Marxist model is liberating for black intellectuals in that it promotes critical consciousness and attitudes toward the dominant bourgeois paradigms and research programs. Marxism provides attractive roles for black intellectuals—usually highly visible leadership roles—and infuses new meaning and urgency into their work. On the other hand, the Marxist model is debilitating for black intellectuals because the cathartic needs it satisfies tend to stifle the further development of black critical consciousness and attitudes.

The Marxist model, despite its shortcomings, is more part of the solution than part of the problem for black intellectuals. This is so because Marxism is the brook of fire—the purgatory—of our postmodern times. Black intellectuals must pass through it, come to terms with it, and creatively respond to it if black intellectual activity is to reach any recognizable level of sophistication and refinement.

The Foucaultian Model:
Black Intellectual as Postmodern Skeptic

As Western intellectual life moves more deeply into crisis and as black intellectuals become more fully integrated into intellectual life—or into "the culture of careful and critical discourse" (as the late Alvin Gouldner called it)—a new model appears on the horizon. This model, based primarily upon the influential work of the late Michel Foucault, unequivocally rejects the bourgeois model and eschews the Marxist model. It constitutes one of the most exciting intellectual challenges of our day: the Foucaultian project of historical nominalism. This detailed investigation into the complex relations of knowledge and power, discourses and politics, cognition and social control compels intellectuals to rethink and redefine their self-image and function in our contemporary situation.

The Foucaultian model and project are attractive to black intellectuals primarily because they speak to the black postmodern predicament, defined by the rampant xenophobia of bourgeois humanism predominant in the whole academy, the waning attraction to orthodox reductionist and scientific versions of Marxism, and the need for reconceptualization regarding the specificity and complexity of African American oppression. Foucault's deep antibourgeois sentiments, explicit post-Marxist convictions and profound preoccupations with those viewed as radically "Other" by dominant discourses and traditions are quite seductive for politicized black intellectuals wary of antiquated panaceas for black liberation.

Foucault's specific analyses of the "political economy of truth"—the study of the discursive ways in which and institutional means by which "regimes of truth" are constituted by societies over space and time—result in a new conception of the intellectual. This conception no longer rests upon the smooth transmittance of "the best that has been thought and said," as in the bourgeois humanist model, nor on the engaged utopian energies of the Marxist model. Rather the postmodern situation requires "the specific intellectual" who shuns the labels of scientificity, civility and prophecy and instead delves into the specificity of the political, economic and cultural matrices within which regimes of truth are produced, distributed, circulated and consumed. No longer should intellectuals deceive themselves by believing—as do humanist and Marxist intellectuals—that they are struggling "on behalf" of the truth; rather the problem is the struggle over the very status of truth and the vast institutional mechanisms which account for this status. The favored code words of "science," "taste," "tact," "ideology," "progress" and "liberation" of bourgeois humanism and Marxism are no longer applicable to the self-image of postmodern intellectuals. Instead, the new key terms become those of "regime of truth," "power/knowledge" and "discursive practices."

Foucault's notion of the specific intellectual rests upon his demystification of conservative, liberal and Marxist rhetorics which restore, resituate and reconstruct intellectuals' self-identities so that they remain captive to and supportive of institutional forms of domination and control. These rhetorics authorize and legitimate, in different ways, the privileged status of intellectuals, which not only reproduces ideological divisions between intellectual and manual labor but also reinforces disciplinary mechanisms of subjection and subjugation. This self-authorizing is best exemplified in the claims made by intellectuals that they "safeguard" the achievement of highbrow culture or "represent" the "universal interests" of particular classes and groups. In African American intellectual history, similar self-authorizing claims such as "the talented tenth," "prophets in the wilderness," "articulators of a black aesthetic," "creators of a black renaissance" and "vanguard of a revolutionary movement" are widespread.

The Foucaultian model promotes a leftist form of postmodern skepticism; that is, it encourages an intense and incessant interrogation of power-laden discourses in the service of neither restoration, reformation nor revolution, but rather of revolt. And the kind of revolt enacted by intellectuals consists of the disrupting and dismantling of prevailing "regimes of truth"—including their repressive effects—of present-day societies. This model suits the critical, skeptical, and historical concerns of progressive black intellectuals and provides a sophisticated excuse for ideological and social distance from insurgent black movements for liberation. By conceiving intellectual work as oppositional political praxis, it satisfies the leftist self-image of black intellectuals, and, by making a fetish of critical consciousness, it encapsulates black intellectual activity within the comfortable bourgeois academy of postmodern America.

The Insurgency Model:
Black Intellectual as Critical Organic Catalyst

Black intellectuals can learn much from each of the three previous models, yet should not uncritically adopt any one of them. This is so because the bourgeois, Marxist and Foucaultian models indeed relate to, but do not adequately speak to, the uniqueness of the black intellectual predicament. This uniqueness remains relatively unexplored, and will remain so until black intellectuals articulate a new "regime of truth" linked to, yet not confined by, indigenous institutional practices permeated by the kinetic orality and emotional physicality, the rhythmic syncopation, the protean improvisation and the religious, rhetorical and antiphonal repetition of African American life. Such articulation depends, in part, upon elaborate black infrastructures which put a premium on creative and cultivated black thought; it also entails intimate knowledge of prevailing Euro-American "regimes of truth" which must be demystified, deconstructed and decomposed in ways which enhance and enrich future black intellectual life. The new "regime of truth" to be pioneered by black thinkers is neither a hermetic discourse (or set of discourses), which safeguards mediocre black intellectual production, nor the latest fashion of black writing, which is often motivated by the desire to parade for the white bourgeois intellectual establishment. Rather it is inseparable from the emergence of new cultural forms which prefigure (and point toward) a post-Western civilization. At present, such talk may seem mere dream and fantasy. So we shall confine ourselves to the first step: black insurgency and the role of the black intellectual.

The major priority of black intellectuals should be the creation or reactivation of institutional networks that promote high-quality critical habits primarily for the purpose of black insurgency. An intelligentsia without institutionalized critical consciousness is blind, and critical consciousness severed from collective insurgency is empty. The central task of postmodern black intellectuals is to stimulate, hasten and enable alternative perceptions and practices by dislodging prevailing discourses and powers. This can be done only by intense intellectual work and engaged insurgent praxis.

The insurgency model for black intellectual activity builds upon, yet goes beyond, the previous three models. From the bourgeois model, it recuperates the emphasis on human will and heroic effort. Yet the insurgency model refuses to conceive of this will and effort in individualistic and elitist terms. Instead of the solitary hero, embattled exile and isolated genius—the intellectual as star, celebrity, commodity—this model privileges collective intellectual work that contributes to communal resistance and struggle. In other words, it creatively accents the voluntarism and heroism of the bourgeois model, but it rejects the latter's naiveté about the role of society and history. From the Marxist model it recovers the stress on structural constraints, class formations and radical democratic values.

Yet the insurgency model does not view these constraints, formations and values in economistic and deterministic terms. Instead of the a priori privileging of the industrial working class and the metaphysical positing of a relatively harmonious socialist society, there is the wholesale assault on varieties of social hierarchy and the radical democratic (and libertarian) mediation, not elimination, of social heterogeneity. In short, the insurgency model ingeniously incorporates the structural, class and democratic concerns of the Marxist model, yet it acknowledges the latter's naiveté about culture.

Lastly, from the Foucaultian model, the insurgency model recaptures the preoccupation with worldly skepticism, the historical constitution of "regimes of truth," and the multifarious operations of "power/knowledge." Yet the insurgency model does not confine this skepticism, this truth-constituting and detailed genealogical inquiry to micronetworks of power. Instead of the ubiquity of power (which simplifies and flattens multidimensional social conflict) and the paralyzing overreaction to past utopianisms, there is the possibility of effective resistance and meaningful societal transformation. The insurgency model carefully highlights the profound Nietzschean suspicion and the illuminating oppositional descriptions of the Foucaultian model, though it recognizes the latter's naiveté about social conflict, struggle and insurgency—a naiveté primarily caused by the rejection of any form of utopianism and any positing of a telos.

Black intellectual work and black collective insurgency must be rooted in the specificity of African American life and history; but they also are inextricably linked to the American, European and African elements which shape and mold them. Such work and insurgency are explicitly particularist though not exclusivist—hence they are international in outlook and practice. Like their historical forerunners, black preachers and black musical artists (with all their strengths and weaknesses), black intellectuals must realize that the creation of "new" and alternative practices results from the heroic efforts of collective intellectual work and communal resistance which shape and are shaped by present structural constraints, workings of power and modes of cultural fusion. The distinctive African American cultural forms such as the black sermonic and prayer styles, gospel, blues and jazz should inspire, but not constrain, future black intellectual production; that is, the process by which they came to be should provide valuable insights, but they should serve as models neither to imitate nor emulate. Needless to say, these forms thrive on incessant critical innovation and concomitant insurgency.

The Future of the Black Intellectual

The predicament of the black intellectual need not be grim and dismal. Despite the pervasive racism of American society and anti-intellectualism of the black community, critical space and insurgent activity can be expanded. This expansion will occur more readily when black intellectuals take a more candid look at themselves, the historical and social forces that shape them, and the limited though significant resources of the community from whence they come. A critical "self-inventory" that scrutinizes the social positions, class locations and cultural socializations of black intellectuals is imperative. Such scrutiny should be motivated by neither self-pity nor self-satisfaction. Rather this "self-inventory" should embody the sense of critique and resistance applicable to the black community, American society and Western civilization as a whole. James Baldwin has noted that the black intellectual is "a kind of bastard of the West." The future of the black intellectual lies neither in a deferential disposition toward the Western parent nor a nostalgic search for the African one. Rather it resides in a critical negation, wise preservation and insurgent transformation of this black lineage which protects the earth and projects a better world.

❈ HAZEL CARBY (b. 1948)

Hazel Carby's work has been instrumental to the black feminist tradition. She writes about issues that affect African American women in particular, often comparing the plight of today's black women to their situation in antebellum times, when black women were often raped by white men. Domestic violence and rape are problems for all women; however, black women in the late nineteenth and early twentieth centuries were lynched as well. Carby seeks to empower women by examining female-related issues in African American literature. Her Reconstructing Womanhood: The Emergence of the Afro-American Woman Novelist *(1987) has become a primary critical text. In* Race Men *(1998), she discusses African American men as race leaders. She is presently Professor of African and American Studies at Yale.*

From Reconstructing Womanhood: The Emergence of the Afro-American Woman Novelist (1987)

"Hear My Voice, Ye Careless Daughters"

Narratives of Slave and Free Women Before Emancipation

A survey of the general terrain of images and stereotypes produced by antebellum sexual ideologies is a necessary but only preliminary contribution to understanding how the ideology of true womanhood influenced and, to a large extent, determined the shape of the public voice of black women writers. What remains to be considered is how an ideology that excluded black women from the category "women" affected the ways in which they wrote and addressed an audience. The relevance of this question extends beyond the writing of slave narratives, and I will first examine texts written by free black women living in the North before turning to a slave narrative, Harriet Jacobs's *Incidents in the Life of a Slave Girl.*

In 1850, Nancy Prince published in Boston her *Life and Travels.* A free woman, Nancy Prince declared that her object in writing was not "a vain desire to appear before the public"; on the contrary, her book was the product of her labor by which she hoped to sustain herself. In other words, Prince regarded her writing as her work. The publication of her *Life and Travels* was the occasion for an assertion of Prince's intention to retain and maintain her independence:

> The Almighty God our heavenly father has designed that we eat our bread by the
> sweat of our brow; that all-wise and holy Being has designed and requires of us
> that we be diligent, using the means, that with his blessing we may not be bur-
> densome, believing we shall be directed and go through.

But this statement was double-edged: it was at once an assertion of her present
condition and a comment on her history which was retold in the main body of the
text. Prince's assertion appealed to the values of the "Protestant ethic," while the
opening pages of her text were an apt demonstration of economic racial discrimination; however hard the young Nancy and her family labored in the North, the
fruits of that society were not granted to them. At fourteen years old, Nancy
replaced a sick friend in service and "thought herself fortunate" to be with a religious family, as she herself had received religious instruction and had been taught
"right from wrong" by her grandfather. Prince recounted the details of her arduous duties and cruel treatment and then interrogated the hypocritical religion of
her employers:

> Hard labor and unkindness were too much for me; in three months, my health
> and strength were gone. I often looked at my employers, and thought to myself,
> is this your religion? I did not wonder that the girl who had lived there previous
> to myself, went home to die. They had family prayers, morning and evening. Oh!
> yes, they were sanctimonious! I was a poor stranger, but fourteen years of age,
> imposed upon by these good people.

After seven years of "anxiety and toil," Prince married and went to live in Russia,
where her husband was employed and where there was "no prejudice against
color." Prince established her international perspective in a section which detailed
life in Russia and then condemned the racism which permeated the United States,
North and South. In a direct address to her audience, which Prince considered to
be primarily a Northern readership, she described how, upon her return to her
own country, "the weight of prejudice . . . again oppressed [her]," even while she
retained her belief in ultimate justice:

> God has in all ages of the world punished every nation and people for their sins.
> The sins of my beloved country are not hid from his notice; his all-seeing eye sees
> and knows the secrets of all hearts; the angels that kept not their first estate but left
> their own habitations, he hath reserved in everlasting chains unto the great day.

By extending the logic of religious conviction, Prince revealed the hypocrisy at
the heart of American society. Her thinly veiled threat of revenge gained additional power from her earlier, obviously sympathetic response to those she had
witnessed rebelling against the injustices of Russian society.

The dignity and power of Prince's narrative was gained from her position at
once inside and outside the society she wished to condemn. Her narrative voice
was given strength through her presentation of herself as a true practitioner of
Christian principles who was able to comment on the hypocritical attitudes and
forms of behavior that she saw practiced throughout the country. Prince used her
knowledge of other societies to compare and contrast with her own. Somewhat

ironically, she commented that she "may not see as clearly as some" because of the weight of oppression, but, of course, this rhetorical device revealed exactly how appropriate a witness and how effective a narrator of racist practices she was. Prince made clear her double position inside U.S. society as a citizen and outside it as an outcast because of her color; her final narrative position, however, was above "this world's tumultuous noise," at the side of the ultimate judge.

In her narrative, one action in particular used, but also questioned, a fundamental attribute of true womanhood: the possession of sexual purity. Having discovered that her eldest sister had been "deluded away" into a brothel and become a prostitute, Prince responded: "[t]o have heard of her death, would not have been so painful to me, as we loved each other very much." This statement was in accord with conventional expectations of the importance of sexual purity; death was easier to accept than loss of virtue. However, Prince did not continue to follow the conventional pattern of regarding her sister as "lost" forever but searched for, found, and rescued her. Far from seizing the narrative opportunity to condemn her sister, Prince claimed her "soul as precious" and revealed the contradiction of a sexual ideology that led her sister to feel she was neither "fit to live, nor fit to die." Returning her sister to the bosom of a family Prince declared not shame but a sense of "victory." As author, Prince used the structure of spiritual autobiography not to conform to a conventional representation of experience but to begin to question the limits of those conventions as they contradicted aspects of her own experience. *A Narrative of the Life and Travels of Mrs. Nancy Prince. Written by Herself* is an early example of a black woman who attempted to use a conventional narrative form, spiritual autobiography, in unconventional ways. Prince's adoption of a public voice assumed and asserted the authority of her experience.

The conviction that writing was work was attested to by another free black woman, Harriet Wilson, in her narrative *Our Nig; or, Sketches from the Life of a Free Black* (1859). A comparison of Wilson's motives for writing with those of Prince is fruitful. Wilson stated in her preface:

> In offering to the public the following pages, the writer confesses her inability to minister to the refined and cultivated, the pleasure supplied by abler pens. It is not for such these crude narrations appear. Deserted by kindred, disabled by failing health, I am forced to some experiment which shall aid me in maintaining myself and my child without extinguishing this feeble life.

Prince established that her book was the product of her labor, and Wilson appealed to her audience to buy her narrative as a product of her labor so that she and her son could survive. But, unlike Prince, Wilson sought her patronage not from a white Northern audience but from her "colored brethren." Wilson attempted to gain authority for her public voice through a narrative that shared its experience with a black community which she addressed as if it were autonomous from the white community in which it was situated.

In his introduction to Wilson's text, Henry Louis Gates, Jr., calls it the first novel by a black writer because of its use of the plot conventions of sentimental novels. But the use of these particular conventions can be found not only in the novel but also in many slave narratives. I would argue that *Our Nig* can be most usefully regarded as an allegory of a slave narrative, a "slave" narrative set in the "free" North. The first indication of the possibility of an allegorical reading occurs in the subtitle, "Sketches from the Life of a Free Black, in a Two-Story White House, North. Showing That Slavery's Shadows Fall Even There." Wilson used her voice as a black woman addressing a black audience to condemn racism in the North and criticize abolitionists. This placed Wilson in a position similar to that of Prince, both inside and outside the society subject to critique. Whereas Prince gained narrative dignity and power from her experience of other countries, her outcast status, and her "true" religious principles, Wilson's narrative authority derived from an assertion of independence from the patronage of the white community. Her narrative was written apart from any links to the abolitionist movement, and her direct appeal to the black community marginalized a white readership.

The "two-story white house" can be interpreted initially as the equivalent of the Southern plantation, in which the protagonist, Frado, was held in virtual slavery. Scenes of punishment and brutality, whippings, and beatings were evoked, as in a conventional slave narrative, to document the relentless suffering and persecution to which the slave was subject. The Northern house, like its Southern counterpart, was the sovereign territory of a tyrant, ruled by a mistress whom Wilson described as being "imbued with *southern principles.*" Mrs. Bellmont, the white mistress, was described as having power over the whole family—husband, sons, daughters, and Frado—and was symbolic of the power of the South. The domestic realm, within which Wilson represented Mrs. Bellmont as the ultimate power, was the terrain of struggle over the treatment of Frado in which debates about the position and future of blacks in the United States are re-created. Sensitivity and compassion were to be found in some members of the family, including Mr. Bellmont and one of his sons, but their protests were ignored; the power of the mistress, like the power of the South, was never effectively challenged. The actions of Mrs. Bellmont determine and structure the overall pattern of her slave's life in the house; a house which increasingly resembles the nation, as the resolve of Mrs. Bellmont's opponents to improve Frado's conditions disintegrated at the slightest possibility of conflict. Mr. Bellmont was portrayed as preferring to leave the house to the tyrannical rages of his wife, hiding until the recurring ruptures receded and Frado had again been punished. In a close resemblance to the position of many abolitionists, Mr. Bellmont and his son offered sympathy and loud protestations but were unwilling to assert the moral superiority of their position by fighting the mistress, the South, and imposing an alternative social order. Both men merely dressed Frado's wounds and turned their backs when battles were renewed. The two-story house was an allegory for the divided nation in which the object of controversy and subject of oppression was *Our Nig*. Like Prince, Wilson gained her narrative authority from adapting literary conventions to more adequately conform to a narrative representation and re-creation of black experience. It is important to identify the source of many of these conventions in the sentimental novel and also to recognize that Wilson's particular use of sentimental conventions derives from the sentimental novel via slave narratives to produce a unique allegorical form. That

Our Nig did not conform to the parameters of contemporary domestic fiction can be attributed to this cultural blend.

The issue of conformity to conventions has been linked to questions concerning the authenticity of slave narratives by historians, particularly in the case of Harriet Jacobs's narrative, *Incidents in the Life of a Slave Girl* (1861). Arguing, convincingly, that historians need to recognize both the "uniqueness" and the "representativeness" of the slave narrative, John Blassingame, in *The Slave Community*, concluded that Jacobs's narrative is inauthentic because it does not conform to the guidelines of representativeness. Blassingame questioned the narrative's orderly framework and the use of providential encounters and continued:

> the story is too melodramatic: miscegenation and cruelty, outraged virtue, unrequited love, and planter licentiousness appear on practically every page. The virtuous Harriet sympathizes with her wretched mistress who has to look on all of the mulattoes fathered by her husband, she refuses to bow to the lascivious demands of her master, bears two children for another white man, and then runs away and hides in a garret in her grandmother's cabin for seven years until she is able to escape to New York. . . . In the end, all live happily ever after.

With regard to internal evidence and the question of the authority of the public voice, the critique that Blassingame offers focuses heavily, though perhaps unconsciously, on the protagonist, Linda Brent, as conventional heroine.

In comparing slave narratives to each other, historians and literary critics have relied on a set of unquestioned assumptions that interrelate the quest for freedom and literacy with the establishment of manhood in the gaining of the published, and therefore public, voice. The great strength of these autobiographies, Blassingame states, is that, unlike other important sources, they embody the slaves' own perception of their experiences. Yet it is taken for granted that this experience, which is both unique and representative, is also male:

> If historians seek to provide some understanding of the past experiences of slaves, then the autobiography must be their point of departure; in the autobiography, more clearly than in any other source, we learn what went on in the minds of *black men*. It gives us a window to the "inside half" of the slave's life which never appears in the commentaries of "outsiders." Autobiographers are generally so preoccupied with conflict, those things blocking their hopes and dreams, that their works give a freshness and vitality to history which is often missing in other sources.

The criteria for judgment that Blassingame advances here leave no room for a consideration of the specificity and uniqueness of the black female experience. An analogy can be made between Blassingame's criticism of *Incidents* as melodrama and the frequency with which issues of miscegenation, unrequited love, outraged virtue, and planter licentiousness are found foregrounded in diaries by Southern white women, while absent or in the background of the records of their planter husbands. Identifying such a difference should lead us to question and consider the significance of these issues in the lives of women as opposed to men, not to the conclusion that the diaries by women are not credible because they deviate from the conventions of male-authored texts. Any assumption of the representativeness of patriarchal experience does not allow for, or even regard as necessary, a gender-specific form of analysis. Indeed, the criteria chosen by Blassingame as the basis for his dismissal of the narrative credibility of Jacobs's narrative are, ideologically, the indicators of a uniquely female perspective.

Jean Fagan Yellin, a literary historian, critic, and biographer of Jacobs, has (from external evidence) established the authenticity of Jacobs's narrative. Jacobs wrote under the pseudonym Linda Brent. *Incidents in the Life of a Slave Girl* was first published in Boston in 1861, under the editorship of Lydia Maria Child, and a year later it appeared in a British edition. In the discussion that follows, the author will be referred to as Jacobs, but, to preserve narrative continuity, the pseudonym Linda Brent will be used in the analysis of the text and protagonist.

Incidents in the Life of a Slave Girl is the most sophisticated, sustained narrative dissection of the conventions of true womanhood by a black author before emancipation. It will be the object of the following analysis to demonstrate that Jacobs used the material circumstances of her life to critique conventional standards of female behavior and to question their relevance and applicability to the experience of black women. Prior to a close examination of the text itself, it is necessary to document briefly the conditions under which Jacobs wrote her autobiography and gained her public voice.

At the time of writing, Jacobs worked as a domestic servant for and lived with Nathaniel P. Willis and his second wife, the Mr. and Mrs. Bruce of the text. Unlike either his first or second wife, Nathaniel Willis was proslavery. Against Jacobs's wishes but to protect her from the fugitive slave law, the second Mrs. Willis persuaded her husband that Jacobs should be purchased from her owners and manumitted by the family. Because of her suspicions of Nathaniel Willis, Jacobs did not want him to be aware that she was writing of her life in slavery; the need for secrecy and the demands of her domestic duties as nurse to the Willis children forced Jacobs to write at night. Jacobs recognized that the conditions under which she lived and wrote were very different from those under which other female authors were able to write and under which her audience, "the women of the North," lived. In her preface, Linda Brent stated:

> Since I have been at the North, it has been necessary for me to work diligently for my own support, and the education of my children. This has not left me much leisure to make up for the loss of early opportunities to improve myself; and it has compelled me to write these pages at irregular intervals, whenever I could snatch an hour from Household duties.

Unlike her white female audience or contemporary authors, Jacobs had neither the advantages of formal education nor contemplative leisure. She contrasted both her past life as a slave and her present condition, in which the selling of her labor was a prime necessity, with the social circumstances of her readership. Jacobs thus established the context within which we should understand her choice of epigram, from Isaiah (32:2): "Rise up, ye women that are at ease! Hear my voice, Ye careless daughters! Give ear unto my speech." Jacobs had achieved her freedom from slavery, but she was still bound to labor for the existence of herself and her children.

The closing pages of *Incidents* contrasted the "happy endings" of the conventional domestic novel with the present condition of the narrator, Linda Brent:

> Reader, my story ends with freedom; not in the usual way with marriage. . . .We are as free from the power of slaveholders as are the white people of the north; and though that, according to my ideas, is not saying a great deal, it is a vast improvement in *my* condition.

Contrary to Blassingame's interpretation, *Incidents* does not conform to the conventional happy ending of the sentimental novel. Linda Brent, in the closing pages of her narrative, was still bound to a white mistress.

Jacobs's position as a domestic servant contrasted with the lives of the white women who surrounded and befriended her. Mrs. Willis, though she was instrumental in gaining her manumission, had the power to buy her and remained her employer, her mistress. Jacobs's letters to Amy Post, although to a friend, revealed her consciousness of their different positions in relation to conventional moral codes. Desiring a female friend who would write some prefatory remarks to her narrative, Jacobs consulted Post, but the occasion led her to indicate that the inclusion of her sexual history in her narrative made her "shrink from asking the sacrifice from one so good and pure as yourself." It was as if Jacobs feared that her own history would contaminate the reputation of her white friend. Lydia Maria Child, who became Jacobs's editor, and Harriet Beecher Stowe, with whom Jacobs had an unfortunate brush, were both described by her as "satellite[s] of so great magnitude." This hierarchy in Jacobs's relations with white women was magnified through the lens of conventional ideas of true womanhood when they appeared in print together, for Jacobs's sexuality was compromised in the very decision to print her story and gain her public voice. As she wrote to Post, after Post had agreed to endorse her story, "Woman can whisper her cruel wrongs into the ear of a very dear friend much easier than she can record them for the world to read." Jacobs had children but no husband and no home of her own. In order to be able to represent herself in conventional terms as a "true" woman, Jacobs should have had a husband to give meaning to her existence as a woman. . . . Any power or influence a woman could exercise was limited to the boundaries of the home. Linda Brent, in the concluding chapter of her narrative, recognized that this particular definition of a woman's sphere did not exist for her, and this factor ensured her dependence on a mistress. She stated, "I do not sit with my children in a home of my own. I still long for a hearthstone of my own, however humble. I wish it for my children's sake far more than my own."

The ideological definition of the womanhood and motherhood of Linda Brent (and Jacobs) remained ambivalent as Linda Brent (and Jacobs) were excluded from the domain of the home, the sphere within which womanhood and motherhood were defined. Without a "woman's sphere," both were rendered meaningless. Nevertheless, the narrative of Linda Brent's life stands as an exposition of her womanhood and motherhood contradicting and transforming an ideology that could not take account of her experience. The structure of Jacobs's narrative embodied the process through which the meaning of Linda Brent's and Jacobs's motherhood and womanhood were revealed. Jacobs, as author, confronted an ideology that denied her very existence as a black woman and as a mother, and, therefore, she had to formulate a set of meanings that implicitly and fundamentally questioned the basis of true womanhood. *Incidents* demystified a convention that appeared as the obvious, commonsense rules of behavior and revealed the concept of true womanhood to be an ideology, not a lived set of social relations as she exposed its inherent contradictions and inapplicability to her life.

Jacobs rejected a patronizing offer by Harriet Beecher Stowe to incorporate her life story into the writing of *The Key to Uncle Tom's Cabin*. This incorporation would have meant that her history would have been circumscribed by the bounds of convention, and Jacobs responded that "it needed no romance." The suggestion that Stowe might write, and control, the story of Jacobs's life raised issues far greater than those which concerned the artistic and aesthetic merit of her narrative; Jacobs "felt denigrated as a mother, betrayed as a woman, and threatened as a writer by Stowe's action." Jacobs knew that to gain her own public voice, as a writer, implicated her very existence as a mother and a woman; the three could not be separated. She also knew from experience, as did Prince and Wilson, that the white people of the North were not completely free from the power of the slaveholders, or from their racism. To be bound to the conventions of true womanhood was to be bound to a racist, ideological system.

Many slave authors changed the names of people and places in their narratives to protect those still subject to slavery. However, Jacobs's need for secrecy in the act of writing and her fear of scorn if discovered meant that her pseudonym, Linda Brent, functioned as a mechanism of self-protection. The creation of Linda Brent as a fictional narrator allowed Jacobs to manipulate a series of conventions that were not only literary in their effects but which also threatened the meaning of Jacobs's social existence. The construction of the history of Linda Brent was the terrain through which Jacobs had to journey in order to reconstruct the meaning of her own life as woman and mother. The journey provided an alternative path to the cult of true womanhood and challenged the readers of *Incidents* to interrogate the social and ideological structures in which they were implicated and to examine their own racism. Jacobs denied that she wrote to "excite sympathy" for her own "sufferings" but claimed that she wanted to "arouse the women of the North to a realizing sense of the condition of two millions of women at the South, still in bondage, suffering what I suffered, and most of them far worse." Jacobs established that hers was the voice of a representative black female slave, and in a contemporary interpretation this appeal is defined as being an appeal to the sisterhood of all women:

> Seen from this angle of vision, Jacobs' book—reaching across the gulf separating black women from white, slave from free, poor from rich, reaching across the chasm separating "bad" women from "good"—represents an attempt to establish an American sisterhood and to activate that sisterhood in the public arena.

However, these bonds of sisterhood are not easily or superficially evoked. "Sisterhood" between white and black women was realized rarely in the text of

Incidents. Jacobs's appeal was to a potential rather than an actual bonding between white and black women. The use of the word *incidents* in the title of her narrative directs the reader to be aware of a consciously chosen selection of events in Jacobs's life. Many of the relationships portrayed between Linda Brent and white women involve cruelty and betrayal and place white female readers in the position of having to realize their implication in the oppression of black women, prior to any actual realization of the bonds of "sisterhood."

The narrative was framed by Linda Brent's relationships to white mistresses. The relationship to Mrs. Willis with which the narrative concluded has already been discussed. The opening chapter, "Childhood," described Linda's early disillusion with a mistress whom she loved and trusted. Linda's early childhood was happy, and only on the death of her mother did Linda learn that she was a slave. *Sister* and *sisterhood* were made ambiguous terms for relationships which had dubious consequences for black women. Early in the text Linda referred to her mother and her mother's mistress as "foster sisters" because they were both fed at the breast of Linda's grandmother. This intimate "sisterhood" as babes was interrupted by the intervention of the starkly contrasting hierarchy of their social relationship. Linda's grandmother, the readers were told, had to wean her own daughter at three months old in order to provide sufficient food for her mistress's daughter. Although they played together as children, Linda's mother's slave status was reasserted when she had to become "a most faithful servant" to her "foster sister." At the side of the deathbed of Linda's mother, her mistress promised her that "her children [would] never suffer for anything" in the future. Linda described her subsequent childhood with this mistress as "happy," without "toilsome or disagreeable duties." A diligent slave, Linda felt "proud to labor for her as much as my young years would permit," and she maintained a heart "as free from care as that of any free born white child."

Unlike Kate Drumgoold in *A Slave Girl's Story*, Linda Brent did not attempt to replace this mistress as surrogate mother. The phrase carefully chosen by Jacobs was "almost like a mother." The juxtaposition of the concepts of a carefree childhood with laboring registered an experience alien to that of the readership. This gentle disturbance to middle-class ideas of childhood moved toward a climactic shock at the death of the mistress, when Linda was bequeathed to the daughter of her mistress's sister. Linda and her community of friends had been convinced that she would be freed, but, with bitterness, Linda recalled the years of faithful servitude of her mother and her mistress's promise to her mother. In a passage that used a narrative strategy similar to that used by Prince in her *Life and Travels*, Jacobs's narrator indicted the behavior of her mistress according to conventional moral codes. Linda Brent reasserted the religious doctrine espoused by her mistress to condemn her action and reveal the hypocrisy of her beliefs:

> My mistress had taught me the precepts of God's word: "Thou shalt love thy neighbor as thyself." "Whatsoever ye would that men should do unto you, do ye even so unto them." But I was her slave, and I suppose she did not recognize me as her neighbor.

The disparity between "almost a mother" and the lack of recognition as "neighbor" highlighted the intensity of Jacobs's sense of betrayal. Having taught her slave to read and spell, this mistress had contributed to the ability of Jacobs to tell her tale, but the story Jacobs told condemned the mistress, for it was her "act of injustice" that initiated the suffering in Linda Brent's life.

Because of the hierarchical nature of their social, as opposed to emotional, relationships, white mistresses in the text were placed in positions of power and influence over the course of the lives of slave women, an influence that was still being exerted at the close of the narrative after Linda's emancipation. Linda did not recount the actions of her mistress as if they were only an individual instance of betrayal but placed them within a history of acts of betrayal toward three generations of women in her family: herself, her mother, and her grandmother. Each served as faithful servant, each trusted to the honor of her mistress, and each was betrayed. The reconstruction of these acts through time and over generations was an attempt to assert their representative status within a historical perspective of dishonesty and hypocrisy.

The polarization between the lives of white sisters and black sisters was a recurring motif. The material differences in their lives that determined their futures and overwhelmed either biological relation or emotional attachment were continually stressed in the text. Linda Brent told the reader:

> I once saw two beautiful children playing together. One was a fair white child; the other was her slave, and also her sister. When I saw them embracing each other, and heard their joyous laughter, I turned sadly away from the lovely sight. I foresaw the inevitable blight that would fall on the little slave's heart. I knew how soon her laughter would be changed to sighs. The fair child grew up to be a still fairer woman. From childhood to womanhood her pathway was blooming with flowers. . . . How had those years dealt with her slave sister, the little playmate of her childhood? She was also very beautiful; but the flowers and sunshine of love were not for her. She drank the cup of sin, and shame, and misery, whereof her persecuted race are compelled to drink.

Any feminist history that seeks to establish the sisterhood of white and black women as allies in the struggle against the oppression of all women must also reveal the complexity of the social and economic differences between women. Feminist historiography and literary criticism also need to define the ways in which racist practices are gender-specific and sexual exploitation racialized. The dialectical nature of this process is reconstructed in the "incidents" that Jacobs reconstructed between the slave woman and her mistress.

Linda Brent described her second mistress, Mrs. Flint, in ways that utilized the conventions of an antebellum ideal of womanhood while exposing them as contradictory:

> Mrs. Flint, like many southern women, was totally deficient in energy. She had not strength to superintend her household affairs; but her nerves were so strong, that she could sit in her easy chair and see a woman whipped, till the blood trickled from every stroke of the lash.

Mrs. Flint forced Linda Brent to walk barefoot through the snow because the "creaking" of her new shoes "grated harshly on her refined nerves." In these and other passages the conventional figure of the plantation mistress is ironically undermined. The qualities of delicacy of constitution and heightened sensitivity, attributes of the Southern lady, appear as a corrupt and superficial veneer that covers an underlying strength and power in cruelty and brutality.

Linda Brent realized that because of Dr. Flint's overt sexual advances and intentions she represented an actual as well as potential threat to the dignity and pride of Mrs. Flint. Jacobs demonstrated the slave's capacity to analyze the grief and pain of her mistress; the slave, however, waited in vain for a reciprocal display of kindness or sympathy. The sisterhood of the two abused women could not be established, for Mrs. Flint, who "pitied herself as a martyr . . . was incapable of feeling for the condition of shame and misery in which her unfortunate, helpless slave was placed."

In an attempt to appeal directly to the compassion of her white Northern readers, Jacobs contrasted the material conditions of black female slaves with their own lives:

> O, you happy free women, contrast *your* New Year's day with that of the poor bond-woman! With you it is a pleasant season, and the light of the day is blessed. . . . Children bring their little offerings, and raise their rosy lips for a caress. They are your own, and no hand but that of death can take them from you. But to the slave mother New Year's day comes laden with peculiar sorrows. She sits on a cold cabin floor, watching the children who may all be torn from her the next morning; and often does she wish that she and they might die before the day dawns.

Linda Brent was a demonstration of the consequences for motherhood of the social and economic relations of the institution of slavery. Jacobs recognized that plantation mistresses were subject to forms of patriarchal abuse and exploitation, but because they gave birth to the heirs of property they were also awarded a degree of patriarchal protection. Slave women gave birth to the capital of the South and were therefore, in Linda Brent's words, "considered of no value, unless they continually increase their owner's stock." Upon this hierarchical differential in power relations an ideology was built which ensured that two opposing concepts of motherhood and womanhood were maintained. As Linda Brent argued, "that which commands admiration in the white woman only hastens the degradation of the female slave." If a slave woman attempted to preserve her sexual autonomy, the economic system of slavery was threatened: "[I]t [was] deemed a crime in her to wish to be virtuous."

The barriers to the establishment of the bonding of sisterhood were built in the space between the different economic, political, and social positions that black women and white women occupied in the social formation of slavery. Their hierarchical relationship was determined through a racial, not gendered, categorization. The ideology of true womanhood was as racialized a concept in relation to white women as it was in its exclusion of black womanhood. Ultimately, it was this racial factor that defined the source of power of white women over their slaves, for, in a position of dependence on the patriarchal system herself, the white mistress identified her interests with the maintenance of the status quo. Linda Brent concluded:

> No matter whether the slave girl be as black as ebony or as fair as her mistress. In either case, there is no shadow of law to protect her from insult, from violence, or even from death; all these are inflicted by friends who bear the shape of men. The mistress, who ought to protect the helpless victim, has no other feelings towards her but those of jealousy and rage.

Jacobs thus identified that mistresses confirmed their own social position at the expense of denying the humanity of their slaves particularly when they were insecure in their own relation to patriarchal power: "I knew that the young wives of slaveholders often thought their authority and importance would be best established and maintained by cruelty."

The Northern women who formed Jacobs's audience were implicated in the preservation of this oppression in two ways. In a passage that directly addressed the reader, Linda Brent accused Northerners of allowing themselves to be used as "bloodhounds" to hunt fugitives and return them to slavery. More subtly, Linda Brent also illustrated how Northerners were not immune to the effects of the slave system or to the influence of being able to wield a racist power when she described how, "when northerners go to the south to reside, they prove very apt scholars. They soon imbibe the sentiments and disposition of their neighbors, and generally go beyond their teachers. Of the two, they are proverbially the hardest masters." *Incidents* also documented the numerous acts of racist oppression that Linda Brent had to suffer while in the Northern states. A major motive for her escape from the South was her determination to protect her daughter, Ellen, from the sexual exploitation she herself had experienced. However, Ellen was subject to sexual harassment in the household in which she lived and worked as a servant in New York, which made Linda Brent question the nature and extent of her freedom in the "free" states of the North. Described as being in a position of "servitude to the Anglo-Saxon race," Linda Brent urged the whole black community to defy the racism of Northerners, so that "eventually we shall cease to be trampled underfoot by our oppressors."

This spirit of defiance characterized Jacobs's representations of all Linda Brent's encounters with her master. Conventional feminine qualities of submission and passivity were replaced by an active resistance. Although Flint had "power and law on his side," she "had a determined will," and "there was might in each." Her strength and resourcefulness to resist were not adopted from a reservoir of masculine attributes but were shown to have their source in her "woman's pride, and a mother's love for [her] children." Thus, Jacobs developed an alternative set of definitions of womanhood and motherhood in the text which remained in tension with the cult of true womanhood.

The slave became the object of the jealousy and spite of her mistress; Jacobs wrote that Mrs. Flint even vented her anger on Linda Brent's grandmother for offering Linda and her children protective shelter: "She would not even speak to her in the street. This wounded my grandmother's feelings, for she could not retain ill will against the woman who she had nourished with her milk when a babe." In an effective adaptation of convention it was Linda Brent's grandmother who was portrayed as a woman of genuine sensitivity. The two women were polarized: the grandmother exuded a "natural" warmth, but Mrs. Flint, as Jacobs's choice of name emphasized, displayed an unnatural, cold, and hard heart. For the grandmother, the act of nurturing gave rise to sustained feelings of intimacy; Mrs. Flint's rejection of this mothering relationship implied that she was an unnatural woman. Linda Brent stated that she was "indebted" to her grandmother for all her comforts, "spiritual or temporal." It was the grandmother's labor that fed and clothed her when Mrs. Flint neglected her slave's material needs, and it was the grandmother who stood as the source of a strong moral code in the midst of an immoral system. In a considerable number of ways, Jacobs's figure of the grandmother embodied aspects of a *true* womanhood; she was represented as being pure and pious, a fountainhead of physical and spiritual sustenance for Linda, her whole family, and the wider black community. However, the quality of conventional womanhood that the grandmother did not possess was submissiveness, and Linda Brent was portrayed as having inherited her spirit. Her love for her grandmother was seen to be tempered by fear; she had been brought up to regard her with a respect that bordered on awe, and at the moment when Linda Brent needed the advice of another woman most desperately she feared to confide in her grandmother, who she knew would condemn her. Out of the moment of her most intense isolation Jacobs made her narrator forge her own rules of behavior and conduct of which even her grandmother would disapprove.

Dr. Flint was characterized by Jacobs as the epitome of corrupt white male power. He was a figure that was carefully dissected to reveal a lack of the conventional qualities of a gentleman. His lack of honor was established early in the text when he defrauded Linda Brent's grandmother. Presented as a representative slaveholder, Dr. Flint embodied the evil licentiousness that was the ultimate threat to virtue and purity. He whispered foul suggestions into Linda's ears when she was still an innocent girl and used his power to deny her the experience of romance, preventing her from marrying her first, true love. In the chapter entitled "The Lover," a free-born black carpenter was described as possessing the qualities that were absent in Dr. Flint. Honor was posed against dishonor, respect for Linda's virtue against disrespect and insult. The lover Jacobs described as both "intelligent and religious," while Dr. Flint appeared as an animal watching a young girl as his prey. The "base proposals of a white man" were contrasted with the "honorable addresses of a respectable colored man." But, despite the fact that Dr. Flint was the embodiment of the corruption of the slave system, as his prey Linda Brent was not corrupted by him, and her struggle was an aggressive refusal to be sexually used and compromised or to succumb to the will of the master.

Instead, hoping to gain a degree of protection from Dr. Flint, Linda Brent decided to become the lover of a white "gentleman," a Mr. Sands. She thought that in his fury Dr. Flint would sell her to her newly acquired lover and that it would be easier in the future to obtain her freedom from her lover than from her master. Linda's reasoning was shown to be motivated by consideration not only for her own welfare but also for improving the chances of survival for any children she might bear. From her experience she knew that Dr. Flint sold his offspring from slave women and hoped that if her children were fathered by Sands he could buy them and secure their future.

The struggle of Linda Brent to retain some control over her sexuality climaxed in a confession of her loss of virtue. It was at this point in the narrative that Jacobs most directly confronted conventional morality. In order to retain narrative authority and to preserve a public voice acceptable to an antebellum readership, Jacobs carefully negotiated the tension between satisfying moral expectations and challenging an ideology that would condemn her as immoral. Jacobs's confession was at once both conventional and unconventional in form and tone. The narrator declared in a direct address to her readers that the remembrance of this period in her "unhappy life" filled her with "sorrow and shame" and made no reference to sexual satisfaction, love, or passion, as such feelings were not meant to be experienced or encouraged outside of marriage and were rarely figured to exist within it. Yet Jacobs refused to follow convention in significant ways. In contrast to the expected pattern of a confessional passage, which called for the unconditional acceptance of the judgment of readers, Linda Brent's act of sexual defiance was described as one of "deliberate calculation": the slave actively chose one fate as opposed to another. Jacobs attempted to deflect any judgmental response of moral condemnation through consistent narrative reminders to the reader that the material conditions of a slave woman's life were different from theirs. Readers were the "happy women" who had been "free to choose the objects of [their] affection." Jacobs, through Linda Brent, claimed the same right in her attempt to assert some control over the conditions of her existence: "It seems less degrading to give one's self, than to submit to compulsion. There is something akin to freedom in having a lover who has no control over you, except that which he gains by kindness and attachment." Jacobs argued that the practice of conventional principles of morality was rendered impossible by the condition of the slave. Her own decision to take a lover was not described as immoral or amoral but as outside conventional ethical boundaries. In a key passage for understanding the extent to which Jacobs challenged ideologies of female sexuality, Linda Brent reflected, "in looking back, calmly, on the events of my life, I feel that the slave woman ought not to be judged by the same standard as others." Within the series of "incidents" that Jacobs represented, this decision was pivotal to the structure of the text and to the development of an alternative discourse of womanhood. Previous events focused on the disruption to a normative journey through childhood, girlhood, and romantic youth; following incidents established the unconventional definitions of womanhood and motherhood that Jacobs, herself, tried to determine.

Linda Brent's decision as a slave, to survive through an act that resulted in her loss of virtue, placed her outside the parameters of the conventional heroine. Barbara Welter has described how heroines who were guilty of a loss of purity, in novels or magazines, were destined for death or madness. According to the doctrine of true womanhood, death itself was preferable to a loss of innocence; Linda Brent not only survived in her "impure" state, but she also used her "illicit" liaison as an attempt to secure a future for herself and her children. Jacobs's narrative was unique in its subversion of a major narrative code of sentimental fiction: death, as preferable to loss of purity, was replaced by "Death is better than slavery." *Incidents* entered the field of women's literature and history transforming and transcending the central paradigm of death versus virtue. The consequences of the loss of innocence, Linda Brent's (and Jacobs's) children, rather than being presented as the fruits of her shame, were her links to life and the motivating force of an additional determination to be free.

Linda Brent's second child was a girl, and the birth caused her to reflect on her daughter's possible future as a slave: "When they told me my new-born babe was a girl, my heart was heavier than it had ever been before. Slavery is terrible for men; but it is far more terrible for women. Superadded to the burden common to all, *they* have wrongs, and sufferings, and mortifications peculiarly their own." The narrative that Jacobs wrote was assertively gender-specific and resonated against the dominant forms of the male slave narrative. But the sexual exploitation that Linda Brent confronted and feared for her daughter was, at the same moment, racially specific, disrupting conventional expectations of the attributes of a heroine. Death became the price that Linda Brent was prepared to pay to free her daughter from slavery: "I knew the doom that awaited my fair baby in slavery, and I determined to save her from it, or perish in the attempt." The slave mother made this vow by the graves of her parents, in the "burying-ground of the slaves," where "the prisoners rest together; they hear not the voice of the oppressor; the servant is free from his master." Jacobs added the voice of her narrator to a history of slave rebels but at the same time completed a unique act. The transition from death as preferable to slavery to the stark polarity of freedom or death was made at this narrative moment. "As I passed the wreck of the old meeting house, where, before Nat Turner's time, the slaves had been allowed to meet for worship, I seemed to hear my father's voice come from it, bidding me not to tarry till I reached freedom or the grave." Freedom replaced and transcended purity. Linda Brent's loss of innocence was a gain; she realized the necessity of struggling for the freedom of her children even more than for herself. Thus, the slave woman's motherhood was situated by Jacobs as the source of courage and determination.

In order to save her children, Linda Brent apparently had to desert them. To precipitate a crisis and persuade Dr. Flint that he should sell the children to their father, Sands, Linda escaped and hid. The children were sold and returned to their great-grandmother's house to live, where, unknown to them, their mother was in hiding. However, Linda Brent's hopes for emancipation for her children were shattered when her daughter, Ellen, was "given" as a waiting maid to Sands's relatives in New York. After years in hiding, Linda escaped to New York and found employment. Her daughter was neglected, inadequately fed and clothed, and when Benjamin, her son, was finally sent north to join her, Linda realized that in order to protect her children she must own herself, freeing them all from the series of white people's broken promises that had framed her life.

Having obtained Ellen's freedom, Linda Brent confided her sexual history to her daughter as the one person whose forgiveness she desired. As opposed to the earlier confession, which was directly addressed to readers, Jacobs portrays Linda as in need of the unmediated judgment of Ellen. Ellen refused to condemn her mother and told her that she had been aware of her sexual relations with Sands, rejected her father as meaning nothing to her, and reserved her love for Linda. The motherhood that Jacobs defined and shaped in her narrative was vindicated through her own daughter, excluding the need for any approval from the readership. Jacobs bound the meaning and interpretation of her womanhood and motherhood to the internal structure of the text, making external validation unnecessary and unwarranted. Judgment was to be passed on the institution of slavery, not on deviations from conventions of true womanhood.

Jacobs gained her public voice and access to a sympathetic audience through the production of a slave narrative, a cultural form of expression supported and encouraged by the abolitionist movement. She primarily addressed the white Northern women whom she urged to advocate the abolition of the system of slavery. However, Jacobs's narrative problematized assumptions that dominated abolitionist literature in general and male slave narratives in particular, assumptions that linked slave women to illicit sexuality. Jacobs's attempt to develop a framework in which to discuss the social, political, and economic consequences of black womanhood prefigured the concerns of black women intellectuals after emancipation. For these intellectuals the progress of the race would be intimately tied to and measured by the progress of the black woman.

Black women writers would continue to adopt and adapt dominant literary conventions and to challenge racist sexual ideologies. Like Prince, Wilson, and Jacobs, they would explore a variety of narrative forms in the attempt to establish a public presence and continue to find ways to invent black heroines who could transcend their negative comparison to the figure of the white heroine. The consequences of being a slave woman did not end with the abolition of slavery as an institution but haunted the texts of black women throughout the nineteenth century and into the twentieth. The transition from slave to free woman did not liberate the black heroine or the black woman from the political and ideological limits imposed on her sexuality. In the shift from slave narrative to fiction, . . .

GAYL JONES (b. 1949)

Gayl Jones grew up in Kentucky and began writing at an early age. Her first novel, Corregidora *(1975), deals with the difficulties that African Americans often experience because of racism and sexism.* Eva's Man *(1976) deals with similar themes; in the novel, a woman strikes back at her male antagonist. Jones is consistent to her focus in her book of short stories,* White Rat *(1977). She is concerned about the denial of freedom and the consequences that stem from it. In addition to fiction, she has published several books of poetry, including* The Hermit-Woman *(1983). One of her major texts examines the African American oral tradition:* Liberating Voices: Oral Tradition in African American Literature *(1991).*

From Liberating Voices: Oral Tradition in African American Literature (1991)

Dialect and Narrative: Zora Neale Hurston's Their Eyes Were Watching God

Their Eyes Were Watching God (1937) is a transitional novel in the dialect tradition. Though a small work, it is not about a little world of dialect; it is a hypercharged little book which coordinates and resolves certain early dialect problems while initiating and anticipating many of the concerns and conceptions of contemporary writers. Like a shining hummingbird, it flies backwards (as only the hummingbird can) and forwards, pointing to the past and anticipating the future dialect novel.

A glimpse of dialect's function in the nineteenth century African American novel reveals the same presuppositions of the minstrel mode we found in Dunbar's "The Lynching of Jube Benson," with similar effects on the interplay of dialect and personality. William Wells Brown's *Clotel* (1853) is a well of such presuppositions. Chapter XII, "A Night in the Parson's Kitchen," illustrates the author's and the age's attitude toward dialect. In this important chapter, for the first time in African American literature the reader is introduced to slaves in a social and communicative context. Here dialect follows one of James Weldon Johnson's tenets: it enters only as comic relief. Therefore, the chapters which dramatize the relationships between blacks exist chiefly as amusing interludes. This stylistic attitude and its consequence—like the aesthetics of the central character Clotel, "indistinguishable from a white woman" and the leading victim of slaveholders' duplicity and sexual abuse—appear to contradict the purpose of the book: that is, to show (prove?) the humanity of blacks as well as expose the cruel conditions of slavery as an abolitionist argument. None of the Blacks in the book is given full portrayal, either in character, scene, or language. This treatment resembles the European literary tradition (and hence Brown's literary model) of treating servants and the lower classes comically, or as background figures (even when they were pulled to the foreground as in *Don Quijote,* they remained essentially comedians, when not villains, though Cervantes modifies tradition somewhat by Sancho's Quixotic metamorphosis). In *Clotel* both the black slaves and the Southern poor whites are treated to a similar pattern of comic relief or minstrel humor. Likewise, in nineteenth-century European-American literature the routine opinion was that " 'low' scenes and characters could appropriately be dealt with only as comic," as seen in the mining stories of Bret Harte. Walt Whitman, the only pre-Twain writer who thought otherwise, felt that "vernacular [was] adequate to meet any demand a serious writer might make on it."

Chapter XIII of *Clotel,* "A Slave Hunting Parson," scenically parallels Chapter XII; here, treated like the Blacks in the previous chapter, the poor whites assume the role of Mr. Bones to the white parson's Interlocutor. Moreover, the dialect of the poor whites is virtually indistinguishable from the slaves' diction. Rather than liberating the dialect, Brown's intention is perhaps to allow it to become a part of the antislavery argument too: the refusal to educate the poor white and the general low condition of these people, linguistically and otherwise, are yet another consequence of slavery. To show the "despicable language" of slavery being used by whites as well as Blacks was precisely one of the antislavery techniques, and the fact that the chapters are annexed verifies this tactic. The novel's purpose aside, the scene in the kitchen registers the adverse influence of the minstrel tradition on the use of dialect in the novel, and discloses its human and experiential limitations. Without quoting the scene, the bit of verse that precedes the chapter serves to crystallize its function:

> And see the servants met,
> Their daily labour's o'er;
> And with the jest and song they set
> The kitchen in a roar.

The only nineteenth-century black novel which admits intelligent and complex speakers of dialect and "elevated uses" is Martin Delany's *Blake*, but Delany notably departs from many other obdurate conventions. According to Black Aesthetic critic Addison Gayle, the writer's paradigmatic hero is "handsome, black, intelligent." But even though Delany admits and displays a variety of characters using dialect, his central character—an educated man—speaks standard; indeed, a very rarified, formal, stylized, impeccable English. This is another variation in the dialect-standard ambivalence. Many African American writers hesitate between dialect and standard. For some the standard language becomes precious, that is, too respectful, observant, and attentive to the rules, too meticulous, too punctilious and seemingly "derivative" without the versatility and easy informality of writers who take their tradition and language for granted. This can also happen to European writers from different social groups: those who take their cultural modes for granted often more freely innovate and originate, are less modest and moderate in what they will do with the standard and its forms. There are exceptions, of course, such as D. H. Lawrence and James Joyce, but Joyce after all had an elitist, Jesuit education. Still Joyce could do nothing to please certain of his "social betters" such as Virginia Woolf, who called *Ulysses* "illiterate" and "underbred." Even D. H. Lawrence had at least moral if not social objections to the "deliberate, journalistic dirty-mindedness" of the book. Ulysses, as we know, is neither illiterate nor journalistic, and if dirty-minded, it is rarified, exalted, stellar dirty-mindedness. Yet perhaps his social placement did make for Joyce's *push*, to prove that he could do anything and everything in the language.

But to get back to that other punctiliousness: it often carries into characterization itself, where even virtue is formalized—what Sterling Brown called "plaster of Paris saints." Yet this formality, more noticeable perhaps in black writers because of both the dialect stereotyping and the linguistic reality of many speakers, is really no different from that of other writers who come from dialect regions. Standard language often acquires a rare elegance, and actors and writers from St. Louis are often mistaken for (upperclass) Englishmen (even Virginia Woolf would approve). One is more attentive to the standard. One listens deeper. One becomes at times, too literate. (It is interesting that in French a sign of the educated speaker is the *liaison*—the running-on of letters, whereas in many Southern American communities—black and white—the educated speaker pronounces *all his letters*—occasionally those not meant to be pronounced.)

Delany's *Blake* speaks standard. Even in scenes with other slaves the minstrel pattern is absent. He does not assume the role of Mr. Interlocutor with his "ignorant fellows." Blake's interchanges with speakers of dialect are not for comic relief; indeed very complex situations are often recognized and recreated. Here a dialect-speaking woman is introduced in a way that contrasts significantly with the traditional pattern: "'How de do, sir!' saluted she, a modest and intelligent, very pretty young black girl, of good address." In *Blake*, intelligent personalities are still visible through dialect, are allowed to speak it, and may still be moral, serious, and complex human beings.

In nineteenth-century pre-Hurston fiction, it was generally simply taken for granted that the central character, along with his moral and intellectual superiority, would also be a speaker of standard English (and his language proof of these other qualities); this was unquestioned and unquestionable. This is not the case in Hurston's work. Janie does not speak standard, yet she is the central character. She does not speak standard, yet she is intelligent and complex, and her dialect is part of what Whitman would call the "taste of identity." I might add here, however, that one of my students who was reading Hurston's *Their Eyes Were Watching God* laughed when he got to the dialect—Janie's speaking dialect was unexpected. We talked about his reaction and possible reasons for it. I suggested two: that he was used to the leading black character's speaking standard in the participant-observer novels of earlier black writers; and that his was a conditioned response to *any* dialect, and marked the persistence of the minstrel attitude. For instance, we continue to see the usage of not only ethnic but regional dialect in the media, even though many of the literary writers have long since abandoned that comic or satirical intention. In films especially, unless they are comedians or villains, even white Southerners do not speak like Southerners, perhaps because this would trigger too much laughter when the intent is dramatic. Usually the leading characters whom the audience must identify with speak standard. White Southern writers, on the other hand, have liberated their own voices, so that they at least bring authentic American voices into their fiction, often to the forefront of American letters. Nor are these voices restricted to dialogue, but enter every mode of expression. Occasional movies and television shows, taking their cue from the literature, also allow these voices (for their "flavor"), but I believe most audiences still *hear* them as quaint, picturesque, or minor; and speakers of regional dialects are often described, no matter how loquacious, as "inarticulate," (this is how a New York critic referred to the garrulous characters in the stories of Bobbie Ann Mason). And as I mentioned in the chapter on Hurston's short story, it could have been the attitude of the reader, not the writer, that cued Wright to dismiss Hurston's intent out of hand as minstrel.

Hurston's dialect, however, is linked both to her concern with the authentic possibilities of the black voice in literature and to variegated dimensions of character. *Their Eyes Were Watching God* is a transitional dialect novel because it extends the innovations in the dialect tradition the author began in her short story "The Gilded Six-Bits," and because it more fully actualizes the potential of literary dialect than did the fictions of Dunbar or Chesnutt, or the antecedent novels of William Wells Brown and even Martin Delany, though *Blake* provides a sturdier bridge to Hurston's work and its aims than do any of the others.

As with Hurston's short story, the dramatic focus of Hurston's novel is *within* an African American community. The theme is a woman's search for love that leads to a new conception of freedom and identity. Hurston stresses the psychology of character and complexity of relationships, all providing a background of fictional value to complement the linguistic innovation—an innovation which perhaps again seems slight to contemporary readers, but is noteworthy for the emotional and experiential range and sense of human possibilities released by both Hurston's redefining perspective and literary dialect. Though she is not talking specifically of Zora Neale Hurston here, novelist and poet Alice Walker defines this necessary, important shift in perspective:

> even black critics have assumed that a book that deals with the relationships between members of a black family—or between a man and a woman—is less important than one that has white people as a primary antagonist. The consequence of this is that many of our books by "major" writers (always male) tell us little about the culture, history, or future, imagination, fantasies, etc. of black people, and a lot about isolated (often improbable) or limited encounters with a nonspecific white world. Where is the book, by an American black person (aside from *Cane*) . . . that exposes the subconscious of a people, because the people's dreams, imaginings, rituals, legends, etc. are known to be important, are known to contain the accumulated collective reality of the people themselves.

To receive the full weight of this observation, one must compare Walker's statement with two other critical perspectives: first, the black protest tradition, concentrating on interracial conflict at the expense of intricate character relationships, and second, the white critical perspective, assuring black writers that the "broader perspective" was never their own, militated against this "accumulated collective reality" in black fictional imaginings.

Below, Rebecca Chalmers Barron's praise throws light on her view of a black writer's perspective: "Nor does the boundary of color bar the promising new writer, Ann Petry, from the broader perspective. Her latest book, *Country Place*, exposes plenty of seaminess in New England small town life without recourse to racial questions. In fact, there is only one Negro character, and she is cast in a minor role." In an otherwise well-written and astute book, Barron here manifests the critical atmosphere of her time (and ours?). To deal with whites in a small town is "broad," even laudatory, but to deal with Blacks in a small town (à la *Winesburg, Ohio* or *Dubliners;* even *Madame Bovary* is provincial, but "French provincial") is "narrow" and a "recourse to racial questions." Unfortunately, not a few black readers themselves share this sensibility, and works where only Blacks are visible or have the major visibility in the text are dismissed by themselves as racial material. A simple test would be to repaint some of the faces without changing the work technically and see how instantly "racial material" becomes universalized (meaning improved) or vice versa.

Ideally, the black writer, like any writer, should be able to write about *anyone anywhere anytime*—Greek farmers, Swedish businessmen, Bolivian mathematicians, Chinese professors of Italian literature, African astronauts—including his own, to show that sort of human as well as technical diversity and dexterity; but to confuse the issue, as it is still being confused, is to suggest that an Irish writer *must* write about Spaniards to be universal. Indeed, if black writers are castigated for writing about Blacks, mainstream white American writers should be castigated for writing about mainstream, middle-class white Americans (in their major roles). The only time I've seen this was when reading a book on science fiction writing; aspiring writers were informed that most of the world was *not* middle-class, white American and were advised to consider putting some Indians, Africans—or—let's not be too difficult—at least some Italians in outer space! (That is, as space *heroes*.) It is refreshing to hear middle-class white American writers being called to such a high standard, since they have so often accused others of not being universal if they do not include *them*, preferably in *their* leading roles. But enough of this—racial material and political motive and social psychology will probably continue to be confused with objective literary criticism. As black sculptor Mildred Thompson once said, "gallery personnel could not look at the work for looking at me!"

The black writer needs, in spite of others' confusion, to control and restore his own perspective as the norm. Michael S. Harper has expressed this well: "for me, Blacks are the norm, the individual context from which all can extrapolate. The particular is always the key to the universal, so I've never thought I had to get away from anything." In *Their Eyes Were Watching God*, dialect voicings break the boundaries of convention to restore perspective and tell us about "culture, history, future, imagination, fantasies," the internal and external reality of the characters in Hurston's world. For Hurston, too, "Blacks are the norm."

Dialect in Hurston's world has "the beauty and power of heard speech and lived experience." It is not restricted to the comic in any of its forms: grotesque, parody, burlesque, satire, or the pathos. Hurston's dialect demonstrates its capacity for a broad communicative range, through a variety of emotional transformations in many scenes, in shifts of mood and atmosphere, and in the quality and depth of assorted relationships. Here, as in Hurston's short story, dialect is still capable of humor, but it is the imaginative humor of the oral tradition—such as the storytelling on the store porch; it is the humor that one laughs *with*, the humor of boast and tall tale and comic balladry. Or it is a dialect capable of wit and biting satire, but never denying the intelligence or full humanity of its users. It is also a language that can go beyond pathos to the tragedy of Tea Cake's death and the incidents surrounding it; to express the heroism of Tea Cake's saving Janie during the hurricane, and the magic of their whole relationship. There are no fixed conventions. Like condensed energy suddenly made articulate, it can express any wonder, voice any meaning.

For Hurston, Janie is an articulate woman who "happens to" use dialect. The folk heroine, no longer quaint like Charles W. Chesnutt's "The Wife of His Youth," has become the complicated center of the work. However, Hurston maintains certain dialect conventions. For example, though Janie tells her story to her friend Phoeby, Hurston does not let her narrate the whole story in her own voice. She sets up the storytelling, then returns to the standard authorial voice. Let's refer again to John Wideman's comment that the framed story legitimizes and gives authority to black speech. Wideman goes on to discuss different frames and how they dramatize the assumptions of dialect, locking it into formulaic molds, determining the kinds of experiences, subject matter, and emotions it is allowed to express. And though the technique of the frame-story is old in Western litera-ture (Chaucer and Boccaccio used it; Joseph Conrad later employed it widely) we can see how a seemingly innocuous stylistic technique in African American liter-ature transcends itself to say something (or not say something) about human value and possibility.

In *From Behind the Veil*, Robert Stepto speaks further of this aspect of *Their Eyes Were Watching God* and the wider thematic implications regarding the articulate heroine: "Hurston's curious insistence on having Janie's tale—her personal his-tory in and as a literary form—told by an omniscient third person, rather than by a first-person narrator, implies that Janie has not really won her voice and self after all—that her author (who is, quite likely, the omniscient narrating voice) cannot see her way clear to giving Janie her voice outright." Stepto's discussion rivets the connection between voice and character liberation. And it also suggests a contrary standard regarding Western and African American literature. In Western literature, as I believe Oliver Wendell Holmes noted in an essay on writ-ing novels, most "great books" (he said *all*) have been third-person narratives; in African American literature from the slave narrative on, the importance of telling one's own story has been the thrust (*Invisible Man* is often distinguished in this tradition). I think this is an important instance where the higher technique in one tradition is not recognized as the higher technique in another. Its influence on how most African American literature is read and received outside the tradition is probably greater than suspected. (All well and good, but what can you do in third person? says one standard. Yes, but I'm winning my—or my character's—voice and self, says another.) What this could imply for contemporary work could be something like judging English drama by Racine's dramatic method: oh what loose, illogical, flighty, chaotic dramatists the English are!

Janie's grandmother's slave narrative—"Ah was born back due in slavery and it wasn't for me to fulfill my dreams of what a woman oughta be and to do"—pref-aces and foreshadows Janie's own story and provides the dramatic and revelatory pattern for it. Thus the slave narrative is also framed within a novel that drama-tizes a modernized version of it, although freedom here involves not only physi-cal escape, but spiritual renewal and escaping constricting ideas of self. Therefore, Janie searches for a new freedom, a new idea of what a woman should be and do, and she creates her own values, through patterns of illusion and disillusion, until, after her fulfilling, emancipating relationship with Tea Cake, she grows into whole womanhood. Though their relationship is important, as Robert Hemenway notes, Tea Cake is not the *cause* of Janie's growth but a complement for it: "While Jody would not let her take part in storytelling sessions, with Tea Cake it is perfectly natural for her to be a participant . . . It is important to note that Janie's partici-pation comes after she has learned to recognize sexism, a necessary preliminary to her self-discovery." Because there are no models for Janie of what she must be, she must more or less create herself. With Tea Cake that self-creation can develop wholly, after she has redefined her own horizon as distinct from that of her grandmother, her first two husbands, and perhaps her whole community: "She had been getting ready for her great journey to the horizons in search of *people; it was* important to all the world that she should find them and they find her. But she had been whipped like a cur dog, and run off down a back road after *things* . . . Nanny had taken the biggest thing God ever made, the horizon—for no matter how far a person can go the horizon is still way beyond you—and pinched it in to such a little bit of a thing that she could tie it about her granddaughter's neck tight enough to choke her."

Often, as here, fiction in the African American tradition contains models not of what one might be or become but the reverse: examples of what one must escape, nets to avoid in order to achieve wholeness. While some works contain examples of autonomous, self-realized characters who provide moral revelations or possibilities for the unrealized ones, central characters are often like Janie, emerging to recreate or create themselves without guideposts or blueprints except their own, or signs telling them where not to go. Of course this latter method can be tricky. A writer generally has three options for moral revelation: (1) representing characters as they should be (romanticism, idealism); (2) representing them as they are, or as he believes them to be (realism), or (3) representing them as they should *not* be (sometimes but not always in the context of naturalism, satire, irony, and so on). The black writer who chooses the third option is often misread and accused not of exposing the human condition but of stereotyping it (there is always a fine line, for example, between stereotyping and satire or satirical irony, which often distort or exaggerate in order to characterize; moreover, most readers end up understanding the character as negative if Black and stereotype are synonymous). Black writers who write linguistically and stylistically composite novels are also moved to some composite form of character portrayal in which the romantic ideal and its opposite or variants coexist. (Isn't this *Don Quijote* again or those marvelous nineteenth-century Russian novels?) Yet often one writer's romantic idea, even here, can be another's stereotype; certainly the masculine ideal as conceived by a woman writer, for example, might seem unlikely to a masculine reader. For example, Janie's (and Hurston's) "heroic, handsome, sensitive, generous-spirited" Tea Cake appeared to some (male) critics as merely another variant of the "guitar-strumming, irresponsible" (not free-spirited) black man stereotype. It is often the case that characterization is especially ambiguous among groups that have been the victims of unrelenting and even vicious stereotyping by others (like the Irishman in English literature). For such writers the dominant literary traditions and the creative act are often at variance. Again, my students provide an accessible example. Like most "revolutionary reformers," the students who had been the most vocal in denouncing the apparent stereotypes in the works of black writers (including Hurston) and specifying how those characters (and writers) erred, would quite often produce fictional works that others found equally questionable in their portrayals. Possibly lack of craft (necessary in creating any whole character), lack of fictional models (in or outside tradition), or inexorable "subliminal conditioning" (media) produced this result. But the reasons for the gulf between creative theory and creative act are not easy to explain in any tradition and it is always easier to talk the work to be done than to produce it.

Perhaps the only workable ideal black masculine character to have appeared in the literature is again Delany's Blake, a man capable of holding what are often seen as opposing or contradictory virtues: "He was bold, determined and courageous, but always mild, gentle, and courteous, though impulsive when occasion demanded his opposition." Unlike many one-dimensional ideals, Blake can be multidimensional without being contradictory: he adds up to a whole. Still, this remains on the level of description, which is easy, and though Blake achieves much of this characterization in fine and diverse scenes, they are not as skillfully dramatized as one would like, not as skillful as Hurston's or later writers (Wright, Ellison) with even more controversial characters. To be sure, Wright's Bigger Thomas is not meant to represent anyone's ideal, but rather the unrealized personality comparable to Joyce's *Dubliners* (and their implications vis à vis the Englishman's "Paddy"), who are unrealized versions of what Joyce, to his lights, might have been if he had stayed in Ireland. (Joyce later moved to the composite portrayal, the impressive intellect of Stephen Daedalus and the warmth and humanity of Leopold Bloom, in the midst of a multitude of Dubliners as they should not be.)

After Janie succeeded in realizing herself, her story as told to Phoeby assumes the patterns of revelation, the episodic scenic structures, and the geographical movements of the slave narrative, although, unlike the traditional narrative in the genre, Hurston, as we have seen, does not maintain Janie's voice throughout. But although Hurston does not go as far as later writers in breaking the frame and freeing Janie's whole voice as self, we should notice a narrative tension between the two linguistic traditions, a sense of new foundations being laid against an old wall. *Their Eyes Were Watching God* extends the instances that we first noticed in "The Gilded Six-Bits," where the vocabulary, syntax, metaphors, and thought processes of the characters invade the language and authorial voice of the narrative. Hurston's first attempt at breaking the frame occurs when she reports Joe Starks's initial conversation with Janie. The narrative breaks into the rhythms, vocabulary, and world view of Starks:

> Joe Starks was the name, yeah Joe Starks from in an through Georgy. Been working for white folks all his life. Saved up some money—round three hundred dollars, yes indeed, right here in his pocket. Kept hearin' 'bout them buildin' a new state down heah in Floridy and sort of wanted to come. But he was makin' money where he was. But when he heard all about 'em makin' a town all outa colored folks, he knowed dat was de place he wanted to be. He had always wanted to be a big voice, but de white folks had all do sayso where he come from and every where else, exceptin' dis place dat colored folks was buildin' theirselves. Dat was right too. De man dat built things oughta boss it. Let colored folks build things too if dey wants to crow over somethin'. He was glad he had his money all saved up. He meant to git dere whilst de town wuz yet a baby. He meant to buy in big. It had always been his wish and desire to be a big voice and he had to live nearly thirty years to find a chance. Where was Janie's papa and mama?

Here Hurston uses indirect dialogue to break into the integuments of narrative. She modifies the narrative by paraphrasing Joe's speech to Janie. He also in a manner of speaking—though intended ironically here—becomes a "big voice" in the narrative. (And Joe could be someone's romantic idea; Janie—illusively in this text—initially sees him as one.)

Hurston modifies and revivifies the text on other occasions by using the language that Janie might have used—imagery, vocabulary, rhythms, sentence structure, and so on. Though maintaining the third person, she approximates the transcription techniques of contemporary writers who have broken out of the frame. Unlike Joe's monologue, the language isn't distorted with "eye dialect" but is transposed by rhythm, word choice, and syntax much like a contemporary text. In the following excerpt, Hurston breaks into the narrative suggesting Janie's voice and imaginings, her thought processes:

> She rather found herself angry at imaginary people who might try to criticize. Let the old hypocrites learn to mind their own business, and leave other folks alone. Tea Cake wasn't doing a bit more harm trying to win hisself a little money than they was always doing with their lying tongues. Tea Cake had more good nature under his toe-nails than they had in their so-called Christian hearts. She better not hear none of them old backbiters talking about her husband! Please, Jesus, don't let them nasty niggers hurt her boy. If they do, Master Jesus, grant her a good gun and a chance to shoot 'em. Tea Cake had a knife it was true, but that was only to protect hisself. God knows, Tea Cake wouldn't harm a fly.

And here is an instance of Janie's syntax and vocabulary organizing and embellishing the narrative:

> She looked hard at the sky for a long time. Somewhere up there beyond blue ether's bosom sat He. Was He noticing what was going on around here? He must be because He knew everything. Did He mean to do this thing to Tea Cake and her? It wasn't anything she could fight. She could only ache and wait. Maybe it was some big tease and when He saw it had gone far enough He'd give her a sign. She looked hard for something up there to move for a sign. A star in the daytime, maybe, or the sun to shout, or even a mutter of thunder. Her arms went up in a desperate supplication for a minute. It wasn't exactly pleading, it was asking questions. The sky stayed hard looking and quiet so she went inside the house. God would do no less than He had in His heart.

Of course this is one of the narrative writing techniques in which oral tradition and literary again coincide (co-mingle?). In the works of James Joyce and Gustave Flaubert readers frequently assume the narrative territory to be exclusively the territory of authorial voice in diction, vocabulary, and articulation. Hence Joyce and Flaubert are often accused of possessing the romantic sentimentality that they were satirizing. (Joyce's attitude toward Stephen Daedalus might more precisely be called ironic.) Other writers, such as Elizabeth Bowen, make sure that the reader "gets it" by parenthetically stressing that the narrative renderings are the way the character would see, think, or express a thing. She announces what she is doing as part of the ironic structure of the narrative. Irony and satire, not solely dramatic characterization, are often motivations in Western literature for this technique. J. F. Power's "Dawn" does it through Father Udovic's thought processes, vocabulary, and mawkish logic restructuring narrative; another example is Henry James's "central intelligence" method in which much of the verbosity and circumlocutions that we take simply for James's style are third-person narratives that center in the minds of characters and indirectly reproduce their personalities, their rhythms, prolix thoughts, and parlance. The depiction of Gerty in *Ulysses* makes this technique clearer. Because Gerty is a woman, so there are no autobiographical parallels, and because the architecture of *Ulysses* is more multifaceted than that of *A Portrait of the Artist as a Young Man*, it is easier for the reader to know that the intent is satirical, the attitude ironic. On the other hand, if a woman had written a book entitled *Gerty* using this method of indirect dialogue and monologue, many readers would suspect the author and narrator were one; the ironic attitude would have been more difficult to convey and sustain; the author might have had to announce what she is doing. However, Hurston's intent here is not satirical or ironic. She is not satirizing Janie's way of expressing things or organizing thoughts. Nor is she Janie. She is simply allowing us to enter Janie's world.

The author also brings oratory from the African American folk sermon into Janie's and the narrative's vocabulary, amplifying and ornamenting the folk voice and interior revelation. The same thrust and narrative dynamics permeate nearly all of James Baldwin's fictions. James R. Bennett in *Prose Style* found it odd that Baldwin might share this vernacular expression with Southern white writers: "Although Southern writing can be as laconic as other American colloquial prose, it also indulges in that public oratory we habitually associate with the Southern politician, and which we often hear in the prose of Thomas Wolfe and William Faulkner, of Robert Penn Warren and William Styron, and even, ironically, of James Baldwin . . . the oratorical mode shares the characteristics of the colloquial. Its exclamations, repetitions, uncertain backings and fillings, accumulation of synonyms, and rhetorical emphases all originate in the extemporaneousness of speech, the spontaneous jetting of language that maintains its equilibrium by constant movement forward." Knowing that oratorical flourishes are migratory, this does not seem odd to this reader/listener, especially because of the invisible linkings in Southern black and white races and textual relationships (Baldwin's ancestors were transplanted Southerners; nor do we always know in this Southern tradition who is influencing whom in rhetorical strategy). It is what Ellison would call the "true interrelatedness of blackness and whiteness."

Hurston admits Janie's language, imagination, and perspective in many places. However, these are probably places where, says Robert Hemenway, "the narrative shifts awkwardly from first to third person." This narrative awkwardness or tension may be read as Hurston's attempt to give a certain validity and articulate authority to Janie's expression, thought, and experiences; her attempt to make Janie's language do even in small ways, the things that other languages, taken for granted as literary languages, can do.

Not until James Baldwin, Ernest Gaines, Ellease Southerland, Toni Cade Bambara, Ntozake Shange, to name but a few contemporary writers, did the folk language become flexible enough to enter the fabric of the narrative to tell the whole story. Southerland, for instance, breaks into the third-person narrative with the syntax, vocabulary, and metaphors of Abeba's speech community without feeling it necessary to first make the shift to the first-person storyteller, and she resolves the narrative tension in a more shimmering, malleable prose:

> Jackson didn't have good sense. He had all the sense he was born with, but that wasn't enough. He was a great big boy, sixteen years old and what'd he do all day? Go on up the road to the midwife's place and play just as content with the little girl there. Playing tea party. That ain't no way for a grown boy to be. Just two years ago, the little girl fix mud cakes and all. Took weeds and fixed it sos it looked like greens and laid a twig beside the dinner for a fork then called Jackson to the table to eat and that great big boy picked up the little mud cakes and bit right into them. And Abeba Williams that's the little girl, put her hand on her hip just as she see the midwife do and said, "Jackson, you to play eat, not to eat mud sure enough." And Jackson got it straight after that.

Like Ernest Gaines's *The Autobiography of Miss Jane Pittman*, Ellease Southerland's *Let the Lion Eat Straw* extends the work Hurston began in breaking down some of the barriers between dialect and narrative in fiction. Nevertheless in her territory there is still the problem of the look of ease and apparent lack of complexity and implication. (Also, what is innovative in one tradition often appears conventional from the point of view of another where freeing one's voice is not the issue. In American popular music, for instance, the so-called innovations and breakings-out of early rock 'n' roll were not distinguishable from conventional black music, for jazz had already been there and gone. Conventional literature in one culture may likewise surprise another culture while "innovative" literature might hold nothing new. From the point of view of the frame then, we speak of innovation.)

This "look of ease" is something that must be addressed in the African American tradition as in all other literary traditions. How to render the colloquial voice authentically, break out of the frame, and yet be impressive literarily? For instance, the colloquial voices in *The Waste Land* or the interior monologue of Molly Bloom still impress us; is it because these colloquial, natural voices play against the more elaborate unnatural voicings? But if first-person voice is seen as the higher standard, how could a convincing contrast be devised? Perhaps more of the expansiveness and opulence of the sermonic mode could be used to play against the colloquial. But first one seizes authority over one's own voice (and voices), then develops, cultivates, enhances, heightens, intensifies, sets a style.

In Western literature there are essentially two stylistic streams, often interfaced as in *The Waste Land;* one of clarity and one of complexity. Some writers and traders see style as superior the easier it is to understand (decode?). Others deem superior styles that one must work to penetrate, that reveal significant unity or coherence. The more difficult the writing the more the allure. This is the distinction between Frost and Eliot, Hemingway and James (or Joyce). One either tries, like Frost, to "make little orders," or to make profound secret puzzles—

evoke a fictional reality that is as incoherent as the real one. The world itself is not a simple notion. Contemporary African American writers with oral motives in the latter stream are Leon Forest, Ishmael Reed, Steve Cannon (interestingly, they are all men). They produce the difficult texts, something the reader must decode, as if the text were an arena not simply of creation, to use Kimberly Benson's term, or simply of communication, but of intellectual combat. This is not the place to explore the implications of this differing perspective. At its best the masculine text has an impressive adventuresomeness. Even among student writers, the men more often tend to use satire or irony, the more difficult tones and styles which demand more visible displays of cleverness or wit. The women's texts tend to be more low-keyed and to have more of a surface conventionality, with subtler textual subversions, often unnoticed, and which must be pointed out. However, before any adventure, the territory was first seized; the voice first freed.

Seizing some of her territory, then, Hurston, even in the final paragraph of *Their Eyes Were Watching God*, makes the reader feel the oral tradition breaking through—colloquial and heightened—here, as in Toomer's *Cane*, in narrative made to be heard and felt as well as read. Janie's voice welds sermonic rhetoric and oratory with the musical traditions of blues and spiritual:

> The day of the gun, and the bloody body, and the courthouse came and commenced to sing a sobbing sigh out of every corner in the room; out of each and every chair and thing. Commenced to sing, commenced to sob and sigh, singing and sobbing. Then Tea Cake came prancing around her where she was an the song of the sign flew out of the window and lit the top of the pine trees. Tea Cake, with the sun for a shawl. Of course he wasn't dead. He could never be dead until she herself had finished feeling and thinking. The kiss of his memory made pictures of love and light against the wall. Here was peace. She pulled in her horizon like a great fish-net. Pulled it from around the waist of the world and draped it over her shoulder. So much of life in its meshes! She called in her soul to come and see.

AFRICAN AMERICAN LITERARY CRITICISM

Topics for Research

1. What brought about the first African American literary criticism? Who was the first writer to contribute to this body of work? Why was there a need for critical approaches that focused on African American literature? How does African American literary criticism differ from other literary criticism?

2. How do African American literary critics define the role of the black writer? How would you define the black writer's role? Place your definition within the context of the existing work on this topic.

3. In addition to defining the role of the African American artist, what other issues do African American literary critics address?

4. Test the validity of African American critical works by applying them to African American literature. How useful are these theories for readers of black literature?

5. Examine the dual role of critic and creative writer. How prominent is this duality among African American writers? How do the roles complement or clash with each other? Determine the necessity for this duality and identify other roles that African American literary critics assume. What are the implications of these roles for female writers as opposed to male writers of African American literature?

6. Examine the application of theories such as the following to African American literature: structuralism, deconstruction, romanticism, realism, naturalism, and modernism and postmodernism. Assess the usefulness of one or more critical approaches.

PART 9

WRITING ABOUT AFRICAN AMERICAN LITERATURE

WHEN WRITING ABOUT AFRICAN AMERICAN LITERATURE, STUDENTS should be aware of key terms and concepts associated with literary analysis. These include the following: genre, narrative voice, character, theme and symbols, plot, sociohistorical context, aesthetics, and critical theory. Students must view African American literary works in context of a tradition spanning from the 1700s to the present. Students should examine the rhetorical strategies writers use in conveying their main points, taking genre into account and noting how the literary work's form shapes the other aforementioned elements, as described in detail below. By making connections, building bridges, and tracing common threads in literary works, students gain a sense of the complexity of African American literature. Nevertheless, in order to avoid making false judgments or generalizations based on their readings, students must also be aware of diversity within the African American literary tradition. More important, students must realize that even within a single author's body of work, there are often varieties of opinion and thought.

Genre

In their writing, students should incorporate elements of classroom discussion, information gleaned from lectures, their own thoughts about the works, and secondary sources (when needed) to refine and hone their critical skills. Major genres include the slave narrative, dramas, short stories, novels, spirituals, poetry, and the nonfiction essay. Most of these genres appear in other types of literary traditions, but the slave narrative represents a uniquely African American tradition. Common features include an emphasis on identity, rites of passage (literal and figurative), the quest for freedom, and authenticating documents that validate the narrative. Slave narratives were most prevalent in the eighteenth and nineteenth centuries, with examples such as *The Interesting Narrative of the Life of Olaudah Equiano, or Gustavus Vassa, the African, Written by Himself; The Narrative of the Life of Frederick Douglass, an American Slave, Written by Himself;* and *Incidents in the Life of a Slave Girl, Written by Herself.* However, the slave narrative genre continues in the twentieth century, as exemplified by Ernest Gaines's *The Autobiography of Miss Jane Pittman*, which features as its protagonist a female slave in quest of freedom.

Another important genre, drama, includes texts such as William Wells Brown's abolitionist play *The Escape; or, A Leap for Freedom* and later plays such as Marita Bonner's *The Purple Flower,* Lorraine Hansberry's *A Raisin in the Sun*, and August Wilson's *The Piano Lesson.* Playwrights dramatize the black experience for the theatergoing audience.

The short story is another important genre. Short stories such as Frances E. W. Harper's "The Two Offers" and Charles Chesnutt's "Po' Sandy" and "The Goophered Grapevine" highlight concerns of the antebellum and Reconstruction eras, while tales such as Jessie Redmon Fauset's "The Sleeper Wakes" highlight the emphasis on race, class, and gender relations in early-twentieth-century America. More contemporary authors, like Alice Walker in "To Hell with Dying," focus on emerging black nationalism, feminism, and the black family in their tales. The short story illustrates the dexterity of African American writers who articulate the black experience in this form.

When writing about autobiography, drama, and the short story, students should consider the correlation between literary form, content, and intended audience as well as the strategies authors employ in their works. These elements are vital as well when writing about the novel, an important development in the African American literary tradition. The novel serves as an extended form of response to the African American experience, developing certain themes through time. The selections here, ranging from antebellum works like Harper's *Iola Leroy; or, Shadows Uplifted* to more contemporary texts such as Gaines's *Autobiography of Miss Jane Pittman*, Charles Johnson's *Middle Passage*, and Gloria Naylor's *Linden Hills*, provide a means for students to make connections.

Other key genres include poetry and the nonfiction essay. Spirituals (religious songs sung by slaves) and work songs serve as a basis for African American poetry. Stylistically, African American poetry runs the gamut from the folk and dialect poems of Paul Laurence Dunbar in the nineteenth century and Langston Hughes during the Harlem Renaissance to the more formalized poetry of Hughes's counterpart Countee Cullen and the black feminist consciousness of contemporary poets such as Sonia Sanchez. When writing about poetry, students should examine the language, common themes, and recurrent symbols in the work.

The nonfiction essay, popularized by individuals such as W. E. B. Du Bois with *The Souls of Black Folk*, also reflects an important avenue of African American literary expression. Du Bois comments on issues of race and class in America through his poetic prose.

Narrative Voice

Standard narrative voices in literature include first person (*I*) and third person (*he/she/it*). Another narrative voice, the omniscient (all-knowing) narrator, views and transmits the thoughts of all the characters to the reader. When writing about narrative voice, students should consider the following issues: How do various characters' voices differ? What does the voice reveal about a character's motivations, education, social background, and worldview? What does the character's use of standard or nonstandard English reveal about him or her? What type of narrative voice predominates? Are there multiple voices in a text, and if so, why? Would the story change if another voice were used?

Character

Character and voice work together as they provide insight into the motivations of the protagonists in literary works. When writing about character, students should address the following topics: Are the characters static (unchanging) or dynamic (changing) during the course of the work? Who are the major characters? the minor characters? Are the characters active or passive? Do they have distinct personalities, or are they similar? Do the characters tell their own story, or is there an omniscient or third person narrator? Are the characters realistic or unrealistic, and why? Other issues to address are how the character's motivations, concerns, and personalities reflect or defy social historical conditions.

Themes

Characters shape the theme in a work. Themes, or the main ideas, often appear in terms of oppositions in African American literature. Common themes often have a basis in historical and social phenomena, including slavery versus freedom, the quest for an identity, the divided self, and the quest for voice. When writing about African American literature, students should trace the development of recurrent themes and should compare and contrast the strategies authors employ in presenting these thematic concerns. Students must also examine how these themes relate to other elements, including symbols. Recurrent symbols appear in African American literature. For example, the caged bird in Dunbar's "Sympathy," Jacobs's *Incidents in the Life of a Slave Girl*, and Angelou's *I Know Why the Caged Bird Sings* represents the theme of slavery versus freedom. Recurrent symbols reflect important attributes of black literature and history.

Plot

Plot (the sequence of events in a work) may be chronological, or it may defy standard linear chronology. In African American literature, writers often deviate from a linear chronology and opt for a plot structure that shifts between past, present, and future. Individuals acquainted with more linear concepts of time may find the narrative difficult to follow. Shifts between past, present, and future often reflect a sense that the past influences the present and the future and that therefore these times cannot be distinguished from one another. Shifts in chronology, sometimes coupled with shifts in narration, make works such as Naylor's *Linden Hills* and Octavia Butler's *Kindred* both realistic and neorealistic in their conceptions of history, time, and place.

Sociohistorical Context

African American texts reflect the time periods in which they were written. Students should analyze texts in relation to the prevailing social, cultural, and political attitudes of these periods. For example, viewing the poetry of writers such as Phillis Wheatley and Jupiter Hammon in the context of the colonial period and the evolution of slavery in America provides insight into their work. Examining the tensions in antebellum society regarding the abolition of slavery proves necessary in understanding *The Escape; or, A Leap for Freedom* by William Wells Brown. Harlem Renaissance works such as Zora Neale Hurston's *Their Eyes Were Watching God* and W. E. B. Du Bois's *The Souls of Black Folk* show emerging African American consciousness. The racial politics of the 1940s and 1950s serve as a backdrop for Richard Wright's *Native Son* and Ann Petry's electrifying *The Street*. The black aesthetics movement, coupled with civil rights legislation, presents a quest for African American civil rights reflected in the poetics of Martin Luther King's "Letter from Birmingham Jail" and Haki R. Madhubuti's "Possibilities: Remembering Malcolm X." The feminist movement and the establishment of African American studies programs at the university level serve as the backdrop for post-1970s neorealist voices, including prominent African American women such as Maya Angelou, Audre Lorde, and Alice Walker. Male authors such as Ernest Gaines in *The Autobiography of Miss Jane Pittman* and John Edgar Wideman in *Damballah* also wrote compelling texts of African American life, often recalling the legacy of slavery and its impact on African Americans today.

Aesthetics

African American literature consists of a triangularity of aesthetics, ranging from folk to bourgeois and proletarian. The "folk" aesthetic reflects works which often have a rural setting with characters who speak nonstandard American English and who are from the lower social and economic levels. They often feel closely connected to the African past and heritage. Examples of the folk aesthetic include the poetry of Paul Laurence Dunbar in "When Malindy Sings" and the short stories of Charles Chesnutt, such as "Po' Sandy." The bourgeois aesthetic represents literature that focuses on characters with middle- or upper-class backgrounds and formal education who speak standard American English. Novels such as Naylor's *Linden Hills*, which critiques middle-class blacks in suburbia, represent this aesthetic, as does the poetry of Countee Cullen, who models British Romantic poets. The proletarian aesthetic includes works with a protest theme in which the writers overtly critique race, class, and/or gender oppression. Slave narratives such as *The Narrative of the Life of Frederick Douglass*, written in the nineteenth century, and texts such as *Native Son*, written in the twentieth century, represent the protest aesthetic in African American literature. As students write about these texts, they should raise questions like these: Are the works representative of folk, bourgeois, or proletarian aesthetics, or are they a blending of the three? Which aesthetics predominate in a given period or in an author's work? Why? How do these aesthetics connect with the sociocultural background of the texts?

Critical Theory

Students must be aware of the variety of critical approaches in relation to African American literature, ranging from the sociohistorical to feminist approaches. Literary criticism can help in framing students' responses to texts. Earlier examples, such as Langston Hughes's "The Negro Artist and the Racial Mountain" and Zora Neale Hurston's "What White Publishers Won't Print," should frame an examination of the debate regarding historical representations of blacks in American literature. Larry Neal's "The Black Arts Movement" examines the relation between black consciousness in the 1960s and the works that sprang from it. Similarly, Alice Walker's "In Search of Our Mothers' Gardens" and Hazel Carby's *Reconstructing Womanhood: The Emergence of the Afro-American Woman Novelist* examine the wide-ranging implications of race, class, and gender on the female writer, while Henry Louis Gates's *Loose Canons: Notes on the Culture Wars* addresses the question of what constitutes "black" literature. In writing about African American literature, students should use literary criticism as a means of grounding their readings. Students can freely respond to, critique, and analyze the works within the contexts of the work of these theoreticians as they build their own emerging theories of African American literature.

It is vitally important to take these elements into consideration when reading a given work. More important, by viewing all the elements that make up literary works and the contexts in which they were written, students will be able to take a more holistic approach to writing about African American literature. African American literature is a gold mine of material for the writer and the student to explore.

TIMELINE

THE COLONIAL PERIOD 1746–1800

1773   Phillis Wheatley's *Poems on Various Subjects, Religious and Moral* is published. Her book is the first written and published by an African American.

1775–1781   The American Revolutionary War occurs when colonists desire freedom from the rule of British monarchy and succeed in defeating the British Army.

1789   Olaudah Equiano publishes *The Interesting Narrative of the Life of Olaudah Equiano, or Gustavas Vassa, the African*—considered the first major slave autobiography in American literature.

THE ANTEBELLUM PERIOD 1800–1865

1829   George Moses Horton's *The Hope of Liberty* is published and becomes the first book of poetry published by a black Southern writer.

1830   Antislavery advocates develop the Underground Railroad, a network of people who assist fugitive slaves from the South in their escape to the North for freedom.

1831   Nat Turner leads a slave rebellion in Virginia, resulting in many deaths.

1845   *Narrative of the Life of Frederick Douglass, An American Slave, Written By Himself* is published.

1850   The Fugitive Slave Law requires individuals in free states to return escaped slaves to their owners.

1863   President Abraham Lincoln releases the Emancipation Proclamation.

1861–1865   The American Civil War occurs. The Northern (Union) Army defeats the Southern (Confederate) army, and slavery is abolished.

THE RECONSTRUCTION PERIOD 1865–1900

1865   The Thirteenth Amendment to the Constitution formally abolishes the institution of slavery in the United States of America.

1896   The *Plessy v. Ferguson* U.S. Supreme Court decision legalizes racial segregation.

THE HARLEM RENAISSANCE 1900–1940

1902   Paul Laurence Dunbar publishes *The Sport of the Gods.*

1903   W. E. B. Du Bois publishes *The Souls of Black Folk.*

1909   The NAACP is created by blacks and whites. The organization proves instrumental in the Harlem Renaissance, publishing *The Crisis.*

1929 The stock market crash occurs, leading to financial ruin for many and to the Great Depression of the 1930s.

1914–1918 World War I (The United States is directly involved from 1917 to 1918.)

1937 Zora Neale Hurston's *Their Eyes Were Watching God* is published.

1939–1945 World War II (The United States is directly involved from 1941 to 1945.)

THE PROTEST MOVEMENT 1940–1959

1940 Marcus Garvey, head of the Universal Negro Improvement Organization, leader of the Back-to-Africa campaign, and advocate of racial separatism, dies.

1940 Richard Wright's *Native Son* is published.

1944 The Supreme Court rules that skin color cannot be a determinant for voting rights.

1945 Richard Wright's *Black Boy* is published.

1948 President Harry Truman bans segregation in the military.

1950 Gwendolyn Brooks wins a Pulitzer Prize for *Annie Allen*.

1950–1953 The Korean War occurs.

1953 Ralph Ellison receives a National Book Award for *Invisible Man*.

1954 In *Brown v. Board of Education of Topeka, Kansas*, the Supreme Court rules against racial segregation in public schools, overturning the *Plessy v. Ferguson* decision of 1896.

1955 Rosa Parks refuses to give up her seat to a white man on a bus in Montgomery, Alabama; her resistance leads to a bus boycott.

James Baldwin's *Notes of a Native Son* is published.

1956 The Supreme Court rules that segregated seating on buses is unconstitutional.

1957 The Southern Christian Leadership Conference (SCLC) is formed.

The Voting Rights Act is passed.

BLACK AESTHETICS MOVEMENT 1960–1969

1961–1975 The Vietnam War occurs.

1963 The March on Washington—the largest civil rights demonstration—takes place at the Lincoln Memorial; Martin Luther King, Jr., delivers his famous "I Have a Dream" speech.

1964 The Nobel Peace Prize is awarded to Martin Luther King, Jr.

The Civil Rights Act bans segregation in public establishments.

1965 Malcolm X is assassinated in New York City.

1966 The Black Panther party is founded.

1968	Martin Luther King, Jr., is assassinated in Memphis, Tennessee.
1969	A Supreme Court decision demands an end to racial segregation in school districts.

NEOREALISM MOVEMENT 1970–PRESENT

1978	James Alan McPherson is awarded a Pulitzer Prize for *Elbow Room*, a book of short stories.
1983	Gloria Naylor receives an American Book Award for *The Women of Brewster Place*.
	Alice Walker wins a Pulitzer Prize and an American Book Award for *The Color Purple*.
1984	Jesse Jackson becomes the first African American to run for president of the United States.
1985	Sonia Sanchez receives an American Book Award for *homegirls and handgrenades*.
1986	Martin Luther King Day becomes a national holiday.
1987	Rita Dove is awarded a Pulitzer Prize for *Thomas and Beulah*.
	August Wilson receives a Pulitzer Prize for *Fences*.
1988	Toni Morrison receives a Pulitzer Prize for *Beloved.*
	Terry McMillan wins an American Book Award for *Mama*.
1990	Charles Johnson receives a National Book Award for *Middle Passage*.
	August Wilson wins a Pulitzer Prize for *The Piano Lesson*.
	The Persian Gulf War occurs.
1992	Randall Kenan is nominated for a National Book Critics Circle Award for *Let The Dead Bury Their Dead*.
	Derek Walcott wins the Noble Prize in Literature.
	Riots occur in Los Angeles.
1993	Maya Angelou reads her poem "On the Pulse of Morning" at Bill Clinton's inauguration.
	Toni Morrison receives the Nobel Prize in Literature, being the first African American woman to win the award.

IMPORTANT AFRICAN AMERICAN LITERARY, CULTURAL, AND HISTORICAL EVENTS 1994–1998

1994	Rita Dove is named United States Poet Laureate.
	Yusef Komunyakaa is awarded a Pulitzer Prize for his poetry collection *Neon Vernacular*.
	Gwendolyn Brooks receives the National Book Foundation's Medal for Distinguished Contribution to American Letters for her poetry

collection *Annie Allen*. She is also named Jefferson Lecturer by the National Endowment for the Humanities, the highest honor bestowed by the United States Government.

Ernest Gaines's *A Lesson Before Dying* is awarded the National Book Critics Circle Award for fiction.

February 5—Byron De La Beckwith is convicted of the 1963 murder of civil rights activist Medgar Evers.

O. J. Simpson is arrested and tried for the murder of Nicole Brown Simpson and Ronald Goldman.

May 9—The first South African all-race election is held; National Congress presidential candidate Nelson Mandela wins by a landslide.

August 14—Alice Childress dies.

Whoopi Goldberg hosts the 66th Annual Academy Awards ceremony and is the first African American and woman solo host.

1995   Gwendolyn Brooks receives the National Medal of the Arts from President Bill Clinton.

September 4–15—The United Nations sponsors the International Women's Conference in Beijing, China.

October 16—The Million Man March is held in Washington, D.C.

Maya Angelou reads "A Brave and Startling Truth" at the United Nation's Fiftieth Anniversary ceremony.

Howard University awards Toni Morrison an honorary doctorate.

August Wilson's *The Piano Lesson* is filmed for television.

November—Rita Dove receives the Kennedy Center Fund for New American Plays Award for *The Darker Face of the Earth*.

November 1—*Ebony* magazine celebrates its fiftieth anniversary.

November 8—Colin Powell declines to run for president and also declines an invitation to run as Republican Bob Dole's vice-presidential running mate.

December—A screen adaptation of Terry McMillan's *Waiting to Exhale* becomes a box office hit.

1996   April 9—George Walker receives a Pulitzer Prize for *Lilacs*, a voice and orchestra composition.

June 15—Ella Fitzgerald dies.

September—Presidential Medal of Freedom awards are given to civil rights pioneer Rosa Parks and to John H. Johnson, the founder of *Jet* and *Ebony* magazines.

Tupac Shakur, rap artist, is murdered.

Television host Oprah Winfrey establishes Oprah's Book Club.

1997   January—The Oakland school board votes to recognize Black English as a second language.

Seven African American soldiers are awarded the Medal of Honor for their heroism in World War II.

Ennis Cosby is murdered.

February—Anna Deavere Smith named first artist in residence for the Ford Foundation in New York.

March—Martin Luther King's family appeals for a new trial for James Earl Ray, Dr. King's convicted murderer.

The Notorious B.I.G., rap artist, is murdered.

April—Wynton Marsalis becomes the first jazz musician to be awarded a Pulitzer Prize for his epic jazz opera, *Blood on the Fields.*

Cuba Gooding, Jr., awarded an Oscar for best supporting actor in *Jerry Maguire.*

Baseball season honors the fiftieth anniversary of Jackie Robinson's entering the major leagues.

Detroit's Museum of African American History, the nation's largest museum of African American history, opens.

Tiger Woods becomes youngest winner of the Masters golf tournament.

May—Ann Petry dies.

June—The United States apologizes for Tuskeegee syphilis experiment, carried out from 1932 to 1972.

Clinton establishes a seven-person race relations panel.

July—Betty Shabazz, widow of Malcolm X, dies.

Macarthur Foundation fellowships are awarded to artists Kerry James Marshall and Kara Elizabeth Walker and to anthropologist Brackette F. Williams.

Duke Ellington memorial statue unveiled in Harlem.

The Women's National Basketball Association (WNBA) debuts.

November—The Million Woman March is held in Philadelphia.

December—President Clinton holds first town hall meeting on race relations.

Henry Louis Gates, Jr., is elected to the Pulitzer Prize board. The *Norton Anthology of African American Literature*, edited by Gates, is released.

1998 Jazz musicians Ron Carter, James Moody, and Wayne Shorter are named National Endowment for the Arts "American Jazz Masters."

David Barr wins the 12th annual Theodore Ward Prize for African American playwriting for his play *Black Caesar.*

Coretta Scott King presents Myrlie Evers-Williams with the NAACP's 83rd annual Springarn Medal, the highest award in the civil rights arena.

CREDITS

THE HARLEM RENAISSANCE 1900–1940

Marita Bonner, *The Purple Flower* from *Frye Street & Environs: The Collected Works of Marita Bonner*. Copyright © 1987. Reprinted with the permission of Beacon Press, Boston.

Arna Bontemps, "A Black Man Talks of Reaping" and "Close Your Eyes!" Copyright by Arna Bontemps. Reprinted with the permission of the Harold Ober Associates.

Sterling Brown, "Odyssey of Big Boy," "Old Lem," and "Memphis Blues" from *The Collected Poems of Sterling A. Brown*, edited by Michael S. Harper. Copyright 1932 by Harcourt, Brace & Co.; renewed © 1960 by Sterling Brown. Copyright © 1980 by Sterling A. Brown. Reprinted with the permission of HarperCollins Publishers, Inc.

Countee Cullen, "Heritage," "Incident," "Yet Do I Marvel," and "To John Keats, Poet. At Spring Time," from *Color* (New York: Harper, 1925). Copyright 1925 by Harper & Brothers; renewed 1953 by Ida M. Cullen. Reprinted with the permission of the Estate of Countee Cullen. Copyrights administered by Thompson and Thompson, New York, NY.

Langston Hughes, "Mother to Son," "Harlem," "I, Too," "Dream Boogie: Variation" and "Theme for English B" from *The Collected Poems of Langston Hughes*, edited by Arnold Rampersad and David Roessel. Copyright © 1994 by the Estate of Langston Hughes. Reprinted with the permission of Alfred A. Knopf, Inc.

Zora Neale Hurston, from *Their Eyes Were Watching God*. Copyright 1937 by Zora Neale Hurston. Reprinted with the permission of HarperCollins Publishers, Inc. "How It Feels to Be Colored Me" from *The World Tomorrow*, 11 (May 1928). Copyright 1928 by Zora Neale Hurston, renewed © 1956 by John C. Hurston. Reprinted with the permission of the Estate of Zora Neale Hurston.

James Weldon Johnson, "O Black and Unknown Bards" and "The Creation" from *God's Trombones*. Copyright 1927 by The Viking Press, Inc.; renewed © 1955 by Grace Nail Johnson. Reprinted with the permission of Viking Penguin, a division of Penguin Putnam, Inc. Excerpt from *The Autobiography of An Ex-Colored Man*. Copyright 1927 by Alfred A. Knopf, Inc. and renewed © 1955 by Carl Van Vechten. Reprinted with the permission of Alfred A. Knopf, Inc. Excerpt from *Black Manhattan* (New York: Alfred A. Knopf, 1930). Copyright 1930 by James Weldon Johnson. Reprinted with the permission of the Estate of Grace Johnson.

Anne Spencer, "Dunbar" and "The Wife-Woman" from *Times's Unfading Garden*, edited by J. Lee Greene. Copyright © 1977. Reprinted with the permission of Louisiana State University Press.

Wallace Thurman, "Harlem," excerpt from *The Blacker the Berry*. Copyright 1929 by Wallace Thurman. Reprinted by permission.

Jean Toomer, "Bona and Paul," excerpt from *Cane*. Copyright 1923 by Boni & Liveright; renewed 1951 by Jean Toomer. Reprinted with the permission of Liveright Publishing Corporation.

Dorothy West, "The Typewriter" from *The Richer, The Poorer: Stories, Sketches, and Reminiscences*. Copyright © 1995 by Dorothy West. Reprinted with the permission of Doubleday, a division of Random House, Inc.

THE PROTEST MOVEMENT 1940–1959

Margaret Walker, "For My People," "Ex-Slave," and "Lineage" from *This Is My Century: New and Collected Poems*. Copyright © 1989 by Margaret Walker Alexander. Reprinted with the permission of The University of Georgia Press.

James Baldwin, excerpt from *Go Tell It on the Mountain*. Copyright 1953 by James Baldwin. Reprinted with the permission of Doubleday, a division of Random House, Inc.

Gwendolyn Brooks, "The Mother," "The Sundays of Satin-Legs Smith," and "The Rites for Cousin Vit" from *Blacks*. "What Shall I Give My Children?" Copyright © 1991 by Gwendolyn Brooks Blakely. Reprinted with the permission of the author.

Ralph Ellison, excerpt from *Invisible Man*. Copyright 1952 by Ralph Ellison. Reprinted with the permission of Random House, Inc.

BLACK AESTHETICS MOVEMENT 1960–1969

NEOREALISM MOVEMENT 1970–PRESENT

AFRICAN AMERICAN LITERARY CRITICISM

AN AUDIO CD OF AFRICAN-AMERICAN ORAL TRADITIONS
BY KEVIN EVEROD QUASHIE AND STUART L. TWITE

CONTENTS

1. "Ghana: Ewe-Atsiagbekor" from *Roots of Black Music in America*

2. "I Just Come from the Fountain" by Michael LaRue

3. "Bars Fight" (poem by Lucy Terry; read by Arna Bontemps)

4. "Go Down Moses"

5. "On Being Brought from Africa to America" (poem by Phillis Wheatley; read by Jean Brannon)

6. "Pick a Bale of Cotton" from "Pete Seeger at Carnegie Hall"

7. "Backwater Blues" from "Lead Belly's Last"

8. "Come by Hyar" (traditional; sung by Bernice Reagon)

9. *Remembering Slavery*—newly released recordings of former slaves talking about slavery. Interview #1

10. *Remembering Slavery*—newly released recordings of former slaves talking about slavery. Interview #2

11. "The Rebirth of Sojourner Truth" (read by Jean Brannon)

12. "Harriet Tubman" (read by Jean Brannon)

13. "What If I Am a Woman" (speech by Maria W. Stewart; read by Ruby Dee)

14. "If There Is No Struggle, There Is No Freedom" (excerpt; speech by Frederick Douglass; read by Ossie Davis)

15. "Swing Low Sweet Chariot" (traditional; sung by Paul Robeson)

16. "Address at the Atlanta Exposition" (Booker T. Washington)

17. "I Couldn't Hear Nobody Pray" (The Fisk Jubilee Singers)

18. "Dawn" (poem by Paul Laurence Dunbar; read by Arna Bontemps)

19. "Crisis Magazine" (W. E. B. Du Bois)

20. "The Creation" (poem by James Weldon Johnson; read by Arna Bontemps)

21. "If We Must Die" (poem and reading by Claude McKay)

22. "I've Known Rivers" (poem and reading by Langston Hughes)

23. "I Too" (poem and reading by Langston Hughes)

24. "Song in the Front Yard" (poem and reading by Gwendolyn Brooks)

25. "I Sing Because I'm Happy" (sung by Mahalia Jackson)

26. "He's Got the Whole World in His Hands" (sung by Marian Anderson)

27. "Mass Meeting" (speech by Martin Luther King, Jr.)

28. "Wade in the Water" from "Voices of the Civil Rights Movement: Black American Freedom"

29. *Angela Davis*

30. "liberation/poem" (poem and reading by Sonia Sanchez)

31. "Woman" (poem and reading by Nikki Giovanni)

32. "Zum Zum" (Street and Gangland Rhythms) from "Beats and Improvisations by Six Boys in Trouble"